PS 320-321,
327-336,
438
PS

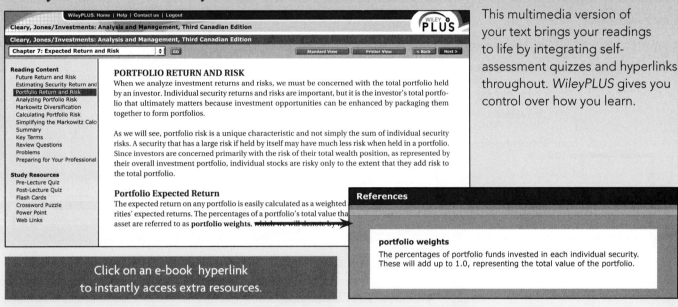
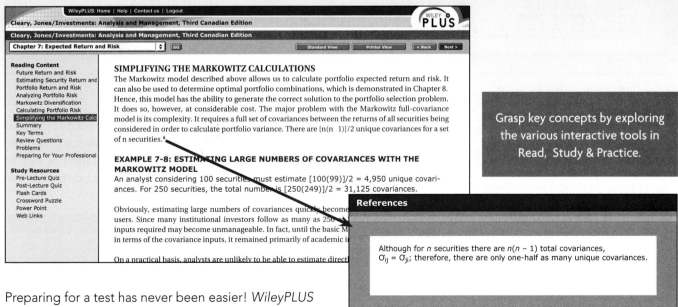

WILEY PLUS *for Investments:* Analysis and Management

Complete and Submit Assignments On-line Efficiently

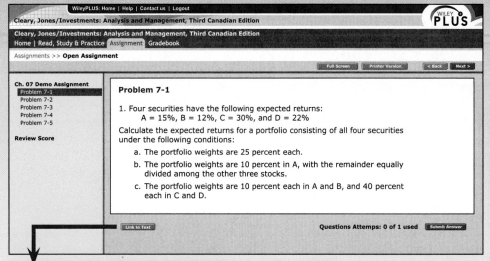

Your homework questions contain links to the relevant section of the multimedia text, so you know exactly where to go to get help solving each problem. In addition, use the Assignment area of *WileyPLUS* to monitor all of your assignments and their due dates.

Your instructor can assign homework on-line for automatic grading and you can keep up-to-date on your assignments with your assignment list.

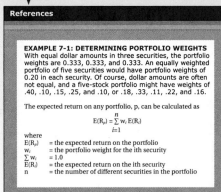

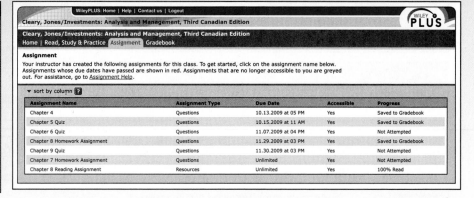

Keep Track of Your Progress

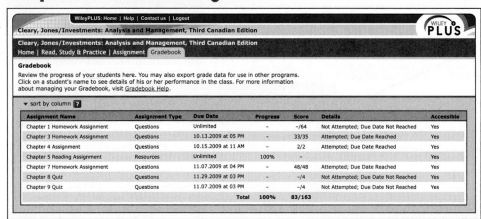

Your personal Gradebook lets you review your answers and results from past assignments as well as any feedback your instructor may have for you.

Keep track of your progress and review your completed questions at any time.

Technical Support: http://higheredwiley.custhelp.com
Student Resource Centre: http://www.wileyplus.com

For further information regarding *WileyPLUS* and other Wiley products, please visit www.wiley.ca.

INVESTMENTS

ANALYSIS AND MANAGEMENT

THIRD CANADIAN EDITION

W. SEAN CLEARY

Queen's University

CHARLES P. JONES

North Carolina State University

JOHN WILEY & SONS CANADA, LTD.

Library and Archives Canada Cataloguing in Publication

Cleary, W. Sean (William Sean), 1962–
Investments: Analysis and Management / W. Sean Cleary,
Charles P. Jones. — 3rd Canadian ed.

ISBN 978-0-470-15759-6
1. Investments—Textbooks. 2. Investment analysis—Textbooks.
I. Jones, Charles Parker, 1943- II. Title.
HG4521.C48 2008   332.6   C2008-904396-0

Production Credits

Acquisitions Editor: Darren Lalonde
Vice President & Publisher: Veronica Visentin
Vice President, Publishing Services: Karen Bryan
Creative Director, Publishing Services: Ian Koo
Marketing Manager: Aida Krneta
Editorial Manager: Karen Staudinger
Developmental Editor: Gail Brown
Editorial Assistant: Tamara Capar
Editorial Assistant/Permissions Coordinator: Rachel Coffey
Typesetting: Interrobang Graphic Design
Interior Design: Natalia Burobina
Cover Design: Ian Koo
Cover Image: Lloyd Sutton/Masterfile
Printing & Binding: Quebecor World Inc.

Printed and bound in the United States.
1 2 3 4 5 QW 12 11 10 09 08

John Wiley & Sons Canada, Ltd.
6045 Freemont Blvd.
Mississauga, Ontario L5R 4J3
Visit our website at: www.wiley.ca

ABOUT THE AUTHORS

W. Sean Cleary, CFA is BMO Professor of Finance at Queen's University in Kingston, Ontario. Dr. Cleary graduated with his MBA from Saint Mary's University, and with his PhD in finance from the University of Toronto. He was awarded the Chartered Financial Analyst (CFA) designation in 2001. He has also completed the Canadian Securities Course (CSC), the Professional Financial Planning course (PFPC), as well as the Investment Funds Institute of Canada (IFIC) Mutual Fund Course. Dr. Cleary has taught numerous university finance courses, including investments, introductory finance, corporate finance, and financial institutions at various institutions. He has also taught seminars preparing students to write the Canadian Securities Course and all three levels of the CFA program for several years. Dr. Cleary has published articles in *The Journal of Finance*, *The Journal of Financial and Quantitative Analysis*, the *Journal of Banking and Finance*, *The Journal of Financial Research*, the *Journal of Multinational Financial Management*, the *Canadian Journal of Administrative Sciences*, and the *Canadian Investment Review*, in addition to receiving several major research grants from the Social Sciences and Humanities Research Council of Canada (SSHRC). He has also prepared chapters for professional courses offered by the Canadian Securities Institute.

Charles P. Jones is Edwin Gill Professor of Finance in the College of Management, North Carolina State University. A graduate of UNC-Chapel Hill, he has taught investments, managerial finance, risk management, and financial institutions and capital markets courses for almost 35 years. Dr. Jones has published numerous articles in the leading finance journals, including *The Journal of Finance*, *The Journal of Financial Economics*, *The Journal of Financial and Quantitative Analysis*, *The Journal of Business*, *The Journal of Portfolio Management*, and *The Financial Analysts Journal*. His current research continues a lengthy stream of papers analyzing the returns and risks of major financial assets. Dr. Jones is a Chartered Financial Analyst. He has served as a consultant in several capacities and is a former co-director of the Financial Analysts Review, which offers instructional programs to CFA candidates. Dr. Jones has received two different outstanding teaching awards from his university.

This book is designed to provide a solid foundation in the theory of investments with the practical application that students require to make real-life investment decisions. It is also intended to serve as a useful resource for students intending to pursue a career in the financial services industry. With these objectives in mind, much attention has been devoted to describing the investment environment that presently exists in Canada, as well as globally, with particular emphasis on the United States, since this represents an important and readily accessible market for Canadian investors. In addition, we place great emphasis on topics that are included in the Chartered Financial Analysts (CFA) program.

Students should benefit from the intuitive approach applied to topics throughout. Descriptive material is first covered thoroughly, then, the analytics of investments are presented throughout every discussion to help students reason out investment issues for themselves. To improve topic flow, more technical or rigorous material is covered in footnotes and appendices. This also allows instructors to increase the level of the course, if desired. The analytics are applied in illustrative examples to actual Canadian companies or financial instruments to the greatest extent possible. Real-world examples are included from various publications such as *The Globe and Mail*, the *Canadian Investment Review*, *CFA Magazine*, *MoneySense*, and *The Wall Street Journal*, to reinforce the application aspects of the concepts. Finally, an abundance of review questions and problem material is included at the end of every chapter, including numerous CFA practice and exam questions.

The book has several distinct features that contribute to achieving the above objectives:

- It brings a clear accessible approach that focuses on the more applied/practical aspects of investments.
- It provides up-to-date information regarding the Canadian and global investment environments, with a strong emphasis on Canada.
- Many real-world examples are used to apply concepts discussed in the text to Canadian companies. These can be found in the illustrative examples found throughout the text, as well as in the "Real-World Returns" features.
- There is a strong reference to CFA Institute material throughout the book, including the introduction of a "CFA Practice Questions" section, which includes a selection of Dr. Cleary's own practice questions, selected questions from past CFA Sample Questions that are provided for Level I CFA candidates, as well as past CFA exam questions. In addition, CFA material is included in much of the text, and two appendices are devoted to specific CFA topics. Finally, many of the Real-World Returns boxes have been obtained from the *CFA Magazine*, a publication of the CFA Institute that discusses many "cutting edge" investment issues.

The book is written for the first course in investments at universities and colleges, and is a useful supplement for students planning to enroll in the CFA Program or in the Canadian Securities Course (CSC). Standard prerequisites include basic accounting, economics, and introductory finance. A course in statistics is very useful but not absolutely essential. We have sought to minimize formulas and to simplify difficult material, consistent with a presentation of the subject that takes into account current ideas and practices. Relevant, state-of-the-art material has been simplified and structured specifically for the benefit of the student.

Organization of the Text

The text is divided into seven parts, organized around background, portfolio and capital market theory, the analysis of different types of securities, and portfolio management.

Part 1 provides the needed background for students before encountering the specifics of security analysis and portfolio management. The goal of this section is to acquaint beginners with an overview of what investing is all about. After a general discussion of the subject in Chapter 1, the next five chapters describe the variety of securities available when investing directly and indirectly (investment funds), the markets in which they are traded, the mechanics of securities trading, and a careful and complete analysis of the important concepts of risk and return that dominate any discussion of investments.

Part 2 is concerned with portfolio management, capital market theory, and the concept of efficient markets. Chapter 7 contains a complete discussion of modern portfolio concepts, centring on expected return and risk. The primary emphasis is on the essentials of Markowitz portfolio theory and the single-index model. Chapter 8 continues the discussion of portfolio concepts by concentrating on portfolio selection, based on the concept of efficient portfolios. The separation theorem and systematic and non-systematic risk are discussed. Chapter 9 discusses capital market theory, a natural extension of portfolio theory. This discussion focuses on the Capital Asset Pricing Model, and, to a lesser extent, on the Arbitrage Pricing Theory. Part 2 concludes with a discussion of Market Efficiency in Chapter 10, which provides some insight into the controversy and investing implications that arise from discussion of this topic.

Parts 3 and 4 focus on the basic approach to security analysis and valuation by presenting "how to" tools and techniques for bonds and stocks, respectively. Part 3 examines the analysis, valuation, and management of bonds, a logical starting point in learning how to value securities. Part 4 builds on these concepts in discussing the analysis, valuation, and management of common stocks.

Parts 4 and 5 are devoted to common stocks, a reasonable allocation given investor interest in common stocks. Part 5 covers fundamental analysis, the heart of security analysis. Because of its scope and complexity, three chapters are required to adequately cover the fundamental approach. The sequencing of these chapters—market, industry, and company—reflects the belief that the top-down approach to fundamental analysis is the preferable one for students to learn, although the bottom-up approach is also discussed. Part 5 also discusses the other approach to common stock selection—technical analysis. Technical analysis is a well-known technique for analyzing stocks that goes back many years.

Part 6 discusses the other major category of securities available to investors—derivative securities. Chapter 19 analyzes call and put options, which are popular investment alternatives in recent years. Stock-index options are also covered. Chapter 20 is devoted to financial futures, an important topic in investments. Similar to options, investors can use these securities to hedge their positions and reduce the risk of investing.

Part 7 concludes the text with a discussion of portfolio management and the issue of evaluating portfolio performance. Chapter 21 is structured around the CFA Institute's approach to portfolio management as a process and concludes with some illustrative examples. Chapter 22 discusses portfolio evaluation, which is a logical conclusion to the text, because all investors are keenly interested in how well their investments have performed. Actual Canadian mutual funds are used as examples of how to apply these portfolio performance measures and how to interpret the results.

Pedagogical Features

- **Learning Objectives** identify what students should know after reading each chapter. They are reviewed in the **Summary** at the end of the chapter.

- **Key Terms** are defined in the margin and are listed at the end of each chapter with page references, and also compiled in the glossary at the end of the textbook.

- **Real-World Returns** boxes feature articles from the business news media and demonstrate how points discussed in the book are applied in the real world.

- **Investing Tips** help students understand the logic behind important investment concepts.

- **Check Your Understanding** review questions help students check that they have understood the key concepts discussed throughout each chapter; answers are provided at the end of the textbook.

- **Demonstration Problems** and **Problems** give students the opportunity to apply what they have learned.

- The end-of-chapter section entitled **Preparing for Your Professional Exams** includes a selection of Dr. Cleary's own CFA practice questions developed through years of instructing CFA preparatory courses and selected questions from past CFA exams.

New to this Edition

In response to feedback from students and instructors who used the first two editions, we have maintained the same reader-friendly, application-based format. However, based on this same feedback, improvements have been made, including the following:

1. All material, such as financial statistics, examples using actual companies, and topics included in the Real-World Returns boxes, have been updated and enhanced.

2. Updated **CFA curriculum questions** in the "Preparing for Your Professional Exams" sections.

3. New spreadsheet problems of increasing complexity, which force students to apply a greater understanding of key topics, have been added. In this regard, the problem sections have been expanded dramatically in certain critical chapters, including Chapters 7 to 9, 11 to 13, and 17.

4. **WileyPLUS**, a powerful yet easy-to-use technology solution, provides instructors and students with a suite of interactive resources, including a complete on-line version of the text and tools that allow instructors to assign and grade homework and quizzes.

5. **Ethics & Corporate Governance**, a feature found in each part of the text, includes an item discussing ethics and corporate governance and how these issues affect corporations today. These items are accompanied by questions to help launch in-class analysis and discussion.

Supplements

The *Investments: Analysis and Management,* Third Canadian Edition website at www.wiley.com/canada/cleary provides a wealth of on-line resources, including:

Instructor's Manual: chapter objectives, chapter overview, and chapter outline

Solutions Manual: answers to all questions and problems in the text

Test bank: numerous multiple-choice and true-false questions for each chapter as well as short discussion questions and problems; the test bank is also available in a computerized format

PowerPoint slides: available for each chapter

Appendices Tables: additional appendices tables are available on-line

Web links: links to investment-related material including links to company websites and investment news media

ACKNOWLEDGEMENTS

I would like to thank my children (Jason, Brennan, Brigid, and Siobhan) and my father (Bill) for their never-ending support.

In addition, I am grateful to the following reviewers whose thoughtful comments contributed to the quality, relevancy, and accuracy of all three editions of this text:

Syed Ahmed, University of Toronto

Ben Amoako-Adu, Wilfrid Laurier University

Tov Assogbavi, Laurentian University

Glenn Baigent, Long Island University

Dean Banman, Malaspina University-College

Steve Beveridge, University of Alberta

Abraham Brodt, Concordia University

Wayne Campbell, Sheridan College

Chris Duff, Royal Roads University

Carol Edwards, British Columbia Institute of Technology

Carmine Fabiilli, Algonquin College

M. Nauman Farooqi, Mount Allison University

Alex Faseruk, Memorial University of Newfoundland

Iraj Fooladi, Dalhousie University

Dave Galotta, Algoma University

Larry Gould, University of Manitoba

Don Hamilton, First Nations University

Shahriar Hasard, Thompson River University

Yunke He, Okanagan University College

Sean Hennessey, University of Prince Edward Island

Christopher Higgins, Saint Mary's University

Mike Inglis, Ryerson University

Keith Jensen, Vancouver Island University

Gene Karlik, Red River Community College

Patrick Latham, Northern Alberta Institute of Technology

Michael Leonard, Kwantlen Polytechnic University

Stephen Mullins, St. Clair College

Peter Ostrowski, University of Northern British Columbia

Eben Otuteye, University of New Brunswick

Geoffrey Poitras, Simon Fraser University

Charles Schell, University of Northern British Columbia

Ian Skaith, Fanshawe College

Michael Stevulak, Royal Roads University

Khalil Torabzadeh, University of Lethbridge

Ganesh Vaidyanathan, University of Saskatchewan

Chris Watson, George Brown College

Semih Yildirim, York University

Ayse Yuce, Ryerson University

Marie Zukowski, Seneca College

I would especially like to thank the contributors who revised and updated the text's supplements: Alex Faseruk (test bank), Stephen Mullins (instructor's manual), and Khalil Torabzadeh (PowerPoint slides).

Finally, I would like to thank Wiley Canada's editorial team, including Darren Lalonde and especially Gail Brown for her tireless efforts in producing this new edition, as well as Laurel Hyatt, Ross Meacher, and Leanne Schultz for their combined copy editing and proofreading expertise.

W. Sean Cleary,
Queen's University
January 2009

UNDERSTANDING INVESTMENTS

Chapter 1 provides the foundation for the study of investments by analyzing what investing is all about. The critically important trade-off between expected return and risk is explained, and the major issues that every investor must deal with in making investment decisions are analyzed. An organizational structure for the entire text is provided.

Learning Objectives

After reading this chapter, you should be able to

1. Define investment and discuss what it means to study investments.
2. Explain why risk and return are the two critical components of all investing decisions.
3. Outline the two-step investment decision process.
4. Discuss key factors that affect the investment decision process.

CHAPTER PREVIEW

This chapter lays the foundation for the study of investments. You will learn what an investment is and why it is important to study the investment process. We introduce the concept of a trade-off between expected return and risk—the basis for all investment decisions—and outline the two-step investment decision process of security analysis and portfolio management. Finally, we discuss some of the key factors that affect the investment decision process such as global markets and institutional investors.

THE PURPOSE OF THIS TEXTBOOK

The objective of this text is to help you understand the investments field as it is currently understood, discussed, and practised so that you can make sound investment decisions that will enhance your economic welfare. Key concepts are presented to provide an appreciation of the theory and practice of investments. After reading this text, you will be able to intelligently answer questions such as the following:

- The S&P/TSX Composite Index, which is the major Canadian stock index measuring stock performance on the Toronto Stock Exchange (TSX), fell 604.99 points (or 4.75 percent) on January 21, 2008, which combined with previous losses that week to produce an 11.4 percent decline for the TSX for that week's trading. The next day (January 22, 2008), the Index increased 509 points (or 4.2 percent). What causes this type of extreme volatility? With volatility such as this, should investors avoid common stocks altogether, particularly for retirement plans?

- The average return on Canadian equity mutual funds was 15.0 percent for the five-year period ending December 31, 2007.[1] This is below the 18.4 percent return achieved over this period by the S&P/TSX Total Return Index. Why is this?

- In 2007, the average returns earned on Canadian Emerging Market and Global Equity mutual funds were 18.9 percent and –3.2 percent respectively, while the average return for Canadian equity funds was 5.5 percent. Should Canadian investors be participating in developed and/or emerging global equity markets? If so, what investment options are available to them and how much wealth should they allocate to such investments?

- Is it possible to have earned 30 percent or more investing in low-risk Treasury bills in a single year?

- In January of 2008, the French bank Société Générale announced losses of €4.9 billion, or $7.14 billion (US), resulting from the fraudulent actions of a single futures trader who implemented a series of unauthorized trades that spiraled out of control. Given that such potential losses can be caused by futures trading, how is it that investors use these instruments to actually reduce or control risk?

- What is the historical average annual rate of return on common stocks and what can an investor reasonably expect to earn from stocks in the future?

Both descriptive and quantitative materials on investing are readily available in a variety of forms. Some of this material is very enlightening, much of it is entertaining but debatable because of the many controversies in investments, and some of it is simply worthless. This text seeks to cover what is particularly useful and relevant for today's investment climate. It offers some ideas about what you can reasonably expect to accomplish by using what you learn and therefore what you can realistically expect to achieve as an investor in today's investment world. Many investors have unrealistic expectations, which ultimately lead to disappointment or worse.

Learning to avoid the many pitfalls awaiting you as an investor by clearly understanding what you can reasonably expect from investing your money may be the single most important benefit to

---

[1] www.globefund.com, May 12, 2008.

be derived from this text. For example, would you entrust your money to someone offering 36 percent annual return on riskless US government Treasury securities? Some 600 investors did and lost approximately $10 million to a former Sunday school teacher. Intelligent investors learn to say no and to avoid many of the mistakes that can thus be prevented.

THE NATURE OF INVESTMENTS

Some Definitions

The term investing can cover a wide range of activities. It often refers to putting money in GICs, bonds, common stocks, or mutual funds. More knowledgeable investors would include other paper assets, such as income trusts, warrants, puts and calls, futures contracts, and convertible securities, as well as tangible assets, such as gold, real estate, and collectibles. Investing can range from very conservative to aggressive speculation. Whether you are a university graduate starting out in the workplace or a senior citizen concerned with how to get by in retirement, investing decisions will be very important to you.

An **investment** can be defined as the commitment of funds to one or more assets that will be held over some future time period. The field of **investments**, therefore, involves the study of the investment process. The study of investments is concerned with the management of an investor's wealth, which is the sum of current income and the present value of all future income. (This is why present value and compound interest concepts have an important role in the investment process.) Although the field of investments encompasses many aspects, it can be thought of in terms of two primary functions: analysis and management.

In this text, the term investments refers in general to **financial assets** and in particular to marketable securities. Financial assets are paper (or electronic) claims on some issuer such as the federal or provincial government or a corporation; on the other hand, **real assets** are tangible physical assets such as precious metals (gold, silver), gems (diamonds), art, and real estate. **Marketable securities** are financial assets that are easily and cheaply traded in organized markets. Technically, investments include both financial and real assets, and both marketable and non-marketable assets. Because of the vast scope of investment opportunities available to investors, our primary emphasis is on marketable securities; however, the basic principles and techniques discussed in this text are applicable to real assets as well.

Even when we limit our discussion primarily to financial assets, it is difficult to keep up with the proliferation of new products. One such product that was relatively unimportant a few years ago is exchange-traded funds (ETFs) (discussed in Chapter 3). Real-World Returns 1-1 refers to the recent growth of ETFs.

Investing as Part of Personal Financial Planning

The investment of funds in various assets is only part of the overall financial decision making and planning that most individuals must do. Before investing, each individual should develop a financial plan that should include the decision on whether to purchase a house, a major investment for most individuals. In addition, decisions must be made about insurance of various types—life, health, disability, and protection of business and property. Finally, the plan should provide for emergency reserve funds.[2]

This text assumes that investors have established their overall financial plan and are now interested in managing and enhancing their wealth by investing in an optimal combination of financial assets. The idea of an "optimal combination" is important because our wealth, which we hold in the form of various assets, should be evaluated and managed as a unified whole. Wealth should be evaluated and managed within the context of a **portfolio**, which is made up of the asset holdings of an investor.

Investment
The commitment of funds to one or more assets that will be held over some future time period.

Investments
The study of the investment process.

Financial Assets
Paper or electronic claims on some issuer such as the federal or provincial government or a corporation.

Real Assets
Physical assets, such as gold or real estate.

Marketable Securities
Financial assets that are easily and cheaply traded in organized markets.

Portfolio
The securities held by an investor taken as a unit.

[2]Personal finance decisions of this type are discussed in personal finance texts.

REAL-WORLD RETURNS 1-1

When It Comes to Paying Fund Fees, the Price Is Right with ETFs

One of the first things I ever read about exchange-traded funds was a *Wall Street Journal* piece that described them as being 2007's "It" investment. Now that's a characterization you've got to love—the investing equivalent of fashion "must-haves" like Louboutin heels or spring's bright florals and trench coats.

The problem, though, is that no one really expects to be wearing those flirty florals or bright orange trench coats in five years' time. You want more from your investments than fads: You want the equivalent of a classic tailored suit or winter coat, something that will be in your wardrobe for decades. Like Louboutins, though, once in a while a fad becomes a trend with staying power.

Last weekend, I had a chance to poll more than 10 of my friends and not one of them knew what exchange-traded funds, or ETFs, are. For the uninitiated, ETFs are like mutual funds that trade like a stock. But they are different from mutual funds in that they are baskets of stocks or bonds put together to mirror indexes, such like, say, the S&P/TSX composite index. There is no portfolio manager actively buying and selling the stocks. In theory, if the S&P/TSX composite rises 10 percent in a year, so should your TSX ETF.

In the last few years, the number of ETFs in Canada and particularly the US has skyrocketed to about 700. They have moved from covering the large indexes to zeroing in on the smallest of niches. It's fun to see how small a niche can be: For example, in the US, you can buy ETFs that track the health care sector, but you can also narrow that down further to funds that focus on just cardiology or dermatology. But that explosion in the number of ETFs, particularly in niche funds, concerns Heather Pelant, the head of business development for Barclays Global Investors in Canada. Her company runs many of the most widely traded ETFs in Canada. She worries that the investor who is looking at ETFs for the first time may be put off by all the "noise and confusion."

Ms. Pelant admits that the average investor still doesn't know much about ETFs, but predicts that will change over the next five years, probably at the expense of mutual funds. "Our belief is that this is just a better investment tool."

There is a lot to like about ETFs, the major selling point being lower fees. While the typical mutual fund has a management-expense ratio of 2.6 percent and the average money market fund, more than 1 percent, ETFs have ratios generally below one-half of 1 percent. Just how much can fees cost you? Take this example published in this paper last month: A $1,000 investment in mutual funds with an annual return of 8 percent over 20 years would produce a profit of $3,661 without fees—but only $1,807 after a typical 2.6-percent management-expense ratio.

ETFs have lower fees because management of their funds is passive, although it certainly isn't without risk. Take, for instance, a fund that aims to replicate the S&P/TSX composite. The basket wouldn't contain the exact same stocks, but a mixture of stocks or futures contracts that when put together try to achieve the same results as the index.

According to a study by Morgan Stanley reported this week in the *Wall Street Journal*, which looked at 330 ETFs south of the border, funds that tracked broad US stock market indexes last year on average delivered returns that were 0.32 of a percentage point less than those of the indexes after fees.

But, especially in niche funds, there were some whopping misfires—Vanguard Telecommunication Services ETF returned 5.5 percent, compared with the benchmark's 10.5 percent, a difference of five percentage points.

Which means, like all stock market-related investments, there's no such thing as a sure thing. The other thing to consider about ETFs is that even when they do replicate indexes, most people want their funds to do better. Everybody wants to beat the market, but maybe that's a fool's game.

To that point, Barclays' Ms. Pelant cites the Standard & Poor's Indices Versus Active Funds Scorecard, which was released last week. It found that in the five-year period ending in 2007, only 8.4 percent of actively managed Canadian equity mutual funds have outperformed the S&P/TSX composite index. In other words, just meeting the index was doing better than 90 percent of equity funds over the five-year period.

A disadvantage of ETFs is that because they are bought and sold on exchanges, you have to pay brokerage commissions. That makes it hard for the many people who set aside small amounts each month—say $200 a month—for their mutual funds. It just wouldn't make sense to buy ETFs in such small quantities.

For now, Ms. Pelant says that ETFs are only 2 percent of the total fund market, but growing at twice the pace of mutual funds. My feeling is that the numbers will continue to climb. It may be because RRSP season has just recently passed, but I've been hearing a lot of grumbling lately from friends who worry about low returns and high fees with their mutual funds.

I can't help but think that when they come to know ETFs, the low fees will be a huge lure. Whether they'll be excited by a dermatology fund is a whole other issue.

Source: Rasbach, Noreen, "When it comes to paying fund fees, the price is right with ETFs," *The Globe and Mail*, March 8, 2008, CTVglobemedia Publishing, Inc. All Rights Reserved.

Why Do We Invest?

Although everyone would agree that we invest to make money, we need to be more precise. We invest to improve our welfare, which for our purposes can be defined as monetary wealth, both current and future. Funds to be invested come from assets already owned, such as savings or inheritances, borrowed money, or "foregone consumption." By foregoing consumption today and investing the savings, investors expect to enhance their future consumption possibilities by increasing their wealth.

Investors also seek to manage their wealth effectively, obtaining the most from it while protecting it from inflation, taxes, and other factors. There are three primary investment objectives:

1. Safety

2. Income

3. Growth of capital.

These objectives are mutually exclusive to some extent in the sense that a single security cannot maximize two or more of these primary objectives. In other words, trade-offs exist, so if you wish to maximize safety, you have to be willing to make some sacrifices with respect to income and growth potential.

Secondary investment objectives include liquidity or marketability and tax minimization. They are considered secondary in the sense that investors should not allow them to dominate primary investment considerations. For example, it would be imprudent to alter an investment portfolio designed to maximize safety, simply to avoid taxes. On the other hand, it makes good sense to devise and follow tax avoidance strategies within the context of any investment plan. The point is that they should not be the overriding factor determining investment decisions.

Investors face several constraints that will affect the objectives of their investment policy and determine how effectively these objectives can be attained. The most obvious factors are the level and stability of income and the level of financial obligations faced by an investor, both now and in the future. The individual's level of investment knowledge and general tolerance for risk should also play an important role in the design of an investment policy. Some investors will be constrained by legal, moral, and ethical considerations. In addition, miscellaneous factors such as illness or a pending divorce may become an overriding factor in the investment decision. These issues are discussed in detail in Chapter 21.

CHECK YOUR UNDERSTANDING

1-1. All financial assets are real assets, but only some marketable securities are real assets. Do you agree, or disagree? Explain.

1-2. What term is used to refer to all the securities held by an investor? Why is it important to think of asset holdings taken as a unit rather than individually?

1-3. Is tax minimization one of the three primary investment objectives? If not, should this factor ever be considered when making investment decisions?

THE IMPORTANCE OF STUDYING INVESTMENTS

The Personal Aspects

It is important to remember that all individuals have wealth of some kind; if nothing else, they have the value of their services in the marketplace. Most individuals must make investment decisions sometime in their lives. These include day-to-day decisions such as how to improve the return from savings accounts by investing funds in alternative financial instruments. In fact, the decision to enroll at a postsecondary educational institution represents a significant investment decision, since it requires a large sacrifice of your time and money. The future benefits are uncertain, although they include an increase in earnings potential; intangible benefits include the sense of accomplishment individuals feel as they learn and/or achieve academic success.

A good example of the critical importance of making good investment decisions is deciding how much to contribute to a Registered Retirement Savings Plan (RRSP) (discussed in Chapter 3), and what types of assets these should include. Working taxpayers can make tax-deductible contributions up to specified limits per year (depending on their income and their contributions to other registered plans). The earnings on the contributions are not taxed until they are withdrawn, as long as the assets are RRSP-eligible.

RRSP funds can be invested in a wide range of assets, from the very safe to the very speculative. Since these funds may be invested for long periods of time, good investment decisions are critical. Over many years, the differences in the investment returns earned can be staggering. Table 1-1 demonstrates how $4,000 invested every year for 40 years will grow to over $7 million if the funds earn 15 percent per year; they will grow to $1.78 million at 10 percent and $483,200 at 5 percent— quite a large variation in final wealth.

Table 1-1 also demonstrates the importance of investing early. This is obvious from the great difference in ending wealth values that accrue after 20 years, which are dramatically smaller than the corresponding 40-year values listed in the bottom row of that table.

With so much individual investor money flowing into mutual funds, and with individual investors owning a large percentage of all stocks outstanding, the study of investments is more important than ever. After being net sellers of stocks from 1968 through 1990, individual investors have swarmed into the financial markets. Individual investor interest in the stock market since 1990 is best expressed by the power of mutual funds (explained in Chapter 3), their favourite investment vehicle. Mutual funds, pension funds, and other institutional investors are now the driving forces in the marketplace, and over half of all trades on the TSX and on the NYSE are block trades by institutional investors. In fact, the total

Table 1-1 ━━

Possible Payoffs from Long-Term Investing

Amount Invested per Year	Number of Years	Final Wealth if Funds Are Invested at		
		5%	10%	15%
$4,000	20	$132,264	$229,100	$409,760
$4,000	30	$265,756	$657,960	$1,739,000
$4,000	40	$483,200	$1,770,360	$7,116,400

assets in mutual funds in Canada grew from $24.9 billion at the end of 1990, to $697.3 billion by December 31, 2007.[3]

In the final analysis, we study investments in the hope of earning better returns in relation to the risk we assume when we invest. A careful study of investment analysis and portfolio management principles can provide a sound framework for both managing and increasing wealth. Furthermore, this knowledge will allow you to sift through and properly evaluate the many articles on investing that appear daily in newspapers and magazines, which in turn will increase your chances of reaching your financial goals.

Many of the issues discussed regularly in the financial media and by average investors are covered in the text, and learning about them will make you a much smarter investor, including the following list of topics:

1. Financial assets available to investors

2. Total rate of return versus yield

3. Compounding effects and terminal wealth

4. Realized returns versus expected returns

5. Index funds and mutual fund expenses

6. How diversification works to reduce risk

7. The asset allocation decision

8. The significance of market efficiency to investors

Investments as a Profession

In addition to the above reasons for studying investments, the world of investments offers several rewarding careers, both professionally and financially. At the end of 2005 there were 201 firms in the securities industry in Canada employing more than 39,000 individuals.[4] This number is significant but it pales in comparison to the numbers employed by the big Canadian banks. For example, the **Royal Bank of Canada** alone employed over 60,000 people in 2005. A study of investments is an essential part of becoming a professional in these fields.

Investment professionals who arrange the sale of new securities and assist in mergers and acquisitions enjoyed phenomenal financial rewards in the booming 1980s and in the latter part of the 1990s. The total value of mergers in Canada reached an all-time high of $257 billion in 2006. Experienced merger and acquisition specialists can earn over a million dollars a year, and even someone with just a few years' experience can earn $200,000 to $400,000 in this area.

Top security traders and registered representatives (investment advisors) commonly earn six-figure salaries, which escalate during periods of strong market activity, such as that displayed during the mid-1990s until early 2001, and over the 2003 to mid-2007 period. Bond traders can also

---

[3]The Investment Funds Institute of Canada (IFIC) website: www.ific.ca.
[4]Investment Industry Regulatory Organization of Canada (IIROC) website: www.iiroc.com, formerly Investment Dealers Association of Canada (IDA).

commonly earn in the six-figure range, with the salaries increasing with experience. A relatively inexperienced bond salesperson selling to institutional investors can earn $200,000 or more and, if experienced, the figure rises to the $600,000 to $700,000 range.

Although less glamorous and less profitable for the firms involved, there are good paying jobs on Bay Street and Wall Street in research. Analysts with a few years of experience can earn well over $100,000, while those with 10 years or more of experience can earn up to $500,000. A range of financial institutions—including securities firms, banks, investment companies, and insurance companies—need the services of investment analysts. Securities firms need them to support their registered representatives who in turn serve the public, for example, by preparing the research reports provided to customers. They also need analysts to assist in the sale of new securities and in the valuation of firms as possible merger or acquisition candidates. Banks, insurance companies, and investment companies need analysts to evaluate securities for possible purchase or sale from their investment portfolios.

The firms mentioned above all need portfolio managers to manage the portfolios of securities handled by these organizations. Portfolio managers are responsible for making the actual portfolio buy and sell decisions—what to buy and sell, when to buy and sell, and so forth. Portfolio performance is calculated for these managers, and their jobs typically depend on their performance relative to other managed portfolios and to market averages.

Finally, the number of financial planners continues to grow. While most provinces do not regulate the term "financial planner," many planners pursue professional designations, including the Certified Financial Planner (CFP). The CFP designation has been sanctioned by the Financial Planners Standards Council (FPSC), which was formed in 1995 to develop a set of minimum standards for financial planners in terms of education, experience, and ethical and moral conduct. The FPSC establishes and enforces uniform professional standards for financial planners who choose to recognize the internationally recognized CFP™ designation. Today, there are nearly 17,000 CFP professionals in Canada and almost 100,000 in 19 countries around the world. CFP professionals work in every segment of the financial services industry. In addition, the FPSC strives to continue to develop and regulate standards that are relevant to the current financial planning needs of Canadians.

Individuals interested in careers in the investments field, rather than financial planning, should consider studying to become a **Chartered Financial Analyst** (CFA). This is a professional designation for people in the investments area, not unlike the CA, CMA, or CGA designations for accountants. The CFA designation is widely recognized in the investments industry. It serves as an indication that areas of knowledge relevant to investing have been studied and that high ethical and professional standards have been recognized and accepted. Details of the CFA program are included in Appendix 1A. Throughout this text we will use relevant parts of the CFA curriculum, procedures, and philosophy because it directly relates to a study of investments.

UNDERSTANDING THE INVESTMENT DECISION PROCESS

learning objective 2
Explain why risk and return are the two critical components of all investing decisions.

An organized view of the investment process involves analyzing the basic nature of investment decisions and organizing the activities in the decision process.

Common stocks have produced, on average, significantly larger returns over the years than savings accounts or bonds, but these higher returns mean larger risks. Underlying all investment decisions is the trade-off between expected return and risk. Therefore, we first consider these two basic parameters that are of critical importance to all investors and the trade-off that exists between expected return and risk.

Given the foundation for making investment decisions—the trade-off between expected return and risk—we next consider the decision process in investments as it is practised today. Although numerous separate decisions must be made, for organizational purposes this decision process has traditionally been divided into a two-step process: security analysis and portfolio management. Security analysis involves the valuation of securities, whereas portfolio management involves the management of an investor's investment selections as a portfolio (package of assets), with its own unique characteristics.

The Basis of Investment Decisions
Return

Stated in simplest terms, investors wish to earn a return on their money. Cash has an opportunity cost. By holding cash, you forego the opportunity to earn a return on that cash. Furthermore, in an inflationary environment, the purchasing power of cash diminishes, with high rates of inflation (such as that in 1980) bringing a rapid decline in purchasing power.

In investments it is critical to distinguish between an **expected return** (the anticipated return for some future period) and a **realized return** (the actual return over some past period). Investors invest for the future—for the returns they expect to earn—but when the investing period is over, they are left with their realized returns. What investors actually earn from their holdings may turn out to be more or less than what they expected when they first made the investment. This point is the essence of the investments process: investors must always consider the risk involved in investing.

Risk

Investors would like their returns to be as large as possible; however, this objective is subject to constraints, primarily risk. The Toronto Stock Exchange had a reasonably good year in 2007, with total returns for the S&P/TSX Composite Index of 9.8 percent. During the same period, the returns earned by professionally managed Canadian equity mutual funds varied from as low as –27.0 percent to as high as 35.1 percent.[5] This demonstrates the riskiness associated with marketable securities that offer variable rates of return. The investment decision, therefore, must always be considered in terms of both risk and return. The two are inseparable.

There are different types, and therefore different definitions, of risk. We define **risk** as the chance that the actual return on an investment will be different from its expected return.[6] Using the term risk in this manner, the nominal (current dollar) return on a long-term Government of Canada bond can be considered free of default risk, since it is virtually assured that the government will redeem these obligations as they mature. On the other hand, there is some risk, however small, that the Royal Bank or BCE will be unable to redeem an issue of long-term bonds when they mature. And there is a very substantial risk of not realizing the expected return on any particular common stock over some future holding period.

Do investors dislike risk? In economics in general, and investments in particular, the standard assumption is that investors are rational and prefer certainty to uncertainty. It is easy to say that investors dislike risk, but more precisely, we should say that investors are risk averse. A **risk-averse investor** is one who will not assume risk simply for its own sake and will not incur any given level of risk unless there is an expectation of adequate compensation for having done so. Note carefully that it is not irrational to assume risk, even very large risk, as long as we expect to be compensated for it. In fact, investors cannot reasonably expect to earn larger returns without assuming larger risks.

Investors deal with risk by choosing (implicitly or explicitly) the amount of risk they are willing to incur. Some investors choose high levels of risk with the expectation of high levels of return. Other investors are unwilling to assume much risk at all, and they should not expect to earn large returns.

We have said that investors would like to maximize their returns. Can we also say that investors, in general, will choose to minimize their risks? No! The reason is that there are costs to minimizing the risk—specifically a lower expected return. Taken to its logical conclusion, the minimization of risk would result in everyone holding risk-free assets such as savings accounts, CSBs,

Expected Return
The anticipated return by investors for some future period.

Realized Return
Actual return on an investment for some previous period of time.

Risk
The chance that the actual return on an investment will be different from the expected return.

Risk-Averse Investor
An investor who will not assume a given level of risk unless there is an expectation of adequate compensation for having done so.

[5]www.globefund.com, March 12, 2008.
[6]As we shall see in Chapter 7, expected return is a precise statistical term, not simply the return the investor expects. As indicated in our definition, risk involves chances or probabilities, which will also be discussed in Chapter 7 along with measures of the dispersion in the expected return.

and Treasury bills. Thus, we need to think in terms of the expected risk–return trade-off that results from the direct relationship between the risk and the expected return of an investment.

The Expected Return–Risk Trade-Off

Within the realm of financial assets, investors can achieve virtually any position on an expected risk–return spectrum such as that depicted in Figure 1-1. The line RF to B is the assumed trade-off between expected return and risk that exists for all investors interested in financial assets. This trade-off always slopes upward, because the vertical axis is expected return, and rational investors will not assume more risk unless they expect to be compensated for doing so. The expected return must be large enough to compensate for taking the additional risk.

Figure 1-1
The Expected Return–Risk
Trade-Off Available to
Investors

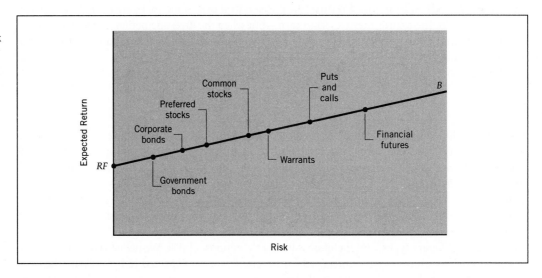

RF in Figure 1-1 is the return on a riskless asset such as Government of Canada T-bills. Since these assets have no risk, the expected return will equal (approximately) the realized return, which equals the current rate of return offered by these assets. This **risk-free rate of return**, which is available to all investors, will be designated as RF throughout the text. Using this as a starting point, we can say the following relationship will hold for expected returns on risky assets:

Risk-Free Rate of Return
The return on a riskless asset, often proxied by the rate of return on Treasury securities.

Expected return = Risk-free rate (RF) + Expected risk premium

This figure shows the relative positions for some of the financial assets that will be discussed in Chapter 2. As we move from riskless securities to more risky corporate bonds, equities, and so forth, we assume more risk in the expectation of earning a larger return. Common stocks are quite risky in relation to bonds, but they are not as risky as uncovered positions in options or futures contracts. (All of these terms are defined in Chapter 2.)

Obviously, we are using broad categories here. Within a particular category, such as common stocks, a wide range of expected return and risk opportunities exists at any time. The important point is that it is the trade-off between expected return and risk that should prevail in a rational environment. Investors unwilling to assume risk must be satisfied with the risk-free rate of return, RF. If they wish to try to earn a larger rate of return, they must be willing to assume a larger risk as represented by moving up the expected risk–return trade-off into the wide range of financial assets available to investors. Although all rational investors like returns and dislike risk, they are satisfied by quite different levels of expected return and risk. Put differently, investors have different limits on the amount of risk they are willing to assume and, therefore, the amount of return that can realistically be expected. In economic terms, the explanation for these differences in preferences is that rational investors strive to maximize their utility, the perception of which varies among investors.[7]

It is important to remember that the risk–return trade-off depicted in Figure 1-1 is *ex ante*, meaning "before the fact." That is, before the investment is actually made, the investor expects higher returns from assets that have a higher risk, and the expected risk premium is positive. This is the only sensible expectation for risk-averse investors, who are assumed to constitute the majority of all investors. *Ex post* (meaning "after the fact" or when it is known what has occurred), for a given period of time, such as a month or a year or even longer, the trade-off may turn out to be flat or even negative. For example, the 2002 return on Canadian stocks as measured by the S&P/TSX Composite Index was –12.4 percent, while the return on long-term Government of Canada bonds that year was 10.1 percent. This implies that the actual (*ex post*) returns on the riskier common stocks were well below the realized returns on the relatively safer bonds. Such is the nature of risky investments!

Structuring the Decision Process

Investors can choose from a wide range of securities in their attempt to maximize the expected returns from these opportunities. They face constraints, the most pervasive of which is risk. Traditionally, investors have analyzed and managed securities using a broad two-step process: security analysis and portfolio management.

learning objective 3
Outline the two-step investment decision process.

Security Analysis

The first part of the investment decision process involves the valuation and analysis of individual securities, which is referred to as **security analysis**. Institutional investors usually employ professional security analysts. Of course, there are also millions of amateur security analysts in the form of individual investors.

The valuation of securities is a time-consuming and difficult job. First of all, it is necessary to understand the characteristics of the various securities and the factors that affect them. Second, a valuation model must be applied to these securities to estimate their price or value. Value is a combination of the expected future returns on a security and the risk attached. Both of these parameters must be estimated and then brought together in a model.

For bonds, the valuation process is relatively straightforward because the returns are known and the risk can be approximated from currently available data. This does not mean, however, that all the problems of bond analysis are easily resolved. Interest rates are the primary factor affecting bond prices, and no one can consistently forecast changes in these rates.

The valuation process is much more difficult for common stocks than for bonds. The investor must take into account the overall economy, the industry, and the individual company. With common stocks, estimating the expected return and the risk is not easy, but despite the difficulties, investors serious about their portfolios must perform some type of analysis. Unless this is done, one has to rely on personal hunches, suggestions from friends, and recommendations from brokers—all of which may be dangerous to one's financial health.

Security Analysis
The first part of the investment decision process, involving the valuation and analysis of individual securities.

Portfolio Management

The second major component of the decision process is **portfolio management**. After securities have been evaluated, portfolio composition must be determined. The concepts associated with building a portfolio are well known and are discussed at some length in Chapters 7 to 10, and in Chapter 21.

Portfolio Management
The second step in the investment decision process, involving the management of a group of assets (i.e., a portfolio) as a unit.

---

[7]Utility theory is a complex subject; however, for our purposes we can equate maximization of utility with maximization of welfare. Because welfare is a function of present and future wealth, and wealth in turn is a function of current and future income discounted (reduced) for the amount of risk involved, in effect, investors maximize their welfare by optimizing the expected risk–return trade-off. In the final analysis, expected return and risk constitute the foundation of all investment decisions.

Having built a portfolio, the astute investor must consider how and when to revise it. This raises a number of important questions. Portfolios must be managed, regardless of whether an investor is active or passive. If the investor pursues an active strategy, the issue of market efficiency must be considered. If prices reflect information quickly and fully, investors should consider how this would affect their buy and sell decisions. Even if investors follow a passive strategy (which involves designing or purchasing a portfolio that mirrors the performance of some market benchmark), questions to be considered include taxes, transaction costs, maintenance of the desired risk level, and so on.

Finally, all investors are interested in how well their portfolio performs. This is the bottom line of the investment process, but measuring portfolio performance is an inexact procedure and needs to be carefully considered.

CHECK YOUR UNDERSTANDING

1-4. Historically, stocks have outperformed other asset classes such as bonds, on average. Should all intelligent investors own stocks?

1-5. Rational investors always attempt to minimize their risks. Do you agree or disagree?

1-6. Investors should always seek to maximize their returns from investing. Do you agree or disagree?

1-7. The valuation and analysis of individual securities is a difficult and time-consuming task. Does this activity represent the full scope of the investment decision process?

IMPORTANT CONSIDERATIONS IN THE INVESTMENT DECISION PROCESS

learning objective 4
Discuss key factors that affect the investment decision process.

Intelligent investors should recognize that the investment decision process described above can be lengthy and involved. Regardless of individual actions, certain factors in the investment environment affect everyone. Investors should be aware of these factors as they work through the investment decision process.

The Great Unknown

"You have to understand that being wrong is part of the process." This statement by Peter Bernstein, one of the world's most prominent investment experts, illustrates the paramount factor that all investors must come to grips with—uncertainty. Investors buy various financial assets, expecting to earn certain returns over some future holding period. These returns are only what can be expected; they may never be realized. The simple fact that dominates investing is that the realized return on a risky asset is likely to be different from what was expected—sometimes, quite different.

At best, estimates are imprecise; at worst, they are completely wrong. Some investors try to handle uncertainty by building elaborate quantitative models, and others simply keep it in the back of their mind. All investors, however, are affected by it, and the best they can do is make the most informed return and risk estimates they can, act on them, and be prepared for changing circumstances. Regardless of how careful and informed investors are, the future is uncertain, and mistakes will be made. This will always be true for everyone involved with financial markets and, in fact, for anyone at all, since life itself is uncertain. For example, many experts predicted the Canadian dollar would remain stable or increase slightly during 2007, yet by the end of that year the value of the dollar had increased dramatically by 17.6 percent from $0.8581 US to $1.0088 US.

Investors often use historical data to make their estimates and modify this to incorporate what they believe is most likely to happen. It is important to remember that basing investment decisions solely on the past may lead to serious errors. Just because stocks had a 10 percent average return over the last 10 years is no guarantee of the same return next year, or 10 years from now.

Anyone can tell you what you should have bought or sold in the past—it's a matter of record. For example, the **Altamira** Canadian Equity mutual fund produced a 20-year compound average return of 12.8 percent for the period ending December 31, 2007, well above the 10.0 percent average return for the **S&P/TSX Total Return Index** over the same period. That fund outperformed the TSX in 2007 (10.82 percent versus 9.8 percent), yet underperformed in both 2006 (15.6 percent versus 17.3 percent) and in 2005 (22.5 percent versus 24.1 percent). The point is that while the past provides important information, no one can guarantee you a successful portfolio for next year or any other specified period of time. Unanticipated events will affect financial markets. No one can consistently forecast what will happen with interest rates or in financial markets, including the professionals who are paid to make recommendations.

Although uncertainty is always present, all is not lost. It is often possible to make reasonable and informed judgments about the outcomes of many investment opportunities. Investment decisions are both an art and a science. To succeed, we must think in terms of what we expect to happen. We know what has happened, but the past may or may not repeat itself. Although the future is uncertain, investors can attempt to manage it intelligently by developing a thorough understanding of the basic principles of investing. In addition, new tools and techniques are constantly being developed that may help investors to make better decisions.

The Global Investments Arena

Now more than ever, investors must think of investments in a global context. Although foreign investments have been possible for a number of years, many investors have not bought and sold on an international basis. However, astute investors can no longer afford to limit themselves to domestic investment only.

An international perspective is becoming increasingly important to all investors as we find ourselves operating in a global marketplace of round-the-clock investing. Since the Canadian stock and bond markets comprise only about 2 percent of their respective world markets, Canadian investors who ignore these markets will be cutting themselves off from a large number of investment alternatives.

Foreign markets have grown rapidly, and several are now large by any measure. The Japanese market is well known, having reached very high levels followed by very low levels. Western European markets are well developed and offer investors numerous alternatives in what some observers feel will be the premier economic power of the future.

A hot investment concept in recent years is the potential rewards of investing in **emerging markets**.[8] Indeed, much of the strength in Canadian markets can be attributed to strong commodity prices, which have been driven to a large extent by the tremendous economic growth in China and India. During 2007, the returns for the Chinese stock market were 63.1 percent, those in India were 71.2 percent, while returns in Peru were 86.0 percent. Consistent with the volatile nature of emerging markets, from January 1 to March 11, 2008, the Chinese and Indian markets had declined 21.3 and 24.5 percent respectively, while the returns in Peru were positive 11.5 percent.

Emerging Markets
Markets of less developed countries characterized by high risks but potentially large returns.

The impact of the US economy for Canadian investors is apparent on a daily basis, as we routinely observe large swings in Canadian bond and stock price levels in response to announcements by the US Federal Reserve Board, or the release of other US economic statistics. Given that the United States accounts for well over 70 percent of Canadian exports and imports, it is not surprising that the returns on Canadian stock markets are tightly tied to those on US markets. Real-World Returns 1-2 demonstrates this relationship clearly, as fears of a US recession in January of 2008 triggered a stock market selloff in global stock markets, including Canada. Indeed, the turmoil in Canadian markets that began in the summer of 2007 and has persisted throughout much of 2008 can be mainly attributed to the subprime debt market crisis in the US, and the economic fallout resulting from this crisis.

---

[8]The World Bank classifies a stock market as "emerging" if its country's economy had less than $7,910 in US dollars per capita gross domestic product (GDP) in 1991.

REAL-WORLD RETURNS 1-2

US Recession Fears Spark Global Sell Off

The looming threat of a US recession that could infect the rest of the world dealt Canadian stocks their biggest one-day blow since 9/11 yesterday as share prices plunged from London to Frankfurt to Tokyo.

In Canada, markets that had been skidding for several days fell off a cliff, with the S&P/TSX composite index tumbling 605 points or 4.75 percent. In the past week, the index has shrunk by more than 1,500 points, or 11.4 percent. Energy and mining stocks, buoyed in recent months by high commodity prices, fell the furthest yesterday.

"The market is finally starting to wake up to some realities out there," said Murray Leith, director of research at investment adviser Odlum Brown Ltd. in Vancouver. "The rest of the world is not going to decouple from the United States," which is likely headed for recession, he said.

"To think that the United States and the developed world can have a slowdown and it will not have any impact on emerging markets is really ridiculous," he said. "A big part of this correction is the world waking up to that reality."

Many analysts suggested that one reason for the worldwide decline is a feeling that the US stimulus package unveiled by President George W. Bush and Federal Reserve chief Ben Bernanke last week is insufficient.

But more action is coming. The Bank of Canada is almost certain to lower interest rates today to bolster the economy.

And the Federal Reserve Board in the United States is expected to lower its key interest rate when it makes its next setting on Jan. 30. It's now under pressure to make the move even earlier.

All this happened while US markets were closed for the Martin Luther King Day holiday. This morning, all eyes will be on Wall Street to see how the biggest and most important market reacts to what took place outside the US borders.

Trading in stock futures, which change hands when the market is closed, suggests the US markets could see losses today that will be larger than yesterday's, and the global rout was continuing last night when markets opened sharply down in Asia.

Among the hardest hit Canadian stocks was BCE Inc. It has come under increasing pressure since rumours emerged that the takeover by a group led by the Ontario Teachers' Pension Plan could get scuttled. At yesterday's close of $34.42, BCE stock is 19 percent below the takeover price of $42.75 a share.

Source: Excerpted from Blackwell, Richard, "The market is finally starting to wake up to some realities," *The Globe and Mail*, January 22, 2008, page A1.

In addition to the US, the performance of Canadian investment assets is also greatly affected by global economic activity outside North America, as alluded to above with respect to the growth in the economies in China and India, and the resulting impact on world commodity prices. In addition, we routinely observe large volatility in domestic markets being caused by international events such as concerns over the ability of Russia to meet its external debt payments in 1998 or the war in Iraq that began in 2003.

There are several reasons why global events have such a significant impact on Canadian investors. One is the very nature of Canada's economy, which consists of a relatively large proportion of commodity-based industries such as oil, mining, and forestry. Since the price of these commodities is determined in the global marketplace, our economy is greatly influenced by global supply and demand. In addition, many Canadian firms (even those that are not commodity-based) derive a large proportion of their revenues from abroad. As a result, adverse movements in foreign exchange rates can have unhappy consequences for Canadian multinational companies whose foreign currency profits are translated into fewer Canadian dollars. On the other hand, many Canadian companies benefit from a decline in the value of the dollar because their products become relatively less expensive in foreign markets, which increases demand for their products abroad.

Another important reason for Canadian investors to think in a global context is that the rates of return available in foreign securities are often higher than those available from Canadian markets. Finally, the addition of foreign securities allows investors to achieve beneficial risk reduction, since many foreign markets move differently from Canada's. For example, when Canadian stocks are doing poorly, some foreign stocks may be doing well, which would help offset the poor domestic performance. This risk reduction is a result of diversification. The simple point is that if domestic diversification in a portfolio reduces risk (as discussed in Chapter 7), which it clearly does, foreign diversification should provide even greater risk reduction—and it does! Given the increased attention paid to international investing, it is not surprising that many studies of international equity have found that global portfolio diversification does not contribute to performance as much as it did in the past; however, it still offers substantial benefits.

Thus, we should consider foreign markets as well as the domestic financial environment. We will do so throughout this text as an integral part of the discussion rather than in a separate chapter, because although the details may vary, the principles of investing are applicable to financial assets and markets wherever they exist.

The New Economy Versus the Old Economy

Investors must now cope with a changed investing environment. In the past there was one large market of securities, ranging from the tiny company to the giant company, from very shaky companies to the very successful companies, from the purely domestic company to the multinational firms. These days, investors talk about Old Economy stocks and New Economy stocks, and the same rules and analysis procedures may not apply to both.

Old Economy stocks refer to the traditional "smokestack" companies and the traditional service, consumer, and financial companies. Examples include Molson, Magna International Inc., Procter & Gamble, Imperial Oil Limited, and McDonald's Corporation. They produce and sell goods and services, show a profit, and reward their stockholders fairly consistently. These companies may be successful and have a lengthy history, but they are not considered exciting. The New Economy stocks such as Research In Motion (RIM), Nortel Networks, 724 Solutions, Cisco Systems Inc., and AOL have a heavy focus on technology. The New Economy includes many stocks that had meteoric rises and very dramatic declines, resulting in the Internet bubble of the late 1990s and subsequent burst in the early 2000s. We use the graph of the stock price of Nortel to summarize this phenomenon, as shown in Figure 1-2.

Nortel used to be a simple, telecommunications manufacturer controlled by BCE Inc. However, in the Internet mania of the late 1990s, investor interest shifted to companies making the equipment for the backbone of the Internet. Two Canadian companies, Nortel and JDS Uniphase, attracted a huge amount of interest. As can be seen from the graph that follows, Nortel's stock price jumped from the $20 to $40 range to peak at over $170, before collapsing to the penny stock range. The prices of JDS and other IT companies followed similar patterns over this time frame. At one point, Nortel and JDS combined to make up over one-third of the market value of the S&P/TSX Composite Index, and they dragged it up along with them when they soared, and dragged it back down again when they crashed.

What does this mean to investors? It illustrates that the world in general and the investing world in particular is changing faster than ever today. Investors often have to change their views and sometimes their procedures. Many of the new e-commerce companies have no earnings or cash flows, and

Figure 1-2
Nortel Stock Price
(1987–2005)

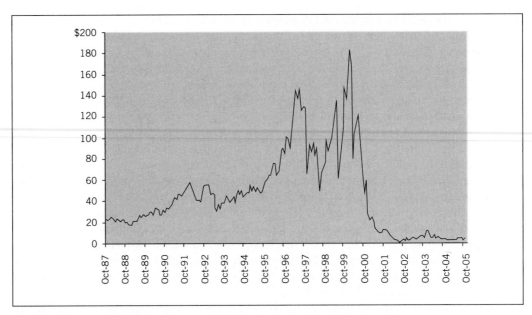

therefore traditional valuation approaches do not work very well, if at all. At one point, investors paid $500 per share for Amazon, a company with no profits, while eBay has sold for a P/E ratio in the thousands. This is a brave new world and one that investors must consider. After all, if they simply ignore the new technologies and trends, they will miss opportunities to acquire stocks in companies such as RIM, Cisco Systems Inc., Dell Inc., Microsoft Corporation, and Intel Corporation—all of which have rewarded their shareholders tremendously in the past.

As discussed above, during the 2001–2002 period, technology stocks in general suffered dramatic declines in value and the markets were significantly off from their previous highs. However, many technology stocks made solid recoveries during 2003. This illustrates that learning about rational investment principles that have held up over long periods of time is important. Ultimately, investors return to basic valuation principles, such as those discussed in this text.

The Role of the Internet

Any discussion of the investment decision process must focus on the role of the Internet, which has significantly changed the investments environment. Investors can access a wealth of information about investing, trade cheaply and quickly in their brokerage accounts, obtain real-time quotes throughout the day, and monitor their portfolios.

This is a true revolution. The Internet has democratized the flow of investment information. Any investor—whether at home, at work, or on vacation—can download an incredible amount of information, communicate with other investors, do security analysis, manage portfolios, check company filings with government agencies, and carry out numerous other activities not thought possible for a small investor only a few years ago. Although some of these information sources and/or services carry a fee, most are free.

Institutional Investors
Pension funds, investment companies, bank trust departments, life insurance companies, and so forth that manage huge portfolios of securities.

Institutional Investors

There are two broad categories of investors: individual and **institutional investors**. The latter group, consisting of banks, pension funds, investment companies, insurance companies, and so forth, includes professional money managers who are frequently publicized in the popular press. The amount of money managed by these institutions is staggering. For example, by October of 2007, **IGM Financial** (Investors, MacKenzie Financial) managed total net assets of $111 billion, while

RBC Asset Management Inc., a subsidiary of the Royal Bank Financial Group, managed total net assets exceeding $81 billion. At this time, IGM offered investors over 380 funds to choose from, while RBC offered over 80 funds.

The amount of assets managed by institutional investors has continued to escalate in both Canada and the United States. In addition to the rapid growth in mutual fund assets in Canada in recent years (to $697 billion by December 31, 2007), banks, pension funds, and life insurance companies are important participants in Canadian (and international) financial markets. These institutional investors do not constitute a monolithic bloc of investors, but are composed of thousands of different organizations, most of which have multiple money managers.

The first issue to note about institutional investors is that their relative importance has changed. Mutual funds became the primary buying force in North American stock markets in the 1990s, due to the large growth in popularity of these investment vehicles. The role of pension funds has also changed significantly in both Canada and the United States in recent years. Canadian pension funds have historically invested very conservatively, primarily in fixed income securities such as bonds and money market instruments. However, in recent years, they have become more aggressive and have become more important players in Canadian and foreign equity and derivative security markets. Real-World Returns 1-3 alludes to the changes in Canadian pension plan activity, and the Canada Pension Plan (CPP) in particular, over the last two decades.

REAL-WORLD RETURNS 1-3

The Changing Face of Pension Plans

What do Canadians have in common with New Zealand air travelers? More than one might expect, as a result of this week's $1.3 billion (Canadian) offer by the Canada Pension Plan Investment Board (CPPIB) to purchase New Zealand's largest airport (Auckland).

Should we be concerned about such an announcement? After all, isn't this a risky place to invest our hard earned dollars that we have contributed to the CPP?

Indeed, such an announcement would have been unheard of 20 years ago when Canadian pension fund assets were comprised almost entirely of high quality fixed income securities (mainly government bonds). In fact, the CPP's assets in particular, were entirely comprised of said fixed income securities as recently as 1999. However, in today's investing environment, announcements such as the one above are far from extraordinary.

So what has changed? It turns out that it all has to do with a change in the regulations guiding pension fund management. In particular, fund managers are bound to a duty of care to the plan beneficiaries, which was historically guided by something referred to as the ***prudent man rule***. This rule required that they determine whether a prospective investment would be considered prudent based on its own individual merits, in isolation from the existing investments held by the fund.

This rule effectively prohibited pension funds from holding common stock, real estate, etc. As a result, pension fund assets were entirely invested in low-risk, low-return investments, thus restricting their return potential. In response to this important shortcoming, the current version of the ***prudent investor rule*** has been adopted in various provincial jurisdictions since 1990, and was officially incorporated into the Uniform Trustee Investment Act of 1997.

The new rule is based upon the basic tenets of modern portfolio theory (MPT), which asserts that that the risk of a well diversified portfolio is determined by the interaction of individual assets in that portfolio, and is therefore distinct from the risk of any one particular investment. Therefore many investments that might be viewed as high risk in isolation may in fact be suitable for inclusion in a given portfolio. Indeed, the rule specifically stipulates that it

(continued)

REAL-WORLD RETURNS 1-3 *continued*

is the duty of fund managers to adequately *diversify* the fund's assets. These ideas are not new by any stretch of the imagination, having originated in the 1950s. Why it took so long to put them into practice is anybody's guess...

So what have been the results of these changes? As of June 2007, the $120.5 billion in CPP assets were comprised of approximately 58 percent public equities, 7 percent private equities, 10 percent in inflation sensitive assets (such as real estate and commodities), and only 25 percent in bonds—quite a change indeed. In fact, the CPP was one of the last Canadian pension plans that was able to adapt to changing rules. Others including the Ontario Teachers Pension Plan ($106 billion in assets as of December 31, 2006) and La Caisse de Depot in Quebec ($143.5 billion in assets as of December 31, 2006) have been well diversified across the various asset classes and have been major "players" in domestic and global equity markets since the early 1990s.

How has this worked out so far? Over the four year-period ending March 31, 2007, the CPP provided an average annual return of 13.6 percent, and the plan assets more than doubled from $55.6 billion to $116.6 billion. Over $37 billion of this growth can be attributed to investment returns, with the rest being attributed to contributions. By comparison, long-term Canada bonds provided an average annual return of approximately 9.1 pecent over this period, which would have caused the plan assets to grow by about $23 billion. So we can say that over this brief period of time, the change in policy contributed an additional $14 billion (approximately) or more to the fund.

The new asset mix may not always perform better than holding all bonds, especially over short or even intermediate horizons. However, in the long run, there is no doubt that adding equities and other potential investments to a portfolio will enhance the expected returns. For example, since 1938, bonds have provided an average annual return of approximately 6 percent, versus 11 percent on equities.

While there have been several other factors at work, there is no doubt that the manner in which the plan's assets are now being managed is an important reason why the general consensus today is that Canadians can count on CPP payments when they retire. We may take this for granted, but as little as 10 or 15 years ago many financial planners were advising their clients to plan for retirement based on the premise that they would not receive any CPP payments. And perhaps we should not judge each investment decision until we know the whole picture.

Source: Cleary, Sean, CFA and MacKinnon, Greg, CFA, "The changing face of pension plans," *Halifax Daily News*, November 10, 2007.

The second issue to note about institutional investors is their dual relationship to individual investors. On the one hand, individuals are the indirect beneficiaries of institutional investor actions, because they own or benefit from these institutions' portfolios. On a daily basis, however, they are competing with these institutions in the sense that both are managing portfolios of securities and attempting to do well financially. Both groups are trying to make intelligent trading decisions about securities. Can individual investors hope to compete fairly with institutions, and how do these large portfolios affect the individual investor's decision process?

Institutional investors are indeed the professional investors, with vast resources at their command. They generally pay lower commission fees on security transactions than those paid by retail investors. In addition, there is evidence to suggest that some companies disclose important information selectively to some institutional investors. According to a survey by the National Investor Relations Institute (an association for investor-relations professionals), perhaps one-third of public companies disclose sensitive information concerning their stock that may put individual investors at a disadvantage.

Another advantage that institutional investors have is that they can trade in the "aftermarket" (negotiated trades conducted electronically among institutions) following exchange closings. (The

TSX closes at 4 p.m. Eastern Time.) By the time a stock opens the next morning, the price may have adjusted significantly.

Does the average investor, then, have a reasonable chance in the market? Yes, in the sense that he or she can generally expect to earn a fair return for the risk taken. On average, the individual investor may do just as well as the big institutional investors, because markets are usually quite efficient and securities fairly priced.

Some individual investors do even better than professionals due to superior skill, insight, or luck. Furthermore, some opportunities can more easily be exploited by individual investors, who have greater flexibility in adjusting their portfolio composition, than by institutional investors.

The question of how well individual investors do relative to institutional investors raises the issue of market efficiency, which we consider next. All intelligent investors who seek to do well when investing must ultimately come to grips with the issue of market efficiency.

The Issue of Market Efficiency

One of the most profound ideas affecting the investment decision process, and indeed all of finance, is the idea that the securities markets, particularly the equity markets, are efficient. In an efficient market, the prices of securities do not depart for any length of time from the justified economic values that investors calculate for them. Economic values for securities are determined by investor expectations about earnings, risks, and so on, as investors grapple with the uncertain future. If the market price of a security does differ from its estimated economic value, investors act to bring the two values together. Thus, as new information arrives in an efficient marketplace, causing a revision in the estimated economic value of a security, its price adjusts to this information quickly and, on balance, correctly. In other words, securities are efficiently priced on a continuous basis. We discuss the full implications of this statement in Chapter 10.

Efficient Market Hypothesis (EMH)
The proposition that securities markets are efficient, with the prices of securities reflecting their economic value.

Obviously, the possibility that the stock market is efficient has significant implications for investors. In fact, one's knowledge of and belief in this idea, known as the **Efficient Market Hypothesis (EMH)**, will directly affect how one views the investment process and makes investment decisions. Those who are strong believers in the EMH may adopt, to varying degrees, a passive investment strategy, because of the likelihood that they will not be able to find underpriced securities. These investors will seek to minimize transaction costs and taxes, as well as the time and resources devoted to analyzing securities, which, if the EMH is correct, should be correctly priced to begin with.

Investors who do not accept the EMH, or have serious doubts, pursue active investment strategies, believing they can identify mispriced securities and/or lags that exist in the market's adjustment of securities' prices to new information. These investors generate more search costs (both in time and money) and more transaction costs but believe the marginal benefits outweigh the marginal costs incurred.

Corporate Governance

The issue of corporate governance has garnered a tremendous amount of attention in recent years in light of such financial debacles as Enron and WorldCom, and more recently Nortel in Canada. Some of the main issues that have been brought to "centre stage" as a result of these and similar abuses of the financial system include:

- The accountability of the Board of Directors and Management

- A re-examination of accounting and auditing practices

- Management compensation arrangements such as executive stock option plans, which are designed to align the interests of management and shareholders

INVESTING

An efficient market does not have to be perfectly efficient to have a profound impact on investors. All that is required is that the market be economically efficient. That is, after acting on information to trade securities and subtracting all costs (transaction costs and taxes, to name two), the investor would have been as well off with a simple buy-and-hold strategy. If the market is economically efficient, securities could depart somewhat from their true economic values, but it would not pay investors to take advantage of these small discrepancies.

- Disclosure requirements

- The effectiveness of existing regulatory bodies

Many changes have already been put in place on a number of these fronts including many regulatory changes, the imposition of stricter auditing standards, and increased accountability for top executives and company directors. More changes are still in the works. Real-World Returns 1-4 discusses the Sarbanes-Oxley (SOX) Act of 2002 that was implemented in the US in response to a complete collapse in public confidence as a result of the Enron and WorldCom fallout.

As the key provisions of SOX indicate, the main targets are the company and its auditors. There was significant belief that Enron's auditor, Arthur Andersen, was too tight with Enron, as many former Andersen people worked with Enron and the local auditors overruled head office in several key areas. In the future, the company's auditor has to be rotated every five years to ensure their objectivity. Further,

REAL-WORLD RETURNS 1-4

Sarbanes-Oxley Act of 2002

The Sarbanes-Oxley Act is a piece of legislation that combines Bills written by Senators **Paul Sarbanes** (D-MD) and **Michael G. Oxley** (R-OH) that addressed corporate auditing accountability and reporting practices. Simply put, it comprises regulations intended to control financial abuses at large public companies. The law now requires that companies boost their accounting oversight and adopt strict internal controls.

The full text of the **Sarbanes-Oxley Act** is lengthy. A few quick focal points are:

- Section 101 – Establishment of the Public Accounting Oversight Board (PCAOB) and Board Membership
- Section 102(a) – Public Accounting Firm Mandatory Registration
- Section 107 – SEC has authority over the PCAOB
- Section 201 – Services Outside The Scope Of Practice Of Auditors; Prohibited Activities
- Section 301 – "Whistleblower" procedure
- Section 402(a) – Prohibition on Personal Loans to Executives
- Section 404 – Internal controls
- Section 409 – Real-time disclosure
- Section 807 – Criminal penalties for defrauding shareholders of publicly traded companies
- Section 1350 – Failure of corporate officers to certify financial reports

Sarbanes-Oxley has passed into the vernacular as Sarbox or SOX, and has come to the forefront of many CEO and CFO task lists. Besides the beneficial, protective effects of SOX, the Act's certification requirements have also had other less-predicted effects. For example, CFOs may be reluctant to join a company and be prepared to certify its past financial statements, being criminally liable for any inaccuracies. Some smaller companies have considered returning the business to private operations to avoid the cost of SOX compliance. Adhering to SOX rules can be time-consuming and expensive, many times without a clear return on investment. The Act itself does not include best practices for complying with its rules. Internal guidelines must be set by the company.

Source: www.fiercesarbox.com/topics/sarbanesoxleyact, March 12, 2008.

the non-auditing functions of the major accounting firms were separated from their audit functions, since many felt the accounting firms were in a severe conflict of interest. This was because many felt the accounting firms were treating auditing as a "loss leader" to get consulting contracts. Consequently, they were not sufficiently objective in their audit responsibilities. This judgment is confirmed by the fact that the US government set up an oversight body to regulate audit firms and take direct control of many accounting areas.

For US companies, the major change is the requirement of stronger internal controls. One of the failures at Enron was apparently a weak audit committee that did not exercise proper oversight of the company's financial statements. In the future, the audit committee has to be composed of independent and unrelated members of the board of directors (BOD) with the power to engage external consultants and to have the external auditors report to them. Further, management has to report on and the auditor comment on the firm's internal controls with the CEO and CFO certifying the statements as fair.

SOX has had a major impact in the US in improving the public confidence in the objectivity of the financial statements of US companies. It also affects a significant number of Canadian companies (especially the large ones) that issue securities in the US and have to comply with US securities laws. Indeed, while accounting scandals in Canada have been fewer in number, and of a smaller scale than those in the US, concerns over such misrepresentations and their impact on our business environment have dictated that Canadian regulatory authorities maintain strict controls over the auditing process, similar to those employed in the US.

CHECK YOUR UNDERSTANDING

1-8. Individual investors make investing decisions under conditions of uncertainty, while professional investors make such decisions under conditions of controlled risk taking, thereby eliminating the uncertainty. Do you agree or disagree? Explain your reasoning.

1-9. Canadian investors should hold foreign securities primarily because they offer higher expected returns than domestic securities. Do you agree with this statement?

SUMMARY

This summary relates to the learning objectives for this chapter.

1. **Define investment and discuss what it means to study investments.**
   An investment is the commitment of funds to one or more assets that will be held over some future time period. The field of investments involves the study of the investment process and is concerned with the management of an investor's wealth. We study investments for both personal and professional reasons.

2. **Explain why risk and return are the two critical components of all investing decisions.**
   Risk is defined as the chance that what you expect to gain from an investment will differ from its actual return. The basis of all investment decisions is the trade-off between expected return and risk. Expected return and risk are directly related; the greater the risk, the greater the expected return, and the smaller the risk the smaller the expected return. Rational investors are risk averse, meaning they are unwilling to assume risk unless they expect to be adequately compensated.

3. **Outline the two-step investment decision process.**
   The investment decision process is generally divided into two categories: securities analysis and portfolio management. Security analysis involves the valuation and analysis of individual securities. Portfolio management involves building a portfolio of individual securities after they have been evaluated and maintaining that portfolio.

4. Discuss key factors that affect the investment decision process.
Major factors affecting the investment decision process include uncertainty, the global nature of investing, the role played by institutional investors, and the efficiency of markets. Investors should consider these factors carefully as they evaluate information and claims and make decisions.

KEY TERMS

Canadian Securities Course™ (CSC) (Appendix 1B), p.23
Chartered Financial Analyst® (CFA) (Appendix 1A), p.24
Efficient Market Hypothesis (EMH), p.19
Emerging markets, p.13

Expected return, p.9
Financial assets, p.3
Institutional investors, p.16
Investment, p.3
Investments, p.3
Marketable securities, p.3
Portfolio, p.3

Portfolio management, p.11
Real assets, p.3
Realized return, p.9
Risk, p.9
Risk-averse investor, p.9
Risk-free rate of return, p.10
Security analysis, p.11

REVIEW QUESTIONS

1-1. Define the term investments. Why study investments?

1-2. Distinguish between a financial asset and a real asset. Give two examples of each.

1-3. List three primary investing objectives and two secondary investing objectives.

1-4. Briefly describe three constraints that have an impact on the design of an investment policy.

1-5. With respect to Figure 1-1, when would an investor expect to earn the risk-free rate of return?

1-6. Distinguish between expected return and realized return.

1-7. Why should the required rate of return be different for a corporate bond and a Government of Canada bond?

1-8. A marketable security is said to be liquid if it can be easily and cheaply traded. Why is the liquidity of a marketable security an important thing for investors to consider?

1-9. Differentiate between an active investment strategy and a passive investment strategy.

1-10. List at least four categories of institutional investors. Give examples of Canadian corporations that fit in each category.

1-11. Describe the broad two-step process involved in making investment decisions.

1-12. Why is the study of investments important to most individuals?

1-13. Carefully describe the risk–return trade-off faced by all investors.

1-14. "A risk-averse investor will not assume risk." Do you agree or disagree with this statement? Why?

1-15. Summarize the basic nature of the investment decision in one sentence.

1-16. Are all rational investors risk averse? Do they all have the same degree of risk aversion?

1-17. What are institutional investors? How are individual investors likely to be affected by institutional investors?

1-18. What is meant by the expression efficient markets?

1-19. Of what significance is an efficient market to investors?

1-20. Discuss at least three reasons why Canadian investors should be concerned with global investing. Do you think the exchange rate value of the Canadian dollar will have any effect on the decision to invest globally?

1-21. Although a Treasury bill is said to be "risk free," there actually is some risk associated with investing in one. What do you think the risk (or risks) would be?

1-22. Define risk. How many specific types can you think of?

1-23. What other constraints besides risk do investors face?

1-24. What are four external factors that affect the decision process? Which do you think is the most important, and why?

1-25. What is meant by the terms *ex ante* and *ex post*?

1-26. Explain why risk and return are the two critical components of all investing decisions.

1-27. How has Internet technology influenced the nature of investing?

1-28. Construct a chart to show how the following typical investments compare in terms of expected return and expected risk: Coins and stamps, common shares, commercial real estate, residential real estate, corporate bonds, government bonds, options/futures, treasury bills, preferred shares, art objects.

1-29. What is meant by an investor's risk tolerance? What role does this concept play in investor decision making?

APPENDIX 1A

THE CHARTERED FINANCIAL ANALYST® PROGRAM

Individuals interested in careers in the investment analysis field should consider seeking the **Chartered Financial Analyst®** (**CFA®**) designation, which is, for people in the investment area, not unlike the CA, CGA, or CMA for accountants. The CFA charter, granted exclusively by CFA Institute, is widely recognized in the investments industry today.

> **Chartered Financial Analyst®(CFA®)**
> A professional designation for people in the investment field.

Candidates enrolled in the CFA program must show that they have mastered important material in economics, quantitative analysis, ethical and professional standards, financial accounting, fixed income securities, equity securities analysis, and portfolio management. Candidates must successfully complete three examinations, referred to as Level I, Level II, and Level III, and meet certain work experience and membership requirements, in order to be awarded the CFA designation.

The basis of the CFA study and examination program is a candidate body of knowledge (CBOK). The CBOK is organized along functional and topical lines and is structured around the investment decision-making process. The CBOK functional areas are ethics and professional standards, investment tools, asset valuation, and portfolio management.

For each level of the exam, the curriculum is organized around a functional area:

Level I study program—emphasizes tools and inputs

Level II study program—emphasizes asset valuation

Level III study program—emphasizes portfolio management

Ethical and professional standards are considered an integral part of all three functional areas and are included in all levels of the curriculum.

Six-hour examinations are given throughout Canada, the United States, and around the world once a year, around June 1, and must be completed in sequence. Level I exams are also offered in December. As a result, completion of the CFA program requires a minimum of two and a half years.

By 2008 over 81,000 investment professionals from 126 countries and territories had earned the CFA charter since it was first awarded in 1963. The most common occupations of CFA charter holders include the following:

- CEO/Principal
- Chief Investment Officer
- Equity Analyst
- Fixed Income Analyst
- Investment Banker

- Investment Counselor
- Investment Firm Manager
- Portfolio Manager
- Portfolio Strategist
- Sales/Marketing Professional

What does it mean to be awarded the CFA charter? Increasingly, employers are recognizing the value of this designation and the potential benefits that an employee with it can offer a company. The CFA charter represents a combination of academic achievement and professional experience along with a commitment to a stringent code of professional and ethical standards. CFA charter holders must renew their pledge to abide by the code every year and violations can carry severe sanctions.

The investments profession, like many others, involves lifelong learning. After receiving the CFA designation, investment professionals can participate in the CFA Professional Development program in order to remain current on investment issues. This program allows them to earn continuing education credits a number of ways including workshops, seminars, and reading on their own.

For more information about the CFA program, call its toll-free number at 1-800-247-8132 or 1-434-951-5499, or visit the CFA Institute website at www.cfainstitute.org.

APPENDIX 1B

THE CANADIAN SECURITIES INSTITUTE (CSI)

The Canadian Securities Institute (CSI) has been providing education for financial professionals and the general public since 1970, and has trained over 700,000 global professionals. CSI serves the broad financial services industry with an emphasis on securities. CSI courses, seminars, and specialized programs are recognized by regulators as the proficiency benchmarks for all levels of industry professionals.

Canadian Securities Course™ (CSC)

This course is offered by the Canadian Securities Institute (CSI) and is a mandatory requirement for individuals who wish to become licensed to sell financial securities in Canada and to register to sell mutual funds.

The **Canadian Securities Course™ (CSC)**[9] is a prerequisite for many other CSI courses and is a starting point for earning sought-after professional designations. Completion of certain CSI courses is mandatory to meet the requirements for various registration categories. Individuals who wish to become licensed to sell securities must pass the CSC as well as the Conduct and Practices Handbook (CPH). Completion of the CSC also allows individuals to become registered to sell mutual funds.

CSI's approach to professional investment education is based on extensive research and consultation with the financial services industry, regulators, and end-users. Rather than single-course offerings, CSI programs focus on career streams that lead students to specialized designations. For more information about CSI and its programs, call 1-866-866-2601 or visit its website at www.csi.ca.

---

[9]The Canadian Securities Course™ (CSC) and other courses discussed here are trademarks of the Canadian Securities Institute.

CHAPTER 2

INVESTMENT ALTERNATIVES

Chapter 2 explains the most important investment alternatives available to investors, ranging from money market securities to capital market securities—bonds and stocks—to derivative securities. It organizes the types of financial assets available in the money and capital markets, and it provides the reader with a good understanding of the securities that are of primary interest to most investors, particularly bonds and stocks. The emphasis is on the basic features of these securities, providing the reader with the knowledge needed to understand the investment opportunities of interest to most investors. Recent trends such as securitization are considered, as is international investing.

Although our discussion is as up to date as possible, changes in the securities field occur so rapidly that investors are regularly confronted with new developments. Investors in the twenty-first century have a wide variety of investment alternatives available, and it is reasonable to expect that this variety will only increase. However, if investors understand the basic characteristics of the major existing securities, they will likely be able to understand new securities as they appear.

Learning Objectives

After reading this chapter, you should be able to

1. Describe the major types of financial assets and how they are organized.
2. Explain what non-marketable financial assets are.
3. Describe the important features of money market securities.
4. Describe the important features of capital market securities.
5. Distinguish among preferred stock, income trusts, and common stock.
6. Understand the basics of options and futures.

CHAPTER PREVIEW

Changes in the securities field occur so rapidly that investors are regularly confronted with new developments. However, if investors understand the basic characteristics of the major existing securities, they will likely be able to understand new securities as they appear. This chapter explains the most important investment alternatives available to investors, ranging from non-marketable financial assets to marketable investments in money market, capital market, and derivative securities. You will learn the basic features of securities that are of primary interest to most investors, particularly bonds and stocks. We also discuss recent trends such as "securitization" and international investing.

ORGANIZING FINANCIAL ASSETS

learning objective 1
Describe the major types of financial assets and how they are organized.

The emphasis in this chapter (and in the text in general) is on financial assets, which, as explained in Chapter 1, are financial claims on the issuers of securities. We focus in particular on marketable securities, which are claims that are negotiable, or saleable, in various marketplaces, as discussed in Chapter 4.

This chapter concentrates on investment alternatives available through direct investing, which involves securities that investors buy and sell themselves, primarily capital market securities and derivative securities. The taxation of income earned from these financial assets in Canada is discussed in Appendix 2A at the end of the chapter. In Chapter 3, we examine **indirect investing**. Rather than invest directly in securities, investors can invest in a portfolio of securities by purchasing the units of a financial intermediary that invests in various types of securities on behalf of its shareowners. Perhaps the most common method of indirect investing involves mutual funds. Indirect investing is a very important alternative for all investors to consider and has become tremendously popular in the last few years with individual investors.

Indirect Investing
The buying and selling of the shares of investment companies that themselves hold portfolios of securities.

People who invest directly in financial markets have a wide variety of assets from which to choose. Non-marketable investment opportunities, such as savings accounts at financial institutions, are discussed briefly at the beginning of the chapter since investors often own these assets and are familiar with them. Henceforth, we will consider only marketable securities, which may be classified into one of three categories:

1. The money market

2. The capital market

3. The derivatives market

Investors should understand money market securities, particularly Treasury bills, but they typically will not own these securities directly, choosing instead to own them through the money market funds explained in Chapter 3. Within the capital market, securities can be classified as either fixed-income or equity. Finally, investors may choose to use derivative securities in their portfolios. The market value of these securities is derived from underlying securities such as common stock.

Figure 2-1 organizes the types of financial assets to be analyzed in this chapter (under the heading of direct investing) using the above classifications. It also indicates various indirect investment alternatives, which will be discussed in more depth in Chapter 3. Although we cover direct investing and indirect investing in separate chapters, it is important to understand that investors can, and often do, both. Many individuals invest directly through the use of a brokerage account and indirectly in one or more investment companies. Furthermore, brokerage accounts that accommodate the ownership of investment company shares are becoming increasingly popular, thereby combining direct and indirect investing into one account.

Non-marketable	**DIRECT INVESTING** • Savings deposits • GICs • Canada Savings Bonds (CSBs)
Money market	• Treasury bills • Commercial paper • Eurodollars • Repurchase agreements • Bankers' acceptances (B/As)

Capital market	• Fixed-income
	   Government bonds
	   Government agency bonds (e.g., Ontario Hydro)
	   Corporate bonds
	• Mortgage-backed securities (MBS)/
	   Asset-backed securities (ABS)
	• Income trusts
	• Equities
	   Preferred stock
	   Common stock

Derivatives market	• Options • Futures contracts

Investment funds	**INDIRECT INVESTING**
	• Open end
	   Money market mutual fund
	   Stock, bond, and income funds
	• Closed end

Figure 2-1
Major Types of Financial Assets

An International Perspective

As noted in Chapter 1, investors should adopt an international perspective in making their investment decisions. The investment alternatives analyzed in this chapter, in particular some money market assets, bonds, and stocks, are available to Canadian investors from many foreign markets. Thus, the characteristics of these basic securities are relevant if we invest in domestic or foreign financial assets, or both. Canadian investors usually invest internationally indirectly through investment companies, many of which offer a wide variety of global asset funds.

CHECK YOUR UNDERSTANDING

2-1. What is the main difference between direct and indirect investing?

2-2. List the two main classifications of capital market securities, and one example of each.

NON-MARKETABLE FINANCIAL ASSETS

We begin our discussion of investment alternatives by mentioning those that are non-marketable because most individuals will own one or more of these assets regardless of what else they do in the investing arena. Furthermore, these assets represent useful contrasts to the marketable securities we will concentrate on throughout the text.

learning objective 2
Explain what non-marketable financial assets are.

A distinguishing characteristic of these assets is that they represent personal transactions between the owner and the issuer. That is, as the owner of a savings account at a bank, you must open the account personally and deal with the bank in maintaining the account or in closing it. In contrast, marketable securities trade in impersonal markets where the buyer and seller do not know one another and do not care.

Most non-marketable instruments are safe investments available from insured financial institutions or issued by the Canadian government. Most of these assets offer the ultimate in **liquidity**, which can be defined as the ease with which an asset can be converted to cash. An asset is liquid if it can be disposed of quickly with no more than small price changes, assuming no new information in the marketplace. Thus, we know we can get all of our money back from a savings account or a Canada Savings Bond very quickly.

The most familiar form of non-marketable assets is savings accounts (or demand deposits) with financial institutions such as chartered banks, trust and mortgage companies, and credit unions or caisses populaires. The funds invested here are available on demand, which guarantees the liquidity of these investments. The safety of these deposits is further enhanced through the existence of deposit insurance, as discussed in Real-World Returns 2-1.

Liquidity

The ease with which an asset can be converted to cash. An asset is liquid if it can be bought or sold quickly with relatively small price changes.

REAL-WORLD RETURNS 2-1
Protecting Canadian Investors

Most chartered banks and trust companies are members of the Canada Deposit Insurance Corporation (CDIC), an agency of the federal government. The CDIC insures qualifying deposits with member institutions, up to a maximum of $100,000 of total deposits with one financial institution. Individuals wishing to have more than $100,000 in insured deposits must maintain deposits with several institutions and ensure the total deposits with any particular institution do not exceed $100,000.

Insurance companies, credit unions and caisses populaires, and investment dealers are not eligible for CDIC membership, but generally provide other forms of protection for their clients. Credit unions generally offer protection through provincial deposit insurance or guarantee programs. For example, deposits with credit unions in British Columbia are protected through the Credit Union Deposit Insurance Corporation of BC. This corporation guarantees the total savings, chequing, and term deposits by an individual with one credit union up to a maximum of $100,000. The $100,000 maximum per individual per credit union also applies to both RRSP and RRIF plans, in addition to the $100,000 limit for savings accounts.

The maximum deposit protection and the qualifying criteria for investment protection varies across the provinces. The maximum protection per individual per institution is $60,000 of the total of savings, chequing, and term deposits in New Brunswick and Prince Edward Island. The caisses populaires in Quebec offer $60,000 coverage per investor. Coverage is limited to $100,000 in Ontario and to $250,000 in Nova Scotia. Alberta, Manitoba, and Saskatchewan all offer unlimited protection.

The Canadian Life and Health Compensation Corporation (CompCorp) came into existence in 1990 to provide protection for customers of companies that sell life and/or health insurance to the Canadian public, and became Assuris in 2005. The Property and Casualty Insurance Compensation Corporation (PACICC) performs a similar function for customers of property and casualty insurance companies. Finally, customers of investment dealers are afforded protection by the Canadian Investor Protection Fund (CIPF), which is discussed in greater detail in Chapter 5.

Guaranteed Investment Certificates (GICs) are non-transferable time deposits with chartered banks and trust companies that offer investors higher returns than those available on savings accounts. These differ from demand deposits because they are locked in for a fixed period of time, and early withdrawals are not permitted, or else are often accompanied by penalties and/or the loss of accrued interest.

Another widely used non-marketable financial asset is the Canada Savings Bond (CSB), with over $45 billion in these bonds having been sold since their introduction in 1946. Unlike other bonds, CSBs can be cashed out by the owner at full par value plus eligible accrued interest at any bank in Canada at any time. They are not transferable, and their prices do not change over time. They are only available for six months of the year (between early October through April 1st each year) and require a minimum $100 investment. They are sold in registered form to provide protection against loss, theft, or destruction. In recent years, only individuals, estates of deceased persons, and trusts governed by certain types of deferred savings and income plans have been allowed to acquire CSBs.

The published rate of return on CSBs is not always fixed. This is done to avoid having holders cash out in times of rising interest rates. However, the government often guarantees minimum rates for the future. An effective program for selling CSBs is administered through the payroll savings plans of over 12,000 organizations. The various options available to investors, as well as some of the features of these instruments, are described in Real-World Returns 2-2.

REAL-WORLD RETURNS 2-2
Bonds

Canada Savings Bonds are a safe and secure way to reach your savings and investment goals, and are also ideal for gift giving. They are issued by the Government of Canada and can be purchased with an RRSP or RRIF option from the Bank of Canada. You can choose either the Canada Savings Bond (CSB), which is cashable at any time, or the Canada Premium Bond (CPB), which is cashable once a year. Both the CSB and the CPB offer a variety of features:

The Canada Premium Bond
The CPB is fully backed by the Government of Canada and offers a higher rate of interest at the time of issue than the Canada Savings Bond on sale at the same time. The CPB can be redeemed once a year on the anniversary of the issue date and during the 30 days following.

The Canada Savings Bond
The CSB is a safe, secure investment enjoyed by millions of Canadians for over 60 years. It provides both maximum flexibility and security. It is backed by the Government of Canada and offers a minimum guaranteed rate that will be increased should market conditions warrant. It can also be purchased through payroll deduction where available at sponsoring employers.

The Canada RSP
The Canada Retirement Savings Plan is a no-fee RRSP created to allow Canadians to hold compound interest Canada Savings Bonds as RRSP investments without the need for a self-directed plan. The Canada RSP option is available where you bank or invest, through direct telephone and online purchase and via the Payroll Savings Program.

The Canada RIF
The Canada Retirement Income Fund is a no-fee RRIF, designed to hold compound interest Canada Savings Bonds as retirement income investments without the need for a self-directed plan. The Canada RIF option is available where you bank or invest.

(continued)

REAL-WORLD RETURNS 2-2 *continued*

Other Retail Products

Treasury Bills, Marketable Bonds, and Real Return Bonds have a guaranteed return if held to maturity but can be bought or sold prior to maturity at market prices, which vary from day to day. These products are available only through investment dealers.

How to Buy

The Canada Premium Bond and the Canada Savings Bond can be purchased online for ease and convenience. The site is encrypted for security, and provides a fast and easy way to become a bondholder. The CPB and the CSB can also be bought wherever you bank or invest, or by contacting us. The CSB can also be purchased through payroll deduction where available at sponsoring employers.

How to Redeem

Bonds with certificates may be redeemed at most financial institutions in Canada. CSBs purchased through the Payroll Savings Program may be redeemed online or by calling Customer Service. Bonds held within The Canada RSP and The Canada RIF may be redeemed by writing to the Trustee.

Source: www.csb.gc.ca/eng/bonds.asp, March 12, 2008.

CHECK YOUR UNDERSTANDING

2-3. Marketable securities may be referred to as impersonal assets, whereas non-marketable financial assets are not. Why is this?

2-4. Do individuals who make deposits at most chartered banks and trust companies in Canada have any risk of losing their funds?

MONEY MARKET SECURITIES

Describe the important features of money market securities.

Money Market
The market for short-term, highly liquid, low-risk debt instruments sold by governments, financial institutions, and corporations. Canadian government Treasury bills are an example.

Money markets include short-term, highly liquid, relatively low-risk debt instruments sold by governments, financial institutions, and corporations to investors with temporary excess funds to invest. The returns on these instruments exceed those offered by savings accounts; however, the size of transactions is generally large ($100,000 or more). On the other hand, several financial institutions purchase large blocks of these instruments and break them up into smaller denominations (as low as $1,000) in order to make them available for their retail customers. The rates on these smaller denominations will be lower than those available on the larger blocks, which is how the intermediaries make their profits.

The money market is dominated by financial institutions (particularly banks) and governments. The maturities of money market instruments range from one day to one year, and are often less than 90 days. Some of these instruments are negotiable and actively traded, and others are not. Most of them are sold on a discount basis. For example, 91-day Treasury bills with a face (or maturity) value of $100,000 may be sold to investors for $98,500. The investor receives $100,000 at maturity, which means they have earned $1,500 in interest on their original investment of $98,500. Investors may invest directly in some of these securities, but more often they do so indirectly through money market mutual funds offered by investment companies.

Another reason that knowledge of these securities is important is the use of government **Treasury bills (T-bills)** as a benchmark asset. Although in some pure sense there is no such thing as a risk-free financial asset, on a practical basis Government of Canada Treasury bills are risk-free since there is virtually no chance of default by the federal government, and the length of the investment period is very short. The T-bill rate, denoted RF, is used throughout the text as a proxy for the nominal risk-free rate of return available to investors (e.g., the RF shown and discussed in Figure 1-1 in Chapter 1).

In summary, money market instruments are characterized as short-term, highly marketable investments, with an extremely low probability of default. Because the minimum investment is generally large, money market securities are normally owned by individual investors indirectly in the form of investment funds known as money market mutual funds, or, as they are usually called, money market funds.

Money market rates tend to move together and most rates are very close to each other for the same maturity, as can be seen in the Real-World Returns 2-3. Notice that T-bill rates are lower than those for other money market securities because of their risk-free nature.

Treasury Bill (T-bill)

A short-term money market instrument sold at discount by Canadian governments.

REAL-WORLD RETURNS 2-3

Money Markets

MONEY MARKET	24/01/08	25/01/08	+/-
Overnight rate	4.0019%	4.0137%	+ 0.0118
Target for the overnight rate	4.00%	4.00%	0.00
Overnight repo rate (CORRA)	4.0054%	4.0264%	+ 0.0210
Corporate paper, 1 month	4.05%	4.04%	- 0.01
Treasury bill, 1 month	3.48%	3.46%	- 0.02
Bankers' Acceptances, 1 month	4.05%	4.06%	+ 0.01

Source: www.globeinvestorgold.com, January 28, 2008.

The following are the major money market securities of most interest to individual investors.

1. *Treasury bills*. The premier money market instrument, a fully guaranteed, very liquid IOU from the Government of Canada or provincial governments. Government of Canada Treasury bills are sold by auction every two weeks at a discount from face value in denominations ranging from $1,000 to $1 million. The greater the discount at the time of purchase the higher the return earned by investors. Standard maturities are 91, 182, and 364 days, although shorter maturities are also offered. New bills can be purchased by investors on a competitive or non-competitive bid basis. Outstanding (i.e., already issued) bills can be purchased and sold in the secondary market, an extremely efficient market where government securities dealers stand ready to buy and sell these securities.

2. *Commercial paper*. A short-term, unsecured promissory note issued by large, well-known, and financially strong corporations (including finance companies). Denominations start at $100,000 with maturities of 30 to 365 days. Commercial paper (CP) is usually sold at a discount either directly by the issuer or indirectly through a dealer, with rates slightly above T-bills. There is an important distinction between bank-backed CP, which as the name suggests consists of CP that is guaranteed or backed by a bank (or banks), and non-bank-backed CP. This distinction came to the forefront of investor attention in the summer of 2007, as the trading in non-bank based asset backed commercial paper (ABCP) ceased entirely, and as of March 2008, trading had not resumed. This issue

is discussed in Real-World Returns 2-4, with a potential resolution in sight, but one that would still result in significant losses for those who had participated in this market. The secondary market for commercial paper has become more active in recent years. Similar to bonds, commercial paper is rated by a rating service as to quality (relative probability of default by the issuer).

3. *Eurodollars*. Dollar-denominated deposits held in foreign banks or in offices of Canadian banks located abroad. Although this market originally developed in Europe (hence the name), dollar-denominated deposits can now be made in many countries, such as those of Asia. Eurodollar deposits consist of both time deposits and certificates of deposit (CDs), with the latter constituting the largest component of the Eurodollar markets. Maturities are mostly short-term, often less than six months. The Eurodollar market is primarily a wholesale market, with large deposits and large loans. Major international banks transact among themselves with other participants including multinational corporations and governments. Although relatively safe, Eurodollar yields exceed those of other money market assets because of the lesser regulation for Eurodollar banks. In addition, Eurodollar CDs are not covered by CDIC.

4. *Repurchase agreement (RP)*. An agreement between a borrower and lender (generally institutions) to sell and repurchase money market securities. The borrower initiates an RP by contracting to sell securities to a lender and agreeing to repurchase these securities at a pre-specified (higher) price on a stated future date. The effective interest rate is given by the difference between the repurchase price and the sale price. The annual interest rate implied by these transactions is referred to as the repo rate. The maturity of RPs is generally very short, from three to 14 days, and sometimes overnight. The minimum denomination is typically $100,000.

5. *Bankers' acceptance (B/A)*. A time draft drawn on a bank by a customer, whereby the bank agrees to guarantee payment of a particular amount at a specified future date. B/As are negotiable instruments that are sold for less than face value (i.e., at a discount) in the money market. They are traded on a discount basis, with a minimum denomination of $100,000. Maturities range from 30 to 180 days, with 90 days being the most common.

REAL-WORLD RETURNS 2-4

Players in ABCP Drama Agree on Terms

The group of investors and banks working to restructure Canada's frozen $33-billion asset-backed commercial paper market is one step closer to a solution after all players signed off late Thursday night on a proposal that's set to go before a judge as soon as Friday morning for approval.

All the players in the contentious negotiations agreed on terms of a deal late last night, sources said. Canada's big banks have all agreed to back a credit line to support the restructuring, one key to the proposal.

While a framework had been in place for months to swap the frozen paper for new longer-term notes, worsening credit markets made it tough for all the parties involved to agree on how exactly to do it.

Now, with time running out before a standstill agreement that kept peace between the players expires at midnight, the restructuring committee will ask a judge to sign off on the plan.

JPMorgan, the investment bank that is advising the committee, has prepared estimates of the values of the assets underlying the ABCP, which average about 80 cents on the dollar, sources said.

However, it's unlikely that the new notes will fetch that much in the open market after the swap, which could happen as soon as May. That means holders who are looking to sell the new notes and free up cash that has been frozen since the ABCP market seized up in August will be looking at sizable losses.

The committee's official spokesman was not available to comment Friday morning.

The support of Canada's big banks was one of the final issues that had to be nailed down. Toronto-Dominion Bank had balked at the idea of being involved with the credit line, saying that it didn't sell affected ABCP so it shouldn't be required to help. Similarly, Bank of Montreal was leery of participating because the bank is dealing with potential losses on other areas of its balance sheet and was looking to conserve capital.

However, both came to the table.

"We have been firm in our support of stability in the Canadian commercial paper market," said BMO spokesan Paul Deegan, who confirmed his bank's participation.

TD spokesman Simon Townsend declined to confirm his firm would be involved, saying Thursday that while TD was participating in talks and those had been productive, "until the committee finalizes its plan, I'm not in a position to comment."

Source: Erman, Boyd, www.globeinvestorgold.com, March 14, 2008.

CHECK YOUR UNDERSTANDING

2-5. Holding maturity constant, why would you expect the yields on money market securities to be close to each other?

2-6. Why does the Treasury bill serve as a benchmark security?

CAPITAL MARKET SECURITIES

learning objective 4
Describe the important features of capital market securities.

Capital markets encompass fixed-income and equity securities with maturities greater than one year. Risk is generally much higher than in the money market because of the time to maturity and the very nature of the securities sold in the capital markets. Marketability is poorer in some cases. The capital market includes both debt and equity securities, with equity securities having no maturity date.

Fixed-Income Securities

We begin our review of the principal types of capital market securities owned directly by individual investors with **fixed-income securities**. All of these have a specified payment schedule and, in most cases, such as with a traditional bond, the amount and date of each payment are known in advance. Some of these securities deviate from this format, but all fixed-income securities have a specified payment or repayment schedule—they must mature at some future date.

Bonds

Bonds can be described simply as long-term debt instruments representing the issuer's contractual obligation or IOU. The buyer of a newly issued coupon bond is lending money to the issuer who, in turn, agrees to pay interest on this loan and repay the principal at a stated maturity date.

Bonds are fixed-income securities because the interest payments (if any) and the principal repayment for most bonds are specified at the time the bond is issued and fixed for its life. At the time of purchase, the bond buyer knows the future stream of cash flows to be received from buying and holding the bond to maturity. Barring default by the issuer, these payments will be received at specified intervals until maturity, at which time the principal will be repaid. However, if the buyer decides to sell the bond before maturity, the price received will depend on the interest rates at that time.

Capital Markets
The markets for long-term securities such as bonds and stocks.

Fixed-Income Securities
Securities such as bonds with specified payment dates and amounts.

Bonds
Long-term debt instruments representing the issuer's contractual obligation or IOU.

Bond Characteristics

Par Value (Face Value)

The redemption value of a bond paid at maturity, generally $1,000.

The **par value (face value)** of most bonds is $1,000, and we will use this number as the amount to be repaid at maturity.[1] The bond generally matures (terminates) on a specified date and is technically known as a term bond.[2] Most bonds are coupon bonds, where coupon refers to the periodic interest that the issuer pays to the holder of the bonds.[3] Interest on bonds is generally paid semi-annually.

EXAMPLE 2-1: GOVERNMENT OF CANADA COUPON BOND

A three-year, 9.00 percent Government of Canada coupon bond was listed in the bond listings at www.financialpost.com/markets/market_data/bonds-canadian.html on March 17, 2008. Assuming the bond has a par value of $1,000, it has a dollar coupon of $90.00 (9.0 percent of $1,000); therefore, knowing the percentage coupon rate is the same as knowing the coupon payment in dollars.[4] If the interest on the bond is paid semi-annually, this bond would pay interest (the coupons) of $45.00 on a specified date every six months. The $1,000 principal would be repaid three years hence at the maturity date (hence we say the term-to-maturity is three years).

Zero Coupon Bond

A bond sold with no coupons at a discount and redeemed for face value at maturity. Also known as a strip bond.

An important innovation in the format of traditional bonds is the **zero coupon bond** (or strip bond), which does not pay any coupons, or interest, during its life. The purchaser pays less than par value for "zeroes" and receives par value at maturity. The difference in these two amounts generates an effective interest rate or rate of return. Similar to Treasury bills, the lower the price paid for the coupon bond, the higher the effective return.

Zeroes are usually created when financial intermediaries purchase traditional bonds, strip the cash flows from them, and sell the cash flows separately. These bonds first appeared in Canada in 1982. In the United States, the US Treasury created STRIPS, or Separate Trading of Registered Interest and Principal of Securities, in 1985. Under this program, all new **treasury bonds** (i.e., bonds issued by the US government) and notes with maturities greater than 10 years are eligible to be stripped to create zero coupon Treasury securities that are direct obligations of the US Treasury Department.

Treasury Bond

Long-term bonds sold by the US government.

By convention, bond prices are quoted as a proportion of par value using 100 as par rather than 1,000. Therefore, a price of 90 represents $900, and a price of 55 represents $550, using the normal assumption of a par value of $1,000. The easiest way to convert quoted bond prices to actual prices is to remember that they are quoted in percentages, with the common assumption of a $1,000 par value.

EXAMPLE 2-2: PRICE OF A GOVERNMENT OF CANADA COUPON BOND

The bid price of the three-year 9.00 percent Government of Canada coupon bond was 117.70 on March 14, 2008. This quoted price represents 117.70 percent of $1,000, or $1,177.00.

The above example suggests that an investor could purchase the bond for $1,177.00 on that day. Actually, bonds trade on an accrued interest basis. That is, the bond buyer must pay the bond seller the price of the bond as well as the interest that has been earned (accrued) on the bond since the last interest payment. This allows an investor to sell a bond any time without losing the interest that has accrued. Bond buyers should remember this additional cost when buying a bond because prices are quoted in the paper without the accrued interest.[5]

---

[1]The par value is almost never less than $1,000, although it easily can be more.

[2]The phrase term-to-maturity is used to denote how much longer the bond will be in existence. In contrast, a serial bond has a series of maturity dates. Thus, one issue of serial bonds may mature in specified amounts year after year, and each specified amount could carry a different coupon.

[3]The terms interest income and coupon income are interchangeable.

[4]The coupon rate on a traditional, standard bond is fixed at the bond's issuance and cannot vary.

[5]The invoice or cash price is the price the bond buyer must pay and will include the accrued interest.

The price of the bond in the above example is above 100 (i.e., $1,000) because market yields on bonds of this type were below the stated coupon rate of 9.00 percent on this bond (in fact, the yield associated with this price for this bond is 2.72 percent). The coupon on this particular bond became more than competitive with the going market interest rate for comparable newly issued bonds, and the price increased to reflect this fact. At any point in time some bonds are selling at premiums (above par value), reflecting a decline in market rates after that particular bond was sold. Others are selling at discounts (below par value), because the stated coupons are less than the prevailing interest rate on a comparable new issue.

The **call provision** gives the issuer the right to "call in" the bonds, thereby depriving investors of that particular fixed-income security. Exercising the call provision becomes attractive to the issuer when market interest rates drop sufficiently below the coupon rate on the outstanding bonds for the issuer to save money. Costs are incurred to call the bonds, such as a "call premium" and administrative expenses. However, issuers expect to sell new bonds at a lower interest cost, thereby replacing existing higher interest-cost bonds with new, lower interest-cost bonds.

Call Provision

Gives the issuer the right to call in a security and retire it by paying off the obligation.

INVESTING *tip*

The call feature is a risk to investors who must give up the higher yielding bonds. Consistent with our discussion of risk and return in Chapter 1, we generally observe that callable bonds offer investors a higher yield than similar non-callable bonds as compensation for this risk. The wise bond investor will note the bond issue's provisions concerning the call, carefully determining the earliest date at which the bond can be called, and the bond's yield if it is called at the earliest date possible. This calculation is shown in Chapter 11.

Callable bonds give the issuer the option to call or repurchase outstanding bonds at predetermined "call prices" (generally at a premium over par) at specified times. This feature is detrimental to the bondholders who are willing to pay less for them (i.e., they demand a higher return) than for similar non-callable bonds. Generally, the issuer agrees to give 30 or more days' notice that the issue will be redeemed. Most callables have a time period (referred to as call protection) prior to the first call date during which they cannot be called. The redemption price often declines on a graduated scale, reflecting the fact that the hardship to the investor of having an issue called is reduced as the time to maturity declines. Most Government of Canada and US Treasury bonds are non-callable.[6] Provincial bonds are usually callable at 100 plus accrued interest. Usually corporate issues have a mandatory call feature for sinking fund purposes.

Retractable bonds allow the bondholder to sell the bonds back to the issuer at predetermined prices at specified times, while **extendible bonds** allow the bondholder to extend the maturity date of the bond. Both of these bonds offer investors an additional privilege, which implies they will pay more for these bonds (i.e., accept a lower return). They both tend to trade similar to short-term bonds during periods of rising interest rates, as it is likely that they will be redeemed (or not extended). Similarly, they tend to behave like long-term bonds during periods of decreasing interest rates. The holders generally must state their intentions to extend or redeem during the election period (which occurs six to 12 months prior to the extendible or retractable dates).

Retractable Bonds

Bonds that allow the bondholder to sell the bonds back to the issuer at predetermined prices at specified times.

Extendible Bonds

Bonds that allow investors to extend the maturity date of the bond.

A sinking fund provision provides for the orderly retirement of the bond issue during its life. The provisions of a sinking fund vary widely. For example, it can be stated as a fixed or variable amount and as a percentage of the particular issue outstanding or the total debt of the issuer outstanding. All or part of the bond issue may be retired through the sinking fund by the maturity date. One procedure for carrying out the sinking fund requirement is simply to buy the required amount of bonds on the open market each year. A second alternative is to call the bonds randomly. Again, investors should be aware of such provisions for their protection.

Convertible bonds may be converted into common shares at predetermined conversion prices. This privilege is afforded to the investor in order to make the issue more saleable and to reduce the interest rate that must be offered to purchasers. The conversion price is often graduated upward through time to encourage early conversion. Most convertibles are callable. Certain convertibles include a forced conversion clause, which forces conversion by affording the issuer the right to redeem the issue once the common share price goes above pre-specified levels. Convertibles typically trade

Convertible Bonds

Bonds that are convertible, at the holder's option, into shares of common stock of the same corporation at predetermined prices.

---

[6] US Treasury bonds issued after February 1985 cannot be called.

INVESTING *tip*

Investors should not expect to receive the conversion option free. The issuer sells convertible bonds at a lower interest rate than would otherwise be paid, resulting in a lower interest return to investors.

similar to straight debentures when the conversion price is well below the market price of the common shares. A "premium" appears as market price approaches conversion price, and it is said to "sell off the stock" once market price exceeds the conversion price.

Floating rate bonds (or floaters) are an alternative to traditional fixed coupon bonds. They have adjustable coupons that are generally tied to T-bill rates or some other short-term interest rate. They are attractive for the protection offered in times of volatile interest rates (and/or during inflationary periods) and behave like money market securities in an investment portfolio. An example of a floating-rate bond that provides protection against increases in inflation (which is generally accompanied by an increase in interest rates) is Government of Canada Real Return Bonds. These were introduced in 1991 to provide investors with a real yield of about 4.25 percent. The variants now exist with longer terms to maturity that provide real yields of 4.0 percent and 3.0 percent respectively. The real yields are achieved by pegging the face value to the Consumer Price Index (CPI) and having the coupon rate of 4.25 (4.0 or 3.0) percent apply to the inflation-adjusted face value.

Types of Bonds

Bond certificates may be in either bearer or registered forms. Bearer bonds are presumed to be owned by the party holding them. Coupons are numbered and dated and may be clipped and redeemed for cash. Registered bonds have the name of the owner on their face and interest is paid to the registered owner by the issuer. If lost or stolen, it is difficult for anyone other than the owner to cash them. Most bonds are traded through dealers in the over-the-counter market, which is described in Chapter 4.

Bonds may be classified as domestic, foreign, or Eurobonds. Domestic bonds are issued in the currency and country of the issuer, while foreign bonds are issued primarily in a currency and country other than the issuer's. Eurobonds are issued in any number of currencies in the Euromarket or the international bond market (if issued in Canadian dollars they would be called EuroCanadian bonds, and if issued in US dollars they would be called Eurodollar bonds).

While government bonds constitute the majority of the bond market in Canada, corporate bonds are growing in importance. For example, at the end of 1995, there was $452 billion US in Canadian government bonds outstanding versus $50 billion US outstanding in Canadian corporate bonds (approximately 10 percent of the Canadian total). However, by June 2007, the corporate bond market grew in size to $418.1 billion US (or 38.4 percent of the total Canadian bond market), while the amount of Canadian government bonds outstanding stood at $670.4 billion.

Government Bonds

The Government of Canada is the largest single issuer of bonds in Canada. Like Treasury bills, they are sold at competitive auctions, but unlike bills, they are sold at approximately face value with investors submitting bids on yields (for example, 4.3 percent). Interest payments (coupons) are usually paid semi-annually. Face value denominations are $1,000, $5,000, $10,000, $100,000, $500,000, and $1 million. These bonds are considered an extremely safe credit risk because the government's ability to print money and increase taxes implies the risk of default is minimal for these securities. An investor purchases them with the expectation of earning a steady stream of interest payments and with full assurance of receiving the par value of the bonds when they mature.

Provincial governments also participate in Canadian and global bond markets through direct bond issues as well as by guaranteeing bond issues of provincially appointed authorities and commissions (e.g., Hydro Québec may have outstanding bonds that are guaranteed by the Province of Quebec). Finally, municipal governments also raise debt capital through bond markets. In recent years, municipalities have relied primarily on instalment debentures or serial bonds (described in footnote 2) to raise debt capital from the markets.

US government agencies are the second-largest issuers/guarantors of bonds in the world, with over $6.35 trillion US in outstanding debt securities by June 2007, and lagging only the Japanese government ($6.58 trillion). The US federal government issues numerous notes and bonds with maturities greater than one year through the Treasury Department (hence the name Treasury notes or Treasury bonds).[7] Various US credit agencies also compete for funds in the marketplace by selling government agency securities. Securities issued by federal agencies that are legally part of the federal government are fully guaranteed by the Treasury. The most important agency for investors is the Government National Mortgage Association (often nicknamed "Ginnie Mae"). In addition to these federal agencies, there exist several other federally sponsored credit agencies in the United States that are privately owned institutions that sell their own securities in the marketplace. They have the right to draw on Treasury funds up to some approved amount; however, their securities are not guaranteed by the government. Some of the more important federally sponsored credit agencies include the Federal Home Loan Mortgage Corporation ("Freddie Mac"), the Federal Home Loan Bank, the Farm Credit System, and the Student Loan Marketing Association. Perhaps the best known of these federally sponsored agencies is the Federal National Mortgage Association (FNMA, referred to as "Fannie Mae"), which is designed to help the mortgage markets.[8]

Corporate Bonds

Several of the larger corporations issue **corporate bonds** to help finance their operations. An investor can find a wide range of maturities, coupons, and special features available from corporate bonds. The average corporate bond pays semi-annual interest, is callable, carries a sinking fund provision, and is sold originally at a price close to par value, which is usually $1,000.[9]

Corporate bonds are **senior securities**. That is, they are senior to any preferred stock and to the common stock of a corporation in terms of priority of payment and in case of bankruptcy and liquidation. However, within the bond category itself there are various degrees of security. Mortgage bonds are secured by real assets, which means that holders have legal claim to specific assets of the issuer. **Debentures** are generally unsecured and are backed only by the issuer's overall financial soundness. In addition, debentures can be "subordinated," resulting in a claim on income that stands below (subordinate to) the claim of the other debentures.[10]

Corporate bonds carry a greater risk of default by the issuer than government bonds, and as a result, their indentures (or contracts) often include protective covenants, which are clauses that restrict the actions of the issuer. Negative covenants prohibit certain actions (e.g., restrict dividend payments or prevent pledging of any assets to lenders). Positive covenants specify actions that the firm agrees to undertake (e.g., furnish quarterly financial statements or maintain certain working capital levels).

Rating services perform detailed analysis of bond issuers to determine their ability to maintain uninterrupted payments of interest and repayment of principal. The Dominion Bond Rating Service (DBRS) and the Canadian Bond Rating Service (CBRS) are the two major Canadian **bond rating** services. Standard & Poor's (S&P) Corporation and Moody's Investors Service Inc. are two major US rating agencies that rate bond issuers (both government and corporate) across the world.

Corporate Bonds
Long-term debt securities of various types sold by corporations.

Senior Securities
Those securities that are senior, because they are ahead of common and preferred stock in terms of payment in case of liquidation or bankruptcy.

Debenture
An unsecured bond backed by the general financial worthiness of the firm.

Bond Rating
Letters assigned to bonds by rating agencies to express the relative probability of default.

---

[7]US Treasury securities with maturities greater than one year and less than 10 years technically are referred to as Treasury notes, while those with maturities greater than 10 years are referred to as Treasury bonds.

[8]At the time of writing, Fannie Mae and Freddie Mac held approximately $5 trillion in secured and unsecured mortgages in default, and were being bailed out by the US government.

[9]There are various exceptions to this generalization, of course, including bonds with warrants attached, mortgage-backed bonds, collateral trust bonds (which are backed by financial assets), and zero coupon bonds.

[10]Other types of corporate bonds exist, including collateral trust bonds, which are backed by other securities. For example, a parent firm may pledge the securities of one of its subsidiaries as collateral. Equipment obligations (or equipment trust certificates) are backed by specific real assets such as railway engines or airplanes. A trustee is used to hold the assets involved with both collateral trust bonds and equipment obligations.

The following are the debt ratings categories for CBRS and DBRS:

CBRS		DBRS	
A++	highest quality	AAA	highest credit quality
A+	very good quality	AA	superior credit quality
A	good quality	A	upper medium grade credit quality
B++	medium quality	BBB	medium grade credit quality
B+	lower medium quality	BB	lower medium grade credit quality
B	poor quality	B	speculative credit quality
C	speculative quality	CCC	highly speculative credit quality
D	default	CC	in default
Suspended	rating suspended	C	second tier of debt of an entity in default

Ratings may also be modified by high or low to indicate the relative ranking or the trend within the category, such as high A+ or low A+. Investment grade bonds are defined as those with bond ratings of BBB (DBRS and S&P), B++ (CBRS), or Baa (Moody's), or higher. Generally, institutional investors such as insurance companies must confine themselves to investment grade bonds. Other things being equal, bond ratings and bond coupon rates are inversely related. Junk (or high-yield or low-grade) bonds have bond ratings below these. These bonds are regarded as speculative securities in terms of the issuer's ability to meet its contractual obligations.

Despite their widespread acceptance, bond ratings have their limitations, and debt rating agencies have come under extreme criticism in light of their inability to predict many of the problems that arose as a result of the US sub-prime crisis that began in 2007. Real-World Returns 2-5 elaborates.

REAL-WORLD RETURNS 2-5

DBRS to Roll Out a New Road Map on Risk

Canadian bond-rating firm **DBRS Ltd.** is planning new disclosure demands designed to help investors better understand the risks of complex securities, a response to a blowup in credit markets that led to heavy criticism of rating companies for not giving enough warning.

The idea is to give investors a simple, easy-to-follow outline of the risks and the setup of so-called "structured" securities that are based on large pools of underlying assets such as mortgages. Toronto-based DBRS has been consulting with regulators, investors, issuers and banks since March and may unveil the disclosure proposal as soon as next month, said Huston Loke, head of global structured finance at DBRS.

"In the credit crunch it became clear that a number of investors weren't aware of all the risks they were entering into in acquiring their investments, and the disclosure frameworks demanded by the regulators and what the issuers were willing to put out were not always sufficient," Mr. Loke said.

Rating agencies around the world are revamping their ratings and policies to address criticism and demands from regulators after the collapse in the US subprime loan market created a domino effect that led to hundreds of downgrades of securities based on the loans.

Many investors were blindsided when securities that were triple-A-rated had their ratings slashed as defaults on mortgages piled up. DBRS itself has come under fire for giving top ratings to some of the asset-backed commercial paper that ended up frozen last August when the credit crunch hit.

"What we want to see is investors having a shot at getting the right information, where they can look at it, do some of their own analytics, get an appreciation for the risk and then decide, yes, I will invest in this."

(continued)

REAL-WORLD RETURNS 2-5 *continued*

DBRS rival **Standard & Poor's Corp.** yesterday announced a 27-step plan to increase investor confidence in ratings. Another big US player in bond ratings, **Moody's Investors Service Inc.**, is considering switching ratings of complex debt securities from letter grades that are also used for standard corporate bonds and government debt to numerical grades, driving home to investors that the debt is different.

S&P's proposals encompass enhanced disclosure, including a "flag" to help investors differentiate between traditional corporate or government bonds and structured securities. The firm also introduced broader reforms focused on governance, such as creating an ombudsman to watch for conflicts of interest and rotating analysts periodically so they do not become too close to bond issuers.

A key plank in S&P's plan is to educate investors about credit ratings, both how they work and what they mean.

"Part of the misunderstanding in the market is that when you assign a triple-A, people believe it's never going to change," said Vickie Tillman, an executive vice-president at S&P.

"Ratings do change. They change with circumstances, and they change with economic changes."

S&P consulted with regulators and central banks around the world, Ms. Tillman said, before settling on the package of reforms. Indeed, Canada's central bank has been vocal in calls for more clarity in ratings of structure products.

"Whatever helps to improve transparency and give investors confidence, that's just good for the market," said Mr. Loke of DBRS.

However, DBRS isn't planning a wholesale revamp of its governance structure like S&P. Mr. Loke said ratings agencies are better off focusing on ensuring that securities are structured robustly enough to withstand market turmoil, rather than on "pretty complicated governance frameworks. Because ultimately these transactions were unable to withstand the stress of the slump in the US housing market because they didn't have adequate amounts of credit enhancements to protect them against the unknown."

S&P'S PLANS

- Create an ombudsman to watch for potential conflicts of interest and analysis problems.
- Rotate analysts periodically to keep them from getting too close to issuers.
- Focus on training.
- Simplify ratings criteria.
- Add "What if" scenarios that help investors judge risks.
- Publish a manual to explain what ratings are for and how they should be used.
- Launch "market outreach" to promote understanding of complex securities.

Source: Erman, Boyd, www.globeinvestorgold.com, March 17, 2008.

We conclude by noting that while the Canadian market for corporate bonds has grown in importance in recent years, it is still smaller than the Canadian government bond market, as discussed above. In addition, the $418 billion US in Canadian corporate bonds outstanding in June 2007 is very small relative to corporate bond markets in other countries. For example, the United States, Japan, France, Italy, and Germany had $17.0 trillion, $1.6 trillion, $1.1 trillion, $1.1 trillion, and $1.01 trillion US of corporate debt outstanding at that time. In fact, the Canadian figure accounts for only approximately 1.5 percent of the world corporate debt market.

Asset-Backed Securities

The money and capital markets are constantly adapting to meet new requirements and conditions. This has given rise to new types of securities that were not previously available. "Securitization" refers to the transformation of illiquid, risky individual loans into more liquid, less risky securities referred to as **asset-backed securities (ABS)**. The best example of this process is mortgage-backed securities (MBS). These are created when a financial institution purchases (or originates) a number of mortgage loans that are then repackaged and sold to investors as mortgage pools. Investors in MBSs are, in effect, purchasing a piece of a mortgage pool. MBS investors assume little default risk because most mortgages are guaranteed by a federal government agency, as described below.

The Canada Mortgage and Housing Corporation (CMHC) introduced MBSs in Canada in 1987. Similar to the GNMA in the United States (which fully supports Ginnie Mae issues), the CMHC issues fully guaranteed securities in support of the mortgage market. These securities have attracted considerable attention in recent years because the principal and interest payments on the underlying mortgages used as collateral are "passed through" to the bondholder monthly as the mortgages are repaid. However, these securities are not completely riskless because they can receive varying amounts of monthly payments depending on how quickly homeowners pay off their mortgages. Although the stated maturity can be as long as 40 years, the average life of these securities has actually been much shorter.

ABSs are created when an underwriter, such as a bank, bundles some type of asset-linked debt (usually consumer oriented) and sells investors the right to receive payments made on that debt. As a result of the trend to securitization, other asset-backed securities have proliferated as financial institutions have rushed to securitize various types of loans.

Marketable securities have been backed by car loans, credit-card receivables, railway car leases, small-business loans, leases for photocopiers or aircraft, and so forth. The assets that can be securitized seem to be limited only by the imagination of the packagers, as evidenced by the fact that new asset types include items such as royalty streams from films, student loans, mutual fund fees, tax liens, monthly hydro bills, and delinquent child support payments!

The original use of securitization was to enhance the liquidity of the residential mortgage market, and MBSs grew from about 15 percent of mortgages in 1980 to more than 63 percent in 2003. In fact, the market value of global MBSs exceeded $8 trillion in 2006, which begs the question: Why do investors like these securities? The attractions are relatively high yields and relatively short maturities (often five years) combined with investment-grade credit ratings, typically the highest two ratings available. Investors are often protected by a bond insurer. Institutional investors, such as pension funds and life insurance companies, have become increasingly attracted to these securities because of the higher yields; the same is true of foreign investors.

As for risk, securitization works best when packaged loans are homogeneous, so that income streams and risks are more predictable. This is clearly the case for home mortgages, for example, which must adhere to strict guidelines, but for some of the newer loans being considered for packaging—such as loans for boats and motorcycles—the smaller amount of information results in a larger risk from unanticipated factors.

However, as we have seen in 2007 and 2008, investors underestimated the risks associated with many of these investments. Indeed, the market value of MBSs had fallen to $6.5 trillion by February of 2008, as a result of the massive market write-downs emanating from the sub-prime crisis fallout. This decline in value occurred despite the fact that the actual number of low grade (i.e., sub-prime) mortgages comprising MBSs was "supposed to be" relatively small. Indeed, many investors (mainly institutional investors—the so-called "experts") holding various MBSs and ABSs experienced severe losses as the market values of these instruments declined substantially. Investors in the Canadian non-bank backed ABCP market are still waiting to see how large will be their losses, when (and if) trading begins again in this market. As alluded to in Real-World Returns 2-5, the utter collapse of these markets has caused massive damage to the reputations of the debt rating agencies, since they failed to identify the inherent risks in these types of investments, and many market participants relied heavily (too heavily) on these ratings.

Asset-Backed Securities (ABS)

Securities issued against some type of asset-linked debts bundled together, such as credit card receivables or mortgages.

Rates on Fixed-Income Securities

Interest rates on fixed-income securities have fluctuated widely over the years as inflationary expectations as well as supply and demand conditions for long-term funds change. As one would expect on the basis of the return–risk trade-off explained in Chapter 1, corporate rates generally exceed government rates because of the higher risk, and lower-rated corporate securities yield more than do higher-rated ones.

Equity Securities

learning objective 5
Distinguish among preferred stock, income trusts, and common stock.

Unlike their fixed-income counterparts, equity securities represent an ownership interest in a corporation. These securities provide a residual claim—after payment of all fixed-income obligations—on the income and assets of a corporation. There are three forms of equities: preferred stock, income trusts, and common stock. Investors have traditionally been more interested in common stocks; however, income trusts have attracted a lot of attention from investors in recent years.

Preferred Stock

Most preferred shares in Canada are traded on the TSX and in the United States on the NYSE. They generally offer fixed monthly or quarterly dividends and are rated as to credit risk (similar to bonds and commercial paper). Although technically an equity security, **preferred stock** is often referred to as a hybrid, because it resembles both equity and fixed-income instruments.

Preferred Stock
A hybrid security that is part equity and part fixed-income because it increases in value but also pays a fixed dividend.

As an equity security, preferred stock has an infinite life and pays dividends. It resembles fixed-income securities in that the amount of the dividend is fixed and known in advance, providing a stream of income very similar to that of a bond. The difference is that the stream continues forever, unless the issue is called or otherwise retired. Similar to bonds, the prices of preferreds are very sensitive to interest rates, but their price fluctuations often exceed those in bonds due to their long-term nature.

Preferred shareholders rank below creditors but above common shareholders in terms of priority of payment of income and in case the corporation is liquidated. While payment of preferred dividends is not obligatory like interest payments, payment to common shareholders has to wait until preferred shareholders receive full payment of the dividends to which they are entitled. Most preferred shares are non-voting; however, once a stated number of dividend payments have been omitted, it is common practice to assign voting privileges to the preferred. In addition, failure to pay anticipated preferred dividends weakens investor confidence in the issuer, which has an impact on its general credit and borrowing power. Finally, preferred shares usually have a "cumulative" feature associated with their dividends. This requires the firm to pay all preferred dividends (both current and arrears) before paying any dividends to common shareholders, and that makes the preferred less risky than common shares from the investor's point of view.

Preferred dividends are paid from after-tax earnings, and, unlike interest payments, they do not provide the issuer with a tax-deductible expense. However, individual investors receive relief in the form of a dividend tax credit, which implies they will pay lower taxes on a dollar of dividend income than on interest income. In addition, dividends received by one Canadian corporation from another Canadian corporation are not taxable. As a result of this tax incentive many Canadian financial institutions (banks and insurance companies, in particular) used to be large participants in the market for preferred shares. However, tax laws were changed in 1987, which required specified financial institutions (including banks and insurance companies) to treat preferred dividend payments as the equivalent to interest (which is fully taxable). The result of this change in tax laws is that fewer new issues of preferred shares have occurred since then.

Companies issue preferred shares as a compromise between the demands created by debt, and the dilution of common equity caused by the issuance of additional common shares, or when market conditions are unfavourable for new common share issues. Investors may be attracted to them if they want dividend income, which offers tax advantages over interest income. In addition, some issues have special features that make them attractive to investors. For example, some preferred issues are convertible into common stock at the owner's option. Similar to convertible debt, most convertible preferred shares are callable at a premium over par value.

Other types of preferred shares include

1. Retractable preferreds, which can be tendered by the holder to the issuer for redemption;

2. Variable-rate or floating-rate preferreds, which have the dividend rate tied to current market interest rates;

3. Participating preferreds, which have certain pre-specified rights to a share in company earnings over and above their specified rate.

In addition, some preferreds require the company to purchase a specified amount in the open market if they are available at or below the stipulated price. This provides built-in market support for these shares. Sinking fund provisions are less common for preferred share issues. They have the potential disadvantage to investors that the required purchases may be called in by lot at the sinking fund price plus accrued and unpaid dividends if the fund's open market operations are unsuccessful.

Income Trusts

Income Trusts

Investment instruments that pay out a substantial portion of cash flows generated from the underlying revenue-generating assets.

While **income trusts** have been around for a long time, they have grown in importance dramatically over the last few years, as discussed in Chapter 1. They are usually structured so that the trust itself invests in the shares and debt obligations of an underlying operating company. Since it is a trust, all the income is passed through to trust unitholders without any tax consequences to the trust. Further, since the trust owns both the debt and equity of the company, the use of debt can be maximized to reduce (or eliminate) any corporate income tax, provided the trust pays out most (or all) of its income to unitholders. Obviously this structure provides the businesses with the ultimate incentive to pay out most of their earnings in order to avoid paying taxes. This feature, in turn, made trusts very popular among investors.

The tax efficient structure of trusts, along with their popularity among investors, led to dramatic growth in this market. As of March 31, 2006, there were 238 income trusts listed on the Toronto Stock Exchange (TSX), up from 73 in 2001, and only a handful in the mid 1990s. In fact, the total market capitalization of these instruments grew from $1.4 billion in 1994 to $192 billion by March of 2006, representing approximately 10 percent of the quoted market value of the TSX.[11] Income trusts became the major source of equity initial public offerings (IPOs) in Canada during the 2000s, often accounting for over half of all new equity IPOs. Some of these trust IPOs provided financing for new businesses, while others were associated with existing companies "converting" to the trust structure. As a result of this growth, the TSX fully incorporated income trusts into the S&P/TSX Composite Index as of March 2006.

On October 31, 2006, Finance Minister Jim Flaherty announced unexpectedly, and in contradiction of a key election promise, that the distributions made by newly created trusts would be taxed at prevailing corporate tax rates, and that this new tax would apply to existing trusts beginning in 2011. This announcement was made just as Canadian telecommunications giants TELUS Corp. and BCE Inc. were in the midst of preparing to convert from the traditional corporate structure to the income trust structure, which would have added another $50 billion or so in market cap to the income trust market.

Not surprisingly, both BCE Inc. and TELUS Corp. subsequently cancelled their plans to convert to the trust structure, and many other planned income trust IPOs were also cancelled. Indeed, the October 31 announcement brought a dramatic end to the growth of income trusts, and severely damaged the Canadian equity IPO market, as can be seen in Real-World Returns 2-6.

---

[11]TSX website: www.tsx.com.

REAL-WORLD RETURNS 2-6

Income Trust Tax Slowed Canada's IPO Pace in 2007

The value of Canadian initial public offerings was down substantially last year despite a fourth-quarter surge, PricewaterhouseCoopers said in a report Monday.

It said there were 90 IPOs last year on the Toronto Stock Exchange and the TSX Venture, worth a total of $3.4 billion in 2007. That was down from 109 new offerings in 2006, worth $5.6 billion.

"A host of different factors conspired against the IPO market last year," Ross Sinclair, national leader of PricewaterhouseCoopers' IPO and income-trust services, said in a statement, noting the impact of the federal government announcing in October 2006 it would start taxing new income trusts as corporations in the new year.

"The environment in 2007 was anything but predictable and stable," he added. "The impact of the loss of income trusts in the market was felt most of the year, as potential issuers tried to chart a course for the future."

In the fourth quarter of 2007, PricewaterhouseCoopers counted 19 IPOs, worth $2.1 billion. That compared with five launches in the same quarter a year earlier for $987 million.

One particular IPO that made the difference last in the year was the one for Franco-Nevada Corp. for $1.1 billion. PricewaterhouseCoopers said without that deal, the annual total for IPOs would have been $2.3 billion. That's close to the $2.1 billion worth of IPOs in 2001, which was the lowest level in a decade.

Source: Retrieved from www.financialpost.com, *Financial Post*, January 7, 2008. Reprinted by permission. Copyright © 2007 CanWest Interactive, a division of CanWest MediaWorks Publications, Inc. All rights reserved.

Common Stock

Common stock represents the ownership interest of corporations or the equity of the shareholders, and we can use the term equity securities interchangeably. If a firm's shares are owned by only a few individuals, the firm is said to be closely held. Many companies choose to go public, or they sell common stock to the general public, primarily to let them raise additional capital more easily. If a corporation meets certain requirements, it may choose to be listed on one or more exchanges such as the TSX. Otherwise, it will be listed in the over-the-counter market (this process is discussed in Chapter 4).

As the residual claimants of the corporation, shareholders are entitled to income remaining after the fixed-income claimants such as the preferred shareholders have been paid; also, in case of liquidation of the corporation, they are entitled to the remaining assets after all other claims (including preferred stock) are satisfied.

As owners, the holders of common stock are entitled to elect the directors of the corporation and vote on major issues.[12] Each shareholder is allowed to cast votes equal to the number of shares owned when such votes take place at the annual meeting of the corporation, which each shareholder is allowed to attend.[13] Most stockholders vote by proxy, meaning that they authorize someone else

Common Stock
An equity security representing the ownership interest in a corporation.

---

[12]The voting rights of the shareholders give them legal control of the corporation. In theory, the board of directors controls the management of the corporation, but in many cases the effective result is the opposite. Shareholders can regain control if they are sufficiently dissatisfied.

[13]Most shareholders do not attend, often allowing management to vote their proxy. Therefore, although technically more than 50 percent of the outstanding shares are needed for control of a firm, effective control can often be exercised with considerably less because not all of the shares are voted.

(most often management) to vote their shares. Sometimes proxy battles occur, whereby one or more groups unhappy with corporate policies seek to bring about changes.

The amount of protection afforded shareholders by this right to vote is a matter of debate. The value of this privilege is in fact a function of several elements of corporate governance, including the effectiveness of the board of directors in serving in the best interests of shareholders.

There often exists a clause in a corporation's charter that grants existing shareholders the first or pre-emptive right to purchase any new common stock sold by the corporation. The right is a piece of paper giving each stockholder the option to buy a specified number of new shares, usually at a discount, during a specified short period of time. These rights are valuable and can be sold in the market.

Finally, shareholders also have limited liability, meaning they cannot be held responsible for the debts of the company or lose more than their original investment. In the event of financial difficulties, creditors have recourse only to the assets of the corporation, leaving the stockholders protected. This is perhaps the greatest advantage of the corporation and the reason why it has been so successful.

Characteristics of Common Stocks

The par value for a common stock, unlike that of a bond or preferred stock, is generally not a significant economic variable. Corporations can make the par value any number they choose and an often-used par value is $1. New stock is usually sold for more than par value, with the difference recorded on the balance sheet as "capital in excess of par value" or "additional paid-in capital." Canadian corporations incorporated under the Canada Business Corporations Act (CBCA) and under most provincial acts can no longer issue shares with par value.

Book Value

The accounting value of common equity as shown on the balance sheet.

The **book value** of a corporation is the accounting value of the common equity as shown on the books (i.e., balance sheet). It is the total value of common equity for a corporation, represented by the sum of common stock outstanding, capital in excess of par value and/or contributed surplus, and retained earnings. Dividing this sum—total book value—by the number of common shares outstanding, produces the book value per share. In effect, book value is the accounting value of the stockholders' equity. Although book value per share plays a role in making investment decisions, market value per share is the critical item of interest to investors.

EXAMPLE 2-3: BOOK VALUE FOR MAGNA INTERNATIONAL INC.

Magna International Inc. reported $7.157 billion in common shareholders' equity for fiscal year end 2006. This is the book value of common equity. Based on the year-end common shares outstanding of 109.880 million for that year (a figure obtained from the company's annual report), the book value per share was $65.13.

The market value or price of the equity is the variable of concern to investors. The aggregate market value for a corporation is calculated by multiplying the market price per share of the stock by the number of shares outstanding. This represents the total value of the firm as determined in the marketplace. The market value of one share of stock, of course, is simply the "observed" current market price. At the time the observation for Magna's book value was recorded, the market price was in the $93.87 range. This implies that Magna's market-to-book ratio (discussed in Chapter 13) was $93.87/$65.13 = 1.44.

Dividends

Cash payments declared and paid by corporations to stockholders.

Dividends are the only cash payments regularly made by corporations to their stockholders. They are decided upon and declared by the board of directors quarterly and can range from zero to virtually any amount the corporation can afford to pay (up to 100 percent of present and past net earnings). Roughly half of the companies listed on the TSX (and three-fourths of the companies listed on the NYSE) pay dividends. However, the common stockholder has no specific promises to receive any cash from the corporation since the stock never matures and dividends do not have to be paid. Therefore, common stocks involve substantial risk because the dividend is at the company's discretion and stock prices can fluctuate sharply, which means that the value of investors' claims may rise and fall rapidly over relatively short periods of time.

The two dividend terms dividend yield and payout ratio are important considerations for investors.

The **dividend yield** is the income component of a stock's return stated on a percentage basis. It is one of the two components of total return, which is discussed in Chapter 6. Dividend yield is commonly calculated as the most recent annual dividend amount divided by the current market price.

The **payout ratio** is the ratio of dividends to earnings. It indicates the percentage of a firm's earnings paid out in cash to its stockholders. The complement of the payout ratio is the retention ratio, and it indicates the percentage of a firm's current earnings retained by it for reinvestment purposes.

EXAMPLE 2-4: PAYOUT RATIO FOR MAGNA INTERNATIONAL INC.

Magna's 2006 earnings were $4.86 per share, and it paid an annual dividend on its common shares of $1.52 per share. Assuming a price for Magna of $93.87, the dividend yield would be $1.52/$93.87, or 1.62 percent. The payout ratio was $1.52/$4.86, or 31.28 percent, and the retention ratio was 68.72 percent (i.e., 100 percent – 31.28 percent).

Dividends are commonly declared and paid quarterly, but to receive a declared dividend, an investor must be a holder of record on the specified date that a company closes its stock transfer books and compiles the list of stockholders to be paid (which is generally done two to four weeks before the payment date). The ex dividend date is set at the second business day before the record date, and shares trade without the right to the associated dividend on and after this date. Since stock trades settle on the third business day after a trade, a purchaser of the share two days before the record date would not settle until the day after the record date, and would thus not be entitled to receive the dividend. Shares are said to trade cum dividend up to the ex dividend date, and trade ex dividend thereafter. This will be reflected in the share price, which typically falls by an amount close to the dividend amount on the ex rights date.

EXAMPLE 2-5: ANNOUNCING DIVIDENDS FOR MAGNA INTERNATIONAL INC.

Assume that the board of directors of Magna meets on April 24 and declares a quarterly dividend, payable on June 30. April 24 is called the declaration date. The board will declare a holder-of-record date, say, June 9. The books close on this date, but Magna goes ex-dividend on June 7 (assuming June 7 and June 8 are regular business days). To receive this dividend, an investor must purchase the stock by June 6. The dividend will be mailed to the stockholders of record on the payment date, June 30.

Stock dividends and stock splits attract considerable investor attention. A **stock dividend** is a payment by a corporation in shares of stock instead of cash.[14] A **stock split** involves the division of a corporation's stock by issuing a specified number of new shares while simultaneously lowering the face value of outstanding shares. With a stock split, the book value and par value of the equity are changed; for example, each would be cut in half with a 2-for-1 split. However, on a practical basis, there is little difference between a stock dividend and a stock split since the net result of both actions is an increase in the number of shares outstanding.

Dividend Yield

The income component of a stock's return, generally calculated by dividing the current annual dividend by the prevailing market price.

Payout Ratio

The percentage of a firm's earnings paid out in cash to its stockholders, calculated by dividing dividends by earnings.

Stock Dividend

A payment by a corporation of a dividend in shares of stock rather than cash.

Stock Split

The division of a corporation's stock by issuing a specified number of new shares while simultaneously lowering the face value of outstanding shares.

---

[14]The amount of the stock dividend received by an investor equals the number of shares he or she receives, times the prevailing market price per share. The amount is taxable in the same manner as a cash dividend for this dollar amount.

EXAMPLE 2-6: SPLITTING STOCK 2-FOR-1

A 5 percent stock dividend would entitle an owner of 100 shares of a particular stock to an additional five shares. A 2-for-1 stock split would double the number of shares of the stock outstanding, double an individual owner's number of shares (e.g., from 100 shares to 200 shares), and cut the price in half at the time of the split.

Stock data, as reported to investors in most investment information sources and in the company's reports to stockholders, are adjusted for all stock dividends and stock splits. These adjustments must be made when splits or dividends occur in order for legitimate comparisons to be made for the data.

The important question to investors is the value of the distribution, whether a dividend or a split. It is clear that the recipient has more shares (i.e., more pieces of paper), but has anything of real value been received? Other things being equal, these additional shares do not represent additional value because proportional ownership has not changed. Quite simply, the pieces of paper—stock certificates—have been repackaged. For example, if you own 1,000 shares of a corporation that has 100,000 shares of stock outstanding, your proportional ownership is 1 percent; with a 2-for-1 stock split, you now own 2,000 shares out of a total of 200,000 shares outstanding, but your proportional ownership is still 1 percent.

Regardless of the above, some evidence does suggest that the stock price receives a boost following a split. A recent study by a university professor, David Ikenberry, finds that such stocks tend to outperform the market in the first year following a split by an average eight percentage points and that the effect continues for some three years following the split. According to S&P data, split shares tend to outperform the market for some 18 months following the split. Typically, the dividend is raised at the time of the split, which would have a positive effect by itself. If the above findings are correct, it suggests that management signals with splits and dividends that they are confident about future prospects, which in turn should boost investor confidence.

P/E Ratio

The ratio of stock price to earnings, using historical, current, or estimated data. Also known as earnings multiplier. (*See also* E/P Ratio.)

The **P/E ratio**, also referred to as the earnings multiplier, is generally calculated as the ratio of the current market price to the firm's most recent earnings, although it can also be based on expected future earnings. It is an indication of how much the market as a whole is willing to pay per dollar of earnings. It is standard investing practice to refer to stocks as selling at, say, 10 or 15 times earnings. Investors have traditionally used such a classification to categorize stocks. Growth stocks, for example, generally sell at high multiples, compared with the average stock, because of their expected higher earnings growth.

The P/E ratio is a widely reported variable, appearing in daily newspapers and websites carrying stock information, in brokerage reports covering particular stocks, in magazine articles recommending various companies, and so forth. It is usually reported in the media as the current price divided by the latest 12-month earnings. For example, the P/E ratio for Magna International Inc. based on the information above would be $93.87/$4.86 = 19.31. However, variations of this ratio are often used in the valuation of common stocks. In fact, the P/E ratio in its various forms is one of the best-known and most often cited variables in security analysis and is familiar to almost all investors.[15] The P/E ratio is discussed in great detail in Chapters 13 through 17, which deal with common stock valuation.

Investing Internationally in Equities

Canadians can invest internationally in a variety of ways. First, they may purchase shares of foreign companies that list directly on Canadian exchanges or in the Canadian over-the-counter market. Alternatively, they may purchase shares of foreign companies in the country of origin or purchase options or

---

[15]In calculating P/E ratios on the basis of either the latest reported earnings or the expected earnings, problems can arise when comparing P/E ratios among companies if some of them are experiencing, or are expected to experience, abnormally high or low earnings. To avoid this problem, some market participants calculate a normalized earnings estimate. Normalized earnings are intended to reflect the "normal" level of a company's earnings; that is, transitory effects are presumably excluded, thus providing the user with a more accurate estimate of "true" earnings.

futures contracts on foreign stock indexes. Finally, they can purchase foreign securities indirectly by purchasing units (or shares) of investment companies (mutual funds, closed-end funds, or exchange traded funds) specializing in foreign securities, as discussed in Chapter 3. The latter method is the approach used by the vast majority of Canadians wishing to invest globally.

CHECK YOUR UNDERSTANDING

2-7. Consider two corporate bonds: one rated AAA, the other rated BBB. Could you say with confidence that the first bond will not default while for the second bond there is some reasonable probability of default?

2-8. Should risk-averse investors avoid junk bonds?

2-9. Why might investors opt to hold preferred stocks rather than bonds in their portfolios?

2-10. Is it fair to say that income trusts became popular investment vehicles primarily because of the tax efficiency of the payments they make to investors?

2-11. Suppose you own common stock in a company that has just declared bankruptcy because it cannot pay the amounts owing to its bondholders. Can the bond investors expect you to pay off the debt? Why or why not?

DERIVATIVE SECURITIES

We focus our attention here on the two types of derivative securities that are of interest to most investors. Options and futures contracts are **derivative securities**, so named because their value is derived from their connected underlying security. Numerous types of options and futures are traded in world markets. Furthermore, there are different types of options other than the puts and calls discussed here. For example, a **warrant** is a corporate-created, long-term option on the underlying common stock of the company. It gives the holder the right to buy the stock from the company at a stated price within a stated period of time, often several years. They are often issued as "sweeteners" attached to a debt, preferred share, or common share issue to make the issue more attractive to investors.

Options and futures contracts share some common characteristics. Both have standardized features that allow them to be traded quickly and cheaply on organized exchanges. In addition to facilitating the trading of these securities, the exchange guarantees the performance of these contracts and its clearing house allows an investor to reverse his or her original position before maturity. For example, a seller of a futures contract can buy the contract and cancel the obligation that the contract carries. The exchanges and associated clearing houses for both options and futures contracts have worked extremely well.

Options and futures contracts are important to investors because they provide a way for them to manage portfolio risk. For example, investors may incur the risk of adverse currency fluctuations if they invest in foreign securities, or they may incur the risk that interest rates will adversely affect their fixed-income securities. Options and futures contracts can be used to limit some, or all, of these risks, thereby providing risk-control possibilities.

Options and futures contracts have important differences in their trading, the assets they can affect, their risk factor, and so forth. Perhaps the biggest difference to note now is that a futures contract is an obligation to buy or sell, but an options contract is only the right as opposed to an obligation to do so. The buyer of an option has limited liability, but the buyer of a futures contract does not.

Options

In today's investing world, the word **options** refers to **puts** and **calls**. Options are created not by corporations but by investors seeking to trade in claims on a particular common stock, stock index, or futures contract. A standard equity call (put) option gives the holder (buyer) the right to purchase (sell) 100 shares of a particular stock at a specified price (called the exercise price) within a specified time.[16] The maturities on most new puts and calls are available up to several months away, although **LEAPs** have maturity dates of several years. Many exercise prices are created for each underlying common stock, giving investors a choice in both the maturity and the price they will pay or receive.

LEAPs

Options to buy (calls) or sell (puts) securities with longer maturity dates of up to several years, also known as long-term options.

Holders (buyers) of calls receive the right to purchase a specified number of shares at a specified price. These investors are betting that the price of the underlying common stock will rise, making the call option more valuable. Put buyers receive the right to sell a specified number of shares at a specified price. They are betting that the price of the underlying common stock will decline, making the put option more valuable. Both put and call options are written (created) by other investors who are betting the opposite of their respective purchasers. The sellers (writers) receive an option premium for selling each new contract while the buyer pays this option premium.

Once the option is created and the writer (seller) receives the premium from the buyer, it can be traded repeatedly in the secondary market. The premium is simply the market price of the contract as determined by investors. The price will fluctuate constantly, just as the price of the underlying common stock changes. This makes sense, because the option is affected directly by the price of the stock that gives it value. In addition, the option's value is affected by the time remaining to maturity, current interest rates, the volatility of the stock, and the price at which the option can be exercised.

Puts and calls allow both buyers and sellers (writers) to speculate on the short-term movements of certain common stocks. Buyers obtain an option on the common stock for a small, known premium, which is the maximum that the buyer can lose. If the buyer is correct about the price movements on the underlying assets, gains are magnified in relation to having bought (or sold short) the assets because a smaller investment is required. However, the buyer has only a short time in which to be correct. Writers (sellers) earn the premium as income, based on their beliefs about a stock. They win or lose, depending on whether their beliefs are correct or incorrect.

Options can be used in a variety of strategies, giving investors opportunities to manage their portfolios in ways that would be unavailable in the absence of such instruments. For example, since the most a buyer of a put or call can lose is the cost of the option, the buyer is able to truncate the distribution of potential returns. That is, after a certain point, no matter how much the underlying stock price changes, the buyer's position does not change. Some basic options strategies are discussed in Chapter 19.

Forward and Futures Contracts

Forward Contracts

Commitments today to transact in the future.

Forward contracts are commitments today to transact in the future. Two parties agree to exchange an underlying asset, such as gold, in the future at a price that is determined today. Both parties have agreed to a deferred delivery at a sales price that is currently determined. These contracts are sold through the over-the-counter market, with no funds being exchanged initially.

Forward contracts are centuries old, while organized futures markets, on the other hand, only go back to the mid-nineteenth century in Chicago. Futures markets are, in effect, organized and standardized forward markets. An organized futures exchange standardizes the non-standard forward contracts, establishing such features as contract size, delivery dates, and condition of the items that can be delivered. Only the price and number of contracts are left for futures traders to negotiate. Individuals can trade without personal contact with each other because of the centralized marketplace. Performance is guaranteed by a clearing house, relieving one party to the transaction from worry that the other party will fail to honour its commitment.

Futures contracts have been available on commodities such as corn and wheat for a long time. Today, they are also readily available on several financial instruments, including stock market indexes, currencies, Treasury bills, bankers' acceptances, and government bonds.

---

[16]Option expiry dates are expressed in terms of the month in which they expire. Option contracts expire on the Saturday following the third Friday of the month, so the third Friday is the last trading day for these instruments.

A **futures contract** is an agreement that provides for the future exchange of a particular asset between a buyer and a seller. The seller contracts to deliver the asset at a specified delivery date in exchange for a specified amount of cash from the buyer. Although the cash is not required until the delivery date, a "good faith deposit," called the margin, is required to reduce the chance of default by either party. The margin is small compared with the value of the contract.

Most futures contracts are not exercised. Instead, they are "offset" by taking a position opposite to the one initially undertaken. For example, a purchaser of a May Government of Canada bond futures contract can close out the position by selling an identical May contract before the delivery date, while a seller can close out the same position by purchasing that contract.

Most participants in futures are either hedgers or speculators. Hedgers seek to reduce price uncertainty over some future period. For example, by purchasing a futures contract, a hedger can lock in a specific price for the asset and be protected from adverse price movements. Similarly, sellers can protect themselves from downward price movements. Speculators, on the other hand, seek to profit from the uncertainty that will occur in the future. If prices are expected to rise, contracts will be purchased, and if prices are expected to fall, contracts will be sold. Correct anticipations can result in very large profits because only a small margin is required. Futures are discussed at length in Chapter 20.

In addition to traditional options and futures contracts, there also exist options on futures. Calls on futures give the buyer the right, but not the obligation, to assume the futures position.

Futures Contracts
Agreements providing for the future exchange of a particular asset between a buyer and seller at a specified date for a specified amount.

CHECK YOUR UNDERSTANDING

2-12. What is the most significant conceptual difference between a futures contract and an options contract?

2-13. Suppose you believed that the price of a particular common stock would soon fall dramatically. Which type of derivative contract would be best suited to allowing you to profit from the situation?

SUMMARY

This summary relates to the objectives for this chapter.

1. **Describe the major types of financial assets and how they are organized.**
   Investors may invest either directly in non-marketable assets, money market instruments, capital market securities (divided into fixed-income and equity securities), and derivative securities, or indirectly in the form of investment company shares (e.g., mutual funds).

2. **Explain what non-marketable financial assets are.**
   Non-marketable financial assets are highly liquid, safe investments available from insured financial institutions or issued by the Canadian government. In contrast to marketable securities, these assets represent personal transactions between the owner and the issuer. Non-marketable financial assets are widely owned by investors and include savings deposits, GICs, and Canada Savings Bonds.

3. **Describe the important features of money market securities.**
   Money market investments are characterized as short-term, highly liquid, very safe investments. These include (but are not limited to) Treasury bills, commercial paper, Eurodollars, repurchase agreements, and banker's acceptances.

4. **Describe the important features of capital market securities.**
   Capital market securities have maturities in excess of one year and are of two types: fixed-income securities and equity securities. Fixed-income securities have a specified payment and/or

repayment schedule and are issued by governments and corporations. Equity securities represent an ownership interest in a corporation or trust and are of three forms: preferred stock, common stock, and income trusts.

5. **Distinguish among preferred stock, income trusts, and common stock.**
Preferred stock, while technically an equity security, is often regarded by investors as a fixed-income type of security because of its stated (and fixed) dividend. Preferred stock has no maturity date but may be retired by calls or other means. Common stock (equity) represents the ownership of the corporation. The stockholder is the residual claimant in terms of both income and assets.

6. **Understand the basics of options and futures.**
Options allow both buyers and sellers (writers) to speculate on and/or hedge the price movements of stocks for which these claims are available. Calls are multiple-month rights to purchase a common stock at a specified price, while puts are the same rights to sell. Futures contracts provide for the future exchange of a particular asset between a buyer and a seller. A recent innovation is options on futures.

KEY TERMS

Asset-backed securities (ABS), p.40	Dividends, p.44	Payout ratio, p.45
Bonds, p.33	Dividend yield, p. 45	P/E ratio, p.46
Bond rating, p.37	Extendible bonds, p.35	Preferred stock, p.41
Book value, p.44	Fixed-income securities, p.33	Puts, p.47
Calls, p.47	Forward contracts, p.48	Retractable bonds, p.35
Call provision, p.35	Futures contract, p.49	Senior securities, p.37
Capital markets, p.33	Income trusts, p.42	Stock dividend, p.45
Common stock, p.43	Indirect investing, p.26	Stock split, p.45
Convertible bonds, p.35	LEAPs, p.48	Treasury bill (T-bill), p.31
Corporate bonds, p.37	Liquidity, p.28	Treasury bond, p.34
Debenture, p.37	Money market, p.30	Warrant, p.47
Derivative securities, p.47	Options, p.47	Zero coupon bond, p.34
	Par value (Face value), p.34	

REVIEW QUESTIONS

2-1. Outline the classification scheme for marketable securities used in the chapter. Explain each of the terms involved.

2-2. What is the difference between a savings deposit and a GIC?

2-3. What does it mean for Treasury bills to be sold at a discount?

2-4. Why is the common stockholder referred to as a "residual claimant"?

2-5. Do all common stocks pay dividends? Who decides?

2-6. Distinguish between a serial bond and a term bond.

2-7. What is meant by "indirect" investing?

2-8. Why should we expect that the six-month Treasury bill rate will be less than the six-month commercial paper rate?

2-9. What types of securities are traded on the money markets? What types are traded on the capital markets? Give examples of each type obtained from a daily business newspaper.

2-10. From the investor's perspective, what is the difference between a warrant and a call option?

2-11. What are the advantages and disadvantages of investing in Government of Canada bonds versus corporate bonds?

2-12. What are the differences between a Canada Savings Bond and a Government of Canada long-term bond?

2-13. Why is preferred stock referred to as a "hybrid" security?

2-14. What is meant by the term derivative security? What is the major determinant of the price of a derivative security?

2-15. What is meant by the term securitization? Give at least two examples of asset-backed securities.

2-16. Why are convertible and retractable features generally advantageous for bondholders? How do they pay for these privileges?

2-17. What is the value to investors of stock dividends and splits?

2-18. What are the advantages and disadvantages of being a holder of the common stock of Bombardier Inc. as opposed to owning a Bombardier bond?

2-19. Assume that a company whose stock you are interested in will pay regular quarterly dividends soon. Looking at the stock listings on-line, you observe a dividend figure of $3.20 listed for this stock. The board of directors has declared the dividend payable on September 1, with a holder-of-record date of August 15. When must you buy the stock to receive the dividend, and how much will you receive if you buy 150 shares?

2-20. List three types of derivative securities. Explain the difference between each type.

2-21. Under what conditions might a bondholder utilize the convertible feature of a bond?

2-22. Under what conditions might a bondholder utilize the retractable feature of a bond?

2-23. How is it possible that an investor who buys shares in a company may make a profit even if the share price drops?

2-24. Do you think that a stock with a high dividend yield will be more or less risky than a stock that does not pay any dividend? Why?

2-25. Is the call provision on a bond an advantage to the investor or an advantage to the issuing corporation? Given your knowledge of risk and return, what effect should the call feature have on the pricing of a bond; in other words, will the bond offer a higher or lower rate of interest? Why?

2-26. From the corporation's perspective, what are the differences between a warrant and a call option? If the call option is exercised, what will happen to the share price of the underlying company? If the warrant is exercised, what might happen to the share price of the underlying company?

2-27. What do you think some of the contributing factors might be when a company's management determines what the dividend payout ratio will be?

2-28. Name and briefly describe four types of money market securities.

2-29. Give at least two examples of asset-backed securities.

2-30. What kind of investment would be attractive to an individual who is in a high tax bracket?

2-31. Why might an individual be interested in investing in a strip bond?

2-32. What kind of issuers would you expect to offer the lowest yield for their long-term bonds?

2-33. Why do junk bonds offer high yields?

2-34. What are bearer bonds? What are the advantages and disadvantages of holding this type of bond?

2-35. What are Eurobonds? Why might these be attractive to an investor?

2-36. Name the four issuers of bonds discussed in this chapter. Which do you think would be most risky as a general proposition?

2-37. Why is the call provision on a bond generally a disadvantage to the bondholder?

2-38. With regard to bond ratings, which of the following statements is incorrect?

    a. The first four categories represent investment-grade securities.

    b. Ratings reflect the absolute probability of default.

    c. Both corporates and municipals are rated.

    d. Ratings are current opinions on the relative quality of bonds.

2-39. Choose the statement that best completes the sentence: Preferred stocks and common stocks are similar in that

    a. Both are equity securities.

    b. Both pay a stated and fixed dividend.

    c. The expected return for each can be estimated with precision for the next period.

    d. Both have an equal claim on the income stream of the company.

PROBLEMS

2-1. Suppose a resident of Ontario will earn an extra $100 of investment income in 2008. For the various levels of taxable income shown below, determine how much of the $100 the investor will keep (the after-tax income) if it is earned as: (a) dividends from a large Canadian company; (b) interest from a Government bond; and (c) profit from selling some stock (a capital gain).

    The federal and provincial tax rates are provided in Appendix 2A. Note that in addition to the federal dividend tax credit, there is also an Ontario dividend tax credit of 6.75 percent of the taxable amount of the dividend (145 percent of the dividend received). You may want to lay out your spreadsheet as follows:

Taxable Income	Marginal Tax Rate		Dividends		After-Tax Income		
	Federal	Ontario	Tax	Tax Credit	Dividends	Interest	Capital Gain
12,500							
37,500							
50,000							
75,000							
87,500							
112,500							
125,000							

APPENDIX 2A

TAXATION OF INVESTMENT INCOME IN CANADA

General Information

The basic federal tax rates (as of 2008) are:

1. 15 percent for taxable income up to $37,885

2. 22 percent on the next $37,884 up to $76,769

3. 26 percent on the next $47,415 up to $123,184

4. 29 percent on any amount above $123,184

In addition, each province operates a separate provincial tax system. It used to be that provincial taxes were a simple multiple of federal taxes, so that Ontario for example would add on 52 percent (at its peak) of the federal taxes. However, things have changed over the last 10 years and each province except Quebec has developed a parallel tax system that works similar to the federal system. The 2008 provincial/territorial tax rates[17] are provided in Table 2A-1.

Table 2A-1

Provincial and Territorial Tax Rates

Province/Territories:	Rates
Newfoundland and Labrador	8.2% on the first $30,215 of taxable income, + 13.3% on the next $30,214, + 16% on the amount over $60,429
Prince Edward Island	9.8% on the first $31,984 of taxable income, + 13.8% on the next $31,985, + 16.7% on the amount over $63,969
Nova Scotia	8.79% on the first $29,590 of taxable income, + 14.95% on the next $29,590, + 16.67% on the next $33,820 + 17.5% on the amount over $93,000
New Brunswick	10.12% on the first $34,836 of taxable income, + 15.48% on the next $34,837, + 16.8% on the next $43,600, + 17.95% on the amount over $113,273
Ontario	6.05% on the first $36,020 of taxable income, + 9.15% on the next $36,021, + 11.16% on the amount over $72,041
Manitoba	10.9% on the first $30,544 of taxable income, + 12.75% on the next $35,456, + 17.4% on the amount over $66,000
Saskatchewan	11% on the first $39,135 of taxable income, + 13% on the next $72,679, + 15% on the amount over $111,814
Alberta	10% of taxable income
British Columbia	5.24% on the first $35,016 of taxable income, + 7.98% on the next $35,017, + 10.5% on the next $10,373, + 12.29% on the next $17,230, + 14.7% on the amount over $97,636
Yukon	7.04% on the first $37,885 of taxable income, + 9.68% on the next $37,884, + 11.44% on the next $47,415, + 12.76% on the amount over $123,184
Northwest Territories	5.9% on the first $35,986 of taxable income, + 8.6% on the next $35,987, + 12.2% on the next $45,038, + 14.05% on the amount over $117,011
Nunavut	4% on the first $37,885 of taxable income, + 7% on the next $37,885, + 9% on the next $47,414, + 11.5% on the amount over $123,184

Source: Reproduced with permission of the Canada Revenue Agency and the Minister of Public Works and Government Services Canada, 2008.

Interest, Dividend, and Capital Gains Income

Interest income from debt securities (including bonds and money market securities) is taxable at the full marginal rate; however, dividends and capital gains afford investors a tax break. Dividends (whether they are cash, stock, or reinvested dividends) received from Canadian corporations are taxable in the following manner for all provinces except Quebec. First, the amount of the dividend is "grossed-up" by 45 percent (as of the May 2006 budget) to obtain the taxable amount of dividend that is used in determining net income. The taxpayer is then able to claim a federal tax credit of 18.97 percent of the taxable amount of the dividend. The investor then claims a provincial tax credit that varies with the province or territory of residence. This is done to reduce the amount of "double taxation," which refers to the fact that dividends are paid by companies out of after-tax earnings (i.e., these earnings have been taxed), and then investors pay taxes on the dividends they receive from the businesses.

---

[17]www.cra-arc.gc.ca/tx/ndvdls/fq/txrts-eng.html#provincial, March 18, 2008.

The marginal tax rates on dividends are lower than on interest and are lower on capital gains for investors in lower marginal tax brackets, with the cut-off points varying by province. This lower effective tax rate enhances the investor's after-tax return.

In response to the 2008 federal budget, which will reduce corporate taxes from 19.5 percent in 2008 to 15 percent in 2012, the amount of the federal dividend gross-up will be reduced from 45 percent to 38 percent, and the credit will be reduced to 15 percent from 19 percent by 2012. This will effectively increase the marginal rate on dividends from 14.55 percent to 19.29, assuming no further changes.

Foreign dividends are usually taxed by the source country and there is an allowable credit, which is essentially the lower of the foreign tax paid and the Canadian tax payable on foreign income subject to certain adjustments.

A capital gain arises from the disposition of capital assets for proceeds in excess of their cost. Only 50 percent of the capital gain is taxable, provided the transaction involved a taxpayer whose ordinary business does not involve the trading of securities, or that Canada Revenue Agency did not determine the trading to be speculative in nature. The general rule is that capital gains equal the proceeds from distribution minus the adjusted cost base (which includes commission costs, etc.) plus any costs of disposing of assets.

The adjusted cost base is complicated when shares were purchased at different prices and is based on the average cost method. For example, if 200 shares were purchased for $5 (including commission) and an additional 300 shares were purchased for $6 (including commission), then the average adjusted cost per share would be ($1,000 + $1,800) ÷ 500 = $5.60 per share. Taxes on disposition of debt securities are applied as above; however, the accrued interest portion of a bond purchase price is not included as part of the adjusted cost base and is treated as taxable income in the hands of the bond seller.

Capital losses cannot be claimed by the security holder unless ownership is transferred in writing to another person. One exception to this rule is where the security becomes worthless due to bankruptcy of the underlying company. Superficial losses are those that result from the sale and purchase of the same security within a given time frame and are not tax deductible. However, the taxpayer eventually receives the tax benefit since the amount of the superficial loss is added to the cost base of the repurchased shares, which lowers the ultimate capital gain. A superficial loss occurs when securities are sold at a loss but are repurchased and still held 30 days after the sale. They do not apply to losses resulting from leaving Canada, death of a taxpayer, expiry of an option, or a deemed disposition of securities by a trust or to a controlled corporation.

Certain items related to investment income are tax deductible including carrying charges such as interest on borrowed funds, investment counselling fees, fees paid for administration or safe custody of investments, safety deposit box charges, and accounting fees paid for recording investment income. Interest on borrowed funds is deductible only if the investor had a legal obligation to pay the interest, the purpose of the borrowing was to earn income, and the income earned from the investment is not tax exempt. (Note: it does not need to be an arm's-length transaction.) In addition, the interest charge:

1. Cannot exceed the amount of interest earned on debt securities unless they are convertible

2. Is disallowed as a deduction if it exceeds the grossed-up amount of preferred dividends

3. Is for the most part deductible if it is for the purchase of common shares

Table 2A-2 breaks down the various marginal provincial and territorial tax rates on ordinary income (i.e., interest income), dividends, and capital gains for a taxable income of $75,000 as of 2008.

Table 2A-2

Personal Tax Calculator

Province/ Territory	Tax Payable	After-Tax Income	Average Tax Rate	Marginal Tax Rate	Marginal Rate on Capital Gains	Marginal Rate on Eligible Dividends*	Marginal Rate on Ineligible Dividends
B.C.	$17,077	$57,923	22.77%	32.50%	16.25%	4.40%	17.58%
Alberta	$18,291	$56,709	24.39%	32.00%	16.00%	5.85%	17.71%
Sask.	$20,391	$54,609	27.19%	35.00%	17.50%	7.30%	19.58%
Manitoba	$20,948	$54,052	27.93%	39.40%	19.70%	13.68%	28.65%
Ontario	$17,923	$57,077	23.90%	39.41%	19.71%	13.81%	22.59%
Quebec	$21,818	$53,182	29.09%	38.37%	19.19%	15.42%	24.05%
N.B.	$21,370	$53,630	28.49%	38.80%	19.40%	11.36%	25.21%
N.S.	$21,590	$53,410	28.79%	38.67%	19.34%	15.74%	22.04%
P.E.I.	$21,043	$53,957	28.06%	38.70%	19.35%	13.39%	23.58%
Nfld.	$20,615	$54,385	27.49%	38.00%	19.00%	17.96%	24.58%
N.W.T.	$17,266	$57,734	23.02%	34.20%	17.10%	5.42%	18.58%
Yukon	$17,992	$57,008	23.99%	31.68%	15.84%	4.40%	17.37%
Nunavut	$16,067	$58,933	21.42%	29.00%	14.50%	5.50%	14.58%

Source: Ernst & Young, www.ey.com/GLOBAL/content.nsf/Canada/Tax_-_Calculators_-_2008_Personal_Tax, June 19, 2008.

Derivative Securities

When convertible features are exercised, it is not deemed to be a disposition of property, so no capital gain or loss is recorded. Instead, the adjusted cost base of the new shares will be that of the original securities. For example, if 100 preferred shares are purchased for a total cost of $5,000 and each share is convertible into 10 common shares, the adjusted cost base of one common share (after conversion), will be $5,000/100/10 or $50/10 = $5 per share.

Warrants and rights may be acquired through direct purchase, by owning shares, or by purchasing units with rights or warrants attached. When they are purchased they are treated the same as convertibles; however, if they are the result of owning underlying shares, the adjusted cost base of the original shares is altered. When warrants or rights are not exercised, a capital gain or loss may result, unless they were acquired at zero cost.

There are two basic types of options—calls and puts. At the time of the sale of either option, the seller receives consideration for the option and has disposed of a right. This sale of a right generates a capital gain calculated as the cost of the option, which is nil or zero subtracted from the consideration received. As with all capital gains, only one-half of it is included in income. The buyer or purchaser of either option has acquired a right with a cost equal to the amount of consideration paid.

There are no further tax consequences to the buyer until the option is either exercised or allowed to expire.

If either option expires, then the buyer has disposed of it for no consideration. Since the disposition has occurred, the selling price is zero and the buyer has a capital loss equal to the amount paid to acquire the option subtracted from the selling price, which is zero.

If a call option is exercised, then the price paid to acquire the option is added to the price paid to acquire the underlying asset. The option holder now owns the underlying asset with a cost calculated as the price paid for the underlying asset plus the price paid for the option to acquire the asset. The seller of the underlying asset through the call option contract (the call seller) must add the price received for the option to the selling price of the asset that was sold. This increased selling price becomes the proceeds of disposition of the asset and a capital gain (or loss) is calculated by subtracting the original cost of the asset from these increased proceeds of disposition. When the original option was sold, the seller included a capital gain in their income as described by the above paragraph. This seller must now file an amended tax return if the option was sold in a year previous to the year the actual underlying asset was sold.

If a put option is exercised, the tax consequences are similar to the above. The purchaser of the asset (the put seller) has received consideration for the put option. Therefore the purchaser of the underlying asset deducts the amount received for the option and the cost of the underlying asset is calculated as the actual consideration paid to acquire the asset minus the amount received for the option to sell. Since the buyer of the asset through the put option (the put seller) has already reported a capital gain on the sale of the put option, an amended tax return must be filed to remove this income from the previous year. The seller of the underlying asset (the put buyer) has paid an amount for the put option and has received consideration for the actual sale of the asset. The selling price of the asset is reduced by the amount paid for the option. The seller calculates a capital gain (or loss) equal to the selling price of the asset minus the amount paid for the option minus the purchase price of the asset through exercise of the put option.

Profits or losses on hedging futures contracts, which is normally part of risk management for businesses, are considered normal business income or loss and are included, or deductible, in the annual financial statements.

For the general investor, speculating in futures contracts can generate either capital gains or losses or normal income. The choice of which approach to take is left open to the speculator. The only requirement is that once a choice has been made, that selection must be adhered to in the future. One of the main considerations in this selection is that if the investor is using borrowed funds for the purpose of speculating in futures contracts, the interest on the borrowed funds is deductible against the income that is being generated. Therefore, the normal investor must select income treatment for speculation purposes. If capital gains treatment was selected, and the investor was using borrowed funds, the interest on these funds is not deductible.

CHAPTER 3

INVESTMENT FUNDS

Chapter 2 was primarily concerned with direct investing, meaning investors make decisions to buy various securities, typically in a brokerage account, and eventually sell them. The investor makes the decisions and controls the actions involving the investments. Chapter 3, in contrast, discusses the very important alternative of indirect investing used by many investors—buying and selling mutual funds, closed-end funds, unit investment trusts, and exchange-traded funds.

All four types of funds are analyzed in this chapter, with primary emphasis on mutual funds and on the increasingly popular exchange-traded funds. The key point about indirect investing is that the investor turns his or her money over to one of these types of funds, thereby relinquishing direct control of the securities in the portfolio. In contrast, an investor with a portfolio of 10 stocks in his or her brokerage account can decide exactly how long to hold each one before selling, when to realize capital losses for tax purposes, or what to do with any dividends generated by the portfolio, as examples.

Learning Objectives

After reading this chapter, you should be able to

1. Distinguish between direct and indirect investing.
2. Define open-end and closed-end investment funds.
3. State the major types of mutual funds and give their features.
4. Explain the transactions behind indirect investments.
5. Define exchange-traded funds (ETFs).
6. Understand how the performance of investment funds is measured.
7. Discuss the opportunities for investing indirectly internationally.

CHAPTER PREVIEW

Investors may choose to invest either directly or indirectly in the instruments that we described in Chapter 2. In this chapter, we focus on investing indirectly through investment funds, chiefly through the buying and selling of mutual funds. You will learn about the two major types of investment funds (open-end and closed-end), the transactions behind them, and how we measure the performance of these funds. Finally, we turn to opportunities for investing indirectly internationally and discuss hedge funds.

INVESTING INDIRECTLY

learning objective 1
Distinguish between direct and indirect investing.

Basically, households have three choices with regard to savings:

1. Hold the liabilities of traditional intermediaries, such as banks, trust companies, and insurance companies. These include savings accounts, GICs, and so forth.

2. Hold securities directly by purchasing stocks and bonds through brokers and other intermediaries.

3. Hold securities indirectly through investment companies and pension funds.

There has been a pronounced shift toward indirect investing in North America in recent years. Individuals have increasingly turned away from the direct holding of securities and the liabilities of traditional intermediaries and toward indirect holdings of assets through pension funds and mutual funds.

A substantial proportion of Canadian families own investment funds of some type. Mutual fund assets reached an all-time high of $697.3 billion by the end of 2007. In fact, mutual fund assets in Canada have increased approximately 30 times over the 19-year period ending December 31, 2007—from $23.5 billion in 1989. In the United States, mutual funds grew tenfold during the 1980s to $1 trillion, and by 2005 the amount approximated $8.9 trillion. The dramatic growth in mutual fund assets in Canada is clearly demonstrated in Figure 3-1. This may well be the most important trend in recent years affecting the average household with regard to its investing activities and programs.

Figure 3-1
Net Assets—Canadian
Mutual Funds ($billions)
1989–2007

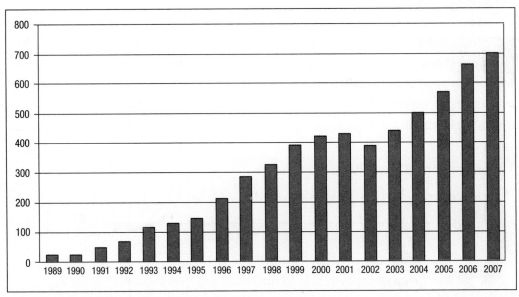

Source: The Investment Funds Institute of Canada (IFIC)

The rising ownership of pension fund assets and mutual fund shares, an alternative to the direct investing methods discussed in Chapter 2, is very important to every investor in accomplishing his or her investing goals. Investors now rely heavily on indirect investing. A significant contributor to the growth in investment fund assets in Canada has been the steady increase in contributions to

Registered Retirement Savings Plans (RRSPs) by Canadian investors throughout the 1990s and through the early 2000s. The nature of RRSPs is discussed in detail in the following Investing Tip.

In 1997, Canadians contributed $27.4 billion to RRSPs, representing a 71 percent increase over 1991. However, by 2004, RRSP contributions were only $25.2 billion, with the average contribution being $6,402 per person. In fact, despite a record 6.2 million contributors during 2007, they only used about 7 percent of their total contribution room, as discussed in Real-World Returns 3-1.

INVESTING *tip*

Registered Retirement Savings Plans (RRSPs)

Registered Retirement Savings Plans (RRSPs) are important tax deferral investment alternatives that allow Canadian taxpayers to make annual tax-deductible contributions up to predetermined limits. The income earned on the plan is tax-free as long as it remains in the plan, and provided the plans are registered with Canada Revenue Agency.

Most individuals contribute to their RRSPs by purchasing one or more pooled or mutual funds that are managed by fund managers. However, some investors choose to contribute through self-directed RRSPs. Under these arrangements, the investor funds or contributes certain acceptable securities into a registered plan that is administered for a fee; however, the investment transactions are directed by the investor.

RRSPs are trust accounts for the investor's benefit upon retirement and access to funds cannot be gained immediately without paying a withholding tax. In addition, RRSPs cannot be used as collateral for loan purposes. RRSP contributions must be made within 60 days of year end. Contributions are limited to the lesser of 18 percent of the previous year's earnings or the dollar limit (presently $20,000, and scheduled to increase to $21,000 in 2009 and to $22,000 in 2010) less the previous year's Pension Adjustment and Past Service Pension Adjustment plus the unused RRSP deduction room.

A penalty tax of 1 percent per month is levied on "overcontributions" of $2,000 or more. When a planholder contributes securities already owned to an RRSP (referred to as a "contribution in kind"), the taxpayer pays taxes on any capital gains but is unable to claim any capital losses that result.

A married taxpayer may contribute to an RRSP with the spouse named as the beneficiary, to the extent it does not use the maximum contribution to the contributor's plan. The contribution does not affect the contribution limits of the spouse. For example, if a wife contributes $9,000 of her $12,000 available contribution room to her own plan, she may also contribute $3,000 to her husband's plan without affecting his contribution limits. The proceeds from de-registering a spousal plan are taxable income for the spouse (not the contributor), except for contributions made in the year of de-registration and the two calendar years before the plan is de-registered.

An RRSP holder may de-register the plan at any time, but mandatory de-registration is required at the age of 71 (which was increased from 69 in 2007). There are several available options for de-registering RRSPs upon retirement. The least desirable from a tax perspective is to withdraw the full lump sum amount, which is then fully taxable. To spread out the taxes paid on withdrawn funds, the proceeds from the plan may be used to purchase a life annuity with a guaranteed term or a fixed term annuity that provides annual benefits to age 90. Similarly, the funds may be used to purchase a Registered Retirement Income Fund (RRIF) that provides annual income to age 90 or life.

Subsequent to retirement, if a plan owner dies, remaining benefits on an annuity or RRIF can be transferred to a spouse or child, or else the value is included in the deceased's income in the year of death and is fully taxable. RRIF holders must withdraw and pay income tax on a set fraction of the total assets in the fund (the annual minimum amount). The annual fraction is determined by a formula designed to provide benefits for a desired term; however, the payout may be accelerated if the owner elects. A taxpayer may own more than one RRIF and these may be self-directed if desired.

There are several advantages associated with RRSPs, some of which are discussed in Real-World Returns 3-1. First, they allow taxpayers to reduce taxable income during high taxation years. Second, they allow investors to shelter certain types of income from taxation by transferring them into an RRSP. Third, RRSPs are tax-efficient mechanisms for accumulation of retirement funds, with the funds earning income on a tax-free basis, thus allowing deferment of some taxes. Finally, RRSPs provide investors with an opportunity to split retirement income (through spousal RRSPs), which may result in lower total tax payments.

REAL-WORLD RETURNS 3-1

RRSP Contribution Tips for Your Clients

For some clients, contributing to their RRSP is harder to do than visiting the dentist. Last year Canadians used just 7 percent of the total room available to eligible tax filers, despite a record 6.2 million Canucks contributing.

Why aren't people saving more? Because Canadians like their stuff. "It doesn't come as second nature to go put money in an RRSP when you can buy something with those funds," says Gena Katz, executive director at Ernst & Young. "But it makes good sense. The earlier your clients start, the better off they are. It's something advisors should always encourage clients to do."

To help advisors convince their clients that making an RRSP contribution is beneficial, the company put out its list of "Eight Tips to Tackle RRSP Crunch Time."

One of the suggestions on the list deals with a problem that's likely common to many of your clients: they don't have enough cash to contribute this year.

Katz says borrowing money to put into an RRSP is a good option for those Canadians lacking funds. "The borrowing often comes up because people go on their merry way all year and don't put money in an RRSP."

However, she adds that using borrowed money is not for everyone. The benefits depend on a number of things, including age. If a client is 60, contributing with loaned money doesn't make much sense, as the investment will not likely grow significantly before he or she retires. It's a different story for someone who's 30 and will see his or her investment grow substantially over 40 years.

Borrowing also makes sense if the client can pay off the loan in a reasonable amount of time. "If the funds are going to be there for quite a number of years, and the client can repay the loan in a reasonable amount of time, like one to four years, then borrowing does make sense," Katz says.

Clients can also make contributions with non-registered investments, but there will be an accrued gain if that contribution is in the form of stocks. "The client will be paying tax up front right now, and later on they'll be taxed on the full amount coming out," says Katz.

But with equity markets in turmoil, dumping your lower-priced stocks into an RRSP might be a wise move, as your gains could be less than they would be in an up market.

Another tip that Ernst & Young offers is contributing to a spousal RRSP. Katz says a lot of people think pension splitting, which was introduced in 2007, replaces spousal RRSPs, but that is not the case.

"Spousal RRSPs still make sense because there's no limitation," she says. "Income splitting is only half of eligible pension income. For spousal RRSPs, individuals can potentially put all contributions in the plan and they can get more income in their spouse's hand. And they're not limited by eligible pension income."

Ernst & Young lists several other ways to maximize your clients' RRSP contributions, like suggesting they pay the $2,000 penalty-free excess contribution so they can contribute less down the road or, if they're making a large "catch-up" contribution, spread the deduction over a couple of years to increase the related tax benefit.

But more important than any of these strategies is to make sure your client contributes sooner rather than later.

"The final suggestion is 'now that you know that your RRSPs are so wonderful, instead of just doing 2007 now, how about contributing for 2008 too?'" says Katz.

Source: Borzykowski, Bryan, Advisor.ca. Retrieved from www.advisor.ca, January 29, 2008.

INVESTING INDIRECTLY THROUGH INVESTMENT FUNDS

An investment fund such as a mutual fund is a clear alternative for an investor seeking to own stocks and bonds. Rather than purchase securities and manage a portfolio, investors can, in effect, indirectly invest by putting their money into an investment fund, and allowing their investment advisor to do all the work and make all the decisions (for a fee, of course). Investment funds are ideal for investors

• with small capital bases who cannot properly diversify on their own

• who do not have adequate time to manage their own investments

• who do not wish to manage their own portfolio

Indirect investing in this discussion refers to the buying and selling of the units of investment funds that consist of portfolios of securities. Investors who purchase units of a particular fund managed by an investment company are buying an ownership interest in the fund portfolio and are entitled to a portion of the dividends, interest, and capital gains generated. Shareholders must also pay a share of the fund expenses and its management fee, which will be deducted from the portfolio's earnings as it flows back to the shareholders.

The contrast between direct and indirect investing is illustrated in Figure 3-2, which shows that indirect investing essentially accomplishes the same thing as direct investing. The difference is that the investment companies that manage and sell the fund units stand between investors and the portfolio of securities. Although technical qualifications exist, the point about indirect investing is that investors gain and lose through the investment fund's activities in the same manner that they would gain and lose from holding a portfolio directly. The differences are the costs (any sales charges plus the management fee) and the additional services gained from the investment fund, such as record-keeping and cheque-writing privileges.

The choice between direct or indirect investing is very important to all investors. Since each has advantages and disadvantages, the choice may not be straightforward. Investors can be classified as active (those who are interested in participating in managing their portfolios), or passive (those who do not get involved in managing their portfolios). Moreover, it is possible to have both classes of investors invest directly or indirectly.

The line between direct and indirect investing is becoming blurred. For example, investors can invest in investment funds directly through their brokerage accounts, generally at no additional expense. In addition, brokerage firms offer alternatives to mutual funds in several forms, which will be discussed in Chapter 5.

Figure 3-2
Direct Versus Indirect
Investing

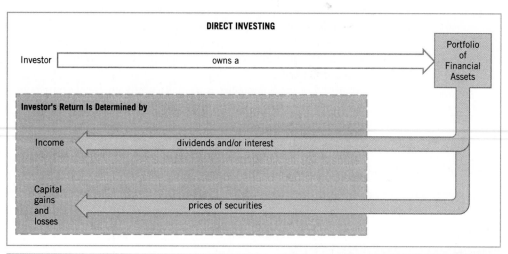

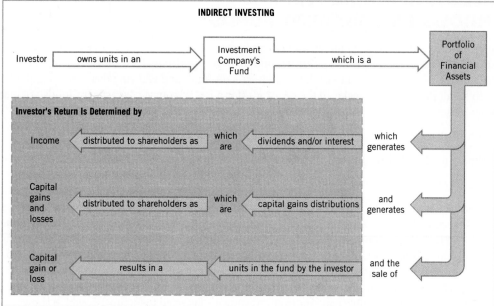

CHECK YOUR UNDERSTANDING

3-1. What trend is felt to be a significant factor in the growth of investment fund assets in Canada?

3-2. Why do many investors choose the indirect investing route when there are significant costs (fees to an advisor or investment company) to doing so?

3-3. Although there is not always a clear distinction, who would you expect to be more likely to invest indirectly through an investment company: active or passive investors?

Investment Fund

A financial company or trust fund that sells shares in itself or units of the trust fund to the public and uses the funds to invest in a portfolio of securities such as money market instruments, stocks, and bonds.

WHAT IS AN INVESTMENT FUND?

An **investment fund** sells shares or units in a trust fund to the public and invests these funds in a portfolio of securities such as money market instruments, stocks, and bonds. By pooling the funds of thousands of investors, a widely diversified portfolio of financial assets can be purchased. Investment companies usually manage several funds simultaneously and offer their customers a variety of services.

EXAMPLE 3-1: RBC ASSET MANAGEMENT INC.

RBC Asset Management Inc. had the largest dollar amount of mutual fund assets under its management in Canada in September 2008 at $101.8 billion. Real-World Returns 3-2 includes excerpts from its June 27, 2008 "Simplified Prospectus" for RBC Funds, which refers to the basic characteristics of mutual funds and the general risks associated with investing in mutual funds.

REAL-WORLD RETURNS 3-2

What Is a Mutual Fund and What Are the Risks of Investing in a Mutual Fund?

A mutual fund is a pool of investments made on behalf of people with a similar investment objective. When you invest in a mutual fund, your money is working together with that of many other investors. A professional investment manager invests this money on behalf of the whole group.

Investors share a mutual fund's income, expenses, gains and losses in proportion to their interest in the mutual fund. Mutual funds can give individuals the advantages of a simpler, more accessible, less expensive and less time-consuming method of investing in a portfolio of securities.

Mutual funds own different kinds of investments, depending on their objectives. These include equities like stocks, fixed income securities like bonds and cash or cash equivalents like treasury bills. The value of these investments will change from day to day, reflecting changes in interest rates, economic conditions, financial markets and company news.

When you invest in a mutual fund trust, you are buying a portion of the fund called a unit. Mutual funds keep track of all the individual investments by recording how many units each investor owns. The more money you put into a mutual fund, the more units you get. The price of a unit changes every day, depending on how the investments are performing. When the investments rise in value, the price of a unit goes up. When the investments drop in value, the price of the unit goes down.

Some mutual funds offer units in more than one series. A multi-series structure recognizes that different investors may seek the same investment objective, yet require different investment advice and/or service. Each series represents an investment in the same investment portfolio of each fund. However, each series may charge a different management fee and and incur its own specific expenses. As a result, a separate net asset value per unit is calculated for each series on a daily basis.

Your investment in any mutual fund is not guaranteed. Unlike bank accounts or guaranteed investment certificates (GICs), mutual fund units are not covered by the Canada Deposit Insurance Corporation or any other government deposit insurer.

Under exceptional circumstances, you may not be able to redeem your units.

Risk and Return

As an investor, there is always a risk you could lose money. Mutual funds are no exception, but the degree of risk varies considerably from one mutual fund to the next. As a general rule, investments with the greatest risk also have the greatest potential return. The key is to recognize the risk involved with your investment, understand it, and decide whether it is a risk you are comfortable accepting.

Although the value of your investments may drop in the short term, a longer investment horizon will help to lessen the effects of short-term market volatility. A shorter investment horizon may result in you having to sell your investments in adverse conditions. Ideally, investors in equity funds have a five- to 10-year investment horizon, which generally provides enough time for their investments to overcome any short-term volatility and grow.

(continued)

REAL-WORLD RETURNS 3-2 *continued*

The following chart shows the relationship between risk and potential return. As you can see, money market funds are the least volatile and generally have the lowest returns. At the other end of the scale, equity funds are usually the most risky, but also tend to have the highest potential return.

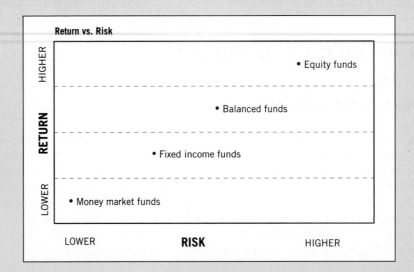

Source: RBC Asset Management Inc., 2008 Simplified Prospectus (June 27, 2008), pp. 3-4.

An investment fund acts as a conduit, flowing dividends, interest, and realized capital gains through to its unitholders, who pay taxes on this income at their own marginal tax rates. In effect, fund owners are treated as if they held the securities in the fund's portfolio. During the year, funds make capital gains and losses when they sell securities. These gains are taxable in the hands of the investor. Therefore, investors should determine if a capital gains distribution is pending before purchasing a fund, since this will result in a decline in the fund's value corresponding to the amount of the tax liability incurred.

In addition to taxes on income earned by the investment fund, when a fund owner redeems the shares or units in a fund, the transaction is considered a disposition for tax purposes and is subject to capital gains or losses. A complication arises due to the reinvestment of interest and dividends, which implies that investors (or their investment advisors) must keep track of the actual purchase prices of all units in a fund.

Most Canadian investment funds fall under the jurisdiction of the securities acts of the provinces in which they operate. While management of mutual funds is regulated by the securities commissions, distribution of funds is regulated by the Mutual Fund Dealers Association (MFDA), which is the mutual fund industry's self-regulatory organization (SRO). Since most funds continually issue new shares, they are in a continuous state of primary distribution, and must annually file a prospectus or simplified prospectus. Usually, funds file simplified prospectuses similar to the one provided by RBC Asset Management Inc. referred to in Real-World Returns 3-2. The prospectus must contain all material information and must be amended when material changes occur. Fund buyers must receive copies of this document no later than two business days after an agreement of purchase has been made.

Investment fund managers, distributors, and their sales personnel must be registered with the securities commissions in which they do business, and must adhere to industry code of practice guidelines. Salespeople must have successfully completed the CSC or the education program offered by the Investment Funds Institute of Canada (IFIC).

TYPES OF INVESTMENT FUNDS

All investment funds begin by selling shares or units in the associated trust fund to the public. Most are managed by investment companies that offer professional supervision of the portfolio as one of the benefits.

Unit Investment Trusts

An alternative form of investment company that deviates from the normal managed type is the **unit investment trust**, which typically is an unmanaged, fixed-income security portfolio put together by a sponsor and handled by an independent trustee. Redeemable trust certificates representing claims against the assets of the trust are sold to investors at net asset value plus a small commission. All interest (or dividends) and principal repayments are distributed to the holders of the certificates. Most unit investment trusts hold tax-exempt securities. The assets are almost always kept unchanged and the trust ceases to exist when the bonds mature, although it is possible to redeem units of the trust.

In general, unit investment trusts are passive investments. They are designed to be bought and held, with capital preservation as a major objective. They enable investors to gain diversification, provide professional management that takes care of all the details, permit the purchase of securities by the trust at a cheaper price than if purchased individually, and ensure minimum operating costs. If conditions change, however, investors lose the ability to make rapid, inexpensive, or costless changes in their positions. Assets of unit investment trusts currently represent a very small part of total investment company assets.

Closed-End Investment Funds

A **closed-end investment fund** usually sells no additional shares after the initial public offering (IPO). Therefore, the fund capitalization is fixed unless a new public offering is made. The shares of a closed-end fund trade in the secondary markets—that is, on the exchanges—exactly like any other stock. To buy and sell, investors use their brokers, paying the current price at which the shares are selling plus brokerage commissions, or receiving that price less the commissions.

Because shares of closed-end funds trade on stock exchanges, their prices are determined by the forces of supply and demand. Interestingly, however, the market price is seldom equal to the actual per-share value of the closed-end shares. We examine the issue of closed-end discounts and premiums later in the chapter.

Closed-end funds have been around for a long time; in fact, they were a popular investment before the great crash of 1929. After that, they lost favour and were relatively unimportant until they started to attract significant investor interest again following the crash of 1987. By 2005, for example, the amount of fund assets in closed-end funds in the United States had grown to approximately $275 billion. There were approximately 240 closed-end funds in Canada by March of 2008.

Open-End Investment Funds (Mutual Funds)

Open-end investment funds (or **mutual funds**) account for a large majority of aggregate funds invested in Canada. As stated earlier, the growth in mutual funds and their assets has been one of the important developments in recent years. The number of mutual funds has grown rapidly as well. At the beginning of 1988, there were 294 Canadian mutual funds, with assets totalling $20.4 billion, and by the end of 2007 there were 2,038 funds, with total assets of $697.3 billion. Growth in the United States was even more spectacular, where the number of mutual funds increased from 564 in 1980 to more than 7,000, with total assets exceeding $8.9 trillion by 2005.

As mentioned, mutual funds are formed either by creating a mutual fund company and selling shares in it, or by creating a mutual fund trust and selling "units" in the mutual fund trust. Mutual funds continue to sell their treasury shares or units to investors after the initial sale that starts the fund. The capitalization of an open-end investment fund is frequently changing as it continually

Unit Investment Trust
An unmanaged form of investment company, typically holding fixed-income securities, offering investors diversification and minimum operating costs.

learning objective 2
Define open-end and closed-end investment funds.

Closed-End Investment Fund
An investment fund with a fixed capitalization whose shares trade on exchanges and over-the-counter (OTC) markets.

Open-End Investment Fund
An investment fund whose capitalization constantly changes as new shares or trust units are sold and outstanding units are redeemed. Popularly known as mutual funds.

Mutual Funds
The popular name for open-end investment funds whose capitalization constantly changes as new shares are sold and outstanding shares are redeemed.

issues and redeems shares or units on demand. This right of redemption is the hallmark of open-end funds. In fact, that is what makes it open-ended, as new investors buy additional shares or units and owners cash in by selling their shares or units back to the company.

Mutual funds are purchased in two ways:

1. Directly from a fund company by mail, telephone, or at office locations;

2. Indirectly from a sales agent, including securities firms, banks, life insurance companies, and financial planners.

Mutual funds may be affiliated with an underwriter, who usually has an exclusive right to distribute shares to investors. Most underwriters distribute shares through broker/dealer firms.

Most mutual funds are corporations or trusts formed by an investment advisory firm that selects the board of trustees (directors) for the company. In turn, the trustees hire a separate management company, normally the investment advisory firm, to manage the fund. The management company is contracted by the investment company to perform necessary research and to manage the portfolio, as well as to handle the administrative chores. For that it receives a fee.

There are economies of scale in managing portfolios—expenses rise as assets under management increase, but not at the same rate as revenues. Because investment managers can oversee various amounts of money with few additional costs, management companies seek to increase the size of the fund(s) being managed. Most investment companies operate several different funds simultaneously. Investors can choose from a large number of mutual fund complexes. A fund complex is a group or family of funds managed by the same fund management company.

EXAMPLE 3-2: IGM FINANCIAL AND RBC ASSET MANAGEMENT INC.

As of October 2007, IGM Financial (**Investors Group, MacKenzie**) was the largest mutual fund company in Canada with total net assets exceeding $111.0 billion, while **RBC Asset Management Inc.**, a subsidiary of the Royal Bank of Canada, was the second largest, with assets of $81.8 billion. As of March 2008, IGM offered investors a choice of 387 funds (many through subsidiaries), while RBC offered 81. These included a variety of the categories of funds described in the subsequent sections of this chapter.

Mutual funds are the most popular form of investment funds for the average investor. One reason is the small minimum investment requirements. Most funds require a minimum initial investment of $1,000 to get started, although some larger funds only need as little as $200. In addition, most funds that are RRSP-eligible have a lower required initial investment for RRSP contributions. After the initial investment, minimum contributions are typically much lower.

EXAMPLE 3-3: RBC CANADIAN EQUITY FUND

RBC Asset Management Inc.'s Canadian Equity Fund requires a minimum initial investment of $1,000, but only $500 if the fund is purchased for an RRSP. Subsequent contributions must be in amounts of $25 or more (whether for an RRSP or not). Most funds will accept less than $500 if a monthly commitment is made (e.g., commit to contribute $50 per month).

Net Asset Value (NAV)
The total market value of the securities in an investment company's portfolio divided by the number of investment fund units currently outstanding.

Owners of fund units can sell them back to the company any time they choose; the mutual fund is legally obligated to redeem them. Investors purchase new units and redeem their existing ones at the **net asset value** (NAV) plus (less) commission fees. The NAV for any investment fund unit is computed by calculating the total market value of the securities in the portfolio, subtracting any accounts payable, and dividing by the number of fund shares or units currently outstanding.[1]

---

[1]Total market value of the portfolio is equal to the sum of the product of each security's current market price multiplied by the number of shares of that security owned by the fund.

EXAMPLE 3-4: RBC CANADIAN EQUITY FUND

Using the numbers from RBC Asset Management Inc.'s June 2007 semi-annual report for the RBC Canadian Equity Fund, the year-end NAV is calculated as follows (all numbers are in 000's except for the per unit NAV figures):

Total assets	$5,015,725
Total liabilities	69,770
Net assets	$4,945,955
Net Assets (series A)	$4,933,523
Units outstanding series A	169,261
NAV series A	$29.15

(i.e., $4,933,523/169,261)

As this example shows, the net asset value is the per unit value of the portfolio of securities held by the investment fund. Over the course of the year, this will change as the value of the securities held changes and as income from the securities is received.

CHECK YOUR UNDERSTANDING

3-4. Which regulatory agency guarantees the money entrusted to investment funds?

3-5. Why do you think mutual funds are by far the most popular type of investment with investors?

3-6. Why is the number of outstanding shares (or units) of a mutual fund continually changing?

MAJOR TYPES OF MUTUAL FUNDS

learning objective 3
State the major types of mutual funds and give their features.

There are two major types of mutual funds:

1. Money market mutual funds (short-term funds)
2. Equity and bond & income funds (long-term funds)

These two types of funds parallel our discussion in Chapter 2 of money markets and capital markets. Money market funds concentrate on short-term investing by holding portfolios of money market assets, whereas equity and bond & income funds concentrate on longer term investing by holding mostly capital market assets. We will discuss each of these types of mutual funds in turn.

Money Market Funds

A major innovation in the investment company industry has been the creation, and subsequent phenomenal growth, of **money market funds (MMFs)**, which are open-end investment funds whose portfolios consist of money market instruments. Created in 1974, when interest rates were at record-high levels, MMFs grew tremendously in 1981–82 when short-term interest rates were again at record levels. Investors seeking to earn these high short-term rates found they generally could not do so directly because money market securities were only available in large denominations, and so they turned to MMFs. By October 2007, the total assets of Canadian MMFs was $50 billion, accounting for 7.0 percent of the total assets of all Canadian mutual fund assets ($710 billion at that time).

The objective of MMFs is to achieve a high level of income and liquidity through investment in short-term money market instruments such as Treasury bills, commercial paper, and short-term government bonds. These funds are attractive to investors seeking low risk and high liquidity. The average maturity of money market portfolios ranges from one to three months.

Investors in money market funds earn and are credited with interest daily. The shares can be redeemed at any time by phone or wire. Money market funds (MMFs) provide investors with a chance to

Money Market Funds (MMFs)

Open-end investment (mutual) funds that invest in short-term money market instruments such as Treasury bills, commercial paper, and short-term government bonds.

earn the going rates in the money market while enjoying broad diversification and great liquidity. The rates have varied as market conditions changed. The important point is that their yields correspond to current market conditions. Although investors may assume little risk because of the diversification and quality of these instruments, money market funds are not insured. Banks and other financial institutions have emphasized this point in competing with money market funds for the savings of investors.

Equity and Bond and Income Funds

The board of directors (or trustees) of an investment fund must specify the objective that the fund will pursue in its investment policy. The companies try to follow a consistent investment policy, according to their specified objective(s), which may have a great deal of influence on the typical investor's purchase decision.

EXAMPLE 3-5: RBC CANADIAN DIVIDEND FUND

The objective of the RBC Canadian Dividend Fund is "To achieve long-term total returns consisting of regular dividend income and modest long-term capital growth by investing primarily in common and preferred shares of major Canadian companies with above average dividend yields."

Given these objectives, it is not surprising to see the fund's holdings as of November 30, 2007, were heavily weighted in sectors that traditionally pay substantial amounts of dividends (e.g., 44 percent in financial services). At that time, the fund had 7.8 percent of its holdings in cash and 3.8 percent in bonds at that time.

EXAMPLE 3-6: RBC BALANCED FUND

The investment objective for RBC's Balanced Fund is stated below:[2]

"This "one-decision" Fund seeks potential for moderate interest income, dividends and capital appreciation. The Fund invests primarily in Canadian equities, bonds and short-term debt securities and may also invest up to 20 percent of its assets in foreign equities. The proportion of the Fund invested in each asset type is periodically changed to respond to changes in the market outlook for that asset."

The holdings of this fund as of November 30, 2007, reflected this objective of balancing growth and income. At that time, the portfolio was composed of 55.1 percent equities, 30.1 percent bonds, and 14.7 percent cash and short-term securities.

The following list identifies and describes several of the major categories of investment objectives, most of which relate to equity and bond and income funds. Investors in these funds have a wide range of investment objectives from which to choose. Traditionally, investors have favoured growth funds, which strive for capital appreciation, or balanced funds, which seek both income and capital appreciation. Today's investors can choose from global funds (either bonds or stocks), precious metal funds, mortgage funds, bond funds, and so forth.

- **Money Market Funds:** Objective is to achieve a high level of income and liquidity through investment in short-term money market instruments such as T-bills, commercial paper, and short-term government bonds. These funds will be attractive to investors seeking low risk and high liquidity.

- **Mortgage Funds:** Riskier than money market funds since terms of investments may be five years or greater, so there is more interest rate risk (although it is less than most bond funds, which have longer maturities).

---

[2]www.globefund.com, March 19, 2008.

- **Bond Funds:** Primary goals are income and safety. However, they are still subject to capital gains and losses due to inherent interest rate risk.

- **Dividend Funds:** Objective is to benefit from the tax advantage afforded by dividends. Therefore, they are not that appropriate for RRSPs or RRIFs where the credit cannot be applied. Price changes tend to be driven by changes in interest rates and general market trends.

- **Balanced Funds:** Main objective is to provide a mixture of safety, income, and capital appreciation. Usually, the prospectus stipulates minimum and maximum weighting in each asset class.

- **Asset Allocation Funds:** Similar objectives to balanced funds, but they are usually not restricted to holding specified minimum percentages in any class of investment.

- **Equity or Common Stock Funds:** Primary objective is capital gains. The bulk of assets are in common shares, although they maintain limited amounts of other assets for liquidity, income, and diversification purposes. Equity funds may vary greatly in degree of risk and growth objectives.

- **Index Funds:** Their objective is to mirror the performance of a market index such as the S&P/TSX Composite Index, or the ScotiaMcLeod Bond Index. The management fees are generally much lower than for actively managed funds. An alternative to these are exchange-traded funds (ETFs), which are discussed later in this chapter.

- **Specialty Funds:** These funds seek capital gains and are willing to forego broad diversification benefits in the hopes of achieving them. They typically concentrate on companies in one industry, one segment of the capital market, or in one geographical location.

- **International or Global Funds:** These can be considered subsets of the specialty funds, and invest in markets that offer the best prospects, regardless of location. They carry the additional risk of foreign exposure.

- **Real Estate Funds:** Invest in income-producing property in order to achieve long-term growth through capital appreciation and the reinvestment of income. The valuation of real estate funds is done infrequently (monthly or quarterly) and is based on appraisals of properties in the portfolio. They are less liquid than other funds and may require investors to give advance notice of redemption.

- **Hedge Funds:** Professionally managed portfolios that are traditionally sold to "sophisticated," wealthy investors. Minimum investments are usually between $90,000 and $150,000. Hedge fund managers often pursue strategies not available to traditional mutual fund managers, which may involve additional risks. These funds may try to hedge against a variety of factors such as market risks (domestic or foreign), foreign exchange risk, commodity price risk, or inflation. Some of the more aggressive funds may use leverage to magnify gains or losses, further contributing to their risk.

- **Ethical Funds:** These funds are guided by moral criteria that may prevent the funds from investing in companies that produce tobacco, for example.

Figure 3-3 shows that Canadian and foreign equity funds constituted close to half of the assets of Canadian mutual funds in October 2007. The nature of these equity funds can vary significantly and it is common to categorize equity funds based on investment objectives such as "growth" and "growth and income." These categorizations may change in the future as many observers believe it is more important to describe a fund's investment style and actual portfolio holdings rather than state that the fund is seeking "growth of capital," which could be accomplished in several different ways. As part of this new trend, Morningstar Inc., a well-known Chicago mutual fund research firm, uses nine categories for equity funds. These categories, such as large cap, mid cap, small cap, value, blend, and growth, are intended to describe investment styles, as shown in Figure 3-4, where Morningstar categorizes the Altamira Growth Portfolio as a Large Cap, Growth style equity fund.[3]

---

[3] "Cap" refers to capitalization, or market value for a company, calculated as the price of the stock times the total number of shares outstanding. A mutual fund that invests in stocks with large market capitalizations would be a large cap fund, while a small cap fund is one that invests in companies with small market capitalizations.

Figure 3-3
Mutual Fund Assets
(October 2007)

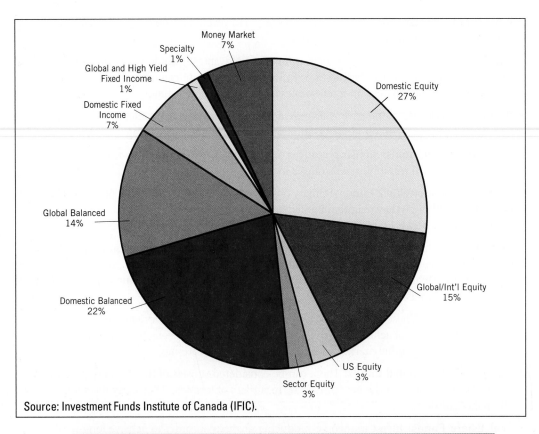

Source: Investment Funds Institute of Canada (IFIC).

Figure 3-4
Morningstar Classification
of Altamira Growth
Portfolio

	Value	Blend	Growth
Large			X
Mid			
Small			

Source: Retrieved from www.morningstar.ca, March 18, 2008.

Most stock funds can be divided into two categories based on their approach to selecting stocks—value funds and growth funds. A value fund generally looks for stocks that are cheap on the basis of standard fundamental analysis yardsticks, such as earnings, book value, and dividend yield. Growth funds, on the other hand, seek companies that are expected to show rapid future growth in earnings, even if current earnings are poor or even non-existent.

Value funds and growth funds tend to perform well at different times. Therefore, fund investors should distinguish between the two types, which is not always easy to do. A more risk-averse investor worrying about a market decline may wish to emphasize value funds, while more aggressive investors seeking good performance in an expected market rise might favour growth funds. Given the evidence on efficient markets, the best strategy could be to buy both types of funds. However, there is some evidence to suggest that value stocks outperform growth stocks over the long run. These and other issues relating to market efficiency are considered in Chapter 10.

While Figures 3-3 and 3-4 and the discussion above provide some useful guidelines for investors regarding what particular types of funds are all about, one must be wary of reading too much into the classification of a fund into a particular category. For example, it may be surprising to some readers to observe that close to 12 percent of the holdings of the RBC Canadian Dividend Fund referred to in the example above consisted of cash and short-term securities and bonds (which pay interest and not dividends). This is not uncommon among funds and it is typical to see funds composed of securities that do not appear to be obvious choices for inclusion in that portfolio based upon the fund name or objectives. This illustrates two important points regarding mutual funds and other professionally managed portfolios:

1. The name of the fund does not always provide a sufficient description of the nature of the securities that are found within the portfolio.

2. There is a great deal of variation in the composition of the portfolio holdings across funds, even when they are classified within the same fund category.

CHECK YOUR UNDERSTANDING

3-7. Why are money market funds the safest type of mutual fund an investor can hold?

3-8. Why might investors prefer a balanced fund to either a stock fund or a bond fund?

INDIRECT INVESTMENT TRANSACTIONS

Investors transact indirectly via investment companies by buying, holding, and selling shares of closed-end funds, mutual funds, exchange-traded funds (ETFs), segregated funds, and Labour Sponsored Venture Capital Corporations (LSVCCs). In this section, we analyze some of the details involved in these transactions.

learning objective 4
Explain the transactions behind indirect investments.

Closed-End Funds

Historically, the market prices of closed-end funds have varied widely from their net asset values (NAVs). A discount refers to the situation in which the closed-end fund is selling for less than its NAV. If the market price of the fund exceeds the NAV the fund is said to be selling at a premium. That is,

If NAV > market price, the fund is selling at a discount.

If NAV < market price, the fund is selling at a premium.

Although several studies have addressed the question of why these funds sell at discounts and premiums, no totally satisfactory explanation has been widely accepted by all market observers. On average, closed-end funds tend to sell at a discount from their NAV. For example, on March 18, 2008, the average discount on the 241 closed-end funds in Canada was 6.8 percent from their NAV per share, with only 24 (or 10 percent) of these funds not trading at a discount.

Some explanations that have been cited to explain discounts in various closed-end funds include illiquidity (either for the fund's holdings or in the fund's shares themselves) high expenses, poor performance, and unrealized capital gains. Another of these explanations—anti-takeover provisions—would prevent investors from taking over the fund and liquidating it in order to realize the full NAV.[4]

By purchasing a fund at a discount, an investor is actually buying shares in a portfolio of securities at a price below their market value. Therefore, even if the value of the portfolio remains unchanged, an investor can gain or lose if the discount narrows or widens over time. That is, a difference exists between the portfolio's return, based on net asset values, and the shareholder's return, based on closing prices.

While most of these funds trade at a discount, some also trade at premiums, and the amount of the discounts or premiums vary through time. For example, as of March 18, 2008, SL Split Corp shares sold at a 32 percent premium to their NAV of $45.64, while the shares in Global Diversified Inv Grade Inc Tr I traded at a 66.5 percent discount from their NAV of $7.77.

Mutual Funds

Some mutual funds use a sales force to reach investors, with shares or units available from brokers and financial planners. In an alternative form of distribution called direct marketing, the company uses advertising and direct mailing to appeal to investors.

---

[4]As for premiums such as those enjoyed by several closed-end funds that hold foreign securities, it is hard to short these funds because of the difficulty in borrowing the shares to do so. Thus, they end up selling at premiums.

INVESTING *tip*

Initial public offerings (IPOs) of closed-end funds typically involve brokerage commissions of 6 or 7 percent. Brokers often support the price in the after-market temporarily, but then the price drops to NAV or below. Many small investors would do well not to purchase the IPOs of closed-end funds.

Most mutual funds permit purchase of fractional shares or units. Purchase methods include lump sum cash purchases, accumulation purchase plans, and buying by reinvesting dividends. Lump sum purchases generally involve initial and subsequent minimum purchase amounts as discussed previously. Accumulation purchase plans may be voluntary or contractual arrangements, although the latter have declined in popularity due to their restrictive nature. In addition, many funds automatically reinvest dividends and interest to acquire new shares or units, unless instructed otherwise.

Mutual funds can be subdivided into load funds (those that charge a sales fee) and no-load funds (those that do not). Load funds charge investors a sales fee for the costs involved in selling the fund. Investors either pay the fee initially when the fund units are purchased (front-end sales charges), or in the future when the shares are redeemed by the investors (back-end or redemption charges). When an investor purchases units in a fund that charges an upfront sales charge, the offering or purchase price relates the sales charge to the net asset value (NAV) in the following manner:

Offering or purchase price = (NAV) ÷ (100 percent less the sales charge)

EXAMPLE 3-7: CALCULATING OFFERING PRICE

For example, the offering price for a fund that has a NAV of $10 and a 5 percent upfront sales charge is

Offering price = $10 ÷ (1.0 − 0.05) = $10.53

Notice that $0.53 is 5.3 percent of the NAV (or net amount invested). Regulators require that firms report sales charges in prospectuses as both the percentage of amount paid by investor (i.e., 5 percent), and the percentage of net amount invested (i.e., 5.3 percent).

The load or sales charge goes to the marketing organization selling the shares, which could be the investment company itself or brokers. The fee is split between the salesperson and the company employing that person. The load fee percentage usually declines with the size of the purchase. The old adage in the investment company business is that "mutual fund shares are sold, not bought," meaning that the sales force aggressively sells the shares to investors. The current norm for front-end loads is 5 percent of the offering price or less, as a result of increased competitiveness.

Figure 3-4 shows that 71 percent of Canadian mutual funds charged loads in 2008, with 8 percent having front-end sales charges, 19 percent back-end (redemption) charges, and 44 percent giving the investor the option of front- or back-end loads. The other 29 percent of funds were no-loads, which did not charge direct selling charges. However, no-load funds typically levy modest administration fees and charge other management fees that may add up. Investors should read the prospectus carefully to determine the net cost of these services. In addition, some funds are subject to an early redemption fee (often 2 percent) if the funds are redeemed within 90 days of purchase. Finally, some funds charge a distribution charge to pay commissioned salespeople, while trailer fees (or service fees) are those paid by a manager to the selling organization.

The level of management fees paid to compensate mutual fund managers in Canada varies widely depending on the fund, from 1 percent for some money market and index funds to 3 percent for some equity funds. It is normally expressed as a percentage of fund assets. Other fund expenses such as brokerage fees, audit, legal, safekeeping and custodial, and informational fees are also included in the management expense ratio (MER) calculation. These expenses decrease the returns to fund holders, and both management fees and expense ratios for the past five years must be included in the fund prospectus. Generally, sales charges are higher for mutual funds than for a bond or stock, but they offer much more in the package.

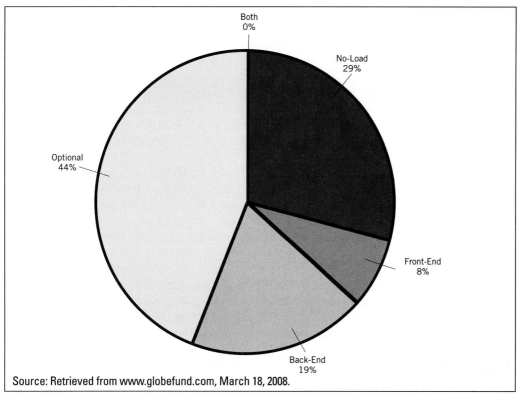

Figure 3-4
Load Versus No-Load
Funds (March 18, 2008)

Source: Retrieved from www.globefund.com, March 18, 2008.

Mutual funds redeem their shares or units on written request at a price that is either equal or close to the fund's net asset value per share (NAVPS). All funds must compute the NAVPS at least once a month (once a week for equity funds and once a year for real estate funds), and most of the larger ones do so on a daily basis (quarterly for real estate funds). Payment must be made for redeemed shares within five business days from the determination of NAVPS, although most funds reserve the right to suspend redemptions under certain highly unusual or emergency conditions—for example, if trading is suspended on securities comprising more than 50 percent of portfolio value.

There is normally no charge to redeem funds unless they are back-end loads, in which case the charge is usually a stated percentage of market value at the time of redemption (although some funds charge a percentage of the original amount invested). Systematic withdrawal plans may be arranged to meet investors' cash flow requirements. There are four general types of withdrawal plans:

1. Ratio withdrawal plan—a specified percentage of fund shares are redeemed at fixed intervals (amounts will vary according to prevailing market values).

2. Fixed dollar withdrawal plan—a specified dollar amount is withdrawn at regular intervals.

3. Fixed period withdrawal plan—a specified amount is withdrawn over a predetermined period of time with the intent that all capital will be exhausted when the plan ends.

4. Life expectancy adjusted withdrawal plan—a variation of number 3 designed to provide as high an income as possible during the holder's expected life; the amounts withdrawn vary in relation to the amount of capital remaining in the plan and the plan holder's revised life expectancy.

Exchange-Traded Funds (ETFs)

A new investing trend of increasing importance is the emergence of **exchange-traded funds (ETFs)**. An ETF is an index fund holding a diversified portfolio of securities, priced and traded on public exchanges. Most ETFs are passively managed funds owning a basket of stocks (or bonds) designed to mimic the performance of a market index such as the S&P/TSX 60 Index, the S&P 500, or the DJIA.

learning objective 5
Define exchange-traded funds (ETFs).

Exchange-Traded Funds (ETFs)
An index fund holding a diversified portfolio of securities, priced and traded on public exchanges.

However, unlike mutual funds, investors are not buying shares from an investment company directly, but rather from another investor. Therefore, ETFs involve regular brokerage transactions and brokerage fees. This makes the ETF resemble a closed-end fund in many respects.

Canadian ETFs trade on the TSX while US-based ETFs trade on US exchanges. Most ETFs are priced continually during the day, can be sold short, and can be purchased on margin (margin and short selling are explained in Chapter 5), unlike mutual funds.

The number of ETFs continues to grow rapidly in Canada and internationally. There was over US $450 billion in Global ETF assets in 2005, up from under $80 billion in 2000. In Canada, IShares (Barclays Canada) offered 24 ETFs in Canada as of January 17, 2008, with total NAV of approximately $15 billion.[5]

The most widely traded Canadian ETFs are the **I-60s**, which represent units in the S&P/TSX 60 Index. They trade on the TSX (ticker: XIU) and units are valued at 1/10th the value of the S&P/TSX 60 Index. For example, if the index is valued at 450, each unit is valued at approximately $45. Dividends are paid every quarter. The MER is currently 0.17 percent. The **TD S&P/TSX Index Fund** has the S&P/TSX Composite Index as its underlying index. In addition, there is a large and growing number of small-cap, mid-cap, industry-based, style-based, and bond ETFs available on the TSX.

Probably the best-known US-based ETF is the "Spider" (Standard & Poor's Depositary Receipt), introduced in 1993 to reflect the S&P 500 Index. Other US ETFs include "Diamonds" (the DJIA), "Cubes" (Nasdaq-100 Index Tracking Stock), "iShares" (S&P 500 as well as other S&P indexes for small-cap, mid-cap, and growth and value indexes, various Russell indexes, various Dow Jones Sector funds, and various country funds), and "HOLDRS" (various sector funds). Most of the global-focused iShares MSCI (formerly WEBS) track Morgan Stanley International indexes of various countries, providing investors with an opportunity to hold well-diversified country portfolios.

What happens when an investor wishes to sell his or her ETF? The shares are simply sold to another investor, thereby having no direct effect on the fund. As a result, it is important to ensure there is adequate liquidity in the form of trading volume (at least a few thousand shares traded daily). This is a direct result of the unique feature of ETFs involving discounts. Recall that many closed-end funds sell at discounts, meaning the price of the shares is less than the NAV of the fund. ETFs, in turn, have devised an unusual process to ensure that the shares always sell for the approximate value of the portfolio holdings. This is accomplished by granting special trading rights to institutional investors interacting with the ETF company. ETF companies include the Bank of New York, Barclays Global Investors, State Street, and Vanguard. If the ETF share price is less than the actual value of the underlying assets, an institutional investor can buy the ETF shares and turn them in to the sponsoring company for an equivalent amount of the underlying stocks, which the institution then sells for an immediate profit. If the ETF share price is greater than the underlying assets, the process is reversed. This unique process essentially ensures that the price of the ETF shares will approximate very closely the value of the underlying assets.

The "in-kind" feature described earlier, involving special trading rights for institutions, also leads to some tax efficiency. The ETF manager does not have to sell shares to pay for redemptions; therefore, redemptions do not create capital gains that must be distributed to the shareholders. Redemptions do not involve the fund at all, but rather one investor selling to another. Therefore, even though both index funds offered by an investment company and ETFs avoid capital gains as a result of no active trading, the ETF also avoids redemptions and the capital gains that could result from this activity. Note, however, that ETFs may still distribute capital gains as well as income as a part of holding a particular set of stocks.

We know that index funds have much lower operating expenses than do actively managed funds because they are passively managed. ETFs have even lower expenses. Although the average domestic stock index fund charges about 0.50 percent a year, the average ETF charges about 0.34 percent, and some (such as the I-60s) charge even less. This is because even though the investment company is responsible for the index fund and for sending investors statements, a brokerage firm does that in the

---

[5]www.ishares.ca.

case of ETFs, leaving the fund itself with very low expenses. ETFs are not for all investors. Regular purchases will incur ongoing brokerage fees, while trading ETFs on a short-term basis leads to taxable capital gains.

Distinguishing Among ETFs, Closed-End Funds, and Mutual Funds

Due to the rise of ETFs, it is sometimes difficult to distinguish them from the typical investment company products such as closed-end funds and mutual funds. It is worthwhile to remember the following:

1. Both closed-end funds and ETFs trade all day on exchanges, can be bought on margin, and can be shorted. Mutual funds, on the other hand, are bought and sold at the end of the trading day when the NAV is calculated. Thus, an investor urgently wanting to buy or sell such assets during the day would be out of luck with the typical mutual fund.

2. Closed-end funds and most mutual funds (exceptions are index funds) are actively managed, for better or for worse. ETFs, in contrast, are currently passive in nature, following an index.

3. Mutual funds trade at NAV (although buyers of load funds pay a sales charge).Closed-end funds typically trade at discounts and premiums, with discounts predominating in many years. ETFs can trade at discounts or premiums, but their mechanics are such that they are very likely to trade close to their NAV.

4. ETFs offer an important advantage over funds with regard to flexibility on taxes. Mutual fund managers may have to sell shares to pay those who want to leave the fund, thereby generating capital gains. Market makers in ETFs, in contrast, are paid for ETFs with a swap of the underlying shares. In these transactions, no capital gains occur. However, ETFs can generate taxable distributions.

Segregated Funds

Segregated funds are offered by insurance companies as alternatives to conventional mutual funds. They are legally considered to be insurance products and the funds must be separated from other assets of the insurance company. They have the unique feature of guaranteeing that, regardless of how poorly the fund performs, investors are entitled to at least a minimum percentage of their total contributions to the fund after a certain period of time. The minimum required by law is 75 percent after 10 years, although most funds guarantee 100 percent. They may also be structured so that the assets within the fund cannot be seized by creditors if the investor declares bankruptcy.

These funds have grown in popularity in recent years, with assets growing from $20 billion in 1991 to $89 billion in 2002, to over $310 billion by 2007. Much of this growth has been fuelled by investor concerns about growing volatility in financial markets. As a result of this demand, investment companies and banks have begun to offer similar products referred to as guaranteed funds or protected funds. While these funds represent attractive alternatives to the risk-averse investor who wishes to participate in increasing stock market prices without exposing themselves to an undue amount of risk, there are a couple of things investors should keep in mind. The first point to recognize is that the guarantee is only good after a certain period of time, and if investors sell their fund units before this date, they could end up receiving less than the guaranteed percentage of their investment. The second important point is that segregated funds (as well as the similar funds offered by investment companies and banks) tend to have higher load fees and some firms insist they be purchased through a contractual purchase plan.

Labour Sponsored Venture Capital Corporations (LSVCCs)

Labour Sponsored Venture Capital Corporations (LSVCCs) offer investors a tax credit and are usually provincially based. They must be sponsored by labour organizations and their specific mandate is to invest in small to medium-size businesses. Their main purposes are to create and protect jobs, promote economic growth and diversification, increase the supply of venture capital, and encourage greater participation in share ownership and business development. They presently account for approximately 40 percent of all venture capital raised in Canada. Eligible investments for LSVCCs include shares, ownership interests, or certain debt securities of eligible corporations or partnerships. Eligibility is restricted to taxable Canadian businesses that are active in Canada and meet specific criteria. These investments may be considered hybrid securities since they are speculative investments that also provide tax benefits.

LSVCC investors are eligible to receive a federal tax credit of 15 percent and provincial credits that are usually in the 15–20 percent range. While there is no maximum amount an investor may invest in an LSVCC, the total tax credit cannot exceed $1,500 in any year; therefore the maximum investment eligible for tax credits is $5,000 (since $1,500 is 30 percent of $5,000). These tax credits are subject to recapture by tax authorities if they are redeemed before they have been held for a certain period of time.

Aside from the available tax credits and foreign content advantages, LSVCCs provide other advantages to investors. In particular, most LSVCCs are RRSP and RRIF eligible, which implies the potential for a double tax advantage. For example, an investor in the 50 percent tax bracket who purchases $5,000 worth of LSVCCs for RRSP purposes can deduct $2,500 (50 percent of $5,000) from their taxable income, in addition to receiving the $1,500 in federal and provincial tax credits (as described above). Hence, an investor could potentially invest $5,000 in LSVCCs, at a net after-tax cost of $1,000.

The potential for higher after-tax returns offered by these investments does not come without the assumption of additional risk. Investors must be aware of the highly speculative and illiquid nature of these investments, which make them suitable only for investors with a high risk tolerance. The portfolios are generally not well diversified geographically and/or across industries and are composed of venture capital investments in small to medium-size companies that often lack an established track record. The companies are typically private companies that may not have been analyzed by a large number of outsiders, and they are not subject to the disclosure requirements of public companies. In fact, their financial statements may not even be audited. The nature of these investments implies that not only are they speculative in nature, but since the companies likely do not trade publicly, there is a great deal of illiquidity associated with the investments. Indeed, Real-World Returns 3-3 discusses the poor performance of these funds over the last decade.

REAL-WORLD RETURNS 3-3
Labour-Sponsored Funds

What Are We Looking For?
Top-performing, labour-sponsored investment funds over the long haul. These investments—now called retail venture funds—were marketed on their long-term potential and juicy tax credits.

Today's Search
We looked at their performance over the decade to the end of 2007—specifically, average annual returns over one, three, five and 10 years.

So What Did We Turn Up?
Ugly returns. Dead funds. Funds reinventing themselves. Many took a hit after the technology bubble burst. And high management fees have taken a big bite from returns.

GrowthWorks Canadian, formerly Working Ventures Canadian Fund, posted an average annual loss of 3 percent over the decade.

Canadian Medical Discoveries (series I), formed from the merger of the first two original series, fared even worse. It suffered an average annual loss of 6.6 percent. And VenGrowth Investment Fund Class A (series E) declined an average of 1.1 percent a year.

(continued)

REAL-WORLD RETURNS 3-3 *continued*

Some funds managed to stay in the black. At the lower end was BEST Discoveries, up 1 percent annually. Dynamic Venture Opportunity (series I) posted a 6.8 percent average annual return—the best in the group. Still, they underperformed the 9.8 percent average for Canadian small-to-mid-capitalization equity funds.

While Crocus Investment Fund is listed as active, it's on life support. The scandal-ridden fund has been mired in legal woes, and its assets are still being liquidated.

Sportfund merged with Retrocom Growth Fund, which filed for bankruptcy protection in 2006 and proceedings are continuing. And Covington Fund I was wound down last year.
Out of 20 funds, 13 are listed as non-active. Some of them are under new managers, or have merged with other funds.

Triax Growth I merged with the Covington Venture Fund Inc. (series I). York Labour Fund, formerly Centerfire Growth, has become Lawrence Enterprise V Fund.

Impax Venture Income Fund, formerly DGC Entertainment Ventures, merged with Impax Venture Fund to become Horizons Advantaged Equity Fund (series I).

Capital Alliance Ventures, Canadian Science & Technology Growth and First Ontario (which took over Trillium Growth Capital and FESA Enterprise Venture Capital) merged with Growth-Works Canadian to start a new series. ENSIS Growth will soon amalgamate with GrowthWorks Canadian too. Workers Investment Fund has merged with GrowthWorks Atlantic Venture Fund.

When funds start a new life, the performance clock often starts all over again. So much for long-term potential.

Labour-Sponsored Funds Existing in 1998

Fund Name*	Inception date	Net assets (millions) as of Dec. '07	% return as of Dec. 2007					Active/Not active fund as of today	MER effective date	Last re-ported MER
			1-year	3-year	5-year	10-year	Since inception			
GrowthWorks Canadian	2/8/1990	227.4	−0.19%	2.87%	3.76%	−2.96%	0.12%	Active	2/28/2005	4.9
Working Opportunity Balncd Ser 1	4/1/1992	154.9	−2.84%	−2.48%	−1.90%	1.62%	2.66%	Active	9/30/2005	2.63
Crocus Investment Fund	3/1/1993								1/30/2004	4.04
Dynamic Venture Opport Series 1	2/28/1994	61.9	−6.52%	5.78%	5.22%	6.79%	1.78%	Active	6/29/2007	3.99
Impax Venture Income Fund Inc.	3/1/1994							Not Active		
Canadian Medical Discoveries	10/7/1994	156.4	−19.84%	−13.93%	−9.93%	−6.60%	−4.32%	Active	5/31/2005	3.71
Trillium Growth Capital Inc.	10/25/1994							Not Active		
First Ontario LSIF Ltd.	1/31/1995							Not Active		
Covington Fund 1	2/28/1995							Not Active		
Capital Alliance Ventures	2/28/1995							Not Active		
Sportfund	2/28/1995							Not Active		
FESA Enterprise Venture Capital	3/1/1995							Not Active		
VenGrowth Invst Fund Inc.	3/1/1995	95.7	−9.57%	−2.70%	−4.35%	−1.12%	0.58%	Active	8/31/2007	4.17
Retrocom Growth	4/13/1995							Not Active		
Triax Growth-I	1/10/1996							Not Active		
Canadian Science & Tech Growth	12/2/1996							Not Active		
B.E.S.T. Discoveries I	12/31/1996	56.9	20.32%	6.59%	1.38%	0.97%	0.70%	Active	9/28/2007	5.72
Workers Investment Fund Inc.	1/10/1997							Not Active		
York Labour Fund Inc.	3/1/1997							Not Active		
ENSIS Growth Fund Inc.	1/5/1998	96.0	2.15%	−3.13%	−2.13%		−2.10%	Active	10/29/2004	4.95
Avg Return - Canadian Small-Mid Cap Equity Fund			7.23%	12.46%	16.95%	9.78%				
Median Return - Canadian Small -Mid Cap Equity Fund			8.02%	11.61%	16.24%	10.47%				
BMO Nesbitt Burns Cdn Small Cap Index			2.01%	12.51%	18.33%	9.68%				

*Note: The list does not include the Quebec Solidarity Fund because it is valued semi-annually and data is incomplete. Source: Globefund.
Source: Won, Shirley. "The ugly truth about labour-sponsored funds," *The Globe and Mail*, February 16, 2008, p. B15.

Disclosure requirements for LSVCCs are similar to those for mutual funds, through a prospectus offering, since shares are continually being issued. Registered salespeople must have passed the CSC exam and follow the IFIC Code of Conduct guidelines. However, LSVCCs differ from mutual funds in several ways. Unlike mutual funds, LSVCCs

1. Are not restricted to 10 percent ownership in given companies (in fact, they may exceed 20 percent)

2. Have restrictions on transferability and redemption

3. May not be valued based exclusively on the market, but rather, may require valuation by independent qualified persons that are to be updated by management

In short, LSVCCs are only suitable as long-term investments due to their speculative and illiquid nature, as well as to restrictions regarding the provision of tax credit benefits.

CHECK YOUR UNDERSTANDING

3-9. ETFs and closed-end funds both trade on exchanges. Why, then, have ETFs become so popular while closed-end funds, as a group, have languished?

3-10. Given the wide availability of no-load funds, why do many investors choose to buy load funds and pay sales charges?

3-11. The tax credits available on LSVCCs are a very appealing feature. Why do you suppose these funds have not surpassed other investment funds in popularity?

INVESTMENT FUNDS PERFORMANCE

learning objective 6
Understand how the performance of investment funds is measured.

Few topics in investments are as well reported on a regular basis as the performance of investment funds, and in particular mutual funds. *The Globe and Mail, National Post, Business Week, Forbes,* and *Money,* among other popular publications, regularly cover the performance of mutual funds, emphasizing their returns and risks. Real-World Returns 3-4 provides an example of fund performance reports available at www.globefund.com.

We will discuss the calculation of investment returns in much more detail in Chapter 6, but the primary focus in that chapter is on individual securities and indexes of securities and the actual mechanics involved. Furthermore, we discuss the evaluation of portfolio performance in detail in Chapter 22 and therefore do not consider the evaluation of mutual fund performance in depth now. Nevertheless, it is instructive at this point to consider some of the basic points about mutual fund returns.

Throughout this text we will use total return (explained in detail in Chapter 6) to measure the return from any financial asset, including a mutual fund. Total return for a mutual fund includes reinvested dividends, interest payments and/or capital gains, and therefore includes all of the ways investors make money from financial assets. It is stated as a percentage and can cover any time period—one day, one month, one year, or several years.

Standard practice in the mutual fund industry is to calculate and present the average annual return, a hypothetical rate of return that, if achieved annually, would have produced the same cumulative total return if performance had been constant over the entire period. The average annual return is a geometric mean (discussed in Chapter 6) and reflects the compound rate of growth at which money grew over time.

Average annual total returns allow investors to make direct comparisons among funds as to their performance, assuming they do so legitimately, as explained in Chapter 22 when we discuss the evaluation of performance. In particular, the risk of the funds being compared should be equivalent, and the funds should have the same general objectives. In addition to various average return figures, Real-World Returns 3-4 includes two measures of risk (3-year risk, which is actually the standard deviation; and beta) that will be discussed in subsequent chapters. For example, we expect equity funds to outperform bond funds and money market funds on average. Another complexity arising in the comparison of fund performance is that, as discussed above, funds with the same stated objectives often have significant variation in the nature of the assets included in their portfolios.

REAL-WORLD RETURNS 3-4

Average Total Returns RBC Asset Management Inc.'s Canadian Equity Fund

Returns as at February 29, 2008

	Fund	Index*
1 Month	3.62%	3.45%
3 Months	-1.31%	-0.12%
6 Months	-0.41%	0.70%
1 Year	4.92%	6.75%
2 Year Avg	9.74%	10.52%
3 Year Avg	13.77%	14.58%
5 Year Avg	16.56%	18.11%
10 Year Avg	8.95%	8.67%
15 Year Avg	11.21%	11.72%
20 Year Avg	9.26%	10.05%
Since Inception	10.19%	-
2007	9.37%	9.83%
2006	17.54%	17.26%
2005	22.99%	24.13%
3 year risk	11.02	10.99
3 year beta	0.99	1.00

*S&P/TSX Total Return

Source: Retrieved from www.globefund.com, February 29, 2008.

Benchmarks

Investors need to relate the performance of a mutual fund to some benchmark in order to judge relative performance with (hopefully) a comparable investment alternative. RBC Asset Management Inc.'s Canadian Equity Fund, presented above, was compared to the S&P/TSX Total Return Index. Other funds are compared to different benchmarks based on their objectives and asset allocation parameters. For example, small-cap funds are compared to small-cap indexes, and bond funds are compared to bond indexes.

How Important Are Expenses?

An important issue for all fund investors is that of expenses. Should they be overly concerned about the load charges, given the large number of no-load funds? What about annual operating expenses, as reflected in MERs? There is considerable evidence that funds with lower MERs provide better returns for investors in the long run, which makes sense to the extent that this expense is passed on to investors (i.e., it reduces their returns). While this will not always be the case, it certainly makes sense to be aware of the level of MER when purchasing funds.

Mutual Fund Ratings

Many agencies provide ratings for mutual funds. One of the best known rating systems is provided by Morningstar. Globefund is a major provider of information and ratings of Canadian mutual funds. Real-World Returns 3-5 shows Globefund's reports for selected RBC funds. Real-World Returns 3-6 describes Globefund's five-star rating system and lists some of the 547 funds that had a five-star rating as of March 18, 2008.

Mutual fund ratings such as those provided by Morningstar and Globefund are widely used by investors as a screening device when searching for a fund to buy. However, it is important to note the measures reflect historical performance, which is no guarantee of "future" performance, as discussed in the next section.

REAL-WORLD RETURNS 3-5

Global Fund Reports

Selected RBC Funds

Fund Report – Standard

Fund name	Price $	1 day $ Chg	30 day %	3 mo %	6 mo %	1 yr %	3 yr %	Incep (mm/yy)
RBC $U.S. Income (US$)	10.275	-0.011	0.83	-0.34	1.75	2.93		3.87 (05/05)
RBC Advisor Canadian Bond	11.215	0.028	2.62	2.41	5.25	4.03	4.28	5.97 (11/99)
RBC Asian Equity	8.631	-0.138	-10.59	-13.44	-12.08	-12.62	4.73	3.91 (07/02)
RBC Balanced	11.785	-0.171	-2.37	-3.29	-1.94	-0.30	7.46	7.87 (01/88)
RBC Balanced - T	12.681	-0.184	-2.37	-3.28	-1.92			-3.49 (07/07)
RBC Balanced Growth	12.038	-0.112	-2.83	-4.79	-3.70	-2.95	6.68	5.27 (04/98)
RBC Balanced Growth - T	12.598	-0.117	-2.83	-4.78	-3.67			-5.37 (07/07)
RBC Bond	6.023	0.026	2.09	1.75	4.11	1.55	3.33	8.32 (11/72)
RBC Canadian Bond Index	11.419	0.024	2.74	2.75	6.15	5.66	4.59	5.81 (06/00)
RBC Canadian Dividend	43.209	-0.846	-5.33	-4.65	-4.80	-0.20	10.51	13.35 (01/93)
RBC Canadian Dividend - T	12.192	-0.239	-5.33	-4.64	-4.79			-6.35 (07/07)
RBC Canadian Index	23.473	-0.784	-5.30	-0.24	0.50	6.31	13.97	11.49 (10/98)
RBC Canadian Money Market	10.000	0.000	0.30	1.00	2.03	3.81	3.01	4.98 (12/86)
RBC Canadian Short-Term Income	10.827	0.001	1.36	2.46	4.20	4.37	2.79	5.20 (01/92)
RBC Canadian T-Bill	10.000	0.000	0.25	0.83	1.72	3.45	2.83	3.81 (01/91)
RBC Cash Flow Portfolio	9.689	-0.036	-0.61	-0.12	1.61	2.06	4.06	4.82 (08/04)
RBC Cdn Diversified Income Trust	16.671	-0.401	-2.77	4.80	4.92	8.39		5.45 (08/06)
RBC Cdn Equity	24.891	-0.811	-4.73	-1.31	-0.41	4.92	13.77	10.19 (04/67)
RBC DS Aggressive All Eq Global Prt	11.002	-0.208	-4.36	-8.08	-6.66	-4.82		5.50 (09/05)

As of March 19, 2008

Fund Report – Key Facts

Fund name	Asset Class	Assets ($M)	MER %	Load Type	Minimum Investment	RSP
RBC $U.S. Income (US$)	Global Fixed Income Balanced	53.0	1.85	NL	1000	Yes
RBC Advisor Canadian Bond	Canadian Fixed Income	157.6	0.88	FE	10000	Yes
RBC Asian Equity	Asia Pacific Equity	592.4	2.69	NL	1000	Yes
RBC Balanced	Canadian Neutral Balanced	8886.5	2.28	NL	1000	Yes

Fund Report – Key Facts (continued)

Fund name	Asset Class	Assets ($M)	MER %	Load Type	Minimum Investment	RSP
RBC Balanced Growth	Canadian Neutral Balanced	1135.0	2.36	NL	1000	Yes
RBC Bond	Canadian Fixed Income	3869.2	1.46	NL	1000	Yes
RBC Canadian Bond Index	Canadian Fixed Income	189.4	0.70	NL	1000	Yes
RBC Canadian Dividend	Canadian Dividend and Income Equity	9268.3	1.73	NL	1000	Yes
RBC Canadian Index	Canadian Equity	485.3	0.71	NL	1000	Yes
RBC Canadian Money Market	Canadian Money Market	4913.2	0.98	NL	500	Yes
RBC Canadian Short-Term Income	Canadian Short Term Fixed Income	1849.2	1.45	NL	1000	Yes
RBC Canadian T-Bill	Canadian Money Market	1425.8	0.97	NL	500	Yes
RBC Cash Flow Portfolio	Canadian Fixed Income Balanced	706.2	1.54	NL	5000	Yes
RBC Cdn Diversified Income Trust	Canadian Equity	13.1	2.14	OPT	1000	Yes
RBC Cdn Equity	Canadian Equity	4919.2	1.99	NL	1000	Yes
RBC DS Aggressive All Eq Global Prt	Global Equity	69.3	2.44	NL	1500	Yes

Source: Retrieved from www.globefund.com, March 18, 2008.

REAL-WORLD RETURNS 3-6
Globefund 5-Star Ratings

Globefund.com in conjunction with Algorithmics Inc. is pleased to introduce the Globefund 5-Star Ratings service, a simple rating for most mutual funds in Canada. Globefund 5-Star Ratings will help you understand how well each fund has been doing relative to similar funds. The ratings are available on the new 5-Star Rating Fund Report, on the Annual and Long-Term Fund Reports and on the Fund Profile. You can also use the Fund Filter to screen funds based on their Globefund 5-Star Rating.

Funds are ranked from one to five stars, with the top ranked funds getting five stars and the lowest ranked funds getting one star. While past performance does not guarantee future performance, our historical testing of this rating system has shown that on average, top-rated funds have tended to outperform their peers over a six-month to two-year horizon.

Our rating system provides a useful gauge of the funds we follow. However, we do not suggest you use it as the single decision point for the suitability of a fund for your needs. Be sure to study all of the information you can gather on any fund before you invest.

(continued)

REAL-WORLD RETURNS 3-6 *continued*

Globefund 5-Star Funds
as of March 19, 2008

Fund Name	Globefund 5-Star Rating	1 Yr Return%	2 Yr Return%	3 Yr Return%	Asset Class
AGF American Growth Class (US$)	★★★★★	5.30	6.31	9.29	International Growth
AGF Canada Class (US$)	★★★★★	22.73	18.36	20.18	Growth
AGF Canadian Balanced	★★★★★	1.11	7.33	8.87	Growth and Income
AGF Canadian Balanced D	★★★★★	1.61	7.88	9.43	Growth and Income
AGF Canadian Conservative Income	★★★★★	1.70	2.58	2.06	Growth and Income
AGF China Focus Class (US$)	★★★★★	45.82	40.89	33.11	Aggressive Growth
AGF Emerging Markets Value (US$)	★★★★★	26.61	24.82	31.79	Aggressive Growth
AGF Glo Government Bond (US$)	★★★★★	14.83	8.46	4.87	Income
AGF Global Equity Class (US$)	★★★★★	5.42	9.32	11.85	International Growth
AGF Global High Yield Bond (US$)	★★★★★	11.26	9.60	10.81	Income
AGF Global Resources Class	★★★★★	24.41	24.14	26.22	Aggressive Growth
AGF Global Resources Class (US$)	★★★★★	47.80	33.48	36.04	Aggressive Growth
AGF Precious Metal	★★★★★	12.21	29.27	31.30	Aggressive Growth
AGF Short Term Income (US$)	★★★★★	22.44	10.81	10.56	Income
AGF World Companies (US$)	★★★★★	5.13	9.64	12.73	International Growth
AGF World Opportunities (US$)	★★★★★	3.85	7.03	10.85	International Growth
AIC Global Focused (US$)	★★★★★	9.37	10.98		International Growth
AIC Global Focused Corp Cl (US$)	★★★★★	9.56	11.63		International Growth
AIC PPC Global Fixed Inc Pool (US$)	★★★★★	10.50	7.11		Income
AIC World Equity (US$)	★★★★★	1.21	8.59	8.01	International Growth
AIC World Equity Corporate Cl (US$)	★★★★★	0.87	8.33	7.64	International Growth
AIM European Growth (US$)	★★★★★	1.26	13.38	14.34	International Growth
AIM European Growth Class (US$)	★★★★★	1.57	13.08	14.18	International Growth
AIM International Growth Class(US$)	★★★★★	4.28	13.08	15.40	International Growth
AIM Short-Term Income 'A' (US$)	★★★★★	22.11	10.27	9.99	Capital Preservation
AIM Short-Term Income 'B' (US$)	★★★★★	21.80	9.96	9.63	Capital Preservation
APEX Balanced (AGF)	★★★★★	2.84	6.62	7.30	Growth and Income
APEX Canadian Value (Dynamic)	★★★★★	2.15	13.95	16.31	Growth
Acuity Pooled Fixed Income	★★★★★	4.27	3.52		

How It Works

We have divided mutual funds into six broad fund categories that closely match the asset allocation categories used by financial planners, as follows:

- Growth (primarily mid-size and large cap Canadian equity funds)
- Growth and Income (primarily balanced, dividend, and asset allocation funds)
- International Growth (foreign equity funds)
- Aggressive Growth (primarily small cap, geographic, and specialty funds)
- Income (fixed income and mortgage funds)
- Capital Preservation (Canadian and foreign money market funds)

The only qualification for including a fund in the rating system is that it must have at least two years of history. Currently, that means we compute a rating for approximately 80 percent of the 6,000 Canadian mutual funds that we track.

Once classified into one of these broad categories, all the funds within that category compete with each other in terms of the best score, and hence the best rating. A fund's score is a combination of return and regret and is determined as follows. On a monthly basis, for each fund, we compute month-by-month returns and subtract from these the return of the 90-day Canadian T-Bill to get what is known as the risk-free return for each month. If this result is positive for any one month, it contributes to the fund's return. If it is negative, it contributes to the fund's regret. We then use an averaging method across each of these returns and regrets (with increasing weight on the most recent data) to derive a final measure for return and for regret for each fund. The final score for a fund is then computed as the return score minus an adjusted regret score, where the adjustment factor for the regret component is unique for each broad asset category. Using the final scores for each of the funds in a category, we rank them and then allocate a star rating for each. The top 10 percent of funds receive a five-star rating, the next 22.5 percent a four-star rating, the middle 35 percent a three-star rating, the next 22.5 percent a two-star rating and the bottom 10 percent of funds a one-star rating.

The Globefund 5-Star Ratings use many of the elements of the Mark-to-Future methodology pioneered by Algorithmics: www.mark-to-future.com. Algorithmics, www.algorithmics.com, was founded in 1989 in response to the complex issues surrounding financial risk management for the enterprise. Today, as the leading provider with the largest and most experienced team in the industry, Algorithmics continues to focus its efforts on creating and implementing enterprise risk management software that meets the evolving needs of its customers. Continuing its tradition of leading the way in risk measurement and management tools and processes, Algorithmics recently introduced Mark-To-Future™ (MtF), an open and comprehensive framework for measuring risk and reward. Headquartered in Toronto, with 14 offices around the world, Algorithmics serves more than 90 global financial institutions with 140 installations worldwide.

Source: Retrieved from www.globefund.com, March 19, 2008. Globefund 5-Star ratings provided by *The Globe and Mail*. Methodology provided by Algorithmics Inc.

Consistency of Performance

Can the returns numbers above, widely available for mutual funds, help investors choose this year's, or next year's, winner? The consistency of performance of mutual funds has long been a controversy, and this continues to be true. Early studies tended to find no consistency in fund performance, but some recent studies did find some. For example, in the 1990s, Grinblatt and Titman found persistence in differences between funds over time. More recently Elton, Gruber, and Blake also found evidence of performance differences.[6]

Princeton University professor Burton Malkiel has also found evidence of such differences, although he found that the historical period had an effect, with differences persisting in the 1970s but not in the 1980s.[7] Malkiel, famous for many years as a strong believer in market efficiency, would have a difficult time saying past performance matters in selecting a fund. However, in a recent interview, Malkiel suggests that investors may gain when selecting funds by relying on recent good performance; however, there are no guarantees when investing, but a possible advantage is to be appreciated.

---

[6]Mark Grinblatt and Sheridan Titman, "The Persistence of Mutual Fund Performance," *The Journal of Finance* 47 (December 1992), pp. 1977–1984; Edwin Elton, Martin J. Gruber, and Christopher Blake, "The Persistence of Risk-Adjusted Mutual Fund Performance," *Journal of Business* 69 (April 1996), pp. 133–157; and Martin J. Gruber, "Another Puzzle: The Growth in Actively Managed Mutual Funds," *The Journal of Finance* 51 (July 1996), pp. 783–810.
[7]Burton G. Malkiel, "Returns from Investing in Equity Mutual Funds: 1971 to 1991," *The Journal of Finance* 50 (June 1995), pp. 549–572.

A study by MPL Communications Inc. of Toronto also documents a lack of persistence in Canadian mutual fund performance. They find that none of the 76 Canadian equity funds that were in existence for the 10-year period ended September 30, 1997, were able to surpass the category average for all 10 years. Further, only one fund was able to beat the average nine times, only three beat the average eight times, while only four could beat the average seven times. In fact, less than half (34) of the funds were able to beat the average in five or more years.[8]

Evidence compiled from www.globefund.com confirms this lack of persistence in Canadian equity fund performance over the 1993–2007 period, as shown in Table 3-1. The table is based on the number of Canadian equity funds that existed throughout the 10- and 15-year periods ending in 2007.

Referring to column two of Table 3-1, we can see that no funds were able to beat the group average for 12, 13, 14, or 15 years, while only two funds were able to outperform for 10 years or 11 years. Closer examination shows that only 16 of the 46 funds (or 34.8 percent) were able to outperform more than half the time (i.e., 8 years or more). Similar results are evident if we look at column three, where we can see that none of the funds were able to outperform in 9 or 10 years, and only 27 of the 82 funds (or 32.9 percent) were able to outperform more than half the time.

In conclusion, although past fund performance provides useful information to investors, strong past performance is no guarantee of strong future performance.

Table 3-1

Canadian Equity Funds Performance

Number of Times Fund Performed Above Average	Number of Funds (1993–2007; 15-year period)	Number of Funds (1998–2007; 10-year period)
0	0	0
1	0	2
2	1	10
3	2	10
4	1	15
5	6	18
6	11	15
7	9	8
8	7	4
9	5	0
10	2	0
11	2	n/a
12	0	n/a
13	0	n/a
14	0	n/a
15	0	n/a
Total number of firms during period	46	82

Source: www.globefund.com, March 19, 2008.

INVESTING INTERNATIONALLY THROUGH INVESTMENT FUNDS

learning objective 7
Discuss the opportunities for investing indirectly internationally.

The mutual fund industry has become a global industry. Open-end funds around the world have grown rapidly, including those in emerging market economies. Worldwide assets were approximately $14.4 trillion US by mid-2004.

---

[8]Peter Brewster, "Better than average: Not very often," *The Globe and Mail/Report on Mutual Funds*, November 6, 1997, p. C1.

Canadian investors can invest internationally by buying and selling investment funds that specialize in international securities. These funds have become both numerous and well-known in recent years. By March 2008, Canadians could choose from a large number of foreign funds, including 649 US equity funds; 94 small- and mid-cap US equity funds; 125 European equity funds; 1,001 global equity funds; 324 international equity funds; 78 North American equity funds; 37 Japanese equity funds; 38 Asia Pacific (excluding Japan) equity funds; 67 emerging market equity funds; 980 global balanced funds; 90 global fixed income funds; and 32 US money market funds.

So-called international funds tend to concentrate primarily on international stocks, while global funds tend to keep a minimum percentage of their total in domestic assets. Another alternative in indirect investing, the single-country funds, concentrate on the securities of a single country. International closed-end funds usually sell at either a discount or a premium to their net asset value as do their domestic counterparts. Some developing countries restrict access to foreign equity ownership, with the result that a single-country fund may be an investor's only readily available alternative for investing in that particular country.

Another alternative for international fund investing is through country funds, which concentrate on each of several different countries. The typical single-country fund is closed-end, and is usually passively managed—geared to match a major stock index of a particular country. Each of these offerings will typically be almost fully invested, have little turnover, and offer significantly reduced expenses to shareholders. For example, Morgan Stanley offers iShares (formerly WEBS), which tracks a pre-designated index (one of Morgan Stanley's international capital indices) for many countries.

THE FUTURE OF INDIRECT INVESTING

One of the hottest new movements concerning indirect investing is the fund "supermarket" in which investors can buy the funds of various mutual fund families through one source, such as a brokerage firm. Supermarket refers to the fact that an investor has hundreds of choices available through one source and does not have to go to other sources to obtain his or her choices. The funds participating in the supermarket pay the firms offering the funds distribution fees (0.25 percent to 0.40 percent of assets per year). Investors often use the Internet to access these supermarkets, with Schwab and Fidelity reporting that about 60 percent of mutual fund trades are done online.

Hedge Funds

We close our discussion of investment companies by considering an offshoot, an unregulated investment company. The Investment Company Act of 1940 gave primacy to the open-end investment company (or mutual fund) as the way to protect investors from the excesses of the unregulated companies of the 1920s. The key was that such companies would be heavily regulated as to investor protections. However, the Act also left open the possibility of a money manager handling funds for a small group of sophisticated investors in an unregulated format. In 1949, a fund was started to "hedge" market risk by both buying and selling short, thus initiating the hedge fund industry.

Hedge funds are unregulated companies that seek to exploit various market opportunities and thereby earn larger returns than are ordinarily available. For example, they may use leverage or derivative securities, or they may invest in illiquid assets, strategies not generally available to the typical mutual fund. They require a substantial initial investment from investors, and may have restrictions on how quickly investors can withdraw their funds. Unlike mutual funds, they traditionally do not disclose information to their investors about their investing activities. Hedge funds charge substantial fees and take a percentage of the profits earned, typically at least 20 percent.

Over time, the average performance of hedge funds has been good, with larger returns and less risk than the typical mutual fund. However, there have been some well-known failures, such as Bayou in 2005 whereby the principals are alleged to have drained investor monies for their own purposes. The most spectacular failure was Long Term Capital in 1998, which got in trouble as a result of Russia defaulting on its debt. In this case, the Federal Reserve had to step in to calm the waters.

In Canada, by 2006, it was estimated there were over 250 funds and $30 billion in assets. Globally, by 2005 there were more than 8,000 hedge funds, with an estimated $1 trillion under management. A legitimate issue to consider is whether there are enough talented managers to run this many funds. Furthermore, are more and more funds competing for the same opportunities in the market? If so, does this not diminish the returns to be expected from hedge funds?

THOSE WHO LIVE IN GLASS HOUSES

In late 2003, Edward D. Jones & Co., a large retail brokerage firm with offices in the US, Canada, and UK, took out ads criticizing the "anything goes" approach that led to abuses in the US mutual fund industry. In late 2004, the US Securities and Exchange Commission finalized a US$75-million settlement agreement with the company. The company was charged with accepting tens of millions of dollars secretly from seven preferred mutual fund groups, which could lead its brokers to favour those funds with their clients even if it were not in the best interest of the clients. Brokers received bonuses and other incentives to sell these particular funds.

It was also found that the brokerage firm did not have in place the proper systems to prevent late trading of mutual funds from taking place. Late trading occurs when fund buyers are able to execute mutual fund orders after 4 p.m. using the 4 p.m. closing price. Thus, favourable market-moving developments after 4 p.m. could cause a fund's value to go up the next day, and buying the shares at the same-day 4 p.m. price can allow favoured clients to earn profits at the expense of long-term fund shareholders.

DISCUSSION QUESTIONS

1. Should Edward Jones have told clients that its brokers were given incentives to sell particular funds, or should it have stopped the practice altogether?

2. Financial advisors not connected with brokerage firms often receive commissions for selling mutual funds. Is that unethical?

3. If customers were to profit from buying mutual funds their broker was receiving incentives for selling, would that make it less unethical?

CHECK YOUR UNDERSTANDING

3-12. If a mutual fund were purchased and held for exactly one year, would the change in unit price represent the total return on the investment?

3-13. Can you be confident that mutual funds with a 5-star Globefund rating will perform well in the future? Would you recommend that investors only invest in these highly rated funds?

3-14. Would an International fund or a Global fund likely be the better choice for an investor seeking a single investment fund to provide broad geographic diversification including both domestic stocks and those from around the world?

3-15. Why are most investors restricted from investing in hedge funds, despite their strong performance records?

SUMMARY

This summary relates to the learning objectives for this chapter.

1. **Distinguish between direct and indirect investing.**

   As an alternative to purchasing financial assets themselves, all investors can invest indirectly, which involves the purchase of shares (or trust units) of an investment fund.

2. **Define open-end and closed-end investment funds.**

   Investment funds are composed of portfolios of securities that are held on behalf of their shareholders. Investment funds are classified as either open-end or closed-end, depending on whether their own capitalization (number of shares or units outstanding) is constantly changing or relatively fixed.

3. **State the major types of mutual funds and give their features.**

   Open-end funds, or mutual funds, can be divided into two categories: money market funds and stock and bond & income funds. Money market mutual funds concentrate on portfolios of money market securities, providing investors with a way to own these high face value securities indirectly. Stock, bond, and income funds own portfolios of stocks and/or bonds, allowing investors to participate in these markets without having to purchase these securities directly.

4. **Explain the transactions behind indirect investments.**

   Investors transacting indirectly in closed-end funds encounter discounts and premiums, meaning that the price of these funds is unequal to their net asset values. Mutual funds can be load or no-load funds, depending on whether they have a sales charge (load) or not. All investment companies charge a management fee.

5. **Define exchange-traded funds (ETFs).**

   An exchange-traded fund is an index fund holding a diversified portfolio of securities designed to mimic the performance of a market index such as the S&P/TSX 60 Index. They are priced and traded on public exchanges.

6. **Understand how the performance of investment funds is measured.**

   Total return for a mutual fund includes reinvested dividends, interest payments, and/or capital gains. A cumulative total return measures the actual performance over a stated period of time, such as the past three, five, or 10 years. The average annual return is a hypothetical rate of return that, if achieved annually, would have produced the same cumulative total return if performance had been constant over the entire period.

7. **Discuss the opportunities for investing indirectly internationally.**

   International funds concentrate primarily on international stocks, while global funds keep a minimum percentage of their total in domestic assets. Single-country funds concentrate on the securities in a single country.

KEY TERMS

Closed-end investment fund, p.65	Investment fund, p.62	Net asset value (NAV), p.66
Exchange-traded funds (ETFs), p.73	Money market funds (MMFs), p.67	Open-end investment fund, p.65
	Mutual funds, p.65	Unit investment trust, p.65

REVIEW QUESTIONS

3-1. What is meant by indirect investing?

3-2. What is a money market fund? Why would it appeal to investors?

3-3. Distinguish between a value fund and a growth fund.

3-4. Distinguish between the direct and indirect methods by which mutual fund units are typically purchased.

3-5. What are passively managed country funds?

3-6. What is the difference between the management fee and the management expense ratio for a mutual fund?

3-7. What is an investment fund? Distinguish between an open-end and a closed-end fund.

3-8. It has been said that many closed-end funds are worth more dead than alive. What is meant by this expression?

3-9. What is meant by an investment fund's objective? What are some of the objectives pursued by an equity, bond, and income fund?

3-10. What is the difference between the average annual return for a fund and the cumulative total return?

3-11. How would the owner of some units of RBC Asset Management Inc.'s Canadian Equity Fund "cash out" when he or she was ready to sell the shares?

3-12. Who owns a mutual fund? Who determines investment policies and objectives?

3-13. What does it mean when someone says "Mutual funds involve investment risk"?

3-14. What is the difference between a load fund and a no-load fund?

3-15. Distinguish between segregated funds and mutual funds.

3-16. Identify three ways in which LSVCCs differ from other mutual funds.

3-17. How does the NAVPS affect the price of an open-end investment fund (mutual fund) as compared to the price of a closed-end fund? Explain.

3-18. As a small investor, what are the major benefits of indirect investing (in a mutual fund, for example) as compared to investing directly in stocks or bonds? What are the drawbacks?

3-19. The Crabtree Canadian Equity Fund has 500,000 units issued to investors. The fund currently has liabilities of $100,000. If the fund's portfolio is composed of the three securities listed below, calculate the fund's NAVPS.

Security	# of Shares	Price / Share
Evergreen Inc.	100,000	$10
Atlantic Fisheries Ltd.	500,000	8
Great Northern Gas Inc.	1,000,000	1.10

3-20. How is the net asset value for a mutual fund calculated?

3-21. Identify the risks associated with investments in LSVCCs.

3-22. Does a closed-end fund normally trade at a discount or a premium from its NAVPS?

3-23. List at least four reasons why it is believed that the situation in Question 22 occurs. How does this phenomenon impact on the concept of market efficiency?

3-24. Although most closed-end funds trade at a discount to their NAVPS, this is not always the case. Why do you think that some closed-end funds trade at a premium (sometimes a substantial premium) to their NAVPS?

3-25. List the benefits of a money market fund for investors. List the disadvantages.

3-26. List some reasons an investor might prefer a closed-end fund to an open-end fund.

3-27. Distinguish between a global fund and an international fund.

3-28. How have investors' preferences with regard to mutual fund investing changed over time?

3-29. What is meant by a "family of funds"?

3-30. List and briefly describe three differences between ETFs and mutual funds.

3-31. What does the term open-end mean with regard to an investment company?

3-32. What is the value to investors of Morningstar and Globefund ratings? What is the weakness of these ratings?

3-33. What does it mean to say an index fund is related to passive investing?

3-34. How does a hedge fund differ from a mutual fund?

3-35. What is a fund supermarket?

PROBLEMS

3-1. The years 2001 to 2008 witnessed some big increases and some significant declines in the Canadian stock market. The data below show the percentage annual returns for two mutual funds in the Mackenzie Financial family of funds: the Focus Canada Fund and the Maxxum Canadian Equity Growth Fund. Note that the figures for 2008 reflect performance for the first eight months of the year, but we will assume they are full-year figures.

	Focus	Maxxum
2001	-6.64	-6.79
2002	-12.00	-8.60
2003	13.38	15.48
2004	14.48	7.78
2005	6.18	25.98
2006	16.61	14.46
2007	7.73	2.01
2008	-7.46	1.34

a. Calculate the average performance for each fund for the eight-year period. Use the spreadsheet function { = average(B4:B11)} where B4:B11 represents the cells holding the annual returns for the fund.

b. Now calculate how much $1,000 invested in each fund at the beginning of 2001 would have grown to by the end of 2004, when the market was entering a growth phase. To do this calculation, construct two new columns, one for each fund, showing the decimal equivalent of the fund's return added to 1.0 (call this the *return relative*—to find it, divide each return by 100 and add 1.0). For example, for Focus, the first entry would be 0.9336. Then for each fund multiply $1,000 by each of the first four return relatives in turn. How much money would an investor in each fund have at the end of 2004? Which fund performed better up to that point?

c. Using the answer determined in (b), calculate the amount of money an investor would have in each fund at the end of 2008. Do this in a manner similar to compounding the result you found at the end of 2005 by each of the four remaining return relatives.

d. What is the difference in ending wealth between the two funds, having started with $1,000 in each fund?

e. Now calculate the average annual total return (geometric mean) for each fund using the spreadsheet function {= geomean (D4:D11)} assuming, for example, that the return relatives for one fund are in the cells D4:D11.

f. How does the difference in the average annual total returns for each fund compare to the arithmetic averages for each over the eight-year period?

PREPARING FOR YOUR PROFESSIONAL EXAMS

CFA PRACTICE QUESTIONS

3-1. An open-ended fund holds three stocks at the end of the business day: 500,000 shares of A valued at $20 each; 100,000 shares of B valued at $10 each; and 200,000 shares of C valued at $15 each plus $1 million in cash. The fund currently has one million shares outstanding. What is the NAV per share?

    a. $10

    b. $13

    c. $14

    d. $15

3-2. Which of the following statements about load funds is true?

    a. Trade their shares on the registered exchanges.

    b. Offer shares at the fund's net asset value plus a sales charge.

    c. Guarantee returns consistent with the fund's systematic risk.

    d. Deduct up to 1.25 percent of average assets per year to cover marketing expenses.

CHAPTER 4

SECURITIES MARKETS

Chapter 4 outlines the structure of the markets where investors buy and sell securities. Although primary markets, including the role of investment bankers, are considered here, the emphasis is on secondary markets where most investors are active. Equity markets are covered in detail because most investors are primarily interested in stocks; bond markets and derivative markets are also discussed. Changes in the securities markets are considered, including globalization. The structure and operating mechanisms of the securities markets in the United States have changed drastically in the last 20 years. Accordingly, this chapter concludes with a look at some of these changes and what the future may hold.

Learning Objectives

After reading this chapter, you should be able to

1. Distinguish between primary and secondary markets.
2. Describe how the equity markets are organized and how they operate.
3. State the major stock market indicators.
4. Describe, briefly, the bond and derivatives markets.
5. Discuss some of the factors behind rapid change in the securities markets.

CHAPTER PREVIEW

Whether you choose to invest directly or indirectly through investment funds, you need to understand the structure of the markets where securities are bought and sold. Financial markets are of two main types: primary markets (new securities are issued, often through investment dealers) and secondary markets (existing securities are traded among investors). In this chapter, we focus on secondary markets in Canada and the United States, as Canadian investors are active mostly in these markets. Secondary markets include the equity, bond, and derivatives markets. We concentrate on equities, because these are the securities that investors most often buy and sell. Bond and derivatives markets are discussed in greater detail in later chapters. We close this chapter with a look at how the structure and operating mechanisms of the securities markets have changed drastically in the past 20 years. Notably, we consider the dramatic changes that have occurred to the structure of Canadian stock markets.

THE IMPORTANCE OF FINANCIAL MARKETS

In order to finance their operations as well as expand, business firms must invest capital in amounts that are beyond their capacity to save in any reasonable period of time. Similarly, governments must borrow large amounts of money to provide the goods and services that people demand of them. Financial markets permit both business and government to raise the needed funds by selling securities. Simultaneously, investors with excess funds are able to invest and earn a return, enhancing their welfare.

Financial markets are absolutely vital for the proper functioning of capitalistic economies, since they serve to channel funds from savers to borrowers. Furthermore, they provide an important allocative function by channelling the funds to those who can make the best use of them—presumably, the most productive users of these funds. In fact, the chief function of a capital market is to allocate resources optimally.[1]

The existence of well-functioning secondary markets, where investors come together to trade existing securities, assures the purchasers that they can quickly sell their securities if the need arises. Of course, such sales may involve a loss, because there are no guarantees in the financial markets. A loss, however, may be much preferred to having no cash at all if the securities cannot be sold readily.

In summary, secondary markets are indispensable to the proper functioning of the primary markets, which are, in turn, indispensable to the proper functioning of the economy.

learning objective 1
Distinguish between primary and secondary markets.

THE PRIMARY MARKETS

Primary Market
The market for new issues of securities such as government Treasury bills or a corporation's stocks or bonds often involving investment dealers. The issuers of the securities receive cash from the buyers who in turn receive financial claims on the issuing organization.

A **primary market** is one in which a borrower issues new securities in exchange for cash from an investor (buyer or lender). New sales of, for example, T-bills, Bank of Montreal common stock, or Hydro-Québec bonds all take place in the primary markets. The issuers of these securities—the Canadian government, the Bank of Montreal, and Hydro-Québec—receive cash from the buyers of these new securities, who, in turn, receive financial claims that previously did not exist. Note that in all three examples, each of these organizations already had outstanding securities before the latest new sales occurred. In other words, these were offerings of *new* securities but they were *not* initial public offerings (IPOs).

Corporate bonds are issued through public offerings or private placements, which are described in the following section. Federal government debt securities are issued in the primary market by the minister of finance through the Bank of Canada using the competitive tender system, which is described below.

The auction or competitive tender system is used for most issues (i.e., Treasury bills and coupon bonds) by the federal government. Primary distributors that are eligible to tender include the chartered banks, investment dealers, and active foreign dealers. Competitive bids may consist of one or

[1]A securities market with this characteristic is said to be allocationally efficient. An operationally efficient market, on the other hand, is one with the lowest possible prices for transactions services.

more bids in multiples of $1,000 (minimum $100,000 per individual bid). The bid must state the yield to maturity to three decimal places. A primary distributor may also submit one non-competitive tender in multiples of $1,000, which is subject to a $1,000 minimum and a $3 million maximum. This bid will be executed at the average price of the accepted competitive tenders.

If a new maturity of bond is being offered, the coupon rate is set to within 25 basis points of the average yield of the accepted competitive tenders, which produces an average issue price at or below par (100). In addition to bidding for its own requirements, the Bank of Canada stands ready to absorb the entire tender if required, which implies that the Bank theoretically could set the yield at each tender.

On the day of tender, the Bank releases complete information about the tender so that bidders can determine their net position. No commissions are paid to dealers who purchase the bonds, and there are no selling price restrictions for the successful buyers.

New issues of provincial direct and guaranteed bonds are usually sold at a negotiated price through a fiscal agent (i.e., an underwriting syndicate). Direct bonds are issued directly by the government (e.g., Province of Manitoba bonds), while guaranteed bonds are issued in the name of a Crown corporation, but are guaranteed by the provincial government (e.g., Hydro-Québec).

Municipal bond and debenture issues are more likely to be placed in institutional portfolios and pension accounts. Non-market sources of investment capital that purchase municipal securities include: (i) the Canada Pension Plan (CPP) and Quebec Pension Plan (QPP), which commit a pro-rata portion of each province's obligation to the purchase of municipal securities; (ii) provincial and municipal pension funds, which directly invest in municipal securities; and (iii) the federal government, which often loans funds to municipalities for specific projects.

Sales of common stock of a publicly traded company are called "seasoned" new issues. If the issuer is selling securities for the first time, this is referred to as an **initial public offering (IPO)**. Once the original purchasers sell the securities, they trade in secondary markets. New securities may trade repeatedly in the secondary market, but the original issuers will be unaffected in the sense that they receive no additional cash from these transactions.

Initial Public Offering (IPO)

Common stock shares of a company being sold for the first time.

It is generally argued that firms would want to issue securities when they have good uses for the funds and when market prices are high. The latter observation is consistent with the observed record levels of IPOs on the TSX in 2000, in response to high stock market price levels at the beginning of that year, which carried over from the high levels of 1999. Table 4-1 shows the Canadian IPO levels over the 2000 to 2007 period. During 2000, the TSX set a record of $5.3 billion raised by initial public offerings (IPOs). On the other hand, IPO activity declined to $2.1 billion in 2001 before recovering to $5.8 billion in 2002 and reaching a high of $6.8 billion in 2005 in response to favourable market conditions during those years. As discussed in Real-World Returns 2-6, IPO activity was hampered by the government's October 31, 2006, decision to alter the tax structure that applies to income trusts. As a result, many planned income trust IPOs were cancelled, with a corresponding impact on IPO activity during the last quarter of 2006 and throughout 2007, when IPOs declined to $3.4 billion.

Table 4-1

Canadian IPO Activity

Year	Amount ($ billions)
2000	5.3
2001	2.1
2002	5.8
2003	4.6
2004	6.2
2005	6.8
2006	5.4
2007	3.4

Sources: Stewart, Sinclair, "IPO activity set to tumble in the wake of trust crackdown," *The Globe and Mail*, January 5, 2007, p. B5. "Income trust tax slowed Canada's IPO pace in 2007," *Financial Post*, January 7, 2008. Retrieved from ww.financialpost.com.

Pricing of initial offerings is an extremely important and complex decision. Firms do not want to set their offering price too low, since the higher the price obtained by the firm per share, the fewer shares have to be issued to raise the same amount of money. However, they do not want to overprice the issue and have it "undersubscribed," thus not raising the required funds. The following well-known example of IPO underpricing illustrates the difficulties associated with determining a fair issue price for companies with no previous trading history.

EXAMPLE 4-1: 724 SOLUTIONS INC.

During January 2000, 724 Solutions Inc. went public at $37 a share. The shares closed their first day of trading at three times the issue price, and then skyrocketed to $345 before falling back to the $55 range by October 2000.

This example indicates the complexity and high degree of uncertainty involved in the pricing of some IPOs, particularly for companies with new products or those operating in rapidly changing industries. Other IPOs for well-known companies in well-defined industries are easier to price with relative accuracy.

There is substantial Canadian, US, and global evidence that, on average, IPOs are underpriced. Underpricing is generally measured as the difference between the first trading day closing price minus the issue price, divided by the issue price. For the 724 Solutions Inc. example, this implies underpricing of $(111 - 37) / 37 = 200.0\%$. Loughran, Ritter, and Rydqvist provide summary evidence for international IPOs and find that average underpricing ranged from a low of 4.2 percent in France to highs of 78.5 percent in Brazil and 166.6 percent in Malaysia (during the 1970s and 1980s).[2] Loughran et al. also show that average underpricing in Germany (1978–92), the United Kingdom (1959–90), the US (1960–92), and Japan (1970–91) was 11.1 percent, 12.0 percent, 15.3 percent, and 32.5 percent respectively.

Jog and Riding provide Canadian evidence for 100 IPOs over the 1971–83 period and find average underpricing of 11.0 percent. However, the degree of underpricing varied significantly and approximately 40 percent of the new issues were actually overpriced.[3] Jog and Srivastava extend Canadian evidence to the 1984–92 period and find that average underpricing falls to 5.67 percent during this period, with only 47.4 percent of the issues being underpriced.[4] It is important to note that not all IPOs are underpriced—some are overpriced. There is also substantial Canadian and US evidence that the subsequent performance of IPOs is below average, which implies that investors could lose any short-term gains in the long run.

Investment Dealers

Investment Dealer

An organization specializing in the sale of new securities, usually by purchasing the issue and reselling it to the public. Known as investment bankers in the US.

In the course of selling new securities, issuers often rely on an **investment dealer** (or an investment banker in the US) for the necessary expertise as well as the ability to reach widely dispersed suppliers of capital. Along with performing activities such as helping corporations in mergers and acquisitions, investment dealers specialize in the design and sale of securities in the primary market while operating simultaneously in the secondary markets. For example, **BMO Nesbitt Burns** offers investment services while operating a large retail brokerage operation throughout the country.

Investment dealers act as intermediaries between issuers and investors. For firms seeking to raise long-term funds, the investment dealer can provide important advice to their clients during the planning stage preceding the issuance of new securities. This advice includes providing information about the type of security to be sold, the features to be offered with the security, the price, and the timing of the sale.

---

[2]Loughran, T., J. Ritter, and K. Rydqvist, "Initial Public Offerings: International Insights," *Pacific-Basin Finance Journal* 2 (May 1994), pp. 165–200.
[3]Jog, V., and A. Riding, "Underpricing in Canadian IPOs," *Financial Analysts Journal* 43 (Nov–Dec 1987), pp. 48–55.
[4]Jog, V., and A. Srivastava, "Underpricing in Canadian IPOs 1971–1992 — An Update," 3 *FINECO* (November 1995).

Investment dealers participate in primary markets as principals when they take on the task of **underwriting** new issues by purchasing the securities (once the details of the issue have been negotiated) and assuming the risk of reselling them to investors. Investment dealers provide a valuable service to the issuers at this stage. The issuer receives its cheque and can spend the proceeds for the purposes for which the funds are being raised. The investment dealers own the securities until they are resold. Although many issues are sold out quickly—sometimes on the first day they are offered to the public—others may not be sold for days or even weeks. Investment dealers are compensated by a spread, which is the difference between what they pay the issuer for the securities and what they sell them for to the public. The securities are purchased from the issuer at a discount.

In addition to having expertise in these matters and closely scrutinizing any potential issue of securities, investment dealers often protect themselves by forming an underwriting syndicate or group of investment dealers. This allows them to diversify their risk and enhance the marketability of the issue. One investment dealer serves as the lead underwriter overseeing the underwriting syndicate. This syndicate becomes part of a larger group that sells the securities. A primary offering of securities through this process is referred to as a syndicated offering.

Investment dealers may also assume the role of agents in primary markets when they market newly issued securities on a "best efforts" basis. Under these arrangements, they receive compensation in the form of a commission, and it is the issuer that assumes the risk of the issue not selling. This arrangement is more common for issues of smaller or more speculative companies, or for "private placements" (discussed below) for large companies with good credit ratings where the risk of the issue not selling is negligible.

All public offerings are regulated by the Canada Business Corporations Act (CBCA) and provincial securities regulations. They require that a **prospectus** be prepared that includes "full, true, and plain disclosure of all material facts relating to the securities offered." A material fact is one that significantly affects, or would reasonably be expected to have a significant effect on, the securities' market price.

Prospectuses are lengthy, legal documents that contain relevant financial statements, proposed use of funds from the issue, future growth plans, and the relevant information regarding the share issue. Normally, before a final prospectus may be issued, it is necessary to prepare and distribute copies of a "preliminary prospectus" to the securities commission and prospective investors. This contains most of the information to be included in the final prospectus except the price to the dealers and public, and sometimes the auditor's report. Because the prospectus is for information only and does not solicit the selling of securities, it is often referred to as a "red herring." A statement, in red, must be displayed on the front page to the effect that it is not final and is subject to completion or amendment before shares can be issued. The dealer may also prepare a "greensheet," which is an information circular, for in-house use only. It includes salient features of the issue, both pro and con, and would be used by the sales department to solicit interest in the new issue.

During the waiting period (between the issuance of red herrings and the receipt of final prospectuses), dealers are prohibited from activities considered to be furthering the issuance of securities (such as entering into purchase and sale agreements), other than solicitation of expressions of interest. However, the dealer will proceed along other lines, attempting to formalize the details of items such as the trust deed or indenture (for debt issues); the underwriting or agency agreement between issuer and distributor; the banking group agreement; the selling group agreement; and final price to the public and to the dealer.

Once the prospectus has been prepared, it will be filed with the relevant securities commissions, and approval generally takes three weeks. Any changes must be agreed upon with the issuers before final approval. The issue is then "blue skied" and may be distributed to the public. It must be accompanied by the consent of all experts whose opinions are referred to in the prospectus. This process prevents investors from investing in companies with few or no assets—that is, from purchasing "the blue sky." The prospectus must be mailed or delivered to all purchasers of the securities, not later than midnight on the second business day after the trade.

Underwriting
The process by which investment dealers purchase an issue of securities from a firm and resell it to the public.

Prospectus
Legal documents that contain relevant financial statements about the proposed use of the funds raised by the stock issue, future growth plans and other relevant information regarding the share issue. Provides information about a public offering of securities to potential buyers.

The Underwriting Process

A typical example of the underwriting process is depicted in Figure 4-1. The first step in the process has the issuing company selling the securities to the financing group (also known as managing underwriters or syndicate managers), which consists of one or two firms. The financing group accepts the liability of the issue on behalf of the banking group members, which includes themselves, as well as other dealers who have agreed to participate based on certain terms.

Figure 4-1
A Primary Offering of Securities

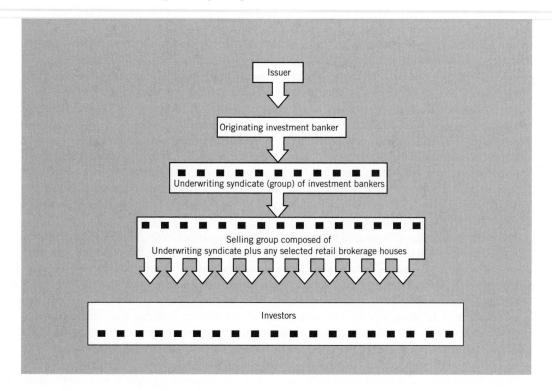

Second, the financing group sells the securities to the marketing group at a "draw down" price, which provides a differential that enables the financing group to recover expenditures undertaken on behalf of the entire banking group.

Third, the securities are distributed for sale to the public, with a certain proportion being allocated to

1. The banking group (the largest proportion)

2. The exempt list, which usually includes only large professional buyers, mostly financial institutions, who are exempt from prospectus requirements

3. The selling group, which consists of other dealers who are not part of the banking group

4. Casual dealers, who are not members of the banking or selling groups, and may be brokers, broker dealers, foreign dealers, banks, etc.

5. Special groups, which may include the issuer's banker or dealer, etc.

Prompt Offering Qualification (POP) System

Allows qualifying senior reporting issuers to put out short form prospectuses in lieu of full ones.

The Prompt Offering Qualification (POP) System

The **Prompt Offering Qualification (POP) System** allows senior reporting issuers, who have made public distributions and who are subject to continuous disclosure requirements, to issue "short form" prospectuses. The rationale is that there is already a great deal of information available on the company that would normally be included in a prospectus. These short form prospectuses save issuers a great deal of time and money, and generally focus on details of the securities being issued such as price, distribution spread, use of proceeds, and security attributes.

Issuers under the POP System

1. Have been filing annual and interim statements for 12 months prior to the issue
2. Have filed or will file an annual information form (AIF) with the appropriate administrator
3. Are not in default of any requirements under the relevant securities legislation
4. Have a large public float (equity shares listed on an exchange and held by non-insiders with a market value of at least $75 million)

Issuers satisfying the first three conditions may also use the POP System for issues of high quality non-convertible debt and/or preferred shares.

Short form prospectuses are commonly used for "bought deals" and have contributed to the growth of these arrangements. Bought deals are the most popular form of underwriting in Canada. The issuer sells the entire issue to one investment dealer or to a group that attempts to resell it and accepts all of the price risk. Generally, the dealer has pre-marketed the issue to a few large institutional investors. Issuers are usually large, well-known firms that qualify for the use of POP. Therefore, bought deals are usually executed very swiftly.

An additional option available to Canadian companies since 1991 is to register securities in advance of issuance, which is referred to as "shelf registration." This alternative, which has been available in the United States since 1982, permits companies to "place on the shelf" securities to be sold. The issuing company can sell the new securities over time by auctioning pieces of the issue, which provides flexibility and savings.

The Listing Process

New share issues are usually initially traded over-the-counter (OTC) and are considered for listing on an exchange only after proof of satisfactory distribution is available. Often, the underwriting agreement will require the underwriters to provide some market support for the new security issue for a specified time period. Sometimes a market develops for new issues prior to their actual listing, and trading is handled by dealers in what is known as the "grey market." This is an unofficial OTC market composed of dealers wishing to execute customers' orders and support an issue until official listing occurs.

Global Security Issues

The global perspective now in place allows companies in various countries to raise new capital in amounts that would have been impossible only a few years earlier because these companies were often limited to selling new securities in their own domestic markets. The global equity offering has changed all that. An important new development for investment dealers is the emphasis on managing the global offerings of securities. A lead investment dealer can act as a "global coordinator," linking separate underwriting syndicates throughout the world in selling equity issues. Many Canadian companies issue bonds in the United States or in the Euromarket.

A number of Canadian companies are "interlisted" on more than one stock market, primarily markets in the United States, such as Nasdaq or the New York Stock Exchange (NYSE). The motivation for Canadian firms to interlist on US markets is to increase the stock's potential market and enhance its visibility. However, empirical evidence is inconclusive regarding share price benefits obtained from interlisting in the United States.

Private Placements

An increasing number of corporations have executed private placements, whereby new securities issues are sold directly to financial institutions, such as life insurance companies and pension funds, bypassing the open market. While private placements have been very common for debt issues for quite some time, they have been used more frequently for equity issuances. For example, in the first quarter of 2004, $2.898 billion (56 percent) of total equity issues were raised through private placements. One advantage is that the firm does not have to prepare a full prospectus, only a specific contract (or offering memorandum).[5] Investment dealer fees are also reduced because the dealer usually acts as an agent for the issuer for a finders fee, which is well below normal underwriting spreads. The disadvantages of private placements include a higher interest cost, because the financial institutions usually require a higher return than would be required from a public subscription, and possible restrictive provisions on the borrower's activities.[6]

Secondary Markets

Markets where existing securities are traded among investors; the TSX is the largest stock market in Canada.

CHECK YOUR UNDERSTANDING

4-1.   In a typical underwriting, the procedure is referred to as a firm commitment. What do you think this means?

4-2.   It is said that IPOs are often underpriced relative to the price at which they could be marketed. What are some possible reasons for this?

4-3.   If a company with publicly traded stock issues more shares through a seasoned offering, would the sale of these securities occur in the primary or secondary market?

---

learning objective 2
Describe how the equity markets are organized and how they operate.

THE SECONDARY MARKETS

Once new securities have been sold in the primary market, an efficient mechanism must exist for their resale if investors are to view securities as attractive opportunities. **Secondary markets** give investors the means to trade existing securities.[7]

Secondary markets exist for the trading of common and preferred stock, rights, warrants, bonds, and puts and calls. Figure 4-2 diagrams the structure of Canadian secondary markets in 2008, which is discussed below in the following order: equities, bonds, and derivative securities.

Auction Market

A securities market with a physical location, such as the Toronto Stock Exchange, where the prices of securities are determined by the bidding (auction) actions of buyers and sellers.

Equity Securities—Auction Markets

Common stocks, preferred stocks, income trusts, and warrants are traded in the equity markets. Some secondary equity markets are **auction markets**, involving an auction (bidding) process in a specific physical location. Investors are represented by **brokers**, intermediaries who represent both buyers and sellers and attempt to obtain the best price possible for either party in a transaction. Brokers collect commissions for their efforts and generally have no vested interest in whether a customer places a buy order or a sell order, or, in most cases, in what is bought or sold (holding constant the value of the transaction).

Brokers

Intermediaries who represent both buyers and sellers and attempt to obtain the best price possible for either party in securities transactions; they receive a commission for this service.

---

[5]The savings in time can sometimes be important, for market conditions can change rapidly between the time an issue is registered and sold.
[6]In addition, a lack of marketability exists because the issue is unregistered. Therefore, the buyer may demand additional compensation from the issuer in the form of a higher yield.
[7]Again, this does not directly affect the issuer, who sells new securities in the primary market in order to raise funds.

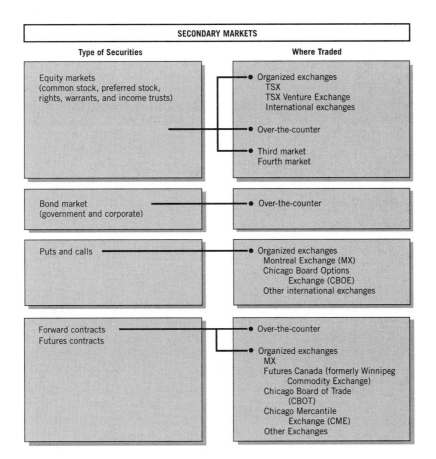

Figure 4-2
The Structure of
Secondary Markets

Canadian Exchanges

Canadian stock exchanges have undergone significant changes. At the start of 1999, there were five stock exchanges in Canada: the **Toronto Stock Exchange (TSX)**, the Montreal Exchange (MX), the Vancouver Stock Exchange (VSE), the Winnipeg Stock Exchange (WSE), and the Alberta Stock Exchange (ASE). A complete overhaul of that structure occurred during 1999 and 2000, and as a result of this restructuring, there are two remaining stock exchanges in Canada: the TSX and the TSX Venture Exchange. In addition, by March 2000 the Montreal Exchange (MX) assumed its role as the Canadian national derivatives market, and it now carries on all trading in financial futures and options that previously occurred on the TSX, the MX, and the now-defunct Toronto Futures Exchange. On May 1, 2008, the TSX Group and the MX merged to create the TMX Group Inc. The February announcement, which describes the process leading up to May 1, is described in Real-World Returns 4-1. This merger is a Canadian example of a broader global trend toward exchange mergers, several of which are discussed in the next sections.

Toronto Stock Exchange (TSX)

Canada's national stock market for senior companies.

REAL-WORLD RETURNS 4-1

Key Milestone Achieved in TSX Group Inc. and MX Combination

Shareholders of Montréal Exchange Inc. today voted 99.6 percent in favour of the combination with TSX Group Inc. to form TMX Group Inc., as announced December 10, 2007.

"This is a significant step towards completing the transaction," said Michael Ptasznik, Interim Co-CEO, TSX Group. "Our efforts are now focused on obtaining the necessary regulatory approvals needed to finalize the combination."

(continued)

On February 1, 2008, the Autorité des marchés financiers (AMF) published MX's application for an amendment to its recognition order to permit the transaction to be completed. TSX Group has provided important undertakings in conjunction with that process. The comment period is open until March 3, 2008 and will be followed by public hearings in Montreal on March 26 and 27, 2008.

"We believe the combination will provide great benefits for shareholders, Quebec and Canadian capital markets", added Mr. Ptasznik. "We are pleased that the AMF comment period is open and hearings have been scheduled. While we may not be able to close by March 31, 2008, we do hope to complete the transaction as soon as possible after the public hearings and receiving the AMF's decision and all other approvals."

Source: News release, TSX Group Inc. Retrieved from www.tsx.com, February 13, 2008.

The TSX is the official exchange for trading of Canadian senior stocks—big companies with solid histories of profits. The TSX, which was incorporated in 1878, is one of the 10 largest stock exchanges in the world, and is the third-largest stock market in North America, behind the New York Stock Exchange (NYSE) and Nasdaq.It was the seventh-largest stock market in the world in 2006, based on the market value of securities traded on the market. Table 4-2 shows the total dollar value of trading on the TSX was close to $1.7 trillion in 2007, with 96.1 billion shares traded. There were more than 1,600 listed companies on the TSX in 2007, and the total market capitalization (which is defined as the total number of shares outstanding times the market price per share) was approximately $2.1 trillion.[8] The requirements for companies wishing to list their companies on the TSX are much more stringent than for the TSX Venture Exchange and tend to preclude smaller companies. These listing requirements are provided later in the chapter in Table 4-3.

Table 4-2

TSX and TSX Venture Exchange Trading Statistics (2006–2007)

	2006	2007
TSX		
Trading volume (millions)	82,050	96,109
Trading value ($ billions)	1,416	1,697
Market capitalization ($ billions)	2,061	2,093
Number of listed companies	1,598	1,613
TSX Venture Exchange		
Trading volume (millions)	37,364	53,147
Trading value ($ billions)	33.3	45.0
Market capitalization ($ billions)	55.3	58.5
Number of listed companies	2,244	2,338

Source: Retrieved from www.tsx.com, March 23, 2008.

[8]Retrieved from www.tsx.com, March 23, 2008.

The TSX Venture Exchange is Canada's public venture capital marketplace, and like the TSX, it is part of the TSX Group. It provides emerging companies with access to capital while offering investors a well-regulated market for making venture investments. By the end of 2007, the TSX Venture Exchange had 2,338 companies listed and the total market capitalization of this market had reached $58.5 billion. TSX Venture Exchange-listed companies are active primarily in the mining, oil and gas, manufacturing, technology, and financial services sectors. It provides the Canadian economy with a capital-raising infrastructure for the small and medium-size businesses that are driving economic growth in Canada. With offices in Vancouver, Calgary, Winnipeg, Toronto, and Montreal, the TSX Venture Exchange provides corporate finance and business development expertise in key markets across the country.

Trading operations for both the TSX and the TSX Venture Exchange are conducted by TSX Markets, also a member of the TSX Group. The TSX closed its trading floor on April 23, 1997, and trading is now completely computerized. Trading occurs through continuous electronic auction markets, with all trades being settled through the Canadian Depository for Securities Limited (CDS). Stock exchange memberships (in the form of stock exchange "seats") are sold to individuals, which permits them to trade on the exchange. These seats are valuable assets that may be sold, subject to certain exchange conditions.

Exchange member firms must be publicly owned, maintain adequate capital requirements, and key personnel must complete required courses of study. Exchanges are governed by bodies that consist of at least one permanent exchange official (e.g., the president), plus governors selected from member firms, as well as two to six highly qualified public governors appointed or elected from outside the brokerage community. Exchanges qualify as non-profit associations and are not subject to corporate income tax.

Exchanges have the power to suspend the trading or listing privileges of an individual security temporarily or permanently. Temporary withdrawals of trading and/or listing privileges include

1. Delayed opening (which may arise if there exist a large number of buy and/or sell orders)

2. Halt in trading (to allow significant news such as merger activity to be reported)

3. Suspension of trading, which may occur for more than one session until an identified problem is rectified by the company to the exchange's satisfaction (if the company fails to meet requirements for continued trading or does not comply with listing requirements)

A listed security can be cancelled or delisted for a variety of reasons:

1. It no longer exists (e.g., a preferred share issue that has been redeemed)

2. The company has no assets or is bankrupt

3. Public distribution of the security is no longer sufficient

4. The company has failed to comply with the terms of its listing agreement

US Exchanges

The US auction markets include two national exchanges and several regional ones. The national exchanges include the **New York Stock Exchange (NYSE)** and the American Stock Exchange (Amex). The NYSE was founded in 1792 and is the oldest and most prominent secondary market in the United States. It is generally regarded as the best regulated exchange in the world and has proven its ability to function in crisis. On Black Monday in October 1987, for example, this exchange handled some 600 million shares when other exchanges were experiencing significant problems.

The NYSE has historically been a not-for-profit corporation and members could transfer seats, by sale or lease, subject to the approval of the exchange. The number of seats remained constant at 1,366 for over 50 years; however, their price varied sharply in response to market conditions. The value of a seat was less than $100,000 in the mid-1970s but had increased to $2 million by February 1998, before eventually falling to $1,225,000 by the end of that year. On December 1, 2005, $4 million was paid for a seat, which was the all-time maximum.

New York Stock Exchange (NYSE)
The largest secondary market for the trading of equity securities in the world.

On December 30, 2005, member seat sales officially ended and were replaced by the sale of annual trading licences, in anticipation of the NYSE's transformation into a publicly held company. This transformation occurred on March 7, 2006, as the NYSE Group Inc. was formed out of the merger of the New York Stock Exchange and Archipelago Exchange. The merger was the largest-ever among securities exchanges up to this time. Shares in the NYSE Group Inc. began trading under the symbol NYX on March 8, 2006.

The changes did not stop there, as the NYSE Group Inc. combined with Euronext N.V. to create NYSE Euronext (a holding company) on April 4, 2007, thereby creating "...the world's largest and most liquid exchange group... NYSE Euronext, which brings together six cash equities exchanges in five countries and six derivatives exchanges, is a world leader for listings, trading in cash equities, equity and interest rate derivatives, bonds and the distribution of market data."[9]

Specialists

Members of an organized exchange who are charged with maintaining an orderly market in one or more stocks by buying or selling for their own accounts.

Professionals with trading licences for the exchange can combine with others to operate as a member organization and do business with the public. Market **specialists** play an important role on the NYSE and are assigned to trading posts on the floor of the NYSE, where they handle one or more of the stocks traded at that post. Specialists are responsible for maintaining an orderly market in one or more stocks by buying or selling shares for his or her own account. Some specialists firms are part of well-known brokerage operations, while many others are virtually unknown to the public. (Specialists are discussed in more detail in Chapter 5.)

As mentioned previously, a number of Canadian companies are interlisted on the NYSE. Table 4-3 shows that the qualifying criteria for TSX-listed companies pale in comparison to those that must be satisfied by NYSE-listed companies.[10] As a result, only the largest Canadian companies are able to list their shares on this exchange.

Table 4-3

TSX* versus NYSE Initial Listing Requirements

Criteria	TSX (Cdn $)	NYSE (US $)
Net Tangible Assets	> = $2M	> = $40M
Pre-Tax Income	> = $200,000 in most recent year	> = $10M in the aggregate the last three years and > = $2m in the two most recent fiscal years (positive amounts in all three years) OR
Pre-Tax Cash Flow	> = $500,000 previous year	(1) > = $50M in global market capitalization (2) > = $100M in revenues during the most recent year (3) > = $25M aggregate cash flows for the last three fiscal years with positive amounts in all three years
Market Value of Publicly Held Shares	> = $4M	> = $60M (companies that list either at the time of their IPOs or as a result of spin-offs or under the Affiliated company standard)
	> = $10M (technology companies)	> = $100M for other companies
Number of Outstanding Shares	1M	1.1M
Number of shareholders of "board" (Can.) or "round" (US) lots (generally 100 shares)	300	400, OR 2,200 total shareholders, AND 100,000 in monthly trading volume; OR,

[9]Retrieved from www.nyse.com, March 23, 2008.
[10]Continuing listing requirements must also be met, or a firm could be delisted from the exchange.

Criteria	TSX (Cdn $)	NYSE (US $)
		500 total shareholders, AND 1,000,000 in monthly trading volume.
Working Capital (W/C) Requirements	Adequate W/C and capitalization to carry on the business	N/A

*The TSX requirements are for "profitable" Canadian industrial companies. Requirements vary for Industrials that are: (i) forecasting profitability; (ii) technology companies; or, (iii) research and development companies. They are also different for mining, oil and gas, and non-Canadian companies, as well as for junior companies.

Sources: Toronto Stock Exchange, www.tsx.com and New York Stock Exchange, www.nyse.com.

The NYSE is the dominant capital market in the world based on trading volume and on the market capitalization of its firms (which is defined as the total number of shares outstanding multiplied by the market price per share). During 2007, the NYSE had 2,805 listed companies and trading volume was $21.9 trillion US (about $87.1 billion US per trading day). The market value of NYSE-listed companies was $17.5 trillion US as of December 2007.[11]

A trend of potential significance that is often discussed in the popular press is **program trading**, which may be defined as the computer-generated trading of large blocks of securities. It is used to accomplish certain trading strategies, such as arbitrage against futures contracts and portfolio accumulation and liquidation strategies. The NYSE published its first report on program trading activities in 1988. During 2007, program trading volume accounted for over 30 percent of total NYSE volume.

The American Stock Exchange (Amex) is the only other national organized exchange in the United States. Relative to the NYSE, the Amex is much smaller and the listing requirements for stocks on the Amex are less stringent than the NYSE. Trading volume is significantly below that of the NYSE (the NYSE generally does more trading in the first hour than the Amex does during the entire day). The Amex does a large business in ETFs, offering over 380 in 2007, comprising over $250 billion in assets, as well as options and other derivative securities. NYSE Euronext is in the process of acquiring Amex, as discussed in Real-World Returns 4-2.

Program Trading
The computer-generated trading of large blocks of securities. It is often implemented to take advantage of price discrepancies between markets (arbitrage opportunities).

REAL-WORLD RETURNS 4-2

NYSE Euronext and Amex Announce Early Termination of the Hart Scott-Rodino Waiting Period for NYSE Euronext's Acquisition of Amex

NYSE Euronext (NYSE Euronext: NYX) and the American Stock Exchange® (Amex®) today announced that the two companies received notification from the Federal Trade Commission that early termination of the waiting period under the Hart-Scott-Rodino (HSR) Antitrust Improvements Act of 1976 has been granted in connection with the proposed acquisition of Amex by NYSE Euronext. The proposed acquisition remains subject to the satisfaction of other conditions including the approval of Amex seat owners and the U.S. Securities and Exchange Commission. The parties expect the transaction to close in the third quarter of this year.

Source: News release retrieved from www.amex.com, March 23, 2008.

---

[11]www.nyse.com.

The United States also has several regional exchanges, although their listing requirements are considerably more lenient. Some of the largest of these are the Chicago Exchange, the Pacific Stock Exchange, the Philadelphia Exchange, the Boston Stock Exchange, and the Cincinnati Stock Exchange. In 2001, the Pacific Exchange combined with an Electronic Communications Network (ECN) (which are discussed below) to form the Archipelago Exchange, which subsequently merged with the NYSE in 2006, as discussed above. Regional exchanges accounted for a very small percentage of both share volume and dollar volume in the United States.

Global Stock Markets

There are numerous stock markets in nations all over the world. The New York, Tokyo, Nasdaq, London, and Euronext markets are the largest, and the TSX is one of the top 10 in terms of market capitalization.

As noted, investors have become increasingly interested in equity markets around the world. Important global equity markets exist in developed countries including the United Kingdom, France, Germany, Italy, Switzerland, Japan, Hong Kong, and Australia. Investors are also interested in emerging markets such as Mexico, Brazil, and Indonesia.[12] Because of the large number and variety of foreign markets, we will consider only a few highlights here.

Western Europe has several mature markets that are mostly electronic. The London Stock Exchange (LSE) is an important equity market, with $3.8 trillion US in market cap as of December 2006. Euronext is Europe's leading cross-border exchange, providing an integrated trading platform for Brussels, Amsterdam, and Paris. Switzerland is home to some of the largest global companies in the world, including Nestlé (food and beverage) and Hoffman La Roche (drugs).

Europe's emerging markets include the Czech Republic, Hungary, and Poland, where potential profits are great but risks are also. Illiquidity is a common problem, corporate information is difficult to obtain, and political risk can be an important factor. Turkey is another example of an emerging market.

The Far East is the fastest growing region in the world, with growth rates twice that of Canada and the United States. North American investors have been particularly active in the Far Eastern markets. These markets also have been very volatile, with large gains and losses because of illiquidity (a scarcity of buyers at times) as well as political and currency risks.

Japan, the dominant Asian economic power, had the second-largest stock market in the world in 2006 based on market capitalization. Although Japan has eight stock exchanges, the Tokyo Stock Exchange with a 2006 market cap of $4.6 trillion US dominates that country's equity markets. Both domestic and foreign stocks are listed on the Tokyo Exchange, and among domestic issues, relatively few are traded on the floor of the exchange; the rest (as well as foreign stocks) are handled by computer.

Hong Kong is the second-largest Asian market in terms of market capitalization. Other Asian markets include India, Indonesia, Japan, South Korea, Malaysia, Pakistan, the Philippines, Singapore, Sri Lanka, Taiwan, and Thailand. Of course, some of these markets are quite small. The Four Dragons—Hong Kong, Singapore, South Korea, and Taiwan—dominate these markets when Japan is excluded.

The big unknown in Asian markets is, of course, China. An emerging economy of potentially great importance, China is booming as an economy but with great risks, for politics strongly affects investments in China. Its financial markets are still tiny by other countries' standards. Chinese companies do trade on the Hong Kong exchange as well as on exchanges in China such as Shanghai and Shenzen.

Latin America is the remaining emerging marketplace that has been of great interest to investors. The markets in Latin America include Argentina, Brazil, Chile, Colombia, Mexico, Peru, and Venezuela. Mexico's market is the largest, followed by Brazil, with the others small by comparison in terms of market capitalization. As we would expect in emerging markets, profit potentials are large, but so are risks—volatile prices, liquidity problems, and political risks such as the assassination of Mexico's leading presidential candidate in 1994. Brazil (1999) and Argentina have also suffered financial crises.

---

[12]There is no precise definition of an emerging market, but generally it involves a stable political system, fewer regulations, and less standardization in trading activity.

Equity Securities—Negotiated Markets

Unlike the exchanges, **over-the-counter (OTC) markets** or dealer markets do not have a physical location but consist of a network of dealers who trade with each other over the phone or over a computer network. It is a **negotiated market**, where only the **dealers'** bid and ask quotations are entered by those dealers acting as "market makers" in a particular security. Market makers execute trades from their inventories of securities in which they have agreed to "make a market" (discussed in Chapter 5). This market essentially handles securities that are not listed on a stock exchange, although some listed securities are now traded in this market.

The Canadian OTC Market

The volume of unlisted or OTC equity trading in Canada has traditionally been much smaller than the volume of exchange-traded equity transactions. From 1991 to 2000, Canadian OTC trading for unlisted securities occurred through the Canadian Dealing Network Inc. (CDN), a subsidiary of the TSX. The CDN consisted of a large network linking dealers across Canada, where trading went on longer than exchange hours. In 2000, OTC stocks began trading on the Canadian Venture Exchange, which has since been replaced by the TSX Venture Exchange as Canada's national junior stock market. Today, the TSX Venture Exchange handles trades in all junior stocks except for those of issuers that do not meet its ongoing listing standards. These stocks trade OTC on the NEX board, a separate board of the TSX Venture Exchange. As one would expect, this market is more speculative in nature than the exchanges and is also generally referred to as a "thin" or illiquid market, since it is characterized by low trading volume and relatively few bids or offers.

The US OTC Market

Thousands of stocks trade in the OTC market in the United States. Many of these are small, thinly traded stocks that do not generate much interest.[13] The most important part of the negotiated market is the **Nasdaq Stock Market**, or **Nasdaq**. Nasdaq represents a national and international stock market consisting of communications networks for the trading of thousands of stocks.

The Nasdaq Stock Market consists of a network of market makers or dealers linked together by communications devices who compete freely with each other through an electronic network of terminals, rather than on the floor of an exchange. These dealers conduct transactions directly with each other and with customers. Each Nasdaq company has a number of competing dealers who make a market in the stock, with a minimum of two and an average of 11 dealers. (Some large Nasdaq companies have 40 or more dealers.)

Nasdaq features an electronic trading system as the centrepiece of its operations. This system provides instantaneous transactions as Nasdaq market makers compete for investor orders. An investor who places an order with his or her broker for a Nasdaq security will have this order executed in one of two ways:

1. If the broker's firm makes a market in the security, the order will be executed internally at a price equal to, or better than, the best price quoted by all competing market makers.

2. If the broker's firm is not a market maker in this security, the firm will buy from or sell to a market maker at another firm.

The **Nasdaq National Market System (Nasdaq/NMS)** is a component of the Nasdaq market. The NMS is a combination of the competing market makers in OTC stocks and the up-to-the-minute reporting of trades. The system uses data similar to that shown for the exchanges (specifically, high, low, and closing quotations, volume, and the net change from one day to the next). The vast majority of the roughly 4,000 Nasdaq-listed securities trade as NMS securities, and on a volume basis NMS issues account for over 90 percent of all Nasdaq volume.

[13]Traditionally, the prices of these stocks were reported only once a day on what are called Pink Sheets. Current prices on these stocks are now available electronically.

Over-the-Counter (OTC) Market
A network of securities dealers linked together by phone and computer to make markets in securities.

Negotiated Market
A market involving dealers such as the OTC.

Dealer
An individual or firm who makes a market in a stock by buying from and selling to investors.

Nasdaq Stock Market (Nasdaq)
A national and international OTC stock market consisting of communication networks for the trading of thousands of stocks.

Nasdaq National Market System (Nasdaq/NMS)
The largest secondary market for the trading of equity securities in the world.

The other distinct segment of Nasdaq is the Nasdaq SmallCap Market, which involves trading in smaller stocks that have not yet reached a suitable size for the NMS, and those that no longer qualify for trading on the NMS. More than 800 companies trade in this market. Several thousand US OTC stocks trade via the OTC Bulletin Board or through the "Pink Sheets" market, which are markets for very thinly traded securities, many of which trade infrequently.

When we think of the Nasdaq market, we typically think of it as a network of market makers. However, today the Nasdaq network connects other trading systems such as Alternative Trading Systems (ATSs) / Electronic Communications Networks (ECNs). These systems allow investors to trade electronically with each other at preset prices and are described later in the chapter. They do not involve a market maker and are simply order-matching systems.

The Nasdaq Stock Market has become a major player in the securities markets. In 2007, there were more companies listed on Nasdaq (over 3,900) than on the NYSE (2,805), and the volume of shares traded exceeded that on the NYSE. However the market capitalization was $5.3 trillion, well below the $17.5 trillion market capitalization of NYSE firms.[14] In November of 2007, they entered into an agreement to acquire the Philadelphia Stock Exchange, and in 2008, Nasdaq combined with OMX AB to form the Nasdaq OMX Group Inc., as discussed in Real-World Returns 4-3.

REAL-WORLD RETURNS 4-3

Nasdaq Completes OMX Transaction to Become The Nasdaq OMX Group, Inc.

The Nasdaq Stock Market, Inc. (Nasdaq:NDAQ) (NASDAQ(r)) has completed its combination with OMX AB, creating the world's largest exchange company, The NASDAQ OMX Group, Inc. (NASDAQ OMX Group).

NASDAQ OMX Group has operations around the world, spanning developed and emerging markets. Its global offerings include trading across multiple asset classes, capital formation solutions, financial services and exchanges technology, market data products, and financial indexes.

"NASDAQ OMX Group is a new type of exchange company. It is unique in its ability to serve customers at multiple levels, from trading platforms supporting multiple asset classes to listings, financial services technology, and data and financial products," said Bob Greifeld, Chief Executive Officer of The NASDAQ OMX Group.

As part of the transaction, NASDAQ OMX Group also became a 33 1/3 percent shareholder in DIFX, Dubai's international financial exchange. As previously announced and approved, Borse Dubai is a 19.9 percent shareholder of NASDAQ OMX Group.

Greifeld added, "We are grateful for the support of OMX shareholders. We look forward to executing on our plan that will benefit all of our constituencies, including investors, shareholders and customers." The NASDAQ OMX Group, Inc. is the world's largest exchange company. It delivers trading, exchange technology and public company services across six continents, and with over 3,900 companies, it is number one in worldwide listings among major markets. NASDAQ OMX offers multiple capital raising solutions to companies around the globe, including its US listings market; the OMX Nordic Exchange, including First North; and the 144A PORTAL Market. The company offers trading across multiple asset classes including equities, derivatives, debt, commodities, structured products and ETFs. NASDAQ OMX technology supports the operations of over 60 exchanges, clearing organizations and central securities depositories in more than 50 countries. OMX Nordic Exchange is not a legal entity but describes the common offering from Nasdaq OMX exchanges in Helsinki, Copenhagen, Stockholm, Iceland, Tallinn, Riga, and Vilnius. For more information about NASDAQ OMX, visit www.nasdaqomx.com.

Source: The Nasdaq Stock Market, Inc. news release, February 27, 2008, PrimeNewswire via COMTEX News Network.

[14]World Federation of Exchanges (formerly International Federation of Stock Exchanges) website: www.world-exchanges.org.

In summary, the common stock issues traded on Nasdaq vary widely in size, price, quality, and trading activity. These stocks range from small start-up companies to huge successful companies that have chosen to remain Nasdaq companies rather than move on to the NYSE.

The Third and Fourth Markets

The **third market** is an OTC market for the trading of securities that are listed on organized exchanges. This market has traditionally been important in the United States for block trades or extremely large transactions. This was done in order to avoid minimum exchange-regulated commission fees, although with the abolition of these fees this market has become less important.

The **fourth market** refers to transactions made directly between large institutions (and wealthy individuals), bypassing brokers and dealers. Essentially, the fourth market is a communications network among investors interested in trading large blocks of stock, often referred to as Electronic Communications Networks. Several different privately owned automated systems exist to provide current information on specific securities that the participants are willing to buy or sell.

Electronic Communications Networks (ECNs) (or alternative trading systems (ATSs)) are taking business away from Nasdaq, the NYSE, and the TSX (having been permitted in Canada as of December 1, 2004). An ECN is a computerized trading network that matches buy and sell orders electronically entered by customers. If no match is currently possible, the ECN acts sort of like a broker, posting its best bid and ask offer (under its own name) on Nasdaq's trading screen. Another party who sees these prices and wants to perform transactions may enter the appropriate buy or sell order. Trading was initially limited to members only, meaning institutional investors or large traders. However, day traders can now link to them through direct-access brokers and Instinet (described below), which began to allow retail access in 2001.

ECNs offer automation, lower costs, and anonymity to buyers and sellers. There are no spreads, or conflicts of interest with a broker (as explained in Chapter 5). Costs are about one cent a share. **Instinet (Institutional Network)**, which is owned by Reuters, is the original electronic trading network. It started in 1969 long before the ECNs. It is a system offering equity transactions and research services to brokers, dealers, exchange specialists, institutional fund managers, and plan sponsors who pay commissions of about one cent a share and who also receive free proprietary terminals. Instinet is always open for trading stocks on any of the exchanges worldwide to which Instinet belongs.

Instinet offers anonymous trading, thereby allowing large traders to bypass brokers with their often attendant leaks on who is transacting. Trades are often less than 10,000 shares each, and an institution can do multiple trades to get into or out of a position in a stock without others knowing.

The prospect is for these electronic networks to grow and consolidate, as seen with the merger of Instinet and Island in 2002. Since April 1999, ECNs have been allowed to register as exchanges under Securities and Exchange Commission (SEC) rules. This led to the development of a new exchange (the Archipelago Exchange), which was formed by combining an ECN and the Pacific Exchange, before merging with the NYSE in 2006. Similar to the US experience, ATSs have grown in Canada, with the TSX offering its own ATS, called NEX, as discussed in Real-World Returns 4-4.

Third Market
An OTC market for the trading of securities that are listed on organized exchanges.

Fourth Market
Transactions made directly between large institutions or wealthy individuals bypassing brokers and dealers. It is a communications network among these large institutional investors.

Electronic Communications Networks (ECNs)
Computerized trading networks for institutions and large traders.

Instinet (Institutional Network)
An electronic trading network that has become the largest computerized brokerage. It is part of the fourth market and only open to those brokers and institutions who pay to use it.

REAL-WORLD RETURNS 4-4

TSX Group's NEX Market Shows Strong Trading Growth

Alternative marketplaces continue to launch in Canada but it is TSX Group's own NEX market that is showing the fastest trading growth of any of these marketplaces.

According to current TSX Group trading data during Q1 2008, NEX activity has recently grown to over 2.6 million shares a day. That's up from the Q4 2007 daily average of 1.3 million shares—and accounts for a growth of 100 percent. NEX is a separate board of TSX Venture Exchange. It provides an alternative trading forum for listed companies that have fallen below

(continued)

REAL-WORLD RETURNS 4-4 *continued*

TSX and TSX Venture Exchange's ongoing listing standards, which otherwise would no longer be eligible to trade on a TSX Group exchange or seek listing on a competitive Canadian exchange.

Comparatively, CNQ's average trading volume is at 1.5 million shares per day. As a percentage of overall Canadian trading, NEX's market share by volume is also greater than each of the competitive Alternative Trading Systems operating in Canada including Pure, Chi-X, CNQ, Triact, Liquidnet, and Blockbook for the month of February.

"NEX meets the needs of the investor community for those trading this segment of issuers and its trading structure was designed with customer needs in mind," said Thomas Kalafatis, Vice-President, Sales and Trading with TSX Markets. "Our most recent changes to NEX streamlined the fee structure to be in-line with a volume based trading fee model, like the TSX and TSX Venture Exchange. The lower rate per share for NEX trading fee reflects smaller market cap of issuers. This fee structure has aided in adding liquidity. We continue to believe that TSX focus on the specific needs of customers will reinforce the growth of markets and address competitive forces. We are excited at continuing to develop new products for the marketplace."

NEX companies benefit from the support and visibility provided by a listing and trading environment tailored to their needs, while the profile and reputation of TSX Venture Exchange companies will be enhanced as a result of the overall improved quality of the main TSX Venture Exchange stock list.

Source: Retrieved from www.tsx.com, March 23, 2008.

After-Hours Trading

ECNs allow investors to trade after exchange hours, which primarily means 4 to 8 p.m. ET, and sometimes early in the morning. Instinet, however, operates around the clock.

On-line brokerage firms offer their clients access to this trading using the computerized order matching systems of the ECNs. It is important to note that such trading is completely independent from the standard trading during market hours. Investors must, in effect, find someone willing to fill their orders at an acceptable price. Liquidity may be thin, although heavily traded NYSE stocks are good candidates for trading, as are most Nasdaq 100 stocks. Limitations exist on the types of orders that can be placed and the size of the orders. As of the beginning of 2001, less than half of on-line brokerage firms allowed customers this option.

In-House Trading

Along with the electronic networks, a new trend that has significant implications for the NYSE is the internal trading, or in-house trading, by fund managers without the use of a broker or an exchange. At a large institution with several funds or accounts, traders agree to buy and sell in-house, or cross-trade, perhaps at the next closing price. For example, at a large bank with several pension fund accounts, the manager of Account A might wish to buy Inco stock at the same time that the manager of Account B is selling a position in Inco.

Fidelity Investments, the largest mutual fund company, operates an in-house trading system for its own funds because of the tremendous amount of buying and selling it does every day. In addition, it has set up the Investor Liquidity Network, which is now used by other brokerage firms and institutional clients. This electronic routing system is said to handle 5 percent of the NYSE's volume, and Fidelity's in-house trading accounts for at least that much more.

Comparison of International Equity Markets

Figure 4-3 shows the market capitalization for the top 10 major world stock markets for 2005 and 2006. As we can see by this measure, New York was by far the largest market, followed by Tokyo, Nasdaq, London, Euronext, and so forth. The Toronto Stock Exchange ranked seventh in 2006 and was sixth in 2005. Based on market capitalization (and on trading volumes), the TSX is the dominant Canadian stock market, while the NYSE remains the dominant market in the United States, followed by Nasdaq.

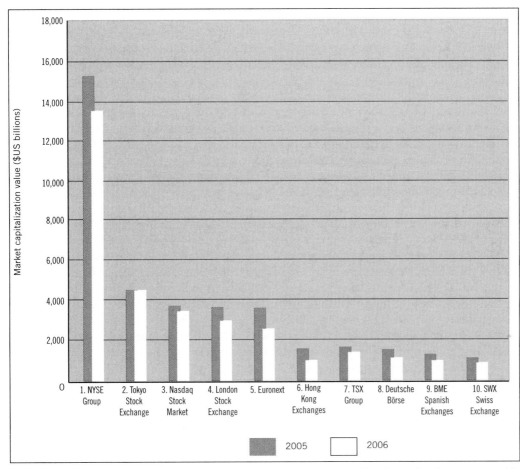

Figure 4-3
The Ten Biggest Stock Markets in the World by Market Capitalization (in Billions of US Dollars, 2005–2006)

Source: World Federation of Exchanges (formerly International Federation of Exchanges) website: www.world-exchanges.org.

Stock Market Indicators

learning objective 3
State the major stock market indicators.

The most popular question asked about stock markets is probably, "What did the market do today?" To answer this question, we need a composite report on market performance, which is what stock market averages and indexes are designed to provide. Because of the large number of equity markets, both domestic and foreign, there are numerous stock market indicators.

An index is a series of numbers that represent a combination of stock prices in such a manner that percentage changes in this series may be calculated over time. They are used primarily for performance comparisons and to gauge the overall direction of movements in the stock market. An average is used in the same manner as an index but differs from it because it is composed of equally weighted items. In this section, we outline only some basic information on these averages and indexes, with subsequent chapters containing more analysis and discussion as needed. The appendix at the end of this chapter provides additional details on these indicators, including composition and construction details.

Canadian Market Indexes

S&P/TSX Composite Index

The S&P/TSX Composite Index measures changes in market values of a portfolio of 300 Canadian stocks due to alterations in the total market capitalization (the number of common shares outstanding multiplied by the market price per share) of these stocks.

The TSE 300 Composite Index, which was widely considered to be the benchmark for Canadian equities, was renamed the **S&P/TSX Composite Index** effective May 1, 2002. The S&P/TSX Composite Index is a capitalization-weighted index (as are all the TSX indexes) and is designed to measure market activity of stocks listed on the TSX. It was developed in conjunction with Standard & Poor's (S&P), which maintains several major market indexes including the S&P 500 Composite Index in the United States (which is discussed below). The index was developed with a base level of 1,000 as of 1975, the same as its predecessor, and there should not be any major impact for former end users of the TSE 300 Composite Index. The index level after May 1, 2002, is completely comparable to its historical data as its constituents and the index calculation method are exactly the same as before. As of December 31, 2007, the index was composed of 258 companies representing 68.5 percent of the market capitalization for Canadian-based, TSX-listed companies. Stocks included in this index are reviewed on a quarterly basis, as is the case for all TSX indexes. The TSX also maintains a Total Return Index based on the total returns provided by stocks included in this index.

The **S&P/TSX Capped Composite Index** was created in response to the extraordinary weighting of Nortel Networks and BCE in the TSE 300 Composite Index during 2000, when Nortel represented 37 percent of that index. The capped composite limits the relative weight of any single index constituent to 10 percent. Currently there are no TSX-listed companies with a weighting of higher than 10 percent.

The **S&P/TSX 60 Index** was introduced on December 31, 1998, and replaced the TSE 35 Index and the TSE 100 Index as the basis for derivative products, including index funds and index-linked GICs. It is designed to mimic the performance of the broader S&P/TSX Composite Index. The index base value was set equal to 100 as of January 29, 1982 (which differs from the base year of 1975 for the S&P/TSX Composite Index). On the day it was introduced, the S&P/TSX 60 Index closing value was reported as 375.98. The stocks included in the S&P/TSX 60 Index represent 60 of the largest and most actively traded stocks comprising the S&P/TSX Composite Index, and as such it is commonly used as a benchmark for large-cap stock performance in Canada. Figure 4-4 provides a listing of the stocks included in this index as of December 31, 2007.

Figure 4-4
The S&P/TSX 60
(December 2007)

1. Research in Motion Ltd.	18. Manulife Financial Corp.	32. Cdn. Tire Corp. Ltd. A	48. Talisman Energy Inc.
2. Potash Corp. of Sask.	19. Shaw Comm. Inc. B	33. Nexen Inc.	49. Biovail Corp.
3. Alcan Inc.	20. Kinross Gold Corp.	34. Nova Chemicals Corp.	50. Thomson Corp.
4. EnCana Corp.	21. Husky Energy Inc.	35. TransCanada Corp.	51. Cdn. National Railway Co.
5. Suncor Energy Inc.	22. TransAlta Corp.	36. Enbridge Inc.	52. Bank of Nova Scotia
6. BCE Inc.	23. Novelis Inc.	37. Toronto-Dominion Bank	53. National Bank of Canada
7. Cdn. Natural Resources Ltd.	24. ACE Aviation Holdings Inc.	38. MDS Inc.	54. Penn West Energy Trust
8. Rogers Comm.	25. Agnico-Eagle Mines Ltd.	39. Domtar Inc.	55. Cameco Corp.
9. Barrick Gold Corp.	26. Shoppers Drug Mart Corp.	40. Celestica Inc.	56. Teck Cominco Ltd. B
10. Agrium Inc.	27. Cognos Inc.	41. Cott Corp.	57. Royal Bank of Canada
11. Sun Life Financial Inc.	28. Tim Hortons Inc.	42. George Weston Ltd.	58. Bank of Montreal
12. Imperial Oil Ltd.	29. Yellow Pages Income Fund	43. Brookfield Asset Management Inc.	59. Nortel Networks Corp.
13. Bombardier Inc.	30. Goldcorp Inc.	44. Lundin Mining Corp.	60. Cdn. Imperial Bank of Commerce
14. Cdn. Oil Sands Trust	31. Cdn. Pacific Railway Ltd.	45. TELUS Corp.	
15. Petro-Canada		46. Loblaw Companies Ltd.	
16. IPSCO Inc.		47. Magna Intl. Inc. A	
17. Fording Cdn. Coal Trust			

Source: "Market Statistics & Returns," TD Newcrest, January 2008.

In addition to the three indexes above, the TSX also maintains several other indexes such as the S&P/TSX 60 Capped Index (which is capped similar to the S&P/TSX Capped Composite Index), the S&P/TSX Mid-Cap Index, and the S&P/TSX Small-Cap Index. The Mid-Cap Index and the Small-Cap Index contain mid-cap and small-cap stocks respectively that meet specific inclusion criteria and are included in the S&P/TSX Composite Index. The TSX also maintains 13 capped industry indexes and one income trust index, as well as two income trust sub-indexes.

The S&P/TSX Venture Index is a broad market indicator for the Canadian venture capital market, which replaced the CDNX Index in December 2001. As of March 2008, it was composed of 484 companies. However, the number of companies included in the index can vary from one period to the next.

US Market Indexes

The **Dow Jones Industrial Average (DJIA)** is the most widely quoted measure of NYSE stock performance, despite the fact that it includes only 30 stocks that trade on the NYSE and Nasdaq. The DJIA is computed from 30 leading industrial stocks whose composition changes slowly over time to reflect changes in the economy. This average is said to be composed of **blue chip stocks**, meaning large, well-established, and well-known companies.

The DJIA is price-weighted and is therefore affected more by changes in higher priced stocks. It is calculated by adding the prices of the 30 stocks together and dividing by a divisor. The divisor was initially 30, but has been revised downward through the years to reflect the impact of stock splits. It is now below 1.0 and was approximately 0.135 by early 2005. The DJIA includes only blue chip stocks with a low-risk profile and it tends to underperform broader based indexes in the long term as a result of this lower risk. Other Dow Jones indexes include the Transportation Average (20 companies), a Utility Average (15 companies), and a Composite Average (65 companies), which are all price-weighted.

There are several other US indexes, of which the **Standard & Poor's 500 Composite Index (S&P 500)** is the most important. The S&P 500 Index is a broadly based market-weighted index that measures US stock performance. The S&P 500 is obviously a much broader measure than the Dow, and it should be more representative of the general market. However, it consists primarily of NYSE stocks, and it is clearly dominated by the largest corporations.[15] Nevertheless, the S&P 500 Index is typically the measure of the market preferred by institutional investors who most often compare their performance to this market index.

Other US indexes include NYSE-maintained market-valued indexes that include all listed equities for a given group: composite, industrials, transportation, finance, real estate, and utilities. The Amex Index includes all stocks that trade on the American Stock Exchange and is value-weighted. The Nasdaq Composite Index was set equal to 100 as of January 1971, and is market-valued. The Russell Indexes are well known. The Russell 1000 is closely correlated with the S&P 500 because it is largely composed of "large-cap" stocks, with the stocks in the index having an average market cap of about $4 billion. The Russell 1000 comprises 90 percent of the market cap of the Russell 3000 Index, with the remaining 10 percent being composed of 2,000 small-cap stocks, with an average market cap of $200 million. The Dow Jones Equity Market Index is capitalization-weighted and consists of 700 stocks covering about 80 percent of the US equity market. Finally, the Wilshire 5,000 Equity Index is a market-valued index that attempts to measure all stocks for which quotations are available; it is the most broadly based US index.

Foreign Stock Market Indicators

Stock market indexes are available for most foreign markets, but the composition, weighting, and computational procedures vary widely from index to index. This makes it difficult to make comparisons. To deal with these problems, some organizations have constructed their own set of indexes on

Dow Jones Industrial Average (DJIA)

A price-weighted series of 30 leading industrial stocks that trade on the US markets, used as a measure of stock market activity and of changes in the economy in general.

Blue Chip Stocks

The stocks of large, well-established, and well-known companies that have long records of earnings and dividends.

Standard & Poor's 500 Composite Index (S&P 500)

Broadly based, market-weighted index of US stock market activity covering 500 stocks. It is generally the measure of the market preferred by institutional investors.

---

[15] The S&P 500 contains some stocks traded on Nasdaq.

a consistent basis to facilitate international market performance comparisons. The largest provider of international indexes is Morgan Stanley Capital International (MSCI). They maintain several global indexes including the MSCI World Index, which is a market-valued index that includes stocks from 21 developed countries. MSCI also maintains 45 country and numerous regional indexes including the **EAFE Index** (the Europe, Australia, and Far East Index), the Emerging Markets Index, and several others.

EAFE Index

The Europe, Australia, and Far East Index is a value-weighted index of the equity performance of major foreign markets.

Similar to the MSCI World Index, the Dow Jones World Stock Index covers Canada, Mexico, and the United States, as well as the Pacific Region and Europe. It is designed to be a comprehensive measure and represents approximately 80 percent of the world's stock markets. Unlike the DJIA, the World Stock Index is a capitalization-weighted index.

The best-known measure of the Japanese stock market is the Nikkei 225 Average, an arithmetic average of prices for 225 actively traded stocks on the Tokyo Stock Exchange. Similar to the Dow Jones Average, it traditionally has been a price-weighted series. In contrast, the Financial Times Actuaries Share Indexes are market-value indexes covering stocks on the London Stock Exchange, the most widely followed being the FT London FT-SE 100 Index. These indexes, as well as those for other foreign markets, can be seen daily in the media.

Bond Markets

learning objective 4
Describe, briefly, the bond and derivatives markets.

Just as stockholders need good secondary markets to be able to trade stocks and thus preserve their flexibility, bondholders need a viable market in order to sell before maturity. Otherwise, many investors would be reluctant to tie up their funds for up to 30 years. At the very least, they would demand higher initial yields on bonds, which would hinder raising funds by those who wish to invest productively.

Investors can purchase either new bonds being issued in the primary market or existing bonds outstanding in the secondary market. Yields for the two must be in equilibrium. If, for example, **Loblaw Co. Ltd.'s** existing bonds are trading to provide a 5 percent yield over a 15-year period, comparable, new Loblaws bonds will be sold with approximately the same yield.

Although some bonds trade on the exchanges (convertible bonds only on the TSX), the secondary bond market is primarily an OTC market, with a large network of dealers making markets in the various bonds. Investors can buy and sell bonds through their brokers, who, in turn, trade with bond dealers. The volume of bond trading in the OTC market in Canada dwarfs the volume of bonds traded on all the exchanges combined. The situation is similar in the United States where OTC trading of bonds dominates, although a few thousand bonds are traded on the NYSE and a very few on the Amex.

The Canadian bond market represents a relatively small percentage of the global bond market. For example, in June 2007, there was approximately $1.09 trillion US in outstanding domestic debt or 2.1 percent of the global market. The size of the Canadian market pales in comparison to several international bond markets such as those in the United States and Japan, where there was $23.4 and $8.1 trillion US in outstanding debt in June 2007.

Government bonds comprised about 61.6 percent of the Canadian bond market at that time, with Government of Canada bonds representing the major component. These are widely purchased, held, and traded, resulting in a broad and deep market, with a large volume of transactions. The market is not as deep for provincial, municipal, or corporate bonds, despite an increase in trading in corporate issues over the past few years. By June 2007, the amount of Canadian corporate bonds outstanding was $418.1 billion US, accounting for approximately 2 percent of the world corporate market. At the same time, there was over $17 trillion US in outstanding corporate bonds in the United States.

Corporate issues are not traded as actively as government issues, which is likely attributable to the fact that over 40 percent of these bonds are held by institutional investors. Most corporate bond trades by institutions involve large amounts. As a result, liquidity is not always good for small transactions in corporate bonds, with delays occurring in the trade, and price concessions often have to be made. Investors should be careful in trading small amounts of corporate bonds and be prepared for delays and costs.

Derivatives Markets

We discuss the details of derivatives markets in their respective chapters. However, at this point we note that options can be bought or sold through an exchange facility or privately arranged (OTC options). All exchange-traded options or financial securities in Canada trade on the Montreal Exchange (Canada's national derivatives market), as shown in Figure 4-5. As discussed previously, the MX agreed to merge with the TSX Group to form the TMX Group in 2008.

Derivative Type	Underlying Asset	Symbol	Contract Specifications
Options	Equities (individual stocks)	Vary	American style 100 shares of underlying stock
Options	S&P/TSX 60 Index	SXO	European style Cash settlement based on $100 × S&P/TSX 60 Index value
Options	S&P/TSX 60 iShare Fund Units	XIU	American style 100 iShares (i.e., S&P/TSX 60 Index Fund units)
Options	Barclays iShares Sector Funds	XEG, XFN, XGD, XGI, XIT	American style 100 iShares for one of the following funds: XEG, XEX: iShares S&P/TSX Capped Energy Index Fund XFN: iShares S&P/TSX Capped Financials Index Fund XGD, XGL: iShares S&P/TSX Capped Gold Index Fund XIT: iShares S&P/TSX Capped Information Technology Index Fund
Futures	S&P/TSX 60 Index	SXF	Cash settlement C$200 times the future value
Futures	Sectoral Index	SXA, SXB, SXH, SXY	Cash settlement SXH (Information Technology): C$500 times the futures value SXY (Energy): C$200 times the futures value SXB (Financials): C$200 times the futures value SXA (Gold): C$200 times the futures value
Futures	Three-Month Canadian Bankers' Acceptance Futures	BAX	Cash settlement C$1,000,000 nominal value of Canadian Bankers' Acceptance with a three-month maturity

Figure 4-5
Montreal Exchange
Product Offerings
(March 2008)

Derivative Type	Underlying Asset	Symbol	Contract Specifications
Options	Options on Three-Month Canadian Bankers' Acceptance Futures	OBX	American style One three-month Canadian Bankers' Acceptance futures
Futures	30-day Overnight Repo Rate Futures	ONX	Cash settlement Each contract shall be for a nominal value of C$5,000,000
Futures	Two-Year Government of Canada Bond Futures	CGZ	Physical delivery C$200,000 nominal value Government of Canada bond with 4% notional coupon
Futures	Ten-year Government of Canada Bond Futures	CGB	Physical delivery C$100,000 nominal value of Government of Canada bond with 6% notional coupon
Futures	Ten-year Government of Canada Bond Futures	CGB	Physical delivery C$100,000 nominal value of Government of Canada bond with 6% notional coupon
Futures	30-year Government of Canada Bond Futures	LGB	Physical delivery C$100,000 nominal value of Government of Canada bond with 4% notional coupon
Options	One Ten-year Government of Canada Bond Futures	OGB	American style
Options	US dollars	USX™	Cash settlement American exercise style Based on $10,000 US trading units
Options	Sponsored Options	Vary	Cash settlement European exercise style

Source: *The Montreal Exchange website: www.m-x.ca.*

In 1973, the Chicago Board of Options Exchange (CBOE) was formed to begin trading in options. It is the best-known options market in the world and operates using a system of market makers. Bid and ask prices are quoted by the market maker, and floor brokers can trade with the market maker or with other floor brokers. Liquidity problems, which had plagued the OTC options markets, were overcome by

1. Standardizing option contracts
2. Introducing a clearing corporation that would guarantee the performance of the seller of an options contract (it effectively becomes the buyer and seller for each option contract)

In Canada, all equity, bond, and stock index option positions are issued and guaranteed by a single clearing corporation, the Canadian Derivatives Clearing Corporation (CDCC), which is wholly owned by the ME. In the US, all listed options are cleared through the Options Clearing Corporation (OCC).

Exercise of options is accomplished by submitting an exercise notice to the clearing corporation, which assigns it to a member firm, which then assigns it to one of its accounts.

In contrast to options, futures contracts are traded on exchanges in designated "pits," using an open-outcry process as a trading mechanism. Under this system, the pit trader offers to buy or sell contracts at an offered price and other pit traders are free to transact if they wish. This open-outcry system is unique in securities trading. There are few sights in the financial system that can rival frenzied trading activity in a futures market pit. Another unique feature of these markets is that the delivery time period can vary, from four to six weeks for commodities such as corn or wheat, to one day for an index contract.

In Canada, the only commodity exchange is the ICE Futures Canada™, which resulted from the Winnipeg Commodity Exchange being acquired by the IntercontinentalExchange Inc. in August of 2007, and was officially renamed as of January 1, 2008. Canola futures are by far the most active product on this exchange, as can be seen in Figure 4-6. The ME trades a wide variety of futures contracts on interest rate products, stock indexes, and even on individual stocks, as seen in Figure 4-5.

Figure 4-6
Futures Canada (formerly Winnipeg Commodity Exchange) Options and Futures Trading (2002–2006)

Options

Year		2006	2005	2004	2003	2002
Canola	Calls	14,295	6,929	10,718	16,650	16,138
	Puts	12,228	20,182	4,871	11,718	19,332
	Total	26,523	27,111	15,589	28,368	35,470
Feed Wheat	Calls	0	0	0	4	92
	Puts	0	1,460	0	0	9
	Total	0	1,460	0	4	101
Flaxseed	Calls	0	0	0	10	97
	Puts	0	0	0	0	0
	Total	0	0	0	10	97
Western Barley	Calls	484	28	411	66	1,668
	Puts	596	848	1,496	2,712	151
	Total	1,080	876	1,907	2,778	1,819
Total	Calls	14,779	6,957	11,129	16,730	17,995
	Puts	12,824	22,490	6,367	14,430	19,492
Total Options		27,603	29,947	17,496	31,160	37,487

Futures

Year	2006	2005	2004	2003	2002
Canola	2,427,697	1,661,463	1,591,039	1,422,794	1,710,345
Canola Meal*	0	0	0	0	155
Feed Wheat	65,802	81,348	84,151	56,186	84,042
Field Peas**	0	0	0	0	729
Flaxseed	0	0	70	3,358	21,206
Western Barley	193,324	133,460	196,973	190,120	203,1049
Total Futures***	2,686,823	1,876,271	1,872,233	1,672,458	2,019,581

* The WCE Canola Meal futures contract was listed on June 26, 2001 and de-listed September 16, 2003.

** The WCE Field Peas futures contract was listed on April 5, 1999 and de-listed October 15, 2002.

*** Totals include volume from de-listed contracts.

Source: ICE Futures Canada (formerly Winnipeg Commodity Exchange) website: www.theice.com.

The centre of commodity futures trading in North America is the Chicago Board of Trade (CBOT) and the Chicago Mercantile Exchange (CME). However, there are several other important exchanges in New York including the Commodity Exchange, the New York Mercantile Exchange, the New York Coffee, Sugar, and Cocoa Exchange, the New York Cotton Exchange, and the New York Futures Exchange.

CHECK YOUR UNDERSTANDING

4-4. The TSX and the NYSE are both secondary markets for equities. How else are they similar? How do they differ (other than country of origin)?

4-5. Distinguish between Nasdaq and the over-the-counter market.

4-6. Why might a company opt to have its shares traded on Nasdaq rather than the NYSE? What about the reverse?

4-7. Is the S&P/TSX Composite Index affected by the size of the companies in the index?

THE CHANGING SECURITIES MARKETS

learning objective 5
Discuss some of the factors behind rapid change in the securities markets.

Over the last two decades, the securities markets have been changing rapidly, with more of the same expected over the coming years. In Canada, a massive restructuring of the security exchanges has resulted in drastic changes to Canadian secondary markets. Globally, there have been numerous combinations of markets, and most markets have also been transformed into for-profit, publicly listed businesses.

Several factors explain why markets have undergone such rapid changes. First, institutional investors have different requirements and often different views from individual investors, and their emergence as the dominant force in the market has necessitated significant shifts in market structure and operation.

Blocks
Transactions involving at least 10,000 shares or $100,000 in value; block trades are usually executed by institutional investors.

Institutional investors often trade in large **blocks**. Large-block activity is an indicator of institutional participation, and the average size of trades on the TSX and NYSE has grown sharply over the years.

Another factor stimulating changes in our markets is the growth of computerized trading of securities, which has made possible the inter-market trading of securities. Inter-market trading permits brokerage houses to electronically route orders to whatever market is offering the best price to a buyer or a seller. This system should enhance market efficiency, by promoting competition and lowering bid-ask spreads, because the dealers with the most attractive prices would automatically receive the orders.

Most of the world's major stock exchanges have moved to computerized trading (including the TSX), the most notable exception being the largest exchange in the world, the NYSE. It continues to justify its nearly 200-year-old specialist system, despite criticisms that it is not attuned to the needs of the modern market. The NYSE defends the specialist system vigorously, citing such evidence as the 1987 market crash, when the specialists stayed at their posts to handle orders while many over-the-counter dealers refused to answer the phone. ECNs will likely have an even larger impact on traditional security markets as we move forward. Finally, the global nature of security markets in today's world has put extreme pressure on all markets to compete aggressively for security listings.

The Globalization of Securities Markets

The move toward around-the-clock trading—which many expected to be the wave of the future—began in the early 1990s. Through such sources as Instinet, stock prices can change quickly even though the exchanges themselves are closed. The after-hours trading is particularly important when significant news events occur, or when an institutional investor is simply anxious to trade a position. Such activity could, in a few years, lead to the 24-hour trading of stocks, just as currency trading now does.

What about bonds? In today's world, bonds increasingly are being traded at all hours around the globe, more so than stocks. The emergence of global offerings means that bonds are traded around the clock and around the world. The result of this global trading in bonds is that bond dealers and investors are having to adapt to the new demands of the marketplace, being available to react and trade at all hours of the day and night. This includes new employees in various locales, expanded hours, and computer terminals in the home.

Foreign markets are changing rapidly, with many merging or simply forming alliances. This is done to reduce costs and attract business as electronic trading costs are lower than those on an exchange. Most stock markets around the world are almost totally computerized, with the remaining ones moving in that direction.

INVESTMENT DEALER FINED FOR LACK OF CONTROLS

The Investment Industry Regulatory Organization of Canada (IIROC) regulates members of the profession to ensure they uphold strict standards when acting on behalf of clients. Violations can result in steep penalties.

In 2007, IIROC's predecessor, the Investment Dealers Association of Canada (IDA), reached a settlement with member National Bank Financial Inc., whereby the firm would pay $795,000 in fines for violating IDA regulations, bylaws, and policies. One violation involved two staff members in one branch, who began to open options accounts for their clients. But neither representative was trained in or approved to trade in options contracts.

The IDA found that a colleague who was approved to trade in options approved the opening of the accounts and entered options trades without ever communicating with the clients or verifying whether the trades matched their actual risk tolerance and investment objectives. Most clients wanted to reduce risk in their portfolio, yet some trades involved high-risk options. For nearly a year, about 100 options accounts were created, with more than 1,100 options trades performed.

The IDA said that National Bank Financial acknowledged its responsibility and took the necessary steps to remedy the situation, including paying "substantial amounts" to clients to compensate them, and stepping up supervision, controls, and approvals. The IDA determined there was little risk the violations would reoccur.

DISCUSSION QUESTIONS

1. What ethics, if any, were breached?

2. If National Bank Financial had not fully cooperated with the IDA investigation, should the penalty have been higher?

3. If the violations had concerned investments less risky than options, would the ethical situation have changed?

SUMMARY

This summary relates to the learning objectives for this chapter.

1. **Distinguish between primary and secondary markets.**

   Financial markets include primary markets, where new securities are sold, and secondary markets, where existing securities are traded. Primary markets involve investment dealers who specialize in selling new securities. They offer the issuer several functions, including advisory, underwriting, and marketing services. Secondary markets consist of equity, bond, and derivative markets. The Toronto Stock Exchange (TSX) is the largest stock market in Canada, and trading on it has been completely computerized since April 1997. The New York Stock Exchange (NYSE) is the world's premier stock market and operates using a specialist system.

2. **Describe how the equity markets are organized and how they operate.**

   The equity markets consist of auction markets (exchanges) and negotiated markets (over-the-counter—OTC—markets). Brokers act as intermediaries, representing both buyers and sellers; dealers make markets in securities, buying and selling for their own account. The OTC market is a network of dealers making markets in unlisted securities.

3. **State the major stock market indicators.**

   The best-known market indicator in Canada is the S&P/TSX Composite Index, a market-weighted index. The best-known stock market indicator in the United States is the Dow Jones Industrial Average (DJIA), a price-weighted average computed from 30 leading industrial stocks. The S&P 500 Composite Index (which is value-weighted, similar to the S&P/TSX Index), is carried in the popular press, and investors often refer to it as a good measure of what the overall US stock markets are doing, at least for large NYSE stocks.

4. **Describe, briefly, the bond and derivatives markets.**

   Although some bonds are traded on the exchanges, most bond trading occurs in the OTC market. Federal government bonds enjoy broad markets, while the markets for provincial, municipal, and corporate bonds are often less liquid. Derivatives markets involve options and futures contracts. Puts and calls are traded on option exchanges using market makers or on the OTC market, while futures contracts are traded in pits using an open-outcry system.

5. **Discuss some of the factors behind rapid change in the securities markets.**

   The securities markets are changing rapidly, stimulated by the demands of institutional investors and by computerized and inter-market trading of securities. The markets are increasingly linked globally.

KEY TERMS

Auction market, p.98

Blocks, p.116

Blue chip stocks, p.111

Brokers, p.98

Dealer, p.105

Dow Jones Industrial Average (DJIA), p.111

EAFE Index, p.112

Electronic Communications Networks (ECNs), p.107

Fourth market, p.107

Initial public offering (IPO), p.93

Instinet (Institutional Network), p.107

Investment dealer, p.94

Nasdaq National Market System (Nasdaq/NMS), p.105

Nasdaq Stock Market (Nasdaq), p.105

Negotiated market, p.105

New York Stock Exchange (NYSE), p.101

Over-the-counter (OTC) market, p.105

Primary market, p.92

Program trading, p.103

Prompt offering qualification (POP) system, p.96

Prospectus, p.95

Secondary markets, p.98

Specialists, p.102

Standard & Poor's 500 Composite Index (S&P 500), p.111

S&P/TSX Composite Index, p.110

Third market, p.107

Toronto Stock Exchange (TSX), p.98

Underwriting, p.95

R E V I E W   Q U E S T I O N S

4-1. Distinguish between the third market and the fourth market.

4-2. What are two primary factors accounting for the rapid changes in securities markets?

4-3. What is the S&P/TSX Composite Index?

4-4. What is the Dow Jones Industrial Average? How does it differ from the S&P 500 Composite Index?

4-5. What is meant by the term blue chip stocks? Cite three examples.

4-6. What is the EAFE Index?

4-7. What is meant by block activity? How important is it on the TSX and NYSE?

4-8. What is meant by the statement "The bond market is primarily an OTC market"?

4-9. What does it mean to say an IPO has been underwritten by BMO Nesbitt Burns?

4-10. Briefly describe the POP system. What kind of companies qualify to use this system?

4-11. What are "bought deals"?

4-12. What are the advantages and disadvantages of private placements?

4-13. What might cause an investment dealer to market newly issued securities on a "best efforts" basis instead of underwriting them?

4-14. What is the chief function of a capital market?

4-15. Why do some large Canadian firms want to be interlisted on US stock exchanges?

4-16. Discuss the importance of financial markets to the Canadian economy. Can primary markets exist without secondary markets?

4-17. Discuss the functions of an investment dealer. How do they serve as principals and how do they serve as agents in primary markets?

4-18. Outline the process for a primary offering of securities involving investment dealers.

4-19. Outline the structure of equity markets in Canada. Distinguish between auction markets and negotiated markets.

4-20. What is Instinet? How does it affect the over-the-counter market?

4-21. What is a prospectus?

4-22. What are some of the concerns that the issuing company takes into account when deciding on the pricing of an initial public offering (IPO)?

4-23. Comment on the global evidence of underpricing in IPOs. How is underpricing measured? Why do you think this phenomenon exists, given your understanding of efficient markets?

4-24. Explain the difference between a price-weighted index and a market-weighted index.

4-25. In what way is an investment dealer similar to a commission broker?

4-26. Describe the roles performed by specialists. How do they maintain an orderly market?

4-27. Is there any similarity between an over-the-counter dealer and a specialist on an exchange?

4-28. What is meant by "in-house trading"? Who is likely to benefit from this activity?

4-29. Explain what an ECN is.

4-30. What advantages do ECNs offer?

4-31. Assume that Pfizer and Altria, both of which are in the DJIA and in the S&P 500, have approximately equivalent market values (price multiplied by the number of shares outstanding) but very different market prices (which in fact is the case). Would a 5 percent move in each stock have about the same effect on the S&P 500 Index?

PROBLEM

4-1. Appendix 4A provides details on how the S&P/TSX Composite Index (a value index) and the Dow Jones Industrial Average (a price index) are constructed. Create both a price index and a value index for a group of 10 imaginary stocks (labelled "Stock 1" through "Stock 10"). In the base case, each stock has a price of $10 per share. Stock 1 has 100 shares outstanding; Stock 2 has 200 shares, and so on up to 1,000 shares outstanding for Stock 10. Use a divisor of 1.0 for the price index so that the starting index value is 100.00; for the value index use a multiplier (or base number) of 100 so that the index also starts at 100.00.

Determine the value of each of the two indices for the following three scenarios. Observe how the different indexing methods are impacted by different types of changes in the stocks.

Case A: The price of Stocks 1 to 5 increases by 10% (to $11 each) but the price of Stocks 6 to 10 fall by 10% (to $9 per share).

Case B: Stock 1 splits its shares 2 for 1 (so there are now 200 outstanding); its price therefore is cut in half. No other stock changes at all from the base case. For the price index, your divisor should now change to 0.95 to account for the stock split.

Case C: The changes from Cases A and B both occur. Note that the price of Stock 1 will now be $5.50 per share with 200 shares outstanding.

PREPARING FOR YOUR PROFESSIONAL EXAMS

CFA PRACTICE QUESTIONS

Use the table below to answer the following three questions.

	Price			Shares		
Company	A	B	C	A	B	C
Day 1	10	25	50	500	350	250
Day 2	10	20	55	500*	350	250
Day 3	9	25	51	1,000	350	250**
Day 4	8	25	17	1,000	350	750

* 2:1 Split on Stock A after Close of Day 2
** 3:1 Split on Stock C after Close of Day 3

4-1. The price-weighted index for Day 1, 2, 3, and 4 respectively, is closest to:

    a. 28.34   13.34   30.10   16.67
    b. 28.33   28.33   30.10   29.51
    c. 88.34   13.43   28.66   29.51
    d. 88.34   28.33   2.82   16.67

4-2. Assuming that the initial index value is 100, a value-weighted index for Day 1 would be closest to:

    a. 1
    b. 100
    c. 98.10
    d. 112.38

4-3. Assuming that the initial index value is 100, a value-weighted index for Day 4 would be closest to:

    a. 1
    b. 100
    c. 98.10
    d. 112.38

4-4. Which of the following statements is false?

    a. The Nikkei 225 is a price-weighted index.
    b. The Standard & Poor's indexes are equal-weighted indexes.
    c. A market-weighted index automatically adjusts for stock splits.
    d. Because of stock splits the denominator of a price-weighted index will decrease over time.

CFA CURRICULUM AND SAMPLE EXAM QUESTIONS (©CFA INSTITUTE)

4-1. The divisor for the Dow Jones Industrial Average (DJIA) is *most likely* to decrease if a stock in the DJIA:

    a. has a stock split.
    b. has a reverse split.
    c. pays a cash dividend.
    d. is removed and replaced.

APPENDIX 4A
STOCK MARKET INDEXES

Several issues must be dealt with in the construction of a stock market index or average. The most important involve its composition, the weighting procedure used, and the method of calculation.

What is the composition of the market measure? Is it a sample of one exchange to be used or a sample from the major exchanges? Should a sample from the over-the-counter (OTC) market be included? Alternatively, should every stock on an exchange(s) be used, and if so, how should OTC stocks be handled? (Do you include every active OTC stock or just those for which daily quotes are available?)

If investors need a broad measure of stock performance, several markets (TSX, TSX Venture Exchange, and OTC) need to be included. If investors want to know the performance of the largest stocks, a measure of TSX performance may be sufficient. Some market measures use sub-samples of one or more markets, whereas others use every stock on one or more markets. It is important to be aware of compositional differences among the various market measures.

A second issue involves the weighting procedure used in constructing the index or average. Does each stock receive equal weight or is each weighted by its market value (i.e., market price multiplied by shares outstanding)? Alternatively, the measure could be price-weighted, resulting in higher priced stocks carrying more weight than lower priced ones.

The third issue is the calculation procedures used. The primary question here is whether an index or an average is being used. A market average is an arithmetic mean of the prices for the sample of securities being used, showing the arithmetic average of the prices at a given time.

A market index measures the current price behaviour of the sample in relation to a base period established for a previous time. Indexes, therefore, are expressed in relative numbers, whereas averages are simply arithmetic means (weighted or unweighted). The use of an index allows for more meaningful comparisons over long periods of time because current values can be related to established base period values.

The Dow Jones Averages are arithmetic averages, but virtually all the other market measures are indexes.

The S&P/TSX Composite Index

To determine the index, the market value of all firms is calculated (current market price multiplied by number of shares), and this total value is divided by the market value of all the securities for the base period. This relative value is multiplied by 1,000, representing the base period value.[16] In equation form, the S&P/TSX Composite Index is calculated as:

(4-1)
$$\text{S\&P/TSX Index} = \frac{\Sigma P_{it}Q_{it}}{\Sigma P_{ib}Q_{ib}}(k)$$

P_{it} = the price of a stock i at time t
Q_{it} = number of shares of stock i at time t
P_{ib} = the price of a stock i at the base period time b
Q_{ib} = number of shares of stock i at the base period time b
b = the base period
k = the base number

A current value of 13,000 for the S&P/TSX Index indicates that the average price of the stocks in the index has increased by a factor of 13 in relation to the base period. If the Royal Bank of Canada was included in the index and had a market value that was seven times as great as that of the National Bank of Canada, a 1 percent change in Royal's price would have more than seven times the impact of a 1 percent change in National's price.

The Dow Jones Industrial Average

In principle, calculation of the DJIA involves adding up the prices of the 30 stocks and dividing by 30 to obtain the average, but it is not that simple because of stock splits and dividends. Instead, the number is adjusted to reflect the stock splits and dividends that have occurred and today is much less than 1.0. As a result, a one-point change in the DJIA does not represent a change of $1 in the value of an average share; rather, the change amounts to only a few cents. You should keep this in mind the next time someone gets excited about a 10- or 20-point rise in one day in the DJIA.

The DJIA is calculated as:

$$\text{DJIA}_t = \Sigma P_{it}/n^*$$

where P is the price of a stock i at time t and n^* indicates an adjusted divisor.

---

[16]Before multiplying by 1,000, the S&P/TSX Index at any point can be thought of as the price, in relation to the beginning price of $1, of all stocks in the index weighted by their proportionate total market values.

CHAPTER 5

HOW SECURITIES ARE TRADED

In Chapter 4 we considered how securities markets are organized. In this chapter we learn the mechanics of trading securities, which investors must know in order to operate successfully in the marketplace. Chapter 5 discusses various details involved in trading securities, critical information for every investor. Brokerage firms and their activities are analyzed, as are the types of orders to buy and sell securities, and the handling of these orders. The regulation of the securities markets is discussed. Finally, the various aspects of trading securities that investors often encounter are considered. Although the details of trading, like the organization of securities markets, continue to evolve, the basic procedures remain the same.

Learning Objectives

After reading this chapter, you should be able to

1. Explain the role of brokerage firms and stockbrokers.
2. Describe how brokerage firms operate.
3. Outline how orders to buy and sell securities are executed.
4. Discuss the regulation of the Canadian securities industry.
5. Explain the importance of margin trading and short selling to investors.

CHAPTER PREVIEW

Now that we have explained the basic types of securities and the markets where they are traded, we turn to the mechanics of trading—that is, what actually happens when a trade takes place. Similar to the organization of securities markets, the details of trading continue to evolve, but the basic procedures remain the same. In this chapter, you will learn about brokerage firms and stockbrokers and how they operate. We introduce the three major types of orders—market orders, limit orders, and stop orders—and explain how they are executed on the exchanges and in the over-the-counter market. (Appendix 5A features the specialist system used by the NYSE.) We discuss the regulation of the Canadian securities industry and its role in protecting investors (Appendix 5B considers regulation in the United States). Finally, you will learn about the importance of margin trading and short selling to investors.

BROKERAGE TRANSACTIONS

Brokerage Firms

learning objective 1
Explain the role of brokerage firms and stockbrokers.

In general, it is quite easy for any responsible person to open a brokerage account. An investor selects a broker or brokerage house by personal contact, referral, reputation, and so forth. Licensed traders of the exchanges are supposed to learn certain basic facts about potential customers, but only minimal information is normally required. Actually, personal contact between broker and customer seldom occurs, with transactions carried out by telephone, in writing, or increasingly, by computer.

Full-Service Brokers

Brokerage firms offering a full range of services, including information and advice.

Customers can choose the type of broker they wish to use and brokers can be classified according to the services offered and fees charged. **Full-service brokers** offer a variety of services to investors, particularly information and advice. Thus, investors can obtain a wide variety of information about the economy, particular industries, individual companies, and the bond market, for example. Full-service brokers in Canada are primarily owned by the large banks. Familiar names include RBC Dominion Securities, Scotia Capital Markets, CIBC World Markets (formerly CIBC Wood Gundy), and BMO Nesbitt Burns.

Discount Brokers

Brokerage firms offering execution services for buying and selling securities at prices significantly less than full-service brokerage firms. They provide little, if any, investing information and give no advice.

In contrast to the full-service brokers, **discount brokers** concentrate on executing orders and are able to charge lower fees. Most offer services frequently used by investors in a manner similar to the full-service brokers, but they provide little, if any, investing information and give no advice. Thus, investors pay less and receive less. Most of the full-service brokerage firms also maintain discount brokerage operations. Familiar names include Bank of Montreal Investor Line, ScotiaBank Discount Brokerage, Royal Bank Action Direct Discount Brokerage, TD Waterhouse (formerly TD Greenline), and CIBC Investor's Edge Discount Brokerage.

Today, there are numerous on-line discount brokerage firms—including E*TRADE Canada and most of the traditional discount brokerage firms—that allow reduced commissions for trading of securities using the Internet. This provides many investors with an attractive option for investing.

Stockbrokers or Financial Consultants?

Traditionally, investors dealt with stockbrokers at large retail brokerage firms who executed their customers' orders, provided advice, and sent them publications about individual stocks, industries, bonds, and so forth. These brokers earned most of their income from their share of the commissions generated by their customers. The key to being a successful broker was to build a client base and to service the accounts, making money as customers traded.

As noted above, investors can now choose to use a discount broker who will provide virtually all of the same services except advice and publications and will charge less for the execution of trades. Smart investors choose the alternative that is best for them in terms of their own needs. Some investors need and want personal attention and research publications and are willing to pay higher brokerage commissions. Others, however, prefer to do their own research and to pay only for order execution.

What about today's full-service stockbrokers? In the first place, they go by different titles, such as financial consultants or investment advisors (or simply registered representatives). This change in title reflects the significant changes that have occurred in the industry. Brokerage firms now derive a smaller percentage of their revenues from commissions paid by individual investors than in the past. And the typical full-service stockbroker, whatever he or she is called, now derives less of their income from customer commissions.

How do brokers earn the rest of their income? One alternative is to sell mutual funds owned by their own firms. These funds carry a load or sales charge, and the broker selling shares in these funds earns part of this sales charge. Although a large brokerage firm may sell dozens or hundreds of different funds, there is evidence that brokers are pressured to put their customers into the in-house funds.

Another alternative involves "principal transactions," or brokerage firms trading for their own accounts. When these firms want to sell some shares from their own account, brokers are often encouraged to sell these securities to their customers, with some additional financial incentives provided. Smart investors, when given a recommendation to buy a security by their broker, ask if the firm has issued a public buy recommendation or if the broker is being compensated to sell this security. This activity now accounts for an increasingly important source of income for brokerage firms.

Yet another source of income is the sale of new issues of securities (IPOs), discussed in Chapter 4. Underwriting new issues is a profitable activity for brokerage firms, and brokers may have an incentive to steer their customers into the new issues.

Other sources of revenue today that were non-existent or much smaller in the past include administrative fees resulting from imposing charges on customer accounts. For example, fees for inactive accounts, transfers, and maintenance may be imposed on customers. Obviously, commissions on products sold by brokers will vary depending on the product. Government bonds or T-bills may carry commissions of less than 1 percent, whereas limited partnerships, which are more complicated instruments, may carry commissions of 8 percent or more.

Types of Brokerage Accounts

The most basic type of account is the **cash account**, whereby the customer pays the brokerage house the full price for any securities purchased. Many customers open a **margin account**, which allows the customer to borrow from the brokerage firm to purchase securities. (Margin is explained in some detail later in this chapter.) An alternative to these accounts is for clients of investment dealers to maintain discretionary or managed accounts. Managed accounts are client portfolios that are managed on a continuing basis by the dealer, usually for a management fee. Discretionary accounts are similar but are generally opened as a convenience to clients who are unwilling or unable to attend to their own accounts (for example, if they are seriously ill or are out of the country). Managed accounts may be solicited, whereas discretionary accounts may not. Both accounts require written consent of the client, and the authorization must include investment objectives. These accounts generally require minimum account balances of $100,000 or $200,000 and charge management fees in the 2 percent range.

In an important development in brokerage accounts, brokers now act as middlemen, matching clients with independent money managers. Brokerage houses offer **wrap accounts** to investors with a minimum of $100,000 to commit. Using the broker as a consultant, the client chooses one or more outside money managers from a list provided by the broker. Under this wrap account, all costs—the cost of the broker-consultant and money manager, transactions costs, custody fees, and the cost of detailed performance reports—are wrapped in one fee. For stocks, fees are typically in the 2 to 3 percent range of the assets managed, dropping as the size of the account gets larger.[1]

learning objective 2
Describe how brokerage firms operate.

Cash Account
The most common type of brokerage account in which the customer pays the brokerage house the full price of any securities purchased.

Margin Account
A brokerage account that allows the customer to borrow from the brokerage firm to purchase securities.

Wrap Account
A type of brokerage account where all costs are wrapped in one fee.

[1]Fees are generally lower for bond portfolios or combinations of stocks and bonds.

Commissions

For most of their long history, North American exchanges have required their members to charge fixed (and minimum) commissions (although on transactions involving more than $500,000, they were negotiable in Canada). In the United States, the requirement of fixed commissions applied to all trades and fuelled the growth of the third market for block trading, as discussed in Chapter 4. The United States eliminated fixed commissions requirements in 1975, and Canada followed suit in 1983. The result of these changes is that in today's environment, fees are supposed to be negotiated, with each firm free to act independently.

These changes have lead to lower commission fees, as well as the growth of discount brokerage firms. Today's investors can attempt to negotiate with their brokers, and different brokers charge different commissions. In practice, the larger full-service brokerage houses have specified commission rates for the small investor. However, the overall competition in the industry has an effect on the rates that are set. Customers are free to shop around, and smart ones do so because differences in commissions among major firms can be substantial in some cases.

In contrast, negotiated rates are the norm for institutional customers, who deal in large blocks of stock. The rates charged institutional investors have declined drastically, from an average of 25 cents a share in 1975 to only a few cents a share for exchange-listed stocks. Institutional investors also receive a better deal when trading in OTC stocks.

Electronic Trading and the Internet

Obviously, we are now in the age of electronic trading. In addition to contacting brokerage firms the traditional way by phone, many investors now trade with dedicated software using their personal computer. In 1992, E*TRADE (and **E*TRADE Canada**) became the first brokerage service to offer on-line trading, and by December 2003, Canadian investors could make equity trades for as low as $6.99. As one would expect, other firms rushed to offer their services on the Internet, and investors now have a wide variety of brokerage firms to choose from. Real-World Returns 5-1 provides a report card for 14 on-line brokerages surveyed by *The Globe and Mail* in October 2007.

While discount brokerages offer on-line trading, full-service firms do not. Such firms do not want to give up their higher commissions, nor break the direct link between broker and client that currently exists. Full-service brokers claim that regardless of the information investors can obtain on the Internet, "Technology can't replace advice."

Individual investors now have three choices when executing trades:

1. Full-service brokers: example, BMO Nesbitt Burns
2. Large discount brokers: example, TD Waterhouse (formerly TD Greenline)
3. Internet discount brokers: example, E*TRADE Canada.

Brokerage costs have changed rapidly because of competition and the rise of the Internet. The following example is only one illustration, and fees are continually changing. Investors need to check out various brokers themselves for brokerage and other costs and the services provided.

REAL-WORLD RETURNS 5-1

Rating Canada's On-line Brokerages

Investors have the on-line brokerage business right where they want it.

To start with, stock-trading commissions are plunging. After years of being stuck in the $24-to-$29 range, more and more brokers are charging just under $10 as long as your accounts have at least $50,000 to $100,000 in total assets. At the same time, these firms are giving clients more for their money with better tools for finding investments and managing their accounts.

(continued)

REAL-WORLD RETURNS 5-1 *continued*

Pay less, get more. The brokers that best followed this line are the front-runners in the 2007–08 version of *The Globe and Mail's* annual ranking of on-line brokers. Qtrade Investor takes top honours for the second year in a row after chopping commissions and revamping its research offerings. E*Trade Canada, TD Waterhouse, BMO InvestorLine and Credential Direct filled out the other top spots.

A total of 14 brokers were included in this year's ranking, including a pair of newcomers called Questrade and TradeFreedom. As always in this ranking, the focus is strictly on on-line services and the target audience is the mainstream investor who has a registered retirement account and is interested in more than stocks.

Costs and fees are a key criterion in this year's ranking because investors rate it as their top concern when choosing a broker. That bit of intelligence comes from an on-line survey we ran on *Globe and Mail* websites last month in which participants were asked to choose what issue matters most to them in choosing an on-line broker. The other rating criteria are the following.

Customer satisfaction: Based on three questions in our on-line survey about customer perceptions of their broker.

Tools and research: An evaluation of resources for choosing securities and also for broader financial planning matters.

Website utility: Does a broker's website help you save time and effort in managing your money?

Website security: A guarantee that clients won't lose money if a hacker accesses their account gets a broker an easy five points in this survey.

Trading: Focuses mainly on how efficient a broker's stock-trading platform is; bonds and funds are also considered.

Trading scores were tweaked slightly to address one of the most contentious issues for on-line brokerage customers today: the treatment of US cash in registered retirement accounts. The background here is that on-line brokers don't yet have computer systems capable of allowing clients to hold US cash in registered accounts. Net result: investors can be dinged on foreign exchange fees.

To help alleviate this problem, a few brokers allow US cash to be channelled in and out of US-dollar money market funds without any currency conversion.

The 14 players in the 2007/2008 *Globe and Mail* ranking of on-line brokers were rated in seven different categories. Here's how they did.

How They Rank

Rank	Broker	Fees & Commisions (/25)	Trading (/25)	Tools & research (/20)	Customer satisfaction (/10)	Website/ account info (/10)	Investment selection (/5)	Security (/5)	Total (/100)
1	Qtrade Investor	19	19	16	10	8.5	4	5	81.5
2	E*Trade Canada	23.5	20	14.5	6.4	6.5	3	5	78.9
3	TD Waterhouse	17.5	17	17	7.2	4.8	4	5	72.5
4	BMO InvestorLine	17.5	17.5	14	4.8	9.8	3.5	5	72.1
5	Credential Direct	16	14	15	8.8	8.8	2.5	5	70.1
6	RBC Direct Investing	17.5	14.5	17	2.8	5.3	3	5	65.1
7	ScotiaMcLeod Direct Investing	11	18.5	15	3.6	4.8	1.5	5	59.4
8	Questrade	23.5	13	8	10	2.8	1	0	58.3
9	TradeFreedom	22	15	6	6.4	5	1.5	0	55.9
10	Disnat	11	16	11.5	6	6	3	0	53.5
11	CIBC Investor's Edge	14.5	13.5	13	5.2	4.3	3	0	53.5
12	National Bank Direct Investing	10.5	13	13	2.4	4.3	3	5	51.2
13	HSBC InvestDirect	11.5	16	13	2.8	4	2.5	0	49.8
14	eNorthern	11.5	12	3	8	3	1	0	38.5

(continued)

REAL-WORLD RETURNS 5-1 *continued*

1. Qtrade Investor

qtrade.ca

Ownership: Privately held

Comments

Qtrade is what you might end up with if you built an on-line brokerage by adopting the best features and practices of all the competitors in the sector. The net result is a low-cost broker that does things right on matters big and small. Qtrade has lots of stock research, it's much better than most at showing you how your portfolio is doing, it removes any worries about hackers getting into your account with a security guarantee and it allows clients trading US stocks to stash their cash in US-dollar money market funds. Last word: Qtrade's customers seem to love the service.

2. E*Trade Canada

canada.etrade.com

Ownership: E*Trade Financial Corp.

Comments

E*Trade used to fancy itself a service for aggressive traders, and it still puts a lot of importance in this market. But in many ways, E*Trade is the friend of the mainstream investor who only trades occasionally, and even beginners. You can trade for $9.99 flat if you have $50,000 in assets with the firm or make at least 30 trades per quarter; otherwise, the minimum charge is a reasonable $19.99. There are no fees of any kind for registered accounts and all funds are commission-free. Looking for a high-interest savings account to park some cash? E*Trade's Cash Optimizer Investment Account now pays an impressive 4.15 percent.

3. TD Waterhouse

tdwaterhouse.ca

Ownership: Toronto-Dominion Bank

Comments

After years of clinging to its $29 minimum commission, TD became a cost-cutting leader among bank-owned firms last month by introducing stock trades for a flat $9.99 if you have $100,000 in any number of accounts with the firm (with less you pay $29). Couple this price cut with TD's solid trading platform and you have a strong package. What would make it better is more attention to small things like showing clients how their portfolios are doing. Note: TD's in the minority of brokers that let clients direct cash from US stock trades into US-dollar money market funds without conversion fees.

4. BMO InvestorLine

bmoinvestorline.com

Ownership: Bank of Montreal

Comments

BMO has been among the top-ranked brokers since this survey began in 1999 and the reason is that it has a unique vision of helping clients invest successfully, even while not providing any advice. Just recently, a feature called MyLink has been introduced to send reminders to clients about developments they need to attend to in their portfolios. BMO is also a leader in account performance reporting and in helping clients build portfolios of mutual funds and exchange-traded funds to suit their needs. BMO is improving on costs now that it has announced it will emulate TD's commission cut starting Nov. 1.

(continued)

REAL-WORLD RETURNS 5-1 *continued*

5. **Credential Direct**
credentialdirect.com
Ownership: The credit union movement

Comments

The credit union bloodline is evident in Credential through its user-friendly website, reasonable fees and well-satisfied clients. It's also apparent in the sometimes bland look of Credential's website and its lack of resources and tools that would get sophisticated investors excited. So big deal. This is a broker that offers an unflashy but well-rounded service ideal for the masses. Much like credit unions.

6. **RBC Direct Investing**
rbcdirectinvesting.com
Owner: Royal Bank of Canada

Comments

A broker on the rise, even if it's still in the middle of the pack. RBC is building a premier stock research centre, and it has introduced a new low-fee class of mutual fund in the RBC family for do-it-yourself investors. Some day, all brokers will sell funds this way. RBC's weak spot is corner-cutting in areas such as helping clients track their personal returns. On the other hand, RBC is addressing its high-cost status by matching TD's commission deal as of Dec. 22.

7. **ScotiaMcLeod Direct Investing**
Scotiamcleoddirect.com
Owner: Bank of Nova Scotia

Comments

SMDI is out of step on stock-trading commissions, it still doesn't offer on-line bond trading (it says its clients aren't interested) and its website, long a sore spot in this ranking, remains as navigationally impaired as ever. The reason why you shouldn't write off SMDI is that it does as good a job as anyone at feeding clients a bracing diet of analyst research on stocks, bonds and funds. If you're looking for guidance in selecting investments, SMDI delivers.

8. **Disnat**
disnat.com
Owner: Groupe Desjardins

Comments

Canada's oldest discount broker—Disnat dates back to 1982, long before the Internet let brokers go on-line—may well be the most improved as well. Disnat used to be dismal—so neglected was this broker that using its website was like an archeological expedition back to the Internet's prehistoric days. Today, Disnat is revitalized with improved stock research tools, on-line bond trading and a much crisper website. Still missing are competitive stock-trading commissions and proper tools for monitoring your account. A security guarantee would be nice, too.

9. **CIBC Investor's Edge**
investorsedge.cibc.com
Owner: Canadian Imperial Bank of Commerce

Comments

There's one flash of originality at this otherwise middling broker. Through a deal called Edge Advantage, clients can pay a flat $395 a year for 50 on-line trades of any type, which works out to $7.90 a crack. After that, you pay $6.95 for any additional trades. The question is whether an investor who trades enough to be interested in this deal would be happy with

(continued)

REAL-WORLD RETURNS 5-1 *continued*

Investor's Edge. The answer is yes, if you plan to take advantage of CIBC's offering of on-line bonds and guaranteed investment certificates and its reservoir of stock research from CIBC World Markets.

10. National Bank Direct Brokerage
nbdb.ca
Owner: National Bank of Canada

Comments

The quintessential "nothing special but still adequate" on-line broker. The rudiments are here—including plenty of stock market and mutual fund research, some good portfolio planning and monitoring tools and an on-line bond trading platform that differs from most other bank-owned firms in offering high-yield, speculative bonds. What would really help are lower commissions. Active traders get attractive rates, but regular clients pay a minimum of $28.95.

11. HSBC InvestDirect
investdirect.hsbc.ca
Owner: HSBC Group

Comments

E*Trade's US parent introduced on-line trading on six global stock markets. Given HSBC's status as one of the most global banks, this is exactly the kind of service that HSBC InvestDirect should be offering, but isn't. There's an attempt to play up the global angle, but there's on-line access only to the Hong Kong Stock Exchange and telephone trades are required for other global markets. Blah is the word to describe InvestDirect's service for investors focusing on Canada and the US market, although it is one of the better ones for helping clients avoid currency costs.

12. enorthern
enorthern.com
Owner: Northern Securities

Comments

A skeletal service where the main attraction is a minimum stock-trading commission of $24. That used to be cheap.

13. Questrade
Questrade.com
Owner: Privately held

Comments

A service for active traders that is reaching out to mainstream investors with commissions as low as $4.95, no matter how often you trade or how big your account is. The website is as basic as they come, but a planned redesign should help.

14. TradeFreedom
Tradefreedom.com
Owner: Bank of Nova Scotia

Comments

Another service for active traders, this one offering mainstream investors a deal where they can trade for $9.95 on orders of up to 1,000 shares. Low commissions are the main story here, and they undercut Scotiabank's SMDI by a big margin. How long will that last?

Source: *The Globe and Mail's* On-Line Broker Survey, retrieved from http://gold.globeinvestor.com, March 25, 2008. © *The Globe and Mail*.

Investing without a Broker

Hundreds of North American companies now offer **dividend reinvestment plans (DRIPs)**. There are over 60 in Canada. For investors, the company uses the dividends paid on shares owned by investors enrolled in these plans to purchase more of the company's shares, and there is usually no brokerage or administrative fees. One of the advantages of such plans is dollar cost averaging, whereby more shares are purchased when the stock price is low than when it is high. In addition, some of the plans (approximately 30 percent of the Canadian plans) offer a 3 to 5 percent discount for share purchases.[2]

In order to be in a company's dividend reinvestment plan, investors buy the stock through their brokers, although some companies do sell directly to individuals. On becoming shareholders, investors can join the dividend reinvestment program and invest additional cash at specified intervals. DRIPs are starting to resemble brokerage accounts. Investors can purchase additional shares by having money withdrawn from bank accounts periodically, and shares can even be redeemed by phone at many companies.

It is possible to invest in the market without a stockbroker or a brokerage account in the traditional sense. As an outgrowth of their dividend reinvestment plans, a number of companies now offer no-load stock purchase programs to first-time investors. By early 2008, close to half of all Canadian companies offering DRIPs also offered direct stock purchase programs.

Dividend Reinvestment Plans (DRIPs)
Plans offered by a company that allow shareholders to reinvest dividends to purchase additional shares of stock at no additional cost.

EXAMPLE 5-1: NATIONAL BANK

National Bank permits investors to buy, each quarter, up to $5,000 worth of their common or preferred stock from the company itself by reinvesting their cash dividend, with no brokerage commissions or administrative charges. Some other well-known Canadian companies offering similar plans in 2008 included Aliant, CIBC, Magna, and Imperial Oil Company.

Investors make their initial purchase of stock directly from the company for purchase fees ranging from zero to about 7 cents a share. The price paid is normally based on the closing price of the stock on designated dates, and no limit orders are allowed. The companies selling stock by this method view it as a way to raise capital without underwriting fees and as a way to build goodwill with investors.

CHECK YOUR UNDERSTANDING

5-1. On-line trading has made investing easier and cheaper, as it has been accompanied by reduced commissions. A more significant reduction in commission fees actually occurred well before the advent of the Internet, however. What prompted this fee reduction?

5-2. State two reasons why an investor establishing a brokerage account might prefer a wrap account to the more traditional asset management account.

HOW ORDERS WORK

Orders on the Organized Exchanges

learning objective 3
Outline how orders to buy and sell securities are executed.

The TSX introduced the world's first computer-assisted trading system (CATS) in 1977, and most exchanges in the world have followed in its footsteps. On April 23, 1997, the TSX closed all floor trading, and all TSX and TSX Venture Exchange trades are now handled electronically. The trading system consists of a central computer terminal that links traders from licensed traders with the TSX. The central terminal processes, records, and monitors all trades.

[2]Stingy Investor website: www.ndir.com.

An order from an investor for 100 shares of **Bombardier** might be handled as follows: The investor phones his or her broker and asks how Bombardier is doing. The broker has immediate access to information regarding the last trade for Bombardier, as well as other information such as the high and low for the day and the number of shares traded.

Assuming that the investor is willing to pay the last trade price or a price close to that, the broker can be instructed to buy 100 shares of Bombardier "at the market." For example, if the last trade price was $5.55 and the investor placed a market order for 100 shares of Bombardier, the order will be transmitted to the firm's registered trader who is responsible for trading in that stock (both for customers and on the member firm's behalf). The purchase order will then be executed immediately, at the best available ask price, which could be $5.55, but might be higher, at $5.60. Confirmation of the transaction details will be sent immediately to the brokerage firm, which will then convey the information to the client.

Had the investor indicated a specific price (the bid price) that he or she was willing to pay for the 100 shares of Bombardier, the order would be considered a limit order (discussed below). Under these circumstances, the limit order would be executed immediately if the bid price was at or above existing ask prices for Bombardier. However, if the bid price is below the existing ask prices, it would be included in the limit order book, and would only be executed when potential sellers were willing to accept that price. Limit orders are executed in order of price. For example, a limit purchase order with a bid of $35 is filled before one with a bid of $34.50, while a limit sell order with an ask price of $36 is filled before one with an ask price of $36.50.

As mentioned in Chapter 4, the NYSE has resisted the move to complete trading automation. The NYSE continues to carry on trading activity on the floor of the exchange using its specialist system, which is described in Appendix 5A. It is often called an agency auction market because agents represent the public at an auction where the interactions of buyers and sellers determine the price of stocks traded on the NYSE.

Orders in the Over-the-Counter Market

Traditionally, market makers (dealers) in the OTC market arrive at the prices of securities by both negotiating with customers specifically and making competitive bids. They match the forces of supply and demand, with each market maker making a market in certain securities. They do this by standing ready to buy a particular security from a seller or to sell it to a buyer. Dealers quote bid and ask prices for each security; the **bid price** is the highest price offered by the dealer, and the **ask price** is the lowest price at which the dealer is willing to sell. The dealer profits from the spread between these two prices. Market makers are required to provide continuous bid and ask quotations throughout the trading day, and there may be more than one market maker for any particular stock.

Types of Orders

Investors can buy or sell stocks in "board lots" ("round lots" in the United States) or "odd lots," or a combination of both. Canadian exchanges define board lots as orders in multiples of 100 shares in most cases. A trade for less than 100 shares is considered to be an odd lot. Thus, an order for 356 shares would be for three board lots and one odd lot of 56 shares.

Investors use three basic types of orders: market orders, limit orders, and stop orders.

1. **Market orders**, the most common type of order, instruct the broker to buy or sell the securities immediately at the best price available. As a representative of the buyer or seller, it is incumbent upon the broker to obtain the best price possible. A market order ensures that the transaction will be carried out, but the exact price at which it will occur is not known until its execution and subsequent confirmation to the customer.

2. **Limit orders** specify a particular price to be met or bettered. They may result in the customer obtaining a better price than with a market order or in no purchase or sale occurring because the market price never reaches the specified limit. The purchase or sale will occur only if the broker obtains

Bid Price

The price at which the specialist or dealer offers to buy shares.

Ask Price

The price at which the specialist or dealer offers to sell shares.

Market Order

An order to buy or sell at the best price when the order reaches the trading floor.

Limit Order

An order that is executed only if the buyer (seller) obtains the stated bid (ask) price.

that price or betters it (lower for a purchase, higher for a sale). Limit orders can be tried immediately or left with the broker for a specific time or indefinitely. In turn, the broker leaves the order with the specialist, who enters it in the limit book.

EXAMPLE: Assume the current market price of a stock is $50. An investor might enter a buy limit order at $47; if the stock declines in price to $47, this limit order, which is on the specialist's book, will then be executed. Similarly, another investor might enter a sell limit order for this stock at $55; if the price of this stock rises to $55, this investor's shares will be sold.

3. **Stop orders** specify a certain price at which a market order takes effect. For example, a stop order to sell at $50 becomes a market order to sell as soon as the market price reaches (or declines to) $50. However, the order may not be filled exactly at $50 because the closest price at which the stock trades may be $49⅞. The exact price specified in the stop order is therefore not guaranteed and may not be realized.

Stop Order
An order specifying a certain price at which a market order takes effect.

EXAMPLE 1: A sell stop order can be used to protect a profit in the case of a price decline. Assume, for example, that a stock bought at $32 currently trades at $50. The investor does not want to limit additional gains, but may wish to protect against a price decline. To lock in most of the profit, a sell stop order could be placed at $47.

EXAMPLE 2: A buy order could be used to protect a profit from a short sale. Assume an investor sold short at $50, and the current market price of the stock is $32. A buy stop order placed at, say, $36 would protect most of the profit from the short sale.

Because market orders specify the buying or selling of a certain number of shares at the best price available, investors are often advised to enter limit orders that name a particular price whenever possible in order to avoid the range of prices that may result from a market order. Investors can enter limit orders as day orders, which are effective for only one day.[3] Alternatively, they may enter good-until-cancelled (GTC) orders or open orders, which remain in effect unless cancelled or renewed.[4] "Good through" orders are good for a specified number of days and then are automatically cancelled if unfilled. There is no guarantee that all orders will be filled at a particular price limit when that price is reached because orders are filled in a sequence determined by the rules of the various exchanges.

Limit orders can be filled in whole or in part until completed (involving more than one trading day) in several ways. All or none (AON) orders are only executed if the total number of shares specified in the order can be obtained or sold, and are often referred to as "fill or kill" orders. An order may be given under this heading that states the minimum number of shares that is acceptable to the client. The advantage of this type of order is that it prevents accumulation of odd lots, which can be more expensive to trade and/or less marketable since most investors prefer to purchase shares in board lots. Any part orders are the opposite of AON orders, and may be more costly to execute since they may entail the purchase of all stock in odd, broken, or board lots.

Stop orders are used to buy and sell after a stock reaches a certain price level. A buy stop order is placed above the current market price, while a sell stop order is placed below the current price. Stop loss orders are orders to sell (as market orders) if the price drops below a certain level. They are used to limit losses on long positions. Stop buy orders are the opposite of stop loss orders. A market buy order is generated if the price rises above a certain level to limit losses on short positions.

Clearing Procedures

Clients who do not wish to or are unable to obtain credit from the securities firm open cash accounts and are expected to make full payment for purchases by the settlement date. The settlement date is the same day for government T-bills; two business days after for other Government of Canada direct liabilities and guarantees up to three years; and three business days after for all other securities

---

[3]A market order remains in effect only for the day.
[4]Many firms limit GTC orders for a specified time period such as 30, 60, or 90 days.

(including long-term government bonds and common shares). On the settlement date, the customer becomes the legal owner of any securities bought (or gives them up if sold) and must settle with the brokerage firm by that time.[5]

Street Name

When customers' securities are held by a brokerage firm in its own name.

Most customers allow their brokerage firm to keep their securities in a **street name**—that is, the name of the brokerage firm. If the certificate is in registered form, the seller must properly endorse and deliver it. Customers receive monthly statements showing the position of their accounts in cash, securities held, any funds borrowed from the broker, and so on.

Brokerage houses must settle all transactions with the other party to the transaction, who may be another brokerage house, a market specialist, or market maker. A clearing house facilitates this process by taking the records of all transactions made by its members during a day, verifying both sides of the trades, and netting out the securities and money due or to be paid each member. Members of clearing houses include brokerage houses, banks, and others involved with securities. Once the transaction is completed on the floor (or electronically), the details of the trade are reported to the exchange, and the buying and selling firms are provided with specific details of the trade such as price, time, and the identity of the other party. The firms phone their clients to confirm the transaction and then mail written confirmation to them.

Today, in Canada, most stock and bond certificates are cleared through the Canadian Depository for Securities (CDS). The CDS is a clearing corporation that electronically settles all transactions between members on a daily basis without physically moving the certificates. When an investment dealer trades from its own account, the trade occurs at current market value as determined by the exchange. There are detailed regulations that licensed traders must observe to avoid potential conflicts of interest. In the United States, the National Securities Clearing Corporation operates a central clearing house for trades on the New York and American stock exchanges and in the OTC markets.

Use of stock certificates as part of the settlement process is dying out in both Canada and the United States, since computers handle most transactions. Members (brokers and dealers) who own certificates (in street name) deposit them in an account and can then deliver securities to each other in the form of a bookkeeping entry. This book-entry system, as opposed to the actual physical possession of securities in either registered or "bearer" form, is essential to minimize the tremendous amount of paperwork that would otherwise occur with stock certificates. Such a system also reduces the potential for securities to be lost or stolen.

CHECK YOUR UNDERSTANDING

5-3. Suppose you purchased some shares in a company for $40 each. The stock has now increased in price to $60. While you think the price may go higher (hence you are unwilling to sell the shares right now), you want to protect most of your gain if the price were to fall. What type of order could you place to accomplish this?

5-4. How do market makers or dealers in the OTC market earn a profit, regardless of what happens to the price of the stock they are trading?

INVESTOR PROTECTION IN THE SECURITIES MARKETS

learning objective 4
Discuss the regulation of the Canadian securities industry.

Investors should be concerned that securities markets are properly regulated for their protection. Our financial system depends heavily on confidence in that system. In the late nineteenth and early twentieth centuries, significant abuses in securities trading did occur; at the same time there was a lack of information disclosure, and trading procedures were not always sound. The market crash in

---

[5]The purchaser of securities usually will not be able to take physical delivery of the securities on the settlement date because they will not be available by then.

1929 and the Great Depression served as catalysts for reforms that effectively began in the 1930s. As mentioned in Chapters 1 and 2, debacles such as the Enron and WorldCom scandals have led to a preoccupation with investor protection, and many regulatory changes have occurred.

Investor protection can be divided into government regulation, at the federal and provincial level, and self-regulation by the industry. Real-World Returns 5-2 discusses a new organization that has been organized to help protect small investors.

REAL-WORLD RETURNS 5-2

Protection for Small Investors

There's almost no job more mystifying and intimidating than going after an investment professional who lost your money through bad or unscrupulous advice.

Lawyers can help, but they're expensive and it's not easy to find one conversant in securities law. Solution: Join the Small Investor Protection Association (SIPA) and take advantage of the free lawyer referral service it set up last month for aggrieved members.

For close to a decade, SIPA has quietly worked to organize individual investors and help them pursue complaints against the financial industry. A few years ago, the non-profit group set up an information-sharing database that helps link up members with complaints against the same adviser.

The lawyer referral service originates in SIPA founder Stan Buell's belief that investors should get legal advice before going after an adviser to recover losses. "The idea is for our members to go in and sit down with a lawyer, or talk to him on the telephone, and get some advice on what their options are," Mr. Buell said.

The options in most cases are these:

Try and get the firm to fix the problem: This may work in egregious cases of investor abuse, but you're just as likely to get the runaround.

Try an ombudsman: Clients of bank-owned investment firms should try the bank's own ombudsman office; for other firms, and if the bank ombudsman doesn't see things your way, there's the Ombudsman for Banking Services and Investments (OBSI).

Try regulators: The Investment Dealers Association of Canada, Mutual Fund Dealers Association of Canada and provincial securities commissions will look into whether an adviser has broken the rules, but they won't try to get your money back.

Try arbitration: The IDA offers an arbitration plan for claims of less than $100,000 and member firms must participate if a client initiates action.

Try legal action: A growing number of lawyers are specializing in representing investors trying to recover losses.

Mr. Buell believes legal action is the best way, although the heavy costs make it prohibitively expensive for some people. Even if you don't end up suing, it's still worth consulting a lawyer before trying to get redress for a serious loss.

"You need to know what you're going to be up against and what the process is," Mr. Buell said. "If you go to see your adviser with a complaint, he'll say, 'Oh, yeah, we'll get that sorted out' and suddenly you're being led down the garden path. Suddenly, you discover you've gone a year and you're no further ahead."

One of the most important matters a lawyer will discuss has to do with a limitation period in Ontario and some other provinces that blocks you from suing if two years or more have gone by since you suffered the loss prompting your legal action. The relevance of these limitation periods is that pursuing a complaint against a broker through regular channels can easily take more than two years, Mr. Buell said.

(continued)

REAL-WORLD RETURNS 5-2 *continued*

There are five lawyers with experience in securities litigation on the SIPA referral roster and they all have agreed to work on a pro bono basis, which means they're donating the time. Mr. Buell said it's possible that the lawyers will pick up business if SIPA members choose them to pursue a legal case. All the lawyers are located in Toronto or Southern Ontario, but Mr. Buell said members across the country can easily deal with them by phone.

To see one of the lawyers, SIPA members have to submit a short summary of their case along with some supporting documents. If the case is legitimate, the information is then forwarded to the lawyer.

SIPA membership costs $20 a year, which is a very small investment to make if you've run into trouble with an adviser. In addition to the information-sharing and lawyer-referral services, SIPA maintains a list of 25 or so lawyers across the country who handle investor cases. These lawyers are not SIPA-endorsed, but they have been recommended by the group's members.

Mr. Buell set up SIPA after a costly run-in with a rogue broker in the 1980s and has been fighting ever since to advance the cause of investor protection. Lately, he's become a touch more optimistic that regulators are starting to take investor concerns seriously. Specifically, he mentioned the IDA's proposals that would give member firms five business days to acknowledge a client complaint and 90 days to issue a final decision.

Long delays are but one of the obstacles to getting your money back when you've been victimized by a bad adviser. For a full list of these complications, and some ideas for surmounting them, consult one of SIPA's lawyers.

The goods on SIPA

Full Name: Small Investor Protection Association
Mission: Advocate for better investor protection and act as a voice for small investors
Founded: 1998
Home Base: Markham, Ont.
Membership cost: $20 a year
Members: 600, up from 22 at the beginning
Services: Assists individuals trying to recoup money lost due to bad investment advice
Website: sipa.ca

Source: Carrick, Rob, "Protection for small investors just got a bit stronger," Globeinvestor.com. Retrieved from www.globeinvestor.com, March 25, 2008.

The Canadian Regulatory Environment

The Office of the Superintendent of Financial Institutions was established in 1987 by legislation that amalgamated the Department of Insurance and the Office of the Inspector General of Banks. It regulates and supervises banks, insurance, trust, loan and investment companies, and cooperative credit associations that are chartered federally. It also supervises over 900 federally regulated pension plans. However, it does not regulate the Canadian securities industry.

The 1987 legislation also established the Financial Supervisory Committee, which is composed of the superintendent (the committee chair), the governor of the Bank of Canada, the deputy minister of finance, and the chairman of the Canada Deposit Insurance Corporation (CDIC). Its purpose is to simplify the confidential exchange of information among its members on all matters relating to supervising financial institutions.

Figure 5-1 provides an overview of the regulatory environment in the Canadian securities industry, discussed below.

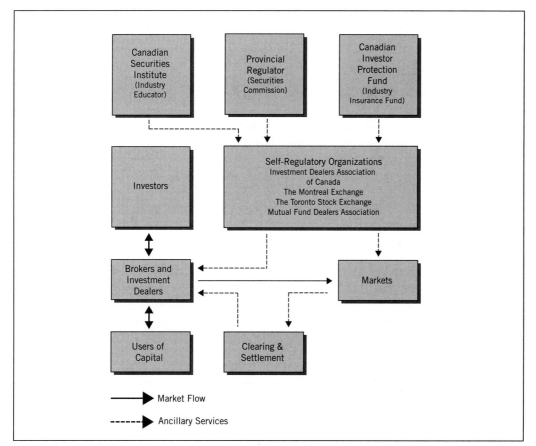

Figure 5-1
Securities Industry
Flowchart

Source: *Canadian Securities Course Textbook* (Toronto: Canadian Securities Institute, Fall 2001); pp. 1–2.
© Fall 2001 Canadian Securities Institute. Modified version. Reprinted with permission.

The Provincial Regulators

Canada has no central federal regulatory agency for the securities industry, unlike the Securities and Exchange Commission (SEC) in the United States. (US regulators are discussed in Appendix 5B.) This is because regulation of the securities business is a provincial responsibility that is delegated to securities commissions in most provinces and is handled by appointed securities administrators in others. The provincial regulators work closely with the Canadian Investor Protection Fund and self-regulatory organizations to maintain high standards.

The Canadian Securities Administrators (CSA), a group representing the 13 provincial and territorial securities regulators, has proposed the adoption of a common "platform" of rules for the investment industry to follow. Many involved parties, including the Minister of Finance, as well as spokespeople for the TSX Group and for the CFA Institute's Canadian Advocacy Committee, recommend the adoption of a "national" securities regulator. Only time will tell how this plays out.

Due to the dominance of the TSX for Canadian stock trading activity, the Ontario Securities Commission (OSC) is one provincial regulatory body of particular importance. The OSC's mandate is to

- protect investors from unfair, improper, or fraudulent practices

- foster fair and efficient capital markets

- maintain public and investor confidence in the integrity of those markets

Self-Regulatory Organizations (SROs)

Organizations in the Canadian securities industry that regulate their own activities. They include the Investment Industry Regulatory Organization of Canada (IIROC), TSX, MX, and the MFDA.

Canadian Investor Protection Fund (CIPF)

A fund established by the Canadian stock exchanges and other organizations to protect investors in the event of the insolvency of any of its members.

Investment Industry Regulatory Organization of Canada (IIROC)

The Canadian investment industry's national self-regulatory organization, which oversees all investment dealers and trading activity on debt and equity marketplaces in Canada.

Part of their responsibility in this context is the oversight of the **self-regulatory organizations (SROs)** that are discussed next.[6]

Canadian Investor Protection Fund (CIPF)

The **Canadian Investor Protection Fund (CIPF)** was established to protect investors in the event of insolvency of a member of any of the sponsoring self-regulatory organizations (SROs), which include the Investment Industry Regulatory Organization of Canada (IIROC) TSX, MX, TSX Venture Exchange, and Mutual Fund Dealers' Association (MFDA). The fund is administered by a nine-member board of governors, which includes one representative from each of the SROs, and governors representing the general investing public. The president and chief executive officer of the fund is also a governor.

The role of this fund is to anticipate and solve financial difficulties of licensed traders in order to minimize the risk of insolvency, and to attempt to bring about an orderly wind-down of a business if necessary. Fund assets are funded by contributions from the securities industry, as well as an operating line that is provided by a chartered bank.

From the moment an investor becomes a customer of any of the SROs, the accounts are automatically covered by the fund. The fund covers separate accounts for individuals, provided they are not held for the same purpose. For example, the accounts of a customer maintaining two personal holding corporation accounts would be combined into one. The coverage limit is $1 million for losses related to securities holdings and cash balances combined. The fund does not cover losses that result from changing market values or from the bankruptcy of an issuer of a security or deposit instrument held in your account. It also rejects claims from parties that are not dealing at arm's length with the insolvent firm or those whose dealings contributed to the insolvency.

Self-Regulatory Organizations (SROs)

SROs deal with member regulation, listing requirements, and trading regulation.

The **Investment Industry Regulatory Organization of Canada (IIROC) (formed through the merger of the Investment Dealers' Association of Canada and Market Regulation Services Inc.)** is the Canadian investment industry's national self-regulatory organization. Its mission is to "set high quality regulatory and investment industry standards, protect investors and strengthen market integrity while maintaining efficient and competitive capital markets." These dual roles as both industry regulator and trade association are complementary.

The responsibilities of the IIROC include monitoring licensed traders for capital adequacy and business conduct, as well as regulating the qualifying and registration process of these firms. As Canada's only national SRO, it has the additional responsibility of ensuring that national policies and rules reflect the various perspectives of people in all parts of the country. In its efforts to foster more efficient capital markets, the IIROC serves as a market regulator by

1. Playing a key role in formulating policies and standards for primary debt and equity markets

2. Monitoring activities of licensed traders, and developing trading and sales practices

The IIROC also serves as an international representative and as a public policy advocate by striving to provide accurate information and practical advice to government agencies on matters related to the securities industry.

The IIROC strives to ensure the integrity of the marketplace and protection of investors. This requires that licensed traders maintain financial standards and conduct their business within appropriate guidelines. The IIROC conducts financial compliance reviews as well as business conduct compliance reviews.

---

[6]OSC website: www.osc.gov.on.ca.

The Canadian Securities Institute (CSI)

The **Canadian Securities Institute (CSI)** was created in 1970 as the national educator of the Canadian securities industry. Completion of CSI courses is mandatory to meet the requirements for various registration categories.

Canadian Securities Institute (CSI)
The national educational body of the Canadian securities industry.

CHECK YOUR UNDERSTANDING

5-5. If an investor purchases shares of a company that subsequently goes bankrupt (resulting in a total loss of the investment), the Canadian Investor Protection Fund (CIPF) will cover the loss, up to $1 million. Do you agree or disagree?

5-6. What reasons might be used to support the adoption of a national securities regulator in Canada? Why do some parties oppose such a move?

MARGIN

As previously noted, accounts at brokerage houses can be either cash accounts or margin accounts. Opening a margin account requires some deposit of cash or securities such as T-bills, bonds, or other equity securities. With a margin account, the customer can pay part of the total amount due and borrow the remainder from the broker, who charges the customer the "margin interest rate." The rate charged to the customer is usually based on the prime lending rate plus a percentage added on by the brokerage firm.[7] Investment firms are allowed the use of customers' free credit balances but must give them written notice to this effect.

A margin account can be used to purchase additional securities by leveraging the value of the eligible shares to buy more. They also permit investors to borrow money from a brokerage account for personal purposes, at the margin interest rate, which is comparable to a bank's prime rate.

The **margin** is that part of the total value of a security transaction that a customer must pay to initiate the transaction; that is, the part that cannot be borrowed from the broker. Cash has 100 percent loan value, which means that $100,000 in cash deposits constitutes a $100,000 margin. Other assets such as stock securities may have 50 percent (or lower) loan value because of potential fluctuations in their market value. This means you would have to deposit $200,000 (market value) of common stocks to satisfy a $100,000 margin requirement.

Margin requirements for stocks traded in Canada with exchange and licensed traders range from 30 percent to 100 percent, depending on the price at which the stock is selling.[8] The margin requirements increase as the stock price decreases, reflecting the additional risk associated with lower-priced stocks. The word margin refers to the amount of funds the investor must personally provide in a margin account, with the balance being provided by the investment dealer in the form of a loan. Maximum loan values by exchange and IIROC members for long positions in securities other than bonds and debentures, expressed as maximum percentages of market value, are provided in Table 5-1.

Initial margin requirements for stocks trading in the US have historically ranged between 40 and 100 percent, with a current level of 50 percent since 1974.[9]

learning objective 5
Explain the importance of margin trading and short selling to investors.

Margin
The part of the total value of a sale of securities that a customer must pay to initiate the transaction with the other part being borrowed from the broker.

---

[7]The prime lending rate is the rate at which banks will lend short-term funds to their best customers. It is usually set at a rate slightly above the bank rate, which is the rate the Bank of Canada lends short-term funds to the chartered banks.

[8]Securities firms can demand more initial margin than required by the SROs if they wish.

[9]In addition, US margin purchases require investors to sustain a "maintenance margin," below which the actual margin cannot go. Maintenance margin requirements for NYSE firms require an investor to maintain equity of 25 percent of the market value of any securities held (and in practice brokers usually require 30 percent or more) on long positions.

Table 5-1

Canadian Margin Requirements

On listed securities selling:	Maximum Loan Values
Securities eligible for reduced margin	70% of market value
At $2.00 and over	50% of market value
At $1.75 to $1.99	40% of market value
At $1.50 to $1.74	20% of market value
Under $1.50	No loan value

Figure 5-2 describes the eligibility criteria to be considered "eligible for special margin."

Figure 5-2
List of Securities Eligible
for Reduced Margin

Eligibility Criteria

For the selection of securities eligible for a reduced margin rate, the securities must meet the following criteria.

General Inclusion Requirements

Price volatility measures
- Calculated price volatility margin interval <= 25%
- Market value per share >=$2.00 per share

Liquidity measures
- Dollar value of public float greater than $50 million
- Average daily trade volume for each month in the quarter >= 10,000 shares per day for at least two out of the three months in the quarter

  OR
- An equivalent average daily traded value amount for each month in the quarter ended >= $500,000 per day [to accommodate high price securities]

Listing requirements
- Listed on a Canadian exchange for six months
  OR
- Listed on a Canadian exchange less than six months, with:
  - Market value per share >= $5.00 per share
  - Dollar value of public float greater than $500 million and
  - In the discretion of IDA staff, the issuer company is in an industry sector known for low price volatility

Other Inclusion Requirements
- A new security listing resulting from an issuer reorganization that:
  - is substantially the same as a previous security listing,
  - has a combined calculated price volatility margin interval for the old and the new listings of <=25%, and
  - meets all the other General Inclusion Requirements for ongoing listings.

For the purposes of this requirement, the term "substantially the same" means a new security listing that represents between 80% and 120% of the public float of a previous security listing.

- A Canada/United States inter-listed security against which options issued by The Options Clearing Corporation are traded
- A security that is senior to or convertible into a security that meets the General Inclusion Requirements or Other Inclusion Requirements above

Source: "List of Securities Eligible for Special Margin," The Investment Dealers Association of Canada December 2003. Retrieved from www.iiroc.ca.

EXAMPLE 5-2: MEETING MARGIN REQUIREMENT

If the margin requirement is 30 percent on a $10,000 transaction (100 shares at $100 per share), the customer must put up $3,000, borrowing $7,000 from the broker.[10] The customer could satisfy their margin requirement by putting up $3,000 in cash or by depositing $6,000 in marginable securities that qualify for 50 percent loan value.

As the stock price changes, so does the investor's equity. This is calculated as the market value of the collateral stock minus the amount borrowed. The market value of the stock is equal to the current market price multiplied by the number of shares. Securities firms calculate the actual margin in their customers' accounts daily to determine whether a "margin call" is required. This is known as having the brokerage accounts "marked to market." If the investor's equity exceeds the required margin, the excess margin can be withdrawn from the account or used to purchase more stock. Conversely, if the investor's equity declines below the required margin, an investor may receive a margin call (described below).[11]

A **margin call** (or maintenance call) occurs when the market value of the margined securities less the debit balance (amount owed) of the margin account declines below the required margin. This type of call is payable on demand, and the brokerage house may reserve the right to take action without notice if market conditions are deteriorating badly enough. In other words, the firm may sell enough shares from the margin account to satisfy the margin requirements.

Margin Call
A demand from the broker for additional cash or securities as a result of the actual margin declining below the margin requirement.

EXAMPLE 5-3: CALCULATING MARGIN

Assume that the required margin is 30 percent, and that the price of the 100 shares of stock (from the previous example) declines from $100 to $95 per share. The following equation is used to calculate actual margin:

$$\text{Actual Margin} = \frac{\text{Market value of securities} - \text{Amount borrowed}}{\text{Market value of securities}}$$

$$26.32\% = (\$9{,}500 - \$7{,}000) \div \$9{,}500$$

Notice that the investor's equity position is now $2,500 (down from $3,000), while the dealer's loan is still for $7,000. The actual margin is now below the required 30 percent and the customer will receive a margin call to restore the investor's equity to the required margin. Thus, the investor should have an equity position of 30 percent of $9,500 (or $2,850), and the broker's maximum loan value is only 70 percent of $9,500 (or $6,650). In order to restore the margin, the investor can contribute $350, which will reduce the loan from $7,000 to the required $6,650, and increase the equity position from $2,500 to the required $2,850.

---

[10] If the margin requirement was 50 percent, the customer would have to initially put up $5,000.
[11] In the United States, investors would only be able to withdraw funds if the actual margin exceeded the initial margin requirement—not just the maintenance margin. On the other hand, they would only receive a margin call when the actual margin fell below the maintenance margin—not the initial margin.

EXAMPLE 5-4: MARGIN REQUIREMENTS

An investor purchases common shares of two companies on margin. The first share (A) is eligible for special margin and is presently trading for $10, while the second share (B) is trading at $2.

  a. What is the total margin requirement if the investor purchases 1,000 shares of A and 1,000 shares of B?

  b. If the price of A immediately increases to $11 and the price of B falls rapidly to $1.50, how much (if any) will be the required deposit in your margin account?

Solution:

a. Total cost A = $10 × 1,000 = $10,000   Total cost B = $2 × 1,000 = $2,000
Less: Maximum loan (@70%) = $7,000   Less: Maximum loan (@50%) = $1,000
Equals: Margin requirement (A) = $3,000   Equals: Margin requirement (B) = $1,000

Total margin requirement (A + B) = $3,000 + $1,000 = $4,000

b. Original cost A = $10,000   Original cost B = $2,000
Less: Revised maximum loan A (@70%)   Less: Revised maximum loan B (@20%)
= 0.70 × $11 × 1,000 = $7,700   = 0.20 × $1.50 × 1,000 = $300
Gross Margin Requirement = $2,300 $1,700

Margin deficit (surplus)   surplus ($700)   deficit $700

Therefore, the net required deposit is zero, since your margin surplus in one account ($700) offsets your deficit in the other.

While margin requirements for common stocks may be as low as 30 percent, the margin option does not have to be fully employed. That is, investors could limit their borrowing to less than 70 percent to reduce the volatility of the investment returns, as well as reducing the probability of ever encountering a margin call.

The traditional appeal of margin trading to investors is that it magnifies any gains on a transaction by the reciprocal of the margin requirement (i.e., 1/margin percentage). Unfortunately, the use of margin also magnifies any losses. This magnification is generally referred to as creating "leverage."

We refer to the example "Meeting Margin Requirement" above to demonstrate this relationship. Commission fees and interest costs on margin loans are ignored for the sake of simplicity. In the example, the margin requirement is 30 percent (which magnifies gains or losses by a factor of $1/0.3 = 3.33$). First, let's consider the profits to an investor who purchased 100 shares for $100 each, for a total investment of $10,000. If the share price increased (decreased) 10 percent to $110 ($90), that investor would have gained (lost) $1,000 ($10 per share price change multiplied by 100 shares). This gain (loss) represents 10 percent of the original investment. Consider another investor who purchased 100 shares at $100 per share on margin, at the 30 percent margin rate. This investor's initial investment was $3,000 (30 percent of the $10,000 total cost). If the share price increased (decreased) by $10 to $110 ($90), the total gain (loss) would still be $1,000. However, since the original cash outlay was only $3,000, the investor's gain (loss) is 3.33 times greater, at 33.3 percent of the original investment (or $1,000/$3,000).

Regardless of what happens, the margin trader must pay the interest costs on the margin account. An investor considering a margined stock purchase should remember that the stock price can go up, remain the same, or go down. In two of these three cases, the investor loses. Even if the stock rises, the break-even point is higher by the amount of the interest charges.

SHORT SALES

The purchase of a security technically results in the investor being "long" in the security. The security is bought and owned because the investor believes the price is likely to rise. But what if the investor thinks that the price of a security will decline? If he or she owns it, it would be wise to sell. If the security is not owned, the investor wishing to profit from the expected decline in price can sell the security short. **Short sales** are a normal part of market transactions.

How can an investor sell short, which is to say sell something he or she does not own? Not owning the security to begin with, the investor will have to borrow from a third party. The broker, on being instructed to sell short, will make these arrangements for this investor by borrowing the security from those held in street-name margin accounts and, in effect, lending it to the short seller.[12]

The short seller's broker sells the borrowed security in the open market, exactly like any other sale, to some investor who wishes to own it. The short seller expects the price of the security to decline. Assume that it does. The short seller instructs the broker to repurchase the security at the currently lower price and cancel the short position (by replacing the borrowed security). The investor profits by the difference between the price at which the borrowed stock was sold and the price at which it was repurchased.

Short Sales
The sale of a stock not owned by the investor but borrowed from a third party in order to take advantage of an expected decline in the price of the stock.

EXAMPLE 5-5: SELLING SHORT ON POWER FINANCIAL CORP.

An investor named Helen believes that the price of **Power's** shares will decline over the next few months and wants to profit from her conviction. She calls her broker with instructions to sell 100 shares of Power short (she does not own Power) at its current market price of $36 per share. The broker borrows 100 shares of Power from another client, Kellie, who has a brokerage account with the firm and currently owns Power ("long"). The broker sells the 100 shares at $36 per share, crediting the $3,600 proceeds (less commissions, which we will ignore for this example) to Helen's account.[13]

Six months later, the price of Power has declined, as Helen predicted, and is now $30 per share. Satisfied with this drop in the price of Power, she instructs the broker to purchase 100 shares of Power and close out the short position. Her profit is $3,600 minus $3,000, or $600 (again, ignoring commissions). The broker replaces Kellie's missing stock with the just-purchased 100 shares, and the transaction is complete.[14]

Several technicalities are involved in a short sale, which are outlined in Table 5-2. Keep in mind that to sell short, an investor must be approved for a margin account because short positions involve the potential for margin calls. The margins are expressed in terms of the liability arising from the "borrowing" of the securities from another investor, as outlined in the example, "Margin Requirement for Selling Short on Power Financial Corp.," on the following page. Short selling is defined as

---

[12]The securities could be borrowed from another broker. If the lending firm calls back the stock loan, the broker may be forced to close the short position. Also, individuals sometimes agree to lend securities to short sellers in exchange for interest-free loans equal to the collateral value of the securities sold short. Collateral value equals the amount of funds borrowed in a margin transaction.

[13]Note that Kellie knows nothing about this transaction, nor is she really affected. Kellie receives a monthly statement from the broker showing ownership of 100 shares of Power. Should Kellie wish to sell the Power stock while Helen is short, the broker will simply borrow 100 shares from Elizabeth, a third investor who deals with this firm and owns Power stock, to cover the sale. It is important to note that all of these transactions are book entries and do not involve the actual stock certificates.

[14]Notice that two trades are required to complete a transaction or "round trip." Investors who purchase securities plan to sell them eventually. Investors who sell short plan to buy back eventually; they have simply reversed the normal buy-sell procedure by selling and then buying.

the sale of securities that the seller does not own. The investor is said to be in a short position since he or she must repay it in the future (hopefully it can be repurchased after prices have fallen). The investor must leave the proceeds of the short sale with the dealer (who then has free use of these funds), and deposit a certain portion of the market value in addition to the proceeds.

Required margin amounts for trades with dealers and exchange members in Canada, expressed as percentages of market value, are provided in Table 5-3.

Table 5-2

The Details of Short Selling

1. Dividends declared on any stock sold short must be covered by the short seller. After all, the person from whom the shares were borrowed still owns the stock and expects all dividends paid on it.

2. Short sellers must have a margin account to sell short and must put up margin as if they had gone long. The margin can consist of cash or any restricted securities held long.

3. The net proceeds from a short sale, plus the required margin, are held by the broker; thus, no funds are immediately received by the short seller. The lender must be fully protected. To do this, the account is marked-to-the-market (as mentioned earlier in connection with margin accounts.) If the price of the stock declines as expected by the short seller, he or she can draw out the difference between the sale price and the current market price. If the price of the stock rises, however, the short seller will have to put up more funds.

4. There is no time limit on a short sale. Short sellers can remain short indefinitely. The only protection arises when the lender of the securities wants them back. In most cases the broker can borrow elsewhere, but in some situations, such as a thinly capitalized stock, this may not be possible.

5. Short sales are permitted only on rising prices or an uptick. A short seller can sell short at the last trade price only if that price exceeded the last different price before it. Otherwise, they must wait for an uptick. Although the order to the broker can be placed at any time, it will not be executed until an uptick occurs.

Table 5-3

Canadian Short Sale Margin Requirements

On listed securities selling:	Maximum margin required
Securities eligible for reduced margin	130% of market value
At $2.00 and over	150% of market value
At $1.50 to $1.99	$3.00 per share
At $0.25 to $1.49	200% of market value
Under $0.25	100% of market + $0.25 per share

EXAMPLE 5-6: MARGIN REQUIREMENT FOR SELLING SHORT ON POWER FINANCIAL CORP.

Suppose Power Financial Corp. is eligible for special margin and requires a margin of 130 percent. When Helen short sells the 100 shares of Power for $36 each, the sale proceeds of $3,600 (which represent 100 percent of Helen's liability at that time) will remain in an account with her securities firm. In addition, she will be required to deposit 30 percent of her liability (or $1,080) with the firm in order to bring the margin account up to 130 percent (with a total of $4,680).

Should the price of Power rise to $42, Helen's liability increases to $4,200 ($42/share × 100 shares), and she would be required to have 130 percent of $4,200, or $5,460, in the account. Since there was only $4,680 in the account, Helen would be required to deposit an additional $780 ($5,460 − $4,680) to restore the margin. Alternatively, if the price of Power fell to $30, her liability would be $3,000, and her required margin would be $3,900 (1.30 × $3,000). Hence, Helen would find herself in an excess margin position and be able to withdraw $780.

There is no time limit on the maintenance of a short position. However, the client must buy the necessary shares to cover the position if the broker is unable to borrow sufficient shares to do so. Because of this potential problem, many experienced traders confine short sales activities to stocks that are actively traded. Members are required to disclose which trades are short sales, and the TSX compiles and publicly reports total short positions regularly.

Difficulties and hazards of short selling include problems in borrowing a sufficient number of shares; responsibility of maintaining an adequate margin; liability for any dividends paid; threat of being required to purchase shares at undesirable prices if the margin is not maintained and/or if originally borrowed stock is called by its owners and cannot be replaced; difficulty in obtaining up-to-date information on total short sales; possibility of volatile prices should a rush to cover occur; and unlimited potential loss.

EXAMPLE 5-7: SHORT SALE MARGIN REQUIREMENTS

a. What amount must an investor put in a margin account, if he or she short sells 1,000 shares of an option-eligible security trading for $10?

b. What will happen if the price of the shares, which were sold short immediately, increases to $12?

Solution:

a.			
Minimum account balance (@130%)	= 1.30 × $10 × 1,000	= $13,000
Less: Proceeds from short sale	= $10 × 1,000	= $10,000
Equals: Minimum margin requirement		= $ 3,000

b.			
Minimum account balance (@130%)	= 1.30 × $12 × 1,000	= $15,600
Less: Proceeds from short sale	= $10 × 1,000	= $10,000
Equals: Minimum margin requirement		= $ 5,600

Required deposit = margin deficit = $5,600 − $3,000 = $ 2,600

CHECK YOUR UNDERSTANDING

5-7. As an investor you should be concerned with the rate of return you earn on the amount of money you actually invest (your equity). Write out an equation that allows you to calculate your return on invested capital, taking into account the following five items: the amount of your equity at purchase, the value of the stock at time of purchase, the value of the stock at time of sale, the total income received while holding the stock, and the total margin interest paid on the transaction.

5-8. What benefits do brokerage firms derive from offering margin accounts?

5-9. What does it mean to say the losses from short selling are infinite while the gains are finite?

DO YOU HAVE AN OBLIGATION FOR GOOD ADVICE UNSOLICITED?

Investors have a choice of brokers, ranging from those providing advice and recommendations (and typically charging more), and those offering little or no advice (and typically charging less). While we generally think of an investor seeking out a broker, brokers often seek out customers. Assume you as an investor have a brokerage account of your own choosing where you transact your investing decisions. Out of the blue one day a broker you have never met, employed at a brokerage firm you are not familiar with, calls you. (For obvious reasons, this is referred to in the business as "cold-calling.") He offers to send you free some investing ideas. You accept the offer. You later decide to invest in one of the stocks he has recommended because after thinking about it and checking further, you decide this stock has merit. You execute the transaction in your regular brokerage account rather than through a new account with the broker who called. Is this ethical behaviour on your part?

Most observers would agree that in this situation you are under no obligation to transact with the broker who sought you out as a potential customer. Had you solicited the recommendation, you would have an obligation, but in this case you do not. Of course, you may not receive any more recommendations from this broker.

DISCUSSION QUESTIONS

1. If you were a broker, would you make cold calls to potential clients? What if some attractive commissions were offered?

2. If you had to make cold calls and you found out that someone took your advice but made a transaction with another broker, how would you react?

3. Is there such a thing as objective financial advice?

SUMMARY

This summary relates to the learning objectives for this chapter.

1. **Explain the role of brokerage firms and stockbrokers.**
   Brokerage firms consist of full-service brokers, discount brokers, and/or Internet brokers who execute stock trades for clients. Full-service stockbrokers earn their incomes from a variety of sources including individuals' trades, in-house mutual fund sales, principal transactions, new issues, and fees.

2. **Describe how brokerage firms operate.**
   With a cash brokerage account, the customer pays in full on the settlement date, whereas with a margin account money can be borrowed from the broker to finance purchases. Wrap accounts, where all costs are wrapped in one fee, are becoming increasingly popular. Brokerage commissions are negotiable. Full-line brokerage houses charge more than discount brokers but offer advice and recommendations, while Internet brokers tend to charge the least. Investors can also invest without a broker through dividend reinvestment plans (DRIPs), whereby companies sell shares directly to investors through share purchase plans.

3. **Outline how orders to buy and sell securities are executed.**
   The TSX was the first stock exchange in the world to go electronic and now handles all trades electronically. Most exchanges are now highly automated, although the NYSE still handles orders using its specialist system. Specialists on the NYSE are charged with maintaining a continuous, orderly market in their assigned stocks. Market orders are executed at the best price available, whereas limit

orders specify a particular price to be met or bettered. Stop orders specify a certain price at which a market order is to take over.

4. **Discuss the regulation of the Canadian securities industry.**

   Investor protection includes government regulation, primarily at the provincial level, and self-regulation by the industry. Self-regulatory organizations (SROs) deal with member regulation, listing requirements, and trading regulation. SROs include the Investment Industry Regulatory Organization of Canada (IIROC), TSX, TSX Venture Exchange, MX, and the MFDA. The IIROC is the Canadian investment industry's national self-regulatory organization.

5. **Explain the importance of margin trading and short selling to investors.**

   Margin is the equity an investor has in a transaction. Required margins are set by the appropriate SROs. The appeal of margin to investors is that it can magnify any gains on a transaction, but it can also magnify losses. An investor sells short if a security's price is expected to decline. The investor borrows the securities sold short from the broker, hoping to replace them through a later purchase at a lower price.

KEY TERMS

Ask price, p.132
Bid price, p.132
Canadian Investor Protection Fund (CIPF), p.138
Canadian Securities Institute (CSI), p.139
Cash account, p.125
Discount brokers, p.124

Dividend reinvestment plans (DRIPs), p.131
Full-service brokers, p.124
Investment Industry Regulatory Organization of Canada (IIROC), p.138
Limit order, p.132
Margin, p.139

Margin account, p.125
Margin call, p.139
Market order, p.132
Self-regulatory organizations (SROs), p.138
Short sales, p.143
Stop order, p.133
Street name, p.134
Wrap account, p.125

REVIEW QUESTIONS

5-1. What is the normal settlement date for common stocks? For long-term government bonds? For T-bills?

5-2. What are the maximum loan values applicable to IIROC and exchange licensed traders in establishing margin accounts for clients who wish to purchase common shares at various price levels?

5-3. What conditions result in a margin call?

5-4. How can an investor sell a security that is not currently owned?

5-5. What is a wrap account? How does it involve a change in the traditional role of the broker?

5-6. Distinguish between a full-service broker and a discount broker.

5-7. How can investors invest without a broker?

5-8. What is the difference between a day order and an open order?

5-9. Why are investors interested in having margin accounts? What risk do such accounts involve?

5-10. Given the lower brokerage costs charged by discount brokers and Internet brokers, why might an investor choose to use a full-service broker?

5-11. Explain the role of the specialists on the NYSE, describing the two roles they perform. How do they act to maintain an orderly market?

5-12. Is there any similarity between an over-the-counter dealer and a specialist on an exchange?

5-13. Discuss the advantages and disadvantages of a limit order versus a market order.

5-14. How does a stop order differ from a limit order?

5-15. What is the role of SROs in the regulation of securities markets?

5-16. What are the risks associated with short selling?

5-17. What role is performed by the Canadian Investor Protection Fund (CIPF)? What losses does it cover, and what losses does it not cover?

5-18. What conditions must be met for an investor to sell short?

5-19. Explain the difference, relative to the current market price of a stock, between the following types of orders: sell limit, buy limit, buy stop, and sell stop.

5-20. How has technology influenced how securities are traded?

5-21. What is an all or none order and what are the advantages of this type of order?

5-22. What is meant by having margin accounts "marked to the market" daily?

5-23. Is there any link between margin accounts and short selling?

PROBLEMS

5-1.   a. Consider an investor who purchased a stock at $100 per share. The current market price is $125. At what price would a limit order be placed to ensure a profit of $30 per share?

   b. What type of stop order would be placed to ensure a profit of at least $20 per share?

5-2. Assume an investor sells short 200 shares of stock at $75 per share. At what price must the investor cover the short sale in order to realize a gross profit of $5,000? Of $1,000?

5-3. Assume that an investor buys 100 shares of stock at $50 per share and the stock rises to $60 per share. What is the gross profit, assuming a margin requirement of 30 percent? Of 50 percent? Of 60 percent?

5-4. An investor buys 100 shares of an option eligible stock on margin at $60 per share. The price of the stock subsequently drops to $50.

   a. What is the actual margin at $50? Is there a margin call?
   b. If the price declines to $45, what is the amount of the margin call? At $35?
   c. If the price increased to $70, how much, if any, funds would the investor have available to them from this account?

5-5. An investor short sells 200 shares of a stock trading at $3. How much must he or she deposit in order to complete the transaction? Suppose the price subsequently falls to $2. How much money can the investor withdraw? If the price rises to $4.50, how much must the investor deposit?

5-6.   a. What is your required margin deposit if you short sell 200 shares of a common stock for $20 per share, and the required margin is 130 percent?

   b. If the price of the common stock above rises to $25 per share, how much cash will you be required to deposit in order to restore your margin position?
   c. What is the leverage factor associated with the margin purchase of 100 shares of a $5 stock if the initial margin requirement is 40 percent?
   d. What will be your annualized return (expressed as a percentage) if you purchase 1,000 shares of a stock for $12 per share on margin and hold them for two months before eventually reselling them for $15 per share? Assume the required margin is 50 percent, and that your broker charges you interest at an annual rate of 8 percent, and you do not receive any margin calls during the two-month period. Ignore transaction costs.

5-7. You open a margin account at Chas. Pigeon, a discount broker. You subsequently short Exciting.com at $286, believing it to be overpriced. This transaction is done on margin, which has an annual interest rate cost of 9 percent. Exactly one year later Exciting has declined to $54 a share, at which point you cover your short position. You pay brokerage costs of $20 on each transaction you make.

    a. The margin requirement is 50 percent. Calculate your dollar gain or loss on this position, taking into account both the margin interest and the transaction costs.

    b. Calculate the percentage return on your investment (the amount of money you put up initially, counting the brokerage costs to buy).

5-8. Using your same brokerage account as in Problem 5-7 (same margin rate and transaction costs), assume that you buy IBM at $156 a share, on 60 percent margin. During the year IBM pays a dividend of $1.30 per share. One year later you sell the position at $233.

    a. Calculate the dollar gain or loss on this position.

    b. Calculate the percentage return on your investment.

5-9. An investor buys 100 shares of Altria at $82 per share on margin. The initial margin requirement is 50 percent, and the maintenance margin is 30 percent.

    a. The price of Altria drops to $61 per share. What is the actual margin now?

    b. The price of Altria declines further to $59.50. Show why a margin call is generated, or is not warranted.

    c. The price declines yet again to $55.25. Show by calculations why a margin call is generated.

    d. Using the information in (c), how much cash must be added to the account to bring it into compliance with the margin requirements?

5-10. You have been watching six stocks (call them "Stock 1" through "Stock 6") and now believe that three of them are poised to move upward, while the other three are likely to fall in price. Therefore, you intend to take a long position (buy 100 shares each) in Stocks 1, 2 and 3 and a short position (sell 100 shares each) in Stock 4, 5, and 6. Each stock is currently trading at $10 per share; you may ignore trading commissions.

    First determine the amount of cash you will have to deposit to your brokerage account (margin) to make the six investments. Now assume you have made this minimum cash deposit and taken the desired positions (made the investments). For the following two scenarios, determine whether your cash balance is now in surplus or deficit as compared to the updated minimum margin amount. Also calculate the total value of the account assuming you do not make any further deposits or withdrawals. Note: margin requirement is 50 percent.

    Scenario 1 ("Good" price changes): Stocks 1 and 2 increase by 10 percent, as expected; Stocks 3 and 4 do not change in price; Stocks 5 and 6 fall by 10 percent.

    Scenario 2 ("Bad" price changes): Stocks 1 and 2 decrease by 10 percent (to $9 per share); Stocks 3 and 4 do not change; Stocks 5 and 6 increase in price by 10 percent.

PREPARING FOR YOUR PROFESSIONAL EXAMS

CFA PRACTICE QUESTIONS

5-1. An investor sold a stock short and is worried about rising prices. To protect against rising prices, the investor would place a

    a. Stop order to sell

    b. Stop order to buy

    c. Limit order to sell

    d. Limit order to buy

5-2. A stock is purchased on margin at $20 per share (assume 50 percent margin requirement). At what price would you receive a margin call if the maintenance margin is 25 percent?

    a. $13.33
    b. $15.00
    c. $18.67
    d. $24.00

5-3. Which of the following rules does not apply to short sale transactions?

    a. They are only permitted on an uptick.
    b. The short position must be closed out within 60 days.
    c. Any dividends declared must be covered by the short seller.
    d. The margin account is "marked-to-the-market"

5-4. You purchase 100 shares of a stock for $30 per share and immediately initiate a stop-loss order at a price of $25 per share. Ignoring transaction costs, your maximum loss:

    a. is $500.
    b. is $600.
    c. is $400.
    d. cannot be determined exactly.

5-5. What difficulties and hazards are associated with short selling a stock?

    i. There can be difficulties borrowing the required quantity of the security sold short to cover the short sale.
    ii. The short seller is not liable for any dividends paid during the period the account is short.
    iii. There are difficulties in obtaining up-to-date information on total short sales on a security.
    iv. The short seller is responsible for maintaining adequate margin in the short account.

    a. i, ii, iii, iv
    b. i, ii, iv
    c. ii, iii
    d. i, iii, iv

APPENDIX 5A
TRADING ON THE NYSE
NYSE Trading and the Specialist System

Assume an investor places an order to buy or sell shares of a NYSE-listed company and that the brokerage firm transmits the order to the NYSE trading floor. The Common Message Switch/SuperDot system used by the NYSE will transmit the order to either a broker's booth or directly to the specialist assigned to that stock. Having received the order, the firm's floor broker would take the order to the trading post, compete for the best price, and make the trade. The specialist will expose the order and make the trade, and will seek the best price for the customer. Upon completion of the trade, a report is sent back to the originating brokerage firm and to the Consolidated Tape Displays worldwide. The brokerage firm processes the transaction electronically, settling the investor's account.

NYSE trades appear on the NYSE consolidated tape, which prints transactions for all NYSE-listed securities on participating markets. This involves several stock exchanges (in addition to the NYSE), the over-the-counter market, and Instinet. Daily papers such as *The Wall Street Journal* report the high and low prices for each stock wherever they occur.

The role of the specialist is critical on the NYSE. Also referred to as NYSE-assigned dealers by the NYSE and discussed in Chapter 4 in connection with the NYSE, specialists are expected to maintain a fair and orderly market in those stocks assigned to them. They act as both brokers and dealers:

• As brokers, specialists maintain the limit book, which records all limit orders, or orders that investors have placed to buy or sell a security at a specific price (or better) and that will not be executed until that price is reached. The commission brokers leave the limit orders with the specialist to be filled when possible; therefore, the specialist receives part of the broker's fee.

- As dealers, specialists buy and sell shares of their assigned stock(s) to maintain an orderly market. The stock exchanges function essentially as a continuous market, assuring investors that they can almost always buy and sell a particular security at some price. Assuming that public orders do not arrive at the same time, so that they can be matched, the specialist will buy from commission brokers with orders to sell and will sell to those with orders to buy, hoping to profit by a favourable spread between the two sides.

Since specialists are charged by the NYSE with maintaining a continuous, orderly market in their assigned stocks, they often must go "against the market," which requires adequate capital. The NYSE demands that specialists be able to assume a position of 5,000 shares in their assigned stocks.[15] However, the NYSE does not require specialists to fund all the liquidity for the market at a particular time, and these stabilization trades are only a small part of total trading.

Most of the NYSE volume results from public orders interacting directly with other public orders. Using NYSE data, in 2005, specialist participation—measured as the total shares bought and sold by specialists divided by twice total volume—accounted for about 15 percent of the share volume traded. This implies that 85 percent of share volume resulted from public and licensed trader orders meeting directly in the NYSE market. It is important to note that specialists are not on both sides of any trade.

How well does the system work? According to NYSE figures, in one year, some 98.2 percent of all transactions occurred with no change in price or within the minimum change permissible on the NYSE. The quotation spread between bid and asked prices was one-fourth of a point or less in 93 percent of NYSE quotes. As an indication of market depth, for volume of 3,000 shares or more, the average stock price showed no change, or one-eighth point change, 91 percent of the time.

Automation of the NYSE

Given the volume of shares handled by the NYSE, trading must be highly automated. About 99 percent of orders and almost half of the volume is handled electronically. An electronic system matches buy and sell orders entered before the market opens, setting the opening price of a stock. SuperDot is the electronic order routing system for NYSE-listed securities. Licensed traders send orders directly to the specialist post where the securities are traded, and confirmation of trading is returned directly to the member firm over the same system. The system's peak capacity has been increased to an order processing capability of 2 billion shares per day.

As part of SuperDot, the Opening Automated Report Service (OARS) automatically and continuously scans the licensed traders' preopening buy and sell orders, pairing buy and sell orders and presenting the imbalance to the specialist up to the opening of a stock. This helps the specialist determine the opening price. OARS handles preopening market orders up to 30,099 shares.

SuperDot also includes a postopening market order system designed to accept postopening market orders of up to 3 million shares. These market orders are executed and reported back to the member firm, sending the order within 17 seconds, on average.

The specialist's volume-handling and volume-processing capabilities have been enhanced electronically by creating the Specialist's Electronic Book, which is yet another part of the SuperDot system. This database system assists in recording and reporting limit and market orders. Not only does it help eliminate paperwork and processing errors, but it now also handles about 98 percent of all SuperDot orders.

The NYSE now allows large institutional investors to avoid trading on the floor of the exchange under certain conditions. The "clean-cross" rule now permits brokers to arrange trades of 25,000 shares or more between customers without considering orders at the same price from other investors

---

[15]Specialists must be approved by the Board of Governors of the NYSE and must have experience, ability as dealers, and specified minimum capital.

on the NYSE floor. However, orders at a better price would have to be accepted.

Financial markets are changing as new techniques and processes are developed. ECNs are an obvious example. Long-standing institutions such as the NYSE must also change, and it is doing so.

APPENDIX 5B

SECURITIES REGULATION IN THE UNITED STATES

Since many Canadian institutional and individual investors transact in securities that are traded in US markets, and since many Canadian companies list their securities in US markets, it is important for Canadians to be familiar with US regulatory practice. The Securities and Exchange Commission (SEC) was created by the US Congress in 1934. It is an independent, quasi-judicial agency of the US government. Its mission is to administer laws in the securities field and to protect investors and the public in securities transactions. The commission consists of five members appointed by the SEC president for five-year terms. Its staff consists of lawyers, accountants, security analysts, and others divided into divisions and offices (including nine regional offices). The SEC has approximately 200 examiners.

The SEC is required to investigate complaints or indications of violations in securities transactions. In general, the SEC administers all securities laws. Thus, under the Securities Act of 1933, the SEC ensures that new securities being offered for public sale are registered with the commission, and under the 1934 Act it does the same for securities trading on national exchanges. The registration of securities in no way ensures that investors purchasing them will not lose money. Registration means only that the issuer has made adequate disclosure. In fact, the SEC has no power to disapprove securities for lack of merit.

Investment advisors and companies must also register with the SEC and disclose certain information. The SEC ensures that these two groups will meet the requirements of the laws affecting them.

Similar to Canada, self-regulation is a defining characteristic of the US securities industry. Stock exchanges regulate and monitor trading for the benefit of investors and the protection of the financial system. The NYSE in particular has a stringent set of self-regulations and declares that it "provides the most meaningful market regulation in the world." The NYSE regulates itself as part of a combined effort involving the SEC, itself, and licensed traders, and NYSE rules and regulations are self-imposed and approved by the SEC. Together, this triad enforces federal legislation and self-regulation for the benefit of the investing public.

In 2007, the National Association of Securities Dealers (NASD) and the member regulation committee of the New York Stock Exchange (NYSE) merged to form the Financial Industry Regulatory Authority (FINRA), the largest non-governmental regulator for securities firms in the US. FINRA, which oversees nearly 5,000 brokerage firms, about 174,000 branch offices and approximately 677,500 registered securities representatives, is "dedicated to investor protection and market integrity through effective and efficient regulation and complementary compliance and technology-based services."[16]

FINRA is involved in almost every area of the securities business including registering and educating industry professionals; examining securities firms; writing rules; enforcing those rules and US federal securities laws; promoting investor protection by educating the investing public; and administering a dispute resolution forum for investors and registered firms. FINRA also performs market regulation under contract for The NASDAQ Stock Market and the American Stock Exchange.

Similar to the CIPF in Canada, the Securities Investor Protection Corporation (SIPC), a quasi-government agency, insures each customer account of member brokers against brokerage firm failure.[17]

---

[16]www.finra.org/AboutFINRA

[17]In addition, many brokerage firms carry additional insurance, often for several million dollars, to provide even more protection for customers.

THE RETURNS AND RISKS FROM INVESTING

Chapter 6 analyzes the returns and risks from investing. We learn how well investors have done in the past investing in the major financial assets. Investors need a good understanding of the returns and risk that have been experienced to date before attempting to estimate returns and risk, which they must do as they build and hold portfolios for the future.

Learning Objectives

After reading this chapter, you should be able to

1. Define "return" and state its two components.
2. Explain the relationship between return and risk.
3. Identify the sources of risk.
4. Describe the different methods of measuring returns.
5. Describe the different methods of measuring risk.
6. Discuss the returns and risks from investing in major financial assets in the past.

CHAPTER PREVIEW

Before you can begin to build a portfolio of investments, you must have a good understanding of the returns and risks from investing that have been experienced to date. Return and risk are described, measured, and estimated throughout this text in relation to the various securities. Our goal in this chapter is to give you a basic working knowledge of these concepts. You will learn about the components of return and risk, and how to measure them. You will have the opportunity to examine *realized* returns on major Canadian financial assets based on the historical record. (In Part II, we turn our attention to *expected* return, which is subject to uncertainty and may or may not occur over some future period.) As you read this chapter, keep in mind that what has occurred in the past should be viewed as a useful, but not guaranteed, guide to the future.

RETURN

learning objective 1
Define "return" and state its two components.

As noted in Chapter 1, the objective of investors is to maximize expected returns, although they are subject to constraints—primarily risk. Return is the motivating force in the investment process. It is the reward for undertaking the investment.

Returns from investing are crucial to investors; they are what the game of investments is all about. An assessment of return is the only rational way (after allowing for risk) for investors to compare alternative investments that differ in what they promise. The measurement of realized (historical) returns is necessary for investors to assess how well they have done or how well investment managers have done on their behalf. Furthermore, the historical return plays a large part in estimating future, unknown returns.

The Components of Return

Return on a typical investment consists of two components: yield and capital gain (loss).

Yield

Yield

The income component of a security's return.

The basic component that usually comes to mind when discussing investing returns is the periodic cash flows (or income) on the investment, either interest or dividends. The distinguishing feature of these payments is that the issuer makes the payments in cash to the holder of the asset. **Yield** measures relate these cash flows to a price for the security, such as the purchase price or the current market price.

Capital Gain (Loss)

Capital Gain (Loss)

The change in price on a security over some period of time.

The second component is also important, particularly for common stocks but also for long-term bonds and other fixed-income securities. This component, commonly called the **capital gain (loss)**, is the appreciation (or depreciation) in the price of the asset. We will refer to it simply as the price change. In the case of a long position, it is the difference between the purchase price and the price at which the asset can be, or is, sold. For a short position, it is the difference between the sale price and the subsequent price at which the short position is closed out. In either case, a gain or a loss may occur.[1]

Given the two components of a security's return, we need to add them together (algebraically) to form the total return, which for any security is defined as

---

[1]This component involves only the difference between the beginning price and the ending price in the transaction. An investor can purchase or short an asset and close out the position one day, one hour, or one minute later for a capital gain or loss. Furthermore, gains can be realized or unrealized. See Appendix 2A: Taxation of Investment Income in Canada at the end of Chapter 2 for a more detailed discussion of capital gains and losses and their taxation.

$$\text{Total return} = \text{Yield} + \text{Price change} \qquad \textbf{(6-1)}$$

where
The yield component can be 0 or +
The price change component can be 0, +, or −

Equation 6-1 is a conceptual statement for the total return for any security. The important point here is that a security's total return consists of the sum of two components—yield and price change. Investor returns from assets can come only from these two components—an income component (the yield) and/or a price change component, regardless of the asset.

EXAMPLE: CALCULATING YIELDS AND PRICE CHANGES

A regular coupon bond purchased at par and held to maturity provides a yield in the form of a stream of cash flows or interest payments. A bond with a maturity value of $1,000 that is purchased for $800 and held to maturity provides both a yield (the interest payments) and a price change. The purchase of a non-dividend-paying stock that is sold six months later produces either a capital gain or loss but no income. A dividend-paying stock produces both a yield component and a price change component (a realized or unrealized capital gain or loss).

RISK

It is not sensible to talk about investment returns without talking about risk because investment decisions involve a trade-off between the two. Investors must constantly be aware of the risk they are assuming, know what it can do to their investment decisions, and be prepared for the consequences.

Risk was defined in Chapter 1 as the chance that the actual outcome from an investment will differ from the expected outcome. Specifically, most investors are concerned that the actual outcome will be less than the expected outcome. The more variable the possible outcomes that can occur (i.e., the broader the range of possible outcomes), the greater the risk.

Investors should be willing to purchase a particular asset if the expected return is adequate to compensate for the risk, but they must understand that their expectation about the asset's return may not materialize. If not, the realized return will differ from the expected return. In fact, realized returns on securities show considerable variability. Although investors may receive on average their expected returns on risky securities in the long-run, they often fail to do so in the short-run.

learning objective 2
Explain the relationship between return and risk.

Sources of Risk

What makes a financial asset risky? Traditionally, investors have talked about several sources of total risk, such as interest rate risk and market risk, which are explained below because these terms are used so widely. Following this discussion, we will define the modern portfolio sources of risk, which will be used in Part II when we discuss portfolio and capital market theory.

learning objective 3
Identify the sources of risk.

Interest Rate Risk

The variability in a security's return resulting from changes in the level of interest rates is referred to as **interest rate risk**. Such changes generally affect securities inversely; that is, other things being equal, security prices move inversely to interest rates. The reason for this movement is tied up with the valuation of securities. Interest rate risk affects bonds more directly than common stocks and is a major risk faced by all bondholders. As interest rates change, bond prices change in an inverse direction.

Interest Rate Risk
The variability in a security's returns resulting from changes in interest rates.

Market Risk

Market Risk

The variability in a security's returns resulting from fluctuations in the aggregate market.

The variability in returns resulting from fluctuations in the overall market—that is, the aggregate stock market—is referred to as **market risk**. All securities are exposed to market risk, although it primarily affects common stocks.

Market risk includes a wide range of factors exogenous to securities themselves, including recessions, wars, structural changes in the economy, and changes in consumer preferences.

INVESTING *tip*

It is important to remember how risk and return go together when investing. An investor cannot reasonably expect larger returns without being willing to assume larger risks. Consider the investor who wishes to avoid any risk (on a practical basis). Such an investor can deposit money in an insured savings account thereby earning a guaranteed return of a known amount. However this return will be fixed and the investor cannot earn more than this rate. Although risk is effectively eliminated, the chance of earning a larger return is also removed. To have the opportunity to earn a larger return, investors must be willing to assume larger risks.

Inflation Risk

A factor affecting all securities is purchasing power risk, or the chance that the purchasing power of invested dollars will decline. With uncertain inflation, the real (inflation-adjusted) return involves risk even if the nominal return is safe (e.g., a T-bill). This risk is related to interest rate risk, since interest rates generally rise as inflation increases because lenders demand additional inflation premiums to compensate for the loss of purchasing power.

Business Risk

The risk of doing business in a particular industry or environment is called business risk. For example, as one of Canada's largest steel producers, Dofasco faces unique problems. Similarly, Shell Canada faces unique problems as a result of developments in the global oil situation.

Financial Risk

Financial risk is associated with the use of debt financing by companies. The larger the proportion of assets financed by debt (as opposed to equity), the larger the variability in the returns, other things being equal. Financial risk involves the concept of financial leverage.

Liquidity Risk

Liquidity risk is the risk associated with the particular secondary market in which a security trades. An investment that can be bought or sold quickly and without significant price concession is considered liquid. The more uncertainty about the time element and the price concession, the greater the liquidity risk. A T-bill has little or no liquidity risk, whereas a small OTC stock may have substantial liquidity risk.

An extreme illustration of liquidity risk is the recent cessation of all trading in the non-bank backed asset-backed commercial paper (ABCP) market in Canada, as discussed in Real-World Returns 6-1.

REAL-WORLD RETURNS 6-1

Liquidity Risk

When you add it all up, the commercial paper in Canada's frozen $32-billion market has lost more than 40 percent of its face value because of market conditions, according to one analyst.

While the figure does not represent the amount that investors might recoup from their holdings, it is indicative of the troubles facing the committee that's been working to fix this market.

RBC Dominion Securities analyst André-Philippe Hardy based his estimate, which he released in a note to clients yesterday, on court documents that were recently made public.

They show that a $17.2-billion portion of the market—leveraged super senior swap transactions—were worth about 30 percent of face value as of March 4, Mr. Hardy noted.

He believes that a further $3-billion portion of the market that's tied to US subprime is probably worth about 20 percent.

Assuming that all of the other assets underlying this paper are still worth their full face value, that "implies a valuation of 56 percent for the ABCP," Mr. Hardy wrote.

Determining exactly how much of their money investors in this paper will recoup is somewhat more complicated, because the restructuring plan for the market involves dividing it up into three types of new investments that will each have different values, because some will be riskier than others.

But Mr. Hardy now believes that National Bank of Canada, which holds more than $2-billion of third-party asset-backed commercial paper, could be forced to take a further $300-million pretax writedown on its holdings.

That would equate to a 38-percent writedown. National Bank has currently shaved 25 percent of the value of the ABCP holdings on its books.

However, Mr. Hardy also pointed out that investment-grade debt spreads have tightened since March 4, meaning the commercial paper could be worth more now than it was then.

The committee led by Toronto lawyer Purdy Crawford has come up with a plan that involves trading in the commercial paper for longer-term notes to fix this market. It has said investors should be able to recoup much of their money if they hold those notes until they mature, which could be up to nine years.

Many investors say they can't wait that long, and the committee is hopeful an over-the-counter market will develop so investors can trade their shares soon after the plan is in place.

According to court documents, the committee considered proposals designed to promote liquidity in that market, and had asked a number of Canadian and international financial institutions about establishing a lending facility or contributing to other "market-making initiatives."

For now, no specific market-making measures are in place that would ensure investors can sell their notes in the short term.

The committee is hoping that it will bring transparency to the market by giving out full details on the new notes. That, combined with ratings that they believe the notes will receive from DBRS, should be enough to ensure that some investors are willing to buy the notes, the committee believes.

It has so far been unable to convince a second rating agency to rate the new notes.

Source: Perkins, Tara, "Frozen paper may have lost 40 percent," Globeinvestor.com. Retrieved from www.globeinvestor.com, March 25, 2008. © Copyright The Globe and Mail.

Exchange Rate Risk

All investors who invest internationally in today's increasingly global investment arena face the prospect of uncertainty in the returns after they convert the foreign gains back to their own currency. Unlike the past when most investors ignored international investing alternatives, investors today must recognize and understand **exchange rate risk**, which can be defined as the variability in returns on securities caused by currency fluctuations.

For example, a Canadian investor who buys a German stock denominated in euros must ultimately convert the returns from this stock back to dollars. If the exchange rate has moved against the investor, losses from these exchange rate movements can partially or totally negate the original return earned. Many Canadian investors learned this lesson the hard way during 2007, when the Canadian dollar appreciated approximately 17.5 percent (from 0.8581 to 1.0088) against the US greenback, wiping out any investment gains they had made on their US investments.

Exchange Rate Risk
The variability in returns on securities caused by currency fluctuations.

Canadian investors who invest only in Canadian stocks on Canadian markets do not face this risk directly; however, many Canadian companies are multinational corporations that derive large amounts of their profits from foreign countries. As a result, even these investors must be concerned with fluctuations in the value of the local currency. In addition, currency risk affects international mutual funds, global mutual funds, closed-end single country funds, foreign stocks, and foreign bonds.

Country Risk

Country risk, sometimes referred to as political risk, is an important risk for investors today. With more investors investing internationally, both directly and indirectly, the political (and therefore economic) stability and viability of a country's economy need to be considered. Countries are often judged on a relative basis using the United States as a benchmark, and they require careful monitoring of country risk, which changes continuously.

Types of Risk

Thus far, our discussion has concerned the total risk of an asset, which is one important consideration in investment analysis. However, modern investment analysis categorizes the traditional sources of risk identified previously as causing variability in returns into two general types: those that are pervasive in nature, such as market risk or interest rate risk; and those that are specific to a particular security issue, such as business or financial risk. Therefore, we must consider these two categories of total risk. The following discussion introduces these terms. We discuss these two sources of risk in more detail in Chapters 8 and 9.

Dividing total risk into its two components—a general (market) component and a specific (issuer) component—we have systematic risk and non-systematic risk, which are additive:

(6-2)

$$\begin{aligned} \text{Total risk} &= \text{General risk} + \text{Specific risk} \\ &= \text{Market risk} + \text{Issuer risk} \\ &= \text{Systematic risk} + \text{Non-systematic risk} \end{aligned}$$

Systematic Risk

Systematic (Market) risk
Risk attributable to broad macro-factors affecting all securities.

As is shown in Part II dealing with portfolio management, an investor can construct a diversified portfolio and eliminate part of the total risk—the diversifiable or non-market part. What is left is the non-diversifiable portion or the market risk. Variability in a security's total returns that is directly associated with overall movements in the general market or economy is called **systematic (market) risk**.

Virtually all securities have some systematic risk—whether bonds or stocks—because systematic risk directly encompasses interest rate, market, and inflation risks. The investor cannot escape this part of the risk because no matter how well he or she diversifies, the risk of the overall market cannot be avoided. If the stock market declines sharply, as it did during the first three months of 2008, most stocks will be adversely affected; if it rises strongly, as it did between 2003 and 2007, most stocks will appreciate in value. These movements occur regardless of what any single investor does. Clearly, market risk is critical to all investors.

Non-Systematic Risk

Non-Systematic (Non-Market) Risk
Risk attributable to factors unique to a security.

The variability in a security's total returns not related to overall market variability is called the **non-systematic (non-market) risk**. This risk is unique to a particular security and is associated with such factors as business and financial risk as well as liquidity risk. Although all securities tend to have some non-systematic risk, it is generally connected with common stocks.

learning objective 4
Describe the different methods of measuring returns.

MEASURING RETURNS

Total Return

Total Return (TR)
Percentage measure relating all cash flows on a security for a given time period to its purchase price.

A correct return measure must incorporate the two components of return, as discussed earlier: yield and price change. Returns across time or from different securities can be measured and compared using the total return concept. Formally, the **total return (TR)** for a given holding period is a decimal (or percentage) number relating all the cash flows received by an investor during any designated time period to the purchase price of the asset. Total return is defined as

$$TR = \frac{\text{Any cash payments received} + \text{Price changes over the period}}{\text{Price at which the asset is purchased}} \qquad \textbf{(6-3)}$$

All the items in Equation 6-3 are measured in dollars. The dollar price change over the period—defined as the difference between the beginning (or purchase) price and the ending (or sale) price—can be either positive (sales price exceeds purchase price), negative (purchase price exceeds sales price), or zero. The cash payments can be either positive or zero. Netting the two items in the numerator together and dividing by the purchase price results in a decimal return figure that can easily be converted into percentage form. Note that in using TR, the two components of return—yield and price change—have been measured.[2]

The general equation for calculating TR is

$$TR = \frac{CF_t + (P_E - P_B)}{P_B} = \frac{CF_t + PC}{P_B} \qquad \textbf{(6-4)}$$

where
CF_t = cash flows during the measurement period t
P_E = price at the end of period t or sale price
P_B = purchase price of the asset or price at the beginning of the period
PC = change in price during the period, or P_E minus P_B

The cash flow for a bond comes from the interest payments received, and for a stock, it comes from the dividends received. For some assets, such as a warrant, there is only a price change. Part A of Figure 6-1 illustrates the calculation of TR for a bond, a common stock, and a warrant. Although one year is often used for convenience, this calculation can be applied to periods of any length.

---

[2]This can be seen more easily by rewriting Equation 6-3 to show specifically its income and price change components.

$$TR = \frac{\text{Cash payments received}}{\text{Purchase price}} + \frac{\text{Price change over the period}}{\text{Purchase price}}$$

The first term is the yield component, while the second term measures the price change.

Figure 6-1
Examples of
Total Return
and Return
Relative
Calculations

A. TOTAL RETURN (TR) CALCULATIONS

I. Bond TR

$$\text{Bond TR} = \frac{I_t + (P_E - P_B)}{P_B} = \frac{I_t + PC}{P_B}$$

I_t = the interest payment(s) received during the period
P_B and P_E = the beginning and ending prices, respectively
PC = the change in price during the period

Example: Assume the purchase of a 10 percent-coupon government bond at a price of $960, held one year, and sold for $1,020. The TR is

$$\text{Bond TR} = \frac{100 + (1020 - 960)}{960} = \frac{100 + 60}{960} = 0.1667 \text{ or } 16.67\%$$

II. Stock TR

$$\text{Stock TR} = \frac{D_t + (P_E - P_B)}{P_B} = \frac{D_t + PC}{P_B}$$

D_t = the dividend(s) paid during the period

Example: 100 shares of **DataShield** are purchased at $30 per share and sold one year later at $26 per share. A dividend of $2 per share is paid.

$$\text{Stock TR} = \frac{2 + (26 - 30)}{30} = \frac{2 + (-4)}{30} = -0.0667 \text{ or } -6.67\%$$

III. Warrant TR

$$\text{Warrant TR} = \frac{C_t + (P_E - P_B)}{P_B} = \frac{C_t + PC}{P_B} = \frac{PC}{P_B}$$

Where C_t = any cash payment received by the warrant holder during the period. Because warrants pay no dividends, the only return to an investor from owning a warrant is the change in price during the period.

Example: Assume the purchase of warrants of **DataShield** at $3 per share, a holding period of six months, and the sale of $3.75 per share.

$$\text{Warrant TR} = \frac{0 + (3.75 - 3.00)}{3.00} = \frac{0.75}{3.00} = 0.25 \text{ or } 25\%$$

B. RETURN RELATIVE CALCULATIONS

The return relative for the preceding bond example shown is

$$\text{Bond return relative} = \frac{100 + 1020}{960} = 1.1667$$

The return relative for the stock example is

$$\text{Stock return relative} = \frac{2 + 26}{30} = 0.9333$$

The return relative for the warrant example is

$$\text{Warrant return relative} = \frac{3.75}{3.00} = 1.25$$

To convert from a return relative to a TR, subtract 1.0 from the return relative.

In summary, the total return concept is valuable as a measure of return because it is all-inclusive, measuring the total return per dollar of original investment. It facilitates the comparison of asset returns over a specified period, whether the comparison is of different assets, such as stocks versus bonds, or different securities within the same asset category, such as several common stocks. Remember that using this concept does not mean that the securities have to be sold and the gains or losses actually realized.

Table 6-1 shows the S&P/TSX Composite Index for the years 1986 through 2007. Included in the table are end-of-year values for the index, from which capital gains and losses can be computed, and dividends on the index, which constitute the income component.

EXAMPLE 6-1: TOTAL RETURN CALCULATIONS

The TRs for each year can be calculated as shown at the bottom of Table 6-1, where, as a demonstration of these calculations, the TR for 2007 is calculated. In 2007, the market, as measured by the S&P/TSX Composite Index, had a TR of 9.83 percent. In 2006, the same market index showed a TR of 17.28 percent.

Table 6-1

S&P/TSX Composite Index, Dividends in Index Form and Total Returns (TRs), 1986–2007, End-of-Year Values

Year	Index Value	Dividends	TR %
1986	3066.18	91.67	—
1987	3160.05	97.32	6.23545
1988	3381.75	113.96	10.62198
1989	3969.79	129.01	21.20352
1990	3256.75	124.90	−14.81539
1991	3512.36	111.98	11.28702
1992	3350.44	102.34	−1.69630
1993	4321.43	97.81	31.90029
1994	4213.61	100.76	−0.16337
1995	4713.54	107.44	14.41448
1996	5927.03	108.63	28.04941
1997	6699.44	110.27	14.89245
1998	6485.94	108.05	−1.57401
1999	8413.75	110.46	31.42598
2000	8933.68	113.42	7.52756
2001	7688.41	119.12	−12.60567
2002	6614.54	126.32	−12.32439
2003	8220.89	134.95	26.32534
2004	9,246.65	154.42	14.35559
2005	11,272.26	224.32	24.33238
2006	12,908.39	312.38	17.28589
2007	13,833.06	344.44	9.83167

To calculate TR: $TR\% = \frac{(P_t - P_{t-1}) + D_t}{P_{t-1}} \times 100$

Example: For 2007 $TR\% = \frac{(13{,}833.06 - 12{,}908.39) + 344.44}{12{,}908.39} \times 100 = 9.83\%$

Source: *TSX Annual Review*, 1986–2007. Reprinted with permission from the Toronto Stock Exchange.

Return Relative

It is often necessary to measure returns on a slightly different basis than total returns. This is particularly true when calculating either a cumulative wealth index or a geometric mean (both of which are explained below) because negative returns cannot be used in the calculation. The **return relative** solves this problem by adding 1.0 to the total return. Although return relatives may be less than 1.0, they will be greater than zero, thereby eliminating negative numbers.

Equation 6-4 can be modified to calculate return relatives directly by using the price at the end of the holding period in the numerator rather than the change in price, as in Equation 6-5.

$$\text{Return relative} = \frac{CF_t + P_E}{P_B}$$

(6-5)

Return Relative
The total return for an investment for a given time period plus 1.0.

Notice that this is equivalent to adding 1.0 to the total return, since:

$$TR + 1 = \frac{CF_t + (P_E - P_B)}{P_B} + 1 = \frac{CF_t + (P_E - P_B)}{P_B} + \frac{P_B}{P_B} = \frac{CF_t + P_E - P_B + P_B}{P_B} = \frac{CF_t + P_E}{P_B}$$

Examples of return relative calculations for the same three assets as the preceding are shown in Part B of Figure 6-1.

EXAMPLE 6-2: CALCULATING RETURN RELATIVE

A TR of 0.10 for some holding period is equivalent to a return relative of 1.10, and a TR of –0.15 is equivalent to a return relative of 0.85.

Cumulative Wealth Index

Cumulative Wealth Index
Cumulative wealth over time, given an initial amount and a series of returns on some asset.

Return measures, such as TRs, measure changes in the level of wealth. At times, however, it is more desirable to measure levels of wealth (or prices) rather than changes. In other words, we measure the cumulative effect of returns over time given some stated beginning amount, such as $1. To capture the cumulative effect of returns, we use index values. The value of the **cumulative wealth index**, CWI_n, is computed as

(6-6)
$$CWI_n = WI_0 (1 + TR_1) (1 + TR_2)...(1 + TR_n)$$

where
CWI_n = the cumulative wealth index as of the end of period n
WI_0 = the beginning index value, typically $1
TR_1 = the periodic TRs in decimal form (when added to 1.0 as in Equation 6-6, they become return relatives)

EXAMPLE 6-3: CALCULATING THE CUMULATIVE WEALTH INDEX

For the S&P/TSX Index total returns in Table 6-1, the cumulative wealth index for the period 2003–2007 would be, using return relatives,

CWI_{2007} = 1.00 (1.2632534) (1.1435559) (1.2433238) (1.1728589) (1.0983167)

= 2.31369

Thus, $1 invested at the end of 2002 (the beginning of 2003) would have been worth approximately $2.31 by the end of 2007.

Note that the values for the cumulative wealth index can be used to calculate the rate of return for a given period, using Equation 6-7.

(6-7)
$$TR_n = \frac{CWI_n}{CWI_{n-1}} - 1$$

where
TR_n = the total return for period n
CWI = the cumulative wealth index

EXAMPLE 6-4: USING THE CUMULATIVE WEALTH INDEX TO CALCULATE

Using the total returns illustrated above for the years 2003–2007, we can make the following calculations.

CWI_{2007} = 1.00 (1.2632534) (1.1435559) (1.2433238) (1.1728589) (1.0983167)

= 2.31369

CWI_{2006} = 1.00 (1.2632534) (1.1435559) (1.2433238) (1.1728589)

= 2.10658

TR_{2007} = (2.31369/2.10658) − 1

= 0.0983167

Thus, the total return for 2007 was 0.0983167, or 0.0983 rounded.

International Returns

When investors buy and sell assets in other countries, they must consider exchange rate risk. This risk can convert a gain from an investment into a loss or a loss from an investment into a gain. An investment denominated in an appreciating currency relative to the investor's domestic currency will lead to a gain from the currency movement, while an investment in a currency that depreciates relative to the investor's own will mean a decrease in the return.

To calculate the return from an investment in a foreign country, we use Equation 6-8. The foreign currency is stated in domestic terms—that is, the amount of domestic currency necessary to purchase one unit of the foreign currency.

$$\text{Total return in domestic terms} = \frac{[\text{RR} \times \text{Ending value of foreign currency}]}{\text{Beginning value of foreign currency}} - 1.0 \qquad \textbf{(6-8)}$$

EXAMPLE 6-5: INTERNATIONAL RETURN ON WAL-MART

Consider a Canadian investor who invests in Wal-Mart (which trades on the New York Stock Exchange) at $46.18 US when the value of the US dollar stated in Canadian dollars was $1.1654. One year later, Wal-Mart is at $47.53 US and the stock paid a dividend of $0.88 US. The US dollar is now at $0.9913, which means that the Canadian dollar appreciated against it.

Return relative for Wal-Mart   = (.88 + 47.53) / 46.18 = 1.0483

Total return to the Canadian investor after currency adjustment is

TR denominated in Canadian $ = [1.0483 × ($0.9913 / $1.1654)] − 1.0

= [1.0483 × 0.8506] − 1.0

= 0.8917 − 1.0

= .1083 or −10.83%

In this example, the Canadian investor earned a 4.83 percent total return in US currency, yet lost 10.83 percent in Canadian dollars because the US dollar decreased in value significantly against the Canadian dollar. With the weakening of the US dollar, the US dollars from the investment in Wal-Mart buy fewer Canadian dollars when the investment is converted back from US dollars, driving down and negating the return an investor would have earned from +4.83 to −10.83 percent.

Summary Statistics for Returns

The total return, return relative, and wealth index are useful measures of return for a specified period of time. Also needed in investment analysis are statistics to describe a series of returns. For example, investing in a particular stock for 10 years or a different stock in each of 10 years could result in 10 TRs, which must be described by one or more statistics. Two such measures used with returns data are described below.

Arithmetic Mean

The best-known statistic to most people is the arithmetic mean. Therefore, the word mean will refer to the arithmetic mean unless otherwise specified. The arithmetic mean, customarily designated by the symbol $\overline{X}$ (X-bar), is

(6-9)
$$\overline{X} = \frac{\Sigma X}{n}$$

or the sum of each of the values being considered divided by the total number of values n.

EXAMPLE 6-6: CALCULATING THE ARITHMETIC MEAN

Based on data from Table 6-2 for the 21 years from 1987 to 2007, the arithmetic mean is calculated in Table 6-2.

$\overline{X}$ = [6.23 + 10.62 + 21.20 + (−14.81) ... + 9.83] /21

= 227.22/21

= 10.82%

Table 6-2

Calculation of the Arithmetic and Geometric Means for the Years 1987–2007 for the S&P/TSX Composite Index

Year	S&P/TSX TRs (%)	S&P/TSX Return Relatives
1987	6.23	1.0623
1988	10.62	1.1062
1989	21.20	1.2120
1990	−14.81	0.8519
1991	11.28	1.1128
1992	−1.70	0.9830
1993	31.90	1.3190
1994	−0.16	0.9984
1995	14.41	1.1441
1996	28.05	1.2805
1997	14.89	1.1489

Year	S&P/TSX TRs (%)	S&P/TSX Return Relatives
1998	−1.57	0.9843
1999	31.43	1.3143
2000	7.53	1.0753
2001	−12.61	0.8739
2002	−12.32	0.8768
2003	26.33	1.2633
2004	14.36	1.1436
2005	24.33	1.2433
2006	17.29	1.1729
2007	9.83	1.0983

$$\text{Arithmetic mean} = \frac{6.23 + 10.62 + 21.20 + \dots + 9.83}{21} = 10.82\%$$

$$
\begin{aligned}
\text{Geometric mean} &= [(1.0623)(1.1062)(1.2120)\dots(1.0983)]^{1/21} - 1 \\
&= (7.5041125)^{1/21} - 1 \\
&= 1.1007 - 1 \\
&= 0.1007 \text{ or } 10.07\%
\end{aligned}
$$

Source: *TSX Annual Review* 1987–2007

Geometric Mean

The arithmetic mean return is an appropriate measure of the central tendency of a distribution consisting of returns calculated for a particular time period, such as a year. However, when percentage changes in value over time are involved, the arithmetic mean of these changes can be misleading. A different mean, the geometric mean, is needed to describe accurately the "true" average rate of return over multiple periods. The geometric mean return measures the compound rate of growth over time. It is often used in investments and finance to reflect the steady growth rate of invested funds over some past period—that is, the uniform rate at which money actually grew over time, per period. Therefore, it measures the realized change in wealth over multiple periods.

The **geometric mean (G)** is defined as the *n*th root of the product resulting from multiplying a series of return relatives together, as in Equation 6-10.[3]

$$G = [(1 + TR_1)(1 + TR_2)\dots(1 + TR_n)]^{1/n} - 1 \tag{6-10}$$

Geometric Mean
The compound rate of return over time.

where TR is a series of total returns in decimal form. Note that adding 1.0 to each total return produces a return relative. Return relatives are used in calculating geometric mean returns because TRs, which can be negative, cannot be used.[4]

[3]Obviously, in most situations a calculator or computer is needed to calculate the geometric mean. Calculators with power functions can be used to calculate roots.
[4]An alternative method of calculating the geometric mean is to find the log of each return relative, add them, divide by *n*, and take the antilog.

EXAMPLE 6-7: CALCULATING THE GEOMETRIC MEAN

Continuing the example from Table 6-2, consisting of the 21 years of data ending in 2007 for the S&P/TSX Index, we find that the geometric mean would be as shown in Table 6-2:

$$G = [(1.0623)(1.1062)(1.2120)(0.8519) \ldots (1.0983)]^{1/21} - 1$$
$$= (7.5041125)^{1/21} - 1$$
$$= 1.1007 - 1$$
$$= 0.1007 \text{ or } 10.07\%$$

The geometric mean reflects compound, cumulative returns over more than one period. Thus, $1 invested in the S&P/TSX Composite Index would have compounded at an average annual rate of 10.07 percent over the period 1987–2007, producing a cumulative ending wealth of $7.50. In other words, the 1987–2007 cumulative wealth index equals $(1.1007)^{21}$ or 7.50. Notice that the geometric average rate of return in Example 6-7 is lower than the arithmetic average rate of return of 10.82 percent because it reflects the variability of the returns. The geometric mean will always be less than the arithmetic mean unless the values being considered are identical. The spread between the two depends on the dispersion of the distribution: the greater the dispersion, the greater the spread between the two means.

Arithmetic Mean versus Geometric Mean

When should we use the arithmetic mean, and when should we use the geometric mean to describe the returns from financial assets? The answer depends on the investor's objective:

• The arithmetic mean is a better measure of average (typical) performance over single periods.

• The geometric mean is a better measure of the change in wealth over time (multiple periods).

EXAMPLE 6-8: CONTRASTING THE ARITHMETIC AND GEOMETRIC MEANS

As an illustration of how the arithmetic mean can be misleading in describing returns over multiple periods, consider the data in Table 6-3, which shows the movements in price for two stocks over two successive holding periods. Both stocks have a beginning price of $10. Stock A rises to $20 in Period 1 and then declines to $10 in Period 2. Stock B falls to $8 in Period 1 and then rises 50 percent to $12 in Period 2. For stock A, the indicated annual average arithmetic rate of change in price is 25 percent. This is clearly not sensible because the price of stock A at the end of Period 2 is $10, the same as the beginning price. The geometric mean calculation gives the correct annual average rate of change in price of 0 percent per year.

For stock B, the arithmetic average of the annual percentage changes in price is 15 percent. However, if the price actually increased 15 percent each period, the ending price in Period 2 would be $10 (1.15) (1.15) = $13.23. We know that this is not correct because the price at the end of Period 2 is $12. The annual geometric rate of return, 9.54 percent, produces the correct price at the end of Period 2: $10(1.0954)(1.0954) = $12.

Table 6-3

Contrasting the Arithmetic and Geometric Means

Stock	Period 0	Period 1	Period 2	Annual Arithmetic Rate of Return	Annual Geometric Rate of Return
A	$10	$20	$10	[100% + (−50%)]/2 = 25%	$[2.0(0.5)]^{1/2} - 1 = 0\%$
B	$10	$8	$12	[−20% + (50%)]/2 = 15%	$[.8(1.5)]^{1/2} - 1 = 9.54\%$

As these simple examples demonstrate over multiple periods, the geometric mean shows the true average compound rate of growth that actually occurred—that is, the rate at which an invested dollar has grown. On the other hand, we should use the arithmetic mean to represent the likely or typical performance for a single period. Consider the TR data for the S&P/TSX Composite Index for the years 1987–2007 as described earlier. Our best representation of any one year's performance would be the arithmetic mean of 10.82 percent because it was necessary to average this rate of return for a particular year, given the wide spread in the yearly numbers, in order to realize an actual growth rate of 10.07 percent after the fact. Thus, the annual returns of 31.43 percent in 1999 and 26.33 percent in 2003 were offset to a large extent by the annual returns of –12.61 percent for 2001 and –12.32 percent in 2002.

EXAMPLE 6-9: CONTRASTING THE ARITHMETIC AND GEOMETRIC MEANS (CONTINUED)

Assume that the returns for two consecutive years for a particular stock were 16.76 percent and –2.0 percent. The arithmetic mean return for these two years would be exactly 7.38 percent; however, $1 invested at these rates of return would have grown to $1 × 1.1676 × 0.98 = $1.1442, a geometric mean rate of return of only 6.97 percent. Based only on these two observations, our best estimate of the average return for next year would be 7.38 percent, not 6.97 percent.

Inflation-Adjusted Returns

All of the returns discussed above are nominal, or money returns. They measure dollar amounts or changes but say nothing about the purchasing power of these dollars. To capture this dimension, we need to consider real returns, or inflation-adjusted returns. To calculate inflation-adjusted returns, we divide 1 + total nominal return, by 1 + the inflation rate, as shown in Equation 6-11. This calculation is sometimes simplified by subtracting rather than dividing, producing a close approximation.

$$TR_{IA} = \frac{(1 + TR)}{(1 + IF)} - 1$$ **(6-11)**

where
TR_{IA} = the inflation-adjusted total return
IF   = the rate of inflation

This equation applies to both individual years and average total returns.

EXAMPLE 6-10: INFLATION-ADJUSTED RETURN FOR CANADIAN SMALL-CAP COMMON STOCKS

The total return for Canadian small-cap common stocks (according to the Barra Small Cap Index) during 2007 was 1.44 percent. The rate of inflation was 2.38 percent. Therefore, the real (inflation-adjusted) total return for small-cap common stocks was actually negative:

1.0144 / 1.0238 = 0.9908

0.9908 − 1.0 = –0.0092 or –0.92%

Now consider the period 1996 to 2007. The geometric mean for small-cap Canadian common stocks for the entire period was 11.65 percent, and for inflation, 2.05 percent. Therefore, the real (inflation-adjusted) geometric mean rate of return for small-cap common stocks for this period was:

1.1165 / 1.0205 = 1.0941

1.0941 − 1.0 = .0941 or 9.41%

The Consumer Price Index (CPI) typically is used as the measure of inflation. The resulting total returns are in real or constant purchasing-power terms. The compound annual rate of inflation over the period 1996 to 2007 was 2.05 percent. This means that a basket of consumer goods purchased for $1 in January 1996 would cost approximately $1.2757 in December 2007. This is calculated as $(1.0205)^{12}$ (the 2.05 percent inflation rate is rounded, making the $1.2757 approximate).

EXAMPLE 6-11: REAL CUMULATIVE WEALTH INDEX FOR CANADIAN SMALL-CAP COMMON STOCKS

For the period 1996 to 2007, the cumulative wealth index for Canadian small-cap common stocks was $3.7536, while inflation had a total index of $1.2757. Therefore, the real total return index, or equivalently, the real cumulative wealth index, was

$$\$3.7536 \, / \, \$1.2757 = \$2.9424$$

CHECK YOUR UNDERSTANDING

6-3. The cumulative wealth index can be calculated for nominal stock returns, but it cannot show the impact of inflation. Do you agree or disagree?

6-4. What does it mean to say that when you buy a foreign asset, you are selling the Canadian dollar?

6-5. Why must return relatives rather than total return figures be used to calculate the geometric mean?

MEASURING RISK

learning objective 5
Describe the different methods of measuring risk.

Risk is often associated with the dispersion in the likely outcomes. Dispersion refers to variability. Risk is assumed to arise out of variability, which is consistent with our definition of risk as the chance that the actual outcome of an investment will differ from the expected outcome. If an asset's return has no variability, it has, in effect, no risk. Thus, a one-year T-bill purchased to yield 4 percent and held to maturity will, in fact, yield (a nominal) 4 percent. No other outcome is possible, barring default by the Canadian government, which is not considered a reasonable possibility.

Consider an investor analyzing a series of returns (TRs) for the major types of financial assets over some period of years. Knowing the mean of this series is not enough; the investor also needs to know something about the variability in the returns. A histogram presents a frequency distribution pictorially, using a vertical bar for each class in a frequency distribution. The vertical axis shows the frequency (or relative frequency), and the horizontal axis represents the value of the class.

Histograms (distributions) of returns for major financial assets for the period 1938–2007 are shown later in this chapter in Table 6-5. Relative to the other assets, common stocks show the largest variability (dispersion) in returns. Long-term bonds have a smaller variability and therefore a more compact distribution, while T-bills are the least risky assets.

Standard Deviation

Standard Deviation
A measure of the dispersion in outcomes around the expected value.

The risk of distributions can be measured with an absolute measure of dispersion or variability. The most commonly used measure of dispersion over some period of years is the **standard deviation**, which measures the deviation of each observation from the arithmetic mean of the observations. It is considered to be a reliable measure of variability because all the information in a sample is used.[5]

---

[5]The variance is the standard deviation squared. The variance and the standard deviation are similar and can be used for the same purposes; specifically, in investment analysis, both are used as measures of risk. The standard deviation, however, is used more often.

The standard deviation is a measure of the total risk of an asset or a portfolio. It captures the total variability in asset or portfolio return, whatever the source(s) of that variability. The standard deviation can be calculated as

$$s = \sqrt{\frac{\Sigma (X - \overline{X})^2}{n - 1}}$$

(6-12)

where

s = standard deviation
X = each observation in the sample
$\overline{X}$ = the mean of the observations
n = the number of returns in the sample

    Knowing the returns from the sample, we can calculate the standard deviation fairly easily.

EXAMPLE 6-12: CALCULATING THE STANDARD DEVIATION

The standard deviation of the 21 TRs (1987–2007) for the S&P/TSX Composite Index, as shown in Table 6-2, can be calculated as shown in Table 6-4.

Table 6-4

Calculating the Historical Standard Deviation

Year	S&P/TSX TRs (%), X	$X - \overline{X}$	$(X - \overline{X})^2$
1987	6.23	−4.59	21.07
1988	10.62	−0.20	0.04
1989	21.28	10.38	107.74
1990	−14.81	−25.63	656.90
1991	11.28	0.46	0.21
1992	−1.70	−12.52	156.75
1993	31.90	21.08	444.37
1994	−0.16	−10.98	120.56
1995	14.41	3.59	12.89
1996	28.05	17.23	296.87
1997	14.89	4.07	16.56
1998	−1.57	−12.39	153.51
1999	31.43	20.61	424.77
2000	7.53	−3.29	10.82
2001	−12.61	−23.43	548.96
2002	−12.32	−23.14	535.46
2003	26.33	15.51	240.56
2004	14.36	3.54	12.53
2005	24.33	13.51	185.52
2006	17.29	6.47	41.86
2007	9.83	−0.99	0.98

$$\Sigma (X - \overline{X})^2 = 3{,}946.09$$

$$\frac{3717.95}{21 - 1} = 197.30$$

$$(197.30)^{1/2} = 14.05\%$$

In summary, the standard deviation of return measures the total risk of one security or a portfolio of securities. The historical standard deviation can be calculated for individual securities or portfolios of securities using TRs for some specified period of time. This *ex post* value is useful in evaluating the total risk for a particular historical period and in estimating the total risk that is expected to prevail over some future period.

The standard deviation, combined with the normal distribution, can provide some useful information about the dispersion or variation in returns. In a normal distribution, the probability that a particular outcome will be above (or below) a specified value can be determined. For normal distributions, within one standard deviation on either side of the arithmetic mean of the distribution, 68.3 percent of the outcomes will be encompassed; that is, there is a 68.3 percent probability that the actual outcome will be within one (plus or minus) standard deviation of the arithmetic mean. The probabilities are 95 percent and 99 percent that the actual outcome will be within two or three standard deviations, respectively, of the arithmetic mean.

Risk Premiums

Risk Premium

That part of a security's return above the risk-free rate of return. The greater the risk of the asset, the greater the associated risk premium.

A **risk premium** is the additional return that investors expect to receive, or actually do receive, by taking on increasing amounts of risk. It measures the payoff for taking various types of risk. Such premiums can be calculated between any two classes of securities. Two well-known risk premiums are

1. The difference between stocks and a risk-free rate (proxied by the return on T-bills), referred to as the **equity risk premium**;

Equity Risk Premium

The difference between stock returns and the risk-free rate (measured as the return on T-bills).

2. The difference between long-term government bonds and the risk-free rate as measured by the return on T-bills, referred to as the bond horizon premium.

In order to maintain consistency with our other series, these risk premiums are measured as the geometric differences between pairs of return series. Therefore:

(6-13)
$$ERP = \frac{(1 + TR_{CS})}{(1 + RF)} - 1$$

where
ERP = the equity risk premium
TR_{CS} = the total return on stocks
RF = the risk-free rate (the T-bill rate)

and,

(6-14)
$$BHP = \frac{(1 + TR_{GB})}{(1 + TR_{TB})}\overline{X} - 1$$

where
BHP = the bond horizon premium
TR_{GB} = the total return on long-term government bonds
TR_{TB} = the total return on T-bills

Other risk premiums can also be calculated. For example, the bond default premium is measured by the difference between the return on long-term corporate bonds and on long-term government bonds. This premium reflects the additional compensation for investing in risky corporate bonds, which have some probability of default, rather than government bonds, which do not.

REALIZED RETURNS AND RISKS FROM INVESTING

learning objective 6
Discuss the returns and risks from investing in major financial assets in the past.

We can now proceed to examine the returns and risks from investing in major financial assets that have occurred in Canada. We also will see how the preceding return and risk measures are typically used in presenting realized return and risk data of interest to virtually all financial market participants.

Table 6-5 shows the average annual geometric and arithmetic returns, as well as standard deviations, for major financial assets for the 1938–2007 period.

Total Returns and Standard Deviations

Table 6-5 indicates that Canadian common stocks had a geometric mean annual return over this 70-year period of 10.68 percent. Hence, $1 invested in the market index at the beginning of 1938 would have grown at an average annual compound rate of 10.68 percent over this period. In contrast, the arithmetic mean annual return for stocks was 11.79 percent. The best estimate of the "average" return for stocks in any one year, using only this information, would be 11.79 percent, not the 10.68 percent geometric mean return.

Table 6-5

Summary Statistics of Annual Total Returns for Major Financial Assets, 1938–2007

Series	Geometric Mean	Arithmetic Mean	Standard Deviation	Distribution
Canadian Common Stocks	10.68%	11.79%	16.22%	
US Common Stocks	11.47%	13.15%	17.54%	
Long-Term Government of Canada Bonds	6.18%	6.62%	9.32%	
91-Day Government of Canada Bonds	5.09%	5.20%	4.32%	
Inflation (CPI)	3.88%	3.94%	3.55%	

Source: The Canadian Institute of Actuaries (CIA) website: www.actuaries.ca. Reprinted with permission from the Canadian Institute of Actuaries. The 2003–2007 figures were obtained from the media and from the Datastream database.

The difference between these two means is related to the variability of the stock return series. Given the data in Table 6-5, the linkage between the geometric mean and the arithmetic mean is approximated by Equation 6-15:

(6-15)
$$(1 + G)^2 \approx (1 + AM)^2 - (SD)^2$$

where

G   = the geometric mean of a series of asset returns
AM   = the arithmetic mean of a series of asset returns
SD   = the standard deviation of the arithmetic series of returns

Using the data in Table 6-5 for common stocks:

$$(1.1068)^2 \approx (1.1179)^2 - (0.1622)^2$$
$$1.225 \approx 1.250 - 0.026$$
$$1.225 \approx 1.224$$

Thus, if we know the arithmetic mean of a series of asset returns and the standard deviation of the series, we can approximate the geometric mean for this series. As the standard deviation of the series increases, holding the arithmetic mean constant, the geometric mean decreases.

Table 6-5 also reports statistics for US stocks, long-term Government of Canada bonds, as well as 91-day T-bills, and the inflation rate. As we would expect, the returns are lower for bonds and T-bills than for stocks. Notice the smaller differences between the geometric and arithmetic means for bonds, T-bills, and inflation, reflecting the much lower levels of variability in these series.

The standard deviations for each of the major financial assets in Table 6-5 reflect the dispersion of the returns over the 70-year period covered in the data. The standard deviations clearly show the wide dispersion in the returns from common stocks compared with bonds and T-bills. Canadian common stocks had a standard deviation of returns of 16.22 percent, about 1.74 times that of long-term bonds and about 3.75 times that of T-bills. Therefore, common stocks were riskier, with more variable returns (greater dispersion), as reflected in their standard deviation.

Cumulative Wealth Indexes

Figure 6-2 shows the cumulative wealth indexes for the major financial assets and the corresponding index number for inflation, as measured by the Consumer Price Index. The series starts at the end of 1938 and shows the cumulative results of starting with $1 in each of these series and going through the end of 2007.

EXAMPLE 6-13: CALCULATING CUMULATIVE ENDING WEALTH FOR COMMON STOCKS

The ending wealth value of $1,218.36 for common stocks in Figure 6-2 is the result of compounding at 10.68341 percent for 70 years, or

$$CWI_{2007} = WI_0 (1.1068341)^{70} = \$1.00 (1218.36) = \$1,218.36$$

As Figure 6-2 shows, the returns on Canadian stocks dominated the returns on long-term Government of Canada bonds over this period. In Example 6-13, we use the geometric mean for 1938–2007 from Table 6-5 (carried out to five decimal places to 10.68341 percent) to calculate cumulative ending wealth for common stocks that is shown in Figure 6-2.

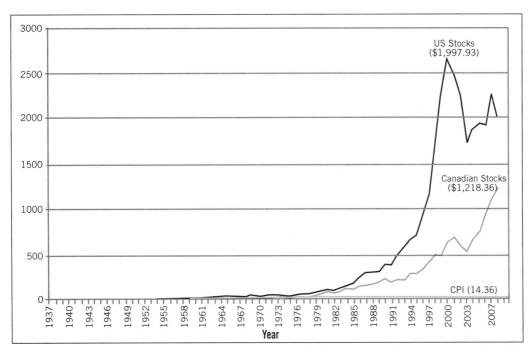

Figure 6-2
Wealth Indexes for
Financial Instruments,
1938–2007

Data Source: CIA website: www.actuaries.ca and Datastream database. Reprinted with permission from the Canadian Institute of Actuaries and Datastream database.

The large cumulative wealth index value for US common stocks (as measured by the Canadian dollar return on US stocks) is also presented in Figure 6-2. One Canadian dollar invested in these stocks would have grown to $1,997.93, which is calculated in the manner demonstrated in the example above. Notice the large difference in ending wealth as a result of the additional 0.79 percent in annual geometric average returns offered by US stocks (i.e., 11.47 percent for US stocks versus 10.68 percent for Canadian stocks).

On an inflation-adjusted basis, the cumulative ending wealth for any of the series can be calculated as

$$CWI_{IA} = \frac{CWI}{CI_{INF}}$$ **(6-16)**

where

CWI_{IA} = the cumulative wealth index value for any asset on an inflation-adjusted basis
CWI = the cumulative wealth index value for any asset on a nominal basis
CI_{INF} = the ending index value for inflation, calculated as $(1 + \text{geometric rate of inflation})^n$, where n is the number of periods considered

EXAMPLE 6-14: ADJUSTING COMMON STOCK CUMULATIVE WEALTH INDEX FOR INFLATION

The cumulative wealth index for common stocks for the period 1938–2007 was $1,218.36. The geometric average annual rate of inflation over this period was 3.88 percent. The ending index number for inflation was, therefore, $(1.0388)^{70} = 14.34$. On an inflation-adjusted basis, the common stock cumulative wealth index value as of 2007 was

$$CWI_{IA} = \frac{\$1,218.36}{14.34}$$

$$= \$84.96$$

This number indicates that, on an inflation-adjusted basis, an investor in common stocks would have multiplied his or her real wealth by a factor of about 84.96 during the period 1938–2007.

Also note that the cumulative wealth index is equivalent to a cumulative total return index and, as such, can be decomposed into the two components of total return: the yield component and the price change component. Because the CWI is a multiplicative relationship, these two components are multiplicative. To solve for either one, we divide the CWI by the other, as in Equation 6-17 and Equation 6-18.

(6-17)
$$CPC = \frac{CWI}{YI}$$

(6-18)
$$YI = \frac{CWI}{CPC}$$

where
CPC = the cumulative price change component of total return on an index number basis
CWI = the cumulative wealth index or total return index for a series
YI   = the yield component of total return on an index number basis

Of course, the single most striking feature of Figure 6-2 is the tremendous difference in ending wealth between US and Canadian stocks. This difference reflects the impact of compounding substantially different mean returns over long periods of time, which produces a dramatic difference in ending results.

Compounding and Discounting

The use of compounding in the previous section points out the importance of this concept and of its complement—discounting. Both are important in investment analysis and are used often. Compounding involves determining the future values resulting from compound interest—earning interest on interest. As we saw, the calculation of wealth indexes involves compounding at the geometric mean return over some historical period.

Present value (discounting) is the value today of a dollar to be received in the future. Such dollars are not comparable because of the time value of money. In order to be comparable, they must be discounted back to the present. Present value concepts are used extensively in Chapters 11 and 13 and in other chapters as needed. Students who do not feel comfortable with these concepts would be well advised to refer to the appropriate section of their introductory finance textbooks.

Tables are readily available for both compounding and discounting, and calculators and computers make these calculations a simple matter. These tables are available at the end of this text.

CHECK YOUR UNDERSTANDING

6-9. It is well known that the inflation rate has been very low in recent years. Why, then, should investors be concerned with inflation-adjusted returns?

6-10. Why do you suppose that the long-term average return for Canadian common stocks has been slightly lower than for US common stocks?

SUMMARY

This summary relates to the learning objectives for this chapter.

1. **Define "return" and state its two components.**

   The term return can be used in different ways. It is important to distinguish between realized (*ex post*, or historical) return and expected (*ex ante*, or anticipated) return. The two components of return are yield and price change (capital gain or loss).

2. **Explain the relationship between return and risk.**

   Risk and expected return should always be considered together. An investor cannot reasonably expect to earn larger returns without assuming greater risks.

3. **Identify the sources of risk.**

   The general components of risk have traditionally been categorized into interest rate, market, inflation, business, financial, and liquidity risks. Investors today must also consider exchange rate risk and country risk. Modern analysis divides these sources into two categories: systematic (market) risk and non-systematic (non-market) risk.

4. **Describe the different methods of measuring returns.**

   The total return is a percentage return concept that can be used to measure correctly the return for any security. The return relative, which adds 1.0 to the total return, is used when calculating the geometric mean of a series of returns. The cumulative wealth index is used to measure the cumulative wealth over time, given some initial starting wealth (typically $1) and a series of returns for some asset. Return relatives, along with the beginning and ending values of the foreign currency, can be used to convert the return on a foreign investment into a domestic return. The geometric mean measures the compound rate of return over time. The arithmetic mean, on the other hand, is simply the average return for a series and is used to measure the typical performance for a single period. Inflation-adjusted returns can be calculated by dividing 1 + the nominal return, by 1 + the inflation rate (as measured by the CPI).

5. **Describe the different methods of measuring risk.**

   Historical returns can be described in terms of a frequency distribution and their variability measured by use of the standard deviation. The standard deviation provides useful information about the distribution of returns and aids investors in assessing the possible outcomes of an investment.

6. **Discuss the returns and risks from investing in major financial assets in the past.**

   Canadian common stocks over the period 1938 to 2007 had an annualized geometric mean total return of 10.68 percent, compared to 6.18 percent for long-term bonds and 5.09 percent for T-bills. Over the same period, common stocks had a standard deviation of returns of approximately 16.22 percent, about 1.74 times that of long-term bonds and 3.75 times that of T-bills.

KEY TERMS

Capital gain (loss), p.154
Cumulative wealth index p.162
Equity risk premium p.170
Exchange rate risk p.157
Geometric mean p.165

Interest rate risk p.155
Market risk p.156
Non-systematic (non-market) risk p.158
Return relative p.161

Risk premium p.170
Standard deviation p.168
Systematic (market) risk p.158
Total return (TR) p.159
Yield p.154

REVIEW QUESTIONS

6-1. How long must an asset be held to calculate a TR?

6-2. Define the components of total return. Can any of these components be negative?

6-3. When should the arithmetic mean be used when talking about stock returns?

6-4. What is an equity risk premium?

6-5. Distinguish between TR and holding period return.

6-6. According to Table 6-5, common stocks have generally returned more than bonds. How, then, can they be considered more risky?

6-7. Distinguish between market risk and business risk. How is interest rate risk related to inflation risk?

6-8. Explain what is meant by country risk. How would you evaluate the country risk of Canada and Mexico?

6-9. Assume that you purchase a stock in yen on a Japanese market. During the period you hold the stock, the yen weakens relative to the Canadian dollar. Assume you sell at a profit on the Japanese market. How will your return, when converted to dollars, be affected?

6-10. Define risk. How does the use of the standard deviation as a measure of risk relate to this definition of risk?

6-11. Explain how the geometric mean annual average inflation rate can be used to calculate inflation-adjusted stock returns over the 1938–2007 period.

6-12. Explain the two components of the cumulative wealth index for common stocks. If we know one of these components on a cumulative wealth basis, how can the other be calculated?

6-13. Common stocks have returned close to twice the compound annual rate of return for bonds over long periods of time. Does this mean that common stocks are about twice as risky as bonds?

6-14. When should the geometric mean return be used to measure returns? Why will it always be less than the arithmetic mean (unless the numbers are identical)?

6-15. What is the mathematical linkage between the arithmetic mean and the geometric mean for a set of security returns?

6-16. Classify the traditional sources of risk as general sources or specific sources of risk.

6-17. Explain verbally the relationship between the geometric mean and a cumulative wealth index.

6-18. As Table 6-5 shows, the geometric mean return for Canadian stocks over a 70-year period has been around 10.68 percent. The returns on bonds over a 15-year period (1989–2003) has averaged approximately 13.3 percent, leading some to recommend that investors avoid stocks and purchase bonds because the returns are similar (or even better on bonds) and the risk is far less. Critique this argument.

6-19. What does it mean if the cumulative wealth index for government bonds over a long period is 0.85?

DEMONSTRATION PROBLEMS

6-1. **Calculation of Total Return:** Calculate total returns using the following information for XPO, a hypothetical company.

Year	(1) End-of-Year Price (P_t)	(2) Calendar-Year Dividends (D_t)	(3) Capital Gain ($P_t - P_{t-1}$)	(4) Total Return in $ (2) + (3) = TR	(5) TR% [100 (4) / P_{t-1}]
20X3	$24.70	$1.105	—	—	—
20X4	27.20	1.26	$2.50	$3.76	15.22
20X5	36.30	1.42	9.10	10.52	38.68
20X6	35.75	1.58	−0.55	1.03	2.84
20X7	38.25	1.62			

20X7 income or yield component is the calendar-year dividend of $1.62. The 20X7 capital gain (loss) is the end-of-year price in 20X7 minus the end-of-year 20X6 price—$38.25 2 $35.75 5 $2.50. The total dollar return for calendar-year 20X7 is equal to income 1 capital gain 5 $1.62 + $2.50 5 $4.12.

The total return (r) in percentage form (r%) for 20X7 was

$$TR = \frac{\$TR}{P_{t-1}} = \frac{\$4.12}{\$35.75} = 0.1152 = 11.52\%$$

The same result is obtained as

$$r = \frac{D_t}{P_{t-1}} + \frac{PC}{P_{t-1}} = \frac{\$1.62}{\$35.75} + \frac{\$2.50}{\$35.75} = 0.0453147 + 0.069930 = 0.1152 = r,$$

$r\% = 11.52$

With the additional information that the price at the end of calendar-year 20X2 was $25.50, we can calculate the values for 20X3 as capital gain 52$0.80, and total return is $0.31. The TR percent is equal to 1.216 percent.

6-2. **Calculation of Arithmetic Mean and Geometric Mean:**

Year(t)	(1) End-of-Year Price (P_t)	(2) Calendar-Year Dividends (D_t)	TR%
20X0	$74.60	$2.88	—
20X1	64.30	3.44	−9.2%
20X2	67.70	3.44	10.6
20X3	56.70	3.44	−11.2
20X4	96.25	3.44	75.8
20X5	122.00	3.71	30.6

The arithmetic mean of the holding period for WSC 20X3–20X7:

$$\frac{\Sigma(TR\%)}{n} = \frac{96.6}{5} = 19.32\%$$

The geometric mean in this example is the fifth root of the product of the $(1 + r)$ version of the TR percent. We formed the TR percent by multiplying the decimal by 100 to get r percent. Now back up to the $(1 + r)$:

Year	TR% = r%	r	(I + r)
20X3	−9.2%	−0.092	0.908
20X4	10.6	0.106	1.106
20X5	−11.2	−0.112	0.888
20X6	75.8	0.758	1.758
20X7	30.6	0.306	1.306

The geometric mean is $GM = [(1 + R_1)(1 + R_2) \ldots (1 + R_n)]^{1/n} - 1$. Therefore, take the fifth root of the product

$$(0.908)(1.106)(0.888)(1.758)(1.306) = 2.047462654, \text{ and}$$

$$(2.047462654)^{1/5} = 1.1541 = (1 + r), r = 0.1541 = 15.41\%$$

6-3. **The Effects of Reinvesting Returns:** The difference in meaning of the arithmetic and geometric mean, holding WSC stock over the period January 1, 20X3 through December 31, 20X7 for two different investment strategies, is as follows:

Strategy A — keep a fixed amount (say, $1,000) invested and do not reinvest returns.

Strategy B — reinvest returns and allow compounding.

First, take WSC's TRs and convert them to decimal form (r) for Strategy A, and then to $(1 + r)$ form for Strategy B.

	Strategy A				Strategy B		
Jan. 1 Year	Amt. Inv. ×	r_i =	Return	Jan. 1 Year	Amt. Inv. ×	$(1 + r_t)$ =	Terminal Amt.
20X3	$1000	−0.092	−92.00	20X3	$1000.00	0.908	$908.00
20X4	1000	0.106	106.00	20X4	908.00	1.106	1004.25
20X5	1000	−0.112	−112.00	20X5	1004.25	0.888	891.77
20X6	1000	0.758	758.00	20X6	891.77	1.758	1567.74
20X7	1000	0.306	306.00	20X7	1567.74	1.306	2047.46
20X8	1000			20X8	2047.46		

Using Strategy A, keeping $1,000 invested at the beginning of the year, total returns for the years 20X1–20X5 were $966, or $193.20 per year average ($966/5), which on a $1,000 investment is $193.20/1000 = 0.1932, or 19.32 percent per year—the same value as the arithmetic mean in Demonstration Problem 6-2.

Using Strategy B, compounding gains and losses, total return was $1,047.46 (the terminal amount $2,047.46 minus the initial $1,000). The average annual rate of return in this situation can be found by taking the nth root of the terminal/initial amount:

$$[2047.46/1000]^{1/5} = (2.04746)^{1/5} = 1.1541 = (1 + r), r\% = 15.41\%$$

which is exactly the set of values we ended up with in Demonstration Problem 6-2 when calculating the geometric mean.

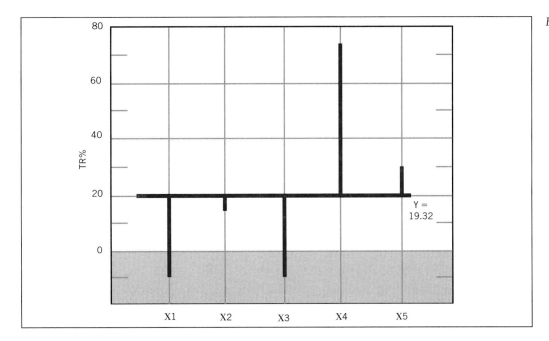

Figure 6-3

6-4. **Calculating the Standard Deviation:** Using the TR values for WSC for the five years 20X3–20X7, we can illustrate the deviation of the values from the mean (Y) graphically.

The numerator for the formula for the variance of these Y_t values is $S(Y_t - Y)^2$, which we will call SS_y, the sum of the squared deviations of the Y_t around Y. Algebraically, there is a simpler alternative formula.

$$SS_y = \Sigma(Y_t - Y)^2 = \Sigma Y_t^2 - \frac{(\Sigma Y_t)^2}{n}$$

Using WSC's annual total returns, we will calculate the SS_y both ways.

Year	$Y_t = TR$	$(Y_t - \overline{Y})$	$(\overline{Y}_t - Y)^2$	Y_t^2
20X1	−9.2%	28.52	813.3904	84.64
20X2	10.6	−8.72	76.0384	112.36
20X3	−11.2	−30.52	931.4704	125.44
20X4	75.8	56.48	3189.9904	5745.64
20X5	30.6	11.28	127.2384	936.36
Sum	96.6	-0-	5138.1280	7004.44

$$\overline{Y} = 19.32\%$$
$$SS_y = \Sigma(Y_t - \overline{Y})^2 = 5138.128, \text{ and also}$$
$$SS_y = \Sigma Y_t^2 - \frac{(\Sigma Y_t)^2}{n} = 7004.44 - \frac{(96.6)^2}{-5} = 5138.128$$

The variance is the "average" squared deviation from the mean:

$$s^2 = \frac{SS_y}{(n-1)} = \frac{5138.128}{4} = 1284.532 \text{ "squared percent"}$$

The standard deviation is the square root of the variance:

$$s = (s^2)^{1/2} = (1284.532)^{1/2} = 35.84\%$$

The standard deviation is the same units of measurement as the original observations, as is the arithmetic mean.

6-5. Calculation of Cumulative Wealth Index and Geometric Mean: By using the geometric mean annual average rate of return for a particular financial asset, the cumulative wealth index can be found by converting the TR on a geometric mean basis to a return relative by adding 1.0, and raising this return relative to the power representing the number of years involved. Consider the geometric mean of 6.18 percent for long-term Government of Canada bonds for the 1938–2007 period. The cumulative wealth index, using a starting index value of $1, is, for the 70 years involved here,

$$\$1\ (1.0618)^{70} = \$66.53$$

Conversely, if we know the cumulative wealth index value, we can solve for the geometric mean by taking the *n*th root and subtracting out 1.0.

$$(\$66.53)^{1/70} - 1.0 = 1.0618 - 1.0 = 6.18\%$$

6-6. **Calculation of Inflation-Adjusted Returns:** Knowing the geometric mean for inflation for some time period, we can add 1.0 and raise it to the *n*th power. We then divide the cumulative wealth index on a nominal basis by the ending value for inflation to obtain inflation-adjusted returns. For example, given a cumulative wealth index of $66.53 for long-term Canada bonds for the 1938–2007 period, and a geometric mean inflation rate of 3.88 percent, the inflation-adjusted cumulative wealth index for this 70-year period is calculated as

$$\$66.53/(1.0388)^{70} = \$66.53/14.34 = \$4.64$$

PROBLEMS

6-1. Using the data for WSC from Demonstration Problem 6-2, calculate the capital gain (loss) and total return for the years 20X3–20X7 and confirm the 20X5 and 20X6 TRs.

6-2. Assume that an investor in a 28 percent marginal tax bracket buys 100 shares of a stock for $40, holds it for five months, and sells it at $50. What tax, in dollars, will be paid on the gain?

6-3. Calculate the future value of $100 at the end of 5, 10, 20, and 30 years, given an interest rate of 12 percent. Calculate the present value of $1 to be received at the end of those same periods, given the same interest rate.

6-4. Calculate the TR and the return relative for the following assets:
   a. A preferred stock bought for $70 per share, held one year during which $5 per share dividends are collected, and sold for $63.
   b. A warrant bought for $11 and sold three months later for $13.
   c. A 12 percent bond bought for $870, held two years during which interest is collected, and sold for $930.

6-5. Show that the geometric mean return for XPO (Demonstration Problem 6-1) for the five years 20X3 to 20X7 is 13.15 percent.

6-6. a. Using a calculator, calculate the arithmetic and geometric mean rate of return for the S&P/TSX Composite Index (Table 6-1) for the years 2003–2007.

b. Using a calculator, calculate the standard deviation of TRs (from Table 6-1) for the years 2003 through 2007.

6-7. Calculate the index value for the S&P/TSX Index (Table 6-2) assuming a $1 investment at the beginning of 2003 and extending through the end of 2007. Using only these index values, calculate the geometric mean for these years.

6-8. Replicate Demonstration Problem 6-3 for the XPO data, showing Strategy A (not investing returns) and Strategy B (reinvest returns and allow compounding).

6-9. Show that the standard deviation for XPO's five annual TRs is equal to 15.042 percent.

6-10. Calculate the cumulative wealth index for government bonds for the period 1926–2007 assuming a geometric mean annual average rate of return of 5 percent.

6-11. Given a cumulative wealth index for corporate bonds of $54.15 for the period 1930–2007, calculate the geometric mean annual average rate of return.

6-12. Given an inflation rate of 3.13 percent over the period 1930–2007 (geometric mean annual average), calculate the inflation-adjusted cumulative wealth index for "small" common stocks as of year-end 2007, assuming that the nominal cumulative wealth index for this asset class was $3,056.26.

6-13. If a basket of consumer goods cost $1 at the end of 1928 and $11 at the end of 2007, calculate the geometric mean annual average rate of inflation over this period.

6-14. Using the TRs for the years 1987–2007 from Table 6-1, determine the geometric mean for this period.

6-15. Using data for three periods, construct a set of TRs that will produce a geometric mean equal to the arithmetic mean.

6-16. According to Table 6-5, the standard deviation for common stocks for the period 1938–2007 was 16.22 percent. Using data from Table 6-1, calculate the standard deviation for the years 2003–2007 and compare your results.

6-17. Listed below are the end-of-year prices and annual dividends for XYZ Corp.

Year	End-of-Year Price	Annual Dividends
2003	$65	$1.20
2004	$72	$1.50
2005	$67	$1.50
2006	$70	$1.60
2007	$72.50	$1.60

a. Calculate the total return (in percentages) for 2004, 2005, 2006, and 2007, and also calculate the return relatives for these years.
b. Calculate the arithmetic average return over the 2004–2007 holding period.
c. Calculate the annualized geometric average return over the 2004–2007 holding period.
d. Determine the cumulative wealth index for the 2005–2007 period.
e. Based solely on the historical information above, what is your best estimate for the return on this portfolio for 2008? Briefly explain.

6-18. Consider a corporate bond that matured on January 1, 2008, and paid a 5 percent coupon ($50) on the first day of each year. The table below shows the market price for this bond at the start of each year from 2003 to 2008. Assume you purchased the bond on January 1, 2003 at the price shown (you would not receive a coupon interest payment until 2004). For each of the five years from 2004 to 2008, calculate your total annual return on this bond investment, as well as the cumulative wealth index (start with a value of 1.00 for 2003).

The table also shows the exchange rate (Canadian dollars required to purchase one US dollar.) over the same period. Assume you are a Canadian investor, but this is a US corporate bond (all prices and coupons denominated in US dollars). What would your total return and cumulative wealth index values be for each year?

	Bond Price ($)	Exchange Rate ($CAD/$US)
2003	1044.52	1.5747
2004	1017.94	1.2900
2005	1006.84	1.2252
2006	1018.86	1.1571
2007	1016.95	1.1649
2008	1000.00	0.9927

6-19. The following data for stock of the Royal Bank of Canada (stock symbol = RY on the TSX) are the December ending prices (adjusted for stock splits) and the annual dividend. This information was obtained from the bank's website and annual reports. Place these data in columns A to C in a spreadsheet. Use three decimal places and calculate results in decimal form (not percentages) for each year from 1993 to 2007 for the following.

   a. Calculate in column D the return relative for the price change only.
   b. Calculate in column E the total return based on price change only.
   c. Calculate in column F the return relative for the price change and dividends.
   d. Calculate in column G the total return based on price change and dividends.
   e. Calculate the arithmetic and geometric means for the return figures (above) for the period from 1993 to 2007.
   f. Calculate the ending wealth as of December 31, 2007 for $100 invested in Royal Bank stock as of the beginning of 1993. Be sure to include the dividends in your calculation.
   g. Calculate the standard deviation of the total returns for the years 1993 to 2007. (Note: Use the total returns, not the return relatives.)

Royal Bank Year-End Prices and Dividends

Year	Closing Price	Dividends
2007	50.74	1.82
2006	55.50	1.44
2005	45.41	1.175
2004	32.13	1.01
2003	30.90	0.86
2002	28.93	0.76
2001	25.92	0.69
2000	25.43	0.57
1999	15.88	0.47
1998	19.14	0.44
1997	18.90	0.38
1996	12.03	0.335
1995	7.78	0.295
1994	7.03	0.29
1993	7.22	0.29
1992	6.16	

PREPARING FOR YOUR PROFESSIONAL EXAMS

CFA PRACTICE QUESTIONS

6-1. Given the following series of returns for an investment: R1 = 10%, R2 = 15%, R3 = −10%, R4 = 20%, and R5 = 5%, what is the arithmetic and geometric mean of this series of returns?

    a. 7.5 percent   8 percent
    b. 8 percent   7.5 percent
    c. 8 percent   8.5 percent
    d. 10 percent   10.5 percent

6-2. A portfolio realized a 10 percent return in Year 1 and a −10 percent return in Year 2. The geometric mean return over the two-year period is:

    a. 0.99 percent.
    b. −0.50 percent.
    c. 0.995 percent.
    d. 0.00 percent.

6-3. A US investor who buys Japanese bonds will most likely maximize his return if interest rates:

    a. fall and the dollar weakens relative to the yen
    b. fall and the yen weakens relative to the dollar
    c. rise and the dollar weakens relative to the yen
    d. rise and the yen weakens relative to the dollar

6-4. An analyst developed the following probability distribution of the rate of return for a common stock:

Scenario	Probability	Rate of Return
1	0.25	0.08
2	0.50	0.12
3	0.25	0.16

The standard deviation of the rate of return is closest to:

    a. 0.0200
    b. 0.0267
    c. 0.0283
    d. 0.0400

CHAPTER 7

EXPECTED RETURN AND RISK

Chapter 7 analyzes expected return and risk, the two key components needed to construct portfolios. The critically important principle of Markowitz diversification is explored, focusing primarily on the concepts of the correlation coefficient and covariance as applied to security returns. In Chapter 8 we will complete the basics of Markowitz portfolio theory.

Learning Objectives

After reading this chapter, you should be able to

1. Explain how expected return and risk for securities are determined.
2. Explain how expected return and risk for portfolios are determined.
3. Describe the Markowitz diversification model for calculating portfolio risk.
4. Simplify Markowitz's calculations by using the single-index model.

CHAPTER PREVIEW

In Chapter 6, we discussed the returns and risks from financial assets that investors have realized in the past. In this chapter, we consider how investors estimate and manage the expected returns and risks from future investments. You will learn how to estimate return and risk for both individual securities and portfolios. We introduce the Markowitz diversification model for calculating portfolio risk, focusing primarily on the concepts of the correlation coefficient and covariance. Finally, we present the single-index model, which simplifies Markowitz's calculations.

FUTURE RETURN AND RISK

As stated in Chapter 1, this text is concerned primarily with investing in marketable securities. An investment in financial assets represents the current commitment of an investor's funds (wealth) for a future period of time in order to earn a flow of funds that compensates for two factors: the time the funds are committed and the risk involved. In effect, investors are trading a known present value for some expected future value that is not known with certainty.

When we invest, we defer current consumption in order to increase our expected future consumption. We are concerned with the increase in wealth from our investments, and this increase is typically measured as a rate of return in order to adjust for differing dollar amounts of investment.

Risk is the chance that the actual return from an investment will differ from its expected return. In an uncertain world, risk is the opposite side of the coin from return. Investors are concerned primarily with how to achieve the highest possible returns without bearing unacceptable risk. Real-World Returns 7-1 provides an interesting discussion of risk and how best to understand it. In this essay, Peter Bernstein, one of the most prominent observers of the investing environment over many years, argues that when approaching risky decisions three elements should be considered: (1) the balance between the consequences of being wrong and the probability of being wrong; (2) expecting the unexpected; and (3) control over the outcomes.

REAL-WORLD RETURNS 7-1

Risk: The Whole versus the Parts

Many years ago, in the middle of a staff meeting, a colleague passed me a scrap of paper on which he had written, "When all is said and done, more things are said than done." When I consider the plethora of books, articles, consultants, and conferences on risk in today's world, my friend's aphorism has never seemed more appropriate. Are we never going to nail risk down and bring it under control? How much more can anyone reveal to us beyond what we have already been told?

In a very real sense, this flood of material about risk is inherently risky. Sorting out the pieces and searching for main themes has become an escalating challenge. The root of the matter gets lost in the shuffle while we are analyzing all the elegant advances in risk measurement and the impressive broadening of the kinds of risks we seek to manage. More is said than is done, or what is done loses touch with what has been said.

If we go back to first principles for a moment, perhaps we can put the multifarious individual pieces into some kind of a larger framework and optimize the choices among the masses of information we are attempting to master.

Professor Elroy Dimson of the London Business School once said risk means more things can happen than will happen. Dimson's formulation is only a fancy way of saying that we do not know what is going to happen—good or bad. Even the range of possible outcomes remains indeterminate, much as we would like to nail it down. Remember always: Risk is not about uncertainty but about the unknown, the inescapable darkness of the future.

If more things can happen than will happen, and if we are denied precise knowledge of the range of possible outcomes, some decisions we make are going to be wrong. How many, how often, how seriously? We have no way of knowing even that. Even the most elegant model, as Leibniz reminded Jacob Bernouilli in 1703, is going to work "only for the most part." What lurks in the smaller part is hidden from us, but it could turn into a load of dynamite.

The beginning of wisdom in life is in accepting the inevitability of being wrong on occasion. Or, to turn that phrase around, the greatest risks we take are those where we are certain of the outcome—as masses of people are at classic market bottoms and tops. My investment philosophy has always been that victory in the long run accrues to the humble rather than to the bold.

This emphasis on ignorance is the necessary first step toward the larger framework we need if we hope to sort out the flood of information about risk that assails us. Now we can break down the problem of risk into what appear to me to be its three primary constituent parts.

First, what is the balance between the consequences of being wrong and the probability of being wrong? Many mistakes do not matter. Other mistakes can be fatal. No matter how small the probability you will be hit by a car when you cross against the lights, the consequences of being hit deserve the greater weight in the decision. This line of questioning is the beginning, and in some ways the end, of risk management. All decisions must pass through this sieve. It is the end if you decide not to take the risk, but it is also the end in the sense that distinguishing between consequences and probabilities is what risk management is all about.

Second, expect the unexpected. That sounds like an empty cliché, but it has profound meaning for risk management. It is easy to prepare for the risks you know—earnings fail to meet expectations, clients depart, bonds go sour, a valued associate goes to a competitor. Insurance and hedging strategies cover other kinds of risks lying in wait out there, from price volatility to premature death.

But preparation for the unexpected is a matter of the decision-making structure, and nothing else. Who is in charge here? That is the critical question in any organization. And if it is just you there when the unexpected strikes, then you should prepare in advance for where you will turn for help when matters seem to be running out of control.

Finally, note that word "control." With an exit strategy—when decisions are easily reversible—control over outcomes can be a secondary matter. But with decisions such as launching a new product or getting married, the costs of reversibility are so high that you should not enter into them unless you have some control over the outcome if things turn out differently from what you expect. Gambling is fun because your bet is irreversible and you have no control over the outcome. But real life is not a gambling casino.

These three elements are what risky decisions are all about—consequences versus probabilities, preparation for dealing with unexpected outcomes, and the distinction between reversibility and control. These are where things get done, not said.

Source: Bernstein, Peter. "Risk: The Whole Versus the Parts," *CFA Magazine*, March/April 2004. Copyright 2004, CFA Institute. Reproduced and republished from *CFA Magazine* with permission from CFA Institute. All rights reserved.

In this chapter, we outline the nature of risk and return as it applies to investment decisions. Unlike Chapter 6, we are talking about the future, which involves expected returns and not the past, which involves realized returns. Investors must estimate and manage the returns and risk from their investments. They reduce risk to the extent possible without affecting returns by building portfolios. Therefore, we must be concerned with the investor's total portfolio and analyze investment risk accordingly. As we shall see, diversification is the key to effective risk management.

At the conclusion of this analysis, we will be able to understand the two key characteristics of every investment decision—its expected return and risk—on both an individual security basis and, more importantly, on a portfolio basis. This will allow us to concentrate on the selection of optimal portfolios in Chapter 8 using Markowitz portfolio theory, a very well-known investment concept.

ESTIMATING SECURITY RETURN AND RISK

In Chapter 6, we discussed the average returns—both arithmetic and geometric—that investors have experienced over the years from investing in the major financial assets available to them. We also considered the risk of these asset returns as measured by the standard deviation. Analysts often refer to the realized returns for a security, or class of securities, over time using these measures, as well as others such as the wealth index.

Realized returns are important for several reasons. For example, they can show investors how their portfolios have performed, and they can also be important in helping investors form expectations about future returns. How do we go about estimating returns, which is what investors must actually do in managing their portfolios? First of all, note that we will use the return and risk measures developed in Chapter 6. The total return measure (TR) is applicable whether one is measuring realized returns or estimating future (expected) returns. Because it includes everything the investor can expect to receive over any specified future period, the TR is useful in conceptualizing the estimated returns from securities.

Similarly, the variance, or its square root—the standard deviation—is the accepted measure of variability for both realized and expected returns. We will calculate both the variance and the standard deviation below and use them interchangeably as the situation dictates. Sometimes it is preferable to use one and sometimes the other.

To estimate the returns from various securities, investors must estimate the cash flows these securities are likely to provide. The basis for doing so for bonds and stocks will be covered in their respective chapters. For now, it is sufficient to remind ourselves of the uncertainty of estimates of the future, a problem emphasized at the outset of Chapter 1.

Dealing with Uncertainty

The return an investor will earn is not known and must be estimated. Future return is an expected one that may or may not actually be realized. An investor may expect the TR on a particular security to be 0.10 for the coming year, but in truth, this is only a "point estimate." Risk, or the chance of an unexpected return, is involved whenever investment decisions are made.

Probability Distributions

To deal with the uncertainty of returns, investors need to think explicitly about a security's distribution of probable TRs. In other words, investors need to keep in mind that, although they may expect a security to return 10 percent, this is only a one-point estimate of the entire range of possibilities. Given that investors must deal with the uncertain future, a number of possible returns can, and will, occur.

In the case of a Government of Canada bond paying a fixed rate of interest, the interest payment will be made with virtual certainty barring a complete collapse of the economy. This implies that the probability for receiving those fixed payments is 1.0—that is, 100 percent—or very close to it.

With two or more possible outcomes (the norm for common stocks), each one must be considered and its probability assessed. The result of considering these outcomes and their probabilities together is a probability distribution consisting of the specification of the likely returns that may occur and the probabilities associated with these likely returns. Probabilities represent the likelihood of various outcomes and are typically expressed as decimals or fractions. The sum of the probabilities of all possible outcomes must be 1.0 because they must completely describe all the (perceived) likely occurrences.

How are these probabilities and associated outcomes determined? In the final analysis, investing for some future period involves uncertainty and therefore subjective estimates. While past occurrences and historical frequency distributions may be useful for estimating probabilities, there is no guarantee the past will repeat itself. Hence, it is important to monitor current economic and company variables that affect security returns and forecast the future values of these variables.

Probability distributions can be either discrete or continuous. With a discrete probability distribution, a probability is assigned to each possible outcome. In Figure 7-1a, five possible TRs are assumed for a stock for next year. Each of these five possible outcomes has an associated probability, with the sum of the probabilities equal to 1.0. With a continuous probability distribution, as shown in Figure 7-1b, an infinite number of possible outcomes exist. Because probability is now measured as the area under the curve in Figure 7-1b, the emphasis is on the probability that a particular outcome is within some range of values.

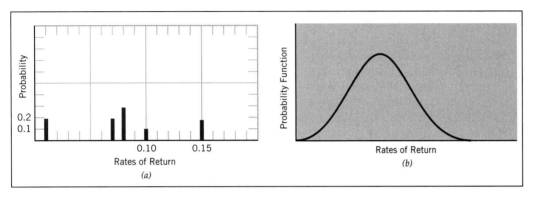

Figure 7-1
(a) A Discrete Probability Distribution
(b) A Continuous Probability Distribution

REAL-WORLD RETURNS 7-2
Using Risk Measures

Risk is a slippery thing. In good times it is often an afterthought. But it looms large in bad times. Advisors can add real value by carefully measuring and dealing with risk in client portfolios.

Problem is, risk is easy to spot with the benefit of hindsight. It is much harder to uncover risk ahead of time. But it's a skill well-worth honing, just ask the clients of advisors who spotted trouble before the Internet bubble burst (these advisors helped save their clients vast sums of money).

Modern risk measurement relies on some rather intimidating mathematics. Never fear, however, as I've put away the complicated formulas and I'll do my best to walk you through the basics.

To stay grounded in the practical world, I start with the past performance of the S&P 500. In this case, I focus on the market's daily price movements from 1950 through to the end of February 2008. My goal is to provide you with some intuition when using the risk measurements provided by Morningstar. You don't need to know how to do the calculations, Morningstar does that job for you, but it is good to know how to interpret the numbers.

Chart Analysis Offers Perspective
Let's start with the accompanying graph, which shows two curves. Focus, first, on the curve made up of all the individual data points. These points indicate how often the S&P 500 achieved various percentage returns each day as indicated by the bottom axis.

Most often the S&P 500 ekes out a very modest daily gain. Indeed, the very highest data point on the graph represents the 1,985 days on which the S&P 500 gained between 0.0% and 0.2% since 1950. Moving to the right side of the graph, the data point just past the +2% mark represents the 66 times that the S&P 500 was observed to gain between 2.0% and 2.2% since 1950.

(continued)

REAL-WORLD RETURNS 7-2 *continued*

Most of the time, the index doesn't change much day to day. It usually returns somewhere between –2% and +2% a day. Now, you may have missed it, but that's a crude risk measurement. Based on the historical record, we've observed that daily changes of more than 2% (up or down) are relatively rare. Indeed, there were only 242 days since 1950 when the S&P 500 lost more than 2%. That's an average of about one horrible day every two months.

Use of the Bell Curve

To model all of the individual data points, the mathematically inclined turn to the bell curve (or more formally the Gaussian distribution). The bell curve is much favoured by students and mathematicians alike. Students like it because it often boosts their grades. I have fond memories of being 'belled' up from a near pass to an A in a particularly horrible course. Mathematicians like the bell curve because it is easy to work with and, as we shall see, allows us to summarize a whole bunch of data by using only two numbers.

Look back to the graph. The solid line represents the bell curve that best fits the index's daily return pattern. You'll notice that it's hardly an exact fit. The bell curve doesn't always fall on top of the data points. Generally speaking, the bell curve isn't quite as spiky as the real observations near the top. It is a little fat around the middle. Near the bottom, the bell curve trails off toward zero too quickly.

Despite its faults, the bell curve yields two interesting numbers. The first can be found at its peak, which represents an estimate of the average daily return of the S&P 500. In this case, the top of the bell is just on the positive side of the centre line at 0.03%. Thankfully, even a tiny average daily return of 0.03% can yield significant gains when compounded over the course of a year.

Let's now turn to the middle part of the bell curve. It is here where we find something called the standard deviation, which is a measure of the bell curve's girth. It also represents a very common risk measurement. Thanks to my handy calculator, the daily standard deviation of the S&P 500 is about 0.89 percentage points. Here the interpretation gets a little complicated. But the bell curve estimates that the S&P 500's daily return was within one standard deviation of its average return about 68% of the time. That's a mouthful. Put another way, 68% of the time the S&P 500's daily return was between –0.86% and +0.92%. The low end of the range is found by subtracting the standard deviation of 0.89 from the average return of 0.03. The high end of the range is found by adding 0.89 to 0.03.

Personally, I have an easier time remembering that 95% of the time the gains fall within two standard deviations of the average. The S&P 500's daily two standard deviations range is between –1.75% and +1.81%. Look back to the graph and you'll remember that the vast majority of the time the S&P 500's daily gains were in the range between –2% and +2%. Using the bell curve we've developed a more precise measurement than we got by simply eyeballing the data. It also lets us condense a great deal of information into only two numbers—the average and standard deviation.

Use of Annual Standard Deviation

Now let's look at the annual standard deviation of a few funds. The Trimark Fund has a long history and Morningstar's PALTrak reports the fund's annualized standard deviation based on data from the last 3, 5, 10, and 15 years. Most people stick with 3 or 5 year figures. The annual standard deviation based on the last five years worth of data for the Trimark Fund happened to be 11.3. Assume the fund gained an average of 6.3% a year over the same period. Put the two numbers together and 95% of the time the fund's annual gains fell within two standard deviations of its average return. In this case, that's between –16.3% and +28.9% (i.e., between 6.3 minus 2 times 11.3, and 6.3 plus 2 times 11.3). If past is prologue, and we all know that's a mighty big if, then the fund's return next year should fall between –16.3% and +28.9% some 95% of the time.

(The standard deviation of a diversified portfolio which includes many funds that cover different asset classes will likely be lower. You can use PALTrak to easily calculate the standard deviation of an entire portfolio.)

Old Rules of Thumb

Standard deviations also tend to confirm old rules of thumb. For instance, the relatively safe Scotia Money Market fund has a standard deviation of only 0.23 percentage points. (That's an annualized number based on 3 years of past return data.) Plain bond funds tend to be a little higher. PH&N's Bond fund clocks in at 2.8. Dividend funds are usually among lower risk equity funds. True to form, the Standard Life Canadian Dividend Growth fund has a standard deviation of 9.6. Specialty stock funds tend to be more volatile. For instance, the Sprott Energy Fund has a standard deviation of 28.8.

Standard deviations are a reasonable way to measure risk, but you've probably already noticed a few potential problems. Most importantly, it is a profoundly backward-looking method. As we all know, past results may not be predictive of future results. The same goes for risk as measured by standard deviation.

More subtly, there might not be much history available for number crunching when it comes to individual funds. Few funds have been around for many decades and most have not been tested during very stressful periods. Even worse, past returns may have been achieved by a different portfolio manager or investment policy. If a new manager is in charge or if the mandate changes, then the fund's risk characteristics may have changed.

Yet, I alluded to an even more concerning caveat early on. If you look back at the graph again, in most cases the bell curve is a little wider than the actual returns from the S&P 500. It is thick in the middle. As a result, standard deviation tends to overestimate risk slightly. That's a good thing if you want to err on the conservative side. But the real problem is hidden way down in the tails of the curve. Variations more than two standard deviations away from the average should happen only 5% of the time. It turns out that they are more frequent and can be far larger than expected.

Biggest Problem Is in the Extremes

You might remember a dark day in October of 1987 when the S&P 500 plunged 20.5%. Yes, that's a 20.5% drop in only one day, which is way off the edge of the chart. Indeed, the bell curve predicts that such an event is a practical impossibility.

Standard deviation can do a fairly good job of measuring risk during normal times, but it fails on occasion. Nonetheless, it represents a good starting point and can help you to gauge common risks. But it is also important to go further and marry the figures with good old-fashioned common sense when building portfolios for your clients.

Source: Rothery, Norman, "Doing the Math: Using risk measures in turbulent times," *Advisor's Edge Report*, March 2008, p. 27.

The most familiar continuous distribution is the normal distribution depicted in Figure 7-1b. This is the well-known bell-shaped curve often used in statistics. The normal distribution is symmetrical, with the mean = mode = median of the distribution, and with the two "halves" of the distribution on either side of the mean being "mirror images" of one another, which means that 50 percent of the observations fall above the mean, and 50 percent below. It is a two-parameter distribution in the sense that the mean and the variance (or standard deviation) fully describe it. In other words, if we know the mean and variance of any normal distribution, we can draw its graph accurately without any additional information. For example, approximately 68 percent of the observations will lie plus or minus one standard deviation from the mean, 95 percent +/− 2 standard deviations, and 99 percent within +/− 3 standard deviations. Real-World Returns 7-2 discusses how averages and standard deviations may provide useful information about the probability distributions of security returns.

Calculating Expected Return

Expected Return

The *ex ante* return anticipated by investors for some future period.

To describe the single most likely outcome from a particular probability distribution, it is necessary to calculate its expected value. The expected value is the average of all possible return outcomes, where each is weighted by its respective probability of occurrence. Since investors are interested in returns, we will call this expected value the expected rate of return, or simply **expected return**, and for any security, it is calculated as

(7-1)

$$E(R) = \sum_{i=1}^{m} R_i pr_i$$

where

$E(R)$ = the expected return on a security
R_i = the ith possible return
pr_i = the probability of the ith return R_i
m = the number of possible returns

The expected return associated with the discrete probability distribution depicted in Figure 7-1a is 0.08. Refer to columns two and three of Table 7-1 for calculations.

Calculating Risk

Investors must be able to quantify and measure risk. To calculate the total risk associated with the expected return, the variance or standard deviation is used. As we know from Chapter 6, the variance and its square root, standard deviation, are measures of the spread or dispersion in the probability distribution; that is, they measure the dispersion of a random variable around its mean. The larger this dispersion, the larger the variance or standard deviation.

To calculate the variance or standard deviation from the probability distribution, we must first calculate the expected return of the distribution using Equation 7-1. Essentially, the same procedure used in Chapter 6 to measure historical risk applies here, but now the probabilities associated with the outcomes must be included, as in Equation 7-2.

(7-2)

$$\text{the variance of returns} = \sigma^2 = \sum_{i=1}^{m} [R_i - E(R)]^2 \, pr_i$$

and

(7-3)

$$\text{the standard deviation of returns} = \sigma = (\sigma^2)^{\frac{1}{2}}$$

where all terms are as defined previously.

Calculating a standard deviation using probability distributions involves making subjective estimates of the probabilities and the likely returns. We cannot avoid making estimates because future returns are uncertain since the prices of securities are based on investors' expectations about the future. The relevant standard deviation in this situation is the *ex ante* standard deviation and not the *ex post* based on realized returns. In other words, we are interested in the variability associated with future expected returns.

Although standard deviations based on realized returns are often used as proxies for *ex ante* standard deviations, investors should be careful to remember that the past cannot always be extrapolated into the future without modifications since standard deviations change through time. Hence, while *ex post* standard deviations provide convenient proxies, they should not be relied upon exclusively to estimate future risk.

The variance and standard deviation of the hypothetical stock returns shown in Figure 7-1a are calculated in columns four, five, and six of Table 7-1.

Table 7-1

Calculating the Standard Deviation Using Expected Data

(1) Possible Return	(2) Probability	(3) (1) × (2)	(4) $R_i - E(R)$	(5) $(R_i - E(R))^2$	(6) $(R_i - E(R))^2 pr_i$
0.01	0.2	0.002	−0.070	0.0049	0.00098
0.07	0.2	0.014	−0.010	0.0001	0.00002
0.08	0.3	0.024	0.000	0.0000	0.00000
0.10	0.1	0.010	0.020	0.0004	0.00004
0.15	0.2	0.030	0.070	0.0049	0.00098
	1.0	0.080 = E(R)			0.00202

$s = (0.00202)^{1/2} = 0.0449 = 4.49\%$

One important point about the estimation of standard deviation is the distinction between individual securities and portfolios. Standard deviations for well-diversified portfolios are reasonably steady across time, and therefore historical values may be fairly reliable in projecting future values. However, when we move from well-diversified portfolios to individual securities, historical calculations become much less reliable. Fortunately, the number one rule of portfolio management is to diversify and hold a portfolio of securities, and the standard deviations of well-diversified portfolios may be relatively stable. Therefore, we focus most of our discussion on the expected return and risk for portfolios.

CHECK YOUR UNDERSTANDING

7-1. Is there a difference between the terms "uncertainty" and "risk"?

7-2. The expected return for a security is typically different from any of the possible outcomes (returns) used to calculate it. How, then, can we say it is the security's expected return?

7-3. Having calculated a security's standard deviation, do we have enough information to fully describe (i.e., draw) the probability distribution of returns?

PORTFOLIO RETURN AND RISK

learning objective 2 °
Explain how expected return and risk for portfolios are determined.

When we analyze investment returns and risks, we must be concerned with the total portfolio held by an investor. Individual security returns and risks are important, but it is the investor's total portfolio that ultimately matters because investment opportunities can be enhanced by packaging them together to form portfolios.

As we will see, portfolio risk is a unique characteristic and not simply the sum of individual security risks. A security that has a large risk if held by itself may have much less risk when held in a portfolio. Since investors are concerned primarily with the risk of their total wealth position, as represented by their overall investment portfolio, individual stocks are risky only to the extent that they add risk to the total portfolio.

Portfolio Expected Return

The expected return on any portfolio is easily calculated as a weighted average of the individual securities' expected returns. The percentages of a portfolio's total value that are invested in each portfolio asset are referred to as **portfolio weights**, which we will denote by *w*. The combined portfolio

Portfolio Weights
The percentages of portfolio funds invested in each individual security. These will add up to 1.0, representing the total value of the portfolio.

weights are assumed to add up to 100 percent of total investable funds, or 1.0, indicating that all portfolio funds are invested.[1]

EXAMPLE 7-1: DETERMINING PORTFOLIO WEIGHTS

With equal dollar amounts in three securities, the portfolio weights are 0.333, 0.333, and 0.333. An equally weighted portfolio of five securities would have portfolio weights of 0.20 in each security. Of course, dollar amounts are often not equal, and a five-stock portfolio might have weights of .40, .10, .15, .25, and .10, or .18, .33, .11, .22, and .16.

The expected return on any portfolio, p, can be calculated as

(7-4)
$$E(R_p) = \sum_{i=1}^{n} w_i \, E(R_i)$$

where

$E(R_p)$ = the expected return on the portfolio

w_i = the portfolio weight for the ith security

$\sum w_i$ = 1.0

$E(R_i)$ = the expected return on the ith security

n = the number of different securities in the portfolio

EXAMPLE 7-2: CALCULATING PORTFOLIO EXPECTED RETURN

Consider a three-stock portfolio consisting of stocks G, H, and I, with expected returns of 12, 20, and 17 percent, respectively. Assume that 50 percent of investable funds is invested in security G, 30 percent in H, and 20 percent in I. The expected return on this portfolio is

$$E(R_p) = 0.5(12\%) + 0.3(20\%) + 0.2(17\%) = 15.4\%$$

Regardless of the number of assets held in a portfolio, or the proportion of total investable funds placed in each asset, the expected return on the portfolio is always a weighted average of the expected returns for individual assets in the portfolio.

INVESTING *tip*

The expected return for a portfolio with positive (long) positions in all of the underlying securities must fall between the highest and lowest expected returns for the individual securities making up the portfolio. Exactly where it falls is determined by the percentages of investable funds placed in each of the individual securities in the portfolio.

Portfolio Risk

The remaining computation in investment analysis is that of the risk of the portfolio. We measure risk as the variance (or standard deviation) of the portfolio's return, exactly as in the case of each individual security.

It is at this point that the basis of modern portfolio theory emerges, which can be stated as follows: *Although the expected return of a portfolio is a weighted average of its expected returns, portfolio risk (as measured by the variance or standard deviation) is less than the weighted average of the risk of the individual securities in a portfolio of risky securities.* Symbolically,

---

[1]For now, we ignore the possibility of short-selling, which can create negative weights in securities. In other words, we assume that all of the weights are positive, which implies we are talking about long positions in the individual securities. This assumption can be relaxed without affecting our results.

$$E(R_p) = \sum_{i=1}^{n} w_i E(R_i)$$

But

$$\sigma_p < \sum_{i=1}^{n} w_i \sigma_i \qquad \textbf{(7-5)}$$

Precisely because Equation 7-5 is an inequality, investors can reduce the risk of a portfolio below the weighted average of the individual securities' risk. We will now analyze portfolio risk in detail in order to see how this risk reduction can be accomplished.

ANALYZING PORTFOLIO RISK

Risk Reduction in Stock Portfolios

To begin our analysis, let's first assume that all risk sources in a portfolio of securities are independent. As we add securities to this portfolio, the exposure to any particular source of risk becomes small. Risk reduction in this manner represents an application of the insurance principle, named for the idea that an insurance company reduces its risk by writing many policies against many independent sources of risk.

If we assume that rates of return on individual securities are statistically independent, such that any one security's rate of return is unaffected by another's rate of return and also assume each of these individual securities has the same level of risk (as measured by standard deviation), the standard deviation of the portfolio is given by

$$\sigma_p = \frac{\sigma_i}{n^{1/2}} \qquad \textbf{(7-6)}$$

Notice that the risk of the portfolio will quickly decline as more securities are added, since the denominator of Equation 7-6 gets larger as n increases.

EXAMPLE 7-3: CALCULATING PORTFOLIO RISK

If we combine several securities that each have a standard deviation of 0.20, the risk of the portfolio will quickly decline as more and more of these securities are added. Equation 7-6 indicates that for the case of 100 securities, the risk of the portfolio is reduced to 0.02:

$$\sigma = \frac{0.20}{(100)^{1/2}} = .02$$

Unfortunately, the assumption of statistically independent returns on stocks is not representative of the real world. Going back to the definition of market risk in Chapter 6, we find that most stocks are positively correlated with each other; that is, the movements in their returns are related. Most stocks have a significant level of co-movement with the overall market of stocks, as measured by market indexes such as the S&P/TSX Composite Index. Risk cannot be eliminated because common sources of risk affect all firms.

Diversification

The insurance principle illustrates the concept of attempting to diversify the risk involved in a portfolio of assets (or liabilities). In fact, diversification is the key to the management of portfolio risk because it allows investors to minimize risk without adversely affecting return. Throughout our discussion in both this chapter and the next, we will be focusing on the diversification principle. We begin with random diversification and move to efficient diversification.

Random Diversification

Random or naive diversification refers to the act of randomly diversifying without regard to relevant investment characteristics such as expected return and industry classification. An investor simply selects a relatively large number of securities randomly (i.e., the proverbial "throwing a dart at the newspaper page containing the stock quotes"). For simplicity, we assume equal dollar amounts are invested in each stock.

Figure 7-2 plots the actual monthly data for Canadian stocks for 1993–97 as reported in Table 7-2 to illustrate naive diversification. The reported results are average standard deviations obtained from randomly selecting 5,000 portfolios of each size. As we can see, portfolio risk for a randomly selected portfolio was reduced below 5 percent per month over this period. As securities are added to the portfolio, the total risk associated with the portfolio of stocks declines rapidly. The first few stocks cause a large decrease in portfolio risk. Based on this data, 47 percent of portfolio standard deviation is eliminated as we go from 1 to 10 securities. Unfortunately, the benefits of random diversification do not continue indefinitely. As more and more securities are added, the marginal risk reduction per security added becomes progressively smaller, eventually producing an almost negligible effect on total portfolio risk.

Figure 7-2
Risk Reduction Using
Naive Diversification

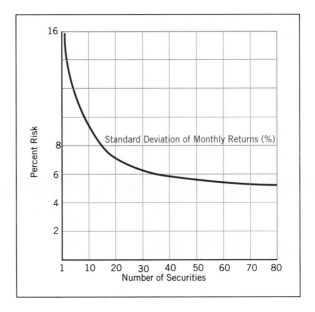

EXAMPLE 7-4: REDUCING RISK THROUGH RANDOM DIVERSIFICATION

Based on the data in Table 7-2, going from 10 to 20 securities eliminates an additional 8 percent of the monthly portfolio standard deviation, but going from 20 to 30 securities eliminates only 4 percent of the monthly standard deviation.

A large number of securities are not required to achieve substantial diversification benefits. On the other hand, note that the monthly portfolio risk reported in Table 7-2 levels out at approximately 5.5 percent once there are 80 securities in the portfolio and beyond. Therefore, no matter how many

Table 7-2

Standard Deviations of Monthly Portfolio Returns (1993–97)

Number of Stocks in Portfolio	Standard Deviation of Monthly Portfolio Returns	Ration of Standard Deviation to Standard Deviation of a Single Stock
1	15.97	1.00
2	13.10	0.82
4	10.94	0.69
6	9.76	0.61
8	8.98	0.56
10	8.44	0.53
12	8.03	0.50
14	7.74	0.49
16	7.50	0.47
18	7.29	0.46
20	7.12	0.45
25	6.78	0.42
30	6.52	0.41
35	6.35	0.40
40	6.18	0.39
45	6.06	0.38
50	5.95	0.37
60	5.77	0.36
70	5.64	0.35
80	5.53	0.35
90	5.45	0.34
100	5.37	0.34
150	5.09	0.32
200	4.95	0.31
250	4.86	0.30
300	4.79	0.30
400	4.70	0.29
481	4.66	0.29

Source: Sean Cleary and David Copp, "Diversification with Canadian Stocks: How Much Is Enough?," *Canadian Investment Review*, Fall 1999, pp. 21–25.

additional securities are added to this portfolio, the risk does not decline by any significant amount. The declining relationship between portfolio risk and the number of securities in a portfolio illustrated in Figure 7-2 for Canadian stocks is a well-known result that holds for diversification among domestic stocks in all developed domestic stock markets around the world. As a result, most finance textbooks contain similar diagrams, with the number of stocks required to achieve diversification varying depending upon the market and particular empirical study referred to in the diagram. For example, a 1987 study of US stocks found that the annual standard deviation of US stocks levelled out at approximately 19 percent after 100 or more stocks were randomly included in the portfolio.[2]

[2]Meir Statman, "How Many Stocks Make a Diversified Portfolio?" *Journal of Financial and Quantitative Analysis* 22 (September 1987), pp. 353–363.

Figure 7-2 highlights the benefits of holding a well-diversified portfolio in terms of risk reduction when diversification is achieved by random security selection. Not surprisingly, we will see that diversification can be achieved more efficiently when we take a more structured approach to forming portfolios.

How Many Securities Are Enough to Diversify Properly?

Table 7-2 indicates that with 20 securities, the standard deviation of monthly returns has dropped from 15.97 to 7.12 percent, and going to 30 securities changes the standard deviation to only 6.52 percent, which is not all that much different. In fact, based on studies over the years, it has become commonplace for investors to believe that having 15 or 20 stocks provides adequate diversification. However, a study by Campbell, Lettau, Malkiel, and Xu showed that, between 1962 and 1997, the market's overall volatility did not change whereas the volatility of individual stocks increased sharply.[3]

However, correlations between stocks tended to decrease, thereby enhancing the benefits of diversification. This study suggests that investors need more stocks today to adequately diversify. According to one of the authors, investors may now need 40 rather than the 20 previously advocated.

Another study examined the period 1993–1999 inclusive and found that with a portfolio of 15 stocks, the probability of underperforming the market benchmark by 100 percent or more was 13.5 percent, a substantial risk.[4] With a portfolio of 40 stocks, however, the probability declines to only 2.4 percent, and with 75 stocks it is virtually zero (0.2 percent). Putting the advantages of diversification in a different perspective, "about one in six stocks reflected total returns in excess of 300 percent. The likelihood of getting one of these super performers increases as you add additional stocks."

International Diversification

Our discussion above assumed random diversification in domestic securities such as stocks traded on the TSX or NYSE. However, we have learned about the importance of taking a global approach to investing. What effect would this have on our diversification analysis?

Considering only the potential for risk reduction and ignoring the additional hazards of foreign investing such as currency risk, we could reasonably conclude that if domestic diversification is good, international diversification must be better. Figure 7-3, which illustrates the benefits of international diversification in reducing portfolio risk, is taken from a classic article by a noted researcher Bruno

Figure 7-3
Domestic vs. International Diversification in Reducing Portfolio Risk

Source: Bruno Solnik, "Why Not Diversify Internationally Rather Than Domestically." Reprinted with permission from *Financial Analysts Journal* July/August 1974, © 1974. Association for Investment Management and Research, Charlottesville, VA. All rights reserved.

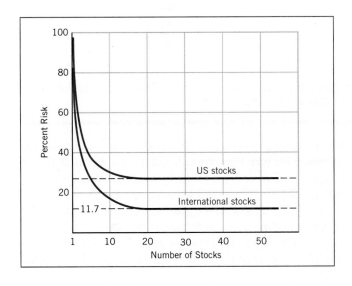

Solnik. Throughout the entire range of portfolio sizes, the risk is reduced when international investing is compared to investing in only domestic stocks (US stocks in this example), and the difference is dramatic—about one-third less. Marmer documents similar risk reduction benefits for Canadian investors who diversify internationally.[5]

Research suggests that the benefits to international diversification have declined, although they are still significant. Real-World Returns 7-3 discusses this issue.

REAL-WORLD RETURNS 7-3
International Diversification

Ever since the removal of the foreign property rule, Canadian investors have been urged to "go global" with their portfolio. Taking a global approach to investing, it was argued, would provide access to broader industry diversification, but also because the markets in different countries behave differently.

While the former remains true—if anything the Canadian market has become even shallower—the latter argument could be fading, especially when it comes to equity markets in the developed world. A recent study entitled *Dispersion, Equity Returns Correlations and Market Integration*, found that between 1973 and 2005, equity market returns for developed economies had become increasingly correlated, with global risks having a greater influence and the impact of country-specific risk lessening.

Over the same period, however, the impact of country-specific risk became increasingly important in emerging markets, with the influence of regional risk fading, and global risk becoming only slightly more important.

Conducted by Esther Eiling, assistant professor of finance at University of Toronto's Joseph L. Rotman School of Management and Bruno Gerard, senior strategist with Mellon Capital Management, the study analyzed the movements of 50 equity markets—24 in developed economies, and 26 in emerging markets—and tracked which forces moved the markets in a given trend.

"The benefits of international diversification strategies across developed markets, within or across regions may have decreased over time," Eiling and Gerard wrote. "In sharp contrast, for emerging markets, we do not detect any significant time trends in cross-country correlations in Eastern Europe, nor in the Asian and Latin American emerging markets." At the start of the study period, 70 percent of the movement in developed European markets could be attributed to country risk, with global risk accounting for less than 10 percent of excess returns, and the remaining 20 percent or more was attributable to regional risk.

Fast forward to 2005, the end date of the study period, and global risks now accounted for about 45 percent of market returns, with country-specific risk effects now limited to 35 percent of market movements.

In developed Asia/Pacific, the influence of country risk contracted from about 65 percent to little more than 40 percent, while the global risk influence rose from about 10 percent to nearly 40 percent. It should be noted that these are not straight-line movements, but the trend indicates increasing global correlation.

North American markets showed the weakest trend toward increased global correlation, but it is also the region with the strongest global correlation to begin with, so growth would be difficult.

It is not hard to fathom why North America would have the strongest global correlation. For decades leading up to the study, the US was the driver of the global economy, and between 1973 and 2005, where the US equity markets went, so did the world.

Eiling and Gerard did find a massive dip in US-global correlation, however, between the mid-1980s and mid-1990s, but the strong correlation to global risk returned, with roughly 60 percent of returns aligned with global risk by the end of the study. *(continued)*

---

[5]H.S. Marmer, "International Investing: A New Canadian Perspective," *Canadian Investment Review* 4 (Spring 1991), pp. 47–53.

REAL-WORLD RETURNS 7-3 *continued*

"The increasing level of co-movements between developed markets has important implications for international investment strategies as it negatively affects the regions' diversification potential," they concluded. "Our evidence suggests as well that extending the investment set with emerging markets equities may deliver some of the benefits of international diversification previously offered by developed markets, although this issue merits further investigation."

While the importance of country-specific risk diminished across all emerging markets in the study, it still accounted for about 60 percent of returns in Eastern Europe, Latin America and emerging Asia. Country-specific risk has remained steady in the Middle East/Africa, accounting for more than 70 percent of returns since 1996, with average correlations falling by 0.5 percent per year.

"Over the last decade, while global factors have supplanted regional factors as drivers of emerging markets co-movements, the importance of country-specific factors has not diminished," Eiling and Gerard write. "Hence, while the aggregate degree of integration of emerging markets has not increased, it has taken a more global than regional nature over that time period."

William Hoyt, manager of the Fidelity Global Dividend Fund, agrees with the report findings as they support the findings of Fidelity's quantitative analysis group. The group calculates correlations "a couple times a year" and has found that Latin America, emerging Asia, and Eastern Europe are behaving very similarly to each other.

"The globalization of economies and industries within those economies has led to a certain amount of homogenization in some industries that are more open," he says. "That has tied the fortunes of these companies more closely together, decreasing the ability to diversify even within the industry... There are several emerging market nations around the world that want to be the next dominant economic power of this century, just as the US was for the bulk of the last century and the UK was for the bulk of the century before that," Hoyt says. "You have entire sovereign nations that are making it their business to invest in their own economies, not with any short-term objective, but with a multi-decade and multigenerational objective."

Essentially, when an investor buys into a developed market, they are simply buying the industries that are contained in a mature, slow-growth economy. Investing in emerging markets also gives the investor exposure to the underlying growth of the economy itself.

"I would agree, if you're looking at correlations over a long period of time, that there is tighter correlation," says Brent Smith, chief investment officer of Fiduciary Trust of Canada. "Over shorter periods, I think the correlation is not as strong."

Global diversification may be of more importance to Canadian investors than others in developed economies, due to industry concentration in the domestic markets. Smith points out that Canadian equity returns have been far greater than those of the US over the past five years, despite the close integration of the two economies.

"The Canadian stock market is nowhere near as diversified [as most industrialized nations]," he says. Particularly since 50 percent of our economy is in two sectors that are really dependent on global economic growth. "Emerging markets should play a role in a well-diversified portfolio. There is a risk premium associated with emerging markets but as they become more developed in nature, that risk premium will disappear," Smith says.

Source: Lamb, Steven, "Markets in Motion," *Advisor's Edge Report*, March 2008, p. 24.

CHECK YOUR UNDERSTANDING

7-4. Why can we say that portfolio returns are a linear measure, but the standard deviation is non-linear?

7-5. What does it mean to an investor that the benefits of diversification kick in immediately but are limited?

7-6. What might explain the fact that the benefits to international diversification have declined?

MARKOWITZ DIVERSIFICATION

Now that we have an understanding of how random diversification works, we need to be more sophisticated and take advantage of information that we can calculate, such as the expected return and risk for individual securities and measures of how stock returns move together. This will provide us with a better understanding of the true nature of portfolio risk and why Equation 7-5 is an inequality.

Harry Markowitz, the father of modern portfolio theory, was awarded the 1990 Nobel Prize in Economics as a result of his work in this field. In the 1950s, he originated the basic portfolio model that underlies modern portfolio theory. Before Markowitz, investors dealt loosely with the concepts of return and risk. Investors have known intuitively for many years that it is smart to diversify, that is, not to put all of your eggs in one basket. However, Markowitz was the first to develop the concept of portfolio diversification in a formal way. He showed quantitatively why and how portfolio diversification works to reduce the risk of a portfolio to an investor.

Markowitz sought to organize the existing thoughts and practices into a more formal framework and to answer a basic question: Is the risk of a portfolio equal to the sum of the risks of the individual securities comprising it? Markowitz was the first to develop a specific measure of portfolio risk and to derive the expected return and risk for a portfolio based on covariance relationships, which we consider in detail in the following discussion.

Measuring Co-Movements in Security Returns

In order to develop an equation that will calculate the risk of a portfolio as measured by the variance or standard deviation, we must account for two factors:

1. Weighted individual security risks (i.e., the variance of each individual security, weighted by the percentage of investable funds placed in each individual security)
2. Weighted co-movements between securities' returns as measured by the covariance between the securities' returns, again weighted by the percentage of investable funds placed in each security

Covariance is a measure of the co-movements between security returns used in the calculation of portfolio risk. Before considering covariance, however, we first analyze how security returns move together by considering the correlation coefficient—a measure of association learned in statistics.

The Correlation Coefficient

As used in portfolio theory, the **correlation coefficient** (ρ_{AB} pronounced "rho") is a statistical measure of the relative co-movements between the returns on securities A and B. It measures the extent to which the returns on any two securities are related; however, it denotes only association, not causation. In other words, it measures how security returns move in relation to one another, but does not provide information regarding the cause of this relationship. It is a relative measure of association that is bounded by +1.0 and −1.0, with

Correlation Coefficient
A statistical measure of the extent to which two variables, such as the returns on two securities, are associated.

$$\rho_{AB} = +1.0$$
= perfect positive correlation
$$\rho_{AB} = -1.0$$
= perfect negative (inverse) correlation
$$\rho_{AB} = 0.0$$
= zero correlation.

With perfect positive correlation, the returns have a perfect direct linear relationship. Knowing what the return on one security will do allows an investor to forecast perfectly what the other will do. In Figure 7-4, stocks A and B have identical return patterns over the six-year period 2003–2008. When stock A's return goes up, stock B's does also; when stock A's return goes down, stock B's does also.

Consider the return and standard deviation information in Figure 7-4. Notice that a portfolio combining stocks A and B, with 50 percent invested in each, has exactly the same return as does either stock by itself since the returns are identical. The risk of the portfolio, as measured by the standard deviation, is identical to the standard deviation of either stock by itself. There is no variation in this return series.

With perfect negative correlation, the securities' returns have an inverse linear relationship to each other. Therefore, knowing the return on one security provides full knowledge about the return on the other. When one security's return is high, the other is low.

In Figure 7-5, stocks A and C are perfectly negatively correlated with each other. Notice that the information given for these two stocks states that each stock has exactly the same return and standard deviation. When combined, however, the deviations in the returns on these stocks around their average return of 12 percent cancel out, resulting in a portfolio return of 12 percent. This portfolio has no risk. It will earn 12 percent each year over the period measured, and the average return will be 12 percent.

With zero correlation, there is no relationship between the returns on the two securities. Knowledge of the return on one security is of no value in predicting the return of the second security.

When does diversification pay?

1. Combining securities with perfect positive correlation with each other provides no reduction in portfolio risk. The risk of the resulting portfolio is simply a weighted average of the individual risks of the securities. As more securities are added under the condition of perfect positive correlation, portfolio risk remains a weighted average. There is no risk reduction.

2. Combining two securities with zero correlation (statistical independence) with each other reduces the risk of the portfolio, which is the foundation for the insurance principle discussed above. If more securities with uncorrelated returns are added to the portfolio, significant risk reduction can be achieved. However, portfolio risk cannot be eliminated in this case.

Figure 7-4
Returns for the Years 2003–2008 on Two Stocks, A and B, and a Portfolio Consisting of 50% A and 50% B, When the Correlation Coefficient is +1.0

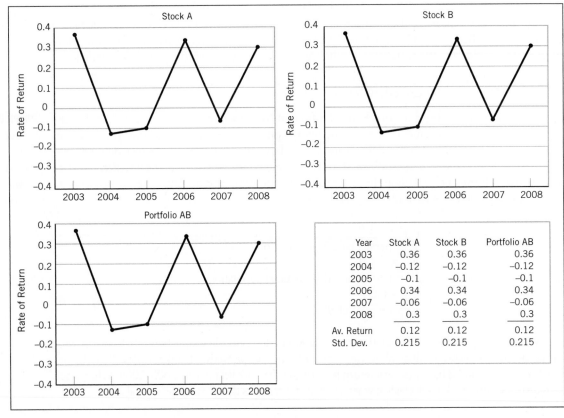

Year	Stock A	Stock B	Portfolio AB
2003	0.36	0.36	0.36
2004	−0.12	−0.12	−0.12
2005	−0.1	−0.1	−0.1
2006	0.34	0.34	0.34
2007	−0.06	−0.06	−0.06
2008	0.3	0.3	0.3
Av. Return	0.12	0.12	0.12
Std. Dev.	0.215	0.215	0.215

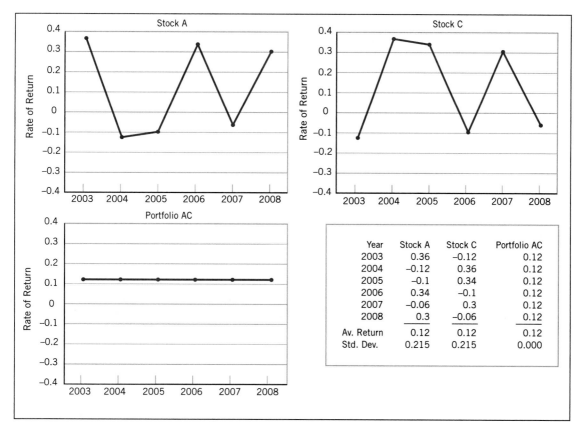

Figure 7-5
Returns for the Years 2003–2008 on Two Stocks, A and C, and a Portfolio Consisting of 50% A and 50% C, When the Correlation Coefficient is −1.0

Year	Stock A	Stock C	Portfolio AC
2003	0.36	−0.12	0.12
2004	−0.12	0.36	0.12
2005	−0.1	0.34	0.12
2006	0.34	−0.1	0.12
2007	−0.06	0.3	0.12
2008	0.3	−0.06	0.12
Av. Return	0.12	0.12	0.12
Std. Dev.	0.215	0.215	0.000

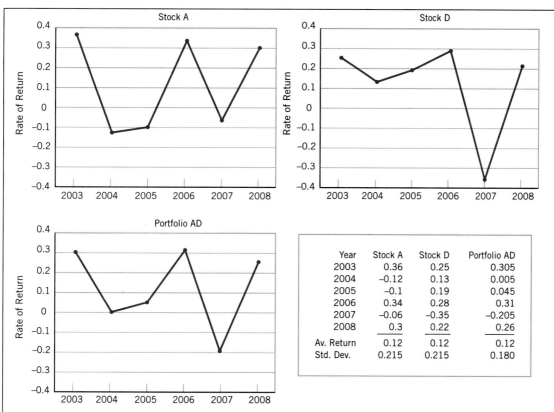

Figure 7-6
Returns for the Years 2003–2008 on Two Stocks, A and D, and a Portfolio Consisting of 50% A and 50% D, When the Correlation Coefficient is +0.55

Year	Stock A	Stock D	Portfolio AD
2003	0.36	0.25	0.305
2004	−0.12	0.13	0.005
2005	−0.1	0.19	0.045
2006	0.34	0.28	0.31
2007	−0.06	−0.35	−0.205
2008	0.3	0.22	0.26
Av. Return	0.12	0.12	0.12
Std. Dev.	0.215	0.215	0.180

3. Combining two securities with perfect negative correlation with each other could eliminate risk altogether if the correct portfolio weights are chosen. This is the principle behind hedging strategies, some of which are discussed in Chapter 20.

4. Finally, we must understand that in the real world, these extreme correlations are rare. Rather, securities typically have some positive correlation with each other. Thus, although risk can be reduced, it usually cannot be eliminated. Other things being equal, investors wish to find securities with the least positive correlation possible. Ideally, they would like securities with negative correlation or low positive correlation, but they generally will be faced with positively correlated security returns since all security prices tend to move with changes in the overall economy.

Figure 7-6 illustrates the more normal case of stocks A and D positively correlated with each other at a level of $\rho = +0.55$. This is typical of the correlations displayed by domestic common stocks listed on the TSX, the NYSE, or other domestic exchanges, and it thereby represents the "normal" situation encountered by investors. Note that the standard deviation of each security is still .215, with an average return of .12, but when combined with equal weights of .50 into the portfolio AD, the average return remains the same but the risk is reduced to a level of .18. Any reduction in risk that does not adversely affect return has to be considered beneficial.

EXAMPLE 7-5: COMBINING CANADIAN STOCKS AND BONDS

Over the 2004–2007 period, the average monthly return on Canadian stocks (as measured by the S&P/TSX Total Return Index) (S) was 1.31 percent, and the standard deviation of monthly returns was 2.91 percent. During the same period, the average monthly and standard deviation for long-term Government of Canada bond (B) returns were 0.66 percent and 1.57 percent. The correlation between the returns on S and B was 0.00 over this period. If we had formed an equally weighted portfolio of them, the return would have been 0.98 percent, halfway between the 1.31 percent return on S and the 0.66 percent return on B. However, the standard deviation for this portfolio would have been 1.65 percent, well below the weighted average of the individual standard deviations of 2.24 percent, and only slightly above the standard deviation of bond returns.

In general, we would expect correlations to be higher between stock returns for companies that are similar in nature and lower among stock returns for companies that have greater dissimilarities. Over one five-year period, for example, the correlation coefficient between the monthly returns for **Bank of Montreal (BMO)** common stock and **Air Canada** stock was 0.07. Over the same period, the correlation between BMO returns and those on **Bank of Nova Scotia** common stock was 0.28.

Covariance

Given the significant amount of correlation among security returns, we must measure the amount of co-movement and incorporate it into any measure of portfolio risk, because such co-movements affect the portfolio's variance (or standard deviation).

The covariance is an absolute measure of the degree of association between the returns for a pair of securities. **Covariance** is defined as the extent to which two random variables covary, or move together, over time. As is true throughout our discussion, the variables in question are the returns (TRs) on two securities. Similar to the correlation coefficient, the covariance can be:

Covariance

An absolute measure of the extent to which two random variables, such as the returns on two securities, tend to covary, or move together, over time.

1. Positive, indicating that the returns on the two securities tend to move in the same direction at the same time; when one increases (decreases), the other tends to do the same;

2. Negative, indicating that the returns on the two securities tend to move inversely; when one increases (decreases), the other tends to decrease (increase);

3. Zero, indicating that the returns on two securities are independent and have no tendency to move in the same or opposite directions together.

The formula for calculating covariance is [6]

$$\sigma_{AB} = \sum_{i=1}^{m} [R_{A,i} - E(R_A)] \, [R_{B,i} - E(R_B)] \, pr_i \qquad (7\text{-}7)$$

where

σ_{AB} = the covariance between securities A and B
$R_{A,i}$ = one estimated possible return on security A
$E(R_A)$ = the most likely outcome (or expected return) for security A for the period
m = the number of likely outcomes for a security for the period
pr_i = the probability of attaining a given return $R_{A,i}$

Relating the Correlation Coefficient and the Covariance

The covariance and the correlation coefficient can be related in the following manner:

$$\rho_{AB} = \frac{\sigma_{AB}}{\sigma_A \sigma_B} \qquad (7\text{-}8)$$

This equation shows that the correlation coefficient is simply the covariance standardized by dividing by the product of the two standard deviations of returns.

Given this definition of the correlation coefficient, the covariance can be rewritten as

$$\sigma_{AB} = \rho_{AB} \, \sigma_A \sigma_B \qquad (7\text{-}9)$$

Therefore, knowing the correlation coefficient, we can calculate the covariance because the standard deviations of the assets' rates of return will already be available. Knowing the covariance, we can easily calculate the correlation coefficient.

CHECK YOUR UNDERSTANDING

7-7. The numerical values used to represent correlation make it a more intuitive measure of co-movement than the covariance. Explain this statement.

7-8. Why is negative correlation between two securities in a portfolio better than a correlation of zero?

CALCULATING PORTFOLIO RISK

Now that we know how to estimate the covariances that account for the co-movements in security returns, we are ready to calculate portfolio risk. First, we will consider the simplest possible case, using only two securities in order to examine what is happening in the portfolio risk equation. We will then consider the case of many securities, where the calculations soon become too large and complex to analyze with any means other than a computer.

---

[6]Notice the similarity of this equation with Equation 7-2, which estimates the variance of returns on a security. For example, the variance for some security A could be calculated as

$$\sigma_A = \Sigma[R_{A,i} - E(R_A)]^2 pr_i = \Sigma[R_{A,i} - E(R_A)] \, [R_{A,i} - E(R_A)] pr_i$$

If we replace the As with Bs in the second term of this expression, we have Equation 7-7.

The Two-Security Case

The risk of a portfolio, as measured by the standard deviation of returns, for the case of two securities, A and B, is

(7-10)
$$\sigma_P = \sqrt{w_A^2\sigma_A^2 + w_B^2\sigma_B^2 + 2w_Aw_B\sigma_{AB}}$$

Equation 7-10 shows us that the risk for a portfolio encompasses not only the individual security risks but also the covariance between these two securities and that three factors, not two, determine portfolio risk:

1. The variance of each security
2. The covariances between securities
3. The portfolio weights for each security.

Noting that $\sigma_{AB} = \sigma_A\sigma_B\rho_{AB}$, we can re-express Equation 7-10 as

(7-11)
$$\sigma_P = \sqrt{w_A^2\sigma_A^2 + w_B^2\sigma_B^2 + 2w_Aw_B\rho_{AB}\sigma_A\sigma_B}$$

Equation 7-11 shows that the standard deviation of the portfolio will be directly related to the correlation between the two stocks, as discussed previously. The only case where there are no risk reduction benefits to be obtained from two-security diversification occurs when the correlation coefficient is $+1.0$. For this case only, the portfolio standard deviation will be a weighted average of the standard deviations of the individual securities.[7] Since $\sigma_P = w_A\sigma_A + w_B\sigma_B$ when $\rho_{AB} = +1$, and since $+1$ is the maximum value for the correlation coefficient, it must be the case that for all other possible correlation coefficients $\sigma_P < w_A\sigma_A + w_B\sigma_B$, which implies there will be benefits from diversification as long as $\rho_{AB} < +1$. The benefits will be greater as the correlation coefficient approaches -1.

EXAMPLE 7-6: DETERMINING MINIMUM VARIANCE WITH PORTFOLIO WEIGHTS

Assume we have some data for two companies, A and B, and that the estimated TRs are 26.3 percent and 11.6 percent, respectively, with standard deviations of 37.3 percent and 23.3 percent. To see the effects of changing the correlation coefficient, assume weights of 0.5 each (i.e., 50 percent of investable funds is to be placed in each security). With this data, the standard deviation, or risk, for this portfolio is

$$\sigma_P = [(0.5)^2(0.373)^2 + (0.5)^2(0.233)^2 + 2(0.5)(0.5)(0.373)(0.233)\,\rho_{A,B}]^{1/2}$$
$$= [0.0348 + 0.0136 + 0.0435\,\rho_{A,B}]^{1/2}$$

since $2(0.5)(0.5)(0.373)(0.233) = 0.0435$.

The risk of this portfolio clearly depends heavily on the value of the third term, which, in turn, depends on the correlation coefficient between the returns for A and B. To assess the potential impact of the correlation, consider the following cases: $\rho_{A,B}$ of $+1$, $+0.5$, $+0.15$, 0, -0.5, and -1.0. Calculating portfolio risk under each of these scenarios produces the following portfolio risks:

$$\rho = +1.0: \sigma_P = [0.0348 + 0.0136 + 0.0435(1)]^{1/2} = 30.3\%$$

---

[7]This fact is easy to show. Using Equation 7-11 and substituting $+1$ for ρ_{AB}, we obtain

$$\sigma_P = \sqrt{w_A^2\sigma_A^2 + w_B^2\sigma_B^2 + 2w_Aw_B(1)\sigma_A\sigma_B} = \sqrt{(w_A\sigma_A + w_B\sigma_B)^2} = w_A\sigma_A + w_B\sigma_B$$

which represents the weighted average of the individual standard deviations.

Notice that for this case only the portfolio standard deviation is a weighted average of the individual standard deviations (i.e., 0.303 = [0.50][0.373] + [0.50][0.233]).

$$\rho = +0.5: \sigma_P = [0.0348 + 0.0136 + 0.0435(0.5)]^{1/2} = 26.5\%$$
$$\rho = +0.15: \sigma_P = [0.0348 + 0.0136 + 0.0435(0.15)]^{1/2} = 23.4\%$$
$$\rho = +0.0: \sigma_P = [0.0348 + 0.0136]^{1/2} = 22.0\%$$
$$\rho = -0.5: \sigma_P = [0.0348 + 0.0136 + 0.0435(-0.5)]^{1/2} = 16.3\%$$
$$\rho = -1.0 \ \sigma_P = [0.0348 + 0.0136 + 0.0435(-1.0)]^{1/2} = 7.0\%$$

Notice that for all of these values of $\rho < +1$, the standard deviation is less than the weighted average of the individual standard deviations.

These calculations clearly show the impact that combining securities with less than perfect positive correlation will have on portfolio risk. In general, we can see there will always be risk reduction benefits from diversification as long as the correlation coefficient between the returns is less than one, and the lower the correlation coefficient, the greater the benefits. The risk of the portfolio steadily decreases from 30.3 percent to 7 percent as the correlation coefficient declines from +1.0 to -1.0.

We must also recognize the importance of the portfolio weights in the calculation of portfolio risk. Clearly, the proportion of total portfolio funds invested in one security as opposed to another has an effect on portfolio risk. In order to minimize portfolio risk, we must find the minimum variance combination given a level of expected return.

EXAMPLE 7-7: DETERMINING MINIMUM VARIANCE WITH PORTFOLIO WEIGHTS

Assume we have two stocks, C and D, with the same expected returns. The standard deviations for C and D are .20 and .30, respectively. Figure 7-7 shows the effects of portfolio weights on the standard deviation of the portfolio for four different correlations of the pattern of returns over time. If ρ is 1.0, the minimum variance is achieved with 100 percent of funds placed in C. If ρ is –0.5, the minimum variance is achieved with a portfolio weight for C of .6, and the same is true if ρ is 0.0. On the other hand, if ρ is 0.5, the minimum variance combination involves a portfolio weight for C of .80.

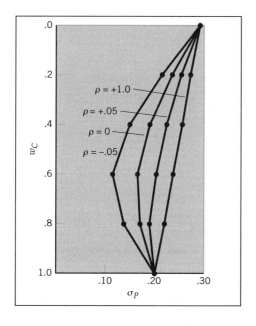

Figure 7-7
The Effects of Portfolio Weights on the Standard Deviation of the Portfolio

The *n*-Security Case

The two-security case can be generalized to the *n*-security case. Portfolio risk can be reduced by combining assets with less than perfect positive correlation. Furthermore, the smaller the positive correlation, the better.

Portfolio risk is a function of each individual security's risk and the covariances between the returns on the individual securities. Stated in terms of variance, portfolio risk for a portfolio composed of "*n*" securities is

(7-12)

$$\sigma_p^2 = \sum_{i=1}^{n} w_i^2 \sigma_i^2 + \sum_{i=1}^{n} \sum_{j=1}^{n} w_i w_j \sigma_{ij}, (i \neq j)$$

where

σ_p^2 = the variance of the return on the portfolio

σ_i^2 = the variance of return for security *i*

σ_{ij} = the covariance between the returns for securities *i* and *j*

w_i = the portfolio weights or percentage of investable funds invested in security *i*

n = the number of securities in the portfolio

$\sum_{i=1}^{n} \sum_{j=1}^{n}$ = a double summation sign indicating that n^2 numbers are to be added together (i.e., all possible pairs of values for *i* and *j*)

Equation 7-12 illustrates the problem associated with the calculation of portfolio risk using the Markowitz mean-variance analysis. The number of relevant covariances for an *n*-security portfolio equals $n(n - 1)$. In the case of two securities, there are two covariances. Since the covariance of A with B is the same as the covariance of B with A, we simply multiply the weighted covariance term in Equation 7-10 by two. In the case of three securities, there are six covariances; with four securities, 12 covariances; and so forth. The number of covariances grows quickly based on the calculation of $n(n - 1)$, where *n* is the number of securities involved. For example, the number of relevant covariances in a 100-security portfolio would equal $100(100 - 1) = 9,900$.

Table 7-3 illustrates the variance–covariance matrix associated with these calculations. For the case of two securities, there are four terms in the matrix—two variances and two covariances. For the case of four securities, there are 16 terms in the matrix—four variances and 12 covariances. The variance terms are on the diagonal of the matrix (i.e., along the grey line) and represent the covariance of a security with itself.

Table 7-3

The Variance–Covariance Matrix Involved in Calculating the Standard Deviation of a Portfolio

Two securities:

$\sigma_{1,1}$	$\sigma_{1,2}$
$\sigma_{2,1}$	$\sigma_{2,2}$

Four securities:

$\sigma_{1,1}$	$\sigma_{1,2}$	$\sigma_{1,3}$	$\sigma_{1,4}$
$\sigma_{2,1}$	$\sigma_{2,2}$	$\sigma_{2,3}$	$\sigma_{2,4}$
$\sigma_{3,1}$	$\sigma_{3,2}$	$\sigma_{3,3}$	$\sigma_{3,4}$
$\sigma_{4,1}$	$\sigma_{4,2}$	$\sigma_{4,3}$	$\sigma_{4,4}$

One of Markowitz's major contributions to portfolio theory was his insight about the relative importance of the variances and covariances. As the number of securities held in a portfolio increases, the importance of each individual security's risk (variance) decreases, while the importance of the covariance relationships increases. In portfolios consisting of a large number of securities, the contribution of each security's own risk to the total portfolio risk will be extremely small, and portfolio risk will consist almost entirely of the covariance risk between securities. For example, in a 100-security portfolio, there will be 9,900 weighted covariance terms and only 100 weighted variance terms.

To see this, consider the first term in Equation 7-12:

$$\sum_{i=1}^{n} w_i^2 \sigma_i^2$$

If we assume equal amounts are invested in each security, the proportions, or weights, will be $1/n$. For example, in a two-security portfolio, the weights will be ½ or 0.50 in each security. Rewriting this term produces

$$\sum_{i=1}^{n}(1/n)^2\sigma_i^2 = \frac{1}{n}\sum_{i=1}^{n}(\sigma_i^2/n)$$

The term in brackets represents an average variance for the stocks in the portfolio. As n becomes larger, this average variance becomes smaller, approaching zero for large values of n (since $1/n$ approaches zero as n approaches infinity). Therefore, the risk of a well-diversified portfolio will be largely attributable to the impact of the second term in Equation 7-12 representing the covariance relationships.

We can rewrite Equation 7-12 into a shorter format:

$$\sigma_p^2 = \sum_{i=1}^{n}\sum_{j=1}^{n} w_i w_j \sigma_{ij}$$ (7-13)

or

$$\sigma_p^2 = \sum_{i=1}^{n}\sum_{j=1}^{n} w_i w_j \rho_{ij} \sigma_i \sigma_j$$ (7-14)

These equations account for both the variance and the covariances because when $i = j$, the variance is calculated; when $i \neq j$, the covariance is calculated.

To calculate portfolio risk using either Equation 7-13 or Equation 7-14, we need estimates of the variance for each security and estimates of the correlation coefficients or covariances. Both variances and correlation coefficients can be (and are) calculated using either *ex post* or *ex ante* data. If an analyst uses *ex post* data to calculate the correlation coefficient or the covariance and then uses these estimates in the Markowitz model, the implicit assumption is that the relationship that existed in the past will continue into the future. The same is true of the variances for individual securities. If the historical variance is thought to be the best estimate of the expected variance, it should be used. However, it must be remembered that an individual security's variance and the correlation coefficient between securities can change over time (and usually does).

CHECK YOUR UNDERSTANDING

7-9. Given the use of the correlation coefficient, which is clear and easy to understand, why do we need to consider covariances?

7-10. Suppose we add a very risky stock to a well-diversified portfolio. Could such an action lower the portfolio's risk?

SIMPLIFYING THE MARKOWITZ CALCULATIONS

learning objective 4
Simplify Markowitz's
calculations by using the
single-index model.

The Markowitz model described above allows us to calculate portfolio expected return and risk. It can also be used to determine optimal portfolio combinations, which is demonstrated in Chapter 8. Hence, this model has the ability to generate the correct solution to the portfolio selection problem. It does so, however, at considerable cost. The major problem with the Markowitz full-covariance model is its complexity. It requires a full set of covariances between the returns of all securities being considered in order to calculate portfolio variance. There are $[n(n - 1)]/2$ unique covariances for a set of n securities.[8]

EXAMPLE 7-8: ESTIMATING LARGE NUMBERS OF COVARIANCES WITH THE MARKOWITZ MODEL

An analyst considering 100 securities must estimate $[100(99)]/2 = 4,950$ unique covariances. For 250 securities, the total number is $[250(249)]/2 = 31,125$ covariances.

Obviously, estimating large numbers of covariances quickly becomes a major problem for model users. Since many institutional investors follow as many as 250 or 300 securities, the number of inputs required may become unmanageable. In fact, until the basic Markowitz model was simplified in terms of the covariance inputs, it remained primarily of academic interest.

On a practical basis, analysts are unlikely to be able to estimate directly the large number of correlations necessary for a complete Markowitz analysis. In his original work, Markowitz suggested using an index to which securities are related as a means of generating covariances. The section below describes one frequently used model that employs this strategy.

The Single-Index Model

Single-Index Model
A model that relates returns on each security to the returns on a broad market index of common stock returns.

Another Nobel laureate, William Sharpe, developed the **single-index model**, which relates returns on each security to the returns on a common index.[9] A broad market index of common stock returns is generally used for this purpose.[10] For example, in Canada, the S&P/TSX Composite Index is commonly used, while in the US, the S&P 500 is often employed.

The single-index model can be expressed using the following equation:

(7-15)

$$R_{it} = \alpha_i + \beta_i R_{Mt} + e_{it}$$

where
R_{it} = the return (TR) on security i at time t

R_{Mt} = the return (TR) on the market index at time t

α_i = that part of security i's return independent of market performance (commonly referred to as the intercept coefficient, since it represents the expected value of R_{it} when $R_{Mt} = 0$)

β_i = a coefficient that measures the expected change in the dependent variable, R_{it}, given a change in the independent variable, R_{Mt} (generally referred to as the slope coefficient)

e_{it} = the random residual error at time t

The coefficients α_i and β_i in Equation 7-15 are generally estimated using a time series of observa-

---

[8]Although for n securities there are $n(n - 1)$ total covariances, $\sigma_{ij} = \sigma_{ji}$; therefore, there are only one-half as many unique covariances.

[9]W. Sharpe, "A Simplified Model for Portfolio Analysis," *Management Science* 9 (January 1963), pp. 277–293.

[10]There is no requirement that the index be a stock index. It could be any variable thought to be the dominant influence on stock returns.

tions for the returns on a stock or portfolio and regressing these returns on the market index returns over the same time period. Based on this regression, α_i is the intercept term, while β_i is the estimated slope coefficient, which measures the average change in R_{it} for a given change in R_{Mt}. For example, a β_i estimate of 1.5 implies that a 1 percent increase in R_{Mt} causes a 1.5 percent increase in R_{it} on average.

The single-index model divides a security's return into two components: a unique part, represented by α_i, and a market-related part, represented by $\beta_i R_{Mt}$. The unique part is a micro-event, affecting an individual company but not all companies in general. Examples include the discovery of new ore reserves, a fire, a strike, or the resignation of a key company figure. The market-related part, on the other hand, is a macro-event that is broad-based and affects all (or most) firms. Examples include a Bank of Canada announcement about the bank rate, a change in oil prices, or an unexpected increase in inflation.

Given these values, the error term is the difference between the left-hand side of the equation (the return on security i) and the right-hand side of the equation (the sum of the two components of return). Since the single-index model is, by definition, an equality, the two sides must be the same.

EXAMPLE 7-9: USING THE SINGLE-INDEX MODEL TO CALCULATE RETURN

Assume the return for the market index for period t is 12 percent, with $\alpha_i = 3$ percent, and $\beta_i = 1.5$. The single-index model estimate for stock i for time t is

$$R_{it} = 3\% + 1.5\,R_{Mt} + e_{it}$$
$$R_{it} = 3\% + (1.5)(12\%) = 21\%$$

If the market index return is 12 percent, the likely return for stock i is 21 percent.

However, no model is going to explain security returns perfectly. The error term e_{it} captures the difference between the return that actually occurs and the return expected to occur given a particular market index return.

EXAMPLE 7-10: CAPTURING THE DIFFERENCE BETWEEN ACTUAL RETURN AND EXPECTED RETURN

Assume in the previous example that the actual return on stock i for period t is 19 percent. The error term in this case $e_{it} = 19\% - 21\% = -2\%$.

This illustrates what we said earlier about the error term. For any period, it represents the difference between the actual return and the return predicted by the parameters of the model on the right-hand side of the equation. The β term, or beta, is important. It measures the sensitivity of a stock to market movements. To use the single-index model, we need estimates of the beta for each stock we are considering. Subjective estimates could be obtained from analysts, or the future beta could be estimated from historical data. We consider the estimation of beta in Chapter 9.

R_{Mt} and e_{it} are random variables, and the single-index model assumes that the market index is unrelated to the residual error. As mentioned above, one way to estimate the parameters of this model is by performing time series regression analysis. Use of this technique ensures that these two variables are uncorrelated. We will use σ_{ei} to denote the standard deviation of the error term for stock i. The mean of the probability distribution of this error term is zero, which implies the equality will hold on average.

The single-index model also assumes that securities are related only in their common response to the return on the market. That is, the residual errors for security i are uncorrelated with those of security j, so that the covariance of their returns is zero, which can be expressed as $COV\,(e_i, e_j) = 0$. This is the key assumption of the single-index model because it implies that stocks covary together only because of their common relationship to the market index. In other words, there are no influences on stocks beyond the market, such as industry effects. Therefore

$$R_{it} = \alpha_i + \beta_i R_{Mt} + e_{it} \text{ for stock } i \text{ at time } t$$

and

$$R_{jt} = \alpha_j + \beta_j R_{Mt} + e_{jt} \text{ for stock } j \text{ at time } t$$

It is critical to recognize that this is a simplifying assumption, and if it is not a good description of reality, the model will be inaccurate.[11]

In the single-index model, all the covariance terms can be accounted for by reference to their common responses to the market index. In other words, the covariance depends only on market risk. Therefore, the covariance between any two securities can be written as

(7-16)
$$\sigma_{ij} = \beta_i \beta_j \sigma_M^2$$

Once again, this simplification rests on the assumption about the error terms being uncorrelated. Alternative models have been derived that consider more than one index.

In the Markowitz model we must consider all the covariance terms in the variance–covariance matrix. The single-index model splits the risk of an individual security into two components, similar to its division of security return into two components. This simplifies the covariance calculations and greatly simplifies the calculation of total risk for a security and for a portfolio. The total risk of a security, as measured by its variance, consists of two components: market risk and unique risk.

(7-17)
$$\sigma_i^2 = \beta_i^2 [\sigma_M^2] + \sigma_{ei}^2$$
$$= \text{Market risk} + \text{Unique risk}$$

The market risk accounts for that part of a security's variance that cannot be diversified away. This part of the variability occurs when the security responds to the market moving up and down. The second term is the security's residual variance, which accounts for that part of the variability due to deviations from the fitted relationship between security return and market return.

This simplification also holds for portfolios, providing an expression to use in finding the minimum variance set of portfolios.

(7-18)
$$\sigma_p^2 = \beta_p^2 [\sigma_M^2] + \sigma_{ep}^2$$

Total portfolio variance = Portfolio market risk + Portfolio residual variance

Some Conclusions about the Single-Index Model

The single-index model greatly simplifies the calculation of the portfolio variance. However, this model makes a specific assumption about the process that generates portfolio returns: the residuals for different securities are uncorrelated. Thus, the accuracy of the estimate of the portfolio variance depends on the accuracy of that key assumption. For example, if the covariance between the residuals for different securities is positive, not zero as assumed, the true residual variance of the portfolio will be underestimated.

The end objective of the single-index model is the same as that of the Markowitz analysis, tracing the efficient frontier (set) of portfolios from which an investor would choose an optimal portfolio. Its purpose is to simplify the calculations necessary to do this. In Chapter 8, we will learn how to derive the efficient frontier.

---

[11]The use of regression analysis does not guarantee that this will be true. Instead, it is a specific simplifying assumption that, in fact, may or may not be true.

CHECK YOUR UNDERSTANDING

7-11. What is the "single index" in the model used to simplify the Markowitz calculations?

7-12. Using the single-index model, how many covariance estimates would be needed for a sample of 50 stocks? How does this compare to the number needed using the Markowitz model?

SUMMARY

This summary relates to the learning objectives for this chapter.

1. **Explain how expected return and risk for securities are determined.**

   The expected return from a security must be estimated and may not be realized. Probability distributions are involved in the calculation of expected return. The standard deviation or variance of expected return for a security is a measure of the risk involved in the expected return; therefore, it also incorporates probabilities.

2. **Explain how expected return and risk for portfolios are determined.**

   Portfolio weights, designated w_i, are the percentages of a portfolio's total funds that are invested in each security, where the weights add up to 1.0. Portfolio risk is less than a weighted average of the individual security risks as long as the correlation coefficient among the individual returns is less than $+1$. To calculate portfolio risk, we must take into account the relationships between the individual securities' returns. The expected return for a portfolio is the weighted average of the individual security expected returns.

3. **Describe the Markowitz diversification model for calculating portfolio risk.**

   Two primary concepts in the Markowitz diversification model are the correlation coefficient and the covariance. The correlation coefficient is a relative measure of the association between security returns. It is bounded by $+1.0$ and -1.0, with zero representing no association. The covariance is an absolute measure of association between security returns and is used in the calculation of portfolio risk. Portfolio risk is a function of security variances, covariances, and portfolio weights. The covariance term captures the correlations between security returns and determines how much portfolio risk can be reduced through diversification. The risk of a well-diversified portfolio is largely attributable to the impact of the covariances.

4. **Simplify Markowitz's calculations by using the single-index model.**

   The major problem with the Markowitz model is the computational burden that arises because it requires a full set of covariances between the returns of all securities being considered in order to calculate portfolio variance. The single-index model simplifies the calculation of portfolio variance by relating the returns on a stock to the returns on a market index. The key assumption of the single-index model is that stocks covary together only because of their common relationship to the market index. The single-index model greatly simplifies the calculation of the portfolio variance.

KEY TERMS

Correlation coefficient, p.201
Covariance, p.204
Expected return, p.192

Portfolio weights, p.193
Single-index model, p.210

REVIEW QUESTIONS

7-1. Distinguish between historical return and expected return.

7-2. How is expected return for one security determined? For a portfolio?

7-3. How would the expected return for a portfolio of 500 securities be calculated?

7-4. What does it mean to say that portfolio weights add up to 1.0 or 100 percent?

7-5. What are the boundaries for the expected return of a portfolio?

7-6. What is meant by naive diversification?

7-7. What is the key assumption underlying the single-index model?

7-8. Evaluate this statement: With regard to portfolio risk, the whole is not equal to the sum of the parts.

7-9. How many factors determine portfolio risk and what are they?

7-10. When, if ever, would a stock with a large risk (standard deviation) be desirable in building a portfolio?

7-11. Many investors have known for years that they should not put all of their eggs in one basket. How does the Markowitz analysis shed light on this old principle?

7-12. What type of risk tells us that the assumption of statistically independent returns on stocks is unrealistic?

7-13. When, if ever, would a stock with a large risk (standard deviation) be desirable as the only position in a portfolio?

7-14. Consider the following information for Shell Canada and Imperial Oil:

Annual expected return for each stock is 15 percent.

Annual standard deviation for each stock is 22 percent.

Covariances with other securities varies.

Everything else being equal, would the prices of these two stocks be expected to be the same? Why or why not?

7-15. Select the true statement from among the following:

   a. The risk for a portfolio is a weighted average of individual security risks.
   b. Two factors determine portfolio risk.
   c. Having established the portfolio weights, the calculation of the expected return on the portfolio is independent of the calculation of portfolio risk.
   d. When adding a security to a portfolio, the average covariance between it and the other securities in the portfolio is less important than the security's own risk.

7-16. Select the correct statement from among the following:

   a. The risk of a portfolio of two securities, as measured by the standard deviation, would consist of two terms.
   b. The standard deviation of returns on a portfolio is a weighted average of the standard deviations of the individual assets in the portfolio.
   c. The risk of a portfolio of four securities, as measured by the standard deviation, would consist of 16 covariances and four variances.
   d. Combining two securities with perfect negative correlation could eliminate risk altogether.

7-17. Select the correct statement from the following statements regarding the Markowitz model:

    a. As the number of securities held in a portfolio increases, the importance of each individual security's risk also increases.

    b. As the number of securities held in a portfolio increases, the importance of the covariance relationships increases.

    c. In a large portfolio, portfolio risk will consist almost entirely of each security's own risk contribution to the total portfolio risk.

    d. In a large portfolio, the covariance term can be driven almost to zero.

7-18. The Markowitz approach is often referred to as a mean-variance approach. Why?

7-19. What is the relationship between the correlation coefficient and the covariance both qualitatively and quantitatively?

7-20. How many covariance terms in total would exist for a portfolio of 10 securities? How many unique covariances?

7-21. How many terms would exist in the variance–covariance matrix for a portfolio of 30 securities? How many of these are variances and how many covariances?

7-22. In explaining diversification concepts and the analysis of risk, why is the correlation coefficient usually more informative than the covariance?

7-23. Should investors expect positive correlations between stocks and bonds? Bonds and T-bills? Stocks and real estate? Stocks and gold?

7-24. Calculate the number of covariances needed for an evaluation of 500 securities using the Markowitz model. Also, calculate the total number of pieces of information needed.

7-25. Using the Sharpe model, how many covariances would be needed to evaluate 500 securities? How many total pieces of information?

7-26. The Markowitz approach is often referred to as a single-period approach. Why?

7-27. Select the false statement from among the following:

    a. Under the Markowitz formulation, a portfolio of 30 securities would have 870 covariances.

    b. Under the Sharpe formulation, a portfolio of 30 securities would require 92 pieces of data to implement.

    c. Under the Markowitz formulation, a portfolio of 30 securities would have 870 terms in the variance–covariance matrix.

    d. Under the Markowitz formulation, a portfolio of 30 securities would require 435 unique covariances to calculate portfolio risk.

7-28. Concerning the riskiness of a portfolio of two securities using the Markowitz model, select the true statements from among the following set:

    a. The riskiness depends on the variability of the securities in the portfolio.

    b. The riskiness depends on the percentage of portfolio assets invested in each security.

    c. The riskiness depends on the expected return of each security.

    d. The riskiness depends on the amount of correlation among the security returns.

    e. The riskiness depends on the beta of each security.

7-29. If you combined two securities that had a zero correlation with each other, would the total portfolio risk increase, decrease, or stay the same? Briefly explain.

7-30. Is it likely, in the real world, to discover two securities with perfect negative correlation with each other?

PROBLEMS

7-1. Four securities have the following expected returns:

$$A = 15\%, B = 12\%, C = 30\%, \text{ and } D = 22\%$$

Calculate the expected returns for a portfolio consisting of all four securities under the following conditions:

  a. The portfolio weights are 25 percent each.
  b. The portfolio weights are 10 percent in A, with the remainder equally divided among the other three stocks.
  c. The portfolio weights are 10 percent each in A and B, and 40 percent each in C and D.

7-2. Calculate the expected return and risk (standard deviation) for Barrick Gold for 2009, given the following information:

  Probabilities: 0.15, 0.20, 0.40, 0.10, 0.15
  Expected returns: 0.20, 0.16, 0.12, 0.05, −0.05

7-3. Assume the additional information provided below for the four stocks in Problem 7-1.

	σ(%)	A	B	C	D
			Correlations with		
A	10	1.0			
B	8	0.6	1.0		
C	20	0.2	−1.0	1.0	
D	16	0.5	0.3	0.8	1.0

  a. Assuming equal weights for each stock, what are the standard deviations for the following portfolios?

  A, B, and C
  B and C
  B and D
  C and D

  b. Calculate the standard deviation for a portfolio consisting of stocks B and C, assuming the following weights: (1) 40 percent in B and 60 percent in C; (2) 60 percent in B and 40 percent in C.

  c. In part a, which portfolio(s) would an investor prefer?

The following data apply to Problems 7-4 through 7-7.

Assume expected returns and standard deviations as follows:

	EG&G	GF
Return (%)	25	23
Standard deviation (%)	30	25
Covariance (%)	112.5	

The correlation coefficient, ρ, is $+.15$.

Proportion in EG&G w_i	GF $w_j = (1 - w_i)$	(1) Portfolio Expected Returns (%)	(2) Variance	(3) Standard Deviation
1.0	0.0	25.0	900	30.0
0.8	0.2	24.6	637	25.2
0.6	0.4	24.2	478	21.9
0.2	0.8	23.4	472	21.7
0.0	1.0	23.0	625	25.0

7-4. Confirm the expected portfolio returns in column 1.

7-5. Confirm the expected portfolio variances in column 2.

7-6. Confirm the expected standard deviations in column 3.

7-7. On the basis of these data, determine the lowest risk portfolio.

7-8. Securities A and B both have expected returns of 20 percent, and standard deviations of 0.42 and 0.28 respectively.

    a. If the securities are equally weighted, what is the total portfolio risk if the correlation coefficient is:

      i. $+1.0$

      ii. $+0.5$

      iii. 0

      iv. -0.5

    b. What does this tell you about the role of correlations in portfolio selection?

7-9. Assume you have a portfolio composed of three stocks, P, Q, and R, which have expected returns of 20 percent, 12 percent, and 16 percent respectively.

    a. If you hold an equally weighted portfolio, what is your expected return?

    b. Assume the standard deviations for the three stocks are 0.377, 0.153, and 0.224 respectively and the correlation matrix looks like the following:

	Correlation with		
	P	Q	R
P	1		
Q	-1	1	
R	0.2	0.6	1

What is the expected portfolio risk if the portfolio is equally weighted?

    c. If you discovered that the correlation matrix in (b) was incorrect, and it actually was supposed to be the following:

	Correlation with		
	P	Q	R
P	1		
Q	-1	-1	
R	0.2	0.6	1

Would your portfolio risk increase, decrease, or stay the same? Why?

7-10. You have $450,000 that you want to invest in a portfolio of five securities, V, W, X, Y, and Z, which have expected returns of 14 percent, 12 percent, 7 percent, 10 percent, and 15 percent respectively. You are considering five different ways of weighing this portfolio:

	V	W	X	Y	Z	Total
1	0.2	0.2	0.2	0.2	0.2	100%
2	0.1	0.1	0.6	0.1	0.1	100%
3	0.1	0.2	0.2	0.1	0.4	100%
4	0.4	0.1	0.2	0.2	0.1	100%
5	0.3	0.1	0.3	0.2	0.1	100%

a. Based on the information given, which scenario would you choose? Why?

b. What other factors might you consider before making a final decision?

7-11. You are given the following information regarding two securities, A and B:

E(Ra)	16%	13%	20%	25%
E(Rb)	18%	10%	12%	19%
Probability	0.4	0.2	0.3	0.1

E(R)a	17%	Std. Dev. A	0.388
E(R)b	14%	Std. Dev. B	0.273

a. Find the covariance between the two securities.

b. What is the correlation coefficient of the portfolio if the securities are equally weighted?

7-12. You are given the following information for stock A and stock B:

State of the economy	Probability of occurrence	Expected return on stock A in this state	Expected return on stock B in this state
High growth	10%	40%	20%
Moderate growth	20%	30%	15%
No growth	50%	10%	8%
Recession	20%	−20%	−5%

a. Estimate the expected return and standard deviation for a portfolio composed of 40 percent invested in stock A and 60 percent invested in stock B.

b. Are there diversification benefits associated with forming the portfolio in part (a)? Briefly explain why or why not.

7-13. You are considering combining two stocks, Peledon and Mexcor, into a portfolio with a standard deviation of 6 percent. The expected return of Peledon is 2 percent with a standard deviation of one percent. The expected return of Mexcor is 25 percent with a standard deviation of 10 percent. The correlation between the two stocks is 0.40.

a. What is the composition (weights) of the portfolio?

b. What is the expected return on the portfolio?

7-14. Calculate the *covariance* and *correlation coefficient* of a portfolio that has 40 percent in Stock X, with an expected return of 40 percent and a standard deviation of 12 percent; and 60 percent in Stock Y, with an expected return of 30 percent and a standard deviation of 15 percent. The portfolio standard deviation is 6 percent.

7-15. Obtain data to examine a "real" efficient frontier involving Research in Motion (RIM.TO) and the Royal Bank (RY.TO).

a. Using monthly data for these two companies from January 2007 to December 2007, graph the relationship between risk and return.

b. Explain the difference between the frontier you developed in part (a) and the efficient frontier.

c. Where do you expect the S&P/TSX index to plot relative to the frontier? Explain.
d. Download the S&P/TSX composite index data for the same period (ticker: ^GSPTSE) and plot the S&P/TSX on your graph.
e. Based on your graph, is the S&P/TSX an efficient portfolio? Explain.
f. What do you expect will happen to the frontier if you increase the number of stocks? Explain your reasoning.

7-16. The data below are annual total returns for Coca-Cola (stock symbol: KO) and Microsoft (stock symbol: MSFT) for the period 1990–2004. Microsoft is highly regarded by many investors. It had a return more than twice as large as that of Coca-Cola. Suppose an investor had placed half her funds in Coca-Cola and half in Microsoft during this 15-year period. Complete the following calculations to determine the resulting portfolio return and risk.

a. Calculate the arithmetic mean returns for each stock.
b. Calculate the standard deviation for each stock using the STDEV function in the spreadsheet.
c. Calculate the correlation coefficient using the CORREL function in the spreadsheet.
d. Calculate the covariance using the COVAR function in the spreadsheet.
e. Calculate the portfolio return assuming equal weights (50 percent) for each stock.
f. Determine the standard deviation of the portfolio (still with 50 percent in each stock). Be sure to use references to the weights and correlation coefficient rather than typing the numbers so that these factors can be changed easily.
g. How does the return and risk of this portfolio compare to the figures for Coca-Cola alone?
h. Assume that the correlation between the two stocks had been –0.10. How much would portfolio risk have changed relative to the result calculated in f?

	KO	MSFT
2004	–0.141	0.222
2003	0.203	0.079
2002	–0.036	–0.220
2001	–0.204	0.527
2000	0.073	–0.628
1999	–0.111	0.684
1998	0.023	1.146
1997	0.291	0.564
1996	0.448	0.885
1995	0.482	0.433
1994	0.196	0.516
1993	0.103	–0.056
1992	0.075	0.153
1991	0.780	1.207
1990	0.254	0.736

7-17. Over the next year, five possible states for the economy may occur. These states and the probabilities of each occurring are shown below. Also shown are the returns that will likely result for two stocks—Stock A and Stock B—in each of these states.

State of Economy	Probability	Stock Returns	
		Stock A	Stock B
Boom	5%	10.0%	-5.0%
Strong Growth	15%	7.5%	0.0%
Weak Growth	40%	5.0%	2.5%
Mild Recession	30%	-2.0%	7.5%
Deep Recession	10%	-5.0%	20.0%

a. Calculate the expected return for each stock.

b. Calculate the variance and the standard deviation for each stock.

c. Calculate the covariance and the correlation coefficient between the returns for these stocks.

d. Create a series of 11 portfolios with various amounts (weights) of these two stocks: 100 percent in Stock A and 0 percent in Stock B; 90 percent in Stock A and 10 percent in Stock B, and so on. For each portfolio, calculate the expected return and standard deviation. Finally, graph the portfolio weights (for Stock A) versus the standard deviation figures. Your resulting graph should be similar to Figure 7-7.

7-18. The table below shows the average monthly return for the five years ending in December 2007 for three large Canadian firms and the S&P/TSX Composite Index (the "market index"). Also shown is the covariance of the returns for each pair of stocks. Note that the covariance of the return on any stock with itself (the diagonal elements in the table) is the variance of that stock's returns.

	Average Return	Covariance with:		
		TELUS	Scotiabank	Teck Cominco
TELUS	0.020	0.005761	0.001270	0.001792
ScotiaBank	0.022	0.001270	0.002284	0.000727
TeckCominco	0.035	0.001792	0.000727	0.010367
Market Index	0.012			

a. You would like to create a portfolio containing these three stocks. TeckCominco appears to be much riskier than the others, so you have decided to put only 20 percent of your funds in that stock, and 40 percent in each of the other two. Calculate the average monthly return you would have received on this portfolio.

b. Finding the risk-level of this portfolio requires including all the variance and co-variance terms. As a start, create a "weighted covariance matrix" by multiplying each covariance (and variance) term by the weight(s) associated with each stock in the portfolio.

c. Calculate the portfolio variance by adding all the terms in the weighted covariance matrix. Find the portfolio standard deviation using the variance just calculated.

d. Use the Single-Index Model to find the monthly return that you should have expected for each of these stocks, as well as for the overall portfolio. Also, calculate the residual error based on the actual returns. Assume that intercept co-efficient Alpha (α) equals 0.0025 per month and the relevant betas (β) are as follows: TELUS = 1.03; ScotiaBank = 0.64; TeckCominco = 2.36; Portfolio = 1.14.

PREPARING FOR YOUR PROFESSIONAL EXAMS

CFA PRACTICE QUESTIONS

7-1. The standard deviation of the rates of return is 0.20 for stock X and 0.12 for stock Y. The covariance between the returns of X and Y is 0.0096. The correlation of the rates of return between X and Y is:

a. 0.40

b. 0.36

c. 0.24

d. 0.20

7-2. Stocks A, B, and C each have the same expected return and standard deviation. Given the following correlations, which portfolio constructed from these stocks has the lowest risk?

Correlation Matrix

Stock	A	B	C
A	+1.9		
B	+0.9	+1.0	
C	+0.1	−0.4	+1.0

a. a portfolio equally invested in stocks A and B
b. a portfolio equally invested in stocks B and C
c. a portfolio equally invested in stocks A and C
d. a portfolio totally invested in stock C

7-3. Which statement about portfolio diversification is correct?

a. Proper diversification can reduce or eliminate systematic risk.
b. The risk-reducing benefits of diversification do not occur meaningfully until at least 10 to 15 individual securities have been purchased.
c. Because diversification reduces a portfolio's total risk, it necessarily reduces the portfolio's expected return.
d. Typically, as more securities are added to a portfolio, total risk is expected to fall at a decreasing rate.

CFA CURRICULUM AND SAMPLE EXAM QUESTIONS (©CFA INSTITUTE)

7-1. An investor has an equal amount invested in each of the following four securities:

Security	Expected Annual Rate of Return
W	0.10
X	0.12
Y	0.16
Z	0.22

The investor plans to sell Security Y and use the proceeds to purchase a new security that has the same expected return as the current portfolio. The expected return for the investor's new portfolio, compared to the current portfolio, will be:

a. lower regardless of changes in the correlation of returns among securities.

b. the same regardless of changes in the correlation of returns among securities.

c. lower only if the correlation of the new security with Securities W, X, and Z is lower than the correlation of Security Y.

d. the same only if the correlation of the new security with Securities W, X, and Z is lower than the correlation of Security Y.

CHAPTER 8

PORTFOLIO SELECTION

Having learned about the importance of diversification, it seems logical that there are limits to its use. How many stocks are enough? How can you know if you have chosen the right portfolio?

If return and risk are the key parameters to consider, how can they be balanced against each other? It seems prudent at this point to learn about optimal portfolios, and in fact the basic principles about optimal portfolios can now be readily understood, given our knowledge to date. Going further, what about an overall plan to ensure that you have evaluated all of your investing opportunities? Someone mentioned that an asset allocation plan is needed when investing, so it seems the time has come to consider this. After all, many of the websites devoted to investing, particularly those associated with financial institutions, refer to asset allocation when discussing what investors should be doing. Therefore, every investor should learn something about this most important concept.

Learning Objectives

After reading this chapter, you should be able to

1. State three steps involved in building a portfolio.
2. Apply the Markowitz efficient portfolio selection model.
3. Describe the effect of risk-free borrowing and lending on the efficient frontier.
4. Discuss the separation theorem and its importance to modern investment theory.
5. Separate total risk into systematic and non-systematic risk.

CHAPTER PREVIEW

In Chapter 7, we demonstrated how to evaluate risky assets and calculate portfolio risk using the Markowitz diversification model. In this chapter, we establish three steps to building a portfolio. First, we consider the Markowitz portfolio selection model, which involves the important concept of efficient portfolios. Second, we analyze the impact of risk-free assets on Markowitz's efficient frontier. Third, we discuss how to select the final portfolio based on risk preferences. We conclude the chapter with a discussion of the separation theorem and the concepts of systematic and non-systematic risk.

INTRODUCING RISKLESS ASSETS

In Chapter 7, we learned that risky assets should be evaluated on the basis of their expected returns and risk, as measured by the standard deviation, and that portfolio expected return and risk can be calculated based on these inputs and the covariances involved. Calculation of portfolio risk is the key issue. The complete Markowitz variance–covariance analysis can be used to calculate portfolio risk, or the single-index model can be used to simplify the calculations, subject to the assumptions of the model.

We analyzed basic portfolio principles, such as diversification, and determined that investors should hold portfolios of financial assets in order to reduce their risk when investing. Clearly, risk reduction through diversification is a very important concept. In fact, diversification is the number one rule of portfolio management and the key to optimal risk management. Every intelligent investor will diversify his or her portfolio of risky assets.

Despite the importance of the diversification principle, our analysis is incomplete because an infinite number of potential portfolios of risky assets exist. Furthermore, investors can invest in both risky and riskless assets and buy assets on margin or with borrowed funds. This chapter completes our portfolio analysis by analyzing how investors select optimal risky portfolios and how the use of a risk-free asset changes the investor's ultimate portfolio position. In effect, we are analyzing the optimal trade-off that exists between risk and expected return. This will allow us in the next chapter to analyze asset pricing and market equilibrium.

BUILDING A PORTFOLIO

learning objective 1
State three steps involved in building a portfolio.

To build a portfolio of financial assets, investors should follow certain steps. Specifically, they should

1. *Use the Markowitz portfolio selection model.* Identify optimal risk–return combinations available from the set of risky assets being considered by using the Markowitz efficient frontier analysis. This step uses the inputs from Chapter 7, the expected returns, variances, and covariances for a set of securities.

2. *Consider borrowing and lending possibilities.* What is the impact of a risk-free asset on the Markowitz efficient frontier? The introduction of borrowing and lending possibilities leads to an optimal portfolio of risky assets and has a significant impact on the way investors think about the investment process.

3. *Choose the final portfolio based on risk preferences.* It should consist of the risk-free asset and the optimal portfolio of risky assets, based on an investor's preferences.

In this chapter, we follow these steps. We first consider the Markowitz analysis, which is used to identify the efficient set of portfolios, and then we discuss the impact of a risk-free asset on this analysis. We show how investors can construct a final portfolio consisting of the risk-free asset and a portfolio of risky assets that is optimal for them.

STEP 1: USE THE MARKOWITZ PORTFOLIO SELECTION MODEL

As we saw in Chapter 7, even if portfolios are selected arbitrarily, some diversification benefits are gained. This results in a reduction of portfolio risk. However, random diversification does not use the entire information set available to investors and does not always lead to optimal diversification.

To take the full information set into account, we use an alternative approach based on portfolio theory as developed by Markowitz. Portfolio theory is normative, meaning that it tells investors how they should act to diversify optimally. It is based on a small set of assumptions, including

1. A single investment period—for example, one year;

2. Liquidity of positions—for example, there are no transaction costs;

3. Investor preferences based only on a portfolio's expected return and risk, as measured by variance or standard deviation.

Efficient Portfolios

Markowitz's approach to portfolio selection is that an investor should evaluate portfolios on the basis of their expected returns and risk as measured by the standard deviation. He was the first to derive the concept of an **efficient portfolio**, defined as one that has the smallest portfolio risk for a given level of expected return or the largest expected return for a given level of risk.

In economics in general, and finance in particular, we assume investors are risk averse. This means that investors will require additional expected return in return for assuming additional risk. Based on this assumption, we can see that rational, risk-averse investors will prefer efficient portfolios because they offer a higher expected return for a given level of risk, or lower risk for a given level of expected return.

Investors can identify efficient portfolios by specifying an expected portfolio return and minimizing the portfolio risk at this level of return. Alternatively, they can specify a portfolio risk level that they are willing to assume and maximize the expected return on the portfolio for this level of risk. Rational, risk-averse investors will seek efficient portfolios because they are optimized on the two dimensions of most importance to investors: expected return and risk.

To begin our analysis, we must first determine the risk–return opportunities available to an investor from a given set of securities. Figure 8-1 illustrates the opportunities available from a given set of securities. A large number of possible portfolios exist when we realize that varying percentages of an investor's wealth can be invested in each of the assets under consideration. Is it necessary to evaluate all the possible portfolios illustrated in Figure 8-1? Fortunately, the answer is no, because investors should be interested in only that subset of the available portfolios known as the efficient set.

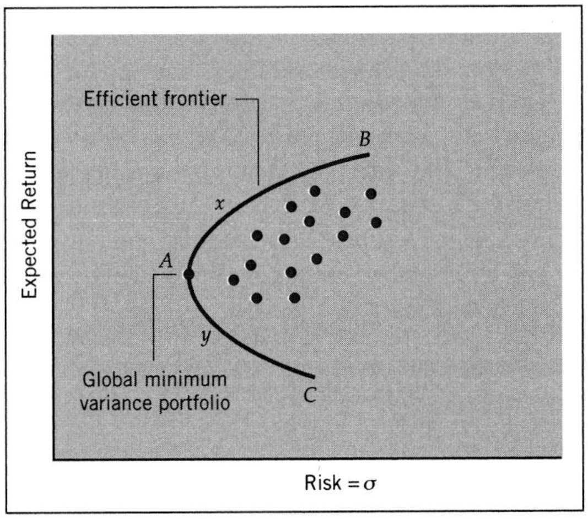

> **learning objective 2**
> Apply the Markowitz efficient portfolio selection model.

> **Efficient Portfolio**
> A portfolio with the highest level of expected return for a given level of risk or a portfolio with the lowest risk for a given level of expected return.

Figure 8-1
The Attainable Set and the Efficient Set of Portfolios

The assets in Figure 8-1 generate the attainable set of portfolios, or the opportunity set. The attainable set is the entire set of all portfolios that could be formed using a group of *n* securities. However, risk-averse investors should be interested only in those portfolios with the lowest possible risk for any given level of return. All other portfolios in the attainable set are dominated by efficient portfolios.

Using the inputs described in Chapter 7—expected returns, variances, and covariances—we can calculate the portfolio with the smallest variance, or risk, for a given level of expected return based on these inputs.[1] Given the minimum variance portfolios, we can plot the minimum variance frontier, which is represented by the entire parabola-shaped curved line in Figure 8-1. Point A represents the global minimum variance portfolio because no other minimum variance portfolio has a smaller risk. Portfolios on the bottom segment of the minimum variance frontier (AC) are dominated by portfolios on the upper segment (AB). For example, since portfolio X has a larger return than portfolio Y for the same level of risk, investors would not want to own portfolio Y.

The segment of the minimum variance frontier above the global minimum variance portfolio, AB, offers the best risk–return combinations available to investors from this particular set of inputs. This segment is referred to as the **efficient set** or **efficient frontier** of portfolios. This efficient set is determined by the principle of dominance.

Efficient Set (Frontier)
The set of efficient portfolios composed entirely of risky securities generated by the Markowitz portfolio model.

Technically, the basic Markowitz model is solved by a complex technique called quadratic programming.[2] Since the model is easily solved by computer, we do not expand on the details. However, we note that the solution involves the determination of optimal portfolio weights or percentages of investable funds to be invested in each security. Because the expected returns, standard deviations, and correlation coefficients for the securities being considered are inputs in the Markowitz analysis, the portfolio weights are the only variable that can be manipulated to solve the portfolio problem of determining efficient portfolios.

Think of efficient portfolios as being derived in the following manner: The inputs are obtained, and a level of desired expected return for a portfolio is specified—for example, 10 percent. Then all combinations of securities that can be combined to form a portfolio with an expected return of 10 percent are determined, and the one with the smallest variance of return is selected as the efficient portfolio. Next, a new level of portfolio expected return is specified, and the process is repeated. This continues until the feasible range of expected returns is processed. Of course, the problem could also be solved by specifying levels of portfolio risk and choosing that portfolio with the largest expected return for the specified level of risk.

Selecting an Optimal Portfolio of Risky Assets

Once the efficient set of portfolios is determined using the Markowitz model, investors must select from this set the portfolio most appropriate for them. The Markowitz model does not specify a single optimum portfolio. It generates the efficient set of portfolios that provide the minimum risk portfolios that are attainable for given levels of expected return, or the maximum expected returns that are attainable for given levels of risk.

The assumption of risk-averse investors means that, if given a choice, they will not take a fair gamble—one with an expected payoff of zero and equal probabilities of a gain or a loss. In effect, with a fair gamble, the disutility from the potential loss is greater than the utility from the potential gain. The greater the risk aversion, the greater the disutility from the potential loss.

Indifference Curves
Curves describing investor preferences for risk and return.

To select the expected return–risk combination that will satisfy an individual investor's personal preferences, **indifference curves** (which are assumed to be known for an investor) are used. These curves, shown in Figure 8-2 for a risk-averse investor, describe investor preferences for risk and return.[3] Each indifference curve represents all combinations of portfolios that are equally desirable to a particular investor.

---

[1]Each investor doing this may use a different set of inputs, and therefore the outputs will differ.
[2]In particular, the problem is to choose optimal weights in the available securities in order to minimize the risk of the portfolio for a given level of expected return. This optimization problem is subject to a wealth constraint (i.e., the sum of the weights in the individual securities must equal total wealth, or 1.0) and is also constrained by the return–risk characteristics of the available set of securities.
[3]Although not shown, investors could also be risk-neutral (the risk is unimportant in evaluating portfolios) or risk seekers. A risk-seeking investor will want to take a fair gamble, and larger gambles are preferable to smaller gambles.

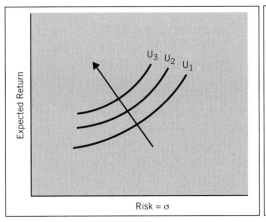

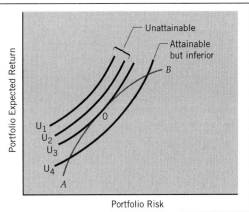

Indifference Curves

Figure 8-3
Selecting a Portfolio
on the Efficient Frontier

A few important points about indifference curves should be noted. They cannot intersect since they represent different levels of desirability. Investors have an infinite number of indifference curves. The curves for all risk-averse investors will be upward sloping, but the shapes of the curves can vary depending on risk preferences. Higher indifference curves are more desirable than lower indifference curves. The greater the slope of the indifference curves, the greater the risk aversion of investors.

The optimal portfolio for a risk-averse investor occurs at the point of tangency between the investor's highest indifference curve and the efficient set of portfolios. In Figure 8-3, this occurs at point 0.[4] This portfolio maximizes investor utility because the indifference curves reflect investor preferences, while the efficient set represents portfolio possibilities. Notice that curves U2 and U1 are unattainable and that U3 is the highest indifference curve for this investor that is tangent to the efficient frontier. On the other hand, U4, though attainable, is inferior to U3, which offers a higher expected return for the same risk (and therefore more utility).

Three important points must be noted about the Markowitz portfolio selection model:

1. The Markowitz analysis generates an entire set, or frontier, of efficient portfolios, all of which are equally "good," and none of these portfolios on the efficient frontier dominates any other.

2. The Markowitz model does not address the issue of investors using borrowed money along with their own portfolio funds to purchase a portfolio of risky assets; that is, investors are not allowed to use leverage. As we will see later in the chapter, allowing investors to purchase a risk-free asset increases investor utility and leads to a different efficient set.

3. In practice, different investors or portfolio managers will estimate the inputs to the Markowitz model differently, leading to different efficient frontiers. This results from the uncertainty inherent in the security analysis part of investments as described in Chapter 1.

INVESTING *tip*

Stated on a practical basis, conservative investors would select portfolios on the left end of the efficient set AB in Figure 8-3 because these have less risk (and, of course, less expected return). Conversely, aggressive investors would choose portfolios toward point B because these offer higher expected returns (along with higher levels of risk).

Alternative Methods of Obtaining the Efficient Frontier

As we saw in Chapter 7, the single-index model provides an alternative expression for portfolio variance, which is easier to calculate than in the case of the Markowitz analysis. This approach can also be used to determine the efficient set of portfolios, but it requires considerably fewer calculations. In the case of the Markowitz analysis, 250 stocks require calculating 31,125 covariances and 250 variances. Using the single-index model as specified in Equation 7-15, we would need 250 estimates of beta (β_i), 250 estimates of the intercept term (α_i), 250 estimates of residual variance, one estimate

[4]The investor is selecting the portfolio with the indifference curve furthest northwest.

of the expected return on the market portfolio, and one estimate for the variance of the market portfolio.[5] In short, the single-index model is a valuable simplification of the full variance–covariance matrix needed for the Markowitz model.[6]

An obvious question to ask is how it performs in relation to the Markowitz model. In his original paper developing the single-index model, Sharpe found that two sets of efficient portfolios—one using the full Markowitz model and the other using his simplification—generated from a sample of stocks were very much alike.[7] Subsequent studies have confirmed the performance of the Sharpe model.

Selecting Optimal Asset Classes

The Markowitz model is generally thought of in terms of selecting portfolios of individual securities; indeed, that is how Markowitz expected his model to be used. As we know, however, it is a cumbersome model to employ because of the number of covariance estimates needed when dealing with a large number of individual securities.

An alternative way to use the Markowitz model as a selection technique is to think in terms of asset classes, such as domestic stocks, foreign stocks of industrialized countries, the stocks of emerging markets, bonds, and so forth. Using the model in this manner, investors decide what asset classes to own and what proportions of the asset classes to hold.

Asset Allocation Decision

The allocation of a portfolio's funds to classes of assets, such as cash equivalents, bonds, and equities.

The **asset allocation decision** refers to the allocation of portfolio assets to broad asset markets—in other words, how much of the portfolio's funds is to be invested in stocks, how much in bonds, money market assets, and so forth. The weights must add up to 100 percent, representing the total amount of investable funds for an investor. Each weight can range from zero percent to 100 percent if we assume that no short selling of securities is allowed.[8] Extending the asset allocation decision to a global setting leads us to ask the following questions:

1. What percentage of portfolio funds is to be invested in each of the countries for which financial markets are available to investors?

2. Within each country, what percentage of portfolio funds is to be invested in stocks, bonds, bills, and other assets?

3. Within each of the major asset classes, what percentage of portfolio funds is to go to various types of bonds, exchange-listed stocks versus over-the-counter stocks, and so forth?

Many knowledgeable market observers agree that the asset allocation decision is the most important decision made by an investor, as alluded to in Real World Returns 8-1. According to some studies, for example, the asset allocation decision accounts for more than 90 percent of the variance in quarterly returns for a typical large pension fund.[9]

---

[5]The single-index model requires $3n + 2$ total pieces of data to implement, where n is the number of securities being considered.

Example:

The 250 securities mentioned earlier would require $3n + 2 = 3(250) + 2 = 752$ estimates, consisting of 250 estimates of α_i; 250 estimates of β_i; 250 variances of the residual errors σ_{ei}; an estimate of the expected return on the market index; and, an estimate of the expected variance on the market index.

In contrast, the full variance–covariance model of Markowitz requires $[n(n + 3)]/2$ estimates for n securities.

In the case of the 250 securities, $[250(253)]/2 = 31,625$ total pieces of data, or

250 expected returns + 250 variances + $[250(249)]/2$ unique covariances = 31,625 total pieces of data.

[6]The single-index model can be used to estimate directly the expected return and risk for a portfolio.

[7]W. Sharpe, "A Simplified Model for Portfolio Analysis," *Management Science* 9 (January 1963), pp. 277–293.

[8]As we shall see, when short-selling is permitted, the weights in the securities sold short will be negative; however, the total weights must still add up to 100 percent.

[9]Gary P. Brinson, L. Randolph Hood, and Gilbert L. Beebower, "Determinants of Portfolio Performance," *Financial Analysts Review* 42 (July/August 1986), pp. 39–44.

REAL-WORLD RETURNS 8-1

Spread It Around

Diversifying May Help Reduce Risk in Your Portfolio

The new millennium certainly provided investors a dramatic lesson in market volatility. As an example, the S&P 500 ended 2002 with a total return of −23.37 percent, but finished 2003 with a flourish, up 26.38 percent, aptly demonstrating how much investment markets can fluctuate. Alas, performance ups and downs—whether over the short or long term—are a given in the world of investing. And in a sharp market downturn, this volatility can significantly shrink your holdings.

Undoubtedly, the last few years' rise in equity values has offered some investor relief after three years of steep stock market declines. But if the volatility lesson got your attention, you may be wondering if you want (or need) to adjust your investment strategy at this point.

When reviewing your portfolio, first realize that you cannot predict how the markets will perform. As a result, trying to "time" the market—attempting to guess which way the markets will move and basing your investment decisions on these predictions—is bound to fail, at least most of the time.

Since market timing is not the answer, you need a better approach for building your portfolio. A tried and true method, based on substantial research, is to diversify your money across different types of investments. "Given the uncertainty of the markets, asset allocation, or dividing holdings among different asset classes like stocks, bonds and real estate, provides a good way to manage risk and to build a portfolio for the long term," says Leonard Govia, participant advice manager, TIAA-CREF. (However, diversification doesn't guarantee against loss.)

The Birth of a Theory

The concept of asset allocation is based on modern portfolio theory, which was developed in the 1950s by the economist Harry M. Markowitz, who later shared a Nobel Prize for his work. Markowitz measured the risk inherent in various types of securities and developed methods for combining investments to maximize the trade-off between risk and return.

Basically, the theory says that investors shouldn't view the prospects of a particular security in isolation, but instead look at each investment and how it fits into an overall portfolio. By combining securities that have a low (or, better yet, negative) correlation with each other—that is, securities that don't perform in the same way under similar market conditions—investors will create a less risky portfolio than if they invested only in securities that perform similarly (i.e., have a high correlation).

"The advantage of diversifying investments is that each type of security won't react to the ups and downs of the market in the same way," says Govia. "So by diversifying, you spread the risk in your portfolio around. The result is a more balanced portfolio that can help you withstand drops in the market."

Other studies demonstrate the impact asset allocation has on volatility. For example, in a notable 10-year study of large pension funds, Gary P. Brinson, L. Randolph Hood, and Gilbert Beebower found that, over time, more than 90 percent of the variability of a portfolio's performance is due to allocation among specific asset classes, while less than 5 percent of the variability of performance results from investment selection.

Create a Portfolio for You

If diversification works, your next question may be "How do I ensure that my portfolio is right for my needs?" Many investment companies give you a simple way to develop an appropriate strategy: model portfolios, diversified among asset classes like stocks, bonds and money market, that are based on different risk tolerances, investment preferences and "time horizons" (the number of years you have to invest before needing to use the money, and how many years you'll need that money to last).

Source: "Spread It Around," *Balance*, Quarterly News and Tools From TIAA-CREF, Summer 2004, pp.10–11. Reprinted by permission.

EXAMPLE 8-1: ASSET MIX AND PORTFOLIO PERFORMANCE

Consider the performance of two Canadian portfolio managers, A and B, between 2004 and 2008. Manager A maintained an equally weighted portfolio with respect to T-bills, long-term government bonds, and common stocks, while manager B was more conservative and allocated 20 percent of funds to each of bonds and stocks, with the remaining 60 percent to T-bills. Assume each manager matched the risk–return performance on the relevant asset class benchmark index for the proportion of their portfolio invested in each of the three asset classes. Over the period, the average annual return and standard deviations for the asset classes were:

	Average Annual Return (%)	Annual Standard Deviation (%)
T-bills	4.01	1.29
Government bonds	5.60	7.96
Common stocks	7.68	20.42

Based on the asset allocation decisions presented above, the annual return earned by manager A would have been 5.76 percent, and the standard deviation of the portfolio would have been 9.89 percent. Over the same period, manager B would have earned 5.06 percent annual return, with a standard deviation of 6.45 percent. In this example, the lower risk and return of manager B's portfolio is completely attributable to her asset allocation decision since we assumed that both managers performed equally well in the management of assets within a given asset class.

The rationale behind the asset allocation approach is that different asset classes offer various potential returns and various levels of risk, and the correlation coefficients may be quite low. As with the Markowitz analysis applied to individual securities, inputs remain a problem because they must be estimated for some uncertain future period. However, the use of diversified portfolios to represent different asset classes requires fewer estimates. In addition, portfolio estimates of expected return and risk are generally much more reliable than those for individual securities, since there will be less unique or company-specific risk involved. Programs exist to calculate efficient frontiers using asset classes. These programs allow for a variety of constraints, such as minimum yield and no short selling. A variety of asset allocation strategies are discussed in Chapters 14 and 21.

Global Diversification

Chapter 7 demonstrated that diversification worked the best when the returns for securities being combined in a portfolio displayed low correlations. Due to differences in overall market performance, economic activity, and industrial structure, the correlation between domestic stock returns and those on stocks trading in other countries will be low in comparison to returns displayed among only domestic stock. Therefore, it is not surprising that diversifying internationally has substantial benefits in terms of risk reduction, which was depicted in Figure 7-3. As discussed in Chapter 7, the benefits associated with international diversification have diminished in recent years as global markets have become more integrated and correlations among international stock returns have increased. However, investors can still benefit by diversifying internationally.

CHECK YOUR UNDERSTANDING

8-1. Various types of data are required to conduct a Markowitz analysis, yet when it comes to finding efficient portfolios, the portfolio weights are the only variables that can be manipulated. Why is this?

8-2. Given the large number of portfolios in the attainable set, why are there relatively few portfolios in the efficient set?

8-3. Why do we consider indifference curves when discussing the efficient frontier? How can we be certain that these indifference curves will always be "upward sloping"?

STEP 2: CONSIDER BORROWING AND LENDING POSSIBILITIES

As we saw above, investors can use the Markowitz analysis as a portfolio optimizer. This analysis determines the best combinations of expected return and risk for a given set of inputs for risky assets. However, investors always have the option of buying a risk-free asset such as T-bills. The portfolio selection question remains the same. Given any set of assets under consideration, what is the best portfolio of assets to hold? To answer this question, as before, we will determine the possibilities and then match them with investor preferences.

A risk-free asset can be defined as one with a certain return and a variance of return of zero. (Note, however, that this is a nominal return and not a real return, which is uncertain because inflation is uncertain.) Since the variance = 0, the nominal risk-free rate in each period will be equal to its expected value. Furthermore, the covariance between the risk-free asset and any risky asset i will be zero, because

$$\sigma_{RF,i} = \rho_{RF,i}\sigma_i\sigma_{RF}$$
$$= \rho_{RF,i}\sigma_i(0)$$
$$= 0$$

ρ denotes the correlation coefficient and σ the respective standard deviation of asset i or the risk-free asset. Therefore, the risk-free asset will have no correlation with risky assets.[10]

The true risk-free asset is best thought of as a government security, which has no risk of default and has a term to maturity matching the holding period of the investor. In this case, the amount of money to be received at the end of the holding period is known with certainty at the beginning of the period.[11] Short-term T-bills are typically taken to be the risk-free asset, and the associated rate of return is referred to here as RF.

Although the introduction of a risk-free asset appears to be a simple step to take in the evolution of portfolio and capital market theory, it is a very significant step. Investors can now invest part of their wealth in this asset and the remainder in any of the risky portfolios in the Markowitz efficient set. It allows Markowitz portfolio theory to be extended in such a way that the efficient frontier is completely changed. This, in turn, leads to a general theory for pricing assets under uncertainty, as discussed in the next chapter.

Risk-Free Borrowing and Lending

Assume that the efficient frontier, as shown by the arc AB in Figure 8-4, has been derived by an investor. The arc AB delineates the efficient set of portfolios composed entirely of risky assets. (For simplicity, we assume these are portfolios of common stocks.) We now introduce a risk-free asset with return RF and standard deviation of zero.

learning objective 3
Describe the effect of risk-free borrowing and lending on the efficient frontier.

---

[10]Alternatively, one could arrive at the conclusion that $\sigma_{RF,i} = 0$ because $\rho_{RF,i} = 0$ since RF is a constant, which by nature has no correlation with the changing returns on risky security i.

[11]If there is no uncertainty about the terminal value of the asset, the standard deviation must be zero and the asset must, therefore, be riskless.

As shown in Figure 8-4, the return on the risk-free asset (RF) will plot on the vertical axis because the risk is zero. Investors can combine this riskless asset with the efficient set of portfolios on the efficient frontier. The section below demonstrates that we can draw a line between RF and any risky portfolio on the efficient frontier to represent obtainable combinations of risk–return possibilities that did not exist previously.

Figure 8-4
The Markowitz Efficient Frontier and the Possibilities Resulting from Introducing a Risk-Free Asset

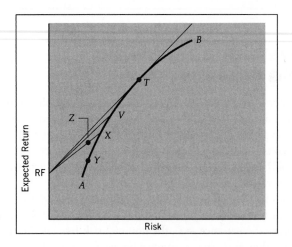

Risk-Free Lending

Consider an arbitrary point on the efficient frontier depicted in Figure 8-4—risky portfolio X. Assume this investor places w_{RF} of investable funds in the risk-free asset and the remainder $(1 - w_{RF})$ in portfolio X. The expected return on this combined portfolio p would be

$$(8-1) \qquad E(R_p) = w_{RF}RF + (1 - w_{RF})\, E(R_X)$$

As always, the expected return of a portfolio is a weighted average of the expected returns of the individual assets. Since portfolio X, consisting of risky assets, would always be assumed to have a larger expected return than the return on the risk-free asset (RF), the greater the percentage of an investor's funds committed to X, $(1 - w_{RF})$, the larger the expected return on the portfolio.

The standard deviation of this portfolio is

$$(8-2) \qquad \sigma_p = (1 - w_{RF})\sigma_X$$

because $\sigma_{RF} = 0$ and the correlation between RF and any risky portfolio is zero, which eliminates the second and third terms of Equation 7-11.[12] Thus, the standard deviation of a portfolio combining the risk-free asset with a risky asset (portfolio) is simply the weighted standard deviation of the risky portfolio. This confirms what one would expect: as a higher proportion of wealth is invested in the risky asset, the portfolio risk increases.

Since both the expected return and standard deviation of a portfolio composed of any portfolio of risky assets X and the riskless asset RF are linear functions of the weights invested in RF and X, the portfolio combinations can be expressed as a straight line. In other words, an investor who combines the risk-free asset with portfolio X of risky assets would have a portfolio somewhere on the line RF-X (e.g., point Z).

---

[12]More formally, Equation 7-11 for this portfolio would equal

$$\sigma_P = \sqrt{(1 - w_{RF})^2\sigma_X^2 + w_{RF}^2\sigma_{RF}^2 + 2(1 - w_{RF})w_{RF}\rho_{RFX}\,\sigma_X\,\sigma_{RF}}$$

$$= \sqrt{(1 - w_{RF})^2\sigma_X^2 + w_{RF}^2(0) + 2(1 - w_{RF})w_{RF}(0)\sigma_X(0)} = \sqrt{(1 - w_{RF})^2\sigma_X^2 + 0 + 0} = (1 - w_{RF})\sigma_X$$

EXAMPLE 8-2: COMBINING RISK-FREE ASSETS WITH RISKY ASSETS (PORTFOLIO)

Assume that portfolio X has an expected return of 15 percent with a standard deviation of 30 percent, and that the risk-free security has an expected return of 3 percent. If 60 percent of investable funds are placed in RF and 40 percent in portfolio X (i.e., $w_{RF} = 0.6$ and $1 - w_{RF} = 0.4$), then

$$E(R_p) = 0.6(3\%) + 0.4(15\%) = 7.8\%$$

and

$$\sigma_p = (1.0 - 0.6)\,30\% = 12\%$$

An investor could change positions on the line RF-X by varying w_{RF}, and hence $1 - w_{RF}$. As more of the investable funds are placed in the risk-free asset, both the expected return and the risk of the portfolio decline.

It is apparent that the segment of the efficient frontier below X (i.e., A to X) in Figure 8-4 is now dominated by the line RF-X. For example, at point Z on the straight line, the investor has the same risk as portfolio Y on the Markowitz efficient frontier, but Z has a larger expected return. Hence, the ability to invest in RF provides investors with a more efficient set of portfolios from which to choose.

In Figure 8-4, a new line could be drawn between RF and the Markowitz efficient frontier above point X, for example, connecting RF to point V. Each successively higher line will dominate the preceding set of portfolios because it will offer higher expected returns for any given level of risk (i.e., they lie northwest of the other lines). This process ends when a line is drawn tangent to the efficient set of risky portfolios, given a vertical intercept of RF. In Figure 8-4, we will call this tangency point T. The portfolio opportunities on this line (RF to T) dominate all portfolios below them.

Portfolio T is important in this analysis. The Markowitz efficient set consists of portfolios of risky assets. In Figure 8-4, no other portfolio connected to the risk-free rate (RF) lies northwest of the straight line connecting RF and portfolio T. This line has the greatest slope (and thereby provides the highest reward per unit of risk).

The straight line from RF to the efficient frontier at point T (RF-T) dominates all straight lines below it and contains the superior lending portfolios, given the Markowitz efficient set depicted in Figure 8-4. The term lending portfolios arises in reference to the fact that purchasing riskless assets such as T-bills to combine with some risky asset is a form of the investor lending money to the issuer of the securities—the federal government. We can think of this risk-free lending simply as risk-free investing.

Through a combination of risk-free investing (investing funds at a rate of RF) and investing in a risky portfolio of securities, T, an investor can improve upon the opportunity set available from the Markowitz efficient frontier, which consists only of portfolios of risky assets. The set of efficient portfolios available to any investor with the introduction of the possibility of risk-free investing now lies along line RF-T.

Borrowing Possibilities

What if we extend this analysis to allow investors to borrow money? The investor is no longer restricted to his or her initial wealth when investing in risky assets. One way to accomplish this borrowing is to buy stocks on margin, which may have margin requirements as low as 30 percent. Of course, investors must pay interest on borrowed money. We will assume initially that investors can also borrow at the risk-free rate RF. Technically, borrowing at the riskless rate can be viewed as short-selling the riskless asset. We will remove the assumption that funds can be invested at the riskless rate later.

Borrowing additional investable funds and investing them together with the investor's own wealth allows investors to seek higher expected returns while assuming greater risk. These borrowed funds can be used to lever the portfolio position beyond the tangency point T, which represents 100 percent of an investor's wealth in the risky asset portfolio T. The straight line RF-T is now extended upward, as shown in Figure 8-5, and can be designated RF-T-L.

Figure 8-5
The Efficient Frontier
when Lending and
Borrowing Possibilities
Are Allowed

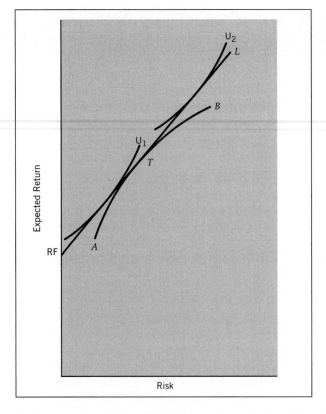

What effect does borrowing have on the expected return and risk for a portfolio? These parameters can be calculated in the usual manner. However, the proportions to be invested are now stated differently. Since the proportions to be invested in the alternatives are stated as percentages of an investor's total investable funds, various combinations must add up to 1.0 (i.e., 100 percent, representing an investor's total wealth). Therefore, the proportion to be borrowed at RF is stated as a negative figure, so that $w_{RF} + (1 - w_{RF}) = 1.0 = 100$ percent of investor wealth.

Assume an investor can borrow an amount equal to all of his or her investable wealth, which, together with that wealth itself, will be invested in risky-asset portfolio T (i.e., 200 percent of investable wealth is invested in portfolio T). The $1 - w_{RF}$ weight must now equal 2.0 to represent the sum of original wealth plus borrowed funds. To obtain this result, the proportion of investable funds associated with w_{RF} is negative; specifically, it is −1.0, representing borrowed funds at the rate RF. Therefore, the proportion to be invested in portfolio T is $[1 - (-1)] = 2$.

Overall, the combined weights are still equal to 1.0, since

$$w_{RF} + (1 - w_{RF}) = 1.0$$
$$-1 + [1 - (-1)] = 1.0$$

The expected return on the investor's portfolio P, consisting of investable wealth plus borrowed funds invested in portfolio T, is now

$$E(R_p) = w_{RF}\, RF + (1 - w_{RF})\, E(R_T) = -1(RF) + 2\, E(R_T)$$

The expected return increases linearly as the borrowing increases. The standard deviation of this portfolio is

$$\sigma_p = (1 - w_{RF})\sigma_T$$
$$= 2\sigma_T$$

Risk will increase as the amount of borrowing increases.

Borrowing possibilities (i.e., leverage) are illustrated by the following example.

EXAMPLE 8-3: BORROWING AND RISK

Assume that the expected return on portfolio T is 10 percent, with σ_T = 20 percent. The expected risk-free rate, RF, is still 3 percent, as earlier. However, it now represents the borrowing rate, or the rate at which the investor must pay interest on funds borrowed and invested in the risky asset T. The expected return on this portfolio would be

$$E(R_p) = -1(3\%) + 2(10\%)$$
$$= -3\% + 20\%$$
$$= 17\%$$

The standard deviation of this leveraged portfolio would be

$$\sigma_p = (1 - w_{RF})\sigma_T$$
$$= [1.0 - (-1.0)]\sigma_T$$
$$= 2(20\%)$$
$$= 40\%$$

The New Efficient Set

The end result of introducing risk-free investing and borrowing into the analysis is to create lending and borrowing possibilities and a set of expected return–risk possibilities that did not exist previously. As shown in Figure 8-5, the new risk–return trade-off can be represented by a straight line that is tangent to the efficient frontier at point T and that has a vertical intercept RF.

The introduction of the risk-free asset significantly changes the Markowitz efficient set of portfolios. Specifically, the following points emerge:

1. The new efficient set is no longer a curve, or arc, as in the Markowitz analysis. It is now linear.

2. Borrowing and lending possibilities, combined with one portfolio of risky assets, T, offer an investor whatever risk-expected return combination he or she seeks; that is, investors can be anywhere they choose on this line, depending on their risk–return preferences.

The critical reader may point out that it is unlikely that the typical investor can borrow at the same rate as that offered by riskless securities because borrowing rates generally exceed lending rates. As a result, the borrowing rate that must be paid to construct the portfolios lying beyond point T in Figure 8-5 will be higher than RF. Obviously, this will make these portfolios less desirable than before. For example, if we recalculate the expected return and standard deviation for the portfolio described in the example "Borrowing and Risk" above, but increase the borrowing rate to 4 percent instead of 3 percent, we would find the expected return for the portfolio would fall to 16 percent, while the standard deviation would remain at 40 percent. Nonetheless, it is obvious that these portfolios will still dominate those formed using risky portfolios only, but the line depicted in Figure 8-5 will be transformed into a line with a "kink" at point T since the borrowing rate exceeds RF. This new line is depicted in Figure 8-6.

CHECK YOUR UNDERSTANDING

8-4. Why is the introduction of risk-free borrowing and lending such an important change relative to the Markowitz analysis?

8-5. One implication of the new linear efficient set is that all investors should choose portfolio "T", and no other risky portfolio. Does this mean that all investors should have exactly the same portfolio?

STEP 3: CHOOSE THE FINAL
PORTFOLIO BASED ON PREFERENCES

Each investor can choose the point on the efficient-set line that corresponds to his or her risk preferences. Formally, this would be where the investor's highest indifference curve is tangent to the straight line RF-T-L in Figure 8-5 (or the kinked line in Figure 8-6). In practical terms, this means that more conservative investors would be closer to the risk-free asset designated by the vertical intercept RF. More aggressive investors would be closer to, or on, point T, representing full investment in a portfolio of risky assets. Even more aggressive investors could go beyond point T by using leverage to move up the line. In order to simplify the following discussion, we assume we can lend and borrow at RF, so Figure 8-5 provides the basis for our analysis. The general conclusions will not be affected materially by the existence of borrowing rates above RF.

Figure 8-6
When Borrowing Rate (R_B)
Exceeds RF

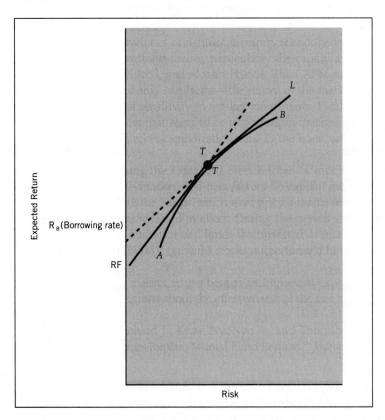

THE SEPARATION THEOREM

learning objective 4
Discuss the separation theorem and its importance to modern investment theory.

We have established that each investor will benefit from holding combinations of the risk-free asset (either lending or borrowing) and the tangency portfolio from the efficient frontier. By combining these two assets into various portfolios, an investor can form efficient portfolios along the line RF-T-L in Figure 8-5. Given the assets under consideration, investors cannot reach a higher risk–return trade-off.

Consider now the case of an investment firm with multiple clients. (Alternatively, we could assume that all investors have identical forecasts of expected returns, standard deviations, and covariances and select the same optimal portfolio of risky assets.) The investment firm, having determined the Markowitz efficient frontier from the set of securities it analyzes for investment purposes, will offer the same portfolio of risky assets to each of its clients. This portfolio is determined as above, where the ray from RF is tangent to the efficient frontier as its highest point.

Unlike the case where we considered the availability of risky assets, it is not necessary to match each client's indifference curves with a particular efficient portfolio because only one efficient portfolio is held by all investors. Rather, each client will use his or her indifference curves to determine where along the new efficient frontier RF-T-L he or she should be. In effect, each client must determine how much of investable funds should be lent or borrowed at RF and how much should be invested in portfolio T. This result is referred to as a separation property.

The **separation theorem** states that the investment decision (which portfolio of risky assets to hold) is separate from the financing decision (how to allocate investable funds between the risk-free asset and the risky asset). The risky portfolio T is optimal for every investor regardless of that investor's utility function; that is, T's optimality is determined separately from knowledge of any investor's risk–return preferences and is not affected by investor risk preferences. All investors, by investing in the same portfolio of risky assets (T) and either borrowing or lending at the rate RF, can achieve any point on the straight line RF-T-L in Figure 8-5. Each point on that line represents a different expected return–risk trade-off. A more conservative investor with utility curve U1 will be at the lower end of the line, representing a combination of lending and investment in T. On the other hand, utility curve U2 represents a more aggressive investor who borrows at the rate RF to invest in risky portfolio T.

The concept of the riskless asset–risky-asset (portfolio) dichotomy is an important one in investments, with several different applications. As we have seen, using the two in combination allows investors to achieve any point on the expected return–risk trade-off that all investors face. This is in sharp contrast to the traditional investing approach where investment firms and money managers tailored a portfolio of stocks to each individual client because of their unique preferences. For example, a retiree living off the income from a stock portfolio would be guided to a portfolio of relatively conservative stocks with an emphasis on their dividend yields. A 35-year-old investor doing well in his or her profession, on the other hand, might be guided to a portfolio with considerably more risk and expected return.

The separation theorem argues that this tailoring process is inappropriate. All investors should hold the same portfolio of risky assets and achieve their own position on the risk–return trade-off through borrowing and lending. The opportunity set is the same because it accommodates investors with different preferences.

Furthermore, some of the new techniques in investments utilize the same two assets. For example, portfolio insurance (see Chapter 19) can be regarded as an asset allocation strategy that seeks to rebalance a portfolio between a risky component and a riskless component in order to keep the portfolio return from declining below some specified minimum return.

Separation Theorem
The idea that the decision of which portfolio of risky assets to hold is separate from the decision of how to allocate investable funds between the risk-free asset and the risky asset.

THE IMPLICATIONS OF PORTFOLIO SELECTION

The construction and selection of optimal portfolios for each investor has implications for the pricing of financial assets. Over one-half of the riskiness of the average stock can be eliminated by holding a well-diversified portfolio. This means that part of the risk of the average stock can be eliminated, but part cannot. Investors need to focus on that part of the risk that cannot be eliminated by diversification because this is the risk that should be priced in the financial markets.

Systematic and Non-Systematic Risk

As Equations 7-17 and 7-18 showed, the single-index model allows us to divide the risk associated with common stocks into two types: (1) a general component, representing that portion in the variability of a stock's total returns that is directly associated with overall movements in general economic (or stock market) activity; and (2) a specific (issuer) component, representing that portion in the variability of a stock's total return that is not related to the variability in general economic (market) activity. These two components, referred to in investment analysis as systematic and non-systematic risk (or by the alternative names shown below), are additive:

learning objective 5
Separate total risk into systematic and non-systematic risk.

$$\text{Total risk} = \text{Systematic risk} + \text{Non-systematic risk}$$
$$= \text{Market risk} + \text{Non-market risk}$$
$$= \text{Non-diversifiable risk} + \text{Diversifiable risk}$$

Variability in a security's total returns that is directly associated with overall movements in the general market or economy is called systematic (market) risk. Whether bonds or stocks, virtually all securities have some systematic risk because it directly encompasses interest rate risk, market risk, and inflation risk. We are concerned here with the systematic risk of common stocks.

The non-systematic risk is the part of the total risk that can be eliminated through diversification. After the non-systematic risk is eliminated, what is left is the non-diversifiable portion, or the market risk (systematic part). Market risk is unavoidable because no matter how well an investor diversifies, the risk of the overall market cannot be avoided. If the stock market declines sharply, most stocks will be adversely affected; if it rises strongly, most stocks will appreciate in value. These movements occur regardless of what any single investor does.

Figure 8-7 illustrates this concept of declining non-systematic risk in a portfolio of securities. As more securities are added, the non-systematic risk becomes smaller and smaller, and the total risk for the portfolio approaches its systematic risk. Since diversification cannot reduce systematic risk, total portfolio risk can be reduced no lower than the total market risk of the portfolio.[13]

Figure 8-7
Systematic and
Non-Systematic Risk

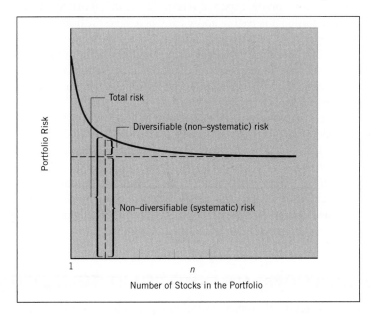

How many securities does it take to eliminate most or all of the non-systematic risk? It has become commonplace to say that approximately 20 to 30 securities will provide a diversified portfolio; however US evidence, discussed in Chapter 7, suggests that holding 40 or more stocks may be optimal. Canadian research suggests that 70 or more stocks are required to obtain a well-diversified portfolio.

Diversification can substantially reduce the unique risk of a portfolio. However, Figure 8-7 indicates that no matter how much we diversify, we cannot eliminate systematic risk. The declining total risk curve in that figure levels off and becomes asymptotic to the systematic risk. Clearly, market risk is critical to all investors. It plays a central role in asset pricing because investors can expect a reward for taking that risk. In addition, there may be disadvantages to being "overly diversified," as discussed in Real-World Returns 8-2.

---

[13]Notice the resemblance of Figure 8-7 to Figure 7-2 of Chapter 7, which was constructed using actual monthly data for Canadian common stocks over the 1993–97 period.

We know that the basic premise of investing is that investors demand a premium for bearing risk. However, we now know the importance of selecting portfolios of financial assets rather than holding individual securities. The relevant risk of an individual stock is its contribution to the riskiness of a well-diversified portfolio. The return that should be expected on the basis of this contribution can be estimated by the capital asset pricing model, which is discussed in the next chapter.

REAL-WORLD RETURNS 8-2
Why to Avoid Excessive Portfolio Diversification

The Merits of Adopting a Focused Approach to Investing

In our years of studying investors, we have found that many of the best ones use concentrated, low turnover approaches. The most obvious is Warren Buffett, CEO of the holding company Berkshire Hathaway, who has achieved extraordinary results by abiding by a high-conviction strategy.

Buffett's commonsense approach to investing involves buying great companies trading at fair prices and holding them for the long haul. A lesser-known but equally important aspect of his philosophy is that lucrative investment opportunities are few and far between, so it's important to patiently wait on the sidelines but act decisively and aggressively when opportunity presents itself.

However, being concentrated doesn't mean you should bet the farm on a handful of attractively valued stocks—that job is usually best handled by the pros. Money managers that subscribe to a focused investment approach—a group that also includes the likes of Tom Stanley, Peter Cundill and Jerry Javasky—spend much of their time sifting through financial statements, reading up on industry trends and talking with management, suppliers and customers of companies they think possess excellent long-term prospects. Clearly, this brand of investing is a full-time endeavour.

It also doesn't mean investors should turn their backs on the basic principles of diversification. When you're building a portfolio, the primary focus should be on diversifying among different asset-classes, sectors and geographies. Without proper diversification, a downturn in those areas could wreak havoc on a portfolio's returns.

Instead, what we're suggesting is that investors follow a focused approach but be mindful of maintaining a certain level of diversification. After all, wouldn't you prefer to have a portfolio devoted to a short list of investments in which you have the highest degree of confidence, which you can hold no matter what the market serves up? True enough, building such a portfolio is easier said than done. This gets even more complicated for those who manage multiple accounts for themselves and others. But by following a few guidelines, investors can strike a careful balance between diversification and concentration.

Less Is More

Diversification can prevent getting caught on the wrong side of a trade. However, one of the most common mistakes of portfolio construction is being overly diversified. After a certain point, adding more funds to your portfolio just creates additional bookkeeping and tax headaches, while doing little to increase returns or lower risk. When too many mutual funds are thrown together, the result tends to be indistinguishable from that of an inexpensive index fund, because any differences among the funds become diversified away.

Unfortunately, there's not a magic number of funds that makes you overly diversified. A lot depends on your goals and types of funds you own. As a rule of thumb, though, we think four or five core funds can adequately provide enough diversification. If you come to realize that you hold too many offerings, it's a good idea to think about trimming that number. Just be aware of any tax implications when selling a fund.

(continued)

REAL-WORLD RETURNS 8-2 *continued*

What You Don't Know Can Hurt You

When you buy stocks, bonds and mutual funds through a variety of different channels, it becomes increasingly difficult to assess the underlying characteristics and, consequently, risks inherent in your portfolio. The most obvious way to familiarize yourself with your investments is through consolidation. If possible, managing money in a single account is probably the best way to stay abreast of your finances.

By the same token, we realize the realities of life make it challenging to manage a portfolio under one umbrella, especially when you're managing RRSPs, RESPs and defined contribution plans, to name a few. This is one reason why people end up with sprawling portfolios. We think a better way to manage accounts that share the same time horizon is as a unified whole. As a result, you'll be able to cut down on the overall number of holdings and focus on the bigger picture.

Sector Funds: Buyer Beware

The proliferation of sector-focused mutual funds and exchange traded funds (ETFs) has made it extraordinarily easy to find a product that's doing better than your boring assortment of core funds. As industry rhetoric goes, "there's always a bull market somewhere." However, the inclusion of these funds could offset the moves made by managers of other offerings in your portfolio.

That said, a sector fund can be practical for those who are informed and bold enough to act decisively. For instance, we have noticed that contrarian investors like Bill Miller of CI Value Trust and the deep value investment team at Brandes Investment Partners have recently been building positions in downtrodden homebuilders. A low-cost ETF that focuses on this unloved area of the market is an example of how investors can invest alongside managers in whom they have confidence.

Overall, the key to making a focused strategy work is to be selective when choosing funds, have an intimate understanding of your portfolio, and take calculated risks. Remember, in order to beat the market, you can't be the market.

Source: Benincasa, Jordan, "Why to avoid excessive portfolio diversification," *Advisor's Edge Report*, February 2008. Retrieved from www.advisor.ca.

CHECK YOUR UNDERSTANDING

8-6. The separation theorem tells us which two decisions can be made independently?

8-7. Which portion of total risk—systematic or non-systematic—is considered most important, and why?

SUMMARY

This summary relates to the learning objectives for this chapter.

1. **State three steps involved in building a portfolio.**

   To build a portfolio, we first use the Markowitz portfolio selection model to identify optimal risk–return combinations available from the set of risky assets being considered. Second, we consider the impact of borrowing and lending possibilities on the Markowitz efficient frontier. Third, we choose the final portfolio based on our risk preferences.

2. **Apply the Markowitz efficient portfolio selection model.**

   Markowitz portfolio theory provides the way to select optimal portfolios based on using the full information set about securities. According to this theory, an efficient portfolio has the highest expected return for a given level of risk or the lowest level of risk for a given level of expected return.

The Markowitz analysis determines the efficient set (frontier) of portfolios composed entirely of risky securities, all of which are equally desirable. The efficient set is an arc in expected return–standard deviation space. The efficient frontier captures the possibilities that exist from a given set of risky securities, while indifference curves can be used to express investor preferences. The optimal portfolio for a risk-averse investor occurs at the *point of tangency* between the investor's highest indifference curve and the efficient set of portfolios.

3. **Describe the effect of risk-free borrowing and lending on the efficient frontier.**

   In addition to owning risky assets, investors can also buy risk-free assets, earning the riskless rate RF. We also assume that borrowing is permitted. Risk-free borrowing and lending changes the efficient set to a straight line that intersects the efficient frontier arc at one point (the tangency point).

4. **Discuss the separation theorem and its importance to modern investment theory.**

   The separation theorem states that the investment decision (what portfolio of risky assets to buy) can be separated from the financing decision (how much of investable funds should be put in risky assets and how much in the risk-free asset). Under the separation theorem, all investors should hold the same portfolio of risky assets and achieve their own position on the return–risk trade-off through borrowing and lending.

5. **Separate total risk into systematic and non-systematic risk.**

   Total risk can be divided into systematic and non-systematic risk. Non-systematic risk, also called diversifiable risk, can be eliminated by diversification. Market risk cannot be eliminated by diversification and is the relevant risk for the pricing of financial assets in the market.

KEY TERMS

Asset allocation decision, p.228   Efficient set (Frontier), p.225   Separation theorem, p.237
Efficient portfolio, p.226   Indifference curve, p.226

REVIEW QUESTIONS

8-1. Using the Markowitz analysis, how does an investor select an optimal portfolio?

8-2. Why do rational, risk-averse investors seek efficient portfolios?

8-3. How is an investor's risk aversion indicated in an indifference curve? Are all indifference curves upward sloping?

8-4. What is meant by the term lending portfolios?

8-5. What is the difference between non-systematic and systematic risk? Explain why proper diversification of a stock portfolio effectively eliminates non-systematic risk but does not reduce systematic risk.

8-6. Given a set of inputs, explain conceptually how efficient portfolios are determined.

8-7. How does the introduction of a risk-free asset change the Markowitz efficient frontier?

8-8. What does the separation theorem imply about the tailored approach to portfolio selection?

8-9. Given the availability of risk-free borrowing and risk-free lending, how would your personal optimal portfolio change if you became very risk-tolerant? In contrast, what would be the composition of your optimal portfolio if you were a very conservative, risk-averse investor? Use a diagram(s) to help illustrate your answer.

8-10. Why would the covariance between a risk-free asset and any risky asset be zero?

8-11. With the Markowitz portfolio selection model, why is it impossible for the efficient frontier to have any "kinks" in it? Phrased another way, why must the efficient frontier be concave rather than convex?

8-12. Most stock returns have positive correlations. Give examples of stocks that you think might have high positive correlations, low positive correlations, or negative ones.

8-13. As an investor's personal level of risk tolerance changes, how (if at all) does the efficient set change? How (if at all) does the investor's indifference curve change? Use diagrams to help illustrate your answer.

8-14. Explain the separation theorem. What are its implications for portfolio managers? For investors?

8-15. In a real-world setting, your cost of borrowing is higher than the interest rate that you can earn on government securities ("risk-free lending"). What effect would this have on the efficient set?

8-16. Given your new-found knowledge of stock portfolios and the efficient frontier, it appears that computers could select the most efficient portfolio(s) for investors to invest in. If this is the case, why do investors pay professional money managers to manage their money? Discuss.

8-17. Select the correct statement concerning the Markowitz model:

  a. The Markowitz model determines the optimal portfolio for each investor.
  b. The efficient frontier expresses preferences while indifference curves express possibilities.
  c. All conservative investors would have the same optimal portfolio.
  d. An investor's optimal portfolio can be found where his or her highest indifference curve is tangent to the efficient frontier.

8-18. Choose the portfolio from the following set that is not on the efficient frontier.

  a. Portfolio A: expected return of 10 percent and standard deviation of 8 percent.
  b. Portfolio B: expected return of 18 percent and standard deviation of 13 percent.
  c. Portfolio C: expected return of 38 percent and standard deviation of 32 percent.
  d. Portfolio D: expected return of 15 percent and standard deviation of 14 percent.

8-19. Select the correct statement from among the following:

  a. Knowing the covariance between two securities and the standard deviation of each, the correlation coefficient can be calculated.
  b. When the total returns for a security are plotted against the total returns for a market index and a regression line is fitted, this line is referred to as the capital market line.
  c. With perfect negative correlation, two securities' returns have a perfect direct linear relationship to each other.
  d. The optimal portfolio for any investor occurs at the point of tangency between the investor's lowest indifference curve and the efficient frontier.

8-20. Choose the statement below that is most closely associated with the work of Markowitz:

  a. Risk-free borrowing and lending can change the efficient frontier.
  b. Non-systematic risk can be identified and assessed.
  c. The efficient frontier can be changed from an arc to a straight line.
  d. Efficient portfolios can be calculated and chosen.

8-21. Why is initial portfolio selection so important?

8-22. Why is the asset allocation decision so important?

8-23. What are some limitations of the Markowitz portfolio selection model?

8-24. Why should Canadian investors look to foreign stock markets?

8-25. Consider a diagram of the efficient frontier. The vertical axis is _____. The horizontal axis is _____ as measured by the _____.

8-26. How many portfolios are on an efficient frontier? What is the Markowitz efficient set?

8-27. With regard to international investing, how has the situation changed in recent years with regard to correlations among the stocks of different countries?

8-28. As we add securities to a portfolio, what happens to the total risk of the portfolio?

PROBLEMS

8-1. Based on the information in the table below, determine which of these portfolio(s) would constitute the efficient set.

Portfolio	Expected Return (%)	Standard Deviation (%)
1	10	20
2	12	24
3	8	16
4	6	12
5	9	21
6	20	40
7	18	36
8	8	15
9	11	19
10	12	22
11	14	26

8-2. Given the following information:

Standard deviation for stock X = 12%   Standard deviation for stock Y = 20%
Expected return for stock X = 16%   Expected return for stock Y = 22%
Correlation coefficient between X and Y = 0.30
The covariance between stock X and Y is
   a. 0.048
   b. 72.00
   c. 3.60
   d. 105.6

8-3. Given the information in Problem 8-2 regarding risk, the expected return for a portfolio consisting of 50 percent invested in X and 50 percent invested in Y can be seen to be
   a. 19%
   b. 16%
   c. less than 16%
   d. more than 22%

8-4. Given the information in Problem 8-2, assume now that the correlation coefficient between stocks X and Y is +1.0. Choose the investment below that represents the minimum risk portfolio.
   a. 100% investment in stock Y
   b. 100% investment in stock X
   c. 50% investment in stock X and 50% investment in stock Y
   d. 80% investment in stock Y and 20% investment in stock X

8-5. Given the following information for four securities:

Security	1	2	3	4
E(R) %	10	12	14	18
σ^2	300	350	400	450

$\rho(1,2) = 0.2$; $\rho(1,3) = 0.4$; $\rho(1,4) = 0.6$; $\rho(2,3) = 0.1$; $\rho(3,4) = 0.9$; $\rho(2,4) = 0.5$.

Calculate five efficient portfolios using the Markowitz analysis, an upper boundary of 50 percent, and a lower boundary of 10 percent for the weights invested in each portfolio.
   a. What is the highest expected return from these four portfolios?
   b. What is the lowest standard deviation from these four portfolios?
   c. Which portfolios involve short sales?
   d. Which portfolio should be preferred by an investor?

8-6. Using the information in Problem 8-5, determine the effects of changing the correlation coefficient between securities 1 and 2 from 0.20 to −0.20.

a. What is the effect on the expected return of the portfolios?

b. What is the effect on the variance of the portfolios?

8-7. Assume that portfolio X has an expected return of 20 percent, a standard deviation of 35 percent, and a risk-free security has an expected return of 7.5 percent.

a. What proportion of invested funds should be placed in the risk-free asset in order to achieve a total portfolio return of 15 percent?

b. What is the standard deviation of this new portfolio?

c. What would happen to the expected return and the risk of the portfolio if you were to increase the weight of invested funds placed in the risk-free security?

d. If you decided that the allocation strategy in (c) better corresponded to your risk preference, would this make you a more aggressive or a more conservative investor?

8-8. You want to borrow an amount equal to all of your investable wealth and invest all of this into a risky-asset portfolio A. Assume that the expected return of this portfolio A is 25 percent with a standard deviation of 40 percent. The expected risk-free rate is 7.5 percent and represents your borrowing rate.

a. What is the expected return on this portfolio?

b. What is the standard deviation of this portfolio?

8-9. You have $100,000 that you want to invest in a risky-asset portfolio M. You also want to borrow an extra $50,000 at a risk-free rate of 8 percent. Portfolio M has an expected return of 20 percent and a standard deviation of 30 percent.

a. What is the expected return on this portfolio?

b. What is the standard deviation of this portfolio?

8-10. You are trying to decide whether to buy Banguard's Large Stock Equity Fund and/or its Treasury Bond Fund. You believe that next year involves several possible scenarios to which you have assigned probabilities. You have also estimated expected returns for each of the two funds for each scenario. Your spreadsheet looks like the following.

Next Year's Possibilities	Probability	Stock Fund Rate of Return	Column D	Bond Fund Rate of Return	Column F
Recession	0.15	−13		15	
Weak Econ.	0.05	5		3	
Moderate Econ.	0.6	10		7	
Strong Econ.	0.2	24		−9	
		Exp Value =		Exp Value =	

a. Fill in columns D and F and calculate the expected return for each fund, given the probabilities for the four possible economic conditions and their associated rates of return.

b. Given the expected value for each fund for next year, fill out the following spreadsheet to calculate the standard deviation of each fund. Note that you need to fill in columns D, E, and F for the stock fund, and columns H, I, and J for the bond fund. The first two columns in each set are labelled; you need to determine what goes in columns F and J, respectively, which will lead to the variance, and then the standard deviation.

Scenario	Probability	Forecast Return	Col. D Deviation from Exp.	Col. E Squared Deviation	Column F	Forecast Return	Col. H Deviation from Exp.	Col. I Squared Deviation	Column J
Recession	0.15	−13				15			
Weak Econ.	0.05	5				3			
Moderate Econ.	0.6	10				7			
Strong Econ.	0.2	24				−9			
	Exp. Ret.	9.1		Variance = Std Dev =				Variance = Std Dev =	

c. Now calculate the covariance between the two funds and the correlation coefficient using the following format.

Scenario	Column B Probability	Deviation from Exp. Return for Stock Fund	Deviation from Exp. Return for Bond Fund	Product of Deviations	Col. B × Col. E
Recession	0.15				
Weak Econ.	0.05				
Moderate Econ.	0.6				
Strong Econ.	0.2				
				Covariance =	Corr. Coeff. =

d. Using the formulas for the expected return and risk of a portfolio, calculate these values for each of the following portfolio weights.

w1 = stock fd % of funds in	w2 = bond fd % of funds in	Portfolio Expected Return	Standard Deviation
0.1	0.9		
0.2	0.8		
0.3	0.7		
0.4	0.6		
0.5	0.5		
0.6	0.4		
0.7	0.3		
0.8	0.2		
0.9	0.1		

e. Which of the portfolios in (d) is the minimum variance portfolio?

f. Based on your analysis, should investors hold a portfolio of 100 percent bonds?

8-11. In one of the Chapter 7 spreadsheet problems we found expected returns and other statistics for two stocks (Stock A and Stock B) given the probabilities for several future states of the economy. The results of those calculations are summarized below.

	Stock A	Stock B
Expected Return	2.53%	5.00%
Standard Deviation	4.56%	5.97%
Correlation		−0.905452

a. As in Chapter 7, create a series of 11 portfolios with various amounts (weights) of these two stocks: 100 percent in Stock A and 0 percent in Stock B; 90 percent in Stock A and 10 percent in Stock B, etc. For each portfolio calculate the expected return and standard deviation. Which of these portfolios has the lowest level of risk?

b. Create a graph of the expected returns versus the standard deviation figures. Your resulting graph should be similar to Figure 8-1. Is the lowest risk portfolio identified in part (a) above actually the best (lowest risk) that can be achieved with these two stocks?

c. Determining the absolute lowest risk portfolio can be accomplished with a little calculus. However spreadsheets, such as in Excel, provide an even easier method to carry out this type of optimization (be sure the "Solver" add-in is installed in Excel). Let us use cell B51 to hold the portfolio weight for Stock A (the weight for Stock B will be 1 minus the Stock A weight); we will enter a starting value, for example 60 percent. In cell D51, enter the formula for the portfolio standard deviation, as you did for the table of portfolios above. When you run Solver, D51 becomes the "target" cell to be minimized (be sure to select "Min"). Cell B51 should be entered in the "By Changing Cells" box. When you click

"Solve", the program will quickly provide the result. Did the weight for Stock A turn out to be a little less than 60 percent as we thought? Is the resulting standard deviation lower than what we found in our table of portfolios?

8-12. The following data was used in Chapter 7 for Problem 7-18. The table shows the average monthly return (for the 5 years ending in December 2007) for three large Canadian firms and the covariance of the returns for each pair of stocks.

	Average	Covariance with:		
	Return	TELUS	Scotiabank	Teck Cominco
TELUS	0.020	0.005761	0.001270	0.001792
Scotiabank	0.022	0.001270	0.002284	0.000727
Teck Cominco	0.035	0.001792	0.000727	0.010367
Market Index	0.012			

a. Using the weight combinations shown below, calculate the average monthly return and the standard deviation for each portfolio.

TELUS	Scotiabank	Teck Cominco
0%	0%	100%
0%	33%	67%
0%	67%	33%
0%	100%	0%
33%	0%	67%
33%	33%	33%
33%	67%	0%
67%	0%	33%
67%	33%	0%
100%	0%	0%

b. Which portfolio weights give the lowest total risk? Why might you not choose to construct your portfolio with those weights?

c. Assume you have selected an equal-weighted portfolio of these stocks (33 percent in each) as your risky asset. There is also a risk-free asset available with a return of 0.5 percent per month. Determine the return and risk (standard deviation) of portfolios created using both the risky and risk-free assets. For the risky asset, use weights of 0 percent, 25 percent, 50 percent, and so on, up to 200 percent. Note that when the weight of the risky asset surpasses 100 percent, the weight for the risk-free asset will be negative (to make the total portfolio weight 100 percent.) This indicates that your portfolio is leveraged or using borrowed funds. Observe how the portfolio risk increases more rapidly than the return.

PREPARING FOR YOUR PROFESSIONAL EXAMS

CFA PRACTICE QUESTIONS

8-1. Portfolio theory as described by Markowitz is most concerned with:

a. the identification of unsystematic risk.
b. the elimination of systematic risk.
c. the effect of diversification on portfolio risk.
d. both a and b.

8-2. An investor puts 40 percent of her investable funds into T-bills earning 5 percent and the other 60 percent of her funds into an equity portfolio yielding 15 percent. The equity portfolio has a standard deviation of returns of 10 percent. What is the expected return and standard deviation of returns of her combined portfolio?

	Expected Return	Standard Deviation
a.	0.09	8%
b.	0.10	7%
c.	0.11	6%
d.	0.12	5%

CFA CURRICULUM AND SAMPLE EXAM QUESTIONS (©CFA INSTITUTE)

8-1. Markowitz Portfolio Theory is most accurately described as including an assumption that:
   a. risk is measured by the range of expected returns.
   b. investors have the ability to borrow or lend at the risk-free rate of return.
   c. investor utility curves demonstrate diminishing marginal utility of wealth.
   d. investment decision-making is based on both rational and irrational factors.

APPENDIX 8A

A MODERN PORTFOLIO THEORY AND THE PORTFOLIO MANAGEMENT PROCESS

The practical relevance of portfolio theory and diversification is demonstrated by its impact on regulations governing the investment behaviour of professional money managers. Guidelines for North American professional money managers require them to adhere to "prudence, loyalty, reasonable administrative cost, and diversification," which alludes to the importance of diversification.

The duty of prudence referred to in the passage above requires fiduciaries to perform their duties "with the care, skill, prudence, and diligence under the circumstances then prevailing that a prudent man acting in a like capacity and familiar with such matters would use in the conduct of an enterprise of a like character and with like aims." The term "familiar with such matters" refers to "the prudent expert rule." This implies the manager's behaviour must meet the standard for trained and experienced investment professionals rather than just that of a "prudent man." This definition of prudence suggests that managers should be responsible for managing the risk of the portfolio as a whole, as opposed to managing the risks associated with each individual investment within the portfolio (which is implied by "the prudent man rule"). This represents an important innovation that can be directly attributable to the concepts underlying modern portfolio theory.

Not surprisingly, the importance attached to taking a portfolio approach to investing is incorporated in educational courses provided for investment professionals. For example, both the CSC and the CFA courses discuss the importance of the portfolio management process. This process stresses the selection of securities based on that security's contribution to the portfolio as a whole, in addition to its individual merit. Security selection and market timing decisions are made within the context of the effect on the whole portfolio. An important feature of portfolio formation (discussed in Chapters 7 and 8) is that portfolio returns will be an average of the returns on all securities within the portfolio, but the risk will be lower than the weighted average of risks as long as the securities are not perfectly correlated. This implies that risk can be eliminated by forming portfolios of securities.

Portfolio management is a continuous process consisting of four parts:

1. Designing an investment policy
2. Developing and implementing an asset mix
3. Monitoring the economy, the markets, and the client
4. Adjusting the portfolio and measuring performance.

We defer an in-depth discussion of the portfolio management process until Chapter 21.

CHAPTER 9

CAPITAL MARKET
THEORY

Although you have postponed dealing with the issue, in the back of your mind you remember from your introductory finance course a well-known model called the CAPM. It occurs to you that this model, which was said to be so important in Finance, probably has a role to play in your investing decisions. And in fact it does because it captures the concept of a required rate of return for a stock, which is important to consider when you are trying to decide which stocks to buy. So the time has come to make your move and review some theory regarding asset prices and markets, and consider the CAPM once again. Knowing about the required rate of return will be important when you start trying to value common stocks, a topic that you are almost ready to tackle. Furthermore, understanding how risk is priced in financial markets can be very valuable to an investor.

Learning Objectives

After reading this chapter, you should be able to

1. Explain capital market theory and the Capital Asset Pricing Model.
2. Discuss the importance and composition of the market portfolio.
3. Describe two important relationships in the CAPM as represented by the capital market line and the security market line.
4. Describe how betas are estimated and how beta is used.
5. Discuss the Arbitrage Pricing Theory as an alternative to the Capital Asset Pricing Model.

CHAPTER PREVIEW

Our discussion of portfolio theory in the last chapter described how to select an optimal portfolio of securities under normal market conditions. In this chapter, we consider capital market theory, which seeks to explain security pricing under conditions of market equilibrium. We focus on the well-known Capital Asset Pricing Model (CAPM) and its application. We conclude the chapter by discussing some of the shortcomings of this model and an alternative model known as the Arbitrage Pricing Theory.

INTRODUCTION TO CAPITAL MARKET THEORY

learning objective 1
Explain capital market theory and the Capital Asset Pricing Model.

Capital Market Theory
Describes the pricing of capital assets in financial markets.

In this chapter we consider **capital market theory**. What happens if all investors seek portfolios of risky securities using the Markowitz framework under idealized conditions? How will this affect equilibrium security prices and returns? In other words, how does optimal diversification affect the market prices of securities? Under these idealized conditions, what is the risk–return trade-off that investors face? In effect, we wish to examine models that explain security prices under conditions of market equilibrium.

One equilibrium model discussed in this chapter is known as the Capital Asset Pricing Model (CAPM). It allows us to measure the relevant risk of an individual security as well as to assess the relationship between risk and the returns expected from investing.

The CAPM is attractive as an equilibrium model because of its simplicity and its implications, but because of serious challenges to the model, alternatives have been developed. An important alternative to the CAPM is Arbitrage Pricing Theory (APT), which allows for multiple sources of risk. Therefore, we conclude the chapter with a discussion of the APT.

The Assumptions of the CAPM

Capital Asset Pricing Model (CAPM)
Relates the required rate of return for any security with the market risk for that security as measured by beta.

The **Capital Asset Pricing Model (CAPM)** is concerned with the equilibrium relationship between the risk and the expected return on risky assets. The traditional CAPM was derived independently by Sharpe and by Lintner and Mossin in the mid-1960s.[1] Although several extensions of this model have been proposed, the original CAPM remains a central tenet of modern financial economics.

The CAPM involves a set of predictions concerning equilibrium expected returns on risky assets. It is derived by making some simplifying assumptions in order to facilitate the analysis and help us to understand the arguments without fundamentally changing the predictions of asset pricing theory.

Capital market theory builds on Markowitz portfolio theory. Each investor is assumed to diversify his or her portfolio according to the Markowitz model, choosing a location on the efficient frontier that matches his or her return–risk preferences. Because of the complexity of the real world, additional assumptions are made to make individuals more alike:

1. All investors have identical probability distributions for future rates of return; they have identical (or homogeneous) expectations with respect to the three inputs of the portfolio model explained in Chapter 7: expected returns, the variance of returns, and the correlation matrix. Therefore, given a set of security prices and a risk-free rate, all investors use the same information to generate an efficient frontier.

2. All investors have the same one-period time horizon.

3. All investors can borrow or lend money at the risk-free rate of return (designated RF in this text).

4. There are no transaction costs.

5. There are no personal income taxes—investors are indifferent between capital gains and dividends.

---

[1]Much of this analysis is attributable to the work of Sharpe. See W. Sharpe, "Capital Asset Prices: A Theory of Market Equilibrium under Conditions of Risk," *The Journal of Finance*, 19 (September 1964), pp. 425–442. Lintner and Mossin developed a similar analysis.

6. There is no inflation.

7. There are many investors, and no single investor can affect the price of a stock through his or her buying and selling decisions. Investors are price-takers and act as if prices are unaffected by their own trades.

8. Capital markets are in equilibrium.

These assumptions appear unrealistic and often disturb individuals encountering capital market theory for the first time. However, the important issue is how well the theory predicts or describes reality. If capital market theory does a good job of explaining the returns on risky assets, it is very useful and the assumptions made in deriving the theory are of less importance. In addition, most of these assumptions can be relaxed without significant effects on the capital asset pricing model or its implications; in other words, the CAPM is robust.[2] Although the results from such a relaxation of the assumptions may be less clear-cut and precise, no significant damage is done. Many conclusions of the basic model still hold.

Most investors recognize that all of the assumptions of the CAPM are not unrealistic. For example, some institutional investors are tax-exempt, and their brokerage costs, as a percentage of the transaction, are quite small. The ability for individual investors to trade through discount brokers and/or the Internet has also reduced their trading costs to extremely low levels. Nor is it too unreasonable to assume that for the one-period horizon of the model, inflation may be fully (or mostly) anticipated and, therefore, not a major factor.

Equilibrium in the Capital Markets

If the assumptions listed previously hold, what is the equilibrium situation that will prevail in the capital markets? In Chapter 8, we demonstrated that rational, risk-averse investors will strive to obtain the highest possible expected return for a given level of risk, or the lowest risk for a given level of expected return. When we introduced the assumption that they could borrow and lend at the risk-free rate, we concluded that investors would all desire to hold some portion of their wealth in one optimal portfolio of risky assets. This optimal portfolio was shown to be the one that is tangent to a line drawn from the risk-free asset to the efficient frontier of risky securities, as was depicted in Figure 8-5. By assuming that all investors have the same time horizon and have homogeneous expectations regarding the expected returns and risks for any given risky asset, we imply they all use identical information for the same time period to determine the composition of the optimal portfolio. As a result, the optimal risky portfolio will be identical for all investors.

Having established that the optimal portfolio will be identical for all investors, we now demonstrate that it will be the aggregate market portfolio, which contains all assets in existence. The value of this portfolio will equal the aggregate of the market values of all the individual assets comprising it. Therefore, the weights of these assets in the market portfolio will be represented by their proportionate weight in the total value of it. We have assumed the existence of market equilibrium, which occurs when prices are at levels that provide no incentive for speculative trading. This implies that markets clear—in other words all assets are assumed to be bought and sold at an equilibrium price that is established by the forces of supply and demand.[3] Since all assets trade, it must mean that they are correctly priced to adequately compensate investors for the associated risks. For example, if an asset was priced too high, then demand would fall, and the price would decline as a result. Market clearing implies that the price would eventually fall to an equilibrium level that would result in the asset being traded.

Since the market consists of all available assets, which are assumed to be priced correctly to reflect adequate compensation for the associated risk, the market portfolio will be the most efficient (or optimal) portfolio with respect to the weights attached to the individual securities comprising it. For

---

[2]For a discussion of changing these assumptions, see E. Elton, M. Gruber, S. J. Brown, and W. N. Goetzmann, *Modern Portfolio Theory and Investment Analysis*, Sixth Edition (New York: John Wiley & Sons, 2003), Chapter 14.

[3]Markets could not be in equilibrium if markets did not clear since this would imply some assets did not trade because buyers and sellers could not agree upon a trading price.

example, consider a market that consists of only two risky assets (A and B) and two investors, each with $1,000 invested in risky assets. This implies the total value of the market would be $2,000. Since each investor will hold the same (optimal) proportions in each of the two assets (say $w_A = 0.80$, and $w_B = 0.20$), these must be the weights for these assets in the market portfolio. In other words, investors A and B will both have $0.80 \times \$1,000 = \$800$ invested in asset A, representing a total of $1,600. This will be the market value of asset A. Each investor will also hold $200 worth of asset B, for a total of $400, which will be its market value. Thus, the market portfolio weights for assets A and B will be 0.80 ($1,600/$2,000) and 0.20 ($400/$2,000). This example produces the same basic result when extended to many investors and many assets.

The implications of this discussion are

1. All investors will choose to hold the risky portion of their portfolio in the aggregate market portfolio, which includes all assets in existence;

2. This market portfolio will be on the Markowitz efficient frontier and will be the optimal risky portfolio to hold;

3. All efficient portfolios will lie along the straight line drawn from the risk-free asset that passes through the point represented by the market portfolio, since this line will represent the optimal trade-off between standard deviation and expected return available from the set of available assets.

We will consider these implications next.

THE MARKET PORTFOLIO

Market Portfolio
The portfolio of all risky assets with each asset weighted by the ratio of its market value to the market value of all risky assets.

In the preceding section, we demonstrated that the market portfolio will be the optimal combination of risky assets available to investors and that all efficient portfolios will lie along the straight line drawn from the risk-free asset that passes through the point represented by the market portfolio. This relationship is depicted graphically in Figure 9-1, which is the same as Figure 8-5 except the point of tangency has been changed from T to M. Portfolio M in Figure 9-1 is called the **market portfolio** of risky securities. It is the highest point of tangency between RF and the efficient frontier and is the

Figure 9-1
The Efficient Frontier with Borrowing and Lending

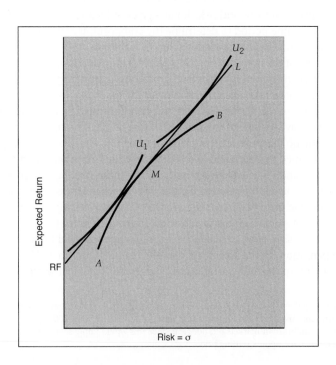

optimal risky portfolio. This optimal risky portfolio from the Markowitz efficient set is found by determining which efficient portfolio offers the highest risk premium, given the existence of a risk-free asset. Because this line produces the highest attainable return for any given risk level, all rational investors will seek to be on this line.

The Importance of the Market Portfolio

All investors would want to be on the optimal line RF-M-L, and, unless they invested 100 percent of their wealth in the risk-free asset, they would own portfolio M with some portion of their investable wealth or they would invest their own wealth plus borrowed funds in portfolio M.[4] This portfolio is the optimal portfolio of risky assets.

All investors hold identical risky portfolios, use the same Markowitz analysis on the same set of securities, have the same expected returns and covariances, and have an identical time horizon. Therefore, they will arrive at the same optimal risky portfolio, and it will be the market portfolio, designated M.

It is critical to note that although investors take different positions on the straight-line efficient set in Figure 9-1, all investors are investing in portfolio M, the same portfolio of risky assets. This portfolio will always consist of all risky assets in existence. The emergence of the market portfolio as the optimal efficient portfolio is the most important implication of the CAPM. In essence, the CAPM states that portfolio M is the optimal risky portfolio.

Composition of the Market Portfolio

In equilibrium, all risky assets must be included in portfolio M because all investors are assumed to arrive at, and hold, the same risky portfolio. Because the market portfolio includes all risky assets, *portfolio M is completely diversified*. Portfolio M contains only systematic risk that cannot be eliminated, even with perfect diversification, because it is the result of macroeconomic factors that affect the value of all securities.

All assets are included in portfolio M in proportion to their market value. For example, if the market value of **Research In Motion (RIM)** common stock constitutes 3.7 percent of the market value of all risky assets at a given point in time, it will account for 3.7 percent of the market value of portfolio M. Therefore, it will also comprise 3.7 percent of the market value of each investor's portfolio of risky assets. As a result, we can state that security i's percentage in the risky portfolio M is equal to the total market value of security i relative to the total market value of all securities.

In theory, the market portfolio should include all risky assets worldwide, both financial (bonds, options, futures, etc.) and real (gold, real estate, etc.), in their proper proportions. The global aspects of such a portfolio imply that international diversification is very important, and a worldwide portfolio, if it could be constructed, would be completely diversified.

For practical purposes, the market portfolio is unobservable, however, we can use proxies to measure its behaviour. Usually, we measure the market portfolio using the portfolio consisting of all common stocks. This common stock portfolio, in turn, is proxied by a market index such as the S&P/TSX Composite Index in Canada, or the S&P 500 Composite Index in the US. Real-World Returns 9-1 discusses some of the limitations associated with using such benchmarks for implementing indexing strategies. For the remainder of our discussion, we will refer to portfolio M as a broad market index such as the S&P/TSX Composite Index. This portfolio is, of course, a risky portfolio, and its risk will be designated σ_M.

---

[4]Keep in mind that a lending investor earns a rate RF, whereas a borrowing investor pays the rate RF on the borrowed funds.

REAL-WORLD RETURNS 9-1

Something about Alpha (and Drags on Beta)

It's hard to beat the market. Net of fees, the average active manager will underperform, because the average active manager (or investor) is the market. It's a zero-sum game. That's the merciless arithmetic delivered by Nobel Prize winner William Sharpe, who contributed to the development of the Capital Asset Pricing Model.

But, CAPM is not the last word. It suggests holding all stocks according to their market capitalization. It has been imperfectly adapted to the investment universe, because it's not quite practicable to own the entire market. Even such titans as Vanguard Group, with its total US market index fund and ETFs, only samples the market.

Second, some of the actions that would keep stocks in equilibrium with other investments —CAPM looks at the risk investors are prepared to assume as against a risk-free alternative such as T-bills—are not actually current practice, such as unlimited shorting or borrowing to maintain a consistent risk profile in a portfolio of stocks, bonds and cash. There are regulatory restrictions on short sales, and margin requirements too for borrowing, that undermine the model.

Finally, some have found that a CAPM portfolio—one that uses the efficient frontier to deliver an optimal trade-off between risk and reward—is suboptimal. It's suboptimal because risk, considered as high beta, is not consistently rewarded. Instead, lower beta stocks often outperform the stocks whose upswings and downswings are magnified because of their high beta.

In part, these criticisms reflect the work of efficient markets proponents Eugene Fama and Kenneth French on enduring value and small-cap premiums in the marketplace. But they also bear on the current construction of indexes that aim to reflect the theoretical market: it turns out that using indexes or ETFs that comprise the bulk of the market capitalization may miss significant investment opportunities, what we generally know as alpha.

This article, one of an occasional series on what indexing and its alternatives contribute to an understanding of the process of investing, tackles Rob Arnott's, former *Financial Analysts Journal* editor and founder of Research Affiliates, controversial challenge to cap-weighted indexes.

"I think traditionally it's fair to divide the investment world into two camps," says Jason Hsu, director of research and investment management at Research Affiliates. "On the one end you have people who believe in market efficiency and therefore the only investment that makes sense is an index, a passive, low-cost investment that simply gets you broad market exposure.

"At the other end of the spectrum, you have people who consider the markets inefficient, that is, that you can get extra additional value by using active managers who determine over and undervaluations and take on active risk against a passive index."

Of course, Hsu acknowledges, fees have to be taken into account. "If you look starkly at the Morningstar or Lipper research, a cross section of the universe, net of fees, it has been demonstrated that it has been very, very difficult for the average manager to outperform. Jack Bogle of Vanguard has been making the same point and saying the same thing to us for 30 years and it's very valid." Indeed, he adds, 70 percent of investors would do well by just following Bogle's advice and buying a broad-based index.

Interestingly, Bogle and Burton Malkiel, author of the classic indexing text *A Random Walk Down Wall Street*, have both jettisoned the efficient market hypothesis pioneered by Fama and French to buttress indexing. Instead, it's largely a matter of cost.

Still, there is an argument for traditional indexing that goes beyond cost, and that is that no one knows in advance whether prices are right. Hsu considers this a fatal flaw.

"We've also seen bubbles," he notes. "We saw the dot-com and telecom bubble, we're potentially seeing a financial and resource bubble in Canada—there's a lot of reasons and certainly now a lot of well-recognized theories from people who study behavioural biases and how that impacts the economy as well as financial worth. So there's a lot of evidence that behavioural reasons lead to pricing inefficiencies, prices that deviate from what one considers rational fundamentally."

As proof, Hsu offers the well known example of Nortel from the late 1990s until 2000. "The underlying fundamentals didn't triple, but prices certainly did, as evidenced by the p/e multiple. So what you had was, as a stock became more and more overvalued, and therefore, I assume, less and less attractive, you were forced to buy more and more of it simply by construction—that is what artificial indexes will do. The passive indexes you look at, they're all cap-weighted; the larger the capitalization, the more weight you give to them.

"That seems entirely counterintuitive: it's the opposite of buy low and sell high. The only way that a cap-weighted index is ever going to be optimal is in a very peculiar environment, that is, if prices are always perfectly efficient—that's what's required when you use CAPM."

Nor have active managers, on the whole, been successful at spotting these bubbles before they pop, Hsu notes. "An easier solution is to delink portfolio weights from prices." He adds that an index where all stocks are equally weighted does accomplish that, and "adjusted for risk, it has outperformed." However, equal weighting is not the best alternative, he explains.

"An equally weighted portfolio, one thing that looks very different from a cap-weighted portfolio would not be very investable. An equally weighted portfolio doesn't have liquidity. It has way too much turnover so if you're cost-sensitive or tax-sensitive, it certainly doesn't work. And, you hold a lot of names that are not representative of the underlying economy."

To Research Affiliates, "the engineering exercise here is move away from market cap but not too far, so that you still preserve capacity, liquidity and low turnover but delink those relationships between price and weight." Fundamental indexing uses four factors as proxies for companies that "would most likely be large and therefore representative of what's going on in the economy, would be likely to have good capacity so that you could deploy a lot of investment dollars into it without affecting prices and would likely have sufficient liquidity to support trading, if necessary."

For those who are still dubious about the merits of fundamental indexing, Hsu has one final word:

"Fundamental indexing is predicated on the market being inefficient. But even if you do believe that the market has a high probability of being efficient, if the markets are perfectly efficient then fundamental indexing collapses to what you could get out of a standard cap-weighted index."

Source: Blythe, Scott, "Something about alpha (and drags on beta)," *Advisor's Edge Report*, September 2007, pages 11, 13.

CHECK YOUR UNDERSTANDING

9-1. What does it mean when we assume that investors have homogenous expectations?

9-2. Why, under capital market theory, do investors not have to make the investment decision?

9-3. How can we be sure that the tangency portfolio, "T", must be the market portfolio?

THE EQUILIBRIUM RISK–RETURN TRADE-OFF

Given the previous analysis, we can now derive some predictions concerning equilibrium expected returns and risk. The CAPM is an equilibrium model that encompasses two important relationships. The first, the capital market line, specifies the equilibrium relationship between expected return and *total risk* for efficient portfolios. The second, the security market line, specifies the equilibrium relationship between expected return and systematic risk. It applies to individual securities as well as portfolios.

The Capital Market Line

The straight line shown in Figure 9-1 traces out the risk–return trade-off for efficient portfolios, is tangent to the Markowitz efficient frontier at point M, and has a vertical intercept RF. We now know that portfolio M is the tangency point to a straight line drawn from RF to the efficient frontier, and that this straight line is the best obtainable efficient-set line. All investors will hold portfolio M as their optimal risky portfolio, and will be somewhere on this steepest trade-off line between expected return and risk because it represents those combinations of risk-free investing/borrowing and portfolio M that yield the highest return obtainable for a given pool of risk. Investors will differ only in the amount of their funds invested in RF versus portfolio M.

Capital Market Line (CML)

The trade-off between expected return and total risk for efficient portfolios.

This straight line is usually referred to as the **capital market line (CML)**. It depicts the equilibrium conditions that prevail in the market for efficient portfolios consisting of the optimal portfolio of risky assets and the risk-free asset. All combinations of risky and risk-free portfolios are bounded by the CML, and, in equilibrium, all investors will end up with efficient portfolios, which must lie somewhere on the CML.

The CML is shown as a straight line in Figure 9-2 without the now-dominated Markowitz frontier. We know that this line has an intercept of RF. If investors are to invest in risky assets, they must be compensated for this additional risk with a risk premium. The vertical distance between the risk-free rate and the CML at point M in Figure 9-2 is the amount of return expected for bearing the risk of the market portfolio; that is, the excess return above the risk-free rate. At that point, the amount of risk for the market portfolio is given by the horizontal dotted line between RF and σ_M. Therefore,

$$\frac{E(R_M) - RF}{\sigma_M} = \text{Slope of the CML}$$

$$= \text{Expected return–risk trade-off for efficient portfolios}$$

Figure 9-2
The Capital Market Line and the Components of Its Slope

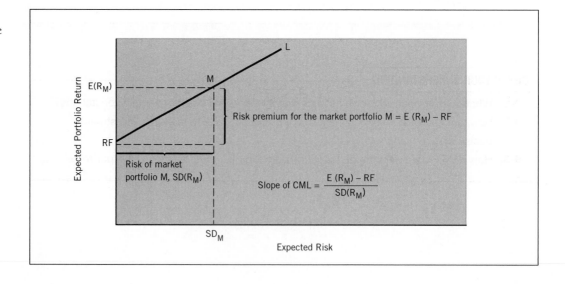

The slope of the CML is the *market price of risk* for efficient portfolios or the equilibrium price of risk in the market.[5] It indicates the additional expected return that the market demands for each percentage increase in a portfolio's risk, as measured by its standard deviation of return.

EXAMPLE 9-1: ESTIMATING THE SLOPE OF THE CML

Assume that the expected return on portfolio M is 13 percent, with a standard deviation of 25 percent, and that RF is 7 percent. The slope of the CML would be

$$(0.13 - 0.07)/0.25 = 0.24$$

In our example a risk premium of 0.24 indicates that the market demands 0.24 percent of return for each one percentage increase in a portfolio's risk.

We now know the intercept and slope of the CML. Since the CML is the trade-off between expected return and risk for efficient portfolios, and risk is being measured by the standard deviation, the equation for the CML is

$$E(R_p) = RF + \frac{E(R_M) - RF}{\sigma_M} \sigma_p \qquad \textbf{(9-1)}$$

where
$E(R_p)$ = the expected return on any efficient portfolio on the CML
RF = the rate of return on the risk-free asset
$E(R_M)$ = the expected return on the market portfolio M
σ_M = the standard deviation of returns on the market portfolio
σ_p = the standard deviation of returns on the efficient portfolio being considered

In other words, the expected return for any portfolio on the CML is equal to the price necessary to induce investors to forego consumption plus the product of the market price of risk and the amount of risk on the portfolio being considered. Note that:

RF is the price of foregone consumption

$\frac{E(R_M) - RF}{\sigma_M}$ is the market price of risk

σ_p is the amount of risk taken on a particular portfolio

The following points should be noted about the CML:

1. Only efficient portfolios consisting of the risk-free asset and portfolio M lie on the CML. Portfolio M, the market portfolio of risky securities, contains all securities weighted by their respective market values—it is the optimum combination of risky securities. By definition, the risk-free asset has no risk. Therefore, all combinations of these two assets on the CML are efficient portfolios.

2. As a statement of equilibrium, the CML must always be upward sloping because the price of risk must always be positive. Remember that the CML is formulated in a world of expected return, and risk-averse investors will not invest unless they expect to be compensated for the risk. The greater the risk, the greater the expected return.

3. On a historical basis, for some particular period of time such as four consecutive quarters, or a year or two, the CML can be downward sloping; that is, the return on RF exceeds the return on the market portfolio. This does not negate the validity of the CML; it merely indicates that returns actually

---

[5]The assumption throughout this discussion is that $E(R_M)$ is greater than RF. This is the only reasonable assumption to make, because the CAPM is concerned with expected returns (i.e., *ex ante* returns). After the fact, this assumption may not hold for particular periods; that is, over historical periods such as a year RF has exceeded RM, which is sometimes negative.

realized differed from those that were expected. Obviously, investor expectations are not always realized. (If they were, there would be no risk.) Thus, although the CML must be upward sloping *ex ante* (before the fact), it can be, and sometimes is, downward sloping *ex post* (after the fact).

4. The CML can be used to determine the optimal expected returns associated with different portfolio risk levels. Therefore, the CML indicates the required return for each portfolio risk level.[6]

The Security Market Line

The capital market line depicts the risk–return trade-off in financial markets in equilibrium. However, it applies only to efficient portfolios and cannot be used to assess the equilibrium expected return on individual securities or inefficient portfolios. Since all investors will hold the risky portion of their portfolio in the market portfolio, the important issue with regards to individual securities is how they contribute to the risk of the market portfolio.

We know from Chapter 7 that the equation for portfolio standard deviation consists of many variance and covariance terms. With respect to the market portfolio, each security in the market portfolio (consisting of n securities) will have a variance term and $n - 1$ covariance terms multiplied by two [since we know that Cov $(1, 2)$ = Cov $(2, 1)$ for securities 1 and 2]. Chapter 7 also shows that for a well-diversified portfolio consisting of a large number of securities, the covariance terms will be the relevant risk factors, with the individual variance terms having little impact on the overall portfolio risk. Based on this observation, the complex variance and covariance terms associated with estimating the risk of the market portfolio can be simplified to the following equation for the standard deviation of the market portfolio:

(9-2)
$$\sigma_M = [w_1 \text{ Cov } (R_1, R_M) + w_2 \text{ Cov } (R_2, R_M) + \dots +]^{1/2}$$
$$= [\text{security 1's contribution to portfolio variance} + \text{security 2's contribution to portfolio variance} + \dots]^{1/2}$$

Equation 9-2 shows that the contribution of each security to the standard deviation of the market portfolio depends on the size of its covariance with the market portfolio. Therefore, investors should consider the relevant measure of risk for any security to be its covariance with the market portfolio. As a result, we can say that in order for market equilibrium to exist, investors will require that the excess reward per unit of covariance risk be equal for all securities. Thus for any two assets i and j, we can say

(9-3)
$$\frac{E(R_i) - RF}{\sigma_{i,M}} = \frac{E(R_j) - RF}{\sigma_{j,M}}$$

Since the covariance of the market portfolio with itself is its variance (i.e., $\sigma_{M,M} = \sigma_M$), we can express the market price of covariance risk as

$$\frac{E(R_M) - RF}{\sigma_{M,M}} \text{ or } \frac{E(R_M) - RF}{\sigma_M^2}$$

Recognizing that the market portfolio is efficient and is held by all investors, this market price of covariance risk must offer adequate compensation for risk and is the excess reward per unit risk required by investors for any asset. Formally, for any asset i, we can say

(9-4)
$$\frac{E(R_i) - RF}{\sigma_{i,M}} = \frac{E(R_M) - RF}{\sigma_M^2}$$

---

[6]This assumes that we can readily compute a portfolio's standard deviation, which is difficult to do in practice.

Equation 9-4 can easily be rearranged to solve for $E(R_i)$, which produces the following equation that shows the expected return on any risky asset is directly proportional to its covariance with the market portfolio

$$E(R_i) = RF + [E(R_M) - RF]\frac{\sigma_{i,M}}{\sigma_M^2}$$

(9-5)

Using Equation 7-9 of Chapter 7, we know that $\sigma_{i,M} = \rho_{i,M}\sigma_i\sigma_M$, which implies we could alternatively express Equation 9-5 as

$$E(R_i) = RF + [E(R_M) - RF]\frac{\rho_{i,M}\sigma_i}{\sigma_M}$$

(9-6)

We now define a new term, the beta coefficient (β_i) or beta, as

$$\beta_i = \frac{\sigma_{i,M}}{\sigma_M^2} = \frac{\rho_{i,M}\sigma_i}{\sigma_M}$$

(9-7)

Substituting beta into the last term of Equation 9-5 or Equation 9-6, we obtain the following expression for determining the expected return of a risky asset

$$E(R_i) = RF + [E(R_M) - RF]\beta_i$$

(9-8)

This equation is referred to as the **security market line (SML)**, which is the key contribution of the CAPM to asset pricing theory.[7] It is depicted as the line RF-Z in Figure 9-3. In this diagram, beta is plotted on the horizontal axis and expected return on the vertical axis, with the intercept on the vertical axis occurring at the risk-free rate of return, RF. The SML represents the trade-off between systematic risk (as measured by beta) and expected return for all assets, whether individual securities, inefficient portfolios, or efficient portfolios.

The SML implies we measure systematic or market risk by a security's beta, which is simply a standardized measure of the security's covariance with the market portfolio. The reason that it is standardized in this manner reflects the fact that beta measures the sensitivity or responsiveness of the stock's returns compared to the returns on the chosen market portfolio. The reasons for measuring the relationship in this manner will be discussed later.

Security Market Line (SML)

The graphical depiction of the CAPM that relates the expected return on an individual security or portfolio to its market risk as measured by beta.

Figure 9-3
The Security Market Line (SML)

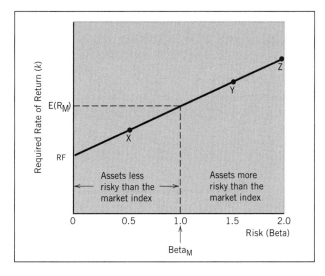

[7]Several alternative derivations of the SML are possible. The one presented in this text would be considered non-technical in nature. For a more rigorous derivation refer to Elton, Gruber, Brown, and Goetzmann, *Modern Portfolio Theory and Portfolio Analysis*, Sixth Edition (New York: John Wiley & Sons, 2003).

Beta

Beta

A measure of volatility for stock or portfolio returns. It is the relative market or systematic risk measured as the sensitivity of returns to that on a chosen market proxy.

Beta is a measure of the systematic risk of a security that cannot be avoided through diversification. Beta is a relative measure of risk—the risk of an individual stock relative to the market portfolio of all stocks. If the security's returns move more (less) than the market's returns as the latter changes, the security's returns have more (less) volatility (fluctuations in price) than those of the market. It is important to note that beta measures a security's volatility, or fluctuations in price, relative to a benchmark, the chosen market portfolio of all stocks.

Securities with different slopes have different sensitivities to the returns of the market index. If the slope of this relationship for a particular security is a 45-degree angle, as shown for security B in Figure 9-4, the beta is 1.0. This means that for every 1 percent change in the market's return, on average this security's returns change 1 percent.

The riskless asset has a beta of 0, since its return is assumed to be known with certainty. The market portfolio has a beta of 1.0, which is intuitive since it moves exactly with itself. It is also obvious computationally, since if we let $i = M$ in Equation 9-7, we obtain

$$\beta_M = \frac{\sigma_{M,M}}{\sigma^2_M} = \frac{\sigma^2_M}{\sigma^2_M} = 1.0$$

INVESTING *tip*

As we would expect, Figure 9-3 again demonstrates that if investors are to seek higher expected returns, they must assume a larger risk as measured by beta, the relative measure of systematic risk. The trade-off between expected return and risk must always be positive. In Figure 9-3, the vertical axis can be thought of as the expected return for an asset. In equilibrium, investors require a minimum expected return before they will invest in a particular security. That is, given its risk, a security must offer some minimum expected return before an investor can be persuaded to purchase it. Thus, in discussing the SML concept, we are simultaneously talking about the required and expected rate of return.

EXAMPLE 9-2: BETAS OF SECURITIES

In Figure 9-4, security A's beta of 1.5 indicates that, on average, its returns are 1.5 times as volatile as market returns, both up and down. A security whose returns rise or fall on average 15 percent when the market return rises or falls 10 percent is said to be an aggressive, or volatile, security. If the line is less steep than the 45-degree line, beta is less than 1.0; this indicates that, on average, a stock's returns have less volatility than the market as a whole. For example, security C's beta of 0.6 indicates that its returns move up or down, on average, only 60 percent as much as the market as a whole.

In summary, the aggregate market has a beta of 1.0. More volatile (risky) stocks have betas larger than 1.0 and less volatile (risky) stocks have betas smaller than 1.0, while the riskless asset has a beta of 0. As a relative measure of risk, beta is very convenient. Beta is useful for comparing the relative systematic risk of different stocks and, in practice, is used by investors to judge a stock's riskiness. Stocks can be ranked by their betas. Because the

Figure 9-4
Illustrative Betas of 1.5 (A), 1.0 (B), and 0.6 (C)

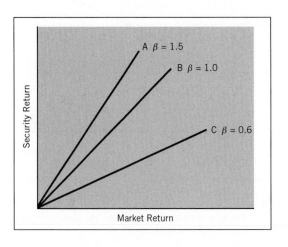

variance of the market is a constant across all securities for a particular period, ranking stocks by beta is the same as ranking them by their absolute systematic risk.[8]

Stocks with high (low) betas are said to be high- (low-) risk securities. Betas may vary widely across companies in different industries and within a given industry. They also change through time as the risk characteristics of the underlying security or portfolio change. Table 9-1 shows beta estimates for some Canadian common stocks in 2008, which provide the reader with some insight into the nature of real-world betas.

Table 9-1

Canadian Betas

Company	Industry Classification	Beta
Breakwater Resources Ltd.	Mining (Zinc)	2.27
Teck Cominco Ltd.	Integrated Mining	1.03
Barrick Gold Corp.	Gold Producer	0.44
Eldorado Gold Corp.	Gold Producer	1.15
Bombardier Inc.	Industrial Products	1.26
Cogeco Cable Inc.	Telecommunications - Cable	1.28
Shaw Communications Inc.	Telecommunications - Cable	0.81
Bank of Montreal	Banks	0.41
Bank of Nova Scotia	Banks	0.60
Canadian Imperial Bank of Commerce	Banks	0.79
Royal Bank	Banks	0.57
Toronto Dominion Bank	Banks	0.92

Source: Retrieved from www.fpinfomart.ca, April 16, 2008.

Intuitively, we might expect the stocks of mining companies such as gold producers to be riskier than other types of firms, since the cash flows generated by these companies are relatively volatile due to several factors including fluctuations in world commodity prices. Table 9-1 confirms that the betas for companies in these industries do tend to be higher than others presented in the table; however, we also note there are significant variations within a given industry. For example, there is a large difference in betas within the firms categorized as gold producers, which range from 0.44 for **Barrick Gold Corp.** to 1.15 for **Eldorado Gold Corp.** In this case, the discrepancy in betas is largely attributable to differences at the firm rather than industry level. In particular, while both firms operate in the same industry, Barrick Gold Corp. is a senior gold producer whose stock is considered to be large-cap, while Eldorado is a small-cap stock with more volatile returns as measured by beta. Finally, we notice that the big five Canadian banks have betas between 0.41 and 0.92, which implies they have displayed below average to average volatility with respect to market prices as a whole in recent years.

The CAPM's Expected Return-Beta Relationship

The Capital Asset Pricing Model formally relates the expected rate of return for any security or portfolio with the relevant risk measure. The CAPM's expected return-beta relationship is the most-often cited form of the relationship. Beta is the relevant measure of risk that cannot be diversified away in a portfolio of securities and, as such, is the measure that investors should consider in their portfolio management decision process.

---

[8]The absolute measure of systematic risk for a stock is the product of the stock's beta squared and the variance of the return for the overall market.

Required Rate of Return
The minimum expected rate of return necessary to induce an investor to purchase a security.

(9-9)

The CAPM in its expected return-beta relationship form is a simple but elegant statement. It says that the expected rate of return on an asset is a linear function of the two components of the **required rate of return**—the risk-free rate and the risk premium. Thus,

$$k_i = \text{Risk-free rate} + \text{Risk premium}$$
$$= RF + \beta_i[E(R_M) - RF]$$

where
k_i = the required rate of return on asset i
$E(R_M)$ = the expected rate of return on the market portfolio
β_i = the beta coefficient for asset i

Market Risk Premium
The difference between the expected return for the equities market and the risk-free rate of return.

This relationship provides an explicit measure of the risk premium. It is the product of the beta for a particular security i and the **market risk premium**, $E(R_M) - RF$. Thus,

$$\text{Risk premium for security } i$$
$$= \beta_i(\text{market risk premium})$$
$$= \beta_i[E(R_M) - RF]$$

The CAPM's expected return-beta relationship formalizes the basis of investments, which is that the greater the risk assumed, the greater the expected (required) return should be. This relationship states that an investor requires (expects) a return on a risky asset equal to the return on a risk-free asset plus a risk premium, and the greater the risk assumed, the greater the risk premium.

EXAMPLE 9-3: REQUIRED RETURN FOR TECK COMINCO LIMITED

Table 9-1 provides a 2008 beta estimate for Teck Cominco Ltd.'s common stock of 1.03. If RF was 0.025 at that time while the expected return on the market was estimated to be 0.10, the required return for Teck Cominco would be estimated as

$$k_{\text{Teck Cominco}} = 0.025 + 1.03(0.10 - 0.025)$$
$$= 10.23\%$$

The required (or expected) return for Teck Cominco is, as it should be, larger than that of the market because Teck Cominco's beta is larger—once again, the greater the risk assumed, the larger the required return.

Over- and Undervalued Securities

The SML has important implications for security prices. In equilibrium, each security should lie on the SML because its expected return should be what is needed to compensate investors for the systematic risk. What happens if investors believe that a security does not lie on the SML? To make this determination, they must employ a separate methodology to estimate the expected returns for securities. In other words, an existing SML can be applied to a sample of securities

INVESTING *tip*

Equation 9-9 indicates that securities with betas greater than the market beta of 1.0 should have larger risk premiums than that of the average stock and therefore, when added to RF, larger required rates of return. This is exactly what investors should expect, since beta is a measure of risk, and greater risk should be accompanied by greater return. Conversely, securities with betas less than that of the market average are less risky and should have required rates of return lower than that for the market as a whole. This will be the indicated result from the CAPM, because the risk premium for the security will be less than the market risk premium and, when added to RF, will produce a lower required rate of return for the security.[9]

---

[9]The risk premium on the security will be less than the market risk premium, because we are multiplying by a beta less than 1.0.

to determine the expected (required) return–risk trade-off that exists. Knowing the beta for any stock, we can determine the required return from the SML. Then, estimating the expected return from an alternative approach, say, fundamental analysis (discussed in Chapter 14), an investor can assess a security in relation to the SML and determine whether it is under- or overvalued.

EXAMPLE 9-4: THE SML AND THE VALUATION OF SECURITIES

In Figure 9-5, two securities are plotted around the SML. Security X has a high expected return derived from fundamental analysis and plots above the SML; security Y has a low expected return and plots below the SML. Which is undervalued?

Security X, plotting above the SML, is undervalued because it offers more expected return than investors require, given its level of systematic risk, as measured by beta. Investors require a minimum expected return of $E(R_X)$, but security X, according to fundamental analysis, is offering $E(R_X^1)$. If investors recognize this, they will purchase security X, because it offers more return than required. This demand will drive up the price of X, as more of it is purchased. The return will be driven down, until it is at the level indicated by the SML.

Security Y, according to fundamental analysis, does not offer enough expected return given its level of systematic risk. Investors require $E(R_Y)$ for security Y, based on the SML, but Y offers only $E(R_Y^1)$. As investors recognize this, they will sell security Y (or perhaps sell it short), because it offers less than the required return. This increase in the supply of Y will drive down its price. The return will be driven up for new buyers because any dividends paid are now relative to a lower price, as is any expected price appreciation. The price will fall until the expected return rises enough to reach the SML, and the security is once again in equilibrium.

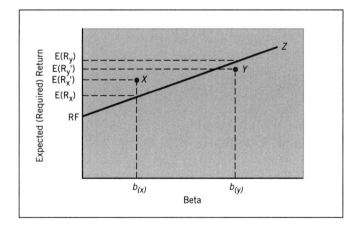

Figure 9-5
Overvalued and
Undervalued Securities
Using the SML

CHECK YOUR UNDERSTANDING

9-4. Explain why the CML applies only to efficient portfolios.

9-5. We can relate the expected return on a security to its covariance with the market portfolio. Why, then, is the CAPM equation written using beta instead of covariance?

9-6. Why do overvalued securities plot below the SML?

ESTIMATING THE SECURITY MARKET LINE (SML)

To use the SML to estimate the required return on an asset, an investor needs estimates of the return on the risk-free asset, the expected return on the market index, and the beta for an individual security. How difficult are these to obtain?

The return on a risk-free asset, RF, should be the easiest of the three variables to obtain. In estimating RF, the investor can use the return on government Treasury bills for the coming period. Estimating the market return is more difficult because the expected return for the market index is not observable. Furthermore, several different market indexes could be used. Estimates of the market return could be derived from a study of previous market returns (such as the S&P/TSX Composite Index data in Table 6-1). Alternatively, expected future market returns could be determined by calculating probability estimates of market returns based on current market conditions and expectations of future market conditions. This would provide an estimate of both the expected return and the standard deviation for the market.

Finally, it is necessary to estimate the betas for individual securities. This is a crucial part of the CAPM estimation process. The estimates of RF and the expected return on the market are the same for each security being evaluated. Since beta is unique with respect to a chosen market proxy, it brings together the investor's expectations of returns for the stock with those for the market. Beta is the only company-specific factor in the CAPM; therefore, risk is the only asset-specific forecast that must be made in the CAPM.

Estimating Beta

learning objective 4
Describe how betas are estimated and how beta is used.

Market Model
Relates the return on each stock to the return on the market using a linear relationship with intercept and slope.

A less restrictive form of single-index model, which was introduced in Chapter 7, is known as the **Market Model**. It is identical to the single-index model except that it does not make the assumption that the error terms of the different securities are uncorrelated. The Market Model equation is the same as Equation 7-15 for the single-index model (again, without the restrictive assumption):

$$R_{it} = \alpha_i + \beta_i R_{Mt} + e_{it}$$

where
R_{it} = the return (TR) on security i at time t
R_{Mt} = the return (TR) on the market index at time t
α_i = the intercept term for security i
β_i = the slope term for security i
e_{it} = the random residual error for security i at time t

The Market Model produces an estimate of return for any stock.

To estimate the Market Model, the TRs for stock i can be regressed on the corresponding TRs for the market index. Estimates will be obtained of α_i (the constant return on security i that is earned regardless of the level of market returns) and β_i (the slope coefficient that indicates the expected increase in a security's return for a 1 percent increase in market return). This is how the estimate of a stock's beta is often derived.

EXAMPLE 9-5: USING THE MARKET MODEL TO ESTIMATE BETA

This example estimates the beta for some company **ABC** to be 0.76 using the Market Model. Total return data for ABC corresponds to the following regression equation estimate using 60 months of return data for 2004–2008, along with corresponding TRs for the S&P/TSX Composite Index:

$$R_{ABC} = -0.004 + 0.76\, R_{S\&P/TSX}$$

When the TRs for a stock are plotted against the market index TRs, the regression line fitted to these points is referred to as the **characteristic line**. Figure 9-6 depicts an example of a characteristic line, based on the monthly return data used in the ABC example.

Characteristic Line

A regression equation used to estimate beta by regressing stock returns on market returns.

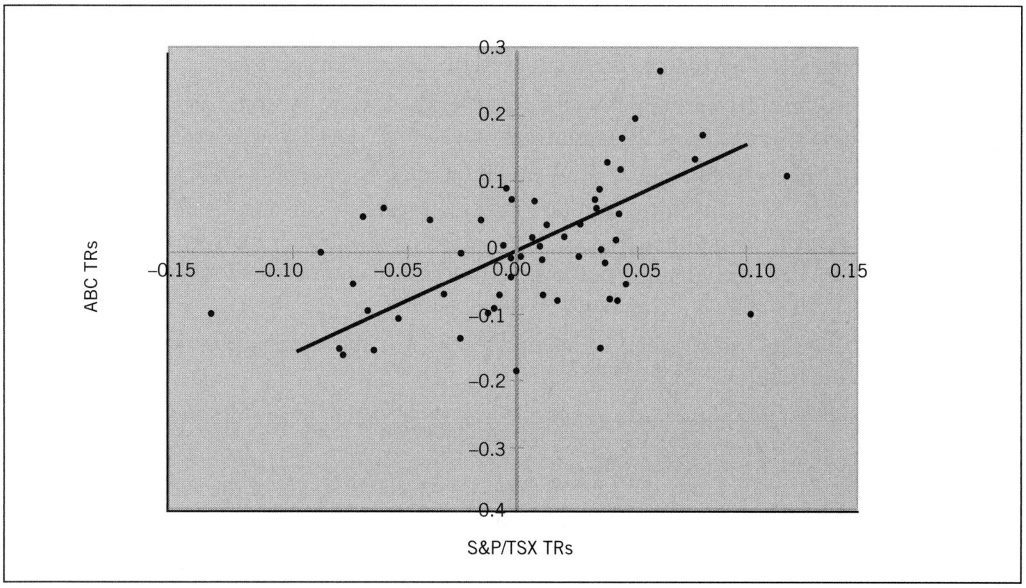

Figure 9-6
A Typical Characteristic Line Based on Monthly Data

The characteristic line is often fitted using excess returns. The excess return is calculated by subtracting the risk-free rate, RF, from both the return on the stock and the return on the market. In excess return form, the same analysis as before applies. The alpha is the intercept of the characteristic line on the vertical axis, which in theory should be zero for any stock. It measures the excess return for a stock when the excess return for the market portfolio is zero. The beta remains the slope of the characteristic line. It measures the sensitivity of a stock's excess return to that of the market portfolio. The variance of the error term measures the variability of a stock's excess return not associated with movements in the market's excess return. Diversification can reduce this variability.

Many brokerage houses and investment advisory services report betas as part of the total information given for individual stocks. For example, the betas reported in Table 9-1 were obtained from the FPinfomart website at www.fpinfomart.ca in April 2008 based on 10 years of return data. The *BMO Nesbitt Burns Research Red Book* and the *Value Line Investment Survey* also report the beta for each stock covered, as do other brokerage firms. Both measures of risk discussed previously, standard deviation and beta, are widely known and discussed by investors.

Whether we use the single-index model or the Market Model, beta can be estimated using regression analysis. However, the values of α_i and β_i obtained in this manner are *estimates* of the true parameters and are subject to error. Furthermore, beta can shift over time as a company's situation changes. A legitimate question, therefore, is how accurate are the estimates of beta?

As noted, beta is usually estimated by fitting a characteristic line to the data. However, this is an estimate of the beta called for in the CAPM. The market proxy used in the equations for estimating beta may not fully reflect the market portfolio specified in the CAPM. Furthermore, several points should be kept in mind:

1. We are trying to estimate the future beta for a security, which may differ from the historical beta, since betas change through time as the risk of the underlying common stock changes.

2. In theory, the independent variable RM represents the total of all marketable assets in the economy. This is typically approximated with a stock market index, which, in turn, is an approximation of the return on all common stocks.

3. The characteristic line can be fitted over varying numbers of observations and time periods. There is no one correct period or number of observations for calculating beta. As a result, estimates of beta will vary. For example, Nesbitt Burns estimates betas based on 54 months of monthly return data, while *The Value Line Investment Survey* calculates betas from weekly rates of return for 60 months (five years). Other analysts may use alternative estimation approaches.

4. The regression estimates of α and β from the characteristic line are only estimates of the true α and β and are subject to error. Thus, these estimates may not be equal to the true α and β.

As mentioned, it is not surprising that we would find that betas change through time, since the fundamental variables (e.g., earnings, cash flow) of a company will change continuously. The fact that beta is not stationary is an important issue that has been examined by many researchers. For example, Blume found that in comparing non-overlapping seven-year periods for various numbers of stock in a portfolio, the following observations could be made:

1. Betas estimated for individual securities are unstable; that is, they contain relatively little information about future betas.

2. Betas estimated for large portfolios are stable; that is, they contain much information about future betas.[10]

In effect, a large portfolio (e.g., 50 stocks) provides stability because of the averaging effect. Although the betas of some stocks in the portfolio go up from period to period, others go down, and these two movements tend to cancel each other. Furthermore, the errors involved in estimating betas tend to cancel out in a portfolio. Therefore, estimates of portfolio betas show less change from period to period and are much more reliable than are the estimates for individual securities. This discussion parallels the one in Chapter 7 about using historical standard deviations to proxy for future standard deviations. At that time, we suggested that historical portfolio standard deviations would provide much better proxies than would individual security standard deviations.

Researchers have found that betas in the forecast period are, on average, closer to 1.0 than the estimate using historical data. This would imply that we can improve the estimates of beta by measuring the adjustment in one period and using it as an estimate for the next period. For example, we could adjust each beta toward the average beta by taking half the historical beta and adding it to half of the average beta. Merrill Lynch, the world's largest brokerage firm, which was acquired by the Bank of America in 2008, reports adjusted betas based on a technique such as this. Other methods have also been proposed, including a Bayesian estimation technique.

TESTS OF THE CAPM

The conclusions of the CAPM are entirely sensible:

1. Return and risk are positively related—greater risk should carry greater return.

2. The relevant risk for a security is a measure of its effect on portfolio risk.

The question, therefore, is how well the theory works, despite all of the assumptions on which it is based. To assess the validity of this or any other theory, empirical tests must be performed. If the CAPM is valid, and the market tends to balance out so that realized security returns average out to equal expected returns, equations of the following type can be estimated:

---

[10]M. Blume, "Betas and Their Regression Tendencies," *Journal of Finance* 10 (June 1975), pp. 785–795; R. Levy, "On the Short-Term Stationarity of Beta Coefficients," *Financial Analysts Journal* 27 (December 1971), pp. 55–62.

$$R_i = a_1 + a_2\beta_i$$

(9-10)

where

R_i = the average return on security i over some number of periods

β_i = the estimated beta for security i

When Equation 9-10 is estimated, a_1 should approximate the average risk-free rate during the periods studied, and a_2 should approximate the average market risk premium during the periods studied.

Extensive literature exists involving tests of capital market theory in general, and the CAPM in particular. Although it is not possible to summarize the scope of this literature entirely and to reconcile findings from different studies that seem to be in disagreement, the following points represent a reasonable consensus of previous empirical results:

1. The SML appears to be linear; that is, the trade-off between expected (required) return and risk is an upward-sloping straight line.

2. The intercept term, a_1, is generally found to be higher than RF.

3. The slope of the CAPM, a_2, is generally found to be less steep than posited by the theory. This implies that CAPM systematically "over predicts" realized returns for low-beta stocks and "under predicts" for high-beta stocks.

4. Although the evidence is mixed, no persuasive case has been made that non-systematic risk commands a risk premium. In other words, investors are rewarded only for assuming systematic risk.[11]

The Fama and French Studies

Evidence by Fama and French contradicts the linear relationship between expected return and beta. They demonstrate that CAPM's sole risk factor, the market risk beta, possesses no explanatory power whatsoever in discriminating among the cross-sectional returns of US stocks.[12]

Fama and French contend that two simple and observable variables, common market equity (ME) and the ratio of book equity to market equity (BE/ME), combine to explain the cross-section of expected returns. Their analysis led them to propose a three-factor pricing model. Specifically, Fama and French suggest that an overall market factor, and factors related to firm size and the book equity to market equity ratio, explain cross-sectional differences in average returns of stocks.[13]

To account for stock return, Fama and French's three-factor model includes the following factors:

1. The expected return to a portfolio of small market capitalization stocks less the return of a portfolio of large market capitalization stocks;

2. The expected return to a portfolio of high book-to-market stocks less the return of a portfolio of low book-to-market stocks;

3. The expected return on the market index.

The Fama and French model has gained increasing acceptance. Its potential importance is evidenced by the fact that Ibbotson Associates (a major provider of financial information) now provides estimates of the required return on equity for companies based on this model, in addition to estimates determined by the more widely recognized CAPM. However, Real-World Returns 9-2 suggests that as a predictive model, it is far from perfect. The article also suggests that market beta provides useful explanatory power for future returns.

---

[11]For a more detailed discussion of empirical tests of the CAPM, *see* Elton, Gruber, Brown, and Goetzmann (2003) Sixth Edition, *Modern Portfolio Theory.*

[12]E. Fama and K. French, "The Cross Section of Expected Stock Returns," *Journal of Finance* 47 (June 1992), pp. 427–465.

[13]E. Fama and K. French, "Size and Book-to-Market Factors in Earnings and Returns," *Journal of Finance* 50 (March 1995), pp. 131–155.

The major problem in testing capital market theory is that it is formulated on an *ex ante* basis but can be tested only on an *ex post* basis. We can never know investor expectations with certainty. Therefore, it should come as no surprise that tests of the model have produced conflicting results in some cases and that the empirical results diverge from the predictions of the model.

REAL-WORLD RETURNS 9-2

The Fama and French Model

This study tests the Fama and French [1993, 1995, 1996] multifactor capital asset pricing model using out-of-sample mutual fund performance data. We find evidence of a reversal effect for two of the factors during the period 1995–2000. Our results raise substantial questions about the out-of-sample performance of the model.

The Fama-French model evolved out of significant empirical and theoretical challenges to the central concepts of modern portfolio theory, particularly the capital asset pricing model (CAPM) of Sharpe [1964], Linter [1965], and Mossin [1966]. The CAPM asserts that stock returns should be a linear function of only one factor—the return of the market, where the beta coefficient of the stock measures its sensitivity to market movements. Further research, however, identifies two additional factors that seem to be important in determining stock returns: 1) company size as measured by market capitalization, and 2) the book value (BV) to market value (MV) ratio.

Tests of mutual fund data using the Fama and French three-factor capital asset pricing model reveal that firm size, book-to-market, and beta factors do explain mutual fund returns. Two results are in sharp contrast with the Fama-French asset pricing model results. Both the firm size and book-to-market factors are reversed in effect. During the period 1995–2000, mutual funds that invested in large stocks outperformed funds that invested in small stocks. Similarly, mutual funds that invested in low BV/MV (growth) stocks outperformed funds that invested in high BV/MV (value) stocks.

Our findings do support the market return beta as an important explanatory variable in stock returns, but raise serious questions about the effectiveness of the size and BV/MV factors.

Source: Excerpted from Curcio, Richard J., Kyaw, NyoNyo A., and Thornton Jr., John H., "Do Size, Book-to-Market, and Beta Factors Explain Mutual Fund Returns?" *Journal of Investing,* Summer 2003, Vol. 12, Issue 2; p. 80.

Difficulties in Testing CAPM

Tests of return predictability over a long period of time using a model such as CAPM inevitably must deal with the "joint-hypothesis problem." This refers to the fact that we can only test whether the asset pricing model (CAPM in this case) fits the data well, if we also assume that assets are priced correctly in the market (i.e., if we assume that markets are efficient). Thus we have two hypotheses that are being tested simultaneously. Evidence that rejects our overall hypothesis may imply a rejection of CAPM, or of market efficiency, or both.

Another important problem with attempting to test CAPM was identified by Richard Roll in his seminal 1977 article.[14] His argument is commonly referred to as Roll's Critique. He argued that CAPM has not been proven empirically, nor will it be. This is because CAPM is untestable since the market

---

[14]R. Roll, "A Critique of the Asset Pricing Theory's Tests; Part I: On Past and Potential Testability of the Theory," *Journal of Financial Economics* 4 (March 1977), pp. 129–176.

portfolio, which consists of all risky assets, is unobservable. This forces researchers or users of CAPM to choose a market proxy that may or may not be mean-variance efficient. In effect, Roll argues that tests of the CAPM are actually tests of the mean-variance efficiency of the chosen market portfolio. He shows that the basic CAPM results will hold whenever the chosen proxy is mean-variance efficient and will not hold if the converse is true.

Despite these and other criticisms, the CAPM remains a logical way to view the expected return–risk trade-off.

ARBITRAGE PRICING THEORY

learning objective 5
Discuss the Arbitrage Pricing Theory as an alternative to the Capital Asset Pricing Model.

Another model of security pricing that has received a great deal of attention is based on **Arbitrage Pricing Theory (APT)** as developed by Roll and enhanced by others. APT represents an alternative theory of asset pricing that it is more general than the CAPM, with less restrictive assumptions. However, like the CAPM, it has limitations, and like the CAPM, it is not the final word in asset pricing.

Similar to the CAPM, or any other asset pricing model, APT posits a relationship between expected return and risk. It does so, however, using different assumptions and procedures. Very importantly, APT is not critically dependent on an underlying market portfolio as is the CAPM, which predicts that only market risk influences expected returns. Instead, APT recognizes that several types of systematic risk may affect security returns.

Arbitrage Pricing Theory (APT)
An equilibrium theory that suggests expected returns for securities are based on their relationship with several underlying risk factors.

APT is based on the *law of one price*, which states that two otherwise identical assets cannot sell at different prices. APT assumes that asset returns are linearly related to a set of indexes, where each index represents a risk factor that influences the return on an asset. Market participants develop expectations about the sensitivities of assets to the factors. They buy and sell securities so that, given the law of one price, securities affected equally by the same factors will have equal expected returns. This buying and selling is the arbitrage process, which determines the prices of securities.

APT states that equilibrium market prices will adjust to eliminate any arbitrage opportunities, which refer to situations where a *zero investment, zero-risk portfolio* can be constructed that will yield a risk-free profit. If arbitrage opportunities arise, a relatively few investors can act to restore equilibrium.

Unlike the CAPM, APT does not assume

1. A single-period investment horizon
2. The absence of taxes
3. Borrowing and lending at the rate RF
4. Investors select portfolios on the basis of expected return and variance

APT, like the CAPM, does assume

1. Investors have homogeneous beliefs
2. Investors are risk-averse utility maximizers
3. Markets are perfect
4. Returns are generated by a factor model

Also similar to CAPM, APT works much better for well-diversified portfolios than for individual securities.

A **factor model** is based on the view that there are *underlying risk factors* that affect realized and expected security returns. These risk factors represent broad economic forces and not company-specific characteristics and, by definition, they represent the element of surprise in the risk factor—the difference between the actual value for the factor and its expected value.

Factor Model
Used to depict the behaviour of security prices by identifying major factors in the economy that affect large numbers of securities.

The factors must possess three characteristics:

1. Each risk factor must have a pervasive influence on stock returns. Firm-specific events are not APT risk factors.

2. These risk factors must influence expected return, which means they must have non-zero prices. This issue must be determined empirically, by statistically analyzing stock returns to see which factors pervasively affect returns.

3. At the beginning of each period, the risk factors must be unpredictable for the market as a whole.[15]

The last characteristic raises an important point. In Example 9-6, we use unexpected inflation and unexpected changes in the economy's output as the two factors affecting portfolio returns. The rate of inflation or economic output per se are not APT risk factors because they are at least partially predictable. In a reasonably stable economy where the quarterly rate of inflation has averaged 1 percent, we can reasonably assume that next quarter's inflation rate will not be 10 percent. On the other hand, unexpected inflation—the difference between actual and expected inflation—is an APT risk factor. By definition, it cannot be predicted since it is unexpected.

What really matters are the *deviations* of the factors from their expected values. For example, if the expected value of inflation is 5 percent and the actual rate for a specific period is only 4 percent, this 1 percent deviation will affect the actual return for the period.

EXAMPLE 9-6: DEVIATION OF FACTORS FROM EXPECTED VALUES

An investor holds a portfolio of stocks that he or she thinks is influenced by only two basic economic factors: inflation surprises and the unexpected changes in the economy's output. Diversification once again plays a role because the portfolio's sensitivity to all other factors can be eliminated by diversification.

Portfolio return varies directly with output and inversely with inflation. Each of these factors has an expected value, and the portfolio has an expected return when the factors are at their expected values. If either or both of the factors deviates from expected value, the portfolio return will be affected. We must measure the sensitivity of each stock in our investor's portfolio to changes in each of the two factors. Each stock will have its own sensitivity to each of the factors. For example, stock 1 (a mortgage company) may be particularly sensitive to inflation and have a sensitivity of 2.0 to deviations of actual inflation from its expected level. On the other hand, stock 2 (a food manufacturer) may have a sensitivity to unexpected inflation of only 1.0.

Understanding the APT Model

Based on this analysis, we can now understand the APT model. It assumes that investors believe that asset returns are randomly generated according to an *n*-factor model.[16] For security *i*, the actual return can be formally stated as

(9-11)
$$R_{it} = E(R_{it}) + b_{i1}f_{1t} + b_{i2}f_{2t} + \ldots + b_{in}f_{nt} + e_{it}$$

where

R_{it} = the actual (random) rate of return on security *i* in any given period *t*

$E(R_{it})$ = the expected return on security *i* for a given period *t*

f_{nt} = the deviation of a systematic factor F_n from its expected value during period *t*

b_i = sensitivity of security *i* to a factor

e_{it} = random error term, unique to security *i* during period *t*

---

[15]M. A. Berry, E. Burmeister, and M. B. McElroy, "Sorting Out Risks Using Known APT Factors," *Financial Analysts Journal* 44 (March–April 1988), pp. 29–41.

[16]It is assumed that all covariances between returns on securities are attributable to the effects of the factors; therefore, the error terms are uncorrelated.

It is important to note that the expected value of each factor (F) is zero. Therefore, the f's in Equation 9-11 are measuring the deviation of each factor from its expected value. Notice in Equation 9-11 that the actual return for a security in a given period will be at the expected or required rate of return if the factors are at expected levels (e.g., $F_1 - E(F_1) = 0$, $F_2 - E(F_2) = 0$, and so forth) and if the chance element represented by the error term is at zero.

A factor model makes no statement about equilibrium. If we transform Equation 9-11 into an equilibrium model, we are saying something about expected returns across securities. APT is an equilibrium theory of expected returns that requires a factor model such as Equation 9-11. The equation for expected return on a security is given by Equation 9-12.

$$E(R_{it}) = a_0 + b_{i1}F_{1t} + b_{i2}F_{2t} + \ldots + b_{in}F_{nt}$$

(9-12)

where
$E(R_{it})$ = the expected return on security i during period t
a_0 = the expected return on a security with zero systematic risk
F = the risk premium for a factor (for example, the risk premium for F_1 is equal to $E(F_1) - a_0$).

With APT, risk is defined in terms of a stock's sensitivity to basic economic factors, while expected return is directly related to sensitivity. As always, expected return increases with risk. The expected return–risk relationship for the CAPM is $E(R_i) = RF + \beta_i$ (market risk premium). The CAPM assumes that the only required measure of risk is the sensitivity to the market. The risk premium for a stock depends on this sensitivity and the market risk premium (the difference between the expected return on the market and the risk-free rate).

The expected return–risk relationship for the APT can be described as: $E(R_{it}) = RF + b_i1$ (risk premium for factor 1) + b_{i2} (risk premium for factor 2) + $\ldots$ + b_{in} (risk premium for factor n). Note that the sensitivity measures (β_i and b_i) have similar interpretations. They are measures of the relative sensitivity of a security's return to a particular risk premium. Also notice that we are dealing with risk premiums in both cases. Finally, notice that the CAPM relationship is the same as would be provided by APT if there were only one pervasive factor influencing returns. For this reason and the others outlined above, APT is more general than CAPM.

The problem with APT is that the factors are not well specified, at least *ex ante*. To implement the APT model, we need to know the factors that account for the differences among security returns. The APT makes no statements about the number of risk factors, or the size or sign of the F_is. Both the factor model and these values must be identified empirically. In contrast, with the CAPM the factor that matters is the market portfolio, a concept that is well understood conceptually. However, as noted earlier, Roll has argued that the market portfolio is unobservable.

Most empirical work suggests that three to five factors influence security returns and are priced in the market. For example, Roll and Ross identify five systematic factors:

1. Changes in expected inflation
2. Unanticipated changes in inflation
3. Unanticipated changes in industrial production
4. Unanticipated changes in the default-risk premium
5. Unanticipated changes in the term structure of interest rates[17]

These factors are related to the components of a valuation model. The first three affect the cash flows of a company while the first two and the last two affect the discount rate. According to this model, different securities have different sensitivities to these systematic factors, and investor risk preferences are characterized by these dimensions. Each investor has different risk attitudes. Investors

[17]Richard Roll and Stephen Ross, "An Empirical Investigation of the Arbitrage Pricing Theory," *Journal of Finance* 35 (December 1980), pp. 1073–1103.

could construct a portfolio depending upon desired risk exposure to each of these factors. Knowing the market prices of these risk factors and the sensitivities of securities to changes in the factors, the expected returns for various stocks could be estimated.

Another study has suggested that an APT model that incorporates unanticipated changes in five macroeconomic variables is superior to the CAPM. These five variables are

1. Default risk
2. The term structure of interest rates
3. Inflation or deflation
4. The long-run expected growth rate of profits for the economy
5. Residual market risk[18]

Using APT in Investment Decisions

Roll and Ross have argued that APT offers an approach to strategic portfolio planning. The idea is to recognize that a few systematic factors affect long-term average returns. Investors should seek to identify the few factors affecting most assets in order to appreciate their influence on portfolio returns. Based on this knowledge, they should seek to structure the portfolio in such a way as to improve its design and performance.

Some researchers have identified and measured, for both economic sectors and industries, the risk exposures associated with APT risk factors such as the five identified previously (default risk, and so forth). These "risk exposure profiles" vary widely. For example, the financial and transportation sectors were found to be particularly sensitive to default risk, while the utility sector was relatively insensitive to both unexpected inflation and the unexpected change in the growth rate of profits.

An analysis of 82 different industry classifications showed the same result—exposure to different types of risk varies widely. For example, some industries were particularly sensitive to unexpected inflation risk, such as the mobile home building industry, retailers, hotels and motels, toys, and eating places. The industries least sensitive to this risk factor included foods, tires and rubber goods, shoes, and breweries. Several industries showed no significant sensitivity to unexpected inflation risk, such as corn and soybean producers and sugar refiners.

Portfolio managers could design strategies that would expose them to one or more types of these risk factors, or "sterilize" a portfolio such that its exposure to the unexpected change in the growth rate of profits matched that of the market as a whole. Taking an active approach, a portfolio manager who believes that he or she can forecast a factor realization can build a portfolio that enhances or reduces sensitivity to that factor. In doing so, the manager will select stocks that have exposures to the remaining risk factors that are exactly proportional to the market. If the manager is accurate with the forecast—and remember that such a manager must forecast the unexpected component of the risk factor—he or she can outperform the market for that period.

CHECK YOUR UNDERSTANDING

9-7. Identify two key problems with testing (or using) the CAPM.

9-8. Can the CAPM be considered simply a special case of APT?

9-9. Although the price of oil can have a significant impact on the cash flows of many companies, it is not a suitable factor for inclusion in a factor model. Why is this, and what similar variable would make a good factor?

---

[18]These factors are based on Berry et al., "Sorting Out Risks."

SOME CONCLUSIONS ABOUT ASSET PRICING

The question of how security prices and equilibrium returns are established—whether as described by the CAPM, or APT, or some other model—remains open. Some researchers are convinced that the APT model is superior to the CAPM. The CAPM relies on the observation of the market portfolio, which, in actuality, cannot be observed. On the other hand, APT offers no clues as to the identity of the factors that are priced in the factor structure.

In the final analysis, neither model has been proven superior. Both rely on expectations that are not directly observable. Additional testing is needed.

S U M M A R Y

This summary relates to the learning objectives for this chapter.

1. **Explain capital market theory and the Capital Asset Pricing Model.**
   Capital market theory, based on the concept of efficient diversification, describes the pricing of capital assets in the marketplace. Capital market theory is derived from several assumptions that may appear unrealistic; however, the important issue is the ability of the theory to predict. In addition, relaxation of most of the assumptions does not change the major implications of capital market theory. The Capital Asset Pricing Model (CAPM) is concerned with the equilibrium relationship between the risk and the expected return on risky assets and is considered a cornerstone of modern financial economics.

2. **Discuss the importance and composition of the market portfolio.**
   Given risk-free borrowing and lending, the new efficient frontier has a vertical intercept of RF and is tangent to the old efficient frontier at point M, the market portfolio. In theory, the market portfolio, M, should include all risky assets, although in practice it is typically proxied by a stock market index such as the S&P/TSX Composite Index. All investors can achieve an optimal point on the new efficient frontier by investing in portfolio M and either borrowing or lending at the risk-free rate RF.

3. **Describe two important relationships in CAPM as represented by the capital market line and the security market line.**
   The new efficient frontier is called the capital market line (CML), and its slope indicates the equilibrium price of risk in the market, where risk is measured as the standard deviation of returns. In effect, it is the expected return–risk trade-off for efficient portfolios. *Ex ante*, the CML must always be upward sloping, although *ex post* it may be downward sloping for certain periods. Based on the separation of risk into its systematic and non-systematic components, the security market line (SML) can be constructed for individual securities (and portfolios). What is important is each security's contribution to the total risk of the portfolio as measured by beta. Using beta as the measure of risk, the SML depicts the trade-off between required return and risk for securities.

4. **Describe how betas are estimated and how beta is used.**
   The Market Model can be used to estimate the alpha and beta for a security by regressing total returns for a security against total returns for a market index. The characteristic line is a graph of the regression involved in the Market Model. Beta, the slope of the characteristic line, is a relative measure of risk. It indicates the volatility of a stock, relative to a market index. If the expected returns for securities can be estimated from security analysis and plotted against the SML, undervalued and overvalued securities can be identified. Problems exist in estimating the SML; in particular, estimating the betas for securities. While all betas change through time, betas for large portfolios are much more stable than those for individual stocks.

5. **Discuss the Arbitrage Pricing Theory as an alternative to the Capital Asset Pricing Model.**
   Tests of the CAPM are inconclusive, which is not surprising since it is an *ex ante* model that makes predictions about the uncertain future, and it is tested with *ex post* data. It has not been proven empirically, nor is it likely to be, but its basic implications seem to be supported. Alternative theories of asset pricing, such as the Arbitrage Pricing Theory (APT), also exist but remain unproven. APT is not critically dependent on an underlying market portfolio as is the CAPM, which predicts that only market risk influences expected returns. Instead, APT—as a risk factor model—recognizes that several types of risk may affect security returns. These risk factors represent broad economic forces and not company-specific characteristics, and, by definition, they represent the element of surprise in the risk factor. APT is more general than the CAPM. If only one factor exists, the two models can be shown to be identical. The problem with APT is that the factors are not well specified, at least *ex ante*. Most empirical work involving APT suggests that three to five factors influence security returns and are priced in the market.

KEY TERMS

Arbitrage Pricing Theory (APT), p.269

Beta, p.260

Capital Asset Pricing Model (CAPM), p.250

Capital market line (CML), p.256

Capital market theory, p.250

Characteristic line

Factor model, p.269

Market model, p.264

Market portfolio, p.252

Market risk premium, p.262

Required rate of return, p.262

Security market line (SML), p.259

REVIEW QUESTIONS

9-1. In terms of their appearance as a graph, what is the difference between the CML and the SML?

9-2. What is the market portfolio?

9-3. What is the major problem in testing capital market theory?

9-4. Why does Roll argue that the CAPM is untestable?

9-5. What is the relationship between the CML and the Markowitz efficient frontier?

9-6. The CML can be described as representing a trade-off. What is this trade-off? Be specific.

9-7. Based on empirical work, how many factors are thought to influence security returns? Name some of these likely factors.

9-8. What does a factor model say about equilibrium in the marketplace?

9-9. What role does the market portfolio play in the APT model?

9-10. What are the three factors included in Fama and French's multifactor model?

9-11. Differentiate between the CML and the SML. What can the SML be used for that the CML cannot be used for?

9-12. How do lending possibilities change the Markowitz model? Borrowing possibilities?

9-13. According to the CAPM, why do all investors hold identical risky portfolios?

9-14. What is the slope of the CML? What does it measure?

9-15. Why does the CML contain only efficient portfolios?

9-16. How can we measure a security's contribution to the risk of the market portfolio?

9-17. How can the SML be used to identify over- and undervalued securities?

9-18. What happens to the price and return of a security when investors recognize it as undervalued?

9-19. The CAPM provides required returns for individual securities or portfolios. What uses can you see for such a model?

9-20. How does an investor decide where to be on the new efficient frontier represented by the CML?

9-21. Draw a diagram of the SML. Label the axes and the intercept.

a. Assume the risk-free rate shifts upward. Draw the new SML.

b. Assume that the risk-free rate remains the same as before the change in (a), but that investors become more pessimistic about the stock market. Draw the new SML.

9-22. What common assumptions do the CAPM and APT share? How do they differ in assumptions?

9-23. What is a factor model?

9-24. What characteristics must the factors in a factor model possess?

9-25. How can APT be used in investment decisions?

9-26. What is meant by an "arbitrage profit?" What ensures that investors could act quickly to take advantage of such opportunities?

9-27. Why is the standard deviation of a security's returns an inadequate measure of the contribution of that security to the risk of a portfolio that is well diversified?

9-28. Given the parameters of CAPM, how is it possible that some stocks in a given year actually have negative returns? Why would an investor have bought these stocks, considering the purchase of the risk-free asset would have presented them with a "guaranteed" positive return with no risk?

9-29. What are some of the difficulties involved in estimating a security's beta?

9-30. How can the CAPM be tested empirically? What are the expected results of regressing average returns on betas?

9-31. Briefly describe three reasons why two different analysts may derive different estimates of beta for the same stock.

9-32. List five of the assumptions underlying the Capital Asset Pricing Model (CAPM).

PROBLEMS

 The expected return for the market is 12 percent, with a standard deviation of 20 percent. The expected risk-free rate is 8 percent. Information is available for five mutual funds, all assumed to be efficient, as follows:

Mutual Funds	SD (%)
Scotia Canadian Balanced	5
PHN Canadian Equity-A	10
AGF Canadian Growth Equity	17
Altamira Special Growth	16
RBC Precious Metals	26

a. Calculate the slope of the CML.

b. Calculate the expected return for each portfolio.

c. Rank the portfolios in increasing order of expected return.

d. Do any of the portfolios have the same expected return as the market? Why?

9-2. Given the market data in Problem 9-1, and the following information for each of five stocks

Stock	Beta	R_i
1	0.9	12
2	1.3	13
3	0.5	11
4	1.1	12.5
5	1.0	12

a. Calculate the expected return for each stock.
b. With these expected returns and betas, think of a line connecting them. What is this line?
c. Assume that an investor, using fundamental analysis, develops the estimates labelled R_i for these stocks. Determine which are undervalued and which overvalued.
d. What is the market's risk premium?

9-3. Assume that RF is 3 percent, the estimated return on the market is 10 percent, and the standard deviation of the market's expected return is 21 percent. Calculate the expected return and risk (standard deviation) for the following portfolios:

a. 60 percent of investable wealth in riskless assets, 40 percent in the market portfolio
b. 150 percent of investable wealth in the market portfolio
c. 100 percent of investable wealth in the market portfolio

9-4. Assume that the risk-free rate is 3 percent and the expected market return is 10 percent. Show that the security market line is

$$E(R_i) = 3.0 + 7.0\beta_i$$

Assume that an investor has estimated the following values for six different corporations:

Corporation	β_i	$R_i(\%)$
A	0.62	9
B	1.16	10
C	0.49	9
D	0.76	8
E	0.76	18
F	0.82	7

Calculate the $E(R_i)$ for each corporation using the SML, and evaluate which securities are overvalued and which are undervalued.

9-5. Assume that Teck Cominco Ltd. is priced under equilibrium conditions. Its expected return next year is 11 percent, and its beta is 0.96. The risk-free rate is 4 percent.

a. Calculate the slope of the SML.
b. Calculate the expected return on the market.

9-6. Given the following information:

Expected return for the market, 12 percent
Standard deviation of market return, 21 percent
Risk-free rate, 8 percent
Correlation coefficient between
Stock A and the market, 0.8
Stock B and the market, 0.6
Standard deviation for stock A, 25 percent
Standard deviation for stock B, 30 percent

a. Calculate the beta for stock A and stock B.
b. Calculate the required return for each stock.

9-7. The equity risk premium for the market is 8 percent. Wilson Products Ltd. has a beta of 1.4. The real risk-free rate is 2 percent and the expected inflation premium is 2 percent. What is the required rate of return for Wilson, according to CAPM?

9-8. You are given the following information for stock A and the market portfolio:

State of the economy	Probability of occurrence	Expected return on stock A in this state	Expected return on the market in this state
High growth	10%	40%	20%
Moderate growth	20%	30%	15%
No growth	50%	10%	8%
Recession	20%	−20%	−5%

a. Estimate the expected return and standard deviation for stock A.

b. Estimate the beta for stock A.

c. If the risk-free rate is currently 4 percent, determine the required rate of return on stock A according to CAPM. Based on your answer, does A lie above or below the SML? Briefly explain.

9-9. Two securities, B and C, are properly priced according to CAPM, with expected returns of 10 percent and 12 percent respectively. If B has a beta of 0.8 and C has a beta of 1.1, what is the expected return on the market?

9-10. Assume expected return on the market portfolio is 16 percent, with a standard deviation of 25 percent. The risk-free rate is 5 percent.

a. What is the slope of the capital market line?

b. What does this slope mean?

c. What is the market risk premium?

9-11. You are investing in a portfolio that consists of four securities, A, B, C, and D, which have betas of 0.32, 1.4, 0.69, and 1.11 respectively.

a. What is the portfolio beta if the securities are equally weighted?

b. What is the portfolio beta if the security weights are 0.5, 0.25, 0.15, and 0.10 respectively?

9-12. Consider two securities, A and B, that have the following estimated expected returns and standard deviations, based on an in-depth company analysis:

$$E(R_A) = 9\%; \sigma_A = 19.46\%; E(R_B) = 7\%; \sigma_B = 12.77\%.$$

a. Suppose that the correlation coefficient between the returns on stock A and market returns is 0.30, while it is 0.70 for stock B. If the standard deviation of the market portfolio is 18 percent, estimate the beta for each security.

b. Estimate the required rate of return on each of the stocks if the expected return on the market is 0.8 percent, and the risk-free rate is 3 percent, and determine whether they appear to be overvalued or undervalued according to CAPM.

c. Estimate the required rate of return for a portfolio formed with 70 percent of wealth invested in A and 30 percent invested in B, and determine if it is undervalued or overvalued.

9-13. The market has an expected return of 11 percent, and the risk-free rate is 5 percent. Pfizer has a beta of 0.9. What is the required rate of return for Pfizer?

9-14. The market has an expected return of 12 percent, and the risk-free rate is 5 percent. Activalue Corporation is 80 percent as risky as the market as a whole. What is the required rate of return for this company?

9-15. Electron Corporation is 50 percent more volatile than the market as a whole. The market risk premium is 7 percent. The risk-free rate is 5 percent. What is the required rate of return for Electron?

9-16. Obtain monthly returns for RIM, the Royal Bank, and the S&P/TSX Composite index for January to December 2008.

a. Which firm do you expect to have a larger beta? Explain your reasoning.

b. Calculate the beta for each company.

c. Create a portfolio consisting of 50 percent in RIM and 50 percent in Royal Bank.

   i. Calculate the monthly returns for the portfolio and calculate the beta of the portfolio using those monthly returns.

   ii. Using Equation 9-7, calculate the beta of the portfolio.

   iii. Compare the two betas.

9-17. Using the following annual price data for Coca-Cola (stock symbol: KO) and the S&P 500, covering the period 1989–2004, calculate the beta for Coca-Cola. Use the ESTLIN function or the SLOPE function in the spreadsheet.

	KO	S&P
2004	40.58	1211.92
2003	48.38	1111.92
2002	40.96	879.82
2001	43.34	1148.08
2000	55.38	1320.28
1999	52.26	1469.25
1998	59.49	1229.23
1997	58.72	970.43
1996	45.93	740.74
1995	32.06	615.93
1994	21.93	459.27
1993	18.67	466.45
1992	17.24	435.71
1991	16.3	417.09
1990	9.29	330.22
1989	7.57	353.4

9-18. The following table shows the average monthly return (for the five years ending December 2007) for three large Canadian firms and the S&P/TSX Composite Index (the "market index"). Also shown is the covariance of the returns for each pair of stocks and the index. Note that the covariance of the return on any stock (or the index) with itself (the diagonal elements in the table) is the variance of that stock's returns.

		Covariance with:			
	Average Return	**TELUS**	**Scotiabank**	**Teck Cominco**	**Market Inex**
TELUS	2.00%	0.005761	0.001270	0.001792	0.000924
Scotiabank	2.19%	0.001270	0.002284	0.000727	0.000576
Teck Cominco	3.47%	0.001792	0.000727	0.010367	0.002111
Market Index	1.21%	0.000924	0.000576	0.002111	0.000893

a. Calculate the beta for each of the stocks and for the market index. If you do this correctly, the market's beta should be exactly 1.0.

b. Assume that the risk-free rate is 0.5 percent per month. Use the CAPM to determine the return for each of the stocks.

c. Create a portfolio containing a 40 percent weighting of TELUS, 40 percent in Scotiabank, and 20 percent in Teck Cominco. What is the beta of this portfolio? What is its return, as predicted by CAPM?

d. In a previous chapter we found that this portfolio would have had an average monthly return of 2.4 percent given the historical returns of the constituent stocks. If the portfolio is currently priced such that the expected return is also 2.4 percent, is the portfolio properly priced, overvalued, or undervalued compared to the CAPM predicted return?

9-19. Suppose that asset returns can be described by a three-factor model where the factors are inflation, GDP growth, and the default risk premium (for corporate bonds over Treasury securities). The levels of sensitivity of stocks A and B to each of these factors are provided below.

Stock	Inflation Beta	GDP Beta	Default Risk Beta
A	0.50	0.75	1.20
B	0.75	0.25	0.85

Forecasters are anticipating inflation of 2 percent, GDP growth of 6 percent, and a default risk premium of 3 percent. Also, analysts have published expected return figures of 6 percent and 5 percent for stocks A and B respectively.

    a. Calculate the actual return on the two stocks using the factor model if the actual values for the factors are: 2.5 percent for inflation, 5 percent for GDP growth, and a default risk premium of 4 percent.

    b. What return should you expect on these stocks if you apply the APT model when the risk free rate (the expected return on a security with zero systematic risk) is 3 percent.

    c. Can you create a portfolio using only these two stocks that is not influenced by inflation? If so, how? (Note that a negative weight is permissible; it indicates that the stock has been sold short.) Using the APT, what would be this portfolio's expected return?

PREPARING FOR YOUR PROFESSIONAL EXAMS

CFA PRACTICE QUESTIONS

9-1. Which of the following statements about the security market line (SML) is false?

    a. Properly valued assets plot exactly on the SML.
    b. The SML applies only to efficient portfolios.
    c. The SML provides a benchmark for evaluating expected investment performance.
    d. The SML is a graphic representation of the relationship between required return and beta.

9-2. An analyst developed the following data on stock X and the market:

- Return on the market	0.1200
- Covariance between return on stock X and return on the market	0.0288
- Correlation coefficient between return on stock X and return on market	0.8000
- Standard deviation of the returns on stock X	0.1800
- Standard deviation of the returns on the market	0.2000

Based on the data above, the beta of stock X is:

    a. 0.889
    b. 0.720
    c. 0.800
    d. 0.144

9-3. A stock has a beta of 0.9 and an expected return of 10 percent. The risk-free rate is 7 percent and the market is expected to return 11 percent. This stock is:

    a. underpriced.
    b. overpriced.
    c. properly priced.
    d. cannot say.

9-4. With a risk-free rate of 5 percent and the expected market return of 15 percent, a portfolio manager is projecting a return of 18 percent on a portfolio with a beta of 1.5. After adjustments for risk are made, this portfolio's return compared to the market is:

    a. safer.
    b. the same.
    c. inferior.
    d. superior.

CFA CURRICULUM AND SAMPLE EXAM QUESTIONS (©CFA INSTITUTE)

9-1. An analyst gathered the following information about a company and the market:

Current market price per share of common stock	$28.00
Most recent dividend per share paid on common stock (D0)	$2.00
Expected dividend payout rate	40%
Expected return on equity (ROE)	15%
Beta for the common stock	1.3
Expected rate of return on the market portfolio	13%
Risk-free rate of return	4%

Using the Capital Asset Pricing Model (CAPM) approach, the cost of retained earnings for the company is closest to:

a. 13.6%.
b. 15.7%.
c. 16.1%.
d. 16.8%.

9-2. Which of the following is least likely to affect the required rate of return on an investment?

a. Real risk-free rate.
b. Asset risk premium.
c. Expected rate of inflation.
d. Investors' composite propensity to consume.

9-3. With respect to the security market line (SML) and the value of a stock, if the stock's estimated return is greater than its expected (required) return, the stock plots:

a. above the SML and is overvalued.
b. below the SML and is overvalued.
c. above the SML and is undervalued.
d. below the SML and is undervalued.

9-4. An investor with a portfolio located on the capital market line to the left of the market portfolio has:

a. a lending portfolio.
b. a borrowing portfolio.
c. lower unsystematic risk than the market portfolio.
d. higher unsystematic risk than the market portfolio.

9-5. Suppose that the risk-free rate is 5 percent and the expected return on the market portfolio of risky assets is 13 percent. An investor with $1 million to invest wants to achieve a 17 percent rate of return on a portfolio combining a risk-free asset and the market portfolio of risky assets. Calculate how much this investor would need to borrow at the risk-free rate in order to establish this target expected return.

9-6. Suppose that the expected return on the stock in the following table is 11 percent. Using a two-factor model, calculate the stock's return if the company-specific surprise for the year is 3 percent.

Variable	Actual Value	Expected Value	Stock's Factor Sensitivity
Change in interest rate	2.0%	0.0%	−1.5
Growth in GDP	1.0%	4.9%	2.0

9-7. A portfolio manager plans to create a portfolio from two stocks. Manumatic (MANM) and Nextech (NXT). The following equations describe the returns for those stocks:

$R_{MANM} = 0.09 - 1F_{INFL} + 1F_{GDP} + E_{MANM}$

$R_{NXT} = 0.12 + 2F_{INF} + 4F_{GDP} + E_{NXT}$

You form a portfolio with market value weights of 50 percent Manumatic and 50 percent Nextech. Calculate the sensitivity of the portfolio to a 1 percent surprise in inflation.

CHAPTER 10

MARKET EFFICIENCY

Having considered the issue of market equilibrium, it occurs to you that while it is relatively easy to discuss, it may be simply that—talk! What matters is how quickly markets digest information, and how well and quickly stock prices reflect information. You have heard some people say investors can beat the market with the right techniques because there are market inefficiencies, while others say the market is efficient and most investors cannot beat the market. You even recall someone telling you about the January effect. So, who is right? With a little reflection, you realize you could end up wasting a lot of time if you employ techniques to pick stocks that have been shown to be of little or no value—and people are always selling a wide variety of services that claim to aid investors in picking stocks. On the other hand, if there really are some apparent exceptions to market efficiency, it could pay to know about them. Also, you have now heard some talk about behavioural finance, which suggests psychology plays a role in investor actions, which would seem to imply investors may not always be acting "rationally." Therefore, it seems logical to you to consider this whole issue of market efficiency.

Learning Objectives

After reading this chapter, you should be able to

1. Explain the concept of efficient markets.
2. Describe the three forms of market efficiency—weak, semi-strong, and strong.
3. Discuss the evidence regarding the Efficient Market Hypothesis.
4. State the implications of market efficiency for investors.
5. Outline major exceptions to the Efficient Market Hypothesis.

CHAPTER PREVIEW

Now that we understand how securities are priced under conditions of market equilibrium, we consider the effects of informational efficiency—that is, how quickly and accurately information about securities is disseminated in financial markets—on the equilibrium relationship. We begin this chapter by discussing the concept of market efficiency and its three forms—weak, semi-strong, and strong. We examine the evidence that supports the Efficient Market Hypothesis as well as major exceptions to it.

THE CONCEPT OF AN EFFICIENT MARKET

"If the markets aren't completely efficient, they're close to it!!" (A quotation in 2002 from a long-time, well-known developer of stock selection techniques—exclamation points added for emphasis).[1]

Market efficiency is an issue that has been debated vigorously for years. Why should you, as an investor, care if the market is efficient? In an informationally efficient market, many traditional investing activities are suspect at best and useless at worst. Why? Because in a truly efficient market, it should be impossible to distinguish between a profitable investment and an unprofitable one, given currently available information. Therefore, you need to carefully consider your investing activities, particularly with regard to how active or passive you are as an investor. Furthermore, if you are interested in a job in the securities business, you need to consider what a truly efficient market would mean. Your expected probability of "beating" the market as a portfolio manager is small, whereas the value of the product of a typical security analyst may be even smaller.

The idea of an efficient market has generated tremendous controversy, as discussed in Real-World Returns 10-1. Many practitioners and academics refuse to accept the notion of market efficiency, which is not surprising in view of the enormous implications that it has for everyone concerned with securities. Some market participants' jobs and reputations are at stake, and they are not going to accept this concept readily.

REAL-WORLD RETURNS 10-1

Efficient Market Hypothesis: Academics and Practitioners Are Still at Odds

If you've ever searched for a pattern in the market's movement, employed fundamental analysis to spot under- or over-valued stocks, or parked your money in an index fund, you've taken a stand on the efficient market hypothesis.

First put forward by Eugene Fama in his landmark doctoral dissertation in 1964, the EMH remains the null hypothesis of academics and active money managers, who have conducted thousands of studies to debunk it. Nothing would challenge the hypothesis more than finding a sustainable anomaly that would lead to an investment strategy. That strategy would enable investors to consistently beat the market to a degree that it would compensate them for the excess risk and transaction costs incurred by trading on the anomaly. Size effect. Day of the week effect. Filter rules. The presidential cycle. Has any research posed a serious challenge to the EMH?

"The momentum effect of Jegadeesh and Titman is the most serious," Fama wrote in response to the question, "though, as they are careful to point out, it cannot be used as the basis of a profitable strategy. Many of the other anomalies are due to bad statistical work, or mistaking rewards for risk with abnormal returns."

Poppycock, says Jeremy Grantham, chairman, of Grantham, Mayo, Van Otterloo & Co. LLC, an active management firm based in Boston, Mass., USA. "I view Fama as the temple

(continued)

---

[1]This quote is from Samuel Eisenstadt, the major player in the development of *Value Line's* famed stock-ranking system, which is more than 40 years old. See Steven T. Goldberg, "Civil Warriors," *Kiplinger's Personal Finance*, August 2002, p. 39.

Because of its significant impact and implications, the idea that markets are efficient deserves careful thought and study. First-time investors should approach it with an open mind. The fact that some well-known market observers and participants reject or disparage this idea does not reduce its validity. Furthermore, the argument that the stock market is efficient is not going to disappear, because too much evidence exists to support this argument. The intelligent approach for investors, therefore, is to learn about it and from it.

In Chapter 9, we considered capital market theory, or how asset prices and returns are determined in equilibrium. The CAPM formulates the equilibrium relationship that should exist between expected return and risk. How markets respond to new information is a very important part of obtaining the equilibrium relationship predicted by capital market theory. Therefore, a direct relationship exists between capital market theory, which specifies the equilibrium relationship, and the concept of informationally efficient markets, which involves how well markets process new information that moves prices toward a new equilibrium.[2]

WHAT IS AN EFFICIENT MARKET?

Investors determine stock prices on the basis of the expected cash flows to be received from a stock and the risk involved. Rational investors should use all the information they have available or can readily obtain. This information set consists of both known information and beliefs about the future (i.e., information that can be reasonably inferred). Regardless of its form, information is the key to the determination of stock prices and therefore is the central issue of the efficient markets concept.

An **efficient market** is one in which the prices of all securities quickly and fully reflect all available information about the assets. This concept postulates that investors will assimilate all relevant information into prices in making their buy-and-sell decisions. Therefore, the current price of a stock reflects:

Efficient Market
A market in which prices of securities quickly and fully reflect all available information.

1. All known information, including:
   - Past information (e.g., last year's or last quarter's earnings)
   - Current information as well as events that have been announced but are still forthcoming (such as a stock split or a dividend)
2. Information that can be reasonably inferred; for example, if many investors believe that interest rates will decline soon, prices will reflect this belief before the actual decline occurs

The early literature on market efficiency made the assumption that market prices incorporated new information instantaneously. The modern version of this concept does not require that the adjustment be literally instantaneous, only that it occur very quickly as information becomes known. Given the extremely rapid dissemination of information in developed countries through electronic means, information is spread very quickly, almost instantaneously, to market participants with access to these sources. For individual investors without this access, important information can be received almost instantaneously on radio, television, and on the Internet, or, at the latest, the following day in such sources as *The Globe and Mail* or the *National Post*.

---

[2]Operational efficiency is concerned with how smoothly orders are transmitted to securities markets and processed. We are concerned here with informational efficiency, or how market prices respond to new information.

The concept that markets are efficient does not claim, or require, a perfect adjustment in price following the new information. Rather, the correct statement involved with this concept is that the adjustment in prices resulting from information is "unbiased."[3] The new price does not have to be the new equilibrium price, but only an unbiased estimate of the final equilibrium price that will be established after investors have fully assessed the impact of the information.

Figure 10-1 illustrates the concept of market efficiency for one company for which a significant event occurs that has an effect on its expected profitability. The stock is trading at $50 on the announcement date of the significant event—day 0 in Figure 10-1 is the announcement date for the event. If the market is fully efficient, the price of a stock always reflects all available information. Investors will very quickly adjust a stock's price to its *fair value*. Assume that the new fair value for the stock is $52. In an efficient market, an immediate increase in the price of the stock to $52 will occur, as represented by the solid line in Figure 10-1. Since, in our example, no additional new information occurs, the price of the stock will continue at $52.

If the market adjustment process is inefficient, a lag in the adjustment of the stock prices to the new information will occur, and it is represented by the dotted line. The price eventually adjusts to the new fair value of $52 as brokerage houses disseminate the new information and investors revise their estimates of the stock's fair value. Note that the time it would take for the price to adjust is not known ahead of time—the dotted line is only illustrative.

Figure 10-1
The Adjustment of Stock Prices to Information: (*a*) If the Market Is Efficient; (*b*) One Possibility if the Market is Inefficient

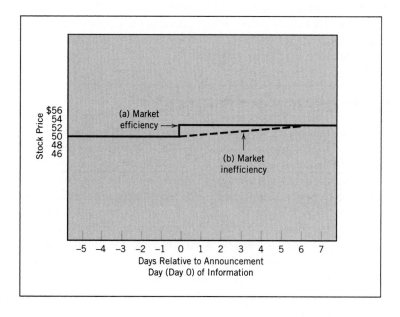

Why the Market Can Be Expected to Be Efficient

If the type of market adjustment described previously seems too much to expect, consider the situation from the following standpoint. It can be shown that an efficient market can exist if the following events occur:

1. A large number of rational, profit-maximizing investors exist who actively participate in the market by analyzing, valuing, and trading stocks. These investors are price takers; that is, one participant alone cannot affect the price of a security.

---

[3]This means that the expected value of the adjustment error is zero—sometimes too large and at other times too small, but on average balancing out and correct.

2. Information is costless and widely available to market participants at approximately the same time.

3. Information is generated in a random fashion such that announcements are basically independent of one another.

4. Investors react quickly and fully to the new information, causing stock prices to adjust accordingly.

These conditions may seem strict, and in some sense they are. Nevertheless, consider how closely they parallel the actual investments environment. There is no question that a large number of investors are constantly "playing the game." Both individuals and institutions follow the market closely on a daily basis, standing ready to buy or sell when they think it is appropriate. The total amount of money at their disposal at any one time is more than enough to adjust prices at the margin.

Although the production of information is not really costless, for institutions in the investments business, generating various types of information is a necessary cost of business, and many participants receive it "free" (obviously, investors pay for such items in their brokerage costs and other fees). It is widely available to many participants at approximately the same time as information is reported on the Internet, radio, television, and specialized communications devices now available to any investor willing to pay for such services.

Information is largely generated in a random fashion in the sense that most investors cannot predict when companies will announce significant new developments—when wars will break out, when strikes will occur, when currencies will be devalued, when important leaders will suddenly suffer a heart attack, and so forth. Although there is some relationship between information events over time, by and large, announcements are independent and occur more or less randomly.

If these conditions are generally met in practice, the result is a market in which investors adjust security prices very quickly to reflect random information coming into the market. Prices reflect fully all available information. Furthermore, price changes are independent of one another and move in a random fashion. Today's price change is independent of the one yesterday because it is based on investors' reactions to new, independent information coming into the market today.

Forms of Market Efficiency

If, as discussed, the conditions necessary to produce market efficiency exist, exactly how efficient is the market, and what does this imply for investors? We have defined an efficient market as one in which all information is reflected in stock prices quickly and fully. Thus, the key to assessing market efficiency is information. In a perfectly efficient market, security prices always reflect immediately all available information, and investors are not able to use available information to earn abnormal returns because it already is impounded in prices. In such a market, every security's price is equal to its intrinsic (investment) value, which reflects all information about that security's prospects.

> **learning objective 2**
> Describe the three forms of market efficiency—weak, semi-strong, and strong.

If some types of information are not fully reflected in prices or lags exist, the market is less than perfectly efficient. In fact, the market is not perfectly efficient any more than it is perfectly inefficient, so it is a question of degree. Therefore, we can think of market efficiency with respect to specific sets of information and ask if investors, on average, can earn abnormal returns using a set of information to buy and sell securities—in other words, exactly how efficient is the market?

Standard practice since Eugene Fama's classic 1970 article reviewing the topic is to discuss the market efficiency concept in the form of the **Efficient Market Hypothesis (EMH)**, which is simply the formal statement of market efficiency previously discussed.[4] The EMH is concerned with the extent to which security prices quickly and fully reflect the different types of available information, which can be divided into the three *cumulative* types as illustrated in Figure 10-2.

Efficient Market Hypothesis (EMH)
The proposition that securities markets are efficient, with the prices of securities reflecting their true economic value.

[4]E. Fama, "Efficient Capital Markets: A Review of Theory and Empirical Work," *Journal of Finance* 25 (May 1970), pp. 383–417. In a sequel some 20 years later, entitled "Efficient Capital Markets: II," Fama refers to a "weaker and economically more sensible version of the efficiency hypothesis" that deals with prices reflecting information to the extent that it is not financially worthwhile to act on any information. See E. Fama, "Efficient Capital Markets: II," *Journal of Finance* 46 (December 1991), pp. 1575–1617.

Figure 10-2
Cumulative Levels of
Market Efficiency and the
Information Associated
with Each

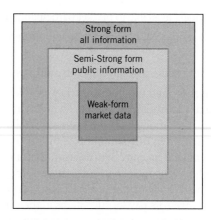

Market Data

Price and volume
information for stocks
or indexes.

Weak Form

That part of the Efficient
Market Hypothesis
stating that prices reflect all
price and volume data.

Semi-Strong Form

That part of the Efficient
Market Hypothesis
stating that prices reflect all
publicly available
information.

Strong Form

That part of the Efficient
Market Hypothesis stating
that prices reflect all
information, public and
private.

1. *Weak form.* One of the most traditional types of information used in assessing security values is **market data**, which refers to all past price (and volume) information. If security prices are determined in a market that is **weak-form** efficient, historical price and volume data should already be reflected in current prices and should be of no value in predicting future price changes. Technical analysis, which relies primarily on the past history of price information, will therefore be of little or no value in markets that are weak-form efficient.

   Tests of the usefulness of price data are called *weak-form tests* of the EMH. If the weak form of the EMH is true, past price changes should be unrelated to future price changes. In other words, a market can be said to be weakly efficient if the current price reflects all past market data. The correct implication of a weak-form efficient market is that the past history of price information is of no value in assessing future changes in price.[5]

2. *Semi-strong form.* A more comprehensive level of market efficiency involves not only known and publicly available market data, but all publicly known and available data, such as earnings, dividends, stock split announcements, new product developments, financing difficulties, and accounting changes. A market that quickly incorporates all such information into prices is said to show efficiency in a **semi-strong form**. Thus, a market can be said to be "efficient in the semi-strong sense" if current prices reflect all publicly available information. Notice that a semi-strong efficient market encompasses the weak form of the hypothesis because market data are part of the larger set of all publicly available information.

   Tests of the semi-strong EMH are tests of the speed of adjustment of stock prices to announcements of new information. A semi-strong efficient market implies that investors cannot act on new public information after its announcement and expect to earn above-average risk-adjusted returns. If lags exist in the adjustment of stock prices to certain announcements and investors can exploit these lags and earn abnormal returns, the market is not fully efficient in the semi-strong sense.

3. *Strong form.* The most stringent form of market efficiency is the **strong form**, which asserts that stock prices fully reflect *all* information—public and non-public. If the market is strong-form efficient, no group of investors should be able to earn, over a reasonable period of time, abnormal rates of return by using information in a superior manner. This applies in particular to all non-public information, including information that may be restricted to certain groups such as corporate insiders and specialists on the exchanges.

   In effect, the strong form of the EMH refers to the successful use of a monopolistic access to information by certain market participants. Strong-form efficiency encompasses the weak and semi-strong forms and represents the highest level of market efficiency.

---

[5]It is not correct to state, as is sometimes done, that the best estimate of price at time $t + 1$ is the current (time t) price, because this implies an expected return of zero. The efficient market in no way implies that the expected return on any security is zero.

EVIDENCE ON MARKET EFFICIENCY

Because of the significance of the efficient market hypothesis to all investors, and because of the controversy that surrounds the EMH, empirical evidence on market efficiency is abundant. Many studies have been conducted over the years and continue to be done. Obviously, we cannot begin to discuss them all, nor is it necessarily desirable to look at several in detail. Our purpose here is to present an idea of how these tests are done, the scope of what has been done, and some results. The empirical evidence will be separated into tests of the three forms of market efficiency previously discussed.

The key to testing the validity of any of the three forms of market efficiency is the consistency with which investors can earn returns in excess of those commensurate with the risk involved. Short-lived inefficiencies appearing on a random basis do not constitute evidence of market inefficiencies, at least in an economic (as opposed to a statistical) sense. Therefore, it makes sense to talk about an economically efficient market, in which assets are priced in such a manner that investors cannot exploit any discrepancies and earn unusual returns after consideration of all transaction costs. In such a market, some securities could be priced slightly above their intrinsic values and others slightly below, and lags can exist in the processing of information, but again not in such a way that the differences can be exploited.

What about the time period involved? In the short run, investors may earn unusual returns even if the market is efficient. After all, you could buy a stock today, and tomorrow a major discovery could be announced that would cause its price to increase significantly. Does this mean the market is inefficient? Obviously not; it means you are either very skilful or, more likely, very lucky. The question is, can you and enough other investors do this a sufficient number of times in the long run to earn abnormal profits? Even in the long run, some people will be lucky given the total number of investors.

INVESTING *tip*

It should be apparent upon reflection that we are talking about price changes and not about the level of price itself. Obviously, a $60 stock has a price on any given day that will be related closely to its price tomorrow since it is unlikely on a typical day to go much above or below $60. In addition, we are not concerned with whether the change in today's price, say +1/2, is related to the change in tomorrow's price, say −1/4. Dollar price changes such as these are also related. The issue centres on percentage price changes over time—are they related or not?

Weak-Form Evidence

As noted, weak-form efficiency means that price data are incorporated into current stock prices. If prices follow non-random trends, stock price changes are dependent; otherwise, they are independent. Therefore, weak-form tests involve the question of whether all information contained in the sequence of past prices is fully reflected in the current price.

The weak-form EMH is related to, but not identical with, an idea from the 1960s called the *random walk hypothesis*. If prices follow a random walk, price changes over time are random (independent).[6] The price change for today is unrelated to the price change yesterday, or the day before,

---

[6]Technically, the random walk hypothesis is more restrictive than the weak-form EMH. Stock prices can conform to weak-form efficiency without meeting the conditions of a random walk.

or any other day. This is a result of the scenario described at the outset of the chapter. If new information arrives randomly in the market and investors react to it immediately, changes in prices will also be random.

One way to test for weak-form efficiency is to test statistically the independence of stock price changes. If the statistical tests suggest that price changes are independent, the implication is that knowing and using the past sequence of price information is of no value to an investor. In other words, trends in price changes do not exist.

A second way to test for weak-form efficiency, after testing the pure statistical nature of price changes, is to test specific trading rules that attempt to use past price data. If such tests legitimately produce risk-adjusted returns beyond that available from simply buying a portfolio of stocks and holding it until a common liquidation date, after deducting all costs, it would suggest that the market is not weak-form efficient.

Statistical Tests of Price Changes

Stock price changes in an efficient market should be independent. Two simple statistical tests of independence are the serial correlation test and the signs test. The serial correlation test involves measuring the correlation between price changes for various lags, such as one day, two days, and so on, whereas the signs test involves classifying each price change by its sign, which means whether it was +, 0, or − (regardless of amount). Then the "runs" in the series of signs can be counted and compared to known information about a random series. If there are persistent price changes, the length of the runs will indicate it.

Fama studied the daily returns on the 30 Dow Jones Industrial stocks and found that only a very small percentage of any successive price change could be explained by a prior change.[7] Serial correlation tests by other researchers invariably reached the same conclusion.

The signs test also supports independence. Although some "runs" do occur, they fall within the limits of randomness since a truly random series exhibits some runs (several + or − observations in succession).

Technical Trading Rules

The statistical tests described previously demonstrate that trends, other than those consistent with a random series, do not appear to exist in stock prices. However, technical analysts believe that such trends not only exist but can also be used successfully. They argue that statistical tests do not detect more sophisticated or realistic strategies. Because an almost unlimited number of possible technical trading rules exist, not all of them can be examined; however, if a sufficient number are examined and found to be ineffective, the burden of proof shifts to those who argue that such techniques have value. This is exactly the situation that prevails. Little evidence exists that a technical trading rule based solely on past price and volume data can, after all proper adjustments have been made, outperform a simple buy-and-hold strategy.[8]

Again, it is important to emphasize the difference between *statistical dependence* and *economic dependence* in stock price changes. Most of the statistical tests discussed earlier detected some small amount of dependence in price changes.[9] Not all of the series could be said to be completely independent statistically. However, they were economically independent in that one could not exploit the small statistical dependence that existed. After brokerage costs, excess returns disappear. After all, this is the bottom line for investors—can excess returns be earned with a technical trading rule after all costs are deducted?[10]

---

[7]E. Fama, "The Behavior of Stock Market Prices," *Journal of Finance* 38 (January 1965), pp. 34–105.
[8]For example, refer to the conclusions found in a study by Mark J. Ready, "Profits from Technical Trading Rules," *Financial Management*, Autumn 2002, pp. 43–62.
[9]Stock returns tend to exhibit a slight positive correlation.
[10]Some studies have indicated that trading rules can produce profits after making the necessary adjustments. For two studies that argue that trading rules may not be so readily implemented under actual conditions, see R. Ball, S. P. Kothari, and C. Wasley, "Can We Implement Research on Stock Trading Rules?" *Journal of Portfolio Management* 21 (Winter 1995), pp. 54–63, and M.J. Ready, "Profits from Technical Trading Rules," *Financial Management* (Autum 2002), pp. 43–61.

Weak-Form Counter-Evidence

DeBondt and Thaler have tested an "overreaction hypothesis," which states that people overreact to unexpected and dramatic news events.[11] As applied to stock prices, the hypothesis states that, as a result of overreactions, "loser" portfolios outperform the market after their formation. DeBondt and Thaler classify stocks as "winners" and "losers" based on their total returns over the previous three- to five-year period. They find that over a half-century, the loser portfolios of 35 stocks outperformed the market by an average of almost 20 percent for a 36-month period after portfolio formation, while the winner portfolios earned about 5 percent less than the market. Their results, expressed in terms of the cumulative average residual (described later in the chapter), are depicted in Figure 10-3.

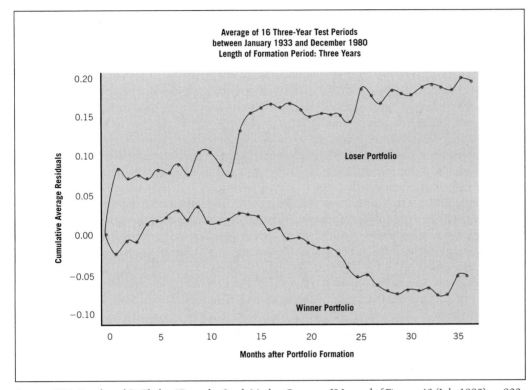

Figure 10-3
DeBondt and Thaler
Results

Source: W. DeBondt and R. Thaler, "Does the Stock Market Overreact?" *Journal of Finance* 40 (July 1985), p. 800.

Interestingly, the overreaction seems to occur mostly during the second and third year of the test period. DeBondt and Thaler interpreted this evidence as indicative of irrational behaviour by investors, or overreaction. Trading strategies designed to exploit this pattern are commonly referred to as "contrarian strategies" since the underlying rationale is to purchase or sell stocks in anticipation of achieving future results that are contrary to their past performance record.

This tendency for stocks that experience extreme returns to go through subsequent return reversals after portfolios are formed, and for the effect to be observed years after portfolio formation, has implications for market efficiency. Specifically, it indicates substantial weak-form inefficiencies because DeBondt and Thaler are testing whether the overreaction hypothesis is *predictive*. In other words, according to their research, knowing past stock returns appears to help significantly in predicting future stock returns.

---

[11]W. DeBondt and R. Thaler, "Does the Stock Market Overreact?" *Journal of Finance* 40 (July 1985), pp. 793–808.

One study of the overreaction hypothesis, which adjusts for several potential problems, found an "economically important overreaction effect" even after adjusting for time variations in beta and for size effects.[12] Using five-year periods to form portfolios, the study revealed that extreme prior losers outperformed extreme prior winners by 5 to 10 percent per year over the following five years. The overreaction effect was considerably stronger for smaller firms (held predominantly by individuals) than for larger firms (held predominantly by institutions).

Interestingly, Kryzanowski and Zhang find no such pattern exists for TSX-listed stocks over a similar period of time (1950–88).[13]

One Canadian study examined the performance of a short-run contrarian strategy (i.e., with monthly reversals). The authors found that the short-term contrarian strategy provides an average excess unrestricted return of 26.25 percent per year. However, the study shows that this abnormal performance is largely driven by small firms and the month of January.[14]

Semi-Strong-Form Evidence

Weak-form tests, of both the statistical and the trading rule types, are numerous and are generally supportive of weak-form efficient capital markets. Semi-strong tests are also numerous but are more diverse in their findings.[15] Although most of these studies support the proposition that the market adjusts to new public information rapidly, some do not.

Semi-strong-form tests are tests of the speed of price adjustments to publicly available information. The question is whether investors can use publicly available information to earn excess returns after proper adjustments. We can use a buy-and-hold strategy with equivalent risk or perhaps the market as a whole as a benchmark.

Event Study

An empirical analysis of stock price behaviour surrounding a particular event.

This empirical research often involves an **event study**, which means that a company's stock returns are examined to determine the impact of a particular event on the stock price. The methodology usually uses an index model of stock returns such as the single-index model discussed in Chapter 7. An index model states that security returns are determined by a market factor (index) and a unique company factor.

Company-unique returns are the residual error terms representing the difference between the security's actual return and that given by the index model. In other words, after adjusting for what the company's return should have been, given the index model, any remaining portion of the actual return is an **abnormal return** representing the impact of a particular event.

Abnormal Return

Return on a security beyond that expected on the basis of its risk.

$$\text{Abnormal return} = AR_{it} = R_{it} - E(R_{it})$$

where
AR_{it} = the abnormal rate of return for security i during period t
R_{it} = the actual rate of return on security i during period t
$E(R_{it})$ = the expected rate of return for security i during period t, based on the equilibrium model relationship[16]

[12]N. Chopra, J. Lakonishok, and J. R. Ritter, "Measuring Abnormal Performance: Do Stocks Overreact?" *Journal of Financial Economics* 31 (1992), pp. 235–268.
[13]L. Kryzanowski and H. Zhang, "The Contrarian Strategy Does Not Work in Canadian Markets," *Journal of Financial and Quantitative Analysis* 27 (September 1992), pp. 389–395.
[14]R. Assoe and O. Sy, "Profitability of the Short-Run Contrarian Strategy in Canadian Markets," *Canadian Journal of Administrative Sciences*, December 2003, p. 311.
[15]In his more recent (1991) survey of efficient capital markets, Fama uses the "now common title, event studies," instead of semi-strong form tests. See Fama, "Efficient Capital Markets II."
[16]For example, according to CAPM, we can express the expected return as $E(R_{it}) = RF_t + [E(R_{Mt}) - RF_t]\beta_i$.
Thus, if we used CAPM to determine the expected return on a security, we could express the abnormal return as
$AR_{it} = R_{it} - [RF_t + [E(R_{Mt}) - RF_t]\beta_i]$.

The **cumulative abnormal return (CAR)** is the sum of the individual abnormal returns over the period of time under examination and is calculated as

$$\text{Cumulative abnormal returns (CAR}_i) = \sum_{t=1}^{n} \text{AR}_{it}$$

where
CAR_i = the cumulative abnormal return for stock i

Cumulative Abnormal Return (CAR)

The sum of the individual abnormal returns over the time period under examination.

Next, we consider a sampling of often-cited studies of semi-strong efficiency without developing them in detail. It is important to obtain a feel for the wide variety of information tested and the logic behind these tests. The methodology and a detailed discussion of the results are not essential for our purposes. At this point, we consider evidence that tends to support semi-strong efficiency.

1. *Stock splits.* An often-cited study of the long-run effects of stock splits on returns was performed by Fama, Fisher, Jensen, and Roll (FFJR), which was the first event study.[17] Theoretically, a stock split adds nothing of value to a company and, therefore, should have no effect on the company's total market value. The FFJR results are depicted in Figure 10-4, which is a diagram format that is frequently used to express the results of any event study. Their results indicate that although the stocks examined displayed sharp increases in price prior to the split announcement, abnormal (i.e., risk-adjusted) returns after the split announcement were very stable. Thus, the split itself did not affect prices. These results indicate that any implications of a stock split appear to be reflected in price immediately following the *announcement* and not the event itself. This supports the semi-strong form of market efficiency because investors could not have earned abnormal returns after the information was made public. Because some subsequent evidence produced conflicting results about stock splits, Byun and Rozeff re-examined the stock split issue in 2003.[18] This study examined 12,747 splits between 1927 and 1996 and found that abnormal performance was not significantly different than zero for splits of 15 percent and larger. Based on their findings, the authors caution against abandoning the concept of market efficiency.

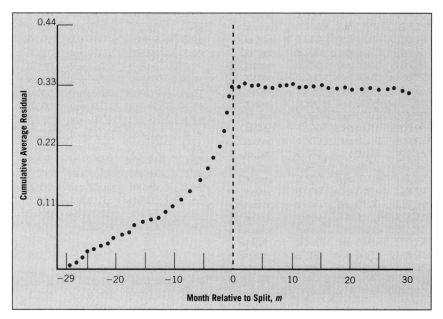

Figure 10-4
The First Event Study

Source: E. Fama, L. Fisher, M. Jensen and R. Roll, "The Adjustment of Stock Prices to New Information," *International Economic Review*, February 1969, pp. 2–21.

---

[17]E. Fama, L. Fisher, M. Jensen, and R. Roll, "The Adjustment of Stock Prices to New Information," *International Economics Review* 10 (February 1969), pp. 2–21.
[18]J. Byun and M. Rozeff, "Long-run Performance after Stock Splits: 1927 to 1996," *The Journal of Finance*, 58, June 2003, pp. 1063–1086.

2. *Dividend announcements.* Several studies have examined the effects of dividend announcements. Isolating the impact of dividend announcements is somewhat troublesome, since they are usually made at the same time as earnings announcements, which may contain earnings surprises. Most of these studies have concluded that the market adjusts rapidly to new information, thus lending support to the notion of market efficiency.

3. *Accounting changes.* Several studies have examined the effects on stock prices of announcements of accounting changes. The accounting changes include depreciation, the investment tax credit, inventory reporting (LIFO versus FIFO), and other items. Essentially, two different types of changes are involved:

   a. The change may affect only the manner in which earnings are reported to stockholders, and therefore should not affect stock prices. The reason for this is that such changes do not affect the firm's cash flows and thus its real economic value.

   b. The change may affect the firm's economic value by affecting its cash flows. This is a true change and should therefore generate a change in market prices. In an efficient market, stock prices should adjust quickly to the announcement of this type of change.

   In general, the studies indicate that the market is able to distinguish the superficial changes described in the first type from the real changes described in the second type.

4. *Initial public offerings.* A company that goes public creates an initial public offering, or IPO. Given the risk the underwriters face in trying to sell a new issue in which the true price is unknown, they may underprice the new issue to ensure its rapid sale. The investors who are able to buy the IPO at its offering price may be able to earn abnormal profits, but if prices adjust quickly, investors buying the new issues shortly after their issuance should not benefit.

   Empirical evidence indicates that new issues purchased at their offering price yield abnormal returns to the fortunate investors who are allowed to buy the initial offering.[19] This is attributed to underpricing by the underwriters. Investors buying shortly after the initial offering, however, are not able to earn abnormal profits because prices adjust very quickly to the "true" values.

5. *Reactions to announcements and news.* Investors are constantly given a wide range of information concerning both large-scale events and items about particular companies. Each of these types of announcements has been examined for the effects on stock prices.

   One form of announcement involves economic news such as money supply, real economic activity, inflation, and the Bank Rate (as determined by the Bank of Canada). A study of these types of announcements found no impact on stock prices that lasted beyond the announcement day.[20] Even an analysis of hourly stock price reactions to surprise announcements of money supply and industrial production found that any impact was accounted for within one hour.[21]

   The "Heard in the Street" column in *The Wall Street Journal* is a daily feature highlighting particular companies and analysts' opinions on stocks. A study of public takeover rumours from the "Heard on the Street" column found that the market is efficient at responding to published takeover rumours.[22] Excess returns could not be earned on average by buying or selling rumoured takeover targets at the time the

[19]For a review of early IPO literature, see R. Ibbotson, J. Sindelar, and J. Ritter, "Initial Public Offerings," *Journal of Applied Corporate Finance* 1 (Summer 1988), pp. 37–45. International evidence can be found in T. Loughran, J. Ritter, and K. Rydqvist, "Initial Public Offerings: International Insights," *Pacific-Basin Finance Journal* 2 (May 1994), pp. 165–200. Canadian evidence is documented by V. Jog and A. Riding, "Underpricing of Canadian IPOs," *Financial Analysts Journal* 43 (Nov–Dec 1987), pp. 48–55; by Craig Dunbar, "IPO Investing—Outlook for IPOs Might Not Be So Bleak, Studies Show," *Canadian Journal of Administrative Sciences*, December 2003, p. 311; and by V. Jog and A. Srivastava, "Underpricing of Canadian IPOs 1971–1992—An Update," working paper, Carleton University, 1994.

[20]D. Pearce and V. Roley, "Stock Prices and Economic News," *Journal of Business* 59 (Summer 1985), pp. 49–67.

[21]P. C. Jain, "Response of Hourly Stock Prices and Trading Volume to Economic News," *Journal of Business* 61 (April 1988), pp. 219–231.

[22]J. Pound and R. Zeckhauser, "Clearly Heard on the Street: The Effect of Takeover Rumors on Stock Prices," *Journal of Business* 63 (July 1990), pp. 291–308.

rumour appeared. No significant excess returns occurred on the day the takeover rumour in *The Wall Street Journal* was published, although a positive cumulative excess return of approximately 7 percent occurs in the calendar month before the rumour appears in the "Heard on the Street" column.

Another study suggests that the recommendations made by panellists during 1997 on "Wall $treet Week with Louis Rukeyser" provided an opportunity for investors to earn modest but significant abnormal one-day returns the day following the broadcast. The study also found that the recommended stocks performed strongly for eight quarters following the broadcast.[23]

Professional Portfolio Manager Performance

Perhaps the strongest evidence of semi-strong market efficiency is the fact that the average professional fund manager does not outperform the market benchmark on a risk-adjusted basis. The most abundant type of managed portfolios examined in the performance literature is US-based equity mutual funds. This category of fund type includes mutual funds with any or all of the following objectives: aggressive growth, growth, growth and income, balanced, income, and venture. The evidence does not support the hypothesis that the average manager outperforms the appropriate equity market indexes.[24] There are also several US studies regarding the performance of pension funds that indicate that these managers consistently underperform the appropriate benchmark.

The table included in Chapter 3 provided statistics suggesting that very few Canadian equity funds have been able to outperform the average fund performance on a consistent basis. In particular, Table 3.1 provided evidence on actively managed Canadian equity funds that existed throughout the entire 10-year and 15-year periods ending in 2007. This evidence showed that no funds were able to beat the group average for 12, 13, 14, or 15 years, while only two funds were able to outperform in 11 years, and another two for 10 years. In fact, only 16 of the 46 funds were able to outperform more than half the time (i.e., 8 years or more). None of the 82 funds examined over the 10-year period were able to outperform in 9 or 10 years, and only 27 funds were able to outperform more than half the time. Unfortunately, there are very few rigorous empirical studies of the performance of Canadian mutual or pension funds. In addition, the existing studies deal with small numbers of funds over relatively short time periods. Overall, the available Canadian evidence is mixed; however, there has been some evidence of superior performance by professionally managed funds in Canada.[25]

On aggregate, the results indicate that the net performance of the average active portfolio manager (after management expenses) is substantially worse than the performance of the standard passive portfolio benchmarks. In fact, the average active portfolio manager may underperform the market index by 50 to 200 basis points. This implies that the gross performance (before management expenses) of the average active portfolio manager at best equals the performance of standard passive benchmarks and is likely marginally lower than these benchmarks.

Strong-Form Evidence

The strong form of the EMH states that stock prices immediately adjust to and reflect all information, including private information.[26] Thus, no group of investors has information that allows them to earn abnormal profits *consistently*, even those investors with monopolistic access to information.

[23]E. J. Ferreira and S. D. Smith, "'Wall $treet Week': Information or Entertainment?" *Financial Analysts Journal*, January/February 2003, pp. 45–53.

[24]M. Grinblatt and S. Titman, "Mutual Fund Performance: An Analysis of Quarterly Portfolio Holdings," *Journal of Business* 62 (July 1989), pp. 393–416; B. Malkiel, "Returns From Investing in Equity Mutual Funds 1971 to 1991," *Journal of Finance* 50 (June 1995), pp. 549–572.

[25]E. Couture, "Investment's Smart Bomb: Passive Management With Style," *Canadian Investment Review* 5 (December 1992), pp. 43–48; R. Heinkel and R. Quick, "The Relative Performance of Canadian Institutional Portfolios and Canadian Indexes," *Canadian Investment Review* 6 (Fall 1993), pp. 33–39.

[26]In his 1991 paper, Fama refers to these tests as "tests for private information" instead of strong-form tests. See Fama, "Efficient Capital Markets II."

Note that investors are prohibited not from possessing monopolistic information, but from profiting from it. This is an important point in light of the studies of insider trading discussed next.

One way to test for strong-form efficiency is to examine the performance of groups presumed to have access to "true" non-public information. If such groups can consistently earn above-average risk-adjusted returns, the strong form will not be supported. We will consider corporate insiders, a group that presumably falls into the category of having monopolistic access to information. This has led investors to turn to index funds, which are discussed in Real-World Returns 10-2.

Corporate Insiders

A corporate insider is an officer, director, or major stockholder of a corporation who might be expected to have valuable inside information. The Ontario Securities Commission (OSC) requires insiders (officers, directors, and owners of more than 10 percent of a company's stock) whose securities trade on the Toronto Stock Exchange to report their monthly purchase or sale transactions to the OSC by the tenth day of the next month. This information is made public in the OSC's weekly publication, the *OSC Bulletin*. Other provinces such as Quebec and Alberta are more demanding and require insiders to report their activity within 10 days of making a trade. In the United States, the Securities and Exchange Commission (SEC) follows an identical procedure to the OSC, except that the information is made public in the SEC's monthly publication, *Official Summary of Security Transactions and Holdings (Official Summary)*.

Insiders have access to privileged information and are able to act on it and profit before the information is made public. Therefore, it is not surprising that several studies of corporate insiders found they consistently earned abnormal returns on their stock transactions.[27] Other studies, however, have found that insiders do only slightly better than chance alone in predicting the direction of a company's stock.

A study of insider trades by chairpersons, presidents, and other top officials of firms over the period 1975–89 found that these groups substantially outperformed the market when they made large trades. Trades by top executives of 1,000 shares or more were "abnormally profitable" for insiders.[28] On the other hand, most insiders did only slightly better than a coin toss. Canadian evidence also suggests that insiders are able to earn abnormal profits.[29]

A later study by Lakonishok and Lee covering the period 1975–1995 found that companies with a high incidence of insider buying outperformed those where insiders did a large amount of selling. The margin was almost eight percentage points for the subsequent 12-month period. Interestingly, the largest differences occurred in companies with a market capitalization of less than $1 billion.[30]

Profitable insider trading is a violation of strong-form efficiency, which requires a market in which no investor can consistently earn abnormal profits. Furthermore, successful use of this information by outsiders (the general public) would be a violation of semi-strong efficiency. Investors without access to this private information can observe what the insiders are doing by studying the publicly available reports that appear in the *OSC Bulletin*. Several investment information services compile this information and sell it to the public in the form of regularly issued reports, and it is available in *The Globe and Mail* and the *National Post*. Furthermore, services such as *The Value Line Investment Survey* report insider transactions for each company they cover.

In their 1988 study, Rozeff and Zaman used the typical abnormal return methodology of previous studies and found that outsiders could earn profits by acting on the publicly available information concerning insider transactions.[31] However, when Rozeff and Zaman used an abnormal returns measure that took into account size and earnings/price-ratio effects, the profits decreased substantially and

---

[27]For example, see K. Nunn, G. P. Madden, and M. Gombola, "Are Some Investors More 'Inside' Than Others?" *Journal of Portfolio Management* 9 (Spring 1983), pp. 18–22.

[28]A. Peers, "Insiders Reap Big Gains from Big Trades," *The Wall Street Journal*, September 23, 1992, pp. C1, C12.

[29]D. J. Fowler and C. H. Rorke, "Insider Trading Profits on the Toronto Stock Exchange, 1967–1977," *Canadian Journal of Administrative Sciences* 5 (March 1988), pp. 13–24.

[30]J. Lakonishok and I. Lee, "Are Insider Trades Informative?" *Review of Financial Studies* 14 (Spring 2001), pp. 79–111.

[31]M. S. Rozeff and M. A. Zaman, "Market Efficiency and Insider Trading: New Evidence," *Journal of Business* 61 (January 1988), pp. 25–45.

disappeared altogether when transaction costs of 2 percent were included. Furthermore, imposition of a 2 percent transaction costs on corporate insiders reduced their abnormal returns to an average of 3 to 3.5 percent per year. Therefore, this study reaffirms semi-strong market efficiency with respect to insider trading and also suggests that corporate insiders do not earn substantial profits from using inside information directly, which in effect supports strong-form efficiency. The Canadian evidence of Lee and Bishara suggests that outsiders can earn abnormal returns based on insider trading information.[32]

There are several reasons why insider transactions can be very misleading or simply of no value as an indicator of where the stock price is likely to go. Selling shares acquired by key executives through options has become commonplace—they need the cash, and they sell shares acquired as part of their compensation. Similarly, acquiring shares through the exercise of options can simply represent an investment decision by the executive.

IMPLICATIONS OF THE EFFICIENT MARKET HYPOTHESIS

learning objective 4
State the implications of market efficiency for investors.

The non-exhaustive evidence on market efficiency presented here is impressive in its support of market efficiency. What are the implications to investors if this evidence is descriptive of the actual situation? How should investors analyze and select securities and manage their portfolios if the market is efficient?

For Technical Analysis

As mentioned earlier, technical analysis and the EMH directly conflict with each other. Technicians believe that stock prices exhibit trends that persist across time, whereas the weak-form EMH states that price (and volume) data are already reflected in stock prices. EMH proponents believe that information is disseminated rapidly and that prices adjust rapidly to this new information. If prices fully reflect the available information, technical trading systems that rely on knowledge and use of past trading data cannot be of value.

Although technical analysis cannot be categorically refuted because of its many variations and interpretations, the evidence accumulated to date overwhelmingly favours the weak-form EMH and casts doubt on technical analysis. The evidence is such that the burden of proof has shifted to the proponents of technical analysis to demonstrate, using a properly designed test procedure (e.g., adjusting for transaction costs, risk, and any other factors necessary to make a fair comparison), that technical analysis outperforms a buy-and-hold strategy.

For Fundamental Analysis

The EMH also has implications for fundamental analysis, which seeks to estimate the intrinsic value of a security and provide buy-and-sell decisions depending on whether the current market price is less or greater than the intrinsic value. If the semi-strong form is true, no form of "standard" security analysis based on publicly available information will be useful. In this situation, since stock prices reflect all relevant publicly available information, gaining access to information others already have is of no value.

Given the evidence on market efficiency, clearly superior fundamental analysis becomes necessary. For example, an investor's estimates of future variables such as earnings must be better, or at least more consistent, than those of other investors. This investor must also derive more and better insights from information that is publicly available to all investors. There is no theoretical reason why an investor could not do a superior job of analysis and profit thereby. However, the EMH suggests

---

[32]M. H. Lee and H. Bishara, "Recent Canadian Experiences on the Profitability of Insider Trades," *Financial Review* 24 (May 1989), pp. 235–249.

that investors who use the same data and make the same interpretations as other investors will experience only average results. The evidence of below-average performance displayed by the average professional money manager supports this notion.

For Money Management

What about money management activities? Assume for a moment that the market is efficient. What would this mean to the money management process; that is, to professional money managers? The most important effect would be a reduction in the resources devoted to assessing individual securities. For the manager to act in this respect, he or she would have to believe that an analyst had come up with some superior insights, and passive strategies would become the norm. One passive investment strategy that is becoming increasingly popular is indexing, as discussed in Real-World Returns 10-2. Indexing involves the construction of portfolios designed to mimic the performance of a chosen market benchmark portfolio such as the S&P/TSX Composite Index. Investors can index using Index Funds or exchange-traded funds (ETFs), as discussed in Chapter 3.

REAL-WORLD RETURNS 10-2

Index Funds: A Cost-Effective Way to Invest

Mutual funds are widely considered a good way to invest without having to learn the intricacies of the stock markets. But with over 4,000 available in Canada, picking the right fund isn't easy.

Balanced funds have long been offered as one way of making an investment that can be made and parked, worry-free, without having to worry about diverse asset mixes and risk distribution. But historically, balanced funds have not produced exciting returns.

And mutual fund managers often under-perform their target index due to advisory fees, transaction costs and operating expenses. According to the Vanguard Group, broad stock market indexes have outperformed the average general equity fund over time.

Reap the Rewards

That's why index funds are getting a lot of attention. Investors can reap the rewards of the stock market through index funds. They are passively managed funds that try to mirror the performance of a specific stock market index, such as the S&P/TSX 60. An index fund holds only the stocks in the index it's trying to mimic. That way, the fund does as well or as poorly as the overall market. Fund management fees are low—because the funds aren't actively managed. It's a no-brainer.

That's music to the ears of investors pained by how management expense ratios (MERs) have eaten into their returns.

"Statistically, the majority of fund managers can't outperform their given index, and that's why they (index funds) are so popular right now," says Scott Miller, a Financial Consultant for Merrill Lynch. "It is generally a broad-based snapshot of what's going on in the economy."

Only five equity index funds were available to Canadians in 1993. A decade later, Canadians have more than 150 to choose from. The most widely followed index in Canada is the S&P/TSX Composite. One of the most popular in the US is the S&P 500.

A Long Term Investment

In its simplest form, an index fund provides maximum diversity with the lowest fees. In actively managed portfolios, the cost of buying and selling can be quite costly, depending on the degree to which the portfolio is traded. The composition of an index fund changes relatively little. Therefore, it incurs a minimal transaction cost.

(continued)

REAL-WORLD RETURNS 10-2 *continued*

These funds are not, however, for those who want to make a 'quick buck' in the market. Short term, they are as volatile an investment as stocks. They are designed to be a long-term investment—for the investor who wants consistent low-cost market returns each year at a minimal expense with lower risk and above average performance.

Historically, over the long term, the market is always up, so an investment should grow with safety. The predecessor of the S&P/TSX Composite, the TSE 300, averaged compounded annual growth of 17.6 percent in the mid 1990s, while Canadian equity funds averaged 16.1 percent.

Miller recommends index funds as part of an investment portfolio. "It's not an ultra-aggressive approach, but over the long-term you are going to do well."

Between 1988 and 1997, the Wilshire 5000 Index—one of the broadest indexes measuring the performance of US stocks—outperformed 71 percent of general equity funds over the 10-year period. And according to Ibbotson Associates, the US stock market has provided investors with an average return of 11 percent.

More US data from Lipper Analytical Service shows that if an investor assumes an 11 percent gross return, a conventional mutual fund in the US will incur 2 percent in management fees and will net that investor only 9 percent. But an index fund with a 0.3 percent management fee can net that investor a return of 10.7 percent.

Canadians can only wish for management fees as low as 0.3 percent at this time. Management fees for Canadian index funds are at least 50 percent higher than US index fund fees.

Low Management Fees

For example, MERs charged on index funds at the Scotiabank range from 0.95 percent for the Canadian Stock Index to 1.92 percent for the most expensive CanAm fund (derivative funds such as the CanAm generally have higher fees). Scotiabank doesn't charge other fees on top of MERs.

A comparable Canadian Index fund at CIBC carries an MER of 0.96 percent. This fee includes the 0.09 percent management fee.

That's still less than Canadian fees for managed funds, however. For comparison, the average MER for Scotiabank's non-index funds is between 1.75 and 2.25 percent. Fees for funds in developing markets can be 4.09 percent or higher. "It generally depends on the area of expertise of the fund," says Trevor Shearmur, Personal Banking/Investment Specialist for the Bank of Nova Scotia.

Shearmur thinks that index funds are the way to go. Scotiabank offers three index funds, the CanAm Stock Index, the Canadian Stock Index and the American Stock Index. The American has a five-year return of almost 12 percent. "People generally really like it, it's an aggressive fund, and easy to follow," says Shearmur.

Choose Funds Designed for You

A variety of index funds are available to Canadians, however, no one representative may sell all the mutual funds offered in Canada. If you are interested in a certain fund or family of funds, you must do a little research to find out who can sell it to you.

Source: Excerpted from DiCintio, Lisa, "Index funds: A cost-effective way to invest," Money-Sense.ca, May 26, 2004. Retrieved from www.moneysense.ca. Reprinted with permission from MoneySense.ca.

Even with passive management, portfolio managers have certain tasks to perform including the following:

1. *Diversification.* As we saw in Chapter 8, the basic tenet of good portfolio management is to diversify the portfolio. The manager would have to be certain that the correct amount of diversification had been achieved.

2. *Portfolio risk.* Depending on the type of portfolio being managed and its objectives, the manager must achieve a level of risk appropriate for that portfolio as well as maintain the desired risk level.

3. *Taxes.* Investors are interested in the amount of return they are allowed to keep after taxes. Accordingly, their tax situation should be kept in mind as investment alternatives are considered. Tax-exempt portfolios have their own needs and interests.

4. *Transaction costs.* Trading costs can have a significant impact on the final performance of the portfolio. Managers should seek to reduce these costs to the extent possible and practical. The index funds discussed earlier provide managers with one alternative.

Before deciding that these tasks may be all that is left to do in the portfolio management process in the face of an efficient market, we should examine some evidence that suggests possibilities for investors interested in selecting stocks. This evidence is in contrast with that discussed thus far and constitutes a good conclusion for our discussion by indicating that, regardless of how persuasive the case for market efficiency is, debate of this issue is likely to persist.

CHECK YOUR UNDERSTANDING

10-4. Assume stock prices are truly random. Is this evidence of market irrationality?

10-5. Which form of the EMH would an "event study" be used to test, and why is such a methodology used?

10-6. Given the overall evidence supporting market efficiency, how might an institutional investor, such as a mutual fund or a pension plan, justify spending significant sums on stock selection techniques?

BEHAVIOURAL FINANCE

Behavioural Finance (BF)
The study of investment behaviour, based on the belief that investors do not always act rationally.

Much of economics and finance is grounded on the proposition that individuals act rationally and consider all available information in the decision-making process. However, markets consist of human beings who have limited information-processing capabilities, who can and do make mistakes, and who often rely on the opinions of brokers, financial advisers, and the financial press.

Peter Bernstein has suggested that a basis in psychology could help to explain stock market behaviour. **Behavioural finance (BF)** does exactly that—it integrates psychology with finance. It analyzes behavioural biases and the effects these biases have on financial markets. Behavioural finance holds that investors' emotions affect stock prices and markets, and that those making investment decisions need to be aware of this.

Simply stated, behavioural finance says investors often make systematic mistakes when processing information about the stock market. Markets overreact, both up and down. Investors are motivated by numerous "irrational" forces, such as overconfidence, regrets about decisions, and aversion to losses. Other investors, recognizing these mistakes in judgment, may be able to profitably exploit them. This means that careful attention to past trends and similar information can be beneficial. Unfortunately, despite several promising research findings, behavioural finance currently does not have a unifying theory that ties everything together.

BF can perhaps be traced back to 1979, when Tversky and Kahneman offered the first significant alternative to the expected utility theory underlying traditional rational financial decision making. Contrary to what the standard theory predicts, they found evidence that people place different weights on gains and losses, being affected adversely more by a loss than pleased with a gain of the same amount. Tversky and Kahneman developed prospect theory as a way to reconcile with the observed behaviour that people exhibited when making decisions under uncertainty.

An important step in the development of behavioural finance is the work of DeBondt and Thaler, discussed earlier. The long-term return reversals they found with stock losers and winners is said to be a result of investor overreaction. For example, investors overreact to information about companies and drive stock prices to unsustainable highs or lows. When investors realize later that they overreacted to the news, prices return to their correct levels. Similar research indicates that investors may underreact to financial news, not driving stock prices high enough in response to good news. As they gradually realize the impact of the good news, stock prices will go up.

Clear recognition of the impact of behavioural finance came in 2002 with the awarding of the Nobel Prize in Economics to Daniel Kahneman, a Princeton psychologist, and to Vernon Smith of George Mason University, whose economic experiments are at odds with the efficient market hypothesis. Furthermore, two John Bates Clark medals in Economics (awarded every two years) have gone to behaviouralists.

David Dreman, a money manager and columnist for *Forbes*, has been a leading proponent of behavioural finance. He particularly espouses the investor overreaction hypothesis, which states that investors overreact to events in a predictable manner, overvaluing the best alternatives and undervaluing the worst. Premiums and discounts are the result, and eventually these situations reverse as assets regress toward the mean, or average valuation.

This behaviour has led Dreman to his **contrarian investing** philosophy, which involves taking positions that are currently out of favour. For example, in 1998, growth investing was much more profitable than value investing (both concepts are explained below), but Dreman continued to recommend stocks that looked promising on a value basis on the assumption that value stocks would once again excel.[33] And Dreman is famous for recommending that investors buy the low P/E ratio stocks (which are often out of favour) rather than the often currently popular high P/E ratio stocks. The ratio P/E as a valuation technique is discussed in Chapter 13.

Contrarian Investing
The theory that it pays to trade contrary to most investors.

MARKET ANOMALIES

Having considered the type of evidence supporting market efficiency, we now can appropriately consider some **market anomalies**. By definition, an anomaly is an exception to a rule or model, as described in Real-World Returns 10-1 at the beginning of this chapter. In other words, the results from these anomalies are in contrast to what would be expected in a totally efficient market, and they cannot be easily explained away.

We will examine several anomalies that have generated much attention and have yet to be satisfactorily explained. However, investors must be cautious in viewing any of these anomalies as a stock selection device guaranteed to outperform the market. There is no such guarantee because empirical tests of these anomalies may not approximate actual trading strategies that would be followed by investors. Furthermore, if anomalies exist and can be identified, investors should still hold a portfolio of stocks rather than concentrating on just a few identified by one of these methods. As we saw in Chapter 8, diversification is crucial for all investors.

learning objective 5
Outline major exceptions to the Efficient Market Hypothesis.

Market Anomalies
Techniques or strategies that appear to be contrary to an efficient market.

Momentum in Stock Returns

The short-term momentum (persistence) in stock returns is a pattern in historical stock returns that has received a great deal of attention in finance literature. In fact, it is the one anomaly singled out by Eugene Fama (in Real-World Returns 10-1 at the start of the chapter) as the most serious challenge to the notion of market efficiency.

Several studies have documented the success attainable by using momentum (or relative strength) indicators. The evidence suggests that stocks that have been top performers over the past six to 12 months will continue to provide superior investment performance in the subsequent six to 12 months. While these results may be surprising to financial economists, it substantiates an old market motto: "the trend is your friend." These sentiments were echoed by John Silva, former chief economist at Kemper

---

[33]In 1998, Dreman published a book called *Contrarian Investment Strategies in The Next Generation*, by Simon and Schuster. He also started a new journal, *The Journal of Psychology and Financial Markets*.

Financial Services of Chicago, who stated "financial markets are driven by expectations and not the real world." Mr. Silva went on to note that North American traders are momentum players.[34]

There is a substantial amount of supporting empirical evidence for the success of momentum trading strategies. One of the most commonly cited studies was performed by Jegadeesh and Titman in 1993, who examined the returns of portfolios formed by ranking stocks based on their past three to 12 month returns.[35] They demonstrated that buying the top-performing decile of NYSE and AMEX stocks and selling the bottom-performing decile of stocks produces very significant positive abnormal returns.

In a follow-up to their initial study, Jegadeesh and Titman (2001) used "out of sample" testing to re-evaluate their original momentum model in order to show that their 1993 results were not influenced by "data snooping." Using US data from 1990 to 1998, they found that their original model still produced excess returns during the new sample period, and that past winners still outperform past losers by about the same magnitude as in their 1993 study. This is striking evidence, since one would surmise that the attention devoted to this pattern in stock returns would have caused it to self-destruct as investors attempted to exploit it.[36] It is interesting to note that the persistence in short-term (six to 12 months) returns contrasts sharply with the longer-term (three to five years) reversals in return performance documented by DeBondt and Thaler.

Foerster, Prihar, and Schmitz, as well as Cleary and Inglis, show that a similar pattern exists in Canadian stock returns.[37] Cleary and Inglis also demonstrate that the abnormal returns generated from momentum trading cannot be accounted for by transaction costs, size effects, or underlying risk characteristics. Figure 10-5 provides further Canadian evidence that demonstrates that momentum continues to persist in Canadian stock returns. The figure shows that over the 1980 to 1999 period, the returns for a portfolio composed of the "Top 30" stocks (based on their past six-month stock performance) produced far superior returns in the subsequent six-month period (averaging 20.76 percent) than those produced by the "Bottom 30" portfolio (5.99 percent), by the S&P/TSX Composite Index (6.10 percent), or by 91-day T-bill returns (RF).[38] Finally, Rouwenhorst demonstrates that momentum performs well in 12 other international markets.[39]

Earnings Announcements

The adjustment of stock prices to earnings announcements has been studied in several papers, opening up some interesting questions and possibilities. The information found in such announcements does affect stock prices, as it should. Two questions need to be answered:

1. How much of the earnings announcement is new information, and how much has been anticipated by the market? In other words, how much of the announcement is a "surprise"?

2. How quickly is the "surprise" portion of the announcement reflected in the price of the stock? Is it immediate, as would be expected in an efficient market, or is there a lag in the adjustment process? If a lag occurs, investors have a chance to realize excess returns by quickly acting on the publicly available earnings announcements.

To assess the earnings announcement issue properly, we must separate a particular announcement into *expected* and *unexpected* parts. The expected part is that portion anticipated by investors by the time the announcement is made and that requires no adjustment in stock prices. The unexpected part is unanticipated by investors and requires a price adjustment.

---

[34]Bud Jorgensen, "Avoiding Shoals as the Tide Turns," *Financial Post*, October 13, 1995, p. 13.

[35]N. Jegadeesh and S. Titman, "Returns to Buying Winners and Selling Losers: Implications for Stock Market Efficiency," *Journal of Finance* 48 (March 1993), pp. 65–91.

[36]N. Jegadeesh and S. Titman, "Profitability of Momentum Strategies: An Evaluation of Alternative Explanations," *Journal of Finance* 56, 2001, pp. 699–720.

[37]S. Foerster, A. Prihar, and J. Schmitz, "Back to the Future: Price Momentum Models and How They Beat the Canadian Equity Markets," *Canadian Investment Review* 7 (Winter 1994/95), pp.9–13; S. Cleary and M. Inglis, "Momentum in Canadian Stock Returns," *Canadian Journal of Administrative Sciences* 15 (September 1998), pp. 279–291.

[38]S. Cleary, J. Schmitz, and D. Doucette, "Industry Factors Do Not Explain Momentum in Canadian Stock Returns," *Investment Management and Financial Innovations* 2 (2005), pp. 49–60.

[39]K. G. Rouwenhorst, "International Momentum Strategies," *Journal of Finance* 53 (February 1998), pp. 267–284.

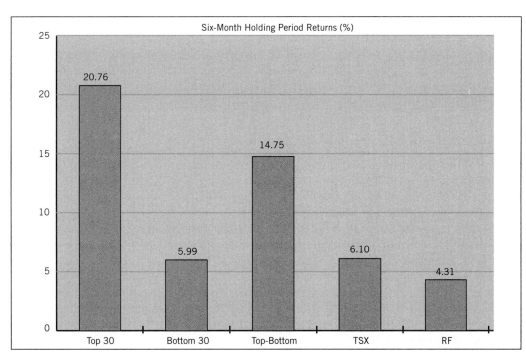

Source: S. Cleary, J. Schmitz, and D. Doucette, "Industry Factors Do Not Explain Momentum in Canadian Stock Returns," *Investment Management and Financial Innovations* 2 (2005), pp. 49–60.

Figure 10-5
Momentum in Canadian
Stock Returns

Latané, Tuttle, and Jones and many subsequent studies have confirmed that earnings announcements are correlated with subsequent short-term price movements.[40] These findings indicate a lag in the adjustment of stock prices to the information in these reports. In 1974, Latané, Jones, and Rieke investigated the earnings surprises in quarterly earnings data. They devised a method for estimating the unexpected part of the earnings announcement, which is commonly referred to as the "earnings surprise." They hypothesized that companies with high (low) unexpected earnings would have a positive (negative) price response.

Latané and Jones have documented the performance of earnings surprises in a series of papers.[41] These surprises were shown to have a definite relationship with subsequent excess holding period returns. Companies displaying the largest positive earnings surprises had superior subsequent performance, while poor subsequent performance was displayed by companies with low or negative earnings surprises. The studies also showed that while a substantial adjustment to the forthcoming earnings announcements occurs before the actual announcement, there is also a substantial adjustment after the announcement. This is the unexplained part of the earnings surprise puzzle. In an efficient market, prices should adjust quickly to earnings rather than with a lag.

By the mid-1980s, considerable evidence had been presented about the relationship between unexpected earnings and subsequent stock returns, and although it is not in any way conclusive, it cannot be easily dismissed. Different researchers, using different samples and different techniques, have examined the unexpected earnings issue and have found similar results. It must be emphasized, however, that these techniques in no way provide a guarantee of major success for investors. The relationships discussed are averages and do not necessarily reflect what any single investor would experience.

---

[40]H. A. Latané, D. L. Tuttle, and C. P. Jones, "E/P Ratios vs. Changes in Earnings in Forecasting Future Price Changes," *Financial Analysts Journal* 25 (January–February 1969), pp. 117–120, 123.
[41]For example: C. P. Jones, R. J. Rendleman, and H. A. Latané, "Stock Returns and SUEs during the 1970s," *Journal of Portfolio Management* 10 (Winter 1984), pp. 18–22.

In two studies, Sean Hennessey demonstrates that portfolios of Canadian stocks that have experienced positive earnings forecast revisions produce excess positive returns subsequent to the revision.[42] The larger the revisions, the greater the excess returns. This implies that investors can earn abnormal returns using publicly available information, which contradicts the semi-strong form of the EMH. Hennessey also shows that this effect is greater for small capitalization firms, which is consistent with less information being publicly available for these stocks.

Value Stocks

Stocks that carry above-average price-earnings (P/E) ratios, market-to-book (M/B) multiples, and below-average dividend yields (DY) are often referred to as "growth" stocks.[43] This is based on the belief that investors are willing to pay a premium for these companies because they expect them to exhibit above-average future growth in earnings and share price. Stocks with below-average price-earnings and market-to-book ratios and above-average dividend yields are referred to as "value" stocks. These stocks can be purchased at relatively inexpensive prices.

Value investing has been a popular investment strategy for many years. For example, this approach was advocated by Graham and Dodd in their 1934 book, *Security Analysis*, which remains the cornerstone of investment policy for several investment professionals to this day. They argued that future growth was difficult to predict; therefore, investors should concern themselves with demonstrated performance. Based on this philosophy, they demonstrate how analysts can identify bargain stocks by analyzing company financial statements.[44]

Figure 10-6
Value versus Growth
Stocks in Canada

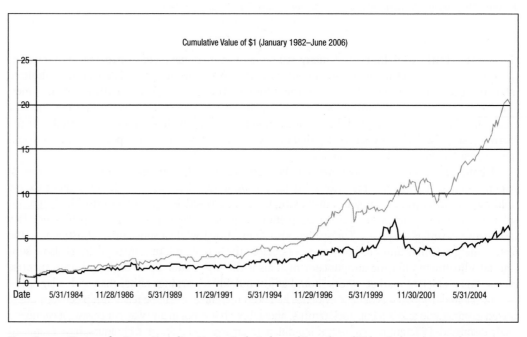

Data Source: Returns for Barra Canadian Equity Style Indexes (Growth and Value Indexes), www.barra.com.

[42]S. Hennessey, "Can Active Managers Profit from Earnings Forecast Revisions?" *Canadian Investment Review* 6 (Spring 1993), pp. 39–45; S. Hennessey, "Get the Drift," *Canadian Investment Review* 8 (Winter 1995/96), pp. 23–28.
[43]Notice that market price is the numerator in both the P/E and M/B multiples, but is the denominator in dividend yield, defined as dividend per share divided by market price per share. Hence, all else being equal, higher market prices lead to higher P/E and M/B ratios and lower dividend yields.
[44]Benjamin Graham and David L. Dodd, *Security Analysis: Principles and Technique* (New York: McGraw-Hill, 1934).

Numerous academic studies have shown that value stocks tend to outperform growth stocks. Figure 10-6 provides evidence demonstrating this pattern. Notice that while value stocks have outperformed growth stocks in the long-run in a given year (or any shorter-term period), this may not be the case, since economic cycles tend to favour one style over another.

Bourgeois and Lussier demonstrate that in Canada, low P/E stocks outperform high P/E stocks and the market as a whole on a risk-adjusted basis, while Chan, Hamao, and Lakonishok find that most of these value measures produce excess returns in the Japanese market.[45] Capaul, Rowley, and Sharpe, as well as Fama and French, demonstrate that the book-to-price effect is strong within other international markets.[46] Lakonishok, Shleifer, and Vishny combine several of the value measures and find even higher average performance.[47]

This evidence seems to contradict the EMH, unless the superior performance of the value portfolios is attributable to greater associated risk levels. However, the results of Fama and French suggest this is not the case. In fact, the exact opposite result arises—value portfolios appear to be less risky than the growth portfolios according to market betas. A study by Bauman and Miller also documents superior performance by value stock portfolios. In addition, their results indicate that the standard deviation of these portfolios is slightly lower than that of the growth portfolios.[48] All of this suggests that value investing is no riskier than growth investing, according to traditional risk measures. These results have lead many to adopt extreme views about market efficiency. For example, Haugen argues that the true risk–return relationship is negative—lower-risk stocks actually provide higher returns, while riskier stocks provide lower returns.[49]

These observations seem to contradict the notion of market efficiency at the semi-strong level, since all of the ratios above (i.e., P/E, DY, M/B) are publicly available and should not allow investors to obtain abnormal profits through their use. It is even more surprising that the pattern has not disappeared in response to its widespread recognition by the investment community. In other words, if investors recognize this pattern and create excess demand for value stocks, their prices will increase, and the excess returns will disappear. Similarly, one would expect investors to reduce demand for growth stocks, which would exert downward pressure on their prices, resulting in increased returns. However, these patterns have persisted for several years, despite their widespread recognition.

Investors need to be careful when following the low P/E strategy. Although a diversified portfolio, as always, is critical, rigid adherence to a low P/E strategy could result in an inadequately diversified portfolio. David Dreman, a well-known financial commentor, has indicated that he takes a minimum of 25 stocks in 15 to 18 industries and that "most (low P/E stocks) have significant problems or very good reasons why you don't want to own them."[50] Only about one in 10 candidates on the basis of low P/E passes his additional screens, such as dividend yields higher than average and accelerating earnings growth over the past. Dreman also suggests an emphasis on large stocks as opposed to small-company stocks.

According to some evidence, the low P/E strategy does well neither in turbulent markets nor in periods of slow economic growth. However, these stocks may perform well in a "full-blown" bear market because of their higher dividend yields. Overall, the low P/E strategy should be viewed as a long-run strategy, to be pursued through both good and bad markets.

---

[45]J. Bourgeois and J. Lussier, "P/Es and Performance in the Canadian Market," *Canadian Investment Review* 7 (Spring 1994), pp. 33–39; L. Chan, Y. Hamao, and J. Lakonishok, "Fundamentals and Stock Returns in Japan," *Journal of Finance* 46 (December 1991), pp. 1739–1764.

[46]C. Capaul, I. Rowley, and William Sharpe, "International Value and Growth Stock Returns," *Financial Analysts Journal* 49 (Jan–Feb 1993), pp. 27–36; Eugene Fama and Kenneth French, "Value Versus Growth: The International Evidence," *Journal of Finance* 53 (December 1998), pp. 1975–1999.

[47]J. Lakonishok, A. Shleifer, and R. Vishny, "Contrarian Investment, Extrapolation and Risk," *Journal of Finance* 49 (December 1994), pp. 1541–1578.

[48]S. Bauman and R. Miller, "Investor Expectations and the Performance of Value versus Growth Stocks," *The Journal of Portfolio Management* 23 (Spring 1997), pp. 57–68.

[49]R. Haugen, *The Inefficient Stock Market: What Pays Off and Why* (Toronto: Prentice Hall, 1995).

[50]David Dreman, "Emotion Versus Logic," *Forbes*, November 7, 1994, p. 351.

The Size Effect

Size Effect

The observed tendency for smaller firms to have higher stock returns than large firms.

The **size effect** is one of the most prominent anomalies documented in the finance literature. The firm size effect literature blossomed in the early 1980s with notable contributions by Banz, Reinganum, and Keim.[51] These authors found that small market capitalization stocks tended to outperform large capitalization stocks, even after adjusting for CAPM market risk. Keim found that 50 percent of the firm size effect occurs in January. Fama and French confirmed the persistence of this pattern for US stocks over the 1963–1990 period.

Tinic, Barone-Adesi, and West, as well as Foerster and Porter, confirmed the existence of a size effect for Canadian stock returns. Similar to US studies, market betas could not account for the returns, and a large portion of the return accrued during the month of January. Foerster and Porter also demonstrated that bid-ask spreads, which are higher for smaller stocks, could not account for the abnormal returns. They suggest that "when trading on the TSE, the small-firm strategy may be a viable strategy for increasing portfolio returns without an offsetting increase in risk."[52]

It is easy today to get confused about the size effect, given all of the research findings and the various definitions of small caps. Many investors today generally accept the notion that small caps outperform large caps, based partly on results from the Ibbotson Associates data, which show that "small" stocks have outperformed the S&P 500 Index by roughly two percentage points on a compound annual average basis. However, "small" as used in this context means the bottom 20 percent of NYSE stocks based on market value.

From 1926 through 1979, US small caps had a mean annualized return of 12.2 percent, while large caps showed 8.2 percent. From 1980 to 1996, small caps had a 13.3 percent return, while large caps showed 15.9 percent. Thus, by this measure, the small-cap "premium" has disappeared. Looking at the Ibbotson Associates data or comparable data from the beginning of 1979 through 1997, small caps and large caps have earned about the same compound annual rate of return. Dreman has argued that the size "myth" is based on stocks that trade thinly or not at all. James O'Shaughnessy, in his book, *What Works on Wall Street*,[53] argues that the returns associated with small stocks are mostly associated with microcap stocks that have very small capitalizations and are not easily bought by individuals or even institutions because of large spreads and commissions.[54]

Seasonality in Stock Returns

January Effect

The observed tendency for returns of small-cap stocks to be higher in January than in other months.

Evidence of seasonal patterns in stock returns has grown out of studies of the size anomaly explained in the previous section. Keim studied the month-to-month stability of the size effect for all NYSE and AMEX firms with data for 1963–79.[55] His findings supported the existence of a significant size effect (a 30.5 percent small-size premium). However, roughly half of this size effect occurred in January, and more than half of the excess January returns occurred during the first five trading days of that month. The first trading day of the year showed a high small-firm premium for every year of the period studied. The strong performance in January by small-company stocks has become known as the **January effect**.[56]

[51]R. Banz, "The Relationship Between Return and Market Value of Common Stocks," *Journal of Financial Economics* 9 (March 1981), pp. 3–18; M. Reinganum, "Misspecification of Capital Asset Pricing: Empirical Anomalies Based on Earnings Yields and Market Values," *Journal of Financial Economics* 9 (March 1981), pp. 19–46; D. Keim, " Size-Related Anomalies and Stock Return Seasonality," *Journal of Financial Economics* 12 (June 1983), pp. 13–32.

[52]S. Tinic, G. Barone-Adesi, and R. West, "Seasonality in Canadian Stock Prices: A Test of the Tax-Loss-Selling Hypothesis," *Journal of Financial and Quantitative Analysis* 22 (March 1987), pp. 51–63; S. Foerster and D. Porter, "Calendar and Size-Based Anomalies in Canadian Stock Returns," in Michael Robinson and Brian Smith, eds., *Canadian Capital Markets* (London, ON: Western School of Business, 1993), pp. 133–140.

[53]James O'Shaughnessy, *What Works on Wall Street: A Guide to the Best-Performing Investment Strategies of All Time* (New York: McGraw-Hill, 1998).

[54]A more detailed discussion of this issue can be found in Marc R. Reinganum, "The Size Effect: Evidence and Potential Explanations," in *Investing in Small-Cap and Microcap Securities*, Association for Investment Management and Research, 1997.

[55]Donald B. Keim, "Size-Related Anomalies and Stock Return Seasonality," *Journal of Financial Economics* 12 (June 1983), pp. 13–32.

[56]Richard Roll, "Vas ist das? The Turn of the Year Effect and the Return Premia of Small Firms," *The Journal of Portfolio Management* 9 (Winter 1983), pp. 18–28. Roll also found a turn-of-the-year effect with abnormal returns for small firms on the last trading day in December.

The January effect is often referred to as the "small firm in January effect" because it is most prevalent for the returns of small-cap stocks. For example, the average US monthly return for January during the 1941–81 period was 1.34 percent for the S&P 500 Index versus an average monthly return of 0.92 percent for the remaining 11 months. During the same period, the average January return was 8.06 percent for the smallest quintile of NYSE stocks, versus 0.88 percent for the other 11 months. During the 1982–90 period, the average January return was 3.20 percent for the S&P 500 Index versus 1.23 percent for the other 11 months, while the January return for the smallest NYSE quintile was 5.32 percent versus 0.17 percent for the remaining 11 months.

Canadian studies have supported the existence of a January effect for Canadian stock returns.[57] For example, Vijay Jog showed that the average January return for the TSE 300 over the 1972–86 period was 3.13 percent, versus an average monthly return of 0.82 percent for the other 11 months over the same time period. The difference in returns was even more pronounced for smaller stocks.

There are several other seasonal effects including the day-of-the-week effect, which was first identified by Cross in the US.[58] He found the average Monday return to be negative and significantly different from the average returns for the other four days, which were all positive. Jaffe and Westerfield have confirmed these results for several international markets, including Canada.[59] Ariel identified a day-of-the-month effect in US stock returns, where returns tend to be higher on the last trading day of each month.[60] The Canadian results of Jog and Riding support the existence of a similar pattern in Canadian stock returns.[61]

The *Value Line* Ranking System

The Value Line Investment Survey is the largest, and perhaps best known, investment advisory service in the world. *Value Line* ranks each of the roughly 1,700 stocks it covers from 1 (best) to 5 (worst) as to its "timeliness"—probable relative price performance within the next 12 months. These timeliness ranks, updated weekly, have been available since 1965.

The performance of the five rankings categories has been very strong, based on *Value Line's* calculations. For example, the complete record of *Value Line* rankings for timeliness from 1965 shows that the ranking system clearly discriminates in a monotonic order. That is, Group 1 stocks perform better than Group 2 stocks, which perform better than Group 3 stocks, and so on. Figure 10-7 shows the record for the *Value Line* ranks without allowing for changes in ranks for the period 1965–2005 (i.e., equal amounts are invested in each stock in each grouping at the beginning of the year and held for 12 months without allowing for subsequent changes in ranking).

Figure 10-7 presents *Value Line's* total record over time, along with both the DJIA and the S&P 500 Index. According to *Value Line*, 2002 was only the fifth time in 41 years that the Group 1 stocks failed to outperform the Group 5 stocks. In other words, over the 41-year period, Group 1 stocks outperformed Group 5 stocks 88 percent of the time.

Allowing for changes in ranks produced spectacular results. For the comparable period shown in Figure 10-7, Group 1 stocks showed a cumulative total return of 21,954 percent (or 14.2 percent per year), not allowing for rating changes. However, such a procedure would have resulted in a prohibitive portfolio turnover rate, generating large transaction costs and short-term capital gains.

According to evidence, for the period from mid-1980 through 1993, Group 1 stocks showed an annualized return of 19.3 percent. According to Mark Hulbert, who tracks the performance of investment letters for his *Hulbert Financial Digest*, this made *Value Line* the best overall performer for this period of all the investment letters tracked.

[57]Tinic et al (1987); V. Jog, "Stock Pricing Anomalies: Canadian Experience," *Canadian Investment Review*, vol 1 (1988), pp. 55–62.

[58]F. Cross, "Price Movements on Fridays and Mondays," *Financial Analysts Journal* 29 (Nov–Dec 1973), pp. 67–69.

[59]J. Jaffe and R. Westerfield, "The Week-End Effect in Common Stock Returns: International Evidence," *Journal of Finance* 40 (June 1985), pp. 433–454.

[60]R. Ariel, "A Monthly Effect in Stock Returns," *Journal of Financial Economics* 18 (March 1987), pp. 161–174.

[61]V. Jog and A. Riding, "The Month-End Effect in Canadian Stock Prices: Some Anomalous Findings," *Canadian Journal of Administrative Sciences* 6 (December 1989), pp. 7–17.

Figure 10-7
Record of *Value Line* Ranks
for Timeliness without
Allowing for Annual
Changes in Rank,
1965–2005

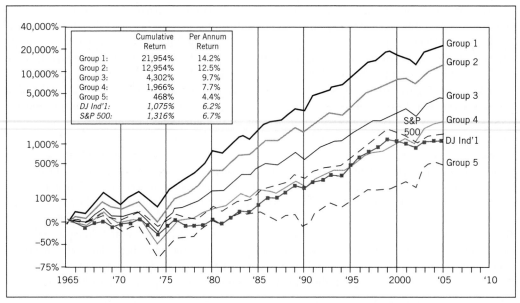

Source: *"Value Line* Selection and Opinion," *The Value Line Investment Survey*, January 27, 2006, p. 1313.
Reproduced with the permission of Value Line Publishing, Inc.

The Value Line Investment Survey now regularly reports a comparison of the performance of its Group 1 stocks with four other strategies: low-P/E, low-cap (small-size), low-price/book value, and low-price/sales. These results provide some information on two of the strategies discussed earlier—low-P/E and the size-effect—as well as two valuation techniques that are discussed in Chapter 13—price/book value and price/sales. These results are shown in Figure 10-8 for the same period, 1965–2005. Figure 10-8 suggests that *Value Line's* Group 1 stocks outperformed the other four strategies by a significant amount. Interestingly, by this comparison the small-cap stocks did better than the other strategies (other than *Value Line's* Group 1), with the low-P/E ratio strategy the next best. The low price/sales and low price/book did particularly poorly in this comparison. It is easy to see from Figure 10-8 why *Value Line* concluded, "The lesson is clear—stay with the Group 1s."

Figure 10-8
Value Line Group 1 Stocks
versus Other Strategies,
1965–2005

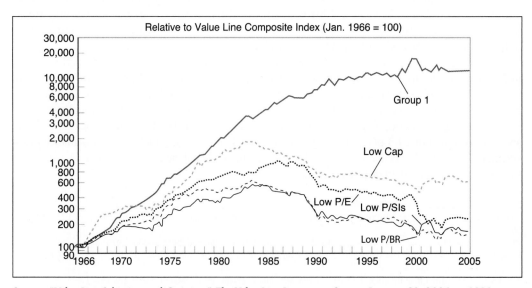

Source: *"Value Line* Selection and Opinion," *The Value Line Investment Survey*, January 31, 2006, p. 1318.
Reproduced with the permission of Value Line Publishing, Inc.

Several studies of the success of *Value Line's* rankings have been done. It appears that the rankings, and changes in the rankings, do contain useful information. However, there is evidence that the market adjusts quickly to this information (one or two trading days following the Friday release) and that true transaction costs can negate much of the price changes that occur as a result of adjustments to this information.[62]

One study by James Choi examined *Value Line's* timeliness rankings from 1965 to 1996 and found evidence that higher ranked stocks offered superior returns. However, he also found that after transaction costs it is doubtful that investors could have earned abnormal returns.[63]

Strong support for the *Value Line* system comes from Mark Hulbert, who has monitored the performance of investing newsletters for 22 years. From January 1989 through the first three quarters of 2002, Hulbert determined that *Value Line's* ranking system outperformed Standard & Poor's *Outlook*, which uses a five-tiered stock-ranking system based on S&P's stock analysts. Over this period, the average *Value Line* top-ranked stock outperformed the average S&P top-ranked stock by more than three percentage points on an annualized basis (13 percent compared to 9.7 percent). For comparison, the Wilshire 5000 produced a 10.2 percent annualized return.[64]

The Value Line Investment Survey is an important source of information for investors and is one of the most used investment advisory services available. We will refer to it again in Chapter 17.

Other Anomalies

The anomalies discussed are not exhaustive. Many others have been reported and discussed. Because it is consistent with the common-sense notion that market efficiency is most likely applied to larger, well-known stocks as opposed to all stocks, one interesting anomaly is the *neglected firm effect*. In this case, neglect means that few analysts follow the stock or that few institutions own it. The area of neglected stocks would appear to be a good opportunity for small investors interested in security analysis and stock selection.

CHECK YOUR UNDERSTANDING

10-7. How does the concept of investor underreaction or overreaction to news and information fit with the concept of behavioural finance?

10-8. Does the existence of market anomalies disprove the efficient market hypothesis?

SOME CONCLUSIONS ABOUT MARKET EFFICIENCY

Given all of the evidence about market efficiency discussed previously—the studies supporting it as well as the anomalies—what conclusions can be drawn? In truth, no definitive conclusion about market efficiency can be stated. The evidence in support of market efficiency is persuasive because of the large amount of research done over many years by numerous investigators. Nevertheless, the evidence of anomalies has yet to be explained satisfactorily. Moreover, many technicians and fundamentalists are convinced that they can outperform the market, or at least provide more benefits than cost. Paradoxically, this belief helps to make the market efficient because it implies there will be many analysts, both amateur and professional, simultaneously scrutinizing the factors that affect any given stock price.

---

[62]S. Stickel, "The Effect of Value Line Investment Survey Changes on Common Stock Prices," *Journal of Financial Economics* 14 (March 1985), pp. 121–143. A good review that attempts to reconcile the various findings about *Value Line* can be found in G. Huberman and S. Kandel, "Market Efficiency and Value Line's Record," *Journal of Business* 63 (April 1990), pp. 187–216.

[63]J. J. Choi, "The Value Line Enigma: The Sum of Known Parts?" *Journal of Financial and Quantitative Analysis* 35 (September 2000), pp. 485–498.

[64]CBS Market Watch website, "Mark Hulbert: The Main Event—S&P vs. *Value Line* 'Machine' over 'Man' in Stock Performance Rankings," October 29, 2002.

INVESTING *tip*

The paradox of efficient markets and active investors is that investors, in an attempt to uncover and use important information about security prices, help to make the market efficient. In other words, in the course of searching out undervalued and overvalued stocks, investors discover information and act on it as quickly as possible. If the information isfavourable, the discoverers will buy immediately, and if it is unfavourable, they will sell immediately. As investors scramble for information and attempt to be the first to act, they make the market more efficient. If enough of this activity occurs, all information will be reflected in prices. Thus, the fact that a number of investors do not believe in the EMH results in actions that help to make the market efficient.

Consider another quote, this one from Charles Ellis, a well-known investment consultant and author who has studied the results of professional managers over many years:

The problem is not that professional managers lack skill or diligence. Quite the opposite. The problem with trying to beat the market is that professional investors are so talented, so numerous, and so dedicated to their work that as a group they make it very difficult for any one of their number to do significantly better than the others, particularly in the long run.[65]

In the final analysis, it is probably best to accept the idea that the market is quite efficient but not totally. Therefore, it is almost a "matter of degree" with respect to how efficient one believes markets are, and this belief will dictate investing philosophy to a certain degree as discussed in Real-World Returns 10-3. Most of the research done to date suggests that information is received and acted on quickly, and generally the correct adjustments are made. In order to outperform the market, superior fundamental analysis must be accomplished. The fundamental analysis that is routinely done every day is already reflected in stock prices. The marginal value of one more investor performing the same calculations that have been done by other investors is zero. Until more evidence to the contrary is forthcoming, the benefits of technical analysis remain questionable at best.

REAL-WORLD RETURNS 10-3

Markets: Efficient or Not? Where You Stand Helps Determine Client Allocation

One of the great debates in the financial services industry surrounds the notion of market efficiency. It has raged for over 40 years, since Eugene Fama wrote his doctoral thesis purporting that markets are sufficiently efficient so it is improbable that a manager can reliably add value over a long time frame (i.e., stock picking is unlikely to yield better-than-market results). Perhaps "raged" is too strong, but the question has festered within the industry for a long time.

Depending on one's stance, Fama's "efficient market hypothesis" leaves almost no middle ground to debate. That's probably why the whole issue is often so explosive. Either markets are efficient or they are not. Like creationism versus evolution, everyone's got an opinion, but at the end of the day, that's all we're left with: opinions.

If markets are inefficient, then active management works. But if active management works, why would proponents settle for a half-baked solution like long-only mutual funds? Wouldn't hedge funds be more appropriate? Diversification could come in the form of style management—distressed capital, convertible arbitrage, long/short strategies, etc. No one worth his salt would agree to a long-only strategy in funds with primarily single asset class mandates as a means of exploiting inefficiencies if, in fact, there were myriad inefficiencies to exploit. Are we trying to make money here or not?

---

[65]See Charles Ellis, *Winning the Loser's Game*, (New York: McGraw Hill, 2002).

If markets are efficient, then fundamental and technical analysis are essentially useless, since market prices would reflect all relevant information instantaneously—with the exception of insiders. If the analysis that underpins security selection yields no additional useful information, then we're left making stock picks based on hunches and trends. As such, security selection based on empirical analysis is not likely to add any value over time.

Still, could there be a middle ground in the form of a more nuanced position? That is the challenge for advisors: how do we make meaningful recommendations to clients in light of this debate? Does it have to be an all or nothing proposition? What about degree? For instance, what if markets are somewhat efficient or mostly efficient, but there are still some opportunities to exploit mispricings that crop up every now and again?

Or perhaps if markets were 96 percent efficient, it might not be worth the trouble to try to beat them. Then again, if markets were only 69 percent efficient, there might be plenty of room to do precisely that. When approached from that perspective, the question then becomes: just how efficient do you think markets are? The corollary is: just how inefficient do markets need to be in order to be able to beat them?

For instance, two people could actually agree that markets are 80 percent efficient. One could conclude that active management should be used to try to "beat the market," while the other could conclude that an 80 percent degree of efficiency is too high a hurdle and thus recommends that clients just "buy the market." Therefore, even if reasonable people could agree on quantification, they could still differ on what to do about it.

Perhaps that's the middle ground in this. Advisors could come up with their own numbers as to how efficient they think markets are and then advise accordingly. Most people in the industry offer their best estimates at somewhere between 80 percent and 92 percent, according to Ken French of Dimensional Fund Advisors.

Obviously, there's no science to this. It is, after all, just a matter of opinion.

Source: De Goey, John, "Markets: Efficient or not? Where you stands helps determine client allocation," *Advisor's Edge Report*, December 2005, p. 12.

Simon Keane has argued that investors must choose between a belief in operational efficiency and inefficiency.[66] In an operationally efficient market, some investors with the skill to detect a divergence between price and semi-strong value earn economic rents. For the majority of investors, however, such opportunities are not available. An operationally inefficient market, on the other hand, contains inefficiencies that the average investor can spot. The evidence to date suggests that investors face an operationally efficient market.

Some anomalies do seem to exist, and since the late 1970s the flow of research reporting on anomalies has accelerated. These anomalies require considerable work to document scientifically and do not represent a guarantee of investment riches. Although they do appear to offer opportunities to astute investors, the reasons why they exist remain unsettled. The quantity and quality of the research in this area has undermined the extreme view that the market is so perfectly efficient that no opportunities for excess returns could possibly exist.

In judging whether a market inefficiency has been uncovered that could be exploited, investors must guard against data mining. This term refers to the search for patterns in security returns by examining various techniques applied to a set of data. With enough effort, patterns will be uncovered, and investing rules and techniques can be found that appear to work in the sense of providing abnormal returns. In most cases, they do not stand up to independent scrutiny or application to a different set of data or time period. The rules and selection techniques resulting from data mining often have no theoretical basis, or rationale, for existing—they simply result from mining the data.

---

[66]Simon Keane, "The Efficient Market Hypothesis on Trial," *Financial Analysts Journal* 42 (March–April 1986), pp. 58–63.

One difficult problem for those who believe in efficient markets is the crash of October 1987. The then TSE 300 Composite Index lost over 11 percent and the S&P 500 Index over 20 percent in one day. In 2008, the TSX Index fell from an all-time high of just over 15,000 in July to below 9,000 in October. Is it really reasonable to argue that investors, efficiently discounting information, decided in one day that the market should be valued some 20 percent less in one day, or some 40 percent less over three months? Not many people, including efficient market proponents, are comfortable making this argument. Another example is the market "bubble" that burst in 2000, with the stock market declining over the next two years. A strict interpretation of the EMH would say that a rational explanation should exist for what happened during the late 1990s as stock prices were bid up to successively higher levels, until they eventually collapsed. But most observers today accept the proposition that a bubble did occur, that it was not based on rational behaviour, and that this is not in agreement with the efficient market view.

In addition to these challenges to the concept of market efficiency that we've discussed, mathematicians are helping a new kind of trader to justify the position that the market is not very efficient, using leading-edge ideas such as chaos theory, neural networks, and genetic algorithms.

What about the behavioural finance view and its current ascendancy in finance thinking? On the one hand, this theory can easily accommodate the notion that some investors can perform better than the market given the irrationalities that exist. On the other hand, ironically, behavioural finance accepts that markets can remain out of kilter for extended periods of time, making it difficult for professionals who manage money to survive the effects of such a market—witness the flight from equities during the last bear market.

Behavioural finance challenges some of the behavioural assumptions underlying the EMH, in particular the assumption that investors are "rational expectations wealth maximizers." Extensive psychological research suggests instead that people tend to be overconfident in their judgments, believe what they want to believe, overweigh evidence that comes easily to mind, and so forth. Through findings such as these, behavioural finance attempts to explain some of the anomalies and inefficiencies that have been reported.

The controversy about market efficiency and behavioural finance remains. Every investor is still faced with the choice between pursuing an active investment strategy or a passive investment strategy, or some combination thereof. Making this choice depends heavily on what the investor believes about efficient markets. Investors who plan, or wish, to pursue some type of active strategy should consider a quote attributed to Warren Buffett, arguably the most famous US investor of our time:

Most investors, both institutional and individual, will find that the best way to own common stocks (shares) is through an index fund that charges minimal fees. Those following this path are sure to beat the net results (after fees and expenses) of the great majority of investment professionals.

For an interesting perspective on the interaction between behavioural activities and market efficiency, see Real-World Returns 10-4. Notice in particular the comments about people finding patterns in the stock market when none may exist.

REAL-WORLD RETURNS 10-4

Market Teaches Math Prof a Valuable Lesson

"It was early 2000, the market was booming, and my investments in various index funds were doing well but not generating much excitement." So began John Allen Paulos's fateful dalliance with WorldCom, the telecommunications giant that collapsed beneath the weight of massive accounting fraud.

Dr. Paulos, a professor of mathematics at Temple University, relates his ordeal as a WorldCom investor in *A Mathematician Plays the Stock Market* (Basic Books, 2003), which explores the stock market's interplay of mathematics, economics, and psychology. *In the Vanguard* spoke to Dr. Paulos at the end of August.

What prompted you to embark on your "illicit affair" with WorldCom?
I had read George Gilder rhapsodizing about the wonders of near-infinite bandwidth and telecommunications. I was particularly vulnerable to his spiel. I spend a lot of time on the Internet, and I knew WorldCom owned UUNET, the backbone of the Internet as well as MCI. So it wasn't a dot-com company. It had $25 billion in revenue. And Jack Grubman, and other so-called stellar telecommunications analysts, were regularly hyping it as well.

I received an unexpected small chunk of money, and investing it in WorldCom seemed like a reasonable thing to do. Thereafter, I became subject to what is often called conformation bias. If you make a decision, it may be tentative at first, but after you make it, you look for all the reasons that it was a brilliant move and ignore all the factors that suggest otherwise. If the stock was great at $40-something, it was even better at $30-something, so I bought more. And continued to buy more as the stock fell.

Your relationship with WorldCom almost bordered on obsession. You e-mailed the CEO to offer him help with making the WorldCom case to investors. You woke up early to check WorldCom trading on the European stock exchanges.
I disdained the hordes who were running away from the stock and thought that I knew better. I didn't know at the time about the various accounting frauds, but those were not a big factor in my WorldCom experience. Too many investors tend to view the shady accounting practices and the long list of villains as somehow determinative of their future and see themselves as victimized. They ignore the fact that they were beneficiaries of the same reviled practices and so-called villains during the late 1990s when investors were making a ton of money.

You've since returned to a primarily index-fund-based portfolio, which you describe as a sensible, inexpensive way to invest. But you also note that index funds have a very real cost.
One must give up the fantasy of being a perspicacious gunslinger/investor outwitting the market. And also the cost of entertainment in a sense. But I think it is a relatively small cost. And it needn't be paid entirely. Even though the bulk of one's assets should be in broad-gauge, low-fee index funds, that doesn't mean every penny you have. If you think you have preternatural insight into a company or sector, put some money there. Just make sure it is a relatively small percentage of your assets.

From a logical perspective, what common errors do investors make?
People tend not to believe that markets move in random ways. Randomness is difficult to recognize. If you have people write down 100 Hs and Ts to simulate 100 flips of a coin, you will always be able to tell a sequence generated by a human from one generated by real coin flips. When humans make up the sequence, they don't put in enough consecutive Hs and consecutive Ts, and they don't make the lengths of these runs long enough or frequent enough. And that is one of the reasons people look at patterns in the stock market and ascribe significance to them.

Have people started asking you for stock tips?
Yes, and I always resist. There aren't any lists of stocks for the first decade of the 21st century, or of how to send your kid to college by investing in the five best funds, or of this or that. The point of the book is to provide a kind of conceptual understanding of the market as a whole, the logic of the market: why it works, what underlies various investing strategies, and whether they work or not. Generally not.

The controversy about market efficiency remains, and every investor is faced with the choice between active and passive investment strategies or some combination of the two. In the final analysis, no one can say exactly how efficient the stock market is. If the market is not fully efficient, it is close. Easy profits are not readily available. Large numbers of investors do not, on average, "beat the market." Perhaps the most telling evidence in favour of market efficiency is the below-average performance of professional investors such as mutual fund managers, as discussed previously.

A good close to this chapter is to quote Samuel Eisenstadt, as we did at the beginning of the chapter. As noted, he was the primary force in developing the *Value Line* ranking system discussed in this chapter. Eisenstadt noted, "…beating the market is difficult and becoming even more so."[67]

WHAT OBLIGATIONS DO FINANCIAL ADVISORS HAVE TO CLIENTS?

Given the evidence cited earlier on the mediocre performance of most professional money managers, should financial advisors explain this information to their clients? These advisors often earn their living by the commissions they receive when investors trade, or from the fees they earn when clients buy load funds.

Would most investors not be better off with an index fund such as RBC's Canadian Index fund, with a management expense ratio (MER) of 0.71 percent, which has outperformed many actively managed funds over time? How can someone justify to a client interested in buying an index equity fund the purchase of Scotiabank's CanAm Stock Index, with a 1.92 percent MER?

Financial advisors often face ethical issues such as these.

DISCUSSION QUESTIONS

1. What would happen if more and more clients opted for no-load funds, index funds, ETFs, and so forth?

2. Should a financial advisor ever stress to a client the benefits of customer service and relationships over actual returns?

3. Given what you've learned about a fund's past performance not being a guarantee of future performance, can a mutual fund and financial advisors always justify higher MERs if the fund has had consistently higher returns?

---

[67]See Steven T. Goldberg, "Civil Warriors," *Kiplinger's Personal Finance*, August 2002, p. 39.

SUMMARY

This summary relates to the learning objectives for this chapter.

1. **Explain the concept of efficient markets.**

   An efficient market is defined as one in which the prices of securities fully reflect all known information quickly and accurately. The conditions that guarantee an efficient market can be shown to hold to a large extent: many investors are competing, information is widely available and generated more or less randomly, and investors react quickly to this information.

2. **Describe the three forms of market efficiency—weak, semi-strong, and strong.**

   To assess market efficiency, three cumulative forms (or degrees) of efficiency are discussed: the weak, semi-strong, and strong form. The weak form involves market data, whereas the semi-strong and strong form involve the assimilation of all public and private information, respectively.

3. **Discuss the evidence regarding the Efficient Market Hypothesis.**

   The weak-form evidence generally supports the hypothesis. Many tests of semi-strong efficiency have been conducted, including stock splits, money supply changes, accounting changes, dividend announcements, and reactions to other announcements, among others. In addition, the performance of professional money managers as a whole has not been better than passive market benchmarks. Although all the studies do not agree, the majority support semi-strong efficiency. Strong-form evidence generally tests the ability of groups presumed to have "private" information to outperform the market. Insiders apparently are able to do well, although the decisions of the managers of mutual funds have not been found to add value. Most knowledgeable observers accept weak-form efficiency, reject strong-form efficiency, and feel that the market is, to a large degree, semi-strong efficient. This casts doubt on the value of both technical analysis and conventional fundamental analysis.

4. **State the implications of market efficiency for investors.**

   Although the EMH does not preclude investors from outperforming the market, it does suggest that this is quite difficult to accomplish and that the investor must do more than the norm. Even if the market is efficient, money managers still have activities to perform, including diversifying the portfolio, choosing and maintaining some degree of risk, and assessing taxes and transaction costs.

5. **Outline major exceptions to the Efficient Market Hypothesis.**

   Several major anomalies that have appeared over the last several years have yet to be satisfactorily explained. These anomalies, which would not be expected in a totally efficient market, include the following:

1. *Momentum in stock returns.* Historical evidence indicates a recurring pattern in stock returns. In particular, stocks that have been top performers over the past six to 12 months will continue to provide superior investment performance in similar, subsequent periods.

2. *Unexpected earnings.* The market appears to adjust with a lag to earnings surprises contained in earnings announcements.

3. *Value stocks.* Value stocks (with low P/E ratios, low market-to-book values, and high dividend yields) appear to outperform growth stocks (with high P/E ratios, high market-to-book values, and low dividend yields) over annual periods, even after adjustment for risk and size.

4. *The size effect.* Small firms have been shown to outperform large firms, on a risk-adjusted basis, over a period of many years.

5. *The January effect.* Much of the abnormal return for small firms occurs in the month of January.

6. Value Line's *performance.* The *Value Line* rankings for timeliness have performed extremely well over time and appear to offer the average investor a chance to outperform the averages.

KEY TERMS

Abnormal return, p.292
Behavioural finance, p.300
Contrarian investing, p.301
Cumulative abnormal return
  (CAR), p.293
Efficient market (EM), p.285

Efficient Market Hypothesis
  (EMH), p.287
Event study, p.292
January effect, p.306
Market anomalies, p.301
Market data, 288

Semi-strong form, p.288
Size effect, p.306
Strong form, p.288
Weak form, p.288

REVIEW QUESTIONS

10-1. What is meant by an efficient market?

10-2. Why is a weak-form efficient market in direct opposition to technical analysis?

10-3. Distinguish between economic significance and statistical significance.

10-4. If the EMH is true, what are the implications for investors?

10-5. What types of events or information, other than those discussed in this chapter, could be used in semi-strong-form tests?

10-6. Do security analysts have a role in an efficient market?

10-7. What is meant by an operationally efficient market?

10-8. Describe the three forms of market efficiency.

10-9. What are the conditions for an efficient market? How closely are they met in reality?

10-10. What do semi-strong market efficiency tests attempt to test for?

10-11. Describe two different ways to test for weak-form efficiency.

10-12. Why could the performance of mutual fund managers be considered a test of semi-strong efficiency?

10-13. Describe the money management activities of a portfolio manager who believes that the market is efficient.

10-14. What are market anomalies? Describe four.

10-15. What is the relationship between earnings surprises and fundamental analysis?

10-16. What are the benefits to society of an efficient market?

10-17. If the market moves in an upward trend over a period of years, would this be inconsistent with weak-form efficiency?

10-18. Evaluate the following statement: "My mutual fund has outperformed the market for the last four years. How can the market be efficient?"

10-19. What are the necessary conditions for a scientific test of a trading rule?

10-20. Assume that you analyze the activities of specialists on the NYSE and find that they are able to realize consistently above-average rates of return. What form of the EMH are you testing?

10-21. How can data on corporate insiders be used to test both the semi-strong and the strong forms of the EMH?

10-22. Assume that the price of a stock remains constant from time period 0 to time period 1, at which time a significant piece of information about the stock becomes available. Draw a diagram that depicts the situation if

a. the market is semi-strong efficient; and
b. there is a lag in the adjustment of the price to this information.

10-23. What would the slope of the demand curve be for stocks in a perfectly efficient market?

10-24. If all investors believe that the market is efficient, could that eventually lead to less efficiency in the market?

10-25. What are some possible explanations for the size anomaly?

10-26. An investment consulting firm has developed and marketed a sophisticated computerized stock trading program. It has been tested using stock market returns for the past 15 years and would have generated economically significant risk-adjusted excess returns after all transaction costs if it had been utilized during those 15 years. Is this consistent with the concept of market efficiency? Explain.

10-27. Given the following information for stocks A and B, determine which is most likely to be purchased by a "value" investor. Justify your answer.

	Stock A	Stock B
Dividend per share	$0.50	$0.20
Price per share	$20	$10

10-28. a. According to studies, in each of the following pairs, which type of stock typically outperforms the other?

   i. Value stocks or growth stocks?
   ii. High dividend yield stocks or low dividend yield stocks?
   iii. Above average P/E ratio stocks or below average P/E ratio stocks?
   iv. Above average M/B ratio stocks or below average M/B ratio stocks?

   b. Why does this contradict the EHM?
   c. Is investing in this type of portfolio [your answer for (a)(iii)] better as a long-term or short-term investment strategy?

10-29. Value investors often form portfolios of stocks that possess:

   a. below average dividend yields.
   b. above average dividend yields.
   c. below average dividend payout ratios.
   d. above average dividend payout ratios.

PREPARING FOR YOUR PROFESSIONAL EXAMS

CFA PRACTICE QUESTIONS

10-1. In an efficient market:

   a. security prices react quickly to new information.
   b. security analysis will not enable investors to realize consistently superior returns on their investments.
   c. security prices are seldom far above or below their justified levels.
   d. All of the above.

10-2. The strong form of the efficient-market hypothesis is based on all of the following assumptions except:

   a. the market consists of a large number of rational, profit-seeking investors.
   b. better informed investors achieved above-average investment returns.
   c. all investors are risk-averse.
   d. all relevant investment information is rapidly and accurately disseminated.

10-3. Earning abnormal profits over a long period of time by executing trades based on information about insider trading that is made public contradicts which level(s) of the EMH?

a. Weak form

b. Semi-strong form

c. Strong form

d. Semi-strong and strong forms

10-4. The fact that stock prices react to "earnings surprises" very quickly

a. contradicts the weak form of the EMH.

b. contradicts the semi-strong form of the EMH.

c. contradicts the strong form of the EMH.

d. does not contradict the EMH.

10-5. A market anomaly refers to:

a. an exogenous shock to the market that is sharp but not persistent.

b. a price or volume event that is inconsistent with historical price or volume trends.

c. a trading or pricing structure that interferes with efficient buying and selling of securities.

d. price behaviour that differs from the behaviour predicted by the Efficient Market Hypothesis.

CHAPTER 11

BOND YIELDS AND PRICES

You have recently inherited $1 million, so you begin studying stocks for potential investment. Following your study of stocks, you realize you also need to understand the basics about bonds. After all, portfolio theory stresses the virtues of diversification, and that includes asset classes. A little math quickly tells you that $1 million invested in bonds returning 6 percent produces an income stream of $60,000 a year, which seems like a nice annual annuity. By now, however, you have learned that when it comes to investing, things are not always what they seem. Maybe bond returns are not as straightforward as they appear. Furthermore, you have heard people say that when interest rates rise, bond prices decline, and you wonder why. It becomes apparent to you that knowing something about bond prices and yields could be useful to you as you manage your inheritance.

Learning Objectives

After reading this chapter, you should be able to

1. Calculate the price of a bond.
2. Explain the bond valuation process.
3. Calculate major bond yield measures, including yield to maturity, yield to call, and horizon return.
4. Account for changes in bond prices.
5. Explain and apply the concept of duration.

CHAPTER PREVIEW

This chapter builds on the background developed in Part I. Having introduced the characteristics of bonds in Chapter 2, we can now examine bond yields and prices. In addition to calculating bond price, in this chapter we lay out the basic principles of valuation, which we will use again when considering other investing alternatives, particularly common stocks (Chapter 13). As part of valuation, you will learn to calculate major bond yield measures such as yield to maturity, yield to call, and horizon return. You will also learn about the factors that affect bond price changes, notably changes in interest rates. Finally, we discuss duration, a concept used by investors to deal with the effect of yield changes.

BOND PRICES

learning objective 1
Calculate the price of a bond.

In addition to the total return concept considered in Chapter 6 (which is applicable to any security), bond investors must also understand specific measures of bond yields. It is traditional in the bond markets to use various yield measures and to quote potential returns to investors on the basis of these measures. However, these gauges can mislead unwary investors who fail to understand the basis on which they are constructed. Investors must understand that bond yields reported daily in various media sources do not necessarily represent the true yield an investor will achieve when he or she buys bonds in the marketplace and holds them to maturity.

The Valuation Principle

What determines the price of a security? The answer is that a security's estimated value determines the price that investors place on it in the open market.

Intrinsic Value

The estimated or true value of a security as determined by an investor after examining a firm's underlying variables.

A security's **intrinsic value**, or estimated value, is the present value of the expected cash flows from that asset. Any security purchased is expected to provide one or more cash flows some time in the future. These could be periodic, such as interest or dividends, or simply a final price or redemption value, or a combination of these. Since these cash flows occur in the future, they must be discounted at an appropriate rate to determine their present value. The sum of these discounted cash flows is the estimated intrinsic value of the asset. Calculating that value, therefore, requires the use of present value techniques. Equation 11-1 expresses the concept:

(11-1)

$$\text{Value}_{t=0} = \sum_{t=1}^{n} \frac{\text{Cash flow (at time } t)}{(1 + k)^t}$$

where
Value$_{t=0}$ = the value of the asset now (time period 0)
Cash flow (at time t) = the future cash flow (at time t) that results from ownership of the asset
k = the appropriate discount rate or rate of return required by an investor for an investment of this type
n = number of periods over which the cash flows are expected

To solve Equation 11-1 and derive the intrinsic value of a security, it is necessary to determine the following:

1. The *expected cash flows* from the security. This includes the size and type of cash flows, such as dividends, interest, face value expected to be received at maturity, or the expected price of the security at some point in the future.

2. The *timing* of the expected cash flows. Since the returns to be generated from a security occur at various times in the future, they must be properly documented for discounting back to time period 0

(today). Money has a time value, and the timing of future cash flows significantly affects the value of the asset today.

3. The *discount rate* or required rate of return demanded by investors will reflect the time value of money and the risk of the security. It is an opportunity cost, representing the rate foregone by an investor in the next best alternative investment with comparable risk.

Bond Valuation

The intrinsic value of any asset is calculated from the present value of its expected cash flows. This is true for short-term instruments such as T-bills, as well as for long-term ones such as bonds or common stocks. Appendix 11A at the end of this chapter discusses the valuation of T-bills, and we focus here on the valuation of traditional bonds.

The interest payments (coupons) and the principal repayment for bonds are known in advance—coupons are paid at regular intervals (either annually or semi-annually) and the principal repayment occurs at the maturity date. The coupons are all for the same amount, which is determined by multiplying the coupon rate (which is stated on an annual basis) by the face value of the bond (F). For example, a bond with a coupon rate of 10 percent and a face value of $1,000 would pay annual coupons of $100 ($50 if paid semi-annually). Hence, the fundamental value of a bond is determined by discounting these future payments from the issuer at an appropriate required yield, r, for the issue. Equation 11-2 is used to solve for the value of a coupon bond.[1]

$$P = \sum_{t=1}^{n} \frac{C_t}{(1 + r)^t} + \frac{F}{(1 + r)^n}$$

(11-2)

where

P = the price of the bond today (time period 0)
C = the regular coupons or interest payments (paid annually or semi-annually)
F = the face value (or par value) of the bond
n = the number of periods to maturity of the bond (the periods may be for a full year or for six months, depending on payment interval)
r = the appropriate period discount rate or market yield (which may be an annual or semi-annual rate depending on how frequently coupons are paid)

Finance students should immediately realize that the stream of interest income to be received in the form of coupons represents an annuity. This is because it represents a series of cash flows that provide the same payment at the same interval (every year or six months), and we are determining the present value of these cash flows using the same discount rate. Recalling some introductory mathematics of finance concepts, we can use the present value annuity (PVA) factor to determine the present value of any cash stream that represents an annuity. Combining this result with the fact that $\frac{1}{(1 + r)^n}$ is generally referred to as the discount or present value factor for a discount rate of r for n periods ($PV_{r,n}$), we can rewrite Equation 11-2 as:

$$P = C \times (PVA_{r,n}) + F \times (PV_{r,n})$$

(11-3)

where

$PVA_{r,n}$ = the present value annuity factor for an n period annuity using a discount rate of r
$PV_{r,n}$ = the present value or discount factor for discounting an amount to be received at time n, using a discount rate of r

---

[1]This formulation is nothing new; John Burr Williams stated it in a book in 1938. *See* J. B. Williams, *The Theory of Investment Value* (Cambridge, MA: Harvard University Press, 1938).

Bond prices can be calculated by referring to the PV and PVA tables at the end of the textbook, or simply using Equation 11-2 and a calculator, or using a computer program such as Excel. Throughout this chapter we will also present solutions calculated using the Texas Instruments BA II Plus financial calculator (which is one of two calculators that CFA candidates are permitted to use in writing the CFA examinations). Although there may be minor variations in the required input procedures, most calculators can be used in a similar fashion to obtain these results (so check your calculator user guide). The present value process for a typical coupon-bearing bond involves three steps, given the dollar coupon on the bond, the face value, and the current market yield applicable to a particular bond:

1. Using the present value of an annuity (PVA) factor (defined in Table A4, which is available in the appendix on the textbook's companion website), determine the present value of the coupons (interest payments).

2. Using the present value (PV) table (Table A-2 in the appendix on the textbook's companion website), determine the present value of the face (par) value of the bond; for our purposes, the face value will usually be $1,000.

3. Add the present values determined in steps 1 and 2 together.

EXAMPLE 11-1: CALCULATING BOND PRICES—ANNUAL COUPONS

To determine the price of a three-year bond with a face value of $1,000 that paid annual coupons at a rate of 10 percent when the appropriate discount rate was 12 percent, we would input the following information into Equation 11-3: C = $100; F = $1,000; n = 3; and r = 12 percent.

$$P = C \times (PVA_{r,n}) + F \times (PV_{r,n}) = \$100 \times (PVA_{12\%,3}) + \$1,000 \times (PV_{12\%,3})$$

$$= \$100 \times (2.40183) + \$1,000 \times (.71178) = \$240.18 + \$711.78 = \$951.96$$

Solution by Financial Calculator (Texas Instruments BA II Plus)

Inputs:
PMT = $100 (i.e., the coupon payment); n = 3 (i.e., the number of payments); FV = 1,000 (i.e., the face value); i = 12 (i.e., the current market rate in percentage terms).

Then compute (CPT) PV, which will give an answer of –$951.96 (ignore the negative sign). This is the present value of the future cash flows (both coupons and face value); therefore, the price is $951.96.

Notice that these bonds sell below their face value (at a discount from par), which is always the case when the discount rate exceeds the stated coupon rate. We will talk about this result in greater detail later in this chapter.

Generally bonds pay interest semi-annually rather than annually, so the discount rate is calculated by dividing the annual discount rate by two, while the number of semi-annual periods to maturity is determined by multiplying the number of years to maturity by two.

EXAMPLE 11-2: CALCULATING BOND PRICES—SEMI-ANNUAL COUPONS

Assume the three-year bond in the Example 11-1 paid semi-annual coupons instead of annual ones and that all the other information above remained the same. To determine its value we would input the following information into Equation 11-3: C = $50; n = 6; and r = 6 percent.

$$P = \$50 \times (PVA_{6\%,6}) + \$1,000 \times (PV_{6\%,6})$$

$$= \$50 \times (4.91732) + \$1,000 \times (0.70496) = \$245.87 + \$704.96 = \$950.83$$

Solution by Financial Calculator (Texas Instruments BA II Plus)

Inputs:

PMT = $50; n = 6; FV = 1,000; i = 6; CPT then PV = –$950.83

So, the price = $950.83.

Thus, while we can see the processes are similar for the annual-pay bonds in Example 11-1 and the semi-annual pay bonds here, they do differ slightly, and it is essential to use the correct equation to obtain the correct answer.

While the PV and PVA factors for various discount rates and periods are found in Appendices A2 and A4 on the textbook's companion website, it is often necessary to use the equations provided at the top of these appendices, which are given below:

$$PV = \frac{1}{(1+r)^n} \quad \text{and,}$$

$$PVA_{r,n} = \frac{1 - \dfrac{1}{(1+r)^n}}{r}$$

EXAMPLE 11-3: CALCULATING BOND PRICES

A bond with 10 years to maturity has an 8 percent coupon rate, with coupons being paid semi-annually. If its face value is $1,000 and the appropriate discount rate is 6.52 percent, we can determine its value as follows:

$$P = \$40 \times (PVA_{3.26\%,20}) + \$1,000 \times (PV_{3.26\%,20}) = \$40 \times \left[\frac{1 - \dfrac{1}{(1.0326)^{20}}}{.0326}\right] + \frac{\$1,000}{(1+.0326)^{20}}$$

$$= \$40 \times (14.52606) + \$1,000 \times (0.52645) = \$581.04 + \$526.45 = \$1,107.49$$

Solution by Financial Calculator (Texas Instruments BA II Plus)

Inputs:

PMT = $40; *n* = 20; FV = 1,000; i = 3.26; CPT then PV = –$1,107.49

So, the price = $1,107.49.

Notice that these bonds sell above their face value (at a premium over par), which is always the case when the discount rate is less than the stated coupon rate. As with Example 11-1 in which we calculated the price for a three-year bond that paid annual coupons, we defer our discussion of this result until later.

Notice that for zero-coupon bonds, the first term of Equation 11-2 is zero, so we are left with the following equation that can be used to determine the price of these bonds:

$$P = \frac{F}{(1+r)^n}$$

(11-4)

In the examples above, the bonds are valued, as are any other assets, on the basis of their future stream of expected benefits (cash flows), using an appropriate market yield. Since the numerator is always specified for coupon-bearing bonds at the time of issue, the only problem in valuing a typical bond is to determine the denominator or discount rate. The appropriate discount rate is the bond's required yield.

The required yield, r, in Equations 11-3 and 11-4 is specific for each particular bond. It is the current market rate being earned by investors on comparable bonds with the same maturity and the same credit quality. (In other words, it is an opportunity cost.) Thus, market interest rates are incorporated directly into the discount rate used to establish the fundamental value of a bond.

Since market interest rates fluctuate constantly, required yields do also. When calculating a bond price it is customary to use the yield to maturity (YTM), which is discussed in the next section, as the appropriate discount rate. If the YTM is used, we can restate Equation 11-3 as

(11-5)

$$P = C \times (PVA_{YTM,n}) + F \times (PV_{YTM,n})$$

Real-World Returns 11-1 contains a list of bond quotations reported on www.financialpost.com. The closing bid prices and corresponding yields are for April 21, 2008, therefore the Newfoundland government bonds that mature on April 17, 2028 have a term to maturity of almost exactly 20 years. These bonds have a 6.15 percent coupon rate, and the reported yield is 4.87 percent (which refers to the yield to maturity). These bonds are selling at a premium over their face value since the coupon rate exceeds the yield. If we assume coupons are paid semi-annually, use Equation 11-3 and the yield of 4.87 percent for this bond, and assume a face (or par) value of $100 (since bond prices are usually reported per $100 of face value), we can determine that the price will equal

$$P = \$3.075 \times \left[\frac{1 - \frac{1}{(1.02435)^{40}}}{.02435}\right] + \frac{\$100}{(1.02435)^{40}} = \$3.075 \times (25.3798) + \$100 \times (0.3820) = \$116.24$$

Solution by Financial Calculator (Texas Instruments BA II Plus)

Inputs:
PMT = $3.075; n = 40; FV = 100; i = 2.435; CPT then PV = −$116.24
So, the price = $116.24

This is exactly the price reported for this bond, because the reported yields are determined based on the day's closing bid prices, which are the reported prices in this case. In other words, once we are given the yields (and the coupon rate and term to maturity), we can determine the corresponding price and vice versa. We deal with the issue of estimating the implied yield from a given price in the next section.

Calculating the price of a bond is an easy procedure in today's financial world using either a financial calculator or personal computer. For example, by using a basic financial calculator, price can be determined after entering the cash flows and required yield.

Before proceeding to the next topic, we would point out that the prices discussed in this section are typically referred to as "quoted" prices. These differ from the actual prices investors pay for bonds whenever bonds are sold at a date other than the one of a coupon. The reason is that interest will accrue to bondholders in between such payment dates, although they will have not actually received the portion of the next coupon to which they are rightfully entitled. As a result, bond purchasers must pay the bond seller the quoted price plus the accrued interest on the bond. This amount is referred to as the cash price of the bond.

Real-World Returns 11-1
Bond Quotes

Canadian Bonds on April 21, 2008

FEDERAL

Issuer	Coupon	Maturity Date	Bid $	Yield %
Canada	5.500	Jun 01/09	102.84	2.87
Canada	3.750	Jun 01/09	100.95	2.87
Canada	11.000	Jun 01/09	108.78	2.87
Canada	4.250	Sep 01/09	101.82	2.87
Canada	10.750	Oct 01/09	111.04	2.87
Canada	4.250	Dec 01/09	102.15	2.87
Canada	5.500	Jun 01/10	105.40	2.84
Canada	3.750	Jun 01/10	101.85	2.84
Canada	9.500	Jun 01/10	113.52	2.84
Canada	4.000	Sep 01/10	102.54	2.88
Canada	9.000	Mar 01/11	116.19	3.04
Canada	8.500	Jun 01/11	116.04	3.04
Canada	6.000	Jun 01/11	108.68	3.05
Canada	3.750	Sep 01/11	102.06	3.10
Canada	3.750	Jun 01/12	102.24	3.16
Canada	5.250	Jun 01/12	107.97	3.16
Canada	5.250	Jun 01/13	109.39	3.24
Canada	3.500	Jun 01/13	101.22	3.24
Canada	10.250	Mar 15/14	136.82	3.32
Canada	5.000	Jun 01/14	109.19	3.32
Canada	11.250	Jun 01/15	149.10	3.41
Canada	4.500	Jun 01/15	106.77	3.42
Canada	4.000	Jun 01/16	103.18	3.55
Canada	4.000	Jun 01/17	102.57	3.67
Canada	4.250	Jun 01/18	103.85	3.79
Canada	10.500	Mar 15/21	165.87	3.94
Canada	9.750	Jun 01/21	158.94	3.95
Canada	9.250	Jun 01/22	156.66	3.97
Canada	8.000	Jun 01/23	144.93	4.01
Canada	9.000	Jun 01/25	160.25	4.07
Canada	8.000	Jun 01/27	150.81	4.13
Canada	5.750	Jun 01/29	122.46	4.14
Canada	5.750	Jun 01/33	125.03	4.14
Canada	5.000	Jun 01/37	114.77	4.12
CHT	4.650	Sep 15/09	102.08	3.11
CHT	3.750	Mar 15/10	100.97	3.22
CHT	3.550	Sep 15/10	100.48	3.34
CMHC	5.500	Jun 01/12	107.05	3.63
EDC	5.000	Feb 09/09	101.70	2.82
EDC	5.100	Jun 02/14	106.75	3.85

PROVINCIAL

Issuer	Coupon	Maturity Date	Bid $	Yield %
B C	6.000	Jun 09/08	100.38	2.87
B C	6.375	Aug 23/10	106.64	3.39
B C	5.750	Jan 09/12	107.18	3.66
B C	8.500	Aug 23/13	122.10	3.87
B C	6.150	Nov 19/27	117.46	4.77
B C	5.700	Jun 18/29	112.06	4.79
B C	4.700	Jun 18/37	98.59	4.79
B C MF	5.900	Jun 01/11	106.31	3.73
HydQue	6.500	Feb 15/11	107.88	3.53
HydQue	10.250	Jul 16/12	124.82	3.83
HydQue	11.000	Aug 15/20	158.30	4.71
HydQue	6.000	Aug 15/31	113.78	4.99
HydQue	6.500	Feb 15/35	122.34	4.98
HydQue	6.000	Feb 15/40	116.18	4.98
HydQue	5.000	Feb 15/45	100.35	4.98
Manit	5.750	Jun 02/08	100.29	2.87
Manit	7.750	Dec 22/25	134.76	4.81
NewBr	5.700	Jun 02/08	100.29	2.88
NewBr	6.000	Dec 27/17	112.25	4.43
Newfld	6.150	Apr 17/28	116.24	4.87
NovaSc	6.600	Jun 01/27	121.88	4.83
Ontario	4.000	May 19/09	100.94	3.09
Ontario	6.200	Nov 19/09	104.52	3.22
Ontario	4.000	May 19/10	101.35	3.32
Ontario	6.100	Nov 19/10	106.46	3.45
Ontario	6.100	Dec 02/11	108.17	3.66
Ontario	4.400	Dec 02/11	102.48	3.66
Ontario	5.375	Dec 02/12	106.56	3.81
Ontario	4.500	Dec 02/12	102.89	3.81
Ontario	4.750	Jun 02/13	104.14	3.85
Ontario	5.000	Mar 08/14	105.49	3.94
Ontario	4.500	Mar 08/15	102.70	4.05
Ontario	4.400	Mar 08/16	101.64	4.15
Ontario	4.300	Mar 08/17	100.17	4.28
Ontario	8.100	Sep 08/23	137.37	4.67
Ontario	7.600	Jun 02/27	134.87	4.79
Ontario	6.500	Mar 08/29	122.15	4.81
Ontario	6.200	Jun 02/31	119.07	4.82
Ontario	5.850	Mar 08/33	114.56	4.84
Ontario	4.700	Jun 02/37	98.18	4.82
OntHyd	5.600	Jun 02/08	100.28	2.87
Quebec	5.500	Jun 01/09	102.52	3.15
Quebec	6.250	Dec 01/10	106.84	3.48
Quebec	6.000	Oct 01/12	108.72	3.84
Quebec	5.250	Oct 01/13	106.26	3.96
Quebec	5.500	Dec 01/14	107.95	4.11
Quebec	5.000	Dec 01/15	105.00	4.22
Quebec	4.500	Dec 01/16	100.96	4.37
Quebec	4.500	Dec 01/17	100.07	4.49
Quebec	4.500	Dec 01/18	99.15	4.60
Quebec	9.375	Jan 16/23	147.89	4.80
Quebec	8.500	Apr 01/26	141.87	4.95
Quebec	6.000	Oct 01/29	113.59	4.96
Quebec	6.250	Jun 01/32	117.54	4.99
Quebec	5.750	Dec 01/36	111.78	4.97
Quebec	5.000	Dec 01/38	100.41	4.97
Saskat	5.500	Jun 02/08	100.27	2.87
Saskat	8.750	May 30/25	145.92	4.79
Toronto	6.100	Dec 12/17	110.96	4.67

CORPORATE

Issuer	Coupon	Maturity Date	Bid $	Yield %
AGT Lt	8.800	Sep 22/25	120.73	6.76
Bell	6.550	May 01/29	74.17	9.39

(continued)

REAL-WORLD RETURNS 11-1 *continued*

Issuer	Coupon	Maturity Date	Bid $	Yield %	Issuer	Coupon	Maturity Date	Bid $	Yield %
BMO	6.903	Jun 30/10	103.17	5.34	HydOne	7.350	Jun 03/30	122.21	5.59
BMO	6.647	Dec 31/10	103.00	5.43	HydOne	6.930	Jun 01/32	117.65	5.59
BMO	6.685	Dec 31/11	102.90	5.80	IntrAm	4.400	Jan 26/26	94.27	4.89
BMO	5.200	Jun 21/12	99.58	5.31	IPL	8.200	Feb 15/24	128.19	5.51
BMO	5.040	Sep 04/12	99.90	5.06	Loblaw	6.650	Nov 08/27	83.86	8.34
BNS	3.930	Feb 18/10	99.15	4.42	MLI	6.240	Feb 16/11	105.01	4.33
BNS	7.310	Dec 31/10	105.88	4.94	MLI	6.700	Jun 30/12	103.99	5.61
BNS	4.580	Feb 15/11	100.08	4.55	Nexen	6.300	Jun 02/08	100.23	4.04
BNS	5.250	Nov 01/12	100.23	5.19	RoyBnk	7.288	Jun 30/10	104.38	5.14
BNS	4.990	Mar 27/13	98.91	5.24	RoyBnk	5.130	Sep 27/10	101.37	4.53
BNS	4.560	Oct 30/13	97.72	5.04	RoyBnk	7.183	Jun 30/11	104.86	5.50
CIBC	3.750	Sep 09/10	97.39	4.93	RoyBnk	4.580	Apr 30/12	97.91	5.16
CIBC	4.400	Mar 07/11	99.13	4.73	RoyBnk	5.200	Aug 15/12	101.21	4.88
CIBC	4.550	Mar 28/11	98.85	4.98	RoyBnk	4.840	Mar 11/13	98.41	5.21
CIBC	4.350	Nov 01/11	98.24	4.90	SNCLav	7.700	Sep 20/10	107.50	4.38
CIBC	5.000	Sep 10/12	99.56	5.11	SunLife	6.865	Dec 31/11	105.51	5.20
Domtar	10.000	Apr 15/11	118.07	3.55	TD Bnk	7.600	Dec 31/09	104.60	4.72
GE CAP	5.730	Oct 22/37	92.56	6.29	TD Bnk	5.382	Nov 01/12	100.67	5.21
GrTAA	6.450	Dec 03/27	107.82	5.78	TD Bnk	5.141	Nov 19/12	100.92	4.91
GWLife	6.750	Aug 10/10	105.23	4.33	TD Bnk	4.779	Dec 14/16	89.39	6.40
GWLife	5.995	Dec 31/12	101.96	5.51	TD Bnk	5.763	Dec 18/17	94.32	6.57
GWLife	5.691	Jun 21/17	93.39	6.67	TorHyd	6.110	May 07/13	107.24	4.49
GWLife	6.140	Mar 21/18	105.50	5.42	UniGas	8.650	Nov 10/25	130.73	5.83
GWLife	6.740	Nov 24/31	108.77	6.04	WelFarg	4.450	Feb 28/11	100.06	4.43
GWLife	6.670	Mar 21/33	108.09	6.04	WelFarg	4.380	Jun 30/15	95.03	5.22
HSBC	7.780	Dec 31/10	106.53	5.14	Wstcoa	6.750	Dec 15/27	108.12	6.04
HydOne	7.150	Jun 03/10	106.75	3.79					
HydOne	6.400	Dec 01/11	107.81	4.05					
HydOne	5.770	Nov 15/12	106.39	4.21					

Source: www.financialpost.com, April 21, 2008.

EXAMPLE 11-4: CASH VERSUS QUOTED PRICES

Consider a bond with a $1,000 face value and an 8 percent coupon rate that is sold on July 15 at a quoted price of $980. If interest payments on this bond are made annually on July 1, the purchaser would have to pay the seller the cash price, equal to $980 plus 15 days of accrued interest at the coupon rate of 8 percent, or

Cash price = Quoted price + Accrued interest

Cash price = $980 + [($1,000) × (0.08) × (15/365)] = $980 + $3.29 = $983.29

CHECK YOUR UNDERSTANDING

11-1. Name the two cash flow components that must be discounted to determine the current price of a traditional bond. When would a bond investor receive these cash flows?

11-2. Why does the quoted price on a bond almost always differ from the "cash price" that an investor actually pays (or receives)?

BOND YIELDS

Bond yields and interest rates refer to the same concept. Therefore, we begin our discussion of the former with a brief consideration of the latter. Interest rates measure the price paid by a borrower to a lender for the use of resources over some time period—that is, interest rates are the price for the funds loaned. The price differs from case to case, based on the supply and demand for these funds, resulting in a wide variety of interest rates. The spread between the lowest and highest rates at any time could be as much as 10 to 15 percentage points. In bond parlance, this would be equivalent to 1,000 to 1,500 basis points, since one percentage point equals 100 **basis points**.

It is convenient to focus on the one interest rate that provides the foundation for other rates. This rate is referred to as the short-term riskless rate (designated RF in this text) and is typically proxied by the rate on short-term government Treasury bills. All other rates differ from RF because of two factors: maturity differentials and risk premiums.

Basis Points
100 basis points is equal to one percentage point.

The Basic Components of Interest Rates

Explaining interest rates is a complex task that involves substantial economics reasoning and study, and it is not feasible in this text. In this chapter, we analyze the basic determinants of nominal (current) interest rates with an eye toward recognizing the factors that affect such rates and cause them to fluctuate. The bond investor who understands the foundations of market rates can then rely on expert help for more details and be in a better position to interpret and evaluate such help.

The basic foundation of market interest rates is the opportunity cost of foregoing consumption, representing the rate that must be offered to individuals to persuade them to save rather than consume. This rate is sometimes called the **real risk-free rate of interest**, because it is not affected by price changes or risk factors.[2] We will refer to it simply as the *real rate* and designate it RR in this discussion.

Nominal interest rates on T-bills consist of the RR plus an adjustment for inflation. A lender who lends $100 for a year at 10 percent will be repaid $110. But if inflation is 12 percent a year, that $110 that the lender receives upon repayment of the loan is worth only $98.21(1/1.12)($110) in today's dollars. Lenders therefore expect to be compensated for the expected rate of price change in order to leave the real purchasing power of wealth unchanged or improved. As a result, interest rates display a strong relationship with inflation as discussed in Real-World Returns 11-2.

Real Risk-Free Rate of Interest
The opportunity cost of foregoing consumption, given no inflation.

Real-World Returns 11-2

Interest Rates and Inflation

Consensus has the Bank of Canada lowering its target overnight bank rate by half a percentage point when it meets tomorrow. But not all economists and market watchers are convinced of the merits of such an aggressive reduction at this time.

What to Keep an Eye On

A 50-basis point lowering would drop the overnight lending rate to 3 percent and bring the decline since the central bank started shaving the rate late last year to 1.5 percentage points. (A basis point is 1/100th of a percentage point.)

The case for a substantial rate cut was boosted last week when it was reported that the March consumer price index dropped to a 14-month low of 1.4 percent annualized, down from 1.8 percent in February, a noteworthy achievement when most other economies are facing

(continued)

[2]The real rate of interest cannot be measured directly. It is often estimated by dividing (1.0 + MIR) by (1.0 + EI), where MIR is the market interest rate and EI is expected inflation. This result can be approximated by subtracting estimates of inflation from nominal (market) interest rates (on either a realized or expected basis).

As an approximation for discussion purposes, this inflation adjustment can be added to the real risk-free rate of interest. Unlike RR, which is often assumed by market participants to be reasonably stable over time, adjustments for expected inflation vary widely. Thus, for short-term, risk-free securities, such as T-bills, the nominal interest rate is a function of the real rate of interest and the expected inflationary premium. This is expressed as Equation 11-6, which is an approximation.[3]

(11-6)
$$RF \approx RR + EI$$

where
RF = short-term T-bill rate
RR = the real risk-free rate of interest
EI = the expected rate of inflation over the term of the instrument

Equation 11-6 is known as the Fisher hypothesis (named after economist Irving Fisher). It implies that the nominal rate on short-term risk-free securities rises point-for-point with anticipated

[3]The precisely correct procedure is to multiply (1 + the real rate) by (1 + the expected rate of inflation), and subtract 1.0. For purposes of our discussion, the additive relationship is satisfactory, provided that levels of inflation are relatively low.

inflation, with the real rate of interest remaining unaffected.[4] Turning Equation 11-6 around, estimates of the real risk-free rate of interest can be approximated by subtracting the expected inflation rate from the observed nominal interest rate.[5] The expected rate of inflation can be determined by reference to various economic projections from the government, banks, and securities firms.

All market interest rates are affected by a time factor that leads to maturity differentials. That is, although long-term government bonds are virtually free from default risk in the same manner as government T-bills, they generally yield more than medium-term bonds, which, in turn, yield more than T-bills. This typical relationship between bond maturity and yield applies to all types of bonds, whether they are corporate, or federal, provincial, municipal, or government debt securities. The term structure of interest rates, discussed in Chapter 12, accounts for the relationship between time and yield—that is, the maturity differentials.

Market interest rates, other than those for riskless government securities, are also affected by a third factor, a risk premium, which lenders require as compensation for the risk involved. This risk premium is associated with the issuer's own particular situation or with a particular market factor. The risk premium is often referred to as the yield spread or yield differential.

Measuring Bond Yields

learning objective 3
Calculate major bond yield measures, including yield to maturity, yield to call, and horizon return.

Several measures of the yield on a bond are used by investors. It is very important for bond investors to understand which yield measure is being discussed and what the underlying assumptions of any particular measure are.

Current Yield

Current yield is defined as the ratio of the coupon interest to the current market price. The current yield is clearly superior to simply citing the coupon rate on a bond because it uses the current market price as opposed to the face amount of a bond (almost always, $1,000). However, current yield is not a true measure of the return to a bond purchaser because it does not account for the difference between the bond's purchase price and its eventual redemption at par value. In effect, it is a one-period rate of return that measures the interest payment return relative to the initial investment.

Current Yield
A bond's annual coupon divided by the current market price.

EXAMPLE 11-5: CALCULATING CURRENT YIELD

Consider one of the bonds listed in Real-World Returns 11-1—the Mar 08/16 Ontario bonds with the 4.4 percent coupon rate, approximately eight years remaining to maturity, and paying coupons semi-annually. The bond is selling at a small premium over par with a current market price of $1,016.40. Because of the inverse relation between bond prices and market yields, it is clear that yields have fallen since the bond was originally issued, because the price is greater than $1,000.

The current yield (CY) on this bond = $44/$1,016.40 = 4.33%

Notice that this CY is less than the coupon rate of 4.4 percent for the bond, which will always be the case for bonds selling at a premium.

Yield to Maturity

Yield to Maturity (YTM)
The promised compounded rate of return on a bond purchased at the current market price and held to maturity.

The rate of return on bonds most often quoted for investors is the **yield to maturity (YTM)**, which is defined as the *promised* compounded rate of return an investor will receive from a bond purchased at

---

[4]Fisher believed that inflation expectations were based on past observations as well as information about the future and that inflation expectations were slow to develop and slow to disappear.
[5]While estimates of the real rate associated with government funds can be made by subtracting actual inflation for the same quarter because government funds are of very short duration, estimates of real rates on instruments with longer maturities require measures of expected inflation over the term of the instrument.

the current market price and held to maturity. This is the yield that was referred to in Real-World Returns 11-1 in the previous section. It captures the coupon income to be received on the bond as well as any capital gains and losses realized by purchasing the bond for a price different from face value and holding to maturity. Similar to the internal rate of return (IRR) in financial management, the yield to maturity is the periodic interest rate that equates the present value of the expected future cash flows (both coupons and face value) to be received on the bond to the initial investment in the bond, which is its current price.

To calculate the yield to maturity for a bond, we use Equation 11-5, where the market price, the coupon, the number of years to maturity, and the face value of the bond are known, and the discount rate or yield to maturity is the variable to be determined.

$$P = C \times (PVA_{YTM,n}) + F \times (PV_{YTM,n})$$

Since both the left-hand side of Equation 11-5 and the numerator values (cash flows) on the right side are known, the equation can be solved for YTM. When the bond pays semi-annual coupons, all terms are expressed in terms of six-month periods. (The resulting semi-annual rate must be doubled to obtain the annual YTM.)

To estimate the YTM requires a trial-and-error process to find the discount rate that equates the inflows from the bond (coupons plus face value) with its current price (cost). Different rates are tried until the left-hand and right-hand sides are equal. It is relatively easy today to find financial calculators or computer programs to solve YTM problems. We illustrate a simple example of the trial-and-error process involved in a yield-to-maturity calculation by referring to the present value tables at the end of the text. The purpose is simply to demonstrate conceptually how to calculate the YTM. Investors will normally use a calculator, computer, or the approximation formula described below to do computations such as these.

EXAMPLE 11-6: CALCULATING YIELD TO MATURITY

Consider the eight-year, 4.4 percent bond in Example 11-5 that was selling for $1,016.40. Because of the inverse relation between bond prices and market yields, it is clear that yields have fallen somewhat since the bond was originally issued, because the price is greater than $1,000. Using Equation 11-5 to determine yield to maturity,

$1,016.40 = $22.00 \times (PVA_{YTM,16}) + $1,000 \times (PV_{YTM,16})$

Trying a semi-annual rate of 2.08 percent for YTM, we get

$1,016.40 = $22.00 \times (PVA_{2.08\%,16}) + $1,000 \times (PV_{2.08\%,16})$

$1,016.40 = $22.00 (13.49206) + $1,000 (0.67362)$

$1,016.40 \approx $1,016.19$ (difference due to rounding error)

In this example, the solution is approximately 2.08 percent on a semi-annual basis, which by convention is doubled to obtain the annual YTM of 4.16 percent. However, since the price calculated using 4.16 percent is too low, we know the true YTM is "slightly" below 4.16 percent (and in fact the reported value is 4.15%).

The example above was simplistic because we were able to approximate a discount rate that equated the present value of the future cash flows almost exactly with its price. In practice, the trial-and-error process will be much more complicated and time consuming.[6]

In practice, every basis point counts and we need to be able to estimate the YTM more precisely. This is where it pays to know how to use your financial calculator! The following example shows how you can use a financial calculator to estimate the YTM of a bond, using the previous example.

[6]One commonly used approach for estimating the appropriate rate involves the use of an estimation technique referred to as linear interpolation, which students may have come across in other quantitative courses.

EXAMPLE 11-7: CALCULATING YIELD TO MATURITY BY FINANCIAL CALCULATOR

Consider again the eight-year, 4.4 percent bond in the previous example that is selling at $1,016.40. We can calculate its YTM using a financial calculator as follows:

Inputs:

PMT = 22.00; n = 16; FV = 1000; PV = −1016.40 (be sure to make the PV negative or make both FV and PMT negative for this calculator; for other calculators it may not be necessary).

Then we compute (CPT) i, which gives i = 2.078 (which is a semi-annual rate).

Annualizing this rate, we get YTM = 2.078% × 2 = 4.156%.

Current Yield, Yield to Maturity, and Coupon Rates

Notice that the YTM of 4.16 percent for the bond in Example 11-7 is below its current yield of 4.33 percent (as calculated for this bond in Example 11-5), which is in turn below the bond's coupon rate of 4.4 percent. This will always be the case for bonds selling at a premium (i.e., coupon rate > current yield > YTM). The relationship will be reversed for bonds selling at a discount, while all three rates will be equal only when bonds are selling at par. These relationships are expressed in the box below:

If: Coupon Rate > Current Yield > YTM	⟶	Bond is selling at a **Premium**
If: Coupon Rate = Current Yield = YTM	⟶	Bond is at **Par**
If: Coupon Rate < Current Yield < YTM	⟶	Bond is selling at a **Discount**

The YTM calculation for a zero-coupon bond is based on the same process shown in Equation 11-5—equating the current price to the future cash flows. Because there are no coupons, the process reduces to Equation 11-7, with all terms as previously defined, and n is generally expressed in semi-annual periods, producing an estimate for the semi-annual YTM:

$$YTM = [F/P]^{1/n} - 1$$

(11-7)

EXAMPLE 11-8 CALCULATING YTM FOR ZERO-COUPON BONDS

A zero-coupon bond has 12 years to maturity and is sold for $300. Given the 24 semi-annual periods to maturity, the power to be used in raising the ratio of $1,000/$300, or 3.333, is 0.04167 (calculated as 1/24). Using a calculator with a power function produces a value of 1.0514. Subtracting the 1.0 and multiplying by 100 leaves a semi-annual yield of 5.145 percent. Because YTM numbers are usually stated on an annual basis, this figure is doubled, which produces an annual yield of 10.29 percent.

It is important to understand that YTM is a promised yield, because investors earn the indicated yield only if the bond is held to maturity and the coupons are reinvested at the calculated YTM. Obviously, no trading can be done for a particular bond if the YTM is to be earned. The investor simply buys and holds. What is not so obvious to many investors, however, is the reinvestment implications of the YTM measure. Because of the importance of the reinvestment rate, we consider it in more detail by analyzing the reinvestment risk.

Yield to Call

Most corporate, as well as some government, bonds are callable by the issuers after some deferred call period. For bonds likely to be called, the yield-to-maturity calculation is an inappropriate measure of

Yield to Call

The promised return on a bond from the present to the date that the bond is first eligible to be called.

its expected return. A better measure in such situations is the promised **yield to call**. The end of the period when a bond can first be called is often used for the yield-to-call calculation. This yield is particularly appropriate for bonds selling at a premium (i.e., high-coupon bonds with market prices above par value) since they are highly likely to be called by the issuer at the first available call date.[7]

To calculate the yield to first call, the YTM formula (Equation 11-5) is used, but with the number of periods until the first call date substituted for the number of periods until maturity and the call price substituted for face value. These changes are shown in Equation 11-8.

(11-8)

$$P = C \times (PVA_{YTC,c}) + CP \times (PV_{YTC,c})$$

where

c = the number of periods until the first call date

YTC = the yield to first call

CP = the call price to be paid if the bond is called

Bond prices are calculated on the basis of the lowest yield measure. Therefore, for premium bonds selling above a certain level, yield to call replaces yield to maturity, because it produces the lowest (and most appropriate) measure of yield.[8]

EXAMPLE 11-9: CALCULATING YIELD TO CALL

Consider the eight-year, 4.4 percent bond used in the previous examples that is selling for $1,016.40. Assuming this bond is callable after four years at a call price of $1,050, we can estimate its first yield to call (YTC) using a financial calculator as follows:

Inputs:
PMT = 22.00; n = 8 (i.e., number of periods to first call date or c); FV = 1050 (i.e., the call price or CP); PV = −1016.40
Then CPT i gives us i = 2.542 (which is a semi-annual rate).
Annualizing this rate, we get YTC = 2.542% × 2 = 5.084%.

Notice that for this example, the bond would be priced using the YTM of 4.16 percent, since it is lower than the YTC. This is because the call price is above the current market price, and thus the bond is not likely to be called unless interest rates decline before the call date.

Reinvestment Risk

Interest on Interest

The process by which bond coupons are reinvested to earn interest.

The YTM calculation assumes that the investor reinvests all coupons received from a bond at a rate equal to the computed YTM on that bond, thereby earning **interest on interest** over the life of the bond at the computed YTM rate. In effect, this calculation assumes that the reinvestment rate is the yield to maturity.

If the investor spends the coupons, or reinvests them at a rate different from the assumed reinvestment rate, the realized yield that will actually be earned at the end of the investment in the bond will differ from the promised YTM. And, in fact, coupons almost always will be reinvested at rates higher or lower than the computed YTM, resulting in a realized yield that differs from the promised yield. This gives rise to **reinvestment rate risk**.

Reinvestment Rate Risk

That part of interest rate risk resulting from uncertainty about the rate at which future interest coupons can be reinvested.

---

[7]That is, bonds with high coupons (and high yields) are prime candidates to be called.

[8]The technical name for the point at which yield to call comes into play is the "crossover point," which is a price and is approximately the sum of par value and one year's interest. For a discussion of this point, see S. Homer and M. Leibowitz, *Inside the Yield Book* (Englewood Cliffs, NJ: Prentice Hall, 1972), Chapter 4.

This interest-on-interest concept significantly affects the potential total dollar return. The exact impact is a function of coupon and time to maturity, with reinvestment becoming more important as either coupon or time to maturity, or both, rises. Holding everything else constant

- the longer the maturity of a bond, the greater the reinvestment risk; and
- the higher the coupon rate, the greater the dependence of the total dollar return from the bond on the reinvestment of the coupon payments.

To illustrate the importance of interest on interest in YTM calculations, Table 11-1 shows the realized yields under different assumed reinvestment rates for a 10 percent non-callable 20-year bond purchased at face value of $1,000. If the reinvestment rate exactly equals the YTM of 10 percent, the investor would realize a 10 percent compound return when the bond is held to maturity, with $4,040 of the total dollar return from the bond attributable to interest on interest. At a 12 percent reinvestment rate, the investor would realize an 11.14 percent compound return, with almost 75 percent of the total return coming from interest on interest ($5,738/$7,738). With no reinvestment of coupons (spending them as received), the investor would achieve only a 5.57 percent return. In all cases, the bond is held to maturity.

Clearly, the reinvestment portion of the YTM concept is critical. In fact, for long-term bonds the interest-on-interest component of the total realized yield may account for more than three-quarters of the bond's total dollar return.

INVESTING *tip*

Consider what happens when investors purchase bonds at high YTMs, such as when interest rates reached exceptionally high levels in the summer of 1982. Unless they reinvested the coupons at the promised YTMs, investors did not actually realize these high promised yields. For that to happen, coupons had to be reinvested at the record rates existing at that time, an unlikely situation especially for a high-YTM bond with a long maturity. The subsequent decline in interest rates during the fall of 1982 illustrates the fallacy of believing that one has "locked up" record yields during a relatively brief period of very high interest rates. On the other hand, if the investor chose to sell the bond before maturity, it would sell at a premium as a result of falling interest rates, resulting in capital gains.

Table 11-1

Realized Yields, Using Different Reinvestment Rate Assumptions, for a 10 Percent 20-Year Bond Purchased at Face Value of $1,000

Coupon Income[a] ($)	Assumed Reinvestment Rate (%)	Amount Attributable to Reinvestment[b] ($)	Total Return[c] ($)	Realized Yields[d] (%)
2000	0	0	2000	5.57
2000	5	1370	3370	7.51
2000	8	2751	4751	8.94
2000	9	3352	5352	9.46
2000	10	4040	6040	10.00
2000	11	4830	6830	10.56
2000	12	5738	7738	11.14

[a]Coupon income = $50 coupon received *semi-annually* for 20 years = $50 × 40 periods.

[b]Amount attributable to reinvestment = total return minus coupon income. This is also known as the interest on interest.

[c]Total return = sum of an annuity for 40 periods, $50 semi-annual coupons (Example: at 10 percent reinvestment rate, $50 × [5 percent, 40 period factor of 120.80] = $6,040.)

[d]Realized yield = [Future Value per Dollar Invested]$^{1/N}$ − 1, where future value per dollar invested = (total return + the selling price of bond) / cost of the bond. The result of this calculation is the potential yield on a semi-annual basis. To put this on an annual basis, this figure must be doubled. This has been done for the yields in Table 11-1.

The realized yield (RY) shown in Table 11-1 can be calculated using the following formula: (Note that RY assumes a constant reinvestment rate.)

(11-9)

$$RY = \left[\frac{\text{Total future dollars}}{\text{Purchase price of bond}} \right]^{1/n} - 1.0$$

EXAMPLE 11-10: CALCULATING REALIZED YIELD

For the bond calculations shown in Table 11-1, consider the yield an investor would achieve at an assumed reinvestment rate of 12 percent. The total future dollars equals the total dollar return shown in Table 11-1, $7,738, plus the selling price of the bond, $1,000, or $8,738. Therefore,

$$RY = [\$8{,}738/1{,}000]^{1/40} - 1.0$$

$$= [8.738]^{.025} - 1 = 1.05569 - 1.0$$

$$= 0.05569, \text{ or } 5.569\% \text{ on a semi-annual basis}$$

$$(= 11.14\% \text{ on an annual basis}).$$

One advantage of a zero-coupon bond is the elimination of reinvestment rate risk because there are no coupons to be reinvested. At the time of purchase, investors know the YTM that will be realized when the bond is held to maturity.

Horizon Return

Horizon Return

Bond returns to be earned based on assumptions about future reinvestment rates.

Bond investors today often make specific assumptions about future reinvestment rates in order to cope with the reinvestment rate problem illustrated earlier. This is sometimes referred to as horizon analysis. Given their explicit assumption about the reinvestment rate, investors can calculate the **horizon return** to be earned if that assumption turns out to be accurate.

The investor makes an assumption about the reinvestment rate expected to prevail over the planned investment horizon. The investor may also make an assumption about the yield to maturity expected to prevail at the end of the planned investment horizon, which in turn is used to estimate the price of the bond at that time. Based on these assumptions, the total future dollars expected to be available at the end of the planned investment horizon can be determined. The horizon return is then calculated as the interest rate that equates the total future dollars to the purchase price of the bond.

CHECK YOUR UNDERSTANDING

11-3. Justify the fact that the coupon rate is greater than the current yield, which in turn is greater than the yield to maturity, whenever a bond sells at a premium.

11-4. "Investors are routinely quoted the yield to maturity on a bond, but the chances of actually earning this quoted yield at the termination of the investment is almost zero." Do you agree with this statement? Explain your reasoning.

11-5. Assume that an investor holds a bond guaranteed not to default. Can the YTM on this bond be described as the actual return the investor will receive rather than a promised return?

BOND PRICE CHANGES

learning objective 4
Account for changes in bond prices.

Bond Price Changes Over Time

We know how to calculate the price of a bond using the cash flows to be received and the YTM as the discount rate. Assume that we calculate the price of a 20-year bond issued five years ago and discover that it is $910. The bond still has 15 years to maturity. What can we say about its price over the next 15 years?

When everything else is held constant, including market interest rates, any bond price that differs from the bond's face value (assumed to be $1,000) must change over time. Why? On a bond's specified maturity date, it must be worth its par or face value. Therefore, over time, holding all other factors constant, a bond's price must converge to $1,000 on the maturity date. In other words, the bond's price is "pulled to par."

After bonds are issued, they sell at discounts from par (prices less than $1,000) and premiums over par (prices greater than $1,000) during their lifetimes. Therefore, holding all other factors constant, a bond selling at a discount will experience a rise in price over time, and a bond selling at a premium will experience a decline in price over time as the bond's remaining life approaches the maturity date.

Figure 11-1 illustrates bond price movements over time, assuming constant yields. Bond 2 depicts a 10 percent coupon, 30-year bond assuming that yields remain constant at 10 percent. The price of this bond does not change, beginning and ending at $1,000. Bond 1, on the other hand, depicts an 8 percent coupon, 30-year bond assuming that required yields start, and remain constant, at 10 percent. The price starts below $1,000 because bond 1 is selling at a discount as a result of its coupon of 8 percent being less than the required yield of 10 percent. Bond 3 illustrates a 30-year bond with a 12 percent coupon, assuming that required yields start and remain constant at 10 percent. The price of bond 3 begins above $1,000 because it is selling at a premium (12 percent is greater than the required yield of 10 percent).

If all other factors are held constant, the price of all three bonds must converge to $1,000 on the maturity date. In actuality, however, other factors do *not* remain constant. In particular, interest rates or yields to maturity change constantly, as do bond prices. Furthermore, the sensitivity of the price change is a function of certain variables, especially coupon and maturity. We now examine these variables.

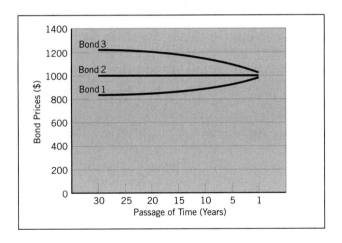

Figure 11-1
Bond Price Movements
Over Time Assuming
Constant Yields of
10 Percent for Three
30-Year Bonds

Bond Price Changes as a Result of Interest Rate Changes

Bond prices change with interest rates and required yields. Understanding how bond prices change in relation to interest rates is critical to successful bond management. The basics of bond price movements as a result of interest rate changes have been known for many years. For example, over 30 years ago, Burton Malkiel derived five theorems about the relationship between bond prices and yields.[9] Using the bond valuation model, he showed the changes that occur in the price of a bond (i.e., its volatility) given a change in yields, as a result of bond variables such as time to maturity and coupon. We will use Malkiel's bond theorems to illustrate how interest rate changes affect bond prices.

[9]B. G. Malkiel, "Expectations, Bond Prices, and the Term Structure of Interest Rates," *Quarterly Journal of Economics*, May 1962, pp. 197–218.

Bond Prices Move Inversely to Interest Rates

Investors must always keep in mind a fundamental fact about the relationship between bond prices and bond yields: Bond prices move inversely to market yields. When the level of required yields demanded by investors on new bond issues changes, the required yields on all bonds already outstanding will also change. For these yields to change, the prices of these bonds must change, since the coupon and maturity payments are fixed when the bond is originally issued. This inverse relationship, which was evident in the bond valuation examples presented earlier in the chapter, is the basis for understanding, valuing, and managing bonds.

Table 11-2 shows prices for a 10 percent coupon bond for market yields from 6 to 14 percent and for maturity dates from one to 30 years. For any given maturity, the price of the bond declines as the required yield increases and increases as the required yield declines from the 10 percent level. Figure 11-2 shows this relationship using data from Table 11-2.

An interesting corollary of the inverse relationship between bond prices and interest rates is as follows: *Holding maturity constant, a decrease in rates will raise bond prices on a percentage basis more than a corresponding increase in rates will lower bond prices.*

EXAMPLE 11-11: BOND PRICES AND INTEREST RATE CHANGES

Table 11-2 shows that for the 15-year, 10 percent coupon bond, the price would be $1,172.92 if market rates were to decline from 10 percent to 8 percent, resulting in a price appreciation of 17.29 percent. On the other hand, a rise of two percentage points in market rates from 10 percent to 12 percent results in a change in price to $862.35, a price decline of only 13.77 percent.

Obviously, bond price volatility can work for, as well as against, investors. Money can be made (and lost) in low-risk government bonds as well as more risky corporate bonds.

Table 11-2

Bond Price and Market Yields for a 10 Percent Coupon Bond

Years to Maturity	Bond Prices at Different Market Yields and Maturities				
	6%	8%	10%	12%	14%
1	$1,038.27	$1,018.86	$1,000	$981.67	$963.84
5	1,170.60	1,081.11	1,000	926.40	859.53
10	1,297.55	1,135.90	1,000	885.30	788.12
15	1,392.01	1,172.92	1,000	862.35	751.82
20	1,462.30	1,197.93	1,000	849.54	733.37
25	1,514.60	1,214.82	1,000	842.38	723.99
30	1,553.51	1,226.23	1,000	838.39	719.22

Although the inverse relationship between bond prices and interest rates is the basis of all bond analysis, a complete understanding of that relationship requires additional information. An increase in interest rates will cause bond prices to decline, but the exact amount of decline will depend on important variables unique to each bond such as time to maturity and coupon. We will examine each of these in turn.

The Effects of Maturity

The effect of a change in yields on bond prices depends on the maturity of the bond. An important principle is that for a given change in market yields, changes in bond prices are directly related to time to maturity. Therefore, as interest rates change, the prices of longer-term bonds will change more than the prices of shorter-term ones, everything else being equal.

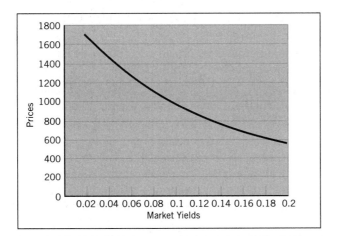

Figure 11-2
The Relationship between
Bond Prices and Market
Yields

EXAMPLE 11-12: MATURITY AND BOND PRICES

Given two 10 percent coupon bonds and a drop in market yields from 10 to 8 percent, we can see from Table 11-2 that the price of the 15-year bond will be $1,172.92, while that of the 30-year bond will be $1,226.23.

The principle illustrated here is simple but important. Other things being equal, bond price volatility is a function of maturity. Long-term bond prices fluctuate more than short-term ones. A related principle regarding maturity can be stated as follows: *The percentage price change that occurs as a result of the direct relationship between a bond's maturity and its price volatility increases at a diminishing rate as the time to maturity increases.*

EXAMPLE 11-13: MATURITY AND PRICE VOLATILITY

As we saw above, a two percentage point drop in market yields (from 10 to 8 percent) increased the price of the 15-year bond to $1,172.92, a 17.29 percent change, while the price of the 30-year bond changed to $1,226.23, a 22.62 percent change.

This example shows that the percentage of price change resulting from an increase in time to maturity increases, but at a decreasing rate. Put simply, a doubling of the time to maturity will not result in a doubling of the percentage price change resulting from a change in market yields.

The Effects of Coupon

In addition to the maturity effect, the change in the price of a bond as a result of a change in interest rates depends on the coupon rate of the bond. We can state this principle as follows (other things being equal): *Bond price fluctuations (volatility) and bond coupon rates are inversely related.* Note that we are talking about percentage price fluctuations; this relationship does not necessarily hold if we measure volatility in terms of dollar price changes rather than percentage price changes. This result is intuitive since a greater proportion of total income on higher coupon bonds is received in earlier periods; therefore the discount rate effect is lower for such bonds.

The Implications of Malkiel's Theorems for Investors

Malkiel's derivations for bond investors lead to the practical conclusion that the two bond variables of major importance in assessing the change in the price of a bond, given a change in interest rates, are its coupon and its maturity. This conclusion can be summarized as follows: A decline in interest rates will cause a rise in bond prices (and vice versa), with the most volatility in bond prices occurring in longer maturity bonds and bonds with low coupons. Therefore

1. A bond buyer, in order to receive the maximum price impact for an expected change in interest rates, should purchase low-coupon, long-maturity bonds.

2. If an increase in interest rates is expected (or feared), an investor contemplating their purchase should consider bonds with large coupons, short maturities, or both.

These relationships provide useful information for bond investors by demonstrating how the price of a bond changes with interest rates. Although investors have no control over the change and direction in market rates, they can exercise control over the coupon and maturity, both of which have significant effects on bond price changes. Nevertheless, it is cumbersome to calculate various possible price changes on the basis of these theorems. Furthermore, maturity is an inadequate measure of the sensitivity of a bond's price change to changes in yields because it ignores the coupon payments and the principal repayment.

Investors managing bond portfolios need a measure of time designed to more accurately portray a bond's "average" life, taking into account all of the bond's cash flows, including both coupons and the return of principal at maturity. Such a measure—called duration—is available and is widely used.

CHECK YOUR UNDERSTANDING

11-6. "The price of a bond is certain to change if it is selling for either a discount or a premium." Do you agree with this statement?

11-7. We know that the prices of long-term bonds are more sensitive to interest rate changes than the prices of short-term bonds. Why then, is maturity alone not sufficient to measure interest rate sensitivity?

Measuring Bond Price Volatility: Duration

learning objective 5
Explain and apply the concept of duration.

In managing a bond portfolio, perhaps the most important consideration is the effect of yield changes on the prices and rates of return for different bonds. The problem is that a given change in interest rates can result in very different percentage price changes for the various bonds that investors hold. We saw earlier that both maturity and coupon affect bond price changes for a given change in yields.

Although maturity is the traditional measure of a bond's lifetime, it is inadequate because it focuses only on the return of principal at the maturity date. Two 20-year bonds, one with an 8 percent coupon and the other with a 15 percent coupon, do not have identical economic lifetimes. An investor will recover the original purchase price much sooner with the 15 percent coupon bond. Therefore, a measure is needed that accounts for the entire pattern (both size and timing) of the cash flows over the life of the bond—the effective maturity of the bond. Such a concept, called duration, was conceived over 50 years ago by Frederick Macaulay.[10] Duration is very useful for bond management purposes because it combines the properties of maturity and coupon.

Duration Defined

Duration
A measure of a bond's economic lifetime based on the weighted present value of expected cash flows over the life of the bond.

Duration measures the weighted average maturity of a bond's cash flows on a present value basis; that is, the present values of the cash flows are used as the weights in calculating the weighted average maturity. Thus,

Duration = number of years needed to fully recover purchase price of a bond, given present values of its future cash flows

= weighted average time to recovery of all interest payments plus principal[11]

---

[10]F. R. Macaulay, *Some Theoretical Problems Suggested by the Movement of Interest Rates, Bond Yields and Stock Prices in the United States Since 1856* (New York: National Bureau of Economic Research, 1938).
[11]This discussion applies only to option-free bonds.

Figure 11-3 illustrates the concepts of both time to maturity and duration for a bond with five years to maturity, a 10 percent coupon, and selling for $1,000. As the figure indicates, the stream of cash flows generated by this bond over the term to maturity consists of $50 every six months, or $100 per year, plus the return of principal of $1,000 at the end of the five years. The last cash flow combines the interest payment of $50 with the principal repayment of $1,000 that occurs at the maturity date.

Although the term to maturity for the bond illustrated in Figure 11-3 is five years, its Macaulay duration is only 4.17 years as indicated by the arrow. This means that the weighted average maturity of the bond's cash flows is 4.17 years from the beginning date. It is important that we understand how this duration value is calculated.

Calculating Duration

To calculate Macaulay duration, it is necessary to consider a weighted time period. The time periods at which the cash flows are received are expressed in terms of years and denoted by CF_t in this discussion. When all of these cash flows (CF_ts) have been weighted and added together, the result is the duration, stated in years.

The present values of the cash flows serve as the weighting factors to apply to the time periods. Each weighting factor shows the relative importance of each cash flow to the bond's total present value, which is simply its current market price. The sum of the weighting factors will be 1.0, indicating that all cash flows have been accounted for. Putting this all together gives us the equation for duration:

$$\text{Macaulay Duration} = D = \sum_{t=1}^{n} \frac{PV(CF_t)}{\text{Market price}} \times t \qquad \textbf{(11-10)}$$

where

t	= the year at which the cash flow is expected to be received
n	= the number of years to maturity
$PV(CF_t)$	= value of the cash flow in period t discounted at the annual yield to maturity
Market price	= the bond's current price (or the present value of all the cash flows)

As Equation 11-10 shows, duration is obtained by multiplying each year's weighted cash receipt (weighted by the price of the bond) by the number of years when each is to be received, and adding. Note that duration is measured in years, and that for ease of exposition, we state the equation on an annual basis although interest on bonds is often paid semi-annually.

EXAMPLE 11-14: CALCULATING DURATION

Table 11-3 provides an example of calculating the duration for a bond, using the same bond as shown in Figure 11-3, except now for ease of exposition, the calculation is done on an annual basis. This is a 10 percent coupon bond with five years remaining to maturity. The bond is priced at $1,000 for simplicity, and the YTM is 10 percent.[12]

---

[12]A shortcut formula can be used for coupon bonds selling at face value:

$$\text{Duration} = \frac{1 + YTM}{YTM}[1 - (1/(1 + YTM)^n)]$$

Using a semi-annual rate and doubling the number of periods, we must divide the answer by 2.0 to put it on an annual basis.

Figure 11-3
Illustration of the
Cash Flow Pattern of a
10 Percent Coupon,
Five-Year Maturity Bond
Paying Interest Semi-
Annually and Returning
the Principal of $1,000
at Maturity

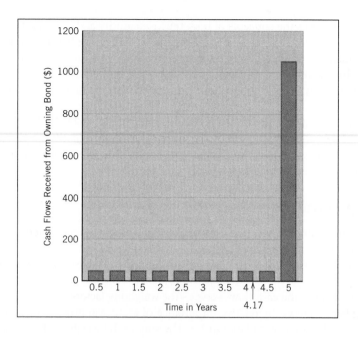

The cash flows consist of five $100 coupons plus the return of principal at the end of the fifth year. Notice that the fifth-year cash flow of $1,100 ($100 coupon plus $1,000 return of principal) accounts for 68 percent of the value of the bond and contributes 3.42 years to the duration of 4.17 years. In this example, the other cash flows combined contributed less than one year to the duration. The duration of 4.17 years is almost one year less than the term to maturity of five years. As we will see, duration will always be less than time to maturity for bonds that pay coupons.

Table 11-3

An Example of Calculating the Duration of a Bond Using a 10 Percent Coupon, Five-Year Maturity Bond Priced at $1,000 and Paying Annual Interest

(1) Years	(2) Cash Flow	(3) PV Factor	(4) $ (2) × (3)	(5) (4) / Price	(6) (1) × (5)
1	$100	.909	90.90	.0909	.0909
2	100	.826	82.60	.0826	.1652
3	100	.751	75.10	.0751	.2253
4	100	.683	68.30	.0683	.2732
5	1100	.621	683.10	.6831	3.4155
					Duration = 4.1701

Understanding Duration

How is duration related to the key bond variables previously analyzed? An examination of Equation 11-10 shows that the calculation of duration depends on three factors:

1. The maturity date of the bond

2. Coupon payments

3. Yield to maturity.

1. *The maturity date of the bond.* Holding the size of coupon payments and the yield to maturity constant, duration expands with time to maturity but at a decreasing rate, particularly beyond 15 years to maturity. Even between five and 10 years time to maturity, duration is expanding at a significantly lower rate than was the case before the five-year mark, where it expands rapidly.[13] Note that for all coupon-paying bonds, duration is always less than maturity. For a zero-coupon bond, duration is equal to time to maturity.

2. *Coupon payments.* Holding maturity and yield to maturity constant, coupon is inversely related to duration. This is logical because higher coupons lead to quicker recovery of the bond's value, resulting in a shorter duration, relative to lower coupons.

3. *Yield to maturity.* Holding coupon payments and maturity constant, yield to maturity is inversely related to duration.

Why is duration important in bond management and analysis? First, it tells us the difference between the effective lives of alternative bonds. Bonds A and B, with the same duration but different years to maturity, have more in common than bonds C and D with the same maturity but different durations. For any particular bond, as maturity increases the duration grows at a decreasing rate.[14]

EXAMPLE 11-15: DURATION AND TERM TO MATURITY

Given the 10 percent coupon bond discussed above with a yield to maturity of 10 percent and a five-year life, we saw that the duration was 4.17 years. If the maturity of this bond was 10 years, it would have an effective life (duration) of 6.76 years, and with a 20-year maturity it would have an effective life of 9.36 years—quite a different perspective. Furthermore, under these conditions, a 50-year maturity for this bond would change the effective life to only 10.91 years. The reason for the sharp differences between the term to maturity and the duration is that cash flows received in the distant future have very small present values and therefore add little to a bond's value.

Second, the duration concept is used in certain bond management strategies, particularly immunization, as explained later in the chapter.

Third, duration is a measure of bond price sensitivity to interest rate movements, a very important part of any bond analysis. Malkiel's bond price theorems are inadequate to examine all aspects of bond price sensitivity. This issue is considered in some detail below because of its potential importance to bond investors.

Estimating Price Changes Using Duration

The real value of the duration measure to bond investors is that it combines coupon and maturity, the two key variables that investors must consider in response to expected changes in interest rates. As noted earlier, duration is related positively to maturity and negatively to coupon. However, bond price changes are directly related to duration; that is, the percentage change in a bond's price, given a change in interest rates, is proportional to its duration. The reason for this relationship is that Macaulay's duration can be derived by taking the first derivative of the bond pricing equation with respect to $(1+r)$. Most students who have studied calculus will recall that the first derivative of a function (in this case the bond pricing equation) is its slope. The slope, in turn, measures the responsiveness of the function value (or the bond price) with respect to changes in the chosen variable [in this case $(1+r)$]. Therefore, duration can be used to measure interest rate exposure.

[13]The duration of a perpetuity is $(1 + YTM)/YTM$. This indicates that maturity and duration can differ greatly since the maturity of a perpetuity is infinite, but duration is not. That is, perpetuities have an infinite maturity but a finite duration.
[14]Deep discount bonds are an exception to the general rule. Their duration first increases with time to maturity, up to some distant point, and then decreases in duration beyond this point. This is because deep discount bonds with very long maturities behave like perpetuities.

Modified Duration
Duration divided by
(1 + yield to maturity).

(11-11)

The term **modified duration** refers to Macaulay's duration in Equation 11-10 divided by $(1+r)$, or

$$\text{Modified duration} = D^* = D / (1 + r)$$

where
D^* = modified duration
r = the bond's yield to maturity

EXAMPLE 11-16: CALCULATING MODIFIED DURATION

Using the duration of 4.17 years calculated earlier and the YTM of 10 percent, the modified duration based on annual interest would be

$$D^* = 4.17 / (1 + 0.10) = 3.79$$

The modified duration can be used to calculate the percentage price change in a bond for a given change in r, using Equation 11-12, which is an approximation:[15]

(11-12)

$$\text{Percentage change in bond price} \approx \frac{-D}{(1 + r)} \times \text{Percentage point change in } r$$

or

(11-13)

$$\Delta P/P \approx -D^*\Delta r$$

where
ΔP = change in price
P = the price of the bond
$-D^*$ = modified duration with a negative sign
Δr = the instantaneous change in yield

EXAMPLE 11-17: MODIFIED DURATION AND CHANGES IN BOND

Using our same bond with a modified duration of 3.79, assume an instantaneous yield change of 20 basis points (+0.0020) in the YTM, from 10 to 10.20 percent. The approximate change in price, based on Equation 11-13, would be

$$\Delta/P = -(3.79)(+0.0020)(100) = -0.758\%$$

Given the original price of the bond of $1,000, this percentage price change would result in an estimated bond price of $992.42. This is very close to the price of $992.32 (0.768 percent decline) that we would get if we determined the bond price based on a YTM of 10.20 percent using the bond valuation equation. For very small changes in yield, Equations 11-12 or 11-13 provide good approximations. However, for larger changes, such as 100 or 200 basis points, the approximate percentage price change is less accurate. This is because the relationship is derived using the first derivative of the bond valuation equation. First derivatives measure the slope of a function (bond prices in this case) accurately over small intervals or for small changes in the variable that is being allowed to vary (interest rates in this case).

An alternative measure of duration, called *effective duration*, is equivalent to modified duration for option-free bonds. It has the additional benefit that it may also be used for measuring price volatility of bonds with options such as callable or retractable features attached. This method of estimating

[15]This formula provides a reasonable approximation for "option-free" bonds if the change in yield is very small, and if the yield curve undergoes a parallel shift in rates.

duration, along with a method for estimating *effective convexity*, is presented in Appendix 11B. These approaches are used extensively in the current CFA curriculum.

Convexity

Although Equation 11-12 is only an approximation for very small changes in the required yield, the approximation is quite close. However, as the changes become larger, the approximation becomes poorer. The problem is that modified duration produces symmetric percentage price change estimates using Equation 11-10 (if *r* had decreased 0.20 percent, the price change would have been +0.758 percent), when, in actuality, the price–yield relationship is not linear. This relationship is, in fact, convex, and calculations of price changes should properly account for the convexity of the price–yield relationship. **Convexity** is the term used to refer to the degree to which duration changes as the yield to maturity changes.[16]

To understand the convexity issue, Figure 11-4 repeats the analysis from Figure 11-2 that shows a 10 percent coupon bond at different market yields and prices. We can think of modified duration graphically as the slope of a line that is tangent to the convex price–yield curve of Figure 11-4 at the current price and yield of the bond, which is assumed to be $1,000 and 10 percent.[17]

In effect, we are using a tangent line to measure the slope of the curve that depicts the inverse relationship between bond price and yield. For a very small change in yield, such as a few basis points, the slope of the line—the modified duration—provides a good approximation for the rate of change in price, given a change in yield. As the change in yield increases, the error that results from using a straight line to estimate a bond's price behaviour as given by a curve increases.[18]

As we move away from the point of tangency in Figure 11-4 in either direction, we underestimate the price of the bond using modified duration; that is, the price change is always more favourable than suggested by the modified duration. Notice that the shaded area in Figure 11-4 captures the convexity areas both above and below the starting point of 10 percent and $1,000. If yields decrease, prices increase, and the duration tangent line fails to indicate the true higher price. Conversely, when yields increase, prices decrease, but the duration tangent line overstates the amount of the price decrease relative to the true convex relationship. This helps illustrate what is meant by the term positive convexity.

Convexity

A measure of the degree to which the relationship between a bond's price and yield departs from the straight line; that is, the degree to which duration changes as the yield to maturity changes.

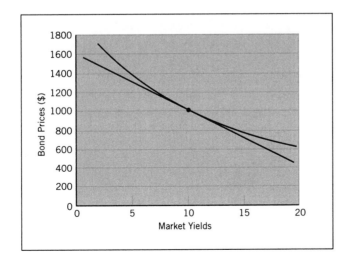

Figure 11-4
Convex Relationship between Yields and Prices and Tangent Line Representing Modified Duration for a 10 Percent, 10-Year Bond

[16]An in-depth discussion of convexity is beyond the scope of this text; however, we would note that it is derived by taking the second derivative of the bond valuation equation with respect to interest rates. For a more detailed discussion, see F. J. Fabozzi and T. D. Fabozzi, *The Handbook of Fixed Income Securities*, Fifth Edition (Irwin Professional Publishing, 1997).
[17]Technically, the slope of the tangent line in Figure 11-4 is equal to the negative of modified duration multiplied by the bond's current market price.
[18]As the yield changes, the tangency line and slope also change; that is, modified duration changes as yield changes.

Convexity is largest for low coupon bonds, long-maturity bonds, and low yields to maturity. If convexity is large, extensive changes in duration are implied, with corresponding inaccuracies in forecasts of price changes. Convexity calculations can be made similar to those with modified duration discussed earlier. These calculations produce an approximate percentage price change due to convexity that can be added to the one based on duration discussed earlier. This total percentage price change is still an approximation, but it is considerably improved over that using only duration.

Some Conclusions on Duration

What does this analysis of price volatility mean to bond investors? The message is simple—to have the maximum (minimum) price volatility from a bond, investors should choose bonds with the longest (shortest) duration. If an investor already owns a portfolio of bonds, he or she can act to increase the duration of the portfolio if a decline in interest rates is expected and the investor is attempting to achieve the largest price appreciation possible. Fortunately, duration is additive, which means that a bond portfolio's duration is a weighted average of each individual bond's duration.

The duration concept has become so popular in today's investment world that it is widely known and discussed in the popular press. Investors can find duration numbers in a variety of sources, particularly with regard to bond funds. As Real-World Returns 11-3 suggests, investors should basically forget maturity and think in terms of duration.

Although duration is an important measure of bond risk, it is not necessarily always the most appropriate one. Duration measures volatility, which is important but is only one aspect of the risk in bonds. If an investor considers price volatility an acceptable proxy for risk, duration is the measure of risk to use along with the correction for convexity. Duration may not be a complete measure of bond risk, but it does reflect some of the impact of changes in interest rates.

REAL-WORLD RETURNS 11-3
Using Duration to Estimate the Risk of a Bond

To predict how your bond fund will perform when the bond market gets walloped, look at its duration.

Duration is the single most important measure of how risky most bond funds are because it measures their sensitivity to interest-rate changes. Duration tells you how a bond or bond fund will react to a one-percentage-point change in interest rates. For example, if a bond has a duration of 8 years, it should lose 8 percent of its value if interest rates on similar bonds rise by one percentage point—and gain 8 percent in value if interest rates fall by one percentage point. A bond with a duration of 5 years should lose only 5 percent of its value if rates go up by one percentage point—and gain only 5 percent if rates drop one percentage point. (Although duration is expressed technically in years, think of it as a percentage change.)

Doubling a bond's duration can give you a good idea of how that bond will react if rates change by two percentage points rather than one. For instance, a bond with a duration of 8 years will lose roughly 16 percent of its value if rates climb two percentage points.

Because it's such a good measure, bond-fund managers almost always keep a tight grip on the duration of their holdings. "Every trade I make, I recalculate the duration of the portfolio," says Jerome Jacobs, manager of Vanguard Municipal Long Term. (Alas, when we called Vanguard's 800 number, we got a garbled definition of duration and a slightly different number from the one Jacobs quoted.)

Investors don't need to analyze their holds with pinpoint accuracy any more than they need to know the precise braking distance on a new car. But it's good to have at least a rough idea of the duration of the bonds and bond funds you own—as well as those that you're considering buying.

Duration is of far more value than the number that many inexperienced investors focus on: yield. "People who buy bond funds tend to do so on the basis of yield, but often the higher the yield the higher the duration," says Kurt Brouwer, a San Francisco investment adviser. A lot of investors who left the safety of certificates of deposit last fall for the higher yields of bond funds have found out the hard way that concentrating too much on yield can be costly.

While many investors don't understand duration, most are at least familiar with a less-precise measure of bond funds' interest-rate risk: maturity. Maturity is simply the number of years until a bond pays back its principal. Measure the maturities of the bonds in a fund and weight each bond according to how big a position it has in the portfolio, and you have the fund's weighted average maturity. The longer a fund's maturity, the more affected it tends to be by interest-rate swings.

But maturity is a flawed measure of interest-rate risk. "Duration is a much better guide for quantifying risk than is maturity," says Tom Poor, portfolio manager of Scudder Short-Term Bond fund. Why? Simply because duration takes into account both the amount paid on maturity and the value of the interest payments made along the way.

Consider two hypothetical 20-year bonds. One, a zero-coupon bond, doesn't pay a penny in interest until the day it matures. The other pays 7 percent interest annually. Common sense tells you that a bond that pays 7 percent annually is less volatile than one that pays nothing for 20 years.

But duration gives a more precise method of comparing the interest-rate sensitivity of the two bonds. Because the zero-coupon bond doesn't pay any interest until it matures, its duration is virtually the same as its maturity—20 years. Meanwhile, the other bond, priced at $100 and yielding 7 percent annually, has a duration of 10.7 years. Other things being equal, the higher a bond's yield, the *shorter* its duration. Take a 20-year bond also priced at $100 but with a 10 percent yield. Its duration is 8.6 years, or more than two years shorter than the duration of the 7 percent bond.

Some of the equations used in determining duration are so complex that without today's computers, duration would be an impractical tool. Fortunately, investors don't have to bother with the math. Even many portfolio managers don't know exactly how durations are figured. "If you call a bond trader and ask him how he calculates a duration, he's going to say he punches up a computer screen and looks at it," says Vanguard's Jacobs.

If you could know only one number about a bond fund, it should be its duration. But there is a second important number to use in choosing a bond fund—total return. While duration measures interest-rate risk, total return shows an investor how much a bond fund has earned, both in yield and in capital gains.

A good general rule in investing is that the more risk you take the higher your potential rewards should be. But the best funds manage to produce top returns without undue risk.

Keeping Names Straight

As good a measure as it is, duration isn't perfect. One flaw is that it changes as interest rates change. When interest rates climb, bond-fund durations shorten. When rates fall, durations lengthen. Unless rates shift dramatically, however, changes in duration should be fairly small, particularly for short- and intermediate-term bond funds. A bond fund's duration can also change when the fund trades the bonds in its portfolio. Check your fund's duration periodically to avoid unpleasant surprises.

There are a few other things to be aware of in using duration as an evaluation tool. It won't tell you anything about the credit quality of your bonds. A high-yield junk bond reacts as much to investor concerns about the stability of the economy and the issuing company as it does to interest rates. For that reason, duration is of less value in assessing junk bonds or funds. Similarly, foreign bonds change in value with currency swings, as well as with changes in interest rates. So duration isn't all that helpful in evaluating foreign bonds, either.

(continued)

REAL-WORLD RETURNS 11-3 *continued*

It also pays to keep in mind that duration is a theoretical measure of interest-rate risk. The ultimate test of a bond's worth is the marketplace. During times of extreme volatility—such as the first quarter of this year—liquidity can dry up and buyers may become scarce, regardless of what duration indicates the price should be. "In a rapidly moving market environment, bonds aren't necessarily going to behave the way bond math suggests," cautions Brad Tank, manager of Strong Short-Term Bond fund. This is particularly true of complex derivatives, used by some bond-fund managers to enhance returns.

Be aware that duration can be expressed in more than one way. The most accurate measure is *effective duration*, which takes into account the impact of bonds being called—that is, redeemed early by the issuer. In the municipal-bond market, bonds are often issued with maturities of 20 or 30 years but contain a provision that allows the issuer to pay them off earlier, typically after ten years. Effective duration also takes into account the prepayment risk in mortgage-backed bonds. If rates decline, many homeowners will refinance, lowering the duration of the bonds in mortgage-securities funds.

Although it's not as accurate, modified duration is the number that funds are most willing to make public. It does not take into account the probable effect of prepayments and calls. In municipal-bond and mortgage funds, especially, modified duration is likely to overstate slightly the interest-rate risk.

Source: Adapted and reprinted with permission from *Kiplinger's Personal Finance Magazine*, June 1994. Copyright © 1994. The Kiplinger Washington Editors, Inc.

JUNK BONDS ARE RISKY BUSINESS

In 2001, credit card company American Express sustained heavy losses because it was overly aggressive in investing in junk bonds. In the second quarter of the year, it reduced pre-tax earnings by US$826 million. After the announcement, company stock traded as low as $37.17, down from a two-year high of $62.00.

American Express CEO Kenneth I. Chenault admitted the firm "did not fully comprehend the risk" in its $3.5 billion portfolio of junk bonds.

Some of the high-yield bonds had ratings as low as single B, which had the potential for huge losses if default rates in the junk bond market increased, which they did.

DISCUSSION QUESTIONS

1. If American Express executives approved the junk bond investments in good faith, hoping to increase shareholder wealth, did that make their actions unethical?

2. What can companies do to better understand and manage investment risk?

3. Should financial advisors steer their clients away from junk bonds?

CHECK YOUR UNDERSTANDING

11-8. Holding maturity constant, a bond with a larger coupon will have a shorter duration than a bond with a smaller coupon. Agree or disagree, and explain your reasoning.

11-9. Using the duration concept, if you expect a decline in interest rates and you want to use this decline to your advantage, how should you adjust your bond portfolio?

SUMMARY

This summary relates to the learning objectives for this chapter.

1. **Calculate the price of a bond.**
   A bond's intrinsic value is its estimated value, or the present value of the expected cash flows from that asset. Bond prices are determined according to Equation 11-2.

2. **Explain the bond valuation process.**
   Bonds are valued using a present value process. The expected future cash flows for a bond—interest payments and principal repayments—are discounted at the bond's required yield. Bond prices change in response to changes in the level of market interest rates on similar instruments.

3. **Calculate major bond yield measures, including yield to maturity, yield to call, and horizon return.**
   The yield to maturity is defined as the promised compounded rate of return an investor will receive from a bond purchased at the current market price and held to maturity. The yield to call is the promised yield to the end of the period when a bond can first be called. The horizon return is the total rate of return earned on a bond over some time period given certain specified reinvestment rates of return.

4. **Account for changes in bond prices.**
   Bond prices move inversely with interest rates; prices increase as the required yield decreases and vice versa. Changes in bond prices are directly related to time to maturity and inversely related to bond coupons. Given a change in interest rates the two most important bond variables in assessing the change in a price of a bond are its coupon and its maturity.

5. **Explain and apply the concept of duration.**
   Duration is the weighted average time to recovery of all interest payments plus principal repayment. Duration expands with time to maturity but at a decreasing rate, and it is inversely related to coupon and yield to maturity. The modified duration can be used to calculate the percentage price change in a bond for a given change in the bond's yield to maturity. The bond price–yield relationship is not linear but convex, and precise calculations of price changes should properly account for this convexity.

KEY TERMS

Basis points, p.327
Conversion premium
  (Appendix 11C), p.356
Conversion price
  (Appendix 11C), p.356
Conversion ratio
  (Appendix 11C), p.356
Conversion value
  (Appendix 11C), p.356

Convertible securities
  (Appendix 11C), p.356
Convexity, p.343
Current yield, p.329
Duration, p.338
Horizon return, p.334
Interest on interest, p.332
Intrinsic value, p.320
Modified duration, p.342

Real risk-free rate of interest,
  p.327
Reinvestment rate risk, p.332
Yield to call, p.332
Yield to maturity (YTM), p.329

REVIEW QUESTIONS

11-1. When a bond is issued, its coupon rate is set at approximately _____.

11-2. Why is current yield an incorrect measure of a bond's return?

11-3. What does it mean to say that YTM is a promised yield?

11-4. What is meant by interest on interest?

11-5. Distinguish between promised yield and realized yield. How does interest on interest affect realized return?

11-6. How is the intrinsic value of any asset determined? How are intrinsic value and present value related?

11-7. How is the price of a bond determined? Why is this process relatively straightforward for a bond?

11-8. What effect does the use of semi-annual discounting have on the value of a bond in relation to annual discounting?

11-9. When is a bond selling at a discount, based on coupon rate, current yield, and YTM? When is it selling at a premium?

11-10. Define YTM. How is YTM determined?

11-11. Why is YTM important?

11-12. If YTM is merely a promised yield, why do investors not use some other measure of yield?

11-13. Which bond is more affected by interest-on-interest considerations?

   a. Bond A — 12 percent coupon, 20 years to maturity
   b. Bond B — 6 percent coupon, 25 years to maturity

11-14. How can bond investors eliminate the reinvestment rate risk inherent in bonds?

11-15. How does duration differ from time to maturity? What does duration tell you?

11-16. Assume that a bond investor wishes to maximize the potential price volatility from a portfolio of bonds about to be constructed. What should this investor seek in the way of coupon, maturity, and duration?

11-17. Is duration a complete measure of bond risk? Is it the best measure? Why?

11-18. What assumptions are involved in calculating the horizon return?

11-19. Differentiate between yield to call and yield to maturity. Will the yield be the same for both? Explain.

11-20. What are the implications of Malkiel's bond price theorems to bond investors? Which two bond variables are of major importance in assessing bond price changes?

11-21. How is duration related to time to maturity? To coupon payments? To the yield to maturity? Do the same relationships hold for a zero-coupon bond?

11-22. What is convexity? Why should bond investors consider it?

11-23. With the exception of zero-coupon bonds, a bond's duration will always be less than the bond's time to maturity. Why?

11-24. Yield to maturity can be thought of as the internal rate of return on a bond investment. Do you agree or disagree? Explain your reasoning.

11-25. Given two bonds with identical risk, coupons, and maturity date, with the only difference between the two being that one is callable, which bond will sell for the higher price?

11-26. What two characteristics of a bond determine its reinvestment rate risk?

11-27. The bond price curve is said to have a convex shape. What does this mean in terms of increases in interest rates relative to changes in bond prices?

11-28. Why is the duration of a zero-coupon bond equal to its time to maturity?

PROBLEMS

11-1.   a. Consider a bond with a coupon rate of 10 percent, a face value of $1,000, and with three years to maturity, while the appropriate discount rate is 8 percent. Show that the price of the bond is $1,051.54 with annual discounting and $1,052.24 with semi-annual discounting. Use a calculator to determine the discount factors.

    b. What would be the price of this bond if both the coupon rate and the discount rate were 10 percent?

11-2. With reference to Problem 1(a), what would be the price of the bond if the coupons were paid quarterly?

11-3. Calculate the price of a 10 percent coupon bond with eight years to maturity, given an appropriate discount rate of 12 percent, using both annual and semi-annual discounting.

11-4. Calculate the price of the bond in Problem 11-3 if the maturity is 20 years rather than eight years, using semi-annual discounting. Which of Malkiel's principles are illustrated when comparing the price of this bond to the price determined in Problem 11-3?

11-5. The YTM on a 10 percent, 15-year bond is 12 percent. Calculate the price of the bond if coupons are paid semi-annually.

11-6. Consider a junk bond with a 12 percent coupon (paid annually) and 20 years to maturity. The current required rate of return for this bond is 15 percent. What is its price? What would its price be if the required yield rose to 17 percent? 20 percent?

11-7.   a. Calculate the YTM for a 10-year zero-coupon bond sold at $400. Recalculate the YTM if the bond had been priced at $300.

    b. Determine the price of a 15-year zero-coupon bond if the required rate of return is 12 percent.

11-8. Calculate the realized compound yield for a 10 percent bond paying semi-annual coupons with 20 years to maturity and an expected reinvestment rate of 8 percent.

11-9. Consider a 12 percent, 10-year bond paying annual coupons purchased at face value. Based on Table 11-1 and assuming a reinvestment rate of 10 percent, calculate

    a. The interest on interest
    b. The total return
    c. The realized return given the 10 percent reinvestment rate

11-10. Consider a 4 percent coupon bond with 15 years to maturity that pays semi-annual coupons. Determine the YTM that would be necessary to drive the price of this bond to $300.

11-11. Calculate the YTM for the following bonds that all pay coupons semi-annually.

    a. A 12 percent, 20-year bond with a current price of $975
    b. A 6 percent, 10-year bond with a current price of $836
    c. A 9 percent, eight-year bond with a current price of $714

11-12. Laurentian Bank's bonds, with a coupon rate of 6.50 percent, are selling at 104.92 and pay semi-annual coupons. Exactly two years remain to maturity. Determine the

    a. Current yield
    b. Yield to maturity

11-13. TD Bank's bonds, with a coupon rate of 6.5 percent, sell to yield 6.66 percent. Exactly 25 years remain to maturity. What is the current market price of the bonds assuming semi-annual coupons? If the YTM had been 5.5 percent, what would the price of the bonds be? Explain why this difference occurs.

11-14. A 12 percent coupon bond has 20 years to maturity and pays annual coupons. It is currently selling for 20 percent less than face value. Determine its YTM.

11-15. Given a 10 percent, three-year bond with a price of $1,052.24 that pays semi-annual coupons, if the market yield is 8 percent, calculate its duration using the format illustrated in Table 11-3.

11-16. A 12 percent coupon bond with 10 years to maturity is currently selling for $913.50. Determine the modified duration for this bond.

11-17. Calculate the yield to first call for a 10 percent, 10-year bond that pays annual coupons and is callable five years from now. The current market price is $970, and the call price is $1,050.

11-18. Using Problem 11-12, assume that 18 years remain to maturity. How would the yield to maturity change? Does the current yield change?

11-19. Using the duration from Problem 11-15, determine:

    a. The modified duration

    b. The percentage change in the price of the bond if r changes 0.50 percent.

11-20. Calculate the duration of a 12 percent coupon bond with 10 years remaining to maturity and selling at par.

11-21. Given the duration calculated in Problem 11-20, calculate the percentage change in bond price if the market discount rate for this bond changes by 0.75 percent.

 11-22. The yield to maturity on a bond can be calculated using the IRR function. Enter the bond price as a negative number, and the coupons (on a semi-annual basis) and face value as cash flows. Use the spreadsheet formula = *IRR (A1:An) where n is the last cell with a cash flow.*

    Calculate, using the spreadsheet, the YTM for a 6-year, 7 percent coupon bond currently selling for $949.75.

 11-23. Using the spreadsheet, calculate the yield to call for a 6 percent, 12-year bond callable in five years at a call price of $1,040.

 11-24. YTM can also be calculated directly in the spreadsheet using the function = YIELD (A1,A2,An) where n is the last cell with inputs for the problem. The user inputs settlement date, maturity date, coupon rate, current bond price, face value (par value), and number of coupons paid per year. You can set the settlement date as the current date, and the maturity date as the same month and day in the year of maturity (5 years from now, 8 years from now, etc.). Price is stated as a percentage of par (e.g., 100 = $1,000). The following format can be used to solve the YTM for the bond.

Settlement date

    1/1/2007 = YEAR (year,month,day)*

Maturity date

    1/1/2010 = YEAR (year,month,day)*

    0.1   Annual coupon rate

    105.242   Bond price

    100   Face value = par value

    2   Coupon payments per year

    0.08   Yield to maturity as a decimal

*Be sure under the Format settings for the spreadsheet (Format, Cells, Number) to select for Date the format m/d/year. Note: Settlement date is not important—use the current date. Maturity date should reflect the number of years to maturity and the same month and day as the settlement date.

 11-25. Using the same basic format as in Problem 11-24, we can solve for bond price by entering the settlement date, the maturity date, the annual coupon rate, the YTM, the par value of the bond expressed as a percentage (100), and the number of coupons per year. Use the function = PRICE (A1, A2, A3, A4, A5, A6). Problem: solve for the price of a 6-year, 7 percent coupon bond if the YTM is 8.25 percent.

 11-26. Duration can be calculated using spreadsheet formulas. Data must be entered as follows (see Problem 11-24 for DATE information):

    Settlement date   Date is entered as DATE(year, month, day)

    Maturity date   Date is entered as DATE(year, month, day)

    Coupon as a decimal

    Required yield as a decimal

    Frequency of payments

Use the formula = DURATION (A1, A2, A3, A4, A5) for duration and = MDURATION (A1, A2, A3, A4, A5) for modified duration. Example—Calculate the duration and modified duration for a 6 percent, 7-year bond with a required yield of 5 percent. This is done as follows (note that the dates are seven years apart; also note the format for the date):

2/16/2006	Settlement date = DATE(year,m,d)
2/16/2013	Maturity date = DATE(year,m,d)
0.06	coupon rate as decimal
0.05	required yield as decimal
2	frequency of coupons
5.86	Macaulay Duration
5.71	Modified Duration

Using this format, calculate the duration for the bond in Table 11-3.

11-27. Real World Returns 11-1 provides data for a large sample of Canadian bonds. Use the data for the first 10 corporate bonds: AGT, Bell, BMO (five bonds) and BNS (three bonds) to complete this problem. You can assume that the settlement date (when the exchange of funds would occur) is April 22, 2008; also assume that all the bonds pay coupon interest semi-annually and that the face value for each is $100.

    a. Use the given yield and the "=PRICE(...)" function to calculate the price for each bond. Do your calculated prices match the quoted prices? (As the given yields are specified to only two decimal places, you will find that several calculated prices differ from the corresponding quote by a few cents.)

    b. Use the given price to calculate the yield-to-maturity for each bond. Do your figures match the given yields?

    c. Use the "=DURATION(...)" function to determine the Macaulay duration for each bond.

    d. Use the "=MDURATION(...)" function to calculate the modified duration value for each of the bonds.

    e. Why do you think the Bell corporate bond has a shorter duration than the AGT bond, even though the latter matures sooner?

11-28. The following bonds all have a face value of $1,000 and pay annual coupons.

Bond	A	B	C	D
Maturity (years)	10	10	5	10
Coupon Rate	6%	8%	7%	7%

    a. Consider bonds A and B, which are identical other than their coupons. Calculate the price of each bond for the following range of market interest rates (yields): 4 percent, 4.5 percent, ..., 9.5 percent, 10 percent. Using the function "= -PV(...)" is the easiest approach here as the maturities are an exact number of years in the future. Next, determine the change in price (in percentage terms) that occurs as the market rate increases (from 4 percent to 4.5 percent, from 4.5 percent to 5 percent, etc.) Graph these price changes (percents) versus the market rate to verify that Bond A (the lower coupon bond) is more sensitive to yield changes.

    b. Consider bonds C and D, which are identical other than their maturities. Calculate and graph the prices and price changes for these bonds as you did above. Does your graph confirm that Bond D (the longer maturity bond) is more sensitive to yield changes?

PREPARING FOR YOUR PROFESSIONAL EXAMS

CFA PRACTICE QUESTIONS

11-1. Which bond has the longest duration?

    a. 8-year maturity, 6 percent coupon
    b. 15-year maturity, 6 percent coupon
    c. 8-year maturity, 11 percent coupon
    d. 15-year maturity, 11 percent coupon

11-2. The interest rate risk of a bond is normally:

    a. lower for higher coupons.
    b. lower for longer duration.
    c. greater for shorter maturities.
    d. all of the above.

11-3. A bond with a call feature:

    a. is attractive because the immediate receipt of principal plus premium produces a high return.
    b. would usually have a higher yield than a similar non-callable bond.
    c. is more apt to be called when interest rates are high, because the interest saving will be greater.
    d. none of the above.

11-4. What would be the market price of a 10 percent non-callable corporate bond with a face value of $1,000 and 14 years to maturity, if it pays interest semi-annually, and the required rate of return on similar bonds is presently 8.4 percent?

    a. $1,129
    b. $1,130
    c. $1,000
    d. None of the above.

11-5. How much accrued interest would have to be paid if you purchased the bond in Question 11-4 on February 8, 2002 and the bond matures on December 31, 2015?

    a. $5.34
    b. $9.56
    c. $10.44
    d. More information is needed.

11-6. In which one of the following cases is the bond selling at a discount?

    a. Coupon rate is greater than current yield, which is greater than yield to maturity
    b. Coupon rate is less than current yield, which is less than yield to maturity
    c. Coupon rate equals current yield, which equals yield to maturity
    d. Coupon rate is less than current yield, which is greater than yield to maturity

11-7. A $1,000 par value, 10 percent semi-annual, 20-year debenture bond is currently selling for $1,100. What is this bond's current yield?

    a. 10.5 percent
    b. 10.0 percent
    c. 9.1 percent
    d. 8.9 percent

11-8. What is the yield to maturity for the bond in Question 11-7?

    a. 8.9 percent
    b. 9.3 percent
    c. 9.5 percent
    d. 10.6 percent

CFA CURRICULUM AND SAMPLE EXAM QUESTIONS (©CFA INSTITUTE)

11-1. An analyst made the following statement: "We should purchase Treasury notes because they are risk-free. Default risk is essentially nonexistent." State whether this analyst's statement is correct with respect to:

	Risk free	Default risk
a.	No	No
b.	No	Yes
c.	Yes	No
d.	Yes	Yes

11-2. An analyst accurately calculates that the price of an option-free bond with a 9 percent coupon would experience a 12 percent change if market yields increase 100 basis points. If market yields decrease 100 basis points, the bond's price would most likely:

    a. increase by 12%.
    b. increase by less than 12%.
    c. decrease by less than 12%.
    d. increase by more than 12%.

11-3. The duration of an option-free bond priced t $900 is 8.5. If yields decrease by 150 basis points, the most accurate statement about the actual price of the bond after the decrease in yields is that the actual price will be:

    a. equal to $1,014.75.
    b. greater than $1,014.75.
    c. lower than $1,014.75 because of the convexity adjustment.
    d. lower than $1,014.75 because the lower level of yields increases the bond's interest rate risk.

11-4. If an investor's required return is 12 percent, the value of a 10-year maturity zero-coupon bond with a maturity value of $1,000 is closest to:

    a. $312.
    b. $688.
    c. $1,000.
    d. $1,312.

APPENDIX 11A

TREASURY BILL YIELDS AND PRICES

Treasury bills are sold in Canada on a discount basis, based on their bond equivalent yield, which is determined using the following equation:

$$r_{BEY} = \frac{Face - P}{P} \times \frac{365}{n} \times 100$$

where
r_{BEY} = the bond equivalent yield
P = the T-bill price
Face = the T-bill face value
n = the number of days to maturity

For example, the yield on an 89-day Government of Canada Treasury bill that is presently selling at a price (P) of 99 per 100 of face value, can be determined in the following manner:

$$r_{BEY} = \frac{100 - 99}{99} \times \frac{365}{89} \times 100 = 4.1425\%$$

Rearranging this equation, we can see that T-bills are priced according to the following relationship:

$$P = \frac{Face}{(1 + r_{BEY} \times \frac{n}{365})}$$

For example, a 91-day T-bill with a $100 face value that is priced to yield 3.20 percent would be selling for $99.2085, as calculated below:

$$P = \frac{100}{[1 + (.0320 \times \frac{91}{365})]} = \frac{100}{1.007978} = 99.2085$$

Yields on US T-bills are quoted based on the bank discount yield, which is determined using a slightly different procedure than that used to calculate the bond equivalent yield in Canada. The differences arise from the use of face value instead of price in the denominator of the first term, and that 360 days, instead of 365, is used to annualize the rate. The resulting equation is given by:

$$r_{BDY} = \frac{Face - P}{Face} \times \frac{360}{n} \times 100$$

where
r_{BDY} = the bank discount yield

APPENDIX 11B

EFFECTIVE DURATION AND EFFECTIVE CONVEXITY

Effective Duration

Effective duration can be estimated using the following equation:

(11-14)

$$\text{Effective Duration} = \frac{B_- - B_+}{2\,B_0\,(\Delta y)}$$

B_0 = initial bond price
Δy = a chosen change in interest rates (such as 50 basis points or 0.005)
B_+ = resulting price for a given increase in yield (Δy)
B_- = resulting price for a given decrease in yield (Δy)

Effective duration is an appropriate measure of interest rate risk for both option-free bonds and those that contain embedded options such as callable and retractable bonds. For option-free bonds, we have the following relationship:

Effective Duration = Modified Duration

Therefore, either measure can be used to approximate price changes in Equation 11-13. However, for bonds with embedded options the relationship is:

$$\text{Effective Duration} \neq \text{Modified Duration}$$

For these bonds, modified duration cannot account for changes in bond cash flows when these bonds are called or redeemed, for example. Therefore, effective duration is the appropriate measure.

Replacing effective duration for modified duration (D*) in Equation 11-13, the duration effect on bond price can be estimated as:

$$\text{Percentage change in bond price (duration effect)} = (-\text{ Effective duration}) (\Delta y)$$

Effective Convexity

As discussed in the chapter, the convexity measure adjusts for the "non-linearity" in the price–yield relationship, which duration does not pick up, since it is a linear approximation. It can be estimated using the following equation, with all terms as defined above:

$$\text{Effective Convexity} \frac{B_+ + B_- - 2V_0}{2V_0 (\Delta y)^2} \tag{11-15}$$

We can use this equation to estimate the convexity effect on bond prices, which is given as:

$$\text{Convexity effect} = (\text{Convexity}) (\Delta y)^2$$

Combining the duration and convexity effect, we obtain the following equation for estimating bond price changes:

$$\begin{aligned} \text{Percentage change in bond price} \ &= \text{Duration effect} + \text{Convexity effect} \\ &= (-\text{ Effective duration}) (\Delta y) + (\text{Convexity}) (\Delta y)^2 \end{aligned} \tag{11-16}$$

This equation is applied in Example 11A-1.

EXAMPLE 11B-1: ESTIMATE DURATION, CONVEXITY, AND BOND PRICE CHANGES

A 20-year, 7 percent semi-annual-pay bond is currently trading at par. If interest rates rise by 50 basis points, the price of the bond will fall to $948.62; if rates fall by 50 basis points, the price will rise to $1,055.52.

a. Calculate the effective duration of this bond.
b. Calculate the effective convexity of this bond.
c. Estimate the price after a 100 basis point increase in market rates using the duration and convexity effects.

Solution:
a. Effective duration = $(1055.52 - 948.62)/[2(1000)(.005)] = 106.9/10 = 10.69$
b. Convexity = $[1055.52 + 948.62 - 2(1000)]/[2(1000)(.005)^2] = 4.14/.05 = 82.8$
c. Percentage price change = $(-10.69)(.01) + (82.8)(.01)^2$
  $= -.1069 + .00828 = -.09862$ or -9.862%
Therefore, the new price = $1,000 \times (1 - .09862) = \$901.38$.

APPENDIX 11C

CONVERTIBLE BONDS

Convertible Securities

Bonds or preferred stock convertible into common stock.

The convertible bond is a form of equity-derivative securities (discussed in Chapter 19) that permits the owner to convert it into common stock under specified conditions. **Convertible securities** or "convertibles," which also encompass convertible preferred stock, carry a claim on the common stock of the issuer, which is exercisable at the owner's initiative. If the option is never exercised, the convertible bond remains in existence until its maturity date, whereas a convertible preferred could remain in existence forever, since preferred stock has no maturity date.[19]

Unlike puts and calls and warrants, convertible securities derive only part of their value from the option feature (i.e., the claim on the underlying common stock). These securities are valuable in their own right, as either bonds or preferred stock. Puts and calls and warrants, on the other hand, are only as valuable as the underlying common stock and have no value beyond their claim on the common stock. Convertibles have increased in popularity because they offer a unique combination of equity and bond characteristics.

Terminology for Convertible Securities

Convertible securities, whether bonds or preferred stock, have a certain terminology.

Conversion Ratio

The number of shares of common stock that the owner of a convertible security receives upon conversion.

1. The **conversion ratio** is the number of shares of common stock that a convertible holder receives on conversion, which is the process of tendering the convertible security to the corporation in exchange for common stock.[20]

2. The **conversion price** is the par value of the bond or preferred divided by the conversion ratio.[21]

Conversion Price

The par value of a convertible security divided by the conversion ratio.

(11-17) $$\text{Conversion price} = \text{Par value/Conversion ratio}$$

3. The **conversion value** is the convertible's value based on the current price of the common stock. It is defined as

(11-18) $$\text{Conversion value} = \text{Conversion ratio} \times \text{Current price of common stock}$$

Conversion Value

A convertible security's value based on the current price of the common stock.

4. The **conversion premium** is the dollar difference between the market price of the security and its conversion value.

(11-19) $$\text{Conversion premium} = \text{Market price of convertible} - \text{Conversion value}$$

Convertible securities are, by construction, hybrid securities. They have some characteristics of debt or preferred stock and some of the common stock on which they represent an option.

Therefore, to value them one must consider them in both contexts.

Conversion Premium

The dollar difference between the market price of a convertible security and its conversion value.

EXAMPLE 11A-2: ESTIMATING CONVERSION PREMIUM

Consider the convertible debentures of a company that mature in nine years and have a coupon rate of 5 percent, with coupons paid semi-annually. Its conversion ratio is $100 worth of par value for 3.49 common shares. The conversion price is $28.63, or approximately $100/3.49.[22] Its common stock is selling at $16.05 while its debentures are selling at $87.00 per $100 par value. The conversion value of these convertibles is therefore 3.49 × $16.05 = $56.01. Thus, the conversion premium is $87.00 – $56.01 = $30.99 (or 55.3 percent of the conversion value of $56.01).

---

[19]Many convertible bonds cannot be converted for an initial period of six to 24 months.

[20]Forced conversion results when the issuer initiates conversion by calling the bonds.

[21]It is obvious that the conversion privilege attached to a convertible can be expressed in either conversion ratio or conversion price terms. Both the conversion price and the conversion ratio are almost always protected against stock splits and dividends.

[22]Many convertible bonds have a conversion price that increases over time.

The Basics of Convertible Bonds

Convertible bonds are issued by corporations as part of their capital-raising activities. Similar to a warrant, a convertible feature can be attached to a bond as a sweetener to make the issue more attractive to investors. They allow the issuer to pay a lower interest rate by offering investors a chance for future gains from the common stock. Convertibles are sometimes sold as temporary financing instruments with the expectation that over a period of months (or years) the bonds will be converted into common stock. The bonds are a cheaper source of financing to the issuer than the common stock, and their gradual conversion places less price pressure on the common stock. Finally, convertibles offer a corporation the opportunity to sell common stock at a higher price than the current market price. If the issuer feels that the stock price is temporarily depressed, convertible bonds can be sold at a 15 to 20 percent premium. The result of this premium is that the price of the stock must rise by that amount before conversion is warranted.

Most bonds, whether convertible or not, are callable by the issuer. This results in additional concerns for the convertible bondholder.

Convertible bonds are typically issued as debentures. They are often subordinated to straight (non-convertible) debentures, increasing their risk. According to bond rating agencies, most convertible bonds are one class below a straight debenture issue. Nevertheless, convertible bonds enjoy good marketability. Large issues are often more actively traded than many non-convertible issues of the same quality.

Analyzing Convertible Bonds

A convertible bond offers the purchaser a stream of interest payments and a return of principal at maturity. It also offers a promise of capital gains if the price of the stock rises sufficiently. To value a convertible bond, it is necessary to account for all of these elements. The convertible bond model is illustrated graphically in Figure 11-5 to provide a framework for analysis. We shall then illustrate the components of value individually.

Graphic Analysis of Convertible Bonds

Figure 11-5 shows the components of the convertible bond model. This diagram depicts the expected relationships for a typical convertible bond. The horizontal line from PV (par value) on the left to the face value (F) on the right provides a reference point; any bond sold at par value would start out at PV, and all bonds will mature at their face value. If such a bond is callable, the call price will be above the par value in the early years because of the call premium; by maturity this price would converge to the face value.

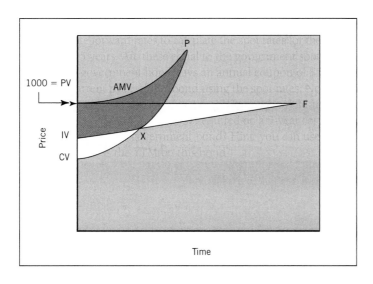

Figure 11-5
Conceptual Model for Understanding Convertible Bonds

Each convertible bond has an investment value (IV) or straight-debt value, which is the price at which a convertible would sell to equal the yield on a comparable non-convertible. In other words, the investment value is the convertible's estimated value as a straight bond. By evaluating the coupons and the face value of the convertible at the going required rate of return for a comparable straight bond, the beginning investment value can be determined. Remember that the straight (i.e., non-convertible) bond has a higher market yield because it does not offer a speculative play on the common stock. The investment value is represented in Figure 11-5 by the line from IV to F, the face value.

Each convertible has a conversion value at any time. The original conversion value (point CV) is established by multiplying together the conversion ratio and the price of the common stock at the time the convertible is issued. The conversion value curve in Figure 11-5 is then drawn on the assumption that the price of the stock will grow at a constant rate, g; that is,

$$P_1 = P_0(1 + g)$$
$$P_2 = P_1(1 + g)$$

and so forth. Obviously, this is an expected relationship and may not occur in this manner. Using this assumption, the conversion value rises above the par value as the price of the stock rises, tracing out the curve CV-P in Figure 11-5.

Finally, because the convertible often sells at a premium, it is necessary to draw an actual market value (AMV) curve, which is shown in Figure 11-5 as AMV-P. This curve eventually approaches the conversion value curve as the conversion value increases. This is primarily because the convertible may be called, forcing conversion. If this occurs, the convertible holder can receive only the conversion value. Therefore, investors are not likely to pay more than this for the convertible.

The shaded area in Figure 11-5 is the premium over conversion value, which declines as the market price of the convertible rises. This reflects the fact that the bond is callable.

Bond Value

Every convertible bond has a *straight bond value* or an investment value, which is the price at which the bond would sell with no conversion option. This price is given by the present value calculations for a bond, as explained in Chapter 11.

(11-20)
$$SBV = C \times (PVA_{r,n}) + F \times (PV_{r,n})$$

where
SBV = straight bond value (or investment value)
C   = the interest payments (coupons)
F   = face value of the bonds
n = number of periods to maturity
r = appropriate required rate of return

EXAMPLE 11A-3: STRAIGHT BOND VALUE

Let's consider again the convertible debentures that were discussed in Example 11A-2. Assuming an appropriate discount rate for similar non-callable bonds at that time of 7.5 percent, and assuming a term to maturity of exactly nine years, we obtain the following estimate of the investment value or straight bond value of these convertibles:

$$SBV = 2.50 \times (PVA_{3.75\%,18}) + 100 \times (PV_{3.75\%,18}) = 32.30 + 51.55 = \$83.85$$

Of course, the bond value fluctuates over time as market interest rates change.

Conversion Value

Every convertible bond has a conversion value that is the value of the common stock received upon conversion. At the time it is issued, a convertible bond has a conversion value equal to the market price of the common stock multiplied by the number of shares of stock that can be received by converting. As noted, the conversion price is usually set 15 to 20 percent above the current market price of the common, so that conversion would not be worthwhile. Over time, if the price of the common stock increases, the conversion value should also grow at the same rate.

Minimum (Floor) Value

Every convertible bond has a minimum or floor value. A convertible will always sell for no less than the greater of (1) its bond (straight) value or (2) its conversion value. In other words,

$$\text{Floor value of a convertible} = \text{Maximum (straight bond value; conversion value)} \qquad \textbf{(11-21)}$$

Even if the value of the conversion feature is zero, with virtually no prospect of a change in this value, a convertible bond would have a minimum price of its investment or straight bond value (i.e., its value as a non-convertible debt instrument). If the price were to decline below this value, bond investors would buy it because its yield would be greater than alternative comparable bonds. The straight bond value for the debentures in Example 11A-3 on the valuation date was $83.85, the absolute minimum price for this bond as of that time.

Actual Bond Value (Price)

Convertible bonds usually sell at prices above their minimum value, and, as we have seen, that is the higher of the bond value or the conversion value. For example, the convertible debentures in the previous example sold for $87.00, $4.15 above its bond value (and floor value), and was $30.99 above its conversion value.

Two of the reasons convertibles sell at premiums are:

1. The conversion option has a positive value because the right to convert any time during the life of the bond is valuable and investors are willing to pay for it. In effect, this is equivalent to owning a call option on the stock, and calls command positive premiums (as explained in Chapter 19).

2. A convertible bond offers investors downside protection, thereby decreasing their risk. If the price of the common stock declines sharply, resulting in a sharp decline in the conversion value, the convertible will still sell as a bond and will have a bond value determined by the present value of interest payments and principal. This dual minimum-price feature of convertibles reduces investors' risk and commands a premium in doing so.

In evaluating convertible bonds, certain details in addition to the preceding factors should be kept in mind. When a convertible bond is converted, the holder loses the accrued interest from the last interest payment date. Furthermore, if a holder converts after the ex dividend date, the common stock dividend on the newly received common shares could be lost. Since the issuer can call the bonds and force conversion, these factors can be important, and it is not unusual for issuers to choose a time favourable to themselves.

INVESTING

In a similar manner, a convertible bond cannot sell below its conversion value. If it did, arbitrageurs would buy the bond, convert it into common stock, and sell the shares, or simply establish a position in the underlying common stock at a cost lower than would otherwise be possible. Since the conversion value of $56.01 in Example 11A-2 was lower than its bond value, the bond value was its minimum, or floor value, at the time of these calculations. In Figure 11-5, the line/curve IV-X-P represents the minimum market value for the convertible bond. This minimum market value is made up of part of the investment value line (IV to X) and part of the conversion value curve (X to P). We can call this the effective market value floor.

A bond is subject to call if the market price exceeds the call price. Investors who pay a premium over the conversion value in these circumstances run a risk of having the bond called as the company forces conversion.

Should Investors Buy Convertible Bonds?

Why should investors consider convertible bonds? As for advantages, convertible bonds offer investors a unique combination of an income stream from a fixed-income security and a chance to participate in the price appreciation of the common stock. Convertibles offer downside protection in relation to owning the common stock, because regardless of what happens to the price of the common stock, the convertible bond will not decline below its value as a straight bond. They offer upside potential, because a convertible bond must always be worth at least its conversion value as the price of the common stock rises. Furthermore, the yield on a convertible bond usually exceeds the dividend yield of the underlying common stock, and interest payments have first order of priority. Compared to common stock owners, convertible bond holders enjoy a yield advantage while awaiting appreciation in the stock price.

As for disadvantages, convertible bonds yield less than do straight bonds of similar risk and maturity. Investors must give up some yield to receive the conversion feature. Convertibles are callable, and in many cases the issuer can and will force conversion. When a convertible bond is called, the holder will choose the better alternative—accept the call price or convert into common stock. If a corporation calls a bond at, say, $1,100 (face value of $1,000 plus one year's interest of $100 for a call premium), and the conversion value is, say, $1,200, the bondholders in effect are forced to convert. They give up their fixed-income security and the chance for future capital gains from the common stock.

CHAPTER 12

BONDS: ANALYSIS AND STRATEGY

As you think about managing your inheritance, you have convinced yourself that at your age you should only be interested in equities and not in bonds. However, you also realize that something could happen to change your mind and that it would be smart to at least learn something now about including and managing bonds in your portfolio. After all, you are familiar enough with sharp stock market declines, such as the ones in 2000–2002 and 2008, to understand that there are times you may wish not to have your inheritance invested only in stocks. Having learned something about managing bonds, you will be in a much better position to evaluate recommendations from brokers, financial advisors, and others as to what you should buy and hold in your portfolio.

Learning Objectives

After reading this chapter, you should be able to

1. Explain why investors buy bonds.
2. Discuss major considerations in managing a bond portfolio.
3. Explain what is meant by the term structure of interest rates.
4. Differentiate between passive and active strategies for managing a bond portfolio.
5. Describe how both conservative and aggressive investors build a fixed-income portfolio.

CHAPTER PREVIEW

In Chapter 11, we learned how to calculate bond prices and yields and identified key factors such as interest rate changes that affect the bond market. In this chapter we conclude our discussion of bonds by examining some of the broader issues involved in the management of a bond portfolio. We consider why investors buy bonds and discuss important issues such as the term structure of interest rates and yield spreads. We differentiate between passive and active strategies of managing a bond portfolio. Finally, we look at the importance of the global bond market to investors.

WHY BUY BONDS?

learning objective 1
Explain why investors buy bonds.

As noted in Chapter 6, the total return on bonds can be separated into two components: income from the coupons, and the capital gains (or losses) due to changes in bond prices. This explains why bonds appeal to both conservative investors seeking steady income and aggressive investors seeking capital gains. A wide range of investors participate in the fixed-income securities marketplace, ranging from individuals who own a few government or corporate bonds to large institutional investors who own billions of dollars of bonds. Most of these investors are presumably seeking the basic return–risk characteristics that bonds offer; however, quite different overall objectives can be accomplished by purchasing bonds.

As fixed-income securities, bonds are attractive for many investors because they offer a steady stream of interest income over the life of the obligation and a return of principal at maturity. An important reason for buying bonds is that they provide "shelter from the storms" that frequently hit equity markets, as alluded to in Real-World Returns 12-1. Buyers know the promised yield on a bond held to maturity, and barring default by the issuer, they will have the bond principal returned to them at maturity. By holding to maturity, investors can escape the risk that interest rates will rise, thereby driving down the price of the bonds, although other risks may not be eliminated.

REAL-WORLD RETURNS 12-1

Fixed Income Weathers Storm

The so-called "smart money"—institutional money—has not fared much better than the rest of the industry. Nearly three out of every four pooled funds in Morningstar Canada's database lost money during the first quarter of 2008, with the best returns coming from fixed-income funds.

It should be noted that the institutional pooled funds universe is very small compared to the retail space, with a handful of names occupying a given category. Therefore, it's not always the best indicator of an asset category. Nevertheless, these funds represent a significant chunk of money since they are included in many institutional portfolios and defined contribution plans.

Overall, 10 of the 41 pooled fund categories had positive median returns in the first quarter of 2008. The worst performer was the Science & Technology Equity category with a 16.3 percent median loss. Two categories are tied for second-worst return of the quarter: Asia Pacific Equity and US Small/Mid Cap Equity, which both lost 9 percent.

The only equity-based categories to post positive median returns were Precious Metals Equity (which contains just one fund) with 1.3 percent and Natural Resources Equity (four funds) with 1.2 percent.

In some of these categories, like the Canadian Equity category, which had a median loss of 3.9 percent, there was not a single fund that had positive returns, according to Morningstar Canada's associate editor Christian Charest.

Charest says the best Canadian equity performer was Manulife/Fidelity Canadian Large Cap at –0.7 percent, and the Fidelity Canadian Large Cap version not sponsored by Manulife was second with –0.8 percent.

(continued)

As an illustration of the return and risk situation for an investor who is seeking steady returns, consider Figure 12-1, which shows total return indexes and total returns for long-term Government of Canada bonds for the period 1938 to 2007. These bonds possess no practical risk of default. At the end of 2007, investors in these government bonds, with coupons reinvested, would end up with $66.57 per dollar invested at the beginning of 1938. This is a compound growth rate of 6.2 percent. As the bottom panel shows, the total annual returns have generally been positive, and if held to maturity, the nominal returns on these bonds would always be positive.

Some investors are interested in bonds precisely because bond prices will change with interest rates. If interest rates rise, bond prices will fall and vice versa. These investors are interested not in holding the bonds to maturity, but rather in earning the capital gains that are possible if they correctly anticipate movements in interest rates. Because bonds can be purchased on margin, large potential gains are possible from speculating on interest rates. (Of course, large losses are also possible.)

To get some idea of the changes in returns that can result from fluctuations in interest rates, consider again Figure 12-1. Notice that some of the total annual returns were very large, far beyond the yield component alone. For example, the total return was 43 percent in 1982, 25 percent in 1985, and 26 percent in 1995. Clearly, successful bond speculation in each of those years resulted in very large returns. Note, however, that returns were also negative in 16 out of 70 years, although there have only been two negative annual returns since 1981 and 11 of the 16 negative returns were –3 percent or less.

Figure 12-1(a)
Long Canada Bonds
Total Return Index
(1938–2007)

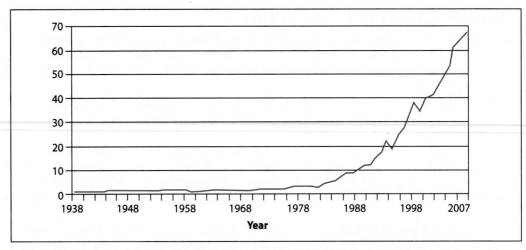

Source: Canadian Institute of Actuaries website (www.actuaries.ca) and Datastream database.

Figure 12-1(b)
Long Canada Bonds
Total Annual Returns
(1938–2007)

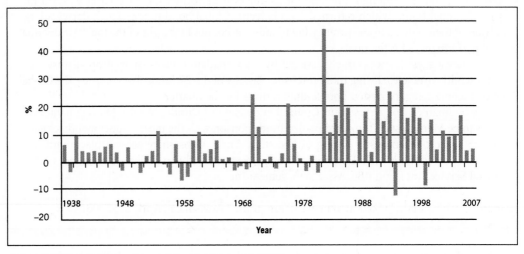

Source: Canadian Institute of Actuaries website: www.actuaries.ca.

Speculation has been heavy in the bond markets. In the past, bonds were viewed as very stable instruments whose prices fluctuated very little in the short run. This situation changed drastically, however, with bond markets becoming quite volatile. Interest rates in the early 1980s reached record levels, with long-term government bonds offering yields over 15 percent in 1981. The high interest rate levels caused large changes in bond prices. The subsequent decline in interest rates throughout the 1990s led to some excellent years for bond returns.

There are many kinds of bond speculators, from financial institutions to individual investors, but they all have one thing in common. Each is trying to take advantage of an expected movement in interest rates. Thus, investors seeking income from bonds, as well as investors attempting to speculate with bonds, are keenly interested in the level of interest rates and any likely changes.

Buying Foreign Bonds

Why do Canadian investors have foreign bonds in their portfolios? One obvious reason is that approximately 98 percent of the fixed-income investment opportunities available in the world exist outside Canada. Canada's bond market is small relative to those in countries such as the US and Japan, as can be seen in Table 12-1. For example, in June 2007, Canada's debt outstanding totalled $1.09 trillion US, which represented only 2.1 percent of all outstanding domestic debt on the world's largest bond markets. On the other hand, US and Japanese bond markets accounted for 44 percent and 15 percent of the world market respectively.

Although the performance of bonds, like equities, changes continuously, foreign bonds may offer higher returns than alternative domestic bonds. Based on historical performance standards, Canada has not had one of the best performing international bond markets. Investing globally increases the likelihood that a portion of the investment will be placed in a high-performing country.

Another important reason for buying foreign bonds is the diversification, which is extremely important for both stock and bond portfolios. Given the relatively small size of the Canadian bond market, taking a global perspective greatly expands the number of available investment opportunities. This increases the likelihood of developing a well-diversified fixed-income portfolio. When Canadian bond prices are declining, those in some foreign countries may be rising.

Table 12-1

Domestic Debt Securities

June 2007	$US billions	Percentage
Canada	1,088.5	2.06
France	2,453.9	4.64
Germany	2,318.2	4.38
Italy	2,792.6	5.27
Japan	8,144.8	15.38
UK	1,299.7	2.45
US	23,380.4	44.16
China	1,368.0	2.58
Spain	1,429.3	2.70
Other	$8,666.7	16.38
TOTAL	**52,942.1**	**100.00**

Source: International Banking and Financial Market Developments, Bank for International Settlements (BIS) website: www.bis.org. Used with permission.

As we now know when considering investment opportunities, investors do not receive something for nothing. First of all, individual investors find it difficult to invest directly in foreign bonds. It is relatively costly and can be time consuming. Furthermore, some brokerage firms do not offer foreign bonds to individual investors, while others require a minimum investment of $10,000 and often much more. Selling foreign bonds that are directly owned also can be a problem, since many foreign secondary markets face liquidity problems. This means that individual investors selling small amounts of foreign bonds abroad generally will not be able to demand the top prices.

Investors who are considering direct investment in foreign bonds face the additional issue of transaction costs. Dollars must be converted into the foreign currency to make purchases and converted back into dollars when they are sold. On small transactions, these costs can significantly eat into returns.

Finally, investors in foreign bonds must deal with exchange rate risk. An adverse movement in the dollar can result in a Canadian investor's return being lower than the actual return on the asset; in some case that return could even be negative.

CHECK YOUR UNDERSTANDING

12-1. In 2006 and 2007 the Canadian dollar strengthened significantly relative to the U.S. dollar. How would this have affected Canadian investors in American bonds?

12-2. Bond investors sometimes react favourably when the Bank of Canada (or any other central bank) tightens monetary policy by increasing interest rates. Why is this the case when we know that higher interest rates cause bond prices to fall?

IMPORTANT CONSIDERATIONS IN MANAGING A BOND PORTFOLIO

Understanding the Bond Market

The first consideration for any investor is to understand the basic nature of the bond market. It has been commonplace to talk about the bond market benefiting from a weak economy. This refers to the fact that if the economy is growing slowly, interest rates may decline and bond prices rise. In effect, a decline in economic growth may lead to fewer investment opportunities, leading savers to increase their demand for bonds, pushing bond prices up and bond yields down. While this result benefits existing bondholders, it may make bond yields unattractive to potential new investors. Nonetheless, talk of a rapidly growing economy is thought to frighten bond investors, since it will increase inflationary and interest rate expectations, thus putting downward pressure on bond prices.

The relationship that really matters in this view is between bond yields and inflation, not between economic growth and bond yields. As we know from Chapter 11, interest rates reflect expected inflation. If investors expect a rise in inflation, they demand more from a bond to compensate for the expected decline in the purchasing power of the future cash flows. Therefore, an increase in expected inflation tends to depress bond prices and increase yields.

Figure 12-2 shows a plot of annual yields on long-term Government of Canada bonds, T-bill yields, and annual growth rates in the Consumer Price Index (CPI), which is a measure of inflation, over the period 1961 to 2005. Notice that bond yields followed an upward trend until 1981 and a downward trend thereafter. The CPI growth rate behaved in similar fashion, and there was a high positive correlation coefficient of over 0.60 between CPI and bond yields. This should not be surprising since CPI measures actual inflation levels, which we would expect to be highly correlated with expected inflation.

Figure 12-2
Inflation, T-Bill Yields, and Long-Term Canada Bond Yields

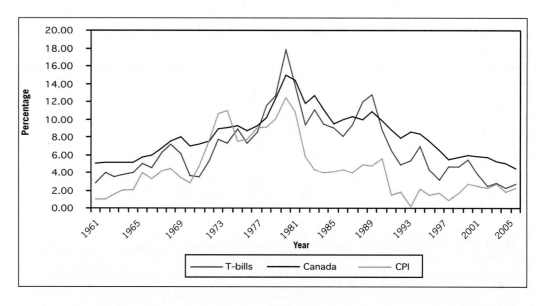

We can say that bond markets clearly dislike inflation because of its negative effect on fixed-income securities, and they favour Bank of Canada actions that temper economic growth and reduce inflation. Thus, bond investors may react quite favourably to a tightening of monetary policy because this helps to calm inflation fears, which is one reason why investors carefully monitor Bank of Canada actions, both realized and prospective.

Given the importance of inflation on bond returns, it is not surprising that many investors have turned to investing in "real return" bonds, which provide inflation protection (as discussed in Chapter 2).

The bond market may also respond favourably to a strengthening of the dollar, as alluded to in Real-World Returns 12-1 at the beginning of the chapter. A stronger dollar increases the value of dollar-denominated assets to foreign investors. The traditional relationships in the bond market may be changing because of the global nature of money management and the increasing use of derivatives. Leverage has become a big factor in the bond markets and has magnified the swings in bond prices.

Other events of a global nature affect the bond market. When the Brazilian crisis erupted around the end of 1998, there was a "flight to safety (or quality)" in the form of purchases of US Treasury securities. As the crisis diminished, this demand for Treasuries decreased. This flight to safety tends to happen whenever there is significant uncertainty in global markets. On the other hand, with Japanese interest rates on the rise, bond investors feared that Japanese investors would liquidate their holdings of foreign bonds in order to buy their own government bonds, which would reduce the demand for foreign bonds, and hence their prices. There are numerous examples of this flight to quality, several of which are discussed later in this chapter in the subsection dealing with yield spreads.

The Term Structure of Interest Rates

learning objective 3
Explain what is meant by the term structure of interest rates.

The **term structure of interest rates** refers to the relationship between time to maturity and yields for a particular category of bonds at a particular time. Ideally, other factors are held constant, particularly the risk of default. The easiest way to do this is to examine Government of Canada securities, which have no practical risk of default, have no sinking fund, and are taxable. By eliminating those that are callable and those that may have some special feature, a quite homogeneous sample of bonds is obtained for analysis.

Term Structure of Interest Rates
The relationship between time to maturity and yields for a particular category of bonds at a particular time.

Yield Curves

The term structure is usually plotted in the form of a **yield curve**, which is a graphical depiction of the relationship between yields and time for bonds that are identical except for maturity. The horizontal axis represents time to maturity, whereas the vertical axis represents yield to maturity.

Figure 12-3 shows the yield curve in Canada as of April 22, 2008, which shows that short-term rates were below 3 percent, while long-term rates exceeded 4 percent. Figure 12-4 shows four historical yield curves for Government of Canada T-bills and bonds in June of 1990, 1994, 1998, and 2004.[1] The upward-sloping curves in 1994 and 2004 are considered typical; that is, interest rates that rise with maturity are considered the "normal" pattern. The downward-sloping curve for 1990 is less common, with short-term rates above long-term rates. These "inverted" yield curves are unusual, and some market participants believe they indicate that short-term rates will fall and, in fact they did decline in the 1991 to 1993 period. Another less common shape is the relatively flat yield curve existing in 1998, which indicates that long- and short-term rates are very similar.

Yield Curve
A graphical depiction of the relationship between yields and time to maturity for bonds that are identical except for maturity.

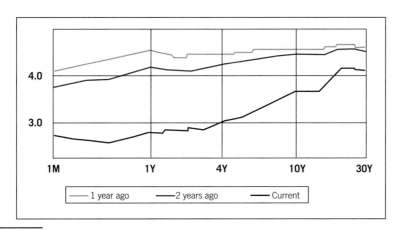

Figure 12-3
Canada Yield Curve (April 22, 2008)

Source: Retrieved from www.gold.globeinvestor.com, April 22, 2008.

[1]These are only four examples—there are numerous other shapes that yield curves can assume.

Figure 12-4
Yield Curves

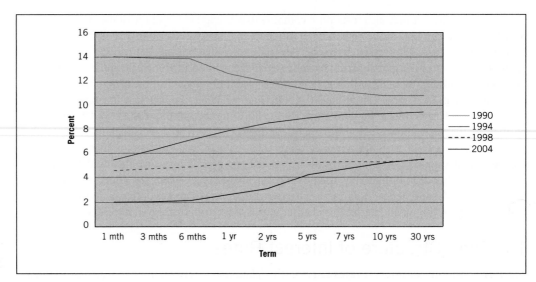

Yield curves are for Government of Canada securities in June for the respective years.

Most observations about yield curves involve tendencies and not exact relationships. For example, there generally is a negative relationship between short rates and the yield spread. A higher short rate is usually associated with a flatter yield curve because long rates do not increase by quite as much. However, this relationship does not always hold, as was the case for 1998 when the yield curve was flat despite the existence of low short-term rates.

Implied Forward Rates

The following yields offered by Government of Canada securities were used to construct the yield curve depicted in Figure 12-4, for June 2004:

Time to Maturity	Yield (%)
1-month T-bills	2.04
3-month T-bills	2.07
6-month T-bills	2.18
1-year T-bills	2.61
2-year Canada bonds	3.14
5-year Canada bonds	4.06
7-year Canada bonds	4.64
10-year Canada bonds	5.33
30-year Canada bonds	5.39

The rates above are referred to as "spot" rates, and we use them to compute implied forward rates. For example, the one-year spot rate is 2.61 percent and the two-year spot rate is 3.14 percent. The implied forward rate is the one that solves the following expression:

$$(_tR_1 + 1)(1 + {}_1f_2) = (1 + {}_tR_2)^2$$

where,
$_tR_1$ = the current known one-year spot rate prevailing at time t
$_tR_2$ = the current known two-year spot rate prevailing at time t
$_1f_2$ = the implied one-year forward rate, from the end of year 1 to the end of year two

In this example,

$$(1 + {_1}f_2) = (1 + {_tR_2})^2 / ({_tR_1} + 1) = (1.0314)^2 / (1.0261) = 1.0367,$$

so ${_1}f_2 = 3.67\%$

Similarly, if the three-year rate was 3.61 percent, then the implied forward rate from year two to year three could be calculated as:

$$(1 + {_2}f_3) = (1 + {_tR_3})^3 / ({_tR_2} + 1)^2 = (1.0361)^3 / (1.0314)^2 = 1.0456,$$

so ${_2}f_3 = 4.56\%$

Term Structure Theories

A theory of the term structure of interest rates is needed to explain the shape and slope of the yield curve and why it shifts over time. Four theories traditionally advanced are the expectations theory, the liquidity premium theory, the preferred habitat theory, and the market segmentation theory.

The pure or "unbiased" **expectations theory** of the term structure of interest rates asserts that financial market participants determine security yields, such that the return from holding an n-period security equals the average return expected from holding a series of one-year securities over the same n periods. In other words, the long-term rate of interest is equal to an average of the present yield on short-term securities plus the expected future yields on short-term securities that are expected to prevail over the long-term period. For each period, the total rate of return is expected to be the same on all securities regardless of time to maturity.

Expectations Theory
The hypothesis that the long-term rate of interest is equal to an average of the short-term rates that are expected to prevail over the long-term period.

In effect, the term structure consists of a set of forward rates and a current known rate. **Forward rates** are those that are expected to prevail in the future; that is, they are unobservable but anticipated future rates. In essence, the pure expectations theory suggests that the implied forward rates calculated previously equal the expected future spot rates.

Forward Rates
Unobservable rates that are expected to prevail in the future.

Under the expectations theory, long rates must be an average of the present and future short-term rates. For example, a three-year bond would carry an interest rate that is an average of the current rate for one year and the expected forward rates for the next two years. The same principle holds for any number of periods; therefore, the market rate for any period to maturity can be expressed as an average of the current rate and the applicable forward rates. Technically, the average involved is a geometric rather than an arithmetic average.

For expositional purposes:

${_tR_n}$ = the current known yield (at time t) on a security with n periods to maturity

${_{t+1}r_n}$ = the yield expected to prevail one year from today (at time $t + 1$) for n periods—these are forward rates

The rate for the three-year bond referred to above must be a geometric average of the current one-year rate (${_tR_1}$) and the expected forward rates for the subsequent two years.

Therefore, in equation form

$$(1 + {_tR_3}) = [(1 + {_tR_1})(1 + {_{t+1}r_1})(1 + {_{t+2}r_1})]^{1/3} - 1.0 \qquad \textbf{(12-1)}$$

where
$(1 + {_tR_3})$ = the rate on a three-year bond $(1 + {_tR_1})$ = the current known rate on a one-year bond
$(1 + {_{t+1}r_1})$ = the expected rate on a bond with one year to maturity beginning one year from now
$(1 + {_{t+2}r_1})$ = the expected rate on a bond with one year to maturity beginning two years from now

EXAMPLE 12-1: USING FORWARD RATES

Assume the current one-year bond rate $(_tR_1)$ is 0.07, and the two forward rates are 0.075 $(_{t+1}r_1)$ and 0.082 $(_{t+2}r_1)$. The rate for a three-year bond, $(1 + {}_tR_3)$, would be

$$(1 + {}_tR_3) = [(1.07)(1.075)(1.082)]^{1/3} - 1.0$$
$$= 1.07566 - 1.0$$
$$= 0.07566 \text{ or } 7.566\%$$

The same principle applies for any number of periods. Any long-term rate is a geometric average of consecutive one-period rates.

Forward rates cannot be easily measured, but they can be inferred for any one-year future period. The expectations theory, however, does not say that these future expected rates will be correct; it simply says that there is a relationship between rates today and those expected in the future.

According to this hypothesis, investors can expect the same return regardless of the choice of investment, because any combination of securities for a specified period will have the same expected return. For example, a five-year bond will have the same expected return as a two-year bond held to maturity plus a three-year bond bought at the beginning of the third year. The assumption under this hypothesis is that expected future rates are equal to implied forward rates. Profit-seeking individuals will exploit any differences between forward rates and expected rates, ensuring that they level out.

Liquidity Preference Theory

The idea that interest rates reflect the sum of current and expected short rates, as in the expectations theory, plus liquidity (risk) premiums.

The second theory, the **liquidity preference theory**, states that interest rates reflect the sum of current and expected short rates, as in the expectations theory, plus liquidity (risk) premiums. Because uncertainty increases with time, investors prefer to lend for the short run. Borrowers, however, prefer to borrow for the long run in order to be assured of funds. Investors receive a liquidity premium to induce them to lend long term, while paying a price premium (in the form of lower yields) for investing short term. The implication of this theory is that longer-term bonds should offer higher yields, which is consistent with the observation that yield curves are generally upward sloping.

The difference between the liquidity preference theory and the expectations theory is the recognition that interest rate expectations are uncertain. Risk-averse investors seek to be compensated for this uncertainty. Forward rates and estimated future rates are not the same; they differ by the amount of the liquidity premiums. In other words, under the liquidity preference theory, the implied n-period forward rate for some future time period t, will equal the expected n-period spot rate at time t, plus a liquidity premium.

Preferred Habitat Theory

Investors have preferred maturity sectors or habitats in which they seek to invest but are willing to shift to other maturities if they can expect to be adequately compensated.

(12-2) $$_t f_{t+n} = {}_t r_n + \text{liquidity premium}$$

A third hypothesis for explaining the term structure of interest rates is the **preferred habitat theory**, which states that investors have preferred maturity sectors or habitats. For example, a financial institution with many five-year debentures to pay off will not want to take the reinvestment rate risk that would result from investing in one-year T-bills.

What if imbalances arise in a given maturity range between the demand and supply of funds? The preferred habitat theory states that borrowers and lenders can be induced to shift maturities if they are adequately compensated by an appropriate risk premium, which distinguishes this theory from the market segmentation theory explained next. The implication of this theory for the term structure is that both expectations concerning future interest rates and risk premiums play a role, and the yield curve can take any shape.

Market Segmentation Theory

Investors confine their activities to specific maturity sectors and are unwilling to shift from one sector to another to take advantage of opportunities.

The preferred habitat theory is related to, but not identical with, the **market segmentation theory**. This theory states that the various investors, having different maturity needs dictated by the nature of their liabilities, confine themselves to specific maturity segments. Investors are not willing to shift from one maturity sector to another to take advantage of any opportunities that may arise. Under the market segmentation theory, the shape of the yield curve is determined by the supply and demand conditions for securities within each of the multiple maturity sectors.

Which of these theories is correct? The issue of the term structure has not been resolved; although many empirical studies have been done, the results are at least partially conflicting. Therefore, definitive statements cannot be made. The empirical evidence on the expectations hypothesis is equivocal at best. The evidence on the liquidity premium hypothesis is the most persuasive. Substantial evidence suggests that risk premiums exist, but their behaviour over time is subject to debate.

In actual practice, market observers and participants do not tend to be strict adherents to a particular theory. Rather, they accept the reasonable implications of all of them and try to use any available information in assessing the shape of the yield curve. For example, many market participants will focus on expectations but allow for liquidity premiums.

Generally, upward-sloping yield curves have been the norm, as would be predicted by the liquidity preference theory. This theory is more compatible than the others with the study of investments since it emphasizes the risk–return trade-off that exists. The liquidity preference theory stresses the idea that because of larger risks, longer maturity securities require larger returns or compensation. In contrast, the expectations theory categorizes investors as return maximizers, whereas the preferred habitat theory categorizes investors as risk minimizers.

Regardless of which of the theories is correct, it seems reasonable to assert that investors demand a premium from long-term bonds because of their additional risk. After all, uncertainty increases with time, and as we have seen, long-term bonds are more sensitive to interest rate fluctuations than are short-term bonds. Furthermore, the typical shape of the yield curve is upward sloping, which indicates that investors are more averse to the risk of long bonds than to short-term securities.

On the other hand, the most reasonable explanation for downward-sloping yield curves is that investors expect short-term rates to decline in the near future. Otherwise, investors could earn higher returns from short-term assets, which have less risk than long-term assets. One could not expect this relationship to persist for long periods of time, since it runs counter to the risk-expected return trade-off we associate with financial assets.

Historical data can be used to provide some insights into bond horizon (maturity) premiums between 1938 and 2007. One simple approximation of the average bond horizon premium is the difference between the average annual returns on long-term government bonds and 91-day government T-bills. The data indicate that the annual arithmetic mean for T-bills was 5.20 percent versus 6.62 percent for long-term bonds, making the average horizon premium for this period 1.42 percent.

The Risk Structure of Interest Rates—Yield Spreads

Assume that market interest rates on risk-free securities are determined as previously discussed. If the expected rate of inflation rises, the level of rates does also. Similarly, if the real rate of interest were to decline, market interest rates would decline; that is, the level of rates would decrease. Furthermore, as seen in the term structure analysis, yields vary over time for issues that are otherwise homogeneous. The question that remains is this: Why do rates differ between different bond issues or segments of the bond market?

The answer lies in what bond analysts call the risk structure of interest rates, or simply yield spreads. **Yield spreads** refer to the relationships between bond yields and the particular issuer and issue characteristics, and constitute the risk premiums mentioned earlier. Yield spreads are often calculated among different bonds holding maturity constant. They are a result of the following factors:

1. Differences in quality or risk of default. Clearly, other things being equal, a bond rated BAA will offer a higher yield than one rated AAA because of the difference in default risk.

2. Differences in call features. Bonds that are callable have higher yields to maturity (YTMs) than otherwise identical non-callable bonds. If the bond is called, bondholders must give it up, and they could replace it only with a bond carrying a lower YTM. Therefore, investors expect to be compensated for this risk.

3. Differences in coupon rates. Bonds with low coupons have a larger part of their YTM in the form of capital gains.

Yield Spreads

The relationship between bond yields and the particular features on various bonds such as quality, callability, coupon rates, marketability, and taxes.

4. Differences in marketability. Some bonds are more marketable—have better liquidity—than others. They can be sold either more quickly, with less of a price concession, or both. The less marketable a bond, the higher the YTM.

5. Differences in tax treatments.

6. Differences between countries.

Other Factors Affecting Yield Spreads

Clearly, yield spreads are a function of the variables connected with a particular issue or issuer. Investors expect to be compensated for the risk of a particular issue, and this is reflected in the risk premium. However, investors are not the only determining factor in yield spreads. The actions of borrowers also affect them. Heavy government financing, for example, may cause the yield spreads between government and corporate bonds to narrow as the large increase in the supply of government securities pushes up the yields on government debt.

The level of interest rates also plays a role in explaining yield spreads. As a general proposition, risk premiums tend to be high when the level of interest rates is high.

Yield Spreads over Time

Yield spreads among alternative bonds may be positive or negative at any time. Furthermore, the size of the yield spread changes over time. Whenever the differences in yield become smaller, the yield spread is said to narrow; as the differences increase, it widens.

One yield spread of interest to investors is the difference between the yields on corporate and government bonds. This spread is often referred to as the default risk premium, which can change for a number of reasons. Real-World Returns 11-1 in Chapter 11 included many examples demonstrating the existence of default spreads. In other words, there were many cases where bonds from different issuers that had similar features with respect to maturity dates and coupon rates were providing quite different yields to investors. For example, the Government of Canada 5.25 percent bonds maturing on June 1, 2012, were providing a yield of 3.16 percent. At the same time, the BMO corporate bonds maturing June 21, 2012, were providing a yield of 5.31 percent. Figure 12-5 provides a visual demonstration of yield spreads, plotting the yield spreads among AA, A, and BBB rated corporate bonds over the 1996 to 2006 period. Notice how these spreads change through time, hitting troughs in stable years such as 1997 and 2005, and hitting peaks in years of economic uncertainty such as 1998 and 2002.

Figure 12-5
Yield Spreads

Source: Datastream database.

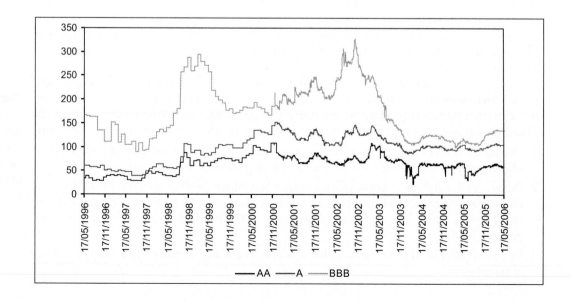

The spread between government and corporate bonds is one that investors monitor closely and typically averages about 1 percent, but it has varied historically from as low as 0.5 percent to as high as 2 percent. Another yield spread that is very important for Canadian investors is the one between the yields on Canadian and US bonds and money market instruments. Generally, US debt instruments have offered lower yields than their Canadian counterparts; however, between 1995 and 1997, Canadian yields (both short-term and long-term) were below those of the US. As of March 2008, T-bill yields were higher while Canadian bond yields were lower. Figure 12-6 depicts the yield spreads for the difference between Canadian and US government T-bills and long-term bonds from 1990 to March 2008.

Notice how the T-bill spread was approximately as high as 6 percent in 1990, then declining steadily and actually hitting –2 percent in 1997, before increasing to over 2 percent in 2003, and then hitting negative territory again in 2006 and 2007. Bond yield spreads followed a similar trend, although it is obvious these spreads displayed much less volatility.

Generally, yield spreads widen during recessions, when investors become more risk-averse, and narrow during times of economic prosperity. Since the probability of default is greater during a recession, investors demand more of a premium. Yield spreads were at their widest during the early 1930s when the Great Depression was at its worst. Real-World Returns 12-2 alludes to the "widening" of junk bond yield spreads to as high as 7 percent during 2008 during the period of economic uncertainty that followed the sub-prime meltdown, which was discussed earlier. In contrast, yield spreads narrow during boom periods because even financially weak companies have a good chance of surviving and paying their debts. Historical evidence supports these trends; thus, we can state that the yield spread varies inversely to the business cycle.

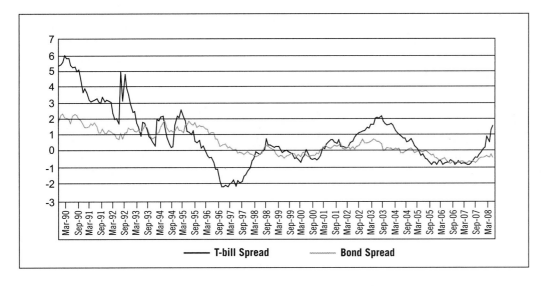

Figure 12-6
Canada–US Interest Rate Spreads

Source: Datastream database.

REAL-WORLD RETURNS 12-2

Junk Bond Yield Spreads

Now's a good time to start buying something that may be lacking in your portfolio.

High-yield bonds, sometimes disparaged as junk bonds, have been crushed at least as badly as stocks since last summer and now offer yields that are double or more what you can get from government bonds. "This is probably one of the best times in the past five to six years to be buying this stuff," said Gavin Graham, chief investment officer at Guardian Group of Funds.

(continued)

REAL-WORLD RETURNS 12-2 *continued*

There's also a diversification argument for buying high-yield bonds. By mixing them with your high-grade government and corporate bonds, you lessen your vulnerability to rising interest rates and enhance your overall returns.

High-yield bonds are issued by companies that aren't financially strong enough to earn the investment-grade credit rating that pension funds, insurance companies and other institutional investors may insist on before buying. Technically speaking, high-yield bonds are all those with ratings below triple-B.

Higher risk levels mean higher returns. The yield from bonds held in GGOF High Yield Bond, the high-yield fund at Mr. Graham's firm, is currently running in the high 7-percent range, and that's after fees. With Government of Canada bonds these days, you'd be lucky to get a yield of 3 percent for terms of five years or so.

To understand what's happening in the high-yield bond market today, you first need to know that bond prices and yields move in opposite directions. In recent months, the price of high-yield bonds has been on the decline, which means yields are rising. There are two reasons for this, one being the risk that the economic slowdown will cause less financially solid companies to default on their bonds. There's also the lingering taint of the US subprime mortgage fiasco, which has driven investors toward more reliable government bonds and away from riskier corporate debt.

There are actually two benefits to buying high-yield bonds at current levels—you stand to benefit from capital gains if bond prices recover from their recent losses, and you tap into an income flow that beats anything else in the bond market or guaranteed investment certificates.

Be cautious if you do make a move into the high-yield sector, however. Rex Chong, manager of the Trimark Advantage Bond, suggests an averaging-in approach, where you buy a little now and then wait and see what happens over the next few months before buying more. The reason is that these bonds have a history suggesting that before they rebound, they could fall significantly further.

The last time high-yield bonds got hammered was about six years ago, when the likes of Enron and WorldCom were disintegrating. Mr. Chong said high-yield bonds traded back then at spreads as high as 10 percentage points, which is the same level they reached in the early 1990s. All of this raises the question of whether high-yield bonds could be headed for more trouble in the near term. "I'm not sure, but it would not surprise me," Mr. Chong said.

If you judge by assets in high-yield bond funds, investors have shown only modest interest in the sector. But in the analysis of many experts, holding 10 to 25 percent of your fixed-income investments in high-yield bonds can improve returns through their higher yields and add stability.

Guardian Group's Mr. Graham notes that high-yield bonds behave in an opposite way to conventional bonds, which means they'll do just fine when interest rates are rising and may struggle when rates fall. If the economy is strong enough to warrant interest rate increases, then that suggests companies issuing high-yield bonds can make their interest payments and redeem their bonds without problem. Falling rates suggest a slowing economy that could weigh heavily on companies with high-yield debt.

No Deals in These Wheels

Retail investors looking for high-yield bonds are likely to come across a lot of choices issued by the financing arms of General Motors of Canada and Ford Motor Co. of Canada. The yields are high by current standards and in some cases hit double digits. For example, a General Motors Acceptance Corp. Canada bond maturing at the end of next year was available this week with a yield of just over 11 percent.

Mr. Chong said he's a holder of a very small amount of Ford Credit Canada debt that matures early in 2009. Generally, though, he's wary of this corner of the high-yield market because

(continued)

REAL-WORLD RETURNS 12-2 *continued*

it's costing car-financing companies more to raise the funds they lend out to individuals. "For the average individual, I think the risk-reward does not make sense," Mr. Chong said.

Fund	MER	Minimum investment	One-year return	Five-year return
PH&N High Yield Bond A Morningstar says: Low fees, and a very good risk–return profile	0.89%	$5,000	0.3%	8.1%
TD High Yield Income Morningstar says: Results have been hurt by US exposure, but TD's fixed income team is strong	1.9%	$100	−10.8%	2.9%
Trimark Global High Yield Bond Morningstar says: Downside protection has been good with this fund, and manager Rex Chong is a favourite	1.75%	$500	−7.7%	3.4%

Sources: Globefund.com and Morningstar.ca

Source: Carrick, Rob, "Looking for yield? Junk bonds may be the answer," www.globeinvestor.com, April 21, 2008. © Copyright *The Globe and Mail* and CTVglobemedia Publishing Inc.

CHECK YOUR UNDERSTANDING

12-3. Assume that the liquidity preference theory is valid and that interest rates are expected to remain unchanged. Will the yield curve still slope upward?

12-4. Why should we expect yield spreads to vary inversely to the business cycle?

BOND STRATEGIES

learning objective 4
Differentiate between passive and active strategies for managing a bond portfolio.

We now consider the basic approaches that investors can use in managing their bond portfolios, or the bond portion of their overall portfolio. An understanding of these strategies requires more than a comprehension of the basic factors affecting the valuation and analysis of bonds.

Bond investing has become increasingly popular, no doubt as a result of the high yields provided by bonds. Unfortunately, the theoretical framework for bond portfolio management has not developed to the same extent as that for common stocks. In some ways common stocks have been more "glamorous," and more attention has been devoted to them. Furthermore, there is generally more data available for common stocks.

Bond investors may adopt a variety of different strategies, depending on their risk preferences, knowledge of the bond market, and investment objectives. For organizational purposes, and because this scheme corresponds to the two broad strategies that any investor can follow with any type of portfolio, we will concentrate primarily on passive and active management of bond portfolios, as well as discussing a hybrid approach referred to as immunization. Active and passive approaches can be distinguished by the types of inputs needed. Active management relies heavily on expectations data, while passive strategies do not.

Passive Management Strategies

Recall the discussion of efficient markets from Chapter 10. Many investors agree that securities are fairly priced in the sense that the expected return is commensurate with the risk taken. This belief can justify a **passive management strategy**, meaning that the investor does not actively seek out trading possibilities in an attempt to outperform the market. Passive bond strategies are based on the proposition that bond prices are fairly determined, leaving risk as the portfolio variable to control. In effect, the inputs are known at the time of the analysis.

The use of passive bond investment strategies is supported by evidence for various periods, which shows that the performance of bond managers during the years examined failed to equal that of a market index. A comprehensive study examining the performance of bond mutual funds, using two samples of bond funds, found that they underperformed relevant indexes from the fixed-income area.[2] The results were robust across a wide choice of models. For the most part, this underperformance approximated the average management fees; therefore, before expenses, funds performed about as well as the indexes. There was no evidence that using past performance will allow us to predict future performance.

Passive management strategies are based on inputs that are known at the time, rather than expectations. These strategies have a lower expected return and risk than do active strategies. *A passive investment strategy does not mean that investors do nothing.* They must still monitor the status of their portfolios in order to match their holdings with their risk preferences and objectives. Conditions in the financial markets change quickly, and investors must also make fast changes when necessary. Passive management does not mean that investors accept changes in market conditions, securities, and so on, if these changes cause undesirable modifications in the securities they hold.

In following a passive management approach, bond investors must first determine whether the bonds to be held are suitable investment opportunities. They must assess default risk and diversify their holdings to protect themselves against changes in the probability of default. Similarly, call risk must be examined at the outset. Ideally, investors may be able to find bonds that are not callable over the period that they will be held. The higher the coupon on a bond, the more likely it is to be called. A third factor affecting investors is the marketability of a bond. Some bonds cannot be readily sold without a price concession, a lag in the time required to sell the bond, or both.

Other factors that the passive bond investor must consider at the outset of the program and monitor during the life of the investment include their current income requirement and taxes. Some bond investors need large current yields. This suggests large coupons, other things being equal. Taxes are also a factor, because the after-tax return is very important.

Strategies for investors following a passive bond management approach include buy and hold, and indexing.

Buy and Hold

An obvious strategy for any investor interested in non-active trading policies is simply to buy and hold. Having considered the factors just mentioned, this investor carefully chooses a portfolio of bonds and does not attempt to trade them in a search for higher returns. An important part of this strategy is to choose the most promising bonds that meet the investor's requirements. Making this selection requires some knowledge of bonds and markets. Simply because an investor is following a basic buy-and-hold strategy does not mean that the initial selection is unimportant. The investor must have knowledge of the yield advantage of corporate securities over government debt instruments, the yield advantage of utilities over industrials, and other factors.

One alternative for the buy-and-hold investor is to try to duplicate the overall bond market by purchasing a broad cross-section of bonds. Bond index funds and bond ETFs have now made it easy to accomplish this strategy. We consider this possibility separately under indexing.

---

[2]C. Blake, E. Elton, and M. Gruber, "The Performance of Bond Mutual Funds," *The Journal of Business* 66 (July 1993), pp. 371–403.

Indexing

In Chapters 1 and 10, we learned that one factor affecting the investments environment is the efficiency of the markets. If capital markets are efficient—meaning that securities prices reflect information fully and quickly—investors may not be able to gain by actively searching for undervalued securities or by attempting to time market movements. The available research on this issue has led many investors to decide that they are unlikely to outperform a market index. Therefore, they are willing to build, or, more likely, buy a portfolio that will match the performance of a well-known bond index such as the SCM Universe Bond Total Return Index in Canada. Two common US bond indexes are the Shearson Lehman Index and the Salomon Brothers Index. Mutual funds designed to match the performance of some index are known as **index funds**, and such funds are available for both bonds and stocks (stock index funds are discussed in Chapter 14).[3]

One example of such an index fund is the CIBC Canadian Bond Index Fund, which is a diversified fund that seeks to match the performance of the SCM Universe Bond Index. Given the performance of bond managers discussed previously, bond index funds have become a popular alternative for investors.

Index Funds
Mutual funds holding a bond or stock portfolio designed to mimic the performance of a particular market index.

Another alternative for bond investors is to purchase exchange-traded funds (ETFs), which were discussed in Chapter 3. Canadian investors can presently purchase five bond ETFs (iShares) traded on the TSX that are offered by Barclay's Global Investors, and are briefly described below:

1. XBB — tracks the DEX Universe Bond Index, which includes both government and investment grade corporate bonds;

2. XCB — tracks the DEX All Canadian Corporate Bond Index, which includes investment grade Canadian corporate bonds;

3. XGB — tracks the DEX All Government Bond Index, which includes Canadian government bonds;

4. XLB — tracks the DEX Long Bond Index, which includes both long-term government and long-term investment grade corporate bonds; and,

5. XRB — tracks the DEX Real Return Bond Index, which includes mainly federal and provincial bonds.

Active Management Strategies

Although bonds are often purchased with the intention of being held to maturity, frequently they are not. Henry Kaufman, a well-known forecaster of interest rates, commented some years ago that bonds are bought for their price appreciation potential and not for income protection. Many bond investors feel this way and use **active management strategies**. Such strategies have traditionally sought to profit from active management of bonds by either

1. Forecasting changes in interest rates, because we know that bond prices will rise or fall as a result of these movements; or

2. Identifying relative mispricing between various fixed-income securities.

Active Management Strategy
A strategy designed to provide additional returns by pursuing active trading activities.

Notice that, unlike the passive strategy, the key inputs are not known at the time of the analysis. Instead, investors have expectations about interest rate changes and mispricings among securities.

We will consider each of these alternatives in turn. We will also examine briefly some of the newer techniques for actively managing a bond portfolio.

---

[3]In practice, it is not feasible to replicate a broad bond index exactly. This is a result of the rebalancing problems that occur as bonds are dropped from the index because their maturities fall below one year and as new bonds are issued. Thus, the bonds used to compute an index change frequently.

Forecasting Changes in Interest Rates

Changes in interest rates are the chief factor affecting bond prices because of the inverse relationship between bond prices and interest rates. When investors project interest rate declines, they should take action to invest in the right bonds for price appreciation opportunities. When interest rates are expected to rise, the objective is to minimize losses by holding bonds with shorter durations or by not holding bonds at all.

While it is difficult for the average investor to forecast interest rates very well on a consistent and accurate basis, it is not an entirely fruitless exercise. Reasonable forecasts can be made about the likely growth rate of the economy and the prospects for inflation, both of which affect interest rates and, therefore, bond investors. Assuming that an investor has a forecast of interest rates, what strategy can be used? The basic strategy is to change the duration of the portfolio. Specifically, an investor should lengthen the duration of a bond portfolio when interest rates are expected to decline, or shorten it when they are expected to rise.

It is important to be aware of the trade-offs in strategies involving maturity:

1. Shorter durations sacrifice price appreciation opportunities, but serve to protect the investor when rates are expected to rise.

2. Longer durations provide for greater price fluctuations; therefore, the chance for bigger gains (and losses) is magnified. However, longer maturity bonds may be less liquid than T-bills.

An important component in forecasting interest rates is the yield curve, discussed earlier in connection with the term structure of interest rates. The shape of the yield curve at any point in time contains potentially valuable information about the future course of interest rates. Bond market participants in particular, and investors in general, pay close attention to yield curves as an aid in forecasting interest rates and as part of deciding what segments of the bond market to invest in.

EXAMPLE 12-2: CHANGING YIELD CURVES AND BOND RETURNS

Consider the situation at the end of June 1994. At that time, one-month T-bills offered a yield of 5.45 percent, while 30-year bonds were almost 4 percentage points higher at 9.42 percent. This difference in yields was high by historical standards, since the difference was usually less than 3 percent, with an average difference of 1.4 percent between 1934 and 1997. This caused many observers to predict a decrease in long-term rates in order to restore the yield curve to a more "normal" shape. Active bond investors sharing this belief would have moved to lengthen the duration of their bond portfolios, by increasing their holdings of longer term (duration) bonds, and selling shorter term (duration) securities. These beliefs turned out to be well founded, and within a year, long-term yields fell over 1 percent. The result of this decline in long-term rates was that long-term bond investors produced some very impressive returns (in excess of 20 percent) over this holding period.

One form of interest rate forecasting, horizon analysis, involves the projection of bond performance over a planned investment horizon. The investor evaluates bonds that are being considered for purchase over a selected holding period in order to determine which will perform the best. To do this, the investor must make assumptions about reinvestment rates and future market rates and calculate the horizon returns for the bonds being considered based on that set of assumptions. Note that this concept is different from yield to maturity, which does not require expectations to be integrated into the analysis. Horizon analysis requires users to make assumptions about reinvestment rates and future yields but allows them to consider how different scenarios will affect the performance of the bonds being considered. Horizon analysis was discussed in Chapter 11.

Identifying Mispricings Among Securities

Managers of bond portfolios attempt to adjust to the constantly changing environment for bonds (and all securities, for that matter) by engaging in what are called **bond swaps**. The term usually refers to the purchase and sale of bonds in an attempt to improve the rate of return on the bond portfolio by identifying relative mispricings among different types of bonds in the market. There are several different types of bond swaps, the best known of which are discussed briefly below.[4]

Bond Swaps
An active bond management strategy involving the purchase and sale of bonds in an attempt to improve the rate of return on the bond portfolio.

1. The **substitution swap** involves bonds that are perfect (or very close) substitutes for each other with regard to characteristics such as maturity, quality rating, call provisions, marketability, and coupon payments. The only difference is that at a particular time, the two bonds sell at slightly different prices (and, therefore, a different yield to maturity). The swap is made into the higher yielding bond, which, if its yield declines to that of the other bond, will provide capital gains as well as a higher current yield.

2. A **pure yield pickup swap** involves no expectations about market changes, as does the substitution swap (where the buyer expects the yield on the higher yielding bond to drop). This swap simply involves selling a lower yielding bond and purchasing a higher yielding one of the same quality and maturity. The motivation is strictly to obtain higher yield.

3. The **rate anticipation swap** is based on a forecast of interest rates. When rates are expected to rise (fall), swaps are made into short (long) duration bonds (or cash).

4. The **intermarket spread (sector) swap** is designed to take advantage of expected changes in the yield spread relationships between various sectors of the bond market. For example, a bond investor may perceive a misalignment between government bonds and utility bonds. If the yield spread between the two sectors is too wide and is expected to narrow, a switch may be made into the higher yielding security.

Use of Newer Techniques

The bond markets have changed rapidly over the years, due to numerous structural alterations. These have been accompanied by new techniques for the active management of fixed-income portfolios.

The distinction between the bond market and the mortgage market is now blurred, with mortgage instruments competing in the capital markets in the same manner as bonds. The mortgage has been transformed into a security, and the mortgage market has become more uniform and standardized. These securities are alternatives to bonds, especially corporate bonds, and can be used in the portfolio as substitutes.

Financial futures are now a well-known part of the investor's alternatives. Their use has grown tremendously, in particular to hedge positions and to speculate on the future course of interest rates. Futures will be discussed in more detail in Chapter 20.

Interest Rate Swaps

One of the newer techniques in bond management that has generated considerable attention is **interest rate swaps**. This term refers to a contract between two parties to exchange a series of cash flows based on different securities, but without actually exchanging the securities directly. This contract involves trading between private parties, typically large institutions, on a global basis.

Interest Rate Swaps
A contract between two parties to exchange a series of cash flows based on fixed-income securities, but without actually exchanging the securities directly.

In a simple interest rate swap, a large institution could commit to pay a fixed interest rate in exchange for receiving payments based on a short-term floating rate. In effect, the institution swaps the cash flow from the fixed interest rate amount of funds for a cash flow generated by the short-term floating rate applied to some amount of funds. No securities are actually traded. Instead, the institution pays interest on a "notational principal" and receives a cash flow based on the amount of that

---

[4]For a complete discussion of these swaps, see S. Homer and M. Leibowitz, *Inside the Yield Book* (Englewood Cliffs, NJ: Prentice Hall, 1972).

principal. In this example, the institution has effectively converted a bond portfolio with a fixed rate into a (synthetic) portfolio with a floating rate.

Interest rate swaps are used primarily to hedge interest rate risk, but they can also be used in other ways. For example, a bond manager could speculate on changing conditions in the bond market or a financial institution could convert its floating-rate liabilities to fixed-rate liabilities. Swaps typically involve a dealer, such as a bank, which quotes swap prices on a regular basis. The spread between what the dealer pays and receives constitutes the dealer's revenue.

Growth in the market for interest rate derivative products has been rapid, as can be seen in Table 12-2, which shows the notional amounts of various over-the-counter (OTC) derivative products over the 2001 to 2007 period, and in Table 12-3, which shows the growth in exchange-traded derivatives from 2005 to 2007. As of June 2007, the notional amount of interest rate swaps outstanding was $271.9 trillion US, representing well over half of the outstanding notional amount of OTC interest rate derivative contracts at that time. This is all the more impressive when one considers that the first swaps occurred in 1982, and that by 1996, the notional principal of all outstanding swaps was around $19 trillion US.

Table 12-2

Amounts Outstanding of Over-the-Counter (OTC) Derivatives by Risk Category and Instrument (in billions of US dollars)

OTC Markets	Notional Amounts				Gross Market Values			
	Jun-01	Jun-03	Jun-05	Jun-07	Jun-01	Jun-03	Jun-05	Jun-07
TOTAL CONTRACTS (in billions of US$)	99,756	169,680	281,492	516,408	3,044	7,907	10,605	11,142
Foreign Exchange	16,910	22,088	31,082	48,621	772	996	1,142	1,344
Forwards & Swaps	10,582	12,332	15,801	24,526	395	476	464	492
Currency Swaps	3,832	5,159	8,236	12,291	314	419	549	617
Options	2,496	4,597	7,045	11,804	63	101	129	235
Interest Rate	67,465	121,800	204,794	346,937	1,573	5,458	6,700	6,058
Forward Rate Agree.	6,537	10,271	13,973	22,809	15	20	31	43
Interest Rate Swaps	51,407	94,583	163,749	271,853	1,404	5,004	6,077	5,315
Options	9,521	16,946	27,072	52,275	154	434	592	700
Equity-Linked	1,885	2,799	4,550	9,202	199	260	382	1,116
Forwards & Swaps	329	488	1,086	2,599	49	67	88	240
Options	1,556	2,311	3,464	6,603	150	193	294	876
Commodity	590	1,041	2,940	7,567	83	110	375	670
Gold	203	304	288	426	21	22	24	47
Other					62	88	351	623
Forwards & Swaps	229	458	1,748	3,447				
Options	158	279	904	3,694				
Credit Default Swaps			10,211	42,580			188	721
Single-name	.	.	7,310	24,239	.	.	136	406
Multi-name	.	.	2,901	18,341	.	.	52	315
Unallocated	12,906	21,952	27,915	61,501	417	1,083	1,818	1,233

Source: Bank for International Settlements website: www.bis.org.

Table 12-3

Amounts Outstanding of Exchange-Traded Derivatives by Category and Instrument (in billions of US dollars)

	Notional Amounts	
	Dec-05	**Jun-07**
TOTAL	**57,789**	**96,683**
Futures	21,601	31,677
Interest Rate	20,709	30,148
Currency	108	202
Equity Index	784	1,327
Options	36,188	65,006
Interest Rate	31,588	55,987
Currency	66	101
Equity Index	4,534	8,918

Source: Bank for International Settlements website: www.bis.org

Immunization—A Hybrid Strategy

Because interest rates change over time, investors face uncertainty about the realized returns from bonds. This, of course, is the nature of interest rate risk. The strategy of protecting a portfolio against interest rate risk (i.e., changes in the general level of interest rates) is called **immunization**.

To see how such a strategy works, think of interest rate risk as being composed of two parts:

1. The price risk, resulting from the inverse relationship between bond prices and required rates of return;

2. The reinvestment rate risk, resulting from the uncertainty about the rate at which future coupon income can be reinvested.

As discussed in Chapter 11, the YTM calculation assumes that future coupons from a given bond investment will be reinvested at the calculated yield to maturity. If interest rates change so that this assumption is no longer operable, the bond's realized YTM will differ from the calculated (expected) YTM.[5]

Notice that these two components of interest rate risk move in opposite directions:

- If interest rates rise, reinvestment rates (and therefore income) rise, whereas the price of the bond declines.

- If interest rates decline, reinvestment rates (and therefore income) decline, whereas the price of the bond rises.

In effect, the favourable results on one side can be used to offset the unfavourable results on the other. This is what immunization is all about, protecting a bond portfolio against interest rate risk by cancelling out the two components of interest rate risk, reinvestment rate risk, and price risk.

The duration concept discussed earlier is the basis for immunization theory. Specifically, a portfolio is said to be immunized (the effects of interest rate risk are neutralized) if the duration of the portfolio is made equal to a pre-selected investment horizon for the portfolio. Note carefully what this statement says. An investor with, say, a 10-year horizon does not choose bonds with 10 years to maturity but bonds with a duration of 10 years, which is something quite different. The duration strategy will usually require holding bonds with maturities in excess of the investment horizon, unless they are zeroes, whose duration exactly equals their maturity.

Immunization

The strategy of protecting or immunizing a portfolio against interest rate risk by cancelling out its two components: price risk and reinvestment rate risk.

---

[5]For additional information on reinvestment rate risk, see R. W. McEnally, "How to Neutralize Reinvestment Rate Risk," *The Journal of Portfolio Management* 6 (Spring 1980), pp. 59–63; and W. L. Nemerever, "Managing Bond Portfolios Through Immunization Strategies," in Donald L. Tuttle, *The Revolution in Techniques for Managing Bond Portfolios* (Charlottesville, VA: Institute of Chartered Financial Analysts, 1983), p. 140.

Figure 12-7 outlines the essential points of immunization. Think of it as a strategy to protect against the adverse consequences of interest rate risk, thereby allowing the portfolio holder to achieve a pre-specified rate of return over a selected period of time.

Figure 12-7
Understanding the
Concept of Immunization

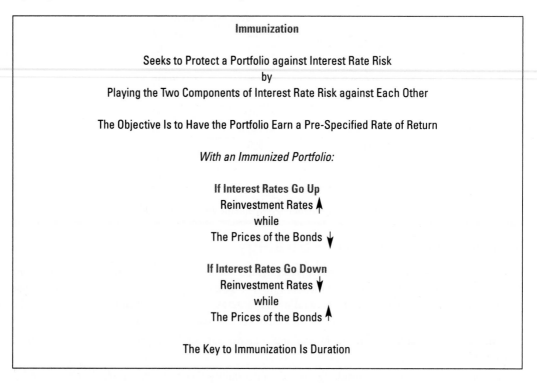

Immunization

Seeks to Protect a Portfolio against Interest Rate Risk
by
Playing the Two Components of Interest Rate Risk against Each Other

The Objective Is to Have the Portfolio Earn a Pre-Specified Rate of Return

With an Immunized Portfolio:

If Interest Rates Go Up
Reinvestment Rates ⬆
while
The Prices of the Bonds ⬇

If Interest Rates Go Down
Reinvestment Rates ⬇
while
The Prices of the Bonds ⬆

The Key to Immunization Is Duration

For an example of the immunization concept, consider Table 12-4, which illustrates for a portfolio of a single bond what ideally could happen with a portfolio of several bonds. Assume an investor has a five-year investment horizon after which she wishes to liquidate her bond portfolio and spend the proceeds. The current yield to maturity for AAA-rated bonds, the only investment grade our investor is willing to consider, is 7.9 percent for both five-year and six-year bonds because of the flatness of the yield curve. In order to simplify the calculations, we will assume that interest is paid annually so that we can concentrate on the immunization principle.

Because the YTM is 7.9 percent, our investor, understanding the reinvestment rate implications of bonds, expects that after five years her investment should yield a ratio of $(1.079)^5$, or 1.46254. That is, if she invests $1,000 in a bond today and the intermediate coupons are reinvested at 7.9 percent each, as the YTM calculation assumes, the ending wealth for this investment in a bond that can be purchased for face value should be $1,000 $(1.079)^5$, or $1,462.54.

Our investor can purchase bond A, with a 7.9 percent coupon and a five-year maturity, or bond B, with a 7.9 percent coupon, a six-year maturity, and a duration of five years. The top panel of Table 12-4 illustrates what happens if bond A is purchased and market yields remain constant for the five-year investment horizon. Because the intermediate cash flows are reinvested at exactly 7.9 percent each year, the amounts cumulate toward the final amount of $1,462.54, a wealth ratio of 1.46254. Notice in these examples that we separate year five from the other four because of the return of principal ($1,000) at the end of year five; obviously, no compound interest is earned on the return of this $1,000 at the end of the year. In a similar manner, no interest is earned on the first year's cash flow of $79, which is assumed to occur at the end of the year.

Now consider what would happen if our investor bought bond A and in the third year of its five-year life, market yields for this and comparable bonds declined to 6 percent and remained at that level for the remainder of the five-year period. As a result, the intermediate cash flows in the last three years

Table 12-4

Ending Wealth for a Bond Following a Change in Market Yields With and Without Immunization

Bond A: Purchased for $1,000, five-year maturity, 7.9 percent coupon, 7.9 percent yield to maturity.

Bond B: Purchased for $1,000, six-year maturity, 7.9 percent coupon, 7.9 percent yield to maturity, duration = 5.00 years

Part A: Ending Wealth for Bond A if Market Yields Remain Constant at 7.9 Percent

Years	Cash Flow	Reinvestment Rate (%)	Ending Wealth
1	$ 79	—	$ 79.00
2	79	7.9	164.24
3	79	7.9	256.22
4	79	7.9	355.46
5	79	—	462.54
5	1000	—	1462.54

Part B: Ending Wealth for Bond A if Market Yields Decline to 6 Percent in Year 3

Years	Cash Flow	Reinvestment Rate (%)	Ending Wealth
1	$ 79	—	$ 79.00
2	79	7.9	164.24
3	79	6.0	253.10
4	79	6.0	347.29
5	79	—	447.13
5	1000	—	1447.13

Part C: Ending Wealth for Bond B if Market Yields Decline to 6 Percent in Year 3 (Bond B has a duration of five years)

Years	Cash Flow	Reinvestment Rate (%)	Ending Wealth
1	$ 79	—	$ 79.00
2	79	7.9	164.24
3	79	6.0	253.10
4	79	6.0	347.29
5	79	—	447.13
5	1017.92[a]	—	1465.05

[a]The price of bond B with one year left to maturity and a market yield of 6 percent is $1,017.92.

of the bond's life would be reinvested at 6 percent rather than at 7.9 percent. Therefore, the reinvestment rate risk present in bond investments has a negative impact on this particular bond investment.

The results of a drop in the reinvestment rate are shown in Part B of Table 12-4, using the same format as before. As this panel shows, at the end of year five the ending amount of wealth for bond A now is only $1,447.13, representing a shortfall for the investor's objective. This result occurred because she did not immunize her bond portfolio against interest rate risk, but instead purchased a bond based on matching the maturity of the bond with her investment horizon. As explained, to protect against this interest rate risk it is necessary to purchase a bond whose duration, not maturity, is equal to the investor's investment horizon.

Assume that a $1,000 bond with a coupon rate of 7.9 percent and a six-year maturity could have been purchased at the same time. The duration of this bond, which we call bond B, is exactly five years, matching the investor's investment horizon. In this case, the bond would be immunized against interest rate risk because any shortfall arising from a declining reinvestment rate would be offset by a higher price for the bond at the end of the investment horizon (because the drop in interest rates produces an increase in the price of the bond). Note that at the end of five years, which is our investor's investment horizon, bond B has one year left to maturity and could be sold in the market.

The bottom panel of Table 12-4 illustrates the same process as before for bond B. Notice that the ending cash flows are the same for the first four years as they were for the previous situation with the five-year bond. At the end of year five, the bond still has one year to go to maturity, but its price has risen because of the drop in interest rates. As the analysis in Table 12-4 demonstrates, the ending wealth of $1,465.05 is more than enough to meet the investor's objective of $1,462.54 per $1,000 invested.

Thus, the example in Table 12-4 illustrates the basic concept of immunization. By choosing a bond or a portfolio of bonds with a duration equal to a predetermined investment horizon, it is possible, in principle, to immunize the portfolio against interest rate risk. Notice that reinvestment rate risk could have been completely eliminated by purchasing a zero-coupon bond with a maturity (and duration) of five years. The usefulness of zeroes for immunization purposes is one reason they have grown in popularity.

EXAMPLE 12-3: IMMUNIZATION

Bond portfolios that will achieve target wealth despite changes in interest rates are said to be immunized. Immunization is possible if the duration of the bond or portfolio equals the investor's horizon. If an investor needed $2,580 at the end of 10 years, he could achieve this by purchasing a 10-year zero-coupon bond with a face value of $2,580. If no suitable zero could be purchased, the investor could immunize himself in the short run using any traditional coupon bond, provided it had a duration of 10 years. For example, suppose the investor purchases a 20-year, 10 percent coupon bond with a duration of 10 years. He would be protected against rate changes in the immediate future. Assuming interest rates are presently at 8 percent, and remain at that level for the next 10 years, the bond would provide the owner with total income of $2,582.86 ($1,448.66 from the coupons reinvested at 8 percent and $1,134.20 from the value the bond would have at that point).

If rates fall to 7.5 percent (and remain at that level) during the first year after the investor buys the bond but before the first coupon payment, the total value after 10 years would be $2,586.31. This total is composed of $1,414.71 from reinvesting the coupons at 7.5 percent and $1,171.60 from the value of the bond in 10 years. The difference in value is only $3.45, because what the investor lost on reinvesting the coupons at only 7.5 percent, is made up in the increased bond value.

Immunization is in many respects a hybrid strategy between passive and active. Although the classical immunization discussed here could be thought of as a passive strategy, we must be aware of the real-world problems involved in implementing such a plan. In truth, this strategy is difficult to implement, and it is not a passive strategy in application. Immunization strategies based on duration matching only work well for small changes in interest rates, and for short periods of time. To achieve immunization as discussed here requires frequent rebalancing because duration should always be equal to the investment horizon. An investor simply cannot set duration equal to investment horizon at the beginning of the process and ignore the bond or portfolio thereafter (unless they hold zeroes). Finally, immunization based on duration matching is based on the assumption of a flat yield curve, and that changes in interest rates are parallel across the yield curve, which is generally not the case in practice.

There are several other variations of the basic immunization strategy. The most popular variation is called horizon matching or combination matching. This involves a portfolio that is duration matched and also cash matched in the first few years. Another variation is contingent immunization, which involves active management plus a lower floor return that is ensured for the horizon period. The portfolio manager must act to earn the floor return by immunizing the portfolio if necessary. Otherwise, the manager can actively manage the portfolio or some portion thereof.

12-5. Why is it that a high-coupon callable bond might not be a good choice for a passively managed portfolio?

12-6. An investor expects to liquidate her bond portfolio in five years. Her target portfolio value can be achieved with the current yields to maturity available on high-grade corporate bonds. Would the best strategy for this investor be to create a portfolio of bonds which mature in five years?

BUILDING A FIXED-INCOME PORTFOLIO

Having reviewed some active and passive strategies for managing a bond portfolio, we will now consider how to build a fixed-income portfolio. The first consideration, which is true throughout the range of investment decisions, is to decide on the risk–return trade-off that all investors face. If investors seek higher expected returns, they must be prepared to accept greater risk. In building a fixed-income portfolio, it is useful to think of the two broad approaches an investor can take—conservative and aggressive. We will use these two broad strategies next to organize the discussion.

learning objective 5
Describe how both conservative and aggressive investors build a fixed-income portfolio.

Conservative Investors

Conservative investors view bonds as fixed-income securities that will pay them a steady stream of income. In order to maintain low levels of risk, they will lean toward government issues that have practically no risk of default. These investors tend to use a buy-and-hold approach. This sort of investor seeks to maximize their current income subject to the risk (quality of issue) they are willing to assume: corporates should return more than government issues, BBB issues more than those rated A or AA, longer durations more than shorter durations, and so on.

Even conservative investors in bonds must consider a number of factors. Assume that an investor wishes to purchase only Government of Canada issues, thereby avoiding the possible risk of default. Careful consideration should be given to the duration of the issue, since the range is from T-bills of a month's duration to bonds maturing well into the twenty-first century. Reinvestment rate risk must be considered. For investors who may need their funds back before the bonds mature, interest rate risk is relevant.

The investor's choice will depend to a large extent on interest rate forecasts. Even conservative buy-and-hold investors should probably avoid long-term issues if interest rates are expected to rise over an extended period of time. Finally, investors may wish to consider the differences in coupons between issues. Previous discussion has shown that the lower the coupon on a bond, the higher the price volatility. Although many investors in this group may plan to hold to maturity, conditions can change, and they may need to sell some of these bonds before maturity.

EXAMPLE 12-4: CONSERVATIVE INVESTORS AND BOND PORTFOLIOS

As an example of what can happen to conservative investors when they are buying and holding a bond portfolio, consider the situation faced by municipal bond investors in the US in mid-1992. Most municipal bonds can be called after 10 years, and many investors had bought municipals in 1982 when interest rates were at record highs. On July 1, 1992, several billion dollars of municipals were redeemed, with more calls expected in the future on the typical call dates, January 1 and July 1. Investors were forced to give up high-yielding municipals at a time when interest rates were quite low. Moreover, in trying to replace the income stream, they had to consider alternatives with lower quality (and therefore greater risk) and/or longer maturity (and therefore subject to interest rate risk as rates rose), or simply resign themselves to a bond portfolio with a new, lower return.

Indirect investing through bond funds is another possibility. In addition to traditional bond funds that hold government securities, corporate bonds, or mixtures of these with a wide range of maturities, investors can consider flexible-income funds. These invest in bonds of all types, convertible securities, and stocks. The emphasis on these funds tends to be on income, but their investment strategies vary greatly.

Aggressive Investors

Aggressive investors are more focused on the capital gains that arise from a change in interest rates. There exists a substantial range of aggressiveness, from the really short-term speculator to the somewhat less aggressive investor who is willing to realize capital gains over a longer period while possibly earning high yields.

The short-term speculator studies interest rates carefully and moves into and out of securities on the basis of interest rate expectations. If rates are expected to fall, this investor can buy long-term, low-coupon issues and achieve maximum capital gains if the interest rate forecast is correct. Government bonds can be bought on margin to further magnify gains (or losses). Alternatively, the aggressive investor can turn to interest rate options or futures contracts on interest rate instruments, which are discussed in Chapter 19 and Chapter 20, respectively.

Another form of aggressive behaviour involves seeking the highest total return, whether from interest income or capital gains. Investors who follow this strategy plan on a long horizon in terms of holding a portfolio of bonds but engage in active trading during certain periods when such actions seem particularly appropriate. One such period was 1982, when bonds were offering record yields to maturity and interest rates were widely expected to decline. Even mildly aggressive investors could purchase government bonds yielding high-coupon income and have a reasonable expectation of capital gains. The downside risk in this strategy at this time was small. These investors still needed to consider maturity and coupon questions, however, because no interest rate decline can be assumed with certainty. This situation is in sharp contrast to today's environment where bond yields are low by historical standards.

The International Perspective

When investors build bond portfolios, they should consider the opportunities available in international markets. Investors can invest directly or indirectly in foreign bonds by making their own decisions and using their broker or by purchasing units in an investment fund holding foreign bonds.

As we know by now, larger returns are associated with larger risks. Speculative investors who purchase foreign bonds are implicitly betting on the future direction of interest rates in these countries, which, in turn, reflects bets on their economies. A slowdown would favour the odds of lower interest rates and higher bond prices. Furthermore, investors in foreign bonds face exchange rate or currency risk. Adverse currency fluctuations can significantly reduce the returns to a cash bond investor and wipe out an investor on margin. Therefore, investors must decide whether to hedge the position against adverse currency movements. Investors who are bearish on the foreign currency would probably choose to hedge their positions while investors who were bullish would not.

In Chapter 2, we noted that investors always have an alternative to direct investing. They can invest indirectly by purchasing units of investment funds that, in turn, invest in the securities in which they are interested. For example, a Canadian investor can purchase units in selected Global Bond Funds that hold diversified portfolios of North American, Asian, European, and some Australian and New Zealand bonds. Other global bond funds focus on the debt securities of only one country or on particular geographic areas such as Europe.

How does the Canadian dollar affect the foreign bond investor? If the Canadian economy improves, the dollar will probably rise, and if it rises against the currencies involved in the foreign bonds, after converting back to dollars, the returns to Canadian investors are negatively impacted. Most global bond funds recognize the importance of fluctuations in exchange rates and adopt a foreign exchange hedging policy, which may involve fully hedged, partially hedged, or completely unhedged positions, relative to a given currency.

SUMMARY

This summary relates to the learning objectives for this chapter.

1. **Explain why investors buy bonds.**

   A wide range of investors are interested in bonds, ranging from those who seek a steady stream of interest income and return of principal to those seeking capital gains by speculating on future interest rate movements.

2. **Discuss major considerations in managing a bond portfolio.**

   The future level of interest rates is the key factor affecting bond portfolio performance. Inflationary expectations play a key role in understanding what drives the bond market since they have a direct influence on interest rates. Yield spreads are the relationship between bond yields and particular bond features such as quality and callability. Differences in type, quality, and coupon account for most of the yield spreads.

3. **Explain what is meant by the term structure of interest rates.**

   The term structure of interest rates denotes the relationship between market yields and time to maturity. A yield curve depicts this relationship graphically, with upward-sloping curves being the most common. None of the prevalent theories proposed to explain term structure—the expectations theory, the liquidity preference theory, the preferred habitat theory, or the market segmentation theory—is dominant.

4. **Differentiate between passive and active strategies for managing a bond portfolio.**

   Bond investment strategies can be divided into passive and active. Passive bond strategies, whereby the investor does not try to outperform the market by actively seeking out trading possibilities, include buy and hold, and indexing. Active management strategies can be broadly divided into forecasting changes in interest rates and identifying relative mispricing between various fixed-income securities. New techniques include the use of mortgage instruments and strategies with financial futures. Interest rate swaps are now a significant item in the management of bond portfolios by institutions. A "hybrid" strategy is immunization, which involves protecting (immunizing) a portfolio against interest rate risk by attempting to have the two components of interest rate risk—reinvestment rate risk and price risk—cancel each other out.

5. **Describe how both conservative and aggressive investors build a fixed-income portfolio.**

   In building a bond portfolio, investors must make a decision on the risk–return trade-off. Conservative investors tend to use a buy-and-hold approach, whereas aggressive investors seek higher returns by speculating on interest rates or trading actively during certain periods.

KEY TERMS

Active management strategy, p.377

Bond swaps, p.379

Expectations theory, p.369

Forward rates, p.369

Immunization, p.381

Index funds, p.377

Interest rate swaps, p.379

Liquidity preference theory, p.370

Market segmentation theory, p.370

Passive management strategy, p.376

Preferred habitat theory, p.370

Term structure of interest rates, p.367

Yield curve, p.367

Yield spreads, p.371

REVIEW QUESTIONS

12-1. Describe two different types of investors interested in bonds.

12-2. List some of the problems involved for Canadian investors in buying and selling foreign bonds.

12-3. Identify and explain at least two passive bond management strategies.

12-4. Why is the yield on Government of Canada bonds used as the benchmark for comparing yields on various types of bonds?

12-5. Explain the difference between the expectations theory and the liquidity preference theory of term structure.

12-6. What is the normal slope of the yield curve for bonds?

12-7. What is the difference between a spot rate and a forward rate?

12-8. How would proponents of the liquidity preference theory explain the existence of a downward-sloping yield curve?

12-9. What is the key factor in analyzing bonds? Why?

12-10. Identify and explain two specific active bond management strategies. Are the two related?

12-11. You have correctly forecast that interest rates will soon decline sharply. Assuming that you will invest only in fixed-income securities and that your time horizon is one year, how would you construct a portfolio?

12-12. When would investors find bonds with long maturities, selling at large discounts, particularly unattractive as investment opportunities?

12-13. How can horizon analysis be used to manage a bond portfolio?

12-14. You are interested in some British government bonds that are currently yielding three percentage points more than comparable Government of Canada securities. If you think the British economy will slow down, is this favourable or unfavourable for your decision to purchase British bonds? If you are bullish on the British pound, does this suggest a hedged or unhedged position when you buy the bonds?

12-15. If you have constructed a bond portfolio that is properly immunized, would you sell the bonds on their maturity dates or before? Why?

12-16. Explain the concept of immunization. What role, if any, does duration play in this concept?

12-17. Describe four types of bond swaps. Indicate the assumption(s) being made by an investor in undertaking these swaps.

12-18. Name three differences in bond characteristics that may lead to "yield spreads."

12-19. What tends to happen to yield spreads during periods of uncertainty? Briefly explain.

12-20. Assume a Canadian investor buys French bonds. If the euro weakens, how does that affect the Canadian investor's dollar-denominated return?

12-21. A Canadian investor buying foreign bonds is selling the dollar. Agree or disagree and explain your reasoning.

12-22. Why would bond yields be expected to move in the same direction as nominal GDP?

12-23. Why would an expected increase in inflation negatively impact bond investors?

12-24. In 2008, why would the Fed's multiple increases in the federal funds rate be expected to lead to increases in the long-term bond rate in the US?

12-25. Under the expectations theory, long rates must be an average of the present and future short-term rates. Explain.

12-26. Why are yield spreads important to an investor?

PROBLEMS

12-1. Assume the current one-year spot rate is 8 percent, and the implied forward rates for one, two, and three years hence are as follows:

$$_1f_2 = 9\%$$
$$_2f_3 = 10\%$$
$$_3f_4 = 11\%$$

    a. What price should a $1,000 face-value zero-coupon bond sell for that has four years until maturity?

    b. Based on the expectations theory, what are the expected one-year interest rates for years 2, 3, and 4?

    c. Based on the liquidity preference theory, are the expected one-year interest rates for years 2, 3, and 4 the same as in part (b)? Why or why not?

12-2. If the yield on a one-year Government of Canada Treasury bill is 7.8 percent, and the yield on a two-year Government of Canada Bond is 8.05 percent, what is the implied one-year forward rate for the second year $(_1f_2)$?

12-3. You are asked to invest $30 million in a bond portfolio consisting of only two bonds. Bond A has a duration of 4.36 years, and bond B has a duration of 6.50 years. The portfolio is expected to have an investment horizon of five years. How much of each bond issue would you have to buy to immunize the portfolio?

12-4. You buy a five-year, 12 percent bond that pays annual coupons at its par value of $1,000. If its duration is four years, compare your ending wealth at the end of four years if interest rates (i) immediately fall to 11 percent or (ii) immediately increase to 13 percent.

12-5. You are managing a diversified bond portfolio that is presently composed of 60 percent government bonds and 40 percent corporate bonds. The current spread between government long-term bonds and corporate bonds is 1 percent, and you believe this spread will narrow in the near future. What actions will you take to attempt to benefit from this belief? Be specific.

12-6. You observe the following spot rates for government (AAA rated) bonds: 1 year = 4%; 2 years = 4.5%; 3 years = 5%; 4 years = 5.5%; 5 years = 6%.

    a. Calculate the implied forward rates for years 2 through 5. Round to three decimal places in all your calculations (e.g. 5.123%)

    b. The spread between the forward rates for government bonds and for corporate bonds (A rated) is currently 0.6 percent in all future years. Determine the forward rates on corporate bonds. Note that the "forward rate" for year 1 is the same as the spot rate for one year.

    c. Use these corporate forward rates to calculate the spot rates for the corporate bonds for maturities from 1 to 5 years. Are these equal to the government spot rates plus the spread?

    d. Suppose a 5-year government bond pays an annual coupon of $50, and has a $1,000 face value. Find the current price of this bond using the spot rates. Now find its price using the forward rates. You should get the same price! What is the yield-to-maturity on this bond?

    e. What annual coupon payment would be required on a 5-year corporate bond for it to have the same price today as the government bond? Hint: you can use Excel's "Solver" utility to get this answer. What is the YTM on this bond?

12-7. The following four bonds are available to be added to your portfolio. You would like to explore how different combinations of these bonds will affect the yield and duration of the portfolio. Each bond matures exactly 10 years from today, and coupon interest is paid annually.

Bond	A	B	C	D
Coupon	8.5%	7.0%	5.5%	0.0%
YTM	7.0%	7.0%	6.5%	6.5%

   a. Calclate the current price for each bond. Assume the face value is $100.

   b. Create a table with the cash flows for each year, for each bond. For example, Bond A's cash flows are $8.50 in years 1 to 9 and $108.50 in year 10.

   c. Determine the cash flows for two different portfolios you are considering: one portfolio will have exactly one of each bond (so the initial investment will be the sum of the prices of the four bonds); the other will be equal weighted (i.e., 25 percent of the portfolio invested in each bond.) You can set the total value of this portfolio to be the same as the cost of the first portfolio. Hint: determine how many of each bond can be purchased with 25 percent of the total portfolio value before working out the portfolio cash flows.

   d. Calculate the yield on these two portfolios. Hint: if you set the total cost (or price) as a negative value (time 0 cash outflow) and years 1 to 10 cash flows as positive figures, the "=IRR" spreadsheet function will give you the desired yield.

   e. Create a table showing the present values for all the cash flows you determined above. Be sure to use the yield (or YTM) for each bond or portfolio to discount the cash flows associated with that item.

   f. Calculate the duration for each bond and portfolio. The built-in spreadsheet function could be used for the individual bonds, but not for the portfolios. You may want to refer to Equation 11-10 for calculating duration. Use the table of present values; multiply each figure by the year (time) at which it occurs (this is easily accomplished using the "=SUMPRODUCT" function); then divide this sum by the cost of the bond or portfolio. If you've done this correctly, the duration for Bond D (a zero-coupon bond) is exactly 10, and the equal-weighted portfolio will have a duration equal to the average (actually a weighted average) of the four bond durations. Note that the higher yielding portfolio (the first one, with one of each bond) has a lower duration, as you should expect.

PREPARING FOR YOUR PROFESSIONAL EXAMS

CFA PRACTICE QUESTIONS

12-1. The table below shows spot rates on US Treasury securities as of January 1, 1993:

Term to maturity	1	2	3	4	5	10
Spot rates	3.50%	4.50%	5.00%	5.50%	6.00%	6.60%

Based on this data, the implied forward one-year rate of interest at January 1, 1996 is:

   a. 2.4 percent.
   b. 5.50 percent.
   c. 7.01 percent.
   d. 6.00 percent.

12-2. In explaining the shape of yield curves, the expectation hypothesis asserts that:

    a. the yield curve is primarily explained by the interest rate anticipations of investors.

    b. once a flat yield curve has been established, it will stabilize.

    c. descending yield curves are typical.

    d. yield curves take an ascending form due to the compounding effect.

12-3. Which theory explains the shape of the yield curve by considering the relative demands for various maturities?

    a. Liquidity premium theory

    b. Relative strength theory

    c. Unbiased expectations theory

    d. Segmentation theory

12-4. A portfolio manager who subscribed to the liquidity preference hypothesis would expect:

    a. long-term rates to be higher than expected due to the existence of a liquidity premium.

    b. that longer-term securities will tend to promise higher returns.

    c. rational investors to pay a price premium for a shorter-term security.

    d. All of the above.

CFA CURRICULUM AND SAMPLE EXAM QUESTIONS (©CFA INSTITUTE)

12-1. An analyst stated that a callable bond has less reinvestment risk and more price appreciation potential than an otherwise identical option-free bond. The analyst's statement most likely is:

    a. incorrect with respect to both reinvestment risk and price appreciation potential.

    b. incorrect with respect to reinvestment risk, but correct with respect to price appreciation potential.

    c. correct with respect to reinvestment risk, but incorrect with respect to price appreciation potential.

    d. correct with respect to both reinvestment risk and price appreciation potential.

12-2. An analyst stated that an amortizing security typically has more reinvestment risk and more interest rate risk than an otherwise identical zero-coupon bond. The analyst's statement most likely is:

    a. incorrect with respect to both reinvestment risk and interest rate risk.

    b. incorrect with respect to reinvestment risk, but correct with respect to interest rate risk.

    c. correct with respect to reinvestment risk, but incorrect with respect to interest rate risk.

    d. correct with respect to both reinvestment risk and interest rate risk.

12-3. All other factors being equal, would bond yield spreads from treasury securities most likely be larger (wider):

	For bond issues that are liquid or illiquid?	For bonds issued with put options or with call options?
a.	Liquid	Put options
b.	Liquid	Call options
c.	Illiquid	Put options
d.	Illiquid	Call options

12-4. In a normal yield curve environment, the relationship between yield and maturity can be best described as:

 a. the longer the maturity, the lower the yield.
 b. the longer the maturity, the higher the yield.
 c. maturity and yield are independent of each other.
 d. the yield is approximately the same for all maturities.

12-5. What are the four types of shapes observed for the yield curve?

12-6. How is the slope of the yield curve defined and measured?

12-7. Based on the broadest interpretation of the pure expectations theory, what would be the difference in the 4-year total return if an investor purchased a 7-year zero-coupon bond or a 15-year zero-coupon bond?

12-8. Based on the local expectations form of the pure expectations theory, what would be the difference in the 6-month total return if an investor purchased a 5-year zero-coupon bond or a 2-year zero-coupon bond?

12-9. Comment on the following statement made by a portfolio manager to a client:

Proponents of the unbiased expectations theory argue that the forward rates built into the term structure of interest rates are the market's consensus of future interest rates. We disagree with the theory because studies suggest that forward rates are poor predictors of future interest rates. Therefore, the position that our investment management firm takes is that forward rates are irrelevant and provide no information to our managers in managing a bond portfolio.

12-10. Based on arbitrage arguments, give two interpretations for each of the following three forward rates:

 a. The 1-year forward rate seven years from now is 6.4%.
 b. The 2-year forward rate one year from now is 6.2%.
 c. The 8-year forward rate three years from now is 7.1%.

12-11. You are the financial consultant to a pension fund. After your presentation to the trustees of the fund, you asked the trustees if they have any questions. You receive the two questions below. Answer each one.

 a. "The yield curve is upward-sloping today. Doesn't this suggest that the market consensus is that interest rates are expected to increase in the future and therefore you should reduce the interest rate risk exposure for the portfolio that you are managing for us?"
 b. "I am looking over one of the pages in your presentation that shows spot rates and I am having difficulty in understanding it. The spot rates at the short end (up to three years) are increasing with maturity. For maturities greater than three years but less than eight years, the spot rates are declining with maturity. Finally, for maturities greater than eight years the spot rates are virtually the same for each maturity. There is simply no expectations theory that would explain that type of shape for the term structure of interest rates. Is this market simply unstable?"

12-12. Below are the key rate durations for three portfolios of US Treasury securities all with the same duration for a parallel shift in the yield curve.

a. For each portfolio describe the type of portfolio (barbell, ladder, or bullet).

Key Rate Maturity	Portfolio A	Portfolio B	Portfolio C
3-month	0.04	0.04	0.03
1-year	0.06	0.29	0.07
2-year	0.08	0.67	0.31
3-year	0.28	0.65	0.41
5-year	0.38	0.65	1.90
7-year	0.65	0.64	0.35
10-year	3.38	0.66	0.41
15-year	0.79	0.67	0.70
20-year	0.36	0.64	1.95
25-year	0.12	0.62	0.06
30-year	0.06	0.67	0.01

b. Which portfolio will benefit the most if the spot rate for the 10-year decreases by 50 basis points while the spot rate for all other key maturities change very little?

c. What is the duration for a parallel shift in the yield curve for the three portfolios?

12-13. Can an inverted (i.e., downward sloping) yield curve occur with the three theories of the term structure of interest rates (pure expectations theory, liquidity preference theory, and market segmentation theory)?

a. Yes.
b. All except pure expectations.
c. All except liquidity preference.
d. All except market segmentation.

12-14. An investor is considering the purchase of four option-free bonds:

Bond	Coupon rate
1	7.0%
2	7.5%
3	8.0%
4	8.5%

All four bonds have the same time remaining to maturity and the same 8.0 percent yield to maturity. If the investor plans to hold the bonds to maturity, the bond with the total dollar return that is most dependent on reinvestment income is bond:

a. 1.
b. 2.
c. 3.
d. 4.

CHAPTER 13

COMMON STOCK VALUATION

The moment you have been waiting for is almost at hand. Having prepared yourself to manage your inheritance by dealing with the numerous issues you have now reviewed, whether it be mutual funds, or selling short, or basic portfolio theory, or the CAPM, what you really want to do is what most people are itching to do—get out there and buy some stocks. After all, you know someone who bought Cisco at $20 and it went to $90, and you know for sure this person is not the brightest bulb in the chandelier. On the other hand, you have read all the horror stories about the folks who bought the technology stocks, which subsequently collapsed, if indeed they even survived—and some of these people were surely smart. So there must be more to it than is at first apparent. Once again you decide you have to bite the bullet and learn about valuation. The bad news, as you are about to learn, is that valuation is as much an art as it is a science—it requires judgement as well as skill. The good news is that learning the basic principles of valuation, though not a guarantee of success, will in fact give you an advantage over many investors.

Learning Objectives

After reading this chapter, you should be able to

1. Name two approaches to the valuation of common stocks used in fundamental security analysis.
2. Explain the present value approach.
3. Use the dividend discount model to estimate stock prices.
4. Explain the P/E ratio approach.
5. Outline other relative valuation approaches.

CHAPTER PREVIEW

In the next few chapters, we explore the approaches that investors use to value and select common stocks. In this chapter, we concentrate on two valuation methods used in fundamental security analysis, which seeks to estimate the intrinsic value of a stock: present value and P/E ratio or earnings multiplier. Under present value, we explain how to use the dividend discount model to estimate stock prices; Appendix 13B discusses another widely used present value approach, the free cash flow model. We then consider the P/E ratio, the approach most widely used by practising security analysts, as well as other valuation methods.

THE PRESENT VALUE APPROACH

learning objective 1
Name two approaches to the valuation of common stocks used in fundamental security analysis.

learning objective 2
Explain the present value approach.

The classic method of calculating intrinsic (estimated or formula) value involves the use of present value analysis, which is often referred to as the capitalization of income method. As explained in Chapter 11, a present value process involving the capitalization (discounting) of expected future cash flows can be used to estimate the value of any security. That is, the intrinsic value of a security can be estimated as the discounted (present) value of the future stream of cash flows that an investor expects to receive from the asset. Repeating from Chapter 11,

(13-1)
$$\text{Estimated value of security} = \sum_{t=1}^{n} \frac{\text{Cash Flows}}{(1 + k)^t}$$

where
k = the appropriate discount rate or required rate of return[1]

To use such a model, an investor must

1. Estimate an appropriate required rate of return.
2. Estimate the amount and timing of the future stream of cash flows.
3. Use these two components in a present value model to estimate the value of the security, which is then compared with the current market price of the security.

Figure 13-1 summarizes the present value process commonly used in fundamental analysis. It emphasizes the factors that go into valuing common stocks. The exact nature of the present value process used by investors in the marketplace depends upon assumptions made about the growth rate in the expected stream of cash flows, as explained later in this chapter.

The Required Rate of Return

An investor who is considering the purchase of a common stock must assess its risk and the associated minimum expected rate of return that will be required to induce the investor to make the purchase. This minimum expected return, or *required rate of return*, is an opportunity cost. It is the same concept as the required yield used in Chapter 11 to value bonds.

The *required rate of return, capitalization rate,* and *discount rate* are interchangeable terms in valuation analysis. Regardless of which term is used, it is challenging to determine the numerical value to use for a particular stock. While in theory we know what this variable is, in practice it is not easy to arrive at the precise number to use. Because of this complexity, we will generally assume that we know the capitalization rate and concentrate on the other issues involved in valuation, which are difficult enough. In the next chapter, we consider the required rate of return in more detail.

---

[1]The concept of required rate of return is explained in more detail in Chapter 14.

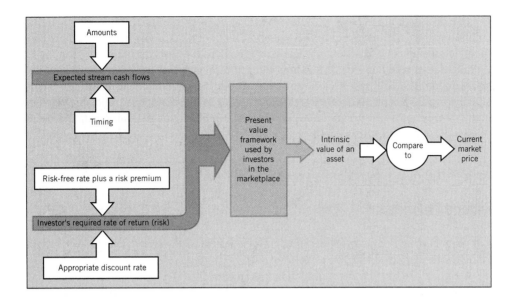

Figure 13-1
The Present Value
Approach to Valuation

The Expected Cash Flows

The other component that goes into the present value framework is the expected stream of cash flows. Just as the value of a bond is the present value of all interest payments plus the present value of the bond's face value that will be received at maturity, the value of a common stock is the present value of all the cash flows to be received from the issuer (corporation). The questions that arise are

1. What are the cash flows to use in valuing a stock?
2. What are the expected amounts of the cash flows?
3. When will the expected cash flows be received?

Shareholders may plan to sell their shares sometime in the future, resulting in a cash flow from the sales price. As we will see later, however, even if investors think of the total cash flows from common stocks as a combination of dividends and a future price at which the stock can be sold, this is equivalent to using the stream of all dividends to be received on the stock.

What about earnings? Are they important? Can they be used in valuing a stock? The answer to both questions is yes. Dividends are paid out of earnings and are clearly important. An alternative approach to fundamental analysis, which is considered later, uses the earnings and a P/E ratio to determine intrinsic value. Therefore, earnings are an important part of fundamental analysis; in fact, earnings receive more attention from investors than any other single variable.

If the corporation retains earnings, they presumably will be reinvested, thereby enhancing future earnings and, ultimately, future dividends. The present value analysis should not count the earnings reinvested currently and paid later as dividends. If properly defined and separated, these two variables produce the same results. This means that more than one present value model is possible.[2] However, it is theoretically correct to use dividends in the present value analysis, and this is what is usually done when investors use the present value approach to valuation.

INVESTING *tip*

To find which cash flows are appropriate in the valuation of a common stock, ask yourself the following question: If I buy a particular common stock and place it in a special trust fund for the perpetual benefit of myself and my heirs, what cash flows will be received? The answer is dividends, because this is the only cash distribution that a corporation actually makes to its shareholders. Although a firm's earnings per share in any year technically belong to the shareholders, corporations generally do not pay out all their earnings but reinvest a portion into the firm.

---

[2]In addition to dividends and earnings, the variable referred to as "free cash flow" (defined later) is often used for these models.

Because dividends are the only cash flow stream to be received directly by investors under normal conditions, it is appropriate to have a valuation model based on dividends. We now consider such a model, the dividend discount model, which provides the basis for understanding the fundamental valuation of common stocks. It is important to recognize that there is an important link between dividends and earnings. Recall from your introductory finance that firms are reluctant to increase dividend payments unless they are confident they can be maintained, and are even more reluctant to cut dividends because of the negative signal it sends to market participants. This issue is discussed in Real-World Returns 13-1.

REAL-WORLD RETURNS 13-1

Dividend Payments

All we keep hearing is how awful things are. Credit is tight. Consumers are nervous. Growth is slowing or threatening to shift into reverse.

Yesterday, Federal Reserve chairman Ben Bernanke didn't help matters, warning that "the outlook for the economy has worsened in recent months, and the downside risks to growth have increased."

But if everything is so terrible, why are so many companies raising their dividends? Do they know something we don't know?

Let's look at the evidence.

Yesterday, EnCana doubled its quarterly dividend to 40 cents (US) a share after fourth-quarter profit leaped 63 percent to $1.08-billion. Canada's biggest oil and gas company—whose dividend is now more than four times as large as it was in 2006—cited "confidence in the sustainability of its business model" for the latest hike.

That doesn't sound like a company bracing for an economic slowdown.

But, you say, energy companies are enjoying an era of high resource prices, so of course they're raising their dividends. They're the exception, right?

Wrong. Two of Canada's biggest life insurers also raised their payouts yesterday. Sun Life Financial boosted its quarterly dividend to 36 cents from 34 cents, even as profit rose less than expected and investors hammered the stock. A few hours later, Great-West Lifeco raised its dividend to 29.25 cents from 27.5 cents, after quarterly profit jumped 9 percent.

What about mutual fund companies? With stock markets in disarray and investors heading for the nearest fallout shelter, you'd think fund companies would be cutting their payouts, or at least not raising them.

Wrong again. Late last month, AGF Management hiked its dividend by a hefty 25 percent. After the close yesterday, the country's biggest mutual fund company, IGM Financial, was also expected to raise its quarterly payout, for the third time in the past 12 months.

What's going on here? Simple: Companies are expressing their confidence that, although the economy may be heading for a slowdown, their profits will keep growing—perhaps not as quickly as before, and maybe with a hiccup here or there, but growing nonetheless.

Companies do not treat dividend increases lightly. After all, when a board declares a dividend, it is not merely a promise to make this quarter's payment. It is an implicit promise to pay at least the same level of dividends in subsequent quarters, too, for there is no greater sin a company can commit than cutting its dividend. To do so means certain death for its stock, not to mention all those executive options tied to the share price.

And while it's true that several US financial institutions, including Citigroup, have cut their dividends because of the subprime debacle, Canadian banks are generally in a much stronger financial position. Bank dividend increases may be smaller this year than in years past, but they're still expected to grow. And that growth will pick up when the economy gets back on track.

(continued)

The Dividend Discount Model

learning objective 3
Use the dividend discount model to estimate stock prices.

Since dividends are the only cash payment a shareholder receives directly from a firm, they are the foundation of valuation for common stocks. In adapting Equation 13-1 specifically to value common stocks, the cash flows are the dividends expected to be paid in each future period. An investor or analyst using this approach carefully studies the future prospects for a company and estimates the likely dividends to be paid. In addition, the analyst estimates an appropriate required rate of return or discount rate based on the risk foreseen in the dividends and given the alternatives available. Finally, he or she would discount to the present, the entire stream of estimated future dividends (properly identified as to amount and timing).

The present value approach to calculating the value of a common stock is conceptually no different from the approach used in Chapter 11 to value bonds or in Appendix 13A at the end of the chapter to value preferred stock. Specifically, Equation 13-1 adapted for common stocks, where dividends are the expected future cash flows, results in Equation 13-2. This equation, known as the **dividend discount model (DDM)**, states that the value of a stock today is the discounted value of all future dividends:

Dividend Discount Model (DDM)
A model for determining the estimated price of a stock by discounting all expected future dividends by the appropriate required rate of return for the stock.

$$\hat{P}_{CS} = \frac{D_1}{(1 + k_{CS})^1} + \frac{D_2}{(1 + k_{CS})^2} + \ldots + \frac{D_\infty}{(1 + k_{CS})^\infty} \qquad \textbf{(13-2)}$$

$$= \sum_{t=1}^{\infty} \frac{D_t}{(1 + k_{CS})^t}$$

$$= \text{Dividend discount model (DDM)}$$

where

$\hat{P}_{CS}$ = intrinsic or estimated value of a common stock today based on the model user's estimates of the future dividends and the required rate of return

$D_1, D_2, \ldots$ = the dividends expected to be received in each future period

k_{CS} = the required rate of return for this stock, which is the discount rate applicable for an investment with this degree of riskiness (again, the opportunity cost of a comparable risk alternative)

There are two immediate problems with Equation 13-2:

1. The last term in Equation 13-2 indicates that investors are dealing with infinity. They must value a stream of dividends that may be paid forever, since common stock has no maturity date.

2. The dividend stream is uncertain:

   a. There are no specified number of dividends, if, in fact, any are paid at all. If dividends are to be paid, they must be declared periodically by the firm's board of directors. (Usually, they are declared quarterly but conventional valuation analysis uses annual dividends.)

   b. The dividends for most firms are expected to grow over time; therefore, investors usually cannot simplify Equation 13-2 to a **perpetuity** as in the case of a preferred stock.[3] Only if

Perpetuity
An annuity with no maturity date.

---

[3]Refer to Appendix 13A at the end of the chapter for details regarding the valuation of preferred stock.

dividends are not expected to grow can such a simplification be made. Although such a possibility exists and is covered below, it is unusual.

How are these problems resolved? The first problem, that Equation 13-2 involves an infinite number of periods and dividends, will be resolved when we deal with the second problem, specifying the expected stream of dividends. However, from a practical standpoint, this problem is not as troublesome as it first appears. At reasonably high discount rates, such as 12, 14, or 16 percent, dividends received 40 or 50 years in the future are worth very little today, so that investors need not worry about them. For example, if the discount rate is 15 percent, the present value of $1 to be received 50 years from now is $0.0009.

The conventional solution to the second problem, that the dollar amount of the dividend is expected to grow over time, is to make some assumptions about the expected growth rate of dividends. That is, the investor or analyst estimates or models the expected percentage rate of growth in the future stream of dividends. To do this, he or she classifies each stock to be valued into one of three categories based on the expected growth pattern in dividends. In summary: We operationalize the dividend discount model by estimating the expected growth rate(s) in the dividend stream.

A timeline will be used to represent the three alternative growth rate versions of the dividend discount model. All stocks that pay a dividend, or that are expected to in the future, can be modelled using this approach. It is critical to remember in using the DDM that an investor must account for all dividends from now to infinity by modelling the growth rate(s). As shown below, the mechanics of this process are such that we don't actually see all of these dividends because the formulas reduce to a simplified form, but nevertheless we are accounting for all future dividends when we use the DDM.

It is necessary in using the DDM to remember that the dividend currently being paid on a stock (or the most recent dividend paid) is designated as D_0 and is, of course, known. However, investors must estimate the future dividends to be paid, starting with D_1, the dividend expected to be paid in the next period.

The three growth rate models for dividends are

1. A dividend stream with a zero-growth rate resulting from a fixed dollar dividend equal to the current dividend, D_0, being paid every year from now to infinity. This is typically referred to as the no-growth rate or zero-growth rate model:

D_0	D_0	D_0	D_0	$+ \ldots +$	D_0	Dividends
0	1	2	3	$+ \ldots +$	∞	Time period

2. A dividend stream that is growing at a constant rate, g, starting with D_0. This is typically referred to as the constant or normal growth version of the dividend discount model:

D_0	$D_0(1 + g)^1$	$D_0(1 + g)^2$	$+ \ldots +$	$D_0(1 + g)^\infty$	Dividends
0	1	2	$+ \ldots +$	∞	Time period

3. A dividend stream that is growing at variable rates, for example, g_1 for the first two years and g_2 thereafter, is referred to as the multiple-growth version of the dividend discount model:

D_0	$D_1 = D_0(1 + g_1)$	$D_2 = D_1(1 + g_1)$	$D_3 = D_2(1 + g_2) + \ldots + D_\infty = D_{\infty-1}(1 + g_2)$	Dividends
0	1	2	3 $+ \ldots +$ ∞	Time period

CHECK YOUR UNDERSTANDING

13-1. What are the two key inputs when using the present value approach to value common stock?

13-2. Why is the required rate of return for a stock critical in the valuation process?

> **13-3.** What does it really mean to say that the estimated value of a stock today is the discounted value of all future dividends?

The Zero-Growth Model

Under the non-growth case, the dividend model reduces to a perpetual annuity or perpetuity. Assuming a constant dollar dividend, Equation 13-2 simplifies to the no-growth model shown as Equation 13-3.

$$\hat{P}_0 = \frac{D_0}{k_{CS}} = \text{Zero} - \text{growth version of the DDM} \tag{13-3}$$

where D_0 is the constant dollar dividend expected for all future time periods and k_{CS} is the opportunity cost or required rate of return for this particular common stock.

The no-growth case is equivalent to the valuation process for a preferred stock discussed at the end of this chapter because, exactly like a preferred stock, the dividend (numerator of Equation 13-3) remains unchanged. Therefore, the dividends arising from a zero-growth rate common stock represent a perpetuity that can be easily valued once k_{CS} is determined.

It is extremely important in understanding the valuation of common stocks using the DDM to recognize that in all cases an investor is discounting the future stream of dividends from now to infinity. This fact tends to be overlooked when using the perpetuity formula involving the zero-growth rate case because the discounting process is greatly simplified. Nevertheless, in this case, as in all others, we are accounting for all dividends from now to infinity. It is simply a mathematical fact that dividing a constant dollar amount by the discount rate, k, produces a result equivalent to discounting each dividend from now to infinity separately and summing all of the present values.

The Constant Growth Model

The other two versions of the DDM indicate that to establish the cash flow stream of expected dividends, which is to be subsequently discounted, it is first necessary to compound some beginning dividend into the future. Obviously, the higher the growth rate used, the greater the future amount, and the longer the time period, the greater the future amount.

A well-known scenario in valuation is the case in which dividends are expected to grow at a constant rate over time. This constant- or normal-growth model[4] is shown as Equation 13-4.

$$\hat{P}_0 = \frac{D_0(1 + g)}{(1 + k_{CS})^1} + \frac{D_0(1 + g)^2}{(1 + k_{CS})^2} + \frac{D_0(1 + g)^3}{(1 + k_{CS})^3} + \dots + \frac{D_0(1 + g)^\infty}{(1 + k_{CS})^\infty} \tag{13-4}$$

where D_0 is the current dividend being paid and growing at the constant rate g, and k_{CS} is the appropriate discount rate.

Equation 13-4 can be simplified to the following equation:[5]

$$\hat{P}_0 = \frac{D_1}{k_{CS} - g} \tag{13-5}$$

where D_1 is the dividend expected to be received at the end of Year 1. Notice that k must be greater than g, or else the results are uninformative.

---

[4]The constant-growth model is often referred to as the Gordon model named after Myron J. Gordon, who played a large part in its development and use.

[5]Equation 13-4 represents a geometric series that is being multiplied by $(1 + g)/(1 + k)$ every period. The sum of this series is represented by Equation 13-5 as the number of periods involved approaches infinity.

Equation 13-5 is used whenever the growth rate of future dividends is estimated to be constant to infinity. It is used quite often in actual practice because of its simplicity and because in many circumstances, it is a reasonable description of the actual behaviour of a large number of companies, as well as the market as a whole.

EXAMPLE 13-1: ESTIMATING PRICE FOR SUMMA CORPORATION

Summa Corporation is currently paying $1 per share in dividends and investors expect those to grow at the rate of 7 percent a year for the foreseeable future. For investments at this risk level, investors require a return of 15 percent a year. The estimated price of Summa is

$$\hat{P}_0 = \frac{D_1}{k_{CS} - g} = \frac{\$1.00(1.07)}{0.15 - 0.07} = \$13.38$$

Note that a current dividend (D_0) must be compounded for one period because the constant growth version of the DDM specifies the numerator as the dividend expected to be received one period from now, which is (D_1). This is consistent with the model's general approach of valuing stocks based on expected future cash flows. In valuation terminology, D_0 represents the dividend currently being paid, and D_1 represents the dividend expected to be paid in the next period. If D_0 is known, D_1 can always be estimated:

$$D_0 = \text{Current dividend}$$
$$D_1 = D_0(1 + g)$$

where g is the expected growth rate of dividends.[6]

To completely understand the constant-growth model, which is widely used in valuation analysis, it is instructive to think about the process that occurs under constant growth. Table 13-1 illustrates the case of Summa's growth stock with a current dividend of $1 per share (D_0), an expected constant growth rate of 7 percent, and a required rate of return, k, of 15 percent.

Table 13-1

Present Value of 60 Years of Dividends
(current dividend = $1 g = 7% k = 15%)

Period	Dollar Dividend	PV Factor	PV of Dollar Dividend
1	1.07	0.8696	0.93
2	1.14	0.7561	0.87
3	1.23	0.6576	0.81
4	1.31	0.5718	0.75
5	1.40	0.4972	0.70
6	1.50	0.4323	0.65
7	1.61	0.3759	0.60
8	1.72	0.3269	0.56
9	1.84	0.2843	0.521
10	1.97	0.2472	0.49
11	2.10	0.2149	0.45
12	2.25	0.1869	0.42
13	2.41	0.1625	0.39
14	2.58	0.1413	0.36

[6]Similarly, D_2 can be determined in the constant growth model as $D_0(1 + g)^2$ or $D_1(1 + g)$.

Period	Dollar Dividend	PV Factor	PV of Dollar Dividend
15	2.76	0.1229	0.34
16	2.95	0.1069	0.32
17	3.16	0.0929	0.29
18	3.38	0.0808	0.27
19	3.62	0.0703	0.25
20	3.87	0.0611	0.24
21	4.14	0.0531	0.22
22	4.43	0.0462	0.20
23	4.74	0.0402	0.19
24	5.07	0.0349	0.18
25	5.43	0.0304	0.16
26	5.81	0.0264	0.15
27	6.21	0.0230	0.14
28	6.65	0.0200	0.13
29	7.11	0.0174	0.12
30	7.61	0.0151	0.11
31	8.15	0.0131	0.11
32	8.72	0.0114	0.10
33	9.33	0.0099	0.09
34	9.98	0.0086	0.09
35	10.68	0.0075	0.08
36	11.42	0.0065	0.07
37	12.22	0.0057	0.07
38	13.08	0.0049	0.06
39	13.99	0.0043	0.06
40	14.97	0.0037	0.06
41	16.02	0.0032	0.05
42	17.14	0.0028	0.05
43	18.34	0.0025	0.05
44	19.63	0.0021	0.04
45	21.00	0.0019	0.04
46	22.47	0.0016	0.04
47	24.05	0.0014	0.03
48	25.73	0.0012	0.03
49	27.53	0.0011	0.03
50	29.46	0.0009	0.03
51	31.52	0.0008	0.03
52	33.73	0.0007	0.02
53	36.09	0.0006	0.02
54	38.61	0.0005	0.02
55	41.32	0.0005	0.02
56	44.21	0.0004	0.02
57	47.30	0.0003	0.02
58	50.61	0.0003	0.02
59	54.16	0.0003	0.01
60	57.95	0.0002	0.01

Sum of dividends = $870.47

Sum of first 60 years of discounted dividends = $13.20

As Table 13-1 shows, the expected dollar dividend for each period in the future grows by 7 percent. Therefore, $D_1 = \$1.07$, $D_2 = \$1.14$, $D_{10} = \$1.97$, and so forth. Only the first 60 years of growth are shown, at the end of which time the dollar dividend is \$57.95. The last column of Table 13-1 shows the discounted value of each of the first 60 years of dividends. Thus, the present value of the dividend for Period 1, discounted at 15 percent, is \$0.93. While the actual dollar amount of the expected dividend in Year 60 is \$57.95, its present value in today's dollars is only \$0.01. Obviously, dividends received far in the future, assuming normal discount rates, are worth very little today.

Figure 13-2 depicts the growth in the dollar dividend for only the first 30 years in order to provide some scale to the process. Because k is greater than g, the present value of each future dividend is declining, since the dividends are growing at a rate (g) that is below the discount rate (k) being used in the denominator of the discount procedure. For example, the present value of $D_1 = \$0.93$, the present value of $D_2 = \$0.87$, and the present value of $D_{10} = \$0.49$. Therefore, the present-value-of-dividends curve at the bottom of Figure 13-2 is declining more rapidly than the estimated-dollar-dividend-over-time curve above it is increasing.

The estimated price of Summa, as illustrated in Table 13-1 and Figure 13-2, is the sum of the present values of each of the future dividends. Adding each of these present values together from now to infinity would produce the correct estimated value of the stock. Note from Table 13-1 that adding the present values of the first 60 years of dividends together produces an estimated value of \$13.20. The correct answer, as obtained from adding all years from now to infinity, was calculated as \$13.38 in the example above, for a difference of only \$0.18. This implies that the dividends received from Years 61 to infinity add a total value of \$0.18 to the stock price (i.e., the present value of all dividends received from Year 61 to infinity is only \$0.18 in year 0). The reason for this is the extremely low values for the PV factors as the number of periods increases.

Figure 13-2
The Constant Growth Model

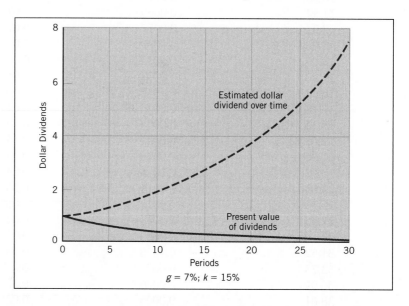

Table 13-1 illustrates the very important point about these valuation models that was explained earlier. The constant-growth version of the DDM given in Equation 13-5 takes account of all future cash flows from now to infinity, although this is not apparent from simply looking at the equation itself. Although Equation 13-5 has no summation or infinity sign, the results produced by this equation are equivalent to the sum that would be obtained by adding together the discounted value of all future dividends (as described in footnote 5). As was the case for the zero-growth model, the mathematics of the process involving a constant growth rate to infinity reduces to a very simple expression, masking the fact that all dividends from now to infinity are being accounted for.

The constant-growth DDM can also provide a useful assessment of the market's perception of growth opportunities available to a company. For example, let's assume that a firm with no profitable growth opportunities should not reinvest residual profits in the company, but rather pay out all its earnings in the form of dividends. This implies $g = 0$, and $D_1 = EPS_1$, where EPS_1 represents the expected earnings per common share in the upcoming year. Under these assumptions, the constant-growth DDM reduces to the following expression:

$$\hat{P}_0 = \frac{EPS_1}{k_{CS}}$$ **(13-6)**

Although we may not find many no-growth firms in practice, the result above can be applied to firms that do have growth opportunities available to them. Thus, at any given time we can view the share price of any common stock (that satisfies the assumptions of the DDM), as being composed of two components: its no-growth component and the present value of growth opportunities (PVGO). This can be expressed as

$$\hat{P}_0 = \frac{EPS_1}{k_{CS}} + PVGO$$ **(13-7)**

EXAMPLE 13-2: ESTIMATING PVGO FOR SUMMA CORPORATION

Assume the expected year one earnings per share (EPS_1) for Summa is $2.00. If their shares were trading at the intrinsic value of $13.38 (estimated in Example 13-1), it implies that only $0.05 for the present value of growth opportunities (PVGO) is factored by market participants into Summa's share price:

$$\hat{PVGO} = P_0 - \frac{EPS_1}{k_{CS}} = 13.38 - \frac{2.00}{0.15} = 13.38 - 13.33 = \$0.05$$

This suggests that very little of Summa's share price is attributable to future growth opportunities.

To fully understand the constant growth rate version of the DDM, it is also important to realize that the model shows that the stock price for any one period is estimated to grow at the same rate as the dividends, which is g. This means that the expected growth rate in price, plus the expected percentage return received in the form of dividends, will equal the required rate of return (k). This is obvious if we rearrange the constant-growth DDM in the following manner, using the present market price in place of intrinsic value, to obtain an estimate of the return required by investors on a particular share:

$$k_{CS} = \frac{D_1}{P_0} + g$$ **(13-8)**

The first term in Equation 13-8 represents the expected dividend yield on the share, therefore, we may view the second term, g, as the expected capital gains yield, since the total return must equal the dividend yield plus capital gains yield. This provides an appropriate approximation for required return, only if the conditions of the constant-growth DDM are met (in particular the assumption regarding constant growth in dividends to infinity must be satisfied). It also assumes that markets are reasonably efficient, by assuming that the market price equals the intrinsic value.

EXAMPLE 13-3: ESTIMATING PRICE CHANGE FOR SUMMA CORPORATION

For Summa, the estimated price today is $13.38, while the estimated dividend at the end of this year (D_1) is $1.07, and the estimated long-term growth rate in dividends, g, is 7 percent. This implies an expected rate of return of 15 percent:

$$k_{CS} = \frac{D_1}{P_0} + g = \frac{1.07}{13.38} + 0.07 = 0.08 + 0.07 = 0.15$$

This suggests that the expected return on Summa is composed of a dividend yield of 8 percent and a capital gains yield of 7 percent. In other words, we expect Summa's share price to increase by 7 percent over this year. We can check this out by using Equation 13-5 to estimate the intrinsic value of Summa at the end of Period 1:

$$\hat{P}_1 = \frac{D_2}{k_{CS} - g} = \frac{\$1.07(1.07)}{0.15 - 0.07} = \$14.31$$

This estimated price at the end of Period 1 is 7 percent higher than the estimated price today of $13.38 (rounding causes slight differences):

$$\text{Price change} = \frac{\text{Ending price} - \text{Beginning price}}{\text{Beginning price}}$$

$$= (\$14.31 - \$13.38) / \$13.38 = 7\%$$

This result is intuitive, since the equation used to determine $\hat{P}_1$ is the same equation used to determine P_0, multiplied by $(1 + g)$.

EXAMPLE 13-4: ESTIMATING IMPLIED RATE OF RETURN FOR SUMMA CORPORATION

Notice that in Example 13-3, our estimate of the expected return exactly equals the required return of 15 percent that we used to determine the intrinsic value of Summa. This is because we assumed the share is trading at its intrinsic value. What if Summa was actually trading in the market at a price of $15? Under these circumstances, we estimate an expected return of 14.13 percent:

$$k_{CS} = \frac{D_1}{P_0} + g = \frac{1.07}{15.00} + 0.07 = 0.0713 + 0.07 = 0.1413$$

At a price of $15, Summa's shares are not attractive investments, since they offer a rate of return of 14.13 percent, which is below our required rate of return of 15 percent. In other words, based on our analysis, they are overpriced at $15.

Similarly, if Summa's shares were trading below $13.38, they would be undervalued according to our analysis, and we would expect to earn above our required rate of return. For example, if they were trading at $12, the expected rate of return would be 15.92 percent, well above 15 percent:

$$k_{CS} = \frac{D_1}{P_0} + g = \frac{1.07}{12.00} + 0.07 = 0.0892 + 0.07 = 0.1592$$

An examination of Equation 13-5 quickly demonstrates the factors affecting the price of a common stock, assuming the constant-growth version of the dividend discount model to be the applicable valuation approach:

1. If the market lowers the required rate of return for a stock, price will rise (other things being equal).
2. If investors decide that the expected growth in dividends will be higher as the result of some favourable development for the firm, price will also rise (other things being equal).

Of course, the converse for these two situations also holds—a rise in the discount rate or a reduction in the expected growth rate of dividends will lower price.

The present value or intrinsic value calculated from Equation 13-5 is quite sensitive to the estimates used by the investor in the equation. Relatively small variations in the inputs can change the estimated price by large percentage amounts.

EXAMPLE 13-5: EFFECT OF THE DISCOUNT RATE ON PRICE FOR SUMMA CORPORATION

For Summa, assume the discount rate used, k, is 16 percent instead of 15 percent, with other variables held constant:

$$\hat{P}_0 = \frac{\$1.00(1.07)}{0.16 - 0.07} = \$11.89$$

In this example, a one-percentage-point rise in k results in an 11.14 percent decrease in price, from \$13.38 to \$11.89.

EXAMPLE 13-6: EFFECT OF THE GROWTH RATE ON PRICE FOR SUMMA CORPORATION

Assume that for Summa the growth rate, g, is 6 instead of 7 percent, with other variables held constant:

$$\hat{P}_0 = \frac{\$1.00(1.06)}{0.15 - 0.06} = \$11.78$$

In this example, a one percentage point decline in g results in an 11.96 percent decrease in price, from \$13.38 to \$11.78.

EXAMPLE 13-7: EFFECT OF MULTIPLE VARIABLES ON PRICE FOR SUMMA CORPORATION

Assume that for Summa the discount rate rises to 16 percent, and the growth rate declines to 4 percent:

$$\hat{P}_0 = \frac{\$1.00(1.04)}{0.16 - 0.04} = \$8.67$$

In this example, the price declines from \$13.38 to \$8.67, a 35.20 percent change.

These differences demonstrate why stock prices constantly fluctuate as investors make their buy and sell decisions. Even if all investors use the constant-growth version of the dividend discount model to value a particular common stock (which in practice they don't), many different estimates of value will be obtained because of the following:

1. Each investor has his or her own required rate of return based on their estimate of the risk associated with the stock and future market conditions, resulting in a relatively wide range of values of k.

2. Each investor has his or her own estimate of the expected growth rate in dividends. Although this range may be reasonably narrow in many valuation situations, small differences in g can produce significant differences in price, everything else held constant. In addition, there are several situations under which there will be large ranges of possible estimates for k and g, which suggests why investors can hold such varied opinions about the true value of common shares.

Thus, at any time, some investors are willing to buy, whereas others wish to sell a particular stock, depending on their evaluation of its prospects. This helps to make markets active and liquid.

The Multiple-Growth Case

Many firms grow at a rapid rate (or rates) for a number of years and then slow down to an "average" growth rate. Other companies pay no dividends for a period of years, often during their early growth period. The constant-growth model discussed earlier is not formulated to deal with these situations. A model that can incorporate such a variation of the DDM is the multiple-growth model.

In addition, short-term earnings and dividend estimates should be much more reliable than those covering a longer period of time, which are often calculated using some very general estimates of future economic, industry, and company conditions. In order to use the best information available at any time, it often makes sense to estimate growth as precisely as possible in the short term before assuming some long-term rate of growth.

Multiple growth is defined as a situation in which the expected future growth in dividends must be described using two or more growth rates. Although any number of growth rates is possible, most stocks can be described using just two or three. It is important to remember that at least two different growth rates are involved; this is the distinguishing characteristic of multiple-growth situations.

A number of companies have experienced rapid growth that could not be sustained forever. During part of their lives their growth exceeded that of the average company in the economy, but later the growth rate slowed. This seems reasonable since we would expect that competitive pressures and/or business cycle influences will prevent firms from maintaining extremely high growth in earnings for long periods of time. Some well-known examples from the past include **McDonald's, Disney, Xerox,** and **IBM**.

To capture the expected growth in dividends under this scenario, it is necessary to model the dividend stream during each period of different growth. It is reasonable to assume that at some point the company's growth will slow down to some steady rate such as that of the economy as a whole. At this time, the company's growth in future dividends can be described by the constant-growth model (Equation 13-5). What remains, therefore, is to model the exact dividend stream up to the point at which dividends slow to a normal growth rate and to find the present value of all the components. This can be described in equation form as

(13-9)
$$\hat{P}_0 = \frac{D_1}{(1 + k_{CS})^1} + \frac{D_2}{(1 + k_{CS})^2} + \ldots + \frac{D_n}{(1 + k_{CS})^n} + \frac{\hat{P}_n}{(1 + k_{CS})^n}$$

where
$$\hat{P}_n = \frac{D_{n+1}}{k_{CS} - g}$$

n = the time at which constant growth in dividends to infinity is assumed to begin[7]

Essentially, we estimate dividends up to the beginning of the period where it is reasonable to assume constant growth to infinity. Then we can use the constant version of the DDM to estimate the intrinsic value or market price of the stock at that point in time ($\hat{P}_n$). Finally, we discount back to the beginning of the evaluation period (time 0): (1) all of the estimated dividends up to the beginning of constant growth period; and (2) the estimated intrinsic value at that time. This provides us with today's estimate of the share's intrinsic value.

How does this approach provide us with the present value of all expected future dividends from Period 1 to infinity? Recall from the constant growth version of the DDM that the intrinsic value determined at time n ($\hat{P}_n$), represents the present value of all expected dividends (at time $t = n$), from $n+1$ to infinity. Because $\hat{P}_n$ is the expected price of the stock at the end of period n, it must be discounted back to the present. When we discount $\hat{P}_n$ back to time 0, and add it to the present value of all dividends from $t = 1$ to $t = n$, we end up with the present value (at time $t = 0$) of all expected future dividends from time $t = 1$ to infinity. This is the estimated value of the stock today, according to the DDM.

Figure 13-3 illustrates the concept of valuing a multiple-growth rate company that is expected to pay a dividend of $1.50 at the end of this year, a $2.00 dividend at the end of Year 2, and a $2.30 dividend at the end of Year 3. It is estimated dividends will grow at a constant rate of 5 percent per year thereafter. To determine the intrinsic value of this company's common shares if the required rate of

---

[7]The dividend at period $n + 1$ is equal to the dividend paid in period n compounded up by the growth rate expected from period n to infinity. The designation $n + 1$ refers to the first period after the years of abnormal growth.

return is 10 percent, the first step is to estimate dividends up to the start of constant growth to infinity—$D_1 = \$1.50$, $D_2 = \$2.00$, $D_3 = \$2.30$. Next, you must estimate the intrinsic value at the beginning of the constant growth to infinity period:

$$\hat{P}_3 = \frac{D_4}{k_{CS} - g} = \frac{(2.30)(1.05)}{0.10 - 0.05} = \$48.30$$

Finally, discount back the relevant cash flows to time 0 and add:

$$\hat{P}_0 = \frac{1.50}{(1.10)^1} + \frac{2.00}{(1.10)^2} + \frac{2.30}{(1.10)^3} + \frac{48.30}{(1.10)^3} = 1.364 + 1.653 + 1.728 + 36.288 = \$41.03$$

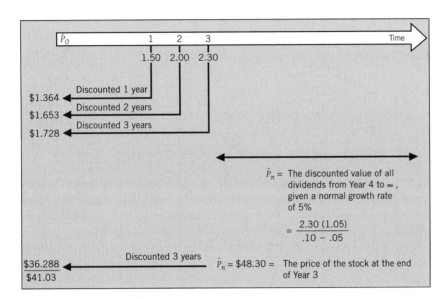

Figure 13-3
Valuing a Multiple-Growth Rate Company

A well-known multiple-growth model is the two-stage growth rate model. This model assumes near-term growth at a rapid rate for some period (typically, 2 to 10 years) followed by a steady long-term growth rate that is sustainable (i.e., a constant-growth rate as discussed earlier).

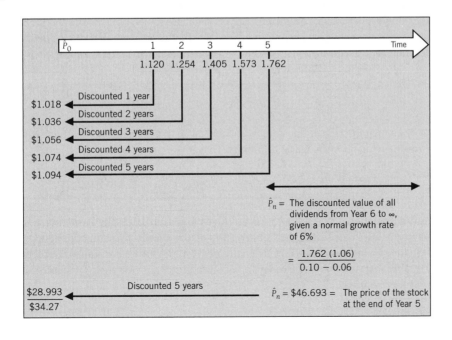

Figure 13-4
Valuing a Two-Stage Growth Rate Company

Figure 13-4 illustrates the concept of valuing a multiple-growth rate company displaying growth in two stages. The current dividend is $1 and is expected to grow at the higher rate (g_1) of 12 percent a year for five years, at the end of which time the new growth rate (g_c) is expected to be a constant 6 percent a year. The required rate of return is 10 percent.

First estimate dividends up to the start of constant growth to infinity, done by compounding the beginning dividend, $1, at 12 percent for each of five years, producing the following: $D_0 = \$1.00$, $D_1 = \$1.00(1.12) = \$1.120$, $D_2 = \$1.00(1.12)^2 = \$1.254$, $D_3 = \$1.00(1.12)^3 = \$1.405$, $D_4 = \$1.00(1.12)^4 = \$1.573$, $D_5 = \$1.00(1.12)^5 = \$1.762$.

Then estimate the price at the beginning of the constant growth to infinity period:

$$\hat{P}_5 = \frac{D_6}{k_{CS} - g} = \frac{(1.762)(1.06)}{0.10 - 0.06} = \$46.693$$

And finally discount back the relevant cash flows to time 0:

$$\hat{P}_0 = \frac{1.120}{(1.10)^1} + \frac{1.254}{(1.10)^2} + \frac{1.405}{(1.10)^3} + \frac{1.573}{(1.10)^4} + \frac{1.762}{(1.10)^5} + \frac{46.693}{(1.10)^5}$$

$$= 1.018 + 1.036 + 1.056 + 1.074 + 1.094 + 28.993 = \$34.27$$

Dividends, Dividends—What about Capital Gains?

In their initial study of valuation concepts, investors often are bothered by the fact that the dividend discount model contains only dividends and an infinite stream of dividends at that. Although this is true, many investors are sure that (1) they will not be here forever, and (2) they really want capital gains. Dividends may be nice, but buying low and selling high is so much better! Since so many investors are interested in capital gains, which by definition involves the difference between the price paid for a security and the price at which it is later sold, a valuation model should seemingly contain a stock price somewhere. Thus, in computing present value for a stock, investors are interested in the present value of the expected price two years from now, or six months from now, or whatever the expected holding period is. How can price be incorporated into the valuation—or should it be?

According to the DDM, the only cash flows that an investor needs to be concerned with are dividends. Expected future price is built into the dividend discount model given by Equation 13-2; it is simply not visible. To see this, ask yourself at what price you can expect to sell a common stock that you have bought. Assume, for example, that you purchase today and plan to hold for three years. The price you receive three years from now will reflect the buyer's expectations of dividends from that point forward (at the end of Years 4, 5, etc.).[8] The estimated price today of the stock is equal to

(13-10)
$$\hat{P}_0 = \frac{D_1}{(1 + k_{CS})^1} + \frac{D_2}{(1 + k_{CS})^2} + \frac{D_3}{(1 + k_{CS})^3} + \frac{\hat{P}_3}{(1 + k_{CS})^3}$$

But $\hat{P}_3$ (the estimated price of the stock at the end of Year 3) is, in turn, equal to the discounted value of all future dividends from Year 4 to infinity. That is,

(13-11)
$$\hat{P}_3 = \frac{D_4}{(1 + k_{CS})^1} + \frac{D_5}{(1 + k_{CS})^2} + \frac{D_6}{(1 + k_{CS})^3} + \cdots + \frac{\hat{P}_\infty}{(1 + k_{CS})^{\infty-3}}$$

Substituting Equation 13-11 into 13-10 produces Equation 13-2, the basic dividend discount model. Thus, the result is the same whether investors discount only a stream of dividends or a combination of dividends and price. Since price at any point in the future is a function of the dividends to be received after that time, the price today for a common stock is best thought of as the discounted value of all future dividends.

---

[8]This is the exact assumption we used to implement the multi-stage growth model. Not surprisingly, Equation 13-10 is identical to Equation 13-9 with $n = 3$.

Intrinsic Value

After making careful estimates of the expected stream of benefits and the required rate of return, the intrinsic value of the stock can be determined using present value analysis via the dividend discount model. Determining the intrinsic value is the objective of fundamental analysis. What does intrinsic value imply? Traditionally, investors and analysts specify a relationship between the estimated intrinsic value (IV) of an asset and its current market price (CMP). Specifically,

If IV > CMP, the asset is undervalued and should be purchased or held if already owned.
If IV < CMP, the asset is overvalued and should be avoided, sold if held, or possibly sold short.
If IV = CMP, this implies an equilibrium in that the asset is correctly valued.

Does the problem of varying estimates of value render valuation models useless? No, because individual investors cannot make intelligent investment decisions without having an intelligent estimate of the value of an asset. If the common shares of **Emera Inc.** are currently priced at $21.42 a share, is it a good buy for you? It may or may not be, depending on your own required rate of return (discount rate), your estimate of the future benefit stream to be derived from owning Emera, and certain other factors.[9]

> ## INVESTING *tip*
>
> Intrinsic value is generally derived from a present value process involving estimates of uncertain (future) benefits and the use of (varying) discount rates by different investors. Therefore, the same asset may have many estimated intrinsic values, depending on who, and how many, are doing the evaluation. This is why, for a particular asset on a particular day, some investors are willing to buy and some to sell. Because future benefits and the required rate of return are uncertain and must be estimated, investors will arrive at different inputs to be used in the valuation process. In addition, it is unlikely that investors will all use the same valuation models. All of these factors result in varying estimates of the intrinsic value of an asset. The market price of an asset at any point is, in this sense, the consensus intrinsic value of that asset for the market.

EXAMPLE 13-8: INTRINSIC VALUE OF EMERA INC.

Assume that you require 9 percent return to invest in Emera; that is, your best estimate of the opportunity cost for alternative investment opportunities of similar risk is 9 percent. Also assume that the most recent dividend was $0.95 and you expect it to grow at the rate of 4 percent a year for the indefinite future. Based on these figures and using the constant-growth dividend discount model, the intrinsic value (justified price) of Emera to you would be estimated at $19.76 per share. Based on the intrinsic value principle, Emera is overvalued at $21.42 and should not be purchased, should be sold if held, or sold short if not held.

Notice that this valuation process tells you that if you pay $19.76 per share for Emera, you will earn your required rate of return of 9 percent, if the assumed dividend growth rate is correct. You can, therefore, pay less, say $19 or $16 per share, and earn more than the required rate of return.[10]

Other investors with different estimates for *k* and *g* may be at the margin valuing this security, with estimated values only slightly higher or lower than $21.42. They are potential traders if the price moves slightly or if a news event causes even slight variations in their *k* or their *g*.

The Dividend Discount Model in Practice

Many money managers and investment services firms use the DDM in various ways to estimate the intrinsic values of stocks. Regardless of who uses the model, and how it is used, estimates are always involved. Investors should always remember this in using or evaluating output from these models.

---

[9]As we know from Part II, securities should be chosen on the basis of a portfolio concept—that is, how they fit together to form a unified whole.

[10]To determine the expected return for an investor who purchases the shares at $16, we can use Equation 13-8, along with an estimate for $D_1 = (\$0.95)(1.04) = \$0.988$ to obtain the following expected annual return: $k_{CS} = (0.988)/(16) + 0.04 = 0.1018$, or 10.18 percent (well above the required return of 9 percent).

The DDM has a great deal of intuitive appeal because it links equity prices to two important fundamentals:

1. Corporate profitability (through their link with dividends)
2. The general level of interest rates (through their impact on the discount rate)

In particular, the model predicts that the intrinsic value of common shares will increase as a result of increases in expected dividends (which are closely related to profitability); increases in the growth rate of these dividends; and/or decreases in the appropriate discount rate. From previous chapters, we know that the discount rate will be an increasing function of the general level of interest rates, as well as the riskiness of the underlying security.

For these reasons, the DDM provides a great deal of insight into the factors affecting the general level of security prices in an economy. While the DDM provides great insight into the valuation process, it has its limitations. A key limitation is the large number of inputs that must be estimated regarding the uncertain future. In addition, the DDM tends to work best for large, stable companies that have positive and growing earnings and that pay a significant portion of these earnings as dividends. Examples of such companies include large utility companies, large manufacturing companies, and banks. However, the DDM does not work at all (without modification) for companies that do not pay dividends (or pay very low dividend amounts), or for those that have very volatile earnings. In other words, the DDM is not likely to work well for small companies in the early stages of growth, new technology companies that have negative or low earnings, or commodity-producing companies (such as mining and oil companies) since they have very volatile earnings, and many do not pay dividends. Real-World Returns 13-2 provides a good overview of the uses and limitations of the DDM.

A present value model that is being used more frequently is the free cash flow valuation model, which is discussed in Appendix 13B. This model overcomes some of the limitations of the DDM, specifically the discretionary nature of dividends, which are determined by a company's board of directors. Rather than focusing on dividends, this model focuses on "free" cash flows or the cash flows that are available to common shareholders after all expenses have been paid and all capital expenditures have been funded. Conceptually, this is the amount of cash that could be paid out in dividends without affecting the company's future growth plans. This model is an important part of the current CFA curriculum, as is the DDM.

REAL-WORLD RETURNS 13-2
Digging into the Dividend Discount Model

It's time to dust off one of the oldest, most conservative methods of valuing stocks—the dividend discount model (DDM). It's one of the basic applications of a financial theory that students in any introductory finance class must learn. Unfortunately, the theory is the easy part. The model requires loads of assumptions about companies' dividend payments and growth patterns, as well as future interest rates. Difficulties spring up in the search for sensible numbers to fold into the equation.

The Dividend Discount Model

Here is the basic idea: any stock is ultimately worth no more than what it will provide investors in current and future dividends. Financial theory says that the value of a stock is worth all of the future cash flows expected to be generated by the firm, discounted by an appropriate risk-adjusted rate. According to the DDM, dividends are the cash flows that are returned to the shareholder. (We're going to assume you understand the concepts of time value of money and discounting.)

To value a company using the DDM, you calculate the value of dividend payments that you think a stock will throw-off in the years ahead. The classic dividend discount model works best when valuing a mature company that pays a hefty portion of its earnings as dividends, such as a utility company.

Assumptions—The Problem of Forecasting

Proponents of the dividend discount model say that only future cash dividends can give you a reliable estimate of a company's intrinsic value. Buying a stock for any other reason—say, paying 20 times the company's earnings today because somebody will pay 30 times tomorrow—is mere speculation.

In truth, the dividend discount model requires an enormous amount of "speculation" in trying to forecast future dividends. Even when you apply it to steady, reliable, dividend-paying companies, you still need to make plenty of assumptions about their future. The model is subject to the axiom "garbage in, garbage out," meaning that a model is only as good as the assumptions it is based upon. Furthermore, the inputs that produce valuations are always changing and susceptible to error.

The first big assumption that the DDM makes is that dividends are steady, or grow at a constant rate indefinitely. But even for steady, reliable, utility-type stocks, it can be tricky to forecast exactly what the dividend payment will be next year, never mind a dozen years from now.

Multi-Stage Models

To get around the problem posed by unsteady dividends, multi-stage models take the DDM a step closer to reality by assuming that the company will experience differing growth phases. Stock analysts build complex forecast models with many phases of differing growth to better reflect real prospects. For example, a multistage DDM may predict that a company will have a dividend that grows at 5 percent for seven years, 3 percent for the following three years and then at 2 percent in perpetuity.

However, such an approach brings even more assumptions into the model—although it doesn't assume that a dividend will grow at a constant rate, it must guess when and by how much a dividend will change over time.

What Should Be "Expected"?

Another sticking point with the DDM is that no one really knows for certain the appropriate expected rate of return to use. It's not always wise simply to use the long-term interest rate because the appropriateness of this can change.

The High-Growth Problem

No fancy DDM model is able to solve the problem of high-growth stocks. If the company's dividend growth rate exceeds the expected return rate, you cannot calculate a value —because you get a negative denominator in the formula. Stocks don't have a negative value. Consider a company with a dividend growing at 20 percent while the expected return rate is only 5 percent: in the denominator $(r - g)$ you would have –15 percent (5% – 20%)!

In fact, even if the growth rate does not exceed the expected return rate, growth stocks, which don't pay dividends, are even tougher to value using this model. If you hope to value a

(continued)

REAL-WORLD RETURNS 13-2 *continued*

growth stock with the dividend discount model, your valuation will be based on nothing more than guesses about the company's future profits and dividend policy decisions. Most growth stocks don't pay out dividends. Rather, they reinvest earnings into the company with the hopes of providing shareholders with returns by means of a higher share price.

Consider Microsoft, which didn't pay a dividend for decades. Given this fact, the model might suggest the company was worthless at that time—which is completely absurd. Remember, only about a third of all public companies bother to pay dividends. Furthermore, even companies that do offer payouts are allocating less and less of their earnings to shareholders.

Conclusion

The dividend discount model is by no means the be-all and end-all for valuation. That being said, learning about the dividend discount model does encourage thinking. It forces investors to evaluate different assumptions about growth and future prospects. If nothing else, the DDM demonstrates the underlying principle that a company is worth the sum of its discounted future cash flows. (Whether or not dividends are the correct measure of cash flow is another question.) The challenge is to make the model as applicable to reality as possible, which means using the most reliable assumptions possible.

Source: Excerpted from McClure, Ben, "Digging into the Dividend Discount Model," Investopedia.com, April 14, 2004. Retrieved from www.investopedia.com. Reprinted with permission from Investopedia.com.

CHECK YOUR UNDERSTANDING

13-4. The equations for the zero-growth and constant-growth rate DDM do not include the discounting factor that we associate with finding a present value. How, then, can the DDM be said to involve a present value process?

13-5. Assume that a group of investors uses the constant-growth version of the DDM to value Power Corp., a Canadian conglomerate. Are they likely to come up with different estimates of value?

13-6. Can the intrinsic value of a stock be determined with a formula, or is it something that can only be estimated?

RELATIVE VALUATION APPROACHES

P/E Ratio (Earnings Multiplier)
The price to earnings (P/E) ratio for a stock measures the stock price relative to the earnings per share.

Relative valuation approaches determine the value of common shares by comparing the market prices of "similar" companies, relative to some common variable such as earnings, cash flow, book values, or sales. Although relatively simple to apply, using multiples based on comparable companies has the potential to build market errors into the value estimation process. This section discusses the application and appropriateness of some of these approaches, with particular emphasis on the P/E ratio, the most commonly cited one for common share valuation.

The P/E Ratio Approach

learning objective 4
Explain the P/E ratio approach.

An alternative fundamental analysis method of valuation frequently used by practising security analysts is the **P/E ratio** or **earnings multiplier** approach. The P/E ratio is the number of times investors value earnings as expressed in the stock price.

Practising security analysts probably use this method more often than dividend discount models as alluded to in Real-World Returns 13-3. Although the P/E ratio model appears easier to use than the DDM, its very simplicity causes investors to forget that estimation of the uncertain future is also involved here. This is an important point to remember. Every valuation model and approach, properly done, requires estimates of the uncertain future.

REAL-WORLD RETURNS 13-3
P/E Ratio

Here's a quotation to live by: "Why not invest your assets in the company you really like? As Mae West said, 'Too much of a good thing can be wonderful.'"

It comes from Warren Buffett, the legendary chairman and CEO of Berkshire Hathaway Inc. I love his quote because of its positive spirit —the idea that you shouldn't have to invest in companies you don't like.

On the other hand, I've learned enough to know that kind of sentiment comes with many caveats, enough, probably, to fill several columns. It's important for me to like the company, but I also have to make sure it's a good investment.

On that subject, I have heard a lot from readers, who fill my inbox every week with e-mails full of advice and reflection, of praise and mild rebuke (like the one that started with "I'm going to try to be kind.") By far, the message experienced investors want to pass on is that in picking stocks, consider price but also look at other indicators of a stock's value.

The most-cited indicator, by readers and experts, is the P/E (price-to-earnings) ratio, the ratio that gives investors an idea of how much they are paying for a company's earnings. (For those like me that are new to this calculation, it is simple: Take the stock price and divide it by the company's earnings per share. But you don't really need to figure out each ratio yourself; most services that provide stock quotes (like globeandmail.com) also offer up the P/E ratio.)

Take Apple, for example, a company I really like and have been watching very closely over the past couple of months. Its P/E ratio is about 27. That is pretty high. In fact, many of the "value investors" who wrote to me indicate that they would never buy a company's shares if the P/E ratio is above 14 or 15.

To put that in perspective, consider this analogy: It's like buying a store and paying a price equivalent to 27 years worth of profits from that store.

But P/E ratios are a little more complicated than that. It's never simple, is it? To take the analogy of the store further, a price equivalent to 27 years worth of profits would not be as crazy if you thought profits were going to soar by 20 or 30 percent a year. High-growth companies— Apple and other technology companies—tend to have higher P/E ratios because they are expected to grow faster than, say, financial institutions.

One way to see if a P/E is high or low is to compare it with similar firms. While Apple's P/E was 27 yesterday, Intel's was 18, Hewlett Packard's stood at 16, Dell at 15 and Research In Motion's was 47. Knowing those numbers helped me put Apple's ratio in context—at the higher end of technology stocks.

I know I have a huge affinity for technology stocks, so this week I also decided to broaden my horizons a little and look at some other companies I really like, although maybe not in Mae West territory. I picked blue-chip Canadian stocks that I know something about—Canadian Imperial Bank of Commerce, Thomson Corp., Imperial Oil and Manulife Financial. Two of the companies' P/E ratios were in the single digits (CIBC at 7 and Thomson at 6), while Manulife Financial's stood at 13 and Imperial Oil, 15.

(continued)

REAL-WORLD RETURNS 13-3 *continued*

After weeks of following technology stocks, with their volatility and high P/E ratios, I was momentarily lulled by these firms and their comparatively low P/E ratios. They seem so comfortable and safe.

It strikes me that I have a decision to make: What kind of investor will I be? Will I pick stocks of companies that are solid but are growing relatively slower, or will I tend to the high-growth, more volatile stocks, like Apple?

Eventually, I think I'll want a mix of both, but I can say this so far: I'm comfortable buying higher P/E stocks. I want to buy a growth stock like Apple, so I'm willing to take the risk that comes with it.

It's just a matter of when to take that risk. I read this paper's report on Warren Buffett's visit to Toronto this week, titled "Buffett sitting on his wallet." The great value investor doesn't see a lot of bargains yet on the equity markets despite the huge declines over the past few weeks.

His words made me feel concerned because the financial news keeps getting worse and experts like Mr. Buffett don't think it will end soon. This week, I noticed that analysts and experts stopped using words like "may" or "likely" or "probable" when referring to a recession in the US. In their minds, it seems to be a done deal.

So if Warren Buffett can't find a bargain, who am I to disagree? I'm sitting on my wallet with Warren.

Source: Rasbach, Noreen, "High P/E, low P/E. I'm sitting still right now… just like Warren," *The Globe and Mail*, February 9, 2008, p. B10.

The conceptual framework for the P/E model is not as solidly based on economic theory as the DDM. However, a P/E ratio model is consistent with the present value analysis because it concerns the intrinsic value of a stock or the aggregate market, exactly as before.

The P/E ratio as reported daily in the financial media is simply an identity calculated by dividing the current market price of the stock by the latest 12-month earnings. As such, it tells investors the price being paid for each $1 of the company's most recent earnings. For example, in April 2008, investors were willing to pay 15.8 times (the most recent 12-month) earnings for **Emera Inc.** but only 12.5 times earnings for **Laurentian Bank**. These P/E ratios, however, provide no basis for valuation other than showing the underlying identity on which the P/E valuation model is based: This identity is[11]

(13-12)
$$P_0 = \text{Current market price} = E_0 \times P_0/E_0$$

To implement the earnings multiplier model and estimate the value of the stock today, we must estimate the values on the right-hand side of Equation 13-12. The typical P/E formulation uses estimated earnings for the next 12 months. The basic equation then becomes

(13-13)
$$P_0 = \text{Estimated earnings} \times \text{Justified P/E ratio}$$
$$= E_1 \times P_0/E_1$$

EXAMPLE 13-9: EFFECT OF P/E RATIO ON PRICE

If investors are willing to pay 15 times expected earnings, a stock with estimated earnings of $3 per share for the next 12 months will sell for $45. This price will change as estimates of earnings or the justified P/E changes.

---

[11] E_0 here refers to the earnings used to calculate the P/E ratio as reported; usually it is the most recent 12-month earnings.

Determinants of the P/E Ratio

What determines a P/E ratio? The P/E ratio can be derived from the dividend discount model, which, as we have seen, is the foundation of valuation for common stocks. We will illustrate this process only for the case of constant growth. If a multiple-period growth model is applicable to the stock being considered, a more complicated formulation than the one presented here is required.

Start with Equation 13-5, the estimated price of a stock using the constant-growth version of the model. We use P_0 to represent estimated price from the model.

$$P_0 = \frac{D_1}{k_{CS} - g} \qquad \textbf{(13-14)}$$

Dividing both sides of Equation 13-14 by expected earnings, E_1,

$$\frac{P_0}{E_1} = \frac{D_1/E_1}{k_{CS} - g} \qquad \textbf{(13-15)}$$

Equation 13-15 indicates those factors that affect the estimated P/E ratio.

1. The expected dividend payout ratio (D_1/E_1)
2. The required rate of return (k_{CS})
3. The expected growth rate of dividends (g)

The following relationships should hold, other things being equal:

- The higher the expected payout ratio, the higher the P/E.
- The higher the expected growth rate, g, the higher the P/E.
- The higher the required rate of return, k, the lower the P/E.

It is important to remember the phrase "other things being equal," because usually other things are not equal and the preceding relationships do not hold by themselves. It is quite obvious, upon reflection, that if a firm could increase its estimated P/E ratio, and therefore its market price, by simply raising its payout ratio, it would be very tempted to do so. However, such an action would in all likelihood reduce future growth prospects, lowering g, and thereby defeating the increase in the payout. Similarly, trying to increase g by taking on particularly risky investment projects would cause investors to demand a higher required rate of return, thereby raising k. Again, this would work to offset the positive effects of the increasing growth rate.

Variables 2 and 3 are typically the most important factors in the preceding determination of the P/E ratio because a small change in either can have a large effect on its value.

EXAMPLE 13-10: EFFECT OF RATE OF RETURN AND GROWTH RATE ON THE P/E RATIO

Assume that the expected payout ratio is 53.5 percent (i.e., $D_1/E1 = 1.07/2.00 = 0.535$). By varying k and g, and therefore changing the difference between the two (the denominator in Equation 13-15), investors can assess the effect on the P/E ratio as follows:

Assume $k_{CS} = 0.15$ and $g = 0.07$

$$\frac{P_0}{E_1} = \frac{D_1/E_1}{k_{CS} - g} = \frac{0.535}{0.15 - 0.07} = 6.69$$

Now assume k increases to 0.16, while g falls to 0.06, the justified P/E ratio falls to 5.35.

$$\frac{P_0}{E_1} = \frac{D_1/E_1}{k_{CS} - g} = \frac{0.535}{0.16 - 0.06} = 5.35$$

This is not surprising since both of these events produce a negative impact on the justified P/E ratio.

Now assume that k falls to 14 percent, while g increases to 8 percent, which are both favourable events.

$$\frac{P_0}{E_1} = \frac{D_1/E_1}{k_{CS} - g} = \frac{0.535}{0.14 - 0.08} = 8.92$$

Think about each of these P/E ratios being used as a multiplier with expected earnings for Summa for next year of $2. The possible prices for Summa would be $13.38, $10.70, and $17.84, respectively, which is quite a range, given the small changes in k and g that were made.

Understanding the P/E Ratio

Most investors intuitively realize that the P/E ratio should be higher for companies whose earnings are expected to grow rapidly. However, it is not easy to determine how much higher. The market will assess the degree of risk involved in the expected future growth of earnings—if the higher growth rate carries a high level of risk, the P/E ratio will be affected accordingly, by the corresponding increase in the required rate of return (k_{CS}). Furthermore, the high growth rate in earnings may be attributable to several different factors, some of which are more desirable than others. For example, rapid growth in unit sales owing to strong demand for a firm's products is preferable to favourable tax situations, which may change, or liberal accounting procedures, which may cause future reversals in the firm's situation.

P/E ratios reflect investors' expectations about the growth potential of a stock and the risk involved. However, evidence provided in Chapter 10 suggests that stocks with low P/E ratios tend to outperform those with higher P/E ratios, on a risk-adjusted basis. Some analysts also make reference to the PEG ratio, which scales the P/E ratio by the company's growth rate in earnings, to adjust for the influence of growth.

Estimating the P/E Ratio

Estimates of the justified P/E ratio ultimately involve a great deal of subjectivity. While the valuation procedure itself is relatively easy, the estimation of an appropriate P/E ratio is difficult. As the discussion in the previous section suggests, determining an appropriate P/E ratio requires much analysis and judgement regarding the firm's growth opportunities, position within the industry, and the riskiness associated with the firm, its industry, and the economy as a whole.

Despite the intuitive appeal of estimating the justified P/E ratio based on Equation 13-15, it is only appropriate under certain conditions, since it is merely a reformulation of the constant-growth DDM. It will only work well for firms that exhibit stable and growing dividends, at a rate below the required return on their common shares (i.e., k_{CS} must be $> g$). An alternative approach is to find "comparable" companies, rate one company relative to the others, and estimate a target P/E ratio for the company being analyzed, based on this comparison, and based on the P/E ratios of the comparable companies. Often this approach involves scaling an industry average P/E ratio up or down, based on the analyst's opinion regarding how well the company stacks up against its peers.

A comparison of one company with its peers also involves a great deal of subjectivity regarding several company-specific characteristics including risk, potential for growth, and overall financial health of the company. Some other approaches to estimating justified P/E multiples include using historical averages for the company or the company's industry. An alternative approach is to determine the ratio based on its historic relationship to P/E multiples in the market as a whole. For example, a company or industry may historically have traded at P/E ratios that average 90 percent of the P/E ratio for the S&P/TSX Composite Index, so you could estimate an appropriate P/E multiple based on 90 percent of the S&P/TSX's current P/E ratio. The problem with any of these ways of estimating justified P/E ratios is that they may build market errors into the value estimation process. For example, we could overestimate the appropriate P/E multiple based on industry averages if the market has systematically overvalued the particular industry that the company is in. Similar results would occur if we scale the S&P/TSX Index multiple by 90 percent but find that the entire market is overvalued.

Aside from the difficulties in estimating an appropriate P/E ratio, there are several other practical concerns regarding how informative P/E ratios are. One important concern is that P/E ratios are uninformative when companies have negative (or very small) earnings. Finally, the volatile nature of earnings implies a great deal of volatility in P/E multiples. For example, the earnings of cyclical companies fluctuate much more dramatically throughout the business cycle than their stock prices. As a result, their P/E ratios tend to peak during recessionary periods (in response to low earnings) and hit low points during the peak of business cycles (in response to high earnings). In response to some of these concerns, there are a number of similar approaches described below, which are often used for valuation purposes.

Market-to-Book Ratio (M/B)

learning objective 5
Outline other relative valuation approaches.

Market-to-Book Ratio (M/B) or Price-to-Book
The ratio of stock price to per share shareholders' equity.

Book value, the accounting value of the firm as reflected in its financial statements, measures the actual values recorded under accounting conventions. As such, book values have the advantages and disadvantages of accounting numbers. The book value of equity is defined as the book value of assets minus the book value of liabilities. It represents an accounting measure of the amount of unencumbered assets to which equity holders are entitled. In Canada and the United States, the book value of assets equals their original cost minus allowable depreciation, while the liability values reflect their values when incurred.

The **market-to-book ratio (M/B)** or **price-to-book value** is determined using the following equation: $M/B = P_0/BV_0$, where P_0 is the market price per common share and BV_0 is the book value per common share (determined by dividing the net book value of the firm by the number of common shares outstanding). This variable is followed closely by investors and analysts. Stocks selling below the book value of equity represent good candidates for "value" portfolios, while stocks trading at high multiples, relative to book value, are often categorized as "growth" stocks.

Estimates of the intrinsic value of a share can be determined by multiplying the justified M/B ratio times the company's book value per share (which is easily determined from the balance sheet). We end up with the following valuation equation, similar to Equation 13-13, which was used for valuing shares based on their justified P/E ratio:

$$P_0 = \text{Book value per share} \times \text{Justified M/B ratio}$$
$$= BV_0 \times M/B$$

(13-16)

There are several reasons why valuing stocks relative to their M/B is attractive. Book value provides a relatively stable, intuitive measure of value relative to market values, which can be easily compared with those of other companies, provided accounting standards do not vary greatly across the comparison group. It eliminates the problems arising from the use of P/E multiples, since book values are rarely negative and do not exhibit the volatility associated with earnings levels. On the other hand, book values are sensitive to accounting standards and practices, which often vary from firm to firm. In addition, they may be uninformative for companies that do not have a large proportion of fixed assets (such as service firms or emerging high-technology firms).

Similar to P/E ratios, the justified M/B ratio can be estimated by comparing with industry ratios, aggregate market ratios and past trends, and by relating to the fundamentals used in the DDM. In order to relate M/B ratios to the constant-growth version of the DDM provided in Equation 13-5, we begin by noting that D_1 may be expressed as: $D_1 = EPS_1 \times$ Payout ratio. Next, we note that EPS_1 can be expressed as $EPS_0 \times (1+g)$, if we assume that earnings and dividends grow at the same rate. Thus we can say that $D_1 = EPS_0 \times (1+g) \times$ Payout ratio. Finally, it is an accounting identity that $EPS_0 = ROE_0 \times BV_0$, so we can say that $D_1 = ROE_0 \times BV_0 \times (1+g) \times$ Payout ratio.[12]

---

[12]It is an accounting identity that $EPS_0 = ROE_0 \times BV_0$, because EPS = net income/number of common shares outstanding, ROE = net income/total common equity, while BV = total common equity/number of common shares outstanding.

When we substitute this expression for D_1 into the numerator of the constant-growth DDM equation, we obtain the following relationship:

$$P_0 = \frac{ROE_0 \times BV_0 \times \text{Payout ratio} \times (1 + g)}{k_{CS} - g}$$

Finally, dividing both sides by book value per share (BV_0), we are left with:

(13-17)

$$\frac{P_0}{BV_0} = \frac{ROE_0 \times \text{Payout ratio} \times (1 + g)}{k_{CS} - g}$$

This equation provides a method of estimating a justified M/B ratio based on underlying fundamentals. It implies that M/B is positively related to its profitability (as measured by ROE), and to its expected growth rate. Similar to the P/E ratio, it will increase as a result of decreases in the discount rate k_{CS}.

EXAMPLE 13-11: ESTIMATING MARKET-TO-BOOK RATIO FOR SUMMA CORPORATION

Suppose that in addition to the previous information, we are given that Summa's most recent return on equity (ROE_0) is 16 percent, while its current book value per share (BV_0) is $12.40. The justified M/B ratio is 1.145.

$$M/B = \frac{P_0}{BV_0} = \frac{ROE_0 \times \text{Payout ratio} \times (1 + g)}{k_{CS} - g} = \frac{(0.16)(0.535)(1.07)}{0.15 - 0.07} = 1.145$$

Using Equation 13-16, we obtain an estimated value of $14.20 for Summa's shares:

$$\hat{P}_0 = M/B \times BV_0 = (1.145)(12.40) = \$14.20$$

Several analysts recommend choosing stocks with low price-to-book value ratios as a stock selection rule. The M/B ratio has received support in empirical tests, several of which were discussed in Chapter 10. The most notable evidence is provided by the 1992 study by Eugene Fama and Kenneth French. They found that two basic variables, size (as measured by the market value of equity) and book-to-market value of equity (which is the reciprocal of the M/B ratio), effectively combined to capture the cross-sectional variation in average stock returns during the period 1963–90. Furthermore, the book-to-market equity ratio had a consistently stronger role in average returns.[13]

Price/Sales Ratio (P/S)

Price/Sales (P/S) Ratio
A company's total common equity market value divided by its sales.

A valuation technique that has received increased attention is the **price/sales (P/S) ratio** calculated by dividing a company's total market value (price times number of shares) by its sales. In effect, it indicates what the market is willing to pay for a dollar of the firm's revenues.

The P/S ratio has several properties that make it attractive for valuation purposes. Unlike earnings and book values, sales are relatively insensitive to accounting decisions and are never negative. Sales are not as volatile as earnings levels, hence, P/S ratios are generally less volatile than P/E multiples. In addition, sales figures provide useful information about corporate decisions such as the impact of pricing and credit policies. On the other hand, sales do not impart much information about cost control and profit margins, which are important determinants of company performance.

The expression for obtaining the share value estimate using this approach is similar to Equation 13-12 for using the P/E ratio and Equation 13-16 for using the M/B ratio:

---

[13]E. Fama and K. French, "The Cross-Section of Expected Stock Returns," *Journal of Finance* 47 (June 1992), pp. 427–465.

$$\hat{P}_0 = \text{Sales per share} \times \text{Justified price-to-sales ratio}$$
$$= \text{Sales}_0 \times \text{P/S}$$

(13-18)

Similar to P/E multiples and M/B ratios, justified P/S ratios can be estimated by reference to industry peers, market ratios, and past trends. We can also alter the DDM to determine an estimate of an appropriate P/S ratio based on fundamentals. We focus on the constant-growth version of the DDM, and begin by noting as we did in the previous section, that D_1 can be expressed as $D_1 = \text{EPS}_0 \times (1+g) \times \text{Payout ratio}$. We also note that $\text{EPS}_0 = \text{Net income margin (NI\%)} \times \text{Sales per share (Sales}_0)$. By making the appropriate substitution for D_1 in the numerator of Equation 13-5, we can rewrite the constant-growth DDM as:

$$P_0 = \frac{\text{NI\%} \times \text{Sales}_0 \times \text{Payout ratio} \times (1 + g)}{k_{CS} - g}$$

Finally, dividing both sides by Sales_0, we get:

$$\frac{P_0}{\text{Sales}_0} = \frac{\text{NI\%} \times \text{Payout ratio} \times (1 + g)}{k_{CS} - g}$$

(13-19)

This calculation shows that the P/S ratio will increase in response to growth in profit margins and the growth rate and decreases in k_{CS}.

EXAMPLE 13-12: ESTIMATING THE PRICE/SALES RATIO FOR SUMMA CORPORATION

Suppose Summa has a net income margin (NI%) of 5 percent, and sales per share (Sales$_0$) of $40. This implies Summa's shares are worth $14.32 each.

$$\frac{P_0}{\text{Sales}_0} = \frac{\text{NI\%} \times \text{Payout ratio} \times (1 + g)}{k_{CS} - g} = \frac{(0.05)(0.535)(1.07)}{0.15 - 0.07} = 0.358$$

$$\hat{P}_0 = \text{Sales}_0 \times \text{P/S} = (40)(0.358) = \$14.32$$

A well-known 1997 book, *What Works on Wall Street*, by James O'Shaugnessy,[14] gives new emphasis to the price/sales ratio. Using Compustat data back to 1951, he analyzed all of the basic investment strategies used to select common stock, such as book value, cash flow, P/E, ROE, yield, and so forth. O'Shaugnessy found that the 50 stocks with the lowest P/S ratios, based on an annual rebalancing of the portfolio, performed at an annual rate of 15.42 percent over the 40 years from 1954 through 1994, compared with 12.45 percent annually for his universe of stocks. Stocks with the highest P/S ratios earned only 4.15 percent annually. Furthermore, combining low P/S stocks (generally, a P/S of 1.0 or lower) with stocks showing momentum (the best 12-month price performance) produced results of 18.14 percent annually over the full 40-year period.

Other Relative Valuation Approaches

Another commonly used ratio is the multiple of price-to-cash flow (P/CF). Generally, cash flow (CF) is estimated as CF = net income + depreciation + deferred taxes.[15]

---

[14]James P. O'Shaugnessy, *What Works on Wall Street: A Guide to the Best-Performing Investment Strategies of All Time* (New York: McGraw-Hill, 1997).

[15]Some analysts focus on "free" cash flow available to equity holders, which is estimated as: net income + non-cash charges (such as depreciation and deferred taxes) $+ -$ capital spending $-$ the change in net working capital $-$ principal repayments + new external finance, as discussed in Appendix 13B.

This ratio alleviates some of the accounting concerns regarding accounting measures of earnings.

Finally, the price-to-earnings before interest and taxes (EBIT) ratio can also be used for valuation purposes. Using EBIT instead of net earnings eliminates a significant proportion of volatility caused in EPS figures by the use of debt. This is useful if we want to reduce the impact of capital structure on our valuation process.

CHECK YOUR UNDERSTANDING

13-7. What problem occurs when using comparable companies to estimate justified P/E ratios?

13-8. The definition of the P/E ratio seems straightforward. Why can it be problematic to use this relative valuation technique?

OTHER VALUATION ISSUES

There is growing interest in two value-added performance measures: economic value added and market value added. These measures are used by a number of companies to evaluate the performance of managers in enhancing firm value. These measures are also being used by security analysts as possible indicators of future equity returns.

Economic Value Added

Economic Value Added (EVA)

A technique for focusing on a firm's return on capital in order to determine if shareholders are being rewarded.

Economic value added (EVA) is a variation of the cash flow valuation approach.[16] In particular, it considers economic profit, which is similar to the net present value (NPV) approach for making capital budgeting decisions. NPV determines asset values based upon the present value of the cash flows it generates during its useful life. However, EVA advocates suggest firm managers cannot be evaluated based on the determination of firm value in this manner. The reason is that it is hard to determine the value impact of cash flows without due regard to their intended use. For example, negative cash flows in a particular period could be detracting from firm value (i.e., when it's losing money), or adding to firm value (i.e., reinvesting in profitable long-term projects). The same can be said of positive cash flows, which could be enhancing value (i.e., increasing profits) or destroying value (i.e., disposing of valuable long-term assets).

EVA addresses these concerns by considering not only profitability, but also the amount of capital resources used to generate these profits. It may be calculated using two approaches: using residual income or refined earnings. The residual income approach determines EVA in the following manner:

(13-20)
$$EVA = (ROC - WACC) \times Capital$$

where ROC is the return on total capital, WACC is the firm's weighted average cost of capital, and Capital is the average total capital (or net assets) employed by the company during the period.

Notice from Equation 13-20 that this measure penalizes decreases in capital (which proxies for growth) as well as decreases in profitability. As a result, managers who are evaluated on this measure will be less likely to enter into short-term, high-return projects if they detract from overall long-term growth in capital assets. In essence, managers are penalized to some extent if they attempt to sacrifice either profitability or growth at the expense of the other.

---

[16]The term economic value added (EVA) has been trademarked by Stern Stewart, a consulting firm that pioneered the use of this concept.

EVA is also calculated using the refined earnings approach in the following manner:

$$EVA = NOPAT - (WACC \times Capital)$$ **(13-21)**

where NOPAT is the firm's net operating profit after taxes. This approach results in a comparison of the dollar cost of capital (i.e., WACC × Capital) with the operating profits generated by the employed capital. Any negative EVA is a bad signal because it means that value is being destroyed; however, even if it is negative, the goal should be to improve upon the value in the previous period.

EXAMPLE 13-13: ESTIMATING EVA FOR SUMMA CORPORATION

Suppose that Summa's ROC is 14 percent, its WACC is 12 percent, its NOPAT is $21 million, and it employs $150 million worth of capital. Equations 13-20 and 13-21 both result in EVA of $3 million:

EVA = (ROC − WACC) × Capital = (0.14 − 0.12) × ($150m) = $3 million

EVA = NOPAT − (WACC × Capital) = $21m − (0.12 × $150m) = $3 million

Some studies have shown that stock price is more responsive to changes in EVA than to changes in earnings, the traditional variable of importance.[17] Some mutual funds are now using EVA analysis as the primary tool for selecting stocks for the fund to hold. One recommendation for investors interested in this approach is to search for companies with a return on capital in excess of 20 percent because this will, in all likelihood, exceed the cost of capital, and, therefore, the company is adding value.

Market Value Added

Unlike EVA, which evaluates internal performance, market value added (MVA) is a measure of external performance. It determines how the market has evaluated the firm's performance as reflected in the market prices of its outstanding debt and equity, relative to the capital invested in the company. MVA can be estimated for any period as follows:

$$MVA = Market\ value\ of\ the\ firm - Capital$$ **(13-22)**

Similar to EVA, it is the changes in this measure that are important. MVA relies on market perceptions and is more forward looking than EVA (which measures the performance in one period only).

EXAMPLE 13-14: ESTIMATING MVA FOR SUMMA CORPORATION

We can determine the MVA for Summa for the most recent period, if we are given a year-end market value for their total equity and debt of $172 million.

MVA = Market value − Capital = $172m − $150m = $22 million

which is a very positive result.

The use of EVA and MVA to evaluate management performance has attracted a great deal of support from the corporate world. Proponents suggest there is an important relationship between EVA and firm market values. On the other hand, detractors criticize EVA for its reliance on accounting measures and for its short-term focus. Empirical evidence regarding the relationship between EVA

---

[17]This discussion is based on Maggie Topkis, "A New Way to Find Bargains," *Fortune*, December 6, 1996, pp. 265–266.

and MVA is fairly limited at this time, and the conclusions offered by prospective researchers are mixed. For example, O'Byrne documents a strong relationship between market values and EVA, while Kramer and Pushner find evidence to the contrary.[18] The relative merit of these approaches will be evaluated in the years to come, but it seems likely they will to continue to grow in importance.

WHICH VALUATION METHOD TO USE?

We have described several valuation procedures here, including two of the most frequently used—the dividend discount model and the P/E ratio (multiplier) model. Which of these should be used?

In theory, the dividend discount model is a correct, logical, and sound position. The best estimate of the current value of a company's common stock is probably the present value of the (estimated) dividends to be paid by that company to its shareholders. However, some analysts and investors feel that this model is unrealistic. After all, they argue, no one can forecast dividends into the distant future with very much accuracy. Technically, the model calls for an estimate of all dividends from now to infinity, which is an impossible task. Finally, many investors want capital gains and not dividends, and some of these investors feel that focusing solely on dividends is not desirable. The discussion in previous sections has dealt with these objections that have been raised about the dividend discount model.

Possibly because of the objections to the dividend discount model cited here, or simply because it is easier to use, the earnings multiplier or P/E model remains the most popular approach to valuation. It is a less sophisticated and more intuitive model. In fact, understanding the P/E model can help investors comprehend the dividend discount model. Because dividends are paid out of earnings, investors must estimate the growth in earnings before they can figure out the growth in dividends or dividends themselves.

Rather than view these approaches as competing alternatives, it is better to view them as complements. Each is useful, and together they provide analysts with a better chance of valuing common stocks. There are several reasons for viewing them as complementary:

1. The P/E model can be derived from the constant growth version of the dividend discount model. They are, in fact, alternative methods of looking at value. In the dividend discount model, the future stream of benefits is discounted. In the P/E model, an estimate of expected earnings is multiplied by a P/E ratio or multiplier.

2. Dividends are paid out of earnings. To use the dividend discount model, it is necessary to estimate the future growth of earnings. The dividends used in the dividend discount model are a function of the earnings of the firm, an estimate of which is used in the earnings multiplier model.

3. Finally, investors must always keep in mind that valuation is no less an art than a science, and estimates of the future earnings and dividends are subject to error. In some cases it may be desirable to use one or the other method, and in other cases both methods can be used as a check on each other. The more procedures investors have to value common stocks, the more likely they are to obtain reasonable results.

In addition, certain techniques will be more appropriate for certain companies and industries.[19] Regardless of which method is used, it is important to remember that valuation employing fundamental analysis, or any other approach, is always subject to error. This is because we are dealing with the uncertain future. No matter who does the analysis, or how it is done, mistakes will be made.

In Chapters 15, 16, and 17, we utilize the overall logic of the fundamental valuation approach—

---

[18]S. O'Byrne, "EVA and the Shareholder," *Financial Practice and Education* 7 (Spring/Summer 1997), pp. 50–54; J. Kramer and G. Pushner, "An Empirical Analysis of Economic Value Added as a Proxy for Market Value Added," *Financial Practice and Education* 7 (Spring/Summer 1997), pp. 41–49.

[19]For an excellent review of the techniques most commonly employed for valuing firms in different industries in Canada, refer to Joe Kan, Editor, *Handbook of Canadian Security Analysis: A Guide to Evaluating the Industry Sectors of the Market, from Bay Street's Top Analysts* Volume 2 (Toronto: John Wiley & Sons Canada, 2000).

namely, that the intrinsic value of a common stock, or the aggregate market, is a function of its expected returns and accompanying risk, as proxied by the required rate of return. The dividend discount model and the P/E ratio model are both used to illustrate the fundamental valuation process.

Bursting the Bubble of New Economy Stocks—
A Lesson in Valuation

At the end of the 1990s and into 2000, investors were caught up in a speculative bubble involving "New Economy" stocks, such as **eToys** and **Dr.Koop.com**. These Internet companies were thought to represent the wave of the future and to be more desirable than "Old Economy" stocks such as **Gillette** or **Procter & Gamble**. In Canada, **Nortel Networks** and **JDS Uniphase** attracted a huge amount of investor interest. Nortel's stock price jumped from the $20 to $40 range to peak at over $170, before collapsing to the penny stock range. The prices of JDS and other IT companies followed similar patterns over this time. At one point, Nortel and JDS combined to make up more than one third of the market value of the S&P/TSX Composite Index, and they pushed it up along with them when they soared, and dragged it back down again when they crashed. There seemed to be no limit on the price of these New Economy stocks as their prices were bid higher and higher. Tremendous fortunes, mostly on paper, were being made.

From early in 1998 through late March 2000, the Amex Interactive Week Internet Index rose to 689 from a starting point of about 87 (split adjusted). Therefore, in just over two years this index showed a gain of almost 700 percent. Because these companies involved revolutionary new technology, many investors argued that they should be valued using revolutionary techniques because the old methods no longer applied. As one of the leading Internet gurus at Merrill Lynch proclaimed in early 2000, "Valuation is often not a helpful tool in determining when to sell hyper-growth stocks." Other star analysts brought up "usage metrics" when discussing these stocks. Usage metrics refers to non-financial metrics such as customer loyalty, website hits, and "engaged shoppers." Many analysts and investors did not want to discuss traditional valuation methods such as EPS, cash flows, and P/E ratios. Of course, for many of these companies these variables did not exist. They had no profitability, and in many cases, little hope of profitability for the foreseeable future.

In the past, companies had to show profitability, or the likely prospect thereof, in order to go public. In 1995, for example, about two-thirds of new companies going public were profitable at the time. In contrast, in the first quarter of 2000, less than 20 percent of companies going public were profitable at the time.

As we now know, the bubble started to burst in March 2000, and continued with horrific declines in early 2001. Many of the hot New Economy stocks dropped 80 percent or more in value and hundreds of Internet companies went out of business. The aggregate dollar loss in the value of investor portfolios was staggering—roughly $4 trillion US from March 2000 to March 2001. The Internet index mentioned above declined to about 280 by the end of 2000 (a 60 percent loss) and declined even further in early 2001.

By early 2001, it became apparent that the old metrics of valuation really did apply. To survive and succeed, companies sooner or later had to generate cash flows and be profitable. Investors no longer believed statements such as that of a major brokerage firm report, which argued that cash burned by dotcom companies was "primarily an investor sentiment issue" and not a long-term risk for the sector.[20]

The bottom line is that valuation standards apply—at least in part—to New Economy stocks, and that stocks must be valued on a rational basis. Revenues and profits do matter and so do P/E ratios, especially when these new economy stocks get too far out of line. For example, at the peak of the Nasdaq market rise, which occurred on March 10, 2000, **Cisco Systems Inc.** had a P/E ratio of about 150, **Yahoo! Inc.** about 650, and **JDS Uniphase Corporation** about 640. One year later, the same companies had P/E ratios of 31, 35, and 41 respectively.

---

[20]This statement and some of the thoughts in this section are based on Gretchen Morgenson, "How Did They Value Stocks? Count the Absurd Ways," *The New York Times*, March 18, 2001.

Some Final Thoughts on Valuation

Valuing stocks is difficult under the best of circumstances. Judgements must be made and variables estimated. No one knows exactly which valuation model should be used for a particular stock. It is almost impossible to prove that an investor's calculations for a valuation model are correct or incorrect (although many calculations could be judged by most people to be "reasonable" or "not reasonable").

In the final analysis, stocks are worth what investors pay for them. Valuations may appear out of line, but market prices prevail.

TRUTH IN THE FINANCIAL MARKETS

Investors seeking to value stocks using valuation principles have a difficult enough job without having to worry about the accuracy of corporate disclosures of important financial information. There have been a number of corporate scandals involving the manipulation of corporate earnings to make them appear more favourable. Prominent cases have included Enron, WorldCom, Nortel, and ImClone.

The manipulation of numbers so that they appear more favourable has serious implications for financial markets, so many hope that these cases and the convictions of a number of top corporate executives will send the message that lying about issues that affect the valuation of a company's shares will not be tolerated. It is unrealistic, of course, to think that the prominent trials and headlines will stop all false statements that are issued by corporate executives, because the potential payoffs are often very large.

DISCUSSION QUESTIONS

1. Why is corporate ethical behaviour and investors' perception of ethical behaviour critical to the orderly functioning of the stock market?

2. Are investors who turn a blind eye to corporate misdeeds in order to earn higher profits just as unethical as the companies they invest in?

3. Will efforts to tighten corporate accountability, such as the Sarbanes-Oxley Act in the US, and a move to adopt international financial reporting standards, help eliminate unethical corporate behaviour?

CHECK YOUR UNDERSTANDING

13-9. What did the extraordinary rise in stock valuations in the late 1990s, ending in March 2000, demonstrate about the valuation of common stock?

SUMMARY

This summary relates to the learning objectives for this chapter.

1. **Name two approaches to the valuation of common stocks used in fundamental security analysis.**

   One commonly employed approach for analyzing and selecting common stocks is fundamental analysis, which should take into account efficient market considerations. Fundamental analysis seeks to estimate the intrinsic value of a stock, which is a function of its expected returns and risk. Two fundamental approaches to determining value are present value and the earnings multiplier (P/E ratio).

2. Explain the present value approach.

The present value approach for common stocks is similar to that used with bonds. A required (minimum) expected rate of return must be determined, based on the risk-free rate and a risk premium. As for expected returns, since dividends are the only cash flows directly paid by a corporation, they are the usual choice for expected future cash flows to be discounted in a present value model. However, in Appendix 13B, we discuss the Free Cash Flow valuation approach, which is growing in popularity.

3. Use the dividend discount model to estimate stock prices.

According to the dividend discount model, the value of a stock today is the discounted value of all future dividends. This model implicitly accounts for the terminal price of a stock. To account for an infinite stream of dividends, stocks to be valued are classified by their expected growth rate in dividends. If no growth is expected, the dividend discount model reduces perpetuity to a valuation problem. If two or more growth rates are expected, a multiple growth model must be used in which the future stream of dividends is identified before being discounted. The constant-growth version of the dividend discount model is used most frequently. It reduces the ratio of the dividend expected next period to the difference between the required rate of return and the expected growth rate in dividends. The dividend discount model is sensitive to the estimates of the variables used in it; therefore, investors will calculate different prices for the same stock while using an identical model.

4. Explain the P/E ratio approach.

The P/E ratio or multiplier approach is based on the identity that a stock's current price is the product of its actual earnings per share and the P/E ratio. It follows that the P/E ratio can be calculated by dividing the current price by the actual earnings per share. To implement the P/E ratio to estimate the value of a stock, we must estimate the earnings and the P/E ratio for the next period. The P/E ratio itself may be expressed as a function of the dividend payout ratio, the required rate of return, and the expected growth rate of dividends (under uncertain conditions). P/E ratios are also inversely related to interest rates because interest rates are directly related to required rates of return.

5. Outline other relative valuation approaches.

Other relative valuation approaches include the use of market-to-book ratios, price-to-sales ratios, price-to-cash flow ratios, and price-to-EBIT ratios.

KEY TERMS

Dividend discount model (DDM), p.399	Market-to-book ratio (M/B) or Price-to-book value, p.419	Perpetuity, p.399 Price/sales (P/S) ratio, p.420
Economic value added (EVA), p.422	P/E ratio (Earnings multiplier), p.414	

REVIEW QUESTIONS

13-1. What is meant by intrinsic value? How is it determined?

13-2. Why can earnings not be used as readily as dividends in the present value approach?

13-3. What problems are encountered in using the dividend discount model?

13-4. Describe the three possibilities for dividend growth.

13-5. Since dividends are paid to infinity, how is this problem handled in the present value analysis?

13-6. Once an investor calculates intrinsic value for a particular stock, how does he or she decide whether or not to buy it?

13-7. Why is the required rate of return for a stock the discount rate to be used in valuation analysis?

13-8. What is the dividend discount model? Write this model in equation form.

13-9. Demonstrate how the dividend discount model is the same as a method that includes a specified number of dividends and a terminal price.

13-10. How valuable are the P/E ratios reported daily in the financial media?

13-11. What factors affect the P/E ratio? How sensitive is it to these factors?

13-12. Assume that two investors are valuing a company and have both decided to use the constant-growth version of the dividend valuation model. Both use $3 a share as the expected dividend for the coming year. Are these two investors likely to derive different prices? Why or why not?

13-13. Some investors prefer the P/E ratio model to the present value analysis on the grounds that the latter is more difficult to use. State these alleged difficulties and respond to them.

13-14. Indicate the likely direction of change in a stock's P/E ratio, and the reason(s) why, if

    a. The dividend payout decreases.
    b. The required rate of return rises.
    c. The expected growth rate of dividends rises.
    d. The riskless rate of return decreases.

13-15. Indicate the likely direction of change in a stock's M/B ratio, and the reason(s) why, if

    a. The dividend payout decreases.
    b. The required rate of return rises.
    c. The expected growth rate of dividends rises.
    d. The riskless rate of return decreases.
    e. The firm's ROE increases.

13-16. Indicate the likely direction of change in a stock's P/S ratio, and the reason(s) why, if

    a. The dividend payout decreases.
    b. The required rate of return rises.
    c. The expected growth rate of dividends rises.
    d. The riskless rate of return decreases.
    e. The firm's net income margin decreases.

13-17. Which of the following statements concerning price-to-book value is true?

    a. There is an inverse relationship between price-to-book values and market prices.
    b. It is calculated as the ratio of price to the book value of assets.
    c. There is supporting evidence that stocks with low price-to-book values significantly outperform the market.
    d. Price-to-book value ratios for many stocks range from 5.5 to 10.5.

13-18. If the dividend growth rate increases for a firm, its P/E will, other things being the same:

    a. increase.
    b. stay the same.
    c. decrease.
    d. increase or decrease but not stay the same.

13-19. Other things being equal, if the:

    a. required rate of return increases, the P/E ratio will rise.
    b. risk premium increases, the P/E ratio will rise.
    c. risk-free rate rises, the P/E ratio will fall.
    d. dividend payout increases, the P/E ratio will fall.

13-20. In general, are P/E ratios and dividend yields positively or negatively related? Briefly explain why, in either case.

13-21. Assume that you are trying to value a company using relative valuation techniques but the company has no earnings. Which techniques could you use?

13-22. List two advantages of using the price/sales ratio as a valuation technique. How is this ratio calculated without using per-share numbers?

DEMONSTRATION PROBLEMS

13-1. Puglisi Pharmaceuticals is currently paying a dividend of $2 per share, which is not expected to change. Investors require a rate of return of 20 percent to invest in a stock with the riskiness of Puglisi. Calculate the intrinsic value of the stock.

Solution:

The first step to solving a common stock valuation problem is to identify the type of growth involved in the dividend stream. The second step is to determine whether the dividend given in the problem is D_0 or D_1.

In this problem it is clear that the growth rate is zero and that we must solve a zero-growth valuation problem (Equation 13-3). The second step is not relevant here because all of the dividends are the same.

$$\hat{P}_0 = \frac{D_0}{k_{CS}} = \frac{2.00}{0.20} = \$10.00$$

13-2. Richter Construction Company is currently paying a dividend of $2 per share, which is expected to grow at a constant rate of 7 percent per year. Investors require a rate of return of 16 percent to invest in stocks with this degree of riskiness. Calculate the implied price of Richter.

Solution:

Since dividends are expected to grow at a constant rate, we use the constant-growth version of the dividend discount model (Equation 13-5). Note carefully that this equation calls for D_1 in the numerator and that the dividend given in this problem is the current dividend being paid, D_0. Therefore, we must compound this dividend up one period to obtain D_1 before solving the problem.

$$D_1 = D_0 (1 + g) = \$2.00 (1.07) = \$2.14$$

and

$$\hat{P}_0 = \frac{D_1}{k_{CS} - g} = \frac{2.14}{0.16 - 0.07} = \$23.78$$

13-3. Baddour Legal Services is currently selling for $60 per share and is expected to pay a dividend of $3. The expected growth rate in dividends is 8 percent for the foreseeable future. Calculate the required rate of return for this stock.

Solution:

To solve this problem, note first that this is a constant-growth model problem. Second, note that the dividend given in the problem is D_1 because it is stated as the dividend to be paid in the next period. To solve this problem for k, the required rate of return, we simply rearrange Equation 13-5:

$$k_{CS} = \frac{D_1}{P_0} + g = \frac{3.00}{60} + 0.08 = 0.13$$

13-4. Wrenn Restaurants has been undergoing rapid growth for the last few years. The current dividend of $2 per share is expected to continue to grow at the rapid rate of 20 percent a year for the next three years. After that time Wrenn is expected to slow down, with the dividend growing at a more normal rate of 7 percent a year for the indefinite future. Because of the risk involved in such rapid growth, the required rate of return on this stock is 22 percent. Calculate the implied price for this stock.

Solution:

We can recognize at once that this is a multiple-growth case of valuation because more than one growth rate is given. To solve for the value of this stock, it is necessary to identify the entire stream of future dividends from Year 1 to infinity, and discount the entire stream back to time period zero. After the third year a constant growth model can be used that accounts for all dividends from the beginning of Year 4 to infinity.

First, estimate dividends up to the start of constant growth to infinity by compounding the beginning dividend, $2, at 20 percent for each of three years, which produces the following:

$$D_1 = \$2.00 \ (1 + 0.20) = \$2.40$$
$$D_2 = \$2.00 \ (1 + 0.20)^2 = \$2.88$$
$$D_3 = \$2.00 \ (1 + 0.20)^3 = \$3.456$$

Second, estimate the price at the beginning of constant growth to infinity period

$$\hat{P}_3 = \frac{D_4}{k_{CS} - g} = \frac{(3.456)(1.07)}{0.22 - 0.07} = \$24.653$$

Third, discount back the relevant cash flows to time 0 and sum

$$\hat{P}_0 = \frac{2.40}{(1.22)^1} + \frac{2.88}{(1.22)^2} + \frac{3.456}{(1.22)^3} + \frac{24.653}{(1.22)^3}$$

$$= 1.967 + 1.935 + 1.903 + 13.577 = \$19.38$$

13-5. Company BDC has an expected dividend payout ratio of 0.43 next year, and their dividends are expected to grow at an annual rate of 8 percent to infinity. The required rate of return on their shares is 11.81 percent, and the expected EPS is $3.45.

a. Using the information above, determine an appropriate P/E multiple based on company fundamentals, and estimate an appropriate share price for BDC.

b. Re-estimate the value of BDC's shares based on their five-year average P/E ratio of 8.62.

c. Repeat using the average industry P/E ratio of 8.83.

Solution:

$$P/E = \frac{D_1/E_1}{k_{CS} - g} = \frac{0.43}{0.1181 - 0.08} = 11.29$$

a. Based on this multiple, BDC's shares are worth

$$P_0 = (P/E) \times (EPS_1) = (11.29) \ (\$3.45) = \$38.95$$

b. Based on BDC's historical P/E multiple of 8.62, BDC's shares are worth

$$P_0 = (P/E) \times (EPS_1) = (8.62) \ (\$3.45) = \$29.74$$

c. Based on the industry average P/E multiple, BDC's shares are worth

$$P_0 = (P/E) \times (EPS_1) = (8.83) \ (\$3.45) = \$30.46$$

PROBLEMS

13-1. Billingsley Products is currently selling for $45 a share with an expected dividend in the coming year of $2 per share. If the growth rate in dividends expected by investors is 5 percent to infinity, what is the implied required rate of return for this stock?

13-2. Assume that Chance Industries is expected by investors to have a dividend growth rate over the foreseeable future of 6 percent a year and that the required rate of return for this stock is 13 percent. The current dividend being paid (D_0) is $2.25. What is the price of the stock?

13-3. Mittra Motors is currently selling for $50 per share and pays $3 in dividends ($D_0$). Investors require 15 percent return on this stock. What is the expected perpetual growth rate of dividends?

13-4. Howe Poultry pays $1.50 a year in dividends, which is expected to remain unchanged. Investors require a 15 percent rate of return on this stock. What is its price?

13-5. Refer to Appendix 13A for this question.

    a. Given a preferred stock with an annual dividend of $3 per share and a price of $40, what is the required rate of return?

    b. Assume now that interest rates rise, leading investors to demand a required rate of return of 9 percent. What will be the new price of this preferred stock?

13-6. The required rate of return for Peterson Industries is 15.75 percent. The stock pays a current dividend of $1.30, and the expected annual growth rate is 5.5 percent to infinity. Calculate the intrinsic value.

13-7. In Problem 13-6, assume that the expected annual growth rate is 7 percent to infinity. Calculate the intrinsic value for this stock.

13-8. Brockbank Computer Suppliers is currently paying a dividend of $1.60 per year, and this dividend is expected to grow at a constant rate of 4 percent a year forever. Investors require a 16 percent rate of return on Brockbank. What is its estimated price?

13-9. Wilson Industries is currently paying a dividend of $1 per share, which is not expected to change in the future. The current price of this stock is $12. What is the implied required rate of return on this stock?

13-10. Cascade Gas is currently selling for $40. Its current dividend is $2, and this dividend is expected to grow at a rate of 7 percent a year forever. What is the expected rate of return for this stock?

13-11. General Foods is currently selling for $50. It is expected to pay a dividend of $2 next period. If the required rate of return is 10 percent, what is the expected perpetual growth rate?

13-12. An investor purchases the common stock of a well-known house builder, DeMong Construction Company, for $25 per share. The expected dividend for the next year is $3 per share, and the investor is confident that the stock can be sold one year from now for $30. What is the implied required rate of return?

13-13. a. The current risk-free rate (RF) is 10 percent, and the expected return on the market for the coming year is 15 percent. Calculate the required rate of return for

      i. stock A, with a beta of 1.0

      ii. stock B, with a beta of 1.7

      iii. stock C, with a beta of 0.8.

    b. How would your answers change if RF in part (a) were to increase to 12 percent, with the other variables unchanged?

    c. How would your answers change if the expected return on the market changed to 17 percent with the other variables unchanged?

13-14. Wingler Company is currently selling for $36, paying $1.80 in dividends, and investors expect dividends to grow at a constant rate of 5 percent a year forever. CEO Tony Wingler believes the stock is undervalued.

   a. If an investor requires a rate of return of 14 percent for a stock with the riskiness of Wingler Company, is it a good buy for this investor?
   b. What is the maximum an investor with a 14 percent required return should pay for Wingler Company? What is the maximum if the required return is 15 percent?

13-15. The Hall Dental Supply Company sells at $32 per share, and CEO Randy Hall estimates the latest 12-month earnings are $4 per share with a dividend payout of 50 percent.

   a. What is Hall's current P/E ratio?
   b. If an investor expects earnings to grow by 6 percent a year forever, what is the projected price for next year if the P/E ratio remains unchanged?
   c. Ray Parker, president of Hall Dental Supply, analyzes the data and estimates that the payout ratio will remain the same. Assume the expected growth rate of dividends is 6 percent per year forever, and an investor has a required rate of return of 16 percent. Would this stock be a good buy? Why or why not?
   d. If interest rates are expected to decline, what is the likely effect on Hall's P/E ratio?

13-16. McEnally Motorcycles is a rapidly growing firm. Dividends are expected to grow at the rate of 18 percent annually for the next 10 years. The growth rate after the first 10 years is expected to be 7 percent annually to infinity. The current dividend is $1.82. Investors require a rate of return of 19 percent on this stock. Calculate the intrinsic value of this stock.

13-17. BSC Ltd. is expected to earn $2 per share next year. BSC has a payout ratio of 40 percent. Earnings and dividends have been growing at a constant rate of 10 percent per year, but analysts are estimating that the growth rate will be 7 percent a year for the indefinite future. Investors require a 15 percent rate of return on BSC. What is its estimated price?

13-18. General Foundries is expected to pay a dividend of $0.60 next year, $1.10 the following year, and $1.25 each year thereafter. The required rate of return on this stock is 18 percent. How much should investors be willing to pay for this stock?

13-19. Griggs Company is not expected to pay a dividend until five years have elapsed. At the beginning of Year 6, investors expect the dividend to be $3 per share and to remain at that amount forever. If an investor has a 25 percent required rate of return for this stock, what should he or she be willing to pay for Griggs?

13-20. Poindexter Industries is expected to pay a dividend of $10 per year for 10 years and then increase the dividend to $15 per share for every year thereafter. The required rate of return on this stock is 20 percent. What is the estimated stock price for Poindexter?

13-21. Roenfeldt Components recently paid a dividend of $1 per share. This dividend is expected to grow at a rate of 25 percent a year for the next five years, after which it is expected to grow at a rate of 7 percent a year forever. The required rate of return for this stock is 18 percent. What is the estimated price of the stock?

13-22. Agrawa Corporation makes advanced computer components. It pays no dividends currently, but it expects to begin paying $1 per share four years from now. The expected dividends in subsequent years are also $1 per share. The required rate of return is 14 percent. What is the estimated price for Agrawa?

13-23. Rader Chocolate Company is currently selling for $60 and is paying a $3 dividend.

   a. If investors expect dividends to double in 12 years, what is the required rate of return for this stock?
   b. If investors had expected dividends to approximately triple in six years, what would be the required rate of return?

13-24. Avera Free Range Poultry is currently paying a dividend of $1.20. This dividend is expected to grow at the rate of 30 percent a year for the next five years, followed by a growth rate of 20 percent a year for the following five years. After 10 years the dividend is expected to grow at the rate of 6 percent a year forever. CEO Bill Avera estimates that the required rate of return for this stock is 21 percent. What is its intrinsic value?

13-25. In Problem 13-24, assume that the growth rate for the first five years is 25 percent rather than 30 percent. How would you expect the value calculated in Problem 13-24 to change? Confirm your answer by calculating the new intrinsic value.

13-26. Rocky Mountain Power and Gas is currently paying a dividend of $1.80. This dividend is expected to grow at a rate of 6 percent in the foreseeable future. Rocky Mountain Power is 10 percent less risky than the market as a whole. The market risk premium is 7 percent, and the risk-free rate is 5 percent. What is the estimated price of this stock?

13-27. Rendleman Software is expected to enjoy a very rapid growth rate in dividends of 30 percent a year for the next three years. This growth rate is then expected to slow to 20 percent a year for the next five years. After that time, the growth rate is expected to level out at 6 percent a year forever. D_0 is $2. The required rate of return is 20 percent. What is the estimated price of the stock?

13-28. Poindexter Industries is expected to pay a dividend of $10 per year for 10 years and then increase the dividend to $15 per share for every year thereafter. The required rate of return on this stock is 20 percent. What is the estimated stock price for Poindexter?

13-29. SLC Ltd. has an expected Year 1 EPS of $3.45, an expected Year 1 payout ratio of 0.456, and an expected annual growth rate in dividends to infinity of 8 percent. Shareholders require a 9.68 percent return on these shares. SLC's five-year average P/E ratio is 26.68, and the present industry average P/E ratio is 27.93. Determine three estimates of SLC's value.

13-30. Using the information for SLC Ltd. provided in Problem 13-29, and assuming the company's most recent ROE was 17.92 percent, and that its current book value per share (BV_0) is $17.86, determine the value of SLC based on the M/B ratio approach.

13-31. Using the information for SLC Ltd. provided in Problem 13-29, and assuming the company's most recent net income margin (NI%) was 3.31 percent, and that its most recent sales per share ($Sales_0$) is $85.71, determine the value of SLC based on the P/S ratio approach.

13-32. Bilco Limited has a policy of paying out 60 percent of its earnings as cash dividends to its shareholders. Bilco recently paid out a $3 per share annual dividend. The required rate of return on stocks with similar risk is 13 percent. Bilco's earnings and dividends are expected to grow at an annual rate of 8 percent forever.

   a. What is Bilco's implied P/E ratio?
   b. If Bilco changed its policy to one where it paid out 80 percent of its earnings as dividends, what would Bilco's implied P/E ratio be?

13-33. Ladslow Incorporated has a required rate of return of 14 percent, and expects that its earnings and dividends will grow at an annual rate of 6 percent forever. Its dividend payout ratio is 40 percent. Ladslow's most recent return-on-equity (ROE) was 20 percent.

   a. What is the implied market-to-book (M/B) ratio?
   b. If the company has assets of $1,000,000 (book value), has 100,000 shares outstanding, and has no debt, what should the price per share be?

13-34. Using the Price/Sales (P/S) ratio approach, what should a company's stock price be, based on the following information: required rate of return of 16 percent; perpetual annual growth rate of earnings and dividends of 6 percent; assets of $100,000,000 (book value); no debt; 20,000,000 shares outstanding; most recent annual sales of $50,000,000; most recent net income of $5,000,000; 50 percent dividend payout ratio.

13-35. The stock for Crazy Horse Corporation is trading at $75. The firm paid out $2.20 in dividends during the last year. If the payout ratio of the firm is 45 percent, what is the price-earnings ratio that will be reported to the pubic?

13-36. The current market price of the stock of Stryker Ltd. is $30 per share. The company just paid a dividend of $0.50 per share last year. If its return on assets (ROA) is 5 percent, its leverage ratio is 2, and its EPS was $2.00 last year, what is the implied rate of return assuming dividends are growing at a constant rate?

13-37. WestTec Corporation, a technology company, has been growing rapidly. After examining the company's operations very carefully, analysts at Meril Link have estimated that dividends and earnings will grow at a rate of 22 percent a year for the next 8 years, followed by 16 percent growth for another 6 years. After 14 years, the expected growth rate is 5 percent. The risk-free rate appropriate for this analysis is 5.5 percent, and the expected return on the market is 10.5 percent. The beta for WestTec is 1.1. It currently pays a dividend of $1.10. Using the spreadsheet format below, estimate the intrinsic value of this stock today. Note the following:

   a. Calculate the required rate of return for WestTec in cell H2 using the CAPM.
   b. Calculate the dollar amount of each dividend for the first 14 years in cells B5 through B18, and the present value of these amounts in cells C5 through C18. Be sure to allow for the change in growth rates in year 9.
   c. In cell G19, calculate the price of the stock at the beginning of year 15 using the then constant-growth rate of 5 percent.
   d. In cell G20, discount the price found in (c) back to today using the proper number of periods for discounting.
   e. Sum the present value of the dividends in cell C21. Add to this the present value of the price found in (d) by putting this value in C22.
   f. In cell C23, add the values found in (e) in cell C24.

Curr div		Ist gr rate	2nd gr rate	normal gr	RF	Exp Mk Rt	Beta	k
	1.1	0.22	0.16	0.05	5.5	10.5	1.1	0.11
		8yrs	6yrs					
Year		Dividend	PV of Div					
1								
2								
3								
4								
5								
6								
7								
8								
9								
10								
11								
12								
13								
14								
				Price at beginning of year 15 =		0.00		
				PV of price today =		0.00		
				Sum of PV of dividends for first 14 years				0.00
				+ PV of price at beginning of year 15				0.00
				Sum of PV of dividends and PV of price				0.00

13-38. Zoom Boards Inc. designs high-end skateboards. Sales have been growing rapidly, and with cash rolling in, the Board of Directors has decided to begin paying dividends to the company's shareholders. Each year, the dividend payout ratio will be 60 percent of net income. Assume that the shareholders have a required return of 12 percent on this stock.

    a. It is now October 1, 2008; Zoom has just declared its first dividend of $0.30 per share to be paid in one year. Analysts expect dividends to increase by $0.15 per year for another two years. After 2011 (when the dividend will be $0.60 per share), dividend growth is expected to settle down to a more moderate long-term rate of 5 percent. How much are the shares worth today?

    b. The management of Zoom is confident that the current level of earnings can be maintained without investing in new assets (i.e., the full amount of earnings could be paid out as dividends). What share price would this no-growth situation imply? What is the value of the growth opportunities (PVGO) built into the share price from part (a)?

    c. Suppose the long-term growth rate is projected to be only 4 percent. What is the impact on the current share price and the value PVGO? What percentage change in these values does the small change in the growth rate create? Repeat these calculations assuming a growth rate of 6 percent.

13-39. Morton's Clothing store has experienced some operating difficulties in recent years. As a result, the stock price has fallen below $20 per share, and the company is thought to be a take-over candidate. The company has 68,200 shares outstanding with a book value of $2,615,200 and no long-term debt. A Pro Forma Income Statement for the upcoming year is presented below.

    a. Use the ratios provided for Elegant Fashions Inc., a comparable firm, to determine a range of share prices that might be justified for Morton's.

    b. Use the free cash flow to the firm (FCFF) method presented in Appendix 13B to find the highest share price that you would be willing to pay for this company. You can make the following assumptions about the company's future operations.

        • In the upcoming year, the increase in net working capital will be $48,000 and capital expenditures will total $140,000.

        • Free cash flow will grow at a perpetual rate of 3.5 percent per year after next year.

        • Risk-free-rate = 4.5%; expected return on market = 10%; beta =1.10.

        • All cash flows occur at the end of the year.

Ratio	Value for Elegant
P/E (forward)	20.8
Price / Sales	0.50
Price / Book	1.25

Pro Forma Income Statement for Morton's Clothing

Revenues	$ 7,300,000
Expenses	6,955,400
EBITDA	344,600
Depreciation	194,620
EBIT	149,980
Income Taxes	37,495
Net Income	112,485

PREPARING FOR YOUR PROFESSIONAL EXAMS

CFA PRACTICE QUESTIONS

13-1. An analyst has gathered the following data about a stock:

The stock paid a $1 dividend last year.
Next year's dividend is projected to be 10 percent higher.
The stock is projected to sell for $25 at the end of the year.
The risk-free rate of interest is 8 percent and the market return is 13 percent.
The stock's beta is 1.2.
What is the value of the stock?
  a. $19.45
  b. $22.89
  c. $24.00
  d. $26.74

13-2. Use the following data to analyze a stock's P/E ratio:
The stock's beta is 1.2.
The dividend payout ratio is 60 percent.
The stock's expected growth rate is 7 percent.
The risk-free rate is 6 percent and the expected rate of return on the market is 13 percent.

Using the dividend discount model, what would you expect the stock's P/E ratio to be?
  a. 5.4
  b. 8.1
  c. 10.0
  d. 12.0

13-3. Assuming all other factors remain unchanged, which of the following would reduce a company's P/E ratio?

  a. The dividend growth rate increases.
  b. The dividend payout ratio increases.
  c. The company's beta increases.
  d. The company's return on equity is expected to increase.

13-4. A company's stock is selling for $45 per share. The firm's earnings and dividends have been growing at an annual rate of 8 percent, and this growth is expected to continue in the future. The firm's earnings per share this past year was $5, and it maintains a 40 percent dividend payout policy. Based on the dividend discount model, what rate of return are stockholders requiring?

  a. 4.5 percent
  b. 8.0 percent
  c. 12.8 percent
  d. 14.2 percent

13-5. A stock is not expected to pay dividends for the next four years. However, it is expected to pay a $0.50 dividend five years from today with dividends expected to grow at 5 percent per year thereafter. What is the price of the stock if the required rate of return is 12 percent?

  a. $7.14
  b. $4.05
  c. $4.54
  d. $4.77

CFA CURRICULUM AND SAMPLE EXAM QUESTIONS (©CFA INSTITUTE)

13-1. An analyst made the following statement: "According to empirical research, differences in both price-to-earnings ratios and price-to-book value ratios may be related to differences in long-run average common stock returns." Is the analyst's statement correct with respect to:

Price-to-earnings ratios?	Price-to-book value ratios?
a. No	No
b. No	Yes
c. Yes	No
d. Yes	Yes

13-2. An analyst gathered the following per-share data about a company for a given year:

Market value of common stock at end of year	$55
Unadjusted book value of common stock at end of year	$25
Adjusted book value of common stock at end of year	$28
Gross sales for year	$48
Net sales for year	$44
Cash flow for year	$7
Earnings for year	$3
Forecasted earnings for next year	$4

What should be the analyst's year-end estimate of the company's

Price-to-sales ratios?	Price-to-book value ratios?
a. 1.15	1.12
b. 1.15	1.96
c. 1.25	1.12
d. 1.25	1.96

13-3. An analyst made the following statement: "When using either price-to-earnings ratios or price-to-cash-flow ratios, differences among companies with respect to quality of earnings are not a major concern." Is the analyst's statement correct with respect to:

Price-to-earnings ratios?	Price-to-cash-flow ratios?
a. No	No
b. No	Yes
c. Yes	No
d. Yes	Yes

13-4. An analyst made the following statement: "Neither price-to-book value ratios nor price-to-sales ratios are useful in valuing firms whose earnings are abnormally high or low." Is the analyst's statement correct with respect to:

Price-to-book value ratios?	Price-to-sales ratios?
a. No	No
b. No	Yes
c. Yes	No
d. Yes	Yes

13-5. An analyst made the following statement: "Compared with price-to-earnings ratios, price-to-sales ratios and price-to-cash-flow ratios are generally less subject to distortion or manipulation." The analyst's statement is correct with respect to:

    a. price-to-sales ratios, but not price-to-cash-flow ratios.

    b. price-to-cash-flow ratios, but not price-to-sales ratios.

    c. both price-to-sales ratios and price-to-cash-flow ratios.

    d. neither price-to-sales ratios nor price-to-cash-flow ratios.

13-6. An analyst gathered the following information about Fallow Corporation:

Current dividend per share	$1.00
Required rate of return	15%
Expected annual growth rate for the next two years	20%
Expected annual growth rate for year three and thereafter	20%

The value of a share of Fallow's common stock is *closest* to:

    a. $10.50.

    b. $12.00.

    c. $13.55.

    d. $15.21.

APPENDIX 13A

THE ANALYSIS AND VALUATION OF PREFERRED STOCK

In Chapter 2, preferred stock was classified for investment analysis purposes as a fixed-income security, although technically it is an equity security. It is best described as a hybrid security, having some characteristics similar to fixed-income securities (i.e., bonds) and some similar to common stocks.

Analysis

Preferred stock can be described as a perpetuity, or perpetual security, since it has no maturity date, and it will pay the indicated dividend forever. Although perpetual, many preferred stock issues carry a sinking fund, which provides for early retirement of the issue, usually over a period of many years. Furthermore, many preferred stocks are callable by the issuer, which also potentially limits the life of preferreds. Finally, roughly half of all preferred stocks issued in recent years are convertible into common stock. Therefore, although preferred stock is perpetual by definition, in reality many of the issues will not remain in existence forever.

Dividends from preferred stock, unlike those from common stock, are fixed when the stock is issued and do not change. These dividends are specified as an annual dollar amount (although paid quarterly) or as a percentage of par value, which is often either $25 or $100. The issuer can forgo paying the preferred dividend if earnings are insufficient. Although this dividend is specified, failure to pay it does not result in default of the obligation, as is the case with bonds. However, most preferred issues have a cumulative feature, which requires that all unpaid preferred dividends, both current and arrears, must be paid before those for common stocks.

Investors regard preferred stock as less risky than common stock because the dividend is specified and must be paid before a common stock dividend can be paid. They regard preferreds as more risky than bonds, however, because bondholders have priority in being paid and in case of liquidation. That is why investors require higher rates of return on preferred stock than on bonds but a smaller required return than on common stocks. However, since most dividends received by individuals qualify for the dividend tax credit, they are taxed at a lower rate than interest income. As a result of this tax advantage, preferred stocks often carry slightly lower yields than bonds of comparable quality.

Valuation

The value of any perpetuity can be calculated as follows:

$$V_p = \frac{C}{(1 + k_p)^1} + \frac{C}{(1 + k_p)^2} + \dots + \frac{C}{(1 + k_p)^\infty}$$ **(13-23)**

$$= \frac{C}{k_p}$$

where

V_p = the value of a perpetuity today
C = the constant annual payment to be received
k_p = the required rate of return appropriate for this perpetuity

Because the dividends provided by a straight preferred share represent a perpetuity, Equation 13-23 is applicable in its valuation. We simply substitute the preferred dividend (D) for C and the appropriate required return (k_{ps}) for k_p, resulting in Equation 13-24.[21]

$$V_{ps} = \frac{D}{k_{ps}}$$ **(13-24)**

A preferred stock, or any perpetuity, is easy to value because the numerator of Equation 13-24 is known and fixed forever. No complex present value calculations are needed for a perpetuity, which simplifies the valuation process considerably. If any two of the values in 13-24 are known, the third can easily be found.

As an example of the valuation analysis, consider preferred shares with a fixed annual dividend of $1.93. To value this preferred, investors need to estimate the required rate of return appropriate for its degree of riskiness. Suppose the required rate of return (k_{ps}), is 10 percent. The value of this preferred would be

$$V_{ps} = \frac{D}{k_{ps}} = \frac{1.93}{0.10} = \$19.30$$

On the other hand, a required rate of return of 11 percent would result in a value of $17.54.

If the current price for this preferred, as observed in the marketplace (P_{ps}), is substituted into Equation 13-24 for V_{ps}, the yield can be solved by using Equation 13-25.

$$k_{ps} = \frac{D}{P_{ps}}$$ **(13-25)**

In the case of the company above, if we observed a price of $27, this implies the yield, or required rate of return, is 7.15 percent.

$$k_{ps} = \frac{D}{P_{ps}} = \frac{1.93}{27.00} = 0.0715$$

Notice from Equation 13-24 that as the required rate of return rises, the price of the preferred stock declines; obviously, the converse is also true. Because the numerator is fixed, the value (price) of a

---

[21]Notice that this equation is identical to the no-growth version of the DDM expressed in Equation 13-3, with D= D_0 and k_{ps} = k_{CS}. This is because the dividend paid on a preferred share is a constant, or given amount.

preferred stock changes as the required rate of return changes. Clearly, investors' required rates of return fluctuate across time as interest rates and other factors change. As rates fluctuate, so do preferred stock prices. In fact, because they are fixed income securities with no maturity date, we observe that their prices will be extremely sensitive to changes in the level of interest rates, similar to long-term bonds.

APPENDIX 13B

THE FREE CASH FLOW VALUATION APPROACH

There are two variations of the Free Cash Flow (FCF) valuation model: the free cash flow to the firm approach and the free cash flow to equity approach. Both of these approaches focus on determining the present value of the future FCFs available to suppliers of capital after all expenses have been paid. Both approaches are discussed below.

The FCF to the Firm Valuation Approach

The FCF to the firm approach focuses on finding the present value of the estimated future FCFs available to all suppliers of capital (both debt and equity suppliers) after all expenses have been paid (denoted as FCF_F). These cash flows are then discounted using the firm's weighted average cost of capital (WACC) to determine the total value of the firm. The value of the firm's equity is then calculated by subtracting the value of the debt from the value of the firm. FCF_F is preferred by many analysts for levered firms that may have negative free cash flow to equity holders (FCF_E).

Estimating FCF_F:

Equation 13-26 can be used to estimate FCF_F:

(13-26)
$$FCF_F = NI + NCC - \text{Cap. Ex.} +/- \Delta WC + I(1-T)$$

where

NI	=	net income;
NCC	=	non-cash charges including depreciation (amortization) expense and deferred taxes;
Cap. Ex.	=	capital expenditures;
$+/- \Delta WC$	=	change in net working capital requirements (if more working capital is required, the number will be negative);
I	=	interest expense; and,
T	=	the firm's estimated marginal tax rate.

Equation 13-26 can also be expressed as:

(13-27)
$$FCF_F = EBIT(1-T) + NCC - \text{Cap. Ex.} +/- \Delta WC$$

where EBIT = earnings before interest and taxes.

Similar to the DDM, the free cash flow models require us to estimate the present value of all FCFs from now to infinity. Similar to the constant-growth DDM, if we assume constant growth in FCFs to infinity and we can estimate the FCF_F for period 1 (i.e., FCF_{F1}), we can proceed in the same fashion as we would using the DDM. In particular, we can use a constant-growth version of the FCF_F model, provided in Equation 13-28 below:

$$V_F = \frac{FCF_{F,1}}{WACC - g}$$

(13-28)

where
WACC = the firm's weighted average cost of capital and
g = the estimated annual growth in FCF_F, to infinity

Equation 13-28 provides an estimate of the value of the total firm. In order to find out the value of the firm's common shares, we must next subtract the value of the firm's debt to find out the value of the firm's common equity. Finally, we would divide the firm's equity value by the number of common shares outstanding to determine the price per common share. This approach is illustrated in Example 13B-1.

EXAMPLE 13B-1: USING THE CONSTANT-GROWTH VERSION OF THE FCF_F MODEL

An analyst determines the following estimates for next year for Kappa Ltd.: Net income = $120 million; non-cash charges = $10 million; capital expenditures = $30 million; additional working capital requirements = $6 million; interest expenses = $10 million; tax rate = 40 percent. Using these estimates, we can determine the firm's free cash flow and estimate the value of its common shares assuming the FCF_F is expected to grow at a 4 percent annual rate indefinitely. The company's weighted average cost of capital is 10 percent, the market value of its liabilities is $1 billion, and it has 20 million shares outstanding.

Solution:

$FCF_{F,1}$ = NI + NCC − Cap. Ex. +/- Δ WC + I (1- T)

= 120 + 10 − 30 − 6 + 10(1 − .40) = 100

Value of Kappa= $V_F = \dfrac{FCF_{F,1}}{WACC - g}$ = ($100 million) / (0.10 – 0.04) = $1,666.67 m

Value of Kappa's equity = $1,666.67 m − $1,000 m = $666.67 m

Price per share of Kappa = $666.67 m / 20 m = $33.33

We can also use this model for two-stage or multi-stage growth situations by applying the same process as we did for the multi-stage DDM cases, except we replace D_t with FCF_t. The multi-stage growth version of the FCF model is illustrated for the FCF to equity approach in the Example 13B-3.

The FCF to Equity Valuation Approach

The FCF to equity approach focuses on finding the present value of the estimated future FCFs available to equity holders after all expenses have been paid and all capital expenditures have been funded (denoted as FCF_E). The value of the equity is calculated by using the required rate of return on the firm's common shares as the appropriate discount rate. If the firm's capital structure is stable, this approach is often preferred by analysts.

Estimating FCF_E:

Equation 13-29 can be used to estimate FCF_E:

$$FCF_E = FCF_F - I\,(1 - T)\; +/- \; \text{Net Debt}$$

(13-29)

where

Net Debt = net amount of new debt issued by the firm (i.e., amount of new debt issues – amount of debt retired).

If we use Equation 13-26, which was used to estimate FCF_F, we see that Equation 13-29 can also be expressed as:

(13-30)
$$FCF_E = NI + NCC - Cap.\ Ex. +/- \Delta\ WC +/- Net\ Debt$$

with all the terms as defined above.

Similar to the DDM and the FCF to the firm approach, we can use a constant-growth version of this model based on the estimate of FCF_E for period 1 (i.e., $FCF_{E,1}$):

(13-31)
$$V_E = \frac{FCF_{E,1}}{k_{CS} - g}$$

where

k_{CS} = required return on the firm's common shares; and,

g = the estimated annual growth in FCF_E to infinity.

Equation 13-31 provides an estimate of the value of the firm's common equity. We would divide the firm's equity value by the number of common shares outstanding to determine the price per common share. This approach is illustrated in Example 13B-2. Alternatively, we could estimate the FCF_E on a per share basis, and estimate the price directly. This is the approach used in Example 13B-3, which illustrates how to apply a multi-stage version of the FCF to equity approach.

EXAMPLE 13B-2: USING THE CONSTANT-GROWTH VERSION OF THE FCF_E MODEL

This example uses the analyst's estimates for Kappa Ltd. in Example 13B-1, and assumes that the required rate of return on Kappa's shares is 18 percent, and that Kappa plans to issue $10 million in new debt this year, and also plans to retire $7 million in old debt. Using these estimates, we can determine the firm's free cash flow to equity, and estimate the value of its common shares, assuming the FCF_E is expected to grow at a 4 percent annual rate indefinitely.

Solution:

Net Debt = 10 − 7 = $3 million

So using Equation 13-30, we get:

$FCF_{E,1}$ = NI + NCC − Cap. Ex. +/- Δ WC +/- Net Debt

= 120 + 10 − 30 − 6 + 3 = 97

Value of Kappa's Equity = $V_F = \dfrac{FCF_{E,1}}{k_{CS} - g}$ = ($97 million) / (0.18 − 0.04) = $692.857m

Price per share of Kappa = $692.857 m / 20 m = $34.64

Example 13B-3 demonstrates how to apply a multi-stage growth version of the FCF to equity model.

EXAMPLE 13B-3: USING THE MULTI-STAGE GROWTH VERSION OF THE FCF_E MODEL

An analyst estimates that a company's FCF_E for this past year is $4 million. She expects these FCFs to grow at 15 percent per year for the next three years before stabilizing at an annual rate of 6 percent. The analyst estimates that 11.2 percent is a reasonable rate of return on this company's shares. We can estimate the company's price per share using the information above, and noting that they have 10 million shares outstanding.

1st Step: Estimate the FCFs up to the start of constant growth to infinity period

$FCF_{E,0}$ $= \$4\ m$

Per share $FCF_{E,0}$ $= \$4\ m\ /\ 10\ m\ shares = \$0.40$

Per share $FCF_{E,1}$ $= 0.40(1.15) = \$0.46$

Per share $FCF_{E,2}$ $= 0.40(1.15)^2 = \$0.529$

Per share $FCF_{E,3}$ $= 0.40(1.15)^3 = \$0.6083$

2nd Step: Estimate the value at the start of constant growth to infinity period

Per share $FCF_{E,4} = 0.40(1.15)^3 (1.06) = \$0.6448$

Intrinsic value (at t = 4) = .6448/(.112 − .06) = \$12.40

3rd Step: Determine the present value of all relevant cash flows

$$P_0 = \frac{.46}{(1.112)} + \frac{.529}{(1.112)^2} + \frac{.6083}{(1.112)^3} + \frac{12.40}{(1.112)^3}$$

$$P_0 = .4137 + .4278 + .4424 + 9.0179 = \$10.30$$

When to Use FCF Models

FCF models are appropriate when the company whose shares are being analyzed does not pay dividends, or if the company pays dividends, but dividends differ significantly from the company's capacity to pay dividends. They are also appropriate if the free cash flows are aligned with profitability.

CHAPTER 14

COMMON STOCKS: ANALYSIS AND STRATEGY

Given your new $1 million portfolio, you will need to manage it. You now realize that the market has a substantial impact on individual stocks and portfolios, and therefore you realize you need to better understand the impact of the overall market on individual stocks. Also, you now appreciate the role the required rate of return plays when evaluating stocks, another issue you decide warrants additional analysis. Both issues are considered here.

One of the most important decisions each investor must make is whether to take an active approach or a passive approach to investing. A passive approach will save costs and will often produce as good or better results as an active approach. Or, if you choose an active approach, you will need to give some thought to whether you want to select stocks or try to time the market. These issues will be covered here.

Learning Objectives

After reading this chapter, you should be able to

1. Discuss the impact of the overall market on common stock investors.
2. Explain the importance of the required rate of return.
3. Distinguish between passive and active investment strategies.
4. Differentiate between technical and fundamental analysis.
5. Describe the bottom-up and top-down approaches in fundamental analysis.

CHAPTER PREVIEW

This chapter covers the analysis and strategy for selecting and holding common stocks. Similar to the passive approach to bond investing, common stock investors can follow a buy-and-hold strategy, or buy index funds or exchange-traded funds that mimic some market index. Under the active approach, we analyze the primary alternatives of stock selection, sector rotation, and market timing and consider the implications of the Efficient Market Hypothesis (which was discussed in Chapter 10). We conclude by considering the two basic methods used in security analysis: technical and fundamental analysis.

TAKING A GLOBAL PERSPECTIVE

In the New Economy, investors cross borders more and more when they invest. And the investing is more sophisticated. Rather than start with a portfolio of Canadian-listed stocks and add selected foreign equities, investors today search for the truly "good" companies (e.g., industry giants, innovative leaders, those with proven track records), regardless of the country in which they are located. What matters today is being a world leader, whether that is Cisco Systems Inc. in the United States or Nokia in Finland. When it comes to important sectors such as pharmaceuticals and telecommunications, globalization is the name of the game.

Many Canadian investors have traditionally been myopic, focusing only on companies they are familiar with, such as Nortel Networks, Bombardier Inc., or The Bank of Nova Scotia. Although this has paid off some of the time, this will not always be the case. Even though Canadian equities have outperformed many foreign equity markets since 1990, they have also underperformed several others. Regardless of this historical performance, we are now in an age of globalization, and investors should therefore take a global perspective.

How much of a Canadian investor's portfolio should be allocated to foreign securities? A general consensus among market observers is that a typical investor should have 10 to 20 percent of his/her portfolio in international markets. However, many suggest that much higher proportions are reasonable. In fact, many experts suggest that it is difficult to construct a portfolio that is well-diversified across industry sectors using only Canadian companies, because of the small number of "quality" companies we have at any given time in a particular industry. Of course, all foreign markets are not the same. Emerging markets are generally much riskier than developed economies and investors should probably not have a large percentage of their portfolio in emerging markets.

SOME IMPORTANT ISSUES INVOLVING COMMON STOCKS

In Chapter 11 we analyzed bonds in terms of interest rates because of the fundamental relationship between interest rates and bond prices. In similar fashion, we now consider the impact of market risk on common stock investors. The impact of the market on every investor in common stocks is pervasive and dominant and must be fully appreciated by investors if they are to be successful.

We also consider the required rate of return in detail. This variable is important in any analysis of common stocks. As we saw in Chapter 13, the required rate of return is a very important component of the valuation process using the dividend discount model, as well as in other valuation approaches.

The Impact of the Overall Market on Individual Stocks

learning objective 1
Discuss the impact of the overall market on common stock investors.

Overall, market risk is the single most important risk affecting the price movements of common stocks. The aggregate market remains the largest single factor explaining fluctuations in both individual stock prices and portfolios of stocks. This is particularly true for a diversified portfolio of stocks, and as we know, the basic tenet of portfolio theory is to diversify into a number of properly chosen securities. For adequately diversified portfolios, market effects often account for 90 percent and more of the variability in the portfolio's return. In other words, for a well-diversified portfolio, the market is the dominant factor affecting the variability of its return. Although any given portfolio may clearly outperform the market, it will usually be significantly influenced by what happens on an overall basis.

EXAMPLE 14-1: MARKET RISK AND AIC ADVANTAGE EQUITY FUND

Consider the performance of **AIC Advantage Equity Fund** over a specific five-year period, as shown in Figure 14-1. This fund, part of the well-known AIC family of funds, invests primarily in Canadian common shares. Notice that although this fund underperformed the aggregate market (as measured by the S&P/TSX Composite Index), with an average annual return of 9.33 percent versus 18.49 percent for the S&P/TSX Total Return Index over this period, its movements roughly paralleled those of the market.

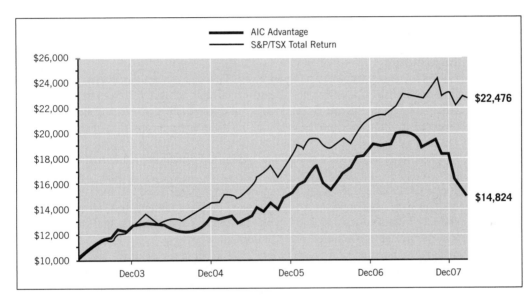

Figure 14-1
Returns for a Well-Diversified Portfolio and the S&P/TSX Composite Index

Source: Globefund website: www.globefund.com. Reprinted with permission from *The Globe and Mail.*

The International Perspective

Canadian investors buying foreign stocks face the same issues as they do at home when it comes to market risk. Some of these markets have performed very well, and some have performed poorly over specified periods of time. The investor fortunate enough to have invested in the Bolivian stock market in 2000 experienced an average gain of more than 160 percent, whereas in the South Korean market he or she would have lost about 51 percent during the same period. Many foreign markets are even more volatile than our own. For example, during 2007, the returns for the Chinese stock market were 63.1 percent and those in India were 71.2 percent; however, from January 1 to late October in 2008, the Chinese and Indian markets had declined 68 and 59 percent respectively.

Perhaps the best foreign example of the impact of the overall market on investors is Japan, clearly an economic superpower. In the 1980s, Japan seemed invincible in its economic performance, and its stock market, as measured by the Nikkei stock index, reflected Japan's success with seemingly unending rises in stock prices. By the 1990s, however, this situation had changed dramatically, with assets in Japan down sharply from the previous record levels.

EXAMPLE 14-2: IMPACT OF FOREIGN MARKETS—THE NIKKEI

The Nikkei stock index described in Chapter 4 peaked at the end of 1989 at a level of almost 39,000. By mid-1992, the index had declined below the 15,000 level, representing a staggering decline of some 60 percent. As one well-known magazine put it, this was the "biggest erasure of wealth in history." The Japanese stock market continued its slump, falling below 8,000 in the spring of 2003. It has recovered a significant amount since then and was just under 14,000 by April 2008.

The Required Rate of Return

Required Rate of Return

The minimum expected rate of return necessary to induce an investor to purchase a security.

The required rate of return was used in the previous chapter as the discount rate for valuing common stocks and in Chapter 11 to determine the price of a bond. Recall that the **required rate of return** for any security is defined as the minimum expected rate of return needed to induce an investor to purchase it. That is, given its risk, a security must offer some minimum expected return before a particular investor can be persuaded to buy it.

This discussion is directly related to the Capital Asset Pricing Model (CAPM) discussion in Chapter 9. The CAPM provides investors with a method of actually calculating a required (expected) rate of return for a stock, an industry, or the market as a whole. Our interest here is to think of the required rate of return on an overall basis as it affects the strategies that investors employ and the management of their portfolios.

What do investors require (expect) when they invest? First of all, investors can earn a riskless rate of return by investing in riskless assets such as Treasury bills. This nominal risk-free rate of return has been designated RF throughout this text. It consists of a real risk-free rate of interest and an inflation premium (to compensate investors for expected inflation).[1] In summary, as an approximation,[2]

(14-1) $$\text{Risk-free rate of return} = \text{Real rate of return} + \text{Inflation premium}$$

Risk Premium

That part of a security's return above the risk-free rate of return. The greater the risk of the asset, the greater the associated risk premium.

In addition to the risk-free rate of return available from riskless assets, rational risk-averse investors purchasing a risky asset expect to be compensated for this additional risk. Therefore, a risky asset must offer a **risk premium** above and beyond the riskless rate of return, and the greater the risk of the asset, the greater the promised risk premium must be.

The risk premium must reflect the uncertainty involved in investing in the asset. Thinking of risk in terms of its traditional sources, such components as the business risk and the financial risk of a corporation would certainly contribute to the risk premium demanded by investors for purchasing the common stock of the corporation. After all, the risk to the investor is that the expected income (return) will not be realized because of unforeseen events.

The particular industry in which a company operates will significantly affect the risk to the investor. For example, data from the S&P/TSX Composite Index showed that information technology companies comprised the worst performing industry in 2002 with a loss of 59.0 percent, while gold companies represented the top-performing industry with a return of 42.5 percent. However, in 2003, information technology was the second-best performing industry category, with a return of +59.3 percent, while gold was the worst performing industry with a return of 13.6 percent, well below the S&P/TSX Composite Index return of 24.3 percent. Similarly, energy stocks were the top performers in 2005 with average returns of 61.3 percent, but were well below average in 2006 and were slightly

[1]The real risk-free rate of interest (i.e., the real time value of money) is the basic exchange rate in the economy or the price necessary to induce someone to forego consumption and save in order to consume more in the next period. It is defined within a context of no uncertainty and no inflation.

[2]The more precise calculation involves adding 1.0 to both the real rate and the inflation premium, multiplying the two together, and subtracting the 1.0 from the product. For example, assuming a real rate of 2 percent and an inflation rate of 5 percent:

$$(1 + RF) = (1 + \text{Real rate})(1 + \text{Inflation premium}) = (1 + 0.02)(1 + 0.05) = (1.071).$$

This implies RF = 0.071, or 7.1%.

below average in 2007, providing returns of 3.2 and 8.2 percent respectively, versus TSX returns of 17.3 and 9.8 percent.

In addition to business risk, the financial decisions that a firm makes (or fails to make) will also affect the riskiness of the stock.

Understanding the Required Rate of Return

The required rate of return for any investment opportunity can be expressed as Equation 14-2. One commonly used version of this equation is the CAPM, and another variation is the Fama and French three-factor model, both discussed in Chapter 9.

$$\text{Required rate of return} = \text{Risk-free rate} + \text{Risk premium}$$ **(14-2)**

It is important to note that there are many financial assets and therefore many different required rates of return. The average required rate of return on bonds is different from that on preferred stocks, and both are different from what is generally required from common stocks, warrants, or puts and calls. Furthermore, within a particular asset category such as common stocks, there are many required rates of return. Common stocks cover a relatively wide range of risk, from conservative utility stocks to small, risky high-technology stocks.

It is also important to be aware that the level of required rates of return changes over time. For example, required rates of return change with inflationary expectations, because the inflation premium is a component of the risk-free rate of return, which, in turn, is a component of the required rate of return. The level also changes as the risk premiums change. Investor pessimism will increase the risk premium and the required rate; investor optimism lowers both.

Risk and the Required Rate of Return

We know from Chapter 9 that the CAPM suggests the trade-off between the required rate of return and risk is linear and upward sloping, as shown in Figure 14-2. In other words, the required rate of return increases as the risk, measured by beta, increases. Taken as a whole, the stock market has a beta of 1.0, indicated by Point M in the diagram. The required rate of return for all stocks is therefore k_m. Stock C, with a beta lower than 1.0, has a required rate of return below k_m because its risk (beta) is less than that of the market. On the other hand, a stock with a beta greater than 1.0 has a required rate of return greater than that of the market. Stock A has a beta of 2.0 and Stock B a beta of 1.5.

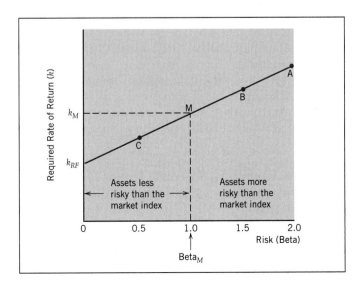

Figure 14-2
Required Rate of Return Versus Risk for Common Stocks

CHECK YOUR UNDERSTANDING

14-1. Suppose you knew with certainty that the next three years would be strong up years for the stock market. Assuming that you are willing to hold common stocks, would you be comfortable letting someone choose for you a broadly diversified subsample of the S&P/TSX Composite Index?

14-2. If you expect a severe gasoline shortage for a period of a few months, what would you predict will happen to the required rate of return for stocks?

BUILDING STOCK PORTFOLIOS

learning objective 3
Distinguish between passive and active investment strategies.

We now consider how investors go about selecting stocks to be held in portfolios. As noted in Chapter 8, individual investors often consider the investment decision as consisting of two steps:

1. Asset allocation

2. Security selection

We will assume that the asset allocation decision has been made so that our focus is only on common stocks. The common stock portion could constitute 100 percent of the total portfolio or some other percentage an investor chooses. For example, the **AIC Advantage Equity Fund** discussed in Example 14-1 consisted of 99.33 percent equity, 0.28 percent other assets, and 0.39 percent cash and short-term securities as of March 31, 2008.

Recall that in our discussion of bond strategies we considered the passive and active approaches. These are also applicable to investors as they select and manage common stock portfolios or select investment company managers who will oversee such portfolios on their behalf. Which of these to pursue will depend on a number of factors, including the investor's expertise, time, and temperament, and, importantly, what an investor believes about the efficiency of the market, as discussed in Chapter 10. We will consider each of these two strategies in turn.

THE PASSIVE STRATEGY

A natural outcome of a belief in efficient markets is to employ some type of passive strategy in owning and managing common stocks. If the market is totally efficient, no active strategy should be able to beat the market on a risk-adjusted basis. The Efficient Market Hypothesis (EMH) has implications for fundamental analysis and technical analysis (discussed in Chapter 18), which are both active strategies for selecting common stocks.

Passive strategies do not seek to outperform the market, but simply to do as well as the market or achieve some other well-defined investment objective. The emphasis is on minimizing transaction costs and time spent in managing the portfolio because any expected benefits from active trading or analysis are likely to be less than the costs. Passive investors act as if the market is efficient and accept the consensus estimates of return and risk, accepting current market price as the best estimate of a security's value. Many investors have adopted passive strategies in light of the inability of active fund managers to beat passive benchmarks. Real-World Returns 14-1 provides evidence in this regard, suggesting that very few active equity fund managers were able to outperform passive index-based ETFs over a recent time period.

Paralleling our discussion of passive approaches to bond management, an investor can simply follow a buy-and-hold strategy for whatever portfolio of stocks is owned. Alternatively, a very effective way to employ a passive strategy with common stocks is to invest in an indexed portfolio. We will consider each of these strategies in turn.

REAL-WORLD RETURNS 14-1

How Canadian Equities Stack Up Against an ETF

What We're Looking For

The performance of mutual funds is best measured against the appropriate benchmark stock or bond index, but let's get practical for a moment. Wouldn't it be more useful to compare mutual funds to low-fee exchange-traded funds (ETFs), which are the best way for individual investors to actually buy an index's returns? This brings us to today's screen, which pits Canadian equity funds against an ETF called the iShares CDN Composite Index Fund (ETFs trade like stocks and the symbol for this one is XIC on the Toronto Stock Exchange).

Today's Search

There are 100 or so funds in the Canadian equity category that have been around for the five years to Sept. 30. Let's compare their compound average annual returns to the composite index ETF. Just for fun, we'll toss another ETF into the mix. It's called the iShares CDN LargeCap 60 Index Fund (XIU-TSX) and it tracks big blue-chip stocks only. We'll also look at a risk measure called beta. The S&P/TSX composite has a beta of one and funds on either side of that number are said to be more or less volatile.

So What Did We Turn Up?

Nothing flattering to the mutual fund industry, that's for sure. Just five funds beat the composite index ETF over the past five years, and one of them was the LargeCap 60 ETF. You might put up with somewhat lower returns from a fund if it had a lower risk profile than an index-hugging ETF, but the beta numbers in our chart suggest that most top-performing funds are similar to the index.

Pay close attention to the effect that management expense ratios have in this comparison. ETFs have ultra-low MERs, while the funds on our list are as high as 2.85 percent. With lower fees, several funds would have put up a much stiffer challenge to ETFs.

We'd ideally use a longer-term comparison for funds and ETFs, but the current selection of Canadian ETFs haven't been around long enough to establish a 10-year track record. Meantime, keep ETFs in mind as an effective way to get some exposure to the same indexes and sectors that mutual funds match up against.

Fund name	As of September 2007 Net assets (000s)	Last reported MER date	MER %	5-yr return	5-yr beta
Acuity All Cap 30 Canadian Equity	347,766	31-Jan-07	2.85	27.96	1.385346
imaxx Canadian Equity Growth	20,179	28-Sep-07	2.76	24.54	0.986167
Altafund Investment Corp.	72,394	28-Sep-07	2.72	22.02	1.042311
TD Canadian Equity	3,091,347	28-Sep-07	2.09	21.39	1.145336
iShares CDN LargeCap 60 Index	9,992,080	28-Sep-07	0.15	21.39	0.980728
TD Canadian Equity-A		28-Sep-07	2.09	21.09	1.130500
iShares CDN Composite Index	451,582	28-Sep-07	0.25	20.94	1.002607
Desjardins Environment	120,715	31-Jan-07	2.35	20.71	0.985526
OTG Diversified		29-Sep-06	1.30	20.51	0.981718
Altamira Precision Cdn Index	199,164	28-Sep-07	0.53	20.45	0.983078
iShares CDN MidCap Index	246,361	28-Sep-07	0.55	20.45	0.983592

(continued)

REAL-WORLD RETURNS 14-1 *continued*

Hartford Canadian Stock D	21,537	28-Sep-07	1.88	20.43	0.949451
Integra Canadian Value Growth	64,937	30-Dec-05	2.24	20.04	0.906116
TD Canadian Index - e		28-Sep-07	0.31	19.93	0.987276
National Bank Canadian Index	17,445	28-Sep-07	1.14	19.84	0.983619
Leith Wheeler Canadian Equity B	169,359	28-Sep-07	1.50	19.72	0.720842
Ferique Equity	368,655	28-Sep-07	0.66	19.58	0.964336
Manulife Sector Rotation Fund	123,915	29-Dec-06	2.69	19.55	1.012749
RBC Canadian Index	500,469	28-Sep-07	0.71	19.55	0.996493
GGOF Canadian Lrg Cap Equ Mutual	168,581	29-Dec-06	2.39	19.54	0.878637
Hartford Canadian Stock B	28,404	28-Sep-07	2.60	19.53	0.952128
Acuity Social Values Canadian Equ	51,189	31-Jan-07	2.85	19.52	1.178193
Sceptre Canadian Equity - A	29,179	29-Dec-06	1.69	19.42	0.939199
TD Canadian Index	884,466	28-Sep-07	0.85	19.41	0.997669
FMOQ Canadian Equity	30,850	28-Sep-07	0.95	19.34	0.933744
CIBC Canadian Index	864,472	29-Dec-06	0.97	19.30	0.995622
Scotia Canadian Stock Index	206,428	28-Sep-07	1.03	19.20	0.997593
BMO Equity Index	478,876	28-Sep-07	1.01	19.12	0.994472
PH&N Canadian Equity-A	1,194,834	28-Sep-07	1.13	19.09	0.870502
Fidelity Cdn Disciplined Equity-B	1,021,928	29-Dec-06	2.24	18.98	1.019771
Fidelity Cdn Disciplined Equity-A	802,546	29-Dec-06	2.45	18.85	1.021164
Meritas Jantzi Social Index	74,262	31-Aug-07	1.94	18.81	0.872850
PH&N Community Values Cdn Equ-A	29,207	28-Sep-07	1.39	18.65	0.815829
Fidelity Cdn Disciplined Equ Cl-B	27,667	31-May-07	2.30	18.65	1.019219
Fidelity Cdn Disciplined Equ Class	38,425	31-May-07	2.50	18.52	1.020240
Manulife Canadian Equity Fund - A	369,908	29-Dec-06	2.23	18.38	1.046150
OTG Growth		29-Sep-06	1.30	18.37	0.933543

Source: Globefund
Source: Carrick, Rob, "How Canadian Equities Stack up against an ETF," *The Globe and Mail*, October 13, 2007, p. B17.

Buy-and-Hold Strategy

A buy-and-hold strategy means exactly that—an investor buys stocks and basically holds them until some future time in order to meet a particular objective. The emphasis is on avoiding transaction costs, additional search costs, and so forth. The investor believes that such a strategy will produce results that are as good as alternatives requiring more active management. Active management will invariably result in greater transaction costs and increase the likelihood of making errors in the stock selection process.

Notice that a buy-and-hold strategy is applicable to the investor's portfolio, whatever its composition. It may be large or small, and it may emphasize various types of stocks. Also note the critical importance of the initial selection decisions that must be made to implement the strategy. The investor must decide to buy stocks A, B, and C and not X, Y, and Z. Once the initial selections have been made, the investor will have to perform certain functions while the buy-and-hold strategy is in existence. For example, any income generated by the portfolio may be reinvested in the same or in other securities. Alternatively, a few stocks may do so well that they dominate the total market value of the portfolio and reduce its diversification. If the portfolio changes in such a way that it is no longer compatible with the investor's risk tolerance, adjustments may be required. The point is simply that even under such a strategy investors must still be ready to take certain actions.

Index Funds and Exchange-Traded Funds

As discussed in Chapter 10, an increasing number of mutual fund and pension fund assets can be described as passive equity investments. Using **index funds**, these asset pools are designed to duplicate as precisely as possible the performance of some market index, similar to bond index funds discussed in Chapter 12.

A stock index fund may consist of all the stocks in a well-known market average such as the S&P/TSX Index. No attempt is made to forecast market movements and act accordingly or to select under- or overvalued securities. Expenses are kept to a minimum, including research costs (security analysis), portfolio managers' fees, and brokerage commissions. Index funds can be run efficiently by a small staff.

While it is relatively straightforward for professional money managers to construct index portfolios, this may pose a problem to the average individual investor who may lack the necessary financial resources and/or investment knowledge. Fortunately, investors currently have a wide selection of index funds to choose from. In addition, as discussed in Chapter 3, the emergence of exchange-traded funds (ETFs) has provided investors with an alternative way of following an indexing strategy.

Recall that an ETF is an index fund holding a diversified portfolio of securities, priced and traded on public exchanges. Most ETFs are passively managed funds that own a basket of stocks (or bonds) designed to mimic the performance of a market index such as the S&P/TSX 60 Index, the S&P 500, or the DJIA. However, unlike mutual funds, investors are not buying shares from an investment company directly, but rather from another investor. Therefore, ETFs involve regular brokerage transactions and brokerage fees. Canadian ETFs trade on the TSX while US-based ETFs trade on US exchanges. Most ETFs are priced continuously during the day, can be sold short, and can be purchased on margin—unlike mutual funds. In addition, they usually have much lower management expense ratios (MERs) than the average index fund.

The most widely traded Canadian ETFs are the **i60s**, which represent units in the S&P/TSX 60 Index. I60s trade on the TSX (ticker: XIU) and currently have an MER of 0.17 percent. In addition, a growing number of Canadian-based small-cap, mid-cap, industry-based, style-based, and bond ETFs are available on the TSX.

Probably the best-known US-based ETF is the "Spider," Standard & Poor's Depository Receipts (SPDR), which was introduced in 1993 to reflect the S&P 500 Index. Other US ETFs include "Diamonds"® (the DJIA), "Cubes" (Nasdaq-100 Index Tracking Stock), "iShares" (S&P 500 as well as other S&P indexes for small-cap, mid-cap, and growth and value indexes, various Russell indexes, various Dow Jones sector funds, and various country funds), and "HOLDRS" (various sector funds). There are currently more than 75 different types of iShares. Most of the global-focused iShares MSCI (formerly WEBS) track Morgan Stanley Capital International indexes of various countries, providing investors with an opportunity to hold well-diversified country portfolios.

Index Funds
Mutual funds holding a bond or stock portfolio designed to mimic the performance of a particular market index.

INVESTING *tip*

Index funds and ETFs have become increasingly popular in response to the large body of evidence concerning the efficiency of the market that has demonstrated the inability of mutual funds to consistently outperform the market on a risk-adjusted basis. If the market is efficient, many of the activities normally engaged in by funds are suspect; that is, the benefits are not likely to exceed the costs. The available evidence indicates that many investment companies have failed to match the performance of broad market indexes. For example, over the 10-year period ending March 31, 2008, the average return for all Canadian equity funds was 6.9 percent, well below the S&P/TSX Total Return Index annual performance of 7.8 percent.

THE ACTIVE STRATEGY

Most of the techniques discussed in this text involve an active approach to investing. In the area of common stocks, the use of valuation models to value and select stocks indicates that investors are analyzing and valuing stocks in an attempt to improve their performance relative to some benchmark such as a market index. They assume or expect the benefits to be greater than the costs.

Pursuit of an active strategy suggests that investors believe they possess some advantage relative to other market participants. Such advantages could include superior analytical or judgement skills, superior information, or the ability or willingness to do what other investors, particularly institutions, are unable to do. For example, many large institutional investors cannot take positions in very small companies, leaving this field for individual investors. Furthermore, individuals are not required to own diversified portfolios and are not prohibited from short sales or margin trading, as are some institutions.

Many investors still favour an active approach to common stock selection and management, despite the evidence from efficient market studies and the published performance results of institutional investors. The reason for this is obvious—the potential rewards are very large, and many investors feel confident that they can achieve such rewards even if other investors cannot.

There are numerous active strategies involving common stocks. We consider the most prominent ones below. Because of its importance, we then consider the implications of market efficiency for these strategies.

Security Selection

The most traditional and popular form of active stock strategies is the selection of individual stocks identified as offering superior return–risk characteristics. Such stocks are selected using fundamental security analysis or technical analysis, or some combination of the two. Many investors have always believed, and continue to believe despite evidence to the contrary from the EMH, that they possess the requisite skill, patience, and ability to identify undervalued stocks.

We know from Chapter 1 that a key feature of the investments environment is the uncertainty that always surrounds investing decisions. Most stock pickers recognize the pervasiveness of this uncertainty and protect themselves accordingly by diversifying. Therefore, the standard assumption of rational, intelligent investors who select stocks to buy and sell is that such selections will be part of a diversified portfolio.

The Importance of Stock Selection

Evidence suggests that 80 to 90 percent of the total return on a portfolio is attributable to asset allocation decisions among various financial asset classes. If this is the case, then how important is stock selection in the overall investment process? Most active investors, individuals or institutions, are, to various degrees, stock selectors. The majority of investment advice and investment advisory services is geared to the selection of stocks thought to be attractive candidates at the time. *The Value Line*

Investment Survey, the world's largest investment advisory service in terms of number of subscribers, is a good example of stock selection advice offered to the investing public.

To gain some appreciation of the importance of stock selection, consider the wide variation observed in the returns across common stocks, referred to as cross-sectional variation in returns. Latané, Tuttle, and Jones were the first to point out the widely differing performances of stocks in a given year using the interquartile range.[3] Examining data through 1972, they found a remarkable constancy from year to year in the spread between the performance of stocks in the upper quartile and the performance of stocks in the lower quartile.[4]

A subsequent study by McEnally and Todd for the period 1946 to 1989 found that investors who successfully confined stock selection to the stocks in the highest quartile would have largely avoided losing years, and even the bad years showed only modest losses.[5] Conversely, for the bottom quarter, results were negative about 55 percent of the time, and about 25 percent of the time even the best stocks would have lost money despite generally favourable market conditions. The implication of these results is that "For those who do attempt to pick stocks, the rewards can be very high, but the risk and negative consequences of poor selection are substantial."[6] An additional finding of this study is that cross-sectional variation of returns has been increasing steadily over the decades, making stock selection even more important.

Although we outline an approach to security analysis below that logically places company analysis last, its importance is obvious. As Peter Lynch, one of the most celebrated portfolio managers and former head of **Fidelity's Magellan Fund**, states: "If it's a choice between investing in a good company in a great industry, or a great company in a lousy industry, I'll take the great company in the lousy industry any day." Lynch goes on to discuss what we can learn from the top 100 winners over the past decade. The basic lesson is that small stocks make big moves—the trick is identifying them. But as Lynch notes, "What do the great successes of the past 20 years tell us? It's the company, stupid."[7]

The Role of the Security Analyst

Two types of investors buy stocks: individuals and institutions. Institutional investors generally have their own analysts (often referred to as "buy-side" analysts), and individual investors may choose to rely on the recommendations of professional analysts ("sell-side" analysts) rather than attempt their own security analysis. An important part of the institutional side of stock selection and recommendation is the role of the security analyst (also called investment analyst or simply analyst) in the investment process.

The security analyst typically works for an institution concerned with stocks and other financial assets, but the analysts' product is often available to the individual investor in the form of brokerage reports and newsletters, reports from investment advisory services, and so forth. Therefore, when considering stock selection it is important to analyze the role of the analyst.

The central focus of the analysts' job is to attempt to forecast stock returns. This task usually involves a direct forecast of a specific company's return. Alternatively, it can involve the inputs to a valuation model such as those we considered in the previous chapter. Investors interested in stock selection use valuation models, and for inputs they can utilize their own estimates or use those provided by analysts.[8]

---

[3]In an ordered set of numbers, the interquartile range is the difference between the value that cuts off the top quarter and the bottom quarter of these numbers. The interquartile range is an alternative measure of dispersion.

[4]H. Latané, D. Tuttle, and C. Jones, *Security Analysis and Portfolio Management*, Second Edition (New York: Ronald Press, 1975), pp. 192–193.

[5]R. McEnally and R. Todd, "Cross-Sectional Variation in Common Stock Returns," *Financial Analysts Journal* 48 (May/June 1992), pp. 59–63.

[6]McEnally and Todd, p. 61.

[7]Peter Lynch, "The Stock Market Hit Parade," *Worth* (July/August 1994), p. 32.

[8]In Chapter 17, we will consider company analysis in detail, and this discussion will be organized around the two valuation models we studied in the previous chapter—the dividend discount model and the P/E ratio model.

What sources of information do analysts use in evaluating common stocks for possible selection or selling?[9] The major sources are presentations from the top management of the companies being considered, annual reports, as well as annual information reports that must be filed by companies with the appropriate regulatory body [such as the Ontario Securities Commission (OSC) for companies listed on the TSX]. According to surveys of analysts, they consistently emphasize the long term over the short term. Variables of major importance in their analysis include expected changes in earnings per share, expected return on equity (ROE), and industry outlook. The important point to note here is that the security analysis process used by financial analysts is the same one that we will examine in Part V.

One of the most important responsibilities of an analyst is to forecast earnings per share for particular companies because of the widely perceived linkage between expected earnings and stock returns. Earnings are critical in determining stock prices, and what matters is expected earnings (what is referred to on Bay Street or Wall Street as earnings estimates). Therefore, the primary emphasis in fundamental security analysis is on expected earnings, and analysts spend much of their time forecasting earnings. Security analyst earnings forecasts are publicly available through a variety of sources including securities firms' research reports, *The Value Line Investment Survey*, Institutional Brokers Estimate System (IBES) International, and Zack's Investment Research.

The information value of analyst reports depends upon a variety of factors and is generally enhanced by

- the amount of recent company information that is used
- the number of analysts following the stock
- the degree of consensus among analysts
- the quality of analysts following the stock

Empirical studies indicate that current expectations of earnings, as represented by the average of the analysts' forecasts, are incorporated into current stock prices. Perhaps more importantly, revisions in the average forecast for year-ahead earnings have predictive ability concerning future stock returns.

Investors should carefully study a company's earnings and estimates of earnings before investing. Estimates are available at many major investing websites. In other words, for better or worse, these estimates are quite widely reported and investors (and hence stock prices) reflect these estimates. For example, in 2002, *Business Week* concluded in an article that analysts still have a major impact on the market, and therefore investors need to pay attention.[10]

In connection with the *Business Week* article mentioned above, StarMine conducted an analysis that measured the impact of analyst changes in recommendations on stock prices. The results are reported in Figure 14-3 and show that on the day following an upgrade by analysts, stocks rise an average of 2.1 percent, while they fall an average of 5.4 percent following a downgrade. Downgrades tend to be more prominent because investors tend to focus more on bad news. StarMine also reports that there is a continued drift in prices for several months following the change in recommendation. This suggests that investors could still benefit from these changes in recommendation after the fact—contrary to the notion of market efficiency.

Intuitively, one would expect analyst earnings predictions to be superior to those obtained using historical data and trends in earnings, since they use more information. However, there is a great deal of evidence that analysts tend to be overly optimistic on average. Supporting US studies include O'Brien, and DeBondt and Thaler, while Canadian evidence is documented by Hennessey, and Ackert and Athanassakos.[11]

---

[9]This discussion is based on T. D. Coggin, "The Analyst and the Investment Process: An Overview," reprinted in *The CFA Candidate Readings*, Level I, Institute of Chartered Financial Analysts, Charlottesville, VA, 1992. The Candidate Readings and other publications issued by the institute are a valuable source of information for any serious investor as well as investment professionals.

[10]"Don't Sell Street Analysts Short," *Business Week*, October 21, 2002.

[11]P. O'Brien, "Analysts' Forecasts as Earnings Expectation," *Journal of Accounting and Economics* 10 (January 1988), pp. 53–83; W. DeBondt and R. Thaler, "Do Security Analysts Overreact?" *American Economic Review* 80 (May 1990), pp. 52–57; S. Hennessey, "Can Active Managers Profit from Earnings Forecast Revisions?" *Canadian Investment Review* 6 (Spring 1993), pp. 39–45; L. Ackert and G. Athanassakos, "Expectations of the Herd," *Canadian Investment Review* 9 (Winter 1996/97), pp.7–11.

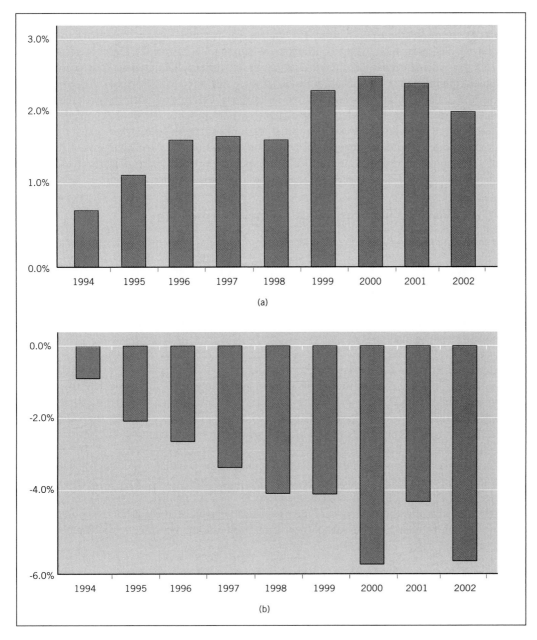

Figure 14-3
Average Percentage Amount a
Stock Moved in a Single Day
Following a Change in Analysts' Recommendations,
1994–2002 (a) Following an
upgrade; (b) Following a
downgrade

Source: StarMine Newsletter.
StarMine website, October
15, 2002. Reprinted with
permission.

The optimism of analysts is not surprising since they have greater incentive to issue buy rather than sell recommendations. They are under pressure by the companies they follow to avoid issuing sell recommendations. In fact, sell recommendations have traditionally been extremely rare, although changes to this practice are evolving, as discussed in the section below. This pressure will be greater if the brokerage firm they work for is trying to sell shares of the company being analyzed, or if there exists an investment banking relationship with the company. In addition, analysts may prefer to make estimates that do not stand out from the crowd. These notions are supported by the results of Ackert and Athanassakos, who find that analysts are "more optimistic when there is greater disper-sion in earnings forecasts."[12]

Several empirical studies, including the 1993 Canadian study by Hennessey, suggest that investors can benefit from earnings estimate revisions. In particular, portfolios of stocks that have experienced

---

[12]L. Ackert and G. Athanassakos, "Expectations of the Herd," *Canadian Investment Review* 9 (Winter 1996/97), pp. 7–11.

positive earnings forecast revisions produce excess positive returns subsequent to the revision. The larger the revisions, the greater the excess returns. This implies that investors can earn abnormal returns using publicly available information, which contradicts the semi-strong form of the EMH. In a subsequent study, Hennessey demonstrates that this effect is greater for small capitalization firms, which is consistent with less information being publicly available for these stocks.[13]

The profitability of a trading strategy based on earnings revisions supports the notion that stock prices are affected not only by the level of and growth in earnings, but also by the market's expectations of earnings. Latané and Jones point out that "earnings surprises" (i.e., when actual EPS is different than expected) represent unexpected new information that will affect share prices.[14] Positive surprises cause price increases, while negative surprises cause price decreases. The magnitude of the resulting price changes is directly proportional to the size of the surprise.

The Controversy Surrounding Security Analysts

During the course of analyzing and recommending companies, analysts supposedly present their recommendations in the form of "buy," "hold," and "sell." However, until recently, investors who received brokerage reports typically saw recommendations for specific companies as "buy," "hold," "speculative hold," or words similar to these. Traditionally, analysts were under great pressure from the companies they followed to avoid the word "sell." One study reported that two-thirds of analysts surveyed felt that a negative recommendation on a company would severely impact their access to the company's management.

Analysts have also been under significant pressure from their own firms, which are seeking to be the underwriter on lucrative stock and bond underwritings. The firms want the analysts to support the stock by making positive statements about it in the hopes of winning the investment banking business. This generates massive conflicts of interest, which have been widely discussed. Analysts lose their objectivity by being at least partly rewarded on the basis of investment banking business. Supposedly, reprisals by companies against brokerage firms, in terms of cutting off investment banking business, have often been widespread.

Several articles have appeared in the financial press that are less than flattering to analysts, such as Real-World Returns 14-2. The market declined sharply in 2000, 2001, and 2002, and investors discovered that analysts continued to recommend stocks even as their prices declined tremendously. Analysts rapidly became the focus of very intensive negative criticism because of the conflicts of interest with the investment banking side of their firms' business, and because their recommendations were found to be faulty in many cases.

REAL-WORLD RETURNS 14-2

Analysts Recommend Buying? Reach for the Sell Button

These are turbulent times in financial markets. So now, more than ever, we should be putting our faith in analyst recommendations instead of trying to pick stocks ourselves, right?

After all, analysts are paid generously to spend all day scanning company financial statements, so of course they're in a better position to know which stocks will rise and which will sink.

Wrong. As it turns out, doing the opposite of what analysts recommend is often a better strategy than following their advice—a fact that should make investors think twice before blindly following the stock picks of brokerage firms in the hope of striking it rich.

---

[13]S. Hennessey, "Get the Drift," *Canadian Investment Review* 8 (Winter 1995/96), pp. 23–28.
[14]H. Latané and C. Jones, "Standardized Unexpected Earnings—A Progress Report," *Journal of Finance* 32 (December 1977), pp.1457–1465.

In a recent study, Thomson Reuters examined the performance of stocks in the S&P 400 MidCap index, dividing them into groups based on analyst recommendations. Care to guess which group fared the worst? That's right, stocks with the highest analyst ratings.

We're not talking about a short-term aberration, either. The study examined the period from March 31, 1994, to Dec. 31, 2007. Over that time, a group of the 80 lowest-rated stocks— rebalanced quarterly to reflect any changes in recommendations—posted an average annual return of 14.35 percent. The top 80 stocks returned just 10.96 percent—more than three percentage points less.

Thomson Reuters examined other indexes, with similar results. On the Dow Jones industrial average, the 10 stocks with the lowest analyst ratings posted an average annual gain of 13.87 percent. Over the same period, the Dow returned 12.17 percent and the S&P 500 11.04 percent.

The effect was even more dramatic for the S&P 100. "Poorly recommended stocks tend to do much better than highly recommended stocks," Thomson Reuters concluded. "Highly recommended stocks … underperform substantially."

There may be a simple explanation for this: Stocks that are hated on Wall Street are often pushed to unreasonably low levels, setting them up for a rebound. It's the same principle that underlies the "Dogs of the Dow" strategy, which calls for buying the Dow stocks with the highest dividend yields.

Jack Hough, author of Your Next Great Stock, has studied the relationship between analysts' recommendations and stock performance. Much of the academic research is contradictory, he says, but a few themes emerge.

One is that stocks with positive analyst recommendations do sometimes outperform lower-rated stocks, but only during bull markets. In bearish phases, like the one we've been in, highly rated stocks tend to lag the market. That may be because, during bull markets, analysts and investors favour growth stocks that do well in precisely that sort of environment.

Analyst recommendations are useful, but it's all in the way investors use them, he says. Rather than look at the absolute number of "buys," "holds" and "sells" on a stock, it's more important to examine changes in ratings. For example, if a stock has numerous "sells" and "holds" but one or two analysts have recently upgraded the company to "buy," that can be a positive signal.

For his part, when Mr. Hough is looking for value stocks, he deliberately avoids those with a lot of favourable ratings. "I'm looking for companies that have popularity left to gain, and if a company has an average recommendation of 'buy' or 'strong buy,' there's obviously not much more favour to gain on Wall Street," he says.

That's something to remember the next time you read a gushing "buy" report on a stock that's already shot up in price.

Source: Heinzl, John, "Analysts recommend buying? Reach for the sell button," *The Globe and Mail*, April 29, 2008, p. B16.

In mid-2002, the Attorney General of New York went to court to force Merrill Lynch, at the time the United States' largest retail brokerage, to change the procedures followed by its analysts in rating stocks (some Merrill Lynch analysts reportedly sent email among themselves castigating some stocks that the firm was recommending to its clients). Merrill Lynch agreed to a $100 million fine to settle charges that its analysts were overly optimistic in their research recommendations in order to win investment banking business. Some other large firms followed suit in changing their practices, primarily because of this action.

Merrill Lynch announced a new system of stock recommendations in mid-2002, with all stocks being rated "buy," "neutral," or "sell." Its stock recommendations would be tied to projections of total return and risk. The firm also provided investors with more disclosure on when it changes the ratings on a company. Many other firms have since followed suit.

Merrill Lynch's changes were in line with new rules adopted by the New York Stock Exchange (NYSE) and Nasdaq in May 2002, which were approved by the Securities and Exchange Commission (SEC). These changes—forcing analysts to limit and disclose contacts with the investment banking side—were a direct result of the enormously negative criticism the brokerage industry has received as a result of the above-mentioned problems.

In 2002, the SEC adopted new rules that should allow investors to understand more thoroughly what analysts are saying and what conflicts of interest may exist. The new rules include the following:

- Analysts must be clear about their recommendations, and use words such as "buy" or "sell."

- Reports must indicate the percentage of recommendations that are buy, hold, or sell.

- Reports must show the author's track record.

- Analysts must indicate for a stock when they initiated coverage and when they changed opinions.

- Price targets for a stock are to be shown, including if and when they change.

- Research must disclose any recent investment banking ties.

Sector Rotation

An active strategy that is similar to stock selection is group or sector rotation. This strategy involves shifting sector weights in the portfolio in order to take advantage of those sectors that are expected to do better, and avoiding or reducing emphasis on those that are expected to do worse. Investors employing this strategy are betting that particular sectors will repeat their price performance relative to the current phase of the business and credit cycle.

INVESTING *tip*

Perhaps because of their rarity, sell recommendations have a pronounced effect. According to one study, sell recommendations result in an average two-day decline of almost 5 percent and an additional 9 percent decline in the next six months. Another study confirmed the six-month decline but found that such stocks had a turnaround and subsequently beat the market.

An investor could think of larger groups as the relevant sectors, shifting between cyclicals, growth stocks, and value stocks. It is quite standard in sector analysis to divide common stocks into four broad sectors: interest-sensitive stocks, consumer durable stocks, capital goods stocks, and defensive stocks. Each of these sectors is expected to perform differently during the various phases of the business and credit cycles. For example, interest-sensitive stocks would be expected to be hurt during periods of high interest rates, and such periods tend to occur at the latter stages of the business cycle. As interest rates decline, the earnings of the companies in this sector—banks and other financial institutions, utilities, and residential construction firms—should improve.

The term "defensive stocks" needs some explanation. Included here are companies in such businesses as food production, soft drinks, beer, pharmaceuticals, and so forth, that often are not hurt as badly as other companies during the downside of the business cycle because people will still purchase bread, milk, soft drinks, and the like. As the economy worsens and more problems are foreseen, investors may move into these stocks for investment protection. These stocks often do well during the late phases of a business cycle.

Investors may view industries as they do sectors and act accordingly. For example, if interest rates are expected to drop significantly, increased emphasis could be placed on the interest-sensitive industries such as housing, banking, and utilities. Effective strategies involving sector rotation depend heavily on an accurate assessment of current economic conditions. A knowledge and understanding of the phases of the business cycle are important, as is an understanding of political environments, international linkages among economies, and domestic and international credit conditions.

Peter Gibson shows that while industry moves are generally in the same direction, relative differences in changes are often dramatic.[15] He suggests the key to industry timing is to identify the best

---

[15]P. Gibson, "Strategy," in Joe Kan, Editor, *Handbook of Canadian Security Analysis: A Guide to Evaluating the Industry Sectors of the Market from Bay Street's Top Analysts* (Toronto: John Wiley & Sons Canada, 1997), pp. 537–644.

industry leadership at each stage of the market cycle. In this regard, for purposes of industry analysis, industry groups should be formed on the basis of factors such as type of business, degree of economic sensitivity, and exposure to international markets.

Chapter 16 provides a detailed discussion of industry analysis; however, at this point we provide some general principles that must be kept in mind. First, prices for industries with similar economic sensitivity tend to move together (and hence display positive correlations among returns), which reduces the potential benefits of rotation gains. Second, it is important to focus on industry activity and not size. Third, be aware that diversification within and across industries is not a straightforward task in Canada. In particular, a few industries within the S&P/TSX Composite Index make up the majority of its total market capitalization. In addition, many S&P/TSX Composite Index industries are dominated by one or two companies, with the notable exceptions of the banks, the paper and forest producers, and the oil and gas producers.

The success of sector rotation strategies depends heavily on forecasting overall market activity, as well as activity within several industry categories. There are great potential benefits to this approach. However, as always, it is easy to say what should have been done after the fact, but it is a very difficult thing to predict which sectors will excel, ahead of time. The bottom line is that forecasting economic and market activity is a daunting task, and there is little evidence that it can produce superior results on a consistent basis.

Indirect Investing in Sectors

Investors can invest in sectors using mutual funds and ETFs. This indirect sector investing offers the potential of large returns, but the risks are also large. For example, for the year ending March 31, 2008, the Altamira Health Sciences fund produced a loss of 13.42 percent, while the Altamira Resource fund produced a 15.05 percent gain.

Market Timing

Market timers attempt to earn excess returns by varying the percentage of portfolio assets in equity securities. When equities are expected to do well, timers shift from cash equivalents, such as money market funds, to common stocks. When equities are expected to do poorly, the opposite occurs. Alternatively, market timers could increase the betas of their portfolios when the market is expected to rise and carry most stock prices up, or decrease them when the market is expected to go down. One important factor affecting the success of a market timing strategy is the amount of brokerage commissions and taxes paid with such a strategy as opposed to a buy-and-hold strategy. Some of the more common asset allocation strategies, based on the ability to time changes in the market, are discussed at the end of this section.

Market timing means that managers invest more aggressively in anticipation of strong markets and more conservatively in anticipation of slow markets. Robert Merton illustrated the astonishing profit potential associated with perfect market timing ability.[16] He showed that an investor with $1,000 to invest in 1927 could have accumulated $5.36 billion after 52 years (at the end of 1978), by correctly investing in either T-bills or the NYSE index (whichever produced a higher return during a given month). This amount dwarfs the $3,600 that would have been accumulated had the investor remained in T-bills the entire period, as well as the $67,500 that would have accumulated, had the investor held the market index the entire period.

Canadian evidence provided in Table 14-1 shows the results from following the monthly rebalancing strategy used by Merton in his study over the 1956–2003 period. An investor with perfect market timing would have experienced an average annual return of 32.99 percent, and would have seen $1,000 grow to over $581 million over that period, versus an annual return of 10.34 percent and accumulated wealth of only $57,793 had the investor remained fully invested in the stock market.

[16]R. Merton, "On Market Timing and Investment Performance: An Equilibrium Theory of Market Forecasts," *Journal of Business* 54 (July 1981), pp. 363–406.

Table 14-1

Canadian Market Timing Evidence
(February 1956 to March 2003)

	Average Annual Return	Ending Wealth of $1,000 Invested Initially
TSX	10.34%	$57,793
T-Bills	6.71%	$21,316
Perfect Market Timing (monthly)	32.99%	$581,642,466
Always Wrong	−11.78%	$2.12
TSX minus the best 5 months	8.91%	$32,359
TSX minus the best 10 months	7.80%	$20,423
TSX minus the best 15 months	6.82%	$13,545
TSX minus the best 20 months	5.90%	$9,137
TSX minus the best 40 months	2.81%	$2,375

The example above illustrates the importance of market timing ability for investors. However, like many issues in the investing arena, the subject of market timing is controversial. Can some investors regularly time the market effectively enough to provide excess returns on a risk-adjusted basis? The available evidence on the subject is mixed, and it is important to keep in mind that market timing is a broad topic and that it is difficult to summarize all viewpoints.

Much of the empirical evidence on market timing comes from studies of mutual funds. A basic issue is whether fund managers increase the beta of their portfolios when they anticipate a rising market and reduce it when they anticipate a declining market. Several studies found no evidence that funds were able to time market changes and change their risk levels in response. Veit and Cheney, for example, found in a study of 74 mutual funds that they were not able to successfully change their risk levels based on their timing strategies.[17]

Chang and Lewellen examined the performance of mutual funds and found little evidence of any market timing ability; furthermore, the average estimated downmarket beta turned out to be slightly higher than the average estimated up-market beta.[18] Overall, this study supported the conclusion that mutual funds do not outperform a passive investment strategy. This conclusion was also supported by Henriksson in a study of 116 mutual funds using monthly data.[19] He found that mutual fund managers are not able to successfully employ strategies involving market timing, and they were not even successful with market timing involving large changes in the market.

On the other hand, Weigel examined the market timing performance of 17 US managers who used a tactical asset allocation approach and found they had reliable market timing skills.[20] Studies by both Foerster and Turnbull, and Beveridge and Bauer have demonstrated the potential benefits of using market timing approaches in Canada.[21] There is also a great deal of evidence that international portfolio managers using dynamic asset allocation strategies can add considerable value to international portfolios.[22]

Mark Hulbert, publisher of a service that monitors the performance of investment advisory letters called the *Hulbert Financial Digest*, believes that the popularity of market timing follows a cycle

---

[17]E. T. Veit and J. M. Cheney, "Are Mutual Funds Market Timers?" *Journal of Portfolio Management* 8 (Winter 1982), pp. 35–42.

[18]E. Chang and W. Lewellen, "Market Timing and Mutual Fund Investment Performance," *Journal of Business* 57, Part 1 (January 1984), pp. 57–72.

[19]R. D. Henriksson, "Market Timing and Mutual Fund Performance: An Empirical Investigation," *Journal of Business* 57, Part 1 (January 1984), pp. 73–96.

[20]E. Weigel, "The Performance of Tactical Asset Allocation," *Financial Analysts Journal* 47 (Sept/Oct 1991), pp. 63–70.

[21]S. Foerster and A. Turnbull, "The Key to Effective Tactical Asset Allocation," *Canadian Investment Review* 6 (Spring 1993), pp. 13–19; S. Beveridge and L. Bauer, "How to Market Time Using Interest Rate Signals," *Canadian Investment Review* 7 (Summer 1994), pp. 13–16.

[22]For example, refer to R. Arnott and R. Henriksson, "A Disciplined Approach to Global Asset Allocation," *Financial Analysts Journal* 45 (Mar/Apr 1989), pp.17–28; M. Keppler, "The Importance of Dividend Yield in Country Selection," *Journal of Portfolio Management* 17 (Winter 1991), pp. 24–29; and, W. Fouse, "Allocating Assets Across Country Markets," *Journal of Portfolio Management* 18 (Winter 1992), pp. 20–27.

of its own.[23] If the market is strongly up, market timing falls into disrepute, and buying and holding is the popular strategy. Following a market decline, however, market timing comes into vogue and the buy-and-hold strategy is not popular. According to Hulbert, on a pure timing basis only 3 percent of the stock timing strategies tracked over the most recent five- and eight-year periods outperformed a buy-and-hold approach.[24]

Many successful portfolio managers such as Warren Buffet and Peter Lynch suggest that market timing is one of the most difficult things for an investor to accomplish. Based on this belief, they establish their investment policies with long-term objectives in mind in order to avoid having to continually make market timing decisions. On the other hand, there are several studies that indicate the potential benefits of market timing strategies. In fact, most funds employ market timing strategies to a certain degree, which is reflected in the varying cash ratios exhibited by their portfolios.

Considerable research suggests that the biggest risk of market timing is that investors will not be in the market at critical times, thereby significantly reducing their overall returns. Investors who miss only a few key months may suffer significantly. For example, over a recent 40-year period, investors who missed the 34 best months for stocks would have seen an initial $1,000 investment grow to only $4,492 instead of $86,650. Even T-bills would have been a better alternative in this situation.[25]

If you are still considering market timing as a strategy suitable for the average individual investor, consider the following US evidence. For the 10-year period 1986 to 1995, inclusive, returns on the S&P 500 Composite Index were as follows:

Fully invested annualized rate of return = 14.8 percent
Take out the 10 best days = 10.2 percent
Take out the 20 best days = 7.3 percent
Take out the 30 best days = 4.8 percent
Take out the 40 best days = 2.5 percent

Table 14-1 also provides Canadian evidence regarding the costs of missing out on some of the best months in the market. For example, we can see that $1,000 left invested in the market from 1956 to 2003 would have grown to $57,793 (an average annual return of 10.34 percent). However, if an investor was attempting to time the market and missed the best 20 months, the investor's ending wealth would have been only $9,137 (average annual return of 5.90 percent).

Asset Allocation Strategies

Asset allocation strategies are based on the ability to time the performance of the major financial asset categories, which include short-term money market instruments (such as T-bills and commercial paper), long-term bonds, and equity securities. The most commonly referred to strategy is tactical asset allocation (TAA), a moderately active asset allocation approach that allows managers short-term deviations from longer-term asset mixes to take advantage of market timing skills. Evidence was presented above regarding the relative success of such strategies.

Several other asset allocation techniques may be employed. Strategic asset allocation involves adhering to a long-term mix by monitoring and rebalancing the portfolio as necessary. In order to achieve a desired asset mix of, say, 60 percent equity and 40 percent bonds, rebalancing is necessary as equity and bond prices change through time, which alters the portfolio asset mix. The asset mix can be returned to the strategic long-term position by buying bonds (or stocks) when they become cheap and selling them when they increase in value. For example, suppose stock prices fell and bond prices rose, so that the actual asset mix changed to 55 percent equity and 45 percent bonds. This would require the manager to sell bonds, which had risen in price, and buy equities, whose prices had fallen. This buy low and sell high strategy is consistent with the notion underlying contrarian or value investment strategies.

---

[23]M. Hulbert, "New Tool for Contrarians," *Forbes*, November 18, 1996, p. 298.
[24]*Ibid*
[25]J. D. Pond, "The Harsh Reality of Market Timing," *Worth* (May 1994), pp. 117–118.

Insured asset allocation allows managers discretion in deciding asset amounts only if they exceed a base portfolio value that must be guaranteed by formula. This involves maintaining a predetermined amount in riskless securities or by using put options or futures contracts to "immunize" the portfolio value (i.e., portfolio insurance). Dynamic asset allocation is an active management technique that adjusts the mix between risk-free and risky assets as market conditions change by selling equities when markets fall and buying them when they rise. This strategy is consistent with the rationale underlying growth investment strategies.

Finally, integrated asset allocation represents an all-encompassing strategy including several of the approaches above. It examines market conditions and investor objectives and constraints separately, and based on this analysis, the optimal asset mix is determined. That asset mix is adjusted at regular intervals to reflect the fact that both market conditions and investor needs change through time.

Efficient Markets and Active Strategies

One of the most significant developments is the proposition that securities markets are efficient. This idea has generated considerable controversy concerning the analysis and valuation of securities because of its significant implications for investors. Regardless of how much (or how little) an investor learns about investments, and regardless of whether an investor ends up being convinced by the efficient markets literature, it is essential to be aware of the implications of market efficiency early in one's study of investments.

Much evidence exists to support the basic concepts of the Efficient Market Hypothesis (EMH), and it cannot be ignored simply because one is uncomfortable with the idea or because it sounds too improbable. It is appropriate to consider this concept with any discussion of active strategies designed to produce excess returns—that is, returns in excess of those commensurate with the risk being taken. After all, if the evidence suggests that active strategies are unlikely to be successful over time after all costs have been assessed, the case for a passive strategy becomes much more persuasive.

As we learned in Chapter 10, the EMH is concerned with the assessment of information by investors. Security prices are determined by expectations about the future. Investors use the information available to them in forming their expectations. If security prices fully reflect all the relevant information that is available and usable, a securities market is said to be efficient.

If the stock market is efficient, prices reflect their fair economic value as estimated by investors. Even if this is not strictly true, prices may reflect their approximate fair value after transaction costs are taken into account, a condition known as economic efficiency. In such a market, where prices of stocks depart only slightly from their fair economic value, investors should not try to employ trading strategies designed to beat the market by identifying undervalued stocks. Nor should they attempt to time the market in the belief that an advantage can be gained. Sector rotation also will be unsuccessful in a highly efficient market.

The implications of an efficient market are extremely important for investors. They include one's beliefs about how to value securities in terms of the two approaches to selecting common stocks discussed below—the fundamental and the technical—which, in turn, encompasses questions about the time and effort to be devoted. Other implications include the management of a portfolio of securities. Again, in terms of the above discussion, should management be active or passive? Efficient market proponents often argue that less time should be spent on deciding which securities to include in a portfolio and more on considerations such as reducing taxes and transaction costs and maintaining the chosen risk level of a portfolio over time.

Suffice it to say that an intelligent investor must be aware of this issue and form some judgement about its implications if he or she is to formulate a reasonable investment strategy. An investor's beliefs about market efficiency will have a significant impact on the type of stock strategy implemented. The efficiency of the market, and how investors should act in selecting portfolios of stocks, remains controversial.

Investors are constantly being bombarded with reports of techniques and procedures that appear to offer above-average returns, thereby contradicting the idea that the market is so efficient that they should not attempt to outperform it. Intelligent investors examine such claims and strategies carefully before using them.

14-4. Security analysts have often been accused of having a serious conflict of interest. What is the cause of this conflict?

14-5. Given the evidence supporting market efficiency, can investors have any confidence that really good security analysis will prove to be profitable year after year?

14-6. State two reasons why market timing strategies are unlikely to be successful for investors.

WAYS OF ANALYZING AND SELECTING STOCK

The two traditional and well-known ways of analyzing and selecting common stocks are fundamental analysis and technical analysis. Both of these are given careful consideration in Part V, but greater emphasis is placed on fundamental analysis.

These two basic approaches are described briefly here, followed by a consideration of the concept of efficient market and its implications. The fundamental approach is then developed in some detail in the remainder of this chapter, setting the stage for the next three chapters, which analyze the fundamental approach in a specific, recommended order.

learning objective 4
Differentiate between technical and fundamental analysis.

Technical Analysis

One of the two traditional strategies long available to investors is technical analysis, which is examined in detail in Chapter 18. In fact, technical analysis is the oldest strategy and can be traced back to at least the late nineteenth century.

The term **technical analysis** refers to the methodology of forecasting fluctuations in securities prices. This methodology can be applied either to individual securities or to the market as a whole (i.e., forecasting a market index such as the S&P/TSX Composite Index).

The rationale behind technical analysis is that the value of a stock is primarily a function of supply and demand conditions. These conditions, in turn, are determined by a range of factors, from scientific analyses to opinions and guesses, all of which play a part in determining the changes in prices. The price trends persist, or they may change with supply and demand conditions. Technicians seek to detect, and act upon, changes in the direction of stock prices.

In its purest sense, technical analysis is not concerned with the underlying economic variables that affect a company or the market; therefore, the causes of supply and demand shifts are not important. The basic question to be asked is: Does excess supply or demand exist for a stock, and can such a condition be detected by studying either the patterns of past price fluctuations or the movements of certain technical indicators or rules? Technicians study the market using graphical charting of price changes, volume of trading over time, and a number of technical indicators.

Technical Analysis The use of specific market data for the analysis of both individual and aggregate stock prices for the purpose of identifying recurring price patterns.

Momentum Strategies

One of the most popular technical analysis techniques is that of **momentum investing**, which is basically a relative strength approach (relative strength is examined in Chapter 18). The basic premise of momentum investing is that if a stock has outperformed the market over some recent period, it is likely to continue to do so. In other words, this approach is one of following the trend.

Momentum Investing Investing on the basis of recent movements in the price of a stock, which generally means buying stocks that have outperformed the market recently. In other words, it is following the trend.

Momentum investing is a short-run approach. For example, stocks that are strong for the prior six months tend to outperform the market only over the next six to 12 months. Evidence of the success of momentum investment strategies was discussed in Chapter 10.

Fundamental Analysis

Fundamental Analysis

The estimation of a stock's value using basic data such as its earnings, sales, risk, and so forth.

Intrinsic Value

The estimated or true value of a security as determined by an investor after examining a firm's underlying variables.

Fundamental analysis is based on the premise that any security (and the market as a whole) has an **intrinsic value**, which is the true value as estimated by an investor. This value is a function of the firm's underlying variables, which combine to produce an expected return and an accompanying risk. By assessing these fundamental determinants of the value of a security, an estimate of its intrinsic value can be determined. This estimated intrinsic value can then be compared to the current market price of the security, as discussed in Chapter 11 with regard to bonds, and in Chapter 13 with regard to common stocks.

In equilibrium, the current market price of a security reflects the average of the intrinsic value estimates made by investors. An investor whose intrinsic value estimate differs from the market price is, in effect, disagreeing with the market consensus of the estimate of either expected return or risk or both. Investors who can perform good fundamental analysis and spot discrepancies should be able to profit by acting before the market consensus reflects the correct information.

Efficient Markets and Behavioural Finance

The rise, and increasing acceptance, of the efficient market concept has had an impact on traditional investing practices. Hardest hit has been technical analysis. If prices fluctuate in accordance with the efficient markets model, there is little chance that pure technical analysis is valid.

The EMH also has implications for fundamental analysis. If the market is efficient, prices will react quickly to new information, and with many active investors buying and selling, prices should be close to their fair economic values. However, fundamental analysis is still needed in an efficient market, because without it, the market would be less efficient. One can argue that what makes the market efficient is the very fact that investors do fundamental analysis, based on the belief that the market is not efficient.

Given the widespread discussion of market efficiency, investors sometimes overlook the issue of psychology in financial markets—that is, the role that emotions play. Particularly in the short run, investors' emotions affect stock prices and markets, and those making investment decisions need to be aware of this.

As discussed in Chapter 10, behavioural finance is a hot topic in investing. Although traditional economics is built on the proposition that investors act rationally on the basis of utility theory, behavioural finance recognizes that investors can, and do, behave irrationally. Markets overreact, in both the up and down directions. Investors are motivated by numerous "irrational" forces, such as overconfidence, regrets about decisions, aversion to losses, and so forth. Unfortunately, despite several promising research findings, behavioural finance currently does not have a unifying theory that ties everything together.

CHECK YOUR UNDERSTANDING

14-7. In technical analysis, how useful is a stock's intrinsic value?

14-8. What are the implications of the efficient market hypothesis for technical analysts who make predictions based on charts of stock prices?

A FRAMEWORK FOR FUNDAMENTAL ANALYSIS

With any fundamental analysis, an investor will obviously have to work with individual company data. Does this mean that the investor should plunge into a study of company data first and then consider other factors, such as the industry within which a particular company operates or the state of the economy, or should the reverse procedure be followed? In fact, when doing fundamental analysis investors and security analysts may use each of these approaches, which are referred to as the "bottom-up" and the "top-down" approaches.

Bottom-Up Fundamental Analysis

With the bottom-up approach, investors focus directly on a company's basics or fundamentals. Analysis of such information as the company's products, its competitive position, and its financial status, leads to an estimate of the company's earnings potential and, ultimately, its value in the market.

Considerable time and effort are required to produce the type of detailed financial analysis needed to understand even relatively small companies. The emphasis in this approach is on finding companies with good long-term growth prospects and on making accurate earnings estimates. To organize this effort, bottom-up fundamental research is often broken into two areas, growth investing and value investing.

Value Versus Growth

Growth stocks carry investor expectations of above-average future growth in earnings and valuations as a result of high price/earnings ratios. Investors expect these stocks to perform well in the future, and they are willing to pay high multiples for this. Examples include Microsoft and Intel, as well as the stocks of many Internet-related companies.

Value stocks, on the other hand, feature cheap assets and strong balance sheets. Value investing can be traced back to the value-investing principles laid out by the well-known Benjamin Graham, who wrote a classic book on security analysis that has been the foundation for many subsequent security analysts.[26]

Table 14-2

Annual Returns for Value and Growth Indexes, 1979–2002

Year	Russell 3000 Growth	Russell 3000 Value	Russell Top 200 Growth	Russell Top 200 Value	Russell Mid-Cap Growth	Russell Mid-Cap Value	Russell 1000 Growth	Russell 1000 Value	Russell 2000 Growth	Russell 2000 Value	S&P Index
1979	26.20%	21.85%	NA	NA	NA	NA	23.91%	20.55%	50.83%	35.38%	18.44%
1980	40.74	24.52	NA	NA	NA	NA	39.57	24.41	52.26	25.39	32.42
1981	-11.09	2.49	NA	NA	NA	NA	-11.31	1.26	-9.24	14.85	-4.91
1982	20.51	20.83	NA	NA	NA	NA	20.46	20.04	20.98	28.52	21.41
1983	16.29	29.24	NA	NA	NA	NA	15.98	28.29	20.13	38.64	22.51
1984	-2.75	9.28	NA	NA	NA	NA	-0.95	10.10	-15.83	2.27	6.27
1985	32.69	31.48	NA	NA	NA	NA	32.85	31.51	30.97	31.01	32.16
1986	14.25	18.78	13.99%	21.44%	17.55%	17.87%	15.36	19.98	3.58	7.41	18.47
1987	3.92	-0.13	6.45	2.20	2.76	-2.19	5.31	0.50	-10.48	-7.11	5.23
1988	12.00	23.63	10.88	22.02	12.92	24.61	11.27	23.16	20.37	29.47	16.81
1989	34.68	24.22	37.68	26.66	31.48	22.70	35.92	25.19	20.17	12.43	31.49
1990	-1.31	-8.85	1.37	-3.67	-5.13	-16.09	-0.26	-8.08	-17.41	-21.77	-3.17
1991	41.66	25.41	39.41	18.16	47.03	37.92	41.16	24.61	51.19	41.70	30.55
1992	5.22	14.90	3.89	9.07	8.71	21.68	5.00	13.81	7.77	29.14	7.67

(continued)

---

[26]Benjamin Graham and David Dodd, *Security Analysis: Principles and Technique* (New York: McGraw-Hill, 1934). This topic is discussed at some length in Chapter 10.

(Table 14-2 continued)

Year	Russell 3000 Growth	Russell 3000 Value	Russell Top 200 Growth	Russell Top 200 Value	Russell Mid-Cap Growth	Russell Mid-Cap Value	Russell 1000 Growth	Russell 1000 Value	Russell 2000 Growth	Russell 2000 Value	S&P Index
1993	3.69	18.65	-0.07	19.76	11.19	15.62	2.90	18.12	13.36	23.84	9.99
1994	2.20	-1.95	4.85	-1.90	-2.17	-2.13	2.66	-1.99	-2.43	-1.55	1.31
1995	36.57	37.03	38.65	40.03	33.98	34.93	37.19	38.35	31.04	25.75	37.43
1996	21.88	21.60	25.57	22.31	17.48	20.26	23.12	21.63	11.26	21.37	23.07
1997	28.74	34.83	33.73	35.47	22.54	34.37	30.49	35.18	12.95	31.78	33.36
1998	35.02	13.50	45.09	21.24	17.86	5.08	38.71	15.62	1.23	-6.45	28.58
1999	33.82	6.64	29.68	10.94	51.29	-0.11	33.16	7.35	43.10	-1.49	21.04
2000	-22.42	8.02	-24.51	2.31	-11.75	19.19	-22.43	7.02	-22.44	22.82	-9.11
2001	-19.63	-4.33	-20.50	-8.80	-20.16	2.33	-20.42	-5.59	-9.24	14.02	-11.88
2002	-28.04	-15.18	-27.98	-18.02	-27.41	-9.65	-27.89	-15.52	-30.26	-11.43	-22.10
Geometric Mean 1996–99	29.76	18.69	33.32	22.18	26.58	14.12	31.25	19.52	16.16	10.18	26.42
Geometric Mean 1979–2002	11.57	13.99					11.84	13.93	8.94	14.74	13.25
Standard Deviation 1979–2002	20.71	14.05					20.84	14.16	23.83	17.40	16.42
Geometric Mean 1986–2002	9.73	11.78	10.42	11.82	10.19	12.21	10.18	11.90	5.12	10.92	11.50
Standard Deviation 1986–2002	21.83	15.04	23.15	15.79	21.77	16.10	22.27	15.27	22.13	18.01	17.59
Percentage of years value exceeded glamour		54		53		65		50		67	

NA = not available.

Note: Returns for the Russell Top 200 and Russell Mid-Cap Growth and Value Indexes begin in 1986.

Source: "Value and Growth Investing: Review and Update," L.K.C. Chan and J. Lakonishok, *Financial Analysts Journal*, Jan./Feb. 2004, pp. 71–86.

As discussed in Chapter 10, value stocks have tended to outperform growth stocks over time. Evidence of this is provided in Table 14-2, which shows the performance for various US value and growth Russell indexes over the 1979–2002 period. For example, over the entire period, the mean geometric return on the Russell 3000 Value Index was 13.99 percent, with a standard deviation of 14.05 percent. Over the same period, the Russell 3000 Growth Index produced a geometric mean return of only 11.57 percent, with a standard deviation of 20.71 percent. However, growth stocks and value stocks tend to be in vogue over different periods, and advocates of each tend to prosper and suffer accordingly. For example, in Table 14-2, we can see that despite the long-term superior performance of the Russell 3000 Value Index, it only "beat" the performance of the Russell 3000 Growth Index in 13 out of 24 years (or 54 percent of the time).

In many cases, bottom-up investing does not attempt to make a clear distinction between growth and value. Many companies feature strong earning prospects and a strong financial base or asset value and therefore have characteristics associated with both categories. Real-World Returns 14-3 discusses a particular variation of a value strategy.

REAL-WORLD RETURNS 14-3

Picking Winners, Byte by Byte

Wall Street Journal columnist Jack Hough has devised some novel computer screening programs.

When Jack Hough was in junior high school, he was constantly skipping classes. But unlike most kids, you wouldn't find him slacking off at the video arcade.

He'd be in the library reading *The Wall Street Journal.*

"From a very young age I've always studied the stock market," says the author of *Your Next Great Stock: How to Screen the Market for Tomorrow's Top Performers*.

Mr. Hough's book is a useful guide for investors who want to make the most of the stock-screening tools proliferating on the Internet. It's the culmination of everything he's learned about investing, first as a curious kid scouring the stock tables for promising companies and later as a broker with firms such as Merrill Lynch—an experience that only reinforced his belief that people must learn to invest on their own rather than rely on a professional.

"I couldn't wait to work for a brokerage company. I envisioned it as being a place where everyone learned how to find great stocks. And it turns out it has nothing to do with that. It has entirely to do with staying on the phone all day asking people to buy a lot of [funds] that have a lot of high fees," he says.

At 35, he's returned to his first love: Hunting for great stocks. As a columnist for *Smart-Money* magazine and *The Wall Street Journal*, he's carved out a niche as an expert in stock screening—using computer software to sift through thousands of stocks to find the ones with the best attributes, whether they're young companies with great growth prospects or mature cash machines that return gobs of money to shareholders through dividends and share buybacks.

As if reading *The Wall Street Journal* as a kid wasn't peculiar enough, one of Mr. Hough's other passions is combing through academic papers on investing. As such, the screening methods in *Your Next Great Stock* are based, not on gut feelings or hunches, but on empirical research.

Consider his "New Dogs Screen." Back in 1991, Michael O'Higgins' book, *Beating the Dow*, popularized the strategy of buying the 10 Dow stocks with the highest dividend yields —the so-called "dogs of the Dow." But Mr. Hough takes the strategy a step further by adding share buybacks to the equation.

Why? Because a 2004 paper published in the *Journal of Finance* showed that companies with a combination of high dividend yields and large net share repurchases—in other words, those that return a lot of cash to shareholders—outperformed the market by an even wider margin than those with high dividend yields alone. (You can see results of The New Dogs Screen in the accompanying table; the "net payout yield" represents cash spent on dividends and buybacks over the past year, divided by the company's market value.)

The book covers some fairly challenging concepts, but it doesn't read like a dry academic study. That's a testament not just to Mr. Hough's knack for explaining arcane financial concepts in everyday language, but also to his sense of humour; it's not often that you find an investing author who spent year doing standup comedy in New York.

Take his explanation of herd behaviour:

"People will do some remarkable things simply because everyone else is doing them. They'll speed, yawn, kill, jump nude into icy water, grow mullets, and pretend to like cigars (usually not all at once). Herd behaviour is easy to see in the stock market. Crashes and bubbles happen when investors follow each other and not the facts," he writes.

That last point is central to understanding why stock screening is a useful tool. Contrary to what the efficient-market hypothesis holds—that it's impossible to consistently pick winning stocks because everyone is privy to the same information—Mr. Hough argues that human beings are prone to all sorts of foibles that create opportunities for smart investors.

For example, many investors shy away from stocks that have already doubled or tripled in price. This is because of a process called anchoring: They're looking at the stock in the context of where it used to trade—the anchor—which makes them feel like they've missed the boat and the stock is now too expensive. Instead, they should be judging the stock on its current merits, such as expected sales and profit growth, valuation and so on.

In fact, contrary to what many investors may think, studies have shown that stocks that have already risen sharply in the past six months to a year, and which are trading near their 52-week highs, are "overwhelmingly more likely to beat the market, and for a longer time," Mr. Hough writes.

(continued)

REAL-WORLD RETURNS 14-3 *continued*

That's not to say price momentum alone is enough to put a stock on your "buy" list. It isn't. But screening for high-fliers is a great way to spot companies with good growth prospects, as long as you do further research to determine whether the shares are still fairly priced. How many stocks like Research In Motion Ltd. or Potash Corp. of Saskatchewan have investors passed on because they thought they were too expensive, only to watch them soar even more?

Mr. Hough's "Buy High Sell Higher Screen" is one of his favourite ways to discover such breakout stocks, but it works best during bull markets. In today's volatile markets, his favourite is the "Impatient Value Screen," which looks for stocks that are showing price momentum but which are still trading at bargain levels. To make the cut, the stock must have a PEG ratio—price-to-earnings ratio divided by projected earnings growth—of less than 1.5 and be trading within 5 percent of its 52-week high, among other criteria. (You can run the screen yourself at www.smartmoney.com/jackhough.)

The book contains about 15 screens in all, including some that attempt to mimic the stock-picking prowess of legendary investors such as Warren Buffett and Peter Lynch. Using stock screeners alone won't turn you into to the next Oracle of Omaha; as Mr. Hough stresses, a screen is merely a starting point for further research on individual companies.

But in an age of ever-expanding information, screens are a great way to cut through the clutter—and they're a lot more efficient than scanning the stock tables.

The New Dogs of the Dow

Dow stocks with high dividend yields and large share buybacks—as measured by the net payout yield—have historically outperformed.

Company name	Stock ticker	Industry	Market cap. ($million)	Recent price	Price change yr.-to-date	Forward P/E (Current Yr.)	Return on equity	Yield	Net payout yield
Home Depot	HD	Home Improvement Stores	$46,426	$27.51	+$2.12	11.71	26.6%	3.27%	33.16%
Int'l Business Machines	IBM	Diversified Computer Sys.	$146,242	$106.13	−$1.82	12.96	48.7%	1.51%	11.96%
Pfizer	PFE	Drug Manufacturers /Major	$153,329	$22.45	−$1.23	9.51	11.5%	5.70%	11.11%
Walt Disney	DIS	Entertainment-Diversified	$60,859	$32.32	+$0.12	14.69	13.9%	1.08%	11.05%
Honeywell Int'l	HON	Aerospace/Defence Prd/Svc	$42,947	$57.51	−$6.59	15.34	29.6%	1.91%	9.66%
Citigroup	C	Money Center Banks	$128,214	$25.74	−$12.57	8.25	14.6%	4.97%	8.86%
JPMorgan Chase & Co.	JPM	Money Center Banks	$143,129	$42.61	−$2.38	10.42	12.8%	3.57%	8.37%
Exxon Mobil	XOM	Major Integrated Oil/Gas	$467,413	$85.55	−$8.69	10.86	33.1%	1.64%	8.25%
Hewlett-Packard	HPQ	Diversified Computer Sys.	$110,522	$43.26	−$14.30	12.88	18.9%	0.74%	7.81%
Microsoft	MSFT	Application Software	$265,249	$28.50	−$19.94	15.32	49.2%	1.54%	7.56%

Douglas Coull/*The Globe and Mail*, source: Smartmoney.com

Source: Heinzl, John, "Picking Winners, Byte by Byte," *The Globe and Mail*, February 19, 2008, p. B15.

Top-Down Fundamental Analysis

The top-down approach is the opposite of the bottom-up one. Investors begin with the economy and the overall market, considering such important factors as interest rates and inflation. They next consider industries or sectors of the economy that are likely to do particularly well. Finally, having assessed the effect of macro factors on equity investing, and having determined which parts of the overall economy are likely to perform well, individual companies are analyzed.

There is no "right" answer to which of these two approaches to follow. However, fundamental analysis can be overwhelming in its detail, and a structure is needed. This text takes the position that the better way to proceed is top-down in fundamental analysis:

1. First, analyze the overall economy and securities markets to determine if now is a good time to commit additional funds to equities.

2. Second, analyze industries and sectors to determine which have the best prospects for the future.

3. Finally, analyze individual companies.

This is consistent with the observation that between 80 and 90 percent of the return on a portfolio is determined by the asset allocation decision. Using this structure, the valuation models presented in Chapter 13 can be applied successively at each of the three levels.

Thus, we use the top-down version of fundamental security analysis here for our discussion. Part V explains fundamental security analysis in detail and we consider here only the justification for this approach.

Economy/Market Analysis

It is very important to assess the state of the economy and the outlook for primary variables such as corporate profits and interest rates. Investors are heavily influenced by these variables in making their everyday investment decisions. If a recession is likely or under way, stock prices will be heavily affected at certain times during the contraction. Conversely, if a strong economic expansion is under way, stock prices will be heavily affected, again at particular times during the expansion. Thus, the status of economic activity has a major impact on overall stock prices. It is, therefore, very important for investors to assess the state of the economy and its implications for the stock market.

In turn, the stock market impacts each individual investor. Investors cannot compete very well against market trends. If the market goes up (or down) strongly, most stocks are carried along. Company analysis is unlikely to produce high returns in a year such as 2002, when the stock market lost approximately 12 percent. On the other hand, most equity investors did well in 2003 to 2007 regardless of their specific company analysis, because the market provided approximate returns of 26, 14, 24, 17, and 10 percent respectively during those years, as measured by the S&P/TSX Total Return Index.

Another indication of the importance of the economy/market on common stocks is the impact on the earnings for a particular company. Available evidence suggests that from a quarter to a half of the variability in a company's annual earnings is attributable to the overall economy (plus some industry effect).[27]

The economy also significantly affects what happens to various industries. One has only to think of the effects of import quotas, record high interest rates, and so forth, to see why this is so. Therefore, economy analysis must precede industry analysis.

Industry Analysis

After completing an analysis of the economy and the overall market, an investor can decide if it is a favourable time to increase or decrease the amount invested in common stocks. The next step should

---

[27]E. J. Elton, M. J. Gruber, S. J. Brown, and W. N. Goetzmann, *Modern Portfolio Theory and Investment Analysis*, Sixth Edition (New York: John Wiley, 2003).

be industry analysis, since industry factors are the second most important component (after overall market movements) affecting the variability in stock returns.

Individual companies and industries tend to respond to general market movements, but the degree of response can vary significantly. Industries undergo significant movements over both relatively short and relatively long periods. Industries will be affected to various degrees by recessions and expansions. For example, the durable goods industries will be severely affected in a recession. Consumer goods will probably be much less affected during such a contractionary period. During a severe inflationary period such as the late 1970s and early 1980s, regulated industries such as utilities were severely hurt by their inability to pass along all price increases. Finally, new "hot" industries emerge from time to time and enjoy spectacular (if short-lived) growth (such as the Internet company "boom" and "bust" periods). Refer to Chapter 16 for related examples as well as a more detailed discussion of various industry categories.

Company Analysis

Although the first two steps are important, great attention and emphasis should also be placed on company analysis. Security analysts are generally organized along industry lines, but the reports that they issue usually deal with one specific company (sometimes more).

The bottom line for companies, as far as most investors are concerned, is earnings per share. There is a very close relationship between earnings and stock prices, and for this reason most attention is paid to earnings. After all, dividends are closely tied to past, present, and future earnings.

A number of factors are important in analyzing a company, but because investors tend to focus on earnings and dividends, we need to understand the relationship between these two variables and between them and other variables. We also need to consider the possibilities of forecasting earnings and dividends.

Because dividends are paid out of earnings, we will concentrate on the latter in our discussion of company analysis in Chapter 17. Earnings and interest rates are the real key to the fundamental analysis of a common stock. A good understanding of these concepts is vital if an investor is to understand, and perform, fundamental analysis.

The Framework for Fundamental Analysis in Perspective

It is useful to summarize the framework for fundamental analysis we are using because the following three chapters are based on it. Figure 14-4 depicts the fundamental valuation process. We should examine the economy and market first, then industries, and finally individual companies. Fundamental valuation is usually done within the context of a present value model (such as the dividend discount model) or a relative valuation model (such as the P/E ratio model). In either case, the two components of the value of any security being examined are (1) the expected stream of benefits, either earnings or dividends, and (2) the required rate of return or discount rate and/or the multiplier or P/E ratio. Investors should concentrate on these two factors as they systematically proceed through the three levels of analysis: economy/market, industry, and company.

CHECK YOUR UNDERSTANDING

14-9. As part of your analysis of the economy and market situation, you notice that interest rates have been increasing lately, and the indications are that they will to continue to rise. What impact is this likely to have on stock prices, in general?

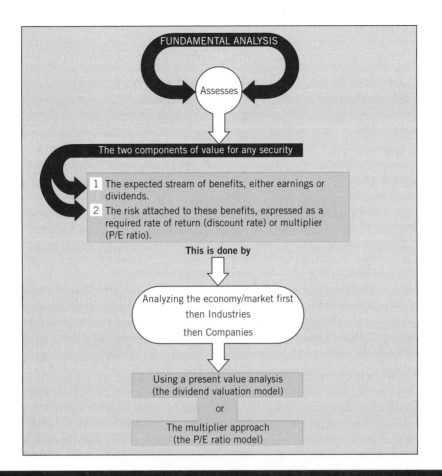

Figure 14-4
A Framework for
Fundamental Security
Analysis

SHOULD BROKERS AND ANALYSTS BE FINED FOR RUMOURS?

In early 2005, the former National Association of Securities Dealers (NASD) in the US announced it had fined a stock analyst $75,000 for spreading a rumour about a small semiconductor manufacturer. It was said to be a "sensational negative rumour" and the stock fell that day, although the company publicly denied the rumour the same day. The company complained to the NASD, which after investigation levied the fine.

The NASD alleged that the broker/analyst in this situation did not adequately investigate to determine if there was a reasonable basis for the rumour. Obviously, the question arises as to what is "adequate." If the rumour had simply been fabricated, or the analyst spread it knowing it was false, there would be clear grounds for a fine. In this case, however, the charge was that the analyst simply circulated it.

Analysts and brokers are not fined for passing on rumours thought to come from a reliable source, or if the rumour is qualified by saying that the accuracy of the rumour could be in serious doubt. Furthermore, rumours are a daily part of trading stocks, happening regularly. Many investors sometimes invest on the basis of rumours or limited information, only later obtaining the actual facts.

DISCUSSION QUESTIONS

1. Should investors hold brokers accountable if rumours the brokers spread (whether or not they know they are false) result in investor losses, or should it simply be a case of 'buyer beware' where investors are concerned?

2. Who determines when an analyst has crossed the line?

3. Many websites offer what they claim to be 'hot stock tips'. Can these be considered a reliable source?

SUMMARY

This summary relates to the learning objectives for this chapter.

1. **Discuss the impact of the overall market on common stock investors.**

   Market risk is the single most important risk affecting the price movements of common stocks. For well-diversified portfolios, market effects account for 90 percent and more of the variability in the portfolio's return.

2. **Explain the importance of the required rate of return.**

   The required rate of return for a common stock, or any security, is defined as the minimum expected rate of return needed to induce an investor to purchase the stock. The required rate of return for any investment opportunity can be expressed as the sum of the risk-free rate of return and a risk premium. The trade-off between the required rate of return and risk is linear and upward sloping, which means that the required rate of return increases as the risk increases. The relevant risk, according to the Capital Asset Pricing Model (CAPM), is measured by beta.

3. **Distinguish between passive and active investment strategies.**

   If the market is totally efficient, no active strategy should be able to beat the market on a risk-adjusted basis, and therefore a passive strategy may be superior. Passive strategies include buy-and-hold and the use of index funds. Pursuit of an active strategy assumes that investors possess some advantage relative to other market participants. Active strategies include stock selection, sector rotation, and market timing.

4. **Differentiate between technical and fundamental analysis.**

   There are two traditional and well-known approaches to analyzing and selecting common stocks: fundamental and technical analysis. The rationale behind technical analysis is that stock prices will move in trends that may persist and that these changes can be detected by analyzing the action of the stock price itself. Fundamental analysis is based on the premise that any security (and the market as a whole) has an intrinsic value that is a function of the firm's (and the market's) underlying variables. This estimated intrinsic value may then be compared to the current market price of the security (and the market).

5. **Describe the bottom-up and top-down approaches in fundamental analysis.**

   Fundamental security analysis can be done following a bottom-up or a top-down approach. With the bottom-up approach, investors focus on information about a company such as products, competitive position, and financial status. The top-down approach used in Part V of this textbook considers, in order: (1) the economy/market, (2) the industry, and (3) the company.

KEY TERMS

Fundamental analysis, p.466   Momentum investing, p.465   Technical analysis, p.465
Index funds, p.453   Required rate of return, p.448
Intrinsic value, p.466   Risk premium, p.448

REVIEW QUESTIONS

14-1. What impact does the market have on well-diversified portfolios? What does this suggest about the performance of mutual funds?

14-2. What is meant by the required rate of return? Explain your answer in the context of an investor considering the purchase of Bombardier's common shares.

14-3. What are the two components of the required rate of return?

14-4. What is the shape of the trade-off between the required rate of return for a stock and its risk? Must this shape always prevail?

14-5. What is the rationale for passive investment strategies?

14-6. What does the evidence cited on market timing suggest about the likelihood of success in this area?

14-7. Identify and differentiate the two traditional approaches to analyzing and selecting common stocks.

14-8. What is the recommended framework for fundamental analysis? Is this a top-down or bottom-up approach? Explain the difference.

14-9. How does this recommended framework relate to the discussion about the impact of the market on investors?

14-10. What is the relationship between fundamental analysis and intrinsic value?

14-11. Explain how technical analysis is primarily based on supply and demand conditions.

14-12. Why is technical analysis inconsistent with the Efficient Market Hypothesis?

14-13. How does an investor in common stocks reconcile the large variability in stock returns, and the big drops that have occurred, with taking a prudent position in owning a portfolio of financial assets?

14-14. Given the drastic—some would say unprecedented—drop in the prices of Japanese stocks, how can Canadian investors justify owning foreign stocks?

14-15. Is there one required rate of return? If not, how many are there?

14-16. What is the required rate of return on the overall market?

14-17. Describe three active strategies that involve the use of common stocks.

14-18. What are the major sources of information used by security analysts in evaluating common stocks?

14-19. How does the cross-sectional variation in common stock returns relate to the issue of stock selection?

14-20. What is meant by sector rotation? What is the key input in implementing effective strategies in sector rotation?

14-21. What is the basic idea behind the Efficient Market Hypothesis?

14-22. What are the implications of the Efficient Market Hypothesis to both stock selectors and market timers?

14-23. What are the advantages and disadvantages to the top-down approach?

14-24. What are the advantages and disadvantages to the bottom-up approach?

14-25. Briefly explain why strategic asset allocation could be classified as a "buy-low, sell-high" strategy. Illustrate with the use of an example.

14-26. List and briefly describe three passive strategies for investing in common stocks.

14-27. For adequately diversified common stock portfolios, market effects often account for __ percent and more of the variability of the portfolio's return.

    a. 60
    b. 70
    c. 80
    d. 90

14-28. If security markets are totally efficient, the best common stock strategy to take is:

    a. an asset allocation approach.
    b. the modern portfolio theory.

c. an active strategy.

d. a passive strategy.

14-29. The equity risk premium for the market is 6 percent. What is the real risk-free rate if the expected return on the market is 11 percent, and expected inflation is 3 percent?

14-30. If more investors became passive investors, how would that affect investment companies?

14-31. How should active investors determine if their efforts are worth the cost relative to passive investing?

14-32. Vanguard's Health Care Fund (VGHCX) outperformed Vanguard's S&P 500 Index fund during the period 2000–2005, although it had a higher operating expense ratio. What is the reason for this outperformance?

PROBLEM

14-1. In Real World Returns 14-1, the five-year return figures for Canadian equity mutual funds and ETFs are presented. Although betas are also given for each fund, these figures are not taken into account when determining how the funds performed relative to the overall market. Let's do that for a selection of the funds; we'll work with the first 15 entries in the table (down to the "National Bank Canadian Index" fund). In a spreadsheet enter the fund name, 5-year return figures, and 5-year beta figures into columns A, B, and C respectively.

a. Assume that the appropriate risk-free rate for this exercise is 4 percent per year. The return figure for the "iShares CDN Composite Index" ETF roughly reflects the overall market (its beta is very close to 1.0). However, this figure is net of the MER. Therefore, let's add the 0.25 percent MER onto that fund's annual return to calculate a more accurate value for the average market return.

b. Using the figures from part (a) and the 5-year beta values along with the CAPM equation, calculate a risk-adjusted return for each fund. These figures will tell us what return was necessary to compensate for the level of risk (the beta) given the return in the overall market. Add a fourth column to your spreadsheet for these figures.

c. Compare the figures in columns B and D. If the actual return (column B) is greater than the risk-adjusted value, then the fund has performed better than the market index, on a risk-adjusted basis. Did any of the funds that were ranked higher than the Composite Index actually have a worse performance (risk-adjusted), or did any of the lower ranked funds actually beat the Index?

PREPARING FOR YOUR PROFESSIONAL EXAMS

CFA PRACTICE QUESTION

14-1. All of the following indicate that the three-step (i.e., top-down) valuation process works *except*:

a. Most changes in a firm's earnings can be attributed to general economic and market factors.

b. There is a relationship between aggregate stock prices and various economic series such as employment.

c. Empirical results show that it is possible to pick underpriced securities regardless of the direction of the economy.

d. Changes in an individual stock's rate of return are best explained by changes in rates of return for the aggregate stock market.

CHAPTER 15

ANALYSIS OF THE ECONOMY AND THE STOCK MARKET

Based on your knowledge of how stocks are valued (Chapter 13), and the impact of the market on stocks in general (Chapter 14), you realize that part of your investments education should be to consider the economy/ market in more detail. After all, a poorly performing economy does not bode well for stocks. You have read enough about recessionary fears that abounded during 2008 and the severe market declines that occurred during the later part of that year. Clearly, it is worthwhile to know something about the overall tone of the stock market and at least be able to intelligently consider likely future outcomes.

Learning Objectives

After reading this chapter, you should be able to

1. Describe the relationship between the stock market and the economy.
2. Analyze the determinants of stock market values.
3. Make basic forecasts of market changes.

CHAPTER PREVIEW

In this chapter, we consider the first step of the top-down approach in fundamental security analysis that was described in Chapter 14—economy/market analysis. Based on our understanding of the relationship between the stock market and the economy, we apply the valuation concepts presented in earlier chapters to the market. We also consider how to make forecasts of changes in the stock market.

THE ECONOMY AND THE STOCK MARKET

learning objective 1
Describe the relationship between the stock market and the economy.

Ultimately, investors must make intelligent judgements about the current state of financial markets as well as changes that have a high probability of occurring in the future. Is the stock market at unusually high or low levels, and what is it likely to do in the next three months, or year, or five years?

A logical starting point in assessing the stock market is to analyze the economic factors that affect stock prices. Understanding the current and future state of the economy is the first step in understanding what is happening and what is likely to happen to the market.

The stock market is, of course, a significant and vital part of the overall economy. Clearly, a strong relationship exists between the two. If the economy is doing poorly, most companies will also be displaying poor performance, which will have an adverse effect on the stock market. Conversely, if the economy is prospering, most companies will also be doing well, and the stock market will reflect this economic strength.

Taking a Global Perspective

As noted throughout this text, investors must now think globally. Canadian investors can invest in equities from over 50 countries, and these equities comprise most of the world's market capitalization and GDP. Therefore, investors should think about economies in other countries and other parts of the world. For example, investors should consider the euro and how expected movements in the euro will affect securities.

The general trend worldwide is to open up economies and deregulate industries. Multinational corporations are restructuring and embracing the New Economy. Therefore, as a general rule, the analysis we consider in this chapter of the Canadian market and economy applies to other countries as well. The equity markets in other countries are going to be driven by earnings growth and interest rate changes, just as Canadian markets are. By understanding the Canadian equity markets, investors are in a better position to understand foreign equity markets despite the cultural, economic, and political differences.

Measures of Economic Activity

Gross Domestic Product (GDP) is the value of all goods and services produced in a country in a given year. It must equal gross domestic income, which will be the same as gross domestic expenditures. Income includes income earned by labour (wages and salaries), business (corporate profits), lenders (interest), and government (taxes). Total expenditures is composed of consumer spending (C), investment in household residences, business investment in inventories and capital equipment (I), government spending (G), and foreigners' spending on Canadian exports (X) minus Canadians' spending on foreign imports (M). The following equation depicts GDP level:

$$GDP = G + C + I + (X - M)$$

Another measure of aggregate economic activity, Gross National Product (GNP), differs slightly from GDP. It is defined as the value of all goods and services produced by Canadian nationals, whether at home or abroad, and it is the preferred measure of economic activity in some countries.

For discussion purposes, we often think of the economy in terms of the **business cycle**. Investors are very concerned about whether the economy is experiencing an expansion or a contraction because stock prices will clearly be affected. This recurring pattern of expansion and contraction, referred to as the business cycle, is described in the section below.

Business Cycle

The recurring patterns of expansion, boom, contraction, and recession in the economy.

The Business Cycle

While the economy has grown over the long run, it typically fluctuates in a series of patterns referred to as business cycles, as depicted in Figure 15-1. The business cycle reflects movements in economic activity as a whole, which is composed of many diverse parts. The diversity of the parts ensures that business cycles are virtually unique, with no two parts identical. However, cycles do have a common framework, with a beginning (a trough), a peak, and an ending (another trough). Thus, economic activity starts in depressed conditions, builds up in the expansionary phase, and ends in a downturn, only to start again.

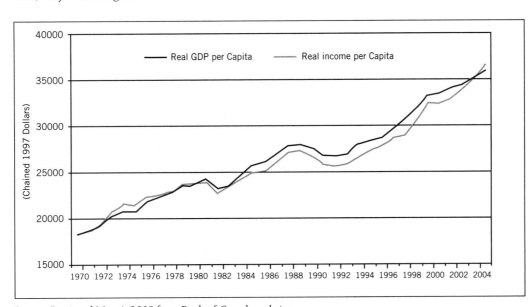

Figure 15-1
Real GDP per Capita and Real Income per Capita (1970–2005)

Source: Retrieved May 4, 2008 from Bank of Canada website: www.bankofcanada.ca/en/speeches/2006/chart1.pdf.

The five major phases of these cycles are

1. **Expansion:** Normal growth stages are characterized by: stable inflation; rises in corporate profits; increased job start-ups and reduced bankruptcies; increasing inventories and investment by business to deal with increased demand; strong stock market activity; and job creation and falling unemployment.

2. **Peak:** Demand has begun to outstrip economic capacity, causing inflationary pressures that lead to rising interest rates and falling bond prices. Investment and sales of durable goods falls, and eventually stock market activity and stock prices decline.

INVESTING *tip*

Why is the market a leading indicator of the economy? Basically, investors are discounting future earnings, because, as the valuation analysis in Chapter 13 showed, the value of stocks today is the discounted value of all future cash flows. Current stock prices reflect investor expectations of the future. Stock prices adjust quickly if investor expectations of corporate profits change. Of course, the market can misjudge corporate profits, resulting in a false signal about future movements in the economy. In other words, when an economic cycle peak or trough has occurred, we generally observe that the stock market had a major move up or down prior to the cycle turn. However, a major stock movement does not always mean a forthcoming business cycle turn.

An alternative explanation for stock prices leading the economy involves an investor change in the required rate of return, which again would result in an immediate change in stock prices. Note that the valuation model allows for a change in confidence (psychological elements) because that alters the required rate of return (in the opposite direction). These psychological elements are often useful in accounting for market movements.

Composite Leading Indicator

An index constructed by Statistics Canada that combines 10 leading indicators in order to predict future economic conditions.

3. **Recession:** Often defined as two consecutive quarters of negative growth. However, this definition is not used by Statistics Canada (StatsCan) or the US National Bureau of Economic Research (NBER). StatsCan judges a recession by the depth, duration, and diffusion of the decline in business activity (i.e., the decline must be of significant magnitude, last longer than two months, and be spread throughout the entire economy).

4. **Trough:** Near the end of a recessionary period, falling demand and excess capacity lead to drops in prices and wages. The resulting decline in inflation leads to falling interest rates, which will begin to rally the economy.

5. **Recovery:** During this period GDP returns to its previous peak. It typically begins with a revival of purchases of interest rate sensitive items such as houses and cars, and then spreads throughout the entire economy. When GDP passes its previous peak, another expansion has begun.

The term "soft landing" refers to a business cycle phase that occurs when economic growth slows sharply but does not turn negative, while inflation falls or remains low. Regulatory authorities attempt to use policies at their disposal to prevent recessions and promote so-called soft landings, although these policies have not always met with a great deal of success.

The business cycle in Canada has historically consisted of an expansion lasting between three and five years. Contractions generally last between six months and two years. However, these are only historical observations and we cannot rely on them exclusively to interpret current or future situations. Business cycles cannot be neatly categorized as to length and turning points at the time they are occurring; such distinctions can be made only in hindsight.

To make good use of business cycle data, an investor needs to monitor indicators of the economy. A good source of help in this regard is StatsCan in Canada and the National Bureau of Economic Research (NBER) in the US. StatsCan and the NBER attempt to identify those components of economic activity that move at different times from each other. Such variables can serve as indicators of the economy in general. Current practice involves the identification and monitoring of leading, coincident, and lagging composite indexes of general economic activity.

Leading indicators tend to peak and trough before the overall economy and provide useful tools for predicting the future direction of the economy. Some of the more important leading indicators include housing starts (which precede construction); manufacturers' new orders, especially for durables (which indicate expected consumer purchases); changes in profits (which generate a general mood of confidence or caution); spot commodity prices (which reflect demand for raw materials); average hours worked per week (which reflect demand for labour); stock prices (which reflect changing levels of profits); and money flows (which represent liquidity).

Statistics Canada's **Composite Leading Indicator** is an index that combines 10 leading indicators, in order to predict future economic conditions. It is composed of

1. The S&P/TSX Composite Index

2. Real Money Supply (M1)

3. The United States Conference Board Leading Indicator

4. New Orders for Durable Goods

5. Shipments to Inventory Ratio—Finished Goods

6. Average Work Week

7. Employment in Business and Services

8. Furniture and Appliance Sales

9. Sales of Other Durable Goods

10. Housing Index

Coincident indicators change at approximately the same time as the economy and are useful for identifying peaks and troughs after the fact. These include GDP, industrial production, personal income, and retail sales.

Lagging indicators change after the economy as a whole has changed. The most notable item is business investment spending. The unemployment rate, labour costs, inventory levels, and inflation levels are also classified as lagging indicators.

An increase in the composite leading indicator generally suggests that our economy will expand over the following three to 12 months, while a decrease indicates the likelihood of an immediate downturn. The coincident and lagging indicators serve to confirm (or negate) the indications of the leading series. If the leading index signal is not confirmed first by the coincident index and then by the lagging index, investors should reconsider the signal.

Real-World Returns 15-1 discusses leading indicators as of December 2007.

REAL-WORLD RETURNS 15-1

Leading Indicators December 2007

The composite leading index dipped 0.1 percent in December after two months of no growth. This was the most protracted period of weakness in the composite index since early 2001, when it fell marginally in five out of six months. The Canadian economy subsequently slowed in 2001, but avoided the recession that gripped the United States.

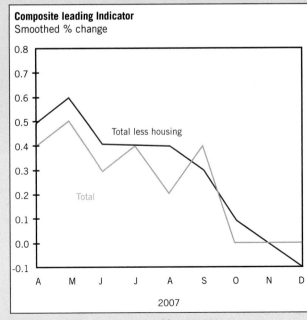

Source: Available on CANSIM: table 377-0003.

There are several reasons to believe that the current slump in the index is not as unsettling as in 2001. Much of the weakness was concentrated in the housing index, where unusually heavy snow storms severely curtailed construction in December. Excluding the drop in housing, the composite index would have been flat in December.

Besides the impact on housing, a snow storm in Eastern Canada during the reference week for the Labour Force Survey also reduced hours worked. This contributed to the sudden downturn in services employment, after 21 straight monthly gains. Consumer spending remained mixed, with increases for furniture and appliances offset by declines for other durable goods. Auto sales were particularly weak, although preliminary data point to a sharp recovery in December.

(continued)

REAL-WORLD RETURNS 15-1 *continued*

But there was less ambiguity about the outlook for the US economy. The US leading indicator fell 0.2 percent for the second consecutive month, led by weakness in housing and consumer confidence. The slowdown in US household demand was reflected in another sharp drop in new orders for goods manufactured in Canada. The ratio of shipments to inventories levelled off, after three straight declines.

Source: Available on CANSIM: table 377-0003.
Definitions, data sources and methods: survey number 1601.
This release was reprinted in the February 2008 issue of *Canadian Economic Observer*. For more information on the economy in December, consult the January 2008 issue of *Canadian Economic Observer*, Vol. 21, no. 1 (11-010-XWB, free).

LEADING INDICATORS

	July 2007	Aug. 2007	Sept. 2007	Oct. 2007	Nov. 2007	Dec. 2007	Last month of data available % change
Composite leading indicator (1992=100)	227.9	228.4	229.2	229.3	229.3	229.1	–0.1
Housing index (1992=100)[1]	148.4	149.6	152.5	150.5	149.7	146.0	–2.5
Business and personal services employment (thousands)	2,850	2,852	2,863	2,868	2,873	2,871	–0.1
S&P/TSX stock price index (1975=1,000)	13,683	13,782	13,918	14,032	13,988	13,981	–0.1
Money supply, M1 ($ millions, 1992)[2]	164,458	165,655	166,937	168,201	168,995	169,513	0.3
US Conference Board leading indicator (1992=100)[3]	126.7	127.0	126.9	126.9	126.7	126.5	–0.2
Manufacturing							
Average workweek (hours)	38.5	38.5	38.4	38.4	38.4	38.4	0.0
New orders, durables ($ millions, 1992)[4]	27,144	26,956	27,125	26,662	26,258	25,987	–1.0
Shipments/inventories of finished goods[4]	1.84	1.84	1.83	1.82	1.81	1.81	0.0[5]
Retail trade							
Furniture and appliance sales ($ millions, 1992)[4]	2,673	2,679	2,701	2,715	2,728	2,745	0.6

Other durable goods sales ($ millions, 1992)[4]	9,150	9,191	9,244	9,290	9,283	9,219	−0.7
Unsmoothed composite leading indicator	229.3	228.4	230.7	229.2	228.9	228.5	−0.2

[1]Composite index of housing starts (units) and house sales (multiple listing service).
[2]Deflated by the Consumer Price Index for all items.
[3]The figures in this row reflect data published in the month indicated, but the figures themselves refer to data for the month immediately preceding.
[4]The figures in this row reflect data published in the month indicated, but the figures themselves refer to data for the second preceding month.
[5]Difference from previous month.

Source: Statistics Canada website, The Daily, January 23, 2008, www.statcan.ca/Daily/English/080123/d080123b.htm.

The Stock Market and the Business Cycle

The relationship between the economy and the stock market is interesting—stock prices lead the economy. Historically, it is the most sensitive indicator of the business cycle. Therefore, we must deal with a complex relationship. The market and the economy are closely related, but stock prices tend to consistently turn before the economy. In other words, equity cycles (i.e., fluctuations in stock prices) tend to lead business cycles. This is why the S&P/TSX Composite Index is included in the composite leading index.

As with any indicator of the future, the stock market is not a perfect forecaster of future economic activity. While it remains an informative measure, it has also been known to provide false signals, and must be used with caution.

Has the Business Cycle Been Tamed?

As of April 2000, the Canadian and US economies had been expanding for almost 10 years. Both stock markets were hitting new highs, with the S&P/TSX Index reaching an all-time high of over 11,000. Some observers were asking if the business cycle was dead, based in part on the belief that slumps are not inevitable but rather are caused by accidents that happen. Also, as one CEO noted, "We are in a global economy … that has changed the paradigm…. We don't see the cyclical events that characterized the past."[1]

The other side of the coin is that as the expansion continues, people tend to forget the lessons learned from previous recessions. As one researcher on business cycles noted, "Who can eliminate herding?," referring to the tendency of people to get collectively carried away. As we know now, the markets in both countries underwent severe declines over the next two years, foreshadowing the decline in economic activity. In fact, by March 2001 the United States entered into an official recession. In Canada, there was also a significant decline over the 2000 to 2002 period; however, it was less severe than in the United States, and the decline never reached official recession status. The fact that business cycles persist has been further confirmed by the worries over recession in the US that dominated the press in the later part of 2007, and throughout 2008.

[1]This quotation and part of the discussion is based on J. M. Schlesinger, "The Business Cycle Is Tamed, Many Say, Alarming Some Others," The Wall Street Journal, November 15, 1996, pp. A1, A16.

CHECK YOUR UNDERSTANDING

15-1. Why do you suppose Average Work Week is included as a leading indicator, whereas the unemployment rate is a lagging indicator of economic activity?

15-2. Assume you have determined that the economy has reached a peak this month, and is headed downward. What conclusions would you draw about stock prices?

Other Factors Affecting the Aggregate Economy

Real-World Returns 15-2 provides an interesting synopsis of some of the major items affecting the Canadian economy and financial markets, including GDP growth, consumer spending, investment, the current account, imports and exports, the unemployment rate, the exchange rate, interest rates, business inventories, the inflation rate, and corporate profits. Some of these items have been discussed above, and the others are discussed in the remainder of this chapter.

Real-World Returns 15-2

The Economy in Brief: April 2008

Overview

- In the fourth quarter of 2007 real gross domestic product (GDP) increased 0.8 percent, the slowest pace of growth since the second quarter of 2003. For the year as a whole real GDP increased 2.7 percent, down slightly from 2.8 percent in 2006.

- Real final domestic demand remained robust in the fourth quarter, rising 6.9 percent, its strongest growth rate in 11 years. Strong household and corporate balance sheets, together with a healthy labour market, continued to underpin domestic demand. Employment rose 2.9 percent in the fourth quarter, up from 1.7 percent in the third quarter. In February 2008, the unemployment rate remained at 5.8 percent, matching a 33-year low.

- Real exports fell while real imports grew strongly in the fourth quarter, contributing to lower GDP growth in the quarter and to a narrowing of the trade surplus. The current account declined from a surplus of $5.3 billion in the third quarter to a deficit of $2.1 billion in the fourth quarter, the first deficit in the current account since the second quarter of 1999. For 2007 as a whole, the current account registered a significant surplus of $14.2 billion or 0.9 percent of nominal GDP.

Real GDP Increases 0.8 percent

Real GDP rose 0.8 percent in the fourth quarter of 2007. With real imports rising and real exports falling, growth in real final domestic demand accounted for the overall gain and outpaced growth in real GDP for the 12th time in the last 13 quarters (Chart 1).

Consumer Spending Grows Sharply

Real consumer expenditure increased 7.4 percent in the fourth quarter, the strongest gain since the third quarter of 1985. Spending in all major categories rose.

Main Economic Indicators
(percent change at annual rates unless otherwise indicated)

	2006	2007	2007: Q2	2007: Q3	2007: Q4	Most recent
Real gross domestic product	2.8	2.7	3.8	3.0	0.8	
Final domestic demand	4.7	4.3	5.2	5.2	6.9	–
Government expenditure						
Goods and services	3.3	3.6	4.1	6.2	6.9	–
Gross fixed capital	8.1	4.5	6.6	9.8	5.9	–

(continued)

Main Economic Indicators *continued*

	2006	2007	2007: Q2	2007: Q3	2007: Q4		Most recent
Consumer expenditure	4.2	4.7	5.8	4.5	7.4		–
Residential investment	2.1	3.2	6.5	5.5	2.4		–
Business fixed investment	9.9	4.4	3.3	5.5	7.2		–
Non-residential construction	12.9	3.9	−2.8	−2.4	0.4		–
Machinery and equipment	7.4	5.1	9.6	13.7	14.3		–
Business inventory investment ($ billion)	10.2	10.8	4.8	16.4	18.7		–
Exports	0.7	0.9	2.3	0.7	−8.5		–
Imports	5.0	5.7	7.3	18.4	10.9		–
Current account balance							
(nominal $ billion)	23.6	14.2	25.6	5.3	−2.1		–
(percentage of GDP)	1.6	0.9	1.7	0.3	−0.1		–
Nominal personal income	6.1	6.1	6.3	2.9	5.3		–
Nominal personal disposable income	6.4	5.6	2.6	4.9	6.4		–
Real personal disposable income	5.0	4.0	0.2	4.4	5.5		–
Profits before taxes	5.0	5.8	5.7	7.9	2.2		–
GDP price deflator	2.4	3.1	3.4	2.8	3.9		–
Consumer price index (CPI)	2.0	2.2	2.2	2.1	2.4	1.8	Feb-2008
Core CPI[1]	1.9	2.1	2.4	2.2	1.6	1.5	Feb-2008
Unit labour costs	3.1	2.9	2.8	−2.4	5.8		
Wage settlements (total)	2.5	3.3	3.0	3.9	3.4	3.3	Jan-2008
Labour market							
Unemployment rate (%)	6.3	6.0	6.1	6.0	5.9	5.8	Feb-2008
Employment growth	1.9	2.3	1.5	1.7	2.9	3.1	Feb-2008
Financial markets (average)							
Exchange rate (US cents)	88.2	93.5	91.1	95.7	101.9	97.90	Mar-2008
Prime interest rate (%)	5.8	6.1	6.0	6.3	6.2	5.25	Mar-2008

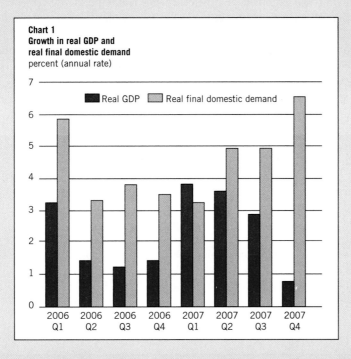

**Chart 1
Growth in real GDP and
real final domestic demand**
percent (annual rate)

■ Real GDP   ■ Real final domestic demand

(continued)

REAL-WORLD RETURNS 15-2 *continued*

Note: Real values are in chained 2002 dollars.

[1]Core inflation excludes eight of the components of the CPI basket that display the greatest volatility, as well as the effect of changes in indirect taxes on the remaining components.

Sources: Statistics Canada, the Bank of Canada and Human Resources Development Canada.

Household spending was supported by personal income growth of 5.3 percent, up sharply from 2.9 percent in the third quarter. With gains in employment and wages, labour income jumped 7.3 percent after a 1.5 percent rise in the previous quarter.

In the fourth quarter, real personal disposable income rose 5.5 percent while per capita real personal disposable income increased 4.1 percent. The personal savings rate was 0.8 percent, down from 1.3 percent in the previous two quarters.

Residential and Business Investment Grow

Residential investment rose 2.4 percent in the fourth quarter, less than half the pace in the third. Housing starts declined in the quarter, moderating growth in new construction activity to 5.4 percent from 10.2 percent in the previous quarter. Spending on renovations rose 5.0 percent. The home resale market, however, softened, reducing transfer expenditures by 10.1 percent.

Business investment in plant and equipment grew 7.2 percent, up from 5.5 percent in the third quarter. Spending on machinery and equipment increased 14.3 percent, a second consecutive double-digit gain, while non-residential construction rose 0.4 percent.

Increased Business Inventory Accumulation

Businesses added $18.7 billion to inventories in the fourth quarter, up from $16.4 billion in the third, thereby contributing to real GDP growth in the quarter. Inventories of retailers and wholesalers rose significantly. With the accumulation in the quarter, the overall inventory-to-sales ratio increased, but remained well below its recent average.

Real Exports Fall While Real Imports Rise, Pushing the Current Account into Deficit

In the fourth quarter, real exports fell 8.5 percent while real imports rose 10.9 percent. Real exports declined across major goods categories, reflecting weaker US demand and the continued strength of the Canadian dollar.

Real imports rose in all major categories, except energy and automotive products. North American vehicle sales at dealers fell, reducing imports of parts for the production and export of cars and trucks. The overall import gain reflected robust domestic spending as well as lower relative prices for imported goods. Imports of services increased 37.1 percent as travel spending abroad by Canadians (including cross-border shopping) soared 84.4 percent.

Although the terms of trade improved in the fourth quarter as export prices fell less than import prices, the sharp decline in net export volumes resulted in a $7.6-billion narrowing in the trade surplus to $14.1 billion. Similarly, the current account declined by $7.4 billion from a surplus of $5.3 billion to a deficit of $2.1 billion, or 0.1 percent of nominal GDP.

Corporate Profits Increase More Slowly

Corporate profits rose 2.2 percent in the fourth quarter after rising 7.9 percent in the third quarter. Stronger consumer spending boosted profits for retailers and wholesalers. However, weak sales hindered motor vehicle and parts manufacturers' profits while lower prices reduced the profits of primary metal manufacturers. Overall, profits as a share of nominal GDP decreased modestly to 13.7 percent in the quarter. While somewhat below the peak at the end of 2005, profit margins remain well above their historical average.

Consumer Price Inflation Remains Subdued

Year-over-year consumer price inflation was 1.8 percent in February 2008, down from 2.2 percent in January, partly reflecting lower prices for fruits and vegetables. Core CPI inflation, which excludes eight of the most volatile items and the effect of changes in indirect taxes, increased to 1.5 percent year-over-year in February from 1.4 percent in January. Core inflation has been below the Bank of Canada's 2 percent target since October 2007.

The GDP deflator, a comprehensive measure of the prices of goods and services produced in Canada (it includes export prices but excludes import prices), rose 4.5 percent in the fourth quarter following a 0.7 percent decrease in the third. The increase in the deflator largely reflects higher energy prices. However, final domestic demand prices (which include the effect of import prices), rose a little over 1 percent, as declining prices for imports dampened the impact of increased prices for domestically produced goods and services.

Unemployment Rate Remains Low

Employment grew 2.9 percent in the fourth quarter, up from 1.7 percent in the third quarter. With further gains in January and February 2008, net job creation stood at a healthy 447,800 since the end of 2006, nearly 90 percent of which was in full-time jobs. In February, the unemployment rate remained at a 33-year low of 5.8 percent. The participation rate was at 67.8 percent, a record high.

Hourly labour productivity for the total economy fell 2.6 percent in the fourth quarter, following growth of 0.8 percent in the previous quarter. Labour costs per unit of output on a total economy basis were up 5.8 percent in the fourth quarter.

Bank of Canada Lowers Policy Rate

On March 4, the Bank of Canada reduced its key policy rate—the target for the overnight rate—by 50 basis points to 3.5 percent. This followed cuts of 25 basis points on both December 4 and January 22. In its announcement following the March cut, the Bank noted that "the deterioration in economic and financial conditions in the United States can be expected to have significant spillover effects on the global economy. These developments suggest that important downside risks to Canada's economic outlook…are materializing and, in some respects, intensifying." The Bank also noted that "the balance of risks…for inflation has…shifted to the downside."

In response to credit market disruptions and a weakening economy, the US Federal Reserve decreased the target for the fed funds rate by 75 basis points on March 18, bringing the total reduction to 300 basis points since September 2007.

Canadian Dollar

High commodity prices, such as those for crude oil, continue to support the Canadian dollar. After hitting a modern-day high of 108.52 US cents on November 6, 2007, the value of the Canadian dollar has since traded between 97 and 103 US cents. It closed at 97.90 US cents on March 28.

Note: Unless otherwise noted, data and percent changes are quoted at annual rates. Incorporates data up to March 28, 2008. The main source of data used in this publication is Statistics Canada.

Source: Department of Finance Canada website: www.fin.gc.ca/ECONBR/ecbr08-04e.html. Reproduced with the permission of the ministers of Public Works and Government Services Canada 2008.

Global Economic Factors

As our previous discussion suggests, global factors play a major role in the Canadian economic environment. The state of the US economy is a very critical factor, since 70 to 80 percent of our merchandise trade is with the US. The impact of the US economy on Canada is discussed in Real-World Returns 15-3.

Real-World Returns 15-3

The Impact of the US Economy on Canada

Canada has avoided being dragged down by US, but that can't last, the central bank says.

Forget the talk that Canada's economy can thrive without help from US consumers.

The Bank of Canada muted that debate yesterday by taking a rare half-percentage-point swipe at its benchmark lending rate that left the cost of overnight loans between commercial banks at 3.5 percent, the lowest in two years.

In making the decision, Governor Mark Carney and his five deputies on the policy-setting Governing Council ignored signs of a thriving domestic economy, including the lowest unemployment rate in three decades.

Their focus was squarely on the deteriorating US economy, which is on the brink of recession amid a collapse in housing prices and tighter credit markets.

The message: There's no way Canada's 33 million people can offset weaker demand from the country's largest trading partner.

"I'm not buying the decoupling story, and the bank is not buying it either," Laurentian Bank Securities' Sebastien Lavoie, a former economist at the Bank of Canada, said from Montreal.

"We're at the mercy of what's going on in the US."

Canada's central bank last slashed borrowing costs by a half point in the wake of the Sept. 11, 2001, terrorist attacks.

That was before Canada emerged as an energy power and emerging economies such as China started bidding up the price of wheat and other commodities.

Over the past year, the wealth generated by record commodity prices led a growing number of economists to suggest that the country's economy might be shielded from a slowdown in the United States.

Many analysts, including HSBC's Stewart Hall, were predicting a milder quarter-point reduction yesterday, citing personal spending that accelerated 1.8 percent in the fourth quarter and wages that grew more than 6 percent in each of the past two years.

Mr. Carney, leading his first policy discussions since taking over from David Dodge last month, adopted the more traditional view of Canada's export-driven economy.

Canada's gross domestic product grew at an annual rate of 0.8 percent in the fourth quarter, the slowest in 4½ years, as exports declined for the first time in 1½ years.

The US economy, which consumes some 80 percent of Canada's exports, was even weaker in the fourth quarter, advancing at a 0.6-percent annual rate.

Faced with that, not only did policy makers ensure money would be cheaper immediately, they said they would likely reduce interest rates again at their next meeting on April 22.

"There are clear signs the US economy is likely to experience a deeper and more prolonged slowdown than had been projected in January," the central bank said in the statement. "These developments suggest that important downside risks to Canada's economic outlook that were identified in [January] are materializing and, in some respects, intensifying."

Mr. Carney is unique among the world's leading central bankers in choosing to follow the lead of Federal Reserve chairman Ben Bernanke, who has carved the US benchmark rate to 3 percent from 4.75 percent since October and is expected to cut it again in March.

The Bank of England, the European Central Bank and the Bank of Japan will likely leave borrowing costs unchanged at meetings this week, according to economists surveyed by Bloomberg News.

Australia's central bank raised its benchmark interest rate a quarter point yesterday to 7.25 percent in order to cool the fastest price increases in 12 years.

The Fed's cuts likely played a role in the Bank of Canada's move. The gap between the US and Canadian rates had widened to the largest since 2004 before yesterday's decision, making Canadian interest-bearing assets more attractive and fuelling demand for the currency.

A stronger dollar only makes selling goods in the US more difficult.

"The dominant theme is that Canada cannot escape the fallout from the US economic slump, which has contributed to the strength in the Canadian dollar and has led to weaker demand for Canadian exports," said Craig Alexander, deputy chief economist at Toronto-Dominion Bank.

Source: Carmichael, Kevin, "As clouds gather, Carney cuts deep: Canada has avoided being dragged down by US, but that can't last," *The Globe and Mail*, March 5, 2008, pp. B1, B4.

In addition to the US economy, Canada is particularly sensitive to world economic conditions because of the importance of commodity-based industries to our economy. This issue is also alluded to in Real-World Returns 15-3, with many economists suggesting that strong commodity prices "shielded" our economy from a US slowdown during the first half of 2008. However, as commodity prices plummeted later that year, they contributed to the rapid declines in our equity markets from over 15,000 in July to around 9,000 by late October. Indeed, despite the trend toward reduced reliance on commodity-based industries, these industries continue to play a major role in Canada's economic performance.

Many analysts suggest that one of the most important pressures exerted on the Canadian dollar is due to changing commodity prices. For example, the decline of the Canadian dollar to $0.63 US in 1998 was attributed in part to declining commodity prices, while its corresponding rebound in 1999 above $0.68 could be attributed to increasing commodity prices. The rationale is that global investors view the Canadian dollar as a "commodity currency," and its price will fall in response to falling commodity prices. After hitting an all-time low of $0.62 US in January of 2002, steady and rising commodity prices through 2003 to the present has contributed to our dollar's continued appreciation to hover around par until the summer of 2008 before being dragged down below 0.80¢ US by plunging commodity prices, later that fall. The fact that cyclical companies comprise a large proportion of the total market capitalization of the S&P/TSX Composite Index, while the S&P/TSX Venture Index is even more dominated by resource-based oil and mining companies, further highlights the importance of world commodity prices to the Canadian economy.

Interest Rates

As discussed in Chapter 13, interest rates are probably the most important financial variables affecting securities markets, since they are essentially the price of credit, as determined by the forces of supply and demand.

High interest rates tend to

1. Raise the cost of capital to firms, which reduces business investment
2. Discourage consumer spending, particularly for durables
3. Reduce disposable income available for net borrowers due to higher debt servicing charges

Some key interest rate determinants include

1. Inflation — rates rise to compensate lenders for loss in purchasing power as inflation rises.
2. Foreign developments and the exchange rate — foreign interest rates and the domestic exchange rate affect the demand for Canadian debt instruments.

3. Government deficits or increases in investment spending cause an increased demand for capital, which increases rates unless there is a corresponding increase in savings.

4. The greater the default risk of the borrower, the greater the rate that must be paid to borrow funds.

5. The Bank of Canada can influence short-term rates directly and may affect long-term rates less directly through its credibility of commitment to controlling inflation.

The Exchange Rate

The exchange rate affects the economy in several ways, most importantly through trade. All else being equal, a higher exchange rate tends to reduce Canada's trade balance. However, there are several other factors at work in determining the impact of a change in the exchange rate on trade. For example, if Canada has a lower inflation rate than the US, the effect of a higher exchange rate would be somewhat offset by Canada's lower costs.

Real-World Returns 15-4 describes the Canadian-dollar effective exchange rate index (CERI), which is a trade-weighted measure of the Canadian dollar exchange rate, with the US dollar being weighted the most heavily for obvious reasons.

Real-World Returns 15-4

Rates and Statistics

Exchange rates: Canadian-dollar Effective Exchange Rate Index (CERI)

What Is CERI?

The Canadian-dollar effective exchange rate index (CERI) is a weighted average of bilateral exchange rates for the Canadian dollar against the currencies of Canada's major trading partners. The CERI replaced the C-6 index in October 2006.

The six foreign currencies in the CERI are the US dollar, the European Union euro, the Japanese yen, the UK pound, the Chinese yuan, and the Mexican peso. Before 1996, the South Korean won was part of the index, but the Chinese yuan was not. Table A gives the weights for the currencies in the CERI.

Unlike the C-6 index, which used bilateral trade-weight calculations, CERI's calculations are based on multilateral trade weights. The weights used in constructing the CERI encompass trade in goods, services, and non-energy commodities, whereas the weights used in constructing the C-6 index were based on merchandise trade.

Table A: Currency Weightings

Currency	Weights based on 1999–2001 trade data[a]	Weights based on 1989–1991 trade data[b]
US dollar	0.7618	0.5886
Euro	0.0931	0.1943
Japanese yen	0.0527	0.1279
Chinese yuan	0.0329	—
Mexican peso	0.0324	0.0217
UK pound	0.0271	0.0368
South Korean won	—	0.0307

[a] These weights are applied to the CERI from 1996 to the present.
[b] These weights are applied to the CERI before 1996.

Formula

The formula uses a weighting scheme that allows percentage changes in currency appreciations and depreciations to be treated symmetrically. An increase in the index represents an effective appreciation of the Canadian dollar, while a decrease represents a depreciation of the Canadian dollar. The index is based to 1992 = 100.

The formula for the CERI is:

$$I_t = I_{t-1} \times \prod_{j=1}^{N(t)} (e_{j,t}/e_{j,t-1})^{w_{j,t}}$$

where I_{t-1} is the idex in the previous period and $e_{j,t}$ and $e_{j,t-1}$ are the prices of foreign currency j per Canadian dollar at times t and $t-1$.
$N(t)$ is the number of foreign currencies in the index at time t, $w_{j,t}$ is the weight of currency j in the index at time t, and $\Sigma_j w_{j,t} = 1$.

Source: Retrieved from Bank of Canada website May 4, 2008 at: www.bankofcanada.ca. Copyright © 1995–2008, Bank of Canada.

The following seven factors affect the exchange rate to varying degrees:

1. Inflation differentials — countries with lower inflation tend to appreciate through time to reflect their increased purchasing power relative to other countries.

2. Interest rate differentials — higher interest rates tend to attract more capital and make a currency value increase, provided the difference is not merely a reflection of higher inflation.

3. Current account — countries that continually run deficits will have excess demand for foreign currencies, which puts downward pressure on the domestic currency.

4. Economic performance — a strong economy attracts investment capital by offering higher returns and thus leads to more favourable exchange rates.

5. Public debt and deficits — countries with large debts are less attractive to foreign investors because: (i) they have higher incentive to allow inflation to grow (and repay in cheaper dollars); (ii) they rely more on foreign investment; and (iii) debt accumulation affects the country's ability to repay.

6. Terms of trade — is the ratio of export prices to import prices, an increase in which suggests increased demand for the local currency.

7. Political stability — capital tends to exhibit a flight to quality, particularly in times of increased uncertainty, and instability exerts downward pressure on exchange rates. We saw evidence of this in the insert above, where the US dollar was appreciating against most world currencies, including Canada's.

Canada, like most countries, maintains a foreign exchange reserve, called the Exchange Fund Account, which belongs to the federal government and is managed by the Bank of Canada. It is composed of foreign currencies (mainly US dollars), gold, and reserves in the IMF. For example, the value of these reserves as of April 23, 2008, was $43.8 billion US. This total amount consisted of $19.6 billion in US dollars (45 percent of total), $22.3 billion in other currencies, $1.1 billion in special drawing rights, a $0.7 billion reserve position in the IMF, and only $0.1 billion in gold. This reserve is used to defend the value of the Canadian dollar in world currency markets. In recent years, Canada and most other countries whose currencies have been under downward pressure have been relatively unsuccessful in preventing the downward trend in the value of their currency.

Inflation

The importance of inflation and inflationary expectations cannot be understated. Inflationary expectations feed into interest rate expectations, which in turn affect stock prices. Inflation is an important indicator for securities markets because it determines the speed at which the real value of investments are eroded. Inflation imposes several costs on an economy:

1. It erodes the standard of living for those on fixed income, which may aggravate social inequities.

2. It reduces the real value of investments such as loans, since they are paid back in dollars that are worth less.

3. It distorts signals to economy participants that are normally given through asset prices (since "relative" prices may be harder to establish).

4. Accelerating inflation may cause rising interest rates, which may lead to recessionary periods.

The generally accepted measure of inflation is the Consumer Price Index (CPI), which tracks the price of a given typical basket of goods and services. It may overstate the true level of inflation by failing to capture improved quality of the basket and consumers' tendencies to switch to less expensive items in response to price increases for goods or services included in the basket. Inflation generally results from too much money chasing too few products. The output gap refers to the difference between the potential full capacity level of output and actual output. When actual output is near full capacity, increased demand will lead to inflation. This is a classic demand side inflationary environment. On the other hand, inflation can be "supply side" induced when the prices of certain goods or inputs in the economy increase dramatically, even when there is no corresponding increase in demand for these products. We faced such a scenario during the first eight months of 2008, with rising oil prices causing inflationary pressures. This has occurred despite weak economic growth and hence weak demand side pressures. This situation caused concerns that global economies, particularly the US economy, would experience a period of stagflation, which refers to the co-existence of stagnant growth and rising prices.

A number of indicators are monitored for signs of changes in inflation, including commodity and wholesale prices, wage settlements, bank credit, and exchange rate movements. Monetary economists argue that monetary supply is the main determinant of inflation, while nonmonetarists argue that money supply increases in response to changes in demand and not vice versa. Standard measures of money supply used by the Bank of Canada include

1. M1 — currency held outside the bank plus demand deposits less private sector float;

2. M2 — M1 plus personal savings deposits plus non-personal notice deposits;

3. M2+ — M2 plus deposits at trust companies and mortgage loan companies, credit unions, caisses populaires, plus money market mutual funds plus insurance annuities; and

4. M3 — M2 plus non-personal fixed term deposits plus foreign currency deposits of residents booked in Canada.

Unemployment

The unemployment rate represents the share of the workforce that is looking for, but hasn't found, employment. It may rise due to decreases in the number of people employed, to increases in the workforce, or both. There are two general types of unemployment: (1) cyclical—which arises due to temporary hirings or layoffs that may be attributable to business cycle influences; and (2) structural—which is caused by a variety of factors. Normal unemployment caused by people in transition between jobs is referred to as frictional unemployment. Other factors such as regulation and general economic health will contribute to the level of structural unemployment that will exist in an economy even if it is healthy. This level of unemployment is sometimes referred to as the natural or full employment unemployment rate.

The unemployment rate is an important factor in assessing economic performance because it affects consumer spending and overall investor confidence. Consumers will spend less, particularly for durable items, when unemployment levels are rising. On the other hand, as unemployment rates approach the full employment rate, upward pressure on wages creates inflationary strains for the economy.

Government Policies

The Government of Canada has two general ways of attempting to influence general economic conditions—monetary policy and fiscal policy. Monetary policy refers to the use of interest rates, the exchange rate, and the rate of money supply growth to influence aggregate demand and the level of inflation. This function is performed by the Bank of Canada in Canada and by the Federal Reserve in the United States. Fiscal policy refers to the use of government taxation, spending, and deficits to affect growth. One of their generally accepted duties is to attempt to "smooth out" the business cycle by spending more and taxing less when the economy is weak. Fiscal policy is discussed below.

Fiscal Policy

Every year (usually in February), the finance minister presents the federal budget to the House of Commons for the coming fiscal year, which runs from April 1 to March 31. The budget contains projected revenues, spending, debt levels, and deficit levels for the coming year (and usually at least one additional year). An important part of the budget is the underlying economic assumptions on which the projections are based.

Fiscal policy affects the economy in four main ways:

1. **Spending:** Governments may purchase goods and services directly as they do when they construct new highways. Alternatively, they can provide direct transfers to citizens, as in the case with social security payments. Both methods increase the amount of spending in the economy; however, only the first kind of spending is included in GDP calculations.

2. **Taxes:** Taxes are levied in a variety of ways, including (i) direct taxes on the income of individuals and corporations; (ii) sales taxes, such as the GST; (iii) payroll taxes, which are levied as a share of wages; (iv) capital taxes, which are levied based on the size of a company's assets; and (v) property taxes, levied on commercial and residential property. All taxes tend to discourage the type of activity being taxed. For example, income taxes reduce the incentive to work, capital taxes discourage capital investment by businesses, and sales taxes discourage consumer spending.

3. **Deficits or Surpluses:** A deficit occurs when spending exceeds revenues, and a surplus means spending is less than revenues. Generally, increasing deficits tend to stimulate the economy in the short run, while falling deficits generally do the opposite. This is because a rising deficit implies greater spending and/or lower taxes, and both of these actions tend to stimulate the economy. However, continually running a deficit over long periods of time can produce negative long-run consequences for an economy, as discussed below.

4. **Automatic Stabilizers:** These stabilizers automatically move counter to the business cycle. For example, the amount of unemployment insurance paid out rises with unemployment, while unemployment insurance premiums paid by individuals falls. As a result, the reduction in disposable income felt by the economy is not as great as it would be otherwise. Income taxes work similarly, falling as economic growth declines, thus lessening the tax burden for spenders in the economy. When the economy is growing, income taxes increase, which can reduce inflationary pressures to a certain extent.

Canada's failure to address deficits from the late 1970s through to the mid-1990s produced several negative consequences. The cost of interest payments grew to be the largest single expenditure of the federal government (26 percent of GDP in 1994–95 versus 10 percent in 1974–75). The combined debt of federal and provincial governments increased to 97 percent of GDP in 1995 from 22 percent in 1977.

In addition, during many periods in the past, fiscal policy has not been synchronized with monetary policy, which has increased the cost to the economy. For example, in the late 1980s, when there was strong economic growth, governments continued to run deficits, which fuelled inflation and lead to higher interest rates on borrowed funds. In the end, large debts restrict government's ability to run countercyclical policies, since it becomes costly (if not impossible) to continue to run large deficits to generate spending.

Canada's federal and provincial governments have devoted a great deal of attention to eliminating fiscal deficits and paying down government debt. The 1997–98 federal budget was balanced for the first time since 1969–70, and all federal budgets have provided surpluses since then. As a result, federal debt as a percentage of GDP declined from an all-time high of 70.9 percent in 1996 to under 35 percent by March of 2007. The string of surpluses may end during the 2008–2009 fiscal year, as the economic tumoils of 2008 continue.

The Relationship between the Bond Market and the Stock Market

Investors today hear much talk about the relationship between bond and stock prices. What is the relationship, if any, and how does it affect stock investors?[2] Despite some claims to the contrary, historically bond and stock investors paid little attention to each other. However, the nature of the bond market has changed dramatically over time with the introduction of mortgage-backed and derivative securities of various types, the explosion of the federal debt in the 1980s, and the sharp swings in the inflation rate since the 1970s. Volatility has become pronounced in today's bond market.

Investors pay attention to the bond market because interest rates are available as a daily indicator of what is happening in the economy. The bond market provides signals of what bond traders and investors think about the economy. Bond traders react to news of unemployment, rising sales, or changes in the money supply, which affect interest rates and bond prices on a daily basis. Thus, in today's investment climate bond investors react to daily information about the economy, and the stock market, in turn, is affected.

Macroeconomic Forecasts of the Economy

Good economic forecasts are of significant value to investors. Since the economy and the market are closely related, good forecasts of macroeconomic variables can be very useful. A variety of economic indicators, such as those discussed in Real-World Returns 15-1, is released on a periodic basis and is tracked closely by economists, market analysts, and investors. Some are published daily in the financial newspapers, while others are released at periodic intervals. Commonly followed indicators represent a variety of measures of the items we have discussed above, including interest rates, foreign exchange rates, economic growth, inflation, unemployment, and US and global economic conditions.

Evidence regarding the success of economic forecasts is mixed. Although well-known forecasters tend to outperform statistical rules of thumb for macro variables, the margin of superiority is small. A major problem facing economic forecasters is the multitude of factors that must be monitored simultaneously. In addition, one of the most important factors influencing the economy in today's environment is the world financial and economic climate, which is difficult to monitor with accuracy. It is even more difficult to predict what will happen in tomorrow's global marketplace, which is facing constant political and economic uncertainty from a number of directions.

When the Monetary Authorities Speak

Regardless of money's current role in forecasting economic activity, many investors keep an eye on the actions of the Bank of Canada and the Federal Reserve because of the impact of monetary policy

---

[2]This discussion is indebted to L. Birinyi Jr., "Coping with volatility," *Forbes*, August 12, 1996, p. 164.

on interest rates, which in turn influence stock prices. Whenever Mark Carney, Governor of the Bank of Canada, or Ben Bernanke, Chairman of the Board of Governors of the US Federal Reserve, make public statements (formal or informal), the financial markets scrutinize every word for clues about the future of the economy and the financial markets. Whenever the Bank of Canada changes the Bank Rate, or the federal government changes its key federal funds rate, financial markets typically react noticeably, both positively and negatively, particularly if the change was unanticipated.

Insights from the Yield Curve

In Chapter 12, we considered the yield curve and its role in the management of bond portfolios. It can also be used in forecasting the economy, reflecting as it does bond traders' views about the future of the economy. Several studies suggest that the yield curve is very useful in making economic forecasts.

A steep yield curve suggests that the economy is accelerating in terms of activity, which could lead to higher inflation, and therefore higher long-term yields. A flat curve suggests moderate growth and moderate inflation. An inverted yield curve, however, carries an ominous message—expectations of an economic slowdown. Studies have shown that inverted yield curves are almost always followed by negative earnings growth, with the warning typically coming about a year in advance of the decline, and therefore providing adequate warning. For example, the US yield curve was inverted in 2000, and the 2000–2001 period was certainly filled with significant problems.

Forecasts from Economic Observers

Investors can obtain forecasts of the economy from various sources. Some of these are what are referred to as "consensus" forecasts, in the same way that we talk about consensus earnings forecasts for stocks. For example, *Blue Chip Economic Indicators* is a publication that compiles consensus forecasts from well-known economic forecasters of such important economic variables as real GDP, consumer prices, and interest rates. Thus, investors can find reputable, consistently done forecasts of the economy for at least the year ahead.

CHECK YOUR UNDERSTANDING

15-3. If the Canadian government were to change its fiscal policies so that its spending increased, how would this be reflected in the country's GDP?

15-4. You observe a downward-sloping yield curve. What significance would this be to you as an investor? How much confidence would you have in the conclusions you would draw from this curve?

UNDERSTANDING THE STOCK MARKET

What Do We Mean by the Market?

How often have you heard someone ask, "How did the market do today?" or "How did the market react to that announcement?" Virtually everyone investing in stocks wants a general idea of how the overall market for equity securities is performing, both to guide their actions and to act as a benchmark against which to judge the performance of their securities. Furthermore, several specific uses of market measures can be identified, as discussed in the next section.

When most investors refer to the "market," they mean the stock market in general as proxied by some market index or indicator. Because the market is simply the aggregate of all security prices, it is most conveniently measured by some index or average of stock prices.

As we know from Chapter 4, the most frequently referred to market index in Canada is the S&P/TSX Composite Index, which tracks the largest stocks trading on the Toronto Stock Exchange. This index tracks the movement of the TSX as a whole, which in turn accounts for most of the dollar volume traded on Canadian stock exchanges. When we refer to the market in Canada, we are usually referring to the S&P/TSX Index. The other major Canadian index is the S&P/TSX Venture Index, which tracks the performance of the TSX Venture Exchange.

In the United States, the two most frequently used indicators of market activity are the Dow Jones Industrial Average and the S&P 500 Composite Index (which is favoured by most institutional investors and money managers). A commonly used index of world equity market activity is the Morgan Stanley World Index, which consists of stocks from 23 developed countries as of June 2007.

Uses of Market Measures

Market measures tell investors how all stocks in general are doing at any time or give them a feel for the market. Many investors are encouraged to invest if stocks are moving upward, whereas downward trends may induce some to liquidate their holdings and invest in money market assets or funds.

The historical records of market measures are useful for gauging where the market is in a particular cycle and may also provide insight into what will happen in the future. Assume, for example, that the market has never fallen more than X percent, as measured by some index, in a six-month period. Although this information is no guarantee that such a decline will not occur, this type of knowledge aids investors in evaluating their potential downside risk over some period of time.

Market measures are useful to investors in quickly judging their overall portfolio performance. Because stocks tend to move up or down together, the rising or falling of the market will generally indicate to the investor how he or she is likely to do. Of course, to determine the exact performance, each investor's portfolio must be measured individually, a topic to be discussed in Chapter 22.

Technical analysts need to know the historical record of the market when they are seeking out patterns from the past that may repeat in the future. Detection of such patterns is the basis for forecasting the future direction of the market using technical analysis, which is discussed in Chapter 18.

Market indexes are also used to calculate betas, an important measure of risk discussed in earlier chapters. An individual security's returns are regressed on the market's returns in order to estimate the security's beta or relative measure of systematic risk.

The Determinants of Stock Prices

learning objective 2
Analyze the determinants of stock market values.

How are stock prices determined? In Chapter 13, we established the determinants of stock prices using the Dividend Discount Model (DDM)—dividends and the required rate of return—and, using the P/E ratio model—earnings and the P/E ratio. Although these are the ultimate determinants of stock prices, a more complete model of economic variables is desirable when we are attempting to understand the stock market, since there is a very strong relationship between the economy and the stock market, and stock prices generally react to information about the state of the economy, as alluded to in Real-World Returns 15-5. Such a model is shown in Figure 15-2, which is a flow diagram of stock-price determination described by US Federal Reserve economist Michael Keran in 1971. It indicates the variables that interact to determine stock prices. Although more than three decades old, this model remains a useful description of the conceptual nature of stock-price determination then, now, and for the future.

Real-World Returns 15-5

The Economy's Effect on the Stock Market

Another key pillar of the US economy appears to have fallen into recession: the insurers, restaurants, hospitals and the like that make up the massive service sector.

The sharpest monthly drop on record in the US service industries unleashed a new round of selling on Wall Street yesterday as investors fret that a recession may have begun.

The sudden decline suggests the overall US economy was likely shrinking in January, economists said. All major US stock indexes fell sharply on the news, including the Dow Jones industrial average (down almost 3 percent), the NYSE (down more than 3.5 percent) and the Nasdaq Stock Market (down 3 percent).

The Institute for Supply Management's (ISM) non-manufacturing index, released yesterday, plummeted to 41.9 from 54.4 in December. It was the steepest drop since the index was launched and the lowest reading since the aftermath of the Sept. 11, 2001, terrorist attack. A reading of less than 50 indicates a contraction of service activity, which accounts for about three quarters of the US economy.

BMO Nesbitt Burns economist Sal Guatieri said the ISM report is "compelling evidence" that the United States is already in recession.

"This is a dire reading ... that portrays the emergence of recession-like conditions in the economy," said Bear Stearns economist John Ryding.

The sharp decline in the ISM index is significant because it suggests a recession could be worse than the relatively mild one experienced in 2001. It's also among the first indications of declining economic activity, not merely hints of problems ahead. Along with lower payrolls and falling auto sales, BMO's Mr. Guatieri said the ISM report is among three key pieces of early recession evidence to emerge from January.

The grim report, which was released an hour earlier than usual because of a suspected leak, surprised many analysts. Economists had expected a reading of 53, according to a poll of analysts by Reuters.

"The number signifies the worst fears that were out there that this is going to be a broader and deeper slowdown than thought," said Matthew Kaufler, a fund manager with Clover Capital Management.

Many analysts now predict that the US Federal Reserve Board will have to respond with even more interest rate relief. The Fed completed the sharpest realignment of monetary policy in nearly two decades last month as it scrambled to deal with a rapidly slowing economy.

Speaking in Charleston, W.Va., Richmond Federal Reserve Bank president Jeffrey Lacker acknowledged that a "mild recession" is now a possibility.

But Mr. Lacker, who does not currently sit on the Fed's monetary policy committee, said a period of sluggish growth is more likely. And he said more rate relief may be needed to offset the growing weight of "downside risks."

The Fed cut its benchmark interest rate by 1.25 percentage points in January, and a total two full percentage points since last summer.

Economists said the Fed could lower the rate, which now stands at 3 percent, by another full percentage point by the summer to spur economic growth.

The Fed isn't slated to meet again until late March. But the central bank has already made two unscheduled rate moves during its current rate-cutting drive.

Ian Shepherdson, chief US economist at High Frequency Economics, said the ISM report should help "keep the pressure" on the Fed to keep cutting rates in the months ahead.

There is very little for the bulls to latch on to in the report. A remarkable 14 of 18 sectors reporting to the ISM said activity shrank in January. The only service sectors to show growth

(continued)

REAL-WORLD RETURNS 15-5 *continued*

were utilities, education and professional services. And three of the four subindexes fell: new orders, jobs and business activity. Only deliveries rose.

The US slump began in the housing sector, where rising foreclosures and slumping prices abruptly ended the housing boom.

But the problem soon spread to the banks and brokers that invested heavily in mortgage securities.

And more recently there has been evidence that US consumers, who make up two-thirds of the economy, may be tapped out.

If there is a bright spot, it is that in its 10-year history the ISM report has not been a particularly good predictor of what's ahead.

And Sam Bullard, an economist at Wachovia Securities, pointed out that service companies, at least, seem to be immune to the credit crunch.

More than 85 percent of the respondents in the survey reported having "no trouble" getting financing.

Source: McKenna, Barrie, "US economic woes point to wider recession: Stocks plunge on signs slump that began with housing has hit several sectors," *The Globe and Mail*, February 6, 2008, pp. B1, B4.

Figure 15-2 shows four exogenous (independent) variables that ultimately affect stock prices: the potential output of the economy (Y^*), which is a non-policy variable, and three policy variables (i.e., variables subject to government policy decisions)—the corporate tax rate (t_x), changes in government spending (G), and changes in nominal money supply (M). All variables to the right of the grey area are determined within the economy and are called endogenous (dependent) variables.

The two primary exogenous policy variables, G and M, affect stock prices through two channels:

1. They affect total spending (Y), which, together with the tax rate (t_x), affects corporate earnings.[3] Expected changes in (real) corporate earnings (E^*) are positively related to changes in stock prices (SP).

Figure 15-2
A Flow Diagram of Stock
Price Determination

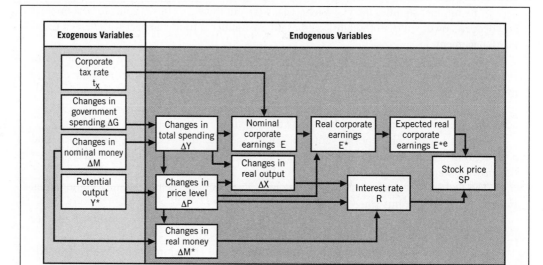

Source: Michael W. Keran, "Expectations, Money and the Stock Market," *Review*, Federal Reserve Bank of St. Louis, January 1971, p. 27.

---

[3]Technically, both the current level and lagged changes in Y affect corporate earnings.

2. They affect total spending, which, together with the economy's potential output (Y*) and past changes in prices, determine current changes in prices (P). Y and P determine current changes in real output (X). Changes in X and P generate expectations about inflation and real growth, which in turn influence the current interest rate (R). Interest rates, a proxy for the discount rate in a valuation model, have a negative influence on stock prices (SP).

The Keran model remains a classic description of stock-price determination because it indicates the major factors that determine stock prices. In this model, the four active policy variables below affect three changes in the economy:

1. Fiscal policy (government spending)
2. Monetary policy (money supply)
3. The corporate tax rate
4. The potential output of the economy

The corresponding changes in the economy are

1. Total spending
2. Price level
3. Real money

These three changes ultimately affect two key stock price determinants:

1. Corporate earnings
2. Interest rates

Investors can find considerable information about the macroeconomy from financial newspapers, and other business and economics publications, as well as from economic reports and forecasts prepared by financial institutions and the government.

Corporate Earnings, Interest Rates, and Stock Prices

As the Keran model in Figure 15-2 shows, the ultimate determinants of stock prices are expected corporate earnings and interest rates (which serve as a proxy for investors' required rate of return). Empirical evidence supports this assertion. For example, Fama found that almost 60 percent of the variance in annual US market returns for the period 1953 to 1987 was explained by changes in industrial production and interest rate factors.[4] Chen, Roll, and Ross identified the following economic factors that are likely to influence stock returns: expected and unexpected inflation; the term structure of interest rates; industrial production; returns on stock market indexes; the risk premium on bonds; consumption prices; and oil prices.[5] Their study found that unexpected inflation, the slope of the term structure, industrial production, and the risk premium on bonds are significant predictors of stock returns. Otuteye obtained similar results for 100 Canadian stocks over the 1970–84 period.[6] In particular, he found that these four variables have predictive power, in addition to the market index.

While the Keran diagram and the DDM were formulated many years ago, the modern explanation of stock prices remains the same. Stocks rise strongly as expected earnings (and dividends) climb and interest rates stay low. In other words, investors must be concerned with expected earnings, growth in earnings (and dividends), and interest rates as they assess the outlook for stocks.

Recall that two factors determine the price or value of the market (or a single stock)—earnings and a P/E ratio (multiplier). Other things often are not equal—earnings may rise, but the discount rate may also rise, leading to

INVESTING tip

If interest rates rise, the riskless rate of return, RF, rises, because it is tied to interest rates, and other things being equal, the required rate of return (discount rate) rises because the riskless rate is one of its two components.

[4]E. Fama, "Stock Returns, Expected Returns, and Real Activity," *Journal of Finance* 45 (September 1990), pp. 1098–1108.
[5]N. Chen, R. Roll, and S. Ross, "Economic Forces and the Stock Market," *Journal of Business* 59 (July 1986), pp. 383–403.
[6]E. Otuteye, "How Economic Forces Explain Canadian Stock Returns," *Canadian Investment Review* 4 (Spring 1991), pp. 93–99.

a decline in the multiplier, which, if strong enough, can cause a decline in stock prices. In some years, stock prices may rise sharply while corporate profits decline significantly. The reason is that the discount rate declines, resulting in an increase in the multiplier.

Interest rates represent the other key variable determining stock prices. This is because they are a basic component of discount rates, as shown in Figure 15-2, with the two usually moving together. There is clearly a relationship between interest rate movements and stock prices just as there is with GDP and corporate profits. In this case, however, the relationship is inverse; that is, as interest rates rise, stock prices fall (or vice versa), other things being equal. This is why analyst recommendations go to such great lengths to incorporate interest rate forecasts into their stock or portfolio recommendations.

Why is there an inverse relationship? Remember from Chapter 13 that the basic fundamental valuation model is given by the following equation (assuming the constant-growth version of the dividend valuation model):

$$P_0 = \frac{D_1}{k - g}$$

The k in the equation above is the required rate of return (discount rate) that investors use in discounting future cash flows. It is the rate of return that investors demand in order to invest in common stocks. This rate can be thought of as the sum of a riskless rate of interest plus a risk premium determined by the riskiness of the stock being valued. Most observers use the rate on government T-bills as a proxy for the riskless rate of return, because they have no practical risk of default and very little maturity risk. Therefore, the discount rate k is intimately tied to interest rates. That is why the Keran model (and others) refer to interest rates in discussing stock-price determination.

Like most relationships involving investing, the relationship between interest rates and stock prices is not exact. It is difficult to estimate the exact impact on stock prices because so many other things are happening simultaneously.

Investors need to understand the role of changes in interest rates in affecting investor expectations. Investors pay close attention to announcements by the Bank of Canada and the US Federal Reserve that could possibly affect interest rates, as well as to any other factors that may play a role. In turn, the popular press reports possible changes in interest rates as they might affect the stock market.

CHECK YOUR UNDERSTANDING

15-5. How might investors purchasing common stocks make use of market measures such as the levels of stock indices?

VALUING THE MARKET

To value the market using the approaches described in Chapter 13, we must refer to the primary variables used in fundamental analysis. Specifically, we focus our analysis on the expected cash flows (dividends) and the rate of return required by investors (or, alternatively, a multiplier or P/E ratio). The following estimates are needed:

1. Dividends or earnings
2. The required rate of return or the earnings multiplier.

These estimates are used in Equations 15-1, 15-2, and 15-3 and were explained in Chapter 13:

$$P_0 = \frac{D_1}{k - g}$$ **(15-1)**

$$P_0 / E_1 = \frac{D_1 / E_1}{k - g}$$ **(15-2)**

$$P_0 = P_0 / E_1 \times E_1$$ **(15-3)**

where
P_0 = present market value
D_1 = expected dividends
E_1 = expected earnings
k = discount rate or required rate of return
g = expected growth rate in dividends or earnings

These equations apply equally to the aggregate market or individual stocks or portfolios. Here we are concerned with an aggregate market index such as the S&P/TSX Composite Index. Conceptually, the value of this index is the discounted value of all future cash flows to be paid (i.e., the index value of dividends). Alternatively, it is the estimated earnings on the S&P/TSX Index multiplied by the estimated forward P/E ratio, or multiplier.[7] In summary,

$$\text{Value of S\&P/TSX Index today} = \frac{\text{Dividends to be paid on index next period}}{\text{Required rate of return} - \text{Expected growth rate in dividends}}$$

or

$$\text{Value of S\&P/TSX Index} = \text{Estimated earnings on the index} \times \text{Estimated forward P/E ratio}$$

We focus our discussion below on the multiplier approach.

The Earnings Stream

Estimating earnings for a market index for a future period is not an easy task. Several steps are involved. The item of interest is the earnings per share for a market index or, in general, corporate profits after taxes. The latter variable is related to GDP, since corporate earnings after taxes are derived from corporate sales, which in turn are related to GDP. A detailed fundamental analysis would involve estimating each of these variables, starting with GDP, then corporate sales, working down to corporate earnings before taxes, and finally to corporate earnings after taxes. Each of these steps can involve various levels of difficulty, as the following points suggest.

• To move from GDP to corporate sales, it may be possible to use a regression equation with percentage change in GDP as the independent variable and percentage change in corporate sales as the dependent variable. Based on this regression equation, a prediction could be made of sales given a forecast of change in GDP.

---

[7]Notice that Equation 15-3 uses the "forward" P/E ratio (P_0 / E_1) and an estimate of future earnings (E_1) to estimate today's price. This differs from the "trailing" P/E ratio (P_0 / E_0), which is the one usually reported in financial newspapers, analyst reports, and other stock-related reports.

- To obtain corporate earnings after tax, it is necessary to estimate a net profit margin, which is a volatile series. After estimating the gross profit margin, multiplying by the sales (per share) would provide an estimate of earnings before depreciation and taxes. Both factors would have to be computed and deducted to obtain an estimate of expected earnings (per share) for the coming year.[8]

For a per share perspective of earnings for the market, consider Table 15-1, which shows prices, earnings, and other selected variables for the S&P/TSX Index for the 1986–2007 period. The table reports trailing P/E ratios (P_0/E_0) for the S&P/TSX, which are determined by dividing the year-end index value by the most recent 12-month earnings (adjusted to the index). Notice that while earnings for the S&P/TSX Index increased over the entire period, the amounts varied, and the percentage changes from year to year can be quite sharp.

Table 15-1

Prices, Earnings, Dividends, and Market Ratios (in Index Form) for the S&P/TSX Composite Index, 1986–2007

Year	End-of-year Index Value (Prices)	Earnings	Dividends	Total Return (%)[a]	P/E[b]	Based on Year-end Prices Dividend Yield (D/P) %	Dividend Payout
1986	3066.18	176.31	91.67	-	17.39	2.99	0.5199
1987	3160.05	220.67	97.32	6.23	14.32	3.08	0.4410
1988	3381.75	312.83	113.96	10.62	10.81	3.37	0.3643
1989	3969.79	268.41	129.01	21.28	14.79	3.25	0.4806
1990	3256.75	202.37	124.9	−14.81	16.09	3.83	0.6172
1991	3512.36	76.63	111.93	11.28	45.83	3.19	1.4606
1992	3350.44	21.4	102.34	−1.69	156.56	3.05	4.7822
1993	4321.43	34.68	97.81	31.9	124.61	2.26	2.8204
1994	4213.61	194.62	100.76	−0.16	21.65	2.39	0.5177
1995	4713.54	342.27	107.44	14.41	13.77	2.28	0.3139
1996	5927.03	245.04	108.63	28.05	24.19	1.83	0.4433
1997	6699.44	293.05	110.27	14.89	22.86	1.65	0.3763
1998	6485.94	227.63	108.05	-1.57	28.49	1.66	0.4747
1999	8413.75	210.18	110.46	31.43	40.02	1.31	0.5255
2000	8933.68	387.76	113.42	7.53	23.03	1.26	0.2925
2001	7688.41	−164.91	119.12	−12.61	N/A	1.54	N/A
2002	6614.54	155.97	126.32	−12.32	42.41	1.91	0.8099
2003	8220.89	416.96	134.95	26.33	19.72	1.64	0.3237
2004	9246.65	491.58	154.42	14.36	18.81	1.67	0.3141
2005	11272.26	565.31	224.32	24.33	19.94	1.99	0.3968
2006	12908.39	818.02	312.38	17.29	15.78	2.42	0.3819
2007	13833.06	750.57	344.44	9.83	18.43	2.49	0.4589

[a]$TR (\%) = \dfrac{(P_t - P_{t-1} + D_t)}{P_{t-1}} \times 100$

[b]P/E is end-of-year price divided by earnings during the most recent calendar year, which is referred to as the trailing P/E ratio (P_0/E_0). The reported dividend yield is calculated similarly.

Source: *TSX Annual Review* for the years 1986 to 2007.

[8]An alternative is to estimate a gross profit margin by considering those factors that affect the gross margin, including unit labour costs, the utilization rate of plant and equipment, and the inflation rate.

The Multiplier

The multiplier to be applied to the earnings estimate is as important as the earnings estimate. Investors sometimes mistakenly ignore the multiplier and concentrate only on the earnings estimate.

Table 15-1 shows that the multiplier is even more volatile than the earnings component, and is therefore even more difficult to predict. For example, the trailing P/E ratios in Table 15-1 vary from a low negative value in 2001, to a high of 156.56 in 1992. The volatility in P/E ratios is likely to be even greater for individual stocks. The average trailing P/E multiple for the S&P/TSX Index over the 22-year period reported in Table 15-1 is 33.79 (ignoring 2001); however, this is a misleading summary statistic due to the impact of the 1992 and 1993 multipliers, which exceed 100. These extreme multipliers are relatively uninformative since they exceed 100 as a result of extremely low corporate profits in those years. Two more meaningful summary statistics for the S&P/TSX P/E ratio over this period are the 22-year median of 19.84 and the 19-year average (excluding the two extreme multiples exceeding 100, as well as the negative 2001 figure) of 22.54.

The lesson from this evidence is that investors cannot simply extrapolate P/E ratios, because dramatic changes occur over time. P/E ratios tend to be high when inflation and interest rates are low. When earnings are growing and the upward profit trend appears sustainable, investors are willing to pay more for today's earnings. In addition, investors must be careful when using P/E ratios to place them in the proper context. This is because P/E ratios can refer to historical data (such as the trailing ratios included in Table 15-1), to an average for a given period, or to a future period such as the year ahead.

Putting the Two Together

Obviously, valuing the aggregate market is not easy, nor will it ever be, because it involves estimates of the uncertain future. If valuing the aggregate market were relatively easy, many investors would become wealthy by knowing when to buy and sell stocks.

As noted, it is difficult to analyze all the complicated details required to perform fundamental market analysis. It involves studying utilization rates, tax rates, depreciation, GDP, and other factors, as well as applying some sophisticated statistical techniques. It is instructive, however, to analyze some general results of our basic valuation techniques. Regardless of the difficulty in doing market analysis and the extent to which an analyst or investor goes, the methodology outlined above is the basis on which to proceed.

As an example of conceptually explaining the market, consider the information in Table 15-1, keeping in mind that these are end-of-year values for the S&P/TSX Composite Index. Be very careful to understand what will be done here. We are going to "explain" the market in hindsight, based on year-end values. We will interpret what *did* happen, which is always much easier than predicting what *will* happen in the future. To value the market in actuality, an investor must forecast the two components of value—earnings and P/E ratios. Nevertheless, the reasoning process we will use is helpful in understanding how to value the market.

First, consider what happened to the market in 1988. Earnings on the S&P/TSX Composite Index increased substantially to 312.83 from 220.67 in 1987 (an increase of approximately 42 percent). As one would expect, market prices increased to 3381.75 in 1988 from 3160.05 in the previous year. This occurred despite increases in interest rates across the entire yield curve, which contributed to a decline in the trailing P/E ratio from 14.32 to 10.81. Thus, for 1988, the positive impact of the increase in profits outweighed the negative impact of an increase in interest rates and a decline in the P/E multiple. Stock prices declined in both 2001 and 2002 despite falling interest rates, due to earnings declines as well as investor uncertainties. In contrast, stock prices increased substantially in 2005 and 2006 despite rising interest rates, which were more than offset by increases in profits and dividends.

Now let's consider the market performance in 1994. Earnings increased substantially from the abnormally low 1993 level of 34.68 to 194.62. However, interest rates rose across the entire yield curve, and investors became increasingly concerned about future profitability. As a result, the required rate of return demanded by investors rose, which had a negative impact on the P/E ratio. Thus, despite a 461 percent increase in earnings, stock prices actually declined slightly, from 4321.43 to 4213.61, because the steep decline in the multiplier more than offset the increase in earnings for the year. The important point of this analysis is that at the beginning of 1994, an investor trying to value the market for the year ahead had to estimate what was likely to happen to the earnings stream for the market and to the P/E ratio (or discount rate). Estimating the earnings is only half the story and the less important half in many cases.

The conclusion of this analysis is that to value the market, an investor must analyze both factors that determine value: earnings (or dividends) and multipliers (or required rates of return). More important, the investor must make some type of prediction of these variables in order to forecast the market. We turn to this issue now.

CHECK YOUR UNDERSTANDING

15-6. You believe you have a precise forecast of what corporate earnings will be for the next year, and expect that most investors will use the forward P/E ratio for valuation. Can you now reliably predict the direction of the market?

FORECASTING CHANGES IN THE MARKET

learning objective 3
Make basic forecasts of market changes.

Most investors want to forecast changes in financial markets. Not only do they want to know what these markets are doing currently and why, but also where they are likely to go in the future. Part of this process requires an analysis of the overall economy and corporate profits.

Accurate forecasts of the stock market, particularly short-term forecasts, are impossible for anyone to do consistently. Chapter 10 provided substantial evidence that the market is efficient, which means that future changes in the market cannot be predicted on the basis of past information. The available evidence on the performance success of professional investors supports the proposition that even professional money managers cannot consistently forecast the market using available information. Such implications are supported by a wealth of anecdotal data.

What investors should search for are clues as to the economy and the market's general direction and the duration of a likely change. For example, to say that we are confident the market will go to 8,000 or 16,000 (as measured by the S&P/TSX Composite Index) one year from now is foolish. Similarly, a strong prediction that corporate earnings will rise or fall next year by 10 percent is a prescription for embarrassment.

In truth, most individual investors—indeed, most professional investors—cannot time the market consistently, as discussed in Chapter 10 and Chapter 14. What, then, should they do? The best approach for most investors is to accept that fact but also to recognize that periodically situations will develop that may warrant portfolio adjustments.

Some evidence suggests that investors lose more by missing a bull market than they gain by dodging a bear market. This point was raised in Chapter 14, which showed that investors who were fully invested in the S&P 500 over the 1986–95 period would have received a 14.8 percent annual return. However, had they missed the best 10 days, the return would have fallen to 10.2 percent, and if they had missed the best 40 days, the return would have fallen to a mere 2.5 percent. The most important point of this discussion is the same as before—the impact of the overall market on an investor's portfolio is enormous.

Using the Business Cycle to Make Market Forecasts

In his 1990 study of US stock returns between 1953 and 1987, Fama found that expected security returns exhibit a clear business cycle pattern.[9] They are high when times have been poor and improvement is anticipated, and are lower when economic conditions are strong. Earlier we established the idea that certain composite indexes can be helpful in forecasting or ascertaining the position of the business cycle. However, stock prices are one of the leading indicators, tending to lead the economy's turning points, both peaks and troughs.

What is the investor who is trying to forecast the market to do? This leading relationship between stock prices and the economy must be taken into account in forecasting likely changes in stock prices. Stock prices generally decline in recessions, and the steeper the recession, the steeper the decline. However, investors need to think about the business cycle's turning points months before they occur in order to have a handle on the turning points in the stock market. If a business cycle downturn appears likely in the future, the market will also turn down some months ahead of the economic downturn.

We can be somewhat more precise about the leading role of stock prices. Because of their tendency to lead the economy, total returns on stocks (on an annual basis) are often negative in years in which the business cycle peaks, due to increasing inflationary pressures, and the corresponding upward pressure on interest rates and downward pressure on future profits. Similarly, stock prices have almost always risen as the business cycle is approaching a trough, as inflation and interest rates decline, and expectations of future profits rise. These increases have been large, so that investors do well during these periods. Furthermore, stock prices often remain steady or even decline suddenly as the business cycle enters into the initial phase of recovery. After a previous sharp rise or as the peak is approached, a period of steady prices or even a decline typically occurs. The economy, of course, is still moving ahead.

Based on the above analysis, an investor can do the following:

1. If the investor can recognize the bottoming out of the economy before it occurs, a market rise can be predicted, at least based on past experience, before the bottom is hit.

2. As the economy recovers, stock prices may level off or even decline. Therefore, a second significant movement in the market may be predictable, again based on past experience.

3. Based on previous economic slumps, the market P/E usually rises just before the end of the slump and remains relatively stable over the next year.

The analysis of business cycle turning points as an aid to market timing is important. Based on historical observations, investors would have increased their returns by switching into liquid assets such as T-bills before the business cycle peaks and into stocks before the cycle reaches its trough.

Using Key Variables to Make Market Forecasts

A number of key market indicators and macro variables have been touted by both individuals and organizations as potential predictors of future movements in the economy and/or the market. Perhaps the best known market indicator is the price-earnings ratio. Table 15-1 showed that the trailing P/E ratio for the S&P/TSX Index has displayed significant volatility, rising above 100 in 1992 and 1993 in response to extremely low corporate earnings and being negative in 2001 in response to negative earnings for the index. The median of 19.84 or the average of 22.54, excluding the three extreme years over the 1986–2007 period, could be thought of as "normal" P/E multiples. Some analysts may view the market as overvalued if the P/E ratio exceeds 20, although we know there are several other factors to consider.

---

[9]E. Fama, "Stock Returns, Expected Returns, and Real Returns," *Journal of Finance* 45 (September 1990), pp. 1098–1108.

Another widely watched indicator of likely market movements is the dividend yield, which averaged 2.32 percent for the S&P/TSX Index between 1986 and 2007, with a median of 2.27 percent. Many market participants believe that when the dividend yield declines below historical levels, the market is in for a downward correction. The logic is that with stock prices high enough to make the dividend yield so low (say below 2 percent), investors will abandon equities in favour of higher returns on safe fixed-income securities. The resulting sale of equities will drive down their prices and drive up the dividend yield, restoring a balance.

Empirical evidence supports the use of dividend yields for predicting future stock returns. For example, dividend yield supposedly has a higher correlation with future S&P 500 changes than any other indicator over the long run.[10] In addition, several studies have shown that lagged aggregate dividend yield is negatively related to equity returns. These results are intuitive if we view dividend yields as measures of general economic conditions. The existence of high dividend yields suggests equity prices have been bid down relative to current dividends, reflecting a decline in economic growth. Conversely, low dividend yields generally occur when the economy is booming and equity prices have been bid up relative to current dividends. This suggests that dividend yields will be negatively correlated with GDP growth, which in turn is negatively correlated with future stock returns. Combining these two factors, we would expect a positive relationship between dividend yields and stock returns. Empirical evidence supports both of the claims above: dividend yields are negatively related to economic growth and are positively related to future stock returns.[11]

The problem with key market indicators is deciding when they are signalling a change and how reliable the signal is, especially given the high volatility in measures such as the P/E ratio, which was discussed above. In addition, we can reasonably assume that the "normal" value of some of these indicators changes over time, so that what is regarded as a low or high signal at one point does not have the same meaning at some other time. Still another problem is how quickly any change signalled by key market indicators and macro variables might occur. In the final analysis, this is an inexact process, subject to considerable interpretations as well as errors.

EXAMPLE 15-1: COMPARING DIVIDEND YIELDS

Consider some of the key indicators and macro variables in past years. On October 1, 1987, a few days prior to the great one-day crash of October 19, 1987, when the TSE 300 Index declined over 11 percent, the trailing P/E ratio was 19.50. While this was high by historical standards at the time, so was the ending 2002 P/E ratio of 42.41, which was followed by an above average S&P/TSX Index return of 26.33 percent in 2003.

A comparison of dividend yields shows that the dividend yield on October 1, 1987, stood at a relatively low level of 2.40 percent prior to the market crash on October 19. However, the ending dividend yield of 1.91 percent at the end of 2002 was also low by historical standards, yet the market performed admirably in 2003. In fact, by the end of 2003 the dividend yield had fallen even further, to 1.64 percent.

Investors attempting to forecast the economy should pay attention to certain important variables. Interest rates are an obvious variable to watch. In fact, one of the most commonly used variables in return predictability studies is the lagged domestic short-term interest rate, which generally mirrors expected future inflation. The short-term interest rate has been shown to be significant in predicting stock returns in many empirical studies.

Two other interest rate variables have also been shown to have predictive power regarding future stock returns. One of these is the term structure variable, which is defined as the lagged long-

[10]"Will Overvaluation Overwhelm Stocks?" *Mutual Funds*, March 1995, pp. 17–19. This discussion is indebted to information in this article.
[11]N. Chen, "Financial Investment Opportunities and the Macroeconomy," *Journal of Finance* 46 (June 1991), pp. 529–554; Fama in footnote 4.

term domestic government bond yield minus the lagged government short-term interest rate. The other is the default spread, which is defined as the difference between the yield on long-term corporate bonds versus the yield on long-term government bonds. This variable is chosen to predict returns based on the fact that default spreads tend to widen during recessionary periods, as investors require additional compensation to hold riskier corporate bonds (i.e., there is a flight to quality during periods of uncertainty).

The direction and levels of commodity prices are also very important, especially for Canada. In addition, unit labour costs are considered by many to be an important economic indicator, with increases exceeding 3 percent signalling a potential problem.

Finally, as you consider the state of the market and whether you should invest now, you might ask if any particular month is riskier than others. Some believe that October is, and the historical evidence seems to support this idea: Many of the largest daily market declines have occurred in October, including huge one-day declines during 2008, as well as the market crashes of 1929 and 1987.

Using Valuation Models to Make Market Forecasts

Based on the valuation models developed earlier, we could use one of two approaches to make market forecasts:

1. Use D_1, k, and g, based on Equation 15-1, $P_0 = D_1/(k - g)$.
2. Use E_1 and P/E, based on Equation 15-3, $P_0 = E_1 \times P_0 / E_1$.

Notice that using Equation 15-3 requires estimates of future earnings (E_1) and the forward P/E ratio (P_0 / E_1), not the trailing P/E ratio (P_0 / E_0) referred to in Table 15-1. The reason forward P/E ratios are seldom reported in public sources such as the newspaper is because of the subjectivity involved in their estimation. In particular, they require estimates of the expected future earnings (E_1), and these will vary from analyst to analyst. For comparison purposes, we have included Table 15-2, which includes forward P/E ratios (P_0 / E_1) for the S&P/TSX Index from 1986 to 2007 based on the actual earnings that resulted in the following year. In other words, the P_0 / E_1 ratios reported in Table 15-2 represent the forward P/E ratios that would have been determined with perfect forecasting ability regarding future earnings at the beginning of each year. The ability to forecast future earnings perfectly is, of course, impossible in the real world, which is why we do not see these ratios reported regularly in the media. The average of these ratios, excluding the negative value for 2000, is 32.23, while the median over all 21 observations is 19.24. Notice that these summary statistics are very close to those observed for the trailing P/E ratios in Table 15-1 and similar to our experience with the trailing ratios: the average is uninformative due to two extreme values (164.13 for 1991 and 96.61 for 1992).

Table 15-2

Forward Price-Earnings ratios (P_0/E_1) for the S&P/TSX Composite Index, 1986–2007

Year	End-of-year Index Value (Prices)	Earnings	Forward P_0 / E_1 Ratio[a]
1986	3066.18	176.31	13.89
1987	3160.05	220.67	10.10
1988	3381.75	312.83	12.60
1989	3969.79	268.41	19.62
1990	3256.75	202.37	42.50
1991	3512.36	76.63	164.13
1992	3350.44	21.40	96.61
1993	4321.43	34.68	22.20
1994	4213.61	194.62	12.31
1995	4713.54	342.27	19.24
1996	5927.03	245.04	20.23

Table 15-2 *continued*

Year	End-of-year Index Value (Prices)	Earnings	Forward P_0 / E_1 Ratio[a]
1997	6699.44	293.05	29.43
1998	6485.94	227.63	30.86
1999	8413.75	210.18	21.70
2000	8933.68	387.76	-54.17
2001	7688.41	-164.91	49.29
2002	6614.54	155.97	15.86
2003	8220.89	416.96	16.72
2004	9246.65	491.58	16.36
2005	11272.26	565.31	13.78
2006	12908.39	818.02	17.20
2007	13833.06	750.57	—

[a]P_0 / E_1 is current end-of-year price divided by earnings during the next calendar year.

Source: *TSX Annual Review* for the years 1986 to 2007.

CHECK YOUR UNDERSTANDING

15-7. Given that earnings and the P/E ratio can be used to determine stock prices, what is the logic for arguing that interest rates are one of the two critical variables in forecasting the direction of the market?

SUMMARY

This summary relates to the learning objectives for this chapter.

1. **Describe the relationship between the stock market and the economy.**

   Macroeconomic forecasts require analysis of several domestic and global factors simultaneously. The recurring pattern of expansion and contraction in the economy is referred to as the business cycle, and stock prices are related to the phases of that business cycle. Leading, lagging, and coincident indicators are used to monitor the economy in terms of business cycle turning dates. It is important to remember that stock prices are leading indicators and generally lead the economy. Therefore, while the market and the economy are clearly related, stock prices usually turn before the economy does.

2. **Analyze the determinants of stock market values.**

   The market is the aggregate of all security prices and is conveniently measured by some average or index of stock prices. To understand the market (i.e., what determines stock prices), it is useful to think in terms of a valuation model. The two determinants of aggregate stock prices are the expected benefits stream (earnings or dividends) and the required rate of return (alternatively, the P/E ratio). Keran's model is useful for visualizing the economic factors that combine to determine stock prices. In trying to understand the market in conceptual terms, it is appropriate to think of corporate earnings and interest rates as the determinants of stock prices. Corporate earnings are directly related to stock prices, whereas interest rates are inversely related to stock prices. To value the market, investors should think in terms of corporate earnings and the P/E ratio, or, dividends and the discount rate.

3. **Make basic forecasts of market changes.**
Forecasting market changes is difficult. The business cycle can be of help in understanding the status of the economy, which investors must then relate to the market (which usually leads the economy). Some intelligent estimates of possible changes in the market can be made by considering what is likely to happen to corporate profits and P/E ratios (or interest rates) over some future period, such as a year.

KEY TERMS

Business cycle, p.479   Composite Leading Indicator, p.480

REVIEW QUESTIONS

15-1. Why should investors be concerned with GDP growth?

15-2. In terms of the Keran model, how can the Bank of Canada affect stock prices?

15-3. List and describe the five phases of the business cycle.

15-4. Differentiate between a leading indicator, a coincident indicator, and a lagging indicator.

15-5. List five key determinants of interest rates.

15-6. Why is market analysis so important?

15-7. What are the two major determinants of stock prices? How are these two determinants related to a valuation model?

15-8. What is the historical relationship among stock prices, corporate profits, and interest rates?

15-9. What was the primary cause of the fall in stock prices in 2001?

15-10. What is the "typical" business cycle–stock price relationship?

15-11. If an investor can determine when the economy will bottom out, when should stocks be purchased—before, during, or after such a bottom? Would stock prices be expected to continue to rise as the economy recovers (based on historical experience)?

15-12. Suppose that you know with certainty that corporate earnings next year will rise 15 percent above this year's level of corporate earnings. Based on this information, should you buy stocks?

15-13. How can the Keran model use interest rates as one of the two determinants of stock prices when the interest rate does not appear in either the dividend valuation model or the earnings multiplier model?

15-14. How can investors go about valuing the market?

15-15. What effect do inflation and interest rates have on P/E ratios?

15-16. Why must an investor analyze both earnings and multipliers when trying to determine the value of the market?

15-17. How is the dividend yield used as a market indicator?

15-18. List some problems or limitations with using the key market indicators.

15-19. When attempting to forecast the economy, which macro variables should an investor pay attention to?

15-20. Why don't public sources report forward P/E ratios?

15-21. What does a steepening yield curve suggest about the economy? What about an inverted yield curve?

15-22. In general, what should be the relationship between corporate earnings growth and the growth rate for the economy as a whole?

15-23. Indicate whether each of the following economic variables are leading, lagging, or coincident economic indicators.

  a. Unemployment
  b. Retail sales
  c. Business investment spending
  d. Housing starts
  e. Inflation

PROBLEMS

15-1. Use the following annual data for a common stock index provided for the years 2003 through 2008. The 2008 values in italics are projected.

Year	End-of-Year Price (P_0)	Earnings (E_0)	Dividends (D_0)	P_0/E_0	Payout (D_0/E_0)	Div. Yield (D_0/P_0)
2003	107.21	13.12	5.35	8.17	40.78	4.99
2004	121.02	16.08	6.04	7.53	37.56	4.99
2005	154.45	16.13	6.55	9.58	40.61	4.24
2006	137.12	16.70	7.00	8.21	41.92	5.11
2007	157.62	13.21	7.18	11.93	54.35	4.56
2008	*186.24*	*15.24*	*6.97*			

  a. Calculate the 2008 values for those columns left blank.
  b. Assuming a projection that 2009 earnings will be 25 percent greater than the 2008 value and assuming that the 2009 dividend-payout ratio will be 0.40, determine the P_0/E_1 ratio for 2008, using the 2008 price in the table above.
  c. Using the projected earnings and dividends for 2009, and $k = 13.2$ percent and $g = 9.5$ percent, use Equation 15-2 to determine the implied P_0/E_1 ratio for 2008.
  d. Recalculate the values for 2008 P_0/E_1 and P_0, using the same $g = 0.095$, but with (1) $k = 0.14$; and (2) $k = 0.12$.

15-2. A common stock index has the following data:

$g = 8\%, k = 12\%$

Assume the payout ratio is held constant. Complete the table below.

Year	Earnings	Dividends	Price	P_0/E_0	Div. Yield
1	14.35	5.74			
2					
3					
4					

15-3. You are studying three Canadian stocks as potential investments. The first is a firm that develops software; the second, a small retail bank; and the third is a regulated natural gas distributor (utility). To begin your top-down analysis, you have collected the following forecasts for the Canadian economy and stock market. We will assume this analysis was conducted at the end of 2008 so those figures are "actuals" not forecasts.

Year	2008	2009	2010	2011	2012	2013
GDP Growth	2.0%	0.5%	-1.0%	1.4%	3.6%	2.1%
Market P/E	12.5	12.2	10.1	12.5	14.6	14.2

a. All three companies had sales of $10 per share in 2008. Use the following estimates to forecast the per share sales of each firm for the years 2009 to 2013. The software firm's sales grow at twice the rate of GDP growth; the bank's revenues grow at the same rate as GDP; the utility firm is largely unaffected by the broader economy so its sales grow at a constant rate of 2.5 percent per year.

b. For this simple analysis, we will move from sales to net income after tax (EPS) in one step using a "net margin" factor. For the software firm deduct $8 per share of fixed costs from sales; its net margin is 50 percent of the remainder (the 2008 figure is $1.00 per share). The bank earned $2.30 in 2008. Its net margin tends to fall when the economy is strong (since that is when interest rates tend to rise and the bank faces higher funding costs). Use a figure of 25 percent less the value of GDP growth. For example, in 2009 the net margin at the bank will be 24.5 percent. The utility firm tends to improve its margins in-line with the economy, so use a net margin of 15 percent plus the rate of growth in GDP (for example, its net margin will be 15.5 percent in 2009); the utility firm earned $1.70 in 2008. Calculate the EPS for each firm for each year in the forecast.

c. Forecast the P/E ratio for each of the firms at the end of each year. The software firm's P/E ratio is now (end of 2008) at 14.0 and this tends to change by twice as much as the overall market P/E changes. The bank ended 2008 with a P/E of 13.5; this figure tends to stay 1.0 higher than the market (so it will be 13.2 in 2009). The utility firm's P/E tends to stay very constant at 11.0.

d. Use the figures from parts (b) and (c) to forecast the share price for each stock at the end of each year from 2009 to 2013. At of the end of 2008, the prices are $14.00, $31.05, and $18.70, for the software firm, the bank, and the utility firm, respectively.

e. Forecast the amount of dividends that these firms are likely to pay in each year. This is simple for the software firm: it has never paid a dividend and doesn't intend to. The bank paid $1.50 per share in dividends in 2008 and has a policy of increasing this figure by 2.5 percent per year. The utility firm usually pays 50 percent of its EPS as dividends ($0.85 in 2008) however, it does not allow the dividend to fall from one year to the next (e.g. in 2009, the dividend will stay at $0.85 even though 50 percent of EPS would be only $0.79).

f. Use the estimated stock prices and dividend figures to determine the total annual return for each stock over the 2009 to 2013 forecast period. Once you have calculated the total annual return, calculate the mean return (arithmetic average), the compound return (geometric average), and the standard deviation of returns for each of the three stocks.

PREPARING FOR YOUR
PROFESSIONAL EXAMS

CFA PRACTICE QUESTION

15-1. An analyst projects the following:
- The market's normalized year-end price-earnings (P/E) ratio will be 12X.
- The ABC Company's normalized year-end P/E ratio will be 16X.
- The market index's value currently stands at $1,000.
- The index is expected to pay a $50 dividend this coming year on projected earnings of $100.

If the analyst buys and holds the market index for the year, what would be the rate of return?
a. 10%
b. 15%
c. 20%
d. 25%

CHAPTER 16

INDUSTRY ANALYSIS

As you prepare to invest your inheritance, you are reminded that you read about the telecom boom and bust of the late 1990s, the strong performance of the energy sector in 2005 and its collapse during the fall of 2008, and so forth. Therefore, it seems obvious to you that you should consider some basic information about sectors and industries that are likely to be important in future years. You already understand that you must think ahead when you invest. Yesterday's performers may very well not be tomorrow's performers. You realize that you cannot become proficient in understanding how to analyze sectors and industries unless you devote a lot of time to the task, but it does seem reasonable that a reasonable effort might pay off. And indeed, it might.

Learning Objectives

After reading this chapter, you should be able to

1. State the importance of industry analysis.
2. Explain how industries are classified.
3. Analyze the life cycle and qualitative factors that affect industries.
4. Evaluate future industry prospects by analyzing the business cycle.

CHAPTER PREVIEW

In this chapter we examine industry analysis—the second step in the top-down approach in fundamental security analysis. After explaining the importance of industry factors to company performance, we describe how industries are defined and classified. We look at the concept of a life cycle and at qualitative factors that are useful in industry analysis. Finally, we evaluate future industry prospects by analyzing the business cycle.

THE IMPORTANCE OF INDUSTRY ANALYSIS

learning objective 1
State the importance of industry analysis.

The second step in the fundamental analysis of common stocks is industry analysis. An investor who is convinced that the economy and the market offer favourable conditions for investing should proceed to consider those industries that promise the best opportunities in the coming years. In the first decade of the 2000s, for example, investors will not view some Canadian industries with the same enthusiasm they would have even 10 years earlier. On the other hand, it is obvious that the telecommunications and computer-related industries such as Internet companies are changing the way most Canadians live.

The actual analysis of industries done by professional security analysts is often a detailed and lengthy process. Numerous factors must be considered, including multiple demand and supply factors, a detailed analysis of price factors, labour issues, government regulation, and so forth.

In this chapter, we concentrate on the conceptual issues involved in industry analysis. The basic concepts of industry analysis are closely related to our previous discussion of valuation principles. Investors can apply these concepts in several ways, depending on the degree of rigor sought, the amount of information available, and the specific models used. What we seek to accomplish here is to learn to think analytically about industries.

The significance of industry analysis can be established by considering the performance of various industries over several periods. This analysis will indicate the value to investors of selecting certain industries while avoiding others at certain times. For example, Real-World Returns 16-1 discusses how the materials and energy sectors benefited from rising gold and oil prices during the first quarter of 2008. We will also establish the need for investors to analyze industries on a continuous basis by showing the inconsistency of industry performance over consecutive periods.

REAL-WORLD RETURNS 16-1

Sector Analysis

If your portfolio has been left in the dust by the S&P/TSX composite index, don't beat yourself up too much. Most professional money managers are having a heck of a time trying to top the benchmark.

Fewer than 20 percent of large-capitalization Canadian institutional fund managers beat the index in the first quarter, according to a survey by Russell Investments Canada. That's down from 41 percent in the fourth quarter and the lowest reading since Russell started monitoring the data in 1999.

"I would describe this environment as the most hostile I've ever seen," said Kathleen Wylie, senior research analyst at Russell in Toronto.

Most small investors would probably agree.

But why did so many pros trail the index?

Two words: energy and materials. These two sectors, which together account for nearly half of the S&P/TSX, were the only ones to generate positive returns in the first quarter.

But most large-cap Canadian equity managers had underweight positions. Some had no exposure at all to gold stocks, which seriously hurt their returns; during the first quarter, the gold sector surged 8.4 percent.

The survey isn't meant to be a definitive look at how professional fund managers have fared. The results are based on the performance of 115 institutional money managers running investment pools that cater to pension funds, foundations and other non-taxable investors. The results are based on total returns, including dividends, but excluding management fees and expenses.

These managers may have different investment styles and objectives than mutual funds, which are not included in the survey. For one thing, the institutional managers in the survey usually hold less cash and have a smaller weighting in foreign stocks than mutual funds. Still, the survey provides a window into the challenges the pros face in beating the benchmark.

It wasn't like the hurdle was set very high. In the first quarter, the S&P/TSX lost 2.8 percent, including dividends. But the median return of large-cap managers in the survey was a loss of 3.9 percent.

Even as most managers trailed the index, some investment styles performed better than others. About 27 percent of value-oriented money managers beat the index, up from 16 percent in the fourth quarter and just 9 percent in the third. Value investors look for stocks that are cheap, based on price-to-earnings, price-to-book and other measures.

But as the performance of value investors was improving, growth managers—who focus on stocks with rapid earnings growth and price momentum—were struggling. Just 24 percent beat the index, down from 53 percent in the fourth quarter and 75 percent in the third.

The improvement in value managers' performance reflects a rebound in financial stocks, which had been beaten down by the credit crisis. Many value investors scooped up the stocks, believing they'd fallen too far.

"Value managers have struggled for the better part of three consecutive years, so this improvement is encouraging," Ms. Wylie said.

"The last time value specialists struggled that much was during the technology bubble, but it's important to note that, following that challenging period, value managers bounced back significantly for the next two years, in 2001 and 2002."

Many value managers have also had a strong April, so the second quarter could see even more improvement, she said. That's something to keep in mind for investors who are wondering when their own portfolios will rebound.

Source: Heinzl, John, "Volatile TSX still beat investment pros," *The Globe and Mail*, May 7, 2008, p. B13.

Performance of Industries over Time

The importance of industry factors for investment managers is irrefutable. For example, Table 16-1 shows that while the 2007 return for the S&P/TSX Composite Index was 9.8 percent, the returns for the industry indexes varied from 48.2 percent for the Information Technology to −24.3 percent for the Health Care Index. Obviously portfolios that were weighted heavily in Information Technology in Health Care would have performed well during this year. In 2002, the S&P/TSX Index fell 14.0 percent, while industry returns ranged from a high of 11.3 percent for Energy to a low of −59.0 percent for Information Technology.

Peter Gibson highlights the potential benefits to predicting future industry performance (based on the 10 largest industries in the TSE 300 in 1996).[1] He shows that an investor using an industry

---

[1]Peter Gibson, "Chapter 14: Strategy," in Joe Kan, ed., *Handbook of Canadian Security Analysis: A Guide to Evaluating the Industry Sectors of the Market, from Bay Street's Top Analysts* (Toronto: John Wiley & Sons Canada, 1997), pp. 537–644.

Table 16-1

Percentage Total Returns of the S&P/TSX Indexes 2002–2007

Sector / Industry	2002	2003	2004	2005	2006	2007	Average
Consumer Discretionary	−21.0	19.5	8.3	8.5	13.2	4.2	5.5
Consumer Staples	1.8	18.9	9.3	−2.2	3.9	−5.3	4.4
Energy	11.3	23.6	28.7	61.3	3.2	8.2	22.7
Financials	−5.0	24.4	16.5	20.5	15.9	−1.6	11.8
Health Care	−33.8	15.1	−17.4	−3.8	−0.7	−24.3	−10.8
Industrials	−31.4	21.5	−2.0	16.5	12.7	10.5	4.6
Information Technology	−59.0	59.3	24.8	−15.8	27.3	48.2	14.1
Materials	5.4	25.8	5.7	13.9	38.0	30.3	19.9
Telecommunications	−12.1	30.4	13.5	9.3	16.4	19.9	12.9
Utilities	−0.3	18.7	5.5	33.4	2.1	11.9	11.9
S&P/TSX Composite	−12.3	26.3	14.4	24.3	17.3	9.8	13.3

Source: TSX Annual Review for the years 2002 to 2007.

rotation strategy (discussed later in this chapter) with perfect foresight could have earned 205 percent per year over the 1973–96 period, by allocating his or her portfolio correctly to the best performing industry sector on a monthly basis. Although perfect foresight is not possible, this example serves to highlight the importance of examining industry factors, as well as the potential benefits of diversifying across industry categories.

Before embarking on industry analysis, we should consider its potential value. To establish the value of industry analysis, we can assess the performance of industry groups over long periods of time. Standard & Poor's provides total return indexes for the 10 industry groups that are reported in Table 16-1. During this same six-year period, performance of the industry groups varied substantially, from the 22.7 average return provided by Energy and 19.9 percent average for Materials, to the −10.8 percent average for Health Care, while the S&P/TSX Composite Index provided an average return of 13.3 percent. Investors who were heavily weighted in Energy and Materials stocks (which combined now comprise about half of the TSX market capitalization) over this period would likely have been very successful. Unfortunately, there is no assurance that strong industry performance in the past will continue in the future.

What about industry performance over shorter periods of time? Should investors screen industries to find those that are currently performing well and are, therefore, likely to be the source of the most promising opportunities from which company analysis will be done? Such a procedure may produce some good results but with wide variance. There are many examples of industries performing at opposite ends of the scale from one period to the next. For example, using data for the S&P/TSX Indexes, information technology companies comprised the worst-performing industry in 2002, with a loss of 59.0 percent. However, in 2003, information technology was the best-performing industry category, with a return of 59.3 percent. Similarly, Energy provided the highest industry return of 61.3 percent in 2005, but the third lowest in 2006 at 3.2 percent, well below the S&P/TSX Composite Index return of 17.3 percent.

Table 16-2 shows the average annual returns and standard deviations for the 10 largest industries in the TSE 300 as of 1996, over the 1973–96 period. This table demonstrates some expected results. For example, we notice that the standard deviation for golds is higher than for the other industries, while other resource-based industries such as oil and gas, integrated oils, paper and forest, and mines also display high volatility in returns. On the other hand, returns to banks have been less volatile, while telephone utilities, as one would expect, display very low return volatility, relative to the other industries.

Table 16-2

TSX Industry Average Annual Returns and Standard Deviations (1973–96)

Industry	Average Return (%)	Standard Deviation (%)
Banks	12.47	20.76
Golds	14.46	48.81
Oil & Gas	6.25	35.59
Mines	10.07	26.85
Telephone Utilities	13.51	14.57
Paper & Forest	9.91	28.82
Chemicals	11.00	25.28
Technology	12.34	28.90
Conglomerates	11.06	25.11
Integrated Oils	8.78	31.17

Source: Peter Gibson, "Chapter 14: Strategy," in Joe Kan, editor, *Handbook of Canadian Security Analysis* (Toronto: John Wiley & Sons Canada, 1997), pp. 537–644.

The lesson to be learned from this discussion is simple: Industry analysis pays because industries perform very differently over time, and investor performance will be significantly affected by the particular industries in which investors select stocks. Investors seek to identify the growing industries of the future, and avoid those industries that are in decline. Industry rankings on some periodic basis (e.g., yearly or quarterly) are not consistent. Investors cannot simply choose those industries that have performed well recently and reliably expect them to continue to do so for the next several periods. While some continuation in performance occurs, so do surprises.

Perhaps just as important, investors should not ignore industries simply because their recent performance has been poor. Their subsequent performance over relatively short periods of time may be, and often is, at the opposite extreme! It is necessary, therefore, to learn the basic concepts of industry analysis. Before we consider these concepts, let us first define exactly what an industry is.

CHECK YOUR UNDERSTANDING

16-1. How important is industry analysis to investors?

16-2. What factors need to be considered when analyzing an industry?

WHAT IS AN INDUSTRY?

At first glance, the term industry may seem self-explanatory. After all, everyone is familiar with the auto industry, the drug industry, and the electric utility industry. But are these classifications as clear-cut as they seem? For example, a consumer can drink beer out of glass containers, aluminum cans, or steel cans. Does this involve one industry, containers, or three—the glass, aluminum, and steel industries (or perhaps two: glass and metals)? The problem becomes even messier because many companies are diversified along several lines of business.

The message is clear. In many cases, industries cannot be casually identified and classified. It seems safe to assert that industries have been, and will continue to become, more mixed in their activities and less identifiable with one product or service. This implies that we must be cautious in our comparisons of companies within a particular industry, since they will often be very different in their underlying nature. Making comparisons across industry groups is also often very difficult, particularly in Canada. This is because many industries are dominated by a few companies.

Classifying Industries

learning objective 2
Explain how industries
are classified.

Regardless of the problems, it is important for analysts and investors to classify industries since company profitability is a function of industry structure and the product that the industry sells. Industry structure results from strategies that companies pursue relative to their competition. Standard & Poor's breaks the S&P/TSX Composite Index into 10 major industry groups, although it should be noted that in Canada several of the industry groups, such as Health Care and Information Technology, are dominated by a few companies.

S&P has been using this system since March of 2002, which is known as the Global Industry Classification Standard (GICS). The objective is to provide "one complete, continuous set of global sector and industry definitions." This system divides everything into 10 economic sectors: Energy, Financials, Information Technology, Consumer Discretionary, Consumer Staples, Health Care, Industrials, Materials, Telecommunications Services, and Utilities. Within the S&P 10-sector framework, there are 23 industry groupings, 59 industries, and 122 sub-industries.

The new S&P system was developed jointly with Morgan Stanley Capital International and provides considerably more detail than S&P's previous classification system. This allows users to more readily customize portfolios and indexes. It is intended to classify companies around the world, and already includes over 25,000 companies.

Standard Industrial Classification (SIC) System

A classification of firms on the basis of what they produce, according to standardized five-digit codes.

One well-known and widely used system for classifying industries is the **Standard Industrial Classification (SIC) System**, which was developed to classify firms on the basis of what they produce. SIC codes have 11 divisions, designated A through K. For example, agriculture-forestry-fishing is industry division A, mining is B, retail trade is G, and K, the last group, is non-classifiable establishments. Within each of these divisions are several major industry groups, designated by a two-digit code. The primary metal industries, for example, are a part of division D, manufacturing, and are assigned the two-digit code 33.

The major industry groups within each division are further subdivided into three-, four-, and five-digit SIC codes to provide more detailed classifications. A specific industry is assigned a three-digit code, as are entire companies.[2] Plants carrying out specific functions (such as producing steel) are assigned four-digit SIC codes. A five-digit code indicates a specific product. Thus, the larger the number of digits in the SIC system, the more specific the breakdown.

SIC codes provide a consistent basis for describing industries and companies. Analysts can use SIC codes to focus on economic activity as broad, or as specific, a manner as desired. Nevertheless, the SIC system has been criticized for not being able to handle rapid changes in the US economy. This led to the development of the North American Industry Classification System (NAICS), which replaced the SIC codes in 1997.

The North American Industry Classification System (NAICS) is a significant change for analyzing economic activities. It was developed using a production-oriented conceptual framework; therefore, companies are classified into industries based on the activity in which they are primarily engaged. Basically, companies that do similar things in similar ways are classified together.

NAICS uses a six-digit hierarchical coding system to classify all economic activity into 20 industry sectors, which provides greater flexibility relative to SIC codes. Fifteen of these sectors are devoted to services-producing sectors, compared to five sectors that are mainly goods-producing sectors. NAICS allows for the identification of 1,170 industries. Nine new service sectors and 250 new service industries are recognized.

---

[2]Companies involved in several lines of activity are assigned multiple SIC codes.

Other sources of information use different numbers of industries in presenting data. The important point to remember is that no one industry classification system is widely used in the standard investment publications.

ANALYZING INDUSTRIES

learning objective 3
Analyze the life cycle and qualitative factors that affect industries.

Similar to markets and companies, industries can be analyzed through the study of a wide range of data, including sales, earnings, dividends, capital structure, product lines, regulations, innovations, and so on. Such analysis requires considerable expertise and is usually performed by industry analysts employed by brokerage firms and other institutional investors.

A useful first step is to analyze industries in terms of their stage in the life cycle. The idea is to assess the general health and current position of the industry. A second step involves a qualitative analysis of industry characteristics designed to assist investors in assessing the future prospects for an industry. Each of these steps is examined in turn.

The Industry Life Cycle

Many observers believe that industries evolve through four stages: the pioneering stage, the expansion stage, the stabilization stage, and the declining stage. There is an obvious parallel in this idea to human development. The concept of an **industry life cycle** could apply to industries or product lines within industries. The industry life cycle concept is depicted in Figure 16-1, and each stage is discussed in the following section.

Industry Life Cycle
The stages of an industry's evolution from pioneering to growth, stabilization, and decline.

Figure 16-1
The Industry Life Cycle

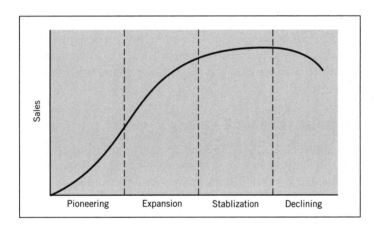

Pioneering Stage

In the pioneering stage, rapid growth in demand occurs. Although a number of companies within a growing industry will fail at this stage because they will not survive the competitive pressures, many will experience rapid growth in sales and earnings, possibly at an increasing rate. The opportunities available may attract a number of companies, as well as venture capital. Considerable jockeying for position occurs as the companies battle each other for survival, with the weaker firms failing and dropping out. Investor risk in an unproven company is high, but so are expected returns if the company succeeds. At the pioneering stage of an industry, it can be difficult for security analysts to identify the likely survivors, never mind future strong performers. By the time the real winners become apparent, the price of their stock will probably have been bid up considerably beyond what they were in the earlier stages of development.

Expansion Stage

In the second period of an industry's life cycle, the expansion stage, the survivors from the pioneering stage are identifiable. They continue to grow and prosper, but at a more moderate rate. At the expansion stage of the cycle, industries are improving their products and perhaps lowering their prices. They are more stable and solid, and at this stage they often attract considerable investment capital. Investors are more willing to invest in these industries now that their potential has been demonstrated and the risk of failure has decreased.

Financial policies become firmly established at this stage. The capital base is widened and strengthened. Companies are often able to pay dividends, further enhancing their attractiveness to a number of investors.

Stabilization Stage

Third, industries evolve into the stabilization (or maturity) stage, at which point the growth begins to moderate. Sales may still be increasing but at a much slower rate than before. Products become more standardized and less innovative, the marketplace is full of competitors, and costs are stable rather than decreasing through efficiency, for example. Industries at this stage continue to move along but without significant growth. Stagnation may occur for considerable periods of time or intermittently.

Declining Stage

Finally, an industry's sales growth can decline as new products are developed and shifts in demand occur. Think of the industry for home radios and black-and-white televisions. Some firms in an industry experiencing decline face significantly lower profits or even losses. Rates of return on invested capital will tend to be low.

Assessing the Industry Life Cycle

This four-part classification of industry evolvement helps investors to assess the growth potential of different companies in an industry. Based on the stage of the industry, they can better assess the potential of different companies within it. However, there are limitations to this type of analysis. First, it is only a generalization, and investors must be careful not to attempt to categorize every industry, or all companies within a particular industry, into neat categories that may not apply. Second, even the general framework may not apply to some industries that are not categorized by many small companies struggling for survival. Finally, the bottom line in security analysis is stock prices, a function of the expected stream of benefits and the risk involved.

The industrial life cycle tends to focus on sales and share of the market and investment in the industry. Although these factors are important to investors, they are not the final items of interest. Given these qualifications to industry life cycle analysis, what are the implications for investors?

The pioneering stage may offer the highest potential returns, but it also poses the greatest risk because many companies in a particular industry will fail or do poorly. Such risk may be appropriate for some investors, but many will wish to avoid it.

Investors interested primarily in capital gains should avoid the maturity stage. Companies at this stage may have relatively high dividend payouts because they have fewer growth prospects. On the other hand, these companies often offer stability in earnings and dividend growth.

It is the second stage—expansion—that is probably of most interest to investors. Industries that have survived the pioneering stage often offer good opportunities, since the demand for their products and services is growing more rapidly than the economy as a whole. Growth is rapid but orderly, an appealing characteristic to investors.

Whether decline is seen in relative or absolute terms, clearly, investors should seek to spot and avoid industries in this stage. In the years to come, with the rapid growth of technology, certain industrial sectors will decline. (In some cases, this decline has already started.)

Qualitative Aspects of Industry Analysis

The analyst or investor must consider several important qualitative factors that can help investors to analyze a particular industry and aid in assessing its future prospects. The four crucial factors examined below are (1) historical performance, (2) competition, (3) government effects, and (4) structural changes.

1. *Historical Performance.* As we have seen, some industries perform well and others poorly over both long and short periods of time. Although performance is not always consistent and predictable on the basis of the past, an industry's track record cannot be ignored.

    Investors should consider the historical record of sales and earnings growth and price performance. Although the past cannot simply be extrapolated into the future, it does provide some useful information.

2. *Competition.* The nature of the competitive conditions existing in an industry can provide useful information in assessing its future. Is the industry protected from the entrance of new competitors as a result of control of raw materials, prohibitive cost of building plants, the level of production needed to operate profitably, and so forth?

    Michael Porter has written extensively on the issue of competitive strategy, which involves the search for a competitive position in an industry. The intensity of competition in an industry determines that industry's ability to sustain above-average returns.[3] This intensity is not a matter of luck but rather a reflection of underlying factors that determine the strength of five basic competitive factors:

    i. Threat of new entrants
    ii. Bargaining power of buyers
    iii. Rivalry among existing firms
    iv. Threat of substitute products or services
    v. Bargaining power of suppliers

    These five competitive forces are shown as a diagram in Figure 16-2. Because the strength of these five factors varies across industries (and can change over time), industries vary from the standpoint of inherent profitability.

    These five competitive forces determine industry profitability because they influence the components of return on investment. The strength of each of these factors is a function of industry structure. The important elements of industry structure are shown in Figure 16-2. This figure shows all the elements of industry structure that affect competition within an industry.

    The central point of the Porter analysis is that industry profitability is a function of industry structure. Investors must analyze industry structure to assess the strength of the five competitive forces, which, in turn, determine industry profitability.

3. *Government Effects.* Government regulations and actions can have significant effects on industries. The investor must attempt to assess the results of these effects or, at the very least, be well aware that they exist and may continue.

---

[3]M. Porter, "Industry Structure and Competitive Strategy: Keys to Profitability," *Financial Analysts Journal* 36 (July–August 1980), pp. 30–41. *See also* M. Porter, *Competitive Advantage: Creating and Sustaining Superior Performance* (New York: Free Press, 1985).

Figure 16-2
Competitive Forces and
Industry Profitability

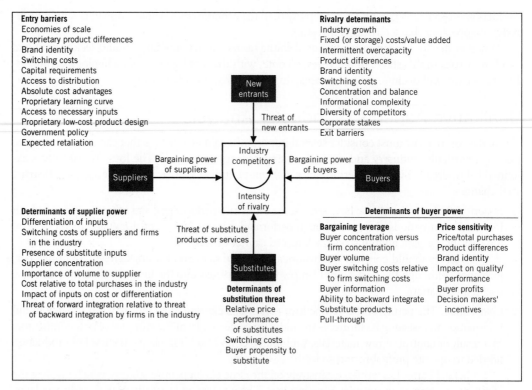

Reprinted with permission from the Free Press, a Division of Simon & Schuster Inc. from *Competitive Advantage: Creating and Sustaining Superior Performance* by Michael E. Porter. Copyright © 1985, 1998 by Michael E. Porter.

Consider the deregulation of the long distance telephone service industry in Canada. This action has changed the Canadian telecommunications industry permanently, and perhaps others as well. As a second example, consider the deregulating of the financial services industries, which allowed banks to own subsidiaries in the securities industry. This has resulted in most of the major securities firms now being wholly owned subsidiaries of the major banks. In December of 1998, the government made a major decision by rejecting the proposed mergers between the Royal Bank of Canada and the Bank of Montreal, and between the Canadian Imperial Bank of Commerce and the Toronto Dominion Bank. Had these mergers been approved, it would have changed the face of the banking industry in Canada as we have come to know it over the past few decades. This debate continues today.

4. *Structural Changes.* A fourth factor to consider is the structural changes that occur in the economy. As Canada continues to move from an industrial society to an information-communications one, major industries will be affected. New enterprises with tremendous potential are, and will be, emerging, whereas some traditional industries, such as steel, may never recover to their former positions.

Structural shifts can occur even within relatively new industries. For example, in the early 1980s, the microcomputer industry was a young, dynamic industry with numerous competitors, some of whom enjoyed phenomenal success in a short time. The introduction of the personal computer by IBM in 1982, however, forever changed that industry. Other hardware manufacturers sought to be compatible with IBM's PC, and suppliers rushed to deliver items such as software, printers, and additional memory boards. IBM's decision to enter this market affected virtually every part of the industry to a significant degree.

Industry Rotation

Industry rotation is an investment strategy that shifts portfolio weights in various industries in order to achieve improved results. The strategy can be profitable if one can successfully predict turning points in economic cycles and their impact on the security prices of various industries.

Industry rotation is concerned with trying to outperform market averages such as the S&P/TSX Composite Index. For example, during the late stages of a recessionary period, bank stocks may recover first in response to declining interest rates. Consumer stocks would improve shortly thereafter, while other industries such as durable goods producers would benefit in the later stages of economic recovery. Successfully shifting between these groups can produce above average results, although it is not as easy as it sounds (as the discussion in this chapter makes clear).

The most basic industry rotation strategy involves shifting back and forth between cyclical and defensive industries. During periods of declining prices, cyclical stocks tend to fall faster, and during times of rising prices, they tend to increase at a more rapid pace. Another strategy is to move in and out of interest rate sensitive industries in response to interest rate forecasts.

Variations in the economic cycle often have a dramatic effect on the timing of industry rotation. Generally, two-thirds of a new economic recovery is driven by increased consumer spending, which tends to precede increases in business spending. During such a period in a normal economic cycle, investors may focus on consumer growth, transportation, consumer cyclical, energy, and capital goods industries in that order.

CHECK YOUR UNDERSTANDING

16-3. What rapid economic changes likely encouraged the development of replacements for SIC codes to classify industries?

16-4. Why would an industry in an expansion phase be of most interest to investors when the pioneering stage tends to offer the highest potential returns?

EVALUATING FUTURE INDUSTRY PROSPECTS

learning objective 4
Evaluate future industry prospects by analyzing the business cycle.

Ultimately, investors are interested in expected performance in the future. They realize that such estimates are difficult to make and are likely to be somewhat in error, but they also know that equity prices are a function of expected parameters and that estimates, therefore, are essential to the valuation process. How, then, is an investor to proceed?

Assessing Longer-Term Prospects

To forecast industry performance over the longer run, investors should ask the following two questions:

1. Which industries are obvious candidates for growth and prosperity over, say, the next decade? (In the early 1980s, such industries as microcomputers, software, telecommunications, and cellular telephones could have been identified; in the early 1990s, it was software and technology firms; in the late 1990s, investors focused a great deal of attention on Internet companies and high technology firms.) In recent years, mining and resource companies have benefited from rising gold and oil prices.

2. Which industries appear likely to have difficulties as Canada changes from an industrial to an information-collecting and -processing economy?

Picking Industries for Next Year

On a shorter-run basis, investors would like to value industries along the lines discussed in Chapter 15 for the market. They would like to be able to estimate the expected earnings for an industry and the expected multiplier, and combine them to produce an estimate of value. However, this is not easy to do. It requires an understanding of several relationships and estimates of several variables. Fortunately, considerable information is readily available to help investors in their analysis of industries. For example, Real-World Returns 16-2 alludes to the importance to Canadian banks of maintaining steady growth in dividends.

REAL-WORLD RETURNS 16-2

Bank Dividends

Are bank dividend hikes drying up?

For years, Canada's banks raked in ever-increasing profits, which they shovelled back to shareholders in the form of rising dividends. Royal Bank of Canada, the largest of the Big Five, raised its dividend at a sizzling 20-percent pace over the past five years. Bank of Montreal, the fifth-biggest bank by market value, raised its dividend by about 18 percent annually.

But suddenly, banks aren't in such a hurry to share the wealth with investors. That's because, with the credit crisis hammering their earnings and the economy in a downward spiral, there's less wealth to share. And it may get worse before it gets better.

Yesterday, after warning it will miss its 2008 profit targets, Bank of Montreal left its quarterly dividend unchanged at 70 cents a share, the third consecutive quarter at the same rate. That broke with its well-established pattern over the past four years, when it raised its dividend at least once every two quarters.

BMO isn't the only bank putting dividend hikes on hold.

Last week, RBC also held its payout steady after first-quarter profit tumbled 17 percent, the first time since 2004 that it went more than two quarters without a hike. As expected, Canadian Imperial Bank of Commerce and Bank of Nova Scotia also didn't raise their dividends.

The only bank to raise its dividend was Toronto-Dominion Bank, which declared a token 2-cent increase.

By forgoing dividend increases, "banks are giving you a message that things are not as good, and that paying out a higher dividend is not the best use of their money right now," said Norman Levine, managing director Portfolio Management Corp., which holds BMO and National Bank of Canada shares.

"In the long run, the Canadian banks are probably your best ... investment in Canada. However, they do go through periods where they're awful, and this is one of those periods," he said.

If the banks are indeed heading into a period of stagnant dividend growth, it wouldn't be the first time. During the recessions of the early 1980s and early 1990s, some banks went for years without raising their payouts. RBC's annual dividend didn't budge from 1982 to 1986, or from 1991 to 1994. And in the 10 years from 1983 to 1992, BMO raised its dividend only twice.

That serves as a reminder to investors that the juicy dividend hikes of recent years aren't necessarily the norm.

David Cockfield, fund manager at Leon Frazer & Associates, remembers the early 1990s when trust companies were imploding because of soured real estate loans and people were worried that one or more of the banks could also bite the dust.

This downturn is relatively mild in comparison, but he thinks it could be up to a year before banks start increasing their dividends again.

"What the lack of increases is telling us is that, looking ahead, the banks are not seeing earnings growing the same way they have over the last five or six years. We're looking at a period of flat to down earnings," he said.

The last thing a bank wants to do is boost its dividend too high, only to find out that its payout ratio—dividends divided by profit—has exceeded the bank's internal target. That could force the bank to cut its dividend to bring the ratio back into line, Mr. Cockfield said.

Bank dividend cuts are rare in Canada, but several US financial institutions, including Citigroup and Washington Mutual, have slashed their payouts because of the subprime loan debacle. According to Standard & Poor's, the number of companies that decreased their payouts in January and February rose to 24, up from eight in the same period a year earlier. That's out of about 7,000 North American-listed companies that report dividends to S & P.

On a brighter note, 382 companies raised their dividends, although that was down from 445 in January and February of 2007.

Source: Heinzl, John, "Don't bank on more payout hikes soon," *The Globe and Mail*, March 5, 2008, p. B14.

To determine industry performance for shorter periods of time (e.g., one year), investors should ask themselves the following question: Given the current and prospective economic situation, which industries are likely to show improving earnings? In many respects, this is the key question for industry security analysis. The investment advisory services provided by Canadian securities firms and banks provide such information on a timely basis. Alternatively, investors can turn to the Institutional Brokers Estimate System (IBES) International and Zack's Investment Research. Both of these entities compile institutional brokerage earnings estimates as well as revisions that occur throughout the year.

Given the importance of earnings and the availability of earnings estimates for industries and companies, are investors able to make relatively easy investment choices? The answer is no, because earnings estimates are notoriously inaccurate. For example, there is a great deal of evidence that analysts tend to be overly optimistic on average. Supporting studies include those by O'Brien and by DeBondt and Thaler in the US, as well as Canadian evidence documented by Hennessey and by Ackert and Athanassakos.[4]

Dreman reports on a study of 61 industries for a 17-year period. Three-quarters of all estimates within industries missed reported earnings by 30 percent or more, and 15 percent showed errors of 80 percent or more. The average forecast error grouped by industries was 50 percent (median error of 43 percent). Only 16 of the 61 industries over the 17 years showed forecast errors of 29 percent or less.[5] These results highlight the point made earlier—even for well-informed and knowledgeable individuals, it is difficult to predict the future performance of industries.

Of course, investors must also consider the likely P/E ratios for industries. Which industries are likely to show improving P/E ratios? Dreman has also tackled the question of whether investors pay too much for favoured companies in an industry. Buying the lowest 20 percent of P/Es in each of 44 industry groups over 25 years (based on the 1,500 largest companies rated by market capitalization in the Compustat database, which contains comprehensive financial data for several thousand US and several hundred Canadian companies) produced an average annual return of 18 percent, compared to 12.4

[4] P. O'Brien, "Analysts' Forecasts as Earnings Expectation," *Journal of Accounting and Economics* 10 (January 1988), pp. 53–83; W. DeBondt and R. Thaler, "Do Security Analysts Overreact?" *American Economic Review* 80 (May 1990), pp. 52–57; S. Hennessey, "Can Active Managers Profit from Earnings Forecast Revisions?" *Canadian Investment Review* 6 (Spring 1993), pp. 39–45; L. Ackert and G. Athanassakos, "Expectations of the Herd," *Canadian Investment Review* 9 (Winter 1996/97), pp. 7–11.
[5] D. Dreman, "Cloudy Crystal Balls," *Forbes*, October 10, 1994, p. 154.

percent for the highest 20 percent P/E group. Dreman also found that buying the lowest P/E stocks across industries produced smaller losses when the market is down relative to the market as a whole and to the highest P/E group.[6]

Other questions to consider are the likely direction of interest rates and which industries would be most affected by a significant change in them. A change in interest rates, other things being equal, leads to a change in the discount rate (and a change in the multiplier). Which industries are likely to be most affected by possible future political events, such as a new federal or provincial government, tax cuts, a vote by Quebec to separate from Canada, and so on?

As with all security analysis, we can use several procedures in analyzing industries. Much of this process is common sense. For example, if you can reasonably forecast a declining number of competitors in an industry, it stands to reason that the remaining firms will be more profitable, other things being equal.

Business Cycle Analysis

A useful procedure for investors to assess industry prospects is to analyze industries by their operating ability in relation to the economy as a whole. That is, some industries perform poorly during a recession, whereas others are able to weather it reasonably well. Some industries move closely with the business cycle, performing better than average in good times and underperforming in bad times. Investors, in analyzing industries, should be aware of these relationships.

Growth Industries
Industries with expected earnings growth significantly above average.

Most investors know about, and are usually looking for, growth companies. In **growth industries**, earnings are expected to grow significantly faster than the average of all industries, and such growth may occur regardless of setbacks in the economy. Growth industries in the 1980s included genetic engineering, microcomputers, and new medical devices. Current growth industries include cellular telephones and Internet companies. Clearly, one of the primary goals of fundamental security analysis is to identify the growth industries of the near and far future.

Growth stocks suffer much less during a recession, such as in 1990, than do the cyclical stocks (explained below). For example, US growth stocks gained 2.5 percent in 1990 while cyclicals lost about 20 percent.

Defensive Industries
Industries least affected by recessions and economic adversity.

At the opposite end of the scale are the **defensive industries**—those that are least affected by recessions and economic adversity. Food has long been considered such an industry. People must eat regardless of the economy. Public utilities would also be considered a defensive industry since they are necessities, and their profits remain relatively stable throughout the business cycle.

Cyclical Industries
Industries most affected, both up and down, by the business cycle.

Cyclical industries are the most volatile—they do unusually well when the economy prospers but are likely to be hurt more when the economy falters. Durable goods are a good example of the products involved in cyclical industries. Automobiles, refrigerators, and stereos, for example, may be avidly sought when times are good, but such purchases may be postponed during a recession because consumers can often make do with the old units.

Cyclicals are said to be "bought to be sold"—that is, investors dump them when the economy turns down. Many professionals advise investors to pursue cyclical industries when the prices of companies in the industry are low, relative to the historical record, and P/Es are high. This seems counterintuitive to many investors, but the rationale is that earnings are severely depressed in a recession and therefore the P/E is high, and this may occur shortly before earnings turn around.

Most S&P/TSX cyclical companies are large international exporters of commodities such as lumber, nickel, copper, and oil. Commodity-based cyclicals include industries such as forestry products, mining, and chemicals. Industrial cyclicals include transportation, capital goods, and basic industries (steel, building materials), while consumer cyclicals include merchandising companies and automobiles.

Countercyclical industries also exist, actually moving opposite to the prevailing economic trend. For example, the gold mining industry has followed this pattern during several periods in the past—rising in price during economic recessions and declining during boom times.

[6]D. Dreman, "A New Approach to Low-P/E Investing," *Forbes*, September 23, 1996, p. 241.

As a rule, the return on equity (ROE) of cyclical industries would vary by at least 100 percent over a complete business cycle, compared to one-third for defensive industries, and 55 percent for the S&P/TSX Index as a whole. The S&P/TSX Index contains a high proportion of deeply cyclical companies based on market capitalization.

These classifications of industries according to economic conditions do not constitute an exhaustive set. For example, people often refer to blue chip stocks, such as IBM or Xerox, which are top investment quality companies that maintain earnings in good times and bad. Their record usually reflects a dominant market position, strong internal financing, and effective management. Another categorization refers to speculative industries, which are so called because there is a great deal of risk and uncertainty associated with them due to the absence of definitive information.

Another important industry classification is the identification of **interest-sensitive industries**, which are particularly sensitive to changes in interest rates. The financial services, banking, and real estate industries are obvious examples of interest-sensitive industries. Another is the construction industry.

The *Handbook of Canadian Security Analysis* classifies the TSX industries into three categories based on their sensitivity to interest rates and the cyclicality of profitability as measured by ROE, which are two of the key factors affecting equity performance. The categories include

1. High Economic Sensitivity (HES) industries

2. Low Economic Sensitivity (LES) industries

3. Emerging Economy (EE) industries

In Chapter 14 of the *Handbook*, Gibson examines industry returns for each TSE 300 industry between 1962 and 1996 and finds that no other fundamental factor contributed more to higher industry returns than falling interest rates. Every industry, regardless of their categorization, displayed higher returns during periods of falling interest rates.

Gibson's results are summarized on the following page in Table 16-3, which is taken from his discussion. He finds that on average, interest rates produce a greater effect on industry share prices than increases in profitability as measured by ROE. This is true for all 20 HES industries and for 11 of the 12 LES industries. On average, the LES industries produced a 3.97 percent higher return during periods of falling rates than during periods of rising ROE, while the comparable number for HES industries was 3.70 percent. What does all of this mean to investors? Obviously, it is desirable to purchase shares in an industry entering into an environment where ROE is increasing or interest rates are falling. It would be even more desirable to purchase shares when both of these events are occurring; however, such forecasting ability is extremely difficult and rare, according to empirical evidence discussed in Chapter 10.

What are the implications of these classifications for investors? To predict the performance of an industry over shorter periods of time, investors should carefully analyze the stage of the business cycle and the likely movements in interest rates. If the economy is heading into a recession, cyclical industries are likely to be affected more than others, whereas defensive industries are the least likely to be affected. With such guidelines, investors may make better buy or sell decisions. Similarly, an expected rise in interest rates will have negative implications for the financial services industry and the home building industry, whereas an expected drop in interest rates will have the opposite effect.

These statements reinforce the importance of market analysis. Not only do investors need to know the state of the economy and market before deciding to invest, but such knowledge is valuable in selecting (or avoiding) particular industries. Furthermore, investors need to consider the possibility of overcapacity as well as global competition.

We end this chapter by referring to Table 16-4, which is also taken from Chapter 14 of the *Handbook of Canadian Security Analysis*. It provides a brief

Interest-Sensitive Industries
Industries particularly sensitive to changes in interest rates, such as financial services, real estate, and the construction industries.

INVESTING *tip*

Clearly, business cycle analysis for industries is a logical and worthwhile part of fundamental security analysis. Industries have varying sensitivities to the business conditions and interest rate expectations at any given time, and the smart investor will think carefully about these factors.

overview of some of the key factors (most of which have been discussed here or in Chapter 15) affecting the profitability and common share performance of a variety of Canadian industries.

Table 16-3

TSE 300 Performance

Sector	Interest Rates		ROE		Relative ROE		Combinations			
	↓ Rates	↑ Rates	↓ ROE	↑ ROE	↓ Rel. ROE	↑ Rel. ROE	↑ ROE ↓ RATES	↓ ROE ↓ RATES	↑ ROE ↑ RATES	↓ ROE ↑ RATES
LOW ECONOMIC SENSITIVITY										
Defensive & Interest Sensitive Utilities	%	%	%	%	%	%	%	%	%	%
Gas/Electrical Utilities	–	–	–	–	–	–	–	–	–	–
Pipelines	13.3	7.7	11.9	10.2	12.4	9.2	10.8	12.7	8.8	9.1
Financials										
Banks & Trusts	17.3	9.8	14.6	12.3	11.3	14.9	13.7	15.8	10.9	11.1
Investment Cos. & Funds	18.2	8.6	18.9	8.7	17.8	9.0	14.9	15.6	7.1	13.8
Insurance	–	–	–	–	–	–	–	–	–	–
Financial Management	12.4	2.6	7.8	6.2	6.9	6.9	9.7	9.0	4.4	4.5
Consumer Staples										
Broadcasting	20.9	10.4	16.5	18.4	16.8	16.5	19.0	17.4	12.6	13.3
Cable & Entertainment	24.0	8.9	12.7	20.5	17.6	14.7	17.4	21.2	14.9	8.8
Food Processing	13.8	8.5	11.3	11.2	10.5	11.9	12.0	12.3	9.4	9.5
Food Stores	13.3	5.6	9.4	10.6	8.9	11.4	11.1	11.6	9.7	5.3
Tobacco	21.5	14.6	16.9	17.3	16.2	17.2	18.4	17.9	14.2	15.4
Distilleries	17.5	10.7	9.3	18.6	10.4	16.8	13.3	16.9	16.9	6.6
Breweries & Beverages	15.0	3.9	8.2	10.0	7.0	11.3	10.1	13.3	7.4	5.0
Communication Services										
Telephone Utilities	13.3	7.2	12.6	8.8	8.7	112.2	12.2	11.1	6.8	10.5
HIGH ECONOMIC SENSITIVITY										
Cyclicals & Profit Growth Sensitive										
Consumer Cyclicals	%	%	%	%	%	%	%	%	%	%
Department Stores	7.9	4.1	4.8	6.9	8.1	5.0	6.6	6.8	4.0	5.7
Specialty Stores	14.3	7.9	10.7	13.1	7.4	17.0	12.8	12.3	8.5	10.2
Household Goods	11.0	4.9	8.3	4.4	4.3	6.8	6.2	11.1	5.7	5.4
Publishing & Printing	21.3	10.2	18.5	14.0	15.5	16.3	17.4	18.3	11.0	13.7
Autos & Parts	26.2	5.6	15.1	18.7	14.5	18.9	18.8	18.6	13.2	11.8
Building Materials	17.4	6.6	9.2	13.6	11.9	10.3	14.0	13.8	9.4	7.6
Industrial Basic										
Transportation	14.6	11.9	9.5	13.5	11.0	11.8	12.8	9.4	12.8	12.0
Conglomerates	18.4	7.6	15.0	12.3	15.9	11.0	15.1	15.8	9.6	10.5
Industrial Capital Goods										
Wholesale Distributors	18.8	7.7	11.0	15.7	9.4	16.9	15.0	15.9	12.5	7.5
Hospitality	–	–	–	–	–	–	–	–	–	–
Transportation Equipment	15.4	5.1	6.4	14.8	6.0	8.8	12.3	12.2	12.8	2.4
Fabricating & Engineering	17.2	8.4	8.6	15.6	9.7	14.5	15.6	12.6	11.7	7.8
Real Estate	4.3	2.9	7.1	0.9	1.7	4.9	4.8	3.6	-0.5	7.7
Commodity Basic										
Integrated Mines	10.6	6.2	8.0	9.9	8.5	6.8	8.6	10.4	8.1	6.5
Mining	11.6	5.6	10.1	5.8	12.0	4.2	8.6	10.4	5.2	7.9
Paper & Forest Products	12.9	7.0	6.1	11.7	6.6	11.1	12.6	8.8	7.6	7.9
Steel	8.2	3.9	6.2	5.3	6.7	4.8	5.7	7.9	4.7	4.6
Chemicals & Fertilizers	14.0	6.8	10.1	7.8	11.0	6.8	10.0	12.5	8.1	7.3
Gold & Precious Minerals	20.8	10.8	12.8	15.1	16.2	11.9	15.1	18.4	12.0	11.6
Energy										
Integrated Oils	15.4	8.8	11.6	10.8	11.5	10.7	13.3	12.5	9.8	9.5
Oil & Gas Producers	13.6	6.5	9.9	9.9	12.9	5.7	9.6	13.2	10.3	5.4
EMERGING ECONOMY										
Technology — Hardware	21.0	9.5	18.4	10.2	14.3	13.6	16.3	17.4	8.3	14.1
Technology — Software	–	–	–	–	–	–	–	–	–	–
Biotechnology/Pharmaceuticals	–	–	–	–	–	–	–	–	–	–

Source: Peter Gibson, "Chapter 14: Strategy," in Joe Kan, editor, *Handbook of Canadian Security Analysis* (Toronto: John Wiley & Sons Canada, 1997), pp. 547–548.

Table 16-4

Key Macroeconomic and Microeconomic Factors Behind the Timing of Profit Cycles

LOW ECONOMIC SENSITIVITY		
Utilities	Pipelines Gas/Electric	1. Interest Rates 2. GDP growth and capital investment 3. Deregulation trends and regulatory environment 4. Franchise and non-franchise growth opportunities 5. Management quality
Financials	Banks	1. Long bond rates — relative valuation 2. Yield curve — borrow short, invest long 3. Competition — margins, consolidation 4. Earnings momentum and dividend growth 5. Growth in book value
	Insurance	1. GDP and wealth growth 2. Population growth 3. Savings rates 4. Disease/epidemics/natural disasters 5. Competitive environment
Consumer Staples	Broadcasting	1. Consumer confidence/spending 2. GDP and economic growth 3. Income growth — especially real wages 4. Advertising volumes 5. Digital technology evolution
	Food Stores	1. Food inflation 2. Demographics (geography) 3. Personal disposable income 4. New product development 5. Consumer confidence
Communication Services	Telephone/Utilities Communications	1. GDP growth 2. Household growth 3. Regulation, marketing effectiveness 4. Ten-year Canada bond yield 5. Technological developments
HIGH ECONOMIC SENSITIVITY		
Consumer Cyclical	Publishing/Printing	1. Consumer confidence/spending 2. GDP and employment growth 3. Income growth — especially real wages 4. Advertising volumes, expenses, paper, and labour 5. Digital technology evolution
	Auto & Retailing	1. Consumer confidence/spending 2. Personal disposable income 3. GDP and employment growth 4. Interest rates 5. Technology and auto outsourcing
Industrial Transportation	Airlines	1. Interest rates 2. Fuel costs 3. Consumer spending/confidence 4. Aircraft purchases 5. Load factors and price wars
	Trucking and Railroads	1. GDP growth 2. Fuel costs 3. Retail shipments 4. Industrial production 5. Commodity mix — grain
Industrial Basic & Capital Goods	Fabricating	1. Canadian capital investment 2. Secular growth of emerging markets 3. Size of firms

(continued)

Table 16-4 *continued*

		4. Private sector financing vehicles
		5. Access to multiple sources of credit
	Real Estate	1. Inflation expectations
		2. Interest rates and GDP growth
		3. Vacancy rates
		4. Building regulations
		5. Availability of funds
Commodity Basic (Specific Commodity Prices Important)	Metals & Minerals	1. OECD industrial production
		2. US dollar
		3. Inventories
		4. Capacity utilization
		5. Consumption
	Golds	1. Reserve growth
		2. Real interest rates
		3. International mining regulations
		4. New technology
		5. Personnel available
	Paper & Forest	1. Global GDP
		2. Real exchange rates
		3. Economic development and trade
		4. Inventory cycle
		5. Capacity additions, input costs
	Chemicals	1. GDP growth
		2. Technological breakthroughs
		3. Harvest quality/quantity
		4. Strategic advantages/disadvantages
		5. Product supply/demand
	Steel	1. GDP growth
		2. Auto sales
		3. Capacity utilization
		4. New capacity
		5. Changes in international cost position of steel markets
Energy	Oil & Gas	1. Exploration success
		2. Technological innovation
		3. Success/failure in production targets
		4. US dollar
		5. Marketing and refining margins
EMERGING ECONOMY		
Biotechnology Technology		1. Machine and equipment spending
		2. International GDP growth
		3. R&D investment and tax credits
		4. Component pricing
		5. Computer sales and consumer confidence

Source: Peter Gibson, "Chapter 14: Strategy," in Joe Kan, editor, *Handbook of Canadian Security Analysis* (Toronto: John Wiley & Sons Canada, 1997), pp. 605–606.

CHECK YOUR UNDERSTANDING

16-5. What two closely related factors are at the heart of business cycle analysis?

16-6. Suppose you found that cross-sectional volatility (the variation in returns) across various industries had been increasing over time. Would this make industry analysis more or less valuable to investors?

SUMMARY

This summary relates to the learning objectives for this chapter.

1. **State the importance of industry analysis.**

   Industry analysis is the second of three steps in a top-down framework of fundamental security analysis, between economy/market analysis and individual company analysis. The objective is to identify those industries that will perform best in the future in terms of returns to stockholders. Industry analysis is valuable because over the long term, some industries perform better than others. Industry performance is not consistent because past price performance does not always predict future price performance. Particularly over shorter periods such as one or two years, industry performance rankings often completely reverse themselves.

2. **Explain how industries are classified.**

   Although the term industry at first seems self-explanatory, definitions and classifications of it are not straightforward, and the trend toward diversification of activities over the years has blurred the lines even more. The S&P/TSX Composite Index classifies stocks into 14 major industry groups based on business activity. The Standard Industrial Classification (SIC) system is a comprehensive scheme for classifying major industry groups, specific industries, specific functions, and specific products.

3. **Analyze the life cycle and qualitative factors that affect industries.**

   To analyze industries, a useful first step is to examine their stage in the life cycle, which in its simplest form consists of the pioneering, expansion, and maturity stages. Most investors will usually be interested in the expansion stage, in which growth is rapid and risk is tolerable. Investors also need to consider qualitative aspects such as historical performance, competition, government effects, and structural changes.

4. **Evaluate future industry prospects by analyzing the business cycle.**

   A second industry analysis approach involves business cycle analysis, since the performance of different industries varies substantially throughout the stages of the business cycle. Investors interested in evaluating future industry prospects have a wide range of data available for their use. These data can be used for a detailed, in-depth analysis of industries using standard security analysis techniques for examining recent ratings of industry performance or for ranking likely industry performance.

KEY TERMS

Cyclical industries, p.526
Defensive industries, p.526
Growth industries, p.526

Industry life cycle, p.519
Interest-sensitive industries, p.527

Standard Industrial Classification (SIC) System, p.518

REVIEW QUESTIONS

16-1. Why is it difficult to classify industries?

16-2. Why is the NAICS coding system said to be superior to the SIC system?

16-3. How consistent is year-to-year industry performance?

16-4. What are the stages in the life cycle of an industry? Can you think of other stages to add?

16-5. Name one industry in each of the three life cycle stages today.

16-6. During which stage of the industry life cycle do investors face the highest risk of losing a substantial part of the investment?

16-7. Name the 14 industry groups that are distinguished within the S&P/TSX Composite Index.

16-8. Why is industry analysis valuable?

16-9. Name some industries that you would expect to perform well in the next five years and in the next 10 to 15 years.

16-10. Which industries are the most sensitive to the business cycle? The least sensitive?

16-11. Explain how aggregate market analysis can be important in analyzing industries in relation to the business cycle.

16-12. Explain the concept used in valuing industries.

16-13. Explain how Figure 16-1 might be useful to an investor doing industry analysis.

16-14.   a. Name and briefly describe the five factors described by Porter that affect industry competitiveness.

   b. Why is it important to use the Porter analysis?

16-15. The important point of the Porter analysis is that industry structure is a function of industry profitability. Agree or disagree with this statement.

16-16. Industry analysis is important because

   a. companies can only do as well as their industry.
   b. industries often have an inverse relationship to the market.
   c. industries perform very differently over time.
   d. companies in declining industries lose money.

16-17. Which life cycle stage generally sees industries improving their products, lowering prices, and starting to attract considerable investment funds?

   a. Pioneering stage
   b. Expansion stage
   c. Stabilization stage
   d. Maturity stage

PREPARING FOR YOUR PROFESSIONAL EXAMS

CFA PRACTICE QUESTIONS

16-1. All of the following statements are true about Porter's five factors except:
   a. Rivalry increases when many firms of relatively equal size compete within an industry.
   b. New entrants to an industry means increased competition.
   c. The presence of substitute products limits the profit potential of an industry.
   d. Profitability is enhanced by increases in the bargaining power of buyers and suppliers to an industry.

16-2. Which of the following statements about industry lifecycles is false?
   a. In the stabilization phase, profit margins tighten and returns on equity approach normality.
   b. In the rapid growth phase, the sales growth rate is high but profit margins are low.
   c. The creation of a new industry is generally brought about by a technological breakthrough.
   d. The industry life cycle refers to the regular pattern of growth, maturity, and decay experienced by most new industries.

CFA CURRICULUM AND SAMPLE EXAM QUESTIONS (©CFA INSTITUTE)

16-1. Industry life cycles are typically categorized by the:

    a. level of competition.
    b. rates of growth in sales.
    c. level of productive capacity.
    d. rates of growth in return on equity.

CHAPTER 17

COMPANY ANALYSIS

The last step in your bid to understand how investors go about doing security analysis is to consider individual companies. You have believed from the outset of your quest to gain some investing knowledge that you will want to own some individual stocks regardless of whether you also plan to hold index funds and ETFs. After all, you have heard several stories about individuals who owned stocks that doubled, tripled, or did even better. And what little you have heard when investors or TV programs discuss stocks has often involved earnings, so you figure this must be important. Finally, you wish to be able to understand what all the fuss is about when it comes to earnings guidance, earnings surprises, and earnings disappointments. While this is more challenging, you can become comfortable with these concepts.

Learning Objectives

After reading this chapter, you should be able to

1. Define fundamental analysis at the company level.
2. Explain the accounting aspects of a company's earnings.
3. Describe the importance of EPS forecasts.
4. Estimate the P/E ratio of a company.
5. Use the beta coefficient to estimate the risk of a stock.

CHAPTER PREVIEW

In this chapter, we consider the third and final step in top-down fundamental analysis: company analysis. Using the valuation framework outlined in Chapter 13, we use earnings per share (EPS) and the price-earnings (P/E) ratio to determine if the stock price for a company is undervalued or overvalued. We touch on the accounting aspects of EPS, examine the impact of earnings announcements and surprises on stock prices, and consider how practising analysts carry out fundamental security analysis. At the end of the chapter, we bring all the pieces together in an analysis of **Empire Company Limited**.

FUNDAMENTAL ANALYSIS

learning objective 1
Define fundamental analysis at the company level.

Once analysis of the economy and the market has indicated a favourable time to invest in common stocks and industry analysis has been performed to find those industries that are expected to perform well in the future, it remains for the investor to choose promising companies within those industries. The last step in top-down fundamental analysis, therefore, is to analyze individual companies. As with the previous two steps, an investor should think in terms of the two components of fundamental value: dividends and required rate of return or, alternatively, earnings and the P/E ratio, and analyze them to the extent practical using the valuation framework presented in Chapter 13.

Fundamental analysis at the company level involves analyzing basic financial variables in order to estimate the company's intrinsic value. These variables include sales, profit margins, depreciation, the tax rate, sources of financing, asset utilization, and other factors. Additional analysis could involve the firm's competitive position in its industry, labour relations, technological changes, management, foreign competition, and so on. The end result of fundamental analysis at the company level is the data needed to calculate the estimated or intrinsic value of a stock using one or more valuation models.

As discussed in Chapter 13, investors can use the dividend discount model (DDM) to value common stocks for companies that maintain relatively stable dividend payments. In some circumstances, it is reasonable to assume that the dividend growth rate for a particular company will be approximately constant over the future, which allows us to use the constant-growth version of the DDM shown as Equation 17-1 (Equation 13-5 from Chapter 13):

(17-1)

$$\text{Intrinsic value} = \hat{P}_0 = \frac{D_1}{k - g}$$

where
$\hat{P}_0$ = the estimated value of the common stock today
D_1 = the expected dollar dividend to be paid next period
k = the required rate of return
g = the estimated future growth rate of dividends expected to continue indefinitely

In fundamental analysis, the intrinsic or estimated value of a stock is its justified price, the price justified by a company's fundamental financial variables.

Alternatively, the earnings multiplier model could be used. Intrinsic value is the product of the estimated earnings per share (EPS) for next year and the multiplier or forward P/E ratio (P_0 / E_1), as shown in Equation 17-2.[1]

(17-2)

$$\text{Intrinsic value} = \hat{P}_0 = \text{Estimated EPS} \times P_0 / E_1 \text{ ratio}$$

$$= E_1 \times P/E$$

---

[1]Technically, to calculate the intrinsic value of a stock using the multiplier method, analysts often determine what is called the normalized EPS, defined as the normal earnings for a company under typical operating conditions. This adjusts for unusual impacts on earnings such as non-recurring or extraordinary earnings.

Using either Equation 17-1 or Equation 17-2, we can compare a stock's calculated intrinsic value to its current market price. If the intrinsic value is larger than the current market price, the stock can be considered undervalued—a buy. If intrinsic value is less than the market price, the stock is considered overvalued and should be sold if owned, and avoided or sold short if not owned.

For purposes of discussion, we concentrate on earnings and P/E ratios for several reasons. First, dividends are paid from earnings. Although the two series are not perfectly correlated, future dividend growth typically must come from future earnings growth. Second, the close correlation between earnings changes and stock-price changes is well documented. The discussion in Real-World Returns 17-1 alludes to the importance of earnings expectations in the valuation process, suggesting that the P/E ratios prevailing in March of 2008 can be attributed to "shaky" earnings forecasts. The article also alludes to the roles played by inflation and interest rates in determining stock prices.

REAL-WORLD RETURNS 17-1

Stocks May Not Be as Cheap as They Seem

With the US economy showing clear signs of recession and the credit markets in turmoil, the floor under stock prices seems to be getting thinner. Here is another reason to worry: Stock prices aren't as cheap as they seem and, based on other periods when inflation was accelerating and the economy weak, the market can struggle for prolonged periods.

Some argue stocks are attractively priced after a 17-percent decline in the Standard & Poor's 500-stock index since October. Based on earnings forecasts for 2008 collected by Reuters Estimates, the S & P 500 is trading at 13.2 times projected earnings, compared with an average of 16.5 times going back to 1989, according to data compiled by Morgan Stanley.

Price-to-earnings ratios reflect the amount investors are willing to pay for future earnings. When these ratios fall below long-term trends, conventional wisdom is stocks are cheap and it's time to buy.

Until 2000, investors feasted on the combination of rising P/E ratios and rising stock prices. At the end of the 1980-1982 bear market, S & P stocks changed hands at a price-to-earnings ratio of 8.7, according to Morgan Stanley's data.

In the next 17 years the ratio moved higher, topping out just shy of 30 in the spring of 1999. During this time, when the S & P rose an average of about 17 percent a year, roughly one-third of returns on the S & P 500 were the result of rising P/E multiples, according to Ibbotson Associates.

That period also featured a long downtrend in inflation and interest rates, which generally lead directly to higher multiples. Now, inflation is quickening and interest rates, while heading down, can't fall much further. This suggests an environment less conducive to rising stock multiples.

That was the case in the most recent bull market, when price-to-earnings multiples actually fell even as the market rose. When the bull market began in early October, 2002, the S & P 500 had finished the previous month at a P/E ratio of 17.6 when measured against the previous 12 months earnings. This past September, just before the market began its descent, the ratio was 16.8.

It is a similar story when looking at expected earnings, the basis on which stocks currently look particularly cheap. At the end of September, 2002, the S & P 500 was priced at 14.5 times the coming 12 months expected earnings, according to Morgan Stanley. This past September, after a five-year run in which the S & P 500 rose an average of more than 15 percent a year, the P/E on the index was 14.8 times the coming year's expected earnings.

"The growth in stock returns came mostly from earnings growth," says Peng Chen, chief investment officer at Ibbotson Associates.

Morgan Stanley analysts contend that stubborn inflation means investors won't be willing to pay big premiums for future earnings. Goldman Sachs Group strategists say that based on typical declines in P/E ratios in the past four recessions, stock multiples can go much lower.

(continued)

REAL-WORLD RETURNS 17-1 *continued*

Nicholas Bohnsack, of Strategas Research Partners, says it is a mistake for investors to assume multiples will head higher. There have been extended periods in which multiples went down or were flat, most recently in the 1970s, he notes.

Friday, the Dow Jones industrial average fell 146.70 points or 1.2 percent to 11,893.69, capping a week in which the average fell 372.70 points or 3 percent. The S & P 500 fell 10.97 points or 0.84 percent to 1,293.37, leaving it down 2.8 percent for the week and 12 percent for the year. The Nasdaq composite fell 8.01 points or 0.36 percent to 2,212.49, off 2.6 percent for the week and 17 percent for the year.

Part of the problem is that the earnings side of the equation is looking shaky. Wall Street analysts predict a double-digit increase in corporate profits for 2008, but forecasts have been pared back. As of Friday, S & P 500 stocks are expected to generate $98.25 in earnings a share this year, down from the $101.87 a share that had been predicted at the end of last year, according to Reuters.

Analysts have taken an especially sharp knife to estimates of first-quarter earnings, which now are expected at $22.58 a share, compared with the $23.64 a share forecast at the end of December. That means that instead of rising at a 5.1-percent rate, first-quarter earnings now are expected to be basically flat.

Another problem is inflation. In a number of recent sessions the stock market has reacted positively to higher commodity prices on the theory that it will boost profits of energy and materials companies. But if inflation stays stubbornly high despite the US economic slowdown, it would be a negative for multiples, because it reduces the value of future earnings.

Abhijit Chakrabortti, Morgan Stanley's chief global and US equity strategist, says inflation is running about 0.8 percentage points above the long-term trend of 3.5 percent, and that value for the S & P 500 should be reduced by the same amount. With that factor taken into consideration, he argues that current fair value for the index is about 17 times trailing earnings, not much above its present reading.

Source: Lauricella, Tom, "Stocks May Not Be as Cheap as They Seem," *The Globe and Mail*, March 10, 2008, p. B5.

THE ACCOUNTING ASPECTS OF EARNINGS

learning objective 2
Explain the accounting aspects of a company's earnings.

If investors are to focus on a company's earnings per share, a critical variable in security analysis, they should understand how EPS is derived and what it represents. For investors, an EPS figure is often the bottom line—the item of major interest—in a company's financial statements. Furthermore, they must understand the components of EPS before they can attempt to forecast it.

The Financial Statements

Financial Statements
The principal published financial data about a company, primarily the balance sheet and income statement.

Investors rely heavily on the **financial statements** of a corporation, which provide the major financial data about companies. Before proceeding with our discussion of how this information can be used by analysts, we note that the information contained in financial statements is generally somewhat dated. This is because of the time involved in compiling financial statements, which implies they will not be available to the public for several days after the end of the reporting period. For annual financial statements, for example, the lag between the fiscal year-end and the public availability of financial statements often exceeds two months, with 90 days being the norm, while the release of quarterly statements is somewhat more timely. In the interim period, companies generally release some highlights (such as earnings per share and sales figures) well before the comprehensive statements are made public.

To illustrate the use of financial statements in doing company analysis, we examine the 2006 and 2007 consolidated financial statements for Empire Company Limited, which owns Sobeys Inc.,

THE ACCOUNTING ASPECTS OF EARNINGS

one of Canada's two national retail grocery and food distributors. Through subsidiaries and franchises, the company operates more than 1,300 corporate and franchised stores in all 10 provinces under retail banners that include Sobeys, IGA, IGA Extra, Foodland, and Price Chopper. Empire also owns chains of convenience stores (e.g., Needs), drug stores (Lawtons), and owns related real estate assets, although the food retailing division accounts for most of its sales (approximately 97.5 percent in fiscal 2007).

The Balance Sheet

The balance sheet shows the portfolio of assets for a corporation, as well as its liabilities and shareholders' equity, at a given time. The amounts at which items are carried on the balance sheet are dictated by accounting conventions. Cash is the actual dollar amount, whereas marketable securities could be at cost or market value. Shareholders' equity and fixed assets are on a book value basis.

The balance sheet for Empire, shown in Table 17-1, shows the company's consolidated financial position for 2006 and 2007, as of May 5, 2007and May 6, 2006, which correspond to the company's fiscal year end. Receivables and inventory accounted for over 75 percent of Empire's 2007 current assets of $1,434.2 million. These items went up by 18.7 percent and 9.1 percent respectively from 2006 to 2007. Also, Empire's property and equipment totalled $2,302.9 million in 2007, or approximately 44 percent of total assets ($5,224.9 million). In terms of the nature of the company, it is not surprising to see high property and equipment levels on the consolidated financial statements.

The liability and equity side of the balance sheet is composed of $1,260.3 million in accounts payable and accrued liabilities, $40.4 million in future tax liabilities, $82.5 million in current portion of long-term debt, $792.6 million in long-term debt, $36.9 million in long-term lease liabilities, $14.0 million in other liabilities, and $2,135.4 million in shareholders' equity. The shareholders' equity consists primarily of its two major components, $196.1 million in capital stock and $1,939.6 million in retained earnings. It is important to recognize that the retained earnings item does not represent "spendable" funds for a company; rather, it designated that part of previous earnings not paid out as dividends.

Several financial ratios that can be calculated from balance sheet data are useful in assessing the company's financial strength (e.g., the current ratio, a measure of liquidity, or the debt-to-total-assets ratio, a measure of leverage). These ratios are part of the standard ratio analysis, which is often performed by managers, creditors, stockholders, and other interested groups, and are covered in most financial management texts and courses. Some of these ratios are demonstrated later in the analysis, and a detailed description of many other financial ratios is included in Appendix 17A at the end of this chapter.

Table 17-1

Consolidated Balance Sheets for Empire Company Limited

Year Ended	May 5, 2007	May 6, 2006
(In millions of Canadian dollars)		
Assets:		
Current		
Cash and cash equivalents	294.9	341.1
Receivables	326.8	275.4
Income taxes receivable	3.6	—
Inventories	757.5	694.3
Prepaid expenses	51.4	51.5
	1,434.2	1,362.3

Table 17-1 *Continued*

Investments, at cost (quoted market value $283.1, 2006 = $398.9)	189.7	359.9
Investments, at equity (realizable value $434.0, 2006 = $425.3)	142.8	157.5
Property and equipment	2,302.9	2,143.6
Assets held for sale	24.1	23.1
Other assets	344.6	273.3
Goodwill	786.6	731.8
Total Assets	**5,224.9**	**5,051.5**
Liabilities and Shareholders' Equity:		
Current:		
Bank indebtedness	30.1	98.6
Accounts payable and accrued liabilities	1,260.3	1,241.8
Income taxes payable	—	35.8
Future income taxes	40.4	46.1
Long-term debt due within one year	82.5	95.4
Liabilities relating to assets held for sale	6.8	7.1
	1,420.1	1,524.8
Long-term debt	792.6	707.3
Long-term lease obligation	36.9	20.8
Other liabilities	14.0	18.9
Employee future benefits obligation	102.1	97.3
Future income taxes	133.6	131.8
Minority interest	590.2	585.4
Total liabilities	3,089.5	3,086.3
Shareholders' Equity		
Capital stock	196.1	195.1
Contributed surplus	0.3	0.2
Retained earnings	1,939.6	1,771.0
Cumulative translation adjustment	(0.6)	(1.1)
Total shareholders' equity	2,135.4	1,965.2
Total Liabilities and Shareholders' Equity	**5,224.9**	**5,051.5**

Source: Empire Company Limited, *Annual Report*, 2007.

The Income Statement

This statement is used more frequently by investors, not only to assess current management performance but also as a guide to the company's future profitability. The income statement represents flows for a particular period, usually one year. Table 17-2 shows the consolidated statements of earnings for Empire for the years 2006 and 2007.

The key item for investors on the income statement is the after-tax net income, which, divided by the average number of common shares outstanding, produces earnings per share. Earnings from continuing operations typically are used to judge the company's success and are almost always the earnings reported in the financial press. Non-recurring earnings, such as net extraordinary items that arise from unusual and infrequently occurring transactions, are separated from income from continuing operations.[2]

---

[2]An extraordinary item is one that is not likely to reoccur, such as a loss due to a disposal of an operating division.

Table 17-2

Consolidated Statements of Earnings for Empire Company Limited

Year Ended	May 5, 2007	May 6, 2006
(In millions of Canadian dollars)		
Revenue	13,366.7	13,063.6
Operating expenses		
Cost of sales, selling and administrative expenses	12,724.0	12,378.2
Depreciation and amortization	243.9	225.8
	398.8	459.6
Investment income	**41.5**	**31.8**
Operating income	**440.3**	**491.4**
Interest expense	60.1	83.8
Capital gains and other items	7.1	109.4
Earnings before income taxes and minority interest	**387.3**	**517.0**
Income taxes:		
Current	104.8	141.8
Future	15.4	11.3
	120.2	153.1
Earnings before minority interest	267.1	363.9
Minority interest	57.0	67.1
Net earnings	**210.1**	**296.8**
Earnings per common share		
Basic	**3.20**	**4.53**
Diluted	**3.19**	**4.51**

Source: Empire Company Limited, *Annual Report,* 2007.

Table 17-2 clearly illustrates the "flow" in an income statement. Operating expenses, which include the cost of sales, selling, and administrative expenses, and depreciation and amortization, are subtracted from total revenue, resulting in operating income, which was $440.3 million for Empire in fiscal 2007. Operating income is often referred to as earnings before interest and taxes, or EBIT for short.

Operating income is then adjusted by adding interest income and subtracting the interest expense, which represents an important item for companies because interest is tax-deductible. Capital losses and other items are then charged. Netting these items with operating income produces Empire's 2007 income before tax and minority interest figure of $387.3 million. Finally, subtracting out income taxes and minority interest produces net income of $210.1 million for Empire in 2007.

Finally, dividing by the average number of shares outstanding produces a Basic EPS of $3.20. The Diluted EPS figure of $3.19 adjusts for the influence on EPS of potentially dilutive securities such as convertible debt or preferred shares, and outstanding warrants and options. Investors trying to understand the financial statements with regard to items such as EPS may need to consult the company's annual report in order to determine the average common shares outstanding, which is not always a straightforward process. Empire reports 2007 net income of $210.1 million, and states that the average number of common shares outstanding during 2007 was 65.6 million. This implies a Basic EPS of ($210.1 million/65.6 million shares) = $3.20 as reported above.

Charges to earnings because of an accounting change or due to extraordinary items are important to investors in trying to understand earnings. What investors seek to determine is the "true" earning power of a company, because ultimately they will be attempting to forecast future earnings. Although no such items are reported for Empire in 2007 or 2006, these items can have large impacts on the reported earnings of companies at various times.

Certifying the Statements

Generally Accepted Accounting Principles (GAAP)

Financial reporting requirements establishing the rules for producing financial statements, developed by the accounting profession on the basis of historical costs and accrual-based income.

The earnings shown on an income statement are derived on the basis of **generally accepted accounting principles (GAAP)**. The company adheres to a standard set of rules developed by the accounting profession on the basis of historical costs and accrual-based income, which can be measured objectively. An auditor from an independent accounting firm certifies that the earnings have been derived according to accounting standards in a statement labelled the "auditor's report."

The auditor's report is required by Canadian corporate law and generally consists of just two or three paragraphs. The first paragraph (or two) describe the scope of the examination, and usually indicates that the examination was made in accordance with generally accepted auditing standards. The final paragraph (or so) of the report gives the auditor's opinion on whether the statements fairly present the firm's financial position and the results of its operations in accordance with GAAP. If the auditor finds discrepancies from GAAP, they may be unable to give an opinion, or may offer a "qualified" opinion that refers to the dubious points. A qualified report can be viewed as a signal that the statements may not fairly represent the company's financial condition and is not allowed in some provinces. Figure 17-1 includes the auditor's report for Empire's 2007 consolidated financial statements.

Note that the auditor's report does not guarantee the accuracy or the quality of the earnings in an absolute sense; rather, it only attests that the statements are a fair presentation of the company's financial position for a particular period. The auditors are in effect certifying that generally accepted accounting principles were applied on a consistent basis. In Canada, the Canadian Institute of Chartered Accountants (CICA) formulates accounting standards, while in the US, the Financial Accounting Standards Board (FASB) performs this function.

Figure 17-1
Auditor's Report for Empire Company Limited

To the Shareholders of **Empire Company Limited**

We have audited the consolidated balance sheets of Empire Company Limited as at May 5, 2007 and May 6, 2006, and the consolidated statements of earnings, retained earnings, and cash flows for the 52 week fiscal years then ended. These consolidated financial statements are the responsibility of the Company's management. Our responsibility is to express an opinion on these consolidated financial statements based on our audits.

We conducted our audits in accordance with Canadian generally accepted auditing standards. Those standards require that we plan and perform an audit to obtain reasonable assurance whether the consolidated financial statements are free of material misstatement. An audit includes examining, on a test basis, evidence supporting the amounts and disclosures in the consolidated financial statements. An audit also includes assessing the accounting principles used and significant estimates made by management, as well as evaluating the overall consolidated financial statement presentation.

In our opinion, these consolidated financial statements present fairly, in all material respects, the financial position of the company as at May 5, 2007 and May 6, 2007, and the results of its operations and its cash flows for the fiscal years then ended in accordance with Canadian generally accepted accounting principles.

Grant Thornton LLP
Chartered Accountants
New Glasgow, Nova Scotia
June 15, 2007, except for Note 27 which is as of July 23, 2007

Source: Empire Company Limited, *Annual Report, 2007.*

The Problem with Reported Earnings

Although earnings in particular—and financial statements in general—are derived on the basis of GAAP and are certified in an auditor's report, a problem exists with earnings. The problem, simply stated, is that reported EPS for a company (i.e., accounting EPS) is not a precise figure that is readily comparable over time, and the EPS figures for different companies often are not comparable to each other.

The problem with earnings is that alternative accounting principles can be, and are, used to prepare the financial statements. Many of the items in the balance sheet and income statement can be accounted for in more than one manner, resulting in what one might call a conservative or a liberal treatment of EPS. Given the number of items that constitutes the financial statements, the possible number of acceptable (i.e., that conform to GAAP) combinations that could be used is large. Holding everything else constant, such as sales, products, and operating ability, a company could produce several legal and permissible EPS figures, depending solely on the accounting principles used. The question that investors must try to answer is, "Which EPS best represents the *true* position of a company?"

Because reported EPS is a function of the many alternative GAAPs in use, it is extremely difficult, if not impossible, for the "true" performance of a company to be reflected consistently in one figure. Since each company is different, is it reasonable to expect one accounting system to capture the true performance of all companies? With the business world so complex, one can make a case for the necessity of alternative treatments of the same item or process, such as inventories or depreciation.

Some EPS figures are better than others in the sense that they have been derived using more conservative principles. In other words, they are of higher quality. In an article on the quality of earnings, Bernstein and Seigel stated:

…a company's reported earnings figure is often taken by the unsophisticated user of financial statements as the quantitative measure of the firm's well-being. Of course, any professional knows that earnings numbers are in large part the product of conscious and often subjective choices between various accounting treatments and business options, as well as of various external economic factors. If he wants to assess the true earning power of each company, the financial statement user must make some determination of the *quality of its earnings* [emphasis added].[3]

As if the problems with reported earnings are not bad enough, in the late 1990s companies introduced a whole new level of confusion by reporting their own version of earnings, with varying labels and varying calculation procedures. One commonly used version of reported earnings during this period was "pro forma earnings." While pro forma earnings have been used for a long time, they had never been as widely reported as they came to be by many "dot-coms" that exploded into the scene in the late 1990s. Of course, many of these companies had no earnings in the traditional sense. Aside from the obvious problem that these represent estimates of future earnings, many other problems are associated with the use of pro forma earnings figures since each company can choose its own method of calculations.

Quality assessments are usually difficult to make and require considerable expertise in accounting and financial analysis. The best advice for the investor is to go ahead and use the reported EPS because it is all that is normally available, and the majority of investors will also have to rely on this figure. Investors should, however, be aware of the potential problems involved in EPS and should constantly keep in mind its nature and derivation. Real-World Returns 17-2 provides some suggestions of what to look for to distinguish between reasonable and unreasonable (or aggressive) reported earnings figures.

INVESTING *tip*

Given the difficulties involved, and the alternative accounting treatments, investors must remember that reported EPS is not the precise figure that it first appears to be. Unless adjustments are made, the EPS of different companies may not be comparable on either a time series or a cross-sectional basis.

---

[3] L. Bernstein and J. Seigel, "The Concept of Earnings Quality," *Financial Analysts Journal* 35 (July–August 1979), p. 72.

REAL-WORLD RETURNS 17-2

Aggressive Accounting: Bad for Company Health?

Aggressive corporate accounting practices (combined with "a game of nods and winks" between many corporate managers, auditors, and analysts) have caused the quality of reported earnings to deteriorate. To avoid pitfalls associated with such problems, analysts need to learn to identify warning signs of potential mischief, such as financial confusion, aggressive revenue recognition, growth through acquisitions, cutting discretionary expenses, and specific accounting problems. Perhaps most important, analysts need to resist "Wall Street misconceptions" about evaluating companies and take a skeptical approach to interpreting the information contained in (or omitted from) earnings reports and financial statements.

Analysts' best defense against aggressive or misleading accounting practices is constant vigilance. At Behind the Numbers, we provide a service that makes only sell recommendations and focuses primarily on quality-of-earnings issues, although we also look at fundamental issues. We believe the analysis of fundamental issues should be combined with the analysis of accounting issues, not to mention common sense. Accounting issues tell a story, and that story needs to be included in the total analytical approach to company analysis.

Prior to the Enron scandal, Arthur Levitt, the former chairman of the US SEC, strongly expressed his concern about the deterioration in reported earnings as a result of managements' sleight of hand in decisions regarding the accounting assumptions or methods chosen for reporting to shareholders:

> We are witnessing an erosion in the quality of earnings. Managing may be giving way to manipulation. Too many corporate managers, auditors, and analysts are participants in a game of nods and winks...Wishful thinking may be winning the day over a faithful representation.[1]

Levitt also said: "It's difficult to hold the line on good practices when...competitors operate in the gray area between legitimacy and outright fraud." He defines the gray area as being "where the accounting is being perverted, where managers are cutting corners, and where earnings reports reflect the desires of management rather than the underlying financial performance of the company." Accounting is the result of a series of estimates. Too many analysts and portfolio managers take companies' financial reports at face value. The reporting of such numbers, however, involves a great deal of latitude and not necessarily a great deal of precision.

What to Look For

Several considerations are paramount in evaluating earnings reports and financial statements.

EPS versus Sales Growth

Analysts need to ask whether earnings per share (EPS) growth is matched by sales growth.

Gross Margin versus EPS

Is gross margin increasing at the same rate as EPS?

Cash Flow versus EPS

Is cash flow growing—and at the same rate as EPS? Although analysts should focus on EPS, they should also look at the cash flow statement.

Charge-Offs

How frequent are charge-offs? Remember, charge-offs represent shareholders' money that was wasted.

Return on Capital

Does the company earn a reasonable return on invested capital? This point is much ignored today.

The Flexibility of GAAP

Generally accepted accounting principles (GAAP) give companies extraordinary flexibility. Read the footnotes to see if the accounting matches economic common sense.

Extrapolation of Trends

Analysts should not extrapolate from the past or the future. Instead, they should assess the current environment and how it is likely to affect the company.

Contrarian Thinking

Analysts need to understand that management always thinks optimistically, which can be deceptive. Management wants to focus on optimistic factors that can be used to market the company.

Sources of Trouble

Sources of trouble: financial confusion, aggressive revenue recognition, unsustainable growth through acquisitions, cutting discretionary expenditures, specific accounting problems, Wall Street misconceptions, and low returns on invested capital.

Financial Confusion

Companies often use frequent acquisitions and charge-offs to disguise unsustainable growth rates. The key task for an analyst in estimating future earnings is to learn about the company's past. This task is complex.

Aggressive Revenue Recognition

Aggressive revenue recognition nearly always foreshadows problems.

Growth through Acquisitions

Growth through acquisitions often leads to consolidation difficulties, unmanageable debt levels, lower returns on capital, and write-offs.

Cutting Discretionary Expenses

Bristol-Myers Squibb Company is a great example of cutting discretionary expenses to improve the bottom line.

Specific Accounting Problems

Accounting practices allow for the distortion of economic reality. As stated in the Enron "Risk Control Manual," specifying a number of GAAP income does not necessarily mean the number reflects economic reality.

Wall Street Misconceptions

At Behind the Numbers, we believe that Wall Street's individual company "bull" premise often makes no sense. It is extremely important for analysts to look beyond financial statements. A good example of the Street's "bull" premise and a great example of the misuse of EBITDA (earnings before interest, taxes, depreciation, and amortization) occurred with the paging companies a few years ago. EBITDA is a great way for Wall Street and management to divert attention away from reported earnings. Therefore, analysts should always be skeptical about the road that both management and Wall Street are trying to lead them down.

Summary

Company management may use aggressive or even misleading accounting practices to tell analysts the story they wish to hear. As Arthur Levitt warned: "Too many corporate managers, auditors, and analysts are participants in a game of nods and winks." The cautious analyst will delve beneath these accounting games to find the true story of a company's health.

[1]Arthur Levitt, "Lifeblood of Our Markets." Speech given at the Economic Club of New York, New York City, October 18, 1999.

Source: Tice, David, W., "Aggressive Accounting: Bad for Company Health?" CFA Institute Conference Proceeding, Equity Research & Valuation Techniques 2002. Reproduced with permission from CFA Institute. Copyright 2002. All Rights Reserved.

The Global Arena—International Accounting

Investors who find Canadian accounting comparisons difficult have often been even more troubled by international accounting practices. Practices can and do vary widely across countries.

There is a current movement toward trying to converge to a common set of standards. The International Accounting Standards Board (IASB) has formulated a set of global rules that eliminate numerous choices and enforce stricter reporting standards. Currently over 100 countries have adopted these international financial reporting standards (IFRS), which resemble GAAP. Although IFRS more closely resemble both Canadian and US GAAP than the accounting standards in most countries, several differences will still exist. Canada plans to adopt the IFRS for financial reports covering periods beginning on or after January 1, 2011, as discussed in Real-World Returns 17-3.

REAL-WORLD RETURNS 17-3

Very Few Ready for Changeover to IFRS According to CA Survey

A survey by the Chartered Accountants of Canada suggests many companies are closer to the starting gate rather than the finish line when it comes to preparing for the country's transition to International Financial Reporting Standards (IFRS).

A total of 550 senior executives in Canadian companies were surveyed in March 2008 and all are Chartered Accountants. Just over half surveyed indicated their company will need to adhere to IFRS. Among those executives only 8 percent have either started (4 percent) or completed (4 percent) the conversion process. Almost three-in-four have either not started to assess the impact (42 percent) or are in the process of assessing the impact (30 percent).

"The results are not surprising," said Ron Salole, Vice-President, Standards with the Canadian Institute of Chartered Accountants. "The changeover date to IFRS was just confirmed in mid-February. Confirmation of the date has brought certainty for business leaders in their planning process making now the right time to start the work to get ready."

The Accounting Standards Board recently released an Exposure Draft of the coming standards. They will apply to Canadian publicly accountable enterprises. In general, these can include publicly-listed companies, certain government corporations and enterprises with fiduciary responsibilities such as banks, insurance companies, credit unions and securities firms. The draft document outlines what will be expected when IFRS is adopted for interim and annual financial statements for fiscal years beginning on January 1, 2011, or thereafter.

"Knowing what the future holds helps companies and individuals plan for the global accounting world of tomorrow," said Salole. "Business leaders are encouraged to take advantage of this excellent opportunity to determine how their operations will be affected. The earlier enterprises begin preparing the smoother the transition."

Moving to IFRS will bring Canada into step with a parade of more than 100 countries that have already completed the transition. Those using IFRS include the European Union, Australia and New Zealand. IFRS is principles-based and is similar to the current Canadian approach in terms of conceptual framework and topics covered. A common international accounting language will help promote comparability for publicly-traded companies world wide.

The Exposure Draft can be downloaded from a dedicated IFRS website launched by the CICA (www.cica.ca/IFRS). The site offers a variety of valuable resources to steer individuals and companies through the IFRS transition process.

In addition, a major conference on IFRS is being staged in Toronto April 23-25, 2008. The conference is a joint presentation by the CICA and the International Accounting Standards Committee Foundation. Sir David Tweedie, Chairman of the International Accounting Standards Board, will be speaking at both the conference and during a luncheon at the Empire Club on

April 25, when Toronto hosts the IFRS gathering. A series of IFRS courses and other events will also be presented by the CA profession across the country throughout the transition process.

The Canadian Institute of Chartered Accountants (CICA), together with the provincial, territorial and Bermuda Institutes/Ordre of Chartered Accountants, represents a membership of approximately 72,000 CAs and 10,000 students in Canada and Bermuda. The CICA conducts research into current business issues and supports the setting of accounting, auditing and assurance standards for business, not-for-profit organizations and government. It issues guidance on control and governance, publishes professional literature, develops continuing education programs and represents the CA profession nationally and internationally. CICA is a founding member of the International Federation of Accountants (IFAC) and the Global Accounting Alliance (GAA).

Source: The Canadian Institute of Chartered Accountants website, www.cica.ca, May 19, 2008.

CHECK YOUR UNDERSTANDING

17-1. Given that the financial statements of a company are certified by its auditors, why should investors be concerned about the information contained therein?

17-2. Assume a company has completed its financial statements for the year and that the income statement shows a large loss. Does this mean the company will not have adequate cash to pay its bills?

17-3. In reporting their results, companies may choose to focus on operating earnings or even EBITDA. Why would they do this?

ANALYZING A COMPANY'S PROFITABILITY

At the company level, EPS is the culmination of several important factors. Accounting variables can be used to examine these determining factors by analyzing key financial ratios. Analysts examine the components of profitability in order to try to determine whether a company's profitability is increasing or decreasing and why. Primary emphasis is on the **return on equity (ROE)**—the accounting net income available to the common stockholders—because it is a key component in determining earnings and dividend growth.

Return on Equity (ROE)
The accounting rate of return on stockholders' equity.

We begin our discussion by noting that EPS = ROE × Book value per share (which is the accounting value of shareholders' equity on a per share basis), which demonstrates the relationship between EPS and ROE. Since book value typically changes rather slowly, ROE is the primary variable on which to concentrate.

ROE can be determined using the following equation:

$$\text{ROE} = \text{Net income/Shareholders' equity} \qquad \textbf{(17-3)}$$

Using Empire's data from Tables 17-1 and 17-2, we would calculate the ROE for 2007 as follows, if we use the year-end equity figure in the denominator:

ROE = Net income/Shareholders' equity = ($210.1)/($2,135.4) = 0.0984 = 9.84%

The ROE is the accounting rate of return that stockholders earn on their portion of the total capital used to finance the company; in other words, it is the return on equity. The figure above differs from the 10.3 percent reported by Empire in their annual report, which divides by the "average" equity figure during the year (estimated as the average of the beginning and ending of year equity figures).

This ROE calculation is common because it accounts somewhat for the fact that the numerator (earnings) is a flow variable throughout the period, while the denominator (equity) is a stock figure that is measured at a single point in time.

Analyzing Return on Equity (ROE)

The ROE is the end result of several important variables that are often analyzed by what is referred to as the DuPont system of analysis because it originated at the DuPont Corporation. The idea is to decompose the ROE into its critical components in order both to identify adverse impacts on ROE and to help analysts predict future trends in ROE.

Return on Assets (ROA)

The accounting rate of return on a firm's assets.

   Different combinations of financial ratios can be used to decompose ROE. One approach is to use a multiplicative relationship that consists of five financial ratios, all multiplied together to produce ROE. The first four can be multiplied together to determine **return on assets (ROA)**, an important measure of a company's profitability. ROA measures only the return on assets, while ROE measures the return to the stockholders who finance only part of the assets (the creditors finance the other part). The five financial ratios are (1) EBIT efficiency, (2) asset turnover, (3) interest burden, (4) tax burden, and (5) leverage.

1. A key component of a company's profitability is its operating efficiency, which is unaffected by interest charges, taxes, or the amount of debt financing used by a company to finance its assets (that is, the leverage). To determine operating efficiency, analyze its components—operating income or EBIT—and asset turnover.

   The EBIT/sales ratio is a measure of the firm's ability to operate efficiently. EBIT reflects the earnings before the financing decision is accounted for as a result of subtracting the interest expense and before the provision for income taxes. The larger the EBIT per dollar of sales, the better in terms of operational efficiency. In effect, the EBIT reflects the operating margin on sales:

$$\text{EBIT/Sales} = \text{Pre-tax, pre-interest profit margin} = \text{EBIT efficiency}$$

2. Asset turnover is a measure of efficiency. Given some amount of total assets, how much can be generated in sales? The more sales per dollar of assets the better it is for a firm, since each dollar of assets has to be financed with a source of funds bearing a cost. The firm may have some assets that are unproductive, thereby adversely affecting its efficiency:

$$\text{Sales/Total assets} = \text{Asset turnover}$$

3. Next, consider the impact of interest charges. Interest expense for most companies is an important tax-deductible item. The "interest burden" can be calculated as the ratio of pre-tax income to EBIT:

$$\text{Pre-tax income/EBIT} = \text{Interest burden}$$

4. The last variable that must be considered as part of the analysis of a company's return on assets is the tax burden. To calculate this amount, divide net income by pre-tax income:

$$\text{Net income/Pre-tax income} = \text{Tax burden}$$

Return on assets (ROA) can now be calculated from these four variables that have important impacts on a company's return on assets:

(17-4) $\text{ROA} = (\text{EBIT/Sales} \times \text{Sales/Total assets} \times \text{Pre-tax income/EBIT} \times \text{Net income/Pre-tax income})$

EXAMPLE 17-1: CALCULATING ROA FOR EMPIRE COMPANY LIMITED

Using the data for Empire for 2007 from Tables 17-1 and 17-2:

EBIT/Sales = $440.3/$13,366.7 = 0.0329
Sales/Total Assets = $13,366.7/$5,224.9 = 2.5583

Pre-tax Income/EBIT = \$387.3/\$440.3 = 0.8796
Net Income/Pre-tax Income = \$210.1/\$387.3 = 0.5425
ROA = 0.0329 × 2.5583 × 0.8796 × 0.5425 = 0.0402 = 4.02%

Return on assets (ROA) is a fundamental measure of firm profitability, reflecting how effectively and efficiently the firm's assets are used. Obviously, the higher the net income for a given amount of assets, the better the return. For Sobeys, the 2007 return on assets is 4.02 percent. The ROA can be improved by increasing the net income more than the assets (in percentage terms) or by using the existing assets even more efficiently.

5. Finally, the effects of leverage must be considered. The leverage ratio measures how the firm finances its assets.[4] Basically, firms can finance with either debt or equity. Debt, though a cheaper source of financing, is a riskier method, because of the fixed interest payments that must be systematically repaid on time to avoid bankruptcy. Leverage can magnify the returns to the stockholders (favourable leverage) or diminish them (unfavourable leverage).

To capture the effects of leverage, use a multiplier rather than a debt percentage.

Leverage = Total assets/Shareholders' equity

INVESTING tip

What this analysis does not show is the impact of leverage on the risk of the firm. Remember that in this analysis we are examining only the determinants of EPS. However, as we know from our discussion of valuation, two factors, EPS and a multiplier, are required to determine value. An increase in leverage may increase the riskiness of the company more than enough to offset the increased EPS, thereby lowering the company's value. Investors must always consider both dimensions of the value of a stock, the return side and the risk side.

EXAMPLE 17-2: CALCULATING LEVERAGE FOR EMPIRE COMPANY LIMITED

In 2007, Empire's ratio of total debt (all sources) to total assets was 59.1 percent. Thus, the creditors were financing over half of the assets and the equity holders were underwriting the remainder. Dividing total assets by equity (5,224.9/2,135.4) produces an equity multiplier of 2.4468, which is used as the measure of leverage.

Finally, the last step in the ROE analysis is to relate ROA and leverage:

$$ROE = ROA \times Leverage$$ (17-5)

EXAMPLE 17-3: RELATING ROA AND LEVERAGE

Combining these two factors, ROA and leverage, for Empire for 2007 produces the following ROE:

$$ROE = 0.0402 \times 2.4468 = 0.0984 = 9.84\%$$

A standard formulation of the ROE analysis often used in the CFA curriculum combines all factors considered above into one long multiplication equation based on these ratios or variations to accommodate the multiplication:

$$ROE = EBIT\ efficiency \times Asset\ turnover \times Interest\ burden \times Tax\ burden \times Leverage$$
$$ROE = EBIT/Sales \times Sales/Assets \times Pre\text{-}tax\ income/EBIT \times Net\ income/Pre\text{-}tax\ income \times Assets/Equity$$ (17-6)

EXAMPLE 17-4: CALCULATING ROE FOR EMPIRE COMPANY LIMITED

For Empire, using 2007 data:

$$ROE = 0.0329 \times 2.5583 \times 0.8796 \times 0.5425 \times 2.4468 = 0.0984 = 9.84\%$$

---

[4]Leverage can be measured in several other ways, such as the ratio of total debt to total assets or the ratio of debt to equity.

An alternative version of the DuPont system, often referred to as the three-point DuPont decomposition, breaks down ROE into three components, as described below:

(17-7)
$$\text{ROE} = \text{Net income/Sales} \times \text{Sales/Total assets} \times \text{Total assets/Shareholders' equity}$$
$$\text{ROE} = \text{Net income margin} \times \text{Asset turnover} \times \text{Leverage}$$
where Net income margin = net income/sales.

Notice that the last two terms are identical to the last two in the five-point decomposition in Equation 17-6. Net income margin, therefore, must equal the product of the first three terms in Equation 17-6, which it does, as shown below: Net income/Pre-tax income × Pre-tax income/EBIT × EBIT/Sales = Net income/Sales = Net income margin

---

EXAMPLE 17-5: THREE-POINT DUPONT DECOMPOSITION

For Empire for 2007, we already know from above that Asset Turnover = 2.5583 and that Leverage = 2.4468.
Empire's Net income margin = Net income/sales = $210.1/$13,366.7 = 0.0157 (or 1.57%).
Combining these numbers in Equation 17-7, we get
ROE = Net income margin × Asset turnover × Leverage = 0.0157 × 2.5583 × 2.4468 = 0.0983 = 9.83% (difference due to rounding)

Estimating the Internal (Sustainable) Growth Rate

Internal (Sustainable) Growth Rate
The estimated earnings growth rate, calculated as the product of ROE and the retention rate.

An important part of company analysis is the determination of a sustainable growth rate in earnings and dividends. Such a growth rate estimate can be used in the dividend discount model or to estimate an appropriate P/E multiple.

What determines the sustainable growth rate? The **internal (sustainable) growth rate** of earnings or dividends, g, can be determined as the product of the ROE and the retention ratio—which is calculated as 1.0 minus the dividend payout ratio—as shown in Equation 17-7.[5]

(17-8)
$$g = \text{ROE} \times (1 - \text{Payout ratio})$$

Equation 17-8 is one of the principal calculations in fundamental security analysis and is often used by security analysts. We can calculate g by using data for a particular year, using long-term averages, or using "normalized" figures for ROE and payout ratio. The intuition behind this measure is that growth in earnings (and dividends) will be positively related to the amount of each dollar of earnings reinvested in the company (as measured by the retention ratio), times the return earned on reinvested funds (ROE). For example, a firm that retains all its earnings and earns 15 percent on its equity would see its equity base grow by 15 percent per year. If the same firm paid out all of its earnings, then it would not grow. Similarly, a firm that retained a proportion (b), would earn 15 percent on that proportion, resulting in $g = b \times \text{ROE}$. A weakness of this approach is its reliance on accounting figures that are based on book values and the accrual method of accounting. As a result, they may not always serve as reliable proxies for market values and cash flows.

---

[5]Technically, g is defined as the expected growth rate in dividends. However, the dividend growth rate is clearly influenced by the earnings growth rate. Although dividend and earnings growth rates can diverge in the short run, such differences would not be expected to continue for long periods of time. The standard assumption in security analysis is that g represents the growth rate for both dividends and earnings.

EXAMPLE 17-6: INTERNAL GROWTH RATE ESTIMATE FOR EMPIRE COMPANY LIMITED

Using the 2007 figures for ROE and payout ratio, we can estimate its sustainable growth rate as 7.99 percent, as shown below.

$$g = \text{ROE} \times (1 - \text{Payout ratio}) = (0.0984) \times (1 - 0.1881) = 0.0799 = 7.99\%$$

Using Empire's average ROE and average payout ratio of 12.18 percent and 15.54 percent respectively for the 2003–2007 period, we estimate its sustainable growth rate as 10.28 percent, which is very high, and thus unlikely to be sustainable indefinitely:

$$g = \text{ROE} \times (1 - \text{Payout ratio}) = (0.1218) \times (1 - 0.1554) = 0.1028 = 10.28\%$$

The earnings growth rate, or persistence in the earnings trend, is seldom easy to predict. Investors cannot blindly use the current or past internal growth rate for EPS to predict the future rate of growth.

The internal growth rate estimate produced by Equation 17-8 is reliable only if a company's profitability as measured by ROE remains in balance and if the company maintains a stable payout ratio. If, for example, the ROE or payout ratio for a company grows significantly in the future or declines significantly, the actual EPS growth rate will turn out to be quite different than the internal growth rate estimate produced by Equation 17-8.

A problem associated with using a particular year to estimate the internal growth rate is that the year used may not be a "normal" one. Basing a projection on one year's results can result in a faulty estimate; this is particularly true for companies in cyclical industries.

Payout ratios for most companies vary over time, but reasonable estimates can often be obtained for a particular company using an average of recent years. Estimating future ROE is more challenging. The previous analysis is useful in analyzing the factors that affect ROE. The challenge for analysts and investors is trying to determine how these factors will change in the future.

What matters is the future expected growth rate, not the actual historical growth rate. If investors expect the growth rate to be different in the future, they should use the expected growth rate and not simply the calculation based on current data.

There are alternative approaches that can be used to determine expected future growth rates. One approach is to examine historic rates of growth in dividends and earnings levels, including long-term trends in these growth rates for the company, the industry, and the economy as a whole. Predictions regarding future growth rates can be determined based on these past trends using arithmetic or geometric averages or using more involved statistical techniques such as regression analysis.

Another important source of information regarding company growth, particularly for the near term, can be found in analyst estimates, which is discussed at length in the following section. Investors may be especially interested in consensus estimates, because it is quite likely that market values are based to a large extent on these estimates. Deviations from these estimates could signal that a security is mispriced in the market, which may represent an exploitable investment opportunity.

When estimating growth rates it is important to distinguish between rates that might be sustainable for the short term from long-term rates (especially when these rates are assumed to be sustainable to infinity). If analysts use growth rates that are too high and assume they will exist to infinity, the suggested values when using the constant growth DDM or free cash flow models will be meaningless. Intuitively, competitive pressures will prevent companies from growing rapidly forever. Technically speaking, it is also easy to show that such growth would result in a company eventually encompassing the global economy, as discussed in the following Investing Tip.

INVESTING *tip*

Many investors get carried away when estimating the expected growth rate in EPS for companies they find attractive. The natural tendency of most investors is to rely on historical rates because that is the only objective evidence available. An immediate problem when one does this is deciding what recent period of time might be relevant in forecasting the future, particularly when significant differences exist. For example, if a company had a 15 percent annual growth rate in EPS for the last 10 years, but a 25 percent annual growth rate for the last 5 years, which (if either) is more likely to be indicative of the future?

When we think about it logically, there must be limits to how fast a company can continue to grow, whether in price or EPS. Clearly, some can grow extremely fast for a few years. But an analysis of companies shows that the outer limit for truly long-term growth is about 20 percent. And most companies do not achieve this growth rate over long periods of time.

Consider this—Cisco, one of the great growth stocks of modern times, grew almost 100 percent a year for a 10-year period through March 2000.[6] Fantastic growth, and it produced great performance for Cisco's stockholders. However, had Cisco grown at that rate for the next 10 years, it would have had a total market value of $520 trillion in 2010. This would have far exceeded the combined value of every stock in the world in 2000. Simply put, very rapid growth cannot last indefinitely. It is not possible for a wide variety of reasons—competition, regulation, changes in technology, poor management decisions, and so forth.

CHECK YOUR UNDERSTANDING

17-4. Assume a company uses no debt to finance its operations. What is the relationship between its ROA and its ROE?

17-5. ROE can be calculated directly from figures on the financial statements (Net Income/Shareholders' Equity). Why then do we go through the trouble of decomposing ROE into (three or five) constituent parts?

17-6. Assume that a company's EPS for the most recent year was $3, but that included $1 of unusual (non-recurring) items. Its ROE is 18 percent with the unusual items, but 12 percent once they are removed. The firm declared a dividend of $1 per share. Calculate two estimates of the internal growth rate (one with the unusual items, one without). Which estimate better reflects the sustainable growth rate for this firm?

EARNINGS ESTIMATES

learning objective 3
Describe the importance
of EPS forecasts.

The EPS that investors use to value stocks is the future (expected) EPS. Current stock price is a function of future earnings estimates and the appropriate P_0/E_1 ratio, not the past. If investors knew what the EPS for a particular company would be next year, they could achieve good results in the market.

When performing fundamental security analysis using EPS, an investor needs to (1) know how to obtain an earnings estimate, (2) consider the accuracy of any earnings estimate obtained, and (3) understand the role of earnings surprises in impacting stock prices. We consider each of these topics in turn.

A Forecast of EPS

Security Analysts' Estimates of Earnings

Among the most obvious sources of earnings estimates are security analysts, who make such forecasts as part of their job. This type of earnings information is widely available. All of the major

---

[6]This example is based on Jason Zweig, "Murphy Was an Investor," *Money*, July 2002, p. 62.

investment dealers in Canada provide such estimates in their research reports. Canadian consensus estimates can be found at sources such as Globe Investors at www.globeinvestor.com or from the *Financial Post* database www.fpinfomart.ca. *The Value Line Investment Survey* is the largest and probably most well-known investment advisory service in the United States. It provides subscribers with quarterly earnings forecasts for several quarters ahead for the more than 1,700 companies that it monitors. Earnings estimates are also available from other companies such as Zacks Investment Research (www.zacks.com).

Several studies suggest that individual analysts are by and large undistinguishable in their ability to predict EPS as discussed in Chapter 14. The practical implication of these findings is that the consensus forecast is likely to be superior to the forecasts of individual analysts.

Mechanical Estimates of Earnings

An alternative method of obtaining earnings forecasts is the use of mechanical procedures such as time series models. In deciding what type of model to use, some of the evidence on the behaviour of earnings over time should be considered.

Time series analysis involves the use of historical data to make earnings forecasts. The model assumes that the future will be similar to the past. The series being forecast, EPS, is assumed to have trend elements, an average value, seasonal factors, and error. The moving average technique is a simple example of the time series model for forecasting EPS. Exponential smoothing, which assigns differing weights to past values, is an example of a more sophisticated technique. A regression equation would represent another technique for making forecasts; the regression equation could handle several variables, such as trend and seasonal factors. More sophisticated models can also be used.

Studies of the behaviour of the time path of earnings have produced mixed results. Most of the early studies indicated randomness in the growth rates of annual earnings. Other studies found some evidence of patterns. More recent studies, particularly those of quarterly earnings, have indicated that the time series behaviour of earnings is not random.

The Accuracy of Earnings Forecasts

Intuitively, one would expect analyst earnings predictions to be superior to those obtained using historical data and trends in earnings, since they use more information. Several studies, including Brown and Rozeff, as well as O'Brien, suggest that analysts provide superior short-term earnings forecasts (one to three quarters ahead) than mechanical methods.[7] The evidence is mixed regarding the superiority of analyst reports for long-term earnings projections.

Even if investors accept the relative superiority of analysts' estimates to mechanical methods, the fact remains that analysts often over- or underestimate the earnings that are actually realized. Analysts are typically far off target on their estimates. According to one study of almost 400 companies, analysts' estimates averaged 57 percent too high in the first month of a fiscal year, and the error was still up by an average 12 percent by year-end.

Another study by Dreman and Berry covered 66,100 analysts' consensus forecasts for the period 1974–90. Analysts were given every advantage in the study—for example, forecasts could be made in the same quarter as earnings were reported, and the forecasts could be changed up to two weeks before the end of the quarter. Nevertheless, the average annual error was 44 percent, and only 25 percent of consensus estimates came within plus or minus 5 percent of reported earnings. Looking at the estimates on the basis of the 61 industries involved, only one industry had forecast errors averaging under 10 percent for the entire time period and, overall, the average forecast error grouped by industries was 50 percent (the median error was 43 percent).[8]

---

[7]L. Brown and M. Rozeff, "Analysts Can Forecast Accurately!" *Journal of Portfolio Management* 6 (Spring 1980), pp. 31–34; P. O'Brien, "Analyst's Forecasts as Earnings Expectation," *Journal of Accounting and Economics* 10 (January 1988), pp. 53–83.
[8]D. Dreman, "Cloudy Crystal Balls," *Forbes*, October 10, 1994, p. 154.

The information value of analyst reports depends upon a variety of factors and is generally enhanced by: the amount of recent company information that is used; the number of analysts following the stock; the degree of consensus among analysts; and the quality of analysts following the stock. However, there is a great deal of evidence that analysts tend to be overly optimistic on average. Supporting studies include the O'Brien study mentioned, as well as Canadian evidence documented by Hennessey, as well as Ackert and Athanassakos.[9]

These results may not be that surprising since analysts have greater incentive to issue buy rather than sell recommendations. They are under pressure by the companies they follow to avoid issuing sell recommendations. In fact, sell recommendations have traditionally been rare, as discussed in Chapter 14. This pressure will be greater if the brokerage firm they work for is trying to sell shares of the company being analyzed or if there exists an investment banking relationship with the company. In addition, analysts may prefer to make estimates that do not stand out from the crowd. These notions are supported by the results of Ackert and Athanassakos, who find that analysts are "more optimistic when there is greater dispersion in earnings forecasts."[10]

Inaccurate earnings estimates can provide opportunities for investors. Analysts are frequently wrong, and if investors can make better estimates of earnings, they can expect to profit from their astuteness. In addition, several empirical studies, such as Hawkins, Chamberlin, and Daniel, and Hennessey, suggest that investors can benefit from earnings estimate revisions.[11] In particular, portfolios of stocks that have experienced positive earnings forecast revisions, produce excess positive returns subsequent to the revision. The larger the revisions, the greater the excess returns.

Earnings Surprises

We have established that changes in earnings and stock prices are highly correlated. We have also discussed the necessity of estimating EPS and how such estimates can be obtained. What remains is to examine the role of expectations about earnings in selecting common stocks.

The association between earnings and stock prices is more complicated than simply demonstrating a correlation between earnings growth and stock-price changes. Elton, Gruber, and Gultekin found that investors could not earn excess returns by buying and selling stocks on the basis of the consensus estimate of earnings growth. (The consensus estimate was defined as the average estimate of security analysts at major brokerage houses.) They also found that analysts tended to overestimate earnings for companies they expected would perform well and to underestimate for companies they expected would perform poorly.[12]

Investors must form expectations about EPS, and these will be incorporated into stock prices if markets are efficient. Although these expectations are often inaccurate, they play an important role in affecting stock prices. Malkiel and Cragg concluded that in making accurate one-year predictions, "It is far more important to know what the market will think the growth rate of earnings will be next year rather than to know the (actual) realized long-term growth rate."[13]

As Latané and Jones have pointed out, new information about a stock is unexpected information.[14] The important point about EPS in terms of stock prices is the difference between what investors in

[9]S. Hennessey, "Can Active Managers Profit from Earnings Forecast Revisions?" *Canadian Investment Review* 6 (Spring 1993), pp. 39–45; L. Ackert and G. Athanassakos, "Expectations of the Herd," *Canadian Investment Review* 9 (Winter 1996/97), pp. 7–11.
[10]L. Ackert and G. Athanassakos, "Expectations of the Herd," p. 7.
[11]E. Hawkins, S. Chamberlin, and W. Daniel, "Earnings Expectations and Security Prices," *Financial Analysts Journal* 40 (Sept/Oct 1984), pp. 24–37; S. Hennessey, "Can Active Managers Profit from Earnings Forecast Revisions?" *Canadian Investment Review* 6 (Spring 1993), pp. 39–45.
[12]E. Elton, N. Gruber, and M. Gultekin, "Expectations and Share Prices," *Management Science* 27 (September 1981), pp. 975–987.
[13]B. Malkiel and J. Cragg, "Expectations and the Structure of Share Prices," *American Economic Review* 60 (September 1970), p. 616.
[14]H. Latané and C. Jones, "Standardized Unexpected Earnings—A Progress Report," *Journal of Finance* 32 (December 1977), pp. 1457–1465.

general are expecting the EPS to be and what the company actually reports. Unexpected information about earnings calls for investors to revise their expectations about the future and therefore an adjustment in the price of the stock. A favourable **earnings surprise**, in which the actual earnings exceed the market's expectation, should bring about an adjustment to the price of the stock as investors alter their beliefs about the company's earnings. Conversely, an unfavourable earnings surprise should lead to a downward adjustment in price; in effect, the market has been disappointed in its expectations.

Earnings Surprise
The difference between a firm's actual earnings and the consensus earnings estimate.

In conclusion, stock prices are affected not only by the level of earnings and their growth, but also by the market's expectations of earnings. Investors should be concerned with both the forecast for earnings and the difference between the actual earnings and the forecast—that is, the surprise. Therefore, fundamental analysis of earnings should involve more than a forecast, which is difficult enough: It should involve the role of the market's expectations about earnings.

What happens when the quarterly earnings are reported and the figures are below analysts' estimates? Obviously, the stock price is likely to drop quickly, and in some cases sharply. In a number of cases, the stock market is very unforgiving about disappointments in the form of negative earnings surprises. Such disappointments, and the accompanying sharp drops in stock price, are a common occurrence on Bay and Wall Streets. Similarly, it is not uncommon to see a stock price increase on news of a negative EPS, if the actual loss is not as great as had been expected.

If the price does drop sharply following the announcement of earnings below expectations, should an investor interested in owning the stock react quickly to take advantage of the price drop? According to one study of 2,000 large companies that experienced single-day price drops of over 10 percent in one particular year, the average decline was 17 percent the first day the stock traded after the bad news.[15] On average, these stocks were 25 percent cheaper 30 days after the report of bad news, and 90 percent of the stocks were lower at that time. Sixty days after the bad news, these stocks were still down an average of 23 percent, and after 90 days almost 20 percent. Why? The initial shock is often followed by additional shocks.

The Earnings Game

Investors need to realize that the process of estimating earnings, announcing earnings, and determining earnings surprises has become much more of a game, or managed process, over time. The way the "game" has been played up until now is as follows:

1. Analysts attempt to guess what a particular company will earn each quarter.

2. The company simultaneously provides "guidance" as to what it thinks earnings will be. According to one survey, about 80 percent of companies provide guidance, as compared to 10 percent only a few years earlier.

3. The "guidance number" plays a major role in the consensus estimate among analysts as to the expected earnings.

4. The variance of the actual reported earnings from the consensus estimate has typically constituted the earnings surprise. However, investors must now contend with "whisper forecasts," which are unofficial earnings estimates that circulate among traders and investors before earnings are announced. One study suggests that these estimates are more accurate than are the consensus estimates.

5. The earnings surprises are increasingly guided by companies in the form of earnings preannouncements, which have increased sharply.

Obviously, investors must try to understand the earnings game and the likely impact it will have on stock prices as a result of earnings surprises. Suffice it to say that it has become more complicated as investors try to figure out which forecast the actual earnings are expected to beat. In the final analysis, however, remember—it is all a game and almost everyone involved knows it.

---

[15]D. Dreman, "Let the Dust Clear," *Forbes*, October 12, 1992, p. 166.

The introduction of Regulation FD in the United States in October 2000 has required that, rather than inform only a few analysts of a significant upcoming change in earnings, companies must now make public disclosure of important information to all investors at the same time. Analysts and portfolio managers claim that Regulation FD has resulted in companies disclosing less information and in stock prices being more volatile, according to a March 2001 survey released by AIMR (now the CFA Institute). Of course, it is hard to document such claims, and these players obviously have a vested interest in the situation. Numerous companies are now releasing corporate information to all investors simultaneously through Internet broadcasts.

A new trend has started among some companies that may have a major impact on how information about earnings is formulated and distributed. Warren Buffett, among others, has argued that companies should not provide guidance. Some companies, such as Coca-Cola, have taken this approach.

Useful Information for Investors about Earnings Estimates

Summarizing our discussion about earnings forecasts, we can note the following useful information about the role of earnings forecasts in selecting common stocks:

1. Earnings reports are a key factor affecting stock prices. However, it is the surprise element in the reports that really matters—the difference between the actual results reported and the results expected by the market.
2. Surprises occur because analyst estimates are often considerably off target.
3. There appears to be a lag in the adjustment of stock prices to earnings surprises.
4. One earnings surprise tends to lead to another; there is a 45 percent chance of repeating an earnings surprise.
5. The best guidelines to surprises are revisions in analyst estimates. If estimates are steadily being adjusted upward, a buy signal is indicated; downward adjustments indicate a sell signal.
6. Stocks with significant revisions of 5 percent or more—up or down—often show above or below average performance.
7. Investors interested in buying stocks that report bad news and suffer a sharp decline should wait a while. Chances are the stock will be cheaper 30 and 60 days after the initial sharp decline.

Sales Growth—An Alternative to Earnings

Given the accounting problems with earnings, and the difficulty in forecasting earnings, it is not surprising that investors look at other fundamental data when selecting stocks. This is particularly true with newer companies that may not have current EPS, or the expectation thereof for several years. Therefore, investors must evaluate other dimensions.

A key company variable is obviously revenues, or sales. After all, a company cannot have earnings without reasonable revenues. Revenues not only lead to the accounting EPS for a company, but also make possible the firm's cash, which it uses to pay its bills and to operate. Most of the major providers of earnings estimates also offer revenue estimates.

CHECK YOUR UNDERSTANDING

17-7. An investor has decided to use an EPS forecast provided by analysts rather than attempting the forecast herself. Why might she be better off using a consensus forecast rather than the figure provided by any one analyst?

17-8. A company you are studying just reported that its EPS for the most recent quarter was lower than the previous quarter's figure. To your surprise, the stock price increased after the announcement. Why would this happen?

THE P/E RATIO

learning objective 4
Estimate the P/E ratio of a company.

The other half of the valuation framework in fundamental analysis is the **price-earnings (P/E) ratio**, or the earnings multiplier. The P/E ratio reported in the financial media indicates how much per dollar of earnings investors currently are willing to pay for a stock; that is, the price for each dollar of earnings. In a sense, it represents the market's summary evaluation of a company's prospects.

In effect, the P/E ratio is a measure of the relative price of a stock. In June 2004, for example, investors were willing to pay about 68.5 times earnings for **Agnico-Eagle Mines**, but only 1.9 times earnings for **Air Canada**. What are the reasons for such a large difference? To answer this question, it is necessary to consider the determinants of the P/E ratio.

Price-Earnings (P/E) Ratio

The ratio of stock price to earnings, using historical, current, or estimated data. Also known as the earnings multiplier.

Determinants of the P/E Ratio

Reviewing our earlier discussion in Chapter 13, we recall that the appropriate forward P/E ratio (P_0 / E_1) is conceptually a function of three factors, as expressed in the following equation:[16]

$$P_0 / E_1 = \frac{D_1 / E_1}{k - g}$$

(17-9)

where
D_1 / E_1 = the expected dividend payout ratio
k = the required rate of return for the stock
g = expected growth rate in dividends

Investors attempting to determine the P/E ratio that will prevail for a particular stock should think in terms of these three factors and their likely changes. Each of these is considered next.

The Dividend Payout Ratio

Dividends are clearly a function of earnings (although accounting earnings are an imprecise measure for cash flow, out of which dividends are paid). The relationship between these two variables, however, is more complex than current dividends being a function of current earnings. Dividends paid by corporations reflect established practices (i.e., previous earnings level) as well as prospects for the future (i.e., expected future earnings).

Many corporations whose stocks trade in Canadian equity markets pay dividends. Most companies behave as if dividends matter significantly to investors, and once dividend payments are established at a certain level, companies strive to maintain them at that level and increase them, if at all possible. Dividends are usually not reduced until and unless there is no alternative. In addition, they are generally not increased until it is clear that the new, higher level of dividends can be supported. For example, many listed companies pay special dividends, instead of increasing their regular dividends when they have particularly good years. As a result of this reluctance to decrease dividends, or to increase them unless they can be maintained, dividends adjust with a lag to earnings.

The P/E ratio can be expected to change as the expected dividend payout ratio changes. The higher the expected payout ratio, other things being equal, the higher the P/E ratio. However, "other things" are seldom equal. If the payout rises, the expected growth rate in earnings and dividends, g, will probably decline, thereby adversely affecting the P/E ratio. This decline occurs because less funds will be reinvested in the business, thereby leading to a decline in the expected growth rate, g.

---

[16]Strictly speaking, this relationship is only appropriate when it is reasonable to assume constant growth in dividends to infinity since this estimate for P_0 / E_1 is derived from the constant-growth version of the DDM.

The Required Rate of Return

As we know, the required rate of return, k, is a function of the riskless rate of return and a risk premium.

(17-10)
$$k = \text{RF} + \text{RP}$$

The riskless rate of return is usually proxied by the short-term government T-bill rate, although some use the rate of return on long-term government bonds. The risk premium is the additional compensation demanded by risk-averse investors before purchasing a risky asset such as a common stock. In Chapter 9, we saw that the CAPM provides a method for estimating the size of the risk premium, based on a stock's (or portfolio's) market risk as measured by beta (refer to Equation 9-9).

As an alternative to using CAPM to estimate "k" (which does not always work well for individual companies, as discussed in Chapter 9), many analysts estimate the return on a company's stock using the bond yield plus risk premium approach, which employs the following equation:

(17-11)
$$k = \text{The Company's Bond Yield} + \text{Equity-Bond Risk Premium}$$

In this equation, the analyst simply finds out the prevailing yield on a company's long-term bonds that are outstanding and adds a risk premium (usually in the 200–600 basis points range) to compensate investors for the additional risk associated with holding a company's equity versus holding its debt. Similar to the risk premium used in the CAPM model, this risk premium will vary across firms (being higher for riskier firms), and will also vary through time (being higher during periods of greater uncertainty).

Based on Equation 17-10 and 17-11, the following two statements can be made about a company's required rate of return:

1. Other things being equal, if the risk-free rate, RF, rises (or bond yields rise), the required rate of return, k, will rise. Thus, in periods of high interest rates such as 1980–81, k will be higher than in recent periods when interest rates had declined.

2. Other things being equal, if the risk premium rises as a result of an increase in risk (which could be caused by an increase in business risk, financial risk, or other risks), k will rise. Conversely, if the risk premium falls as a result of a decrease in risk, k will fall.

As we learned in Chapter 13, the relationship between k and the P/E ratio is inverse: Other things being equal, as k rises, the P/E ratio declines; as k declines, the P/E ratio rises. Because the required rate of return is a discount rate, P/E ratios and discount rates move inversely to each other.

The Expected Growth Rate

The third variable affecting the P/E ratio is the expected growth rate of dividends, g. We know that g = retention ratio × ROE, making the expected growth rate a function of the return on equity and the retention rate. The higher either of these variables is, the higher g will be, all other things being equal. What about the relationship between g and P/E? P/E and g are directly related: The higher the g, the higher the P/E ratio, other things being equal.

Investors are generally willing to pay more for a company with expected rapid growth in earnings than for one with expected slower growth in earnings. A basic problem in fundamental analysis, however, is determining how much more investors should be willing to pay for growth. In other words, how high should the P/E ratio be? There is no precise answer to this question. It depends on such factors as the following:

- The confidence that investors have in the expected growth. For some companies, investors may be well justified in expecting a rapid rate of growth for the next few years because of previous performance, management's ability, and the high estimates of growth described in investment advisory services. This may not be the case for another company, where, because of competitive inroads and other factors, the high growth prospects are at great risk.

- The reasons for the earnings growth can be important. Is it a result of great demand in the marketplace or of astute financing policies that could backfire if interest rates rise sharply or the economy enters a severe recession? Is growth the result of sales expansion or cost cutting (which will be exhausted at some point)? DuPont analysis is designed to provide insight into these issues.

Analyzing the P/E Ratio

In analyzing a particular P/E ratio, we first ask what model describes the expected growth rate for that company. Recent rapid growth and published estimates of strong expected future growth would lead investors not to use the constant-growth version of the dividend valuation model. Instead, we should evaluate the company by using a multiple-growth model. At some point, however, this growth can be expected to slow down to a more normal rate. In such cases it would be more appropriate to use the multi-stage growth version of the DDM, described in Chapter 13.

Why P/E Ratios Vary among Companies

Stock prices reflect market expectations about earnings. Companies that the market believes will achieve higher earnings growth rates will tend to be priced higher than those that are expected to show low earnings growth rates. Thus, a primary factor in explaining P/E ratio differences among companies is investor expectations about the future growth of earnings.

It is important to remember the role of interest rates, which are inversely related to P/E ratios, as discussed in Chapter 13. When interest rates are declining, the largest impact is on the P/E ratios of reliable growth stocks. This is because most of their earnings will occur far into the future, and can now be discounted at lower rates.

In addition, the size of the risk premium will affect "k," and hence the P/E ratio. In other words, the higher the risk premium associated with a particular stock, or with a particular time period, the higher the required rate of return, and the lower the P/E ratio.

The PEG Ratio

Some investors divide the P/E ratio by the earnings growth rate to obtain the following PEG ratio.

$$\text{PEG ratio} = \frac{\text{P/E}}{g} \tag{17-12}$$

where, g = the company's earnings growth rate.

The advantage of this calculation is that it relates the P/E ratio to earnings growth rather than relying on the P/E ratio by itself.

Real-World Returns 17-4 discusses the PEG ratio, surmising that firms with low PEG ratios offer the "cheapest profit growth." According to Peter Lynch, a famous manager of the Magellan Fund when it enjoyed great success, the P/E ratio of a company that is fairly valued will equal its expected growth rate. Therefore, an indication of undervaluation could be a stock with a P/E less than its earning growth rate.

REAL-WORLD RETURNS 17-4

Low PEG Ratio List Reveals Cheapest Profit Growth

What Are We Looking For?

We're spending the week looking at Thomson ONE's Stock Reports Plus, which is a stock ideas feature inside Thomson Reuters' portfolio management tool used by institutional investors. Today we'll look at the Canadian companies trading at the lowest price-to-earnings growth ratio, or PEG ratio.

More about Today's Screen

We'll screen for companies with market capitalizations greater than $1-billion. The PEG ratio is a commonly used valuation measurement that helps investors see if they are paying too high a P/E for a company's earnings growth.

The formula is to take the P/E and divide it by the annual earnings growth. If a company's P/E is 20, then the earnings would have to be growing at 20 percent for the PEG ratio to be 1. If the P/E is 10, then the PEG is 0.5. If the P/E is 40, then the PEG is 2. A lower ratio means the stock is cheaper.

What Did We Find Out?

A number of companies that were on yesterday's cheap P/E list are also on today's low PEG list, including Yellow Pages, Inmet, Lundin, Rona and Nexen.

Lowest PEG ratios for Canadian companies over $1-billion market capitalization

Company Name	Symbol	$ Price May 5	52-wk low $	52 wk high $	% yield	1-yr % price chg	Current Forward PEG	Forward EPS $	Market cap ($ mil)
Inmet Mining	IMN-T	81.31	58.26	111.89	0.3	10.0	0.1	10.42	3,830
TriStar Oil and Gas	TOG-T	17.35	6.00	17.54	0.0	0.2	0.91		1,872
Centerra Gold	CG-T	9.71	3.16	16.08	0.0	−14.4	0.3	0.98	1,960
Galleon Energy	GO.A-T	19.12	11.49	19.46	0.0	12.7	0.4	1.61	1,261
HudBay Minerals	HBM-T	20.18	13.70	29.63	0.0	−16.6	0.4	1.61	2,523
Laurentian Bank of Canada	LB-T	42.98	31.30	45.08	3.0	35.5	0.4	3.52	1,029
Yellow Pages Income Fund	YLO.UN-T	10.71	9.58	14.81	10.6	−25.1	0.4	1.47	5,680
Nexen Inc.	NXY-T	36.40	26.00	38.25	0.6	7.2	0.5	3.75	18,831
WestJet Airlines	WJA-T	16.35	14.11	23.49	0.0	0.9	0.5	1.50	2,128
Lundin Mining	LUN-T	7.39	6.50	15.42	0.0	−48.4	0.6	0.94	2,813
Oilexco Inc.	OIL-T	15.42	8.99	17.92	0.0	63.5	0.6	1.33	3,413
Petrobank Energy and Res.	PBG-T	54.59	23.15	63.03	0.0	124.5	0.6	2.68	4,222
Quebecor Inc.	QBR.B-T	28.70	25.33	41.94	0.7	−29.1	0.6	2.51	1,270
Rogers Communications	RCI.B-T	44.97	32.92	52.20	2.2	2.2	0.6	2.14	23,822
Astral Media	ACM.A-T	34.66	33.40	46.95	1.4	−20.2	0.8	2.91	1,889
CAE Inc.	CAE-T	12.15	9.92	15.25	0.3	-6.8	0.8	0.70	3,114
Canadian Western Bank	CWB-T	25.66	20.89	32.20	1.6	7.0	0.8	1.76	1,621
Rona Inc.	RON-T	14.18	13.00	25.26	0.0	−41.7	0.8	1.59	1,670
Shaw Communications	SJR.B-T	20.83	17.00	28.74	3.5	−3.7	0.8	1.14	8,922
Telus Corp.	T-T	46.00	41.05	66.45	3.9	−26.3	0.8	3.67	8,291
Linamar Corp.	LNR-T	15.00	12.92	26.48	1.6	−10.2	0.9	1.36	1,052

Note: PEG based on last full week's price close. Source: Thomson and Globe Investor

Source: Adams, Scott, "Low PEG Ratio List Reveals Cheapest Profit Growth," *The Globe and Mail*, May 7, 2008, p. B16.

Like most calculations of this type, the PEG ratio is only a rule of thumb. There are no assurances that one is paying too much or too little. One problem with this calculation is that it relates a ratio to a percentage number. Another is that different earnings growth rates can be used to calculate it. Some use recent earnings growth rates while others use estimated earnings.

CHECK YOUR UNDERSTANDING

17-9. Dividends are said to follow earnings "with a lag," that is, dividend changes occur somewhat later than earnings changes. Why is this?

FUNDAMENTAL SECURITY ANALYSIS IN PRACTICE

learning objective 5
Use the beta coefficient to estimate the risk of a stock.

We have examined several important aspects of fundamental analysis as it is applied to individual companies. Obviously, such a process can be quite detailed, involving an analysis of a company's sales potential, competition, tax situation, cost projections, accounting practices, and so on. Regardless of detail and complexity, the underlying process is as described. Analysts and investors are seeking to estimate a company's earnings and P/E ratio and to determine whether the stock is undervalued (a buy) or overvalued (a sell).

In doing fundamental security analysis, investors need to use published and computerized data sources both to gather information and to provide calculations and estimates of future variables such as EPS. There are several sources of information including financial newspapers such as *The Globe and Mail* and the *National Post* in Canada, and international publications such as *The Wall Street Journal* and the *Financial Times*. In addition, there exist a large number of financial magazines including *Forbes, BusinessWeek, Fortune*, and *Money*.

Corporate annual and quarterly reports also provide extensive information about companies. The SEDAR (System for Electronic Document Analysis and Retrieval) website (www.sedar.com) provides on-line access to annual reports and various other information statements that are filed by companies with the appropriate regulatory authority.

Reports from investment dealers provide a current assessment of a number of companies, as does *The Financial Post* (www.fpinfomart.ca).

In the US, there are several large investment advisory services including *The Value Line Investment Survey*, Moody's *Industrial Manual*, and Standard & Poor's *Corporation Records and Industry Surveys*. In addition, there are numerous websites that provide up-to-date information regarding companies.

Real-World Returns 17-5 includes portions of an investor report on Empire Company Limited obtained from the *Financial Post* database at www.fpinfomart.ca. Notice that this report includes several of the items we have discussed in this chapter (and in Chapters 13 to 16) including the P/E ratio, earnings estimates, the dividend yield, the book value per share, the DuPont decomposition, beta, and growth rate estimates, among other items. The price recommendation is $38.20 (with a sell recommendation above $43 and a buy recommendation below $32), which is very close to the May 16, 2008, closing price of $38.32, and as we shall see, it is fairly close to the valuation estimate we arrive at in the concluding section of this chapter, although our analysis is conducted based on the May 2008 time period.

In modern investment analysis, the risk for a stock is often measured by its beta coefficient, as explained in Chapter 9. Beta reflects the relative systematic risk for a stock, or the risk that cannot be diversified away. The higher the beta coefficient, the higher the risk for an individual stock, and the higher the required rate of return. Beta measures the volatility of a stock's returns relative to fluctuations in market returns.

REAL-WORLD RETURNS 17-5

Empire Company Limited Investor Report

Company:	Empire Company Limited
Head Office:	115 King St., Stellarton, Nova Scotia, B0K 1S0
Business:	Operates principally in the business segments of food distribution, real estate, theatre exhibition, and equity investments.
Segmented Data:	52 weeks ended May 5/07
Revenue by Industry:	Food distribution: 97%, Real estate: 2%, Corporate and other: 1%

Recent Price	Recent Daily Vol.	Annual Avg. Daily Vol.	52-wk range	Shares Outstanding
$38.32 at May 16/08	20,470 at May 16/08	56,891	$57.14 – $35.25	65,745,000 at May 5/07

Market Capitalization	IAD	Ex-Dividend Date	Yield	Listed	Price/ Book
$2,519,358,000	$0.66	Apr 10/08	1.7%	TSX/EMP.A	1.10

P/E	% Below High	Book Value	12 mo EPS	3-yr. Return	10-yr Beta
10.40	32.9%	$32.37	$3.70	2.04%	0.41

Recommendation (provided by Value Sciences Inc.)

Valuation Date	Price	P/E	Fundamentals
Mar 14/08	$38.20	8.0	10.3

Valuation	Cost of Capital	Volatility	Fundamentum
–2.3%	9.7%	LOW	–24.4

Most stores including Empire and Sobeys are coming out swinging after the Loblaw's business. The grocery business is competitive and margins are razor thin, which means it is all about management. Empire seems to still be trying to find that consistency and areas of growth.

Buy Below: $32
Sell Above: $43

Based on the copyright General Valuation Model. Copyright © Value Sciences Inc. 2008.

Forecasts provided by *I/B/E/S*

Consensus Recommendation of 4 Analysts	Hold
Consensus Target Price of 4 Analysts	$41.13

Consensus Information - EPS $							
Periods	Date	# Ests.	Mean	High	Low	Up	Down
Quarter Ending:	Apr/08	2	1.11	1.29	0.93	0	0
Quarter Ending:	Jul/08	1	0.94	0.94	0.94	0	0
Quarter Ending:	Oct/08	1	0.91	0.91	0.91	0	0
Quarter Ending:	Jan/09	1	0.60	0.60	0.60	0	0
2008	Apr	2	3.49	3.57	3.41	0	0
2009	Apr	3	3.59	3.99	3.24	0	0

Consensus Information - Cash Flow Per Share $

Periods	Date	# Ests.	Mean	High	Low	Up	Down
2008	Apr	2	9.34	9.84	8.84	0	0
2009	Apr	2	8.94	9.26	8.62	0	0

Fiscal year ended May 5

Revenue	Quarter 1	Quarter 2	Quarter 3	Quarter 4	Total
Fiscal Year	$000s	$000s	$000s	$000s	$000s
May 5/08	3,519,400	3,484,800	3,503,000	–	–
May 5/07	3,373,800	3,313,500	3,281,900	3,350,400	13,366,700
May 6/06	3,361,700	3,285,600	3,264,400	3,249,400	13,161,100
May 7/05	3,073,700	3,022,800	2,978,500	3,360,200	12,435,200
Apr 30/04	2,814,700	2,794,400	2,798,500	2,876,400	11,284,000

EPS	Quarter 1	Quarter 2	Quarter 3	Quarter 4	Total
Fiscal Year	$	$	$	$	$
May 5/08	2.17	0.89	0.74		
May 5/07	0.81	0.87	0.54	0.98	3.20
May 6/06	1.12	0.74	0.86	1.81	4.53
May 7/05	0.67	0.61	0.72	0.83	2.83
Apr 30/04	0.64	0.56	0.81	0.63	2.63

Latest Dividend Declared	$0.165 paid Apr 30/08
Paid 2008	$0.33
Paid 2007	$0.6300001
Paid 2006	$0.58

Short Position	182,242 (Apr 30/08)
	145,850 (Apr 15/08)

Top 3 In Industry (by Market Capitalization)

	Market Capitalization	Yield	P/E
Shoppers Drug Mart Corporation	$12,123,180,032	1.50%	23.80
Loblaw Companies Limited	$9,140,946,944	2.50%	27.10
George Weston Limited	$6,584,092,160	2.80%	12.40

DuPont Model

	2006	2005	2004	2003	2002	2001	2000
Income/Sales	2.00	2.76	2.01	2.06	2.09	1.89	5.23
Sales/Assets	2.56	2.61	2.52	2.41	2.35	2.30	2.71
Assets/Equity	2.46	2.58	2.90	2.99	3.19	3.37	3.85
Return on Equity	10.27	16.21	11.41	11.58	11.39	11.48	69.07

Earnings Quality Model

	2006	2005	2004	2003	2002	2001	2000
EBIT Margin %	3.35	4.56	3.76	3.86	4.09	4.16	7.85
Asset Turnover	2.56	2.61	2.52	2.41	2.35	2.30	2.71

(continued)

REAL-WORLD RETURNS 17-5 *continued*

Earnings Quality Model *continued*

	2006	2005	2004	2003	2002	2001	2000
Interest Burden %	1.15	1.66	1.76	1.96	2.06	2.59	3.34
Retention %	68.96	70.39	65.60	67.52	64.81	65.24	80.54
Leverage	2.46	2.58	2.90	2.99	3.19	3.37	3.85
Book Value/Share $	32.37	29.77	25.90	23.82	21.54	19.47	16.82
Apparent Tax Rate %	31.04	29.61	34.40	32.48	35.19	34.76	19.46

Growth Rates %

	2006	2005	2004	2003	2002	2001	2000
Sales	1.56	5.84	10.20	6.21	7.03	(13.97)	3.35
Sustainable	8.33	14.21	9.47	9.82	9.78	10.29	67.73
Cash Flow	(28.28)	28.77	4.20	31.25	(42.45)	323.42	(46.41)
Book Value/Share	8.74	14.96	8.73	10.58	10.64	15.75	92.80
Dividends/Share	7.14	16.67	20.00	21.21	54.39	25.74	21.43

Latest Results

Periods ended:	39w Feb 2/08 $000	%Chg	39w Feb 3/07 $000
Operating revenue	10,507,200	+5	10,016,300
Net income	249,300	+77	141,000
Earnings per sh.*	$3.79		$2.15

* Class A & B

Restated

The results were attributed to full ownership of Sobeys Inc. following privatization in June 2007, and higher revenue from real estate division and Empire Theatres. The company noted Sobeys same-store sales were up 2% for the quarter

Source: Retrieved from www.fpinfomart.ca, May 19, 2008.

EXAMPLE 17-7: MEASURING RISK FOR EMPIRE COMPANY LIMITED

Using the 0.41 estimate of the beta for Empire provided in Real-World Returns 17-5, we conclude that Empire's systematic risk is much lower than the market as a whole (which has a beta of 1.0 by definition). That is, on average, its price does not fluctuate closely with market fluctuations. If the market is expected to rise 10 percent over the next year, investors could expect Empire to rise approximately 4.1 percent based on its beta of 0.41.

In trying to understand and predict a company's return and risk, we need to remember that both are a function of two components. The systematic component is related to the return on the overall market. The other component is the unique part attributable to the company itself and not to the overall market. It is a function of the specific positive or negative factors that affect a company independent of the market.

It should come as no surprise that because security analysis always involves the uncertain future, mistakes will be made, and analysts will differ in their outlooks for a particular company. As we might expect, security analysis in today's world is often done differently than it was in the past. The reason for this change is not so much that we have a better understanding of the basis of security analysis, because the models we have discussed earlier—value as a function of expected return and risk—remain the basis of security analysis today. Rather, the differences now have to do with the use of technology to perform many calculations quickly and objectively, as well as the timeliness and quantity of relevant information now available to investors and analysts.

PUTTING ALL THE PIECES TOGETHER

We conclude our discussion by illustrating how we could have used the information in the investor report in Real-World Returns 17-5 to estimate the value of Empire's common shares on May 16, 2008, when its share price was $38.32. We will use the following estimates obtained from the investor report:

Sustainable growth rate (g) = 8% (rounding off the 7.99% sustainable growth rate figure we had calculated previously using the 2007 ROE and payout figures)
Dividend payout ratio (2007) = 0.1881
Fiscal 2007 dividend per share = $0.60
Most recent annual dividend per share as of May 2008 (sum of last four quarters) (D_0) = $0.66
Fiscal 2007 earnings per share = $3.19
Most recent annual dividend per share as of May 2008 (sum of last four quarters) (EPS_0) = $4.78
Beta = 0.41

We begin by using the three-month T-bill rate as of May 2008 (approximately 2.3 percent) as the measure of the risk-free rate of return. Using the long-term (1938–2007) average return on Canadian common stocks of 11.8 percent as an estimate for the expected return on the market for the following year, we can determine the required return on Empire's shares using CAPM:

$$\text{Required return } k = 2.3 + (11.8 - 2.3)(0.41) = 6.20\%$$

This rate of return seems to be unreasonably low, given that 30-year Government of Canada bonds were yielding approximately 4.0 percent in May 2008, and given that two companies similar to Sobeys were providing bond yields over 8 percent—Loblaw Companies Limited had 20-year bonds that were yielding 8.39 percent and George Weston had 25-year bonds that were yielding 8.50 percent. In other words, 6.2 percent does not seem to provide a reasonable risk premium for holding Empire's common stock. As mentioned, CAPM does not always work extremely well for individual companies, and judgement and common sense need to be applied when using this model.

Some analysts prefer to use long-term government yields as a proxy for the risk-free rate when estimating a required rate of return for a long period into the future, especially when short-term rates are low, as they were in May 2007. Using the 30-year government yield of 4.0 percent as the risk-free rate, we obtain the following estimate of the required return on Empire's stock:

$$k = 4.0 + (11.8 - 4.0)(0.41) = 7.20\%$$

This estimate is more reasonable, although it is still on the low side.

Finally, if we use the bond yield plus risk premium approach (i.e., Equation 17-11), using Loblaw's long-term bond yield of 8.39 percent and adding 200 basis points (which is reasonable given the low risk associated with Sobeys), we end up with a required rate of return of approximately 10.39 percent, which seems more reasonable. If we compare and combine this to the cost of capital estimate of 9.7 percent found in Real-World Returns 17-5, it seems reasonable to use k = 10 percent for our future analysis.

We begin our analysis based on the assumption that the estimated 8 percent growth rate is sustainable indefinitely. This implies we can use the constant-growth version of the DDM given in

Equation 17-1. Based on this model, we get the following estimate for the value of Empire's shares in May 2008:

$$\hat{P}_0 = \frac{D_1}{k-g} = \frac{(\$0.66) \times (1.08)}{0.10-0.08} = \frac{\$0.713}{0.02} = \$35.65$$

Alternatively, we could have used the P/E ratio approach to estimate the value of Empire's shares. If we again assume constant growth to infinity, we can determine the appropriate forward P/E ratio (P_0/E_1) using Equation 17-9:

$$P/E = \frac{D_1/E_1}{k-g}$$

If we use the last four quarters' EPS as EPS_0 of \$4.78 and combine it with the growth rate, we would estimate next year's EPS to be

$$EPS_1 = EPS_0 \times (1+g) = (\$4.78) \times (1.08) = \$5.16$$

Combining this EPS estimate with our DPS_1 estimate implies the following payout ratio and P/E ratio:

$$P/E = \frac{D_1/E_1}{k-g} = \frac{.713/5.16}{0.10-0.08} = 6.91$$

Combining these results and using Equation 17-2, we get the following estimate for the value of Empire:

$$\hat{P}_0 = \text{Estimated EPS} \times P_0/E_1 \text{ ratio} = \$5.16 \times 6.91 = \$35.66$$

While this price estimate seems reasonable, the EPS estimate seems high given their historical EPS figures, while the P/E ratio seems low, given the analyst consensus EPS estimate for 2008 is \$3.59 (as provided in Real-World Returns 17-5) and that their five-year average P/E ratio is 11.26. If we use the consensus EPS estimate for EPS_1 and combine this with our DPS_1 estimate, we obtain the following payout ratio and P/E ratio:

$$P/E = \frac{D_1/E_1}{k-g} = \frac{.713/3.59}{0.10-0.08} = 9.93$$

Combining these results and using Equation 17-2, we get the following estimate for the value of Empire:

$$\hat{P}_0 = \text{Estimated EPS} \times P_0/E_1 \text{ ratio} = \$3.59 \times 9.93 = \$35.65$$

This estimate is also reasonable, and the inputs are more reasonable.

Finally, notice that if we use the five-year average P/E ratio and the consensus EPS estimate we would obtain the following price estimate:

$$\hat{P}_0 = \text{Estimated EPS} \times P_0/E_1 \text{ ratio} = \$3.59 \times 11.26 = \$40.42$$

Notice that the estimates are very close, which is attributable to the fact that they use the same inputs and both assume constant growth in earnings and dividends at a rate of 8 percent to infinity. This may or may not have been a reasonable assumption, and there are many alternative methods and assumptions available for valuing Empire, many of which were discussed at length in Chapter 13.

For ease of exposition, let's assume these estimates were considered reasonable at the time, and consider their implications. Most of these estimates suggest that Empire was slightly overvalued at $38.32, its May 2008 trading price. Based on this analysis, an investor would have been inclined to sell Empire shares if already held, or short sell them if not held.

The analysis above uses the 2003–2008 accounting figures to estimate future growth in earnings and dividends. One concern with this approach is that the use of historical earnings and dividend measures could provide a misleading estimate of future growth if the chosen period is not representative of the future. As we know, there is never any guarantee that past performance will repeat itself, so there are always problems associated with using historical data to predict future performance (this is an issue we have been forced to deal with at various points throughout the text). In order to avoid these problems, we must obtain future estimates of growth based on other sources of information and analysis.

By the time this text is in print, we may find out the "market" has revalued Empire by a significant amount. This would not mean that fundamental analysis is a waste of time, but merely highlights a fact that we have been stressing throughout the text—it is difficult to predict the future, especially for relatively short periods of time. This is the unavoidable risk associated with investing in common stocks.

In fact, it should come as no surprise that analysts often differ substantially regarding their views for any particular company because security analysis always involves forecasting the uncertain future, and mistakes are inevitable. Real-World Returns 17-6 illustrates two different opinions on Time Warner at the same point in time, with one analyst arguing that Time Warner is an attractive buy while the other argues that the stock is fully valued.

REAL-WORLD RETURNS 17-6

Time Warner: Can the Media Conglomerate Get with the Program?

YES: Henry Ellenbogen, co-manager, T. Rowe Price Media & Telecommunications Fund
AOL is changing from an Internet service provider to a content provider with online advertising; there is risk in this transition, but the price that you're paying for the opportunity is very reasonable.

When we look at the operating and senior management team, we feel very comfortable with the way the company has been run over the past few years. As far as the accounting difficulties, these are all issues that existed under previous management.

On cable systems, we think the Adelphia acquisition gives Time Warner very strong regional clusters, and we think it will continue to perform at the high end of the cable industry. Its cable operation will grow.

The company has pruned its portfolio to focus on higher-return-on-capital businesses. The by-product of this is that now it's in the position of returning substantial cash to shareholders.

NO: Thomas Forte, consumer analyst, Geneva Investment Management of Chicago
The fact that AOL is losing subscribers to broadband Internet services is one reason why the company had to change focus. Even though advertising sales are gravitating toward the Internet, with the exodus of users from AOL that doesn't help Time Warner as much as the loss of revenue hurts its cable properties like TNT and CNN.

(continued)

REAL-WORLD RETURNS 17-6 *continued*

Given the company's history of earnings restatements, there are times when it's difficult to trust its accounting.

The cable distribution business is doing well, but it faces significant competition from AT&T and Verizon on the Internet television side and from Dish Network and DirecTV on the satellite side.

To the extent that shareholder activist Carl Icahn forces the company to sell large stakes in AOL or Time Warner Cable, it may increase the stock price in the short term.

Source: Maudlin, William, "Face-Off," *SmartMoney*, February 2006, p. 28. Copyright © by SmartMoney, a joint venture of the Hearst Corporation and DowJones & Company, Inc. All rights reserved.

We conclude the main text of this chapter by noting that Appendix 17A provides a comprehensive example of company analysis that focuses on ratio analysis (including DuPont analysis), as well as combining this analysis with some of the valuation techniques discussed in Chapter 13.

EARNINGS OVERSTATEMENT CAUSES SHARE DROP

Company earnings, as you have learned, are fundamental to assessing a stock's value and potential. Investors, regulators, and the legal system take corporate financial statements very seriously.

In 2004, Canadian telecommunications giant Nortel Networks surprised the market by announcing that its previously reported earnings would be restated—reduced in half—and that its profits had evaporated into losses. The company blamed "serious accounting errors" for the overstatement. The stock price plunged 30 percent in one day, the equivalent of $9 billion in value.

The Ontario Securities Commission, US Securities and Exchange Commission, and the RCMP all launched probes into Nortel's finances, and shareholders brought lawsuits. Top executives were fired and charged with civil and criminal accounting fraud charges. The company restated its results several times in the following years. In 2007, Nortel agreed to improve its reporting policies.

DISCUSSION QUESTIONS

1. What determines an accounting error versus accounting fraud?

2. Do shareholders have unreasonable expectations for financial statements?

3. Should investors and financial advisors "forgive" a company for past unethical behaviour and buy its shares after it has apparently solved its problems?

SUMMARY

This summary relates to the learning objectives for this chapter.

1. **Define fundamental analysis at the company level.**

   The analysis of individual companies, the last of the three steps in fundamental security analysis, examines the basic financial variables of the company, such as sales, management, and competition. It involves the application of the valuation procedures described in earlier chapters. Intrinsic value (a stock's justified price) can be estimated using a dividend valuation model, an earnings multiplier model, or many other approaches, several of which are discussed in Chapter 13. It is then compared to the current market price in order to determine whether the stock is undervalued or overvalued. An important first step in fundamental analysis is to understand the earnings per share (EPS) of companies. The financial statements can be used to understand the accounting basis of EPS.

2. **Explain the accounting aspects of a company's earnings.**

   The balance sheet shows the assets and liabilities at a specific date, whereas the income statement shows the flows during a period for the items that determine net income. Although these statements must be prepared in accordance with a set of guidelines determined by the accounting profession—generally accepted accounting principles (GAAP)—the use of alternative permissible accounting practices can result in EPS figures that are not always precise, readily comparable figures. EPS is the result of the interaction of several variables. Changes in earnings are directly related to changes in stock prices. To assess expected earnings, investors often consider the earnings growth rate, which is often measured as the product of ROE and the earnings retention rate.

3. **Describe the importance of EPS forecasts.**

   The lack of persistence in growth rates may lead investors to consider EPS forecasts, which are available mechanically or from analysts. All forecast methods are subject to error and the evidence is mixed on which method is better, although studies favour analysts' forecasts. The difference between actual and forecast EPS is important because of the role of the market's expectations about earnings.

4. **Estimate the P/E ratio of a company.**

   The price-earnings (P/E) ratio is the other half of the earnings multiplier model, indicating the amount per dollar of earnings investors are willing to pay for a stock. It represents the relative price of a stock per dollar of earnings, with some companies carrying high P/E ratios and others having low ones at particular times. The P/E ratio is influenced directly by investors' expectations of the future growth of earnings and the payout ratio, and inversely by the required rate of return. P/E ratios vary among companies and for the same company through time, primarily because of investors' expectations about the future growth of earnings. If investors lower their expectations, the price of the stock may drop while actual earnings remain constant or even rise.

5. **Use the beta coefficient to estimate the risk of a stock.**

   The beta coefficient measures the volatility for a stock with respect to fluctuations in market returns. It indicates the average responsiveness of the stock's price to the overall market, with high beta stocks exhibiting larger changes than the overall market; low beta stocks show smaller changes.

KEY TERMS

Earnings surprise, p.555

Financial statements, p.538

Generally accepted accounting

principles (GAAP), p.542

Internal (sustainable) growth

rate, p.550

Price-earnings (P/E) ratio, p.557

Return on assets (ROA), p.548

Return on equity (ROE), p.547

REVIEW QUESTIONS

17-1.   What is the intrinsic value of a stock?

17-2.   How can a stock's intrinsic value be determined?

17-3.   What are the limitations of using Equation 17-1 to determine intrinsic value?

17-4.   What is meant by GAAP?

17-5.   What does the auditor's report signify about the financial statements?

17-6.   How can investors obtain EPS forecasts? Which source is better?

17-7.   What problems do estimating accounting earnings present?

17-8.   What is the concept of earnings quality?

17-9.   Outline, in words, the determination process for EPS.

17-10. Assuming that a firm's return on assets exceeds its interest costs, why would it not boost ROE to the maximum through the use of debt financing since higher ROE leads to higher EPS?

17-11. How can the earnings growth rate be determined?

17-12. How well do earnings growth rates for individual companies persist across time?

17-13. What role do earnings expectations play in selecting stocks?

17-14. How can the unexpected component of EPS be used to select stocks?

17-15. Why would an investor want to know the beta coefficient for a particular company? How could this information be used?

17-16. Is beta the only determinant of a company's return?

17-17. Explain the role of financing in a company's EPS.

17-18. What are the variables that affect the P/E ratio? Is the effect direct or inverse for each component?

17-19. Holding everything else constant, what effect would the following have on a company's P/E ratio?

   a. An increase in the expected growth rate of earnings
   b. A decrease in the expected dividend payout
   c. An increase in the risk-free rate of return
   d. An increase in the risk premium
   e. A decrease in the required rate of return.

17-20. The two components of EPS are:

   a. ROA and leverage.
   b. book value per share and leverage.
   c. ROE and book value per share.
   d. leverage and profit margin.

17-21. The two components of ROE are:

   a. ROA and book value per share.
   b. ROA and leverage.
   c. ROA and profit margin.
   d. leverage and book value.

17-22. The DuPont method breaks down ROA into:

   a. net income margin and turnover.
   b. book value and turnover.
   c. leverage and book value.
   d. net income margin and leverage.

17-23. Which of the following statements concerning dividends is false?

    a. Over half of all NYSE-listed firms pay dividends.

    b. Dividends adjust with a lag to earnings.

    c. Dividends are a function of earnings.

    d. If the dividend payout rises, the risk of the firm rises.

PROBLEMS

17-1. GF is a large producer of food products. In 2008, the percentage breakdown of revenues and profits was as follows:

	Revenues (%)	Profits (%)
Packaged foods	41	62
Coffee	28	19
Processed meat	19	13
Food service — other	12	6
	100	100

International operations account for about 22 percent of sales and 17 percent of operating profit.

For the 2004–2008 fiscal years, ending March 31, the number of shares outstanding (in millions) and selected income statement data (in millions of dollars) were as follows:

Shares Outst.	Year	Revenues	Oper. Inc.	Cap. Exp.	Amort.	Int. Exp.	Net Income Before Tax	Net Income After Tax
49.93	2004	$5472	$524	$121	$ 77	$ 31	$452	$232
49.97	2005	5960	534	262	78	39	470	256
49.43	2006	6601	565	187	89	50	473	255
49.45	2007	8351	694	283	131	152	418	221
51.92	2008	8256	721	266	133	139	535	289

For each year calculate:

    a. Operating income as a percentage of revenues.

    b. Net profits after tax as a percentage of revenues.

    c. After-tax profits per share outstanding (EPS).

The balance sheet data for the same fiscal years (in millions of dollars) were as follows:

Year	Cash	Current Assets	Current Liabilities	Total Assets	Long-Term Debt	Common Equity
2004	$291	$1736	$ 845	$2565	$251	$1321
2005	178	1951	1047	2978	255	1480
2006	309	2019	929	3103	391	1610
2007	163	2254	1215	3861	731	1626
2008	285	2315	1342	4310	736	1872

    d. Calculate the ratio of current assets to current liabilities for each year.

    e. Calculate the long-term debt as a percentage of common equity.

    f. For each year calculate the book value per share as the common equity divided by the number of shares outstanding.

    g. Calculate ROE.

    h. Calculate ROA.

    i. Calculate leverage.

    j. Calculate the net income margin.

    k. Calculate turnover.

    l. Calculate the EBIT.

    m. Calculate the income ratio.

    n. Calculate operating efficiency.

    o. On the basis of these calculations evaluate the current status of the health of GF and the changes over the period.

17-2. Combining information from an analyst's report on GF and some estimated data for 2010, the following calendar-year data, on a per-share basis, are provided:

Year	Price Range		Earnings	Dividends	Book Value	(D/E) (%)	Annual Avg. P/E	ROE = E/Book (%)
	Low	High						
2004	$26.5	$35.3	$4.56	$1.72	$25.98	37.7	7.0	17.6%
2005	28.3	37.0	5.02	1.95	29.15	38.8	6.2	17.2
2006	23.5	34.3	5.14	2.20	32.11	42.8	5.8	16.0
2007	27.8	35.0	4.47	2.20	30.86		7.7	
2008	29.0	47.8	5.73	2.30	30.30		6.8	
2009	36.6	53.5	6.75	2.40	39.85			
2010			6.75	2.60	44.00			

    a. Calculate the D/E, ROE, and TR for 2007, 2008, and 2009. (Use the average of the low and high prices to calculate TRs.)

    b. Show that from 2005 through 2009 the per annum growth rate in dividends was 6.9 percent and for earnings was 8.2 percent.

    c. Using the current price of $47, with estimated earnings for 2010 of $6.75, show that the P/E would be evaluated as 6.96.

    d. On the basis of the annual average P/E ratios provided and your estimate in (c), assume an expected P/E of 7. If an investor expected the earnings of GF for 2010 to be $7.50, show that the intrinsic value would be $52.50.

    e. What factors are important in explaining the difference in the P/E ratios of Empire and GF?

    f. From your calculation of the growth rate of dividends in (b), assume that the annual rate is 7 percent. If the required rate of return for the stock is 12 percent and the expected dividend payout ratio is 0.4, show that P/E = 8.

    g. If the dividend payout ratio is 0.4 and the return on equity is 15 percent, show that g = 0.09.

    h. Using $k = 0.14$ and $g = 0.09$, with expected 2010 dividends of $2.60, show that the intrinsic value is $52.

    i. Assume the beta for GF is 0.8 relative to Empire's beta of 0.41. Is this information of any help in explaining the different P/E ratios of these two companies?

17-3. Information for Company ABC is presented in the following table.

    a. Calculate Company ABC's ROE, using the extended (five-part) DuPont system. (You must show and label the appropriate value for each of the components of ROE).

    b. Estimate the company's sustainable growth rate. (Assume its ROE is 12 percent if you do not complete part (a).

    c. Company XYZ is in ABC's industry. XYZ has an asset turnover ratio of 1.5, a net profit margin of 6 percent, and a debt ratio of 50 percent. Estimate XYZ's ROE, and compare it to ABC's. Comment on the source of differences in the ROE of XYZ relative to the ROE of ABC using a DuPont traditional (three-part) framework.

Company ABC
Income Statement

Total Revenue	$ 1,426,000
Cost of Goods Sold	1,238,700
Depreciation/Amortization	40,100
General, Selling & Admin. Expense	33,100
Earnings before Interest and Taxes	114,100
Interest Expense	5,300
Pre-tax Income	108,800
Income Tax Expense:	
Current	10,900
Deferred	9,000
Net Income	88,900
Dividends — Common Shares	14,700
Market Price per Share (Close)	6.69

Balance Sheet

Assets:	
Cash & Equivalents	$ 150,000
Accounts Receivable	174,000
Inventory	220,200
Total Current Assets	544,200
Fixed Assets — Gross	1,372,700
Less: Accumulated Depreciation	766,200
Fixed Assets — Net	606,500
Total Assets	1,150,700
Liabilities & Equity:	
Bank Loans & Equivalents	147,800
Accounts Payable	347,200
Current Portion of Long-Term Debt	5,400
Total Current Liabilities	500,400
Long-Term Debt	83,500
Deferred Taxes	41,600
Equity:	
Common Stock	348,900
Retained Earnings	176,300
Total Equity	525,200
Total Liabilities & Equity	1,150,700

17-4. What is the sustainable growth rate for a company with a dividend yield of 3 percent, a trailing P/E ratio of 20 that has a net income margin of 5 percent, and a total asset turnover ratio of 2.0, if total liabilities account for 60 percent of the firm's total assets?

17-5. a. Determine the asset turnover ratio for Company ABC, which has an ROA of 5 percent, an EPS of $1.00, and a sales per share figure of $50.
b. Determine ABC's ROE if its leverage ratio (equity multiplier) is 2.0.
c. Determine ABC's sustainable growth rate if its dividend per share figure is $0.30.
d. Estimate the company's justifiable P/E ratio based on the information above if it has a beta of 2.0, and the expected market return is 12 percent, while the risk-free rate is 5 percent.

e. What is ABC's average tax rate if its interest burden ratio is 0.60 and its EBIT efficiency ratio is 0.05?

17-6. Internet Industries expects to earn $5.00 for the coming year, and pay a $2.00 dividend. Its ROA is 13 percent, while its leverage factor is 1.7. Calculate its expected year-end dividend per share for year 2.

17-7. Given the following information for Mighty Manufacturing Company, calculate its ROA and ROE.

> EBIT efficiency: 0.1
> Net income: $50,000,000
> Net income margin: 0.05
> Total asset turnover: 3
> Leverage: 1.5
> Retention rate: 0.3

17-8. A firm has a sustainable growth rate of 5 percent indefinitely, and the required return on its shares is 15 percent.

   a. Estimate the value of this company's shares today using the price-to-sales ratio approach, if the company's most recent EPS was $5.00, while the dividends per share were $2.00. Its sales per share figure is $100.

   b. Repeat part (a) using the market-to-book approach if the firm's book value per share is $60, its ROA is 5 percent, and its leverage ratio (equity multiplier) is 3.0.

17-9. A firm has a book value per share of $20. Its most recent EPS and dividend per share figures were $2.00 and $0.50 respectively. If it has a beta of 1.2, and the expected return on the market is 10 percent, while the current risk-free rate is 3 percent, calculate the price of its shares using the market-to-book ratio approach.

17-10. Sangunk Electronics has net assets of $550 million and shareholders' equity of $330 million. It has total debt of $220 million. ROA is 11.3 percent. What is the ROE for this company?

17-11. The following table provides summary data for the 2007 fiscal year for Empire Corp. and three of its competitors: Shopper's Drug Mart Corp., Loblaw Companies Ltd., and George Weston Ltd. (The data for the competitors was obtained from "Google Finance", a source of free corporate and stock information.) Enter these figures into a spreadsheet and use them to conduct a three-point Dupont decomposition as specified below. (You can check your work against the calculations for Empire Corp. provided in the text).

	Empire	Shopper's	Loblaw	Geo.Weston
Sales	13366.7	8478.4	29384	32815
Net Income	210.1	493.6	330	563
Total Assets	5224.9	5644.0	13674	18388
S/H Equity	2135.4	3097.0	5545	4937
Dividends	39.5	139.0	230.3	185.9

   a. Calculate the net income margin for each firm. Which company has the most efficient operations (highest margin)?

   b. Calculate the asset turnover for each company. Which firm is the best at generating revenues from its assets?

   c. Calculate the leverage ratio for the four firms. Which is the most highly levered? (That is, used the most debt relative to assets.)

   d. Use the results above to find the return on equity for each company in 2007.

   e. Use the dividends paid in 2007 to calculate a sustainable growth rate for each of the companies.

17-12. In the technology boom of the late 1990s, many computing and networking firms traded at very high P/E multiples. Analysts had difficulty valuing these firms and often produced widely different estimates. Let's consider a typical company that is followed by three well-known analysts. Estimates of the appropriate beta for the firm's stock were 1.25, 1.38, and 1.55 for Analyst 1, Analyst 2, and Analyst 3, respectively. At the time, the risk-free rate was 5.5 percent.

   a. Use a spreadsheet to lay out a table of expected return figures (as calculated from the CAPM), that would result from the analysts' beta values and the following estimates of the market risk premium: 4.5 percent, 6.0 percent, 7.5 percent, and 9.0 percent.
   b. The consensus earnings forecast for the company (for the upcoming year) was $2.10 per share. The three analysts also announced P/E ratios that they felt this stock would trade at in one year's time: Analyst 1, 40; Analyst 2, 50; and Analyst 3, 65. Use these figures to determine the value (the price target) each analyst expects for the stock one year from now.
   c. For each of the three future stock prices (from part b) determine the present value (discount by one year), using the range of expected return figures from part a, as the discount rates. This will give you a table of figures (four for each analyst) showing the range of stock prices that these analysts feel are currently justified.

PREPARING FOR YOUR PROFESSIONAL EXAMS

CFA PRACTICE QUESTIONS

17-1. The risk-free rate is 5 percent and the expected return on the market index is 15 percent. A stock has a beta of 1.0, a dividend payout ratio of 40 percent, and an ROE on new investments of 15 percent. If the stock will pay a $2.50 dividend, what is its intrinsic value?

   a. $27.77
   b. $41.67
   c. $50.00
   d. $53.33

17-2. Company ABC just paid an annual dividend of $1.20 per share and had an EPS of $3 per share. Its projected values for net income margin, asset turnover, and the leverage ratio are 5 percent, 1.5, and 1.33 respectively. Its sustainable growth rate is:

   a. 2%.
   b. 3%.
   c. 4%.
   d. 6%.

17-3. You project next year's stock index EPS at $400. You also project that the dividend payout will be 55 percent, ROE will be 15 percent, and that the required rate of return on the market will be 12 percent. What would you project the market index to be next year?

   a. $2,500
   b. $3,200
   c. $3,700
   d. $4,200

CFA CURRICULUM AND SAMPLE EXAM QUESTIONS (©CFA INSTITUTE)

17-1. An analyst gathered the following information about a company and the market:

Current market price per share of common stock	$28.00
Most recent dividend per share paid on common stock (D_0)	$2.00
Expected dividend payout rate	40%
Expected return on equity (ROE)	15%
Beta for the common stock	1.3
Expected rate of return on the market portfolio	13%
Risk-free rate of return	4%

Using the discounted cash flow (DCF) approach, the cost of retained earnings for the company is closest to:

   a. 13.6%.
   b. 15.7%.
   c. 16.1%.
   d. 16.8%.

17-2. An analyst gathered the following information about a company:

2001 net sales $10,000,000
2001 net profit margin 5.0%
2002 expected sales growth –15.0%
2002 expected profit margin 5.4%
2002 expected common stock shares outstanding 120,000

The company's 2002 expected earnings per share is closest to:
   a. $3.26.
   b. $3.72.
   c. $3.83.
   d. $4.17.

17-3. Your supervisor has asked you to evaluate the relative attractiveness of the stocks of two very similar chemical companies: Litchfield Chemical Corp. (LCC) and Aminochem Company (AOC). AOC and LCC have June 30 fiscal year ends. You have compiled the data in Exhibit P-1 for this purpose. Use a one-year time horizon and assume the following:

Exhibit P-1 ▬▬▬▬▬▬▬▬▬▬▬▬▬▬▬▬▬▬▬▬▬▬▬▬▬▬▬▬▬▬▬▬

Selected Data for Litchfield and Aminochem

	Litchfiled Chem. (LCC)	Aminochem (AOC)
Current stock price	$50	$30
Shares outstanding (millions)	10	20
Projected earnings per share (FY 1996)	$4.00	$3.20
Projected dividend per share (FY 1996)	$0.90	$1.60
Projected dividend growth rate	8%	7%
Stock beta	1.2	1.4
Investors' required rate of return	10%	11%
Balance sheet data (millions)		
Long-term debt	$100	$130
Stockholders' equity	$300	$320

- Real gross domestic product is expected to rise 5 percent.
- S&P 500 expected total return of 20 percent.
- U.S. Treasury bills yield 5 percent.
- 30-year U.S. Treasury bonds yield 8 percent.

   a. Calculate the value of the common stock of LCC and AOC using the constant-growth DDM. Show your work.
   b. Calculate the expected return over the next year of the common stock of LCC and AOC using the CAPM. Show your work.
   c. Calculate the internal (implied, normalized, or sustainable) growth rate of LCC and AOC. Show your work.
   d. Recommend LCC or AOC for investment. Justify your choice using your answers to A, B, and C and the information in Exhibit P-1.

17-4. Scott Kelly is reviewing MasterToy's financial statements in order to estimate its sustainable growth rate. Using the information presented in Exhibit P-2,

   a. i. Identify the three components of the DuPont formula.
       ii. Calculate the ROE for 1999 using the three components of the DuPont formula.
      iii. Calculate the sustainable growth rate for 1999.

      Kelly has calculated actual and sustainable growth for each of the past four years and finds in each year that its calculated sustainable growth rate substantially exceeds its actual growth rate.
   b. Cite one course of action (other than ignoring the problem) Kelly should encourage MasterToy to take, assuming the calculated sustainable growth rate continues to exceed the actual growth rate.

Exhibit P-2 ▬▬▬▬▬▬▬▬▬▬▬▬▬▬▬▬

Master Toy Inc. Actual 1998 and Estimated 1999 Financial Statements for FY Ending December 31 ($ millions, except per-share data)

Income Statement	1998	1999e	Change (%)
Revenue	$4,750	$5,140	8.2
Cost of goods sold	$2,400	$2,540	
Selling, general, and administrative	$1,400	$1,550	
Depreciation	180	210	
Goodwill amortization	10	10	
Operating income	$760	$830	9.2
Interest expense	20	25	
Income before taxes	$740	$805	
Income taxes	265	295	
Net income	$475	$510	
Earnings per share	$1.79	$1.96	9.5
Average shares outstanding (millions)	265	260	

Exhibit P-2 *continued*

Balance Sheet	1998	1999ᵉ	Change (%)
Cash	$400	$400	
Accounts receivable	680	700	
Inventories	570	600	
Net property, plant, and equipment	800	870	
Intangibles	500	530	
Total assets	$2,950	$3,100	
Current liabilities	$550	$600	
Long-term debt	300	300	
Total liabilities	$850	$900	
Stockholders' equity	2,100	2,200	
Total liabilities and equity	$2,950	$3,100	
Book value per share	$7.92	$8.46	
Annual dividend per share	$0.55	$0.60	

17-5. The management of Telluride, an international diversified conglomerate based in the United States, believes that the recent strong performance of its wholly owned medical supply subsidiary, Sundanci, has gone unnoticed. In order to realize Sundanci's full value, Telluride has announced that it will divest Sundanci in a tax-free spin-off.

   Sue Carroll, CFA, is Director of Research at Kesson and Associates. In developing an investment recommendation for Sundanci, Carroll has directed four of her analysts to determine a valuation of Sundanci using various valuation disciplines. To assist her analysts, Carroll has gathered the information shown in Exhibits P-3 and P4.

Exhibit P-3

Sundanci Actual 1999 and 2000 Financial Statements for FY Ending May 31
       ($ millions, except per-share data)

Income Statement	1999	2000
Revenue	$474	$598
Depreciation	20	23
Other operating costs	368	460
Income before taxes	86	115
Taxes	26	35
Net income	60	80
Dividends	18	24
Earnings per share	$0.714	$0.952
Dividends per share	$0.214	$0.286
Common shares outstanding (millions)	84.0	84.0

Exhibit P-3 *continued*

Balance Sheet	1999	2000
Current assets	$201	$326
Net property, plant, and equipment	474	489
Total assets	675	815
Current liabilities	57	141
Long-term debt	0	0
Total liabilities	57	141
Shareholders' equity	618	674
Total liabilities and equity	675	815
Capital expenditures	34	38

Exhibit P-4

Selected Financial Information

Required rate of return on equity	14%
Growth rate of industry	13%
Industry P/E	26

Prior to determining Sundanci's valuation, Carroll analyzes Sundanci's return on equity (ROE) and sustainable growth.

    a. i. Calculate the three components of ROE in the DuPont formula for the year 2000.

      ii. Calculate ROE for the year 2000.

      iii. Calculate the sustainable rate of growth. Show your work.

Carroll learns that Sundanci's Board of Directors is considering the following policy changes that will affect Sundanci's sustainable growth rate:

- Director A proposes an increase in the quarterly dividend by $0.15 per share.
- Director B proposes a bond issue of $25 million, the proceeds of which will be used to increase production capacity.
- Director C proposes a 2-for-1 stock split.

    b. Indicate the effect of each of these proposals on Sundanci's sustainable rate of growth, given that the other factors remain unchanged. Identify which components of the sustainable growth model, if any, are directly affected by each proposal.

        Helen Morgan, CFA, has been asked by Carroll to determine the potential valuation for Sundanci using the DDM. Morgan anticipates that Sundanci's earnings and dividends will grow at 32 percent for two years and 13 percent thereafter.

    c. Calculate the current value of a share of Sundanci stock using a two-stage dividend discount model and the data from Exhibits P-3 and P-4. Show your work.

17-6. Peninsular Research is initiating coverage of a mature manufacturing industry. John Jones, CFA, head of the research department, gathers information given in Exhibit P-5 to help in his analysis.

Exhibit P-5 ━━━━━━━━━━━━

Fundamental Industry and Market Data

Forecasted industry earnings retention rate	40%
Forecasted industry return on equity	25%
Industry beta	1.2
Government bond yield	6%
Equity risk premium	5%

a. Compute the price to earnings (P0/E1) ratio for the industry based on the fundamental data in Exhibit P-5. Show your work.

   Jones wants to analyze how fundamental P/Es might differ among countries. He gathers the data given in Exhibit P-6:

Exhibit P-6 ━━━━━━━━━━━━

Economic and Market Data

Fundamental Factors	Country A	Country B
Forecasted growth in real gross domestic product	5%	2%
Government bond yield	10%	6%
Equity risk premium	5%	4%

b. Determine whether each of the fundamental factors in Exhibit P-6 would cause P/Es to be generally higher for Country A or higher for Country B. Justify each of your conclusions with one reason. Note: Consider each fundamental factor in isolation, with all else remaining equal.

17-7. Janet Ludlow's company requires all its analysts to use a two-stage DDM and the CAPM to value stocks. Using these models, Ludlow has valued QuickBrush Company at $63 per share. She now must value SmileWhite Corporation.

   a. Calculate the required rate of return for SmileWhite using the information in Exhibit P-7 and the CAPM. Show your work.

      Ludlow estimates the following EPS and dividend growth rates for SmileWhite:
      First three years: 12% per year
      Years thereafter: 9% per year
      The 1997 dividend per share is $1.72.

   b. Estimate the intrinsic value of SmileWhite using the data above and the two-stage DDM. Show your work.

Exhibit P-7 ━━━━━━━━━━━

Valuation Information December 1997

	QuickBrush	SmileWhite
Beta	1.35	1.15
Market price	$45.00	$30.00
Intrinsic value	$63.00	?
Notes		
Risk-free rate	4.50%	
Expected market return	14.50%	

   c. Recommend QuickBrush or SmileWhite stock for purchase by comparing each company's intrinsic value with its current market price. Show your work.
   d. Describe one strength of the two-stage DDM in comparison with the constant-growth DDM. Describe one weakness inherent in all DDMs.

17-8. Using the dividend discount model, what is the cost of equity capital for Zeller Mining if the company will pay a dividend of $2.30 next year, has a payout ratio of 30 percent, a return on equity (ROE) of 15 percent, and a stock price of $45?

   a. 9.61 percent
   b. 10.50 percent
   c. 15.61 percent
   d. 16.50 percent

17-9. An analyst gathered the following data for a company:

Based on the information above, the most appropriate conclusion is that, over the period 2003 to 2005, the company's

	2003	2004	2005
ROE	19.8%	20.0%	22.0%
Return on total assets	8.1%	8.0%	7.9%
Total asset turnover	2.0	2.0	2.1

   a. net profit margin and financial leverage have decreased.
   b. net profit margin and financial leverage have increased.
   c. net profit margin has decreased, but its financial leverage has increased.
   d. net profit margin has increased, but its financial leverage has decreased.

17-10. FPR is expected to pay a $0.60 dividend next year. The dividend is expected to grow at a 50 percent annual rate for Years 2 and 3, at 20 percent annually for Years 4 and 5, and at 5 percent annually for Year 6 and thereafter. If the required rate of return is 12 percent, what is the value per share?

APPENDIX 17A

FINANCIAL RATIO ANALYSIS: AN OVERVIEW

Interpreting Financial Statements

Analyzing a company's historical financial statements and financial ratios can provide end users with useful information for estimating the magnitude of future cash flows (earnings and dividends) and the riskiness inherent in these estimates. Ratios are commonly used to analyze a company's financial performance. Although a single ratio has limited value, it does provide relative measures of performance/risk characteristics of firms when compared with other ratios.

Trend analysis compares ratios at a particular time with those of a previous period. It provides information regarding how the firm is evolving through time and enables comparison of the firm's most recent performance with that in earlier periods.

External comparisons of company ratios with those of similar companies or industry averages are used as a method of determining how well a company is performing in relation to its competitors. It is important to ensure that the comparison group consists of "similar" firms whose ratios have been calculated according to the same basis. For example, it may be misleading to compare ratios of two firms in the same industry if they have different fiscal year ends, particularly if sales are seasonal. In Canada, the *Financial Post* (www.fpinfomart.ca), Dun and Bradstreet, the Canadian Manufacturers Association, and some banks provide industry ratios for comparison purposes.

There are several limitations of financial statement analysis. A key concern is that it is hard to determine what is "good" performance. Trend analysis may provide uninformative results if the nature of a company changes substantially due to the acquisition of new companies and/or the divestiture of certain operating divisions. It is often difficult to determine comparable companies when examining multinational and/or conglomerate firms. Finding comparable companies is a significant problem for Canadian firms, because in certain industries there may be only one or two large companies.

Another comparability issue arises because comparable companies may not have the same fiscal year ends. This can also bias industry averages; however, companies in a given industry often choose the same fiscal year ends. For example, in Canada all of the large chartered banks have fiscal years ending on October 31. An alternative is to compare a chosen company with similar US companies; however, one must be aware of potential biases that may arise due to the use of different accounting standards (even though the standards are very similar across the two countries). In addition, inflation can distort results in certain situations, such as when trying to compare younger firms with older ones.

Despite some of the limitations of financial statement analysis, it is an excellent tool for analyzing company performance that provides analysts with information that is central to the company valuation process. Ratios provide insight into the performance of a variety of areas of the company's operations.

Five areas of operation that are often analyzed by reference to ratios are:

1. Liquidity—the firm's ability to generate required cash in a hurry to meet its short-term obligations
2. Asset Management—how effectively the company manages its assets to generate sales and profits
3. Debt Management—how well the company is able to deal with its debt obligations with regard to its ability to repay and its ability to assume more debt
4. Profitability—how well the company has made use of its resources
5. Value—shows the worth of the company's shares or the returns for owning them

We present some commonly used ratios next; however, we note that some of the definitions differ from those that students have seen in introductory finance, investments, or accounting textbooks. This is not uncommon. In fact, if you pick up three or four different textbooks or analyst reports, it would be rare to see them all have the exact same definitions for all reported ratios. Despite the variations in the definitions, the ratios generally measure the same type of thing. The important point of this discussion is to make sure that all ratios that are to be compared with others are determined on the same basis. Otherwise, one runs the risk of arriving at erroneous conclusions by comparing apples with oranges.

Ratio Analysis

The following are financial statements and some selected ratios for Company XYZ for the 2004–2008 period, with the calculations for the 2008 ratios also provided. We will use this information, as well as the industry ratios, to provide an illustrative example of ratio analysis, which is then combined with additional information to conduct a valuation analysis of Company XYZ.

XYZ Company

($000's — Year ended December 31)

STATEMENT OF INCOME:	2004	2005	2006	2007	2008
Total Revenue	1426000	2143300	2892300	3058600	4448000
Cost of Sales	1238700	1931400	2559400	2699200	4005800
Depreciation/Amortization	40100	43600	76800	75300	101300
Interest Expense	5300	7500	53200	52600	79000
Research / Exploration	0	0	36300	53700	73100
Other Expense	33100	43600	46100	56400	37900
Unusual Items	0	0	0	0	0
Pre-Tax Income	108800	117200	120500	121400	150900
Income Tax	−19900	−25700	−20400	−13700	−18100
Earnings BEFORE Extra. Items	88900	91500	100100	107700	132800
Extraordinary Items	0	0	0	0	0
Income AFTER Extra. Items	88900	91500	100100	107700	132800
Dividends — Preferred Shares	3500	3800	4000	2900	2600
Income Available to Common Shares	85400	87700	96100	104800	130200
Earnings /Share	0.68	0.68	0.706	0.727	0.85
Common Shares — Year End (1000s)	125658	131398	141443	152337	154280
Common Shares — Average (1000s)	125536	128932	136073	144121	153237
Dividends — Common Shares	14700	22000	28700	27400	32200
Market Price per Share (Close)	6.69	7.63	7.88	17.13	11.63

BALANCE SHEET:

XYZ Company

($000's — Year ended December 31)

ASSETS:	2004	2005	2006	2007	2008
Cash & Equivalent	150000	84000	87500	179200	235100
Accounts Receivable	174000	428800	413700	360100	380400
Inventory	220200	583500	992700	1215700	1803100
Marketable Securities	0	0	0	0	0
Other	0	0	0	0	0
TOTAL Current Assets	544200	1096300	1493900	1755000	2418600
Fixed Assets — Gross	1372700	1650500	1956200	2277600	2914600
less: Accumulated Depreciation	−766200	−809800	−886600	−961900	−1063200
Fixed Assets — Net	606500	840700	1069600	1315700	1851400
TOTAL Assets	1150700	1937000	2563500	3070700	4270000

LIABILITIES AND EQUITY:	2004	2005	2006	2007	2008
Bank Loans & Equivalent	147800	346800	537400	620800	828500
Accounts Payable	347200	684400	831800	901400	1380900
Current Portion of L-T Debt	5400	30000	20800	19300	56400
TOTAL Current Liabilities	500400	1061200	1390000	1541500	2265800
Long-Term Debt & Debentures	83500	211000	425500	586600	963700
Deferred Taxes & Credits	41600	42000	53800	43300	56400
Equity: Preferred Stock	158300	157700	37400	35700	34100
Common Stock	190600	223100	347400	476800	465200
Retained Earnings	176300	242000	309400	386800	484800
Total Equity	525200	622800	694200	899300	984100
TOTAL Liabilities + Equity	1150700	1937000	2563500	3070700	4270000

XYZ Company

FINANCIAL RATIOS:	2004	2005	2006	2007	2008
Current Ratio	1.09	1.03	1.07	1.14	1.07
Acid Test (Quick) Ratio	0.65	0.48	0.36	0.35	0.27
ACP (days)	44.54	73.02	52.21	42.97	31.22
Inventory Turnover	5.63	3.31	2.58	2.22	2.22
Total Asset Turnover	1.24	1.11	1.13	1.00	1.04
Debt Ratio	0.51	0.66	0.71	0.69	0.76
Debt-to-Equity Ratio	1.11	2.04	2.62	2.37	3.28
Equity Multiplier	2.19	3.11	3.69	3.41	4.34
TIE (or Interest Coverage)	21.53	16.63	3.27	3.31	2.91
Net Income Margin	6.23%	4.27%	3.46%	3.52%	2.99%
Return on Assets (ROA)	7.73%	4.72%	3.90%	3.51%	3.11%
Return on Equity (ROE)	16.93%	14.69%	14.42%	11.98%	13.49%
P/E Ratio	9.84	11.21	11.15	23.56	13.68
M/B Ratio	2.29	2.15	1.70	3.02	1.89
Dividend Yield	1.75%	2.24%	2.68%	1.11%	1.81%
Dividend Payout Ratio	0.17	0.25	0.30	0.26	0.25

INDUSTRY AVERAGES

FINANCIAL RATIOS:	2004	2005	2006	2007	2008
Current Ratio	2.12	2.85	2.25	2.01	1.69
Acid Test (Quick) Ratio	1.21	1.97	1.36	1.24	1.09
ACP (days)	35.20	34.09	44.50	45.90	46.90
Inventory Turnover	7.78	8.20	7.68	8.52	8.16
Total Asset Turnover	1.78	1.43	1.37	1.26	1.23
Debt Ratio	0.23	0.33	0.32	0.29	0.32
Debt-to-Equity Ratio	0.36	0.61	0.56	0.49	0.55
Equity Multiplier	1.57	1.82	1.78	1.70	1.74
TIE (or Interest Coverage)	34.41	42.19	5.95	5.53	8.61
Net Income Margin	8.47%	6.03%	4.34%	4.19%	5.68%
Return on Assets (ROA)	15.08%	8.64%	5.95%	5.27%	7.01%
Return on Equity (ROE)	23.68%	15.72%	10.59%	8.96%	12.20%
P/E Ratio	6.42	9.08	12.13	22.38	15.53
M/B Ratio	1.51	1.42	1.28	2.00	1.88
Dividend Yield	1.71%	1.73%	2.86%	2.67%	2.08%
Dividend Payout Ratio	0.13	0.24	0.35	0.39	0.26

We begin by conducting a ratio analysis that examines each of the five areas of firm operations listed.

Liquidity

Commonly used liquidity indicators include the following:

1. Working capital (or net current assets) = Current assets − Current liabilities
2. Current ratio = Current assets ÷ Current liabilities
3. Quick (or acid test) ratio = (Current assets − Inventory) ÷ Current liabilities

The current ratio measures a firm's ability to repay current obligations from current assets, while the quick ratio is a more conservative estimate of liquidity that reflects the fact that inventories are generally not as liquid as other current assets. As with most ratios, there is no absolute standard for these ratios, but higher values suggest greater firm liquidity. Cash forecasts can provide additional insight into the firm's liquidity situation.

The 2008 current and quick ratios for Company XYZ are calculated below.

$$\text{Current ratio for XYZ (2008)} = 2{,}418{,}600/2{,}265{,}800 = 1.07$$

$$\text{Quick ratio for XYZ (2008)} = (2{,}418{,}600 - 1{,}803{,}100)/2{,}265{,}800 = 0.27$$

Asset Management

Some commonly used measures of asset management include the inventory turnover ratio, the average collection period, and the total asset turnover ratio, although there are many others as well. We define these three ratios next.

1. Inventory turnover $= \dfrac{\text{Cost of goods sold}}{\text{Average inventory}}$

The quality of inventories may be reflected in the inventory turnover ratio, which can also indicate the firm's efficiency in inventory management. Because inventories are valued at cost, they should, in theory, be related to the cost of goods sold; however, in practice, cost of goods sold is often replaced by net sales (especially by providers of industry financial ratios, which often form the basis for comparison) due to the difficulty in obtaining information for a large number of companies regarding their cost of goods sold. A high inventory turnover is often regarded as a signal of efficient management whereas a slipping ratio may flag both overstocking and obsolete inventories. Once again, however, caution is advised, as an unusually high inventory turnover could also be associated with too low a level of inventories and corresponding stockouts.

Sometimes analysts focus on the day's inventory figure, rather than the inventory turnover figure, which refers to how long, on average, it takes a company to sell its inventory. It can be calculated as the inventory value divided by the daily cost of goods sold, or simply as 365 divided by the inventory turnover ratio. The 2008 inventory turnover ratio and days inventory figure for Company XYZ are calculated below:

$$\text{Inventory Turnover for XYZ (2008) (using COGS)} = (4{,}005{,}800)/1{,}803{,}100$$
$$= 2.22 \text{ times}$$

$$\text{Days Inventory for XYZ (2008)} = 365/2.22 = 164.4 \text{ days}$$

The annual turnover ratio of 2.22 is equivalent to inventory being replaced once every 365/2.22 = 164.4 days, as reflected in the days inventory ratio.

2. Average collection period (ACP) $= \dfrac{\text{Accounts receivable}}{\text{Average daily sales}}$

Many analysts use the average collection period (ACP) to examine the quality and liquidity of accounts receivable. It indicates the average number of days that sales are outstanding and uncollected. Technically, it would be preferable to use average daily "credit" sales rather than average daily sales. However, the credit sales figure is often unavailable or difficult to ascertain, so most analysts use the simpler version in the equation above, which is reasonable as long as the majority of sales are on credit. In addition, some analysts use the receivables turnover ratio instead of the ACP, which can be calculated as annual sales divided by accounts receivable, or simply as 365 divided by ACP.

The ACP and the receivables turnover ratio indicate the speed of collections, which in turn is influenced by the efficiency of the firm's credit and collection policies. Again, however, too low a figure could stem from excessively restrictive credit policies that jeopardize sales and profitability. As with inventory turnover, seasonal or otherwise uneven sales can also distort the ratios. The 2008 ACP and receivables turnover ratio for Company XYZ are calculated below:

$$\text{ACP for XYZ (2008)} = 380{,}400/(4{,}448{,}000/365) = 31.22 \text{ days}$$

$$\text{Receivables turnover for XYZ (2008)} = 365/31.22 \text{ days} = 11.69 \text{ times}$$

3. Asset turnover $= \dfrac{\text{Sales}}{\text{Total assets}}$

The asset turnover ratio measures the sales generated by each dollar invested in assets. It is a broad indicator of the efficiency achieved in employing assets to produce a given level of output. Once again, values computed for this ratio must be interpreted in their particular context. What may be an inadequate asset turnover for a food store or department store might be unattainable by an electric utility. Furthermore, an older firm may show a better turnover than a newer company because its assets are depreciated and carried on the books at values that are low relative to current replacement costs. Similarly, a firm that has expanded rapidly may show heavy investments in new assets and hence a lower turnover than a company that has remained static.

The 2008 asset turnover ratio for Company XYZ is calculated below:

$$\text{Total Asset Turnover for XYZ (2008)} = 4{,}448{,}000/4{,}270{,}000 = 1.042$$

Debt Management

Four commonly used measures of debt management are discussed next. The first three are similar in that they relate to the firm's capacity to assume additional debt, while the fourth is a common measure of a firm's ability to service its debt. There are many other ratios that are used to measure similar characteristics.

1. Debt ratio = Total debt / Total assets

The debt ratio is defined in several different manners, depending on the analyst. The definition above estimates the proportion of the firm's total assets that is financed through debt and other liabilities.[17] A higher ratio indicates greater risk and a lower capacity for a firm to assume additional debt.

The 2008 debt ratio for Company XYZ is calculated below:

$$\text{Debt ratio for XYZ (2008)} = (2{,}265{,}800 + 963{,}700)/4{,}270{,}000 = 0.756$$

This indicates that the firm financed 75.6 percent of its assets with debt in 2008.

---

[17]It is common not to include Deferred Taxes as part of the debt total, although in some instances it may make sense to include it in the debt total.

2. Debt-to-equity = Total debt/Total equity

The debt-to-equity ratio estimates the proportion of debt financing to equity financing for a firm. Similar to the debt ratio, a higher ratio indicates greater risk, and a lower capacity for a firm to assume additional debt.

The 2008 debt-to-equity ratio for Company XYZ is calculated below:

$$\text{Debt-to-equity} = (2,265,800 + 963,700)/984,100 = 3.282$$

This indicates that the firm has approximately $3.28 in debt financing for every $1 of equity financing.

3. Leverage Ratio (or Equity Multiplier) = Total assets/Equity

The leverage ratio (or equity multiplier) is another measure of the amount of assets a firm finances with debt. It is not as commonly used as the debt ratio or the debt-to-equity ratio; however, you will recall from Chapter 17 that it is part of the DuPont decomposition. The higher the ratio, the lower the proportion of the firm's assets that is financed through equity, and therefore the higher the proportion financed through debt.

The 2008 leverage ratio for Company XYZ is calculated below:

$$\text{Leverage ratio for XYZ (2008)} = 4,270,000/984,100 = 4.339$$

4. Times interest earned (TIE) ratio = $\dfrac{\text{Earnings before interest and taxes (EBIT)}}{\text{Interest expense}}$

While borrowing may enhance financial performance, the firm has to ensure that it is not jeopardized by excessive leverage. A widely used indicator of the "safety" of periodic interest payments (i.e., the firm's ability to cover its required interest payments) is the times interest earned ratio (or interest coverage ratio). It represents how many times the firm's earnings could cover its interest payments, before excluding the interest payments and taxes. Earnings are taken before taxes and interest payments, because interest payments are tax-deductible expenses.

The 2008 TIE ratio for Company XYZ is calculated below:

$$\text{TIE for XYZ (2008)} = (150,900 + 79,000)/79,000 = 2.91 \text{ times}$$

Profitability

Analysts use profitability ratios in an attempt to assess the overall managerial efficiency and profitability of a firm. Profitability measures often relate profits to sales, assets, and to shareholder equity. There are numerous commonly used measures of profitability, some of which were discussed in the main part of this chapter; however, we present only three of the more commonly used ones here.

1. Net income (or profit) margin = Net income/Sales

The net income margin figure is a summary measure of the overall profitability of a firm, relative to sales, after accounting for all expenses. Obviously higher numbers are preferred. The 2008 net income margin ratio for Company XYZ is calculated below:

$$\text{Net income margin} = 132,800/4,448,000 = 2.99\%$$

2. Return on assets (ROA) = Net income/Total assets

As discussed in the chapter, the return on assets (ROA) measures the dollar return per dollar invested in assets, and can be viewed as a broad measure of how well management is employing assets to earn profits. The 2008 ROA for Company XYZ is calculated below:

$$\text{ROA for XYZ (2008)} = 132,800/4,270,000 = 3.11\%$$

3. Return on equity (ROE) = Net income/Equity

As discussed in the chapter, a firm's return on equity (ROE) is a measure of how well management serves shareholder interest, which determines the profits generated per dollar of equity invested in the company. The DuPont system described in the chapter demonstrates that the ROE figure is the result of both the firm's operating performance (as measured by profitability and asset turnover) and the leverage afforded by the use of debt in the capital structure. The 2008 ROE for Company XYZ is calculated below:

$$\text{ROE for XYZ (2008)} = 132{,}800/984{,}100 = 13.49\%$$

Value

Market value ratios relate data from the firm's financial statements to financial market data, thereby providing some insights into investors' perceptions of the firm and its securities. Four value ratios that are commonly used in this analysis are provided below:

1. $\text{Dividend payout} = \dfrac{\text{Common share dividends}}{\text{Earnings available to common shareholders}}$

   $\text{or} \qquad = \dfrac{\text{Dividends per common share}}{\text{Earnings per common share}}$

The dividend payout ratio is a measure of a firm's dividend policy. It indicates the percentage of earnings paid to shareholders in the form of dividends. The 2008 payout ratio for Company XYZ is calculated below:

$$\text{Payout for XYZ (2008)} = 32{,}200 / 130{,}200 = .2473 = 24.73\%$$

This ratio indicates that XYZ paid out approximately 25 cents of every dollar it earned to common shareholders, or alternatively that it reinvested approximately 75 cents out of every dollar earned.

2. $\text{Dividend yield} = \dfrac{\text{Dividends per common share}}{\text{Price per common share}}$

Dividend yield is a commonly used market value ratio by investors and analysts. It relates the dividend income received by shareholders to the price investors are willing to pay for the shares. It measures how much investors are willing to pay for the firm's dividends. The market price is in the denominator of this ratio, and hence a lower dividend yield implies investors are willing to pay more for $1 of a company's dividends, and a higher value indicates they are willing to pay less.

The 2008 dividend yield for Company XYZ is calculated below:

$$\text{Dividend yield for XYZ (2008)} = (32{,}200 / 153{,}237) / 11.63 = 0.21 / 11.63$$
$$= 1.81\%$$

This ratio indicates that investors purchasing XYZ for $11.63 would receive a dividend return (i.e., yield) of 1.81 percent over the year, if they received $0.21 in dividend payments per share.

3. $\text{Price-earnings ratio} = \dfrac{\text{Price per common share}}{\text{Earnings per common share}}$

The price-earnings (P/E) ratio (or earnings multiplier) is widely used and reflects what investors are prepared to pay for each dollar of reported annual earnings available on a common share. A higher number indicates that investors are willing to pay more for $1 of the company's earnings. This may be due to expected growth in earnings, or lower riskiness associated with the earnings. This ratio was discussed in detail in Chapter 13.

The P/E ratio is typically reported using the earnings per share figure over the last 12 months in the denominator, and the current market price in the numerator. This is sometimes referred to as the "trailing" P/E ratio, since it relates today's market price to the firm's most recent earnings figures. As we saw in Chapter 13, analysts often use the "forward" P/E ratio, which uses expected earnings in the coming period, to try to establish a reasonable price for common shares.

The 2008 P/E ratio for Company XYZ is calculated below:

$$\text{P/E ratio for XYZ (2008)} = 11.63/0.85 = 13.68$$

This means that the market was willing to pay $13.68 for each $1 of XYZ's earnings, based on its present market price per share of $11.63.

4. Market-to-book (M/B) ratio $= \dfrac{\text{Market price per share}}{\text{Book value per share}}$

The market-to-book (M/B) ratio is based on recognition that the numerator (i.e., market value per share) reflects the present value of the firm's stream of future cash flows, as determined in competitive security markets. It is often viewed as a measure of future growth opportunities for the firm. This is because it relates market prices (which are determined based on future expectations) to the book value of existing assets. Higher values for this ratio are associated with higher future growth opportunities, and vice versa.

The 2008 M/B ratio for Company XYZ is calculated below:

$$\text{M/B ratio for XYZ (2008)} = 11.63/[(984,100 - 34,100)/154,280]$$
$$= 11.63/6.16 = 1.89$$

Ratio Analysis Summary

A brief assessment of XYZ's current situation is provided below based on an examination of the ratios for XYZ and the industry ratios.

Liquidity: XYZ currently displays below average liquidity. Its current and quick ratios of 1.07 and 0.27 in 2008 are both well below the industry averages of 1.69 and 1.09. In addition, its liquidity ratios exhibit a bad trend. While the current ratio has been steady, the quick ratio has deteriorated significantly. The low and deteriorating quick ratio is due to high levels of inventory, which indicates a potential problem with inventory management.

Asset Management: XYZ's collections of receivables, as measured by ACP, is below average (31 days versus 47 days) and is improving, which is a positive sign. However, its inventory turnover ratio is very low (2.2 versus industry average of 8.2), and has been continually deteriorating, reflecting the fact that they are currently maintaining high inventory levels. This is a problem area that was noted above. Finally, its asset turnover ratio is below average, has been over the entire period, and continues to deteriorate.

Debt Management: XYZ's debt levels have increased steadily and its coverage has deteriorated, which indicates a bad trend with respect to debt management. For example, in 2008, its debt ratio is 0.76 (up from 0.51 in 2004), its debt-to-equity is 3.28 (up from 1.11 in 2004), and its interest coverage is 2.91 (down from 21.53 in 2004). In terms of both debt capacity and coverage, it is well below average in 2008, with a debt ratio of 0.76 versus the 0.32 industry average, a debt-to-equity ratio of 3.28 versus the 0.55 industry average, and an interest coverage ratio of 2.91 versus the 8.61 industry average. Debt is obviously an area of concern for this company.

Profitability: While XYZ is a profitable company, its ratios indicate a steady decline in net income margin, ROA, and ROE over the 2004–2008 period. All of its profitability ratios are below industry averages, except for ROE; however, as the DuPont analysis below suggests, this is due to the use of greater leverage than the average firm in the industry (as noted above).

DuPont Analysis: The ROE is the end result of several important variables, which can be isolated using the DuPont system of analysis, as discussed in the chapter. For the purposes of our present analysis, we will use the three-point DuPont decomposition to examine Company XYZ for 2008, and compare it to its industry averages.

XYZ (2008) ROE   = (Net income margin)(Asset turnover)(Leverage)
                      = (.0299)(1.042)(4.339)= 13.51%

Industry averages (2008)   ROE = (.0568)(1.23)(1.74) = 12.16%

This analysis suggests that XYZ displays an above average ROE due to its higher leverage factor (4.339 versus 1.74), which is not desirable, and despite the fact it has below average profitability and asset turnover, which are also not desirable.

Value: XYZ's P/E and M/B ratios are close to the industry average, which is also the case for its dividend yield, and these ratios have been close to or slightly above average over the entire period. This suggests the market views XYZ as an "average" company despite some of the problems we have observed. Whether this means it is overvalued by the market or that we have been unduly hard on XYZ is a matter to be decided by valuation analysis.

Conclusion: Based on the analysis above we can see that XYZ is below average and deteriorating in terms of liquidity, inventory turnover, and debt management. However, it is profitable, even if it is not up to industry standards, and even if its profitability is dwindling. The market views XYZ as an "average" company despite its problems. XYZ will probably have to deal with its debt, inventory, and liquidity problems in order to maintain an average valuation in the market in the future.

Valuation Analysis

We will now combine the ratio analysis above with some additional inputs to determine the value of XYZ's shares.

Estimating "k"
Let's assume that we have determined the following estimates based on our analysis of XYZ and present market conditions:
Beta for Company XYZ: 1
Expected market return: 9%
Risk-free rate: 3%:

Using CAPM, we can estimate the required return on XYZ's shares as: $k = 3 + 1.0(9 - 3) = 9\%$

Estimating "g"
We will use a variety of methods to attempt to estimate the future growth rate in dividends and earnings for Company XYZ. Note that we are using "historical-based" methods, which as we know can often provide incorrect implications regarding the future.

We begin by estimating the geometric average growth rate in dividends over the 2004–2008 period:

XYZ's dividend per share (DPS) figures for 2008 and 2004 are:
DPS(2008) = 32,200/ 153,237 = 0.21
DPS(2004) = 14,700/125,536 = 0.117

So we can estimate the growth rate as follows:
$0.117 \times (1 + g)^4 = 0.210$
$(1 + g)^4 = 0.210/0.117$
$g = (0.210/0.117)^{1/4} - 1 = 0.1575 = 15.75\%$

This estimate is very high, and is unreasonable as a long-term growth rate. The arithmetic average growth rate for growth in DPS is even higher at 17.5 percent, which is also unreasonably high.

Next, let's consider the growth rate in earnings, as measured by the geometric average growth rate in EPS over the 2004–2008 period. Given that the 2008 EPS = 0.85 and that the 2004 EPS = 0.68, we can estimate the growth rate as

$0.68 \times (1 + g)^4 = 0.85$
$(1 + g)^4 = 0.85/0.68$
$g = (0.85/0.68)^{1/4} - 1 = 0.0574 = 5.74\%$

This estimate seems reasonable. While it may seem inappropriate at first glance to use the growth rate in EPS to estimate the growth rate in dividends, it is in fact a very common practice and it is intuitive. This is because dividends must be paid from earnings, and it would be unreasonable for them to grow at rates significantly different from earnings over the long run. In the short run, dividends often grow at rates different than earnings due to the fact that companies tend to adjust dividends with a lag to earnings, as discussed in the chapter.

Finally, let's estimate the sustainable growth rate using the 2008 figures for ROE and payout, and using the 2004–2008 averages for these ratios:

Using 2008 figures $g = (1 - 0.25)(0.1349) = 10.12\%$
Using 2004–2008 averages $g = (1 - 0.246)(0.1430) = 10.78\%$

Once again, these estimates seem unreasonably high for long-term growth rates. Finally, let's assume that after more investigation, we choose $g = 6$ percent (which is close to the five-year growth rate in EPS) for the long-term growth rate.

Valuation Approaches
We will now use some of the valuation techniques discussed in Chapter 13 to estimate the price of XYZ's common shares.

Constant-Growth DDM:
    Price = (0.21)(1.06) / (.09 − .06) = $7.42

P/E Approach (using fundamentals and 2008 payout ratio):
    P/E = payout / (k − g) = (0.25) / (.09 − .06) = 8.33
    EPS (2009) = 0.85 (1.06) = $0.901
    Price = (8.33)($0.901) = $7.51

P/E Approach (using five-year company average P/E ratio):
   Price = (13.89)($0.901) = $12.51

P/E Approach (using 2008 industry average P/E ratio):
   Price = (15.53)($0.901) = $13.99

M/B Approach (using fundamentals and 2008 payout ratio):
   M/B = (ROE)(payout)$(1 + g) / (k - g)$ = (.1349)(.25)(1.06) / (.09 − .06) = 1.19
   Price = (1.19)($6.16) = $7.33

M/B Approach (using five-year company average M/B ratio):
   Price = (2.21)($6.16) = $13.61

M/B Approach (using 2008 industry average M/B ratio):
   Price = (1.88)($6.16) = $11.58

P/Sales Approach (using fundamentals and 2008 payout ratio):
   P/Sales = (net income margin)(payout)$(1 + g) / (k - g)$
      = (.0299)(.25)(1.06) / (.09 − .06) = 0.264
   Sales per share = 4,448,000 / 153,237 = $29.03
   Price = (0.264)($29.03) = $7.66

Multi-Stage Growth DDM:
   Using g = 10% for three years, and then 6% thereafter:

1st D_1 = (0.21)(1.10) = 0.231
      D_2 = (0.231)(1.10) = 0.254
      D_3 = (0.254)(1.10) = 0.279

2nd D_4 = 0.279(1.06) = 0.296

$$P_3 = \frac{D_4}{k - g} = \frac{0.296}{0.09 - 0.06} = \$9.87$$

$$3rd \quad P_0 = \frac{0.231}{(1.09)} + \frac{0.254}{(1.09)^2} + \frac{0.279 + 9.87}{(1.09)^3}$$

$$= 0.212 + 0.214 + 7.837 = \$8.26$$

Valuation Summary
While we conclude our estimation process at this point, we note that many other valuation approaches may also be used (some of which may be more appropriate for certain companies and particular circumstances), including price-to-cash flow, price-to-EBIT, and price-to-free cash flow.

XYZ's shares were trading at $11.63 at year end. According to fundamental approaches, they are overvalued and should be trading in the $7.33 to $8.26 range. According to comparable ratios such as five-year averages and industry averages, they should be trading between $11.58 and $13.99; however, according to our financial statement analysis, they seem to be in worse shape than they were five years ago, and they also seem to be below average relative to their competitors. Therefore, we choose to rely more heavily on the estimates based on fundamentals, and conclude that XYZ's shares appear to have been overvalued at $11.63. By our estimates these shares are worth between $7.33 and $8.26.

CHAPTER 18

TECHNICAL ANALYSIS

As you complete your study of how to select and analyze common stocks, you decide you should take a look at technical analysis because some of your friends have mentioned it, and you have read about charting in the popular press. Technical analysis—studying the price patterns of stocks across time and using these patterns to predict future price changes—sounds intriguing. After all, when you look at a chart of stock prices some patterns seem to clearly stand out. Alternatively, you could use some so-called technical indicators to aid you in your buy/sell decisions. However, having considered the efficient market hypothesis, you suspect it might not be as easy and rewarding as it sounds. After all, if it easy to do, and it works, would not many investors be using it successfully on a regular basis?

Learning Objectives

After reading this chapter, you should be able to

1. Define technical analysis and explain why it is used.
2. Describe the major techniques used in technical analysis.
3. Discuss the limitations of technical analysis.

CHAPTER PREVIEW

In this chapter, we explore an alternative approach to security analysis—technical analysis—which differs substantially from fundamental analysis. After a brief explanation of the differences between these two types of analysis, we describe some of the major techniques used by technical analysts. We conclude the chapter with an assessment of the limitations of technical analysis.

INTRODUCTION

As discussed in Chapter 14, technical analysis is the other traditional approach for selecting stocks. It differs from the fundamental approach to security analysis discussed in the last three chapters. Although the technical approach to common stock selection is the oldest used by analysts (dating back to the late 1800s), it remains controversial.[1] It has come under constant criticism from those espousing the merits of the efficient market hypothesis (EMH), since the use of technical analysis flies in the face of the notion that markets are efficient in the weak-form sense of the EMH.[2] However, it is important to recognize that analysis of any type, fundamental or technical, is essentially a waste of time if we accept the assumptions of the EMH. Thus, just as fundamental analysis was examined under the premise that it can help improve investment results if done properly, the same argument can be made for technical analysis. Indeed there are numerous examples of technicians earning superior returns, just as there are numerous examples of disappointing results obtained by following similar strategies. The primary objective of this chapter is to make students aware of the various technical strategies and available tools so that they can make informed decisions regarding how to integrate technical analysis into their investment program, if at all.

Anyone learning about investments will be exposed to technical analysis, because numerous investors, investment advisory firms, and the popular press talk about it and use it. As noted, it has been around for a long time and is widely known. Furthermore, it may produce some insights into the psychological dimension of the market. While it is likely that the debate regarding its usefulness will continue, many investors use technical information when making their investment decisions. Therefore, the prudent course of action is to study this topic, or indeed any other recommended approach to making investing decisions, and try to make an objective evaluation of its validity and usefulness. Real-World Returns 18-1 compares technical analysis with fundamental analysis.

REAL-WORLD RETURNS 18-1

Fundamental vs. Technical Analysis

"It's an old Wall Street tale," says John Bollinger, CFA, CMT. "Fundamental analysts would get their list of top stocks and, when no one was looking, would pull out their charts to decide when to buy or sell. Yet most fundamental analysts tend to think of technical analysis as chicanery and charlatanism."

Bollinger runs the Manhattan Beach research and asset management firm that bears his name. He is one of the 380 investment professionals who have straddled the subjects of fundamental and technical analysis and achieved both the designation of chartered financial analyst as well as chartered market technician. The Market Technicians Association administers the CMT designation.

"In general, I believe that fundamental analysis has more value than technical analysis because it provides a much deeper framework for valuing stocks or bonds than just looking at

---

[1]Technical analysis itself can be traced back to the rice markets in seventeenth century Japan.
[2]Recall from Chapter 10 that the weak-form version of the EMH states that in efficient security markets, prices will accurately reflect all historical price and trading volume information.

patterns in past price movements," says Andreas Sauer, Ph.D., CFA, managing director & CIO of UNION PanAgora in Frankfurt, Germany.

Sauer belongs to the community of fundamental analysts who readily admit the use of both sets of tools. "We employ momentum and reversal factors in all of our own equity and bond models."

Christopher Orndorff, CFA, managing principal, head of equity strategy, Payden & Rygel, Los Angeles, Calif., USA, is also an unabashed member. "We use both technical and fundamental analysis for both fixed income and equity," he says. "Fundamental analysis really drives the decision of which securities we want to own. But the timing of purchase and sale decisions is split pretty evenly between technical and fundamental."

Like Sauer, Orndorff's group at the US$40 billion asset and mutual fund manager employs a couple of technical indicators. "We try not to outsmart ourselves," says Ornorff. "We use moving averages, moving average crosses, and oscillators. We believe that with just these three factors we get 80 percent of the usefulness of technical analysis."

Bollinger coined the term for the juncture of technical and fundamental analysis almost 20 years ago. He calls it "rational analysis." "If you've got two toolboxes, one labelled 'tools for red cars' and the other labelled 'tools for blue cars,' what would you do if you wanted to work on a white car? The rational approach would be to use the best tools from each box," he says. "Rational analysis is made up of the finest fundamental tools and the finest technical tools."

Not all professionals stand in the middle where technical and fundamental analyses coexist, however. Adherents to one school of thought assume a much more warlike stance toward the other. "There are forces polarizing fundamental and technical analysts," explains Bollinger. "The whole idea of the efficient market hypothesis is most often what fundamentals use to attack technicals. If the market is efficient after all, then there is no opportunity to find the inefficiencies that technical analysts look to find."

Technicians are also faced with a new opponent—that of quantitative analysis. "The technical analysis community has split in the last 20 years with a great big piece cleaving off and calling themselves quants," says Bollinger. "If you go down the halls in big institutions today, you will find lots of doors labelled 'quantitative analyst.' They're getting highly paid, unlike technical analysts.

"They took a large body of knowledge from the technical approach, made it rigorous, fired it up with higher math and statistical power and incorporated parts of fundamental analysis. Some use relative strength with ideas like alpha, earnings growth, and cash flow."

"A pure 'technical analyst' is looking for specific price patterns in the past to predict the future and builds his analysis solely on these factors," Sauer says. "A quant usually relies on a more diversified set of information. I'm a strong proponent of quantitative analysis based on a diversified set of information because I believe that relying on one kind of information to find superior stocks or bonds carries too much risk."

While the controversy continues to grow, at least one person believes that more fundamental analysts are checking their charts these days. "Lots of analysts are more cynical today. More are agreeing with the technical analysts who say that financial numbers don't mean a thing and the books have always been cooked," admits Orndorff.

"But to say that all they need to pick stocks and bonds is to see price movements doesn't seem to be enough either. That method is no different than trading wheat, corn, or cattle futures," he says. "Most CFA charterholders differ with that approach, or we did all that studying for nothing."

Key Points

- Technical analysis is based on the belief that the market is not efficient.
- Technical analysts use indicators that are independent of the company's financial condition.
- Fundamental analysts focus on the financial health of companies.

(continued)

REAL-WORLD RETURNS 18-1 *continued*

- Fundamental analysis chooses stocks to buy; technical analysis chooses when to buy for analysts who use both.

- Proponents of strong form efficient market theory and technical analysts are at opposite ends of the philosophical spectrum.

Tools of the Trade

Technical Analysis Trading Rules and Indicators	Fundamental Analysis Valuation Models and Factors
Trend channels	Dividend discount models
Support and resistance levels	Free cash flow models
Moving average lines	Residual income models
Relative strength	Price to earnings ratio
Charting of prices and volume	Price to book ratio
Contrary opinion indicators	Price to sales ratio
Mutual fund cash positions	Price to cash flow ratio
Credit balance brokerage accounts	Enterprise value to EBITDA
Investment advisory opinions	Dividend yield
OTC versus NYSE volume	Return on equity
CBOE put/call ratio	Operating and profit margins
Traders bullish on stock index futures	Asset turnover ratios
Follow the smart money	Leverage ratios
Barron's confidence index	Earnings growth rates
T-bill/euro spread	Free cash flow growth rates
Short sales by specialists	Growth rates of dividends, cash flow, and earnings
Breadth of market	Risk free rate and risk premium
Short interest	
Stocks above 200-day moving average	From Reilly, F. K., Brown, K. C., and Reilly, F., *Investment*
Block uptick-downtick ratio	*Analysis and Portfolio Management*, Sixth Edition,
	published by South-Western Educational Publishing,
	and Stowe, J. D., Robinson, T. R., Pinto, J. R., and
	McLeavey, D. W., *Analysis of Equity Investment: Valuation*,
	published by Association for Investment Management.

Source: Copyright 2003, CFA Institute. Reproduced and republished from "Fundamental vs. Technical Analysis: Controversy between the Two Schools Is Still Alive and Well" by Cynthia Harrington, *CFA Magazine*, Jan/Feb 2003, with permission from CFA Institute. All Rights Reserved.

Although technical analysis can be applied to bonds, currencies, and commodities as well as to common stocks, technical analysis typically involves the aggregate stock market, industry sectors, and/or individual common stocks. Therefore, we restrict our discussion in this chapter to common stocks.

WHAT IS TECHNICAL ANALYSIS?

Define technical analysis and explain why it is used.

Technical Analysis
The use of specific market data for the analysis of both individual and aggregate stock prices for the purpose of identifying recurring price patterns.

Technical analysis can be defined as the use of specific market-generated data for the analysis of both aggregate stock prices (market indexes or industry averages) and individual stocks. Martin J. Pring, in his book *Technical Analysis Explained*, states

> The technical approach to investing is essentially a reflection of the idea that prices move in trends which are determined by the changing attitudes of investors toward a variety of economic, monetary, political and psychological forces. The art of technical analysis—*for it is an art*—is to identify trend changes at an early stage and to maintain an investment posture until the weight of the evidence indicates that the trend is reversed.[3]

---

[3]Martin J. Pring, *Technical Analysis Explained* (New York: McGraw-Hill Publishers), 1991.

Technical analysis is sometimes called market or internal analysis because it utilizes the record of the market itself to attempt to assess the demand for, and supply of, shares of a stock or the entire market. Thus, technical analysts believe that the market itself is its own best source of data—as they say, "let the market tell its own story."

Economics teaches us that prices are determined by the interaction of demand and supply. Technicians do not disagree, but argue that it is extremely difficult to assess all the factors that influence demand and supply. Since not all investors are in agreement on price, the determining factor at any time is the net demand (or lack thereof) for a stock based on how many investors are optimistic or pessimistic. Furthermore, once the balance of investors become optimistic—or pessimistic—this mood is likely to continue for the near term and can be detected by various technical indicators. As the chief market technician of one investment firm says, "All I care about is how people feel about those particular stocks as shown by their putting money in and taking their money out."[4]

Technical analysis is based on published **market data** as opposed to fundamental data, such as earnings, sales, growth rates, or government regulations. Market data includes the price of a stock or the level of a market index, volume (number of shares traded), and technical indicators (explained later), such as the short interest ratio. Many technical analysts believe that only such market data, as opposed to fundamental data, are relevant.

Market Data
Price and volume information for stocks or indexes.

Recall that in fundamental analysis, the dividend discount model, the earnings multiplier model, or some other valuation model uses fundamental company data regarding future earnings, dividends, and company risk to determine an estimate of a stock's intrinsic value, which is then compared to the market price. Fundamentalists believe that their data, properly evaluated, indicate the worth or intrinsic value of a stock. Technicians, on the other hand, believe that it is extremely difficult to estimate intrinsic value and virtually impossible to obtain and analyze good information consistently. In particular, they are dubious about the value to be derived from an analysis of published financial statements. Instead, they focus on market data as an indication of the forces of supply and demand for a stock or the market.

Technicians believe that the process by which prices adjust to new information is one of a gradual adjustment toward a new (equilibrium) price. As the stock adjusts from its old level to its new one, the price tends to move in a trend. The central concern is not why the change is taking place, but rather the very fact that it is taking place at all. Technical analysts believe that stock prices show identifiable trends that can be exploited by investors. They seek to identify changes in the direction of a stock and take a position in the stock to take advantage of the trend.

The following three points summarize technical analysis:

1. Technical analysis is based on published market data and focuses on internal factors by analyzing movements in the aggregate market, industry average, or stock. In contrast, fundamental analysis focuses on economic and political factors that are external to the market itself.

2. The focus of technical analysis is identifying changes in the direction of stock prices, which tend to move in trends as the stock price adjusts to a new equilibrium level. These trends can be analyzed, and changes in trends detected, by studying the action of price movements and trading volume across time. The emphasis is on likely price changes.

3. Technicians attempt to assess the overall situation concerning stocks by analyzing breadth indicators, market sentiment, and momentum.

A Framework for Technical Analysis

Technical analysis can be applied to both an aggregate of prices (the market as a whole or industry averages) and individual stocks. It includes the use of graphs or charts, and technical trading rules and indicators. Figure 18-1 depicts the technical analysis approach to investing.

---

[4]Jonathan Butler, "Technical Analysis: A Primer," *Worth*, October 1995, p. 128.

Figure 18-1
The Technical Analysis
Approach to Common
Stock Selection

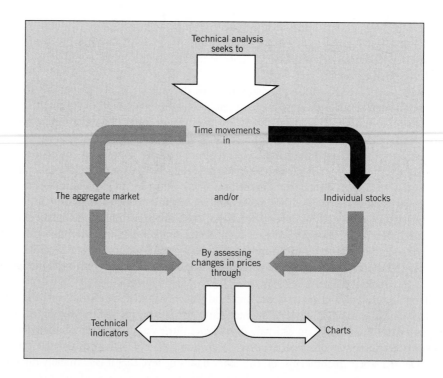

Price and volume are the primary tools of the pure technical analyst, and the chart is the most important mechanism for displaying this information. Technicians believe that the forces of supply and demand result in particular patterns of price behaviour, the most important of which is the trend or overall direction in price. Using a chart, the technician hopes to identify trends and patterns in stock prices that provide trading signals.

Volume data are used to gauge the general condition in the market and to help assess its trend. The evidence seems to suggest that rising stock prices are usually associated with rising volume and falling prices with falling volume. If stock prices rose but volume activity did not keep pace, technicians would be sceptical about the upward trend. An upward surge on contracting volume would be particularly suspect. A downside movement from some pattern or holding point, accompanied by low volume, would be taken as a bearish sign.

We first consider stock price and volume techniques, often referred to as charting. However, technical analysis has evolved over time, so that today it is much more than the charting of individual stocks or the market as a whole. In particular, technical analysts use indicators to assess market conditions and investor sentiment. They also engage in contrary analysis, which suggests investors should go against the crowd.

CHECK YOUR UNDERSTANDING

18-1. What would a technical analyst mean by the phrase, "Let the market tell its own story."?

18-2. Some technical analysts have said they do not need to know the name of the stock they are analyzing in order to make recommendations about it. Explain.

18-3. How would a pure technical analyst make use of a stock's intrinsic value?

STOCK PRICE AND VOLUME TECHNIQUES

learning objective 2
Describe the major techniques used in technical analysis.

The Dow Theory

The oldest and best-known theory of technical analysis is the **Dow Theory**. It was originally developed in the late l800s by the editor of *The Wall Street Journal*, Charles H. Dow, who many regard as the father of technical analysis. Although Dow developed the theory to describe past price movements, William Hamilton followed up by using it to predict movements in the aggregate market. The Dow Theory was very popular in the 1920s and 1930s. Articles offering support for it still appear periodically in the literature and several investment advisory services are based on the Dow Theory.

The theory is based on the existence of three types of price movements:

1. Primary moves, a broad market movement that lasts several years;

2. Secondary (intermediate) moves, occurring within the primary moves, which represent interruptions lasting several weeks or months; and

3. Day-to-day moves, occurring randomly around the primary and secondary moves.

The term **bull market** refers to an upward primary move, whereas **bear market** refers to a downward primary move. A major upward move is said to occur when successive rallies penetrate previous highs, whereas declines remain above previous lows. A major downward move is expected when successive rallies fail to penetrate previous highs, whereas declines penetrate previous lows.

The secondary or intermediate moves give rise to the so-called technical corrections, which are often mentioned in the popular press. These corrections supposedly adjust for excesses that have occurred. These movements are of considerable importance in applying the Dow Theory.

Finally, the day-to-day ripples occur often and are of minor importance. Even ardent technical analysts do not usually try to predict day-to-day movements in the market.

Figure 18-2 illustrates the basic concept of the Dow Theory, although numerous variations exist. The primary trend, represented by the dotted line, is up through time Period 1. Although several downward (secondary) reactions occur, these corrections do not reach the previous low. Each of these reactions is followed by an upward movement that exceeds the previously obtained high. Trading volume continues to build over this period.

Although prices again decline after time Period 1 as another correction occurs, the price recovery fails to surpass the last peak reached. (This process is referred to as an abortive recovery.) When the next downward reaction occurs, it penetrates the previous low. This movement could suggest that a primary downturn or new bear market has begun, although it is subject to confirmation. As originally conceived, the Dow Jones Industrial and Rail Averages (which was later replaced by the Transportation Average) must confirm each other for the movement to be validated.

Dow Theory
A technique for detecting long-term trends in the aggregate stock market.

Bull Market
An upward trend in the stock market.

Bear Market
A downward trend in the stock market.

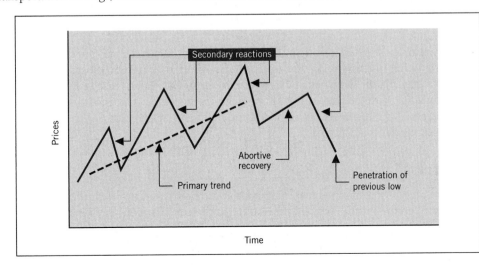

Figure 18-2
The Basic Concept of the Dow Theory

The Dow Theory is intended to forecast the start of a primary movement, but it does not tell us how long the movement will last. The trend will continue as long as the averages confirm each other. Only these averages matter, and extensive records are not required, nor are chart patterns examined.

It is obvious that today's economy is vastly different from the one that existed when the Dow Theory was developed. Many studies of its success rate have been disappointing; for example, over periods of as much as 25 years, investors would have been more successful with a buy-and-hold policy in the same stocks. In addition, confirmations are slow to arrive and are often unclear when they do, while the amount of price movement needed for a confirmation is ambiguous. Its users interpret the theory in various ways, and so it may predict different (and conflicting) movements at the same time. On the other hand, several investment letters have achieved various degrees of success based upon the Dow Theory and it is still widely used by practitioners. In short, investors today are still debating its merits.

Charts of Price Patterns

To assess individual stock-price movements, technicians often rely on charts or graphs of price movements and on relative strength analysis. The charting of price patterns is one of the classic technical analysis techniques. Technicians believe that stock prices move in trends, with price changes forming patterns that can be recognized and categorized. By visually assessing the forces of supply and demand, technicians hope to be able to predict the likely direction of future movements.

Support Level

A price range at which a technician expects a significant increase in the demand for a stock.

Technicians seek to identify certain signals in a chart of stock prices and use certain terminology to describe the events. A **support level** is the level of price (or, more correctly, a price range) at which a technician expects a significant increase in the demand for a stock—in other words, a lower boundary on price where it is expected that buyers will act, supporting the price and preventing additional price declines. A **resistance level**, on the other hand, is the price level at which a technician expects a significant increase in the supply of a stock—in other words, an upper boundary on price where sellers are expected to act, providing a resistance to any further rise in price.

Resistance Level

A price range at which a technician expects a significant increase in the supply of a stock.

Figure 18-3 illustrates support and resistance levels. As the stock approaches $10 per share, it encounters a resistance level and drops back below this price. Conversely, as it approaches slightly less than $6 per share, it gains supports and eventually rises. If the stock price breaks through the resistance level on heavy volume, this is taken as a very bullish sign and is referred to as a *breakthrough*.

Support levels tend to develop when profit taking causes a reversal in a stock's price following an increase. Investors who did not purchase earlier are now willing to buy at this price, which becomes a support level. Resistance levels tend to develop after a stock declines from a higher level. Investors are waiting to sell the stocks at a certain recovery point. At certain price levels, therefore, a significant increase in supply occurs, and the price will encounter resistance moving beyond this level.

As noted above, a trend line is a line drawn on a chart to identify a trend. If a trend exhibits support and resistance levels simultaneously that appear to be well defined, the trend lines are referred to as channel lines, and price is said to move between the upper channel line and the lower channel line. Momentum is used to indicate the speed with which prices are changing, and a number of measures of momentum exist, referred to as momentum indicators. When a change in direction occurs in a short-term trend, technicians say that a reversal has occurred. A correction occurs when the reversal involves only a partial retracing of the prior movement. Corrections may be followed by periods of consolidation, with the initial trend resuming following the consolidation.

Technical analysts rely heavily on bar charts and point-and-figure charts, although other types such as candlestick charts are also used.[5]

Bar charts

Graphs of daily stock price plotted against time.

Bar Charts

Bar charts are probably the most popular chart in technical analysis and are clearly the simplest. These charts plot price on the vertical axis and time on the horizontal axis. Each day's price movement is

---

[5]Technicians also use a basic line chart, which uses only one number—usually the closing price for the day—to reflect the price movement. Another type of chart gaining some popularity is the candlestick. Developed in Japan, the candlestick is similar to the bar chart, although it shows the opening price as well as the high, low, and closing prices.

S&P/TSX Composite Index Price and Volume Chart for the Year Ending May 23, 2008

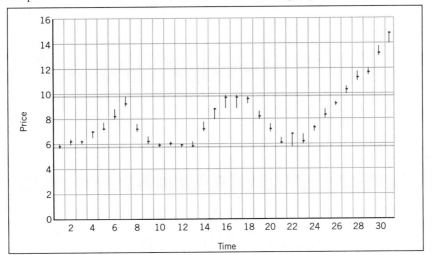

Figure 18-3
Support and Resistance
Levels for a Stock and a
Breakthrough

Dow Jones Industrial Average Price and Volume Chart for the Year Ending May 23, 2008

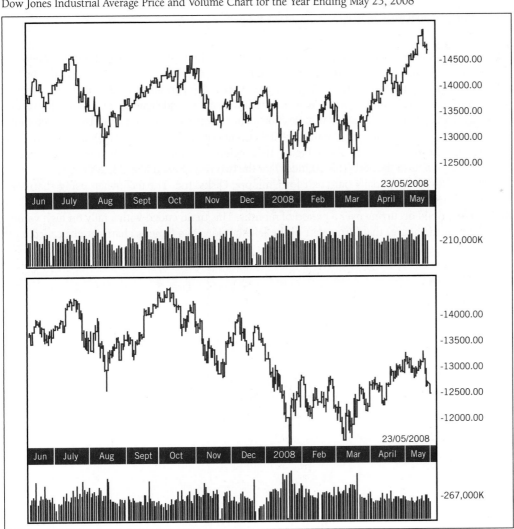

Figure 18-4
Price Graphs and Volume
Bar Charts for S&P/TSX
Composite Index and Dow
Jones Industrial Average

Source: Data retrieved from www.decisionplus.com, May 25, 2008.

Figure 18-5
Weekly Price and Volume
Chart for i60 Shares
(Symbol XIU—Units in the
S&P/TSX 60 Index) for the
Two Years Ended May 23,
2008

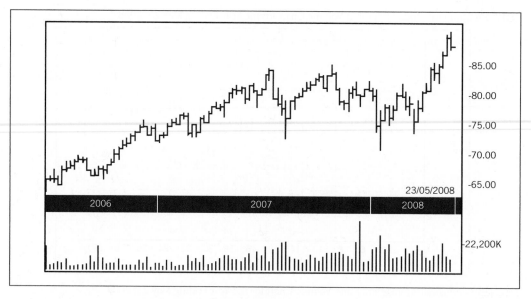

Source: Retrieved from www.decisionplus.com, May 25, 2008

represented by a vertical bar, the top of which represents the high price for the day, and the bottom is the low price. (A small, horizontal tick is often used to designate the closing price for the day.) The bottom of a bar chart usually shows the trading volume for each day, permitting the simultaneous observation of both price and volume activity.[6] Many financial websites provide graphs of bar charts for various market indexes each day with trading volume shown on the bottom—refer to Figure 18-4, which shows price graphs and volume bar charts for the S&P/TSX Composite Index and the Dow Jones Industrial Average for the year ended May 23, 2008. Figure 18-5 includes a more detailed chart for the i60 iShares (symbol XIU—Units in the S&P/TSX 60 Index) for the two years Ended May 23, 2008.

Figure 18-6 shows a daily bar chart for Unfloppy Disks, Inc. The technician using charts will search for patterns in the chart that can be used to predict future price moves. Note in Figure 18-6 the strong uptrend occurring over a period of months. This trend ended with a rally on high volume (at Point 1 in the figure) that forms part of the left shoulder of a famous chart pattern called a top

Figure 18-6
A Bar Chart for Unfloppy
Disk, Inc.

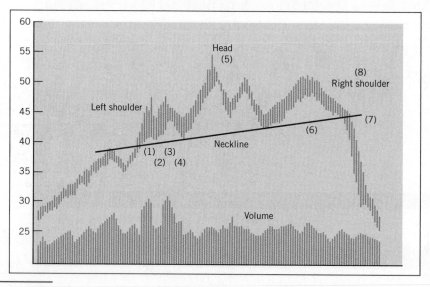

---

[6]The time intervals do not have to be days but could be weeks, months, or anything else a particular analyst might choose.

head-and-shoulders pattern. (The bottom head-and-shoulders pattern is the mirror image of the top pattern, with the logic being reversed for the interpretation of the movements).

The left shoulder shows initially strong demand followed by a reaction on lower volume (Point 2), and then a second rally, with strong volume, carrying prices still higher (Point 3). Profit taking again causes prices to fall to the so-called neckline (Point 4), thus completing the left shoulder. (The neckline is formed by connecting previous low points.) A rally occurs, but this time on low volume, and again prices sink back to the neckline. This is the head (Point 5). The last step is the formation of the right shoulder, which occurs with light volume (Point 6). Growing weakness can be identified as the price approaches the neckline. As can be seen in Figure 18-6, a downside breakout occurs on heavy volume, which technicians consider to be a sell signal.

What about other patterns? Technicians have considered a very large number of such patterns. Some of the possible patterns include flags, pennants, gaps (of more than one type), triangles of various types

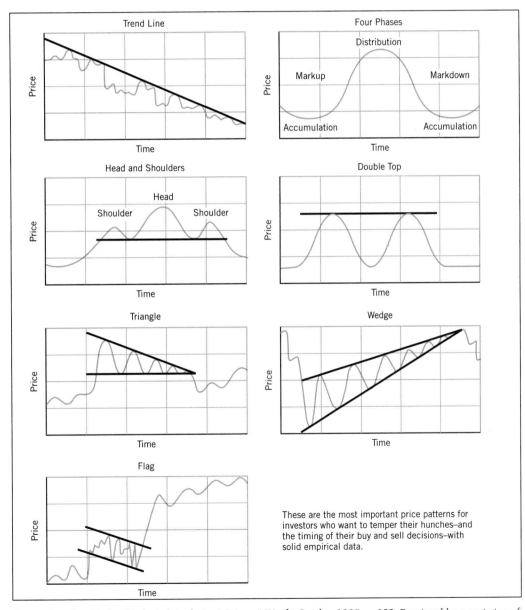

Figure 18-7
Important Price Patterns for Investors Using Charts

These are the most important price patterns for investors who want to temper their hunches—and the timing of their buy and sell decisions—with solid empirical data.

Source: Jonathan Butler, "Technical Analysis: A Primer," *Worth*, October 1995, p. 133. Reprinted by permission of *Worth* magazine.

(e.g., symmetrical, ascending, descending, and inverted), the inverted saucer or dome, the triple top, the compound fulcrum, the rising (and falling) wedge, the broadening bottom, the duplex horizontal, rectangles, and the inverted V. Figure 18-7 shows one set of price patterns said to be the most important for investors to recognize when reading charts of stock prices.

Obviously, numerous patterns are possible and can usually be found on a chart of stock prices. It is also obvious that most, if not all, of these patterns are much easier to identify in hindsight than at the time they are actually occurring. Such is the nature of trying to predict the future.

Point-and-Figure Charts

Point-and-Figure Charts
Graphs of stock prices showing only significant price changes.

Technicians also use **point-and-figure charts** that show only significant price changes and not volume. The user determines what a significant price change is ($1, $2, etc.) and what constitutes a price reversal ($2, $3, $4, etc.). Although the horizontal axis still depicts time, specific calendar time is not particularly important. (Some chartists do show the month in which changes occur.)

An X is used to show upward movements and an O for downward ones. Each X or O on a particular chart may represent $1 movements, $2 movements, $5 movements, and so on, depending on how much movement is considered significant for that stock. An X or O is recorded only when the price moves by the specified amount. Figure 18-8 illustrates a point-and-figure chart for Gigantic Computers.

Figure 18-8
A Point-and-Figure chart for Gigantic Computers.
X = $1 upward price change, O = $1 downward price change (numbers indicate months)

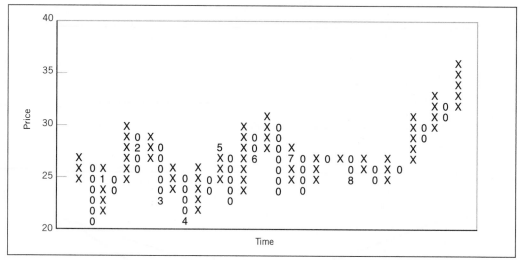

A point-and-figure chart is designed to compress many price changes into a small space. By doing so, areas of "congestion" can be identified. A congestion area is a compacted region of price fluctuations (a closely compacted horizontal band of Xs and Os). The technician studies a congestion area in search of a breakout that will indicate an expected upward or downward movement in stock price.

Point-and-figure charts may be used for a variety of technical strategies such as the application of filter rules or the Dow Theory. For example, a "three rule" filter strategy recommends that an investor does not buy or sell until there are three Xs or three Os in a column.

There are many chart patterns, some of which were mentioned earlier, and numerous technicians analyze and interpret these patterns. Due to the seemingly limitless number of patterns that can be identified in stock price movements, it is impossible to demonstrate conclusively the predictive significance of charting. In fact, very few scientific studies of the ability of chart patterns to predict the future direction of price movements have been conducted, and the conclusions of these studies have varied regarding their effectiveness. As a result, opinions about charting vary widely. Since the evidence is not conclusive, the controversy will continue.

Moving Averages

A moving average of prices is a popular technique for analyzing both the overall market and individual stocks. They are used to detect both the direction and the rate of change. Some number of days of closing prices is chosen to calculate a moving average. A well-known average for identifying major trends is the 200-day moving average (alternatively, a 10-week [50-day] average is used to identify intermediate trends). After initially calculating the average price, the new value for the moving average is calculated by dropping the earliest observation and adding the latest one. This process is repeated daily (or weekly). The resulting moving average line supposedly represents the basic trend of stock prices.

EXAMPLE 16-1: CALCULATING MOVING AVERAGE

Week 1 — $20; Week 2 — $22; Week 3 — $21; Week 4 — $24; and Week 5 — $25.

A five-week moving average could be determined in the following manner:

Moving average (five-week) = (20 + 22 + 21 + 24 + 25)/5 = $22.40

If the next week-end price is $23, the five-week moving average would then be:

Moving average (five-week) = (22 + 21 + 24 + 25 + 23)/5 = $23.00.

Real-World Returns 18-2 discusses how one could interpret the signals associated with the 40-week moving average. Various publications offer plots of moving averages for some index plotted against the index itself.

REAL-WORLD RETURNS 18-2

40-Week Moving Average

A recent article in *The Globe and Mail* quoted William O'Neil, author of *How to Make Money in Stocks*, who suggested to "sell a stock when it's first sensed that it isn't acting right."

Well, if I know the average investor, he will sense that his stock "isn't acting right" when the stock goes 1 cent lower than the price he bought it. Hence, it is probably not a very good way to judge stocks.

Instead of such a subjective emotion, there is a more objective measure that professionals have used for decades—the use of the 40-week moving average.

Before we look at the fantastic power of this tool, let's define the terms. A 40-week average is the sum of the past 40 weeks' closing prices divided by 40. Other averages (10-week, 200-day, etc.) are constructed similarly. When this exercise is repeated week after week, this average will "move" and becomes a "moving average."

In the olden days before computers, charting moving averages was a tedious task, but today any one of these averages could be accessed instantly on chart services such as Globeinvestor.com or GlobeinvestorGold.com.

The above was the mathematical definition. My practical definition is that the average illustrates the rate at which money is flowing in or out of a stock. When buyers want to own the stock and are willing to pay more for this security (bid up the price), the average will rise as a consequence.

The opposite is also true: when there are more anxious sellers who would sell at any price, the 40-week moving average will fall.

Therefore, when a rising 40-week average stops rising and begins to decline it shows that the sellers have gained the upper hand. Of course, since this tool measures the last 40 weeks, this average moves quite slowly, which is both its advantage and its failure.

(continued)

REAL-WORLD RETURNS 18-2 *continued*

The average will never give a sell signal at the top. The average could rise for weeks or even months before it turns and begins to descend. But whenever it reverses direction, whenever it turns down, the signal is clear: Get out of the position.

Losses in Bank of Montreal, Loblaw, Citigroup and Bear Stearns all could have been anticipated and prevented by the use of this simple tool. When the average stopped rising, flattened out and then began to fall for these stocks, it was time to "abandon ship." Did these signals come in time?

Definitely. The 40-week moving average signal for Bank of Montreal (now at $50.25) came at $69 on July 27, 2007 to prevent a potential 27-percent loss.

For Loblaw ($29.44), it was at $71.65 on July 29, 2005 to prevent a potential 59-percent loss. For Citigroup ($26.81) it came at $50.73 on June 29th, 2007, to prevent a potential 47-percent loss and for Bear Stearns ($10.67) at $147.95 on June 18th, 2007 to prevent a whopping 92-percent loss.

Are there any stocks on our watch-list at this time? Any stocks that are close to giving a 40-week moving average sell signal? None at the moment, but we are watching CAE and Gildan here, as well as Altria and AT & T in the United States.

Is this signal infallible? No. There are occasions when the moving average turns down, but the stock reverses soon thereafter and moves to a new high.

However, such occasions are so rare that it is better to act on the signal, than to subject oneself to a huge potential loss by trying to double-guess it.

Source: Meisels, Ron, "Call the downturn with a 40-week moving average," as appeared in *The Globe and Mail*, April 29, 2008, p. B17. Reproduced with permission of Phases & Cycles.

A comparison of the current market price to the moving average produces a buy or sell signal. The general buy signal is generated when actual prices rise through the moving average on high volume, with the opposite applying to a sell signal.

The following are specific signals of a turning point generating a sell signal:

1. The actual price is below the moving average, advances toward it, does not penetrate the average, and starts to turn down again.

2. Following a rise, the moving average flattens out or declines, and the price of the stock or index penetrates it from the top.

3. The stock price rises above the moving average line while the line is still falling.

Buy signals would be generated if these situations were reversed:

1. The actual price is above the moving average, declines toward it, does not penetrate the average, and starts to turn up again.

2. Following a decline, the moving average flattens out or increases, and the price of the stock or index penetrates it from the bottom.

3. The stock price falls below the moving average line while the line is still increasing.

The signals above have been shown in hindsight to have predictive power in some circumstances; however they have failed in others. In other words, the results are inconclusive as to how much we could have profited from this information. Perhaps more experienced technicians would possess better differentiating power regarding which signals are strong enough to dictate action be taken and which signals are inconclusive, but perhaps not. In addition, even if we did profit from this analysis in one period, there is no guarantee that we would experience similar profits in the following period. Once again, this is the risky nature of investing in common stocks—we cannot be sure what will unfold in the future.

Relative Strength

A well-known technique used for individual stocks (or industries) is relative strength analysis. The **relative strength** for a given stock is calculated as the ratio of the stock's price to a market index, or an industry index, or the average price of the stock itself over some previous period. These ratios can be plotted to form a graph of relative price across time. In effect, the graph shows the strength of the stock relative to its industry, the market, or whatever. According to the chief market analyst at Merrill Lynch, "Very often changes in trend, from good to bad or from bad to good, will be preceded by a change in the stock's relative performance.[7]

The relative strength of a stock over time may be of use in forecasting. Because trends are assumed to continue for some time, a rising ratio (an upward-sloping line when relative strength is plotted) indicates relative strength. That is, it indicates a stock that is outperforming the market and that may continue to do so. A declining ratio would have the same implications for the downside. One rule of thumb is that a stock is attractive when the relative strength has improved for at least four months, but as with most technical indicators, technicians interpret some of these signals in different ways.

Relative strength is often used by technicians to identify industry sectors that look attractive, prior to selecting individual stocks. This is in line with our analysis in Part V that supports a top-down approach to security analysis, with industry analysis preceding company analysis. By focusing on the selection of promising industries, investors narrow the number of possibilities to be considered.

This group selection approach may be helpful in supporting the proposition that an individual stock showing relative strength is not an anomaly, but the technique does not protect an investor against the chance that the overall market is weak, and that one or more groups that currently appear strong are next in line to show weakness. Such a possibility once again supports the case for a top-down approach that begins with market analysis in order to assess the likelihood that now is a good time to be investing in stocks. One of the problems with relative strength is that a stock or group could show increasing relative strength because it is declining less quickly than the market, not because it is, in fact, increasing. This suggests that relative strength is not a technique to be used in isolation.

Many sources publish a variety of relative strength indicators. For example, *The Globe and Mail Report on Business* publishes weekly relative strength indicators for the TSX indexes. Numerous investment information services also provide information on relative strength such as The Value Line Investment Survey, which divides a stock's price by the Value Line Composite Average and plots this relative strength ratio for each company it covers at the top of the page. Relative strength analysis lends itself well to computerized stock analysis, which contributes to its popularity among institutional investors who own highly automated and sophisticated data analysis systems. The extent to which a number of institutional investors use relative strength techniques and have the means to observe changes at about the same time can affect the volatility of a stock.

Relative Strength
The ratio of a stock's price to some market or industry index, usually plotted as a graph.

Obtaining Charts to Use in Technical Analysis

In today's computerized world, and with the proliferation of Internet sources of information, investors have many choices for obtaining charts and related information. Many financial magazines and websites offer charts of various degrees of complexity for thousands of companies, updatable in a variety of ways and time frequencies. Some of these publications and websites are included on the textbook's companion website. Real-World Returns 18-3 provides a chartist view on the prospects for IBM based on price patterns, moving averages, and a point and figure diagram.

---

[7]Butler, "Technical Analysis: A Primer," p. 133.

REAL-WORLD RETURNS 18-3

IBM Technical Analysis

IBM Corp. traded within a large horizontal range between $70 and $100 from 2002 to 2007 (see dashed lines). The stock pierced above this base in early 2007 and reached a high of $121.46. The stock subsequently found support at the top of the preceding trading range (ceiling becomes a floor and current prices should provide a good buying opportunity in view of higher targets. Only a sustained decline below $100 would reverse the positive long-term status of this stock.

Point & Figure measurements provide initial targets of $129 and $144. The large base from 2002 to 2007 supports significantly higher targets.

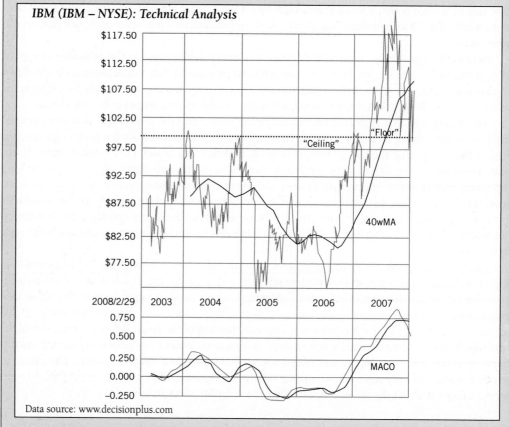

IBM (IBM – NYSE): Technical Analysis

Data source: www.decisionplus.com

Source: Meisels, Ron and Rizk, Monica, "What the charts say," as appeared in *The Globe and Mail*, March 1, 2008, p. B13. Reproduced with permission of Phases & Cycles.

CHECK YOUR UNDERSTANDING

18-4. Suppose someone tells you that they use the Dow Theory regularly and that it provides them with valuable information. They urge you to do the same. What objections might you raise against doing this?

18-5. How might an investor use a stock price charting technique as part of an overall top-down approach to security analysis?

TECHNICAL INDICATORS

The chart remains the technician's most important tool for making buy and sell decisions. However, in addition to looking at the plot of stock prices, technicians also like to examine the overall situation by analyzing such factors as breadth and market sentiment indicators.

Breadth Indicators

Breadth of the Market and the Advance-Decline Line

There are a number of indicators of stock market breadth. For example, *The Globe and Mail Report on Business* reports several of these measures on a daily basis, as depicted in Figure 18-9.

Figure 18-9
Market Breadth

	% change indicators increase/decrease from 13-week average			
	TSX	**Venture**	**NYSE**	**Nasdaq**
Advance	772	540	922	884
% Chg.	1.74	7.66	−44.67	−38.18
Adv. Vol. (000s)	171,877	100,488	570,756	435,338
Decline	789	479	2,516	1,961
% Chg.	26	−15.19	54.35	28.22
Decl. Vol. (000s)	179,907	67,045	3,146,445	1,266,574
Unchanged	710	1,451	257	372
% Chg.	14.21	14.95	−12.03	18.03
Unch. Vol. (000s)	18,556	27,870	14,885	33,367
Total	2,271	2,470	3,695	3,217
New High	27	17	26	20
% Chg.	−37.24	−38.71	−30.75	−75.40
New Low	32	32	56	98
% Chg.	−31.10	1.46	−36.30	−.09
Vol. (000s)	370,340	195,403	3,732,086	1,735,278
% Chg.	.42	8.48	16.32	−16.88

Source: *The Globe and Mail/Report on Business*, May 24, 2008, p. B10.

Figure 18-9 reports the number of issues advancing and the number declining. A common measure of market breadth is the advance-decline line. This line measures, on a cumulative daily basis, the net difference between the number of stocks advancing in price and those declining in price for a group of stocks such as those on the TSX or NYSE. Subtracting the number of declines from the number of advances produces the net advance for a given day (which, of course, can be negative). This measure may include hundreds or thousands of stocks.

The advance-decline line, often referred to as the breadth of the market, results from plotting a running total of these numbers across time. The line can be based on daily or weekly figures, which are readily available from daily newspapers.

The advance-decline line is compared to a stock index such as the S&P/TSX Index in order to analyze any divergence—that is, to determine whether movements in the market indicator have also occurred in the market as a whole. Technicians believe that divergences signal that the trend is about to change. The advance-decline line and the market averages normally move together. If both are rising, the overall market is said to be technically strong. If both are falling, the market is weak. If the advance-decline line is rising while the average is declining, the decline in the average should reverse itself. Particular attention is paid to a divergence between the two during a bull market. If the average rises while the line weakens or declines, this indicates a weakening in the market; the average would therefore be expected to reverse itself and start declining.

New Highs and Lows

Part of the information reported for the TSX and other stock exchanges is the new high and low prices for each stock. Technicians regard the market as bullish when a significant number of stocks each day hit new highs. On the other hand, technicians see rising market indexes and few stocks hitting new highs as a troublesome sign. (Figure 18-9 includes new highs and lows for the TSX, the TSX Venture Exchange, the NYSE, and Nasdaq.)

Volume

Volume is an accepted part of technical analysis. High trading volume on exchanges, other things being equal, is generally regarded as a bullish sign. Heavy volume combined with rising prices is even more bullish.

Sentiment Indicators

Short-Interest Ratio

Short-Interest Ratio
The ratio of total shares sold short to average daily trading volume.

The short interest for a security is the number of shares that have been sold short but not yet bought back.

The short-interest ratio is defined as

(18-1)
$$\text{Short-interest ratio} = \text{Total shares sold short} \div \text{Average daily trading volume}$$

In effect, this ratio indicates the number of days necessary to "work off" the current short interest.[8] It is considered to be a measure of investor sentiment, and many investors continually refer to it.

Investors sell short when they expect prices to decline; therefore, it would appear that the higher the short interest, the more investors are expecting a decline. A large short-interest position for an individual stock should indicate heavy speculation by investors that the price will drop. However, many technical analysts interpret this ratio in the opposite way: A high short-interest ratio is taken as a bullish sign because the large number of shares sold short represents a large number of shares that must be repurchased in order to close out the short sales. If the ratio is low, the required future purchases are lower. In effect, the short seller must repurchase, regardless of whether or not his or her expectations were correct. The larger the short-interest ratio, the larger the potential demand that is indicated. Therefore, an increase in the ratio indicates more pent-up demand for the shares that have been shorted.

The short-interest ratio for a given month should be interpreted in relation to historical boundaries. However, one problem is that the boundaries keep changing. Short-interest figures have been distorted by hedging and arbitrage techniques that have become more popular. For example, if a fund buys Royal Bank and shorts CIBC, how does this affect the interpretation of the short interest? Hedged short sellers are not likely to panic if their short position moves adversely, which otherwise might lead them to buy and push the price up.

---

[8]For example, a ratio of 1.0 means that the outstanding short interest approximates a day's trading volume.

Mutual Fund Liquidity

Several indicators are based on the theory of contrary investing (also known as contrary opinion). The idea is to trade contrary to most investors, who supposedly almost always lose—in other words, to go against the crowd. This is an old idea and over the years technicians have developed several measures designed to capitalize on this concept.

Mutual fund liquidity can be used as a contrary opinion technique. Under this scenario, mutual funds are presumed to act incorrectly before a market turning point. Therefore, when mutual fund liquidity is low because the funds are fully invested, contrarians believe that the market is at, or near, a peak. The funds should be building up cash (liquidity); instead, they are extremely bullish and are fully invested. Conversely, when funds hold large liquid reserves, it suggests that they are bearish. Contrarians would consider this a good time to buy because the market may be at, or near, its low point.

Put/Call Ratio

Some technical analysts believe that people who play the options market are, as a group, consistent losers. Speculators buy calls when they expect stock prices to rise, and they buy puts when they expect prices to fall. Because they are generally more optimistic than pessimistic, the put to call ratio is usually well below 1.0. For example, a ratio of 0.60 indicates that only six puts are purchased for every 10 calls. The rise of this ratio indicates increased pessimism on the part of speculators in options, but this is a buy signal to a contrarian. A low ratio would be a sell signal to a contrarian because of the rampant optimism such a ratio indicates.

While small changes are considered unimportant, extreme readings are said to convey information. According to one well-known analyst, this would correspond to a CBOE put/call ratio below 0.7 or above 0.9.[9]

The Odd-Lot Theory

An odd-lot transaction involves the purchase or sale of shares in less than a round lot, which varies according to stock price but is usually less than 100 shares. According to the odd-lot theory, small investors are more likely to buy or sell odd lots, and they are usually wrong in their actions at market peaks and troughs. Supposedly, such investors typically buy when the market is at or close to a peak and sell when it is near the bottom. In addition, it is assumed that small investors do not get involved with short sales unless they are particularly bearish.

Odd-lot ratios measure the total purchases and sales involving less than a round lot. An increase in odd-lot purchases is bearish, while an increase in odd-lot sales is bullish.

TESTING TECHNICAL ANALYSIS STRATEGIES

What constitutes a fair test of a technical trading rule? The adjustments that should be made include at least the following:

1. *Risk.* If the risk involved in two strategies is not comparable, a fair comparison cannot be made. As we know, other things being equal, a more risky strategy would be expected to outperform a less risky one.

2. *Transaction and other costs (e.g., taxes).* Several technical trading rules may produce excess returns before transaction costs are deducted. However, after such costs are deducted, they may be inferior to a buy-and-hold strategy, which generates much lower trading costs.

---

[9]Butler, "Technical Analysis: A Primer," p. 129.

3. *Consistency*. Can the rule outperform the alternative over a reasonable period of time, such as five or 10 years? Any rule may outperform an alternative for a short period, but it will not be too useful unless it holds up over some longer term.

4. *Out-of-sample validity*. Has the rule been tried on data other than that used to produce the rule? It is always possible to find a rule that works on a particular sample if enough rules are tried; that is, it is possible to torture the data until it confesses.

If we conduct enough tests, we can find a rule that produces favourable results on a particular sample. Therefore, before we conclude that a trading rule is successful, we should conduct a fair test as outlined above. Risks must be comparable, and appropriate costs must be deducted. Finally, the rule should be tried on different samples of stocks over a sufficiently long-term period.

SOME CONCLUSIONS ABOUT TECHNICAL ANALYSIS

learning objective 3
Discuss the limitations of technical analysis.

INVESTING *tip*

No inherent reason exists for stock price movements to repeat themselves. For example, flipping a coin 100 times should on average result in about 50 heads and 50 tails. While it is possible that the first 10 tosses could produce 10 heads the chance of that pattern repeating itself is extremely small.

Technical analysis often appeals to those who are beginning a study of investments because it is easy to believe that stock prices form repeatable patterns over time or that certain indicators should be related to future market (or individual stock) price movements. It is easy to look at a chart of a particular stock and immediately see what we believe to be patterns in the price changes and clear evidence of trends that should be obvious to anyone studying it. How should we view this situation?

On the one hand, most academics, numerous practitioners, and anyone believing in the weak-form version of the EMH are highly sceptical of technical analysis, to say the least. On the other hand, many practitioners, both professional and amateur, use technical information to assist them in their investment decisions. Indeed, it is rare to see any type of analytical report on a stock that does not include some sort of historical price information or a price chart.

One of the contributing factors to this debate is that it is impossible to test all the techniques of technical analysis and their variations and interpretations. The techniques of this approach are simply too numerous, and technical analysis is broader than the use of only price information. As a result, technical analysis has not been tested thoroughly and definitive statements about this subject cannot be made. A good example of the omissions in this area is the use of volume in technical strategies. Although volume is a recognized part of technical analysis, few tests have been conducted on its use in conjunction with the rest of technical analysis.[10]

In addition to the lack of abundance of empirical evidence, the evidence that has been produced has not led to unilateral conclusions on the subject. While a large number of thorough tests of technical analysis techniques have failed to confirm the value of technical trading strategies, several studies have found conflicting evidence. For example, an article by Brock, Lakonishok, and LeBaron demonstrated the profitability associated with the use of some standard technical trading strategies.[11] They used 90 years of daily data over the period 1897 to 1986 to demonstrate the superior returns produced by moving average and trading range breakout strategies.

Jegadeesh found predictable patterns in stock prices based on monthly returns for the period 1934–1987.[12] His study showed that stocks with large losses in one month are likely to show a significant reversal in the following month, and that stocks with large gains in one month are likely to show a significant loss in the next month. Interestingly, in a subsequent study of US stock returns,

---

[10]O. Joy and C. Jones, "Should We Believe the Tests of Market Efficiency?" *Journal of Portfolio Management* 12 (Summer 1986), pp. 49–54.

[11]W. Brock, J. Lakonishok, and B. LeBaron, "Simple Technical Trading Rules and the Stochastic Properties of Stock Returns," *Journal of Finance* 47 (December 1992), pp. 1731–1764.

[12]N. Jegadeesh, "Evidence of Predictable Behavior of Security Returns," *Journal of Finance* 45 (July 1990), pp. 881–898.

Jegadeesh and Titman documented the success associated with "momentum" trading strategies, which involves purchasing stocks that have performed well in the recent time period, and selling those that have performed poorly.[13] These results have been confirmed in Canada by Foerster, Prihar, and Schmitz, and by Cleary and Inglis.[14]

There are several other troubling features of technical analysis for non-believers. First, several interpretations of each technical tool and chart pattern are not only possible, but usual. One or more of the interpreters will be correct (more or less), but it is virtually impossible to know beforehand who these will be. After the fact, we will know which indicator or chart, or whose interpretation, was correct, but only those investors who used that particular information will benefit. Tools such as the Dow Theory are well known for their multiple interpretations by various observers who disagree over how the theory is to be interpreted.

Furthermore, consider a technical trading rule (or chart pattern) that is, in fact, successful. When it gives its signal on the basis of reaching some specified value (or forms a clear picture on a chart), it correctly predicts movements in the market or some particular stock. Such a rule or pattern, if observed by several market participants, will be self-destructive as more and more investors use it. Price will reach its equilibrium value quickly, taking away profit opportunities from all but the quickest. Some observers will start trying to act before the rest on the basis of what they expect to happen. (For example, they may act before a complete head and shoulders pattern forms.) Price will then reach an equilibrium even more quickly, so that only those who act earliest will benefit. Eventually, the value of any such rule will be negated entirely (i.e., the pattern will disappear).[15]

What can we conclude about technical analysis? While technical analysis attempts to measure the psychology behind the forces of supply and demand, it is as much an art as it is a science. While it does not meet several criteria for academic acceptance, it remains popular among many investors. It is important to recognize that no investment system—technical, fundamental, or one based on the use of modern portfolio theory—will work in all markets all the time, since we are dealing with the uncertain future. The important matter is that investors should attempt to gain value added wherever possible, and along these lines, a basic knowledge of the tenets of technical analysis may prove useful.

CHECK YOUR UNDERSTANDING

18-6. Investors who believe a stock's price will fall (a pessimistic view) may sell the stock short. Why then do many technical analysts view an increase in the short-interest ratio as an optimistic sign for a stock price?

18-7. Your broker calls to say that she has developed a trading technique which involves adjusting your portfolio each week based on up-to-date market indicators. Furthermore, she claims that tests of this technique using data from all of last year show that it provides very high returns. Why might you be skeptical of the broker's claims?

SUMMARY

This summary relates to the learning objectives for this chapter.

1. **Define technical analysis and explain why it is used.**

Technical analysis, an alternative to fundamental analysis, is the oldest approach used by investors. Technical analysis relies on published market data, primarily price and volume data, to predict the

---

[13]N. Jegadeesh and S. Titman, "Returns to Buying Winners and Selling Losers: Implications for Stock Market Efficiency," *Journal of Finance* 48 (March 1993), pp. 65–91.

[14]S. Foerster, A. Prihar, and J. Schmitz, "Back to the Future: Price Momentum Models and How They Beat the Canadian Equity Markets," *Canadian Investment Review* 7 (Winter 1994/95), pp. 9–13; S. Cleary and M. Inglis, "Momentum in Canadian Stock Returns," *Canadian Journal of Administrative Sciences* 15 (September 1998), pp. 279–291.

[15]Readers should recognize that having technicians identify and exploit these opportunities will contribute to market efficiency, since the patterns should eventually disappear.

short-term direction of individual stocks or the market as a whole. The emphasis is on internal factors that help to detect demand-supply conditions in the market. The rationale for technical analysis is that the net demand (or lack thereof) for stocks can be detected by various technical indicators, and that trends in stock prices occur and continue for considerable periods of time. Stock prices require time to adjust to the change in supply and demand.

2. Describe the major techniques used in technical analysis.

Price and volume are primary tools of the technical analyst, as are various technical indicators. Technical analysis can be applied to both the aggregate market and individual stocks. Aggregate market analysis originated with the Dow Theory, the best-known technical theory. It is designed to detect the start of major movements. Other technical indicators of the aggregate market include, but are not limited to, the following:

 a. Moving averages, which are used to detect both the direction and the rate of change in prices;
 b. The advance-decline line (breadth of market), which is used to assess the condition of the overall market;
 c. Mutual fund liquidity, which uses the potential buying power (liquidity) of mutual funds as a bullish or bearish indicator;
 d. Short-interest ratio, which assesses potential demand from investors who have sold shares short; and
 e. Contrary opinion, which is designed to go against the crowd. Included here are mutual fund liquidity and the put/call ratio, as well as the odd-lot theory.

Technical analysis also involves the use of charts of price patterns to detect trends that are believed to persist over time. The most frequently used charts are bar charts, which show each day's price movement as well as volume, and point-and-figure charts, which show only significant price changes as they occur. Numerous chart patterns are recognizable to a technician. However, all patterns are subject to multiple interpretations because different technicians will read the same chart differently.

Another well-known technique for individual stocks is relative strength, which shows the strength of a particular stock in relation to its average price, its industry, or the market.

3. Discuss the limitations of technical analysis.

Technical analysis is popular among investors but is not generally accepted by academics who see it as more an art than a science. The techniques of technical analysis are too numerous to test empirically, and the evidence that does exist is inconclusive. Critics point out that the same technical information can lead analysts to several different interpretations.

KEY TERMS

Bar charts, p.600	Market data, p.597	Short-interest ratio, p.610
Bear market, p.599	Point-and-figure charts, p.604	Support level, p.600
Bull market, p.599	Relative strength, p.607	Technical analysis, p.596
Dow Theory, p.599	Resistance level, p.600	

REVIEW QUESTIONS

18-1. Describe the rationale for technical analysis.

18-2. What do technicians assume about the adjustment of stock prices from one equilibrium position to another?

18-3. What role does volume play in technical analysis?

18-4. How does the Dow Theory forecast how long a market movement will last?

18-5. Differentiate between support levels and resistance levels.

18-6. What is relative strength analysis?

18-7. Why is the advance-decline line called an indicator of breadth of the market?

18-8. Why is a rising short-interest ratio considered to be a bullish indicator?

18-9. What is the rationale for the theory of contrary opinion?

18-10. Why are the opinions of investment advisory services considered a contrary opinion signal?

18-11. Why do stock-price movements repeat themselves?

18-12. Differentiate between fundamental analysis and technical analysis.

18-13. What is the Dow Theory? What is the significance of the confirmation signal in this theory?

18-14. Using a moving average, how is a sell signal generated?

18-15. Distinguish between a bar chart and a point-and-figure chart.

18-16. What new financial instruments have caused the short-interest ratio to be less reliable? Why?

18-17. Describe a bullish sign and a bearish sign when using a moving average. Do the same for the advance–decline line.

18-18. Assume that you know a technical analyst who claims success on the basis of his or her chart patterns. How might you go about scientifically testing this claim?

18-19. Is it possible to prove or disprove categorically the validity of technical analysis?

18-20. On a rational economic basis, why is the study of chart patterns likely to be unrewarding?

18-21. Consider the plot of stock X in Figure 18-10. The plot shows weekly prices for one year, based on a beginning price of $30.

    a. Do you see any chart patterns in this figure?
    b. Do any patterns you see in this chart help you to predict the future price of this stock?
    c. What is your forecast of this stock's price over the next three months?

18-22. Which of the following statements about technical analysis is false? Technical analysis:

    a. refers to the methodology of forecasting fluctuations in security prices.
    b. can be applied either to individual securities or to the market as a whole.
    c. must precede fundamental analysis when valuing stocks.
    d. involves the use of charts and graphs.

18-23. Describe the odd-lot theory.

18-24. What constitutes a fair test of a technical trading rule?

18-25. Using a moving average, how is a buy signal generated?

18-26. Draw a chart showing a "bottom head and shoulders" price pattern.

PROBLEMS

18-1. In April 2008, the share price of mining firm BHP Billiton was moving in an upward trend. The table below shows the closing price for the stock, as well as the volume of shares traded (in thousands) for each of the first 15 trading days in the month.

    a. Calculate a 5-day moving average of the stock's closing prices. Note that you will only be able to do this calculation for days 5 through 15
    b. Use Excel's charting capabilities to plot the closing prices and the moving averages. You should be able to put both "line charts" on the same graph by using two "data series". Observe that the moving average levels out but doesn't decrease even when the stock price falls for a few days.

c. Create a bar chart of the trading volume over the 15 day period. Can you identify the day(s) when significant news about the company was released?

Day	Closing Price	Volume ('000)
1	66.91	4,554
2	67.83	4,582
3	70.55	8,102
4	73.22	4,974
5	75.07	5,267
6	79.00	12,835
7	78.31	4,606
8	77.97	2,952
9	77.05	2,111
10	76.81	1,834
11	79.80	4,694
12	82.27	8,052
13	80.58	4,194
14	80.96	4,868
15	83.55	4,835

18-2. Monthly closing prices for stock of the Royal Bank of Canada (RBC) and the level of the S&P/TSX Composite index are shown below for the first nine months of 2008.

Month	Index	RBC
January	13155	50.65
February	13583	49.39
March	13350	47.95
April	13937	48.02
May	14715	50.80
June	14467	45.83
July	13593	47.25
August	13771	48.75
September	11753	50.50

a. Calculate a relative strength indicator for the bank's stock by dividing its price by the level of the index. These will be very small numbers, so scale the values (multiply) by a factor of 1,000.
b. Plot the relative strength using Excel's line chart.
c. Comment on the performance of the bank's stock price relative to the index during the first two quarters (January to June) of 2008. Was the situation different in the third quarter (July to September)?

PREPARING FOR YOUR PROFESSIONAL EXAMS

CFA PRACTICE QUESTIONS

18-1. All the following are valid statements about the assumptions underlying technical analysis except:

a. The laws of supply and demand drive stock prices.
b. Supply is driven by the rational behaviour of firms offering their shares, while demand is driven by the irrational behaviour of investors.

c. Stock prices move in trends that persist for long periods of time.

d. Shifts in supply and demand can be observed in market price behaviour.

18-2. Which of the following is not an example of stock price and volume techniques involving technical analysis?

   a. Dow Theory
   b. Short interest ratio
   c. Moving average lines
   d. Support and resistance levels

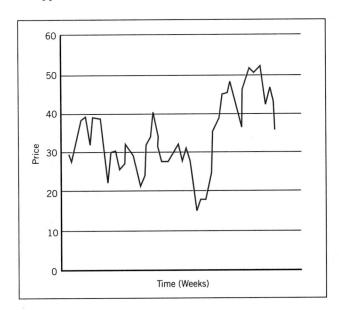

Figure 18-10
Stock X

CHAPTER 19

OPTIONS

Having heard about options from several sources, you decide this is one of those topics that you at least have to be able to talk about. If you are going to manage your inheritance without interference, you don't want to be left standing there looking foolish when someone asks you about writing calls or buying a put to protect against market declines. Even the popular press talks about calls and puts on a regular basis. Therefore, you see no alternative but to plow ahead and learn enough about derivatives in general, and options in particular, to let you hold your own. And, besides, this may turn out to be very valuable information you can use in the future when investing.

Learning Objectives

After reading this chapter, you should be able to

1.   Define options and discuss why they are used.
2.   Describe how options work and give some basic strategies.
3.   Explain the valuation of options.
4.   Identify types of options other than puts and calls.

CHAPTER PREVIEW

Derivatives are contracts between two parties (a buyer and a seller) that have a price and that trade in specific markets. The importance of derivative securities lies in the flexibility they provide investors in managing investment risk. Derivative instruments can also be used to speculate in various markets. Chapter 19 analyzes one of these derivative contracts—options—while Chapter 20 analyzes another: futures. Real-World Returns 19-1 alludes to the risks associated with derivatives when misused, pointing to the recent multi-billion-dollar losses generated by a rogue trader at the French bank, Société Générale. The article goes on to point out that derivatives per se are not bad, but the danger lies in the reckless action of their users.

REAL-WORLD RETURNS 19-1
Derivatives

How's this for timing: The January edition of *Risk* magazine named a certain French bank the Equity Derivatives House of the Year. A week later, that bank—Société Générale—was suddenly short $7.2-billion because of some unfortunate futures bets.

To be fair, not even *Risk* magazine's deep-thinking editors can predict a rogue trader. But still, that amusing little story does highlight an important point about derivatives. They're not dangerous in and of themselves. But in the hands of people who don't understand them or who have the wrong incentives, they're a powder keg. And since greed makes us all blind and stupid, investors should be extremely wary of any company that dabbles in derivatives.

There are too many kinds of derivatives to count, and more are invented all the time. A derivative is a financial position based on an underlying asset. Compared with a stock or a bond or real estate—traditional assets—derivatives are fleeting, with short life spans generally. They're also powerful because they bulge with leverage—a small change in the underlying asset's price usually means a much bigger change in the derivatives' value, up or down.

The Chicago Board Options Exchange has a price calculator for index options that will show you how a one-year option on an index can go up by 33 percent in value if the index moves from $90 to $91. If the index value moves from $90 to $89, the loss is 29 percent. Now you can see why SocGen's junior trader could do so much damage. But we can also start to see how misleading derivatives talk can be.

Lots of people who want to scare investors with talk of financial Armageddon will talk about the value of derivative positions and how they've mushroomed over the years. Measured in notional terms, that's true: JPMorgan's derivatives book has grown to $92-trillion in 2007 from $22-trillion in 1999. The total amount of US commercial bank derivatives was $172-trillion in the third quarter, $20-trillion more than in the second quarter.

Trillion is the best headline word after sex, drugs and Britney Spears, but is it accurate? In our example above, the notional value of a call option would be $90. It's not how much you can lose (or make). Entire indexes don't generally go to zero. They can drop a lot—say 20 percent, which in our example would cause the theoretical price of the option to go to zero. But the loss isn't $90, it's $1.70, the cost of the option.

So don't concentrate on that raw $172-trillion number. Most of that, in fact, is hedged—that is, the banks take a long position, a neutralizing short position and earn a small fee up the middle. SocGen's rogue trader pretended to be doing this but he was in fact making one-sided bets on future index values. If he thought an index would go up, he'd find someone who thought it would go down (or someone trying to lock in portfolio gains) and make a bet.

Back to the notion of notional: By far the most common derivatives that big US banks are involved in are swaps, whereby two investors agree to trade the return on different assets. Banks often use interest rate swaps to protect themselves (or their clients do it). For example, they may agree to pay a floating interest rate on a notional amount of principal in exchange for receiving a fixed rate from the counterparty. The bank isn't betting on the direction of interest rates; rather it's protecting itself because, in our example, it has to pay interest on debt and wants to make sure it has the cash to make the payments.

What we're saying is: Don't panic when you see big headline numbers. That said, don't be naive. While the absolute number of notional exposure isn't really that telling, the growth is a little more so, and so is that growth relative to bank assets. But even that doesn't hint at the real problem with derivatives, which is the computer programs that tell traders how to cobble together supposedly "safe" portfolios of derivatives. SocGen's problem, if you believe management, is straightforward: Thousands of little bets on the direction of stock indexes that went into the red (and that management liquidated in a panic, more than doubling the loss).

Most derivative explosions happen when a trader thinks he understands the co-relationships between a basket of related derivatives and learns, painfully, that his computer models were wrong. When a Calgary trader blew up hedge fund Amaranth in 2006, he wasn't just long or short a futures contract. He was long some and short others, hoping to earn a spread that flawed statistics told him would materialize. In short, he simply didn't know what he was doing.

The same holds true, in part for CIBC which, we note, has hired 40 consultants to help it work through its derivatives mess. Why didn't it employ these experts before plunging headlong into the derivatives world?

And as for greed, last year Wall Street bonuses were $33-billion. Credit-crunch-related losses, a lot of them caused by derivatives, are more than $100-billion. Shareholders lost that money; rest assured the bonuses won't be repaid to them.

To paraphrase the gun lobby, derivatives don't maul investors. People maul investors.

Source: Taylor, Fabrice, "The minefield of derivatives," *The Globe and Mail Report on Business*, January 30, 2008, p. B13.

This chapter briefly introduces the nature of derivatives in general, and then analyzes options, which are important derivative securities that provide flexibility for investors in managing investment risk and the opportunity to speculate in security markets. We explain the advantages of options and provide some basic strategies. We also discuss how options are valued using the Black-Scholes model. Although our focus is on put and call options, we take a look at interest rate, currency, and stock-index options at the end of the chapter.

INTRODUCTION TO OPTIONS

Rather than trade directly in common stocks, investors can purchase securities representing a claim—an option—on a particular stock or group of stocks. This option gives the holder the right to receive or deliver shares of stock under specified conditions. The option need not be exercised (and often will not be worth exercising). Instead, an investor can simply buy and sell these **equity-derivative securities** that derive their value from the equity prices of the same corporation. Gains or losses will depend on the difference between the purchase price and the sales price.

This chapter looks at put and call options. Appendix 11A discussed convertible securities, and Appendix 19B at the end of this chapter examines warrants and rights. All are equity-derivative securities.[1] We concentrate primarily on options on individual stocks and stock indexes, and to a much lesser extent on interest rate options. In Chapter 20, we consider futures contracts, which together with

Equity-Derivative Securities

Securities that derive their value in whole or in part by having a claim on the underlying common stock.

---

[1] Interest rate derivative securities, such as bond options and futures contracts on bankers' acceptances, are also commonly used derivatives, as discussed in Chapters 2 and 4. Interest rate swaps (which are discussed in Chapter 12) are used primarily by financial institutions and large corporations.

options constitute the most commonplace equity-derivative securities used by the average investor. Since we are focusing on investing instruments, we limit our discussion to financial derivatives.

Our emphasis is on how puts and calls work and on their importance to portfolio managers. As derivative securities, options are innovations in risk management, not in risk itself, and as such they should be both welcomed and used by investors and portfolio managers. Since our emphasis is on equity securities, our examples revolve around common stocks.

Options Basics

learning objective 1
Define options and discuss why they are used.

Options
Claims that give the holder the right, but not the obligation, to buy or sell a stated number of shares of stock within a specified period at a specified price.

Call
An option that gives the holder the right, but not the obligation, to buy a specified number of shares of stock at a stated price within a specified period.

Put
An option that gives the holder the right, but not the obligation, to sell a specified number of shares of stock at a stated price within a specified period.

Options, which typically represent claims on an underlying common stock, are created by investors and sold to other investors. The corporation whose common stock underlies these claims has no direct interest in the transaction, being in no way responsible for creating, terminating, or executing put and call contracts.

A **call** option contract gives the holder the right but not the obligation to buy (or "call away") a specified number of shares of a particular common stock at a specified price any time prior to a specified expiration date.[2] Investors purchase calls if they expect the stock price to rise because the price of the call and the common stock will move together. Therefore, calls permit investors to speculate on a rise in the price of the underlying common stock without buying the stock itself. For example, a Canadian Pacific Railway (CP) two-month call option at $74 per share gives the buyer the right (an option) to purchase 100 shares of CP at $74 per share from a writer (seller) of the option anytime during the two months before the specified expiration date.

A **put** option contract gives the buyer the right but not the obligation to sell (or "put away") a specified number of shares of a particular common stock at a specified price prior to a specified expiration date. If exercised, the shares are sold by the owner (buyer) of the put contract to a writer (seller) of the contract, who has been designated to take delivery of the shares and pay the specified price. Investors purchase puts if they expect the stock price to fall, because the value of the put will rise as the stock price declines. Therefore, puts allow investors to speculate on a decline in the stock price without selling the common stock short. For example, the writer (seller) of a CP two-month put at $74 per share is obligated, under certain circumstances, to receive from the holder of this put 100 shares of CP, for which the writer will pay $74 per share.

Why Options Markets?

An investor can always purchase shares of common stock if he or she is bullish about the company's prospects rather than buy a call (or sell a put). Similarly, one can sell a company's shares short if bearish about the stock rather than buy a put (or sell a call). Why, then, should we create these indirect claims on a stock as an alternative way to invest? Several reasons have been advanced, including the following:

1. Puts and calls expand the opportunity set available to investors, making available risk–return combinations that otherwise would be impossible or that improve the risk–return characteristics of a portfolio. For example, an investor can sell a stock short and buy a call. This decreases the risk on the short sale for the life of the call since the investor has a guaranteed maximum purchase price until the call option expires.[3]

2. In the case of calls, an investor can control (for a short period) a claim on the underlying common stock for a much smaller investment than required to buy the stock itself. In the case of puts, an investor can duplicate a short sale without a margin account and at a modest cost in relation to the value of the stock. In addition, the option buyer's maximum loss is known in advance. If an option expires worthless, the most the buyer can lose is the cost (price) of the option.

---

[2]It is important to remember throughout this discussion that the standard option contract on the organized exchanges is for 100 shares of the underlying common stock.

[3]Many stocks do not have puts and calls available in the organized options market exchanges. For example, the active options trading on the Montreal Exchange consists of less than a hundred stocks, while a few hundred stocks dominate the listings and trading activity on large US options markets such as the Chicago Board Options Exchange (CBOE). There are also a large number of stock options that trade in the over-the-counter market through brokers.

3. Options provide leverage by magnifying the percentage gains in relation to buying or short selling the underlying stock. In fact, options can provide greater leverage potential than fully margined stock transactions.

4. Using options on a market index such as the S&P/TSX 60 Index, an investor can participate in market movements with a single trading decision.

UNDERSTANDING OPTIONS

Options Terminology

To understand puts and calls, one must understand the terminology used in connection with them. Our discussion here applies specifically to options on the organized exchanges as reported daily in the financial media.[4] Important options terms include the following:

1. The **exercise (strike) price** is the per-share price at which the common stock may be purchased (in the case of a call) or sold (in the case of a put). Most options are available at several different exercise prices, thereby giving investors a choice. As the stock price changes, options with new exercise prices are added.[5]

2. The **expiration date** is the last date on which an option can be exercised. All puts and calls are designated by the month of expiration, with equity options expiring on the Saturday following the third Friday of the month. This forces clients to make their exercise decisions on the Friday. The expiration dates for options contracts vary from stock to stock.

3. The **option premium** is the price paid by the option buyer to the writer (seller) of the option, whether put or call. The premium is stated on a per-share basis for options on organized exchanges, and since the standard contract is for 100 shares, a $3 premium represents a cost per contract of $300, a $15 premium represents a cost of $1,500, and so forth.

Options exchanges have introduced combinations of standardized expiration dates (known as trading cycles) and standardized exercise prices. For example, Real-World Returns 19-2 describes Equity Option Cycles on the Montreal Exchange.

Exercise (Strike) Price
The per-share price at which the common stock may be purchased from (in the case of a call) or sold to (in the case of a put) a writer.

Expiration Date
The date on which an option expires.

Option Premium
The price paid by the option buyer to the seller (writer) of the option.

REAL-WORLD RETURNS 19-2

Equity Option Cycles

All equity options issued by the Canadian Derivatives Clearing Corporation (CDCC) and listed on the Montréal Exchange have expiry cycles. Expiry cycles are used to establish the length of time that an option will be listed and quoted by the equity option market makers.

Cycles vary in relation to the dividend that is being paid out by the listed underlying company and are comprised of four maturities: two near months and two quarterly months. Exceptions to this rule are the iShares and index options, which fall under cycle 4 having five maturities, as shown hereunder.

Montréal Exchange also has long-term equity options expiring in one-, two- and three-year intervals. These long-term equity options only have one expiry month, i.e. January (or March for long-term index options). Long-term options eventually get included as regular expiries when their cycle approaches nine months to its expiry.

(continued)

---

[4]Puts and calls existed for many years before the existence of organized exchanges. They could be bought or sold in the over-the-counter (OTC) market. The terms of each individual contract (price, exercise date, etc.) had to be negotiated between buyer and seller. This was clearly a cumbersome, inefficient process. The OTC market for options is unregulated, and transactions are not reported. Although specific information is not available, a very large OTC market for options does exist and is widely used by corporations and portfolio managers for hedging purposes.

[5]Options sold on these exchanges are protected against stock dividends and stock splits; both the exercise price and the number of shares in the contract are adjusted for dividends or splits, as necessary.

REAL-WORLD RETURNS 19-2 *continued*

Cycle 1 Four maturities — two near months and the next two months from the January, April, July, October cycle.

Cycle 2 Four maturities — two near months and the next two months from the February, May, August, November cycle.

Cycle 3 Four maturities — two near months and the next two months from the March, June, September, December cycle.

Cycle 4 Five maturities — three near months and the next two months from cycle 3.

Source: Retrieved from Montreal Exchange Equity Option Cycles Publication www.m-x.ca, May 26, 2008.

Figure 19-1 is an excerpt from Globeinvestor.com that shows the most actively traded call options on the Montreal Exchange on May 26, 2008. It reports the symbol for the underlying stock and for the call option, the option expiry date, the strike price, the underlying stock price, the last price for the option, the change in the option price in dollar figures and as a percentage, and the volume and open interest for the call option. The volume shows the number of options contracts that were traded the previous day, while the open interest represents the number of options of a particular series that are presently outstanding. It is usually used as a measure of liquidity, along with the volume of trading.

Figure 19-1
Equity Options

MOST ACTIVE - PRICE INCREASE (CALLS)

Stock	Symbol Option	Expiry Date	Strike Price	Underlying Price	Put/ Call	Last	Change $	Change %	Vol	Open Interest
TLM-T	TLMF2600	2008-06	26.00	24.70	CALL	0.75	0.45	150.00	125	5741
TLM-T	TLMF2800	2008-06	28.00	24.70	CALL	0.35	0.20	133.33	142	105
TLM-T	TLMF2400	2008-06	24.00	24.70	CALL	1.75	0.95	118.75	583	5957
TLM-T	TLMG2600	2008-07	26.00	24.70	CALL	1.10	0.50	83.33	45	1050
TLM-T	TLMG2800	2008-07	28.00	24.70	CALL	0.55	0.25	83.33	50	60
TLM-T	TLMG2400	2008-07	24.00	24.70	CALL	2.05	0.85	70.83	82	156
TLM-T	TLMI2600	2008-09	26.00	24.70	CALL	1.95	0.80	69.57	120	3522
TLM-T	TLMF2200	2008-06	22.00	24.70	CALL	3.10	1.25	67.57	90	3358
TLM-T	TLMG2200	2008-07	22.00	24.70	CALL	3.30	1.10	50.00	20	6
BCB-T	BCBA700	2009-01	7.00	3.61	CALL	0.15	0.05	50.00	40	0
PWF-T	PWFG4200	2008-07	42.00	35.60	CALL	0.15	0.05	50.00	10	526
BCB-T	BCBG500	2008-07	5.00	3.61	CALL	0.15	0.05	50.00	60	357
TLM-T	TLMI2400	2008-09	24.00	24.70	CALL	2.80	0.90	47.37	102	562
TLM-T	TLMF2000	2008-06	20.00	24.70	CALL	4.65	1.30	38.81	52	2447
TLM-T	TLMI2800	2008-09	28.00	24.70	CALL	1.10	0.30	37.50	20	973
TLM-T	TLMG2000	2008-07	20.00	24.70	CALL	4.90	1.30	36.11	14	0
TLM-T	TLMF1900	2008-06	19.00	24.70	CALL	5.75	1.45	33.72	10	1277
TLM-T	ZLMA2600	2009-01	26.00	24.70	CALL	2.45	0.60	32.43	40	861
TLM-T	ZLMA2400	2009-01	24.00	24.70	CALL	3.35	0.80	31.37	63	1185
TLM-T	ZLMA2800	2009-01	28.00	24.70	CALL	1.70	0.40	30.77	98	186
FNX-T	FNXF2600	2008-06	26.00	23.95	CALL	0.45	0.10	28.57	3	125
TLM-T	ZLMA2200	2009-01	22.00	24.70	CALL	4.45	0.95	27.14	86	887
TLM-T	TLMI2200	2008-09	22.00	24.70	CALL	3.55	0.75	26.79	31	1562
MBT-T	MBTF4000	2008-06	40.00	42.20	CALL	2.45	0.50	25.64	13	28

| Symbol | | Expiry | Strike | Underlying | Put/ | | Change | | | Open |
Stock	Option	Date	Price	Price	Call	Last	$	%	Vol	Interest
TLM-T	TLML2800	2008-12	28.00	24.70	CALL	1.50	0.30	25.00	309	779
FTS-T	FTSG3000	2008-07	30.00	27.67	CALL	0.25	0.05	25.00	6	658
TLM-T	ZLMA2000	2009-01	20.00	24.70	CALL	5.80	1.10	23.40	193	1061
TLM-T	TLML2600	2008-12	26.00	24.70	CALL	2.15	0.40	22.86	110	388
TLM-T	TLML2400	2008-12	24.00	24.70	CALL	3.00	0.55	22.45	145	494
TLM-T	TLMI2000	2008-09	20.00	24.70	CALL	5.00	0.90	21.95	25	1206
BNS-T	BNSG5200	2008-07	52.00	48.20	CALL	0.30	0.05	20.00	8	1607
NG-T	NGA900	2009-01	9.00	8.58	CALL	1.85	0.30	19.35	15	0
HXD-T	HXDG1600	2008-07	16.00	16.38	CALL	2.50	0.40	19.05	3	0
FM-T	FMF8000	2008-06	80.00	77.15	CALL	4.15	0.65	18.57	10	21
BNS-T	BNSF4800	2008-06	48.00	48.20	CALL	1.30	0.20	18.18	60	3660
TLM-T	ZLMA1800	2009-01	18.00	24.70	CALL	7.25	1.10	17.89	31	552
CP-T	CPF7400	2008-06	74.00	71.95	CALL	1.00	0.15	17.65	12	346
NCX-T	NCXF2800	2008-06	28.00	27.84	CALL	1.00	0.15	17.65	20	96
TLM-T	ZLMA1600	2009-01	16.00	24.70	CALL	9.00	1.25	16.13	94	328
TLM-T	WLMA2600	2010-01	26.00	24.70	CALL	4.00	0.55	15.94	10	119
PDN-T	PDNF500	2008-06	5.00	5.71	CALL	0.75	0.10	15.38	101	442
TLM-T	TLMI1800	2008-09	18.00	24.70	CALL	6.50	0.85	15.04	5	452
BNS-T	BNSF5000	2008-06	50.00	48.20	CALL	0.40	0.05	14.29	47	1923
MFC-T	MFCG4400	2008-07	44.00	38.14	CALL	0.08	0.01	14.29	10	673
CP-T	CPG7400	2008-07	74.00	71.95	CALL	1.65	0.20	13.79	5	244
TLM-T	WLMA2000	2010-01	20.00	24.70	CALL	7.10	0.85	13.60	3	498
NCX-T	NCXF2600	2008-06	26.00	27.84	CALL	2.25	0.25	12.50	10	65
RY-T	RYF5000	2008-06	50.00	50.15	CALL	1.40	0.15	12.00	14	3993
CCO-T	CCOF4200	2008-06	42.00	40.94	CALL	1.40	0.15	12.00	25	568
TLM-T	WLMA1200	2010-01	12.00	24.70	CALL	13.35	1.40	11.72	5	125

Source: Retrieved from www.globeinvestor.com, May 26, 2008.

Consider the third last row referring to the **Royal Bank of Canada (RBC)** June 2008, $50 call options, reported as:

| Symbol | | Expiry | Strike | Underlying | Put/ | | Change | | | Open |
Stock	Option	Date	Price	Price	Call	Last	$	%	Vol	Interest
RY-T	RYF5000	2008-06	50.00	50.15	CALL	1.40	0.15	12.00	14	3993

We can see that these options expire in June 2008, and they have an exercise price of $50, while the common shares of RBC closed trading on May 26, 2008, at $50.15 per share. The last trade price for these options was $1.40 per option (or $1.40 × 100 = $140 per option contract), the traded volume in this option series that day was 14 contracts, and the open interest was 3993 contracts.

Long-term options or **LEAPs** (short for Long-Term Equity AnticiPation Securities)[6] are options with maturities greater than one year and ranging to two years and beyond. They are available on several stocks, with more being traded all the time. For example, in May 2008, an investor could purchase long-term call options on **RBC** with maturity dates of January 2010 or January 2011.

Long-Term Options (LEAPs)

Options on individual stocks with maturities greater than one year.

---

[6]LEAPs is a registered trademark of the Chicago Board Options Exchange.

How Options Work

learning objective 2
Describe how options work and give some basic strategies.

As noted, a standard call (put) contract gives the buyer the right to purchase (sell) 100 shares of a particular stock at a specified exercise price before the expiration date. Both puts and calls are created by sellers who write a particular contract. Sellers (writers) are investors, either individuals or institutions, who seek to profit from their beliefs about the underlying stock's likely price performance, just as the buyer does.

The buyer and the seller have opposite expectations about the likely performance of the underlying stock and therefore the performance of the option.

- The call writer expects the price of the stock to remain roughly steady or perhaps move down.
- The call buyer expects the price of the stock to move upward and relatively soon.
- The put writer expects the price of the stock to remain roughly steady or perhaps move up.
- The put buyer expects the price of the stock to move down and relatively soon.

EXAMPLE 19-1: BUYING A CALL OPTION ON RBC

Consider an individual named Carl who is optimistic about RBC's prospects. Carl instructs his broker to buy a June 2008 call option on RBC at a strike price of $50. Assume that the negotiated premium is $1.40 (i.e., the Last value reported in Figure 19-1). This implies the cost of one option contract is $140 plus brokerage commissions.

Three courses of action are possible with any option:

1. *The option may expire worthless.* Assume the price of RBC fluctuates up and down but is at $45 on the expiration date. The call gives the buyer (owner) the right to purchase RBC at $50, but this would make no sense when RBC can be purchased on the open market at $45. Therefore, the option will expire worthless.

2. *The option may be exercised.* If RBC appreciates above $50, Carl could exercise the option by paying $5,000 (the $50 exercise price multiplied by 100 shares) and receiving 100 shares of RBC. For example, if the shares appreciated to $60 before expiration, Carl could purchase 100 shares for $5,000 plus commission fees, and resell them in the market for $6,000 less commission fees. His resulting profit would be $6,000 – $5,000 – $140 (the original cost of the option contract) – total commission fees.

3. *The option can be sold in the secondary market.* If RBC appreciates, the value (price) of the call will also. Carl can easily sell the call in the secondary market to another investor who wishes to speculate on RBC because listed options are traded continuously. Most investors trading puts and calls do not exercise those that are valuable; instead, they simply sell them on the open market, exactly as they would the common stock.[7]

Puts work the same way as calls, except in reverse. A writer creates a particular put contract and sells it for the premium that the buyer pays. The writer believes that the underlying common stock is likely to remain flat or appreciate, while the buyer believes that the stock price is likely to decline. Unlike a buyer, a writer may have to take action in the form of taking delivery of the stock.

EXAMPLE 19-2: SELLING A PUT OPTION ON RBC

Assume a writer sells a June 2008 RBC put option contract with an exercise price of $52.00 when the stock price is $50.15. A premium of $2.35 (the Last price as of May 26, 2008) means a total

---

[7]One of the implications of the option pricing model to be considered later is that American calls on stocks that do not pay a cash dividend should never be exercised before the expiration date, but those with dividends might be exercised.

of $235 per option contract, which the buyer of the put pays and the writer receives (brokerage costs would be involved in both cases).

Suppose the price of RBC declines to $45 near the expiration date. The put owner (buyer), who did not own RBC previously, could instruct the broker to purchase 100 shares of RBC in the open market for $4,500. The buyer could then exercise the put, which means that a chosen writer must accept the 100 shares of RBC and pay the put owner $52.00 per share, or $5,200 total (although the current market price has fallen to only $45). The put buyer earns $465 before commission fees ($5,200 received less $4,500 cost of 100 shares less the $235 paid for the put contract). The put writer suffers an immediate paper loss because the 100 shares of RBC are worth $45 per share but have a cost of $52.00 per share, although the premium received by the writer reduces this loss by $235. (Brokerage costs have once again been omitted in the example.)

As in the case of a call, two other courses of action are possible in addition to the exercise of the put. If the market price of the shares was below $52.00 (the exercise price), it is far more likely that the put owner would sell the put in the secondary market for a profit (or a loss), rather than exercising the option. As in the case of calls, most put investors simply buy and sell their options in the open market. Alternatively, if the price of RBC is at or above $52.00, the put would expire worthless because the price of the common stock did not decline enough to justify exercising the put.

The Mechanics of Trading
The Options Exchanges

Most exchange listed equity options are American style, which can be exercised at any time up to and including the expiration date. Index options and over-the-counter (OTC) options are typically European, which means they can only be exercised on the expiration date. Options can be bought or sold through an exchange facility or privately arranged (OTC options).

As mentioned in Chapter 4, all exchange-traded options in Canada trade on the Montreal Exchange (ME), which officially merged with the TSX on May 2, 2008, to form the TMX Group. Five option exchanges constitute the secondary market in the US: the Chicago Board Options Exchange (CBOE), the American, the Philadelphia, the Pacific, and the newer International Securities Exchange (ISE) in New York. Traditionally, the first four exchanges controlled the trading of US options, each handling different options and competing very little. The ISE began trading in May 2000, and now has a substantial share of US trading volume in options. This all-electronic market is extremely efficient, and this competition has led to lower costs and narrower spreads for customers and quicker access to the market.

The options markets provide liquidity to investors, which is a very important requirement for successful trading. Investors know that they can instruct their broker to buy or sell whenever they desire at a price set by the forces of supply and demand. Liquidity problems, which often plague the OTC options markets, are overcome by

1. Offering standardized option contracts

2. Having all transactions guaranteed by a clearing corporation, which effectively becomes the buyer and seller for each option contract.

The same types of orders discussed in Chapter 5, in particular, market, limit, and stop orders, are used in trading puts and calls.[8] Certificates representing ownership are not used for puts and calls; instead, transactions are handled as bookkeeping entries. Option trades settle on the next business day after the trade. The exercise of an equity option settles in three business days, the same as

---

[8]While these orders are available, the manner in which some types of orders are executed on some of the options exchanges varies from that used on the stock exchanges.

with a stock transaction. An investor must receive a risk disclosure statement issued by the clearing corporation (discussed in the following section) before the initial order is executed.

Table 19-1 shows the option volume on the Montreal Exchange for 2006 and 2007.

Table 19-1

Option Product Group

Option Product Group	2006		2007	
	Volume		**Volume**	
Interest Rate Derivatives				
Future Options	605,806	4.7%	748,991	5.3%
Bond Options	2,275	0.02%	13,782	0.01%
Index Derivative				
Options on Index Derivatives	906,677	7.0%	814,880	5.7%
Equity Derivatives				
Equity Options	10,629,749	82.0%	11,903,402	83.6%
Leaps	787,009	6.1%	730,658	5.1%
Totals	**12,962,778**	**100.0%**	**14,246,602**	**100.0%**

Source: Retrieved from www.m-x.ca

While Table 19-1 indicates the volume of options traded in Canada has been increasing, a significant problem with the Canadian options markets has traditionally been thin trading. As a result, many investors have often taken their option trades to US markets, which deal with much larger trading volumes. For example, the largest options exchange in the world is the Chicago Board Options Exchange (CBOE). The volume of trading in all options on this exchange in 2007 was 944.5 million contracts—more than 66 times the volume of all ME option trades that year.

In addition to the equity options that are available on the ME and the OTC markets in Canada and through the US markets, there are a variety of alternative option products available to Canadian investors. Stock-index options on the S&P/TSX Index are available in Canada and options also trade on many of the Canadian-based ETFs discussed in Chapter 3, such as the i60 units, whose values are determined by the levels of the S&P/TSX 60 Index.

Index options on the Standard & Poor's 100 Index plus others in US are also available. Stock-index options are "cash-settled" based on 100 times the value of the index at expiration date. Bond options trade on the ME on Government of Canada bonds, while US dollar options are available on the ME and other currency options are available in US markets.

The Clearing Corporation

Canadian Derivatives Clearing Corporation (CDCC)

The clearing corporation that issues and guarantees all equity, bond, and stock index positions on options exchanges in Canada.

In Canada, all equity, bond, and stock index positions are issued and guaranteed by a single clearing corporation, the **Canadian Derivatives Clearing Corporation (CDCC)**, which is owned by the ME.

In the US, all listed options are cleared through the Options Clearing Corporation (OCC). Exercise on options trading on exchanges is accomplished by submitting an exercise notice to the clearing corporation. The clearing corporation then assigns the exercise notice to a member firm, which then assigns it to one of its accounts.

These clearing corporations perform a number of important functions that contribute to the success of the secondary market for options. They function as intermediaries between the brokers representing the buyers and the writers. That is, once the brokers representing the buyer and the seller negotiate the price on the floor of the exchange, they no longer deal with each other but with the

CDCC (or the OCC in the US). Through their brokers, call writers contract with the CDCC itself to deliver shares of the particular stock, and buyers of calls actually receive the right to purchase the shares from the CDCC. Thus, the CDCC becomes the buyer for every seller and the seller for every buyer, guaranteeing that all contract obligations will be met. This prevents the risk and problems that could occur as buyers attempted to force writers to honour their obligations. The net position of the CDCC is zero, because the number of contracts purchased must equal the number sold.

Investors wishing to exercise their options inform their brokers, who in turn inform the CDCC of the exercise notice. Once the option holder submits the exercise note, the process is irrevocable. The CDCC randomly selects a broker on whom it holds the same written contract, and the broker randomly selects a customer who has written these options to honour the contract. Writers chosen in this manner are said to be assigned an obligation or to have received an assignment notice.[9] Once assigned, the writer cannot execute an offsetting transaction to eliminate the obligation; that is, a call writer who receives an assignment must sell the underlying securities, and a put writer must purchase them.

One of the great advantages of a clearing house is that transactors in this market can easily cancel their positions prior to assignment. Since the CDCC maintains all the positions for both buyers and sellers, it can cancel out the obligations of both call and put writers wishing to terminate their position. For example, a call writer can terminate the obligation to deliver the stock any time before the expiration date (or assignment) by making a "closing purchase transaction" at the current market price of the option. The CDCC offsets the outstanding call written with the call purchased in the closing transaction. A put writer can also close out a position at any time by making an offsetting transaction.

Options cannot be purchased on margin, and buyers must pay 100 percent of the purchase price. With regard to puts and calls, *margin* refers to the collateral that option writers provide their brokers to ensure fulfillment of the contract in case of exercise. This collateral is required by the CDCC of its member firms whose clients have written options, in order to protect the CDCC against default by option writers. The member firms, in turn, require its customers who have written options to provide collateral for their written positions. This collateral can be in the form of cash or marketable securities (including shares in the underlying security).

CHECK YOUR UNDERSTANDING

19-1. Why might an investor prefer to buy a put on a particular stock rather than sell it short?

19-2. What does it mean to say a call buyer has a right but not an obligation? What about the call seller?

19-3. Assume that an investor buys a put on a stock. Describe three different outcomes that could occur for the investor holding this option.

19-4. How does the clearing house (or clearing corporation) help to ensure the fulfillment of put and call contracts?

SOME BASIC OPTIONS CHARACTERISTICS

In the Money, At the Money, and Out of the Money

Special terminology is used to describe the relationship between the exercise price of the option and the current stock price. If the price of the common stock, S, exceeds the exercise price of a call, E, the call is said to be *in the money* and has an immediate exercisable value. On the other hand, if the price of the common is less than the exercise price of a call, it is said to be *out of the money*. Finally,

---

[9]Assignment is virtually certain when an option expires in the money.

calls that are near the money are those with exercise prices slightly greater than current market price, whereas calls that are *at the money* are those with exercise prices equal to the stock price.

These same definitions also apply to puts, but in reverse.

In summary,

If S > E, a call is in the money and a put is out of the money.

If S < E, a call is out of the money and a put is in the money.

If S = E, an option is at the money.

Intrinsic Values

Intrinsic Value (Option)

The value of an option if today was the expiration date.

If a call is in the money (the market price of the stock exceeds the exercise price for the call option), it has an *immediate* value equal to the difference in the two prices. This value will be designated as the **intrinsic value** of the call; it could also be referred to as the option's minimum value, which in this case is positive. If the call is at or out of the money, the intrinsic value is zero and the price of the option is based entirely on its speculative appeal. The intrinsic value can never fall below $0, since exercise is optional. Summarizing, where S_0 = current stock price:

(19-1)

$$\text{Intrinsic value of a call} = \text{Maximum } \{(S_0 - E), 0\}$$

EXAMPLE 19-3: CALCULATING INTRINSIC VALUE OF CP

We observe a closing price of $71.95 for the common shares of CP on May 26, 2008 (as shown in Figure 19-1). An October 2008 call option on CP with a $70 strike price is available at a premium of $6.40 (the last trade price). This option is in the money because the stock price is greater than the exercise price. The intrinsic value of the October 2008 call is

Intrinsic value of CP October 70 call

$$= \text{Maximum } [(\$71.95 - \$70.00), 0] = \$1.95$$

Puts work in reverse. If the market price of the stock is less than the exercise price of the put, the put is in the money and has an intrinsic value. Otherwise, it is at or out of the money and has a zero intrinsic value. Thus,

(19-2)

$$\text{Intrinsic value of a put} = \text{Maximum } \{(E - S_0), 0\}$$

EXAMPLE 19-4: CALCULATING INTRINSIC VALUE OF CP

There was an October 2008 put on CP stock available on May 26, 2008, with an exercise price of $74.00 (with a last trade price of $6.00). Given the market price for CP shares of $71.95 at that time, the intrinsic value for this put can be determined in the following manner:

Intrinsic value of CP October 74 put

$$= \text{Maximum } [(\$74.00 - \$71.95), 0] = \$2.05$$

PAYOFFS AND PROFITS FROM BASIC OPTION POSITIONS

We can better understand the characteristics of options by examining their potential payoffs and profits. The simplest way to do this is to examine their value at expiration. At the expiration date, an option has an investment value, or payoff, which equals the option's intrinsic value at that time. In addition, we can also examine the net profit, which takes into account the price of the stock, the exercise price of the option, and the cost of the option. We consider both variables because option traders are interested in their net profits, but option valuation is perhaps better understood by focusing on payoffs.

As part of this analysis, we use letters to designate the key variables:

$$S_T = \text{the value of the stock at expiration date T}$$
$$E = \text{the exercise price of the option}$$

Calls

Buying a Call

Consider first the buyer of a call option. At expiration, the investment value or payoff to the call holder is

Payoff to call buyer at expiration:
$$= S_T - E \text{ if } S_T > E$$
$$= 0 \text{ if } S_T < E$$

Notice that this payoff is the intrinsic value for a call option at time T, as presented in Equation 19-1. This payoff to a call buyer is illustrated in Figure 19-2(a). The payoff is $0 until the exercise price is reached, at which point the payoff rises as the stock price rises.

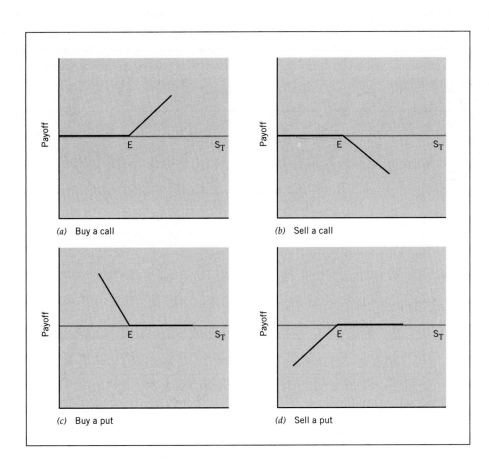

(a) Buy a call *(b)* Sell a call *(c)* Buy a put *(d)* Sell a put

Figure 19-2
Payoff Profiles for Call and Put Options at Expiration

EXAMPLE 19-5: DETERMINING PAYOFF ON AN RBC CALL

Assume an investor buys an RBC July call option with an exercise price of $50. The payoff for the call at expiration is a function of the stock price at that time. For example, at expiration the value of the call relative to various possible stock prices would be calculated as in the following partial set of prices:

RBC stock price at expiration	$40	45	50	55	60
RBC call value (payoff) at expiration	$ 0	0	0	5	10

Notice that the payoff is not the same as the net profit to the option holder or writer. For example, if RBC is at $55 per share, the payoff to the option buyer is $5, but the net profit must reflect the cost of the call. In general, the profit to an option holder is the value of the option less the price paid for it. For the example above, if the cost of the RBC July 50 call option was originally $1.85, the net profit to the option holder (ignoring transactions costs) would be

$$\text{Net profit (option holder)} = \text{Option payoff} - \text{Option cost}$$

$$\text{Net profit (option holder)} = \$5 - \$1.85 = \$3.15$$

EXAMPLE 19-6: DETERMINING NET PROFIT ON CALL AND PUT OPTIONS

Figure 19-3 illustrates the profit situation for a call buyer. The price of the stock is assumed to be $48, and a six-month call is available with an exercise price of $50 for a premium of $4 per option, or $400 per option contract. If this call expires worthless, the maximum loss is the $400 premium. Up to the exercise price of $50, the loss is $4 per option. The break-even point for the investor is the sum of the exercise price and the premium, or $50 + $4 = $54. Therefore, the profit-loss line for the call buyer crosses the break-even line at $54. If the price of the stock rises above $54, the value of the call will increase with it, at least point for point, as shown by the two parallel lines above the $0 profit-loss line.

Figure 19-3
Profit and Losses to the
Buyer of a Call Option

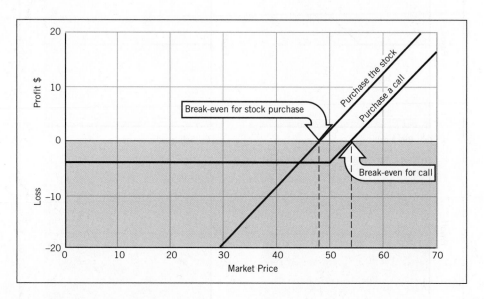

Selling (Writing) a Call

A "naked" or uncovered option writer is one who does not have their position "covered" in the underlying stock—in other words, does not own shares in the underlying stock to make available if the call option is exercised. Naked call option writers (or sellers) incur losses if the stock's price increases, as shown by the payoff profile in part (b) of Figure 19-2. The payoff is flat at the amount of the premium until the exercise price is reached, at which point it declines as the stock price rises. The call writer loses and the call buyer gains if the stock price rises.

Payoff to naked call writer at expiration:
$$= -(S_T - E) \text{ if } S_T > E$$
$$= 0 \qquad \qquad \text{if } S_T < E$$

The net profit line in Figure 19-4 is the mirror image of that for the call buyer, with positive profit levels up to the exercise price because the call writer is receiving the premium. The horizontal axis intercept in Figure 19-4 occurs at the break-even point for the option writer—the sum of the exercise price and the option premium received (note that the break-even point is identical to that of the call buyer). As the stock price exceeds the break-even point, the call writer loses. In fact, there is no conceptual limit to the call option writer's losses, since there is no upward limit on the price of the underlying share.

The mirror images of the payoff and net profit profiles for the call buyer [Figure 19-2(a) and Figure 19-3] and the call writer [Figure 19-2(b) and Figure 19-4] illustrate an important point. Option trading is often referred to as a zero-sum game, because whatever the option buyer gains, the option writer loses and vice versa. With commissions, options trading could be unprofitable for both buyers and sellers and must be unprofitable for both taken together since it is a zero-sum game. However, even though no actual wealth is created, both parties may achieve their investment objectives.

To illustrate this zero-sum game notion, consider the RBC July 50 call option discussed above that had a payoff of $5 to the option holder, when the ending share price was $55. Under the same circumstances, the payoff to the option writer would be –$5. Assuming this option writer had received $1.85 per option (the price paid by the option holder), the option writer's net profit would be the exact opposite of the net profit to the option holder, or

Net profit (option writer) = Option premium − Option payoff

Net profit (option writer) = $1.85 − $5.00 = −$3.15

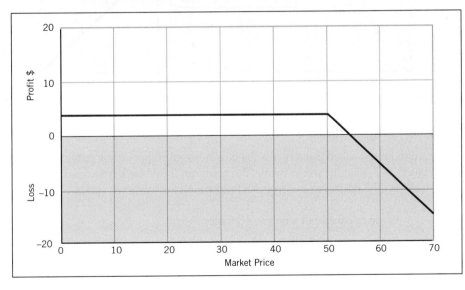

Figure 19-4
Profit and Losses to the Writer of a Call Option

Puts

Buying a Put

A put buyer makes money if the price of the stock declines. Therefore, as part (c) of Figure 19-2 illustrates, the payoff pattern is flat at the $0 axis to the right of the exercise price; that is, stock prices greater than the exercise price result in a $0 payoff for the put buyer. As the stock declines below the exercise price, the payoff for the put option increases. The larger the decline in the stock price, the larger the payoff.

Payoff to put buyer at expiration:
= 0 if $S_T > E$
= $E - S_T$ if $S_T < E$

Notice, as with call options, that this payoff corresponds to the intrinsic value of the option at the expiration date.

Once again, the profit line parallels the payoff pattern for the put option at expiration. As Figure 19-5 illustrates, the investor breaks even (no net profit) at the point where the stock price is equal to the exercise price minus the premium paid for the put. Beyond that point, the net profit line parallels the payoff line representing the investment value of the put.

Figure 19-5
Profit and Losses to the Buyer of a Put Option

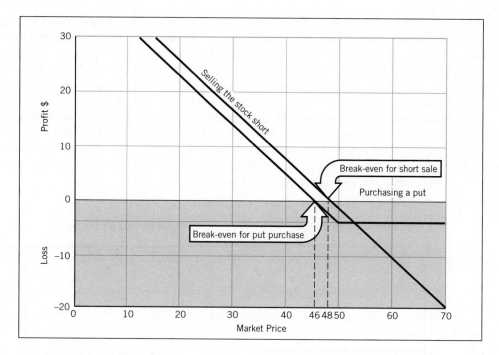

Selling (Writing) a Put

The payoff pattern for the naked put writer is the mirror image of that for the put buyer as shown in part (d) of Figure 19-2. The put writer retains the premium if the stock price rises and loses if the stock price declines. The put writer exchanges a fixed payoff for unknown losses.

Payoff to naked put writer at expiration:
= 0   if $S_T > E$
= $-(E - S_T)$ if $S_T < E$

Writers (sellers) of puts are seeking the premium income exactly as are call writers. The writer obligates himself or herself to purchase a stock at the specified exercise price during the life of the put contract. If stock prices decline, the put buyer may purchase the stock and exercise the put by delivering the stock to the writer, who must pay the specified price.

Note that the put writer may be obligated to purchase a stock for, say, $50 a share when it is selling in the market for $40 a share. This represents an immediate paper loss (less the premium received for selling the put). Also note that the put writer can cancel the obligation by purchasing an identical contract in the market.[10]

EXAMPLE 19-7: DETERMINING PROFITS AND LOSSES

Figure 19-6 illustrates the profit-loss position for the seller of a put. Using the previous figures, we see that a six-month put is sold at an exercise price of $50 for a premium of $4. The seller of a naked put receives the premium and hopes that the stock price remains at or above the exercise price. As the price of the stock falls, the seller's position declines. The seller begins to lose money below the break-even point, which in this case is $50 − $4 = $46. Losses could be substantial if the price of the stock declined sharply. The price of the put will increase point for point as the stock price declines. The maximum loss for the put writer is bounded, unlike that for the call writer, since the price for the underlying share cannot fall below zero. In this example, the most the put writer could lose is $4 − $50 = −$46 (where −$50 is the payoff if the shares became worthless).

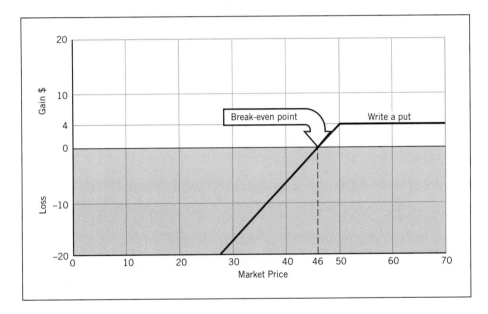

Figure 19-6
Profit and Losses to the Writer of a Put Option

Some Observations on Buying and Selling Options

Options are attractive because of the small investment required and the potentially large payoff. According to the studies that have been done, the odds favour the sellers. Writing calls produces steady, although not extraordinary, returns. Call writing is often profitable, and call buying is often unprofitable. When buying options investors should generally avoid options that expire in a few weeks—about 75 percent of the option premium disappears in the last three weeks of the option's life. Selling uncovered options is very risky. In effect, the reward (premium) does not justify the risk for most investors. Real-World Returns 19-3 discusses one investor's strategy for buying and selling call options.

---

[10]Of course, if the price of the stock has declined since the put was written, the price of the put will have increased and the writer will have to repurchase at a price higher than the premium received when the put was written.

REAL-WORLD RETURNS 19-3

Options

Why buying and selling calls has a place in even a conservative investor's playbook.

I am not much of a gambler. Years ago I was at the Desert Inn in Las Vegas and tried using a "system" for winning big at roulette. I don't recall the fine points, but it involved doubling my bet every time I lost. I was down so far, so fast, it left my head spinning. I spent the rest of the night playing blackjack, determinedly eking out small gains until, many tedious hours later, I was even.

For a long time I shunned options in the stock market as just another form of gambling. But a few years back, I bought some long-term call options, or "Leaps" (for Long-term Equity Anticipation Securities), which worked out quite nicely. Then a broker suggested I sell some calls on stocks I already own. In the process, I learned that selling these "covered calls" is deemed sufficiently conservative to be permitted in tax advantaged retirement accounts. Though I consider myself a cautious investor, I now believe options have a place in every investor's arsenal.

Let's start with the basics, since most people I know, including myself, find options terminology confusing. A call option is the right to buy a share of stock at a fixed price at a fixed date in the future. A put is the opposite, the right to sell a share. Generally speaking, you buy a call when you think the stock price is going to rise and a put when you think it will fall. So why are options considered riskier than stocks? After all, in buying or selling shares, you're also predicting whether the price will rise or fall. The difference is that because calls and puts often expire worthless, you can easily lose all of your investment.

Since options trades are actually contracts, they always have two sides: For every call or put that's bought, there's someone selling it. This is where things get trickier. Selling a call is a bet that the price will drop below the strike price and that you won't have to deliver the shares you promised when you sold someone the right to buy them. Selling a put is a bet the price will rise above the strike price, and therefore the buyer will not exercise the right to sell you the shares. If you sell calls or puts and bet right, you simply keep the sale proceeds. If you bet wrong, you can get into trouble quickly. Say you sold calls on shares you don't own and the price sky rockets. You have to go into the market—and into your pocket—to buy them for delivery, and since there's no limit to how high the price might go (think Qual-comm during the late '90s), there's no limit to your potential loss.

To make this simpler, let's forget about puts entirely. Sure, buying a put can be an insurance policy against a declining market, but it's an expensive one, and selling a put is simply too risky for me.

Calls are another matter. First of all, consider the actual risk. Yes, you can lose 100 percent of your investment. But stocks, too, can go to zero or close to it, as we've learned the hard way the past few years. And because an option price is always a fraction of the share price, you may be putting very little money at risk. If you sell covered calls, your potential losses are also capped by the fact that you already own the shares. Sure, you may have to deliver them at a price far below what they would then fetch in the market, but you're not out any additional money.

I first bought some calls several years ago on shares of Tyco International. The stock had been hammered by short sellers, and then had been really clobbered when the Securities and Exchange Commission announced an investigation. Tyco denied any wrongdoing, and if the company was exonerated, there was potential for big gains. But if it wasn't, the share could go even lower.

I had no idea what the SEC would conclude, but this is a situation where I like to buy calls. The negative sentiment meant that sellers were plentiful, driving down prices on the call options. But I needed an option lasting long enough for the SEC to reach a decision, which is when I discovered Leaps. I was able to buy options expiring more than a year in the future at a strike price barely above where the battered stock was already trading, for about $1 a share. (Finding real time option prices isn't easy. Unless you have something like a Bloomberg terminal, you have to ask a broker, which is a good way to make him actually earn his commission.) I bought 10 contracts, covering 100 shares each, for a total of $1,000. When the SEC exonerated Tyco eight months later, the stock—and option—prices soared, and I scored a big gain—all with just $1,000 at risk.

I had a similar experience buying calls on beleaguered Monsanto after it was attacked by anti-bioengineering activists. I figured the depressed stock would rebound once the benefits of such products as vitamin-enhanced "golden rice" became manifest. Little did I anticipate that Monsanto would be acquired by Pharmacia, which in turn was bought by Pfizer. My stake soared at each juncture. I exercised the options, and when the Pfizer deal closes, I'll own a nice position in the company for an extremely modest investment.

Yes, I've had losses, especially over the past three years in a steeply declining market. My $45 strike price Nortel Networks call options, needless to say, expired worthless this January. Still, with Nortel having plunged to less than $2, my loss was far smaller than if I had bought the shares outright. And as readers of my weekly online column already know, I recently hit a home run with AOL options at a strike price of $7.50. It doesn't take many of these to offset the losses.

So my rules of thumb are quite simple: I reserve buying call options for special situations that have driven a stock price down and soured investor opinion. And I buy only options with a long enough term—so far, at least a year—for the special situation to work itself out.

When I *sell* calls, I put the strategy into reverse. I have found this an excellent way to respond when the market hits one of my selling thresholds, as it did in November's rally. With the market feeling pretty euphoric, I sold covered calls on AIG and Microsoft for a lofty price of about $3.50 per share. Selling options on 500 shares of each stock generated $3,500 in cash right away.

At the time, AIG was trading at about $63, and the strike price was $70, with the contract expiring in January. That meant if AIG shares managed to reach that threshold—and that would require a 10 percent rise in just three months—I would have to deliver the 500 shares. Even if that happened and I wound up having to sell them for less than they were trading for, I figured I would still be happy to realize the $35,000 in proceeds.

After selling call options, you don't have to sit by passively and wait for the contracts to expire. By early December, with the market slumping again, those AIG options I sold for $3.50 were fetching just 20 cents, and the Microsoft options were at 90 cents. I could have stepped in and bought them back, keeping most of my profit and avoiding having to worry about what happened over the next month. But I decided to stand pat and let the hand play out. Odds are these options will expire worthless, and if not—if a sudden rally drives the stocks above the strike prices—I will still benefit from the discipline of selling into a rally, which is in line with my overall investing strategy. As this column went to press, I was still waiting to see whether my bet would pay off.

So here are my rules for selling calls: Sell only covered calls, look for big premiums suggesting a euphoric market sentiment about a stock's prospects, and sell short-term contracts. I have now sold calls on more than a dozen occasions, and every one of them has resulted in a net profit. In other words, I take a cautious, common-sense approach to options trading. Long-term, patient stock ownership remains the backbone of my investment approach, and options are a very small percentage of my portfolio. So far, my options trading has been very profitable. Yet curiously, my approach seems to be very unusual. Most options traders are technophiles and big institutions with sophisticated computerized strategies that seize on minor arbitrage possibilities and volatility aberrations. While I may just be experiencing beginner's luck, I'm beginning to suspect that the professionals have left some big opportunities for the rest of us.

Source: Stewart, James B., "The Options Game," *SmartMoney*, February 2003, pp. 46–48. Copyright 2003 by *SmartMoney*, a joint venture of Hearst Communications, Inc. and DowJones & Company, Inc. All rights reserved.

SOME BASIC OPTIONS STRATEGIES

In the previous section, we examined the payoffs, and profit/losses, for basic uncovered (or naked) positions involving options. These four basic uncovered option positions are buy call, write call, buy put, and write put. In this section we analyze covered positions involving hedges. Spreads and combinations, which are also covered positions, are discussed in Appendix 19A.

Hedge

A strategy using derivatives to offset or reduce the risk resulting from exposure to an underlying asset.

A **hedge** is a combination of an option and its underlying stock designed such that the option protects the stock against loss or the stock protects the option against loss. In the next section, we consider some of the more popular hedges.

Covered Calls

Covered Call

A strategy involving the sale of a call option to supplement a long position in an underlying asset.

A **covered call** involves the purchase of stock and the simultaneous sale (or writing) of a call on that stock; that is, it is a long position in the stock and a short position in a call. The position is covered because the writer owns the stock and could deliver it if called to do so as a result of the exercise of the call option by the holder. In effect, the investor is willing to sell the stock at a fixed price (the exercise price), limiting the gains if the stock price rises, in exchange for cushioning the loss by the amount of the call premium, if the stock price declines.

Using our previous notation, the payoff profile at expiration is:

	$S_T \leq E$	$S_T > E$
Payoff of stock	S_T	S_T
− Payoff of call	-0	$-(S_T - E)$
Total payoff	S_T	E

Figure 19-7 illustrates the payoffs on the covered call hedge by showing all three situations: purchase of the stock, writing a call, and the combined position. Notice that the combined position is identical in shape to the payoff diagram from writing a put option as shown in Figure 19-2(d). The sale of the call truncates the combined position if the stock price rises above the exercise price. In effect, the writer has sold the claim to this gain for the call premium. At expiration, the position is worth, at most, the exercise price and the profit is the call premium received by selling the call.

As Figure 19-7 shows, if the stock price declines, the position is protected by the amount of the call premium received. Therefore, the break-even point is lower compared to simply owning the stock, and the loss incurred as the stock price drops will be less with the covered call position by the amount of the call premium.

EXAMPLE 19-8: CALL PREMIUM ON RBC

Assume that an investor had previously purchased 100 shares of RBC for $40 per share and when the stock price hits $48, writes a (covered) six-month call with an exercise price of $50. The writer receives a premium of $4. This situation is illustrated in Figure 19-8.

If called on to deliver his or her 100 shares, the investor will receive $50 per share, plus the $4 premium, for a gross profit of $14 per share (since the stock was originally purchased at $40 per share). However, the investor gives up the additional potential gain if the price of this stock rises above $50, as illustrated by the flat line to the right of $50 for the covered call position in Figure 19-8. If the price rises to $60 after the call is sold, for example, the investor will gross $14 per share but could have grossed $20 per share if no call had been written. However, should the price fall to $30, the investor would offset the loss of $10 per share held by the amount of the option premium ($4 per option) that was originally received, resulting in a net loss of only $6 per share.

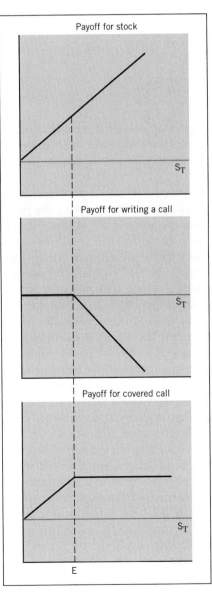

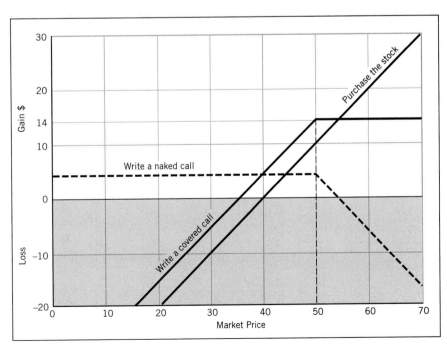

Figure 19-7
Payoff Profiles for a
Covered Call Position

Figure 19-8
Profit and Losses for a
Covered Call Position

Writing a naked call is also illustrated (by the broken line) in Figure 19-8. If the call is not exercised, the writer profits by the amount of the premium, $4. The naked writer's break-even point is $54. This position will be profitable if the price of the stock does not rise above the break-even point. Notice that the potential gain for the naked writer is limited to $4. The potential loss, however, is unlimited. If the price of the stock were to rise sharply, the writer could easily lose an amount in excess of what was received in premium income.

Protective Puts

Protective Put

A strategy involving the purchase of a put option as a supplement to a long position in an underlying asset.

A **protective put** involves buying a stock (or owning it already) and buying a put for the same stock; that is, it is a long position in both the stock and a put. The put acts as insurance against a decline in the underlying stock price, guaranteeing an investor a minimum price at which the stock can be sold. In effect, the insurance acts to limit losses or unfavourable outcomes. The largest profit possible is infinite (although the profit is reduced by the cost of the put option, as discussed below).

The payoff profile is:

Figure 19-9
Payoff Profile and Profit/Losses for a Protective Put Position

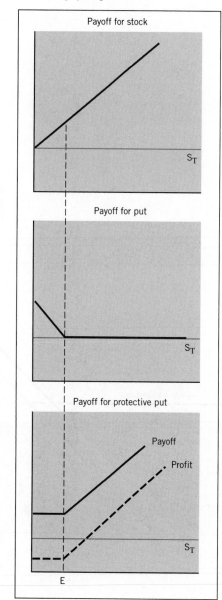

	$S_T < E$	$S_T \geq E$
Payoff of stock	S_T	S_T
+ Payoff of put	$E - S_T$	0
Total payoff	E	S_T

For stock prices at or above the exercise price, the payoff reflects the increase in the stock price. Below the exercise price, the payoff is worth the exercise price at expiration.

Figure 19-9 shows the protective put versus an investment in the underlying stock. As always, the payoff for the stock is a straight line, and the payoff for the option strategy is an asymmetrical line consisting of two segments. The payoff for the protective put clearly illustrates what is meant by the term *truncating* the distribution of returns. Below a certain stock price (the exercise price), the payoff line is flat or horizontal. Therefore, the loss is limited to the cost of the put. Above the break-even point, the protective put strategy shares in the gains as the stock price rises. This is one of the true benefits of derivative securities and the reason for their phenomenal growth—derivatives provide a quick and inexpensive way to alter the risk of a portfolio.

Figure 19-9 illustrates how a protective put offers some insurance against a decline in the stock price. This insurance feature limits losses but at a cost if the insurance turns out not to be needed—the cost of the put. Above the exercise price, the profit is less than the payoff profile for the investment because of the cost of the put. Below the exercise price, losses in the stock price are partially offset by gains from the put, resulting in a constant loss equal to the cost of the put.

This position is identical to purchasing a call except for a different intercept on the vertical axis.

The protective put illustrates a well-known concept called portfolio insurance, which is explained below.

Portfolio Insurance

The potential return–risk modification properties of options, and particularly the insurance aspects discussed above, are well illustrated by the technique known as **portfolio insurance**. This term refers to investment strategies designed to hedge portfolio positions by providing a minimum return on the portfolio while simultaneously providing an opportunity for the portfolio to participate in rising security prices. This asset management technique became very popular in the 1980s, with many billions of dollars of assets insured.

There are several methods of insuring a portfolio, including the use of options, futures, and the creation of synthetic options (which refer to the creation of option-like payoffs by taking positions in other securities such as T-bills and market indexes). In practice, it is common to use futures contracts on market indexes (as discussed in Chapter 20). However, in principal options can be used in portfolio insurance strategies, and their use illustrates the basic nature of a hedge.

The idea behind portfolio insurance with regard to options is simple. A protective put can be purchased that allows the portfolio to be sold for an amount sufficient to provide the minimum return. The remaining portfolio funds are invested in the usual manner. The protective put provides insurance for the portfolio by limiting losses in the event stock prices decline. The portfolio's value at the end of the period must equal or exceed the exercise price of the put.

Portfolio Insurance

An asset management technique designed to provide a portfolio with a lower limit on value while permitting it to benefit from rising security prices.

EXAMPLE 19-9: USING PORTFOLIO INSURANCE TO ENSURE MINIMUM RETURN

For simplicity, we assume an investor starts with $1.00 and purchases one unit of a stock market index that sells for $0.9097.[11] During a subsequent period, the value of the index has increased and the investor wants to lock in a guaranteed selling price of $1.05 for the index. To this end, the investor purchases a European put on this index for $0.0903. Notice the net investment equals $0.9097 + $0.0903 = $1.0000, and the put has a strike price of $1.05.

The investor has used portfolio insurance to ensure a 5 percent minimum return. If the value of the stock index exceeds $1.05 by the end of the investing period, the investor is ahead that much and allows the put to expire worthless. If the value of the index is less than $1.05 by the end of the period, the investor can exercise the option and sell the stock index for $1.05, thereby earning the required 5 percent minimum return on the initial investment of $1.00. Portfolio insurance has provided protection against the downside while allowing the investor to participate in stock price advances.

This example illustrates the conceptual use of puts in portfolio insurance strategies. In practice, however, puts and calls are not used to insure portfolios because those typically available to investors are American and not European. The exercise-at-any-time feature of American options makes them not only more valuable than corresponding European options but also much more costly for portfolio insurance purposes. Furthermore, it generally is not possible to find puts and calls with the exact time to expiration, exercise price, and so on that matches a particular portfolio.

It should also be noted that portfolio insurance is not without cost. The costs include

- The *cost of the option itself*—in our example, the put cost $0.0903. Obviously, if stocks advance and the put expires worthless, the cost of the put has been lost relative to an uninsured strategy. This can be thought of as the insurance premium.

- An *opportunity cost*. An investor who places 100 percent of investment funds in the stock index would participate fully in any market rise. In our example, the insured investor would participate in only 90.97 percent of any market rise.

---

[11]This example is based on R .J. Rendleman and R. W. McEnally, "Assessing the Costs of Portfolio Insurance," *Financial Analysts Journal* (May–June 1987), pp. 27–37.

OPTION VALUATION

learning objective 3
Explain the valuation of options.

A General Framework

In this section, we examine the determinants of the value of a put or call. An option's premium almost never declines below its intrinsic value. The reason is that market arbitrageurs, who constantly monitor option prices for discrepancies, would purchase the options and exercise them, thus earning riskless returns. **Arbitrageurs** are speculators who seek to earn a return without assuming risk by constructing riskless hedges. Short-lived deviations are possible, but they will quickly be exploited.

Arbitrageurs
Investors who seek discrepancies in security prices in an attempt to earn riskless returns.

Suppose a call option with an exercise price of $20 is selling for $2, when the price of the underlying share is $23. Notice that the intrinsic value of this option is $3, since the call enables you to purchase a share that is worth $23 for only $20. An arbitrageur (or anyone else recognizing that the option price is below its intrinsic value) could purchase an option contract for $200 ($2 × 100). The investor could then immediately exercise the option, purchasing 100 shares at a cost of $2,000 ($20 × 100). These shares could be sold in the market at a price of $23 per share, for a total of $2,300. The net result (ignoring transactions costs) would be a profit of $100: $2,300 − $2,000 (cost of exercising the options) − $200 (cost of the options). This profit is earned without assuming any risks and is referred to as arbitrage profit, hence the name arbitrageurs. Clearly, these opportunities should not exist in efficient markets, since rational investors will recognize them, exploit them, and hence eliminate them.

Time Values

Time Value
The difference between the intrinsic value of an option and its market price.

Option prices almost always exceed intrinsic values, with the difference reflecting the option's potential appreciation, referred to as the **time value**. This is somewhat of a misnomer because the actual source of value is volatility in price. However, price volatility decreases with a shortening of the time to expiration, hence the term time value.

Because buyers are willing to pay a price for potential future stock-price movements, time has a positive value—the longer the time to expiration for the option, the more chance it has to appreciate in value. However, when the stock price is held constant, options are seen as a wasting asset whose value approaches intrinsic value as expiration approaches. In other words, as expiration approaches, the time value of the option declines to zero.

The time value can be calculated as the difference between the option price and the intrinsic value:

(19-3)
$$\text{Time value} = \text{Option price} - \text{Intrinsic value}$$

EXAMPLE 19-10: CALCULATING TIME VALUE ON CP OPTIONS

For the CP options referred to in the examples of intrinsic value in the previous section:

Time value of October 70 call = $6.40 − $1.95 = $4.45
Time value of October 74 put = $6.00 − $2.05 = $3.95

We can now understand the premium for an option as the sum of its intrinsic value and its time value, or

$$\text{Premium or option price} = \text{Intrinsic value} + \text{Time value} \qquad \textbf{(19-4)}$$

EXAMPLE 19-11: CALCULATING PREMIUM FOR CP OPTIONS

For the CP options:

Premium for October 70 call = \$1.95 + \$4.45 = \$6.40
Premium for January 30 put = \$2.05 + \$3.95 = \$6.00

Notice an important point about options based on the preceding discussion. An investor who owns a call option and wishes to acquire the underlying common stock will always find it preferable to sell the option and purchase the stock in the open market rather than exercise the option (at least if the stock pays no dividends). Why? Because otherwise, he or she will lose the speculative premium on the option.

Consider the CP October 70 call option, with a market price of the common share of \$71.95. An investor who owned the call and wanted to own the common share would be better off to sell the option at \$6.40 and purchase the common stock for \$71.95, for a net investment of \$65.55 per share. Exercising the call option, the investor would have to pay \$70.00 per share for shares of stock worth \$71.95 in the market, for a net investment of \$70.00 per share. Thus selling the options reduces the required investment to own a share of CP by \$4.45—the amount of the time value. (Brokerage commissions are ignored in this example.)

On the other hand, under some circumstances it may be optimal to exercise an American put early (on a non-dividend-paying stock). A put sufficiently deep in the money should be exercised early because the payment received at exercise can be invested to earn a return. Under certain circumstances it may also be desirable to exercise an American call option on a dividend-paying stock before the expiration date. (This is because dividends reduce the stock price on the ex dividend date, which in turn reduces the value of the call option).

Boundaries on Option Prices

In the previous section we learned what the premium, or price, of a put or call consists of, but we have not considered why options trade at the prices they do and the range of values they can assume. In this section, we learn about the boundaries for option prices, and in the next section we discuss the exact determinants of options prices.

The value of an option must be related to the value of the underlying security. The basic relationship is most easy to understand by considering an option immediately prior to expiration, when there is no time premium. If the option is not exercised, it will expire immediately, leaving the option with no value. Obviously, investors will exercise it only if it is worth exercising (if it is in the money).

Figure 19-10(a) shows the values of call options at expiration, assuming a strike price of \$50. At expiration, a call must have a value equal to its intrinsic value. Therefore, the line representing the value of a call option must be horizontal at \$0 up to the exercise price and then rise as the stock price exceeds the exercise price. Above \$50 the call price must equal the difference between the stock price and the exercise price.

For puts the situation is reversed. At expiration, a put must have a value equal to its intrinsic value. Therefore, the line in Figure 19-10(b) representing the value of a put option must be horizontal at \$0 beyond the exercise price. Below \$50, the put price must equal the difference between the exercise price and the stock price. Note that a put option has a strict upper limit on intrinsic value, whereas the call has no upper limit. A put's strike price is its maximum intrinsic value.

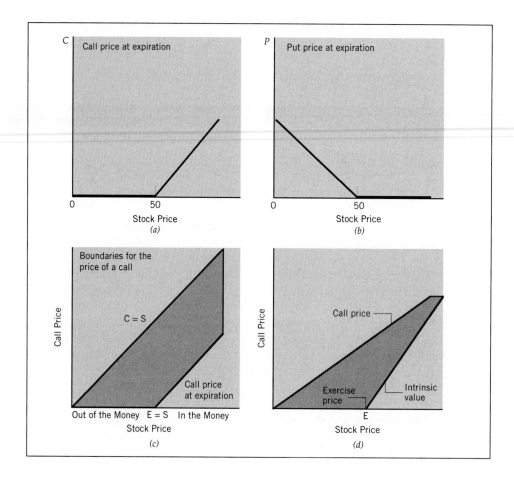

What is the maximum price an option can assume? To see this, think of a call. Since the call's value is derived from its ability to be converted into the underlying stock, it can never sell for more than the stock itself. It would not make sense to pay more for a call on one share of stock than the price of the stock itself. Therefore, the maximum price for a call is the price of the underlying stock.

Based on the preceding, we can establish the absolute upper and lower boundaries for the price of a call option, as shown in Figure 19-10(c). The upper boundary is a 45 degree line from the origin representing a call price equal to the stock price.[12] The lower boundary is the price of the option at expiration, which must be either zero or its in-the-money value. This is represented by the 45 degree line starting at the exercise price. Once again, the lower boundary can be interpreted as the value of the call at the moment the call is exercised, or its intrinsic value.

Finally, Figure 19-10(d) illustrates more precisely and realistically the variation in price for a call option by illustrating how the price of a call varies with the stock price and the exercise price. The call price is always above intrinsic value and rises as the stock price increases beyond the exercise price. The time value, represented by the shaded area in Figure 19-10(d), decreases beyond the exercise price.

To understand fully the price of a call option, we will examine the most common formal model used to estimate call prices, the Black-Scholes model. The price of a put can also be found from this model because of a parity relationship between put and call prices.

---

[12]Think of this as a call with a zero exercise price and an infinite maturity.

The Black-Scholes Model

Fischer Black and Myron Scholes developed a model for the valuation of European call options that is widely accepted and used in the investment community.[13] While the equation estimates the price of European call options on non-dividend-paying stocks, it is also used to evaluate American call options on non-dividend-paying stocks. This is a reasonable application, since we have seen that it is never optimal to exercise such American options before expiration date, so they should be worth approximately the same as the equivalent European option.

The formula itself is mathematical and appears to be very complex; however, it is widely available on calculators and computers. Numerous investors estimate the value of calls using the **Black-Scholes model**. The model is considered to be of such importance that Canadian-born Myron Scholes shared the 1997 Nobel Prize in economics, largely for this work. Black would almost certainly have shared in the award had he not died in 1995.

The Black-Scholes model uses five variables to value the call option of a non-dividend-paying stock.[14] These five variables, all but the last of which are directly observable in the market, are as follows:

1. The price of the underlying stock
2. The exercise price of the option
3. The time remaining to the expiration of the option
4. The interest rate
5. The volatility of the continuously compounded rate of return on the underlying stock

Black-Scholes model

A widely used model for the valuation of call options.

The first two variables are of obvious importance in valuing an option, because, as noted before, they determine the option's intrinsic value, whether it is in the money or not. If it is out of the money, it has only a time value based on the speculative interest in the stock.

Time to expiration (measured as a fraction of a year) is also an important factor in the value of an option because value generally increases with maturity. This is logical, because the longer to the expiration date, the more time is available to profit from price changes. The relationship between time and value is not proportional, however. The time value of an option is greatest when the market price and the exercise price are equal.

The interest rate affects option values because of the opportunity cost involved. Buying an option is a substitute to some degree for buying on margin, on which interest must be paid. The higher interest rates are, therefore, the more interest cost is saved by the use of options. This adds to the value of the option and results in a direct relationship between the value of a call option and interest rates in the market.

The last factor, and the only one not directly observable in the marketplace, is the stock's volatility. The greater the volatility, the higher the price of a call option because of the increased potential for the stock to move up. Therefore, a positive relation exists between the volatility of the stock and the value of the call option.[15]

The Black-Scholes option pricing formula can be expressed as[16]

$$C = S[N(d_1)] - E[N(d_2)] \times \frac{1}{e^{rt}}$$

(19-5)

[13]F. Black and M. Scholes, "The Pricing of Options and Corporate Liabilities," *Journal of Political Economy* 81 (May–June 1973), pp. 637–654.

[14]Options traded on organized exchanges are not protected against cash dividends, and this can have significant effects on option values. When a cash dividend is paid, the stock price should decline to reflect this payment. Any event that reduces the stock price reduces the value of a call and increases the value of a put.

[15]Volatility as used in the options model is not the same concept as a stock's beta as used in Chapter 9. Volatility is used here as a measure of the variability in the stock return (as measured by standard deviation) as opposed to sensitivity to market movements.

[16]This version of the model applies to non-dividend-paying stocks. Adjustments can be made for stocks that pay dividends.

where

C = the price of the call option
S = current market price of the underlying common stock
$N(d_1)$ = the cumulative density function of d_1 (assuming this variable is normally distributed)
E = the exercise price of the option
e = the base of natural logarithms (approximately 2.71828)
r = the continuously compounded riskless rate of interest quoted on an annual basis
t = the time remaining before the expiration date of the option, expressed as a fraction of a year
$N(d_2)$ = the cumulative density function of d_2 (assuming this variable is normally distributed)[17]

To find d_1 and d_2, it is necessary to solve these equations:

(19-6)
$$d_1 = \frac{\ln (S/E) + (r + 0.5\sigma^2)t}{(\sigma[(t)^{1/2}])}$$

(19-7)
$$d_2 = d_1 - (\sigma[(t)^{1/2}])$$

where

ln (S/E) = the natural logarithm of (S/E)
σ = the standard deviation of the annual rate of return on the underlying common stock

The five variables previously listed are needed as inputs. Variables 1 to 4 are immediately available. Variable 5 is not, however, because what is needed is the variability expected to occur in the stock's rate of return. Although historical data on stock returns are generally used to estimate this standard deviation, variability does change over time. A formula user should try to incorporate expected changes in the variability when using historical data. To do so, the user should examine any likely changes in either the market's or the individual stock's variability.

Variables 1 to 3 should be identical for a given stock for everyone using the Black-Scholes model. Variable 4 should be identical or very close among formula users, depending on the exact proxy used for the riskless rate of interest. Variable 5 will vary among users, providing different option values. Empirical studies have shown that estimates of the variance obtained from other than historical data are more valuable than the estimates based on historical data. Because the price of an option can be observed at any time, it is possible to solve the Black-Scholes formula for the implied standard deviation of the stock's return. This is an important application of the Black-Scholes equation that is frequently used by practitioners. Henry Latané and Richard Rendleman found that better forecasts of the actual standard deviation could be obtained by preparing forecasts from the model itself.[18]

EXAMPLE 19-12: USING BLACK-SCHOLES TO CALCULATE OPTION PRICE

The following is an example of the use of the Black-Scholes option pricing formula:

Assume

S = $40

E = $45

r = 0.10

t = 0.5 (6 months)

σ = 0.45

---

[17]This assumption does not mean that stock returns themselves are normally distributed, but that the variables d_1 and d_2 are normally distributed. In fact, one of the technical assumptions of the model is that stock prices are lognormally distributed.
[18]H. Latané and R. Rendleman, Jr., "Standard Deviations of Stock Price Ratios Implied in Option Prices," *Journal of Finance* 31 (May 1976), pp. 369–382.

Step 1: Solve for d_1.

$$d_1 = \frac{\ln(40/45) + [0.10 + 0.5(0.45)^2]\,0.5}{0.45\,[(0.5)^{1/2}]}$$

$$= \frac{-0.1178 + 0.1006}{0.3182}$$

$$= -0.054$$

Step 2: Use a cumulative probability distribution table (such as the one provided on the textbook's companion website) to find the value of $N(d_1)$.

$$N(d_1) \approx 0.4801$$

where $d_1 = -0.054$

Step 3: Find d_2.

$$d_2 = -0.054 - 0.45[(0.5)^{1/2}]$$

$$= -0.372$$

Step 4: Find $N(d_2)$.

$$N(d_2) \approx 0.3557$$

Step 5: Solve for C.

$$C = S[0.4801] - E[0.3557] \times \frac{1}{e^{(.10)(0.5)}}$$

$$= (40)(0.4801) - (45)(0.3557)(0.9512)$$

$$= 19.20 - 15.23$$

$$= \$3.97$$

The theoretical (fair) value of the option, according to the Black-Scholes formula, is $3.97. If the current market price of the option is greater than the theoretical value, it is overpriced; if less, it is underpriced—according to the Black-Scholes model.

Put Option Valuation

To establish put prices, we can take advantage of the principle of put-call parity.

The **put-call parity** principle expresses the relationship between the prices of European puts and calls on the same stock with the same exercise price that must hold if arbitrage is to be ruled out. In other words, unless the price of the put and the call bear a certain relationship to each other, there will be opportunities for earning riskless profits (arbitrage). The put-call parity can be expressed as

$$\text{Price of put} = E/(e^{rt}) - S + C$$

(19-8)

where all terms are as defined before.[19]

Put-Call Parity
The formal relationship between a European call and put on the same item that must hold if no arbitrage is to occur.

---

[19]Refer to Appendix 19C for a more detailed discussion of the no-arbitrage argument.

EXAMPLE 19-13: CALCULATING PUT-CALL PARITY

Use the information for the call given in the previous example. Since the Black-Scholes model uses continuous interest, the discount factor is expressed in continuous form.[20] It is equal to e^{rt} or $e^{10(0.5)}$. Using a calculator, this value is 1.051.
Therefore,

$$\text{Price of put} = 45/1.051 - 40 + 3.97 = \$6.79$$

Summarizing the Factors Affecting Options Prices

If we allow for stocks that pay dividends, we can summarize the factors affecting options prices into a table with six elements, as shown in Table 19-2. The plus sign indicates a direct relation, and a negative sign a negative relation. The assumption behind Table 19-2 is that all other variables remain fixed as we consider any of the six variables.

Table 19-2

Effects of Various Variables on Options Prices

Variable	Calls	Puts
Stock price	+	−
Exercise price	−	+
Time to expiration	+	+
Stock volatility	+	+
Interest rates	+	−
Cash dividends	−	+

The following discussion provides a basis for the intuition regarding how these six factors affect option prices (holding all other factors unchanged). Recall that the Option price = Intrinsic value + Time value (or speculative premium). Based on this framework, we note the following:

1. As share prices increase, the intrinsic value (IV) of calls increase and the IV of puts decrease.

2. As exercise prices increase, the IV of calls decrease and the IV of puts increase.

3. The greater the time to expiration, the greater the chance the option will be in the money, hence the greater the time value (or speculative premium).

4. As share price volatility increases, there is a greater chance that shares will end up in the money, so the time value, or speculative premium, increases.

5. As the riskless rate increases, the advantage of delayed ownership increases for call options. Conversely, the delay of exercising put options, which involves selling assets for cash today, becomes more costly.

6. Share prices fall by roughly the amount of a dividend that is paid. Hence, dividend increases tend to reduce share prices, which reduces the IV of calls and increases the IV of puts.

Hedge Ratios

A key concept with options is their use as a hedging device. Although risky assets themselves, options can be used to control risk. In particular, options can be used to control the riskiness inherent in common stocks.

---

[20]The value e^k is the equivalent of $(1 + r)$ in continuous compounding. If r is 5 percent, the value of e^k is $e^{0.05}$, or 1.051.

To hedge a long stock position with options, an investor would write one call option while simultaneously buying a certain number of common shares. The required number of shares is given by the **hedge ratio**, which is $N(d_1)$ from the Black-Scholes model for call options.[21] The hedge ratio for an option, commonly referred to as the option's delta, indicates the change in the price of the option for a $1 change in the price of the underlying common share. Since the hedge ratio with a call option is $N(d_1)$, for a put option it is $N(d_1) - 1$.

Hedge Ratio
The ratio of options written to shares of stock held long in a riskless portfolio.

EXAMPLE 19-14: DETERMINING THE HEDGE RATIO FOR OPTIONS

In Example 19-12, $N(d_1)$ was 0.48; therefore, for every call option written, 0.48 share of the common stock would be required to hedge the position. For a standard 100-share option contract, 48 shares of stock would be required. A $1 increase in the price of the stock should produce a $0.48 change in the price of the option. The loss on the call options written is 100 × $0.48, or $48, which is offset by the gain on the 48 shares of stock of $48. A perfectly hedged position leaves total wealth unchanged.

Since the maximum value for $N(d_1)$ is 1.0, hedge ratios are usually less than 1.0, except for the case of deep in the money options where the ratio tends to one. This indicates that option values change with stock prices on less than a one-for-one basis. That is, dollar movements in options prices are smaller than dollar movements in the underlying stock. However, percentage price changes on the option generally will be greater than percentage price changes on the stock; this is referred to as the leverage effect.

Using the Black-Scholes Model

What does it mean if we calculate an intrinsic value for an option that is significantly different from the market price? Although this may represent an investment opportunity, we must remember that the original Black-Scholes model is based on some simplifying assumptions, such as the non-payment of dividends, constant volatility, and continuous lognormally distributed stock prices. The standard deviation cannot be observed and must be estimated. Therefore, any observed discrepancies could reflect errors in the estimation of the stock's volatility.

Development of the Black-Scholes model was a significant event and has had a major impact on all options investors, both directly and indirectly. This model has been the basis of extensive empirical investigations into how options are priced. How well does this model work?

The numerous studies that have been conducted offer general support for the Black-Scholes model and the proposition that options are efficiently priced by the market. Some deficiencies have been noted.[22] The deviations and biases that appear to remain in option pricing models may derive from several sources. For example, the true stock-price volatility is unobservable. Despite any statistically significant biases that may exist in the prices generated by the option pricing models, however, the validity of these models remains intact.

CHECK YOUR UNDERSTANDING

19-9. Why does an option's price almost always exceed its intrinsic value?

19-10. What are the boundaries for the price of a call?

---

[21]Technically, the hedge ratio is the slope of the functional relationship between the value of the option (vertical axis) and the value of the stock (horizontal axis), evaluated at the current stock price. It is determined by taking the partial first derivative of the option price with respect to the underlying stock price.
[22]D. Galai, "A Survey of Empirical Tests of Option-Pricing Models," in M. Brenner, Ed., *Option Pricing: Theory and Applications* (Lexington, MA: Lexington Books, 1983), pp. 45–80.

AN INVESTOR'S PERSPECTIVE ON PUTS AND CALLS

What Puts and Calls Mean to Investors

Earlier we examined some simple strategies using puts and calls and briefly considered some more sophisticated strategies. It is important for investors to have an overall perspective on puts and calls and consider what they really add to the investment process.

Option contracts are important to investors in terms of the two dimensions of every investment decision that we have emphasized throughout this book—the return and risk from an asset or portfolio. Options can be used for various types of hedging, which involves the management of risk. Options also offer speculators a way to leverage their investment with a strict limit on downside risk.

The return–risk modification properties of puts and calls vary significantly from other derivative instruments such as futures contracts, which we consider in Chapter 20. The important point about options and portfolio return and risk is that the impact of options is not symmetrical. As discussed earlier, the distribution of payoffs is truncated, because in the case of buying a call the most the investor can lose is the premium, regardless of what happens to the stock price. The same is true when purchasing a put—relative to the profit-loss line when selling short, the distribution of possible profits and losses from purchasing a put is truncated. If the stock price continues to rise, adversely affecting the investor, the most that can be lost from the put purchase is the premium.

The Evolutionary Use of Options

Puts and calls on organized options exchanges have been available to investors since 1973, although financial derivatives were being used long before then. Puts and calls have been popular with individual investors since the beginning of CBOE trading, although the manner in which they are viewed has changed somewhat. At first, options were viewed more or less as speculative instruments and were often purchased for their leverage possibilities. Covered option writing was used to enhance portfolio yields. During the 1980s, many investors were selling puts in order to capitalize on the rising trend in stock prices. This strategy worked well until the famous market crash in October 1987. As a result of the losses, many investors once again viewed options as speculative instruments and options volume did not return to the level reached in 1987 for several years.

The current emphasis by the brokerage industry is on educating investors as to how options can be used efficiently as part of their portfolio. Investors' desire to hedge their portfolios against a market decline as well as the introduction of new products such as options on new indexes, country funds, and LEAPs, has drawn the public back into the market.

Today, options are increasingly valued for their use in strategic portfolio management. Options allow investors to create strategies that expand the set of outcomes beyond what could be achieved in the absence of options. In other words, investors and investment managers sometimes need the nonsymmetric distributions of returns that options can provide. Options strategies increase the set of contingencies that can be provided for.[23]

OTHER TYPES OF OPTIONS

Newer innovations in the options market include **stock-index options**, **interest rate options**, and **currency options**. We briefly discuss interest rate and currency options, before confining our discussion to stock-index options, in keeping with the general theme of the chapter, which is to focus on equity options.

Primary US interest rate options traded on the CBOE include Treasury yield options. Interest rate options trade in Canada in the form of options on Government of Canada bonds, which have traded

learning objective 4
Identify types of options other than puts and calls.

Stock-Index Options
Option contracts on a stock market index such as the S&P/TSX 60 Index.

Interest Rate Options
Option contracts on fixed-income securities such as Government of Canada bonds.

Currency Options
Option contracts whose value is based on the value of an underlying currency, such as the Canadian dollar.

[23]This discussion is based on Richard Bookstaber, "The Use of Options in Performance Structuring," *Journal of Portfolio Management* 11 (Summer 1985), pp. 35–50.

on the ME since 1982. The volume of bond contracts outstanding represents a small proportion of the total options contracts that are traded in Canada. For example, Table 19-1 shows that these bond options accounted for a mere 0.01 percent of ME option trading in 2007. Index options, on the other hand, accounted for 5.7 percent of the 2007 ME option trading, while standard equity options on common shares accounted for approximately 84 percent of ME trading.

The only currency option that trades on the ME is on the US dollar; however, these and other currency options trade actively in the US.

The Basics of Stock-Index Options

Stock-index options presently trade in Canada on the ME and are available on the S&P/TSX 60 Index, and on various ETFs (such as the i60s), which derive their value from the appropriate stock indexes. There are also a variety of US stock-index options on market indexes, including (but not limited to) the S&P 100 Index (OEX), the S&P 500 Index, the NYSE Index, the Russell 2000 Index, the Major Market Index, the Value Line Index, the S&P Midcap Index, the Japan Index, and the OTC Index. Index options are also available on some US industry subindexes, including Pharmaceuticals, Computer Technology, and Semiconductors. In addition, long-term index options (LEAPs) are available for the S&P 100 and 500 indexes and for the DJIA.

Stock-index options enable investors to trade on general stock market movements or industries in the same way that they can trade on individual stocks. Thus, an investor who is bullish on the market can buy a call on a market index, and an investor who is bearish on the overall market can buy a put. The investor need only make a decision about the market as a whole, not on an industry or an individual stock.

Most index options are European style, including the S&P/TSX 60 Index options. Overall, stock-index options are similar to the options listed on the options exchanges. As usual, the exercise price and the expiration date are uniformly established. Investors buy and sell them through their broker in the normal manner. Index option information is read in the same manner as that for stock options. Unlike stock options that require the actual delivery of the stock upon exercise, buyers of index options receive cash from the seller upon exercise of the contract. The amount of cash settlement is equal to the difference between the closing price of the index and the strike price of the option multiplied by a specified dollar amount.

EXAMPLE 19-15: S&P/TSX 60 INDEX OPTION

Assume an investor holds an S&P/TSX Index call option with a strike price of 840 and decides to exercise the option on a day that the S&P/TSX Index closes at 880.75. The investor will receive a cash payment from the assigned writer equal to $100 multiplied by the difference between the option's strike price and the closing value of the index, or

S&P/TSX 60 Index close   = 880.75

S&P/TSX 60 Index option strike price   = 840.00

$$40.75 \times \$100 = \$4{,}075$$

Note the use of the $100 multiplier for the S&P/TSX Index option. The multiplier performs a function similar to the unit of trading (100 shares) for a stock option contract in that it determines the total dollar value of the cash settlement. Since options on different indexes may have different multipliers, it is important to know the multiplier for the stock index being used.

Strategies with Stock-Index Options

The strategies available for use with index options are similar to those for individual stock options. Investors expecting a market rise buy calls, and investors expecting a market decline buy puts. The maximum losses from these two strategies—the option premiums—are known at the outset of the transaction. The potential gains can be large because of the leverage involved with options.

EXAMPLE 19-16: LEVERAGE AND S&P/TSX 60 INDEX OPTIONS

In May, an investor expects the stock market to rise strongly over the next two months. This investor decides to purchase an S&P/TSX 60 Index July 920 call that was selling for $9.40 on a day when the S&P/TSX 60 Index closed at 880.75. The total cost to the investor would be $940 (i.e., $9.40 × 100).

Assume that the market rises, as the investor expected, to a level of 951.21 (an 8 percent increase) on the expiration date. The investor could exercise the option and receive a cash settlement equal to the difference between the index close (951.21) and the exercise price of 920, multiplied by $100, or

S&P/TSX 60 Index close   =   951.21

Call exercise price   = −920.00

$$31.21 \times \$100 = \$3,121$$

The investor's profit for this transaction (excluding commission fees) is:

$$\text{Profit} = \text{Payoff} - \text{Cost of option}$$
$$= \$3,121 - \$940 = \$2,181$$

The leverage offered by index options is illustrated in this example by the fact that an 8 percent rise in the index leads to a 132.0 percent profit on the option position (i.e., ($2,181−$940)/$940 = 232.0 percent). In this example, the investor would have benefited from the use of leverage. However, leverage can, and often does, work against an investor. If the market declined or remained flat, the entire option premium of $940 could be lost, for a 100 percent loss on the investment. As with any option, however, the investor has a limited loss of a known amount—the premium paid.

Investors can use stock-index options to hedge their positions. For example, an investor who owns a diversified portfolio of stocks may be unwilling to liquidate his or her portfolio but is concerned about a near-term market decline. Buying a put on a market index will provide some protection to the investor in the event of a market decline. In effect, the investor is purchasing a form of market insurance. The losses on the portfolio holdings will be partially offset by the gains on the put. If the market rises, the investor loses the premium paid but gains with the portfolio holdings. A problem arises, however, in that the portfolio holdings and the market index are unlikely to be a perfect match. The effectiveness of this hedge will depend on the similarity between the two.

EXAMPLE 19-17: HEDGING WITH S&P/TSX 60 INDEX OPTIONS

Assume an investor has a portfolio of TSX common stocks currently worth $264,000. It is June, and this investor is concerned about a market decline over the next couple of months. The S&P/TSX 60 Index is currently at 880.75 and an S&P/TSX Index July 880 put is available for $26.40. In an attempt to protect the portfolio's profits against a market decline, the investor purchases three of these puts (total cost = 3 × 100 × $26.40 = $7,920), which represents an aggregate exercise price of $264,000 (880 × 100 × 3 = $264,000).[24]

Assume that the market declines 10 percent by the July expiration date, so that the S&P/TSX 60 Index is 792.67 at that point.

Put exercise price   = 880.00

S&P/TSX 60 Index price= 792.67

$$87.33 \times \$100 \times 3 \text{ (puts)} = \$26,199$$

---

[24]The exercise value of an index option, like any stock option, is equal to 100 (shares) multiplied by the exercise price.

If the value of the investor's portfolio declines exactly 10 percent, the loss on the portfolio of $26,400 will be almost exactly offset by the total gain on the three put contracts of $26,199. It is important to note, however, that a particular portfolio's value may decline more or less than the overall market as represented by one of the market indexes such as the S&P/TSX 60 Index.

As before, if the option is held to expiration and a market decline (of a significant amount) does not occur, the investor will lose the entire premium paid for the put(s). In our example, the investor could lose the entire $7,920 paid for the three puts. This could be viewed as the cost of obtaining "market insurance."

Stock-index options can also be useful to institutional investors (or individuals) who do not have funds available immediately for investment but anticipate a market rise. Buying calls will allow such investors to take advantage of the rise in prices if it does occur. Of course, the premium could be lost if the anticipations are incorrect.

Investors can sell (write) index options, either to speculate or to hedge their positions. As we saw in the case of individual options, however, the risk can be large. If the seller is correct in his or her beliefs, the profit is limited to the amount of the premium; if incorrect, the seller faces potential losses far in excess of the premiums received from selling the options. Although the writer of an individual stock call option can deliver the stock if the option is exercised, the writer of a stock-index call option that is exercised must settle in cash and cannot be certain that gains in the stock portfolio will *fully* offset losses on the index option.[25] It would be impractical (or impossible) to write a completely covered stock-index option if one had to buy the appropriate amounts of the individual shares comprising the stock index at all points in time. However, Canadian investors do have this luxury available to them due to the availability of ETFs such as the i60 units. As discussed in Chapter 3, these units can be purchased through a broker, and their value is determined by the value of the S&P/TSX 60 Index.

The Popularity of Stock-Index Options

Stock-index options appeal to speculators because of the leverage they offer. A change in the underlying index of less than 1 percent can result in a change in the value of the contract of 15 percent or more. Given the increased volatility in financial markets in recent years, investors can experience rapid changes in the value of their positions. Since introduced in 1983, stock-index options have grown in popularity and now account for close to 6 percent of options traded through the ME, and approximately 27 percent of CBOE trading. Much of the initial volume was accounted for by professional speculators and trading firms. However, as familiarity with index options has increased, individual investors are assuming a larger role in this market.

CHECK YOUR UNDERSTANDING

19-11. An investor has built a portfolio of Canadian stocks that is well diversified across many industries. She would like to hedge her portfolio against a decline in the price of these stocks, but finds that there are no options traded on most of them. What advice can you offer this investor?

---

[25]Writers of index options are notified of their obligation to make a cash settlement on the business day following the day of exercise.

SUMMARY

This summary relates to the learning objectives for this chapter.

1. **Define options and discuss why they are used.**

   Equity-derivative securities derive their value from the equity price of a corporation. They consist of puts and calls, created by investors, and warrants, rights, and convertible securities, created by corporations. A call is an option to buy a share of a particular stock at a stated price any time before a specified expiration date. Similarly, a put is an option to sell the stock. The seller receives a premium for selling either of these options, and the buyer pays the premium. Advantages of options include a smaller investment than transacting in the stock itself, knowing the maximum loss in advance, leverage, and an expansion of the opportunity set available to investors.

2. **Describe how options work and give some basic strategies.**

   Buyers of calls expect the underlying stock to perform in the opposite direction from the expectations of put buyers. Writers of each instrument have opposite expectations from the buyers. The basic strategies for options involve a call writer and a put buyer expecting the underlying stock price to decline, whereas the call buyer and the put writer expect it to rise. Options may also be used to hedge against a portfolio position by establishing an opposite position in options on that stock. More sophisticated options strategies include combinations of options, such as strips, straps, straddles, and spreads (which include money spreads and time spreads). These strategies are discussed in Appendix 19A.

3. **Explain the valuation of options.**

   Options have an intrinsic value ranging from $0 to the "in-the-money" value. Most sell for more than this, representing a speculative premium, referred to as the time value. According to the Black-Scholes option valuation model, value is a function of the price of the stock, the exercise price of the option, time to maturity, the interest rate, and the volatility of the underlying stock. The available empirical evidence seems to suggest that the options market is efficient, with trading rules unable to exploit any biases that exist in the Black-Scholes or other options pricing models.

4. **Identify types of options other than puts and calls.**

   Interest rate, currency, and stock-index options are also available to investors. Stock-index options are a popular innovation in the options area that allow investors to buy puts and calls on broad stock market indexes. A distinguishing feature of these option contracts is that settlement is in cash. In effect, stock-index options allow investors to make only a market decision and to purchase a form of market insurance. The strategies with index options are similar to those for individual stock options. Investors can both hedge and speculate.

KEY TERMS

Arbitrageurs, p.642
Black-Scholes model, p.645
Call, p.622
Canadian Derivatives Clearing
   Corporation (CDCC), p.628
Covered call, p.638
Currency options, p.650
Equity-derivative securities,
   p.621
Exercise (strike) price, p.623
Expiration date, p.623

Hedge, p.638
Hedge ratio, p.649
Interest rate options, p.650
Intrinsic value (option), p.630
Long-term options (LEAPs),
   p.625
Option premium, p.623
Options, p.622
Portfolio insurance, p.641
Protective put, p.640
Put, p.622

Put-call parity, p.647
Right (Appendix 19B), p.662
Spread (Appendix 19A), p.661
Stock-index options, p.650
Straddle (Appendix 19A),
   p.660
Time value, p.642
Warrant (Appendix 19B),
   p.663

REVIEW QUESTIONS

19-1. State three justifications given for the existence of options.

19-2. What does it mean to say an option buyer has a right but not an obligation?

19-3. How can the writer of a call option cancel his or her obligation?

19-4. Why is the call or put writer's position considerably different from the buyer's position?

19-5. Distinguish between call options, warrants, and rights. (Refer to Appendix 19B for this question.)

19-6. Explain the following terms used with puts and calls:
   a. Strike price
   b. Naked option
   c. Premium
   d. Out-of-the-money option

19-7. Who writes puts and calls? Why?

19-8. What role do clearing corporations play in options markets?

19-9. What is the relationship between option prices and their intrinsic values? Why?

19-10. What is meant by the time value of an option?

19-11. Why do investors write calls? What are their obligations?

19-12. What is an index option? What index options are available in Canada?

19-13. What are the major differences between a stock option and an index option?

19-14. How does writing a covered call differ from writing a naked call?

19-15. What does it mean to say that an option is worth more alive than dead?

19-16. What are the potential advantages of puts and calls?

19-17. Explain the factors used in the Black-Scholes option valuation model. What is the relationship between each factor and the value of the option?

19-18. Give three reasons why an investor might purchase a call.

19-19. What is a straddle? When would an investor buy one? Write one? (Refer to Appendix 19A for this question.)

19-20. What is a spread? What is its purpose? (Refer to Appendix 19A for this question.)

19-21. Explain two types of spreads. (Refer to Appendix 19A for this question.)

19-22. How can a put be used to protect a particular position? A call?

19-23. Which is greater for an option relative to the underlying common share, dollar movements or return volatility? Why?

19-24. Assume that you own a diversified portfolio of 50 stocks and fear a market decline over the next six months.
   a. How could you protect your portfolio during this period using stock-index options?
   b. How effective would this hedge be?
   c. Other things being equal, if your portfolio consisted of 150 stocks, would the protection be more effective?

19-25. Assume that you expect interest rates to rise and that you wish to speculate on this expectation. How could interest rate options be used to do this?

PROBLEMS

Assume the common stock of ABC Company trades on the TSX. ABC has never paid a cash dividend. The stock is relatively risky. Assume that the beta for ABC is 1.3 and that ABC closed at a price of $162. Hypothetical option quotes on ABC are as follows:

Strike Price	Call Apr	Call Jul	Call Oct	Put Apr	Put Jul	Put Oct
140	23.50	s	s	s	s	s
150	16	21	25	1	3.75	r
160	8.88	14	20	3	7	9
170	3	9	13.25	9	10	11
180	1.25	5.25	9	r	20	r

r = not traded; s = no option offered

19-1. Based on the ABC data, answer the following questions:

   a. Which calls are in the money?
   b. Which puts are in the money?
   c. Why are investors willing to pay 1.25 for the 180 April call but only 1.00 for the 150 April put, which has an exercise price that is closer to the current market price?

19-2. Based on the ABC data answer the following:

   a. Calculate the intrinsic value of the April 150 and the October 170 calls.
   b. Calculate the intrinsic value of the April 150 and the October 170 puts.
   c. Explain the reasons for the differences in intrinsic values in parts (a) and (b).

19-3. Using the ABC data, answer the following:

   a. What is the cost of 10 October 150 call contracts in total dollars (excluding commission fees)?
   b. What is the cost of 20 October 160 put contracts in total dollars (excluding commission fees)?
   c. On the following day, assume ABC closed at $164. Which of the options would you have expected to increase? Decrease?
   d. If the new quote on the October 150 call was 26, what would have been your one-day profit on the 10 contracts? What would have been your percentage return?
   e. If the new quote on the October 160 put was 7.50, what would have been your one-day profit on the 20 contracts? What would have been your percentage return?
   f. What is the most you could lose on these 20 contracts?

19-4. You are considering some put and call options and have available the following data (assume no dividends are paid by ABC or DEF):

	Call ABC	Call DEF	Put ABC
Time to expiration (months)	3	6	3
Annual risk-free rate	8%	8%	8%
Exercise price	$50	$50	$50
Option price	$3		$4
Stock price	$45	$45	$45

   a. Comparing the two calls, should DEF sell for more or less than ABC if their shares have the same volatility? Why?
   b. What is the call option time value for call option ABC?
   c. Based on the information for the call and the put for ABC, determine if put-call parity is working.

19-5. Assume that the value of a call option using the Black-Scholes model is $8.94. The interest rate is 8 percent, and the time to maturity is 90 days. The price of the underlying stock is $47.38, and the exercise price is $45. Calculate the price of a put using the put-call parity relationship.

19-6. Using the Black-Scholes formula, calculate the value of a call option given the following information:

Stock price = $50
Exercise price = $45
Interest rate = 7%
Time to expiration = 90 days
Standard deviation = 0.4
What is the price of the put using the same information?

19-7. Using the information in Problem 19-6, determine the sensitivity of the call value to a change in inputs by recalculating the call value if

a. the interest rate doubles to 14 percent but all other values remain the same.
b. the standard deviation doubles to 0.8 but all other values remain the same.
c. Which change causes the greatest fluctuation in the value of the call? What can you infer from this?

19-8. Given the following information, determine the number of shares of stock that must be purchased to form a hedged position if one option contract (covering 100 shares of stock) is to be written.

Stock price = $100
Exercise price = $95
Interest rate = 8%
Time to expiration = 180 days
Standard deviation = 0.6

19-9. Given the information in Problem 8, determine how the value of the call would change if

a. the exercise price is $100
b. the time to expiration is 80 days (use the original exercise price of $95)
c. the time to expiration is 8 days

19-10. Determine the value of Ribex call options if the exercise price is $40, and the option is currently $2 out of the money, the time to expiration is 90 days, the interest rate is 0.10, and the variance of return on the stock for the past few months has been 0.81.

19-11. Using the information in Problem 10, decide intuitively whether the put or the call will sell at a higher price and verify your answer.

19-12. An investor who purchased 100 shares of Stock G for $1,800 sells a six-month call with a strike price of $25 and a $5 call premium.

a. What is the investor's gross profit/loss if the price of the stock rises to $28 and the investor is called to deliver the 100 shares?
b. What is the investor's gross profit/loss if the price drops to $21?
c. What is the investor's gross profit/loss if the price drops to $16?
d. What is the investor's gross profit/loss if the price drops to $11?

19-13. Stock R closes at $16.25 on August 30, 2004. A May 2005 put option on Stock R has an exercise price of $18.05. This put was last traded at a premium of $3.10.

a. What is the intrinsic value of the put?
b. What is the intrinsic value of the put if the exercise price was $16.25?
c. What is the intrinsic value of the put if the exercise price was $14.44?
d. What is the intrinsic value of a March 2005 call option on Stock R, with an exercise price of $18.05?

e. What is the intrinsic value of the call if the exercise price was $16.25?

f. What is the intrinsic value of the call if the exercise price was $14.44?

19-14. Assume an investor buys a put option on Stock C for $4.90, with a strike price of $25. What is the payoff and the net profit for the put option if the price at expiration is $10, $15, $20, $25, or $30?

19-15. Assume an investor purchases a February 2005 call option of Stock B. It has an exercise price of $35 when the stock price is valued at $31.40 in the market, and it carries a premium of $2.15 for this standard contract. What is the investor's total wealth if:

a. The stock price went up to $36.50 and the call was exercised?

b. The stock price went up to $35?

c. The stock price went up to $33.20?

d. The stock price went up to $38.40?

e. What must the stock price be in order for this investor to break even?

f. In each of these cases above, is the call in the money, out of the money, or at the money?

19-16. There are various ways to calculate the price of a call option using the Black-Scholes model. The spreadsheet breaks the required formulas into pieces to make it easy to work with. Column (1) shows the various inputs. The first five cells are the required inputs for a non-dividend-paying stock. The remainder of the cells are the formula parts. Column (2) shows a solved problem for a stock selling for $50, with an exercise price of $45, an interest rate of 6 percent, 90 days (one-quarter of a year), and a standard deviation of .235. Column (3) shows how the cell values in Column (2) were calculated. Once you have this set up in the spreadsheet, you can calculate the price of any call option by substituting the correct values in the first five cells of column (1).

Calculating a Call Price Using the Black-Scholes Model

S	50	
E	45	
r	0.06	
t	0.25	
s	0.235	
$\ln(S/E)$	0.105361	LN(B2/B3)
$r + 0.5\sigma$	0.087613	B4 + (.5)*(B6)∧2
$\sigma(t)^{1/2}$	0.1175	B6*((B5) 0.5)
d_1	1.083095	(B7+(B8*B5))/B9
d_2	0.965595	B10−B9
$N(d_1)$	0.860617	NORMSDIST(B10)
$N(d_2)$	0.832877	NORMSDIST(B11)
$S*N(d_1)$	43.03084	B2*B12
E	2.7183	
$e-r^t$	0.985112	B15∧−(B4*B5)
Call Price	6.109398	B14−(B3*B16*B13)

PREPARING FOR YOUR PROFESSIONAL EXAMS

CFA CURRICULUM AND SAMPLE EXAM QUESTIONS (©CFA INSTITUTE)

19-1. Assume the probability of bankruptcy for the underlying asset is high. Compared to the price of a US put option on the same underlying asset, the price of an equivalent European put option will most likely be:

a. lower.

b. higher.

    c. the same because the probability of bankruptcy does not affect pricing.

    d. the same because the possibility of early exercise only affects the pricing of call options.

19-2. With respect to put-call parity, a protective put consists of a European

    a. put option and the underlying asset.

    b. call option and the underlying asset.

    c. put option and a risk-free bond with a face value equal to the exercise price of a European call option on the underlying asset.

    d. call option and a risk-free bond with a face value equal to the exercise price of a European put option on the underlying asset.

19-3. Unless far out-of-the money or far in-the-money, for otherwise identical call options, the longer the term to expiration, the lower the price for:

    a. European call options, but not US call options.

    b. US call options, but not European call options.

    c. both European call options and US call options.

    d. neither European call options nor US call options.

19-4. A call option with an exercise price of 65 will expire in 73 days. No cash payments will be made by the underlying asset over the life of the option. If the underlying asset price is at 70 and the risk-free rate of return is 5.0 percent, the lower bounds for a US call option and a European call option, respectively, are closest to:

Lower bound for US call option	Lower bound for European call option
a. 5.00	5.00
b. 5.00	5.63
c. 5.63	5.00
d. 5.63	5.63

19-5. A put option with an exercise price of 75 will expire in 73 days. No cash payments will be made by the underlying asset over the life of the option. If the underlying asset price is at 70 and the risk-free rate of return is 5.0 percent, the lower bounds for a US put option and a European put option, respectively, are closest to:

Lower bound for US put option	Lower bound for European put option
a. 4.27	4.27
b. 4.27	5.00
c. 5.00	4.27
d. 5.00	5.00

19-6. Compare a US call with a strike of 50 that expires in 90 days to a US call on the same underlying asset that has a strike of 60 and expires in 120 days. The underlying asset is selling at 55. Consider the following statements. Are they most likely correct or incorrect?

Statement 1: The 50 strike call is in-the-money and the 60 strike call is out-of-the-money.

Statement 2: The time value of the 60 strike call, as a proportion of the 60 strike call's premium, exceeds the time value of the 50 strike call as a proportion of the 50 strike call's premium.

    a. Neither statement is correct.

    b. Statement 1 is incorrect, but Statement 2 is correct.

    c. Statement 1 is correct, but Statement 2 is incorrect.

    d. Both statements are correct.

19-7. Marla Johnson priced both a put and a call on Alpha Numero using standard option pricing software. To use the program, Johnson entered the strike price of the options, the price of the underlying stock, an estimate of the risk-free rate, the time to expiration of the option, and an estimate of the volatility of the returns of the underlying stock into her computer. Both prices calculated by the software program were substantially above the actual market values observed in that day's exchange trading. Which of the following is the most likely explanation?

    a. The strike price was incorrect; most likely too low. a strike price.
    b. The value for time to expiration was too low.
    c. The estimate of volatility was too high.
    d. The estimate of volatility was too low.

19-8. A call with a strike price of $40 is available on a stock currently trading for $35. The call expires in one year and the risk free rate of return is 10 percent. The lower bound on this call's value is:

    a. zero.
    b. $5 if the call is US-style.
    c. $1.36 if the call is European-style.
    d. $3.18 if the call is European-style.

19-9. A silver futures contract requires the seller to deliver 5,000 Troy ounces of silver. An investor sells one July silver futures contract at a price of $8 per ounce, posting a $2,025 initial margin. If the required maintenance margin is $1,500, the price per ounce at which the investor would first receive a maintenance margin call is closest to:

    a. $5.92.
    b. $7.89.
    c. $8.11.
    d. $10.80.

APPENDIX 19A

SPREADS AND COMBINATIONS

Puts and calls offer investors a number of opportunities beyond the simple strategies discussed in Chapter 19. We briefly describe here some combinations of options that can be written or purchased. We also consider the use of spreads.

Combinations of Options

Straddle

A combination of a put and a call on the same stock with the same exercise date and exercise price.

Options can be mixed together in numerous ways. Some typical combinations include a straddle, a strip, and a strap. A **straddle** is a combination of a put and a call on the same stock with the same exercise date and exercise price. A purchaser of a straddle believes that the underlying stock price is highly volatile and may go either up or down. Buying the straddle eliminates the need to predict the direction of the market correctly. The buyer of the straddle can exercise each part separately, and therefore can profit from a large enough move either way. However, the price of the stock must rise or fall enough to equal the premium on both a put and a call; therefore, the straddle buyer must be confident that the underlying stock has a good chance of moving sharply in at least one direction.

    Straddles can also be sold (written). The seller believes that the underlying stock price will exhibit small volatility but could go up or down. Unlike the buyer, the writer does not forecast that a substantial movement in one direction or the other is likely.

    Consider a stock selling at $75 with a six-month straddle available with an exercise price of $75 and, for simplicity, call and put prices of $5 each. The seller of such a straddle is protected (i.e., makes

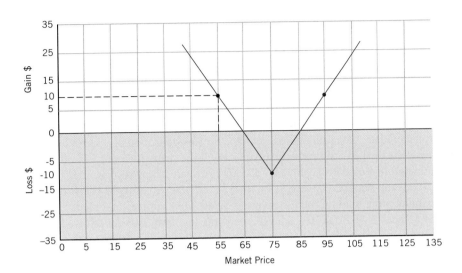

Figure 19-11
Straddle Profit Diagram

a profit) in the range of $65–85 (ignoring commissions). They earn the maximum return of $10, if the price remains at $75, since neither option would be exercised at this price. The buyers hope that the price exceeds one of these boundaries (i.e., $65 or $85) before expiration. In any event, if the price is above or below $75, one of the options would be in the money, and hence be exercised. However, in order for the buyer to achieve a positive profit by exercising the option, the price would have to move up or down by more than $10 (i.e., in order to cover the original cost of $10).[26] The profit diagram for this straddle is shown in Figure 19-11.

A *strip* is a combination of two puts and a call on the same security, again with the same expiration date and exercise price. In this case, the purchaser believes that the price will probably decline rather than rise and therefore wants two puts (but also wants some protection in the opposite direction). The seller obviously believes the opposite.

A *strap* is similar to a strip but combines two calls with a put. Here, of course, the purchaser believes the probability of a price increase exceeds that for a price decrease, and again, the writer expects the opposite.

Spreads

Rather than being only the buyer or the seller of various combinations of puts and calls, an investor can be both simultaneously by means of a spread. A **spread** is defined as the purchase and sale of an equivalent option varying in only one respect. Its purpose is to reduce risk in an option position, and it is a popular practice.

The two basic spreads are the *money spread* and the *time spread*. A money spread involves the purchase of a call option at one exercise price and the sale of the same-maturity option, but with a different exercise price. For example, an investor could buy an October 20 call and sell an October 25 call on the same underlying stock.

A time spread involves the purchase and sale of options that are identical except for expiration dates. For example, an investor could buy an October 25 call and sell a January 25 call on the same underlying stock.

Investors use particular spread strategies, depending on whether they are bullish or bearish. Assume you are bullish about a stock but wish to reduce the risk involved in options. The stock is selling for $22.83, with four-month call options available at exercise prices of $20 and $25 for $3.70 and $1.10, respectively. A bullish money spread consists of buying the $20 call and selling the $25 call.

Spread

The purchase and sale of an equivalent option varying in only one respect.

---

[26] Of course, we know that early exercise is generally less profitable than selling the option in the market, since the seller would receive a time value premium in addition to the intrinsic value (which is the value obtained if the option is exercised).

Your net cost is now $2.60, which is the maximum you could lose if the calls expire worthless because the stock's price dropped sharply. Should the share price rise above $20, however, your $20 call will be worth at least the price of the stock minus the exercise price of $20. This amount is netted against your profit or loss on the $25 call that you wrote. In effect, you give up some potential profit (what could have been earned on the $20 call alone) to reduce your risk (by reducing your net cost) if the stock price declines.

The maximum loss is $2.60, which would occur if the share price was $20 or below on the closing date. For all price levels above $20, this loss would be reduced. For example, if the share price is $22 on the expiration date, the resulting loss would be $0.60—consisting of a $2 payoff from the $20 call option, minus the total cost for the strategy of $2.60. If the share price was $25 on the expiration date, the resulting profit would be $2.40 ($5 – $2.60). For share prices beyond $25, for each $1 you gain on the $20 call you bought, you lose $1 on the $25 call you wrote, so the effects cancel out. As a result, the maximum profit from this bullish spread is $2.40. For example, if the share price is $30, the profit from the $20 call is $6.30 ($10 – $ 3.70), while the loss from the $25 call is –$3.90 ($1.10 – $5.00). This results in a net profit of $2.40 ($6.30 – $3.90). The profit diagram for this bullish money spread is shown in Figure 19-12. (This example ignores commission fees).

Figure 19-12
Bullish Money Spread
Profit Diagram

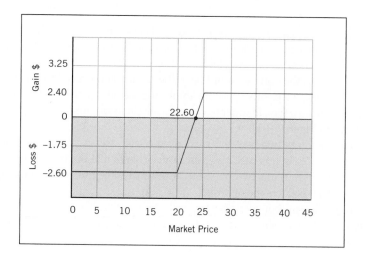

APPENDIX 19B

RIGHTS AND WARRANTS

Rights and warrants are similar to call options because they both give the holder the right to purchase shares at specified prices until the expiration date. Rights are generally short-term in nature, while warrants tend to be issued with maturities of three to five years. Unlike options, they are issued by the corporation itself, and result in dilution of the common equity capital base.

Rights

Right

A corporate-created option to purchase a stated number of common shares at a specified price within a specified time (typically a few months).

A **right** is the term applied to a privilege granted to a shareholder to acquire additional shares at a predetermined (subscription) price that is generally lower than the current market price. This creates value for the shareholder and induces them to exercise this option. Rights generally have short maturities consisting of a few weeks to three months. They are usually transferable, and certificates are mailed to shareholders on the record date. Shares trade ex rights two business days prior to a record date, which means they trade without the right privilege attached. Prior to the ex rights date, the stock is said to trade cum rights, since it trades with the right privilege attached. Typically the share price will drop by the theoretical intrinsic value of the right on the ex rights date.

Rights may be offered because

1. Current market conditions are not conducive to traditional common share issues.

2. Management wants to give existing shareholders the opportunity to acquire shares, possibly at a discount to present market price.

3. It enables new funds to be raised while providing existing shareholders the right to maintain their proportionate ownership of the company.

No commission is levied on the exercise of rights, and a ready secondary market can develop permitting the sale of rights by holders who do not wish to exercise. If the shares trade on an exchange, the rights are listed on the exchange automatically and trading takes place until they expire. Regular delivery requires settlement within three business days, prior to the expiration date of the rights, after which time the rights will trade only on a cash basis. The Exchange will cease trading of rights on the Exchange at 12:00 noon (Toronto time) on the expiration date. Because of their short lifetime, they are often bought and sold on a "when issued" basis, which implies that sellers agree to deliver the rights when they are received.

A rights holder may take four courses of action:

1. Exercise some or all of the rights

2. Sell some or all of the rights

3. Buy additional rights for trading or exercise purposes

4. Do nothing and let the rights expire (which would represent sub-optimal behaviour since the investor would gain nothing through this action)

Usually each shareholder receives one right, and a certain number of rights (N) is required to purchase one share (purchase of fractional shares may or may not be permitted, depending on the details of the issue). The theoretical intrinsic value (IV) of a right, by necessity, is calculated using two methods described below.

During the cum rights period:

$$IV = \frac{(\text{Market price of the stock} - \text{Subscription price})}{N + 1} \qquad \textbf{(19-9)}$$

The addition of 1 to N reflects the fact that the market price of the share includes the value of one right.

During the ex rights period:

$$IV = \frac{(\text{Market price of stock} - \text{Subscription price})}{N} \qquad \textbf{(19-10)}$$

EXAMPLE 19B-1: CALCULATING INTRINSIC VALUE CUM AND EX RIGHTS

A share is trading for $40 cum rights. Four rights are required to purchase a share at the subscription price of $35.

$$IV = (40 - 35) / (4 + 1) = \$1.00$$

Two days after the ex rights date the share price above has fallen to $39.20.

$$IV = (39.20 - 35) / 4 = \$1.05$$

Warrants

Warrants are corporate-issued securities with an option to buy shares from the issuer at a set price for a set period of time. Warrants are generally long-term in nature and tend to be issued with three to five

Warrant
An option created by a corporation to purchase a stated number of common shares at a specified price within a specified time (often several years).

years to maturity, although some have longer lives. They are often attached to debt or preferred share issues as a sweetener (to make the issue more attractive to investors). They are usually detachable either immediately or after a certain holding period, and then trade separately.

Investors may be attracted to warrants because they provide "leverage," which is attractive to speculators. In other words, the market price of a warrant is generally much lower than the price of the underlying security, yet its price moves together with the underlying asset price. The result is greater percentage swings in warrant prices than for the underlying asset, which magnifies gains (or losses) in percentage terms. A ratio that may be used to measure this leverage potential is

(19-11)
$$\text{Leverage potential} = \frac{\text{Market price of the underlying share}}{\text{Market price of the warrant}}$$

Generally speaking, the larger this ratio, the greater the leverage effect; however, other factors such as the amount of overvaluation must also be considered. Other factors to be considered by investors when selecting warrants include marketability and protection against stock splits and/or stock dividends (which is usually provided).

Warrants have an intrinsic value and a time value. The intrinsic value refers to the amount by which the market price of the underlying stock exceeds the exercise price of the warrant. It can never go below zero, since exercise is at the option of the warrant holder. Time value refers to the amount by which the market price exceeds the intrinsic value.

There is also usually an overvaluation associated with warrants, which is calculated as follows:

(19-12)
$$\text{Overvaluation} = \text{Market price of warrant} + \text{Exercise price of warrant} \\ - \text{Market value of underlying asset}$$

This will equal the time value whenever there is a positive intrinsic value but may exceed the time value when the intrinsic value is nil.

EXAMPLE 19B-2: DETERMINING INTRINSIC VALUE, TIME VALUE, OVERVALUATION, AND LEVERAGE

Determine the intrinsic value, time value, percentage overvaluation, and leverage potential of the following warrants:

a. Share price is $50, warrant price is $8, and exercise price of warrants is $52.

b. Share price is $40, warrant price is $15, and exercise price of warrants is $30.

Solution:

a.   IV = Max (50 − 52, 0) = 0

Time Value = 8 − 0 = $8

Overvaluation = 8 + 52 − 50 = 10

Percentage overvaluation = 10/50 = 0.20 or 20%

Leverage potential = 50/8 = 6.25

b.   IV = Max (40 − 30, 0) = 10

Time Value = 15 − 10 = $5

Overvaluation = 15 + 30 − 40 = 5

Percentage overvaluation = 5/40 = 0.125 or 12.5%

Leverage potential = 40/15 = 2.67

Factors to be examined by investors in order to determine the appropriateness of warrant over-valuation include

1. The prospects for the underlying assets
2. Time to expiration
3. Volatility of underlying asset price
4. Higher premiums may be associated with higher price-earnings ratios of underlying shares
5. Lower over-valuations should result for warrants on assets paying higher dividends to compensate the warrant holder for not receiving the dividend

Some special types of warrants include

1. Piggyback warrants—may be received as part of the exercise of original warrants (and typically have higher exercise prices)
2. Put warrants—on stock indices, etc., which result in cash settlement if the price of the underlying is below a specified price
3. Commodity-indexed warrants—where the exercise price is linked to market prices of a specified commodity

APPENDIX 19C

PUT-CALL PARITY: THE NO-ARBITRAGE ARGUMENT

Unless the price of a European put and call on the same non-dividend-paying stock with the same exercise price bear a certain relationship to each other, there will be opportunities for earning riskless profits (arbitrage). We can prove this by using the following no-arbitrage argument, which ignores transactions costs. Consider the following investment portfolios: Portfolio A involves the purchase of a European call option for an underlying share that does not pay dividends (at a cost of C), and investing the present value of the exercise price on this option [PV(E) dollars] in a riskless investment (government T-bills) that will pay off E dollars at the maturity date; portfolio B involves the purchase of one share of the underlying stock (at a cost of S), and also buying one European put on the underlying share (at a cost of P). These actions and their payoffs at expiration date T are depicted below.

Portfolio	Action	Payoff at T $S(T) < E$	$S(T) > E$
A	Buy 1 call	0	$S(T) - E$
	Invest PV(E) in T-bills	E	E
	Total Payoff	**E**	**S(T)**
B	Buy 1 share	S(T)	S(T)
	Buy 1 put	E − S(T)	0
	Total Payoff	**E**	**S(T)**

Notice that portfolios A and B always have the same payoff at T because they will both pay off S(T) at T when S(T) > E, and will both pay off E at T when S(T) < E. Since both the call and the put are European options, we also know that early exercise of either option is impossible. Therefore, since the two strategies must have identical payoffs at the expiration date, and since the options cannot be exercised early, they must have identical costs for constructing the portfolios. If they did not, investors could make riskless (or arbitrage) profits by taking a long position in the undervalued portfolio and taking a short position in the overvalued portfolio. For example, if the cost of constructing A was $10, while the cost of constructing B was $8, one could take a long position in B and a short position in A, and receive $2 today. Since both portfolios have the same payoff at T, the returns from B can always be used to pay off the short position in A, so there is no risk associated with this strategy, yet the payoff is positive. This condition could never exist in efficient markets and would quickly disappear as traders recognized the discrepancy and exploited it. So,

$$\text{Total cost to construct portfolio A} = \text{Total cost to construct portfolio B, or}$$
$$C + PV(E) = P + S$$

This can be rearranged to solve for the price of the put as follows:

$$P = PV(E) - S + C$$

Finally, we note that the present value of E using a continuous discount rate r, and with a time to maturity (in years) equal to t, can be expressed as $PV(E) = E/e^{rt}$, so we are left with Equation 19-8: $P = E/e^{rt} - S + C$.

CHAPTER 20

FUTURES

Quick—there is a freeze in Florida, so buy orange juice futures! You have heard this one before, but you never thought about doing it because you know nothing about futures contracts. Given all that you have had to learn lately as part of your investments education, you are not enthused about learning too much about futures contracts at this time. However, it would be nice to be able to understand what people are talking about when they discuss futures, and even to mull them over in your mind in case one day you want to use futures as part of your portfolio strategy. Therefore, you realize some effort in this area is worthwhile.

Learning Objectives

After reading this chapter, you should be able to

1. Describe the structure of futures markets.
2. Outline how futures work and what types of investors participate in futures markets.
3. Explain how financial futures are used.

CHAPTER PREVIEW

This chapter discusses financial futures, the other derivative security of primary importance to investors. As with options, futures allow investors to manage investment risk and to speculate in the equity, fixed-income, and currency markets. Here we discuss the structure of futures markets, explain the procedures of using futures, and give some basic strategies. We also consider interest rate and stock-index futures.

INTRODUCTION

Futures markets play an important role in today's investments world. New instruments in this area have proliferated, and techniques involving the use of futures, such as program trading, have captured wide media attention. Of particular importance to many investors is the array of financial futures now available. Anyone studying investments should understand what futures contracts are, the wide variety of choices now available, and how financial futures can be used both to hedge portfolio positions and to speculate in fixed-income and equity areas. Futures contracts are an important component of derivative securities and, like options, they represent a major innovation in risk management.

UNDERSTANDING FUTURES MARKETS

Why Futures Markets?

Physical commodities and financial instruments typically are traded in cash markets. A *cash contract* calls for immediate delivery and is used by those who need a commodity now (e.g., food processors). Cash contracts cannot be cancelled unless both parties agree. The current cash prices of commodities and financial instruments can be found daily in the financial media.

There are two types of cash markets: spot markets and forward markets. Spot markets are for immediate delivery.[1] The spot price refers to the current market price of an item available for immediate delivery. Forward markets are for deferred delivery. The forward price is the price of an item that is to be delivered at some specified time in the future.

Suppose that a manufacturer of high school and college class rings is gathering orders to fill for this school year and wishes to ensure an established price today for gold to be delivered six months from now, when the rings will actually be manufactured. The spot price of gold is not the manufacturer's primary concern, because the gold will not be purchased until it is needed for the manufacturing process. However, to reduce its risk, the manufacturer is interested in contracting for gold to be delivered in six months at a price established today. This will allow the manufacturer to price its rings more accurately.

Our manufacturer could find a gold supplier who was willing to enter into a *forward contract*, which is simply a commitment today to transact in the future. The other party to the contract, such as a mining company, agrees to deliver the gold six months from now at a price negotiated today. Both parties have agreed to a deferred delivery at a sales price that is currently determined. No funds have been exchanged. Both parties have reduced their risk in the sense that the mining company knows what it will receive for the gold when it is sold six months from now and the ring manufacturer knows what it will pay for the gold when it actually needs to take delivery six months from now.

Obviously, one of the parties may be disappointed six months later when the price of gold has changed, but that is the advantage of hindsight. If investors could foresee the future, they would know what to do to start with and would not have to worry about risk. The forward and futures markets were developed to allow individuals to deal with the risks they face.

---

[1]"Immediate" means in the normal course of business. For example, it may normally take two days for an item to be delivered after being ordered.

Forward contracts are centuries old, traceable to at least the ancient Romans and Greeks. Organized futures markets, on the other hand, only go back to the mid-nineteenth century in Chicago. Futures markets are, in effect, organized and standardized forward markets. An organized futures exchange standardizes the non-standard forward contracts, establishing such features as contract size, delivery dates, and condition of the items that can be delivered. Only the price and number of contracts are left for futures traders to negotiate. Individuals can trade without personal contact with each other because of the centralized marketplace. Performance is guaranteed by a clearing house, relieving one party to the transaction from worry that the other party will fail to honour its commitment.

The futures markets serve a valuable economic purpose by allowing hedgers to shift price risk to speculators. The risk of price fluctuations is shifted from participants unwilling to assume such risk to those who are. Another economic function performed by futures markets is price discovery. Because the price of a futures contract reflects current expectations about values at some future date, transactors can establish current prices against later transactions.

Current Futures Markets

To most people, futures trading traditionally has meant trading in commodities such as gold, wheat, and oil. However, money can be thought of simply as another commodity, and *financial futures* have become a particularly viable investment alternative for numerous investors. Therefore, futures contracts currently traded on futures exchanges can be divided into two broad categories:

1. Commodities—agricultural, metals, and energy-related
2. Financials—foreign currencies as well as debt and equity instruments.

Each category can be further subdivided as shown in Table 20-1, which shows the futures contracts traded in the United States. As we can see, the futures markets involve trading in a variety of both commodities and financials.

Table 20-1

Futures Contracts Traded in the United States, by Category

The major commodities traded in the United States can be classified into the following categories:

I. Commodities

Grains and oilseeds	Wheat, corn, oats, soybeans, soybean oils, soybean meal, flaxseed, rapeseed, rye, and canola
Livestock and meats	Cattle (both live and feeders), pork bellies, and hogs
Foods	Cocoa, coffee, orange juice, and sugar
Fibres	Cotton
Metals	Copper, gold, platinum, silver, and palladium
Oil	Gasoline, heating oil, crude oil, gas oil, propane, and ethanol
Wood	Lumber

II. Financials

Interest rates	Canadian government bond, Treasury bills, Treasury notes, Treasury bonds, municipal bond index, 30-day federal funds, Eurodollar, 1-month LIBOR, Sterling Long Gilt, Euromark, EuroSwiss, EuroLira, German government bond, Italian government bond, French government bond, 10-year swap, 5-year swap
Stock indexes	S&P/TSX 60 Index, S&P 500 Index, S&P MidCap 400, NYSE Composite Index, Major Market Index, KR-CRB Index, KC Value Line Index, Russell 2000, CAC 40, Nikkei 225 Index, GSCL, FT-SE 100 Index
Foreign currencies	Euro, Japanese yen, Canadian dollar, German mark, British pounds, Swiss franc, Australian dollar, and US dollar index

For each type of contract, such as corn or silver, different delivery dates are available. Each contract will specify the trading unit involved and, where applicable, the deliverable grade necessary to satisfy the contract. Investors can also purchase options on futures contracts (see Appendix 20A).

One of the striking features of Table 20-1 is the proliferation of foreign-based futures contracts on US futures exchanges. This is true for interest rate futures and stock-index futures and is good evidence of the move toward globalization that is occurring throughout the investing world. For example, Real-World Returns 20-1 discusses talks designed to initiate a new futures contract on Canadian crude oil on some US exchanges.

Real-World Returns 20-1

Futures Contract Sought For Canadian Crude

The growing importance of Canadian oil sands production could soon be rewarded with the ultimate status symbol, at least in oil market terms: a heavy crude futures contract.

Canadian oil producers say they're in negotiations with investment banks and commodities exchanges over the development of a futures contract for their heavy crude output. A contract on the New York Mercantile Exchange or the Intercontinental Exchange (ICE) for Western Canadian Select, a blend of heavy Canadian crudes, could be created in the next year if sufficient liquidity can be attained, these people say.

"We've spoken to the ICE and Nymex many times to see how we can set up a contract," said Walt Madro, senior vice-president of crude oil marketing at EnCana Corp., Canada's largest energy company.

"They're chasing this very aggressively. We wouldn't be surprised if they started providing quotes within the next 12 months." At present, Canadian firms trade their crude through private, over-the-counter deals with buyers such as refineries. The lack of transparency inherent in such a system means companies don't know what price their future supplies will achieve, creating uncertainty over revenue projections.

That's a problem producers would like to solve, considering crude output from Alberta's oil sands is expected to triple to three million barrels a day in 2015 and US refiners are showing greater interest in taking Canadian heavy output. ConocoPhillips Co. recently agreed to a huge supply deal with EnCana, while BP PLC and Marathon Oil Corp, have also said they're keen to source supply of more Canadian crude.

"Having a contract provides a great deal more liquidity with respect to moving volumes while providing improved price disclosure," said Rod Wilson, manager of domestic crude supply and natural gas liquids at Petro-Canada. "It's an uncertainty over revenue projections instrument for companies to lay off risk."

Both Nymex and the ICE refused to comment on the possibility of setting up a heavy crude contract. However, Nymex said earlier this month it had obtained authorization to offer the use of its electronic clearing and trading systems in Alberta. Meanwhile, the Toronto Stock Exchange owner, TSX Group Inc., is also mulling the introduction of a Canadian crude oil contract.

To be sure, the strong support in Canada for a heavy crude contract doesn't mean it will happen or be successful. New contracts frequently struggle to take away trading volumes from the traditional West Texas intermediate (WTI) and Brent benchmarks, resulting in an illiquid contract that's unable to attract traders. This month, a heavy crude contract for Russian Export Blend Crude Oil was launched on Nymex, but trading volumes haven't yet taken off.

However, the Canadian producers see a futures contract as a natural progression for their attempts to position Western Canadian Select as a North American benchmark for heavy crude. The blend, which consists of Canadian heavy conventional and bitumen crude oils, blended with sweet synthetic and condensate diluents, was launched by four producers—EnCana, Petrocan, Canadian Natural Resources Ltd. and Talisman Energy Inc—in late 2004. Production runs are at around 250,000 barrels a day, compared with the WTI and Brent benchmarks, both of which are near 350,000 barrels a day.

The level needed to maintain a contract is open to debate. Both EnCana and Canadian Natural, the largest producers of Western Canadian Select, think production of 300,000 barrels a day could sustain a contract, and could be reached within the next 12 months. However, both Petrocan's Mr. Wilson and Craig James, manager of crude and natural gas liquids marketing at Talisman, said a more realistic target is 400,000 barrels a day, which is unlikely to be reached in 2007.

Source: Scott, Norval, "Futures Contract Sought for Canadian Crude," *The Globe and Mail*, November 23, 2006, p. B18.

The only commodity exchange in Canada is ICE Futures Canada, formerly the Winnipeg Commodity Exchange, where trading has taken place in wheat, canola, flaxseed, oats, barley, and rye for several years. Futures on canola are by far the most active commodity futures that are traded in Canada, as shown in Table 20-2.

Table 20-2

Listed Futures Products on ICE Futures Canada for 2006 (formerly Winnipeg Commodity Exchange)

Commodity Futures	Trading Volume
Canola	2,427,697
Feed Wheat	65,802
Western Barley	193,324
Total	2,686,823

Options	Trading Volume
Canola	26,523
Feed Wheat	1,460
Western Barley	1,080
Total	27,603

Source: www.theice.com

Financial futures contracts presently trade in Canada on the ME. The ME trades contracts on three-month bankers' acceptances (which call for cash delivery), as well as on two-year and 10-year Government of Canada bonds. They also offer futures on 30-day overnight Repo Rates. Table 20-3 shows the 2007 volume for Canadian bankers' acceptances was 15.24 million contracts, while the volume for Government of Canada bonds was 9.3 million contracts. The ME trades several equity-based futures contracts, including those based on 200 times the S&P/TSX 60 Index and based on Sectoral Indexes, which all call for cash settlement. The 2007 volumes for the S&P/TSX 60 Index futures was 3.9 million contracts traded.

The centre of commodity futures trading in North America is the Chicago Board of Trade (CBT) and the Chicago Mercantile Exchange (CME); however, there are several other important exchanges in New York, including the Commodity Exchange, the New York Mercantile Exchange, the New York Coffee, Sugar and Cocoa Exchange, the New York Cotton Exchange, and the New York Futures Exchange. Futures markets in Canada are very small and much less developed than those in the US, both in terms of the variety of available products and trading volume. Real-World Returns 20-2 discusses the CME's takeover bid for Nymex Holdings Inc., which is the parent company for the New York Mercantile Exchange.

Table 20-3

Financial Futures Volumes on the ME (2006 and 2007)

Future Product Group	2006 Volume		2007 Volume	
Three-month Canadian Bankers' Acceptance Futures (BAX)	16,702,302	(60.6%)	15,237,958	(53.5%)
Ten-year Government of Canada Bond Futures (CGB)	7,691,797	(27.9%)	9,337,754	(32.8%)
Two-year Government of Canada Bond Futures (CGZ)	85,301	0.3%	6,363	0.0%
S&P Canada 60 Index Futures (SXF)	3,064,695	11.1%	3,885,872	13.6%
Sectoral Index Futures (SXA, SXB, SXH, SXY)	33,964	0.1%	25,507	0.1%
Total	27,578,059	100.00%	28,493,454	100.00%

Source: Montreal Exchange: www.m-x.ca

REAL-WORLD RETURNS 20-2

CME Takeover of Nymex

Chicago Mercantile Exchange parent CME Group Inc. said it had reached, as expected, a definitive agreement to buy New York Mercantile Exchange parent Nymex Holdings Inc. for around $9-billion (US), extending its position as the world's largest derivatives exchange.

CME's next challenge will be to expand its business in over-the-counter derivatives trading. In recent months, regulators have been increasingly worried about opaque trading in the over-the-counter markets, where Wall Street firms have endured billions of dollars in mortgage-related losses.

While trading methods haven't caused these losses, some regulators have explored whether increasing the role of exchanges could boost transparency and reduce volatility in mortgage-debt and credit default swaps markets.

Nymex gives CME an added boost in that area. In the years after Enron and other energy players imploded, the resulting fears about counterparty risk provided opportunity for Nymex to extend its business into over-the-counter energy trading. With the recent credit market meltdown, CME is likely to accelerate this push into financial derivatives that usually trade over-the-counter between large Wall Street firms.

CME and Nymex shares were both hit amid the broader selloff in financial services shares. But because exchanges don't take trading and investment risks like big brokerage firms do, they've held up much better than the worst-hit investment banks. A combined CME-Nymex, for instance, would have a market value of about $32-billion.

CME requires approval from antitrust officials and Nymex members, some of whom have been agitating for richer terms.

The latest exchange deal retains the terms disclosed when the companies revealed they were in exclusive talks in late January, though the value has fallen with CME stock since then, reflecting uncertainty over the regulatory climate for the fast-growing futures and options industry.

Credit Suisse analyst Howard Chen said in a research note that the financial terms are reasonable. He also said the deal makes sense strategically, and that—through CME's acquisition of the Chicago Board of Trade last July—"CME management has proven to be strong integrators."

Nymex holders will receive 0.1323 of CME shares and $36 in cash for each Nymex share, or about $95 each.

CME will also pay up to $500-million to buy the trading rights from 816 Nymex members.

CME officials said they were confident of securing regulatory approval in six to nine months.

Source: Cameron, Doug, and Lucchetti, Aaron, "Derivatives drive CME's takeover of Nymex," *The Globe and Mail*, March 18, 2008, p. B13.

International Futures Markets

European futures exchanges are quite competitive. Most of these systems are now fully automated order-matching systems. Euronext was the first pan-European exchange, created in 2000 by the merger of the Amsterdam, Brussels, and Paris markets. On June 1, 2006, the NYSE and Euronext agreed to combine in a merger of equals. The new NYSE Euronext provides a marketplace for trading cash and derivative securities.

Japan, which banned financial futures until 1985, has been very active in developing futures exchanges. Commodity futures markets account for most of the futures trading. Japan has seven commodity futures exchanges, each of which trades specific contracts. Most foreign brokers concentrate on a small number of financial futures, such as the Nikkei 225 stock index and 10-year government bonds.

Futures Contracts

A **futures contract** is a standardized, transferable agreement providing for the deferred delivery of either a specified grade and quantity of a designated commodity within a specified geographical area or of a financial instrument (or its cash value). The futures price at which this exchange will occur at contract maturity is determined today. The trading of futures contracts means only that commitments have been made by buyers and sellers; therefore, "buying" and "selling" does not have the same meaning in futures transactions as it does in stock and bond transactions. Although these commitments are binding because futures contracts are legal contracts, a buyer or seller can eliminate the commitment simply by taking an opposite position in the same commodity or financial instrument for the same futures month.

> **Futures Contract**
> Agreement providing for the future exchange of a particular asset between buyer and seller at a specified date for a specified amount.

Futures contracts trading on the ME is regulated by provincial securities administrators. Futures trading on the ICE Futures Canada is regulated by the Canadian Grain Commission, which oversees trading on this market under provisions in the Federal Grain Futures Act. Futures trading in the US is regulated by the Commodity Futures Trading Commission (CFTC), a federal regulatory agency that is responsible for regulating trading in all domestic futures markets. In practice, much of the supervisory functions are performed by the self-regulatory organizations, which include the Investment Industry Regulatory Organization of Canada (IIROC) and the exchanges in Canada, and the National Futures Association in the US. In addition, each futures exchange has a supervisory body to oversee its members. In Canada, investment advisors must pass the Derivatives Fundamental Course and the Futures Licensing Course before dealing in futures or options on futures.

CHECK YOUR UNDERSTANDING

20-1. What are the main categories of futures contracts available for trading?

20-2. Forward contracts and futures contracts are conceptually very similar. Distinguish between these two instruments and state one advantage of each.

THE STRUCTURE OF FUTURES MARKETS

> **learning objective 1**
> Describe the structure of futures markets.

Futures Exchanges

As noted, futures contracts are traded on designated futures exchanges, which are voluntary, non-profit associations, typically unincorporated. The exchange provides an organized marketplace where established rules govern the conduct of the members. It is financed by both membership dues and fees charged for services rendered.

There are a limited number of memberships for futures exchanges, which, like stock exchange seats, can be traded at market-determined prices. Members can trade for their own accounts or as agents for others. For example, floor traders trade for their own accounts, whereas floor brokers (or commission brokers) often act as agents for others. Futures commission merchants (FCMs) act as agents for the general public, for which they receive commissions. Thus, a customer can establish an account with an FCM, who, in turn may work through a floor broker at the exchange.

The Clearing Corporation

Similar to options markets, futures markets use a clearing corporation to reduce default risk and to arrange deliveries as required. The clearing corporations also ensure that participants maintain margin deposits or earnest money, to ensure fulfillment of the contract. The Canadian Derivatives Clearing Corporation (CDCC) currently issues and clears futures and futures options contracts traded on the ME, in addition to options contracts (discussed in Chapter 19), while ICE Clear Canada is the designated clearing house for ICE Futures Canada. Futures contracts presently include those on 30-day overnight Repo Rates, the US dollar, two-year and 10-year Government of Canada bonds, 3-month bankers' acceptances, the S&P/TSX 60 Index, the S&P/TSX Sectoral Indexes, and single stock prices. Futures options contracts include options on the 3-month bankers' acceptance futures.

Essentially, the clearing house for futures markets operates in the same way as the one for options, which was discussed in some detail in Chapter 19. Buyers and sellers settle with the clearing house, not each other, and it is actually on the other side of every transaction and ensures that all payments are made as specified. It stands ready to fulfill a contract if either buyer or seller defaults, thereby helping to facilitate an orderly market in futures. The clearing house makes the futures market impersonal, which is the key to its success because any buyer or seller can always close out a position and be assured of payment. The first failure of a clearing member in modern times occurred in the 1980s, and the system worked perfectly in preventing any customer from losing money. Finally, as explained below, the clearing house allows participants to easily reverse a position before maturity because it keeps track of each participant's obligations.

THE MECHANICS OF TRADING

Basic Procedures

Short Position

An agreement to sell an asset at a specified future date at a specified price.

Long Position

An agreement to purchase an asset at a specified future date at a specified price.

Offset

Liquidation of a futures position by an offsetting transaction—buyers sell their positions and sellers buy their positions prior to the settlement of the contract (delivery).

Because the futures contract is a commitment to buy or sell at a specified future settlement date, a contract is not really being sold or bought, as in the case of T-bills, bonds, or stocks, because no money is exchanged at the time the contract is negotiated. Instead, the seller and the buyer simply are agreeing to make and take delivery, respectively, at some future time for a price agreed upon today. As noted above, the terms buy and sell do not have the same meanings here. It is more accurate to think in terms of a

- **Short position** (seller), which commits a trader to deliver an item at contract maturity.
- **Long position** (buyer), which commits a trader to purchase an item at contract maturity.

Selling short in futures trading means only that a contract not previously purchased is sold. For every futures contract, someone sells it short and someone else holds it long. Like options, futures trading is a zero-sum game, because the amount that is gained by one party is lost by the one on the other side of the contract.

Unlike an options contract, which involves the *right* to make or take delivery, a futures contract involves an *obligation* to take or make delivery. However, futures contracts can be settled by delivery or by offset. Delivery, or settlement of the contract, occurs in months that are designated by the various exchanges for each of the items traded. Delivery occurs in less than 1 percent of all transactions.[2]

Offset is the typical method of settling a contract. Holders liquidate a position by arranging an offsetting transaction. This means that buyers sell their positions and sellers buy their positions some-

---

[2]Instruments that can be used in a delivery are explicitly identified in delivery manuals issued by the appropriate exchange.

time prior to delivery. Thus, to eliminate a futures market position, the investor simply does the reverse of what was done originally. As explained above, the clearing house makes this easy to accomplish. It is essential to remember that if a futures contract is not offset, it must be closed out by delivery.

Each exchange establishes price fluctuation limits on the various types of contracts. Typically, a minimum price change is specified. In the case of S&P/TSX 60 Index Futures, for example, it is 0.1 of an index point or $20 per contract. Maximum daily price limits are also in effect for futures contracts. For the S&P/TSX 60 Index futures contracts, a trading halt will be invoked in conjunction with the triggering of "circuit breakers" in the underlying stocks.

With stocks, short-selling can be done only on an uptick, but futures have no such restriction. Stock positions, short or long, can literally be held forever. However, futures positions must be closed out within a specified time, either by offsetting the position or by making or taking delivery.

There are no specialists on futures exchanges and each futures contract is traded in a specific pit, which is a ring with steps descending to the centre. Trading follows an auction market process in which every bid and offer competes without priority as to time or size. A system of open outcry is used, whereby any offer to buy or sell is communicated verbally and/or through the use of hand signals, and must be made to all traders in the pit.

Brokerage commissions on commodities contracts are paid on the basis of a completed contract (both a purchase and sale), rather than being charged for each purchase and each sale, as in the case of stocks. As with options, no certificates exist for futures contracts.

The open interest indicates contracts that are not offset by opposite transactions or delivery. That is, it measures the number of unliquidated contracts at any time, on a cumulative basis.[3] The open interest increases when an investor goes long on a contract and is reduced when the contract is liquidated.

Margin

Recall that in the case of stock transactions the term *margin* refers to the down payment in a transaction in which money is borrowed from the broker to finance the total cost. A **futures margin**, on the other hand, is not a down payment because ownership of the underlying item is not being transferred at the time of the transaction. Instead, it refers to the "good faith" (or earnest money) deposit made by both buyer and seller to ensure the completion of the contract. In effect, margin is a performance bond. In futures trading, unlike stock trading, margin is the norm.[4]

Each clearing house sets its own minimum initial margin requirements (in dollars), which are identical for both buyers and sellers of futures contracts. Furthermore, brokerage firms can require a higher margin and typically do so. The margin required for futures contracts, which is small in relation to the value of the contract itself, represents the equity of the transactor (either buyer or seller). It is not unusual for the initial margin to be in the range of $1,500 to $2,500 per contract, representing some 2 to 10 percent of the value of the contract. Since the equity is small, the risk is magnified.

Assume the initial margin is equal to 5 percent of the total value and an investor holds one contract in an account. If the price of the contract changes by 5 percent because the price of the underlying commodity changes by 5 percent, this is equivalent to a 100 percent change in the investor's equity. This example shows why futures trading can be so risky!

In addition to the initial margin requirement, each contract requires a maintenance margin below which the investor's net equity cannot drop.[5] The net equity is defined as the value of deposited funds (or the marginable value of marketable securities) plus the open profit or minus the open loss. If the market price of a futures contract moves adversely to the owner's position, the equity declines. Margin calls occur when the price goes against the investor causing the investor's equity to fall below the

Futures Margin
The good faith (earnest money) deposit made by the buyer or seller to ensure the completion of a contract.

---

[3]The open interest can be measured using either the open long positions or the open short positions but not both.
[4]Because no credit is being extended, no interest expense is incurred on that part of the contract not covered by the margin, as is the case when stocks are purchased on margin. With futures, customers often receive interest on margin money deposited. A customer with a large enough requirement (roughly, $10,000 and over) can use T-bills as part of the margin.
[5]Maintenance margins are usually set at 75 percent of the initial margin requirements.

maintenance margin level, requiring the transactor to deposit additional cash or to close out the account. Conversely, withdrawal of funds from a futures account can only occur if net equity rises above the initial margin requirement. To understand precisely how this works, we must first understand how profits and losses from futures contracts are debited and credited daily to an investor's account.

Marked to the Market

All profits and losses on a contract are credited and debited to each investor's account every trading day.

All futures contracts are **marked to the market** daily, which means that all profits and losses on a contract are credited and debited to each investor's account every trading day.[6] Those contract holders with a profit can withdraw the gains, whereas those with a loss will receive a margin call when the equity falls below the specified variation margin. This process is referred to as daily resettlement, and the price used is the contract's settlement price.[7]

Table 20-4 illustrates how accounts are marked to the market daily and how a margin call can occur. Consider an investor who buys a stock-index futures contract for 870 and a second investor who sells (shorts) the same contract at the same price. Assume these contracts are on the S&P/TSX 60 Index, where the contract is for $200 times the index value. For example, a price advance from 870 to 871, or one point, represents an advance of $200 on the contract value. Each investor puts up an initial margin of $3,480, representing 2 percent of the contract value of $174,000 ($200 × 870). For purposes of this example, we will assume the maintenance margin is $2,784, or 80 percent of the initial margin requirement.

Table 20-4 traces each investor's account as it is marked to the market daily. At the end of Day 1, the price of the contract has dropped to a settlement price of 869.5, a decrease of one half an index point, causing a change in the futures contracts values of $100. This amount is credited to the seller's account because the seller is short and the price has dropped. Conversely, $100 is debited to the buyer's account because the buyer is long, and the price moved adversely to this position. Table 20-4 shows that the current equity at the end of Day 1 is $3,380 for the buyer and $3,580 for the seller.

Table 20-4

An Example of Investor Accounts, Using Stock-Index Futures, Marked to the Market

	Buyer (Long)	Seller (Short)
Account after one day		
Original equity (initial margin)	$3,480	$3,480
Day 1 mark to the market	(100)	100
Current equity	$3,380	$3,580
Account after two weeks		
Original equity (initial margin)	$3,480	$3,480
Cumulative mark to the market	1,000	(1,000)
Current equity	4,480	2,480
Withdrawable excess equity	$1,000	
Margin call		$1,000

Two weeks have passed, during which time each account has been marked to the market daily. The settlement price on this contract has reached 875.00. The aggregate change in market value for each investor is the difference between the current price and the initial price multiplied by $200, the value of one point in price, which in this example is 875 − 870 = 5.00 × $200 = $1,000.

---

[6]This is not true of forward contracts, where no funds are transferred until the maturity date.
[7]The settlement price does not always reflect the final trade of the day. The clearing house establishes the settlement price at the close of trading.

As shown in Table 20-4, this amount is currently credited to the buyer because the price moved in the direction the buyer expected. Conversely, this same amount is currently debited to the seller, who is now on the wrong side of the price movement. Therefore, starting with an initial equity of $3,480, after two weeks the cumulative mark to the market is $1,000. This results in a current equity of $4,480 for the buyer and $2,480 for the seller. The buyer has a withdrawable excess equity of $1,000 because of the favourable price movement, whereas the seller has a margin call of $1,000, assuming a $2,784 maintenance margin. In other words, the investor would have received a margin call since his or her equity value fell below the required margin of $2,784. The seller would be required to add $1,000 ($3,480 − $2,480) to restore the account to the initial margin level of $3,480.

This example illustrates what is meant by the expression that futures trading, like options trading, is a zero-sum game. The aggregate gains and losses net to zero. The aggregate profits enjoyed by the winners must be equal to the aggregate losses suffered by the losers. This also means that the net exposure to changes in the commodity's price must be zero.

CHECK YOUR UNDERSTANDING

20-3. Suppose you purchased several futures contracts. At the expiration date, the contracts are worth considerably more than when purchased, so that you have a large gain. How can you be assured that the party who sold you these contracts will make good on their obligations?

20-4. The short position's loss is equal to the long position's gain. Explain.

USING FUTURES CONTRACTS

learning objective 2
Outline how futures work and what types of investors participate in futures markets.

Who uses futures and for what purpose? Traditionally, participants in the futures market have been classified as either hedgers or speculators. Because both groups are important in understanding the role and functioning of futures markets, we will consider each in turn. The distinctions between these two groups apply to financial futures as well as to the more traditional commodity futures.

Hedgers

Hedgers are parties at risk with a commodity or an asset, which means they are exposed to price changes. They buy or sell futures contracts in order to offset their risk. In other words, hedgers actually deal in the commodity or financial instrument specified in the futures contract. By taking a position opposite to that of one already held, at a price set today, hedgers plan to reduce the risk of adverse price fluctuations—that is, to hedge the risk of unexpected price changes. In effect, this is a form of insurance.

In a sense, the real motivation for all futures trading is to reduce price risk. With futures, risk is reduced by having the gain in the futures position offset the loss on the cash position and vice versa. A hedger is willing to forego some profit potential in exchange for having someone else assume part of the risk. Figure 20-1 illustrates the hedging process as it affects the return–risk distribution. Notice that the unhedged position not only has a greater chance of a larger loss, but also a greater chance of a larger gain.

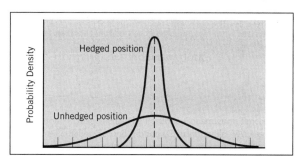

Figure 20-1
Return Distributions for Hedged and Unhedged Positions

The hedged position has a smaller chance of a low return, but also a smaller chance of a high return.

The use of hedging techniques illustrates the trade-off that underlies all investing decisions: Hedging reduces the risk of loss, but it also reduces the return possibilities relative to the unhedged position. Thus, hedging is used by investors who are uncertain of future price movements and who are willing to protect themselves against adverse price movements at the expense of possible gains. There is no free lunch!

How to Hedge with Futures

The key to any hedge is that a futures position is taken opposite to the position in the cash market. That is, the nature of the cash market position determines the hedge in the futures market.[8] A commodity or financial instrument held (in effect, in inventory) represents a long position because these items could be sold in the cash market. On the other hand, an investor who sells a futures contract has created a short position. Since investors can assume two basic positions with futures contracts, long and short, there are two basic hedge positions.

Short Hedge

A transaction involving the sale of futures (a short position) while holding the asset (a long position).

1. *The short (sell) hedge.* A cash market inventory holder must sell (short) the futures. Investors should think of short hedges as a means of protecting the value of their portfolios. Since they are holding securities, they are long in the cash position and need to protect themselves against a decline in prices. A **short hedge** reduces, or possibly eliminates, the risk taken in a long position.

2. *The long (buy) hedge.* An investor who currently holds no cash inventory (holds no commodities or financial instruments) is, in effect, short in the cash market; therefore, to hedge with futures requires a long position. Someone who is not currently in the cash market but who plans to be in the future and wants to lock in current prices and yields until cash is available to make the investment can use a **long hedge**, which reduces the risk of a short position.

Long Hedge

A transaction where the asset is currently not held but futures are purchased to lock in current prices.

Hedging is not an automatic process. It requires more than simply taking a position. Hedgers must make timing decisions as to when to initiate and end the process. As conditions change, hedgers must adjust their hedge strategy.

One aspect of hedging that must be considered is "basis" risk. The basis for financial futures often is defined as the difference between the cash price and the futures price of the item being hedged:[9]

$$\text{Basis} = \text{Cash price} - \text{Futures price}$$

The basis must be zero on the maturity date of the contract. In the interim, the basis fluctuates in an unpredictable manner and is not constant during a hedge period. Basis risk, therefore, is the risk that hedgers face as a result of unexpected changes in basis. Although changes in the basis will affect the hedge position during its life, a hedge will reduce risk as long as the variability in the basis is less than the variability in the price of the asset being hedged. At maturity, the futures price and the cash price must be equal, resulting in a zero basis. (Transaction costs can cause discrepancies.)

The significance of basis risk to investors is that risk cannot be entirely eliminated. Hedging a cash position will involve basis risk.

Speculators

In contrast to hedgers, speculators buy or sell futures contracts in an attempt to earn a return. They are willing to assume the risk of price fluctuations, hoping to profit from them. Unlike hedgers, speculators typically do not transact in the physical commodity or financial instrument underlying the futures contract. In other words, they have no prior market position. Some speculators are professionals who do this for a living; others are amateurs, ranging from the very sophisticated to the

---

[8]The cash position may currently exist (a cash hedge) or may be expected to exist in the future (an anticipatory hedge).
[9]The typical definition for basis is the cash price minus the futures price. For financial futures, the definition is often reversed.

novice. Although most speculators are not actually present at the futures markets, floor traders (or locals) trade for their own accounts as well as others and often take very short-term (minutes or hours) positions in an attempt to exploit any short-lived market anomalies.

Speculators are essential to the proper functioning of the futures market, absorbing the excess demand or supply generated by hedgers and assuming the risk of price fluctuations that hedgers wish to avoid. Speculators contribute to the liquidity of the market and reduce the variability in prices over time.

Why speculate in futures markets? After all, one could speculate in the underlying instruments. For example, an investor who believed interest rates were going to decline could buy Government of Canada bonds directly and avoid the bond futures market. The potential advantages of speculating in futures markets include

1. *Leverage*. The magnification of gains (and losses) can easily be 10 to 1.

2. *Ease of transacting*. An investor who thinks interest rates will rise will have difficulty selling bonds short, but it is very easy to take a short position in a bond futures contract.

3. *Transaction costs*. These are often significantly smaller in futures markets.

By all accounts, an investor's likelihood of success when speculating in futures is not very good and the small investor is up against stiff odds. Real-World Returns 20-3 discusses the benefits of using commodity futures to speculate on commodity prices.

REAL-WORLD RETURNS 20-3
Commodity Futures

One of the most effective ways to play the seemingly inexorable rise in commodity prices is also one of the scariest-sounding to the uninitiated.

Futures contracts present a higher level of complexity than stocks and funds, not to mention the risk of ruinous losses. But they also offer several advantages over traditional investments in energy, gold, metals and agricultural products. If you invest directly in a commodity producer, you're assuming the risk that the firm's management will make decisions that negatively affect returns. And unlike futures contracts, the performance of resource stocks and funds are influenced by the general mood on the stock markets.

You'll be relieved to know that you don't have to trade actual futures contracts to invest in commodity futures. An easier way is to buy an investment fund that tracks an index based on the performance of a diversified basket of commodity futures.

The idea of funds investing in the futures market recalls AGF Managed Futures, which was closed in 2007 after losing half its value in a year. But don't let that turn you off the idea of futures. Today, there is a small but growing collection of other choices in futures-based commodity fund vehicles.

One example is the Criterion Diversified Commodities Currency Hedged Fund, a tiny $20-million mutual fund offered by the mutual fund family Criterion Investments. Several other choices are available in the form of US-listed exchange-traded funds and exchange-traded notes, which are a cousin of the better-known ETF.

Two examples of exchange-traded notes are the iPath Dow Jones-AIG Commodity Index Total Return ETN, which trades on the New York Stock Exchange, and the awkwardly named Elements Linked to the Rogers International Commodity Index–Total Return, listed on the American Stock Exchange. Both of these ETNs track broad commodity indexes, but there are more specialized niche products available.

Commodity-based investments of all types have risen sharply in the past several years, so you're hardly buying low. But with oil and gold both hitting record highs this week, it's clear that

(continued)

REAL-WORLD RETURNS 20-3 *continued*

there's still a lot of momentum in the sector. If you see this continuing, and there are commodity bulls who do, then it's worth looking at funds and ETNs that expose you to commodity futures.

The Criterion diversified commodities fund is noteworthy in that it offers currency hedging, so your returns won't be affected by changes in the Canada–US exchange rate. Returns are linked to the Dow Jones-AIG Commodity Total Return index, which tracks 19 separate commodities. As of the end of January, the index was weighted 31 percent in energy, 21 percent in grains, 20 percent in base metals, 11 percent in gold and silver and the rest in so-called "softs"— sugar, cotton and coffee.

The Dow Jones-AIG Commodity Index is based on futures contracts, which set out a price and delivery date for a commodity at a future date. These contracts are continuously "rolled" or, in other words, sold before they reach their delivery date and replaced with new ones.

A benefit of using commodity futures is that they offer the prized attribute of negative correlation to the stock markets or, in other words, zigging when stocks zag. A study done a few years ago by finance professors at Yale University and the University of Pennsylvania's Wharton School found this to be true over the period stretching from mid-1959 through the end of 2004.

Here's a more recent example: In January, the Criterion diversified commodities fund made 3.3 percent while the S&P/TSX composite total return index fell 4.7 percent. "In the quest for non-correlated assets, commodity futures seem to have a great track record," said Ian McPherson, president of Criterion Investments.

Another benefit of commodity futures is that they insulate you from issues that can prevent the returns provided by resource stocks from mirroring the price of the commodity they produce. Mr. McPherson said an example would be the use of hedging, where a company presells some of its production at a set price and thus doesn't benefit if commodity prices soar. Resource stocks can also be held back by unexpected cost overruns and unforeseen events like Alberta's recent decision to raise the royalties paid by energy producers in the province.

The Yale/Wharton study found other benefits to investing in commodity futures. Returns came in at 5 percentage points higher than risk-free Treasury Bills on an average annual basis, and the risk profile was slightly lower than stocks. Also, commodity futures outperformed spot prices, which apply to immediate payment and delivery. The study's conclusion: Commodity futures are an attractive way to diversify traditional portfolios of stocks and bonds.

Exchange-traded notes are one way to get this diversification. Whereas an exchange-traded fund is a direct investment in a stock index, ETNs are bond-like securities that promise the returns of a particular index. ETNs fluctuate in value according to the value of their underlying index, just like ETFs. One way that they differ is in the fact that an ETN will mature at some point (the range is 15 to 30 years from now) at a value determined by the underlying index. There are no interest payments with ETNs, and no guarantee that you'll get your upfront investment back.

Sonia Morris, an analyst with the investment research firm Morningstar Inc. in Chicago, said there's another key difference between exchange-traded funds and notes. Because the notes are essentially debt, the creditworthiness of the backing financial institution is an important consideration. The iPath ETNs are backed by the giant global bank Barclays, while the Elements products are backed by the Swedish Export Credit Corp.

Ms. Morris said her favourite of the commodity futures ETNs is the broadly diversified iPath Dow Jones-AIG Commodity Index Total Return ETN. "I like it because it's not as energy-heavy as the competition. It caps the energy commodities, or any group, to one-third of assets, whereas some of the other supposedly diversified commodity ETNs have as much as 70 to 75 percent in energy."

If you're more interested in commodity sub-sectors, one to look at is the PowerShares DB Agriculture Fund. This ETF tracks an index called the Deutsche Bank Liquid Commodity

Index–Optimum Yield Agriculture index, which is equally weighted to corn, wheat, soybeans and sugar. Agricultural commodities have been hot lately and this fund has soared by about 25 percent this year, a contrast to the small losses posted by major stock indexes.

This is a classic example of the negative correlation that makes investing in commodities futures so attractive. Tempted to get it working in your portfolio? If so, be wary of commodities overload. Remember, your conventional mutual funds, ETFs and individual stock picks may have lots of exposure to the resource sector already. Also, let's not forget that commodities have come a long way in the past few years. They could go higher, but it's a long way down.

The Futures of Commodities

Here's a selection of investment funds that allow investors to get exposure to commodities through the futures market rather than through the shares of individual companies that produce oil, metals and agricultural products.

Fund	Category	MER	Ticker*	Info
Criterion Diversified Commodities Currency Hedged Fund	Mutual fund	2.65%	n/a	vengrowth.com
iPath Dow Jones-AIG Commodity Index Total Return ETN	Exchange-traded note	0.75%	DJP-N	ipathetn.com
iPath S&P GSCI Total Return Index ETN	ETN	0.75%	GSP-N	ipathetn.com
Elements Linked to the Rogers International Commodity Index - Total Return	ETN	0.75%	RJI-A	elementsetn.com
PowerShares DB Commodity Index Tracking Fund	Exchange-traded fund	0.83%	DBC-A	powershares.com
PowerShares DB Agriculture Fund	ETF	0.91%	DBA-A	powershares.com

*N=New York Stock Exchange; A = American Stock Exchange. Note: the iPath, Elements and PowerShares families also offer products for sector commodity investing. Source: AIG Financial Products Corp.

Source: Carrick, Rob, "Commodity futures can spice up your holdings," *The Globe and Mail*, March 8, 2008, p. B13.

CHECK YOUR UNDERSTANDING

20-5. The maturity date of a futures contract does not dictate realization of an investor's gains and losses. Explain.

20-6. What is the essential difference between a hedger and a speculator when it comes to owning the underlying asset involved in a futures contract?

FINANCIAL FUTURES

learning objective 3
Explain how financial futures are used.

Financial futures are futures contracts on equity indexes, fixed-income securities, and currencies. They give investors a greater opportunity to fine-tune the risk–return characteristics of their portfolios. This flexibility has become increasingly important as interest rates have become much more volatile and as investors have sought new techniques to reduce the risk of equity positions. The drastic changes that have occurred in the financial markets in the last 15 to 20 years could be said to have generated a genuine need for new financial instruments that allow market participants to deal with these changes.

The procedures for trading financial futures are the same as those for any other commodity, with a few exceptions. At maturity, stock-index futures settle in cash because it would be impossible or

Financial Futures
Futures contracts on financial assets such as equity indexes, fixed-income securities, and currencies.

impractical to deliver all the stocks in a particular index.[10] As mentioned previously, the price fluctuations for the S&P/TSX 60 Index contracts are in increments of 0.1 index points. Price fluctuations are limited since a trading halt is invoked in conjunction with the triggering of "circuit breakers" in the underlying stocks. US stock-index futures typically have no daily price limits (although they can be imposed).

We will divide the subsequent discussion of financial futures into the two major categories of contracts: interest rate futures and stock-index futures. Hedging and speculative activities within each category are discussed separately.

Interest Rate Futures

Bond prices are highly volatile, and investors are exposed to adverse price movements. Financial futures allow bondholders and others who are affected by volatile interest rates to transfer the risk. One of the primary reasons for the growth in financial futures is that portfolio managers and investors are trying to protect themselves against adverse movements in interest rates. An investor concerned with protecting the value of fixed-income securities must consider the possible impact of interest rates on the value of these securities.

Today's investors have the opportunity to consider several different interest rate futures contracts that are traded on various exchanges.[11] Available short-term interest rate futures contracts include Three-Month Canadian Bankers' Acceptance (BA) Futures (BAX), which have traded on the ME since April 1988, and 30-day Overnight Repo Rate Futures (ONX). The price fluctuation for BAX is 0.5 basis point (i.e., 0.005) or $12.5 per contract for the nearest three listed contract months, and 1 basis point (i.e., 0.01) or $25 per contract for all other contract months, while the price fluctuation for ONX is 0.5 basis point (i.e., 0.005) or $20.55 (one-half of 1/100 of one percent of $5,000,000 on a 30-day basis) per contract. There is no maximum daily price fluctuation for either contract during regular trading sessions.

Available long-term interest rate futures contracts include 10-year Government of Canada bond futures (CGB), which have traded on the ME since September of 1989, and two-year Government of Canada bond futures (CGZ). The contract unit for the CGBs is $100,000 nominal value of Government of Canada bonds, with a 6 percent coupon rate, while for the CGZs, the unit is $200,000 nominal value of Government of Canada bonds with a 4 percent coupon rate. Prices for 10-year bond futures are quoted per $100 nominal value (e.g., 97.58), just like bonds, while they are quoted per $1,000 par value for the two-year bond futures. The minimum price fluctuation is one basis point for CGB and .005 for CGZ (or $10 per contract for both), and the maximum daily price fluctuation is three points (or $3,000 per contract for CGB and $6,000 per contract for CGZ) above or below the previous day's settlement price.

In the United States, the Chicago Mercantile Exchange trades contracts on US Treasury bills and the one-month London Interbank Offered Rate (LIBOR), as well as Eurodollars. The Chicago Board of Trade (CBT) specializes in longer-maturity instruments, including Treasury notes (of various maturities, such as two-year and five-year) and Treasury bonds (of different contract sizes). Contracts are available on various maturities of US Treasury notes in trading units of $100,000, on Treasury bonds in units of $100,000, and on Treasury bills in trading units of $1 million. The contracts for US Treasury bonds are by far the most important.[12]

Hedging with Interest Rate Futures

We now consider an example of using interest rate futures to hedge an investment position. Our objective here is to illustrate the basic concepts involved in such a hedge. In this example, we concentrate on

---

[10]Gains and losses on the last day of trading are credited and debited to the long and short positions in the same way—marked to the market—as was done for every other trading day of the contract. Therefore, not only is there no physical delivery of securities, but also the buyer does not pay the full value of the contract at settlement.

[11]The Chicago Board of Trade launched financial futures trading in 1975 by opening trading in Government National Mortgage Association (GNMA or Ginnie Mae) bonds. The concept accelerated in 1976, when the International Monetary Market started trading in Treasury bills. Treasury bond futures appeared in 1977.

[12]Futures prices on Treasury bonds are quoted with reference to an 8 percent, 20-year bond. Settlement prices are translated into a settlement yield to provide a reference point for interest rates.

the short hedge since it is by far the more common and discuss the concept of the long hedge later in the chapter.

Short Hedge

Suppose an investor has a bond portfolio and wishes to protect the value of his or her position. This type of hedge is sometimes referred to as the inventory hedge.

EXAMPLE 20-1: SHORT HEDGING ON GOVERNMENT OF CANADA BONDS

On November 1, 2008, a pension fund manager holds $1 million principal (or face) value of 7 percent Government of Canada bonds due June 1, 2018. The manager plans to sell the bonds four months in the future but wishes to protect their value against a rise in interest rates. Since assets are owned (a long position), a short hedge is used.

To protect the position, the manager hedges by going short (selling) in the futures market. As illustrated in Table 20-5, the manager sells 10 March 2009 10-year Government of Canada bond contracts (since each contract is worth $100,000) at a current price of $106.58. In this example, we assume interest rates have risen by March 1, 2009. This produces a loss on the cash side (i.e., in the prices of the bonds held in the cash market) and a gain on the futures side (i.e., the manager can cover the short position at a lower price, which produces a profit). The futures position in this example more than offsets the cash market loss resulting in a net profit.[13]

The manager in this example was able to offset more than 100 percent of the cash market loss because the Government of Canada bond contract is based on 6 percent coupon bonds, whereas the manager was holding 7 percent bonds. In this example, the dollar value of lower coupon bonds changes by a larger amount than the dollar value of higher coupon bonds for the given change in yields. However, if interest rates had fallen, the loss on the futures contract would have exceeded the profit on the long bond position, resulting in a loss. One way to overcome this difference is to execute a "weighted" short hedge, adjusting the number of futures contracts used to hedge the cash position. For example, using the data in Table 20-5, selling 9.5 March contracts would result in a profit on the futures position of $62,510, which is very close to the $63,300 cash market loss.

Table 20-5

Illustration of Hedges Using Interest Rate Futures: A Short Hedge

Cash Market	Futures Market
	Short Hedge
November 1, 2008	November 1, 2018
Hold $1 million principal value of 7% Government of Canada bonds maturing June 1, 2018	Sells 10, 10-year Government of Canada bond futures contracts at a price of $106.58
Current market price: $112.61 (yielding 5.15%)	
March 1, 2009	March 1, 2009
Sells $1 million principal value of 7% bonds at $106.28	Buys 10 bond futures contracts at $100.00 (to close out position)
Loss: $63,300 (i.e., $1,062,800 − $1,126,100)	Gain: $65,800 (i.e., $1,065,800 − $1,000,000)

---

[13]The $65,800 gain on the futures contract in Table 20-5 is calculated as follows: The gain per contract is $6,580 = [(106.58 − 100) × 1,000]. Since each contract is based on par value of $100,000, the gain is: $65,800 = ($6,580 × 10 contracts).

Other Hedges

An alternative hedge is the anticipatory hedge, whereby an investor purchases a futures contract as an alternative to buying the underlying security. At some designated time in the future, the investor will purchase the security and sell the futures contract. This results in a net price for the security position at the future point in time that is equal to the price paid for the security minus the gain or loss on the futures position.

Consider an investor who would like to purchase an interest rate asset now but will not have the cash for three months. If rates drop, the asset will cost more at that point in time. By purchasing a futures contract on the asset now, as a hedge, the investor can lock in the interest rate implied by the interest rate futures contract. This may be a good substitute for not being able to lock in the current interest rate because of the lack of funds now to do so. At the conclusion of this transaction, the investor will pay a net price that reflects the ending cash price minus the gain on the futures contract. In effect, the gain on the futures increases the rate of return earned on the interest rate asset.

Speculating with Interest Rate Futures

Investors may wish to speculate with interest rate futures as well as to hedge with them. To do so, investors make assessments of likely movements in interest rates and assume a futures position that corresponds with this assessment. If the investor anticipates a rise in interest rates, he or she will sell one (or more) interest rate futures, because a rise in interest rates will drive down the prices of bonds and therefore the price of the futures contract. The investor sells a contract with the expectation of buying it back later at a lower price. Of course, a decline in interest rates will result in a loss for this investor, since the price will rise.

EXAMPLE 20-2: SPECULATING ON GOVERNMENT OF CANADA BONDS

Assume that in November, a speculator thinks interest rates will rise over the next month and wishes to profit from this expectation. The investor can sell one December 10-year Government of Canada bond futures contract at a price of 106.58. One month later, the price of this contract has declined to 100.03 because of rising interest rates. This investor would have a gain of 6.55, or $6,550, and could close out this position by buying an identical contract.

The usefulness of interest rate futures for pursuing such a strategy is significant. A speculator who wishes to assume a short position in bonds cannot do so readily in the cash market (either financially or mechanically). Interest rate futures provide the means to short bonds easily.

In a similar manner, investors can speculate on a decline in interest rates by purchasing interest rate futures. If the decline materializes, bond prices and the value of the futures contract will rise. Because of the leverage involved, the gains can be large; however, the losses can also be large if interest rates move in the wrong direction.

Stock-Index Futures

Until recently, futures on individual stocks were not available. Today, they are available in the US, but they only exist on a few stocks and they are traded very thinly, which is the reason they only lasted on the ME for a few years. Stock-index futures trading was initiated in 1982 with several contracts quickly being created. Investors can trade futures contracts on major market indexes such as the S&P/TSX 60 and the S&P/TSX Sectoral Indexes. The contract size of each of these indexes is $200 times the index level. Several other futures contracts are available on other stock indexes around the world

Delivery is not permitted in stock-index futures because of its impracticality. Instead, each remaining contract is settled by cash on the settlement day by taking an offsetting position using the price of the underlying index. For example, the cash settlement price for the S&P/TSX 60 Index is $200 times the official opening index value to the nearest two decimal places, on the final settlement day.

Stock-index futures offer investors the opportunity to act on their investment opinions concerning the future direction of the market. They need not select individual stocks, and it is easy to short the market. Furthermore, investors who are concerned about unfavourable short-term market prospects but remain bullish for the longer run can protect themselves in the interim by selling stock-index futures.

The contract size for each of these indexes is $200 times the index level. Several other futures contracts are available on other stock indexes around the world.

Hedging with Stock-Index Futures

Common stock investors hedge with financial futures for the same reasons that fixed-income investors use them. Investors, whether individuals or institutions, may hold a substantial stock portfolio that is subject to the risk of the overall market; that is, systematic risk. A futures contract enables the investor to transfer part or all of the risk to those willing to assume it. Stock-index futures have opened up new, and relatively inexpensive, opportunities for investors to manage market risk through hedging.

Chapter 8 pointed out the two types of risk inherent in common stocks: systematic risk and non-systematic risk. Diversification will eliminate most or all of the non-systematic risk in a portfolio, but not the systematic risk. Although an investor could adjust the beta of the portfolio in anticipation of a market rise or fall, this is not an ideal solution because of the changes in portfolio composition that might be required.

Investors can use financial futures on stock market indexes to hedge against an overall market decline. That is, investors can hedge against systematic or market risk by selling the appropriate number of contracts against a stock portfolio. In effect, stock-index futures contracts give an investor the opportunity to protect his or her portfolio against market fluctuations.

To hedge market risk, investors must be able to take a position in the hedging asset (in this case, stock-index futures) such that profits or losses on the hedging asset offset changes in the value of the stock portfolio. Stock-index futures permit this action because changes in the futures prices themselves generally are highly correlated with changes in the value of the stock portfolios that are caused by marketwide events. The more diversified the portfolio, and therefore the lower the non-systematic risk, the greater the correlation between the futures contract and the stock positions.

Figure 20-2 shows the price of the S&P 500 Index futures plotted against the value of a portfolio that is 99 percent diversified. That is, market risk accounts for 99 percent of its total risk.[14] The two track each other very closely, which demonstrates that stock-index futures can be very effective in hedging the market risk of a portfolio.

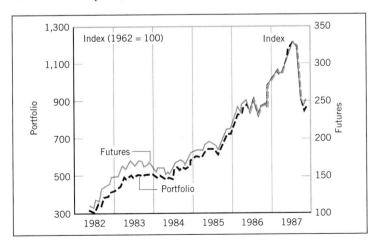

Figure 20-2
The Value of a Well-Diversified Stock Portfolio Versus the Price of the S&P 500 Index Futures

Source: Charles S. Morris, "Managing Stock Market Risk with Stock Index Futures," *Economic Review* 74 (June 1989), p. 9. Reprinted with permission from *Economic Review*.

---

[14]This example is taken from C. S. Morris, "Managing Stock Market Risk with Stock Index Futures," *Economic Review* 74 (June 1989), pp. 3–16.

Short Hedges

Since so much common stock is held by investors, the short hedge represents a natural type of contract for most investors. Investors who hold stock portfolios hedge market risk by selling stock-index futures, which means they assume a short position.

A short hedge can be implemented by selling a forward maturity of the contract. The purpose of this hedge is to offset (in total or in part) any losses on the stock portfolio with gains on the futures position. To implement this defensive strategy, an investor would sell one or more index futures contracts. Ideally, the value of these contracts would equal the value of the stock portfolio. If the market falls, leading to a loss on the cash (the stock portfolio) position, stock-index futures prices will also fall, leading to a profit for sellers of futures.

The reduction in price volatility that can be accomplished by hedging is shown in Figure 20-3, which compares the performance of a well-diversified portfolio (the unhedged one) with the same portfolio hedged by sales of the S&P 500 Index futures. Clearly, there is much less variability in the value of the hedged portfolio as compared to the value of the unhedged one. In fact, the volatility of the returns is 91 percent lower.[15] Notice in particular what happened in the great market crash of October 1987. The value of the unhedged portfolio fell some 19 percent, whereas the value of the hedged one fell only 6 percent.

Figure 20-3
The Value of a
Well-Diversified Portfolio
Versus the Value of the
Same Portfolio Hedged
by Sales of S&P 500
Index Futures

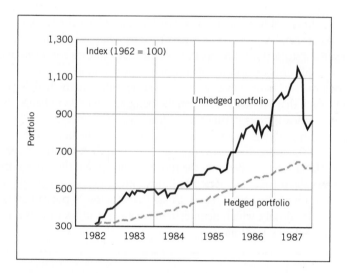

Source: Charles S. Morris, "Managing Stock Market Risk with Stock Index Futures," *Economic Review* 74 (June 1989), p. 10. Reprinted with permission from *Economic Review*.

Table 20-6 illustrates the concept of a short hedge using the S&P/TSX 60 Index futures contract when it is at 870. Assume that an investor has a portfolio of stocks valued at $175,000 that he or she would like to protect against an anticipated market decline. By selling one S&P/TSX 60 stock index future at 870, the investor has a short position of $174,000, because the value of the contract is $200 times the index quote. As the table illustrates, a decline in the stock market of 10 percent results in a loss on the stock portfolio of $17,500 and a gain on the futures position of $17,400 (ignoring commissions). Thus, the investor almost makes up on the short side what is lost on the long side.

---

[15]*Ibid*

Table 20-6

Examples of Short and Long Hedges Using Stock-Index Futures

	Short Hedge		
	Current Position	Position after a 10% Market Drop	Change in Position
(Long position) dollar value of portfolio	$175,000	$157,500	($17,500)
(Short position) sell one S&P/TSX 60 Index futures contract at 870.00	$174,000	$156,600	$17,400
Net gain or loss after hedging			($100)

	Long Hedge		
	Current Position	Position after a 10% Market Increase	Change in Position
(Long position) buy one S&P/TSX 60 Index futures contract at 870.00	$174,000	$191,400	$17,400
Amount of money to be invested in stocks (i.e., cost of stock position)	$175,000	$192,500	($17,500)
Net gain or loss after hedging			($100)

Long Hedges

The long hedger, while awaiting funds to invest, generally wishes to reduce the risk of having to pay more for an equity position when prices rise. Potential users of a long hedge include

- Institutions with a regular cash flow that use long hedges to improve the timing of their positions
- Institutions switching large positions who wish to hedge during the time it takes to complete the process (This could also be a short hedge.)

Assume an investor with $175,000 to invest believes that the stock market will advance but has been unable to select the stocks he or she wishes to hold. By purchasing one S&P/TSX 60 Index future, the investor will gain if the market advances. As shown in Table 20-6, a 10 percent market advance will increase the value of the futures contract $17,400. Although in this example, the investor has to pay 10 percent more (on average) for stocks purchased after the advance, he or she only pays $100 more than $175,000 because of the gain on the futures position.

Limitations of Hedging with Stock-Index Futures

Although hedging with stock-index futures can reduce an investor's risk, generally risk cannot be eliminated completely. As with interest rate futures, basis risk is present with stock-index futures. It represents the difference between the price of the stock-index futures contract and the value of the underlying stock index. A daily examination of Futures prices reported in the financial media will show that each of the indexes quoted under the respective futures contracts differs from the closing price of the contracts.[16]

---

[16]Futures prices are generally more volatile than the underlying indexes and therefore diverge from them. The index futures tend to lead the actual market indexes. If investors are bullish, the futures are priced at a premium, with greater maturities usually associated with greater premiums. If investors are bearish, the futures are normally priced at a discount, which may widen as maturity increases.

Basis risk, as it applies to common stock portfolios, can be defined as the risk that remains after a stock portfolio has been hedged.[17] Note here that stock-index futures hedge only systematic (market) risk. That is, when we consider a stock portfolio hedged with stock-index futures, the basis risk is attributable to nonsystematic (nonmarket or firm-specific) risk.

Figure 20-4a illustrates the effects of basis risk by comparing the value of a relatively undiversified portfolio with the price of the S&P 500 futures contract. In contrast to the 99 percent diversified portfolio in Figure 20-2, this one is only 66 percent diversified. Although the two series are related, the relationship is in no way as close as that illustrated in Figure 20-2. Therefore, stock-index futures will be less effective at hedging the total risk of the portfolio, as shown in Figure 20-4b. In this situation, the variance of returns on the hedged portfolio is only 27 percent lower than the unhedged position. Note that in the crash of October 1987, both portfolios fell sharply, demonstrating that the hedge was relatively ineffective. (It did better than the unhedged position, but not by much.)

From this analysis we can see that stock-index futures generally do not provide a good hedge for relatively undiversified portfolios.

Figure 20-4
(*a*) The Value of a Relatively Undiversified Stock Portfolio and the Price of the S&P 500 Index Futures Contracts (*b*) The Value of the Unhedged Portfolio and the Same Portfolio Hedged by Sales of S&P 500 Futures Contracts

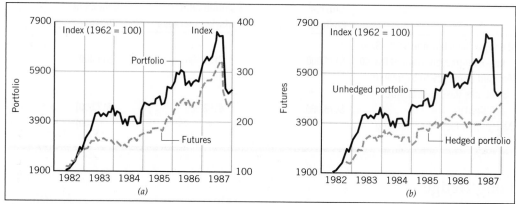

Source: Charles S. Morris, "Managing Stock Market Risk with Stock Index Futures," *Economic Review* 74 (June 1989), pp. 12–13. Reprinted with permission from *Economic Review*.

Index Arbitrage and Program Trading

Program trading (see Chapter 4) hit Bay and Wall Streets in the 1980s, and it has captured much attention and generated considerable controversy. It leads to headlines attributing market plunges at least in part to program trading, as happened on October 19, 1987, when North American and world stock markets plummeted. Because program trading typically involves positions in both stocks and stock-index futures contracts, the topic is within the general discussion of hedging.

Index Arbitrage

Exploitation of price differences between stock-index futures and the index of stocks underlying the futures contract.

Program trading is commonly used for portfolio insurance applications, which were discussed in Chapter 19. It is also used for **index arbitrage**, which refers to attempts to exploit the differences between the prices of the stock-index futures and the prices of the index of stocks underlying the futures contract. For example, if the S&P/TSX 60 Index futures price is too high relative to the S&P/TSX 60 Index, investors could short the futures contract and buy the stocks in the index. In theory, arbitrageurs should be able to build a hedged portfolio that earns arbitrage profits equaling the difference between the two positions. If the price of the S&P/TSX 60 Index futures is deemed too low, investors could purchase the futures and short the stocks, again exploiting the differences between the two prices.

If investors are to be able to take advantage of discrepancies between the futures price and the underlying stock-index price, they must be able to act quickly. Program trading involves the use of

---

[17]This discussion is based heavily on C. S. Morris, "Managing Stock Market Risk with Stock Index Futures," *Economic Review* 74 (June 1989), pp. 11–13.

computer-generated orders to coordinate buy and sell orders for entire portfolios based on arbitrage opportunities. The arbitrage occurs between portfolios of common stocks, on the one hand, and index futures and options, on the other. Large institutional investors seek to exploit differences between the two sides. Specifically, when stock-index futures prices rise substantially above the current value of the stock-index itself (e.g., the S&P/TSX 60 Index), they sell the futures and buy the underlying stocks, in "baskets" of several million dollars. Because the futures price and the stock-index value must be equal when the futures contract expires, these investors are seeking to "capture the premium" between the two, thereby earning an arbitrage profit. That is, they seek high risk-free returns by arbitraging the difference between the cash value of the underlying securities and the prices of the futures contracts on these securities. In effect, they have a hedged position and should profit regardless of what happens to stock prices.

Normally, program traders and other speculators "unwind" their positions during the last trading hour of the day the futures expire. At this time, the futures premium goes to zero, because, as noted, the futures price at expiration must equal the stock-index value.

The headlines about program trading often reflect the results of rapid selling by the program traders. For whatever reason, traders decide to sell the futures. As the price falls, stock prices also fall. When the futures price drops below the price of the stock index, enormous volumes of sell orders can be unleashed, which drive the futures prices even lower.

Speculating with Stock-Index Futures

In addition to the previous hedging strategies (and others not described), investors can speculate with stock-index futures if they wish to profit from stock market volatility by judging and acting on the likely market trends. Stock-index futures are effective instruments for speculating on movements in the stock market because minimal costs are involved in establishing a futures position, and stock-index futures mirror the market, offering just as much risk.

We can refer to one group of speculators as "active traders." These individuals are willing to risk their capital on price changes they expect to occur in the futures contracts. Such individuals are often sophisticated investors who are seeking the opportunity for large gains and who understand the risk they are assuming.

The strategies of active traders basically include long and short positions. Traders who expect the market to rise buy index futures. Because of the high leverage, the profit opportunities are great; however, the loss opportunities are equally great. The same is true for traders expecting a market decline who assume a short position by selling a stock-index futures contract. Selling a contract is a convenient way to go short on the entire market. It can be done at any time. (No wait for an uptick is required, as with stock short sales.)

Another form of speculation involves spreaders, who establish both long and short positions at the same time. Their objective is to profit from changes in price relationships between two futures contracts. There are two major types of spreads:

1. The intra-market spread, also known as a calendar or time spread. This spread involves contracts for two different settlement months, such as buying a March contract and selling a June contract.

2. The inter-market spread, also known as a quality spread. This spread involves two different markets, such as buying an S&P 500 Index contract and selling an S&P/TSX 60 Index contract (both for the same month).

Spreaders are interested in relative price as opposed to absolute price changes. If two different contracts appear to be out of line, the spreader hopes to profit by buying one and selling the other and waiting for the price difference to adjust. This adjustment may require the spread between the two contracts to widen in some cases and narrow in others.

Conclusion

We have focused our discussion of derivatives on options and futures in the last two chapters; however, many other derivatives are used frequently by investors, including swaps, which are discussed in Appendix 20B. The primary roles of most derivatives are hedging, speculation, and in some cases, price discovery.

CHECK YOUR UNDERSTANDING

20-7. Why are stock-index futures "cash settled" contracts?

20-8. If the cash price and the price of a futures contract must be the same at maturity of the contract, why do investors face basis risk? Would this type of risk be considered systematic or non-systematic?

S U M M A R Y

This summary relates to the learning objectives for this chapter.

1. **Describe the structure of futures markets.**

   Futures markets play an important role in risk management. Spot markets are for immediate delivery, while forward markets are markets for deferred delivery. An organized futures exchange standardizes the non-standard forward contracts, with only the price and number of contracts left for futures traders to negotiate.

2. **Outline how futures work and what types of investors participate in futures markets.**

   A futures contract designates a specific amount of a particular item to be delivered at a specified date in the future at a currently determined market price. Buyers assume long positions and sellers assume short ones. A short position indicates only that a contract not previously purchased is sold. Most contracts are settled by offset, whereby a position is liquidated by an offsetting transaction. The clearing house is on the other side of every transaction and ensures that all payments are made as specified. Contracts are traded on designated futures exchanges, which set minimum price changes and may establish daily price limits. Futures positions must be closed out within a specified time. There are no certificates and no specialists to handle the trading, so that each futures contract is traded in an auction market process by a system of open outcry. Margin, the norm in futures trading, is the good faith deposit made to ensure completion of the contract. All futures contracts are marked to the market daily; that is, all profits and losses are credited and debited to each investor's account daily. Hedgers buy or sell futures contracts to offset the risk in some other position. Speculators buy or sell futures contracts in an attempt to earn a return, and their role is valuable to the proper functioning of the market.

3. **Explain how financial futures are used.**

   Interest rate futures, one of the two principal types of financial futures, allow investors to hedge against, and speculate on, interest rate movements. Numerous contracts are available on both domestic and foreign instruments. Investors can, among other transactions, execute short hedges to protect their long positions in bonds. Stock-index futures are presently available on the S&P/TSX 60 and S&P/TSX Sectoral Indexes in Canada and on numerous international indexes. Investors can use stock-index futures to hedge the systematic risk of common stocks- that is, the risk of broad market movements. Short hedges protect a stock position against a market decline, and long hedges protect against having to pay more for an equity position because prices rise before the investment can be made. Index arbitrage refers to attempts to exploit the differences between the prices of the stock-index futures and the prices of the index of stocks underlying the futures contract.

KEY TERMS

Financial futures, p.681
Futures contract, p.673
Futures margin, p.675
Index arbitrage, p.688

Long hedge, p.678
Long position, p.674
Marked to the market, p.676
Offset, p.674

Short hedge, p.678
Short position, p.674
Swap (Appendix 20B), p.697

REVIEW QUESTIONS

20-1. What is a futures contract?

20-2. How do forward contracts differ from futures contracts?

20-3. Explain how futures contracts are valued daily and how most contracts are settled.

20-4. Describe the role of the clearing house in futures trading.

20-5. What determines whether an investor receives a margin call?

20-6. Explain the differences between a hedger and a speculator.

20-7. Given a futures contract on Government of Canada bonds, determine the dollar price of a contract quoted at 98.50.

20-8. Describe the differences between trading in stocks and trading in futures contracts.

20-9. How do financial futures differ from other futures contracts?

20-10. What is meant by basis? When is the basis positive?

20-11. Which side benefits from a strengthening basis? A weakening basis?

20-12. When might a portfolio manager with a bond position use a short hedge involving interest rate futures?

20-13. Is it possible to construct a perfect hedge? Why or why not?

20-14. What is the difference between a short hedge and a weighted short hedge using interest rate futures?

20-15. Why would an investor have preferences among the different stock-index futures?

20-16. What type of risk does stock-index futures allow investors to hedge? Why would this be desirable?

20-17. Explain how a pension fund might use a long hedge with stock-index futures.

20-18. When would an investor likely do the following?

    a. Buy a call on a stock index future.
    b. Buy a put on interest rate futures.

20-19. What is program trading? How does it work?

20-20. (Refer to Appendix 20A for this question.) With regard to futures options, fill in the following blanks with either "less than" or "greater than." The current futures price is 75.

    a. Put options with strike prices _____ 75 are in the money.
    b. Call options with strike prices _____ 75 are out of the money.
    c. Put options with strike prices _____ 75 are out of the money.
    d. Call options with strike prices _____ 75 are in the money.

20-21. How do futures markets serve a valuable economic purpose?

20-22. What are the two broad categories of futures contracts currently traded on futures exchanges?

20-23. How can buyers or sellers eliminate their commitments on a binding futures contract? How often are commitments carried out in the futures market?

20-24. What is meant by marked to market? Why is this done?

20-25. What is meant by the phrase, "futures trading is a zero-sum game"?

20-26. In what way are futures standardized?

PROBLEMS

20-1. An investor buys one March S&P/TSX 60 Index futures contract on February 1 at 870.00. The position is closed out after five days. The prices on the four days after purchase were 868.60, 869.80, 872.20, and 875.00. The initial margin is $7,000.

    a. Calculate the current equity on each of the next four days.
    b. Calculate the excess equity for these four days.
    c. Calculate the final gain or loss for the week.
    d. Recalculate (a), (b), and (c) assuming that the investor had been short over this same period.

20-2. Given the information in Problem 20-1, assume that the investor holds until the contract expires. Ignore the four days after purchase and assume that on the next to last day of trading in March the investor was long and the final settlement price on that date was 876. Calculate the cumulative profit.

20-3. Calculate the dollar gain or loss on Government of Canada bond futures contracts for the following transactions. In each case the position is held six months before closing it out.

    a. Sell 10 bond contracts at a price of 102.80 and buy 10 at 101.50.
    b. Sell 10 bond contracts at a price of 98.60 and buy 10 at 100.
    c. Buy 15 bond contracts at 110.20 and sell 15 at 112.30.
    d. Sell one bond contract at 98.50 and buy one at 105.

20-4. Assume a portfolio manager holds $1 million of 7.5 percent Government of Canada bonds due in two years. The current market price is 104.94, for a yield of 4.88 percent. The manager fears a rise in interest rates in the next three months and wishes to protect this position against such a rise by hedging in futures.

    a. Ignoring weighted hedges, what should the manager do?
    b. Assume two-year Government of Canada bond futures contracts are available at 102.11, and the price six months later is 99.20. If the manager constructs the correct hedge, what is the gain or loss on this position?
    c. The price of the Government of Canada bonds three months later is 101.31. What is the gain or loss on this cash position?
    d. What is the net effect of this hedge?

20-5. An investor buys a stock-index futures contract for $200 and the contract is for 400 times the index value. This contract requires an initial margin of 4 percent of the initial contract value. Assume the maintenance margin requirement is 75 percent of the initial margin. Assume that at the end of day one, the contract drops to a settlement price of $199.25. The price fluctuations for the next five days are as follows: $198.50, $199.75, $200.40, $201.05, $200.50.

    a. What is the initial margin required?
    b. Show how the account would look as it was marked to market daily.
    c. Did the buyer receive any margin calls? At what equity value would the buyer receive a margin call?
    d. What would the contract's settlement price have to drop to on the end of the seventh day for the buyer to receive a margin call?
    e. All other variables the same, show what the marked to market account would look like if the investor had been a seller rather than a buyer of this contract. Show how this contract is a zero-sum game.

20-6. On December 1, 2008, a portfolio manager holds $2 million face value of 10 percent Government of Canada bonds that mature on June 1, 2015. The manager is expecting an increase in interest rates, but he plans to sell the bonds in nine months.

The following is available in the market on December 1, 2008:
September 2009 10-year Government of Canada bond futures, with a contract size of $100,000 at a price of $131.49.
Current market price of 10-year, 10 percent Government of Canada bonds: $146.22

The following is available in the market on September 1, 2009:
March 1, 2010 10-year Government of Canada bond futures, with a contract size of $100,000 at a price of $119.21.
Current market price of 10-year, 10 percent Government of Canada bonds: $134.89

    a. In order to protect the value of the manager's position, show how the manager can hedge against the expected increase in interest rates by investing in 20 bond futures contracts. Did the hedge result in an overall gain or loss?

    b. In order to execute a weighted short hedge, how many futures contracts should have been used to hedge the cash position?

    c. What would you have expected the manager to do if he or she had strongly expected interest rates to decline rather than increase over the period?

20-7. Use a spreadsheet to find the price for the following interest rate swap. Swaps are discussed in Appendix 20B.

XYZ Corp. has a $5 million loan on which it pays a floating interest rate. At the beginning of each year the rate is set equal to the 1-year spot rate for corporate bonds of a similar quality. The company's CFO believes that interest rates will rise over the next few years, and has decided to enter into a 5- year swap agreement which will provide a fixed interest rate of 5.8838 percent per year on the amount of the loan. The spot rates on corporate debt are shown in the following table.

Maturity (Years)	Spot Rate
1	4.0000%
2	4.5000%
3	5.0000%
4	5.5000%
5	6.0000%

    a. Calculate the implied forward interest rate for each year (see Chapter 12).

    b. While the fixed-rate interest payments are known, the future floating rate interest payments cannot be known with certainty. However, their expected value is determined by the implied forward rates computed above. Under the swap contract, the company will pay (or receive) an interest payment at the end of each year based on the difference between the fixed rate and the floating rate set at the start of the year. Calculate the expected amount of each of these payments.

    c. Use the spot rates provided to discount the five expected payments to the present.

    d. Determine the actual cost of the swap by adding the present values of all five expected interest payments.

    e. Your figure in part d should be very small (close to zero). Does this make sense given that the loan amount was $5 million?

PREPARING FOR YOUR PROFESSIONAL EXAMS

CFA PRACTICE QUESTIONS

20-1. Futures contracts differ from forward contracts in the following ways:

   i. Futures contracts are standardized.
   ii. For futures, performance of each party is guaranteed by a clearing house.
   iii. Futures contracts require a daily settling of any gains or losses.
   a. i and iii only
   b. i, ii, and iii
   c. i and ii only
   d. ii and iii only

20-2. Trader A buys 50 contracts of wheat from Trader B. Later, Trader A sells 30 of these contracts to Trader C. Trader B also sells 40 wheat contracts to Trader D. After all of these trades what is the open interest in wheat?

   a. 50
   b. 70
   c. 90
   d. 120

20-3. A silver futures contract requires the seller to deliver 5,000 Troy ounces of silver. An investor sells one July silver futures contract at a price of $8 per ounce, posting a $2,025 initial margin. If the required maintenance margin is $1,500, what is the first price per ounce at which the investor would receive a maintenance margin call?

   a. $5.92
   b. $7.89
   c. $8.11
   d. $10.80

20-4. In futures trading, the minimum level to which an equity position may fall before requiring additional margin is the:

   a. initial margin.
   b. variation margin.
   c. cash flow margin.
   d. maintenance margin.

20-5. Which of the following statements about future contracts is false?

   a. Offsetting trades rather than exchanges for physicals are used to close most futures contracts.
   b. The major difference between forwards and futures is that futures contracts have standardized contract terms.
   c. To safeguard the clearing house, the exchange requires traders to post margin and settle their accounts on a weekly basis.
   d. The futures clearing house allows traders to reverse their positions without having to contract the other side of the initial trade.

CFA CURRICULUM AND SAMPLE EXAM QUESTIONS (©CFA INSTITUTE)

20-1. A private transaction in which one party agrees to make a single fixed payment in the future and another party agrees to make a single floating payment in the future is best characterized as a(n):

   a. futures contract.
   b. forward contract.
   c. exchange-traded contingent claim.
   d. over-the-counter contingent claim.

20-2. A public standardized transaction that constitutes a commitment between two parties to transfer the underlying asset at a future date at a price agreed upon now is best characterized as a(n):

   a. swap.
   b. futures contract.
   c. exchange-traded contingent claim.
   d. over-the-counter contingent claim.

20-3. The party agreeing to make the fixed-rate payment might also be required to make the variable payment in:

   a. an equity swap, but not an interest rate swap.
   b. an interest rate swap, but not an equity swap.
   c. both an equity swap and an interest rate swap.
   d. neither an equity swap nor an interest rate swap.

20-4. Agrawal Telecom is considering issuing $10,000,000 of 6.75 percent fixed coupon bonds to finance an expansion. Alternatively, Agrawal could borrow the funds in the Eurodollar market using a series of 6-month LIBOR contracts. A swap contract matching the maturity of the 6.75 percent coupon bonds is available. The swap uses 6-month LIBOR as the floating rate component. Identify the interest rate swap that Agrawal should use to evaluate the two alternatives.

   a. Agrawal would use a pay fixed, receive floating interest rate swap.
   b. Agrawal would use a pay floating, receive fixed interest rate swap.
   c. Agrawal would use a total return equity payer swaption to evaluate the two borrowing options.
   d. Given that Agrawal is a US corporation and is considering borrowing in the Eurodollar market, Agrawal would need to use a currency swap to evaluate the transaction.

20-5. The current price of an asset is 100. An out-of-the-money American put option with an exercise price of 90 is purchased along with the asset. If the break-even point for this hedge is at an asset price of 114 at expiration, then the value of the American put at the time of purchase must have been:

   a. 0.
   b. 4.
   c. 10.
   d. 14.

APPENDIX 20A

FUTURES OPTIONS

In Chapter 19 we discussed options (puts and calls) on common stocks. In this chapter, we discussed interest rate futures and stock-index futures. Futures options is a combination of the two. The development of this financial instrument is a good example of the ever-changing nature of financial markets, where new instruments are developed to provide investors with opportunities that did not previously exist.

Put and call options are offered on both interest rate futures and stock-index futures. In Canada in 2007, 748,991 option contracts on futures were traded, accounting for 5.3 percent of the total ME exchange-traded options. Available financial futures options in Canada include options on three-month BA futures, which trade on the ME. In addition, options trade on the ICE Futures Canada on canola futures, domestic feed wheat futures, and western domestic feed barley futures.

There are several options on futures contracts available in the United States, including (but not limited to)

- Options on foreign exchange: Pound, mark, Swiss franc, yen, Canadian dollar, and a US dollar index
- Options on interest rate futures: US Treasury bills, notes, and bonds and municipal bonds
- Options on stock-index futures: The S&P 500 Index (traded on the Chicago Mercantile Exchange (CME)), the NYSE Composite Index (traded on the New York Futures Exchange), and the Nikkei 225 Stock Average (CME)
- Options on commodities: Agricultural, oil, livestock, metals, and lumber.

Recall from Chapter 19 that an option provides the purchaser with the right, but not the obligation, to exercise the claim provided by the contract. An option on a futures contract gives its owner the right to assume a long or short position in the respective futures contract. If this right is exercised, the holder's position will be at the exercise (strike) price of the option that was purchased. For example, the exerciser of a call option buys the futures contract at the exercise price stated in the call option.

The key elements of an option contract on a particular futures contract are the exercise price and the premium. As in the case of stock options, premiums are determined in competitive markets. Each put and call option is either in the money or out of the money. With an in-the-money call option, the exercise price is less than the current price of the underlying futures contract. (If the exercise price is greater than the current price, it is out of the money.) For put options, the reverse is true.

Options on futures contracts can serve some of the same purposes as the futures contracts themselves. Specifically, both futures contracts and options can be used to transfer the risk of adverse price movements from hedgers to speculators. For example, a portfolio manager with bond holdings (a long position) who expects a rise in interest rates can hedge against the risk of the capital losses resulting from such a rise by selling futures contracts on government bonds. Alternatively, futures options on government bonds can be used to hedge against this risk because the option's price will change in response to a change in the price of the underlying commodity.

A rise in interest rates is bearish (bond prices will fall), therefore, the portfolio manager would either buy a put or sell a call. The value of these options would rise as the price of the futures contract declined. On the other hand, an investor bullish on bond prices (i.e., one who expects interest rates to decline) would either buy a call or sell a put. In addition to these simple strategies, a number of spreading techniques can be used with options on bond futures.

The general appeal of options on futures contracts is the limited liability assumed by the purchaser. Unlike a futures contract, which has to be settled by some means (say, by offset), once the contract is bought the purchaser has no additional obligation. Moreover, unlike futures, the purchaser is not subject to margin calls. Even if a speculator in futures is ultimately correct in his or her expectations, margin calls in the interim can wipe out all the equity. A writer (seller) of an option on a futures contract, however, does have an obligation to assume a position (long or short) in the futures market at the strike price if the option is exercised. Sellers must deposit margin when opening a position.

APPENDIX 20B

OTHER DERIVATIVE SECURITIES

Swaps

A **swap** is a type of cash settled forward agreement; however, unlike traditional forward agreements, there is a series of predetermined payments. In other words, one could view swaps as a series of forward agreements. The swap market is used extensively by banks for short-term (and to a much lesser extent for long-term) financing. Three types are discussed below: (1) interest rate swaps, (2) foreign exchange or currency swaps, and (3) swaptions.

Swap
A cash settled forward agreement with a series of predetermined payments.

1. *Interest rate swaps* represent agreements to exchange cash flows on an agreed upon formula. It is important to note that the notional or principal amount is not exchanged, either at initiation or maturity of the contract. The most common formula involves the exchange of payments based on a fixed interest rate, for floating rate payments of interest, based on some notional amount of principal. This is often referred to as a "plain vanilla" interest rate swap. Margins are required by both parties (unless one counter-party is a large chartered bank), and the floating rates are reviewed periodically. Floating rates are typically tied to Canadian bankers' acceptance rates or the six-month LIBOR (London Interbank Offered Rate).

EXAMPLE 20B-1: "PLAIN VANILLA" INTEREST RATE SWAP

The notional value for a swap is $10 million and the term is three years. Party A agrees to make fixed annual payments to Party B, based on a fixed interest rate of 4 percent (i.e., A agrees to pay B $400,000 per year). Party B agrees to make payments to Party A based on the prevailing bankers' acceptance rate plus 50 basis points (or 0.50 percent).

On the day the swap was arranged, the BA rate was 3.75 percent, so the floating rate to be paid by Party B would be 4.25 percent (or $10 million $\times$ 0.0425 = $425,000). As a result, the net payment would have B pay A $25,000 ($425,000−$400,000). However, this is subject to change because the BA rate is a floating rate and its level changes on a daily basis. For example, the floating rate paid by Party B could fall to 3 percent (if the BA rate fell to 2.5 percent), or rise to 5 percent (if the BA rate rose to 4.5 percent). Obviously, B feels the floating rate will fall, while A feels it will rise, unless one of the parties has entered into the agreement for hedging purposes.

2. *Foreign exchange swaps or currency swaps* are similar to interest rate swaps; however, there are two important differences:
   i. The cash flows are denominated in two different currencies, and hence the notional amount is actually exchanged at the beginning and end of the contract.
   ii. These swaps do not necessarily have to be fixed for floating, but can be fixed for fixed.

Currency swaps involve two market transactions—for example, the sale of US dollars to buy Canadian dollars today (the near date), and the sale of Canadian dollars and purchase of US dollars at a specified future date (the far date) and price. The difference between the spot price and forward price is referred to as a premium if the forward is greater than the spot. If it is less, it is called a discount. The size of the premium or discount depends on the interest rate differential between the two currencies.

EXAMPLE 20B-2: CURRENCY SWAP

Spot rate is $1.0006 Canadian per US$, term is 30 days, discount is 0.0004, so the forward price is (spot − discount) $1.0002 per US$. Suppose the US funds can be borrowed at a 3.50 percent interest rate.

This implies the equivalent cost of borrowing funds in Canada is: 3.50% − [(discount/spot) × (365/30) × 100] = 3.50% − 0.49% = 3.01%.

3. *Swaptions* are options that give the holder the right, but not the obligation, to enter into a swap agreement. The advantage of swaptions over straight swaps is the limited risk characteristics, as well as the non-obligation by the buyer of the swaption contract. In other words, a swap obligates a party to a future transaction, while a swaption provides the right, but not the obligation, to enter into such future transactions.

Embedded Options

Embedded options include features such as convertible, callable, retractable, and extendible features associated with some debt or preferred share issues. Convertibles enable the holder to convert the bond (or preferred shares) into common shares at a predetermined conversion price—hence they have an embedded call option. The price of this option can be inferred by the difference between the price of a convertible bond, and the price of a similar non-convertible bond (which should sell for less since it has no conversion feature attached).

Callable bonds enable the corporation to buy back the bonds at a predetermined call price, which implies the buyer of a callable bond is selling the bond issuer a call option. The cost of this option would be the difference between the price of a callable and a similar non-callable bond. The non-callable bonds would sell for a greater price because they do not provide the bond issuers with the call privilege (the risk of which is borne by the bondholder).

Retractable bonds enable the bondholder to sell the bond back to the corporation at a predetermined price. This is analogous to the bond issuer writing a put option on the bond, which is held by the bond owner. Once again, the option price can be viewed as the difference in the prices of similar retractable versus non-retractable bonds (which will sell for less because they do not contain the retraction privilege).

An extendible bond allows the bondholder to extend the maturity date of the bonds beyond some more recent maturity date. This can be thought of as a short-term bond, with an option to purchase an additional bond at a predetermined price. Hence they include an embedded call option that is held by the bond owner, and was written by the bond issuer. As a result of this privilege, extendible bonds sell for a greater price than similar non-extendible bonds, the difference representing the cost of the embedded call option.

CHAPTER 21

PORTFOLIO MANAGEMENT

As you near the end of your study of investing, in order to be able to handle your inheritance, you realize that you have covered a number of important topics. However, it sometimes seems that you are seeing the trees but not the forest. It strikes you that all of this might make more sense if there were a clear framework for thinking about all the issues you need to consider. And, in fact, there is. Portfolio management can indeed be thought of as a process, one that is laid out in an orderly, sensible manner. By doing this, you see where the various pieces fit, and you are less likely to overlook one or more important issues.

Learning Objectives

After reading this chapter, you should be able to

1. Discuss why portfolio management should be considered a process.
2. Describe the steps involved in the portfolio management process.
3. Assess related issues such as asset allocation.

CHAPTER PREVIEW

In this chapter, we discuss how and why portfolio management should be thought of as a process. An understanding of the process allows any portfolio manager to apply a consistent framework to the management of a portfolio for any investor, whether individual or institutional. We walk through the steps of the process, from developing an investment policy to measuring and evaluating portfolio performance. We also consider related topics such as taxes, protection against inflation, how expectations about future market returns are formed, and the life cycle of investors.

PORTFOLIO MANAGEMENT AS A PROCESS

learning objective 1
Discuss why portfolio management should be considered a process.

Portfolio management involves a series of decisions and actions that must be made by every investor, individual or institutional. Portfolios must be managed whether investors follow a passive or an active approach to selecting and holding their financial assets such as stocks and bonds. As we saw when we examined portfolio theory, the relationships among the various investment alternatives that are held as a portfolio must be considered if an investor is to hold an optimal portfolio and achieve his or her investment objectives.

Portfolio management can be thought of as a process. Having the process clearly in mind is very important and allows investors to proceed in an orderly manner. In this chapter, we outline the investment management process, making it clear that a logical and orderly flow does exist. This process can be applied to each investor and investment manager. Details may vary from client to client, but the process remains the same. We formalize this process and elaborate in the remainder of this section.

The portfolio management process has been described by Maginn and Tuttle in their book that forms the basis for portfolio management as envisioned by the CFA Institute (formerly AIMR) and advocated in its curriculum for the CFA designation.[1] This is also the approach advocated by the Canadian Securities Course. It is important to develop a standardized framework rather than treating portfolio management on an ad hoc basis, matching investors with portfolios on an individual basis, one by one. Portfolio management should be structured so that any investment organization can carry it out in an effective and timely manner without serious omissions.

Maginn and Tuttle emphasize that portfolio management is a process, integrating a set of activities in a logical and orderly manner. Given the feedback loops and monitoring that are included, the process is both continuous and systematic. It is a dynamic and flexible concept that encompasses all portfolio investments, including real estate, precious metals, and other real assets.

The portfolio management process extends to all types of investment organizations and styles. In fact, Maginn and Tuttle specifically avoid advocating how the process should be organized, who should make the decisions, and so forth. Each investment management organization must decide for itself how best to carry out its activities, consistent with viewing portfolio management as a process.

Having structured portfolio management as a process, any portfolio manager can execute the necessary decisions for an investor. The process provides a framework and a control over the diverse activities involved and allows every investor, individual or institutional, to be accommodated in a systematic, orderly manner.

As outlined by Maginn and Tuttle, portfolio management is an ongoing process by which

1. Objectives, constraints, and preferences are identified for each investor. This leads to the development of explicit investment policies.

2. Strategies are developed and implemented through the choice of optimal combinations of assets. (This step relates to our discussion of portfolio theory in Part II.)

3. Market conditions, relative asset mix, and the investor's circumstances are monitored.

---

[1]John L. Maginn and Donald L. Tuttle, editors, *Managing Investment Portfolios*, Second Edition (Charlottesville, VA: Association for Investment Management and Research, 1990). This chapter follows the format advocated in this book and is indebted to it for much of the discussion.

4. Portfolio adjustments are made as necessary to reflect significant changes that have occurred.

Figure 21-1 explains the portfolio construction, monitoring, and revision process in more detail. Notice that we begin with the specification of investor objectives, constraints, and preferences. This specification leads to a statement of portfolio policies and strategies. Next, capital market expectations for the economy, as well as individual assets, are determined and quantified.

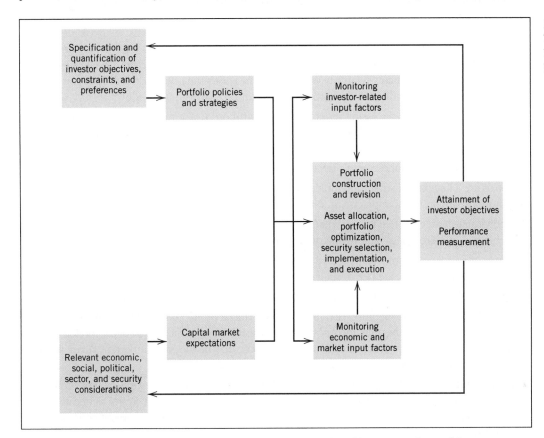

Figure 21-1
The Portfolio Construction, Monitoring, and Revision Process

Source: John L. Maginn, Donald L. Tuttle, Dennis W. McLeavey, and Jerald E. Pinto, "The Portfolio Management Process and the Investment Policy Statement," in *Managing Investment Portfolios*, Third Edition, p.6. Hoboken: John Wiley & Sons, Inc.

The combination of portfolio policies/strategies and capital market expectations provides the investment manager with the basis for portfolio construction and revision. This includes the asset allocation decision (discussed in Chapter 8), a very important determinant of the success of the investment program. Also included here are the portfolio optimization and security selection stages of portfolio management; that is, we must determine appropriate portfolio strategies and techniques for each asset class and the selection of individual securities.

Monitoring is an important part of the process. As indicated in Figure 21-1, the portfolio manager should monitor both investor-related input factors as well as economic and market input factors and rebalance as necessary. For example, the manager may need to respond to any changes in investor objectives and constraints and/or capital market expectations. Finally, the process concludes with the attainment of investor objectives. In order to assess success, we must measure and evaluate portfolio performance, which is discussed in Chapter 22.

We will discuss these steps in more detail below, but first we consider the differences between individual and institutional investors. As we noted in Chapter 2, investors can invest directly and indirectly through institutional investors, and an understanding of both types of investment decision making is important.

Individual Versus Institutional Investors

Significant differences in objectives, constraints, and preferences exist among investors. We are primarily interested in the viewpoint of the individual investor; however, the basic investment management process applies to all investors, individuals and institutions. Furthermore, individuals are often the beneficiaries of the activities of institutional investors, and an understanding of how institutional investors fit into the investment management process is desirable.

A major difference between the two occurs with regard to time horizons. As explained below, for individual investors it is often useful to think in terms of a life cycle as people go from the beginning of their careers to retirement. This approach has little meaning for institutional investors because they generally maintain a relatively constant profile across time. Ronald Kaiser has summarized the differences between individual investors and institutional investors as follows:[2]

1. Individuals define risk as "losing money" while institutions use a quantitative approach, typically defining risk in terms of standard deviation (as in the case of the data presented in Chapter 6).

2. Individuals can be characterized by their personalities, while for institutions we consider the investment characteristics of those with a beneficial interest in the portfolios managed by the institutions.

3. Goals are a key part of what individual investing is all about, along with their assets, while for institutions we can be more precise as to their total package of assets and liabilities.

4. Individuals have great freedom in what they can do with regard to investing, while institutions are subject to numerous legal and regulatory constraints.

5. Taxes often are a very important consideration for individual investors, whereas many institutions, such as pension funds, are free of such considerations.

The implications of all of this for the investment management process are as follows:

• For individual investors: Because each individual's financial profile is different, an investment policy for an individual investor must incorporate that investor's unique factors. In effect, preferences are self-imposed constraints. To investor A, after-tax income may be the most important factor, while for investor B, safety of principal may be the paramount consideration.

• For institutional investors: Given the increased complexity in managing institutional portfolios, it is critical to establish a well-defined and effective policy. Such a policy must clearly delineate the objectives being sought, the institutional investor's risk tolerance, and the investment constraints and preferences under which it must operate.

The primary reason for establishing a long-term investment policy for institutional investors is twofold:

1. It prevents arbitrary revisions of a soundly designed investment policy.

2. It helps the portfolio manager to plan and execute on a long-term basis and resist short-term pressures that could derail the plan.[3]

CHECK YOUR UNDERSTANDING

21-1. Investment management is thought of as a process involving specific steps and decisions. Are investment management firms restricted as to how they structure themselves if they follow this process?

21-2. If individuals are to a large extent free to act as they choose, why do they need an investment policy?

---

[2]Ronald W. Kaiser, "Individual Investors," in John L. Maginn and Donald L. Tuttle, editors, *Managing Investment Portfolios*, Second Edition (Charlottesville, VA: Association for Investment Management and Research, 1990).
[3]"Portfolio Management: The Portfolio Construction Process," in *1997 CFA Level I Candidate Readings* (Charlottesville, VA: Association for Investment Management and Research 1997), p. 177.

FORMULATE AN APPROPRIATE INVESTMENT POLICY

The determination of portfolio policies—referred to as the investment policy—is the first step in the investment process. It summarizes the objectives, as well as the constraints and preferences, for the investor. A recommended approach in formulating an **investment policy** is simply to provide information, in the following order, for any investor, individual or institutional:

1. Objectives:
   - return requirements
   - risk tolerance

2. Constraints and preferences:
   - liquidity   • taxes
   - time horizon   • unique preferences and circumstances
   - laws and regulations

Real-World Returns 21-1 discusses the importance to investors of identifying their risk tolerance, investment horizon, investment knowledge, financial situation, and how to use these inputs to help identify realistic investment objectives. These points are elaborated on in the remainder of this section.

learning objective 2
Describe the steps involved in the portfolio management process.

Investment Policy
The first step in the portfolio management process, involving investor objectives, constraints, and preferences.

REAL-WORLD RETURNS 21-1

What Every Investor Should Know

Defining Your Investment Objectives
Each investor has unique investment objectives that are affected by short- and long-term needs and requirements. This factsheet will help you work with your financial advisor to determine how to best meet your financial goals.

Setting Goals and Identifying Needs: This step provides the foundation of your relationship with a financial advisor. Step back and reflect on your short- and long-term goals, such as funding college for children, business expansion, travel plans, or retirement needs. You should identify these goals with your financial advisor so that his or her recommendations will directly address your needs.

Risk Tolerance: Risk is often defined as portfolio volatility, or the fluctuation in the value of your assets over time. At a personal level, risk can mean the chance you won't achieve your goals or the risk of losing your savings. Understanding your tolerance for risk, which differs for each investor, is key to choosing an investment program.

Your tolerance for risk is a very personal characteristic that may be difficult to determine and may change over time. Your emotional make-up plays a role in your willingness to take risk. But your objective ability to bear risk, given your wealth and financial needs, is important too. Your age may also affect how much risk you can assume. As you become older, there is less time to recover from poor investment results and your appetite to take risk may change—but your wealth and circumstance will probably change too. You may also have different risk tolerances for different parts of your portfolio, for example, money intended for retirement and educational funds for children.

Income: Both your absolute income level and your return requirement may influence your investment decisions. Taxable investors—those who currently pay taxes on their investments rather than those who defer them—need to make decisions based on after-tax returns. Because your income level determines your tax rate, certain investment choices may be more attractive because of their relative after-tax appeal. Income may also influence risk preferences. High-income investors may be more willing to choose riskier strategies because they can more easily contribute additional investment capital should they sustain losses. If you must rely on your portfolio to meet income needs, you may be limited in the size of positions you can take in illiquid non-income producing investments.

Taxes: You should fully inform your financial advisor about your tax situation and any special tax circumstances that may apply to you. These considerations will help determine whether you

(continued)

REAL-WORLD RETURNS 21-1 *continued*

should seek tax-exempt or tax-sheltered securities as part of your portfolio and how to best utilize tax-advantaged investment accounts.

Your overall investment objectives may be influenced by any tax-qualified or tax-deferred assets (such as IRA rollover or 401k plans in the United States, or Registered Retirement Savings Plans and Registered Retirement Income Funds in Canada) that will have separate investment objectives. Your financial advisor should consult with your accountant or attorney to coordinate the management of your tax situation.

Total Wealth: Investment objectives should take into consideration not only the assets that your advisor will manage, but also those you hold outside the portfolio. For example, if a substantial portion of your wealth is in a family owned business then new investments may emphasize diversification. Alternatively, the value of expected pension, deferred compensation, or even Social Security benefits may affect the return objectives and risk tolerances of your security portfolio. Expected inheritance may also have a similar impact. Or, if your asset holdings are largely illiquid, you may seek investments with greater liquidity.

In addition, your level of wealth often impacts your lifestyle. Maintaining a desired standard of living will determine how much risk you can tolerate (i.e., how much you can afford to lose and still maintain your lifestyle) and needs to be factored into your investment objectives.

Time Horizons: Your time horizon is vital in setting investment objectives. Questions to ask include: *When do you expect to draw on the assets in your portfolio? Should you choose assets of short- or long-term maturity? Do you have time to recover from a declining market, or is capital preservation important to meet an immediate financial need?*

Liquidity: Liquidity is the ease with which you can convert your assets to cash at or near current fair market value. Questions to ask include: *Do you require a portfolio that can be liquidated easily, or can you afford to wait?*

Some examples of liquid assets are money market funds and publicly traded securities. Because greater liquidity generally results in lower return, it is necessary to give serious consideration to the inherent trade offs. Your financial advisor can help you in this regard. Illiquid investments—those that cannot be readily converted into cash—include real estate, private equity, and hedge fund investments.

Other Considerations: It is important that your advisor have a full picture of your financial situation. You should provide a full disclosure of your financial assets, expected income streams, and obligations, especially as they affect the portfolio under management. Questions to ask include: *Does your job provide an adequate retirement plan, or must you fund your retirement from your investment portfolio? If your employer provides a stock-purchase plan, is this a substantial part of your personal wealth, and should you consider it as a diversification issue when you make other portfolio choices? If you receive tax-qualified or tax-deferred assets from your job, how will these influence your investment decisions?*

Putting It All Together: A professional financial advisor can work with you to answer all of these questions. Your advisor will use your answers to develop a written investment plan that provides the basis of your investment relationship. Together you should be able to determine a target rate of return and an appropriate mix of assets to place in your portfolio. Regular feedback will enable your advisor to incorporate any changes in your needs or circumstances as they occur. Advisors particularly well qualified to help you with this process may hold the Chartered Financial Analyst® (CFA®) designation, awarded by CFA Institute.

Source: "What Every Investor Should Know," CFA Institute, *Investment Strategies in Turbulent Markets*, CFA North Carolina Society, April 25, 2008, p. 3.

Figure 21-2   New Client Application Form

TABLE 1
New Client Application Form
(to be completed by Investment Advisor)

Account Supervision		
Office	Account	I.A.

(1) (a) Name   Mr
                Mrs
                Miss _
                       (Please Print)

Phones: Home _ _ _ _ _ _ _ _ _ _ _ _ _ _ _ _
         Business _ _ _ _ _ _ _ _ _ _ _ _ _ _ _ .

    Home _
            (Street)

         Other _ _ _ _ _ _ _ _ _ _ _ _ _ _ _ _

    Address _
                (City)   (Province)   (Postal Code)

         Fax _ _ _ _ _ _ _ _ _ _ _ _ _ _ _ _ _ _

    Date of Birth _ _ _ _ _ _ _ _ _ _ _ _ . Client's Social Insurance Number _ _ _ _ _ _ _ _ _ _ _ _ _ _ _ Client's Citizenship _ _ _ _ _ _ _ _ _ _ _ _ _

Type of Account Requested:

(b) Is I.A. registered in the Province or   Yes _ _ _   Cash _ _ _ _ _ _ _ _ _ _ _ _ _ _ _   RRSP/RRIF _ _ _ _ _ _ _ _ _ _   U.S. Funds _ _ _ _ _ _ _ _ _ _
     Country in which the client resides?   No _ _ _   Margin _ _ _ _ _ _ _ _ _ _ _ _ _   Other _ _ _ _ _ _ _ _ _ _ _ _ _
                                                                    D.A.P _ _ _ _ _ _ _ _ _ _ _ _ _ _ _   Pro _ _ _ _ _ _ _ _ _ _ _ _ _   CDN Funds _ _ _ _ _ _ _ _ _ _ _

(2) Special Instructions: Hold in Account _ _ _ _ _ _ _ _ _   Register And Deliver _ _ _ _ _ _ _ _ _ . DAP _
     Duplicate Confirmation _ _ _ _ _ _ _ And/Or Statement _ _ _ _ _ _ _ _

     Name: _   Name: _
     Address: _   Address: _
     _ _ _ _ _ _ _ _ _ _ _ _ _ _ _ _ _ Postal Code: _ _ _ _ _ _ _ _ _ _   _ _ _ _ _ _ _ _ _ _ _ _ _ _ _ _ _ Postal Code: _ _ _ _ _ _ _ _ _ _

(3) Client's   Name _   Type of Business _
     Employer: Address _   Client's Occupation _

(4) Family Information:
     Spouse's Name _   No. of Dependents _
     Occupation _   Employer _ .
                                                                            Type of Business _

(5) How long have you known client? _ _ _ _ _ _ _ _ Advertising Lead _ _ _ _ . Phone In _ _ _ _ _ _ _ _ _ _ _ _ .   Have you met the client face to face?
                                                   Personal Contact _ _ _ _ . Walk In _ _ _ _ _ _ _ _ _ _ _ _ _ _ .   Yes _ _ _ _   No _ _ _ .
     Referral by: _ (name) (if customer, give account no,) _

(6) If yes for Questions 1, 2, or 3, provide details in (11)
     1.   Will any other person or persons: (a) Have trading authorization in this account?   No _ _ _ _   Yes _ _ _ _ .
                                                       (b) Guarantee this account?   No _ _ _ _   Yes _ _ _ _ .
                                                       (c) Have a financial interest in such accounts?   No _ _ _ _   Yes _ _ _ _ .
     2.   Do any of the signatories have any other accounts or control the trading in such accounts?   No _ _ _ _   Yes _ _ _ _ .
     3.   Does client have accounts with other Brokerage firms? (Type_____)   No _ _ _ _   Yes _ _ _ _ .
     4.   Is the account   (a) discretionary or (b) managed   (a) _ _ _ _   (b) _ _ _ _ .
          Insider Information
     5.   Is client a senior officer or director of a company whose shares are traded on an exchange or in the OTC markets?   No _ _ _ _   Yes _ _ _ _ .
     6.   Does the client, as an individual or as part of a group, hold or control such a company? (_____)   No _ _ _ _   Yes _ _ _ _ .

(7) (a)	General Documents	Attached	Obtaining	(b)	Trading Authorization Documents:	Attached	Obtaining
	– Client's Agreement	_ _ _ _ _	_ _ _ _ _		– For an Individual's Account	_ _ _ _ _	_ _ _ _ _
	– Margin Agreement	_ _ _ _ _	_ _ _ _ _		– For a Corporation. Partnership, Trust, etc.	_ _ _ _ _	_ _ _ _ _
	– Cash Agreement	_ _ _ _ _	_ _ _ _ _		– Discretionary Authority	_ _ _ _ _	_ _ _ _ _
	– Guarantee	_ _ _ _ _	_ _ _ _ _		– Managed Account Agreement	_ _ _ _ _	_ _ _ _ _
	– Other	_ _ _ _ _	_ _ _ _ _				

(8) INVESTMENT KNOWLEDGE   Sophisticated _ _ _ _ _   EST. NET LIQUID ASSETS
                            Good   _ _ _ _ _   (Cash and securities less loans
                            Limited   _ _ _ _ _   outstanding against securities)   A _ _ _ _ _ _ _ _ _ _ _ _ _
                            Poor/Nil   _ _ _ _ _   PLUS

     ACCOUNT OBJECTIVES   ACCOUNT RISK FACTORS   EST. NET FIXED ASSETS   B _ _ _ _ _ _ _ _ _ _ _ _ _
     Income   _ _ _ . %   Low   _ _ _ . %   (Fixed assets less liabilities   EQUALS
     Capital Gains   Medium   _ _ _ . %   outstanding against fixed assets)
       Short Term _ _ _ . %   High   _ _ _ . %   EST. TOTAL NET WORTH (A + B = C)   C _ _ _ _ _ _ _ _ _ _ _ _ _
       Medium Term _ _ _ . %   100%   APPROXIMATE ANNUAL INCOME FROM ALL
       Long Term   _ _ _ . %   SOURCES   D _ _ _ _ _ _ _ _ _ _ _ _ _
                   100%
                                                            EST. SPOUSE'S INCOME   E _ _ _ _ _ _ _ _ _ _ _ _ _

(9) Bank Reference: Name _   Bank credit check-acceptable?   Yes _ _ _ _   No _ _ _ .
                     Branch _   Or Credit Bureau check-acceptable?   Yes _ _ _ _   No _ _ _
                     Refer to _ _ _ _ _ _ _ _ _ _ _ _ _ _ _ _ _ _ _ .   Above credit checks considered unnecessary
                     Accounts _ _ _ _ _ _ _ _ _ _ _ _ _ _ _ _ _ _ _   Explain in (11)

(10) Deposit and/or Security Received _ .
     Initial _ _ _ _ _ _ _ _   Buy _ _ _ _ _ _ _ _ _   Solicited _ _ _ _ _ _ _ .   Amount _
     Order _ _ _ _ _ _ _ _   Sell _ _ _ _ _ _ _ _ _   Unsolicited _ _ _ _ _ _   Description _

(11) I.A. Signature _   Designated Officer, Director _
                                                                 or Branch Manager's Approval
     Date: _   Date of Approval _
     Comments: _
     _
     _

Revised April 26, 1994

Source: Investment Industry Regulatory Organization of Canada (formerly Investment Dealers' Association of Canada) website: www.iiroc.ca.

A useful starting point for investment advisors working with individual investors is to have clients fill out the New Client Application Form (see Figure 21-2), and review this with the client. This provides an opportunity for both the advisor and the investor to formalize objectives and identify the relevant constraints and preferences associated with achieving these objectives. Each of these items is discussed in turn below.

Objectives

Portfolio objectives are always going to centre on return and risk because these are the two aspects of most relevance to investors. Investors seek returns, but must assume risk in order to have an opportunity to earn the returns. The best way to describe the objectives is to think in terms of the return–risk trade-off developed in Chapter 1 and emphasized throughout the text. Expected return and risk are related in an upward-sloping manner.

We know from Chapter 7 that investors must think in terms of expected returns, which implicitly or explicitly involves probability distributions. The future is uncertain, and the best that investors can do is to make estimates of likely returns over some holding period, such as one year. Because the future is uncertain, mistakes are inevitable, but this is simply the nature of investing decisions. Estimates of expected returns must be made regardless of the uncertainties, using the best information and investment processes available.

The issue of the life cycle of investors fits into this discussion because of its impact on the individual investor's risk and return preferences. The conventional approach is to think in terms of the risk–return trade-off as discussed throughout this text. This is shown in part (a) of Figure 21-3.

Alternatively, the life cycle approach can be depicted as shown in part (b) of Figure 21-3. Here we see four different phases in which individual investors view their wealth, although it is important to note that the boundaries between the stages are not necessarily clear-cut and can require years to complete. Furthermore, an individual can be in several of these stages at the same time. The four phases are

1. *Accumulation Phase.* In the early stage of the life cycle, net worth is typically small, but the time horizon is long. Investors can afford to assume large risks.

2. *Consolidation Phase.* In this phase, involving the mid-to-late career stage of the life cycle when income exceeds expenses, an investment portfolio can be accumulated. A portfolio balance is sought to provide a moderate trade-off between risk and return.

3. *Spending Phase.* In this phase, living expenses are covered from accumulated assets rather than earned income. While there is still some risk-taking, the emphasis is on safety, resulting in a relatively low position on the risk–return trade-off.

4. *Gifting Phase.* In this phase, the attitudes about the purpose of investments change. The basic position on the trade-off remains about the same as in Phase 3.

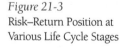
Figure 21-3
Risk–Return Position at Various Life Cycle Stages

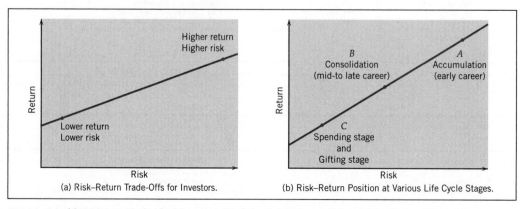

Source: Ronald W. Kaiser, "Individual Investors," in John L. Maginn and Donald L. Tuttle, editors, *Managing Investment Portfolios*, Second Edition. Copyright 1990 CFA Institute.

Inflation Considerations

An investment policy statement often will contain some statement about inflation-adjusted returns because of the impact of inflation on investor results over long periods of time. For example, a wealthy individual's policy statement may be stated in terms of maximum after-tax, inflation-adjusted total return, consistent with the investor's risk profile. Another investor's primary return objective may be stated as inflation-adjusted capital preservation, perhaps with a growth-oriented mix to reflect the need for capital growth over time.

Inflation is clearly a problem for investors. The inflation rate of over 12 percent in 1981 had a horrific impact on investors' real wealth. But even with a much lower inflation, the damage can be substantial. It can persist steadily, eroding values. At a 3 percent inflation rate, for example, the purchasing power of a dollar is cut in half in less than 25 years. Therefore, someone retiring at age 60 who lives to 85 and does not protect him- or herself from inflation will lose half their purchasing power over the years.

Contrary to some people's beliefs, common stocks do not always provide an inflationary hedge. In fact (as discussed in Chapters 13 through 17), high levels of inflation tend to have an adverse effect on stock market returns due to the upward pressure it exerts on interest rates, although the effect is usually less severe for stocks than for bonds. For example, inflation exceeded 12 percent in Canada in both 1974 and 1981, and the returns on the TSE 300 Composite Index in those years were –25.93 percent and –10.25 percent respectively. Obviously, being fully invested in stocks would have only accelerated the deterioration in wealth in those years. The converse is also true—low levels of inflation are good for stock prices. For example, a contributing factor to the strong stock market performance in Canada in 1995 (14.53 percent return) and 1996 (28.35 percent) was the historically low and steady rates of inflation of 1.75 and 2.17 percent respectively.

Constraints and Preferences

To complete the investment policy statement, these items are described for a particular investor as the circumstances warrant. Since investors vary widely in their constraints and preferences, these details may vary widely also.

Time Horizon

Investors need to think about the time period involved in their investment plans. The objectives being pursued may require a policy statement that speaks to specific planning horizons. In the case of an individual investor, for example, this could well be the investor's expected lifetime. In the case of an institutional investor, the time horizon could be quite long. For example, for a company with a defined-benefit retirement plan whose employees are young and that has no short-term liquidity needs, the time horizon would extend several decades.

Liquidity Needs

As noted in Chapter 2, liquidity is the ease with which an asset can be sold without a sharp change in price as the result of selling. Obviously, cash equivalents (money market securities) have high liquidity and are easily sold at close to face value. Many stocks also have great liquidity, but the price at which they are sold will reflect their current market valuations, which can vary substantially.

Investors must decide how likely they are to sell some part of their portfolio in the short run. As part of the asset allocation decision, they must decide how much of their funds to keep in cash equivalents.

Tax Considerations

Unlike some institutional investors, individuals must consider the impact of taxes on their investment programs. Taxes are an important issue because of the differential tax rate, with capital gains and dividends being taxed at a rate lower than ordinary income so that the interest income from bonds is taxed at a higher rate than capital gains or dividend income. Furthermore, the tax laws in Canada are continually changing, making it difficult for investors to forecast the tax rate that will apply in the future. Refer to Appendix 2A at the end of Chapter 2 for a detailed discussion of the Canadian tax environment.

In addition to the differential tax rates and their changes over time, the capital gains component of security returns benefits from the fact that tax is not payable until the gain is realized. This tax deferral is, in effect, a tax-free loan that remains invested for the benefit of the taxpayer.

Retirement programs offer tax sheltering whereby any income and/or capital gains taxes are avoided until such time as the funds are withdrawn. Investors with various retirement and taxable accounts must grapple with the issue of which type of account should hold stocks as opposed to bonds. This is important because bonds generate higher current income in the form of interest payments, which are taxed at a higher rate than capital gains or dividend income.

Real-World Returns 21-2 identifies some important basic considerations in the tax minimization process.

REAL-WORLD RETURNS 21-2

Effective Tax Planning: Deduct, Defer, Divide

Effective tax planning can have a different meaning and emphasis depending upon your personal circumstances. Add in the fact that governments introduce new tax legislation every year and we begin to understand why Albert Einstein said, "The hardest thing in the world to understand is the income tax."

Sometimes tax planning brings immediate benefits, but often the benefits of tax planning take time to be realized. The key building blocks of effective planning are:

1. maintain good records;

2. keep informed and up to date;

3. know your needs and your goals; and

4. assemble a team of good professional advisers.

The Three Ds of Effective Tax Planning

The three Ds to effective tax planning are deduct, defer, and divide. You must understand each of these important functions to plan effectively.

Deduct

A deduction is a claim to reduce your taxable income. A deduction will reduce your tax bill by an amount equal to your marginal tax rate. Some common deductions include:

- Pension plan contributions
- RRSP contributions
- Safety deposit box fees
- Interest expense
- Union/professional dues
- Alimony/maintenance payments
- Employment expenses
- Moving expenses
- Professional fees
- Child care expenses

(continued)

Defer

A deferral strategy attempts to delay when tax will be paid. Deferring tax means you might eliminate the tax this year, but you will have to pay eventually. Generally tax deferral has two advantages: It is better to pay a dollar of tax tomorrow than it is to pay a dollar of tax today; and tax deferral typically puts the control of when to pay the tax in the hands of the taxpayer instead of in the hands of the Canada Revenue Agency (CRA). RRSPs, RESPs, and various investment income strategies are the most common forms of tax deferral for the average Canadian.

Divide

Dividing taxes (or income splitting) implies taking an income and spreading it among numerous taxpayers. For example, it is better to have two people (say a husband and wife) pay tax on incomes of $35,000 each than one person pay tax on an income of $70,000. Unfortunately, you cannot arbitrarily decide who is going to claim what amounts for income. There are, however, strategies to divide income within the rules of the CRA:

1. Contribute to a spousal RRSP to help split income in retirement

2. Split CPP retirement benefits with your spouse

3. Invest non-RRSP savings in the lower income family members

4. Invest the child tax benefit in your children's name

5. Contribute to a registered education fund

6. Pay wages to family members (through a business)

7. Use partnerships or corporations to earn business income

8. Use either inter-vivos or testamentary trusts

Source: Excerpted from Yih, James, "Deduct, Defer, Divide." This article originally appeared on MoneySense.ca, www.moneysense.ca, April 13, 2004. Reprinted with permission from the author.

Legal and Regulatory Requirements

Investors must obviously deal with regulatory requirements growing out of both common law and the rulings and regulations of provincial and federal agencies. Individuals are subject to relatively few such restrictions, unlike institutions, such as pension funds, which must comply with several legal and regulatory requirements.

With regard to fiduciary responsibilities, one of the most famous concepts is the Prudent Man Rule.[4] This rule, which concerns fiduciaries, goes back to 1830, although it was not formally stated until more than 100 years later. Basically, the rule states that anyone, in managing assets for another party, shall act like people of "prudence, discretion and intelligence" act in governing their own affairs.

The important aspect of the Prudent Man Rule is its flexibility, because interpretations of it can change with time and circumstances. In the past, this standard was applied to individual investments rather than the portfolio as a whole, which violates all of the portfolio building principles we learned earlier. Most legislation today requires that plan assets be diversified and that the standards being applied under the act be applied to management of the portfolio as a whole, which affords institutional investors more flexibility in performing their fiduciary duties.

---

[4]This discussion is indebted to "Portfolio Management: The Portfolio Construction Process," in John L. Maginn and Donald L. Tuttle, editors, *Managing Investment Portfolios*, Second Edition (Charlottesville, VA: Association for Investment Management and Research, 1990).

Unique Needs and Circumstances

Once formulated, the investment policy is an operational statement. It clearly specifies the strategies to be taken to try to achieve the investor's goals, or objectives, given the preferences of the investor and any constraints imposed. While portfolio investment considerations are often of a qualitative nature, they help to determine a quantitative statement of return and risk requirements that are specific to the needs of any particular investor.

Investors often face a variety of unique circumstances. For example, a trust established on their behalf may specify that investment activities be limited to particular asset classes or even specified assets. Or an individual may feel that their lifespan is threatened by illness, and wish to benefit within a certain period of time.

EXAMPLE 21-1: ESTABLISHING AN INVESTMENT POLICY

To illustrate the application of the investment management process, consider a question from the Level I CFA Examination.[5] The answer is contained in a succinct but sufficient form.

A. Outline a generalized framework that could be used to establish investment policies applicable to all investors.

B. List and briefly discuss five differences in investment policy that might result from the application of your Part A framework to:

1. The pension plan of a young, fast-growing consumer products company
2. The modest life insurance proceeds received by a 60-year-old widow with two grown children.

Answers:

A. FRAMEWORK

Objectives	Constraints
Return	Time horizon
Risk	Liquidity needs
	Tax considerations
	Legal/regulatory issues
	Unique needs and circumstances

B. APPLICATION DIFFERENCES

	Pension Fund	Widow's Portfolio
Return	Total return objective	Income-oriented objective with some inflation protection
Risk	Above-average capacity; company bears risk	Somewhat below-average capacity indicated; widow bears risk; safety important
Time horizon	Long term; infinite	Medium term
Liquidity	Low; cash flow accrues	Probably medium to high; no reinvestment likely
Tax	Tax-exempt	Income taxes paid on most investment receipts
Legal/regulatory Unique needs and circumstances	Government regulated Cash flow reinvested; opportunity for compounding	Prudent Man Rule applies Widow's needs are immediate and govern now; children's needs should be considered in future planning

---

[5]The question and answer are taken from Question 8 of the 1989 Level I Examination. Reprinted in I: *The CFA Study Guide, 1991* (Charlottesville, VA: CFA Institute), pp. 165 and 173. Used with permission.

CHECK YOUR UNDERSTANDING

21-3. In the context of the life cycle approach, why does the level of expected returns decline as you move through the four phases?

DETERMINE AND QUANTIFY CAPITAL MARKET EXPECTATIONS

Forming Expectations

The forming of expectations involves two steps:

1. *Macro-expectational factors.* These factors influence the market for bonds, stocks, and other assets on both a domestic and international basis. These are expectations about the capital markets.

2. *Micro-expectational influences.* These factors involve the cause agents that underlie the desired return and risk estimates and influence the selection of a particular asset for a particular portfolio.

Rate of Return Assumptions

Most investors base their actions on some assumptions about the rate of return expected from various assets. Obviously, it is important for investors to plan their investing activities on realistic rate of return assumptions.

As a starting point, investors should study carefully the historical rates of return available from a variety of sources (some of which were discussed in Chapter 6). We know the historical mean returns, both arithmetic and geometric, and the standard deviation of the returns for major asset classes such as stocks, bonds, and bills.

Having analyzed the historical series of returns, there are several difficulties in forming expectations about future returns. For example, how much should investors be influenced by recent stock market returns, particularly when they are unusually good returns?

EXAMPLE 21-2: HISTORICAL RATES OF RETURN ON THE S&P/TSX COMPOSITE INDEX

The average annual return on the S&P/TSX Composite Index for the 2003–2007 period was 18.43 percent, approximately 1.6 times the annual average return on the S&P/TSX Index over the 1938–2007 period of 11.79 percent.

Do investors form unrealistic expectations about future returns as a result of such activity? Over the 1938–2007 period, there were 17 years where the return on the S&P/TSX Index was negative or on average about once every four years. In addition, many observers believe that stock returns tend to "revert toward the mean" over time—that is, periods of unusually high returns tend to be followed by periods of lower returns (although not necessarily losses), and the opposite is also true. It is interesting to note that following high average annual returns in the 1996–2000 period of 16.07 percent, the 2001 and 2002 returns on the S&P/TSX Index were −12.57 percent and −12.44 percent respectively. These poor returns were in turn followed by the high returns noted above for the 2003–2007 period.

Investors should recognize some key points about the historical data as they form expectations about future rates of return. The equity risk premium is often defined as the return on a stock index (such as the S&P/TSX Index) minus the return on riskless assets (such as Government of Canada

T-bills or Government of Canada bonds). The expected equity risk premium to be used in this calculation is based on the arithmetic mean of equity risk premiums and not the geometric mean because this is an additive relationship. As stated in the Ibbotson Associates *Yearbook*, "...the arithmetic mean is correct because an investment with uncertain returns will have a higher expected ending wealth value than an investment that earns, with certainty, its compound or geometric rate of return each year."[6]

A second key point that investors should recognize in thinking about expected rates of return, and the returns they can realistically expect to achieve, is that common stock returns involve considerable risk. While the annual geometric average compound rate of return on Canadian common stocks for the 1938–2007 period, according to the S&P/TSX Index data, was 10.68 percent, that does not mean that all investors can realistically expect to achieve this historical rate of return. For example, as mentioned above, 17 out of the 70 one-year S&P/TSX Index returns were actually negative. In addition, returns over longer periods of time, such as five or 10 years, were often well below this average. For example, the average return on the S&P/TSX Index over the 1994–2003 period was a mere 8.4 percent.

The message from this discussion is that, based on the known history of stock returns, the chance that an investor will actually achieve some compound rate of return over time from owning common stocks may not be as high as he or she believes. Common stocks are risky, and expected returns are not guaranteed. Investors must be cognizant of this fact in determining the role common stocks will play in their overall investment plan.

CONSTRUCTING THE PORTFOLIO

learning objective 3
Assess related issues
such as asset allocation.

Having considered the objectives and constraints and formed capital market expectations, the next step is portfolio construction and revision based on the policy statement and capital market expectations. Included here are such issues as asset allocation, portfolio optimization, and security selection. In summary, once the portfolio strategies are developed, they are used along with the investment manager's expectations for the capital market and for individual assets to choose a portfolio of assets.

The portfolio construction process can be viewed from a broad perspective as consisting of the following steps (again, given the development of the investment policy statement and the formation of capital market expectations):

1. Define the universe of securities eligible for inclusion in a particular portfolio. For institutional investors, this traditionally has meant asset classes, in particular stocks, bonds, and cash equivalents. More recently, institutional investors have broadened their investment alternatives to include foreign securities, small stocks, real estate, venture capital, and so forth. This step is really the asset allocation decision, probably the key decision made by investment managers.

2. Utilize an optimization procedure to select securities and determine the proper portfolio weights for these securities.

Both of these steps are discussed in more detail as follows.

Asset Allocation

The asset allocation decision involves deciding the percentage of investable funds to be placed in stocks, bonds, and cash equivalents. It is the most important investment decision made by investors because it is the basic determinant of the return and risk taken. This is a result of holding a well-diversified portfolio, which we know is the primary lesson of portfolio management. Real-World Returns 21-3 discusses the importance of asset allocation during turbulent times.

---

[6]Roger G. Ibbotson and Rex A. Sinquefield, "Stocks, Bonds, Bills, and Inflation (SBBI)," updated in *Stocks, Bonds, Bills, and Inflation 1996 Yearbook™* (Chicago: Ibbotson Associates, 1996), p. 155. All rights reserved.

REAL-WORLD RETURNS 21-3

Asset Allocation

Economic and financial conditions were unusually challenging at the start of 2008. As of first quarter important indicators—the stagnant real estate market, the threat of a full-fledged credit crunch, sluggish corporate profit growth and surging headline inflation—suggested that the US economy rested on the brink of a recession. In response to these sobering portents, US consumer spending dropped, the US dollar weakened, and global equity markets became increasingly volatile.

Difficult investing environments don't remain so forever, of course. Regulators and the market responded promptly to the crisis at hand. Early on in 2008, the Fed slashed interest rates aggressively: asset priced valuations in many equity and some fixed income markets dropped precipitously, and cash on balance sheets (excluding financials) seemed relatively healthy.

So what should an investor be doing today? On a near-term basis, it seems likely that we'll remain in a more defensive investment environment into the summer or early fall 2008. We believe that a risk-neutral portfolio strategy approach is optimal.

Short-term consideration aside, we at U.S. Trust continue to emphasize the critical importance of asset allocation over the long-term.[a]

Many investors, if they allocate assets at all, tend to base their approach on the pioneering work of Harry Markowitz, who introduced modern portfolio theory to the investment world.

But the financial markets have evolved considerably since Markowitz's groundbreaking study was first published. Today, capital markets are global, new markets and asset classes have emerged, investment products and strategies have proliferated and grown more complex, and investors have become more aware of opportunities and more sophisticated in their expectations.

At US Trust we believe that traditional asset allocation methodologies that rely solely on modern portfolio theory have not kept pace with these changes. In our view, effective asset allocation today requires that we rethink the assets under our consideration, the influences on them, and the allocation process we undertake. More specifically, investors should adopt the following principles:

- Seek investment opportunities around the world, including the emerging markets.[b]

- Consider asset classes beyond traditional stocks and bonds. Hedge funds, private equity, real estate and tangible assets offer eligible investors the potential for risk adjusted performance and risk management.[c]

- Combine top-down and bottom-up analysis

- Integrate investment management and financial planning. How does ownership structure impact potential investment performance? How does asset titling impact taxation and ultimate return? What's the best approach to synchronize expected inflows and outflows with asset location, ownership, and titling?

- Consider techniques to minimize income taxes and capitalize on short-term opportunities and thematic investments.

- Adopt a more comprehensive and realistic view of risk.

At all times, but particularly during times of heightened market volatility and uncertainty, US Trust believes that a customized, comprehensive, and up-to-date approach to asset allocation makes sense for most investors.

(continued)

REAL-WORLD RETURNS 21-3 *continued*

   US Trust's seasoned portfolio managers can help you create a highly customized and effective investment plan that follows the above principles. In creating comprehensive and dynamic asset allocations for our clients, we draw upon the extensive investment and planning expertise of our firm—a deep reservoir of insight and experience that informs each step of the asset allocation process.

[a] Asset allocation cannot eliminate the risk of fluctuating prices and uncertain returns. Diversification does not ensure a profit or guarantees against loss.

[b] Investing in emerging markets may involve greater risks than investing in more developed countries. In addition, concentration of investments in a single region may result in greater volatility.

[c] Alternative investments such as derivatives, hedge funds, and private equity funds can result in higher returns potential but also higher loss potential. Changes in economic conditions or other circumstances may adversely affect investments. Before investing in alternative investments, investors should consider their overall financial situation, how much money they have to invest, their need for liquidity, and their tolerance for risk.

Source: Hyzy, Chris, "In Turbulent Times, Effective Asset Allocation is Critical," *Investment Strategies in Turbulent Markets*, CFA North Carolina Society, April 25, 2008, p. 7.

Table 21-1

Asset Mix and Total Return

Asset Group	Index or Average	Portfolio Manager X	Portfolio Manager Y
A. ANNUAL RETURN BY ASSET CLASS			
Cash	10%	11%	9%
Fixed-income securities	6%	8%	4%
Equities	25%	30%	20%
B. ACTUAL ASSET MIX			
Cash		5%	5%
Fixed-income securities		70%	25%
Equities		25%	70%
C. TOTAL RETURN ON A $1,000 PORTFOLIO			
Cash		$5.50	$4.50
Fixed-income securities		56.00	10.00
Equities		75.00	140.00
TOTAL RETURN		$136.50	$154.50
TOTAL % RETURN		13.65%	15.45%

Source: *Canadian Securities Course Textbook* (Toronto: Canadian Securities Institute, August 1998), p. 127. © 1998 Canadian Securities Institute. Reprinted with permission.

   The returns of a well-diversified portfolio within a given asset class are highly correlated with the returns of the asset class itself. Within an asset class, diversified portfolios will tend to produce similar returns over time. However, different asset classes are likely to produce results that are quite dissimilar. Therefore, differences in asset allocation will be the key factor over time causing differences in portfolio performance. This point is demonstrated in Table 21-1, where portfolio manager Y underperforms portfolio manager X in all three asset categories (cash, fixed income, and equities), yet manager Y's overall return exceeds that of manager X due to the asset mix of the two portfolios (Y has 70 percent in equities and 25 percent in fixed income securities, the reverse of X).

The Asset Allocation Decision

Factors to consider in making the asset allocation decision include the investor's return requirements (current income versus future income), the investor's risk tolerance, and the time horizon. This is done in conjunction with the investment manager's expectations about the capital markets and about individual assets, as described above.

How asset allocation decisions are made by investors remains a subject that is not fully understood. What is known is that what investors say and what they do in deciding how to allocate assets are two different things.

According to some analyses, asset allocation is closely related to the age of an investor. This involves the so-called life-cycle theory of asset allocation. This makes intuitive sense because the needs and financial positions of workers in their 50s should differ, on average, from those who are starting out in their 20s. According to the life-cycle theory, for example, as individuals approach retirement they become more risk averse.

Table 21-2 illustrates the asset allocation decision by presenting two examples to show how major changes during life can affect asset allocation. One investor is classified as conservative and another as aggressive. They begin their investment programs and end them with different allocations, but their responses to major changes over the life cycle are similar. For example, both investors have a minimum of 50 percent allocated to stocks at all stages of the life cycle because of the need for growth.

Table 21-2, published in *AAII Journal*, a magazine for individual investors, is illustrative only. Different investors will choose different types of assets. Lifestyle changes could cause investors to move from one stage to the other, but changes in life may not cause a modification in the allocation percentages. Moreover, even among similar age groups, goals can vary substantially. Overall, asset allocation decisions may depend more upon goals than age. Thus while the lifestyle approach may prove useful, it is not always applicable. The important point here is that all investors must make individual asset allocation decisions that will have a major impact on the investment results achieved.

It seems reasonable to assert that the level of risk aversion affects the asset allocation decision. One study examined the risk preferences of households using financial data for a large random sample of US households.[7] The definition of risk used was relative risk aversion, defined as investors' tolerance for risk

---

Table 21-2

How Major Changes Can Affect your Asset Allocation

Asset Category	Conservative			Aggressive		
	Early Career (%)	Late Career (%)	Retirement (%)	Early Career (%)	Late Career (%)	Retirement (%)
Cash	10	10	10	10	10	10
Bonds	20	30	40	0	10	10
Large-cap stocks	40	40	40	30	40	50
Small-cap stocks	15	10	5	30	20	15
International stocks	15	10	5	30	20	15

Source: Maria Crawford Scott, "How Major Changes in your Life Can Affect your Asset Allocation," *AAII Journal* (October 1995), p. 17.

---

[7]William B. Riley, Jr. and K. Victor Chow, "Asset Allocation and Individual Risk Aversion," *Financial Analysts Journal* 48 (December 1992), pp. 32–37.

as measured relative to his or her wealth level. This study found differences in relative risk aversion across three distinct categories of individuals—those 65 and older, those with very high levels of wealth, and those with incomes below the poverty level. The study also found clear patterns for asset allocation over wealth and income levels, with the proportion allocated to risky assets rising consistently with both income and wealth.

There are several approaches to asset allocation, some of which are described in Chapter 14. These strategies are based on the ability to time the performance of the major financial asset categories. The most commonly referred to strategy is tactical asset allocation (TAA), which is a moderately active asset allocation approach that allows managers short-term deviations from longer-term target asset mixes to take advantage of market timing skills.

Strategic asset allocation involves adhering to a long-term mix by monitoring and rebalancing the portfolio as necessary. Integrated asset allocation represents an all-encompassing strategy that examines market conditions and investor objectives and constraints on a separate basis. Based on this analysis, the optimal asset mix is determined. The asset mix is adjusted at regular intervals, to reflect the fact that both market conditions and investor needs change through time.

Portfolio Optimization

Stated simply, portfolio construction involves the selection of securities to be included in the portfolio and the determination of portfolio funds (the weights) to be placed in each security. As we know from Chapters 7 and 8, the Markowitz model provides the basis for scientific portfolio construction that results in efficient portfolios, which are those with the highest level of expected return for a given level of risk, or the lowest risk for a given level of expected return.

MONITOR MARKETING CONDITIONS AND INVESTOR CIRCUMSTANCES

Monitoring Market Conditions

The need to monitor market conditions is obvious. Investment decisions are made in a dynamic marketplace where change occurs on a continuing basis. Key macro variables, such as inflation and interest rates, should be tracked on a regular basis. Information about the prospects for corporate earnings is obviously important because of the impact of earnings on stock prices.

Changes in Investor's Circumstances

An investor's circumstances can change for several reasons. These can be easily organized on the basis of the framework for determining portfolio policies outlined above.

- *Change in wealth.* A change in wealth may cause an investor to behave differently, possibly accepting more risk in the case of an increase in wealth or becoming more risk-averse in the case of a decline in wealth.

- *Change in time horizon.* Traditionally, we think of investors aging and becoming more conservative in their investment approach.

- *Change in liquidity requirements.* A need for more current income could increase the emphasis on dividend-paying stocks or fixed-income securities, while a decrease in current income requirements could lead to greater investment in small stocks whose potential payoff may be years in the future.

- *Change in tax circumstances.* An investor who moves to a higher tax bracket may find common stocks more attractive due to the dividend tax credit, as well as the potential to defer the realization of capital gains.

- *Change in legal/regulatory considerations.* Laws affecting investors change regularly, whether tax laws or laws governing retirement accounts, annuities, and so forth.
- *Change in unique needs and circumstances.* Investors face a number of possible changes during their life, depending on many economic, social, political, health, and work-related factors.

MAKE PORTFOLIO ADJUSTMENTS AS NECESSARY

Even the most carefully constructed portfolio is not intended to remain intact without change. Portfolio managers spend much of their time monitoring and rebalancing existing portfolios. The key is to know when and how to do such rebalancing because a trade-off is involved: the cost of trading versus the cost of not trading.[8]

The cost of trading involves commissions, possible impact on market price, and the time involved in deciding to trade. The cost of not trading involves holding positions that are not best suited for the portfolio's owner, that violate the asset allocation plan, that no longer provide adequate diversification, and so forth. As discussed in Chapters 19 and 20, derivative securities provide efficient mechanisms for making portfolio adjustments without actually buying or selling underlying securities. Using derivatives may offer several advantages over direct trading in the underlying portfolio securities under some circumstances.

PERFORMANCE MEASUREMENT

The portfolio management process is designed to facilitate making investment decisions in an organized, systematic manner. Clearly, it is important to evaluate the effectiveness of the overall decision-making process. The measurement of portfolio performance allows investors to determine the success of the portfolio management process, and of the portfolio manager. It is a key part of monitoring the investment strategy that was developed based on investor objectives, constraints, and preferences.

Performance measurement is important to both those who employ a professional portfolio manager on their behalf as well as to those who invest themselves. It allows investors to evaluate the risks that are being taken, the reasons for the success or failure of the investing program, and the costs of any restrictions that may have been placed on the investment manager. This, in turn, could lead to revisions in the process.

Unresolved issues remain in performance measurement despite the development of an entire industry to provide data and analyses of *ex-post* performance. Nevertheless, it is a critical part of the investment management process, and the logical capstone in its own right of the entire study of investments. We therefore consider this issue next as a separate and concluding chapter of the text.

ILLUSTRATIVE EXAMPLES

We conclude with a few illustrative examples that apply some of the investment planning techniques discussed in the chapter.

[8]This discussion is indebted to Robert D. Arnott and Robert M. Lovell, Jr., "Monitoring and Rebalancing the Portfolio," in John L. Maginn and Donald L. Tuttle, editors, *Managing Investment Portfolios*, Second Edition (Charlottesville, VA: Association for Investment Management and Research, 1990).

EXAMPLE ONE

Brigid is single, 27 years old, and has a steady job in a company with a strong union and solid pension plan. She has no plans to leave her job and her current salary is $36,000 per year. It is reasonable to assume this amount will increase approximately 5 percent per year over the next 30 to 35 years. She has never invested in RRSPs but has contributed to the Canada Pension Plan (CPP) and company pension plan for the past five years. She has recently finished paying off her student loan, and her only remaining debt is a car loan in the amount of $10,000. She rents a modest one-bedroom apartment that costs her $550 per month and feels that she can live comfortably on $1,500 a month.

Discuss what her primary investment objectives should focus on and what type of investment mix she should consider.

Personal Evaluation

Brigid has steady employment, with good earnings potential and an employee registered retirement plan. She has good control over her debt situation and likely has room to borrow additional funds if necessary (for investment, housing, or consumption purposes). If we assume she is adequately insured and that she has no immediate plans to purchase a house, it is reasonable to assume that she is in a position to start investing for retirement. Given the fact that she has quickly paid off her student loan and has not borrowed a great deal of additional funds, it may be reasonable to assume she has a fairly conservative attitude toward managing her finances. In addition, the fact that she has not invested in RRSPs at all suggests that she may not be an extremely knowledgeable investor. Alternatively, it may signal that she is extremely conservative and wished to pay off her debt first, even at the expense of foregoing the tax deduction benefits associated with RRSP contributions.

Investment Objectives

Her primary investment objective should be growth, since she should generate more than sufficient income in the coming years to satisfy her cash flow requirements, and since retirement is some years away. Her secondary objectives would be tax minimization and safety since she is likely to be in the moderate-to-high tax bracket in the coming years, and since she appears to have a fairly conservative attitude toward managing her finances.

Investment Strategy

Brigid's first move should be to take full advantage of her available RRSP contribution limit, which should be substantial due to the carry-over amounts available from previous years. This will minimize her tax obligations and the funds placed in RRSPs should be primarily invested in growth equities to satisfy her primary investment objective of growth. In order to maintain sufficient portfolio diversification, and in light of her apparent conservative disposition, she may want to maintain 5 to 10 percent in money market funds and an additional 10 to 20 percent in fixed income securities. Once she has exhausted her RRSP contribution limits, she may want to invest additional funds into more aggressive equity funds with long-term growth potential, since capital gains will only be realized when the shares are sold, and given the preferential tax treatment associated with any dividends received in the interim.

EXAMPLE TWO

Brennan and Angela have been married for 25 years and their children, Jason and Siobhan, are grown and on their own. Angela and Brennan are both 53 years old and have been teaching high school at the same school for the past 30 years. They both earn $62,000 per year, and they plan to retire in five years. Each of them has invested $3,000 per year in RRSPs for the past 20 years, allocating approximately 20 percent to money market funds and the remaining 80 percent to growth equity funds. They have both also contributed to the CPP and teachers' pension plan for the past 30 years. They recently finished paying off the mortgage on their home, which they plan to live in upon retirement, and their only remaining debt is a car loan in the amount of $20,000. They feel they can live comfortably on $2,800 a month after retirement.

a. Does there appear to be any opportunities for this couple to reduce taxes by using "income splitting" strategies? Briefly explain.

No, they both earn the same amount now and likely will until retirement, therefore, they are probably in the same tax bracket. In addition, they both have contributed about the same amount to registered plans, hence their income (and tax brackets) will remain virtually identical upon retirement.

b. Identify and briefly discuss what their primary investment objectives should focus on and identify any secondary objectives you feel are relevant.

They are both in the peak earnings stage of their life cycle and preservation of capital should be their primary objective, since they plan on retiring in the near future. Since they are in a high tax bracket, tax minimization should be a secondary objective.

c. Prescribe and justify an appropriate investment mix for this couple.

They should begin adjusting their asset mix toward safer securities. Many mixes are possible. For example, an appropriate target might be 40 percent cash (money market instruments), 30 percent fixed income securities, and 30 percent equities (primarily blue chip stocks).

d. Recommend two options available to them if they decide to deregister their RRSPs immediately upon retirement.

They could use the proceeds to purchase a life annuity with a guaranteed term or a fixed term annuity that provides benefits to age 90. Alternatively, or coincidentally, they could purchase a Registered Retirement Income Fund (RRIF), which provides annual income to age 90 or for life. These strategies avoid paying tax on the full amount, which would occur if it were withdrawn upon deregistration of the plan.

CHECK YOUR UNDERSTANDING

21-4. The average annual return on the S&P/TSX Index from 1938 to 2007 was 11.79 percent. Assuming these returns followed the bell-shape of the normal distribution, what was the probability of earning 11.79 percent or more for any one year holding period?

21-5. Why is asset allocation considered to be the most important investment decision?

PENSION MANAGERS EMPHASIZE RISK MANAGEMENT OVER RETURNS

Market volatility is causing pension plan managers in Canada and the United States to swing to the side of risk management instead of making aggressive moves in the hopes of higher returns. A 2008 survey by CFO Research Services and Towers Perrin found that more than three-quarters of senior finance executives in North America planned on reducing risk in their portfolios for defined benefit pensions, where employees are provided certain benefits upon retirement.

"After the highs and lows of the past several years, we're in an economic environment where being ready for storm conditions is the new normal," said Monica McIntosh, national leader of Towers Perrin's asset consulting practice in Canada. "The study shows that in this new world, finance executives are reviewing their pension investment strategy from a broader enterprise risk perspective to avoid undesirable and unacceptable consequences in terms of funded positions and company costs."

Nearly half of those surveyed said they were seriously considering changing their pension asset allocation strategies, such as using duration matching, to better manage risk.

DISCUSSION QUESTIONS

1. With defined benefit pensions, employers contribute to and manage the plans on behalf of employees. Does this give employers a greater ethical obligation to ensure the plans are well-funded when employees retire?

2. With an expected wave of retirements coming, should employers not be trying to increase their returns to ensure there is enough money to provide pension benefits? Is there a possibility of being too cautious?

3. When markets improve, should pension plan managers go back to more aggressive investment strategies in their portfolios?

SUMMARY

This summary relates to the learning objectives for this chapter.

1. **Discuss why portfolio management should be considered a process.**
   Portfolio management should be thought of as a process that can be applied to each investor. It is continuous, systematic, dynamic, and flexible. The portfolio management process can be applied to each investor to produce a set of strategy recommendations for accomplishing a given end result.

2. **Describe the steps involved in the portfolio management process.**
   The entire process consists of
   • Developing explicit investment policies, consisting of objectives, constraints, and preferences
   • Determining and quantifying capital market expectations
   • Constructing the portfolio
   • Monitoring portfolio factors and responding to changes
   • Rebalancing the portfolio when necessary
   • Measuring and evaluating portfolio performance

3. **Assess related issues such as asset allocation.**
   The portfolio construction process can be thought of in terms of the decisions regarding asset allocation and portfolio optimization. Asset allocation is the most important investment decision made

by investors. Some of the more common approaches to asset allocation include tactical, strategic, and integrated.

KEY TERM

Investment policy, p.703

REVIEW QUESTIONS

21-1. What is meant by the portfolio management process?

21-2. Why is asset allocation the most important decision made by investors?

21-3. Differentiate between tactical asset allocation and strategic asset allocation.

21-4. Must each investment management firm be organized the same way in order to carry out the investment process?

21-5. What are some of the differences between individual investors and institutional investors?

21-6. What is meant by the investment policy?

21-7. How can the investment policy be thought of as an operational statement for investment managers to follow?

21-8. How does a well-specified investment policy help institutional investors?

21-9. In forming expectations about future returns from stocks, to what extent should investors be influenced by the more recent past (e.g., the previous 15 years) versus the history of stock market returns from 1938 to 2007?

21-10. How might inflation impact an investor's real wealth?

21-11. What very important constraints and preferences must investors address before investing their wealth?

21-12. Why is asset allocation so closely related to the age of an investor?

21-13. What circumstances or events may cause investors to want to change or rebalance their portfolios?

PREPARING FOR YOUR PROFESSIONAL EXAMS

CFA PRACTICE QUESTIONS

21-1. Which of the following statements reflects the importance of the asset allocation decision to the investment process? The asset allocation decision:

    a. helps the investor decide on realistic investment goals.

    b. identifies the specific securities to include in a portfolio.

    c. determines most of the portfolio's returns and volatility over time.

    d. creates a standard by which to establish an appropriate investment time horizon.

21-2. An individual investor's investment objectives should be expressed in terms of:

    a. risk and return.

    b. capital market expectations.

    c. liquidity needs and time horizon.

    d. tax factors and legal and regulatory requirements.

CFA CURRICULUM AND SAMPLE EXAM QUESTIONS (©CFA INSTITUTE)

21-1. An individual investor's investment objectives should be expressed in terms of:

    a. risk and return.

    b. capital market expectations.

    c. liquidity needs and time horizon.

    d. tax factors and legal and regulatory constraints.

21-2. Which of the following statements best reflects the importance of the asset allocation decision to the investment process? The asset allocation decision:

    a. helps the investor decide on realistic investment goals.

    b. identifies the specific securities to include in a portfolio.

    c. determines most of the portfolio's returns and volatility over time.

    d. creates a standard by which to establish an appropriate investment time horizon.

21-3. Rodolfo Serra is a professional soccer player with FA Milan, a leading soccer team in Italy's Series A league. He has been well paid over his career including an initial, one-time signing bonus of €2 million, which he immediately invested in a start-up company designing training equipment. This aggressive venture eventually went bankrupt. At 34 years old, Serra is now at his professional peak with an annual pre-tax salary of €5 million: €4 million paid throughout the year and a €1 million year-end bonus. His salary is taxed at 40 percent.

Since the beginning of his career Serra has managed his own investments. He has had mixed results in his growth equity portfolio. One of his worst performing equity holdings is B&K, an investment he initially made three years ago. On several occasions, in reaction to an extended decline in B&K's share price, Serra used a portion of his year-end bonus to acquire additional shares in an effort to lower his average cost per share. He avoids the technology sector after incurring severe investment losses in the late 1990s. The remainder of his growth equity portfolio has performed satisfactorily. He also has commercial real estate investments that are expected to be cash-flow neutral this year. A summary of his personal assets is shown in Exhibit 1.

Exhibit 1 ▬▬▬▬▬▬▬

Rodolfo Serra: Personal Assets

(all amounts in €)

Cash savings	4,000,000
Growth equity portfolio*	40,000,000
Commercial real estate investments	14,000,000

*All dividends are reinvested

Serra expects the annual after-tax interest income on his cash savings to be €100,000 at the end of the year.

Serra will retire from professional soccer one year from now at the age of 35. He will pay cash for a personal home costing €4.5 million when he receives his year-end bonus. Having grown up in poverty, Serra recently established a children's welfare foundation. He will legally gift all his commercial real estate investments to the foundation upon his retirement. After retirement, Serra intends to volunteer all of his time to the foundation and does not expect to receive any compensation from other sources.

Serra has been divorced for two years and has a 7-year-old son who lives with his mother in Italy. He makes annual family support payments amounting to €800,000. The annual family support payments will stop when his son reaches age 18. Serra's living expenses are expected to be €1.2 million this year. Both family support payments and living expenses will grow at an average annual inflation rate of 4 percent. All income net of expenses is currently reinvested in his growth equity portfolio. Serra has expressed his desire to maintain the real value of his portfolio during retirement, which is expected to last a minimum of 40 years. Serra recently hired a portfolio manager, Patrick Schneider, CFA, who expects the after-tax nominal annual return for growth equity to be 8.5 percent.

a. i) Formulate the return objective in Serra's investment policy statement.
    ii) Calculate the after-tax nominal rate of return that is required during his first year of retirement. Show your calculations.
    Note: Assume there are no tax benefits or tax liabilities related to Serra's gifting commercial real estate, or paying family support and living expenses.

b. i) Identify two factors in Serra's personal situation that increase his ability to take risk.
    ii) Identify two factors in Serra's personal situation that decrease his ability to take risk.
    iii) Judge, considering all factors, whether Serra has below-average, average, or above-average ability to take risk.

c. Formulate each of the following constraints in Serra's investment policy statement. Support each response with one reason based on Serra's specific circumstances.
    i) Liquidity requirement
    ii) Time horizon

22

EVALUATION OF INVESTMENT PERFORMANCE

At long last you have arrived at the end of your quest to learn enough about investing to manage your inheritance sensibly. Now that you know some basics about how to invest, what to invest in, and what to expect, you must consider how well you are doing as an investor over time. Measuring portfolio performance is the bottom line of investing. Everyone wants to know how they are performing as investors, either in managing their own portfolios or entrusting their money to others to manage for them. Furthermore, if they have others manage their money, they should be aware of what to look for when investment results are presented to them.

Learning Objectives

After reading this chapter, you should be able to

1. Outline the framework for evaluating portfolio performance.
2. Use measures of return and risk to evaluate portfolio performance.
3. Distinguish between the three composite measures of portfolio performance.
4. Discuss problems with portfolio measurement.
5. Explain issues in portfolio evaluation, such as performance attribution.

CHAPTER PREVIEW

This chapter explains what is involved in evaluating investment performance. First, we establish a framework for evaluating portfolio performance that includes a discussion of the CFA Institute's Global Investment Performance Standards (GIPS®). We then focus on the composite measures of portfolio performance developed by Sharpe, Treynor, and Jensen. We conclude the chapter with a look at some of the problems with performance evaluation and other issues, such as performance attribution.

THE BOTTOM LINE

We have now discussed, in an organized and systematic manner, the major components of the investing process. One important issue that remains is the bottom line of this investing process: evaluating the performance of a portfolio. The question to be answered is this: Is the return on a portfolio, less all expenses, adequate to compensate for the risk that was taken? Every investor should be concerned with this issue because, after all, the objective of investing is to increase, or at least protect, financial wealth. Unsatisfactory results must be detected so that changes can be made.

Evaluating portfolio performance is important whether an individual investor manages his or her own funds or invests indirectly through investment companies. Direct investing can be time consuming and has high opportunity costs. If the results are inadequate, why do it (unless the investor simply enjoys it)? On the other hand, if professional portfolio managers (such as those at mutual funds) are employed, it is necessary to know how well they perform. Other things being equal, if manager A consistently outperforms manager B, investors will prefer manager A, and if neither one outperforms an index fund, investors may go elsewhere. The obvious point is that performance has to be evaluated before intelligent decisions can be made.

Portfolio evaluation has changed significantly over time. Prior to the mid-1960s, evaluation was not a major issue, even for investment firms, but in today's highly competitive money-management environment it is. By the end of 2007, Canadian mutual funds had more than $697 billion in assets under management. That is approximately 30 times the money under management as of December 1989, which attests to the growth in these investments throughout the 1990s. In the US, mutual funds are currently managing more than $9 trillion. The pension fund universe is even larger. In addition to these money managers, trusts, discretionary accounts, and endowment funds have portfolios that must be evaluated.

Because of all this complexity, evaluation techniques have become more sophisticated, and the demands by portfolio clients more intense. The broad acceptance of modern portfolio theory has also changed the evaluation process and how it is viewed. In this chapter, we discuss the evaluation of portfolio performance with an eye to understanding the critical issues involved and the overall framework within which evaluation should be conducted. We also review the well-known measures of composite portfolio performance and the problems associated with them.

FRAMEWORK FOR EVALUATING PORTFOLIO PERFORMANCE

learning objective 1
Outline the framework for evaluating portfolio performance.

When evaluating a portfolio's performance, certain factors must be considered. We discuss below some of the obvious factors that investors should consider and describe some of the highlights of the Global Investment Performance Standards (GIPS®) as recommended by the CFA Institute, which will play a prominent role in performance evaluation in the future.

To illustrate our discussion about comparisons, assume that in 2008 the GoGrowth mutual fund earned a total return of 20 percent for its shareholders. It claims in an advertisement that it is the number one performing mutual fund in its category. As a shareholder, you are trying to assess GoGrowth's performance. What can you say?

Some obvious factors to consider are risk levels, time periods, appropriate benchmarks, constraints on portfolio managers, as well as other considerations.

Differential Risk Levels

The risk–return trade-off underlies all investment actions, but with the information we have, we can say relatively little about GoGrowth's performance. Return and risk are opposite sides of the same coin, and both must be evaluated if intelligent decisions are to be made. But we know nothing about the risk levels of this fund, and therefore we can say little about its performance. After all, to achieve this 20 percent return, its managers may have taken twice the risk of comparable portfolios.

Given the risk that all investors face, it is totally inadequate to consider only the returns from various investment alternatives. Although all investors prefer higher returns, they do not like the accompanying higher risk. To evaluate portfolio performance properly, we must determine whether the returns are large enough given the risk involved. If we are to assess performance carefully, we must evaluate performance on a risk-adjusted basis.

Differential Time Periods

It is not unusual to pick up a publication from the popular press and see two different mutual funds of the same type—for example, aggressive equity funds or balanced funds—advertise themselves as the number one performer. How can this be? The answer is simple. Each of these funds is measuring its performance over a different time period. For example, one fund could use the 10 years ending December 31, 2008, while another fund uses the five years ending December 31, 2008. GoGrowth could be using a one-year period ending on the same date or some other combination of years. Mutual fund sponsors can choose any time period they wish in promoting their performance, and funds can also define the group to which comparisons are made. And, to present themselves in the best light, they often stress those periods of highest performance.

Although it seems obvious when one thinks about it, investors tend not to be careful when making comparisons of portfolios over various time periods. As with the case of differential risk, the time element must be adjusted for if valid performance of portfolio results is to be obtained.

Appropriate Benchmarks

A third reason why we can say little about the performance of GoGrowth is that its 20 percent return is meaningful only when compared to a legitimate alternative. Obviously, if the average-risk fund or the market returned 25 percent in 2008, and GoGrowth is average, we would find its performance unfavourable. Therefore, we must make relative comparisons in performance measurement, and an important related issue is the benchmark to be used in evaluating the performance of a portfolio.

The essence of performance evaluation in investments is to compare the returns obtained on some portfolio with those that could have been obtained from a comparable alternative. The measurement process must involve relevant and obtainable alternatives; that is, the **benchmark portfolio** must be a legitimate alternative that accurately reflects the objectives of the portfolio owners.

Benchmark Portfolio
An alternative portfolio against which to measure a portfolio's performance.

An equity portfolio consisting of S&P/TSX Composite Index stocks should be evaluated relative to that index or other equity portfolios that could be constructed from that index, after adjusting for the risk involved. On the other hand, a portfolio of small capitalization stocks should not be judged against the benchmark of the S&P/TSX Composite Index, but against a small-cap index such as the Nesbitt Burns Canadian small-cap index or the S&P/TSX Small Cap Index. Similarly, a predominantly mid-cap fund should be compared with an index such as the S&P/TSX Mid-Cap Index, which consists of mid-cap stocks from the S&P/TSX Composite Index. If a bond portfolio manager's objective is to invest in bonds rated A or higher, it would be inappropriate to compare his or her performance with that of a junk bond manager.

Even more difficult to evaluate are equity funds that consist of some mid-cap and small-cap stocks as well as many from the S&P/TSX Composite Index. Comparisons for this group can be quite difficult. The S&P/TSX Composite Index has been the most frequently used benchmark for evaluating the performance of Canadian institutional portfolios such as those of pension and mutual funds. However, many observers now agree that multiple benchmarks are more appropriate to use when evaluating portfolio returns for various reasons. Customized benchmarks also can be constructed to evaluate a manager's style that is unusual. For example, in addition to several small-cap and mid-cap indexes (some of which were mentioned above), new indexes designed to accommodate portfolio managers' "styles" have been developed, such as the Russell 100 Growth Index and the Russell 100 Value Index.

Constraints on Portfolio Managers

In evaluating the portfolio manager rather than the portfolio itself, an investor should consider the objectives set by (or for) the manager and any constraints under which he or she must operate. For example, if a mutual fund's objective is to invest in small, speculative stocks, investors must expect the risk to be larger than that of a fund invested in S&P/TSX Composite Index, with substantial swings in the annual realized returns.

It is imperative to recognize the importance of the investment policy pursued by a portfolio manager in determining the portfolio's results. In many cases, the investment policy determines the return and risk of the portfolio. For example, authors Brinson, Hood, and Beebower found that for a sample of pension plans, the investment policy accounted for approximately 94 percent of the total variation in the returns to these funds.[1] This obviously leaves little variation to be accounted for by the manager's skills.

If a portfolio manager is obligated to operate under certain constraints, these must be taken into account. For example, if a portfolio manager of an equity fund is prohibited from selling short, it is unreasonable to expect the manager to protect the portfolio in this manner in a bear market. If the manager is further prohibited from trading in options and futures, nearly the only protection left in a bear market is to reduce the equity exposure.

Other Considerations

Of course, other important issues are involved in measuring the portfolio's performance. It is essential to determine how well diversified the portfolio was during the evaluation period, because, as we know, diversification can reduce portfolio risk. If a manager assumes non-systematic risk, we want to know if he or she earned an adequate return for doing so.

All investors should understand that even in today's investment world of computers and databases, there do not exist any precise universally agreed-upon methods of portfolio evaluation. As we will see below, investors can use several well-known techniques to assess the actual performance of a portfolio relative to one or more alternatives. In the final analysis, when investors are selecting money managers to turn their money over to, they evaluate these managers only on the basis of their published performance statistics. If the published "track record" looks good, that is typically enough to convince many investors to invest in a particular mutual fund. However, the past is no guarantee of an investment manager's future, as discussed in Chapter 10 and demonstrated in Table 3-1 in Chapter 3. Short-term results may be particularly misleading.

Global Investment Performance Standards (GIPS®)
Ethical standards to ensure fair representation and full disclosure of investment performance.

CFA Institute's Global Investment Performance Standards (GIPS®)

The CFA Institute (see Appendix 1A), based on years of discussion, has issued minimum standards for presenting investment performance. These **Global Investment Performance Standards (GIPS®)** are a set of guiding ethical principles with several main objectives:

[1]Gary P. Brinson, Randolph Hood, and Gilbert L. Beebower, "Determinants of Portfolio Performance," *Financial Analysts Journal* 42 (July/August 1986), pp. 39–44.

1. To obtain worldwide acceptance of a standard for the calculation and presentation of investment performance in a fair, comparable format that provides full disclosure.

2. To ensure accurate and consistent investment performance data for reporting, record keeping, marketing, and presentation.

3. To promote fair global competition for investment firms from all markets without creating barriers to entry for new firms.

4. To foster the notion of industry self-regulation on a global basis.

While the GIPS are not legal requirements in themselves, many are, in fact, part of legal requirements within many countries. Of course the legal requirements vary from country to country. Real-World Returns 22-1 discusses the "gold" version of these standards. The importance of these standards is alluded to in the article by the CFA Institute's (formerly AIMR's) Vice President.

Some aspects of the standards are mandatory and others are recommended. Table 22-1 summarizes many of the key points of most relevance to this discussion. We will encounter some of these points as we consider how to go about evaluating portfolios.

REAL-WORLD RETURNS 22-1

Going for Gold: IPC Seeks Comment on Updated GIPS Standards

The AIMR Board and the Investment Performance Council (IPC) just released the latest version of the Global Investment Performance Standards (GIPS®) for a six-month public comment period ending August 2004. Called the "gold" GIPS standards, the proposed version will raise the bar for firms claiming GIPS compliance and eliminate the need for separate local standards in many countries.

"The GIPS standards are no longer simply a minimum worldwide standard," says AIMR Vice President Alecia Licata. "With the proposed changes, the GIPS standards now encompass much of what the global industry deems to be best practices in terms of performance presentation and measurement."

The proposed version will certainly impact local versions of the GIPS standards, such as AIMR-PPS® standards, as these versions must incorporate all interpretations and changes to the GIPS standards. As a result, Licata fears that some constituents may miss out on the opportunity to give feedback.

"Although most AIMR members know GIPS standards exist, many don't have a perspective on the relationship between GIPS standards and their local version, and therefore they may gloss over their role in the standard-setting process—to provide feedback—and consequently, the IPC's invitation to comment," Licata says.

Yet Licata maintains that the public commentary process is vital to the success of GIPS standards. "The IPC has broad representation geographically and technically, but it is only so large. Encouraging the public to think about the practicality and applicability of IPC proposals adds significant value to the process," says Licata.

"If we only hear the negative comments, it leaves us wondering whether the majority of the industry agrees with the proposal or whether they just don't know about it," says Licata. All comments received are posted to the AIMR website for others to view.

The proposed updated version of GIPS standards includes new, modified, and deleted provisions for which the IPC requests comments. Provisions anticipated to draw the most feedback include a new provision requiring mandatory verification as of 2010, a new provision requiring firms to provide a compliant presentation to all prospective clients, and a provision that clarifies that firms must provide a list and description of composites to any prospective client that makes such a request.

(continued)

REAL-WORLD RETURNS 22-1 *continued*

Notable modified provisions include postponing the requirement for accrual accounting of dividends and the requirement for carve outs to be managed with their own cash from 2005 to 2010. Licata points out that the decision to push back the effective dates for these requirements is a direct result of industry feedback. "The IPC takes public comment very seriously, and for these two provisions—although they are important and represent best practices—it made sense to give the industry more time to implement these requirements," she explains.

The proposed version also no longer permits two of the three current options for how a firm chooses to define itself for purposes of complying with the *Standards* (based on legal entity or base currency). "These deletions are based on the idea that a firm should be defined by how an entity is actually presenting itself to the public. It's a minor change in the sense that it will not affect most firms' ability to claim compliance. But it is a major change in that it captures the essence of what the GIPS standards are all about," says Licata.

These changes illustrate the great effort made to make the "gold" GIPS standards and process as transparent as possible. Particular attention was given to the structure of the document so that despite changes intended to improve the Standards, such as the addition of a glossary and a section on fundamental concepts, the proposed version looks very similar to the current GIPS standards. Even numbering was kept consistent with the current version.

One of the concentrations over the past five years with the development of the "gold" GIPS standards was adding comparability and transparency to non-standard, mostly private asset classes, such as private equity and real estate. The updated version also incorporates provisions for other technical areas, such as fees and advertising, which already have been released for public comment and finalized by the IPC and AIMR Board.

Following the public comment period, the IPC anticipates adoption of the "gold" GIPS standards early in 2005 with an effective date of 1 January 2006. The IPC's goal is to have updated country versions and translations also adopted by 1 January 2006 so that all firms complying with the GIPS standards, or a version or translation, incorporate the changes by the same date.

"Some of the country versions will lose all their differences once the modifications are adopted. For those countries, the question will be whether there is a need for the country version to have a brand name different from GIPS," says Licata. In the spirit of convergence and transparency, the IPC and the sponsors of each country version are considering the implications of a name change for each market.

While the "gold" GIPS standards represent a triumphant milestone, Licata is quick to remind that the evolution doesn't stop with its adoption. "The GIPS standards are dynamic," says Licata, adding that guidance for leverage and derivatives will be up for public comment in the near future.

Source: Excerpted from Martin, Christine, "Going for Gold: IPC Seeks Comment on Updated GIPS Standards," *CFA Magazine*, March/April 2004. Reprinted with permission from CFA Institute. All Rights Reserved

Table 22-1

CFA Institute's Global Investment Performance Standards (GIPS®)

Some Notable Requirements

1. **Total return**—must be used to calculate performance
2. **Accrual accounting**—use accrual, not cash accounting for fixed-income and all other securities that accrue income
3. **Time-weighted rates of return**—to be used with geometric linking of period returns
4. **Cash and cash equivalents**—to be included in composite returns

5. **All portfolios included**—all actual discretionary portfolios are to be included in at least one composite
6. **No linkage of simulated portfolios with actual performance**
7. **Asset-weighting of composites**—beginning-of-period values to be used
8. **Addition of new portfolios**—to be added to a composite after the start of the next measurement period
9. **Exclusion of terminated portfolios**—excluded from all periods after the period in place
10. **No restatement of composite results**—after a firm's reorganization
11. **No portability of portfolio results**—except under unusual circumstances
12. **All costs deducted**—subtracted from gross performance
13. **Five-year performance record**—minimum period to be presented
14. **Present annual returns for all years**
15. **Convertible and other hybrid securities**—must be treated consistently across and within composite
16. **Asset-only returns**—must not be mixed with asset-plus-cash returns
17. **Full compliance**—there is no such thing as partial compliance; firms must fully comply with GIPS in order to be able to state they are "GIPS compliant"

There are additional requirements for international portfolios, for real estate, and for venture and private placements. In addition, performance presentations must disclose several items of information, such as a complete list of a firm's composites, whether performance results are gross or net of investment management fees, and so on.

Source: Reprinted with permission from Global Investment Performance Standards (GIPs). Copyright 2008 CFA Institute.

CHECK YOUR UNDERSTANDING

22-1. Why is it important to evaluate risk as well as returns when assessing investment performance?

22-2. Assume you are the manager of an investment management firm that has a good record of portfolio performance that is fairly presented to its clients. Will the introduction of GIPS improve the performance results of your firm? If it will not improve performance results, how will its introduction help you as a firm?

RETURN AND RISK CONSIDERATIONS

learning objective 2
Use measures of return and risk to evaluate portfolio performance.

Performance measurement begins with portfolio valuations and transactions translated into rate of return. Prior to the introduction of the performance measures in 1965 (discussed later in this chapter), returns were seldom related to measures of risk. In evaluating portfolio performance, however, investors must consider both the realized return and the risk that was assumed. Therefore, whatever measures or techniques are used, these parameters must be incorporated into the analysis.

Measures of Return

When portfolio performance is evaluated, the investor should be concerned with the total change in wealth. As discussed throughout this text, a proper measure of this return is the total return (TR), which captures both the income component and the capital gains (or losses) component of return. This is the measure reported by investment funds in Canada, as required by security regulators such as the Ontario Securities Commission. It is also required by the CFA Institute, as shown in Table 22-1.

In the simplest case, the market value of a portfolio can be measured at the beginning and end of a period, and the rate of return can be calculated as

$$R_p = \frac{V_E - V_B}{V_B}$$

where V_E is the ending value of the portfolio and V_B is its beginning value.

This calculation assumes that no funds were added to or withdrawn from the portfolio by the client during the measurement period. If such transactions occur, the portfolio return as calculated, R_p, may not be an accurate measure of the portfolio's performance. For example, if the client adds funds close to the end of the measurement period, use of Equation 22-1 would produce inaccurate results because the ending value was not determined by the actions of the portfolio manager. Although a close approximation of portfolio performance might be obtained by simply adding any withdrawals or subtracting any contributions that are made very close to the end of the measurement period, timing issues are a problem.

Dollar-Weighted Returns

Dollar-Weighted Rate of Return (DWR)

Equates all cash flows, including ending market value, with the beginning market value of the portfolio.

Traditionally, portfolio measurement consisted of calculating the **dollar-weighted rate of return (DWR)**, which is equivalent to the internal rate of return (IRR) used in several financial calculations. The IRR measures the actual return earned on a beginning portfolio value and on any net contributions made during the period.

The DWR equates all cash flows, including ending market value, with the beginning market value of the portfolio. Because the DWR is affected by cash flows to the portfolio, it measures the rate of return to the portfolio owner. However, because the DWR is heavily affected by cash flows, it is inappropriate to use when making comparisons to other portfolios or to market indexes, a key factor in performance measurement.

EXAMPLE 22-1: CALCULATING THE DOLLAR-WEIGHTED RATE OF RETURN

An equity portfolio is worth $10,000 at the beginning of the year. After six months the portfolio pays a dividend of $100 and the investor contributes $300 more to the portfolio. Just before the contribution and after paying the dividends, the portfolio was worth $10,050. At the end of the year, the investor receives $100 in dividends and withdraws an additional $150 from the portfolio, which has an ending value of $10,700 after the withdrawal has been made.

To solve for the DWR, we equate the present value of the contributions and the beginning market value, with the present value of withdrawals, cash receipts, and the ending portfolio value, and solve for the corresponding discount rate, as shown below:

Present value (Beginning wealth + Contributions)

= Present value (Cash distributions + Withdrawals + Ending wealth)

$$10,000 + \frac{300}{(1+r)} = \frac{100}{(1+r)} + \frac{150}{(1+r)^2} + \frac{100}{(1+r)^2} + \frac{10,700}{(1+r)^2}$$

which reduces to

$$10,000 + \frac{200}{(1+r)} = \frac{10,950}{(1+r)^2}$$

Solving by financial calculator, we find $r = 3.65$ percent, which is a six-month return; the annual effective return is: $(1 + .0365)^2 - 1 = 0.0743$ or 7.43 percent.

Time-Weighted Returns

Time-Weighted Rate of Return (TWR)
Measures the actual rate of return earned by the portfolio manager.

The **time-weighted rate of return (TWR)** typically is calculated for comparative purposes when cash flows occur between the beginning and the end of a period. TWRs are unaffected by any cash flows to the portfolio; therefore, they measure the actual rate of return earned by the portfolio manager.

Calculating the TWR requires information about the value of the portfolio's cash inflows and outflows. To compute the TWR, we calculate the return to the portfolio immediately prior to a cash flow occurring. We then calculate the return to the portfolio from that cash flow to the next, or to the end of the period. Finally, we link these rates of return together by computing the compound rate of return over time. In other words, we calculate the rate of return for each time period defined by a cash inflow or outflow, and then calculate a compound rate of return for the entire period. If frequent cash flows are involved, substantial calculations are necessary.

EXAMPLE 22-2: CALCULATING THE DOLLAR-WEIGHTED RATE OF RETURN

For Example 22-1, the corresponding TWR would be:

For period one (the first six months) $r_1 = \dfrac{10,050 - 10,000 + 100}{10,000} = 1.50\%$

For period two (the next six months) $r_2 = \dfrac{10,850 - 10,350 + 100}{10,350} = 5.80\%$

So the annual return (based on the geometric average) over the entire period is:

$$r = [(1.0150)(1.0580)] - 1 = 0.0739 \text{ or } 7.39\%$$

Notice that this value differs from the DWR of 7.43%.

Which Measure to Use?

As the examples above illustrate, the dollar-weighted return and the time-weighted return can produce different results. While the difference above is not drastic due to the simplistic nature of the examples, at times these differences are substantial. The time-weighted return captures the rate of return actually earned by the portfolio *manager*, while the dollar-weighted return captures the rate of return earned by the portfolio *owner*.

For evaluating the performance of the portfolio manager, the time-weighted return should be used because he or she generally has no control over the deposits and withdrawals made by the clients. The objective is to measure the performance of the portfolio manager independent of the actions of the client, and this is better accomplished by using the time-weighted return. As we can see in Table 22-1, the GIPS require that returns be computed using the TWR approach. The use of total returns and the TWR approach is required by Canadian mutual funds, according to the Ontario Securities Commission. In particular, they determine total returns based on the change in net asset value of the fund (as defined in Chapter 3).

Risk Measures

Why can we not measure investment performance on the basis of a properly calculated rate of return measure? After all, rankings of mutual funds are often done this way in the popular press, with one-year, three-year, and five-year returns shown. Are rates of return, or averages, good indicators of performance?

As stated in Chapter 1 and restated above, we must consider risk when making judgments about performance. Differences in risk will cause portfolios to respond differently to changes in the overall market and should be accounted for in evaluating performance.

We now know that the two prevalent measures of risk used in investment analysis are total risk (as measured by standard deviation) and systematic or market risk (commonly measured by beta). The standard deviation for a portfolio's set of returns can be calculated easily with a calculator or computer and is a measure of total risk.

Any number of software programs can calculate beta. However, we must remember that betas are only estimates of systematic risk, with respect to a chosen market proxy such as the S&P/TSX Composite Index. Betas can be calculated using weekly, monthly, quarterly, or annual data, and each will produce a different estimate. Such variations in this calculation could produce differences in rankings that use beta as a measure of risk. Furthermore, betas can be unstable, and they change over time.

CHECK YOUR UNDERSTANDING

22-3. You are reviewing the performance of a mutual fund that you already own and wish to compare it with an alternative fund you are considering investing in. Would the TWR or DWR be better for these applications?

22-4. You own a portfolio that has a beta of 1.0 when measured against the S&P/TSX Composite Index. What can you conclude about the risk level and expected performance of this portfolio?

---

learning objective 3

Distinguish between the three composite measures of portfolio performance.

Composite (Risk-Adjusted) Measures of Portfolio Performance

Portfolio performance measures combining return and risk into one calculation.

RISK-ADJUSTED MEASURES OF PERFORMANCE

Based on the concepts of capital market theory, and recognizing the necessity to incorporate both return and risk into the analysis, three researchers—William Sharpe, Jack Treynor, and Michael Jensen—developed measures of portfolio performance in the 1960s. These measures are often referred to as the **composite (risk-adjusted) measures of portfolio performance**, meaning that they incorporate both realized return and risk into the evaluation. These measures are often still commonly used, as seen in Real-World Returns 22-2.

REAL-WORLD RETURNS 22-2

Take a Statistical View of Mutual Funds

There's much more to performance than just annualized performance. If you want to get more technical, you will need to look at some key statistical data on the risk and return of funds.

Sharpe Ratio

The Sharpe ratio measures the return of a mutual fund compared to the risk-free rate of return. The risk-free rate of return is the 91-day T-bill rate. This should be similar to money markets or short-term GICs. Often, this ratio is used to determine if a mutual fund is able to beat GICs.

The Trimark Select Growth Fund has had a Sharpe ratio over the last five years of 0.57. The range of Sharpe ratios for global equity funds went from as low as minus 1.11 to a high of 0.94.

A positive Sharpe ratio means the fund did better on a risk-adjusted basis than the 91-day T-bill rate. In other words, the higher the Sharpe ratio, the better. The Sharpe ratio tells you about history, but it does not tell you anything about the future. Just because a fund has had a positive Sharpe ratio for the last five years does not mean it will outperform GICs for the next five years.

Treynor Ratio

The Treynor ratio is similar to the Sharpe ratio. Instead of comparing the fund's risk-adjusted performance to the risk-free return, it compares the fund's risk-adjusted performance to the relative index. The Trimark Select Growth Fund has a Treynor ratio of 11.52. Just like the Sharpe ratio, the higher the number, the better. The range of ratios for global equity funds is a low of minus 20.91 to a high of 32.

Alpha Ratio

If you are trying to see if a mutual fund has beaten the performance of its relative index, you should take a look at the Alpha ratio. In more simple terms, if you want to see if the Trimark Select Growth Fund beat the MSCI World Index, then you look at the Alpha. The Alpha ratio for the last five years for the Trimark Select Growth Fund is 0.46. If the number is greater than zero, then we say it has a positive Alpha. In this case, over the last five years, the Trimark Select Growth Fund has been able to outperform the MSCI World Index. The greater the number, the greater the outperformance. The range of Alphas for global equity funds is minus 0.87 to 1.72.

Beta Ratio

Where the Alpha looks at excess returns over the index, the Beta looks at excess risk over the index. So we know that the Trimark Select Growth Fund has outperformed the index in the last five years, but how much risk did it take to do so? The Beta for the Trimark Select Growth Fund is 0.61. In context, the benchmark for the Beta measure is one. If you have a Beta of one, we say you have the same risk as the market. With a Beta of 0.61, we say you have experienced about 61 percent of the risk of the market. In other words, you have taken less risk than the market. Betas and Alphas go hand-in-hand. Ideally, you want a fund with a low Beta and a high Alpha. This means you found a fund that has outperformed the index while experiencing less risk than the index.

How Should You Use these Ratios?

Rating and analyzing mutual funds is an imperfect science. Often fund movements cannot be explained by statistics because of random activity. My point is that people place far too much emphasis on performance alone, and the most readily available information is the only information that is used to evaluate performance. If you want to employ better research, you may want to look at some of these ratios to help determine how well a fund has performed in relation to the risk and return of GICs and other benchmark indexes.

Source: Excerpted from Yih, James "Take a Statistical View of Mutual Funds." Article originally appeared on MoneySense.ca website at www.moneysense.ca, June 13, 2002. Reprinted with permission from the author.

The Sharpe Performance Measure

William Sharpe, whose contributions to portfolio theory have been previously encountered, introduced a risk-adjusted measure of portfolio performance called the **reward-to-variability ratio (RVAR)** based on his work in capital market theory.[2] This measure uses a benchmark based on the *ex post* capital market line.[3] This measure can be defined as

$$RVAR = [\overline{TR_p} - \overline{RF}] / SD_p \qquad \textbf{(22-2)}$$
$$= \text{Excess return/Risk}$$

Reward-to-Variability Ratio (RVAR)

Sharpe's measure of portfolio performance calculated as the ratio of excess portfolio return to the standard deviation.

$\overline{TR_p}$ = the average TR for portfolio p during some period of time (we will use annual data)

[2] W. Sharpe, "Mutual Fund Performance," *Journal of Business* 39 (January 1966), pp. 119–138.
[3] Sharpe used it to rank the performance of 34 mutual funds over the period 1954–63.

$\overline{RF}$ = the average risk-free rate of return during the period

SD_p = the standard deviation of return for portfolio p during the period

$\overline{TR}_p - \overline{RF}$ = the excess return (risk premium) on portfolio p

The numerator of Equation 22-2 measures the portfolio's excess return, or the return above the risk-free rate. (RF could have been earned without assuming risk.) This is also referred to as the risk premium. The denominator uses the standard deviation, which is a measure of the total risk or variability in the return of the portfolio. Note the following about RVAR:

- It measures the excess return per unit of total risk (standard deviation).
- The higher the RVAR, the better the portfolio performance, since excess return (which investors desire) is in the numerator and risk (which investors dislike) is in the denominator.
- Portfolios can be ranked by RVAR.

As an example of calculating the Sharpe ratio, consider the data for five Canadian equity mutual funds for the five-year period from May 1, 2003, to April 30, 2008, which were chosen randomly for illustrative purposes only: **AIC Diversified Canadian (AI)**, **Altamira Equity (AL)**, **Investors Canadian Equity—Class A (I)**, **RBC Canadian Equity (R)**, and **TD Canadian Equity (T)**. Table 22-2 shows annual fund returns, the standard deviation of these returns, the beta for the fund, the average return for the S&P/STX Composite Index for those years, and the average yield on 30-day government T-bills, which proxies for RF.[4] On the basis of this data, Sharpe's RVAR can be calculated using Equation 22-2, with the results reported in column two of Table 22-3.

Table 22-2

Return and Risk Data for Five Canadian Equity Mutual Funds
May 1, 2003 to April 30, 2008

Mutual Fund	Average Return (%)	Standard Deviation (%)	Beta
AIC Diversified Canadian	6.99	8.37	0.54
Altamira Equity	16.68	10.53	0.94
Investors Canadian Equity—Class A	13.91	11.28	1.00
RBC Canadian Equity	17.61	11.07	0.99
TD Canadian Equity	21.74	14.26	1.23
S&P/TSX Composite Index	18.65	11.03	
RF (30-day T-bills)	3.31		

Table 22-3

Risk-Adjusted Measures for Five Canadian Equity Mutual Funds
May 1, 2003 to April 30, 2008

Mutual Fund	RVAR	RVOL (%)	Jensen's Alpha (%)*
AIC (AI)	0.44	6.81	−4.60
Altamira (AL)	1.27	14.22	−1.05
Investors (I)	0.94	10.60	−4.74
Royal (R)	1.29	14.44	−0.89
TD (T)	1.29	14.98	−0.44
S&P/TSX Composite Index	1.39	15.34	

*Jensen's differential return measure is discussed below.

[4]While five-year returns are used in Table 22-2 and Table 22-3, the risk measures used are based on three years of data, which is not strictly correct. The five-year returns are used because the three-year returns produced mainly negative Sharpe and Treynor ratios, which give rise to difficulties involved in interpreting these ratios, as is discussed in the respective sections dealing with these measures. Since five-year risk measures were not available, we used three-year measures.

Based on these calculations, we see that none of these five funds outperformed the S&P/TSX Composite Index on an excess return–risk basis during this period. Using only the Sharpe measure of portfolio performance, we would judge the portfolio with the highest RVAR best in terms of *ex post* performance. The RVAR value for the appropriate market index has also been calculated and used for comparison purposes.

As we can see, none of the funds have RVAR ratios that exceed the RVAR of 1.39 for the S&P/TSX Composite Index for the period, even TD, whose average return was above the average S&P/TSX Composite Index return of 18.65 percent. This was because TD's standard deviation was above that of the S&P/TSX Composite Index, resulting in a Sharpe ratio below that of the S&P/TSX Composite Index.

Sharpe's measure for these funds is illustrated graphically in Figure 22-1. The vertical axis is rate of return, and the horizontal axis is standard deviation of returns. The vertical intercept is RF. As Figure 22-1 shows, RVAR measures the slope of the line from RF to the portfolio being evaluated. The steeper the line, the higher the slope (RVAR) and the better the performance.[5] The arrows indicate the slope for the S&P/TSX Composite Index and for RBC, the fund with the greatest slope.

Because of its superior risk-adjusted performance, the S&P/TSX Composite Index has the largest slope, while the slopes for the five funds are lower than that. Because the RVAR for all of these funds are less than the RVAR for the market measure (in this case the S&P/TSX Composite Index), these portfolios lie below the *ex post* capital market line (CML), indicating inferior risk-adjusted performance.

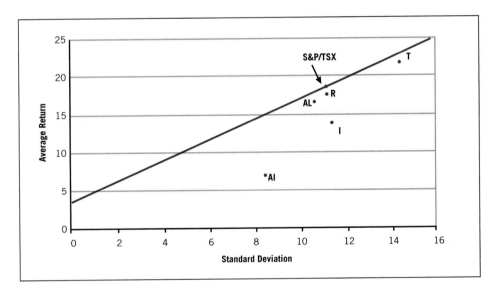

Figure 22-1
Sharpe's Measure of Performance (RVAR) for Five Mutual Funds, May 2003–April 2008

In Figure 22-1 we are drawing the CML when we plot the market's return against its standard deviation and use RF as the vertical intercept. Based on the discussion in Chapter 9, all efficient portfolios should plot on this line, and an investor with the ability to borrow and lend at the rate RF should be able to attain any point on this line. Of course, this is the *ex post* and not the *ex ante* CML.

---

[5]The statement that higher Sharpe ratios imply better performance is true only when we are dealing with positive values. However, this will not always be the case when we have negative Sharpe ratios. For example, consider two funds that provide the same excess "negative" return, but one has higher standard deviation. It will have a higher (i.e., less negative) Sharpe ratio than the other; however, clearly it performed worse than the other fund, since they produced the same negative excess return, but it had higher risk. In short, it is hard to make conclusions regarding performance comparisons when using negative Sharpe ratios.

The Treynor Performance Measure

At approximately the same time as Sharpe's measure was developed (the mid-1960s), Jack Treynor presented a similar measure called the **reward-to-volatility ratio (RVOL)**.[6] Like Sharpe, Treynor sought to relate the return on a portfolio to its risk. Treynor, however, distinguished between total risk and systematic risk, implicitly assuming that portfolios are well diversified; that is, he ignores any diversifiable risk. He used as a benchmark the *ex post* security market line.

In measuring portfolio performance, Treynor introduced the concept of the characteristic line, used in earlier chapters to partition a security's return into its systematic and non-systematic components. It is used in a similar manner with portfolios, depicting the relationship between the returns on a portfolio and those of the market. The slope of the characteristic line measures the relative volatility of the fund's returns. As we know, the slope of this line is the beta coefficient, which is a measure of the volatility (or responsiveness) of the portfolio's returns in relation to those of the chosen market index.

As we learned in Chapter 8, characteristic lines can be estimated by regressing each portfolio's returns on the market proxy returns using either raw returns for the portfolios and raw proxy returns, or by using excess portfolio returns and excess market proxy returns (where the risk-free rate has been subtracted out). The latter method is theoretically preferable and is used here.

Treynor's measure relates the average excess return on the portfolio during some period (exactly the same variable as in the Sharpe measure) to its systematic risk as measured by the portfolio's beta. The reward-to-volatility ratio is

Reward-to-Volatility Ratio (RVOL)

Treynor's measure of portfolio performance calculated as the ratio of excess portfolio return to beta.

(22-3)

$$RVOL = [\overline{TR_p} - \overline{RF}] / \beta_p$$

where
$[\overline{TR_p} - \overline{RF}]$ = average excess return on portfolio p
β_p = the beta for portfolio p

In this case, we are calculating the excess return per unit of systematic risk. As with RVAR, higher values of RVOL indicate better portfolio performance.[7] Portfolios can be ranked on their RVOL, and assuming that the Treynor measure is a correct calculation of portfolio performance, the best performing portfolio can be determined.

Using the data in Table 22-2, we can calculate RVOL for the same five portfolios illustrated and for the S&P/TSX Composite Index, which has a beta of 1.0 by definition. These calculations indicate that all of the funds underperformed the market on the basis of their excess return/systematic risk ratio.

Figure 22-2 illustrates the graph of the Treynor measures in a manner similar to Figure 22-1 for the Sharpe measures. In this graph we are viewing the *ex post* security market line (SML). Again, all of the funds plot below the line. Once again, if we were to draw lines to each fund's return–risk point, the steepest line would be the one drawn to the S&P/TSX Index, which has the largest slope and represents the best risk-adjusted performance.

The use of RVOL, of course, implies that systematic risk is the proper measure to use when evaluating portfolio performance; therefore, it implicitly assumes a completely diversified portfolio. (Similarly, the use of RVAR implies that total risk is the proper measure to use when evaluating portfolios.) As we now know, systematic risk is a proper measure of risk to use when portfolios are perfectly diversified so that no non-systematic risk remains.

---

[6]J. Treynor, "How to Rate Management of Investment Funds," *Harvard Business Review* 43 (January–February 1965), pp. 63–75.

[7]Similar to our comments in Footnote 5 regarding Sharpe ratios, the statement that higher Treynor ratios imply better performance is true only when we are dealing with positive values. However, when we have negative Treynor ratios, this will not be the case. For example, consider two funds that provide the same excess "negative" return, but one has higher beta. It will have a higher (i.e., less negative) Treynor ratio than the other; however, clearly it performed worse than the other fund, since they produced the same negative excess return, but it had higher risk. In short, it is hard to make conclusions regarding performance comparisons when using negative Treynor ratios.

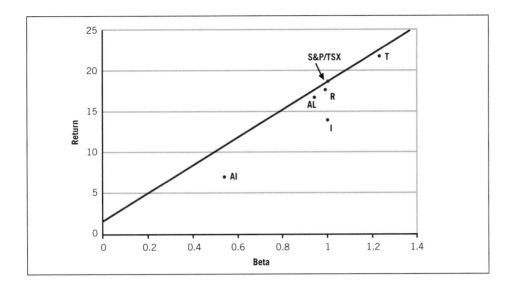

Figure 22-2
Treynor's Measure of
Performance (RVOL) for
Five Mutual Funds,
May 2003–April 2008

Comparing the Sharpe and Treynor Measures

When should RVAR be used and when RVOL and why? Actually, given the assumptions underlying each measure, both can be said to be correct. Therefore, it is usually desirable to calculate both for the set of portfolios being evaluated. The choice of which to use could depend on the definition of risk. If an investor thinks it correct to use total risk, RVAR is appropriate; however, RVOL is appropriate for systematic risk.

What about the rankings of a set of portfolios using the two measures? If the portfolios are perfectly diversified—that is, the correlation coefficient between the portfolio return and the market return is 1.0—the rankings will be identical. For typical large, professionally managed portfolios, such as broad-based equity mutual funds, the two measures often provide identical (or almost identical) rankings as was the case in our example above.

As the portfolios become less well diversified, the possibility of differences in rankings increases. This leads to the following conclusion about these two measures: RVOL assumes portfolios are well diversified while RVAR does not. RVAR takes into account how well diversified a portfolio was during the measurement period. Differences in rankings between the two measures can result from substantial differences in diversification in the portfolio. If a portfolio is inadequately diversified, its RVOL ranking can be higher than its RVAR ranking. The non-systematic risk would not affect the RVOL calculation. Therefore, a portfolio with a low amount of systematic risk and a large amount of total risk could show a high RVOL value and a low RVAR value. Such a difference in ranking results from the substantial difference in the amount of diversification of the portfolio.

This analysis leads to an important observation about the Sharpe and Treynor measures. Investors who have all (or substantially all) of their assets in a portfolio of securities should rely more on the Sharpe measure because it assesses the portfolio's total return in relation to total risk, which includes any non-systematic risk assumed by the investor. However, for those whose portfolio constitutes only one (relatively) small part of their total assets—that is, they have numerous other assets—systematic risk may well be the relevant risk. In these circumstances, RVOL is appropriate because it considers only systematic or non-diversifiable risk.

Jensen's Differential Return Measure

A measure related to Treynor's RVOL is Jensen's **differential return measure** (or alpha). Jensen's measure of performance, like Treynor's, is based on the capital asset pricing model (CAPM).

Differential Return Measure (Alpha)

The measure of portfolio performance calculated as the difference between what the portfolio actually earned and what it was expected to earn given its level of systematic risk.

According to CAPM, the expected return for any security (*i*) or, in this case, portfolio (*p*), is given as:

(22-4)

$$E(R_p) = RF + \beta_p [E(R_M) - RF]$$

with all terms as previously defined.

Notice that Equation 22-4, which covers any *ex ante* period, can be applied to *ex post* periods if the investor's expectations are realized, on average. Empirically, Equation 22-4 can be approximated as Equation 22-5.

(22-5)

$$R_{pt} = RF_t + \beta_p [R_{Mt} - RF_t] + e_{pt}$$

where

R_{pt}	= the return on portfolio *p* in period *t*
RF_t	= the risk-free rate in period *t*
R_M	= the return on the market in period *t*
e_{pt}	= a random error term for portfolio *p* in period *t*
$[R_{Mt} - RF_t]$	= the market risk premium during period *t*

Equation 22-5 relates the realized return on portfolio *p* during any period *t* to the sum of the risk-free rate and the portfolio's risk premium plus an error term. Given the market risk premium, the risk premium on portfolio *p* is a function of portfolio *p*'s systematic risk—the larger its systematic risk, the larger the risk premium.

Equation 22-5 can be written in what is called the risk premium (or, alternatively, the excess return) form by moving RF to the left side and subtracting it from R_{pt}, as in Equation 22-6:

(22-6)

$$R_{pt} - RF_t = \beta_p [R_{Mt} - RF_t] + e_{pt}$$

where

$R_{pt} - RF_t$ = the risk premium on portfolio *p*

Equation 22-6 indicates that the risk premium on portfolio *p* is equal to the product of its beta and the market risk premium plus an error term. In other words, the risk premium on portfolio *p* should be proportional to that on the market portfolio if the CAPM model is correct and investor expectations were generally realized (in effect, if all assets and portfolios were in equilibrium).

A return proportional to the risk assumed is illustrated by Fund Y in Figure 22-3. This diagram shows the characteristic line in excess return form, where the risk-free rate each period, RF_t, is subtracted from both the portfolio's return and the market's return.[8] Equation 22-6 can be empirically tested by fitting a regression for some number of periods. Portfolio excess returns (risk premiums) are regressed against the excess returns (risk premiums) for the market. If managers earn a return proportional to the risk assumed, this relationship should hold. That is, there should be no intercept term (alpha) in the regression, which should go through the origin, as in the case of Fund Y in Figure 22-3.

Given these expected findings, Jensen argued that an intercept term, alpha, could be added to Equation 22-6 as a means of identifying superior or inferior portfolio performance. Therefore, Equation 22-6 becomes Equation 22-7 where α_p is the alpha or intercept term:

(22-7)

$$R_{pt} - RF_t = \alpha_p + \beta_p [R_{Mt} - RF_t] + e_{pt}$$

The CAPM asserts that equilibrium conditions should result in a zero intercept term. Therefore, the alpha should measure the contribution of the portfolio manager since it represents the average incremental rate of return per period beyond the return attributable to the level of risk assumed.

---

[8]This version is usually referred to as a characteristic line in risk premium or excess return form.

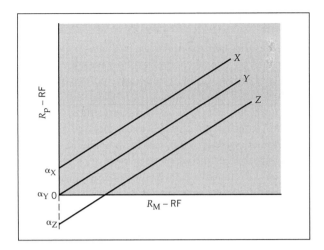

Figure 22-3
Jensen's Measure for
Three Hypothetical Funds

Specifically,

- if alpha is significantly positive, this is evidence of superior performance (illustrated in Figure 22-3 with portfolio X, which has a positive intercept)

- if alpha is significantly negative, this is evidence of inferior performance (illustrated in Figure 22-3 with portfolio Z, which has a negative intercept)

- if alpha is insignificantly different from zero, this is evidence that the portfolio manager matched the market on a risk-adjusted basis (as in the case of portfolio Y)

Note that Equation 22-7 can be rearranged to better demonstrate what α_p really is. Rearranging terms, Equation 22-7 becomes, for the sample time period

$$\alpha_p = (\overline{R}_p - \overline{RF}) - [\beta_p (\overline{R}_M - \overline{RF})]$$ **(22-8)**

where the bars above the variables indicate averages for the period measured.

Equation 22-8 states that α_p is the difference between the actual excess return on portfolio p during some period and the risk premium on that portfolio that should have been earned, given its level of systematic risk and the use of the CAPM. It measures the constant return that the portfolio manager earned above, or below, the return of an unmanaged portfolio with the same (market) risk.

As noted, this difference can be positive, negative, or zero. It is important to recognize the role of statistical significance in the interpretation of Jensen's measure. Although the estimated alpha may be positive or negative, it may not be significantly different (statistically) from zero. If it is not, we would conclude that the manager of the portfolio being evaluated performed as expected. That is, the manager earned an average risk-adjusted return, neither more nor less than would be expected given the risk assumed.

Jensen's performance measure can be estimated by regressing excess returns for the portfolio being evaluated against excess returns for the market (in effect, producing a characteristic line in excess return form).

The alphas for the five mutual funds that are presented in Table 22-3 were estimated using Equation 22-8 and using averages for portfolio returns, market returns, and the risk-free rate. All of the funds reported negative alphas. If significant, these negative alphas would indicate that these funds, on the average, earned annual risk-adjusted rates of return that were below the market performance. In other words, these funds earned negative returns attributable to factors other than the market, which is an indication of the performance of their managers over this period.

Superior and inferior portfolio performance can result from at least two sources. First, the portfolio manager may be able to select undervalued securities consistently enough to affect portfolio performance. Second, the manager may be able to time market turns, varying the portfolio's composition in accordance with the rise and fall of the market. Obviously, a manager with enough ability may be able to do both.

A Comparison of the Three Composite Measures

The Sharpe measure, which uses the standard deviation, evaluates portfolio performance on the basis of both the portfolio's return and its diversification. Treynor's measure considers only the systematic risk of the portfolio and, like Sharpe's, can be used to rank portfolios on the basis of realized performance. Although the Sharpe and Treynor measures rank portfolios, they do not tell us in percentage terms how much a fund outperformed (or underperformed) some benchmark.

Like the Treynor measure, Jensen's alpha uses beta as the measure of risk. Jensen's measure was not designed for ranking portfolio performance, but it can be modified to do so. The Jensen and Treynor measures can produce, with proper adjustments, identical relative rankings of portfolio performance.[9]

If a portfolio is completely diversified, all three measures will agree on a ranking of portfolios. The reason for this is that with complete diversification, total variance is equal to systematic variance. When portfolios are not completely diversified, the Treynor and Jensen measures can rank relatively undiversified portfolios much higher than the Sharpe measure can. Since the Sharpe measure uses total risk, both systematic and non-systematic components are included.

> **CHECK YOUR UNDERSTANDING**
>
> **22-5.** Can the numerator of both the Sharpe and Treynor measures be described as the portfolio's risk premium? If so, what does this mean?
>
> **22-6.** Assume you examine five completely diversified portfolios. Will the Sharpe, Treynor, and Jensen measures agree on how the managers should be ranked? Why or why not?

PROBLEMS WITH PORTFOLIO MEASUREMENT

learning objective 4
Discuss problems with portfolio measurement.

Using the three risk-adjusted performance measures just discussed to evaluate portfolios is not without problems. Investors should understand their limitations and be guided accordingly.

These measures are derived from capital market theory and the CAPM and are therefore dependent on the assumptions involved with this theory, as discussed in Chapter 9. For example, if the T-bill rate is not a satisfactory proxy for the risk-free rate, or if investors cannot borrow and lend at the risk-free rate, this will have an impact on these measures of performance. An important assumption of capital market theory that directly affects the use of these performance measures is the assumption of a market portfolio that can be proxied by a market index. We have used the S&P/TSX Composite Index as a market index, as is often done. However, there are potential problems.

Richard Roll has argued that beta is not a clear-cut measure of risk.[10] If the definition of the market portfolio is changed, the beta can change. This could, in turn, change the rankings of portfolios. In addition, if the proxy for the market portfolio is not efficient, the security market line (SML) used may not be the true SML. When portfolios are plotted against an incorrect SML, benchmark errors can occur.

Although a high correlation exists among most of the commonly used market proxies, this does not eliminate the problem that some may be efficient but others are not. This relates to Roll's major point (mentioned in Chapter 9), that using a market portfolio other than the "true" one does not constitute a test of the CAPM. Rather, it is a test only of whether or not the chosen market proxy is efficient. According to Roll, no unambiguous test of the CAPM has yet been conducted. This point

---

[9]Jensen's alpha divided by beta is equivalent to Treynor's measure minus the average risk premium for the market portfolio for the period.

[10]R. Roll, "Ambiguity When Performance Is Measured by the Securities Market Line," *Journal of Finance* 33 (September 1978), pp. 1051–1069; "Performance Evaluation and Benchmark Error, Part I," *Journal of Portfolio Management* 6 (Summer 1980), pp. 5–12, and Part II, 7 (Winter 1981), pp. 17–22.

should be kept in mind when we consider the Treynor and Jensen performance measures, which are based on the CAPM.

The movement to global investing increases the problem of benchmark error. The efficient frontier changes when foreign securities are added to the portfolio. The measurement of beta will be affected by adding foreign securities. Given that a world portfolio is likely to have a smaller variance than the S&P/TSX Composite Index, any measure of systematic risk is likely to be smaller.

A long evaluation period is needed to successfully determine performance that is truly superior. Over short periods, luck can overshadow all else, but it cannot be expected to continue. According to some estimates, the number of years needed to make such an accurate determination is quite large. As we saw in Table 22-1, the GIPS stipulate at least a five-year performance record.

Theoretically, each of the three performance measures discussed should be independent of its respective risk measure. However, over the years some researchers have found a relationship between them. In some cases the relationship was negative, and in others it was positive. It can be shown that a fundamental relationship does exist between the composite performance measures and their associated risk measure.[11] Given an empirical CML, the relation between Sharpe's measure and the standard deviation can be instantly derived. Similarly, given an empirical SML, the relationship between Jensen's and Treynor's performance measures and beta can be deduced. The only other variable needed to do these calculations is the mean market return for the period.

OTHER ISSUES IN PERFORMANCE EVALUATION

Monitoring Performance

learning objective 5
Explain issues in portfolio evaluation, such as performance attribution.

Evaluation of managed portfolios should be a continuous process using some of the techniques discussed above. In addition, a monitoring process should evaluate the success of the portfolio relative to the objectives and constraints of the portfolio's owners.

Performance Attribution

Most of this chapter has considered how to measure a portfolio manager's performance, but portfolio evaluation is also concerned with the reasons why a manager did better or worse than a properly constructed benchmark with complete risk adjustment. This part of portfolio evaluation, called performance attribution, seeks to determine, after the fact, why a particular portfolio had a given return over some specified time period and, therefore, why it succeeded or failed.

Performance Attribution
A part of portfolio evaluation that seeks to determine why success or failure occurred.

Typically, performance attribution is a top-down approach; it looks first at the broad issues and progresses by narrowing the investigation. Its purpose is to divide the total performance of a portfolio into specific components that can be associated with specific decisions made by the portfolio manager.

Performance attribution often begins with the policy statement that guides the management of the portfolio. The portfolio normally would have a set of portfolio weights to be used, but if the manager uses a different set, this will account for some of the variation in the results. In effect, we are looking at the asset allocation decision referred to in Chapter 14. If a manager chooses to allocate portfolio funds differently than the weights that occur in the benchmark portfolio, what are the results?

After this analysis, performance attribution might analyze sector (industry) selection and security selection. Did the manager concentrate on, or avoid, certain sectors, and if so what were the results? Security selection speaks for itself.

Part of this process involves identifying a benchmark of performance to use in comparing the portfolio's results. This "bogey" is designed to measure passive results, ruling out both asset

---

[11]J. Wilson and C. Jones, "The Relationship Between Performance and Risk: Whence the Bias?," *Journal of Financial Research* 4 (Summer 1981), pp. 109–117.

allocation and security selection decisions. Any differences between the portfolio's results and the bogey must be attributable to one or more of these decisions made by the portfolio manager.

Another way to think about performance attribution is to recognize that performance different from a properly constructed benchmark comes from one or both of these sources:

- Market timing
- Security selection

Techniques are available to decompose the performance of a portfolio into these two components.[12]

Can Performance Be Predicted?

The objective of performance evaluation is to measure the performance of a portfolio and its manager over a certain time period. Having assessed how well a portfolio manager has performed over the past, is such information valuable in predicting future portfolio performance? As discussed in Chapter 10, most studies suggest that the correlation between past relative performance and future performance is weak. For example, the correlation coefficients for the average returns for a five- or one-year period with average returns for the subsequent corresponding period are quite low, usually less than 0.20. Therefore, past relative returns do not successfully predict future returns.

SUMMARY

This summary relates to the learning objectives for this chapter.

1. **Outline the framework for evaluating portfolio performance.**
   Evaluation of portfolio performance, the bottom line of the investing process, is an important aspect of interest to all investors and money managers. The framework for evaluating portfolio performance consists of measuring both the realized return and the differential risk of the portfolio being evaluated, determining an appropriate benchmark portfolio to use to compare a portfolio's performance and recognizing any constraints that the portfolio manager may face. The CFA Institute has issued a set of Global Investment Performance Standards (GIPS®) designed to promote full disclosure by investment managers globally in reporting their investment results and help ensure uniformity in reporting.

2. **Use measures of return and risk to evaluate portfolio performance.**
   The time-weighted, as opposed to the dollar-weighted, return captures the rate of return actually earned by the portfolio manager. Total returns are used in the calculations. The two prevalent measures of risk are total risk (standard deviation) and systematic risk (beta). The most often used composite measures of portfolio performance are those of Sharpe, Treynor, and Jensen, which bring return and risk together in one calculation.

3. **Distinguish between the three composite measures of portfolio performance.**
   The Sharpe and Treynor measures can be used to rank portfolio performance and indicate the relative positions of the portfolios being evaluated, while Jensen's measure is an absolute measure of performance. Both the Sharpe and Treynor measures relate the excess return on a portfolio to a measure of its risk. Sharpe's RVAR uses standard deviation, whereas Treynor's RVOL uses beta. Since RVAR implicitly measures the lack of complete diversification in a portfolio and RVOL assumes complete diversification, portfolio rankings from the two measures can differ if portfolios are not well diversified. The Sharpe measure is more appropriate when the portfolio constitutes a significant portion of an investor's wealth, whereas the Treynor measure is more appropriate when the portfolio constitutes only a small part of that wealth. Jensen's differential return measures the difference between what the portfolio was expected to earn, given its systematic risk, and what it ac-

---

[12]R. Henriksson, "Market Timing and Mutual Fund Performance: An Empirical Investigation," *Journal of Business* 57 (January 1984), pp. 73–96.

tually did earn. By regressing the portfolio's excess return against that of the market index, alpha can be used to capture the superior or inferior performance of the portfolio manager. Based on capital market theory, alphas are expected to be zero. Significantly positive or negative alphas indicate above or below average performance.

4. **Discuss problems with portfolio measurement.**

The composite measures are not without their limitations and problems. The problems associated with capital market theory and the CAPM carry over to performance measurement. One problem in particular is the market portfolio, which cannot be measured precisely. Failure to use the true *ex ante* market portfolio may result in different betas and different rankings for portfolios because of benchmark error.

5. **Explain issues in portfolio evaluation, such as performance attribution.**

Performance attribution is concerned with why a portfolio manager did better or worse than an expected benchmark. It involves decomposing performance to determine why the particular results occurred.

KEY TERMS

Benchmark portfolio, p.727
Composite (risk-adjusted) measures of portfolio performance, p.734
Differential return measure (alpha), p.739

Dollar-weighted rate of return (DWR), p.732
Global Investment Performance Standards (GIPS®), p.728
Performance attribution, p.743
Reward-to-variability ratio

(RVAR), p.735
Reward-to-volatility ratio (RVOL), p.738
Time-weighted rate of return (TWR), p.733

REVIEW QUESTIONS

22-1. How can one construct a characteristic line for a portfolio? What does it show?

22-2. Explain why the steeper the angle, the better the performance in Figures 22-1 and 22-2.

22-3. Outline the framework for evaluating portfolio performance.

22-4. What role does diversification play in the Sharpe and Treynor measures?

22-5. In general, when may an investor prefer to rely on the Sharpe measure? The Treynor measure?

22-6. Explain how Jensen's differential return measure is derived from the CAPM.

22-7. In theory, what would be the proper market index to use?

22-8. Do the Sharpe and Jensen measures always produce the same rankings of portfolio performance?

22-9. Explain how the three composite measures of performance are related to capital market theory and the CAPM.

22-10. How does Roll's questioning of the testing of the CAPM relate to the issue of performance measurement?

22-11. Illustrate how the choice of the wrong market index could affect the rankings of portfolios.

22-12. What are the two different return measures? When should they be used?

22-13. If your portfolio is completely diversified, how will the rankings of portfolios compare when using Sharpe, Treynor, and Jensen's alpha? How will the three measures compare if your portfolio is not completely diversified?

22-14. Discuss some of the problems associated with portfolio measurement.

22-15. What is the purpose of performance attribution? What are the typical issues or components of performance that it investigates?

PROBLEMS

22-1. Consider the five funds shown below:

	α	β
1	2.0	1.0
2	1.6*	1.1
3	3.5	0.9
4	1.2	0.8
5	0.9*	1.20

* Significant at the 5% level.

   a. Which fund had the lowest market risk? The highest?
   b. According to Jensen's alpha, which fund(s) outperformed the market?

22-2. The following data are available for five portfolios and the market for a recent 10-year period:

	Average Annual Return (%)	Standard Deviation (%)	β_p
1	14	21	1.15
2	16	24	1.1
3	26	30	1.3
4	17	25	0.9
5	10	18	0.45
S&P/TSX Composite Index	12	20	
RF	6		

   a. Rank these portfolios using the Sharpe measure.
   b. Rank these portfolios using the Treynor measure.
   c. Compare the rankings of portfolios 1 and 2. Are there any differences? How can you explain these differences?
   d. Which of these portfolios outperformed the market?

22-3. Annual total returns for nine years are shown below for eight mutual funds. Characteristic lines are calculated using annual market returns. The *ex post* values are as follows:

Fund	(1) R_p(%)	(2) σ_p(%)	(3) α_p	(4) β_p
A	17.0	20.0	7.53	0.88
B	19.0	17.8	11.70	0.65
C	12.3	25.0	3.12	0.83
D	20.0	24.5	9.00	1.00
E	15.0	17.4	6.15	0.79
F	19.0	18.0	21.37	0.83
G	8.6	19.0	21.37	0.91
H	20.0	21.5	9.52	0.93

where
R_p = mean annual total return for each fund
σ_p = standard deviation of the annual returns
α_p = the constant of the characteristic line
β_p = the slope

Using an 8.6 percent risk-free return:

  a. Calculate Sharpe's RVAR for each of these eight funds, and rank the eight funds from high to low performance.

  b. Calculate Treynor's RVOL for each fund and perform the same ranking as in part (a).

22-4. Given the following information:

Period	Market	RF	Portfolio 1	Portfolio 2
1	0.12	.07	0.14	0.16
2	0.10	.07	0.18	0.20
3	0.02	.08	0.06	0.04
4	0.20	.08	0.30	0.26
5	0.16	.07	0.21	0.21
6	−0.03	.08	−0.04	−0.06
7	−0.05	.07	−0.04	−0.01
8	0.13	.07	0.14	0.12
9	0.30	.08	0.28	0.32
10	−0.15	.09	−0.20	−0.25

  a. Rank the portfolios on RVAR.
  b. Rank the portfolios on RVOL.
  c. Rank the portfolios on alpha.
  d. Which portfolio had the larger beta?
  e. Which portfolio had the larger standard deviation?
  f. Which portfolio had the larger average return?
  g. How are the answers to (d), (e), and (f) related to the results for the composite performance measures?

22-5. Given the following information for three portfolios for a six-year period:

Period	Market	RF	Portfolio 1	Portfolio 2	Portfolio 3
1	0.10	.05	0.15	0.16	0.17
2	0.02	.06	0.09	0.11	0.13
3	0.20	.08	0.26	0.28	0.18
4	0.30	.09	0.34	0.36	0.42
5	−0.04	.08	−0.02	−0.03	−0.16
6	0.16	.07	0.16	0.17	0.17

Answer (a) through (c) without doing the calculations.

  a. Which portfolio would you expect to have the largest beta?
  b. Which portfolio would you expect to have the largest standard deviation?
  c. Which portfolio would you expect to rank first on the basis of RVAR?
  d. Determine the rankings of the three portfolios based on RVAR and on RVOL.
  e. Which portfolio had the largest alpha?
  f. Which portfolio exhibited the best performance based on the composite measures of performance?

22-6. The following information is available for two portfolios, a market index, and the risk-free rate:

Period	Market Return	RF	Portfolio 1	Portfolio 2
1	0.10	.06	0.10	0.20
2	0.12	.08	0.12	0.24
3	0.20	.08	0.20	0.40
4	0.04	.08	0.04	0.08
5	0.12	.08	0.12	0.24

a. Without doing calculations, determine the portfolio with a beta of 1.0.

b. Without doing calculations, determine the beta of portfolio 2.

c. Without doing calculations, what would you expect the alpha of portfolio 1 to be?

d. What would you expect the RVAR and RVOL to be for portfolio 1 relative to the market?

22-7. A fund had an average annual return of 9 percent with $\sigma = 25$ percent. During the same period, the return on the market was 8 percent, and the standard deviation of the market was 17 percent, while RF averaged 5 percent through the period. The fund also has a correlation coefficient of 0.80 with the market returns.

a. Based on RVAR, did the fund outperform or underperform the market?

b. Based on RVOL, did the fund outperform or underperform the market?

c. Is the portfolio most likely considered to be perfectly diversified?

d. If total risk is relevant, which results should you accept?

e. According to Jensen's alpha, did the fund outperform the market?

22-8. An equity portfolio is worth $80,200 on January 1. On July 1, the portfolio pays a dividend of $60 and is worth $80,300 after paying the dividends. At year end, the portfolio pays a dividend of $60 and has an ending value of $80,800 after paying the dividends and before the investor makes a withdrawl of an additional $200 from the portfolio. Determine your annual effective return on the portfolio if you are the portfolio owner.

22-9. As part of your savings and investing plans you have decided to invest $100 at the start of each month in an equity mutual fund. You do this starting January 1st, and continue until December 1st. On the first anniversary of starting this investment plan, you decide to check the rate of return earned by the mutual fund and your investment. The table below shows the Net Asset Value (NAV) per unit of the mutual fund as of the first day of each month (when your purchases take place. Assume no income distributions are made by the fund.

Month	NAV ($)
January	10.00
February	10.10
March	10.25
April	10.35
May	10.15
June	10.25
July	10.50
August	10.60
September	10.75
October	10.70
November	10.50
December	10.40
January	10.55

a. Calculate the time weighted return (TWR) for the mutual fund.

b. Calculate the dollar weighted return (DWR) which you actually earned. To do this you will need to determine how many units of the mutual fund you purchased each month (January to December) at the NAV per unit. The total units purchased over the year, multiplied by the NAV on the final date ($10.55) gives the total value of your investment. By entering your 12 purchases ($100 each) and the total value of the investment (as a negative figure) into the "=IRR( )" function, Excel will calculate the monthly return you earned. You can then find the effective annual return.

c. Why is your DWR so much lower than the mutual fund's TWR?

22-10. In Chapter 14, Real World Returns 14-1 presents the five-year returns and beta figures for Canadian equity mutual funds and ETFs. We'll work with the first 15 entries in the table (down to the "National Bank Canadian Index" fund). Enter the name, 5-year return figures, and 5-year beta figures into columns A, B, and C respectively of a spreadsheet.

    a. Assume that the return on the iShares Canadian Composite Index fund (ETF) represents the market return, and that the appropriate risk-free rate is 4 percent per year. Calculate Treynor's RVOL and Jensen's Alpha for each of the funds.

    b. Based on the Treynor measure, which of the funds performed best? Which was worst?

    c. To be considered significant (statistically), the Jensen's Alpha must be greater than 1 percent or less than −1 percent. Did the managers of any of these funds actually demonstrate superior (or inferior) skill?

PREPARING FOR YOUR PROFESSIONAL EXAMS

CFA PRACTICE QUESTION

22-1. An analyst gathered the follow information ($ millions) about the performance of a portfolio:

Quarter	Value at Beginning of Quarter (Prior to Inflow or Outflow)	Cash Inflow (Outflow) at Beginning of Quarter	Value at End of Quarter
1	2.0	0.2	2.4
2	2.4	0.4	2.6
3	2.6	(0.2)	3.2
4	3.2	1.0	4.1

The portfolio's annual time-weighted rate of return is *closest* to:

    a. 8%.
    b. 27%.
    c. 32%.
    d. 60%.

CFA CURRICULUM AND SAMPLE EXAM QUESTIONS (©CFA INSTITUTE)

22-1. For an investment portfolio, the Sharpe ratio is used to measure:

    a. risk per unit of mean return.
    b. mean return per unit of risk.
    c. risk per unit of mean excess return.
    d. mean excess return per unit of risk.

CHAPTER 1

1-1. Disagree. Financial assets are claims on an issuer such as a government or corporation, whereas real assets are physical assets such as gold. Therefore, these two terms are mutually exclusive. Marketable securities are financial assets that are easily traded.

1-2. The term "portfolio" refers to the securities held by an investor, taken as a unit. By evaluating and managing asset holdings within the context of a portfolio, investors attempt to find an optimal combination of assets to enhance their wealth.

1-3. No, tax minimization is a secondary investment objective. The primary objectives are safety, income, and growth of capital. Secondary objectives should never be the overriding factor determining investment decisions, but they do form part of a good investment plan.

1-4. Investors should select assets consistent with their risk tolerance. Some investors may not be able to deal with the risks inherent in owning common stocks. Therefore, it is not correct to argue that all intelligent investors should own common stocks.

1-5. Disagree. If rational investors always minimized their investing risk, they would likely own nothing but risk-free investments, such as Treasury bills. The correct statement is that rational investors assume risk if they expect to be compensated adequately for doing so.

1-6. Disagree. In this case, investors would seek the assets expected to return the most, regardless of their risk. The correct statement is that investors should seek to maximize their returns for a given level of risk.

1-7. No, the valuation of individual securities—security analysis—is but one of two parts in the investment decision process. The other part of the process, portfolio management, involves determining the composition of a portfolio and managing the assets held therein.

1-8. Disagree. Uncertainty cannot be eliminated, only reduced. For example, no one—including professional investors—can know what the stock market will do with certainty next year, next month, or even tomorrow.

1-9. Disagree. The primary reason for holding foreign securities is to diversify one's portfolio (although higher returns may also be an attraction). Diversification is a major tenet of portfolio management.

CHAPTER 2

2-1. Direct investing involves investors buying and selling securities themselves. Indirect investing involves buying shares of an investment company, which in turn holds a portfolio of securities.

2-2. The two main classifications of capital market securities are fixed income securities (e.g., government or corporate bonds) and equities (e.g., common stock).

2-3. Marketable securities are traded in financial markets where the buyer and seller are not identified to each other. Non-marketable financial assets must be bought and sold by the owner of the asset, so they represent personal transactions between the owner and the issuer.

2-4. Individuals have no risk of losing funds, up to a limit of $100,000, because the Canada Deposit Insurance Corporation (CDIC) insures deposits (e.g., savings account) made with member institutions such as chartered banks and trust companies.

2-5. You should expect money market securities of similar maturity to have very similar yields because they are all very short-term, very high-quality assets, with little risk of default.

2-6. Treasury bills are considered a benchmark security because they are backed by the federal government, so the rates offered on them reflect current demand and supply conditions for short-term funds without credit risk. Other interest rates are scaled up from this short-term, risk-free rate by adding time and risk premiums.

2-7. No. Bond ratings are a measure of the relative probability of default, so the BBB-rated bond does have a higher likelihood of defaulting. There is, however, some (extremely small) probability that even an AAA bond will default.

2-8. Risk-averse investors can buy junk bonds, or any financial asset, if they expect to be adequately compensated for the risk. The greater the risk, the greater the expected return should be.

2-9. Preferred stocks could have higher expected returns and have no maturity date, so there is no need to worry about reinvesting funds as occurs with bonds. Also, preferred stocks can be much easier to buy and sell than individual bonds.

2-10. Income trusts are certainly tax-efficient structures for businesses; however, investors receiving payments from such a trust will pay taxes just as they would on any other source of interest or dividends. The key feature of income trusts that have made them so popular is the high yield that most of these entities pay.

2-11. No. As a shareholder, you have limited liability. This means that you cannot be held responsible for the corporation's debts. While you will lose your entire investment in this bankrupt firm, the bondholders cannot force you to pay any more to cover the debt.

2-12. Conceptually, the key difference between futures contracts and options contracts is that the former entails an obligation to buy (or sell) the underlying asset, whereas the latter confers a right to buy (or sell) the asset, but not the obligation to do so.

2-13. A put option that gives you the right to sell the stock close to the current price, would allow you to reap a profit if the stock actually falls in price (i.e., you could buy the stock after the price falls and still sell it at the high price by exercising the option). If the stock's price does not fall, you will have lost only the premium paid to purchase the option.

CHAPTER 3

3-1. One of the most significant contributing factors to growth in investment fund assets in Canada has been the steady increase in RRSP contributions.

3-2. The costs of indirect investing are generally viewed as a fair trade-off for the services gained. For example, investors who lack the time or knowledge to manage their own portfolios are willing to pay the fees charged by an investment company to have someone else do the work and make the decisions.

3-3. You would expect passive investors—those who prefer not to be involved in managing their own portfolios—to use indirect investing more so than active investors would.

3-4. Provincial securities commissions oversee the operations of mutual fund companies, and an industry group (MFDA) regulates the distribution of funds (providing protection against fraudulent activity). However, investments in mutual funds are not guaranteed by any agency.

3-5. Mutual funds have existed for many years (as have closed-end funds, but these have fallen out of favour) and are very accessible; that is, minimum investment levels are low enough to be accessible by most investors. Heavy promotion and publicity also account for the popularity of mutual funds.

3-6. Mutual funds—more properly called open-end investment funds—continuously offer shares or units to the public. This means that they will sell new units, or redeem existing ones, at any time.

3-7. Money market funds by definition hold money market assets, which are the safest financial assets because of their high-credit quality and very short maturity. Therefore, the riskiness of these funds simply reflects the type of assets they hold.

3-8. A balanced fund holds both bonds and stocks, thereby offering a combination of assets in one fund. Typically, such funds should have higher returns (on average) than bond funds, while offering lower risk than stock funds.

3-9. ETFs have largely eliminated the issue of discounts and premiums that plague closed-end funds by holding well diversified portfolios that mimic well-known market and/or sector indexes.

3-10. Investors may choose to buy load funds and pay sales charges because of ignorance about the alternatives available or carelessness in seeking out the lower-cost alternative of no-load funds. In addition, many no-load funds have hidden charges, while many load funds have outperformed their no-load counterparts.

3-11. The tax credits available on LSVCC funds have an annual limit such that investments beyond $5,000 do not qualify. These funds tend to hold highly speculative and illiquid (i.e., riskier) assets, making them unsuitable for many investors. Moreover, their long-term performance record has been quite poor, on average.

3-12. No. Any income or capital gains distributions (even if reinvested in the fund) must be included to calculate the total return.

3-13. While the 5-star rating certainly indicates good performance relative to other funds in the same category on a historical basis, it does not guarantee future performance. This type of rating is useful in making investment decisions, but other factors such as the objectives of the fund and management expenses should also be considered.

3-14. International funds tend not to include domestic assets in their portfolios, whereas global funds do. Therefore, an investor seeking to purchase only one fund would likely be better served by a global fund.

3-15. Hedge funds—unregulated investment companies—are only accessible by "sophisticated" investors (high net-worth individuals and institutions) because of securities regulations that aim to protect investors from past abuses by fund companies.

CHAPTER 4

4-1. The term underwriting technically involves a firm commitment, meaning the investment bankers have agreed to purchase the securities outright from the issuer. This is different from a "best efforts" offering, where the risk of the issue not selling rests with the issuer.

4-2. The underwriters have an incentive to quickly sell an issue, thereby reducing their risk as well as enhancing their reputation as successful investment bankers.

4-3. Any time a company (or government) issues securities, the sale occurs in the primary market, even if securities of the same type have been issued previously. The secondary market involves security transactions between investors, independent of the issuer.

4-4. Both the NYSE and the TSX have traditionally functioned in a similar manner—physical exchanges where shares of very well-known, large companies are traded. However, among the top 10 exchanges in the world, trading volume on the TSX is dwarfed by that on the NYSE, the world's largest exchange. Both exchanges sell memberships that permit trading, but some NYSE members are designated as "specialists" and are charged with maintaining an orderly market in certain stocks. The TSX shut its trading floor in 1997; all trading is now computerized. The NYSE continues to use the specialist system, but is also moving toward electronic trading, as evidenced by its 2006 merger with ArcaEx. Whereas the TSX has a near monopoly on stock trades in Canada, the NYSE has a large competitor (Nasdaq), which has pushed it to expand internationally (merging with Euronext in 2007).

4-5. Nasdaq is a marketplace distinguishable by its trading mechanisms and processes. The term over-the-counter market has traditionally referred to the trading of securities not listed on the organized exchanges.

4-6. Companies may have to disclose less information on Nasdaq or may prefer having multiple market makers for their stock. On the other hand, companies may prefer to have their shares traded on the NYSE, which has long been considered the premier secondary market for the trading of equities.

4-7. Yes. The S&P/TSX Composite Index is affected by the size of the companies in the index because it is a capitalization-weighted index. Therefore, each stock's weight in the index is proportionate to its capitalization (total value of all shares outstanding).

CHAPTER 5

5-1. In 1983, fixed commissions were eliminated in Canada (1975 in the US), meaning that each brokerage firm was free to set its own fee level, possibly negotiated with clients. This has lead to the development of discount brokerage firms that provide far less service to customers, but also charge much lower fees.

5-2. A wrap account means that all costs are included in the wrap fee, which some investors prefer. Also, some investors want to have a consultant in the form of a money manager for their account, and a wrap account can provide for this.

5-3. You could place a stop loss order (to sell) at $55. If the price fell to this level, your order would become a market order and be executed close to $55, thereby giving you a profit of approximately $15, since you bought the stock for $40.

5-4. The market maker will "take the other side" of the trade in OTC markets; that is, they buy stock from investors wishing to sell, and sell it to investors wishing to buy. Because there is always a spread—the ask price (at which the dealer sells) is always higher than the bid price (at which the dealer buys)—the market maker earns a profit whether the stock price is rising or falling.

5-5. Disagree. The CIPF protects investors against insolvency of its members (technically, members of the various self-regulatory organizations), principally the brokerage and investment management firms. It does not cover losses resulting from changing market values of securities, or any loss resulting from the bankruptcy of a firm that issued the security.

5-6. The current system of 13 provincial and territorial securities regulators imposes an administrative burden on securities issuers and investment dealers, as they have to abide by 13 sets of rules and regulations, and file documents in all jurisdictions. Reducing this burden is the key argument in favour of a national securities regulator. However, the provincial regulators themselves have generally opposed such a move, fearing loss of control over an area of provincial responsibility (per the Canadian constitution) and an inability to tailor rules to local conditions.

5-7. Ignore purchase and sale commissions: let VP = value of stock at purchase; VS = value of stock at sale; EQ = your equity at purchase; D = dividends (income) received while holding the stock; MI = total margin interest paid.

Return on Equity = $[(VS - VP) + D - MI]$

5-8. Margin accounts may increase the volume of trading that investors undertake (because they effectively have a larger pool of capital to invest), and this would generate additional commissions for brokers. More important, brokerage firms charge interest on funds borrowed in margin accounts. While the interest rate is typically only a little above prime, it is certainly higher than the rate the firm itself pays to borrow, hence the brokerage earns a spread on all margin loans.

5-9. Because there is no theoretical limit to how high a stock price can rise, the losses from short selling are said to be infinite, at least in theory. In practice, most stocks do not increase dramatically in price in short periods of time, so losses can be contained. By contrast, the farthest a stock price can drop is to zero, so the gains from short selling are finite.

CHAPTER 6

6-1. The risk of not receiving the dividend you expect from a stock (or the coupon interest payments from a bond) is related to the company's (or issuer's) ability to make the payment. Therefore, risk in the yield portion of your return would be termed non-systematic risk.

6-2. You would expect to observe five heads and five tails after ten tosses of a fair coin because there is a 50 percent chance of each outcome on a given toss. To make any conclusions about the fairness of the coin would require many more observations. Expected returns from investments are, similarly, meant to be long-term average figures. In the short term, returns can differ greatly from expected figures.

6-3. Disagree. The cumulative wealth index can be calculated for nominal stock returns or inflation-adjusted (real) returns, just as total returns and return relatives can be used on either a nominal or real basis.

6-4. When an investor buys a foreign asset, the investor is in effect selling Canadian dollars to obtain the foreign currency needed to buy the security. When this security is sold in the foreign market, the proceeds will need to be converted back to Canadian dollars.

6-5. We cannot calculate a geometric mean using negative returns. The return relative makes all the return figures positive numbers.

6-6. The spread of the data tells us something about how likely it is that the average, or mean, will be realized. When the data in question are return figures, the spread, as measured by the standard deviation, is a measure of risk.

6-7. In recent years, realized returns on stocks have been fairly high. A number of market observers expect equity returns to be lower in the future based on observation of dividend yields that are currently about half their long-term average. With lower dividend yields, the total return on equities will be reduced (unless price appreciation makes up the difference). Unless interest rates decline (in particular, the risk-free T-bill rate), equity risk premiums will follow equity returns lower.

6-8. Standard deviation figures can be more easily interpreted, as they are written as percentage values, similar to return figures. Variance figures—being the square of the standard deviation—are less easy to understand. For example, a standard deviation of 0.16 = 16%. The equivalent variance would be 0.0256.

6-9. The long-term financial history of Canada shows that inflation is an issue over a period of many years. While it has been very low in recent years, it could be higher in the future. Even at an average inflation rate of 3 percent a year, the purchasing power of money will be cut in half in approximately 24 years. This may seem like too long a time period to be concerned about, but remember that many retirees will live this long after retiring.

6-10. There may be differences in the economies of Canada and the U.S. that might explain differences in returns. However, a simpler answer can be found by looking at the data in Table 6-5. The standard deviation of returns on Canadian stocks has been slightly lower than for U.S. stocks. Consistent with the other assets shown in the table, lower standard deviations (lower riskiness) are associated with lower returns. Canadian stocks have been slightly less risky, and therefore have produced slightly lower returns.

CHAPTER 7

7-1. Yes. The terms "uncertainty" and "risk" are often used interchangeably. However, Peter Bernstein's essay reminds us that these concepts are not quite the same. Uncertainty is the recognition that a range of outcomes may occur. Risk, and therefore risk management, encompasses also the idea that we may not even know the range of outcomes.

7-2. The expected return for a security is a weighted average of the possible outcomes that could occur, with the probability of each outcome used as its weight. It is the best one-point estimate of the return. If this opportunity were to be repeated for a large number of trials, the average return realized would be the expected return.

7-3. Assuming the returns are normally distributed, we do have enough information. In order to calculate the standard deviation, the average (expected) return is required. These two statistics, the average and standard deviation, are sufficient to fully describe a normal probability distribution.

7-4. Security returns are a (weighted) average of the possible outcomes; in a portfolio, the returns of the individual securities are averaged. As no squared (or higher) terms appear in the calculation, returns are a linear measure. On the other hand, the standard deviation for a single security is non-linear because it involves adding squared deviations; the calculation for a portfolio is even more complex.

7-5. The benefits of diversification do kick in immediately. Therefore, two securities provide better risk reduction than one; three are better than two, and so forth. However, at some point very little benefit is to be gained by adding securities (the gains become insignificant), and therefore the benefits of diversification are limited.

7-6. In the same way that decreased correlations between domestic stocks enhanced the benefits of diversification, the benefits of international diversification likely declined because of increased correlations between national and international stock markets.

7-7. Correlation figures are more easily interpreted as they always fall within a range from −1 to +1; this means that we can easily tell how closely the returns of two stocks match each other. Covariance figures are less easy to understand as they do not have a limited range. We cannot say whether a particular covariance is large or small, unless we compare it to the variance of each of the two stocks involved.

7-8. Negative correlation means that security returns move inversely to each other. This provides better risk reduction because the negative movement of one security can be offset by the positive movement of another security.

7-9. Covariances are needed to calculate portfolio risk since it consists of weighted variances and weighted covariances. The correlation coefficient is a component of the covariance, given by $COV_{AB} = \sigma_{AB} = \rho_{AB}\sigma_A\sigma_B$.

7-10. Sometimes when adding a security to a well-diversified portfolio, what matters is its relationship to the other securities and not its own individual risk. If this security is negatively correlated with the other securities in the portfolio, it will work to reduce the overall risk of the portfolio.

7-11. The single-index model assumes that stocks covary together only because of their common relationship to the market index. Thus, the "market" is the single index referred to in the model's name.

7-12. With the single-index model, one covariance estimate is needed for each security: a sample of 50 stocks requires 50 estimated covariances. By contrast, with the Markowitz model, $50 \times 49 = 2,450$ covariance estimates would be required.

CHAPTER 8

8-1. All the information used as inputs to the Markowitz analysis—including asset returns, variances, and covariances—are determined for the individual assets. When it comes to creating portfolios, these inputs are taken as given so the only choice to be made is the weight of each asset in the portfolio.

8-2. Most portfolios (all those in the interior and lower edge of the attainable set) are dominated by another portfolio that has either a higher return for the same level of risk or a lower risk for the same level of return. The efficient set is composed only of the dominating portfolios.

8-3. Indifference curves allow us to talk about preferences with regard to the risk–return trade-off, and therefore find the efficient portfolio best suited to a particular investor. Because all investors are assumed to be risk-averse, they all require some amount of extra return to compensate for higher risk. This implies that an indifference curve must always show higher return as risk increases (i.e., it must be upward sloping).

8-4. The introduction of risk-free borrowing and lending is an important change relative to the original Markowitz analysis because it changes the nature of the efficient frontier. Not only has the efficient frontier been pushed out, but it has been changed from a curve to a straight line.

8-5. Portfolio "T" is the only portfolio of risky assets that investors need to consider because it creates the highest possible (most efficient) linear set. However, investors still have to choose the proportion of this risky portfolio and the risk-free asset they prefer, so their overall portfolios will differ based on their own risk preferences.

8-6. The separation theorem states that the investment decision (what assets to hold) is independent of the financing or allocation decision (how much to invest in risky assets versus the risk-free asset).

8-7. The systematic portion of total risk is considered to be the most important. Non-systematic risk can be very nearly eliminated through diversification, whereas the market (systematic) risk is unavoidable. Therefore, there is no compensation (extra return) for taking on non-systematic risk; only systematic risk provides an opportunity for added returns.

CHAPTER 9

9-1. The notion of homogeneous expectations is one of the key assumptions in the development of the CAPM. It means that all investors have the same beliefs about the expected returns, variances, and correlations for risky assets, and will therefore all generate the same efficient frontier.

9-2. The separation theorem states that the investment decision (what assets to hold) is independent of the financing or allocation decision (how much to invest in risky assets versus the risk-free asset). However, we also know that all investors should hold the tangency portfolio, "T", as the risky asset. Therefore, the investment decision has been made, and only the allocation decision remains.

9-3. All investors should hold only portfolio "T" for the risky-asset portion of their overall portfolios because it is the optimal risky portfolio. If this is true, then every risky asset that is owned by investors must logically be in portfolio "T." Therefore, "T" contains all possible risky assets. Since the aggregate of all risky assets is, by definition, the whole market for risky assets, "T" must be the market portfolio.

9-4. The CML is tangent to the Markowitz efficient frontier. The point of tangency is an efficient portfolio, since only efficient portfolios are on the efficient frontier. All points on the CML are combinations of this efficient portfolio and borrowing and lending.

9-5. Beta is a relative measure of systematic risk (calculated as the covariance with the market relative to the market variance). We use beta rather than the covariance itself because it is more easily understandable: beta for the market as a whole is 1.0, and the betas for individual stocks cluster around 1.0.

9-6. Overvalued securities plot below the SML because they do not offer a large enough expected return given their risk. Thus, investors would prefer a security on the SML. As investors sell these securities, their price will be driven down and their return will go up until they converge on the SML.

9-7. To obtain the required estimates of parameters for use in the CAPM, we typically use historical data; the model actually needs *ex ante* estimates, and beta in particular is known to change over time. Also, the "market portfolio" is not an observable entity; the proxies we use (typically an index of large stocks) may not do a good job of representing the entire market.

9-8. APT is more general than the CAPM in that any number of factors may be used to explain securities' returns. The CAPM is a special case of APT when there is only one factor: the expected return on the market portfolio.

9-9. A risk factor used in a factor model should be unpredictable at the beginning of each period. While we don't know exactly what the price of oil will be in the future, we can make reasonably accurate predictions, at least for short periods of time. Unanticipated changes in the price of oil would be a better factor, as it contains the necessary element of surprise.

CHAPTER 10

10-1. In an efficient market, stock prices should reflect all available information; this includes past information, current information, and information that can reasonably be inferred today. Markets have been shown to be highly—though not perfectly— efficient, and investors should expect that, on average, prices will reflect the available information.

10-2. No. Positive returns are consistent with efficient markets, as are returns that vary with the level of risk undertaken. Efficient markets imply that you cannot use information to earn an abnormal return, which is a return greater than what should be expected given the level of risk.

10-3. The strong form of the EMH would be violated if the CEO can use this "insider" information to make an abnormal return.

10-4. No. Information comes into the market randomly, which, with the other specified conditions, leads to market efficiency. Market efficiency and rationality are related. An irrational market would be one where investors do not react to information quickly and, on balance, accurately.

10-5. The "events" that form the basis of event studies typically involve some form of company announcement (e.g., quarterly earnings), or other occasions when new information becomes public. Therefore, such studies are used to test the semi-strong form of the EMH, which refers to publicly available information.

10-6. An institutional investor—or any investor—can justify spending money on stock selection techniques if it can be shown that the benefits outweigh the costs. In most cases, this cannot be shown, but in some cases it can be. Some institutional investors have a disciplined technique that has been worked out over time, whereas others employ analysts with proven skill and ability.

10-7. Behavioural finance says investors often make systematic mistakes when processing information about the stock market. Markets overreact, both up and down. Investors are motivated by numerous "irrational" forces, such as overconfidence, regrets about decisions, aversion to losses, and so forth. Other investors, recognizing these mistakes in judgment, may be able to profitably exploit them. The long-term return reversals that have been found with stock losers and winners is said to be a result of investor overreaction. For example, investors overreact to information about companies and drive stock prices to unsustainable highs or lows. When investors realize later that they overreacted to the news, prices return to their correct levels.

10-8. The existence of market anomalies does not disprove the EMH. First, only a relatively few anomalies have received wide support over time. Second, some of these anomalies, such as the size effect, have become less apparent over time.

And finally, the anomalies may come about as a result of inadequate means of testing them correctly. It may be the case that researchers have not been clever enough to unravel the true story behind these apparent inefficiencies, with the result that they may not be inefficiencies at all.

CHAPTER 11

11-1. The two cash flow components associated with a traditional bond are the coupon payments, which are received periodically throughout the life of the bond, and the face value amount, which is received when the bond matures.

11-2. The quoted price of a bond does not take into account the fact that coupon interest accrues to a bondholder on a daily basis, but is only paid by the issuer periodically. Therefore, when a bond is purchased, the seller receives the cash price (which is greater than the quoted price) to cover this earned interest.

11-3. A bond sells at a premium whenever market interest rates fall below the coupon rate, leading to an increase in the bond price. The higher price reduces the current yield below the coupon rate, which is fixed. The YTM will be lower (reflecting the market rate) because the bond is being purchased at a premium.

11-4. Yes; agree. The YTM is a promised yield, and to realize this yield an investor must hold the bond to maturity and reinvest the coupons at exactly the calculated yield to maturity. The chance of the reinvestment assumption occurring is practically zero.

11-5. No. The actual return will depend on the rate at which the coupons are reinvested. The YTM is still a promised rate.

11-6. Yes; agree. The price of discount and premium bonds must move toward $1,000 as the bond approaches its maturity date. On that date, the bond will be worth $1,000 because that is what the issuer will redeem it for.

11-7. Taking only maturity into account ignores the coupon on a bond and the existing level of interest rates, both of which also affect the bond's sensitivity to interest rate changes.

11-8. Yes; agree. A relatively larger portion of the cash flow comes earlier in the form of coupon interest payments, reducing the duration of the higher coupon bond.

11-9. You should adjust your portfolio by increasing the average duration of the portfolio, which will increase its interest rate sensitivity.

CHAPTER 12

12-1. Canadian investors experienced a decline in the value of their American bond holdings. The unfavourable currency movement meant that even a bond that had not changed in price (in U.S. dollars) would be worth much less in Canadian dollar terms than it had been.

12-2. The interest rate set by the Bank of Canada is a very short-term rate, whereas bond prices are impacted by interest rates for longer terms. A tightening of monetary policy by a central bank is generally aimed at dampening inflationary pressures. Bond investors are encouraged by such actions, other things being equal, because higher inflation would likely lead to increased interest rates in the future, particularly long-term rates.

12-3. Yes, an upward-sloping yield curve is compatible with the liquidity preference theory. The liquidity preference theory stresses the idea that because of larger risks, longer maturity securities require larger returns or compensation.

12-4. As the economy undergoes recession, or economic difficulties, yield spreads should widen because of the increased risk of lower-quality bonds. Investors demand a greater risk premium to be compensated for the additional risk. In a similar manner, when the economy is enjoying prosperous times, investors will demand a smaller risk premium because most bond issuers will be able to meet their obligations.

12-5. The higher the coupon rate on a bond, the more likely it is that the call feature will be exercised. Besides the reinvestment rate risk, having the bond called would require the investor to search for another suitable investment; this works counter to the notion of passive management.

12-6. No. Falling market interest rates would leave the investor short of her desired portfolio value due to lower earnings on reinvested coupon interest. The investor should instead create a bond portfolio with a duration of five years. This will immunize the portfolio against the re-investment rate risk.

CHAPTER 13

13-1. When valuing common stock (or any security) using the present value approach, the two key inputs are (1) the required rate of return, or discount rate, which must reflect the risk associated with the security; and (2) the expected cash flows for all future periods, which for stocks means estimating future dividends.

13-2. The required rate of return for a stock is the minimum expected rate of return an investor needs to induce him or her to purchase a stock. As such, it takes into account the amount of risk involved.

13-3. Dividends are the only cash payment a common stock owner will receive from the corporation. If all future dividends are discounted back to today at a proper rate of return, it is the most (on a present value basis) the shareholder will receive by owning the stock; therefore, that is the estimated value of the stock.

13-4. Although neither the zero-growth nor the constant-growth rate DDM shows a present value process in its equations, discounting to the present is definitely occurring in both cases. The models presented have been reduced, mathematically, to the indicated forms, while still involving a present value process.

13-5. Yes. Different investors will have different required rates of return, and they may estimate the expected growth rate in dividends differently.

13-6. Both. The intrinsic value of a stock is an estimated value, but those estimates are often made using a formula.

13-7. Using a comparable firm to estimate a justified P/E ratio may build market errors into the value estimation process. If the comparable firm is itself overvalued (or undervalued), the justified P/E derived from it will be too high (or low).

13-8. There are various ways to measure and state P/E ratios. In particular, we could use a known earnings figure (e.g., from the last fiscal year, or the most recent 12 months), or an estimate of future earnings. Also, estimating a justifiable P/E multiplier involves a lot of judgement regarding risks, interest rates, growth opportunities, etc.

13-9. The late 1990s demonstrated that valuations can rise at a rapid rate for several years in a row. Many observers feel there was a bubble in the market for technology stocks, related to investors overvaluing stocks based on their fundamentals.

CHAPTER 14

14-1. You should be comfortable with this approach. A diversified portfolio is always important; with stock values expected to rise, you can expect such a portfolio to perform well.

14-2. The required rate of return would be expected to rise because of investor pessimism. This actually happened in the U.S. in the early 1970s during a gasoline shortage.

14-3. Diversification cannot completely protect your portfolio from the collateral damage that occurs when an overvalued sector declines. After all, this sector will be included in your portfolio (if it is truly diversified), and therefore the portfolio will be adversely affected. However, diversification will limit the damage caused by this sector decline because you will also be exposed to those sectors that perform the best.

14-4. Security analysts have been accused of conflicts of interest because many of them work for firms that also carry out investment banking activities. Analysts may be pressured to not issue negative reports about investment banking clients—both actual and prospective—so as to retain or acquire their business in selling securities.

14-5. Historically, some firms have always performed well in a given year, regardless of what the market does. Even in a highly efficient market, if these top-performing firms can be identified, investors could profit. Another way to say this is that there is always wide cross-sectional variation in stock returns, ranging from very good performance to very poor performance.

14-6. There are two significant issues with regard to market timing. First, although some investors may be able to identify approximate times to get out of the stock market because it is going to decline, it is extremely difficult to determine when to get back in the market. The second but related issue is that studies have shown that much of the market's good performance over a relatively long time period occurs during a few days. Thus, being out of the market greatly increases the chances that one will miss some of these few days when the market enjoys very strong performance, thereby diminishing their overall performance substantially.

14-7. Intrinsic value is of little use in technical analysis. In this approach, stocks are evaluated on the basis of price patterns over time.

14-8. The weak form of the EMH states that stock price changes are essentially independent and therefore cannot be used to predict future price changes. This is in direct contrast to technical analysis, which relies on stock-price changes being dependent or moving in trends that are somewhat predictable.

14-9. Higher interest rates will increase the cost of borrowing for firms, and thus decrease earnings, which would likely depress stock prices. You might also recall that interest rates are an important part of the required return on stocks; a higher required return implies lower intrinsic values. Either way you look at it, interest rates and stock prices generally tend to move in opposite directions.

CHAPTER 15

15-1. Hiring employees takes time, and can be an expensive process. Layoffs can also be very costly, both in direct costs (e.g., severance pay) and indirect ones (e.g., sour relationships and loss of skilled workers). Therefore, hiring and firing, which affect the unemployment rate, tend to occur relatively late compared to economic activity. By contrast, having existing employees work more or fewer hours (e.g., adding shifts or overtime) can usually be accomplished very quickly and cheaply. Thus, many firms will use this approach when their near-term planning indicates changing demand for their products or services.

15-2. Assuming that you are correct in your analysis that the economy has reached a peak this month, it is likely that the stock market has already turned and has been heading lower for some time. Stock prices typically lead the economy, which means the market likely would have anticipated a forthcoming peak in economic activity.

15-3. Government spending on goods and services has a direct impact on GDP. After all, it is the "G" term in the GDP equation: $GDP = G + C + I + (X − M)$. Spending for direct transfers to citizens may also increase GDP if those citizens spend the money (the "C"). Conversely, if the increased spending is accompanied by higher taxes, GDP may be reduced due to lower consumer spending and business investment (the "I").

15-4. A downward-sloping (inverted) yield curve frequently precedes a fall in economic activity or recession. While there are never guarantees about the future, this is one indicator that has been quite reliable in its predictions, and therefore investors should pay close attention to it.

15-5. Stock investors can use market measures in several ways: to get a feel for the mood in the market; to gauge where the market is in a business cycle; as a benchmark for comparing portfolio performance; and to calculate betas for individual stocks.

15-6. It takes two variables to determine a price, whether for one stock or the market. While you may have a reliable estimate of future earnings, you do not know what the P/E ratio will be. Thus, even if you knew corporate earnings would be higher next year, the P/E ratio could decline enough to offset this increase and leave stock prices lower.

15-7. Interest rates are an important part of the required rate of return for stocks, and therefore, affect stock prices. Generally, interest rates and stock prices move in opposite directions.

CHAPTER 16

16-1. Being in the "right" industries over long periods of time has clearly paid off for investors. Substantial differences exist in the performance of industries over time. That said, predicting which industries will perform well in the future remains a difficult task.

16-2. Conducting an analysis of any industry will involve a consideration of many factors. Understanding the drivers of supply, demand, and pricing for the goods or services produced by the industry is critical. It is also important to consider other factors, such as the regulatory environment and labour issues.

16-3. Much of the U.S. and Canadian economies have shifted from goods-producing to services-producing activities in recent decades. This is reflected in the definition of industry sectors in NAICS, where 15 of the 20 sectors are devoted to services. Perhaps an even bigger change in the economy is the trend toward globalization. For example, the auto industry now involves many multinational firms: Toyota is as important a manufacturer as General Motors. GICS attempts to provide a complete and consistent set of industry definitions for global application.

16-4. Along with high potential returns, industries in the pioneering stage also present the greatest risk to investors, as many companies in such industries may fail. By contrast, the expansion phase tends to offer good opportunities for investment in firms that have survived the pioneering phase and whose growth is rapid but orderly.

16-5. Current business conditions (the state of the economy) and expectations for interest rates are the two key factors to be considered in business cycle analysis. Different industries will have varying sensitivities to these factors.

16-6. An increase in the cross-sectional variability of industries would make industry analysis all the more valuable because the differences between good performers and poor performers will be that much greater.

CHAPTER 17

17-1. Auditors certify only that a company's financial statements present fairly the results in compliance with generally accepted accounting principles. Such certification does not ensure the fiscal soundness of the company, or the quality of its earnings, or even provide any guarantee against the possibility of impending problems.

17-2. A company's accounting earnings are only loosely connected to its solvency (ability to pay its bills). A large loss for the year on the income statement does not necessarily have anything to do with the cash position on the balance sheet. Such a firm may still have more than adequate cash with which to operate.

17-3. Companies may choose to report an earnings-related number that places the company in the most favourable light.

17-4. ROE is boosted by leverage and will therefore be higher than ROA for any firm that uses debt. If a company uses no debt, its ROE will equal its ROA.

17-5. The decomposition of ROE allows us to understand how the company achieved its results. Whichever breakdown is used, the components will include some form of operating efficiency, asset turnover, and leverage factors.

17-6. Using the full $3 EPS, the payout ratio is 0.33; therefore, the retention rate is two-thirds. Thus, the estimated growth rate would be two-thirds of 18 percent, or 12 percent. Excluding the unusual items, the EPS is $2; the payout ratio is 50 percent, as is the retention ratio. Now the estimated growth rate is half of the 12 percent ROE, or 6 percent. This lower figure better represents the sustainable rate of growth, as the unusual items that boosted the EPS this year are unlikely to reoccur.

17-7. There is evidence that analysts are frequently wrong in their earnings forecasts (see Chapter 14). Averaging the forecasts of several analysts—the consensus forecast—is likely to provide a more accurate result.

17-8. If other analysts and investors had expected the EPS to fall even further than the reported numbers, the announcement would constitute a favourable earnings surprise. When earnings exceed the market's expectations, the price of the stock often rises.

17-9. Most companies are reluctant to decrease their dividends and will do so only when it becomes apparent that a drop in earnings will not soon be reversed. On the flip side, dividends tend to be increased only when a higher level of earnings is felt to be sustainable. Therefore, dividend changes tend to lag well behind earnings changes.

CHAPTER 18

18-1. This phrase reflects the belief held by technical analysts that the market itself is the best source of data for assessing demand for stocks, and hence the future direction of prices.

18-2. A technical analyst need not know the name of a stock because he or she is not interested in the fundamental data for that company. Instead, the technical analyst is studying the price patterns of the stock over time, and to do this one need not know the name of the company.

18-3. A technical analyst would have little use for the intrinsic value of a stock. In the technical approach, a stock is evaluated only on the basis of its historical price (and volume) patterns.

18-4. There are several versions of the Dow Theory. Even assuming someone is using this theory successfully (and you can't be sure of this without documentation), you might very well use a different version or interpretation if you tried to follow this approach. Furthermore, confirmation signals vary from user to user.

18-5. There are many ways that technical analysis could be combined with fundamental analysis techniques. One means, which is consistent with the top-down approach to security analysis, is to use a relative strength indicator to estimate market prospects, to identify attractive industries, then to analyze the fundamentals of companies within those industries.

18-6. When the short-interest ratio rises, it indicates that a large number of shares will have to be purchased to close out the short sales. A technical analyst would see this as creating extra demand for the stock (sometime in the future), which is likely to cause its price to rise.

18-7. Your broker's technique does not appear to have been adequately tested. First, high returns only tell us half the story—the level of risk must also be quantified. Second, the return calculations may not have taken trading costs into account—making weekly adjustments in your portfolio is likely to incur significant commissions. Finally, data from a one-year period is insufficient to determine the consistency or the validity of any investment technique.

CHAPTER 19

19-1. To sell a stock short, an investor must have a margin account, meet margin requirements, pay interest, make up any dividends on the stock sold short, and worry about possible large losses if the stock price rises sharply. Buying a put, an investor has a maximum loss that is known at the outset. No other requirements have to be met. On the other hand, the put has a relatively short maturity and could expire worthless.

19-2. A call buyer has a right to exercise the option, but has no obligation to do so. Even if the buyer forgets about the option, the worst that can happen is that it will expire worthless. On the other hand, the writer (or seller) of the call is obligated to deliver the underlying stock if the buyer decides to exercise the option.

19-3. The buyer of a put has three alternatives: let it expire worthless, exercise it, or sell it in the options market to another investor. Most investors simply sell their options to another investor.

19-4. The clearing corporation stands between buyers and sellers. It keeps the books on all transactions. Therefore, a seller can offset a position by buying the same option because the clearing house can simply cancel the seller's position.

19-5. An option's payoff is conditional on whether the underlying stock is above or below the exercise price. This is reflected in the payoff diagrams as a "kinked" line (actually two line segments). In contrast, buying (or shorting) a stock involves a linear profile: the payoff increases (or falls) along with the stock price.

19-6. When purchasing a call option, the buyer must pay a premium to the option seller. Therefore, the profit earned on a call option will be lower than the payoff by exactly the amount of this premium (ignoring trading commissions).

19-7. Writing covered calls is considered a conservative strategy because it reduces the cost of stock ownership by the amount of the premium received for writing the calls. In addition, since the writer owns the shares required to be delivered if the option is exercised, this obligation is covered.

19-8. The forms of insurance that most people are familiar with (life, automobile, fire, etc.) involve paying a small fee or premium to gain protection against the possibility of a large loss. In the same way, a put option (purchased for a premium that is generally small relative to the stock price) allows a stock owner to avoid the risk of a large drop in the stock price by guaranteeing a minimum price at which the stock can be sold.

19-9. An option's price generally exceeds its intrinsic value because of the speculative (time) value. Investors are willing to pay an additional amount for the chance that the option will have value before it expires.

19-10. The upper boundary for a call option is the price of the underlying stock. The lower boundary for a call is the price of the option at expiration, which must be either zero or its in-the-money value.

19-11. A well diversified portfolio is likely to follow the overall market very closely. Therefore, this investor could use options on the S&P/TSX 60 Index to hedge the portfolio. Specifically, she could purchase put options (in effect, buying portfolio insurance) on the value of the index.

CHAPTER 20

20-1. Broadly speaking, futures contracts can be categorized as either commodities (e.g., metals, oil, and agricultural products) or financials (e.g., currencies, stock indexes, and interest rates).

20-2. Forwards and futures are both commitments to transact in the future at a price specified today. Futures contracts are standardized with respect to the quantity of the product being traded, the delivery date, etc., and they trade on organized exchanges. These features provide a high level of convenience and ease of access. Although forward contracts do not have a centralized marketplace, their key advantage is that they can be tailored to individual requirements in terms of quantities, time, and so on.

20-3. The clearing corporation acts as the seller to every buyer, and a buyer to every seller. Therefore, it can fulfill a contract if either a buyer or a seller defaults. Furthermore, futures contracts are marked to the market daily, so most of the gains and losses would have been settled prior to the expiration date.

20-4. Trading futures contracts is a zero-sum game. Over the life of a contract, aggregate gains must equal the aggregate losses. In fact, with daily marking to the market, a buyer's gains (losses) must equal the seller's losses (gains) each day.

20-5. With a forward contract, the gains and losses involved are settled only when the contract expires; no money changes hands before then. With a futures contract, the daily marking to the market means that gains and losses are recorded in each investor's account on a daily basis. Therefore, on the maturity date, only the last day of gains or losses needs to be accounted for.

20-6. A hedger typically owns the underlying asset (or expects to own it in the future) and is trying to reduce the risk created by the potential price changes of the asset. A speculator, on the other hand, typically has no intention of ever taking a position in the asset itself. He or she is simply trying to profit from anticipated price changes in the underlying item.

20-7. Stock-index futures are settled with cash (based on the difference between the current level of the index and the level specified in the contract) rather than through actual delivery of the underlying assets. This is because it is impractical to deliver all the stocks that make up a typical stock index.

20-8. Basis risk arises because the futures price will differ from the cash price at all times except at maturity of the contract. Futures contracts allow for hedging of systematic risk, but the basis risk arises from asset-specific (or firm-specific) factors, and is therefore a form of non-systematic risk.

CHAPTER 21

21-1. The process described in this chapter (and detailed by Maginn and Tuttle) avoids specifics regarding how money management companies should be organized, or even who should make the various decisions. Each investment firm must decide for itself how best to carry out its activities, consistent with viewing portfolio management as a process.

21-2. Individual investors need a policy statement in order to avoid the conflicts and inconsistencies that often arise. For example, an investor may say that he or she wants a 10 percent after-tax return while maintaining a very low tolerance for risk. Such an objective is unrealistic, and by having to work through a policy statement, the investor can be shown why such a statement is a problem.

21-3. The four life cycle phases correspond to increasing age, and therefore to ever shorter investment horizons for the investor. With a shorter horizon, there is less time available to recoup losses that may result from higher risk investments, so investors generally want less risk as they age. This desire results in lower expected returns as well, due to the direct association between risk and returns.

21-4. If these historical returns were normally distributed, the 11.79 percent average is also the median return figure. Therefore, the probability of earning 11.79 percent or more in any year was 50 percent. However, the probability of earning 11.79 percent or less in a given year was also 50 percent.

21-5. A portfolio that is well diversified across various asset classes will achieve a great deal of risk reduction. On the flip side, returns can be optimized by weighting asset classes to fit an investor's objectives. Thus, as the basic determinant of both return and risk, asset allocation is the most important decision an investor has to make.

CHAPTER 22

22-1. As we have learned throughout the textbook, risk and return are inextricably linked and differences in risk will cause portfolio returns to differ when the overall market changes. Therefore, a complete assessment of performance must determine whether the returns were sufficient given the level of risk.

22-2. GIPS® is a set of guidelines for the presentation of portfolio performance results. As such, it cannot help a firm improve upon its performance; that is up to the firm itself. However, by requiring other firms to fairly present their performance results, clients and potential clients can fairly judge a firm's performance, and hopefully those firms that might choose to slant their performance results will not be able to do so easily.

22-3. The TWR properly measures a portfolio manager's performance because it removes the impact of cash contributions and withdrawals from the calculated return. It is therefore appropriate for comparing mutual funds to each other, or to a market index. The DWR is the best measure of the performance actually experienced by an investor.

22-4. A portfolio with a beta of 1.0 has a risk level exactly the same as the market index. If the portfolio is well diversified, the beta is unlikely to change, and returns on the portfolio should match those of the market.

22-5. Yes, the numerator of both of the Sharpe and Treynor measures is the portfolio's risk premium. It measures the excess return (above the risk-free rate) per unit of risk. For the Sharpe measure, this means per unit of total risk, whereas for the Treynor measure it means per unit of systematic risk.

22-6. All three measures will agree on how managers should be ranked when the portfolios being evaluated are completely diversified. This is because the total risk (variance) of a completely diversified portfolio is equivalent to its systematic risk. If the portfolio is under or over diversified, then the Sharpe measure may give different rankings than the Treynor or Jensen measures.

A

Abnormal Return Return on a security beyond that expected on the basis of its risk, 292

Active Management Strategy A strategy designed to provide additional returns by pursuing active trading activities, 377

Arbitrage Pricing Theory (APT) An equilibrium theory that suggests expected returns for securities are based on their relationship with several underlying risk factors, 269

Arbitrageurs Investors who seek discrepancies in security prices in an attempt to earn riskless returns, 642

Ask Price The price at which the specialist or dealer offers to sell shares, 132

Asset Allocation Decision The allocation of a portfolio's funds to classes of assets, such as cash equivalents, bonds, and equities, 228

Asset-Backed Securities (ABS) Securities issued against some type of asset-linked debts bundled together, such as credit card receivables or mortgages, 40

Auction Market A securities market with a physical location, such as the Toronto Stock Exchange, where the prices of securities are determined by the bidding (auction) actions of buyers and sellers, 98

B

Bar charts Graphs of daily stock prices plotted against time, 600

Basis Points 100 basis points is equal to one percentage point, 327

Bear Market A downward trend in the stock market, 599

Behavioural Finance (BF) The study of investment behaviour, based on the belief that investors do not always act rationally, 300

Benchmark Portfolio An alternative portfolio against which to measure a portfolio's performance, 727

Beta A measure of volatility for stock or portfolio returns. It is the relative market or systematic risk measured as the sensitivity of returns to that on a chosen market proxy, 260

Bid Price The price at which the specialist or dealer offers to buy shares, 132

Black-Scholes Model A widely used model for the valuation of call options, 655

Blocks Transactions involving at least 10,000 shares or $100,000 in value; block trades are usually executed by institutional investors, 116

Blue Chip Stocks The stocks of large, well-established, and well-known companies that have long records of earnings and dividends, 111

Bond Rating Letters assigned to bonds by rating agencies to express the relative probability of default, 37

Bond Swaps An active bond management strategy involving the purchase and sale of bonds in an attempt to improve the rate of return on the bond portfolio, 379

Bonds Long-term debt instruments representing the issuer's contractual obligation or IOU, 33

Book Value The accounting value of common equity as shown on the balance sheet, 44

Brokers Intermediaries who represent both buyers and sellers and attempt to obtain the best price possible for either party in securities transactions; they receive a commission for this service, 98

Bull Market An upward trend in the stock market, 599

Business Cycle The recurring patterns of expansion, boom, contraction, and recession in the economy, 479

C

Call An option that gives the holder the right, but not the obligation, to buy a specified number of shares of stock at a stated price within a specified period, 47, 622

Call Provision Gives the issuer the right to call in a security and retire it by paying off the obligation, 35

Canadian Derivatives Clearing Corporation (CDCC) The clearing corporation that guarantees all equity, bond, and stock index positions on options exchanges in Canada, 628

Canadian Investor Protection Fund (CIPF) A fund established by the Canadian stock exchanges and other organizations to protect investors in the event of the insolvency of any of its members, 138

Canadian Securities Course (CSC) This course is offered by the Canadian Securities Institute (CSI) and is a mandatory requirement for individuals who wish to become licensed to sell financial securities in Canada and to register to sell mutual funds, 24

Canadian Securities Institute (CSI) The national educational body of the Canadian securities industry, 139

Capital Asset Pricing Model (CAPM) Relates the required rate of return for any security with the market risk for that security as measured by beta, 250

Capital Gain (Loss) The change in price on a security over some period of time, 154

Capital Market The market for long-term securities such as bonds and stocks, 33

Capital Market Line (CML) The trade-off between expected return and total risk for efficient portfolios, 256

Capital Market Theory Describes the pricing of capital assets in financial markets, 250

Cash Account The most common type of brokerage account in which the customer pays the brokerage house the full price of any securities purchased, 125

Characteristic Line A regression equation used to estimate beta by regressing stock returns on market returns, 265

Chartered Financial Analyst (CFA) A professional designation for people in the investments field, 23

Closed-End Investment Fund An investment company with a fixed capitalization whose shares trade on exchanges and over-the-counter (OTC) markets, 65

Common Stock An equity security representing the ownership interest in a corporation, 43

Composite Leading Indicator An index constructed by Statistics Canada that combines 10 leading indicators in order to predict future economic conditions, 480

Composite (Risk-Adjusted) Measures of Portfolio Performance Portfolio performance measures combining return and risk into one calculation, 734

Contrarian Investing The theory that it pays to trade contrary to most investors, 301

Conversion Premium The dollar difference between the market price of a convertible security and its conversion value, 356

Conversion Price The par value of a convertible security divided by the conversion ratio, 356

Conversion Ratio The number of shares of common stock that the owner of a convertible security receives upon conversion, 356

Conversion Value A convertible security's value based on the current price of the common stock, 356

Convertible Bonds Bonds that are convertible, at the holder's option, into shares of common stock of the same corporation at predetermined prices, 35

Convertible Securities Bonds or preferred stock convertible into common stock, 356

Convexity A measure of the degree to which the relationship between a bond's price and yield departs from the straight line; that is, the degree to which duration changes as the yield to maturity changes, 343

Corporate Bonds Long-term debt securities of various types sold by corporations, 37

Correlation Coefficient A statistical measure of the extent to which two variables, such as the returns on two securities, are associated, 201

Covariance An absolute measure of the extent to which two variables, such as the returns on two securities, tend to covary, or move together, over time, 204

Covered Call A strategy involving the sale of a call option to supplement a long position in an underlying asset, 638

Cumulative Abnormal Return (CAR) The sum of the individual abnormal returns over the time period under examination, 293

Cumulative Wealth Index Cumulative wealth over time, given an initial amount and a series of returns on some asset, 162

Currency Options Option contracts whose value is based on the value of an underlying currency, such as the Canadian dollar, 650

Current Yield A bond's annual coupon divided by the current market price, 329

Cyclical Industries Industries most affected, both up and down, by the business cycle, 526

D

Dealer An individual or firm who makes a market in a stock by buying from and selling to investors, 105

Debenture An unsecured bond backed by the general worthiness of the firm, 37

Defensive Industries Industries least affected by recessions and economic adversity, 526

Derivative Securities Securities that derive their value in whole or in part by having a claim on some underlying security, 47

Differential Return Measure (Alpha) The measure of portfolio performance calculated as the difference between what the portfolio actually earned and what it was expected to earn given its level of systematic risk, 739

Discount Brokers Brokerage firms offering execution services for buying and selling securities at prices significantly less than full-service brokerage firms. They provide little, if any, investing information and give no adivce, 124

Dividend Discount Model (DDM) A model for determining the estimated price of a stock by discounting all expected future dividends by the appropriate required rate of return for the stock, 399

Dividend Reinvestment Plans (DRIPs) Plans offered by a company that allow shareholders to reinvest dividends to purchase additional shares of stock at no additional cost, 131

Dividend Yield The income component of a stock's return, generally calculated by dividing that current annual dividend by the prevailing market price, 45

Dividends Cash payments declared and paid by corporations to stockholders, 44

Dollar-Weighted Rate of Return (DWR) Equates all cash flows, including ending market value, with the beginning market value of the portfolio, 732

Dow Jones Industrial Average (DJIA) A price-weighted series of 30 leading industrial stocks that trade on the US markets, used as a measure of stock market activity and of changes in the economy in general, 111

Dow Theory A technique for detecting long-term trends in the aggregate stock market, 599

Duration A measure of a bond's economic lifetime based on the weighted present value of expected cash flows over the life of the bond, 338

E

EAFE Index The Europe, Australia, and Far East Index is a value-weighted index of the equity performance of major foreign markets, 112

Earnings Surprise The difference between a firm's actual earnings and the consensus earnings estimate, 555

Economic Value Added (EVA) A technique for focusing on a firm's return on capital in order to determine if shareholders are being rewarded, 422

Efficient Market A market in which prices of securities quickly and fully reflect all available information, 285

Efficient Market Hypothesis (EMH) The proposition that securities markets are efficient, with the prices of securities reflecting their true economic value, 19, 287

Efficient Portfolio A portfolio with the highest level of expected return for a given level of risk or a portfolio with the lowest risk for a given level of expected return, 225

Efficient Set (Frontier) The set of efficient portfolios composed entirely by the Markowitz portfolio model, 226

Electronic Communications Networks (ECNs) Computerized trading networks for institutions and large traders, 107

Emerging Markets Markets of less developed countries characterized by high risks but potentially large returns, 13

Equity-Derivative Securities Securities that derive their value in whole or in part by having a claim on the underlying common stock, 621

Equity Risk Premium The difference between stock returns and the risk-free rate (measured as the return on T-bills), 170

Event Study An empirical analysis of stock price behaviour surrounding a particular event, 292

Exchange Rate Risk The variability in returns on securities caused by currency fluctuations, 157

Exchange-Traded Funds (ETFs) An index fund holding a diversified portfolio of securities, priced and traded on public exchanges, 73

Exercise (Strike) Price The per-share price at which the common stock may be purchased from (in the case of a call) or sold to (in the case of a put) a writer, 623

Expectations Theory The hypothesis that the long-term rate of interest is equal to an average of the short-term rates that are expected to prevail over the long-term period, 369

Expected Return The *ex ante* return anticipated by investors for some future period, 9, 192

J

January Effect The observed tendency for small-cap stocks to be higher in January than in other months, 306

L

LEAPs Options to buy (calls) or sell (puts) securities with longer maturity dates of up to several years, also known as long-term options, 48

Limit Order An order that is executed only if the buyer (seller) obtains the stated sell (ask) price, 132

Liquidity The ease with which an asset can be converted to cash. An asset is liquid if it can be bought or sold quickly with relatively small price changes, 28

Liquidity Preference Theory The idea that interest rates reflect the sum of current and expected short rates, as in the expectations theory, plus liquidity (risk) premiums, 370

Long Hedge A transaction where the asset is currently not held but futures are purchased to lock in current prices, 678

Long Position An agreement to purchase an asset at a specified future date at a specified price, 674

Long-Term Options (LEAPs) Options on individual stocks with maturities greater than one year, 625

M

Margin The part of the total value of a sale of securities that a customer must pay to initiate the transaction with the other part being borrowed from the broker, 139

Margin Account A brokerage account that allows the customer to borrow from the brokerage firm to purchase securities, 125

Margin Call A demand from the broker for additional cash or securities as a result of the actual margin declining below the margin requirement, 141

Marked to the Market All profits and losses on a contract are credited and debited to each investor's account every trading day, 676

Marketable Securities Financial assets that are easily and cheaply traded in organized markets, 3

Market Anomalies Techniques or strategies that appear to be contrary to an efficient market, 301

Market Data Price and volume information for stocks or indexes, 288, 597

Market Model Relates the return on each stock to the return on the market, using a linear relationship with intercept and slope, 264

Market Order An order to buy or sell at the best price when the order reaches the trading floor, 132

Market Portfolio The portfolio of all risky assets with each asset weighted by the ratio of its market value to the market value of all risky assets, 252

Market Risk The variability in a security's returns resulting from fluctuations in the aggregate market, 156

Market Risk Premium The difference between the expected return for the equities market and the risk-free rate of return, 262

Market Segmentation Theory Investors confine their activities to specific maturity sectors and are unwilling to shift from one sector to another to take advantage of opportunities, 370

Market-to-Book Ratio (M/B) or Price-to-Book The ratio of stock price to per share shareholders' equity, 419

Modified Duration Duration divided by (1 + yield to maturity), 342

Momentum Investing Investing on the basis of recent movements in the price of a stock, which generally means buying stocks that have outperformed the market recently. In other words, it is following the trend, 465

Money Market The market for short-term, highly liquid, low-risk debt instruments sold by governments, financial institutions, and corporations. Canadian government Treasury bills are an example, 30

Money Market Funds (MMFs) Open-end investment (mutual) funds that invest in short-term money market instruments such as Treasury bills, commercial paper, and short-term government bonds, 67

Mutual Funds The popular name for open-end investment funds whose capitalization constantly changes as new shares are sold and outstanding shares are redeemed, 65

N

Nasdaq National Market System (Nasdaq/NMS) The largest secondary market for trading of equity securities in the world, 105

Nasdaq Stock Market℠ A national and international OTC stock market consisting of communication networks for the trading of thousands of stocks, 105

Negotiated Market A market involving dealers such as the OTC, 105

Net Asset Value (NAV) The total market value of the securities in an investment company's portfolio divided by the number of investment fund units currently outstanding, 66

New York Stock Exchange (NYSE) The largest secondary market for the trading of equity securities in the world, 101

Non-Systematic (Non-Market) Risk Risk attributable to factors unique to a security, 158

O

Offset Liquidation of a futures position by an offsetting transaction—buyers sell their positions and sellers buy their positions prior to the settlement of the contract (delivery), 674

Open-End Investment Fund An investment fund whose capitalization constantly changes as new shares or trust units are redeemed. Popularly known as mutual funds, 65

Option Premium The price paid by the option buyer to the seller (writer) of the option, 623

Options Claims that give the holder the right, but not the obligation, to buy or sell a stated number of shares of stock within a specified period at a specified price, 47, 622

Over-the-Counter (OTC) Market A network of securities dealers linked together by phone and computer to make markets in securities, 105

P

Par Value (Face Value) The redemption value of a bond paid at maturity, generally $1,000, 34

Passive Management Strategy A strategy whereby investors do not actively seek out trading possibilities in an attempt to outperform the market, 376

Payout Ratio The percentage of a firm's earnings paid out in cash to its stockholders, calculated by dividing dividends by earnings, 45

P/E Ratio The ratio of stock price to earnings, using historical, current, or estimated data. Also known as earnings multiplier, 46

P/E Ratio (Earnings Multiplier) The price to earnings (P/E) ratio for a stock measures the stock price relative to the earnings per share, 414, 557

Performance Attribution A part of portfolio evaluation that seeks to determine why success or failure occurred, 743

Perpetuity An annuity with no maturity date, 399

Point-and-Figure Charts Graphs of stock prices showing only significant price changes, 604

Portfolio The securities held by an investor taken as a unit, 3

Portfolio Insurance An asset management technique designed to provide a portfolio with a lower limit on value while permitting it to benefit from rising security prices, 641

Portfolio Management The second step in the investment decision process, involving the management of a group of assets (i.e., a portfolio) as a unit, 11

Portfolio Weights The percentages of portfolio funds invested in each individual security. These will add up to 1.0, representing the total value of the portfolio, 193

Preferred Habitat Theory Investors have preferred maturity sectors or habitats in which they seek to invest but are willing to shift to other maturities if they can expect to be adequately compensated, 370

Preferred Stock A hybrid security that is part equity and part fixed income because it increases in value but also pays a fixed dividend, 41

Price-to-Book Value or **Market-to-Book Ratio (M/B)** The ratio of stock price to shareholders' equity, 419

Price-Earnings (P/E) Ratio The ratio of stock price to earnings, using historial, current, or estimated data. Also known as the earnings multiplier, 414, 557

Price/Sales (P/S) Ratio A company's total common equity market value divided by its sales, 420

Primary Market The market for new issues of securities such as government Treasury bills or a corporation's stocks or bonds often involving investment dealers. The issuers of the securities receive cash from the buyers who in turn receive financial claims on the issuing organization, 92

Program Trading The computer-generated trading of large blocks of securities. It is often implemented to take advantage of price discrepancies between markets (arbitrage opportunites), 103

Prompt Offering Qualification (POP) System Allows qualifying senior reporting issuers to put out short form prospectuses in lieu of full ones, 96

Prospectus Legal documents that contain relevant financial statements about the proposed use of the funds raised by the stock issue, future growth plans, and other relevant information regarding the share issue. Provides information about a public offering of securities to potential buyers, 95

Protective Put A strategy involving the purchase of a put option as a supplement to a long position in an underlying asset, 640

Put An option that gives the holder the right, but not the obligation, to sell a specified number of shares of stock at a stated price within a specified period, 47, 622

Put-Call Parity The formal relationship between a European call and a put on the same item that must hold if no arbitrage is to occur, 647

R

Real Assets Physical assets, such as gold or real estate, 3

Real Risk-Free Rate of Interest The opportunity cost of foregoing consumption, given no inflation, 327

Realized Return Actual return on an investment for some previous period of time, 9

Reinvestment Rate Risk That part of interest rate risk resulting from uncertainty about the rate at which future interest coupons can be reinvested, 332

Relative Strength The ratio of a stock's price to some market or industry index, usually plotted as a graph, 607

Required Rate of Return The minimum expected rate of return necessary to induce an investor to purchase a security, 262, 448

Resistance Level A price range at which a technician expects a significant increase in the supply of a stock, 600

Retractable Bonds Bonds that allow the bondholder to sell the bonds back to the issuer at predetermined prices at specified times, 35

Return on Assets (ROA) The accounting rate of return on a firm's assets, 548

Return on Equity (ROE) The accounting rate of return on stockholders' equity, 547

Return Relative The total return for an investment for a given time period plus 1.0, 161

Reward-to-Variability Ratio (RVAR) Sharpe's measure of portfolio performance calculated as the ratio of excess portfolio return to the standard deviation, 735

Reward-to-Volatility Ratio (RVOL) Treynor's measure of portfolio performance calculated as the ratio of excess portfolio return to beta, 738

Right A corporate-created option to purchase a stated number of common shares at a specified price within a specified time (typically a few months), 662

Risk The chance that the actual return on an investment will be different from the expected return, 9

Risk-Averse Investor An investor who will not assume a given level of risk unless there is an expectation of adequate compensation for having done so, 9

Risk-Free Rate of Return The return on a riskless asset, often proxied by the rate of return on Treasury securities, 10

Risk Premium That part of a security's return above the risk-free rate of return. The greater the risk of the asset, the greater the associated risk premium, 170, 448

S

S&P/TSX Composite Index The S&P/TSX Composite Index measures changes in market values of a portfolio of 300 Canadian stocks due to alterations in the total market capitalization (the number of common shares outstanding multiplied by the market price per share) of these stocks, 110

Secondary Markets Markets where existing securities are traded among investors; the TSX is the largest stock market in Canada, 98

Security Analysis The first part of the investment decision process, involving the valuation and analysis of individual securities, 11

Security Market Line (SML) The graphical depiction of the CAPM that relates the expected return on an individual security or portfolio to its market risk as measured by beta, 259

Self-Regulatory Organizations (SROs) Organizations in the Canadian securities industry that regulate their own activities. They include the Investment Industry Regulatory Organization of Canada (IIROC), TSX, MX, and the MFDA, 138

Semi-Strong Form That part of the Efficient Market Hypothesis stating that prices reflect all publicly available information, 288

Senior Securities Those securities that are senior, because they are ahead of common and preferred stock in terms of payment or in case of liquidation or bankruptcy, 37

Separation Theorem The idea that the decision of which portfolio of risky assets to hold is separate from the decision of how to allocate investable funds between the risk-free asset and the risky asset, 237

CFA INSTITUTE MATERIALS USED IN THIS EDITION

Chapter 4

4-1: CFA Level I Examination Sample Question #21

Chapter 7

7-1: CFA Program Curriculum Level I 2009, Vol. 4, Reading 50, #4, p.248

Chapter 8

8-1: CFA Program Curriculum Level I 2009, Vol. 4, Reading 50, #5, p.248

Chapter 9

9-1: CFA Program Curriculum Level I 2009, Vol. 4, Reading 45, #25, p.80
9-2: CFA Level I Examination Sample Question #28
9-3: CFA Level I Examination Sample Question #30
9-4: CFA Level I Examination Sample Question #31
9-5: CFA Program Curriculum Level II 2008, Vol. 6, Reading 68, #9, p.422
9-6: CFA Program Curriculum Level II 2008, Vol. 6, Reading 68, #12, p.422
9-7: CFA Program Curriculum Level II 2008, Vol. 6, Reading 68, #13, p.423

Chapter 11

11-1: CFA Program Curriculum Level I 2009, Vol. 5, Reading 63, #15, p.351
11-2: CFA Program Curriculum Level I 2009, Vol. 5, Reading 66, #19, p.482
11-3: CFA Program Curriculum Level I 2009, Vol. 5, Reading 66, #21, p.483
11-4: CFA Level I Examination Sample Question #27

Chapter 12

12-1: CFA Program Curriculum Level I 2009, Vol. 5, Reading 61, #23, p.269
12-2: CFA Program Curriculum Level I 2009, Vol. 5, Reading 61, #24, p.269
12-3: CFA Program Curriculum Level I 2009, Vol. 5, Reading 63, #14, p.351
12-4: CFA Program Curriculum Level I 2009, Vol. 5, Reading 63, #16, p.351
12-5: CFA Program Curriculum Level II 2008, Vol. 5, Reading 56, #1, p.92
12-6: CFA Program Curriculum Level II 2008, Vol. 5, Reading 56, #2, p.92
12-7: CFA Program Curriculum Level II 2008, Vol. 5, Reading 56, #11, p.92
12-8: CFA Program Curriculum Level II 2008, Vol. 5, Reading 56, #12, p.92
12-9: CFA Program Curriculum Level II 2008, Vol. 5, Reading 56, #13, p.92
12-10: CFA Program Curriculum Level II 2008, Vol. 5, Reading 56, #14, p.93
12-11: CFA Program Curriculum Level II 2008, Vol. 5, Reading 56, #16, p.93
12-12: CFA Program Curriculum Level II 2008, Vol. 5, Reading 56, #17, p.93
12-13: CFA Program Curriculum Level I 2009, Vol. 5, Reading 63, #20, p.352
12-14: CFA Program Curriculum Level I 2009, Vol. 5, Reading 65, #28, p.439

Chapter 13

13-1: CFA Program Curriculum Level I 2009, Vol. 5, Reading 59, #11, p.206
13-2: CFA Program Curriculum Level I 2009, Vol. 5, Reading 59, #12, p.206
13-3: CFA Program Curriculum Level I 2009, Vol. 5, Reading 59, #13, p.206
13-4: CFA Program Curriculum Level I 2009, Vol. 5, Reading 59, #15, p.207
13-5: CFA Program Curriculum Level I 2009, Vol. 5, Reading 59, #17, p.207

Chapter 16

16-1: CFA Level I Examination Sample Question #25

Chapter 17

17-1: CFA Program Curriculum Level I 2009, Vol. 4, Reading 45, #24, p.79
17-2: CFA Level I Examination Sample Question #24
17-3: CFA Program Curriculum Level II 2008, Vol. 4, Reading 46, #17, p.340
17-4: CFA Program Curriculum Level II 2008, Vol. 4, Reading 46, #18, p.341
17-5: CFA Program Curriculum Level II 2008, Vol. 4, Reading 46, #19, p.342
17-6: CFA Program Curriculum Level II 2008, Vol. 4, Reading 46, #20, p.344
17-7: CFA Program Curriculum Level II 2008, Vol. 4, Reading 46, #21, p.344
17-8: CFA Program Curriculum Level I 2009, Vol. 4, Reading 45, #3, p.73
17-9: CFA Program Curriculum Level I 2009, Vol. 3, Reading 39, #11, p.543
17-10: CFA Program Curriculum Level II 2008, Vol. 4, Reading 46, #14, p.340

Chapter 19

19-1: CFA Program Curriculum Level I 2009, Vol. 6, Reading 67, #14, p.27
19-2: CFA Program Curriculum Level I 2009, Vol. 6, Reading 70, #9, p.120
19-3: CFA Program Curriculum Level I 2009, Vol. 6, Reading 70, #10, p.120
19-4: CFA Program Curriculum Level I 2009, Vol. 6, Reading 70, #11, p.120
19-5: CFA Program Curriculum Level I 2009, Vol. 6, Reading 70, #12, p.120
19-6: CFA Program Curriculum Level I 2009, Vol. 6, Reading 70, #13, p.120
19-7: CFA Program Curriculum Level I 2009, Vol. 6, Reading 70, #14, p.121
19-8: CFA Program Curriculum Level I 2009, Vol. 6, Reading 70, #15, p.121
19-9: CFA Level I Examination Sample Question #22

Chapter 20

20-1: CFA Program Curriculum Level I 2009, Vol. 6, Reading 67, #12, p.27
20-2: CFA Program Curriculum Level I 2009, Vol. 6, Reading 67, #13, p.27
20-3: CFA Program Curriculum Level I 2009, Vol. 6, Reading 71, #8, p.143
20-4: CFA Program Curriculum Level I 2009, Vol. 6, Reading 71, #10, p144
20-5: CFA Level I Examination Sample Question #23

Chapter 21

21-1: CFA Level I Examination Sample Question #29
21-2: CFA Level I Examination Sample Question #32
21-3: CFA Level III 2006 Examination Sample Essay Question #1

Chapter 22

22-1: CFA Level I Examination Sample Question #5

INDEX